Publisher	Liz Widdicombe
Acquisitions Editor	Tim Vertovec
Developmental Editor	Glenn E. Martin
Text Designer	Terry Rasberry
Copy Editor	JaNoel Lowe
Indexer	Joyce Teague
Production Manager	Marilyn Williams
Compositor	Typo•Graphics, Inc., Orlando, Florida
Production Services	Seaside Publishing Services, San Diego
Text Type	10/12 Berling
Cover Image	© Steven Hunt/The Image Bank and © 1993/Comstock

Address for Editorial Correspondence
The Dryden Press, 301 Commerce Street, Suite 3700, Fort Worth, TX 76102

Address for Orders
The Dryden Press, 6277 Sea Harbor Drive, Orlando, FL 32887
1-800-782-4479, or 1-800-433-0001 (in Florida)

ISBN: 0-03-029919-5
0-03-094860-6 text with 5 1/4" adVenture software disk
0-03-094861-4 text with 3 1/2" adVenture software disk

Library of Congress Catalog Number: 93-072825
Printed in the United States of America
3 4 5 6 7 8 9 0 1 2 069 9 8 7 6 5 4 3 2 1

The Dryden Press
Harcourt Brace College Publishers

Auditing

Concepts for a Changing Environment

Larry E. Rittenberg
University of Wisconsin—Madison

Bradley J. Schwieger
St. Cloud State University

The Dryden Press
Harcourt Brace College Publishers

Fort Worth Philadelphia San Diego New York Orlando Austin
Toronto Montreal London Sydney Tokyo

The Dryden Press Series in Accounting

Introductory

Bischoff
Introduction to College Accounting
Second Edition

Principles

Hanson, Hamre, and Walgenbach
Principles of Accounting
Sixth Edition

Hillman, Kochanek, and Norgaard
Principles of Accounting
Sixth Edition

Computerized

Bischoff and Wanlass
The Computer Connection
Second Edition

Brigham and Knechel
Financial Accounting Using Lotus 1-2-3

Wanlass
Computer Resource Guide: Principles of Accounting
Fourth Edition

Yasuda and Wanlass
The Real Time Advantage

Financial

Backer, Elgers, and Asebrook
Financial Accounting: Concepts and Practices

Beirne and Dauderis
Financial Accounting: An Introduction to Decision Making

Hanson, Hamre, and Walgenbach
Financial Accounting
Seventh Edition

Kochanek, Hillman, and Norgaard
Financial Accounting
Second Edition

Stickney and Weil
Financial Accounting: An Introduction to Concepts, Methods, and Uses
Seventh Edition

Managerial

Ketz, Campbell, and Baxendale
Management Accounting

Maher, Stickney, and Weil
Managerial Accounting: An Introduction to Concepts, Methods, and Uses
Fifth Edition

Intermediate

Williams, Stanga, and Holder
Intermediate Accounting
Fourth Edition

Advanced

Huefner and Largay
Advanced Financial Accounting
Third Edition

Pahler and Mori
Advanced Accounting
Fifth Edition

Financial Statement Analysis

Stickney
Financial Statement Analysis: A Strategic Perspective
Second Edition

Auditing

Guy, Alderman, and Winters
Auditing
Third Edition

Rittenberg and Schwieger
Auditing: Concepts for a Changing Environment

Theory

Belkaoui
Accounting Theory
Third Edition

Bloom and Elgers
Accounting Theory & Policy: A Reader
Second Edition

Taxation

Everett, Raabe, and Fortin
Income Tax Fundamentals

Sommerfeld, Madeo, Anderson, and Jackson
Concepts of Taxation

Duncan
Essentials of U.S. Taxation

Reference

Miller and Bailey
HBJ Miller GAAS Guide
College Edition

Williams and Miller
HBJ Miller GAAP Guide
College Edition

The Harcourt Brace College Outline Series

Campbell, Grierson, and Taylor
Principles of Accounting I
Revised Edition

Emery
Principles of Accounting II

Emery
Intermediate Accounting I
Second Edition

Emery
Intermediate Accounting II

Frigo
Cost Accounting

Preface

The audit environment is constantly changing. Today's auditors face challenges unlike those of any preceding generation. Users of financial statements continue to expect more expertise from auditors and more safeguarding of the integrity of the entire financial reporting process. Thus, accounting and auditing issues continue to increase in complexity. The work environment of auditors has changed accordingly. Competitive pressures among public accounting firms have created a demand for audit methodologies that enhance the efficiency and effectiveness of the process. These methodologies incorporate better methods of risk analysis, more intelligent use of quantitative tools and expert systems, and, most importantly, better audit judgment.

Recent changes in the economy and in the practice of auditing mean that today's auditors face a need for education throughout their careers. Indeed, the constantly changing auditing environment means that the auditor cannot survive by following a mechanical approach to the task, or by living by static values applicable to a particular point in time. Rather, the auditor must have the educational background to exercise judgment and to understand the rationale underlying current audit approaches and the strengths and weaknesses of those approaches. An effective auditing curriculum must encourage students to develop a questioning attitude and provide them with a thorough understanding of auditing that will allow them to deal with the problems that may confront them as the auditing environment continues to change.

Major Textbook Themes

This textbook is organized around six major themes. Students need to:

1. ***Know how to apply auditing procedures in computerized environments and how to use computers to gain audit effectiveness and efficiency.***
   This theme is developed in two chapters addressing computer control concepts and computerized audit techniques, and receives attention in each succeeding chapter. Examples and cases assume computerized information systems. An integrated case illustrates audit issues for a hypothetical firm using electronic data interchange (EDI) with vendors and customers.
2. ***Develop audit judgment and ethical frameworks to guide their actions throughout their career.***
   These themes are interwoven throughout the text. Complex audit judgment is broken down into identification of problem, analysis of alternatives, and testing the alternatives. Ethics discussions cover utilitarian and ethical theories, providing a backdrop for the consideration of ethical dilemmas facing auditors. Ethical standards are examined as dynamic, rather than static. The philosophies of substance over form, the development of professionalism, and the auditor's role in society are examined in light of the auditor's judgment on "fairness" in financial presentations.
3. ***Understand the client's business environment and how to apply the risk model to each unique client.***
   Understanding a client's business environment is a crucial part of any audit and is emphasized throughout the text. Research questions and cases are presented in each chapter. These help students to understand and analyze risks associated with potential audit clients, and to suggest appropriate

audit approaches. The business analysis approach is integrated with research findings on fraudulent financial reporting.

4. ***Use advanced audit techniques that emulate the real world.***
   In addition to a chapter on regression analysis and other advanced topics, the use of advanced audit tools is integrated throughout the text. adVenture, a user-friendly software system, is included with the text and features data files that link control weaknesses to misstatements of account balances. Students may choose from among attribute, PPS, and nonstatistical sampling and generalized audit software techniques, in making audit judgments when working the computer-assisted problems found in four chapters of the book.
5. ***Know how to audit financial institutions and to evaluate the risks associated with new financial instruments.***
   In an economy dominated by service industries, students need to know how to audit them, particularly financial service companies; some of the more difficult audit problems and most extensive frauds have occurred in financial service companies. This textbook employs numerous examples from this industry, and has a separate chapter on their audits.
6. ***Embark on life-long learning, research challenging issues, and develop new skills as the environment changes.***
   Learning is dynamic, particularly in auditing, and requires a commitment to accounting and audit research. Each chapter of this text encourages the student to pursue knowledge, whether through library research or interviews with practitioners, in an attempt to learn about evolving issues. Several reference databases are described in the text.

Organization of the Text

The textbook is organized into seven major sections as follows:

1. ***Audit Environment: Opportunities and Risks***
   These five chapters introduce the audit environment and cover such topics as professional ethics, auditor liability and exposure, and the opportunities present in the auditor/client relationship. Chapter 3 provides a comprehensive ethical framework, while Chapter 5 presents a unique discussion of the current audit environment, the effect of competition on the auditing profession, the manner in which new clients are obtained, and the relationship of auditing to other services provided by a public accounting firm.
2. ***Fundamental Audit Concepts: Planning, Evidence, Risk Assessment***
   The fundamental framework of auditing is explored in this section. Chapter 6 provides a thorough discussion of the concept of materiality and the need for auditors to understand its dimensions as it affects an audit engagement; the audit risk model is developed and presented in both quantitative and judgmental terms. Chapter 7 develops the assertion approach to gathering audit evidence while presenting an extensive discussion of the types and persuasiveness of audit evidence; and a framework for assessing control risk is given in Chapter 8.
3. ***Auditing in a Computerized Environment***
   Auditing in a computerized environment is explored as a topic in two unique chapters. Chapter 9 is devoted to assessing control risk when using computerized applications, including the need for today's auditors to understand how organizations control their computerized accounting

systems, what those control procedures are, and how auditors identify control strengths and assess risk when working with highly computerized clients. Chapter 10 takes the computer concepts one step further and presents a thorough discussion of alternative computer audit approaches, including some that are well-suited for advanced systems.

4. ***Implementing the Risk Model in the Revenue Cycle: Nature and Extent of Testing***
   The revenue cycle is used to illustrate the application of the concepts developed through the first ten chapters of the book. Approaches for assessing control risk and testing controls in operation are the subject of Chapter 11, while Chapter 12 introduces sampling concepts and discusses their application to revenue cycles. Chapter 13 develops an approach for substantive testing in the revenue cycle and is unique in its coverage of the control environment, audit approaches to assessing inherent risk, and identifying audit problems that arise in the revenue cycle. Chapter 14 covers several important items: sampling concepts for testing account balances and their application to the revenue cycle; probability proportional to size (PPS) sampling; and a section covering various types of classical variables sampling methods.
5. ***Implementing the Risk Model: Developing Audit Approaches for Other Financial Statement Accounts***
   Here the audit framework is applied to conducting the audit. The six chapters included in this section discuss and analyze traditional audit approaches and complement that coverage with a discussion of emerging issues such as new types of financial instruments; electronic cash management techniques and the control/audit implication associated with the techniques; auditing supplemental benefits, such as pensions and other post-retirement benefits; and using automated audit tools throughout each audit area. A separate chapter discusses the unique aspects of auditing financial institutions and provides audit programs for auditing bank loan portfolios and estimating reserves for insurance companies.
6. ***Expanding Reporting Horizons***
   The two chapters in this section are devoted to expanding the student's understanding of audit reporting. Chapter 21 contains numerous real-world examples of audit reports and discusses the difference between audits, compilations, and reviews. Chapter 22 identifies the new types of auditing services that have been developed in the past decade, discusses the demand for these expanded services, and gives examples of audit reports.
7. ***Evolution of the Audit Function***
   This section concludes the text of the book, with two chapters on the continuing evolution of the audit function. Chapter 23 focuses on audit research and advanced audit technology, including coverage of computerized databases that are used in audit research. Chapter 24 provides extensive coverage of governmental and operational auditing.

Suitability for Alternative Presentation Formats

This textbook can be used in a one-term Principles of Auditing course, or it can be easily adapted to a two-term sequence in auditing. It is particularly well-suited to the 150-credit-hour accounting program. Most chapters are divided into three or more distinct sections that can be assigned or omitted at the choice of the instructor.

Those who wish to use the textbook in a two-term sequence will find that more time can be spent on cases, research problems, and computer-assisted problems.

The chapter on advanced auditing techniques and audit research can be covered more thoroughly in a second course. The research problems in this chapter require that students use NAARS or other databases and analyze SEC statements on topics such as revenue recognition.

The appendices on statistical sampling can be used to cover sampling techniques more thoroughly than can be done in one term. The computer-assisted sampling problems provide a wealth of opportunities to study and discuss different misstatement situations, ranging from relatively clean populations to those with specific control problems, as well as potential fraud environments. The effectiveness of sampling can be discussed since each student will select different random samples.

Supplementary Materials

The textbook comes with the following supplementary material to help the instructor and students accomplish the learning objectives outlined above:

1. AdVenture computer software and associated data files emulate many of the features of generalized audit software used by public accounting firms.
2. The Instructor's Manual, prepared by Stephen Willits of Bucknell University, provides a course overview and sample syllabi, and teaching suggestions, homework assignments, a chapter outline, and transparency masters for each chapter. It is also available on disk.
3. The Solutions Manual, prepared by the textbook authors, provides ready access to the solutions for the end-of-chapter problems. It is available in both printed and computerized versions.
4. The Study Guide, written by William Kelting of SUNY/Plattsburgh, provides chapter review notes, review questions, and solutions for the review questions.
5. The Test Bank, prepared by Robert and Katherene Terrell of the University of Central Oklahoma, is available in both a printed and a computerized version. It contains multiple choice, true/false, and essay questions for each chapter.

Computer-assisted problems and instructions are presented in an end-of-book appendix. The adVenture software package is designed to give students experience in using generalized audit software, with a special emphasis on statistical sampling. The software is menu driven, user friendly, and extensively pre-tested. Two features should interest most instructors:

1. Each sampled population has five sets of misstatement situations, ranging from minor errors to a systematic fraud. The assignment of students to a misstatement situation can be made randomly or can be assigned by the instructor.
2. The types and amount of control failures found during the tests of controls in operation tie into the type and amount of misstatements in the related account balance.

The software comes with the textbook and is designed to work with Intel-based personal computers.

Acknowledgments

We gratefully acknowledge and thank Tim Vertovec, Glenn E. Martin, Lynne Bush, and JaNoel Lowe for their fine editorial help, advice, and patience. Marilyn Williams, Production Manager; Terry Rasberry, Designer; Alison Howell, Ancillary Production Manager and her staff; and Becky Rainwater round out the Dryden team, and we thank them for their attentive efforts on behalf of this book. We thank the following professors for their thoughtful reviews of the textbook:

Fred Davis
Hawaii Pacific University
Gordon L. Duke
The University of Minnesota
Rita Hull
Virginia Commonwealth University
Steve Jackson
University of Massachusetts (Amherst)
William Kelting
State University of New York/Plattsburgh
Malcolm H. Latham, Jr.
The University of Virginia
Ronald M. Mano
Weber State University
Tom Oxner
The University of Arkansas
H. Sam Riner, Jr.
Western Kentucky University
Eric E. Spires
The Ohio State University
Robert L. Terrell
The University of Central Oklahoma
Barry Vallee
The Northwood Institute
T. Sterling Wetzel
Oklahoma State University
H. James Williams
Georgetown University
Stephen D. Willits
Bucknell University
Susan Wolcott
The University of Denver

We would also like to thank Anne Lee Bain, doctoral student at the University of Wisconsin, for her editorial assistance, R. Glen Berryman of the University of Minnesota for his review of the ethics chapter, and Jim Williams of Ernst & Young, Dave Ripka of Northern States Power, and Don Espersen of Bremer Financial Services for their reviews of the governmental and operational auditing chapter.

We give a special thank you to Arnold and Jerry Kleinstein of Technical Educational Consultants, Inc., for taking our ideas for the software and making them a reality. Those thanks are also extended to Betty Wolterman of St. John's University, who provided us with a timely review of the software.

We appreciate the permissions granted by the American Institute of Certified Public Accountants and the Institute of Internal Auditors for use of materials from their professional standards and examinations and by the publishers of *The Wall Street Journal*, *Business Week*, and *Accounting Today*.

This book is dedicated to our parents, who encouraged us and provided support for our professional development, and to our wives, Kathleen and Ellen Deane, for their love, patience, and help, which were essential to its completion.

Larry E. Rittenberg
Bradley J. Schwieger
October, 1993.

Table of Contents

PART 1 AUDIT ENVIRONMENT: OPPORTUNITIES AND RISKS

CHAPTER 5 Obtaining Clients and Auditor Responsibilities 170

PART 2 FUNDAMENTAL AUDIT CONCEPTS: PLANNING, EVIDENCE, AND RISK ASSESSMENT

CHAPTER 6 Audit Planning: Materiality and Audit Risk 220

PART 3 AUDITING IN A COMPUTERIZED ENVIRONMENT

PART 4 IMPLEMENTING THE RISK MODEL IN THE REVENUE CYCLE: NATURE AND EXTENT OF TESTING

CHAPTER

1

Learning Objectives

Through studying this chapter, you will be able to:

1. Understand the role auditing plays in promoting the free flow of reliable information.
2. Understand the demand for attestation services.
3. Understand the diversity of services offered by public accounting firms.
4. Understand the unique auditing functions provided by internal auditors and governmental auditors.
5. Identify and understand the role of outside organizations in regulating the auditing profession.
6. Understand the evolutionary nature of the auditing profession.

Introduction to the Auditing Profession

Chapter Contents

Chapter Overview

The public and the management of organizations rely on various services provided by public accounting firms and internal audit departments. This chapter explores the importance of auditing in our society and the requirements to become an auditor. Attention is given to the various types of auditors, the services they provide, and the professional and regulatory organizations that affect them.

[An] enormous job remains to be done in explaining and in educating the broad public just what an independent auditing firm does and does not do and what its audit really can be taken to mean. . . . It is clear that relatively articulate segments of the general public do not have any clear notion of what [a clean opinion represents.]. . . The most serious consequences stemming from such a misunderstanding is that the independent auditor can quickly be portrayed as the force that represents all good in financial accounting and the guarantor of anything positive anyone wants to feel about a given company.[1]

The objective of the ordinary audit of financial statements by the independent auditor is the expression of an opinion on the fairness with which they present fairly, in all material respects, financial position, results of operations, and its cash flows in conformity with generally accepted accounting principles. . . . The independent auditor may make suggestions about the form or content of the financial statements or draft them, in whole or in part, based on information from management's accounting system. However, the auditor's responsibility for the financial statements he has audited is confined to the expression of his opinion on them.[2]*[AU Professional Standards, Vol I, 110.01 and 110.02]*

A–INTRODUCTION

At the heart of a free enterprise system is the free flow of reliable information by which investors, creditors, and regulatory agencies make informed decisions about the allocation of resources or the need for governmental action. Managers—whether of large-scale corporations, privately held businesses, or governmental entities—require reliable information on organizational performance, including compliance with organizational policies and objective analyses of operations. The auditing profession contributes to these vital functions by providing independent evaluations and reports assessing the reliability of an organization's financial statements or the efficiency and effectiveness of various aspects of its performance.

The audit function is "special" in that it exists to serve not merely the auditor's clients but also third parties as well. The importance of this special function as performed by the public accounting profession was reiterated in a 1984 Supreme Court decision. Chief Justice Warren Burger, writing for the Court, noted:

> By certifying the public reports that collectively depict a corporation's financial status, the independent auditor assumes a public responsibility transcending any employment relationship with the client. The independent public accountant performing this special function owes ultimate allegiance to the corporation's creditors and stockholders, as well as to the investing public. This "public watchdog" function demands . . . complete fidelity to the public trust.[3]

Chief Justice Burger's statement captures the essence of public accounting. Those of you who enter the business world as certified public accountants will be serving a number of diverse parties and will be performing a special function. That function requires the highest level of technical competence, freedom from bias in assessing the fairness of financial presentations, and concern for the integrity of the financial reporting process. Auditor failure in meeting these responsibilities leaves virtually no one untouched. Failures in maintaining the integrity of the financial reporting system have led to bank and savings and loan closings, loss of mutual fund investments held for retirement plans, and other losses by investors and creditors.

Indeed, the career many of you are considering is one of the most important and most highly regarded public functions. A survey by Lou Harris and Associates, a noted public opinion research organization, found public accounting to be held in high esteem: "It is a fact that the accounting profession is among the best regarded institutions in the country by the general public. . . . But there is no guarantee that this status is permanent. . . . The profession is no better than what it can do in the future, not what it has done in the past."[4] There is no guarantee of continued success, however, without highly competent individuals with strong personal ethical standards entering the profession.

That future of the profession depends on you and your colleagues. Public accounting will face many new challenges: complex computer systems that facilitate management of every facet of an organization, complex financial transactions that must be evaluated for proper financial presentation, and ever-increasing user expectations that range from detection of fraud to clear communication of the results of a company's financial performance. It is to these challenges, and your ability to meet them, that this book is directed.

B–AUDITING DEFINED

Auditing is both more and less than public accounting. It is more because it encompasses internal and operational auditing, governmental auditing, and other services that evaluate and report on managerial performance measured against prescribed standards. It is less because public accounting encompasses other, nonauditing services. Therefore, it is important to understand the breadth of auditing in this wider context, even though our discussion will necessarily focus on auditing as a service performed by independent public accountants.

One of the broader definitions of auditing is contained in the report of the American Accounting Association's Committee on Basic Auditing Concepts, which has defined **auditing** as

> a systematic process of objectively obtaining and evaluating evidence regarding assertions about economic actions and events to ascertain the degree of correspondence between those assertions and established criteria and communicating the results to interested users.[5]

Auditing, in its broadest context, is the process of attesting to assertions about economic actions and events. It is therefore frequently referred to as an **attestation service.** Attestation is a three-part process: gathering evidence about assertions, evaluating that evidence against objective criteria, and communicating the conclusion reached. Management routinely prepares financial statements and distributes them to third-party users as part of an ongoing process that includes acquiring new capital or debt and negotiating labor or trade contracts.

The public accounting function is unique because, as noted, it results in a communication to third parties about the fairness of a company's financial presentations. Absolute independence and objectivity on the part of the auditor in gathering evidence and formulating an opinion on the financial statements are required to serve the public trust. Auditing exists because third parties need unbiased information on which to assess management performance and make economic decisions.

Potential Problems Associated with Managerial Reporting

Managerial reporting to third parties, in the absence of an audit, provides no outside, independent assurance on the reliability of the information presented. Potential problems with management's communication of financial information may cause users to seek an independent assessment of the financial statement presentation. These potential problems include the following:

- Management bias in providing financial information.
- Remoteness of the user from the organization.
- Complexity of transactions affecting the financial statements.

Existence of Potential Management Bias

Bias may exist because management has a vested interest in the actions of investors, regulatory agencies, and lenders. Management bias may also be present because management compensation contracts may be tied to organizational profitability or because senior managers own large amounts of company stock and stock options.

Remoteness from Users

Remoteness is a potential problem since few users have direct knowledge of a company's operations. Most users cannot interview management, tour a company's plant, or review its financial records firsthand; instead, they must rely on the financial statements to communicate the results of management's performance.

Complexity of Financial Reporting

The types of financial transactions that organizations enter into are complex and therefore require the expertise of professionals who understand the underlying economic substance of those transactions and can account for them properly. Sophisticated computer systems that link data within an organization and, ultimately, between organizations, are also complex. Users rely on the auditor to be without any vested interest, to obtain access to all relevant information, and to cut through the complexity to ensure the fair presentation of results to both them and to management.

The audit function is independent of management's communication to users, but by adding credibility to the financial statements it affects those statements. The auditor gathers evidence by which to judge the fairness of the financial statement presentation (see Exhibit 1.1). If misstatements are noted, the auditor will request that management take appropriate action to correct the errors, properly report any irregularities, and make necessary corrections to the financial statement presentation and/or footnotes. Third-party users receive the financial statements and the auditor's opinion as to whether or not the financial statements are presented fairly. The independent, unbiased opinion of the auditor adds credibility to the financial statements.

Assertions and Established Criteria

An **assertion** is a positive statement about an action, event, condition, or the performance of an entity or product over a specified period of time. When management presents financial statements, it is asserting that those statements are fairly presented as judged by the criterion of fairness within the broad context of generally accepted accounting principles. The assertions embodied in the financial statements provide directions for the design of the audit. For example, by showing inventory valued on the financial statements at $25 million, management is asserting that the inventory is owned, available for use, and properly valued at the lower of cost or market. Auditors can design programs to test those assertions.

To have unbiased and clear communication, criteria must exist whereby independent observers can assess whether or not such assertions are appropriate. Generally accepted accounting principles (GAAP) provide those criteria for financial statement audits.* Other criteria exist for other kinds of audits. An internal auditor performing an operational audit may refer to management's policies and procedures to determine effectiveness and efficiency of operational activities. An internal revenue agent refers to the tax code to assess the appropriateness of assertions contained in a tax return.

Obtaining and Evaluating Evidence

The auditor undertakes a systematic and objective process to obtain and evaluate evidence regarding assertions about an organization's financial transactions. Three of the elements of the process are particularly important to the audit function. First,

*Although GAAP provide criteria, a wide latitude still exists for auditor judgment. There are always new transactions for which authoritative pronouncements have not been issued to establish required accounting. Further, GAAP often provide for alternatives in treating apparently similar transactions.

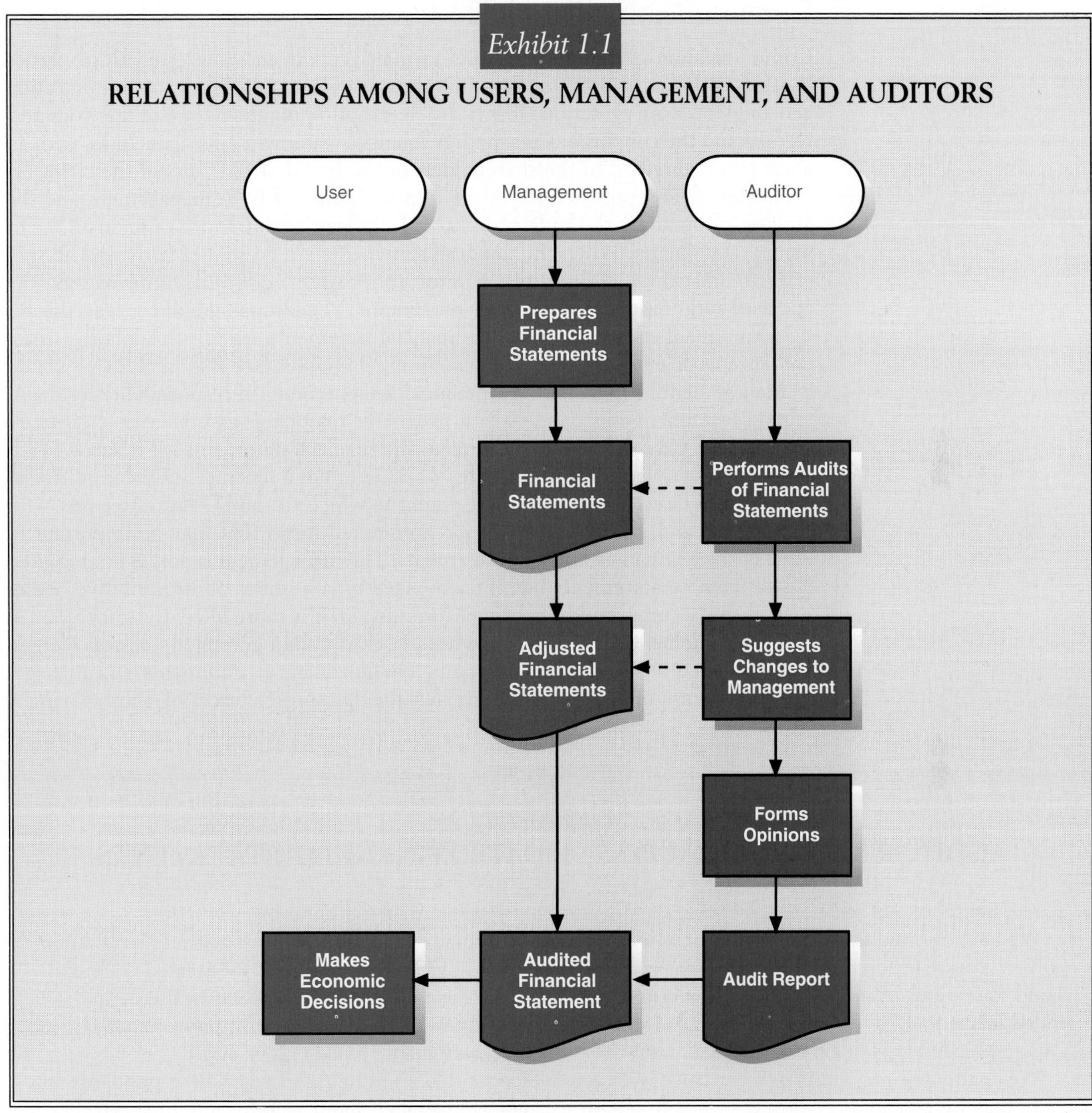

the process of auditing is to *gather evidence* to test assertions. Second, the audit process is *systematic*. A defined methodology is used to gather audit evidence to ensure that a sufficient amount of competent evidence is gathered. Third, an audit must be *objective*—that is, the auditor must be independent and the process unbiased. Unlike a lawyer who gathers evidence and filters through it to present a client's position in the best way possible, the auditor is not the client's advocate, but must objectively gather and evaluate evidence in terms of the assertions tested. Users depend on the auditor to make an unbiased evaluation of the evidence.

Communicating Results to Users

Communication of the audit results to management and interested third parties completes the audit process. To minimize misunderstandings, this communication generally follows a prescribed format by clearly outlining the nature of the work performed and the conclusions reached. A financial statement audit concludes with an audit report directed to the shareholders or the board of directors of the client organization. The report delineates the responsibilities of both management and the auditor, summarizes the audit process, and expresses the auditor's opinion on the financial statements. When the financial statements are presented fairly and no special circumstances require the auditor to provide additional information, the standard audit report includes three paragraphs. The last paragraph contains the auditor's unqualified opinion that the financial statements are presented fairly, in accordance with generally accepted accounting principles (see Exhibit 1.2).

Management's report on the same includes statements of responsibility for maintaining a system of adequate controls to provide reasonable assurance that assets are safeguarded, transactions are authorized, and financial statements are reliable. In addition, management's report indicates whether or not a separate audit committee of the board of directors exists and the extent to which the audit committee met with the internal and external auditors and considered items that may be important to users of the company's financial statements. The management report is not required for all financial statements but is encouraged by a number of authoritative bodies such as the Securities and Exchange Commission. It is more likely to be included in financial statements of companies whose stock is traded on major stock exchanges. The existence of a management report on the financial statements and management's assumption of responsibility for the fair presentation of those financial

Exhibit 1.2

AUDITOR'S REPORT ON CONSOLIDATED FINANCIAL STATEMENTS

To the Shareholders and Board of Directors of Champion International Corporation:

We have audited the accompanying consolidated balance sheet of Champion International Corporation (a New York Corporation) and subsidiaries as of December 31, 1994 and 1993, and the related consolidated statements of income, retained earnings, and cash flows for each of the three years in the period ended December 31, 1994. These financial statements are the responsibility of the company management. Our responsibility is to express an opinion on these financial statements based on our audit.

We conducted our audits in accordance with generally accepted auditing standards. Those standards require that we plan and perform the audit to obtain reasonable assurance about whether the financial statements are free of material misstatement. An audit includes examining, on a test basis, evidence supporting the amounts and disclosures in the financial statements. An audit also includes assessing accounting principles used and significant estimates made by management, as well as evaluating the financial statement presentation. We believe that our audits provide a reasonable basis for our opinion.

In our opinion, the financial statements referred to above present fairly, in all material respects, the financial position of Champion International Corporation and subsidiaries as of December 31, 1994 and 1993, and the results of their operations and their cash flows for each of the three years in the period ended December 31, 1994, in conformity with generally accepted accounting principles.

January 19, 1995 New York, N.Y.

statements does not in any way decrease the auditor's responsibility for gathering sufficient evidence to render an independent opinion on the fairness of those financial statements. Exhibit 1.3 is the management report to accompany the auditor's report in Exhibit 1.2.

Although the preceding discussion emphasizes audits of financial statements, the audit function is much broader. Internal auditors and governmental auditors perform a wide variety of attest functions. These functions, which are described in greater detail in Chapter 24, include operational analyses of company activities, analysis of departmental compliance with company policies, and analysis of the effectiveness of operations. An internal auditor often expresses an opinion on a facet of a company's operations that have been evaluated as to whether they follow the company's policies and procedures. An example of an internal auditor's summary report on an insurance company's medical claims operations is illustrated in Exhibit 1.4.

C–THE IMPORTANCE OF AUDITING IN OUR SOCIETY

The audit function is critical to the success of our economic system. It provides a reliable information base for subjecting management's performance to outside

Exhibit 1.3

MANAGEMENT'S REPORT ON CONSOLIDATED FINANCIAL STATEMENTS

MANAGEMENT REPORT
To Our Shareholders:

The management of Champion International Corporation is responsible for the integrity and objectivity of the financial statements and other information contained in this annual report. The financial statements were prepared in accordance with generally accepted accounting principles and reflect the management's best judgments and estimates.

The company maintains a system of internal controls designed to provide reasonable assurance assets are safeguarded, transactions are executed and recorded in accordance with its authorization, and financial records are maintained so as to permit the preparation of reliable financial statements. The system of internal controls is enhanced by written policies and procedures, an organizational structure providing appropriate segregation of duties, careful selection and training of qualified people, and a program of periodic audits performed by both internal auditors and independent public accountants.

The Audit Committee of the Board of Directors, consisting of directors who are not employees of the company, meets periodically with management, the internal auditors, and the independent public accountants to review the adequacy of corporate financial reporting, accounting systems and control, and internal and independent auditing functions.

Andrew C. Sigler
Andrew C. Sigler
Chairman and Chief Executive Officer

Kenwood C. Nichols
Kenwood C. Nichols
Vice Chairman

Exhibit 1.4

INTERNAL AUDIT REPORT

Transmittal Letter

Morton L. Fepplemeyer, Vice-President
West Coast Operations
Oakland, California

We recently completed an audit of medical claims processed and paid by Metro Health Maintenance Plan (Metro Plan) from May 20, 1994 (date of inception of the plan) to December 31, 1994.

Metro Plan was recently organized as a wholly owned subsidiary to administer all health plans for Hawker Industries' employees living in the Bay Area. Prior to May 20, 1994 health services to employees living in the Bay Area were provided by outside companies.

The audit was made for the initial period of operation to provide a basis for comparing claim costs with past and future periods. It was also made to assess the effectiveness of internal controls pertaining to the processing of medical claims. Our work was limited to analyses of systems, processes, and procedures and audit tests that we considered appropriate under these circumstances.

In general, we found that claim processing and payment procedures are well designed and implemented. Claims are generally paid in conformity with the "new plan," but claim-processing time is excessive. Completed claim files are well designed and generally orderly, but a problem exists in the manner of filing and locating claims in process. Also, the extended absence of a key data-processing employee, as a result of an automobile accident, has strained the system and has resulted in delays in obtaining key reports.

The accompanying report is provided for your information. A copy is also provided to the controller of Metro Plan, who is required by corporate policy to respond to the audit report within 60 days of its receipt.

We acknowledge the full cooperation and helpful assistance given by executives and staff of Metro Plan.

[signature]
Audit Team Leader
[or audit executive]

scrutiny by those to whom management is accountable. Accountability has clearly been the social and organizational backbone of accounting for centuries. Modern society and organizations depend upon intricate networks of accountability based on the recording and reporting of organizational activities. Accounting is essential to the free flow of information that influences resource-allocation decisions in a global economy.

The importance of auditing can best be seen by reviewing the diversity of potential users of an organization's financial statements. The users of an entity's financial statements include shareholders, potential investors, lending institutions, regulatory agencies, labor, academicians, indirect users (such as consumers), and the court system. In many cases, the interests of the various users can conflict. Current shareholders might want management to use accounting principles that result in higher levels of reported income, but lending institutions generally prefer a conservative approach to valuation and income recognition. Exhibit 1.5 presents an overview of potential financial statement users. It is crucial that an auditor know the potential

Exhibit 1.5

USERS OF AUDITED FINANCIAL STATEMENTS

User	Primary Use of Report
Management	Review performance, evaluate the reporting of complex transactions, make decisions affecting future directions of the organization.
Stockholders	Assess management accountability and stewardship; make decisions to increase, decrease, or maintain investment in an enterprise.
Financial Institutions	Determine whether or not to make a loan to the organization and assist in determining the amount and terms of the loan.
Taxing Authorities	Determine taxable income and tax due.
Potential Investors Mutual Funds Insurance Companies Other Organizations Individual Shareholders	Determine whether or not to invest in a company and at what price.
Regulatory Agencies State Insurance Commission Federal Trade Commission Securities & Exchange Commission Federal Deposit Insurance Corporation	Determine whether or not regulatory action is necessary to protect the public.
Labor and Labor Unions	Assess profitability of organization and potential for future wages and/or profit-sharing agreements.
Economists	Assess the effects of economic policies and the potential effect on political constituencies.
Bondholders and Potential Bondholders	Assess riskiness of company and its ability to repay indebtedness
Court System	Assess financial position of a company to assist in cases such as corporate bankruptcy or the valuation of an individual's assets for estate or lawsuit purposes.
Vendors	Assess credit risk
Indirect Users (Consumers)	Indirectly affected by the integrity of the financial reporting system. A breakdown in integrity will affect users as it affects the financial system.

users (and how financial statements may affect their decisions) because the accounting concept of materiality is based on items that would affect the decisions or decision-making processes of users.

The auditor has become an important intermediary in an accountability relationship. If the auditor adopts criteria that serve to maximize reported income at the expense of rational valuation, that action could be seen to result in bias toward some third-party users and against others. Thus, the auditor, the audit function, and the basic criteria for evaluating fairness of presentation (GAAP), must be independent of specific groups of users to lend credibility to the financial statements.

The Need for Unbiased Reporting

The need for unbiased reporting can easily be seen by examining a situation in which a bank is considering a local company's loan request. In preparing its report, the management of the company wishes to obtain the loan and prefers that its auditors agree with its own assessment of its financial accomplishments. Management also realizes the importance of reliable information. The bank relies on the financial statements of the company, among other data, to assess the risk of the loan—the likelihood that the company will be able to repay the loan and its interest in a timely fashion. If the loan is made at a good rate, the bank will prosper and may be able to offer higher savings rates to attract more depositors. The company receiving the loan may be able to expand, hire new workers, and increase the community's work force. All parties benefit. But if this loan and others like it fail, the bank may have insufficient reserves to meet depositor demands. These depositors (ordinary consumers) may not be able to withdraw their funds when they go to the bank. Then the bank may need public assistance from the Federal Deposit Insurance Corporation, or the depositors will lose their savings. Clearly, the more accurate the financial information provided the bank, the more positive the overall results of its decision will be, not merely for the company and the bank but also for society as a whole.

Although reliable financial information is essential, it alone is not a guarantee of success. Banks can still make bad loan decisions, and other economic events can intervene to turn a good loan into a bad one. All parties are best served, however, when the integrity of the financial reporting system is beyond reproach.

Expectations for Auditors

Various elements of society have different expectations of auditors. For example, management may expect different things than users do.

Management Expectations of Auditors

Management regards the independent public accountant as an outside source of expertise on accounting matters. It expects the auditor to make recommendations to improve its accounting system and other operations.

Management often has public accountants provide tax services and perform analyses of various operations similar to those performed by internal auditors. Such analyses assess the efficiency and effectiveness of operations within the organization and evaluate the compliance of departments or divisions with management policies and procedures.

User Expectations of Auditors in Performing Attest Function

Users expect the auditor to gather sufficient evidence to support the audit opinion, to be unbiased in the generation and evaluation of that evidence, and to judge the fairness of the economic presentations so that the reports do not discriminate among potential users. As our economic system and the nature of financial transactions have become more complex and the general public has become more knowledgeable, user expectations of the profession have risen. In 1978, the Commission on Auditor's Responsibilities stated:

> Users expect the auditor to evaluate the measurements and disclosures made by management and to determine whether the financial statements are misleading, even if they technically conform with authoritative accounting pronouncements. . . . Users of financial statements expect auditors to penetrate into company affairs, to exert surveillance over management, and to take an active part in improving the quality and extent of financial disclosure.[6]

The Lou Harris poll cited earlier also refers to a high level of user expectations. Almost half of the users surveyed felt the auditor should be responsible for detecting and reporting management fraud. Although many of the users' expectations seem reasonable, there is a danger that the audit report will be viewed as a "certificate of health" for a company:

> The most serious consequences stemming from such a misunderstanding is that the independent auditor can quickly be portrayed as the force that represents all good in financial accounting and the guarantor of anything positive anyone wants to feel about a given company.[7]

The profession must be responsive to user needs, but users must be aware of exactly what auditors ensure. Auditors ensure that unbiased information is presented so that users can make their own assessment of an organization's health and future prospects. Users can reasonably expect the audited financial statements to be

- Complete and contain all important financial disclosures.
- Free from *material* errors or irregularities.
- Presented fairly according to the substance of generally accepted accounting principles.

Being free from *material* errors is not the same as being free of *all* errors. This concept will be discussed later. The auditing profession strives to heighten user understanding and minimize the level of miscommunication between the auditor and the users.

D–REQUIREMENTS TO ENTER THE PUBLIC ACCOUNTING PROFESSION

Meeting management and user expectations requires considerable expertise. Because of the increasing complexity of the business environment, the demands made on you as a professional auditor certainly will increase. The public accounting profession, in recognition of this trend, has responded in part by recommending that the number of hours required for membership in the American Institute of CPAs be increased to 150 semester hours (225 quarter hours) by the year 2000. Beyond required auditing and accounting skills, today's auditor must be able to identify problems and propose solutions; understand economic and political conditions; utilize computer technology; communicate effectively with management, users, and colleagues; and identify elements of business risk.

Accounting and Auditing Expertise

The complexity of today's environment demands that the auditor be fully versed in the technical accounting and auditing pronouncements. In addition to that technical understanding, the auditor must have a sound conceptual understanding of the basic elements underlying financial reporting. This conceptual understanding is necessary to address the ever-increasing infusion of new types of transactions and contracts for which accounting pronouncements do not exist. Interest rate swaps are one example of such new developments. In these transactions, one entity agrees to swap a variable rate of interest on one liability to another entity for a fixed interest rate liability. The auditor's reasoning must be based on general accounting concepts to determine the most appropriate accounting treatment and disclosure of the economic risks associated with the swaps.

Likewise, tomorrow's auditor must fully understand the fundamental concepts of auditing. Understanding these concepts, in addition to particular rules, is necessary to be able to assess the reliability of the alternative sources of evidence that may be available in the highly complex and integrated computer systems that now permeate businesses.

Knowledge of Business and Its Risks

Financial statements must reflect the underlying substance of accounting transactions and the economic effects of such transactions. To ensure that this objective is being accomplished, the auditor must have a good understanding of the nature of the audit client and the business risks associated with the client's industry. The auditor of a chemical company, for example, must understand the complexity of issues associated with the Environmental Protection Agency's mandate to clean up toxic waste sites and must be able to determine whether or not the client has potential liability for toxic waste cleanup. Similarly, an auditor of a financial institution must be able to assess the risks associated with farm loans, oil loans, or Third World loans. Auditors also must understand a client's industry to be able to comprehend financial transactions unique to that particular industry; for example, an auditor should know whether products of a client's competitor could cause a portion of the client's inventory to become obsolete.

Understanding Accounting System Complexity

Simple, manual accounting systems are things of the past. Instead, depending on the size of the client's enterprise, the auditor will encounter either a small, stand-alone computer system or a large, integrated system. Many such accounting systems are becoming, in whole or in part, paperless. Such systems record original entries for the receipt of goods and the payment of vendor invoices without creating paper documentation. Today's auditors must understand the challenges posed in auditing a system in which traditional source documents do not exist.

E–DIVERSITY OF AUDIT PRACTICE

Auditing is not confined to attesting to financial statements. Auditing services are diverse, from the evaluation of a division's performance for management, to the examination of the economy and efficiency of governmental operations, to the independent attestation of whether a microcomputer program prepares tax returns in compliance with applicable tax law. Although many of these services can be performed by all the audit groups identified below, we will illustrate the breadth of services performed by each professional audit group: certified public accountants, internal auditors, and governmental auditors.

The Public Accounting Profession

The public accounting profession has been granted the sole license to perform the independent audit of a company's financial statements. In performing an audit, the certified public accountant (CPA) must adhere to generally accepted auditing standards (GAAS) in determining whether the financial statements comply with generally accepted accounting principles (GAAP).

Audits of an Organization's Financial Statements

The public accounting profession is unique in that it has been granted the sole license to perform independent audits of an organization's financial statements, therefore, the terms CPA or public accounting profession are often associated with financial statement audits. The profession has established two sets of specific standards to govern the performance of financial statement audits. These standards are referred to as **generally accepted auditing standards (GAAS),** which pertain to the conduct of the audit examination, and generally accepted accounting principles (GAAP), which present criteria by which the auditor judges the fairness of the financial presentation. The certified public accountant must be knowledgeable in both the discipline of auditing and the discipline of accounting. The two are interrelated but separate.

Generally Accepted Auditing Standards

The profession has adopted generally accepted auditing standards to provide overall guidance for the conduct of audits and to set a minimum standard of acceptable practice. The auditor is required to specify whether the audit was performed in accordance with GAAS. These standards—and the practices and procedures mandated under them—are not static. They continue to evolve as the auditing environment itself evolves. As a result, today's auditor is embarking on a career of continual learning. An overview of these guiding standards (GAAS) is presented in Chapter 2.

Generally Accepted Accounting Principles

Generally accepted accounting principles provide the criteria against which the auditor measures the fairness of financial statement presentation. The term *generally accepted accounting principles* is technical; it encompasses the conventions, rules, and procedures that define generally accepted accounting practice at a particular point in time. The auditor looks for authoritative guidance, such as the pronouncements of the Financial Accounting Standards Board (FASB) and long-standing industry practices in evaluating the quality of an organization's financial presentations. When auditors encounter new or unusual transactions for which no authoritative pronouncements exist, they are required to exercise professional judgment to determine the substance of the transaction and then reason by analogy with other accounting principles to determine the appropriate form for financial reporting. Many accounting issues cannot be solved simply by looking for an authoritative pronouncement; professional judgment to analyze a transaction and determine the economic consequences for a client is also required.

Accounting Services Other Than Audits of Financial Statements

Public accounting is not limited to auditing. Public accounting firms have broad areas of expertise that may benefit client organizations. Some clients do not need audits but require the accounting services of a CPA. These other accounting services include the preparation of financial statements for smaller businesses, advice on the appropriate accounting treatment for complex transactions, and the preparation of projected financial results which might occur in conjunction with a proposed project. In such situations, the auditor is not engaged to perform an audit. To prevent others from associating the performance of these services with the financial statement audit, the auditor must disclaim an opinion on the financial statements and state clearly that the scope of the work done was significantly less than an audit.

Attestation Services Other Than Audits of Financial Reports

The dramatic increase in the amount of data contained in large computerized databases is creating a demand for assurances on the validity of the data and the reports generated from them. This demand has led one CPA firm partner to predict that the profession is "on the brink of what could be an explosion of the basic attest function."[8] Examples of **attestation services** other than those of financial statements include audits of financial forecasts, financial projections, computer software performance, contract compliance, and the accuracy of other management reports. The profession demands the same level of professional competence in performing these attestation services as that required in performing financial statement audits.

Other Services Performed by the Public Accounting Profession

Nonattestation services provided by public accounting firms have evolved with changing demands for both accounting and related expertise. Of annual billings in excess of $2 billion generated by some public accounting firms, more than half of this total comes from services that are not audit-related. These other services include tax assistance, consulting, and litigation support.

Tax Services. Many CPAs specialize in performing tax services for their clients, and users have come to recognize CPAs as tax experts. Most CPA firms prepare both corporate and individual tax returns and provide additional assistance in estate planning, merger and acquisition analysis, and corporate restructuring. Tax work represents as much as 20 percent of the annual revenue of large, international CPA firms and can represent as much as 80 to 90 percent of the revenue for smaller CPA firms.

Consulting Services. Consulting has evolved as clients have come to recognize that the breadth of the CPA's expertise could provide significant insight and assistance in dealing with organizational problems. Consulting services initially focused on accounting systems and related financial areas. Today, however, many firms have added specialists to deal with the ever-increasing diversity of problems organizations face in such areas as production management, facility location, systems design, computer-integrated manufacturing, merger and acquisition analysis, and marketing strategy. In some firms, the consulting services represent the area of fastest growth. Consulting revenue ranges from 15 to 45 percent of the total revenue of the largest public accounting firms. To avoid potential impairment of independence, many CPA firms have set up separate divisions to handle consulting engagements.

Litigation Support Services. Litigation is an important part of the business world. As litigation becomes more complex, accountants are often called on to provide detailed analysis of damages or to assist juries in understanding complex accounting or auditing problems. Many firms have adjusted to this challenge by forming litigation support departments.

Public Accounting Firms—Organization and Size

The organization hierarchy of CPA firms has historically been described as a pyramidal structure (see Exhibit 1.6). Partners (or owners) form the top of the pyramid and are responsible for the overall conduct of each audit and the audit reports the firm issues. Next in the hierarchy are the managers, who review the detailed audit work performed by staff personnel (shown at the base of the pyramid). Supervisors are responsible for overseeing the day-to-day activities on an individual audit. Staff personnel typically spend two to four years at a staff level, after which they increasingly assume supervisory responsibilities as seniors, managers, and ultimately partners. Partners and managers will be responsible for many audit engagements being conducted simultaneously while supervisors, seniors and staff will be assigned to only one audit at a time.

Evidence suggests that the organizational structure of CPA firms is beginning to change from the typical pyramid to one better represented by an elongated balloon (see Exhibit 1.6). As audits become more complex, there is a need for more auditors with analytical business skills and experience at the supervisory and middle manager level as well as for greater partner involvement. The detailed work previously performed by staff auditors is increasingly accomplished more quickly and with greater efficiency through the use of computer-assisted audit techniques and microcomputer support systems. Today's auditor, therefore, can spend more time analyzing a client's financial reports. As a result, new auditors will encounter the exciting challenges offered by the profession more quickly than in the past.

Diversity in Size of CPA Firms

As someone about to enter the profession, you are probably aware of the wide differences that exist in the size and scope of firms performing public accounting services. For example, most accounting students have heard of the Big Six international public accounting firms. Although the Big Six firms are significantly larger than

Exhibit 1.6

ORGANIZATIONAL STRUCTURE OF CPA FIRMS

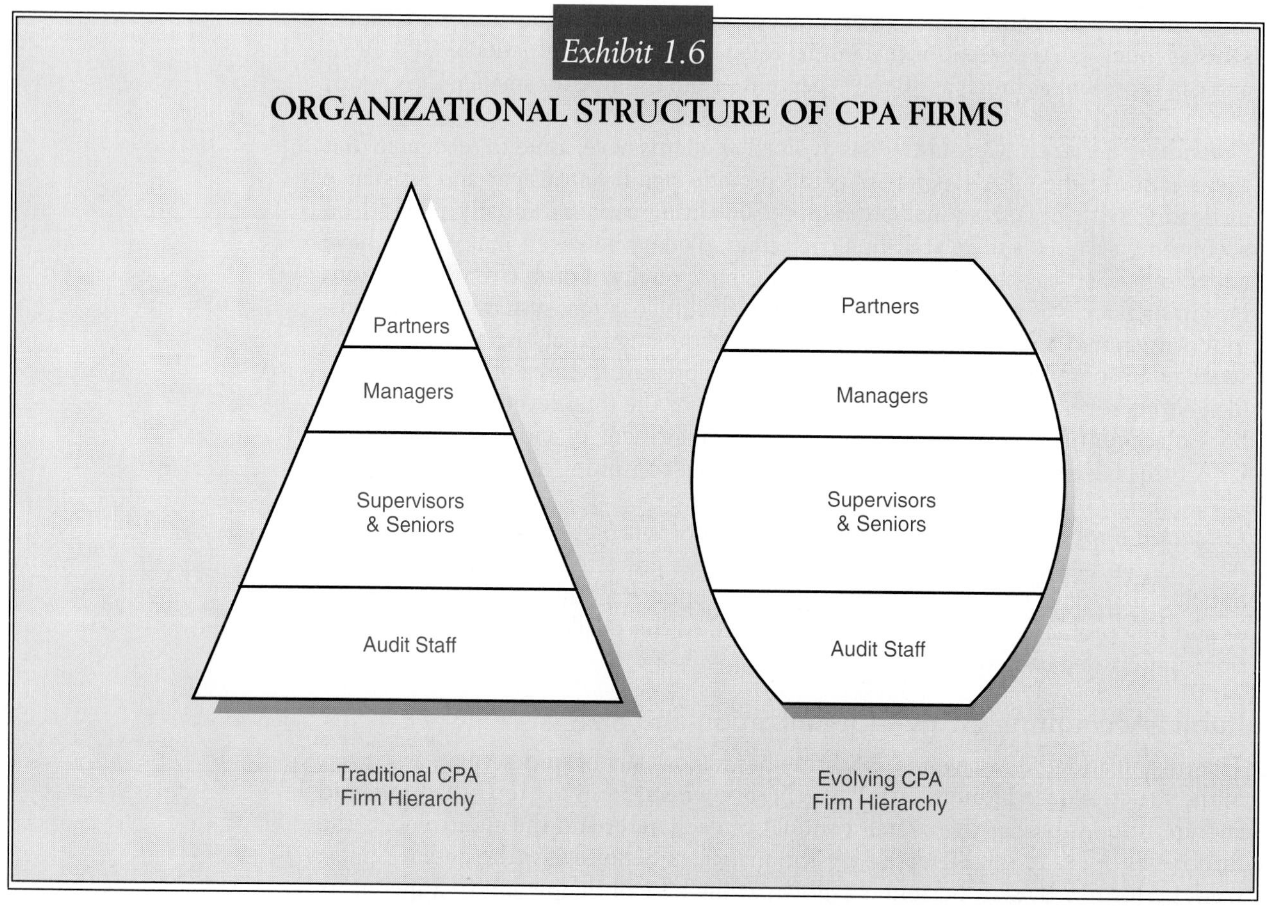

other national firms, there is a diversity among the top 15 national and regional firms headquartered in such areas as Des Moines; South Bend; Los Angeles; New York; and Chicago. In addition to these firms, thousands of local firms with from 1 to 10 offices serve a specific city or portion of a state. The nature of competition among public accounting firms for clients is discussed more thoroughly in Chapter 5.

The size and geographic dispersion of public accounting firms are far from homogeneous. Many have grown to reflect changes in the business environment. As clients have grown, so have they. As businesses have become global in their orientation, CPA firms have merged or planned global growth so they are in a position to better serve large international clients. At the other end of the scale, a number of smaller, local CPA firms have developed special niches by providing accounting, auditing, and other services to smaller businesses in their immediate business community. Some of these smaller local firms perform little or no audit work for their clients but concentrate on providing accounting and other services.

The Internal Audit Profession

Internal auditing is performed throughout the world in diverse environments and within organizations that vary in purpose, size, and structure. The field of internal auditing has experienced dynamic growth in recent years. This rapid growth has been fueled, in part, by three main developments:

- Management's need, in the complex, diversified corporate world for an independent appraisal of organizational or departmental performance.
- Increased internal and external emphasis on effective procedures to detect or prevent fraud.
- Management's need for thorough evaluations of organizational control, with special emphasis on sophisticated computer systems.

The scope of services performed by the internal auditor has expanded the internal auditor's role beyond that of serving as an "internal checker." Today's internal auditor's activities range widely within the major operational divisions and departments of an organization. This expanded scope has led to the recognition that internal auditing provides an excellent training ground for future management positions. The diversity of the **internal audit** profession can be seen in its definition:

> Internal auditing is an independent appraisal function established within an organization to examine and evaluate its activities as a service to the organization. The objective of internal auditing is to assist members of the organization in the effective discharge of their responsibilities. To this end, internal auditing furnishes them with analyses, appraisals, recommendations, counsel, and information concerning the activities reviewed.[9]

The internal audit profession has developed standards through the Institute of Internal Auditors (IIA) to govern the quality of the practice of internal auditing throughout the world. Although the types of audits performed may differ within companies, the standards to follow in performing those audits and in judging the quality remain the same. The types of audits performed by internal auditors can be classified, in general terms, as operational audits, compliance audits, financial audits, and computer system audits.

Operational Audits

Operational audits are designed to evaluate the economy and efficiency with which resources are employed. An operational audit can be applied to virtually every facet of an organization's operations. Such audits offer both challenge and interest because the auditor is charged with developing objective criteria by which an operation can be evaluated, and the auditor by necessity becomes intimately familiar with many operational aspects of an organization. The emphasis is not on historical financial processing but on operational effectiveness about which the auditor is expected to make constructive recommendations for improvement.

Compliance Audits

Management often wants to know whether its organizational policies are being complied with or whether external mandates, such as bond indenture restrictions, are being met. A telephone company policy, for example, stated that all maintenance or service requests should be answered within 24 hours. Management requested that internal auditors perform a **compliance audit** to evaluate the service department in relation to this standard. The internal auditors developed an audit program to determine whether the service department was efficiently meeting management's objectives.

Financial Audits

Financial audits are similar to those performed by the external auditor in the annual audit of a company's financial statements. The internal auditor evaluates the reliability of the financial records as well as the reliability and integrity of important financial processing systems. Since internal auditors are part of the organization, they are not in a position to provide independent attestation services to outside users. Often, however, they will coordinate this financial auditing work with that of the external auditor to provide a broad coverage at an economical cost for the organization.

Computer System Audits

Today's computer systems are becoming increasingly complex and are often integrated with other systems both within the organization and, ultimately, outside it. Because they operate within the organization, internal auditors have the unique ability to conduct regular audits of the computer systems throughout the year. Internal auditors often develop sophisticated techniques to monitor the effectiveness of computer controls and operations throughout the year.

Governmental Auditing Profession

Governmental auditors are employed by various state, local, and federal agencies. The work performed by these auditors ranges from internal audits of a specific agency to audits of other governmental units to audits of reports furnished to the government by outside organizations. The demand for accountability, and thus audits, of governmental agencies is best summarized in *Governmental Auditing Standards*, issued by the Comptroller General of the United States. The requirement of accountability has caused a demand for more information about government programs and services. Public officials, legislators, and private citizens want and need to know not only whether government funds are being handled properly and in compliance with laws and regulations but also whether government organizations, programs, and services are achieving the purposes for which they were authorized and funded and whether they are doing so economically and efficiently.

Governmental auditors perform all the types of audits that internal auditors perform; the major difference is the governmental orientation. The U.S. **General Accounting Office (GAO)** headed by the Comptroller General places a great deal of emphasis on performance audits. These audits have been defined to include audits pertaining to economy and efficiency and program audits. Economy and efficiency audits determine (1) whether the entity is acquiring, protecting, and using its resources economically and efficiently, (2) the causes of inefficiencies or uneconomical practices, and (3) whether the entity has complied with laws and regulations concerning matters of economy and efficiency.[10] Program audits determine (1) the extent to which the desired results or benefits established by the legislature or other authorizing body are being achieved, (2) the effectiveness of organizations, programs, activities, or functions, and (3) whether the entity has complied with laws and regulations applicable to the program.

The three largest audit agencies at the federal level are the GAO, the Internal Revenue Service (IRS), and the Defense Contract Audit Agency. The diversity of audits performed by the GAO is immense; it is responsible for auditing government activities ranging from national defense to health to the environment. The difficulty of GAO work is compounded by the fact that many legislative acts do not include measurable goals or objectives by which a program might be evaluated. As a result, some of the work of GAO auditors involves searching the literature and legislative intent in order to develop objective criteria by which to measure performance. In addition to their regular reports, auditors with the GAO are often asked to testify before Congress on the agency's findings; these can be politically sensitive issues.

F–PROFESSIONAL AND REGULATORY ORGANIZATIONS

Because the auditing profession exists to serve others, there is a need to assure the public that its services are performed competently and in the public interest. A combination of self-policing through professional organizations, such as the American Institute of Certified Public Accountants and regulatory agencies, such as the Securities and Exchange Commission, interact to monitor public practice and ensure high standards of performance.

The American Institute of Certified Public Accountants

The **American Institute of Certified Public Accountants** (more commonly referred to as the AICPA) is the primary governing organization of the public accounting profession. Membership in the AICPA is voluntary; its power derives from actions taken by its predecessor, the American Institute of Accountants (AIA). They convinced Congress and the Securities and Exchange Commission in the 1930s that self-regulation by highly trained professionals dedicated to the public interest would be effective in meeting third-party users' needs. The SEC, therefore, delegated responsibility for both standard-setting and policing of the profession to the AIA, which has been continued by the AICPA. The profession has responded well to self-regulation. Through the Committee on Accounting Principles and, later, the Accounting Principles Board, the AICPA undertook the monumental task of establishing generally accepted accounting principles. Similarly, through the Committee on Auditing Procedures, succeeded by the Auditing Standards Board, the AICPA issues pronouncements establishing generally accepted auditing standards. In the 1970s and 1980s, the profession was criticized for not remaining responsive to third-party needs. It has reacted in several ways, including opening the standard-setting process for financial accounting. In addition, the Auditing Standards Board recently issued a number of new auditing standards to help improve the level of practice. The profession now leaves to the Financial Accounting Standards Board (FASB) and the Governmental Accounting Standards Board (GASB)—independent bodies—the charge for issuing authoritative accounting pronouncements.

Today, the AICPA retains its responsibility for setting not only new auditing standards but also for establishing standards for other attestation services, accounting and review services, consulting services, and tax services. It carries on continuing education programs and, through its Board of Examiners, administers the Uniform CPA Examination.

The AICPA also develops standards for peer reviews and appoints committees to conduct peer reviews of practice units. Public accounting firms must be organized so that both the individuals in the firm and the firm itself achieve the required professional standards of independence, technical competence, and due professional care. Most firms have developed quality control standards to ensure that the profession's standards are met. Because users are generally not in a position to evaluate the competence or independence of a CPA, they must rely on the profession's ability to achieve these standards and to police noncompliance. The profession has taken an active role in "self-policing" by prescribing a peer review program that includes a comprehensive evaluation every three years of the CPA firm's policies, procedures, and audits. Finally, it has a special section to consider disciplinary action against members for breaches of the profession's code of ethics.

State Boards of Accountancy

CPAs are licensed by state boards of accountancy, which are charged with regulating the profession at the state level. Although all state boards require the passage of the Uniform CPA Examination as one of the criteria for licensure, experience requirements vary by state. Some states require candidates to have public accounting audit experience before issuing them a license to practice; other states allow audit experience related to public or governmental accounting. The work experience requirement can also vary with the level of education. A candidate with a graduate degree, for example, may need only one year of auditing experience, but a candidate with a baccalaureate degree may be required to have two years of auditing experience. Most states have reciprocal agreements for recognizing public accountants from other states; in some instances, however, a state may require either additional experience or course work before issuing a license.

The Securities and Exchange Commission

Under the Securities Exchange Act of 1934, the **Securities and Exchange Commission (SEC)** was established by Congress to regulate the capital markets system. The SEC's emphasis has been on full disclosure of financial information so that investors will have an informed basis on which to make judgments about trading in a security. The SEC was given the authority to establish GAAP for companies whose stock is publicly traded, although it has generally delegated this authority to the private sector—first to the AICPA (and its predecessor, the AIA) and then to the FASB. The SEC also has the ability to censure companies and prohibit them from operating before it.

The SEC actively participates in reviewing new accounting and auditing standards and is not reluctant to step in when it believes that the accounting principles a registrant company is using may result in misleading financial statements. In 1988, for example, the commission required Jiffy Lube International to change its accounting for franchise revenue, which reduced Jiffy Lube's earnings by 75 percent.[11] The decision was based on its finding that Jiffy Lube used the premature recognition of the sale of area development rights to increase its reported franchise income. The SEC had reservations about whether the revenue Jiffy Lube recognized was actually earned, and it forced the company to defer the recognition of development right sales as income until the company had performed specific, defined services for its franchisees.

The Institute of Internal Auditors

The Institute of Internal Auditors (IIA) is a voluntary organization dedicated to enhancing the professionalism and status of internal auditing. With currently more than 29,000 members located in 102 countries, the IIA is responsible for issuing standards and interpretations of those standards. In 1976 it issued the most recent revision of the *Statement of Responsibilities of Internal Auditors*, in 1980 the *Standards for the Professional Practice of Internal Auditing*, and in 1988 the revised *Code of Ethics for the Internal Auditor*. In addition, the institute administers the certified internal auditor program, which provides a benchmark measure of competence for the internal auditing profession.

The U.S. General Accounting Office

The U.S. General Accounting Office (GAO) is the nonpartisan audit agency for Congress. Congress has delegated to the GAO the responsibility for developing auditing standards for governmental audits. In 1988 the GAO issued a major revision of *Government Auditing Standards*, setting forth standards for the conduct of audits of governmental organizations, programs, activities, and functions, and of government funds received by contractors, nonprofit organizations, and other nongovernmental entities. The standards cover the auditor's professional qualifications, the quality of the audit effort, and the appropriate audit reports. The standards are similar to those established by the AICPA but relate to the nature of the work performed by governmental auditors and require additional audit procedures and reports appropriate to the funds accounting of governmental organizations and contracts.

The Court System

The court system acts as an effective restraint on the practice of auditing. Third parties may sue accountants under federal securities laws and various state statutes for substandard audit work. Although the profession often becomes alarmed when large damages are awarded to plaintiffs in suits against CPA firms, the courts serve to help ensure that the profession does not fail to meet its responsibilities to third parties. During the past two decades, court cases have led to the codification of additional auditing standards for such areas as related-party transactions, "subsequent events" affecting the financial statements, and clarification of the auditor's report.

Summary

Auditing is a concepts-driven and judgment-based discipline. The auditor must have the ability to define the relevant facts, gather evidence, and use professional judgment to determine fair presentation. Although some audit engagements can seem "routine," the challenge of auditing lies in dealing with a host of problems without clear definition and obvious solutions. Thus, it is important to understand the fundamental concepts of auditing and to develop the ability to apply those concepts to solving complex problems.

Auditing is environmentally influenced by changes in technology (particularly those related to information), changes in the business environment, and changes in user and public demands placed on the profession. Business has become more complex and international in scope. Tomorrow's auditor must understand the risks associated with every aspect of each client's business, which can range from the international economy to changes in product technology to government regulation.

The certified public accountant has been given a position of public trust. The American Institute of CPAs has responded to this through its committees and boards by issuing standards that define the minimum level of practice in this increasingly complex environment. The profession has earned a reputation for quality through its actions, including setting of standards against which you will be measured as a CPA and on which you will build a professional career. If the profession should ever fail to meet user needs, the court system will intervene to protect the public interest.

Significant Terms

American Institute of Certified Public Accountants (AICPA) The primary professional organization for the CPAs, it has a number of committees to develop professional standards for the conduct of audits and other services performed by its members and to self-regulate the profession.

assertion A positive statement about an action, event, condition, or the performance of an entity or product over a specified period of time; the subject of attestation services.

attestation services Provides an expression of an opinion by an auditor to third parties concerning the correctness of assertions contained in financial statements or other reports against which objective criteria can be identified and measured.

auditing A systematic process of objectively obtaining evidence regarding assertions about economic actions and events to ascertain the degree of correspondence between those assertions and established criteria and communicating the results to interested users.

compliance audit A systematic process to determine whether or not an entity's activities are carried out in accordance with standards or policies promulgated by management or in some cases by a regulatory agency for the conduct of the entity's activities.

financial audit A systematic process to determine whether an entity's financial statements or other financial results are fairly presented in accordance with GAAP, if applicable, or another comprehensive basis of accounting.

General Accounting Office (GAO) Governmental organization directly accountable to the Congress of the United States that performs special investigations for the Congress and establishes broad standards for the conduct of governmental audits.

Generally Accepted Auditing Standards (GAAS) Measures adopted by the AICPA to guide the practice of auditing within the public accounting profession in the United States.

internal audit An independent appraisal function established within an organization to examine and evaluate the activities of a division or department within it by providing operational, compliance, computer, and financial audits.

operational audit A systematic appraisal of an entity's operations, usually conducted by an internal auditor, to determine whether an organization's operations are being carried out in an efficient manner and whether constructive recommendations for operational improvements can be made.

Securities and Exchange Commission (SEC) The governmental body with the oversight responsibility to ensure the proper and efficient operation of capital markets in the United States.

Review Questions

A–Introduction

1–1 What is the "special function" that CPAs perform? Whom does the public accounting profession serve in performing this special function?

B–Auditing Defined

1–2 Define the term *auditing*. What are the major elements of the audit process?

1–3 What is an attestation function? What are major factors that create a demand for the performance of attestation services by the public accounting profession?

C–The Importance of Auditing in our Society

1–4 How does complexity affect (1) the demand for auditing services and (2) the performance of auditing services?

1–5 It has been stated that established criteria are necessary for the conduct of an audit. What serves as the primary established criteria against which financial statements are judged? What serves as the primary established criteria against which governmental financial statements are judged?

1–6 Identify five users of audited financial statements. Briefly indicate why independently audited financial statements are important to each user.

1–7 What is the role of the Securities and Exchange Commission in setting accounting and auditing standards?

1–8 In your opinion, is the most important user of an auditor's report on a company's financial statements company management, the company's shareholders, or the company's creditors? Briefly explain your rationale and indicate how potential conflicts in the needs of the three parties should be resolved by auditors.

D–Requirements to Enter the Profession

1–9 Why is it important that a certified public accountant fully understand the client's business and the business risks associated with specific clients?

1–10 Why might the typical pyramid structure of a public accounting firm be changing? What factors might be causing the change? What are the implications of such changes for the profession?

1–11 In what ways does the practice of internal auditing differ from the practice of public accounting?

E–Diversity of Audit Practice

1–12 Why is certification important to the public accounting and internal auditing profession? What are the major certifications of the public accounting and internal auditing professions? In what ways does the internal audit certification differ from the external audit certification?

1–13 In addition to auditing, what are the major services provided by public accounting firms to their clients? Why would a CPA firm expand to provide these additional services? Is it possible for a firm to be referred to as a CPA firm or a public accounting firm if it does not provide audit services?

1–14 What is an operational audit? Why might management want operational audits to be performed by its internal audit department?

1–15 What factors would explain the major differences in the sizes of CPA firms?

1–16 Are small, local CPA firms that serve only small businesses and other local clients subject to the same auditing and accounting standards as the large international CPA firms? If there are differences, what is the rationale for the differences?

1–17 How does an audit enhance the quality of financial statements? Does an audit ensure a fair presentation of a company's financial statements? Explain.

1–18 Why might CPA firms provide accounting and bookkeeping services for clients?

1–19 Compare the responsibility of management for the fair presentation of a company's financial statements with that of the auditor. In what ways does management's acknowledgment of its responsibilities change the auditor's responsibilities?

1–20 Who is primarily responsible for choosing the accounting principles that are used to portray the company's financial position and results? Explain.

F–Professional and Regulatory Organizations

1–21 What is the General Accounting Office (GAO)? What types of audits does it perform? What is its role in setting standards for municipal audits, for example, audits by the local state government?

1–22 What is the role of the AICPA in setting accounting and auditing standards and in policing the profession to ensure the performance of high-quality services by members of the public accounting profession?

1–23 Why is the court system identified as a major regulatory body for the public accounting profession? Does the court system have a role in setting either accounting or auditing standards? Explain.

1–24 What is the communication process as it pertains to the performance of the external auditor's attest function? How does the auditing profession ensure clear communication between auditors and interested third parties?

Multiple Choice Questions

1–25 In determining the primary responsibility of the external auditor for a company's financial statements, the auditor owes primary allegiance to

a. The management of the company being audited because the auditor is hired and paid by management.

b. The audit committee of the company being audited because that committee is responsible for coordinating and reviewing all audit activities within the company.

c. Stockholders, creditors, and the investing public.

d. The Securities and Exchange Commission because the SEC determines accounting principles and auditor responsibility.

1–26 Which of the following would not represent one of the primary problems that would lead to the demand for independent audits of a company's financial statements?

a. Management bias in preparing financial statements.

b. The increasing globalization of business and financial markets.

c. The complexity of transactions affecting financial statements.

d. The remoteness of the user from the organization and thus the inability of the user to directly obtain financial information from the company.

1–27 The independent auditor's unqualified opinion on a company's financial statements contains all of the following except

a. An identification of management's responsibility for the financial statements.

b. An opinion on the fairness of financial presentation as judged by adherence to generally accepted accounting principles.

c. A statement that the auditor assessed significant estimates made by management as a basis for financial statement presentation.

d. A statement that the financial statements have been prepared on a basis consistent with that of the previous period.

1–28 Management's report on a company's financial statements acknowledges management's responsibility for all of the following except

a. Monitoring the independence of the auditor and the completeness of the auditor's work.

b. The objectivity and integrity of the financial statements.

c. The responsibility for designing and maintaining an adequate system of internal controls.

d. Choosing the accounting principles that reflect management's best judgments and estimates.

1–29 According to a 1978 study by the AICPA, users expect auditors to

a. Evaluate whether or not the financial statements are misleading, even if they technically conform with authoritative pronouncements.

b. Evaluate whether management's policies comply with applicable laws and regulations.

c. Communicate whether the organization's controls would allow errors to occur that might not be detected by management.

d. Do all of the above.

1–30 Users can reasonably expect audited financial statements to be all of the following *except*

a. Complete, with adequate disclosures of all items of a material financial nature.

b. Free of all financial fraud.

c. Presented fairly according to the substance of generally accepted accounting principles.

d. Free of all material errors or irregularities that could reasonably be discovered through the application of generally accepted auditing standards.

1–31 An operational audit performed by an internal auditor is best described as

a. An audit of a company's compliance with management's policies and procedures.

b. An evaluation of a company's operations to determine if the company is susceptible to fraud or other material irregularities.

c. Audits of the operations of a company's computer systems.

d. An audit of a company's operations to determine the economy and efficiency with which resources are employed.

e. All of the above.

1–32 The General Accounting Office is responsible for all of the following *except*

a. Developing standards for audits of federal agencies.

b. Developing standards for audits of state agencies.

c. Performing special investigations at the request of Congress.

d. Developing standards for public accounting audits of governmental audits by which the public accounting firm reports to the governmental agency.

e. All of the above.

1–33 The American Institute of CPAs (AICPA) is a private governing organization of the public accounting profession that does all of the following *except*

a. Issues accounting standards dictating acceptable accounting practice for audited financial statements.

b. Issues auditing standards dictating acceptable auditing practice for audits of financial statements.

c. Establishes standards for attestation services other than audits.

d. Prepares and grades the Uniform CPA Examination.

1–34 Which of the following organizations has the ultimate authority to issue accounting pronouncements for publicly traded companies in the United States?

a. AICPA.

b. FASB.

c. SEC.

d. GAO.

Discussion and Research Questions

1–35 (Users of Financial Statements) It has been stated that auditing must be neutral because audited financial statements must serve the needs of a wide variety of users. If the auditor were to favor one group, such as existing shareholders, there might be a bias against another group, such as prospective investors.

Required:

a. What steps has the public accounting profession taken to minimize potential bias toward important users and thereby encourage neutrality in financial reporting and auditing?

b. Who are the primary users of audited financial statements? Identify four or five that you believe are the most important. For each one identified, briefly indicate their primary use of the financial statements. For each user identified, indicate how an accounting treatment might benefit one party and potentially act to the detriment of another user.

1-36 (Purposes of an External Audit) Olson Company, a medium-size manufacturer of products marketed in the Midwest, recently was persuaded by its banker to have its annual financial statements audited. The company has been growing at a rate of 20 percent per year, and the current year's sales volume is approaching $20 million. The company had used an accounting firm to perform some accounting but has not done so since it installed a computer system four years ago.

Required:

a. Briefly describe the objectives of an independent audit.

b. Identify the ways in which the external audit may have specific benefit to Olson Company.

c. Identify some of the points that might be discussed by management in determining whether to have the audit performed by a Big Six firm, a large regional firm, or a local CPA firm.

1–37 (Internal Audit Profession) The internal audit profession has grown rapidly in the last decade and has developed its own certification program. Many companies are developing policies to recruit new personnel into internal audit departments directly from college campuses as opposed to an earlier approach that focused on hiring CPAs.

Required:

a. Briefly describe the audits (operational, compliance, financial, and computer system) performed by internal auditors.

b. Would the internal audit profession have a competitive advantage in performing each of the four types of internal audits over external auditors? Briefly indicate why or why not.

c. What might be the primary arguments for hiring individuals into internal auditing who are not CPAs or who might not even be trained in accounting?

1–38 (Organization of CPA Firms) Numerous authorities have predicted that the organization structure of CPA firms will change dramatically during this decade and that the typical pyramid structure of public accounting firms will be lost.

Required:

a. Briefly explain the rationale for the pyramid organization structure of public accounting firms as it has existed during the past two decades.
b. What forces might be causing that structure to change?
c. Briefly discuss the implications of the change in CPA firm organization structure on (1) the career path for CPAs in public accounting, (2) the nature of the work performed by auditors in public accounting, and (3) technology as a force in changing the organization structure of the firms.

1–39 (Auditor Communication) Many annual reports contain reports from both management and the outside auditors.

Required:

a. Briefly describe the major differences in the reports from management and the reports from the outside auditors.
b. How does the auditor's responsibility for the financial statements differ from management's responsibility?
c. What criteria does the auditor reference as a basis for judging the fairness of a company's financial statements?
d. Based on your reading of the standard audit report, what is an audit?

1–40 (Auditing Professions) Briefly describe the roles and responsibilities of the following professional organizations in developing and maintaining auditing standards and monitoring the quality of the various auditing professions:

a. American Institute of CPAs.
b. Institute of Internal Auditors.
c. General Accounting Office.
d. Securities and Exchange Commission.

1–41 (Audit Skills and Training) You have been talking with one of your close colleagues regarding graduate school. Your colleague has decided to go to graduate school to obtain additional training to become a bank loan officer. You have decided to go to graduate school to further develop your skills for entry into the auditing profession. The discussion eventually focuses on the relative worth of one subject matter to the career of the other area of study.

Required:

a. Briefly explain why additional knowledge in the area of finance and banking would be important in developing your skills as an auditor.
b. Briefly explain to your colleague why knowledge of the audit function would be useful in pursuing a career as a bank loan officer.

c. How might an internal audit department perform (1) an operational audit of procedures related to the loan function and (2) a compliance audit of the loan function?

1–42 (Internal Auditing) You are aware that most of the first courses in auditing focus on the external auditing function and spend very little time on internal auditing. Yet your professor states that most of the concepts related to audit approach and evidence gathering are applicable to both internal and external auditing. However, you have not yet evaluated a potential career in internal auditing as opposed to a career in public accounting.

Required:

a. If you decide to start your career in internal auditing, how do you expect that your first two years of work might differ from your first two years had you started in public accounting?
b. Consider a medium-size manufacturing firm. Describe how an operational audit might be conducted in the following areas: (1) the treasury function, (2) inventory management and control, (3) customer service, and (4) computerized order entry.
c. Assume that you are interested in eventually developing your skills as a manager in a large organization. Explain why beginning a career in internal auditing would be compatible with those objectives.

1–43 (Nature of Auditing and the Public Accounting Profession) You and a colleague are carrying on a heated discussion. The colleague makes a number of statements about the public accounting profession that you believe are in error. Welcoming an opportunity for rebuttal, you are ready to reply.

Required:

a. For each of the statements listed below, develop a brief response indicating erroneous assumptions made by the colleague or your agreement with the statements.
b. Cite relevant evidence in support of your response.

Colleague's Statements

1. "Auditing does not serve a worthwhile purpose in our society. It neither creates goods nor adds utility to existing goods. The only reason for the existence of the auditing profession is that it has been legally mandated."
2. "The failure of the public accounting profession to warn us of the problems that emerged in connection with the savings and loan industry is one more example of a profession not adding utility to society."
3. "The only reason I would hire an auditor is with the expectation that the auditor search for and find any fraud that might exist within my company. Searching for fraud should be the primary focus of an audit."

4. "Auditors cannot legitimately serve the 'user' public because they are hired and fired by the management of the company being audited. If management does not like the opinion given by an auditor, it can simply hire another auditing firm that would be more amenable to the arguments made by management."
5. "Auditors cannot add significant value to financial statements as long as GAAP allows such diversity in accounting principles. How, for example, can the same auditor issue unqualified opinions on identical companies—one that uses FIFO and the other LIFO to account for the same set of transactions—recognizing that the reported income and balance sheets will be materially different? How can both be fairly presented?"
6. "Auditing is narrow—just nitpicking and challenging the organization in an attempt to find mistakes. I would rather pursue a career where I really understand a company's business and would be in a position to make recommendations that would improve it."
7. "The auditor's report is of limited value because the auditor attempts to assign the major responsibility for the financial statements—including errors in the statements—to the management of the firm. If management is responsible, what does the auditor add?"
8. "I might be interested in getting a CPA, but it is just another credential, much like an MBA. The primary reason for obtaining a CPA is to enhance market value and opportunities outside of public accounting."
9. "To be successful in public accounting, an individual must be a cold and calculating type, almost antisocial, in fact, to maintain the needed skepticism to challenge companies and to find fraud."
10. "The auditor's report admits that transactions are evaluated only on a 'test' basis; thus, the results embodied within an auditor's report must be treated with a great deal of skepticism. Test basis, indeed—sounds like a professor attempting to determine how well I will do in my career by writing exams that have very little to do with the real world."

1–44 (Types of Audits) Internal audits, as well as audits conducted by external auditors, can be classified as (1) operational audits, (2) compliance audits, (3) computer system audits, and (4) financial audits.

Required:

a. For each of the audit procedures listed below, briefly indicate which of these four classifications best describes the nature of the audit being conducted.

b. Briefly indicate the type of auditor (public accounting firm, internal auditor, or governmental auditor) that would most likely perform each of the audits.

Audits Procedures Conducted

1. Evaluate the policies of the Department of Housing and Urban Development to determine their adequacy.

2. Determine the presentation in conformity with GAAP of a municipality's statement of operations for the year just ended.
3. Evaluate the procedures used by the service department of a telephone utility to respond to customer maintenance. Determine whether responses are timely and are correctly and completely billed.
4. Determine the costs of a municipality's garbage pickup and disposal and compare these costs to those for similar services that might be obtained by contracting with a private contractor.
5. Determine whether all temporary investments by a company have been made in accordance with company policies and procedures and whether or not cash is handled economically and efficiently to maximize the benefits to the organization.
6. Conduct a tour of a manufacturing plant as a basis for viewing and determining the extent of waste and inefficiency. Study alternatives that might be utilized to cut down waste and inefficiency.
7. Prepare an analysis of projected revenues and expenses associated with the opening of a greyhound racing park. The analysis includes a review of assumptions and similar expenses located at other dog racing parks. The report will be sent to potential investors and lenders.
8. Review the operations of an organization that has received a government grant to assist in training the jobless. The grant specifies criteria that must be utilized in using the grant money for job retraining, and so on. The audit is designed to determine whether such criteria are being utilized by the grantee organization.
9. Analyze the financial statements of a company that has been targeted for a takeover. Present your analysis to management and the board of directors.

1–45 (Public Accounting Profession) The chapter contains the following quote from Lou Harris and Associates regarding the public accounting profession and users' assumption that the audit report can be used as a "certificate of health" for a company:

> "The most serious consequences stemming from such a misunderstanding is that the independent auditor can quickly be portrayed as the force that represents all good in financial accounting and the guarantor of anything positive anyone wants to feel about a given company."

Required:

a. Why is public accounting often viewed as a guarantor of results or even as a provider of assurance that one's investment is of high quality?
b. To what extent is it reasonable to view the auditor as a guarantor? Explain.
c. How does the auditing profession work to create or communicate a reasonable set of expectations that users should hold?
d. To what extent do you believe that user expectations of the public accounting profession appear to you to be unwarranted? Explain.

1–46 **(Research Problem)** User expectations of auditors may differ markedly from goals that the profession is capable of meeting. For example, the

Commission on Auditor's Responsibilities stated that users expect "the auditor to evaluate the measurements and disclosures made by management to determine whether the financial statements are misleading, even if they technically conform with authoritative accounting pronouncements." Similarly, surveys by Lou Harris and Associates indicate that many users expect the auditors to detect fraud.

Required:

a. Review recent studies or news articles that comment on auditor responsibilities. Evaluate the recommendations made regarding audit responsibilities and indicate whether or not you believe the recommendations are reasonable. Briefly support your opinion.

1–47 **(Research Problem)** Users must be confident that the auditing profession is competent and independent in relation to the specific areas being audited. One way in which a profession communicates its commitment to quality services is by requiring auditor certification as an initial indication of competence. Thus, auditors are certified as CPAs, CIAs (certified internal auditors), and CISAs (certified information systems auditors).

Required:

a. Review literature relating to the development of a profession and critique the role of certification as a factor in achieving professionalism.
b. Briefly review the nature of the CPA, CIA, and CISA exams and indicate how they differ in their coverage and nature.
c. In which significant ways does the licensing related to the CPA exam differentiate it from the CIA and CISA exams? Which organizations issue each license or certificate?
d. In what significant ways does the certification program of the CIAs differ from that of the CPA program?

Cases

1–48 In a recent report to Congress entitled: "Superfund: A More Vigorous and Better Managed Enforcement Program is Needed," the GAO made the following observations:

> Because cost recovery has been considered a low priority within EPA [the Environmental Protection Agency] and received limited staff resources, it has faltered.
>
> To provide a systematic approach for implementing its Superfund enforcement initiatives, EPA should establish long-term, measurable goals for implementing the Administrator's Superfund strategy and identify the resource requirements that will be needed to meet these long-term goals. GAO also makes other recommendations to improve EPA's enforcement activities.

Discussion Issues:

a. How would the GAO go about developing evidence to reach the conclusion that cost recovery has been a low priority within the Environmental Protection Agency?

b. Why is it important to the EPA, Congress, and the GAO that the EPA establish long-term, measurable goals? How would the establishment of such goals facilitate future audits of the EPA?

c. Based on the conclusions identified above, would you consider the work performed on the EPA by the GAO to be an audit? Explain why or why not.

d. In what substantive ways does it appear that the audit work of the GAO differs from that of the public accounting profession?

1–49 You recently overheard the following conversation between two auditors:

Auditor 1: "It's impossible to know the needs of all the users of a company's financial statements. For example, how—or even why—should I know how a labor union or a bank might use the financial statements of a company I am auditing?"

Auditor 2: "You have to know the needs of those users; otherwise, you can't determine whether the accounting for a particular transaction might be material to the user."

Auditor 1: "Well, I can't know them all, so I'll concentrate on shareholders and bank lending officers. They're the most important. Besides, management ultimately makes the decision as to what constitutes fair presentation. I'm dealing with their financial statements, not mine. You sometimes just expect too much from us as auditors."

Auditor 2: "It's the public that expects too much. I don't want to be called into court for not meeting user needs. But, I do agree with you; it's certainly difficult to understand all the diverse user needs. Besides, each group seems to want different things, and you can't meet them all. If profits are high, labor wants more wages, and the taxing authorities want more taxes. And management wants to keep reported profits down. I guess we just have to rely on GAAP and if it follows GAAP, we can assume it meets user needs."

Auditor 1: "Now you have finally said something I can agree with. Let's go have lunch."

Discussion Issues:

a. Why is it important that auditors understand the diverse groups that may use the auditor's report and each group's needs?

b. Critique the conclusion of Auditor 2 that because it is impossible to know all user needs, it is best to rely on GAAP.

c. How would an auditor go about obtaining and maintaining knowledge of user needs?

d. Consider the five following groups and indicate how each group's needs for information might create potential conflicts with the needs of the others:

1. Existing shareholders.
2. Potential investors.
3. The company's labor union.
4. A bank lending officer.
5. Company management.

End Notes

1. Louis Harris and Associates, Inc., *A Survey of Perceptions, Knowledge, and Attitudes towards CPAs and the Accounting Profession* (New York: Lou Harris and Associates, 1986), 38.
2. AICPA Professional Standards, Volume I, U.S. Auditing Standards, Attestation Standards, as of June 1, 1993 (Chicago: Commerce Clearing House, 1993).
3. *United States v. Arthur Young & Co. et al.*, U.S. Supreme Court, No. 82-687 [52 U.S.L.W 4355 (U.S. Mar. 21, 1984)].
4. Lou Harris and Associates, *A Survey of Perceptions, Knowledge, and Attitudes towards CPAs and the Accounting Profession*, 11.
5. Auditing Concepts Committee, "Report of the Committee on Basic Auditing Concepts," *The Accounting Review* 47, Supp. (1972), 18.
6. AICPA, *Report of the Commission on Auditor's Responsibilities* (New York: AICPA, 1978), 38.
7. Harris and Associates, *A Survey of Perceptions, Knowledge, and Attitudes towards CPAs and the Accounting Profession*, 38.
8. Robert Mednick, "Our Profession in the Year 2000: A Blueprint of the Future," *Journal of Accountancy* (August 1988), 56.
9. *Codification of Standards for the Professional Practice of Internal Auditing* (Altamonte Springs, Fla.: The Institute of Internal Auditors, 1990), 1.
10. Comptroller General of the United States, *Government Auditing Standards* (Washington, D.C.: U.S.

Government Printing Office, 1988), 2–3.

11. Penelope Wang, "Claiming Tomorrow's Profits Today," *Forbes*, October 17, 1988, 78.

CHAPTER

2

Learning Objectives

Through studying this chapter, you will be able to:

1. Understand the attestation function and how it has evolved.
2. Understand generally accepted auditing standards.
3. Distinguish between financial statement audits and other attestation services.
4. Understand the commonalities and differences between auditing standards and other attestation standards and develop the ability to apply the standards to the underlying situation.
5. Develop an understanding of the basic audit report and modifications necessary to reflect auditor concerns with the fair presentation of the financial statements.

Audit Standards and Responsibilities

Chapter Contents

The value of an attest service lies in its ability to reduce uncertainty or bias. Attest services essentially are appraisals of the signals emanating from given sources and the correspondence between those signals and established criteria for communication of meaning. . . . The shift [in demand for such services] is due, in part, to the economics of information technologies, the long-recognized information needs of absentee owners and enterprise creditors, and the role (and cost) of information in the establishment and accomplishment of social goals and objectives.[1]

Auditing standards differ from auditing procedures in that "procedures" relate to acts to be performed, whereas "standards" deal with measures of the quality of the performance of those acts and the objectives to be attained from the use of the procedures undertaken. Auditing standards is concerned . . . with the judgment exercised in the performance of the audit and the [preparation] of the audit report.[2]

Chapter Overview

A profession that exists to serve the public must ensure that its services are performed at the highest level of technical competence and are designed to protect the public. The public accounting profession is increasingly called on to perform expanded services for its clients and the public at large. This chapter explores the role of the public accounting profession in developing standards to guide the practice of public accounting and the evolving nature of services performed. Attention is paid to the codification of existing standards and their influence on the individual public accounting firm. Finally, the role of the auditor's report in clearly communicating the auditor's responsibility and conclusions reached on an engagement is discussed.

A–INTRODUCTION

The public accounting profession exists because it has special expertise in performing the **attestation function,** particularly for financial reporting. With that expertise alone, the profession would not have been able to attain its current status without the reputation it has achieved for integrity and lack of bias. Users of financial statements have come to respect the profession's status as an intermediary in the financial reporting process and to have confidence in the services it offers. Other groups could perform many of the attestation services that public accountants currently provide. Investment bankers can, and do, report on the fairness of terms for proposed mergers or sales. Data processing specialists could attest to the reliability of computer software for calculating income taxes. What, then, sets public accountants apart from other professionals who might perform attestation services? The answer is that the profession uniquely combines the following four elements:

1. *Technical competence* in the area being audited.
2. *Independence* in conducting an unbiased investigation and communicating an objective assessment to third parties.
3. *Adherence to professional standards* that define how an audit must be performed.
4. A *self-policing mechanism* to ensure that audit engagements meet the profession's standards.

The auditing profession* has developed standards for auditor performance on each type of audit or attest engagement. These standards are complemented by the profession's codes of ethics, which have been further reinforced by the courts. This chapter examines the role of professional standards in shaping the nature of audits and other attestation services. Those standards are not static and have evolved over a period of time in response to the needs of clients, third-party users of financial statements, and the auditors themselves.

Historical Background of the Auditing Profession

The auditing profession as we know it today differs significantly from that in the earlier part of this century. The audit profession 10 to 20 years from now will differ from that of today in many important dimensions, especially with respect to increased computer integration and the globalization of business. The profession acts and reacts to a myriad of forces that cause it to change over time. Understanding how these changes have taken place in the past may provide some guidance as we prepare for the changes we will encounter in the future.

The Profession Prior to 1929

Auditing has its roots in the investment syndicate activities of the 17th and 18th centuries. Investors in overseas trading ventures required each syndicate's management to read the accounts publicly so the investors could audit (literally, could *hear*, from the Latin, *audire*, to hear) the results, that is, learn how well the syndicate had done and judge for themselves the records of account. But auditing in a form we would recognize today emerged in Great Britain in the middle of the 19th century. The evaluations of company performance became more formalized, especially after the passage of the first **Companies Clauses Consolidation Act** in 1845, which required an auditor to be a shareholder of the company. The intent of this original act was to have one shareholder, as a representative of the others, conduct an audit and report its result to all of the owners. The shareholder-auditor could not be an officer of the company; otherwise, the auditor would have a conflict in performing the audit duties. In 1862, the Companies Act was revised to permit—but not require—the auditor to be a shareholder.

During these early years of the formation of the profession, many of today's large international public accounting firms were organized under names such as Messrs. Deloitte & Co. and Price Waterhouse & Co. No formal accounting or auditing stan-

*The term *auditing profession* is used here to broadly indicate all aspects of the profession including internal auditors, external auditors, and governmental auditors. As noted in Chapter 1, these professions are represented by professional groups such as the AICPA, the Institute of Internal Auditors, and the U.S. General Accounting Office. The term public accounting profession refers to the group of external auditors that are licensed to perform attestation services and report to third parties.

dards existed. Rather, auditors from these firms were engaged to examine the financial records and report to shareholders whether or not the accounts contained any errors. Most early audits were particularly oriented to the possibility of fraud—a subject of renewed emphasis today.

As business became more industrialized and the need for information expanded, the profession matured. One scholar has identified four primary developments associated with the growth of public accountancy as a profession:[3]

1. The emergence of large-scale organizations, the railways in particular.
2. The development of the limited liability company (that is, the modern corporate form of business organization).
3. The high rate of business insolvencies during several economic crises in the late 19th and early 20th centuries.
4. The introduction of national income taxation.

These developments were crucial to the growth of the accounting profession in the United States. Exhibit 2.1 highlights selected events in the history of public accountancy in the United States.

U.S. public accounting firms developed somewhat differently, however, from their British counterparts. A British accountant summed it up best: "Accountants in America seem to feel called upon to give advice."[4] In fact, by the turn of the century, public accounting in the United States had already begun to focus on consulting and tax planning as part of the services it offered to clients. The published history of Arthur Andersen & Co., for example, reports that it

> developed financial investigation reports which went into many phases of a business other than financial and accounting, including labor relations, availability of raw materials, plants, products, markets, effectiveness of the organization and future prospects. . . . The risks of this type of work were considerable but the results were helpful in establishing the reputation of the firm . . . for the reports were used by investment banking firms and others as a basis for financing enterprise growth. With the crash of 1929, financing engagements dwindled and this type of work . . . was practically discontinued in 1930 . . . ; however, . . . some of the techniques developed in the financial investigation . . . were adopted in the firm's regular auditing procedures.[5]

The predisposition of U.S. auditors to give advice and assist company management in effective financial control eventually led to considerable debate about the ability of the public accounting profession to maintain its independence and objectivity. That debate still continues and is the subject of review by the Securities and Exchange Commission and the courts on a frequent basis.

The other major development prior to the Great Depression was the enactment of federal income tax legislation. Public accounting firms complemented their expertise in financial reporting with a new-found expertise in tax accounting. Today, taxation work forms a significant portion of the practice for most public accounting firms.

The Profession, 1929–1980

The stock market crash of 1929 served as a catalyst for major changes in the financial reporting requirements of organizations whose stock was traded on national exchanges. From 1929 to 1932, the aggregate value of stocks on the New York Stock

Exhibit 2.1

KEY DATES IN THE EVOLUTION OF THE PUBLIC ACCOUNTING PROFESSION

1845	The Companies Clauses Consolidation Act in Great Britain establishes that an auditor must be a shareholder of the company but cannot hold a managerial position.
1845–50	The predecessors of today's international accounting firms were founded in Great Britain because British companies found it necessary to perform audits of their overseas investments, particularly those in the United States. These early companies included Messrs. Deloitte & Co. and Price Waterhouse & Co.
1862	The Companies Act was revised to permit, but not require, an auditor to be a shareholder.
1866	The board of governors of the New York Stock Exchange (NYSE) required listed corporations to file their financial statements with the exchange. By 1900, the NYSE requirements influenced the development of financial reporting in the United States.
1896	The state of New York enacted the first CPA law. The law required the licensing of certified public accountants to be able to perform the attest function.
1900–20	Several major public accounting firms were formed in the United States under such names as Ernst & Ernst, Haskins & Sells, and Arthur Andersen & Co.
1916	Congress enacted the first U.S. federal income tax legislation, creating additional work for the growing public accounting profession. Tax work developed from this point on to serve as a broad base for the business of many public accounting firms.
1917	The American Institute of Accountants (predecessor to the AICPA) was established and slowly began to work to develop accounting and auditing standards; that work was recognized in the 1930s when the Securities and Exchange Commission delegated much of its rule-making authority to the institute.
1921	The last of the 48 states passed laws to license accountants as certified public accountants and recognize their special function in auditing financial statements.
1929	The stock market crash in October raised serious questions about the adequacy of financial reporting. Prior to the crash, companies could prepare limited financial reports and omit major portions of an earnings (income) statement from those reports.
1933	Congress enacted the Securities Act, which empowered the Federal Trade Commission to oversee the offering of new securities on the market and established strict standards of liability for public accountants who were associated with the prospectuses required for new securities issues.
1934	Congress enacted the Securities Exchange Act to regulate the secondary securities markets and establish the Securities and Exchange Commission, which took over from the FTC the regulation of the primary securities markets and was both given jurisdiction over securities trading on the exchanges, and empowered to promulgate financial reporting and disclosure standards.

Exhibit 2.1

1934	The American Institute of Accountants adopted a rule requiring independence on all audits. Its resolution followed the statutory requirements of the Federal Securities Act of 1933.
1930s	The SEC and the American Institute of Accountants reached an agreement whereby the SEC delegated much of its standard-setting authority for establishing accounting and auditing standards to the profession and gave the profession the opportunity for self-regulation.
1939	The Committee on Auditing Procedures was established by the AICPA (successor to the AIA) to examine auditing procedures; it was soon charged with the responsibility for establishing auditing standards for the profession.
1939	The *McKesson and Robbins* court case highlighted deficiencies in the then existing auditing procedures regarding inventory and accounts receivable. This case was the first of a number of court suits that led to new auditing pronouncements designed to improve the level of practice and meet the public's expectations of auditors.
1940s	Arthur Andersen & Co.; Arthur Young & Co.; Lybrand, Ross Brothers & Montgomery; Haskins & Sells; Ernst & Ernst; Peat, Marwick, Mitchell & Co.; Price Waterhouse; and Touche, Ross, Niven & Co. emerged after World War II as the Big Eight U.S. public accounting firms. These firms would be influential in the development of accounting and auditing standards for the next 40 years.
1949	The Committee on Auditing Procedures issued the first 9 of the 10 generally accepted auditing standards.
1950s	The Accounting Principles Board, a senior technical committee of the AICPA, emerged as the authoritative body for establishing generally accepted accounting principles. It was composed of practicing CPAs with representatives from each of the Big Eight CPA firms along with representatives from smaller firms and one from academia.
1974	The Financial Accounting Standards Board, replacing the AICPA's Accounting Principles Board, was formed as an independent accounting standard-setting body. It was charged with developing a conceptual framework for the establishment of accounting principles and with issuing accounting pronouncements within that framework.
1976	The Senate Subcommittee on Reports, Accounting, and Management (the Metcalf Committee) and the House Subcommittee on Oversight and Investigation (the Moss Committee) issued reports on the accounting establishment that were critical of the profession and called for major changes in the profession as well as more stringent accounting and auditing rules.
1977	Revelations regarding the coverup of political contributions to the campaign of former President Richard Nixon in conjunction with the Watergate investigation resulted in the passage of the Foreign Corrupt Practices Act, which placed increased responsibility on companies that must file with the SEC to maintain adequate systems of internal control.

(Continued)

Exhibit 2.1

1978	The Commission on Auditor's Responsibilities published its *Report, Conclusions, and Recommendations*, which called for bolder action by the public accounting profession in spelling out its responsibilities in audit reports and recommended that the auditor's attest function be extended to reports on internal control.
1978	As a result of the recommendations of the Commission on Auditor's Responsibilities, the AICPA's Auditing Standards Board was created to replace the previous standard-setting committees for auditing and to rationalize the standard-setting process. The board was no longer dominated by the Big Eight U.S. public accounting firms.
1980s	The Governmental Accounting Standards Board was established to promulgate generally accepted accounting standards for governmental entities.
1984–87	Major business failures occurring shortly after companies received unqualified audit opinions led to the establishment of the Commission on Fraudulent Financial Reporting, which called for increased sensitivity within the auditing profession to search for, and report on, fraud.
1985–90	Major failures in the savings and loan industry led to questions concerning the role that the public accounting profession may have played in the industry's downfall. Congress passed a bailout bill to provide billions of dollars to shore up the industry and protect customer deposits.
1988	The Auditing Standards Board issued 10 auditing standards, referred to as the *Expectations Gap Standards*, in an attempt to narrow the gap between user expectations of auditors and the level of audit practice.
1988–90	Several major public accounting firms, formerly members of the Big Eight, merged, reducing the number of the large international public accounting firms to six.
1990–93	Public accounting firms faced a litigation crisis and called for tort reform. Limited liability organization form for CPA firms was accepted in many states.

Exchange dropped from $89 billion to approximately $15 billion. Although the national economy had much to do with this decline, many believed that the abuses represented by misleading or false financial statements contributed to the enormity of the loss.*

Emergence of the SEC. The crash of 1929 provided the stimulus for Congress to pass the **Securities Act of 1933** and the **Securities Exchange Act of 1934.** This legislation has had a profound impact on the public accounting profession. Both

*The alert reader will note how history has a tendency to repeat itself. During the late 1980s, Congress again became concerned about business failures that occurred shortly after an auditor issued an unqualified opinion on the company's financial statements. Several professional groups, including the American Accounting Association, the AICPA, the Institute of Management Accountants, and the IIA, supported a special independent commission to investigate and make recommendations to reduce the incidence of fraudulent financial reporting. The commission issued its comprehensive report on the financial reporting process in October 1987, and the AICPA incorporated some of the commission's recommendations in the auditing standards it issued at the end of the decade.

acts focus on improved disclosure in financial reporting and include stringent standards for accountants' legal liability. The acts also give the SEC the power to censure firms, thus preventing them from practicing before the SEC, and to set financial reporting standards for companies that are subject to SEC jurisdiction.*

In granting the SEC standard-setting power, the Securities Exchange Act of 1934 gives the commission the comprehensive authority

> to prescribe the form or forms in which required information shall be set forth, the items or details to be shown in the balance sheet and earnings statement, and the methods to be followed in the preparation of accounts, . . . in the valuation of assets and liabilities, [and] in the determination of . . . income.

During the late 1930s, the SEC and the American Institute of Accountants (predecessor to the AICPA) reached an agreement in which the commission delegated much of its standard-setting authority to the private sector, specifically to the AICPA. But the SEC retains ultimate control, and it has never been reluctant to specify accounting principles to cover situations in which either no authoritative standards exist or the authoritative literature leads to misleading or inconsistent reporting. In 1979, for example, the SEC required all registrant companies to treat mandatory redeemable preferred stock as a liability even though then-current accounting practice had included it as part of equity.[6]

Over the years, the SEC has developed disclosure standards and has pushed the profession to improve its accountability to the investing public. Through its ***Accounting Series Releases (ASRs)***, the SEC has issued rulings on the appropriate accounting treatment of such items as inventory, preferred stock, and related-party transactions. The *ASR*s have also covered auditing topics in such areas as the detection of fraudulent financial reporting and auditor independence.† Auditor independence, indeed, has been of major interest to the SEC. Because the auditor is paid by the client but is supposed to serve the best interest of the investing public, some conflict and tension are almost inevitable, but the SEC acts as a strong countervailing power and has issued a number of pronouncements specifying minimum independence guidelines, which are often stricter than those the profession has chosen for itself.

The SEC continues to work closely with the accounting profession. The chief accountant of the commission serves on the Emerging Issues Task Force of the Financial Accounting Standards Board.‡ The chief accountant's office reviews all major pronouncements proposed by the FASB, and a former chief accountant of the SEC recently was appointed to the FASB. The SEC continues to push the profession toward greater responsibility in such areas as reporting on internal accounting control and detecting fraud.

---

*The 1934 act specifies that companies with total assets of more than $1 million and a class of equity securities that is held by more than 500 persons at any year-end, or a class of securities registered on a stock exchange, must meet the legal requirements of the SEC, which include (1) filing specified periodic reports, (2) disclosing material facts in proxy statements, (3) restricting insider trading, and (4) disclosing tender offer solicitations.

†In 1982, the Commission began dividing its Accounting Series Releases into two separately titled categories: Financial Reporting Releases and Auditing Enforcement Releases.

‡The Emerging Issues Task Force (EITF) is a body set up by the FASB to provide timely advice on evolving or controversial technical accounting areas. The EITF members are from the FASB, public accounting, industry, and the SEC. Many of the early pronouncements of the EITF addressed technical issues related to financial instruments. The EITF pronouncements indicate a consensus of accepted accounting until such time as the FASB officially addresses the accounting issue.

Litigation Influences. The increasing size of businesses dictates that major corporate failures will result in severe economic losses to the investing public. Investors sue the auditor for damages when they perceive that the auditor has failed to live up to the public trust. Early court rulings generally limited the auditor's responsibility to specifically known classes of users. Over the years, however, the courts have extended the auditor's responsibility to all users who might reasonably rely on audited financial statements for decision-making purposes. Given the increasing litigiousness of society, the increasing complexity of financial transactions, and the increasing expectations of users, the large number of lawsuits against auditors should not be surprising. Some court cases have revealed specific deficiencies in auditing procedures and have contributed to the promulgation of new standards in such areas as auditing inventories, receivables, related-party transactions, events discovered subsequent to the balance sheet date, and communication between predecessor and successor auditors. Chapter 4 treats litigation in some detail.

The Profession in the 1990s

The 1990s to date have been a period of significant change in the accounting profession and in the nature of public accounting firms. This change has largely resulted from the following:

- The increased *globalization* of the world economy and the need for large audit firms to serve clients effectively around the world.
- The emergence of *management consulting,* especially information systems consulting, as a large, profitable, and growing segment of the work of public accounting firms.
- The increased *complexity* and *computerization* of client organizations.
- *Competition* in auditing.
- The increasing cost of *liability insurance* and *litigation.*

Today's audits must be more efficient and even more error-free than they were 10 to 15 years ago. Not only has competition increased, with many companies periodically taking bids from CPA firms for auditing and other services, but also client transactions have become both more complex and more numerous. The auditor faces new kinds of risks everywhere and must devise audit methods and procedures requiring less time to perform and resulting in fewer mistakes.

The public accounting firm mergers of the 1980s represent the most significant change in the profession since the emergence of the Big Eight public accounting firms in the late 1940s. Audits of the largest international companies are performed by only a few firms. But the mergers appear to have strengthened the profession. Small firms seem to have effectively carved out their markets by tending to the special needs of the small- and medium-size companies that have always formed the core of their client base.

Demand for services performed by public accounting firms has shifted. Consulting services are growing at rates exceeding those for auditing services. Auditors are increasingly asked to attest to prospective financial statements or to review financial projections related to proposed projects, not just attest to historical financial statements. Tax work continues to expand as companies face the need to deal with ever-increasing complexity in the tax code and more individuals recognize the need for tax planning. Some members of public accounting firms have become certified as "financial planners." Finally, auditors are increasingly asked to perform attestation services that go well beyond the traditional financial statements.

Standards for Attestation Services—A Framework

Several sets of auditing-related standards have evolved over time: auditing standards for audits of financial statements, accounting and review standards, and most recently, attestation standards covering non-financial statement items that supplement, but do not replace, these other standards. All attestation services, whether they take the form of a traditional audit or of a special engagement, have in common the evaluation of assertions measured against prescribed or agreed-upon criteria and the communication of the attestor's judgment arising from that evaluation. The public accountants can add value—credibility—to the assertions only if they are unbiased, the evaluation is objective, and the report clearly spells out their responsibility. All three elements are essential, and those three elements form the framework for both generally accepted auditing standards and attestation standards.

The standards for audits and other attestation services are categorized into three major parts:

- *General or individual standards,* which cover the characteristics of the accountant, including competence, independence, and due professional care, and the accountant's services.
- *Fieldwork standards,* which present guidance in testing assertions, including the planning for each engagement and an overview of procedures used during it.
- *Reporting standards,* which cover the essential elements of the accountant's communication, including the opinion, the criteria against which the assertions were tested, and an explanation of the basis for the auditor's opinion.

The remainder of this chapter covers generally accepted auditing standards (GAAS), the audit reports mandated under GAAS, attestation standards, and reports issued in conjunction with attestation engagements. It is important to recognize, however, that both sets of standards (GAAS and attestation standards) are consistent in their structure. The broad standards provide the foundation for all Statements on Auditing Standards (SASs) and Statements of Attestation Standards, which prescribe more detailed guidance on the methods, procedures, competencies, and reporting forms for all attestation engagements. Standards for accounting and review services are covered in Chapter 21 and standards related to prospective financial statements are covered in Chapter 22.

B–GENERALLY ACCEPTED AUDITING STANDARDS

The 10 generally accepted auditing standards represent the cornerstone for the conduct of financial statement audits. The more detailed standards referred to as Statements on Auditing Standards (SASs) are derived from the precepts included in the 10 standards. In other words, the 10 generally accepted auditing standards provide the conceptual foundation for the issuance of more detailed Statements on Auditing Standards. When reviewing the standards, it is important to understand that they define a *minimum* level of acceptable conduct for an audit. The basic standards are presented in Exhibit 2.2 and are discussed in more detail below.

The General Standards: Criteria Guiding Auditor Performance

Auditors are entrusted to perform a unique public service. If that service is to be credible, the public must have confidence that practicing auditors are competent in

Exhibit 2.2

TEN GENERALLY ACCEPTED AUDITING STANDARDS

General Standards

1. The examination is to be performed by a person or persons having *adequate technical training and proficiency* as an auditor.
2. In all matters relating to the assignment, an *independence* in mental attitude is to be maintained by the auditor or auditors.
3. *Due professional care* is to be exercised in the performance of the examination and the preparation of the report.

Standards of Fieldwork

1. The work shall be *adequately planned* and assistants, if any, shall be properly supervised.
2. A sufficient understanding of the *internal control structure* is to be obtained to plan the audit and to determine the nature, timing, and extent of tests to be performed.
3. *Sufficient competent evidential matter* is to be obtained through inspection, observation, inquiries, and confirmations to afford a reasonable basis for an opinion regarding the financial statements under examination.

Standards of Reporting

1. The report shall state whether the financial statements are presented in accordance with generally accepted accounting principles.
2. The report shall identify those circumstances in which such principles have not been consistently observed in the current period in relation to the preceding period.
3. Informative disclosures in the financial statements are to be regarded as reasonably adequate unless otherwise stated in the report.
4. The report shall contain either an expression of opinion regarding the financial statements, taken as a whole, or an assertion to the effect that an opinion cannot be expressed. When an overall opinion cannot be expressed, the reasons therefore should be stated. In all cases in which an auditor's name is associated with financial statements, the report should contain a clear-cut indication of the character of the auditor's examination, if any, and the degree of responsibility the auditor is taking.

auditing and accounting, are independent of the client in all aspects of their work, and perform their work carefully with a level of care that would be expected of a professional. Thus, the general standards are designed to guide the profession in the selection and training of its professionals and in maintaining an adequate detachment from the client to meet that public trust. These objectives are addressed under the three topic areas of technical training and proficiency, independence in mental attitude and detachment from the client, and due care by which the profession as a whole can judge the quality of work of practicing auditors. Thus, the general standards supply the conceptual foundation for the conduct of auditing, and all other standards follow from the basic premises in these standards.

Technical Training and Proficiency

The audit is to be performed by individuals having adequate technical training and proficiency as an auditor. The standard does not precisely define what constitutes *adequate technical training and proficiency* because standards of proficiency evolve as the environment changes. Auditors in the 1990s must be proficient in using new technologies to a much greater extent than auditors in the 1950s. The profession has recognized the need for greater knowledge by requiring a five-year degree program in accounting and requiring continuing professional education for membership in the AICPA. Proficiency is an evolving concept that changes with technology, the nature of the assertion being tested, and the complexity of accounting standards.

GAAS require technical knowledge in both auditing and accounting. Today's auditor must dissect complex accounting problems and make judgments on the appropriateness of accounting treatments proposed by clients. Likewise, today's auditor must apply auditing concepts to select audit procedures that will be efficient and have a high likelihood of detecting material errors should they exist in the client's financial statements. More than a detailed knowledge of rules is needed: The auditor also must be able to analyze a problem and use professional judgment to determine the most appropriate accounting treatment within the broad frameworks of accounting and auditing standards.

Independence

Independence is often referred to as the *cornerstone* of auditing—without independence, the value of the auditor's attestation function would be decreased in the eyes of a third party who relies on the auditor's communication. Thus, auditors must not only be independent in their mental attitude toward an audit (independence *in fact*) but also must be perceived by users as independent of the client (independent *in appearance*). Independence requires objectivity and freedom from bias: the auditor must favor neither the client nor third parties in evaluating the fairness of the financial statements.

Due Professional Care

The public expects that an audit will be conducted with the skill and care expected of a professional. Generally accepted auditing standards provide one benchmark for **due professional care.** However, following GAAS is not always sufficient. If a "reasonably prudent person" would have done more, such as investigating for a potential fraud, it is often asserted that the professional should have done at least as much. Public accounting firms use close supervision and review of audit work to ensure that audits are conducted with due professional care.

Practical Experiences

SEEKING HELP IN DETERMINING DUE PROFESSIONAL CARE

As auditing has become more complex, it is increasingly difficult for individual CPAs to be knowledgeable about everything that might be encountered in practice. Therefore, most public accounting firms have industry specialists who are experts in particular industries. Economies of scale can be attained by applying knowledge learned about one client in an industry to audits of other clients in the same industry. Indeed, one national CPA firm audits a large percentage of public utility companies; another audits a substantial proportion of banks and thrift institutions. Recently, one of the major public accounting firms reorganized its practice along six industry lines instead of the traditional functional areas of audit, tax, and consulting. In a like manner, some small public accounting firms choose to develop industry specialties such as the hotel and restaurant industry, and will concentrate their work in that industry.

Most national accounting firms have established internal "help" networks to facilitate the sharing of industry knowledge. For example, an auditor facing a seemingly unique problem dealing with a new financial instrument issued by a client can describe the problem and send it via electronic mail to partners whose work involves the same industry and who might have encountered a similar problem in the past. Many firms are developing electronic databases documenting the handling of unique problems, and the auditor can access the databases to determine firm precedence in handling the accounting or auditing issue.

Many small CPA firms have established associations with firms in other geographic areas whereby they can seek outside expert consultation on audit or accounting questions. Obtaining help can be a problem for CPAs who practice in a sole proprietorship or small partnership and who have not joined an association of firms. The AICPA has a technical information service to help answer practitioner's questions. Some state societies of CPAs have a similar "hotline" service. Many CPAs work hard to maintain channels of communication with other practitioners, not merely for conviviality but also as a problem-solving network.

The Fieldwork Standards: Guiding the Audit Process

The fieldwork standards provide guidance in planning and conducting an audit engagement. The standards are designed to ensure that an engagement is adequately planned and supervised, an organization's control structure is evaluated for the possibility of misstatements occurring and not being detected, and sufficient competent evidence is gathered to support the audit opinion.

Planning and Supervision

Planning an audit is more than developing a scheduling plan and determining when to show up and conduct the audit. A knowledge of the risks associated with a client is necessary, as is a knowledge of the complexity of the client's computerized data processing. Only with such knowledge can an audit be adequately planned. Planning an audit includes the following:

- Developing an understanding of the client's business and the industry within which it operates. The auditor must know how a client is affected by government laws and regulations, changes in the domestic and world economy, and changes in technology.

- Developing an understanding of audit risk and materiality.
- Developing understanding of the client's accounting policies and procedures.
- Anticipating financial statement items likely to require adjustment.
- Identifying factors that may require extension or modification of audit tests, such as potential related-party transactions or the possibility of material errors or irregularities.
- Determining the type of reports to be issued, such as consolidated statements or single-company statements, special reports, or reports to be filed with the SEC or other regulatory agencies.

The most visible product of the planning process is the **audit program,** which lists the audit objectives and the procedures to be followed in gathering evidence. Exhibit 2.3 is an example of a partial audit program for trade receivables. It contains columns for indicating the estimated time to complete the procedure, a reference to

Exhibit 2.3

PARTIAL AUDIT PROGRAM FOR THE AUDIT OF TRADE RECEIVABLES

Trade Receivables

CLIENT ________________________ CLOSING DATE ____________

The objectives of this program are to determine that:

(a) receivables exist, are authentic obligations owed to the entity, contain no significant amounts that should be written off, and the allowance for doubtful accounts is adequate and not excessive;

(b) proper disclosure is made of any pledged, discounted, or assigned receivables; and

(c) the presentation and disclosure of receivables is in conformity with generally accepted accounting principles.

PROCEDURE	Time Est.	Done By	W/P Ref.
1. Foot subsidiary receivable records and select balances for confirmation.	______	______	______
2. Prepare or have client prepare confirmation requests for accounts.	______	______	______
3. Reconcile and evaluate all confirmation replies and clear any exceptions. Non-replies must be verified by use of alternative procedures.	______	______	______
4. Summarize results of confirmation procedures.	______	______	______
Alternate Procedures Performed:			
______________________	______	______	______
______________________	______	______	______

Practice Experiences

WHAT SHOULD AUDITORS DO IF THEY DISAGREE WITH THE APPROACH TAKEN BY THE MANAGEMENT OF THE AUDIT ENGAGEMENT?

Occasionally, a staff auditor may disagree with the audit manager or partner on the engagement about an audit approach or the accounting treatment chosen by the client. For example, the staff auditor may believe that the accounting method chosen by the client seems to be based solely on the *form* of the transaction rather than on the *substance* of the transaction. The staff auditor may believe the accounting treatment is being utilized because of management's desire to mask a short-fall in earnings. Remember, staff auditors are associated with the financial statements, even if they do not sign the audit opinion.

The profession recognizes the need for maintaining the integrity of individual judgment and provides guidance for such a potential disagreement in AU Sec. 322. When such disagreements occur, the audit supervisor has a responsibility to explain the rationale for the audit or accounting approach to the staff auditor. If the staff auditor continues to disagree with the treatment chosen by the client and accepted by the audit manager and partner, the staff auditor should document the disagreement and explain the rationale for the position taken. In a similar manner, the audit manager and partner must document the rationale for the approach taken. The documentation of both views provides an opportunity for reviewing partners to evaluate both sides of the accounting or audit judgment and determine the most appropriate accounting or auditing treatment.

the documentation of the work done, and the initials of the auditor carrying out each audit procedure. The program helps those in charge of the audit to monitor the progress and supervise the work.

Supervision of assistants includes instructing assistants to be sure they know what they are to do and why, keeping informed about significant problems encountered, reviewing their work and work papers, and resolving differences of opinion among the audit staff. The term *assistant* in the context of the standard refers to anyone working on the audit other than the member of the firm who has the authority to issue the opinion on the statements. Therefore, an assistant could be a new staff person, a senior, a manager, or even another partner. The degree of supervision generally depends on the experience of the assistant(s) and the complexity of the work.

Understand the Internal Control Structure

Organizations implement accounting systems and control structures to process large volumes of data in an efficient manner that should also minimize the possibility of misstatements occurring. The controls identified by an organization to ensure that only properly authorized transactions are processed and that the transactions are fully, accurately, and timely recorded are referred to as the organization's **internal control structure.** Analysis of an organization's internal control structure can yield insight into the types of errors or irregularities that might occur without being detected, or alternatively, it might yield insight on the strength of the organization's control procedures to minimize errors.

The internal control structure varies greatly among different entities. In some organizations, few control procedures exist; in others, strong control procedures are in place. Even within a particular company, there may be very good control procedures over some types of transactions—for example, sales—and weak or non-existent control procedures over others—for example, purchases. An analysis of the accounting system and surrounding control procedures might indicate that the client could be creating fictitious invoices without someone independently discovering the misstatement. The knowledge of how the misstatement could occur will assist the auditor in planning audit procedures to detect its potential existence. An understanding of the accounting system and the control structure designed to minimize the possibility of errors is essential to the planning and conduct of an audit. Therefore, the second standard of fieldwork requires the auditor to obtain "a sufficient understanding of the internal control structure . . . to plan the audit and to determine the nature, timing, and extent of tests to be performed."

Evidence

Sufficient (enough) *competent* (reliable and relevant) *evidence* must be obtained to evaluate the assertions embodied in the financial statements, including the related footnotes. Audits depend on the concept of testing because no auditor examines 100 percent of all the transactions entered into by an organization. Sampling is used to gather a sufficient amount of evidence. The exact amount of evidence needed depends on the sampling application and the auditor's assessment of the persuasiveness of the evidence gathered. Fortunately, concepts of audit risk (described more thoroughly in Chapter 6) can be utilized in developing statistically based samples to assist the auditor in planning and evaluating the sufficiency of evidence.

Reporting Standards: Clarifying the Communication Process

Have you ever communicated something explicitly to people only to find out that they did not seem to understand what you said or meant to communicate? Obtaining clear and concise communication is a difficult task. It is even more difficult when the communication involves information on a complex subject such as financial statements. The reporting standards provide a framework for the profession to standardize and improve the quality of its communication with users. Among other things, the profession has found it necessary to communicate explicitly the nature of the work performed and the auditor's responsibility for that work. The reporting standards provide guidelines to (1) standardize the nature of reporting, (2) facilitate communication with users by clearly specifying the auditor's responsibility regarding the report, (3) identify and communicate all situations in which accounting principles have not been consistently applied, and (4) require the auditor to express an opinion on the subject matter examined or indicate all substantive reasons why an opinion could not be rendered.

Presentation in Accordance with GAAP

The auditor is required to state explicitly whether the financial statements are fairly presented in accordance with the agreed-upon criteria for the profession (generally accepted accounting principles). If, upon examining the evidence gathered during the audit, the auditor determines that the statements materially depart from GAAP, the auditor expresses a qualified or an adverse opinion and indicates all substantive reasons, including the dollar effects (whenever determinable) of the departure from GAAP. Such a statement is referred to as a *qualified audit report* because the auditor has expressed reservations regarding the fair presentations of the financial statements.*

Consistency

The consistency standard indicates that once management chooses from among alternative acceptable methods of accounting (such as inventory cost flow assumptions), the same principles will be used from year to year—are *consistent*—to enhance the comparability and usefulness of the financial statements. This does not mean, however, that these principles must be followed rigidly. Two circumstances can lead to justifiable changes in accounting principles. First, the FASB might issue a new pronouncement standardizing the accounting for a previously disparate accounting area, such as accounting for income taxes or research and development. Second, certain circumstances may change, and management may wish to react to them by adopting an alternative principle. As an example, during the 1970s, the new circumstance was rapid inflation, and many companies switched from using FIFO to LIFO on the justification that management believed that LIFO presented a better measure of income.

When a company makes a change in principles, the change must be described in the footnotes to the financial statements and referred to in the audit report. The description should include the dollar effects of the change and management's justification for it.

Disclosures

Readers of the financial statements are usually not in a position to know whether the *disclosures* in the financial statements and related footnotes are adequate. If nothing is mentioned in the auditor's report, the reader can assume that the disclosures are adequate. The auditor is guided by FASB and other authoritative pronouncements to determine whether the required disclosures have been made.

Opinion

The fourth standard of reporting requires the auditor to issue an audit opinion or, if there are reasons why an opinion cannot be issued, to inform the reader of all of the substantive reasons why it cannot be. The type of opinion rendered depends on the results of the auditor's examination. The auditor's report should indicate the type of examination performed and the degree of responsibility taken for it.

---

*In some cases, especially with small businesses, management may prefer to present the financial statements on a different accounting basis than GAAP such as the cash, income tax, or other comprehensive basis of accounting. These alternative reporting formats, referred to in the professional standards as *special reports*, are discussed in detail in Chapter 22.

C–REPORTING AND ATTESTATION STANDARDS

The Audit Report on a Company's Financial Statements

The primary communication of an auditor concerning the audit is an opinion as to the fairness of the presentation of a company's financial statements. We briefly examine the communication content of a typical audit report as a basis for understanding professional standards. (An in-depth discussion of audit and other reports is given in Chapters 21 and 22.)

Standard Unqualified Audit Report

The audit report concisely summarizes the auditor's work performed in conjunction with the audit, the auditor's responsibility for the opinion, the nature of an audit, and the auditor's assessment of the fairness of the financial statements. The major components of the opinion are shown in Exhibit 2.4.

The report is referred to as the *standard* audit report because the Auditing Standards Board has standardized the typical audit report to limit potential misunderstandings related to the auditor's work or the auditor's assessment of the financial statement presentation. This standard report is often referred to as an **unqualified audit report** or as a clean audit report because the auditor has no reservations about the fairness of the client's financial statement presentation. Each paragraph of the audit report has a specific communication function.

Title. Because the auditor's report is typically included in a company's annual report, it should be clearly identified as the auditor's report. The title should include the word *independent* to distinguish it from other reports that may be included in the same document such as reports of management or the audit committee of the board of directors. The word *independent* also identifies the objectivity of the audit report. The report is dated the last date of fieldwork, generally defined as the last date the auditor worked at the client's office conducting the audit.

Addressee. The report is addressed to the board of directors or shareholders of a corporation, or the partners, general partner, or the proprietor of an unincorporated firm. If the report is requested by a specific party, the report is addressed to that party.

Introductory Paragraph. The introductory paragraph communicates the nature of the auditor's engagement and the financial statements covered in the audit. Equally important, the separate and distinct responsibilities of management (the preparation of the financial statements) and the auditor (the expression of an opinion on the fairness of the financial statements) are clearly identified. Thus, the introductory paragraph clearly communicates what the report itself represents: an auditor's opinion on the financial statements specified, as prepared by management.

Scope Paragraph. The scope paragraph describes the overall nature of the audit process. Generally accepted auditing standards are the point of reference to assure

Exhibit 2.4

STANDARD AUDIT REPORT

Report Title	Independent Auditor's Report
Addressee	To the Board of Directors and Stockholders Illustration Company
Introductory Paragraph	We have audited the accompanying balance sheets of Illustration Company as of December 31, 1995 and 1994, and the related statements of income, retained earnings, and cash flows for the years then ended. These financial statements are the responsibility of the Company's management. Our responsibility is to express an opinion on these financial statements based on our audits.
Scope Paragraph	We conducted our audits in accordance with generally accepted auditing standards. Those standards require that we plan and perform the audit to obtain reasonable assurance about whether the financial statements are free of material misstatement. An audit includes examining, on a test basis, evidence supporting the amounts and disclosures in the financial statements. An audit also includes assessing the accounting principles used and significant estimates made by management, as well as evaluating the overall financial statement presentation. We believe that our audits provide a reasonable basis for our opinion.
Opinion Paragraph	In our opinion, the financial statements referred to above present fairly, in all material respects, the financial position of Illustration Company as of December 31, 19X2 and 19X1, and the results of its operations and its cash flows for the years then ended in conformity with generally accepted accounting principles.
Signature	[Signature of the firm—manual or printed]
Date	[Dated as of the end of the audit fieldwork]

the user of the quality of audit work performed. *Reasonable assurance* is a cost/benefit concept; it implies that the auditor performed procedures sufficient to obtain persuasive evidence on which to base the audit opinion. Since the auditor examines evidence on a test basis, the auditor's opinion *does not provide absolute assurance.* Such a "guarantee" could be attained only if the auditor examined 100 percent of an organization's transactions. **Materiality** is a pervasive concept; it is defined as the *magnitude* of a misstatement or omission of information that would affect the judgment of a reasonable person relying on the information.

Opinion Paragraph. The opinion paragraph reflects the best judgment of the auditor as to the fairness of the financial statements as measured by GAAP. Thus, fairly presented statements are statements that follow GAAP and contain all relevant material disclosures.

Signature. The report should be signed in the name of the public accounting firm, not in the name of the individual(s) who performed the audit (unless the firm is a sole proprietorship). The firm is responsible for the opinion; the auditor who signs the firm's name does so as an agent of the firm.

Modifications of the Standard Unqualified Audit Report

The financial statements may be fairly presented, but there may be uncertainties about the ability of the audit client to remain a going concern, there may have been changes in accounting principles during the period that might affect the comparability of financial statements between periods, or the auditor may have relied on another public accounting firm for part of the audit and wants to disclose the division of audit responsibilities. In each of these situations, the audit client receives a *standard, unqualified audit opinion that contains an extra paragraph or sentence describing the additional information that is deemed useful to users of financial reports.*

Going Concern Uncertainties: A Modification of the Unqualified Audit Report. The auditor may have substantial doubt about the ability of the audit client to remain a "going concern." The company may have operating problems or financial difficulties that raise an uncertainty as to whether the historical cost basis is appropriate. When concluding that substantial doubt exists, the auditor should add a fourth paragraph explaining the uncertainty. The paragraph should also refer to a footnote which describes the problem in more detail and lays out management's plans for mitigating the problem. An example of a **going concern report modification** describing an uncertainty is given in Exhibit 2.5.

Inconsistent Application of GAAP. If the client has changed an accounting principle, such as from FIFO to LIFO, and has followed GAAP in accounting for and disclosing this change, an explanatory paragraph is added to direct the user's attention to the relevant footnote disclosure. The description calling the reader's attention to the change (often referred to as a "flag") can be very useful. For example, one company recently highlighted a 22 percent increase in net income throughout its annual report. The auditor's report contained an explanation that, had a change in accounting procedure not occurred, the increase would have been only six percent. The explanatory paragraph is added as a fourth paragraph to the audit report and refers

Exhibit 2.5

GOING CONCERN MODIFICATION

[Paragraph Following the Opinion Paragraph]

The accompanying financial statements have been prepared assuming that the Company will continue as a going concern. As discussed in Note 2 to the financial statements, the Company has suffered recurring losses from operations and has a net capital deficiency that raises substantial doubt about its ability to continue as a going concern. Management's plans in regard to these matters are also described in Note 2. The financial statements do not include any adjustments that might result from the outcome of this uncertainty.

to a detailed note in the financial statements that describes the change and the effect of it on the financial statements, in more detail.

Reliance on Other Auditors. In some situations, the audit firm may utilize the services of another audit firm, especially for global clients. If the amount of work performed by the other audit firm is material to the financial statements, the audit report contains a brief description that part of the work was performed by another audit firm and discloses the percentage of revenues and assets audited by the other firm.

Qualified Reports: Situations Affecting the Auditor's Opinion

Although most audit reports resemble the one in Exhibit 2.4, in some situations, the unqualified opinion is not justified. Generally, the following are the major causes of the opinion change:

- The financial statements contain a material, unjustified departure from GAAP.
- The financial statements lack adequate disclosure.
- The auditor is unable to obtain sufficient, competent evidence (scope limitation).

The opinion is modified to note the auditor's qualification concerning the fairness of presentation or scope limitation and is referred to as a **qualified audit report.** An example of an auditor's qualification due to a departure from GAAP is shown in Exhibit 2.6.

An auditor will qualify for a scope limitation only if the limitation is narrow and is limited to one or two items. In a qualified audit opinion the auditor is stating that overall the financial statements are fairly presented except for (1) the departure from GAAP, (2) the inadequate disclosure, or (3) the lack of sufficient evidence in a particular area to render an opinion about that area or financial statement item.

Exhibit 2.6

QUALIFIED AUDIT REPORT—GAAP DEPARTURE

[Standard Introductory and Scope Paragraphs]

The Company has excluded, from property and debt in the accompanying balance sheets, certain lease obligations that, in our opinion, should be capitalized in order to conform with generally accepted accounting principles. If these lease obligations were capitalized, property would be increased by $10.2 million and $8.7 million, long-term debt by $10.2 million and $8.7 million, and retained earnings would be decreased by $2.8 million and $2.1 million as of December 31, 1995 and 1994, respectively. Additionally, net income would be decreased by $1.4 million and $1.2 million and earnings per share would be decreased by $.40 and $.32, respectively, for the years then ended.

In our opinion, *except for the effects of not capitalizing certain lease obligations as discussed in the preceding paragraph*, the financial statements referred to above present fairly,...

An Adverse Audit Report: Statements Are Not Fairly Presented

On some occasions, the auditor may conclude that the financial statements, taken as a whole, are *not fairly presented* in accordance with generally acceptable accounting principles. In such instances, the work performed is the same that would have been performed to result in an unqualified report. However, the client has chosen to account for transactions on other than a GAAP basis. This occurs, for example, if the client decides to report all property, plant, and equipment and current assets at current appraisal value because management believes such values are more representative of the value of the firm. The auditor also may prefer current appraisal value, but the fact remains that current appraisal values for property, plant, and equipment is not an acceptable accounting alternative. Because the GAAP violation is pervasive, the auditor concludes that the statements as a whole are not fairly presented, leading to an adverse, rather than a qualified, audit report.

An example of an adverse audit report is given in Exhibit 2.7. The **adverse audit report** is similar to the standard unqualified audit report except that the opinion describes the nature of the departures from GAAP and the dollar amounts of the departures (if determinable) and states the auditor's opinion that the financial statements *do not fairly present, in conformity with generally accepted accounting principles,* the financial position or the results of its operations for the years covered in the financial statements.

Disclaimer of Audit Opinion

In some instances, the auditor may be associated with a company's financial statements but that association does not involve performance of an audit of the statements. Or the auditor may be associated with financial statements but is not independent. In such instances, the auditor should issue a **disclaimer** of opinion stating that he or she does not express an opinion on the financial statements. These types of disclaimers of audit opinion are necessary in situations such as when the client wants the auditor to read the financial statements or to act as an adviser to the client in preparing them. This most often occurs with small businesses, which need accounting services but cannot afford to pay for an audit.

In rare cases, the auditor may be engaged to perform an audit but is precluded from doing so because of a limitation on the procedures that could be performed in conjunction with the audit. The limitation is referred to as a *scope limitation*. An example in a disclaimer of opinion because of a scope limitation is shown in Exhibit 2.8. The scope limitation leading to a disclaimer of opinion is more pervasive than a scope limitation that could lead to a qualified audit opinion. Because of legal liability considerations, most auditors, when in doubt as to the appropriate type of opinion for a scope limitation, will issue a disclaimer rather than a qualified audit opinion.

Attestation Services beyond Financial Statement Audits

As the world has become more complex and integrated, information has become crucial to managing organizations and in making investment, lending, and other financially related decisions. Audited financial statements enhance the efficiency of the financial markets. However, significant decisions are not made on the basis of historical financial statements alone. There is a demand for other credible information that has become a significant part of today's decision processes.

Exhibit 2.7

ADVERSE AUDIT REPORT

[Following the Scope Paragraph]

As discussed in Note K to the financial statements, the Company carries its property, plant, and equipment at appraisal values and provides depreciation on the basis of such values. Further, the Company does not provide for income taxes with respect to the differences between financial income and taxable income arising because of the use, for income tax purposes, of the installment method of reporting gross profit from certain types of sales. Generally accepted accounting principles require that property, plant, and equipment be stated at an amount not in excess of cost, reduced by depreciation based on historical cost, and that deferred income taxes be provided.

Because of the departures from generally accepted accounting principles identified above, as of December 31, 1995 and 1994, inventories have been increased by $800,000 and $600,000, respectively, by inclusion in manufacturing overhead the depreciation in excess of that based on cost, and deferred income taxes of $400,000 and $300,000 have not been recorded, resulting in an increase of $1,200,000 and $900,000 in retained earnings and income for the years ended. Additionally, property, plant, and equipment are stated at $18.3 million and $17.6 million in excess of historical cost, and depreciation (other than that charged to cost of sales and inventory) is stated at $1.2 million and $1.1 million in excess of historical cost depreciation. Additionally, $900,000 and $700,000 have been recognized as a credit to income each year to write up assets from historical cost to appraisal values. The write-up has been recognized in income each year.

In our opinion, because of the effects of the matters discussed in the preceding paragraphs, the financial statements referred to above do not present fairly, in conformity with generally accepted accounting principles, the financial position of the Company as of December 31, 1995 and 1994, or the results of its operations or its cash flows for the years then ended.

For example, consider a real estate developer who prepares a prospective financial report projecting the operating results of a proposed shopping center development to be taken to an outside syndicate for financing. Is the developer likely to be unbiased in performing the financial projection? Or consider a firm making a decision to purchase a software program to prepare income taxes. Would the value of the program be enhanced if an expert could attest to whether the program prepares taxes in accordance with the current Internal Revenue code and rules? The public

Exhibit 2.8

DISCLAIMER OF OPINION BECAUSE OF A SCOPE LIMITATION

We were engaged to audit the accompanying balance sheets of the XYZ Company as of December 31, 1995 and 1994, and the related statements of income, retained earnings, and cash flows for the years then ended. These financial statements are the responsibility of the Company's management.

The Company did not make a count of its physical inventory in 1995, or 1994, stated in the accompanying financial statements at $3,765,457 and $2,891,297 as of December 31, 1995, and December 31, 1994, respectively. Further, evidence supporting the cost of property and equipment acquired prior to December 31, 1994, is no longer available. The Company records do not permit the application of other auditing procedures to inventories of property and equipment.

Because the Company did not take physical inventories and we were not able to apply other auditing procedures to satisfy ourselves as to inventory quantities and the cost of property and equipment, the scope of our work was not sufficient to enable us to express, and we do not express, an opinion on these financial statements.

accounting profession has responded to user needs in such areas by developing attestation standards in which the expertise of the auditor as an attestor can be brought to "audit" these types of information. Increasingly, public accounting firms are performing attestation services in such areas as these:

1. Prospective financial statements.
2. Operation of software.
3. Compliance of an entity's operations with applicable governmental regulations.
4. Operations of computer service bureaus and the integrity of controls incorporated into computer applications.

Attestation Standards–An Expansion of the Audit Framework

Audits of a company's financial statements—the predominant form of attestation—are nonetheless just a special subset of attestation engagements. An attest engagement is broadly defined as follows:

> one in which a practitioner is engaged to issue or does issue a written communication that expresses a conclusion about the reliability of a written assertion that is the responsibility of another party.[7]

Attest engagements that do not involve auditing financial statements must follow standards similar to those of audits. The Auditing Standards Board views these attestation standards as a natural extension of generally accepted auditing standards. The attestation standards are summarized in Exhibit 2.9; a comparison of them with auditing standards presented in Exhibit 2.2 should indicate the similarities. The attestation standards are developed around the common framework of general standards, fieldwork standards, and reporting standards, as are the 10 generally accepted auditing standards.

Exhibit 2.9

ATTESTATION STANDARDS

General Standards

1. The engagement shall be performed by a practitioner or practitioners having adequate *technical training* and *proficiency* in the attest function.
2. The engagement shall be performed by a practitioner or practitioners having adequate knowledge in the subject matter of the assertion.
3. The practitioner shall perform an engagement only if he or she has reason to believe that the following two conditions exist:
   - The assertion is capable of evaluation against reasonable criteria that either have been established by a recognized body or are stated in the presentation of the assertion in a sufficiently clear and comprehensive manner for a knowledgeable reader to be able to understand them.
   - The assertion is capable of reasonably consistent estimation or measurement using such criteria.
4. In all matters relating to the engagement, an *independence* in mental attitude shall be maintained by the practitioner or practitioners.
5. *Due professional care* shall be exercised in the performance of the engagement.

Standards of Fieldwork

1. The work shall be *adequately planned* and assistants, if any, shall be properly supervised.
2. *Sufficient evidence* shall be obtained to provide a reasonable basis for the conclusion that is expressed in the report.

Standards of Reporting

1. The report shall identify the assertion being reported on and state the character of the engagement.
2. The report shall state the practitioner's conclusion about whether the assertion is presented in conformity with the established or stated criteria against which it was measured.
3. The report shall state all of the practitioner's significant reservations about the engagement and the presentation of the assertion.
4. The report on an engagement to evaluate an assertion that has been prepared in conformity with agreed-upon criteria or on an engagement to apply agreed-upon procedures should contain a statement limiting its use to the parties who have agreed on such criteria or procedures.

General Standards

The general standards recognize that the auditor must have the technical knowledge and proficiency required of an *auditor* and in the *technical area in which the attest function is being performed.* As an example, an auditor performing an attestation service related to the performance of a computer software package must be knowledgeable about determining the most appropriate audit procedures to gather

Practical Examples

ATTESTATION ENGAGEMENT REGARDING THE TECHNICAL COMPETENCE OF TAX PREPARATION SOFTWARE

A public accounting firm has been requested to perform an attest engagement verifying the completeness and accuracy of a microcomputer software program to compute personal income tax in accordance with the provisions of the IRS code and its interpretations. The software also claims to point out options for the taxpayer to consider when alternative tax treatments might exist.

The auditor considering such an engagement must determine whether the firm has "adequate knowledge in the subject matter of the assertion." The assertion is fairly clear: The software computes income tax in accordance with all the provisions of the IRS code (and interpretations thereof) and identifies potential areas for alternative tax treatments.

To accept the engagement, the auditor must determine that sufficient subject matter competence exists within the firm and the auditor can apply auditing procedures to gather sufficient audit evidence as to the assertion being tested. First, the auditor must reference sufficient subject matter knowledge. Because the engagement clearly defines the appropriate reference for the assertion, a minimum level of knowledge would include knowledge of (1) the IRS code and its interpretations, (2) typical types of tax treatments for which alternatives might be applicable, and (3) tax calculations and the interrelationships that exist between various parts of the tax return. Such knowledge would be necessary to test whether the tax program is complete and whether or not it performs as asserted. Next, the auditor must determine whether special auditing training is necessary in order to test the software. It would not appear that special knowledge is required other than some knowledge of the workings of microcomputer software and methods that might be available to test the software.

sufficient evidence *and* about the type of software being audited. Recall that auditing consists of measuring assertions against prescribed, objective criteria such as GAAP, or other generally accepted criteria related to the item under examination.

An attestation function requires that the opinion be based on objective criteria. The public accountant is not in a position to attest to a financial transaction, such as a prospective takeover of a company, as a "fair" deal because generally accepted criteria for what constitutes "fair" has not been defined.* Likewise, the auditor has been prohibited from providing an opinion on the solvency of a prospective organization that might emerge from a leveraged buyout because criteria for such an evaluation are not clearly defined. Because there will continue to be requests for expanded scope of auditor services, future interpretations of this standard will shape the boundaries of the public accounting profession.

The standards of independence in mental attitude and the performance of the engagement within a framework of due professional care remain the same as with auditing standards. Independence remains the cornerstone of the attestation process; any compromise of independence lessens the value of the attestation process.

*It should be noted that the lack of criteria or explicit definition of what constitutes "fair" has not dissuaded investment banking firms from issuing such opinions on proposed financial transactions.

Standards of Fieldwork

The fieldwork standards are essentially identical to those of GAAS, except that there is no requirement to gain an understanding of the client's control structure. Such an understanding is not required because many attestation engagements require an understanding of only the quality of the product, not of the process by which the report or product was generated. The auditor does not need to understand the process of programming to determine whether the software product referred to in the practical example box correctly computes income taxes.

Standards of Reporting

The standards of reporting for attestation engagements require the auditor to specifically identify (1) the assertion being reported on and (2) the character of the engagement. Both items need to be identified because the types of engagements may vary widely. The auditor then states a conclusion as to whether the assertion is presented in conformity with established or stated criteria against which it was measured. If the auditor has significant reservations about the engagement or the presentation of the assertion, those reservations should be clearly stated in the audit report.

Like auditing standards, the attestation standards are not static. It is expected that they will grow and be refined over time as new types of engagements are encountered and users look for various forms of assurances regarding the engagements. It is expected that the attestation area will present opportunities for significant long-run growth for public accounting firms.

Summary

Auditing standards have evolved over a century in which the scope and nature of the auditor's work has changed significantly. The demand for auditor services has increased—and it is expected to continue to increase. The demand for the CPA's services is directly related to the quality of services rendered by the profession and the high regard in which the profession is held by business and the general public. The generally accepted auditing (or attestation) standards exist to provide a framework for the maintenance of high-quality work. The standards are implemented every day on every engagement.

Significant Terms

Accounting Series Releases (ASRs) Publications by the SEC providing rulings on the appropriate accounting treatment for transactions that have caught the SEC's attention and establishing auditing guidelines for CPA firms practicing before it; as of 1982, ASRs were divided into either *Financial Reporting Releases* or *Auditing Enforcement Releases*.

adverse audit report An audit report whereby the auditor reports an opinion that the financial statements, taken as a whole, are not presented in accordance with generally accepted accounting principles.

attestation function Any function in which one party is engaged to perform an independent examination of an assertion (representation) made by the first party to a third party, resulting in the communication by the independent party of a conclusion as to the fairness of the representation made by the first party to the third party.

audit program An auditor-prepared document which lists the specific procedures and audit tests to be performed in gathering evidence to test assertions.

Companies Causes Consolidation Act of 1845 A British act establishing the requirement for audits that was intended to ensure the fairness of the reporting on a trading company's expeditions and activities by requiring a shareholder to perform an audit of the books of account.

disclaimer An audit report in which the auditor does not express an opinion on the financial statements.

due professional care A standard of care expected to be demonstrated by a competent professional in his or her field of expertise, set by the generally accepted auditing standards but supplemented in specific implementation instances by the standard of care expected by a reasonably prudent auditor.

going concern report modification A fourth paragraph added to the standard unqualified audit report stating the auditor's substantial doubt about the ability of the client to remain operating as a "going concern"; the nature of the client's problems and management's plans for mitigating the problems must be disclosed in footnotes to the financial statements.

independence A state of objectivity and impartiality on the part of the auditor (i.e., an independent mental state) required by general auditing standards; auditors are required to maintain an *independence in fact* and *independence in appearance* in the conduct of all audit and attestation engagements.

internal control structure The controls implemented in an organization to ensure that only properly authorized transactions are processed and that the transactions are fully, accurately, and timely recorded.

materiality The magnitude of a misstatement or omission of financial statement information that would affect the judgment of a reasonable person relying on the information; implies that the auditor must understand users and the uses of financial statements.

qualified audit report Audit report indicating a significant scope limitation or that the auditor has concluded that the financial statements contain material misstatements or omissions that prevent them from being fairly presented in conformance with GAAP.

Securities Act of 1933 Federal statutory law related to the original issuance of securities, imposes a heavy burden on all parties associated with the issuance of the securities to ensure that full and fair disclosure is obtained in the financial reporting.

Securities Exchange Act of 1934 A Congressional act giving the Securities and Exchange Commission broad powers to censure firms practicing before it and to prescribe forms in which information shall be reported to it and the ultimate authority to establish accounting principles for all firms that must file reports with the SEC.

unqualified audit report Term describing the standard audit report in which the auditor states that the results of the audit indicate that the financial statements are fairly presented in conformance with GAAP; sometimes referred to as a *clean opinion*.

Review Questions

A–Introduction

2–1 In what ways have the profession's responsibility and the nature of its activities evolved over the past 100 years?

2–2 What is the role of the Securities and Exchange Commission in setting accounting and auditing standards? How does the SEC traditionally exercise its power?

2–3 The SEC often issues *Accounting Series Releases*. What is the authority of those releases? What companies are explicitly influenced by them?

2–4 What companies are specifically subjected to SEC rule (i.e., what criteria are utilized to determine whether or not a company is subject to SEC oversight)?

2–5 How did the public accounting profession change in the 1980s? What are the major factors influencing the manner in which the work of auditing is conducted today?

2–6 Why did the initial Companies Act originally require the auditor to be a shareholder of the corporation? Why is it likely that such a requirement does not exist today?

2–7 What are the major factors most likely to affect the nature and the work of the public accounting profession during the next decade? Why do you believe the factors selected will be the most important?

2–8 One of the British authors quoted in the chapter commented about the need for the Americans to give advice. Why is this tendency to give advice either good or bad for the U.S. public accounting profession? Explain.

B–Generally Accepted Auditing Standards

2–9 How is the term *due professional care* defined and measured? Identify specific criteria that a court might examine to determine whether a particular audit engagement was conducted with due professional care.

2–10 What role might the concept of due professional care play in litigation that is brought against a public accounting firm?

2–11 What criteria does the auditor use to determine whether or not sufficient audit evidence has been gathered on a particular engagement? How are these criteria measured?

2–12 Why is it important for an auditor to be independent?

2–13 What is an audit program? Who prepares such a program and how is it utilized during an audit?

2–14 What options are open to a new staff auditor who decides that the accounting treatment utilized by the audit client is inappropriate, but the manager and the partner on the engagement take the position that the treatment is appropriate?

C–Reporting and Attestation Standards

2–15 Why were the attestation standards needed when the profession already had generally accepted auditing standards?

2–16 What is an attestation engagement? Give three examples of attestation engagements. For each example, indicate the specific assertion that the auditor investigates.

2–17 How does an attestation engagement differ from an audit engagement?

2–18 What are the major differences between the attestation standards and the 10 generally accepted auditing standards?

2–19 What factors give the public accounting profession a "competitive advantage" in performing auditing and other attestation services? How does the profession ensure individual attainment of these standards?

2–20 What are the primary differences in the reporting standards contained in the attestation standards in contrast to the standards contained in the 10 generally accepted auditing standards?

2–21 What are the major components of a standard unqualified audit report? What is each of the components designed to accomplish?

2–22 What is a qualified audit opinion? Why is it important that the profession clearly distinguish between a qualified and an unqualified audit opinion?

2–23 How does an adverse audit opinion differ from a qualified audit opinion?

2–24 What criteria should a public accounting firm employ in determining whether or not a particular attestation engagement should be accepted?

2–25 The auditor's opinion on financial statements has been standardized for most instances the auditor is likely to encounter. What are the major advantages to the auditor of such standardization?

Multiple Choice Questions

2–26 The application of due professional care in audit engagement by a CPA firm means that the auditor's work at least conforms with all of the following *except:*

a. Current auditing standards as defined by Statements on Auditing Standards.

b. The work that a reasonably prudent auditor would have performed in the same situation.

c. The work that would have been performed by a reasonable person who was not necessarily trained in auditing.

d. The current work was at least equal to that which had been performed on the audit engagement during the preceding year.

2–27 The performance of attestation engagements is limited by all of the following *except:*

a. The competence and knowledge of the attestor in the subject matter of the attestation function.

b. The existence of objective criteria by which objective parties could assess the fairness of management's assertions regarding the item being attested to.

c. The existence of economic criteria by which to judge the assertion.

d. The existence of an information system through which information related to the assertion being examined can be gathered.

2–28 The following assertions have been offered by different companies related to the use of their products. They have approached a CPA firm to perform an attest engagement related to the assertions. Which of the following assertions would the CPA firm be most likely *not* to accept?

a. The software computes income tax in accordance with the IRS code and its interpretations.

b. The software computes income tax in accordance with IRS regulations and is the most efficient software in the business.

c. The software computes income tax in accordance with IRS regulations and prepares a comprehensive schedule of tax planning items related to the nature of the preparer's tax liabilities.

d. The software computes income tax in accordance with IRS regulations and *all* applicable state regulations.

2–29 During the course of an audit, a new staff auditor disagreed with the method the client used to account for an extraordinary item. The staff auditor did not believe that the transaction met the criteria for an extraordinary item, but the partner on the engagement agreed with the client's assessment. The staff auditor should

a. Meet with the corporate controller to convince him that the approach taken is in error and should be changed.

b. Request a meeting with the partner in charge of the office to present her view of the transaction and thereby protect the firm from a potential lawsuit.

c. Document the difference and the rationale for the difference in the working papers.

d. Request a reassignment to another job because the staff auditor should not be forced to be associated with an accounting treatment with which she disagrees.

*2–30 The Securities and Exchange Commission has authority to

a. Prescribe specific auditing procedures to detect fraud concerning inventories and accounts receivable of companies engaged in interstate commerce.

b. Deny lack of privity as a defense in third-party actions for gross negligence against the auditors of public companies.

*Adapted from the Uniform CPA examination or the Certified Internal Auditor examination.

c. Determine accounting principles for the purpose of financial reporting by companies offering securities to the public.

d. Require a change of auditors of governmental entities after a given period of years as a means of ensuring audit independence.

*2–31 An auditor's report includes this statement: "The financial statements do not present fairly the financial position, results of operations, or cash flows in conformity with generally accepted accounting principles." This auditor's report was most likely issued in connection with financial statements that are

a. Inconsistent.

b. Based on prospective financial statements.

c. Misleading.

d. Affected by a material uncertainty.

*2–32 The exercise of due care requires that an auditor

a. Use error-free judgment.

b. Study and review internal accounting control, including compliance tests.

c. Critically review the work done at every level of supervision.

d. Examine all corroborating evidence available.

e. All of the above.

*2–33 A difference of opinion regarding the results of a sample cannot be resolved between the staff auditor who performed the auditing procedures and the in-charge auditor. The assistant should

a. Refuse to perform any further work on the engagement.

b. Accept the judgment of the more experienced in-charge auditor.

c. Document the disagreement.

d. Notify the client that a serious audit problem exists.

*2–34 An auditor may *not* issue a qualified opinion when

a. A scope limitation prevents the performance of an important audit procedure.

b. The auditor's report refers to the work of a specialist from a field outside of accounting.

c. An accounting principle at variance with generally accepted accounting principles is used.

d. The auditor lacks independence with respect to the audited entity.

*2–35 The third general standard states that due care is to be exercised in the performance of an audit. This standard is generally interpreted to require

a. Objective review of the adequacy of the technical training and proficiency of firm personnel.

b. Critical review of work done at every level of supervision.

c. Thorough review of the existing internal control structure.

d. Periodic review of a CPA firm's quality control procedures.

Discussion and Research Questions

*2–36 (Generally Accepted Auditing Standards) Ray, the owner of a small company, asked Holmes, CPA, to conduct an audit of the company's records. Ray told Holmes that the audit must be completed in time to submit audited financial statements to a bank as part of a loan application. Holmes immediately accepted the engagement and agreed to provide an auditor's report within three weeks. Ray agreed to pay Holmes a fixed fee plus a bonus if the loan were granted.

Holmes hired two accounting students to conduct the audit and spent several hours telling them exactly what to do. Holmes told the students not to spend time reviewing the controls but instead to concentrate on proving the mathematical accuracy of the ledger accounts and to summarize the data in the accounting records that support Ray's financial statements. The students followed Holmes' instructions and after two weeks gave Holmes the financial statements that did not include footnotes because the company did not have any unusual transactions. Holmes reviewed the statements and prepared an unqualified auditor's report. The report, however, did not refer to generally accepted accounting principles or to the year-to-year application of such principles.

Required:

Briefly describe each of the generally accepted auditing standards and indicate how the action(s) of Holmes resulted in a failure to comply with each standard.

2–37 (Attestation Standards and New Services) During the 1980s, the investment banking profession began issuing "fairness letters" on proposed mergers or acquisitions. Essentially, the board of directors of an organization that might be a takeover candidate asked the investment banker to assess the terms of proposed buy out and prepare a report to the board assessing the fairness of the proposed transaction.

Required:

a. Could the public accounting profession have performed such an attestation service? Why or why not? Specifically identify factors that might have allowed or prohibited the performance of such services by the public accounting profession.

b. In which ways would the public accounting profession have had a competitive advantage/disadvantage vis-à-vis the investment banker profession in performing such a service?

2–38 (Criteria for Attestation Engagements) Assume that you have been hired to perform an attestation engagement for a new firm called TAXEASY. The company has developed a software package that can be used on microcomputers to assist users in preparing personal tax returns and in tax planning. The company wants the attestation engagement to provide objective evidence as to the completeness and accuracy of the tax software for preparing personal income tax returns and identifying tax planning issues that would be obvious with the preparation of the return. The company would like the attestation report to be included in a brochure that it intends to use as part of its advertising campaign.

Required:

a. Identify the specific assertions the auditor needs to discuss with the client as a basis to determine whether to take the engagement.

b. For each assertion identified above, identify the criteria the auditor might refer to in judging the assertion.

*2–39 (Auditor Reports) The following auditors' report was drafted by a staff accountant of Turner & Turner, CPAs, at the completion of the audit of the financial statements of Lyon Computers, Inc., for the year ended March 31, 1994. It was submitted to the engagement partner, who reviewed matters thoroughly and concluded that Lyon's disclosures concerning its ability to continue as a going concern for a reasonable period of time were adequate.

To the Board of Directors of Lyon Computers, Inc.

We have audited the accompanying balance sheet of Lyon Computers, Inc., as of March 31, 1994, and the other related financial statements for the year then ended. Our responsibility is to express an opinion on these financial statements based on our audit.

We conducted our audit in accordance with standards that required that we plan and perform the audit to obtain reasonable assurance about whether the financial statements are in conformity with generally accepted accounting principles. An audit includes examining, on a test basis, evidence supporting the amounts and disclosures in the financial statements. An audit also includes assessing the accounting principles used and significant estimates made by management.

The accompanying financial statements have been prepared assuming that the Company will continue as a going concern. As discussed in Note H to the financial statements, the Company has suffered recurring losses from operations and has a net capital deficiency that creates substantial doubt about its ability to continue as a going concern beyond a reasonable period of time. The financial statements do not include any adjustments that might result from the outcome of this uncertainty.

In our opinion, subject to the effects on the financial statements of such adjustments, if any, as might have been required had the outcome of the uncertainty referred to in the preceding paragraph been known, the financial statements referred to above present fairly the financial position of Lyon Computers, Inc., and the results of operations and its cash flows in conformity with generally accepted accounting principles applied on a basis consistent with that of the preceding year (which we did not audit).

Turner & Turner
April 28, 1995

Required:

Identify the deficiencies contained in the auditor's report as drafted by the staff accountant. Group the deficiencies by paragraph.

2–40 (Audit Reports) Assume that you are the audit partner for each of the following independent situations. For each situation, indicate the *type of audit report* that should be issued. If additional information is needed to make a decision, indicate the type of information and the types of reports that would be affected by the information. *Assume that all of the situations described below are material to the financial statements.*

Audit Situations

a. You are on the annual audit of OsterWay Company, a client for the past 12 years. The company has experienced severe operating difficulties. Although management believes it can work its way out of the problems if a recession is avoided, you have doubts about its ability to remain in operation for a reasonable period of time.

b. During the audit of Ace Electronics, you become concerned that a significant portion of the inventory is obsolete. Management demonstrates to you that the inventory still works perfectly. However, your analysis of industry trends and recent sales corroborate your opinion that the net realizable value of the inventory is significantly less than historical cost. Management disagrees and will not write the inventory down because there is no proof that there has been an impairment of value since the products still work well.

c. You are engaged to perform a first-year audit of Hastings Manufacturing, but you were not engaged as auditor until after the end of the year. Therefore, you were not able to observe the ending inventory as of the balance sheet date. Although the inventory is highly material, you are able to satisfy yourself by other means that inventory is fairly stated at year-end. No material errors were noted in the rest of the audit, although a number of smaller immaterial errors were noted but were not booked.

d. After completing the audit of Meijer Department Store, you discover that the manager on the audit owns stock in the company. She acquired the stock last year when she married a man who had 500 shares of stock in the company. She and her husband converted all of their assets to joint custody. Meijer is traded on a major stock exchange, and the 500 shares is not considered a material investment by the manager.

e. Weaver Auto Parts has a fleet of several delivery trucks. In the past, Weaver has followed a policy of purchasing all trucks. In the current year, the company decided to lease all new trucks and dispose of all the old trucks. You have concluded that the lease does not meet the criteria of a capital lease. The sale of the old trucks is adequately disclosed in the financial statements and described in a footnote. However, the company shows a significant decline in assets and liabilities due to the change.

f. The Naire Manufacturing Company changed its method of accounting for inventories from FIFO to LIFO. Due to the dramatic increase in inflation affecting the company's products, management believes that LIFO better portrays the economic substance of its operations. The company had not experienced such rapid inflation until the dramatic increase in oil prices over the past few years. The change and the dollar effect of such changes are adequately described in Note J to the financial statements.

2–41 (Audit Reports) Assume that you are the audit partner for each of the following independent situations. For each situation, indicate the *type of audit report* that should be issued. If additional information is needed to make a decision, indicate the type of information and the types of reports that would be affected by the information.

Audit Situations

a. On February 13, just six weeks after year-end, a major customer of Smith Wholesale Company declared bankruptcy. Because the company had confirmed the balance due to Smith at the balance sheet date, management refuses to write off the account for the current year's December 31 audit but is willing to disclose the amounts in a note to the financial statements. The receivable represents approximately 10 percent of net income and 15 percent of earnings. You are convinced that the customer was near bankruptcy at year-end and the receivable was not collectible at that time.

b. A standard audit procedure regarding accounts receivable is to confirm the amount owed by customers by sending them a confirmation at year-end. The controller of Jet Growth will not allow you to confirm the receivables balance from two of its major customers because the customers had requested that they not be "bothered" by year-end audit requests as part of their agreement to do business with Jet Growth. You are unable to satisfy yourself by alternative procedures as to the correctness or collectability of the two receivables.

c. During the past three years, Mid-Continent Oil Company decided to alter its business strategy and expand into the oil drilling business as a source for its refining. Management recognizes that oil drilling is risky and could jeopardize the existing refining business, but the need to ensure a supply of oil was considered too important to not take the risk. During the first three years, the company drilled five oil wells, but only one produced a moderate amount of oil. The drilling results are adequately explained in the footnotes.

d. You have just completed the audit of Tomahawk Specialties, a wholesaler located in a small northern town. The financial statements will be distributed to management and to the local bank as part of a loan agreement with the bank. The company has been very successful, and the owner is a reputable businessperson who also serves on the board of directors of the local bank. The company has requested that footnote disclosures be omitted because they are costly, often confuse rather than amplify, and are not needed because the financial statements will be distributed only to people who are quite familiar with the company's operations anyway.

e. You are finishing the audit of a regional bank. The bank's president has just read about the SEC's encouragement to have all marketable securities stated at market value because such values may better reflect economic reality. Although the SEC has not mandated such reporting, the president wants to be a leader and has mandated that the financial statements reflect all assets and liabilities at current market values.

f. You have audited LBO, Inc., for a number of years. The company has made a large number of acquisitions over the years, and a significant portion of its assets (40 percent) is in goodwill. The company is amortizing the goodwill over 40 years and references APB No. 16 as the authority. A number of acquisitions have been sold, and a significant number of continuing operations are experiencing severe losses. No adjustments have been made to the accounting for, or acquisition of, goodwill because the company understands the financial statements must be consistent with those of the previous years and because goodwill is an intangible whose value is difficult to determine.

2–42 (Audit Reports) The following are independent situations in which you will recommend an appropriate audit report from the types listed below. For each situation, identify the appropriate type of audit report and briefly explain the rationale for selecting the report:

a. Unqualified, standard.
b. Unqualified, explanatory paragraph.
c. Qualified opinion because of departure from GAAP.
d. Qualified scope and opinion.
e. Disclaimer.
f. Adverse.

Audit Situation

a. An audit client has a significant amount of loans receivable outstanding (40 percent of assets) but has an inadequate control system over the loans. The auditor can locate neither sufficient information to prepare an aging of the loans nor collateral for about 75 percent of the loans even though the client states that all loans are collateralized. The auditor sent out confirmations but only 10 of 50 sent out were returned. The auditor attempts to verify the other loans by looking at subsequent payments, but only eight had remitted payments during the month of January and the auditor wants to wrap up the audit by February 15. If only 10 of the 50 loans were correctly recorded, the auditor estimates that loans would need to be written down by $7.5 million.

b. During the audit of a large manufacturing company, the auditor was not able to observe all locations of physical inventory. The auditor chose a random number of sites to visit and the company's internal auditors visited the other sites. The auditor has confidence in the competence and objectivity of the internal auditors. The auditor personally observed only about 20 percent of the total inventory, but neither the auditor or the internal auditor noted any exceptions in the inventory process.

c. During the past year, Network Computer, Inc., devoted its entire research and development efforts to develop and market an enhanced version of its state-of-the-art computer system with an ability to network with all mainframe computer systems and download and process data at the same rate of speed as the mainframe systems even though its products are classified as microcomputers. The costs were significant and were all capitalized as research and development costs. The company plans to amortize these capitalized costs over the life of the new product. The auditor has concluded that the research to date will probably result in a marketable product. A full description of the research and development and the costs are adequately described in a note. The note also describes that basic research costs are expensed as incurred, and the auditor has verified the accuracy of the statement.

d. During the course of the audit of Sail-Away Company, the auditor noted that the current ratio dropped to 1.75 and the company's loan covenant requires the maintenance of a current ratio of 2.0 to 1.0 or the company's debt is all immediately due. The auditor and the company have contacted the bank, which is not willing to waive the loan covenant because the company has been experiencing operating losses for the past few years and has an inadequate capital structure. The auditor has substantial doubt that the company can find adequate financing elsewhere and may encounter difficulties staying in operation. Management, however, is confident that it can overcome the problem and is willing to pledge its personal assets to get a loan from a competing bank. The bank loan is classified as current and the due date is shown on the financial statements, but management does not deem it necessary to include any additional disclosure because it is confident that an alternative source of funds will be found by pledging their personal assets.

e. The Wear-Ever Wholesale Company has been very profitable and has been able to pass on all cost increases to its clients. The company received notice of a 10 percent price increase for a significant portion of its inventory shortly before year-end. The company believes it is important to manage its products wisely and has a policy of writing all inventory up to current replacement cost. This ensures that profits will be recognized on sales to an extent sufficient to replace the assets and realize a normal profit. This operating philosophy has been very successful, and all salespeople reference current cost, not historical cost, in making sales. Only inventory has been written up to replacement cost, but inventory is material because the company carries a wide range of products. The company's policy of writing up the inventory and the dollar effects thereof are adequately described in a footnote to the financial statements. For the current year, the net effect is to increase reported income only by 3 percent, but assets are stated at 15 percent above historical cost.

f. The audit of NewCo was staffed primarily by three new hires and a relatively inexperienced audit senior. The manager found numerous errors during the conduct of the audit and developed very long "to-do" lists for all members of the audit to complete before the audit was concluded. Although the manager had original doubts about the staff's understanding of the audit procedures, he concluded that by the time the audit was finished, the new auditors did understand the company and the audit process and that no material errors existed in the financial statements.

2–43 (Evolving Auditing Procedures) A reference to the history of Arthur Andersen & Co. indicates that very early in that company's history, it was involved in preparing reports on many phases of a company's business. These reports included analysis of availability of raw materials, plants, effectiveness of marketing plans, and financing alternatives. These activities not only served as the basis for the development of a strong consulting practice but also enhanced the audit practice.

Required:

a. Briefly describe how the procedures performed by Arthur Andersen & Co. early in its history might lead to the performance of attestation engagements today. Give some specific examples.

b. Briefly explain how the knowledge developed by understanding the various aspects of a client's business could be used effectively by the auditor in planning and conducting an audit of a company's financial statements.

c. Identify some tools that may have been developed in performing an analysis of a company's operations that might effectively be utilized in the conduct of an audit.

2–44 (Emergence of the Auditing Profession) The auditing profession has changed dramatically over the years. The profession has responded to critical changes in the environment in which it performs services.

Required:

a. How did the nature and practice of auditing differ in the 19th century from that of the early 20th century? What significant events changed the nature of auditing between the 1850s and the early 1900s?

b. How did the profession change with the stock market crash of 1929 and the subsequent legislation developing the Securities and Exchange Commission?

c. How does the public accounting profession in the 1990s differ from that of the 1940s?

2–45 **(Research Question: Attestation Standards)** The rationale for the development of the attestation standards is that the audit function is not limited to performing attestation services on financial statements, but that the public has a demand for an independent assessment of the reliability of all kinds of reports. What are the limits to attestation services that might be performed by the public accounting profession?

Required:

a. Survey some public accounting firms in your area to determine the nature of attestation services performed by those firms.

b. Develop a position paper that would conceptually define the limits of attestation services. In the paper, define criteria the profession might utilize to specifically identify the bounds of such services.

2–46 **(Research Question: The SEC and *Accounting Series Releases*)** The SEC issues *Accounting Series Releases* (ASRs) in response to practice issues it believes are not currently addressed by existing accounting or auditing standards. Some ASRs also follow from the SEC's criticism of particular accounting or auditing which it believes is deficient.

Required:

a. Obtain a copy of a recent *ASR* (either *Financial Reporting Releases* or *Auditing Enforcement Releases*) from your library. Perform a review and answer the following questions:

   1. Why was the *ASR* released (i.e., why was the issue topical)?
   2. In which ways does the *ASR* differ from, or supplement, existing pronouncements by the FASB or the Auditing Standards Board?

3. How many companies or industries are likely to be affected by the *ASR*?

b. What is the authority of the *ASR* pronouncements (i.e., what entities are governed by it)? What type of audit opinion would be given if a client were following GAAP but an *ASR* required the client to follow a different principle for filing with the SEC? Explain the rationale for your answer.

Cases

2–47 (Fairness of Financial Statements) In reporting on the 1982 income of General Motors Corporation, Abraham Briloff reported that General Motors only made $22.8 million from the sale of cars:

> In 1982, General Motors reported only "$22.8 million as the amount earned from the corporation's production and sale of vehicles and related products. The corresponding pre-tax and pre-equity earnings for 1983 amounted to a whopping $4,971.5 million (just shy of $5 billion.)"
>
> Well, then, as the saying goes, "where's the beef?" My response is that the two sets of data are incomparable, even beyond the drastic divergences in their magnitude. Here I want to go back to the $22.8 million toted up for 1982. That "tiny" sum included three items calling for special consideration. To wit:
>
> 1. That operating income included $305 million of LIFO inventory profits, i.e., the amount by which income was injected by reason of the company's decision to refrain from replacing certain of its LIFO inventory pools. For 1983 there was no such surfacing of suppressed LIFO profits.
> 2. For 1982 the company's management opted to stay with FASB Statement No. 8 regarding Foreign Currency Translation (rather than shift to Statement 52). As a consequence that year's income was enhanced by $348.4 million. For 1983 the company's income was actually reduced by $52.3 million. Mind you, GM's decision to "stand pat" on FASB 8 was entirely consistent with the election afforded by the subject of the FASB promulgation; and, it should go without saying, the auditors concurred in that option.
> 3. 1982 Footnote 4, regarding "Other Income" in turn carried a little footnote informing the readers with 20/20 visual acuity that the company enjoyed a $48.7 million "gain" from the early retirement of long-term debt. By such an inclusion that sum was carried down into the $22.8 millon operating income referred to above. . . .
>
> The critical point I am making, essentially as my opening gambit, is that with the auditor's concurrence, which they assured us was all in accordance with GAAP/GAAS, GM's income was swelled by $702.1 million *as a consequence of management's decisions, essentially independent of the underlying "economic realities."* Absent those management-induced injections the company would have been constrained to report a $679.3 million loss (pre-tax and pre-equity in unconsolidated subsidiaries).
>
> . . . I will conclude this David-Goliath saga with the ultimate question, "How unfair may the financial statements be and yet be deemed fair in accordance with GAAP?"[8]

Required:

a. How does the auditor determine whether financial statements are fairly presented when management can choose to manipulate the financial reporting as described above?

b. Is it possible for financial statements to be fairly presented in accordance with GAAP, yet at the same time not really be fairly presented? Explain.

c. A 1978 report by a commission studying the auditor's responsibilities suggested that the auditor needs to step back from a financial presentation to determine whether the financial statements, in their totality, present a misleading financial impression of the economic realities even if the statements are fairly presented according to GAAP. In your view of the accounting profession, what would be the advantages and disadvantages of such a proposal?

2–48 (Fairness and Professionalism) In a 1988 article, Arthur Wyatt, a former member of the Financial Accounting Standards Board, stated:

> Practicing professionals should place the public interest above the interests of clients, particularly when participating in a process designed to develop standards expected to achieve fair presentation. . . . Granted that the increasingly detailed nature of FASB standards encourages efforts to find loopholes, a professional ought to strive to apply standards in a manner that will best achieve the objectives sought by the standards. *Unfortunately, the auditor today is often a participant in aggressively seeking loopholes.* The public, on the other hand, views auditors as their protection against aggressive standard application. (emphasis added)[9]

Required:

a. What does it mean to find "loopholes" in FASB pronouncements? How would finding loopholes be potentially valued by the management of a client?

b. Explain how auditors could be participants in "aggressively seeking loopholes" when the independence standard requires the pursuit of fairness in financial presentation.

c. How is professionalism related to the concept of fairness in financial reporting? Explain.

End Notes

1 Edward Blocher, Roubert Roussey, and Bart Ward, "The Subject Matter of Auditing," *Research Opportunities in Auditing: The Second Decade* (Sarasota, Fla.: American Accounting Association, 1988), 137.

2. AICPA Professional Standards, Volume 1, U.S. Auditing Standards, Attestation Standards, as of June 1, 1993 (Chicago: Commerce Clearing House, 1993).

3. Gary John Previts, *The Scope of CPA Services* (New York, John Wiley, 1985).

4. A. P. Richardson in a 1915 editorial, as quoted in Previts, *Scope of CPA Services*, 39.

5. Arthur Andersen & Co., *The First Fifty Years: 1913–1963* (Chicago: Arthur Andersen & Co., 1982), 32.

6. SEC, *Accounting Series Release* No. 268, "Redeemable Preferred Stock" (Washington, D.C.: Government Printing Office, 1979).
7. AU Sec. 2010.
8. Abraham Briloff, "Standards without Standards/Principles without Principles/Fairness without Fairness," *Advances in Accounting* 3 (1986), 25–50.
9. Arthur Wyatt, "Professionalism in Standard Setting," *CPA Journal* (July 1988), 20–26.

CHAPTER

3

Learning Objectives

Through studying this chapter, you will be able to:

1. Increase awareness of the importance of thoughtfully dealing with ethical dilemmas.
2. Use a framework to resolve ethical dilemmas.
3. Gain an appreciation of the need for professional codes of ethics.
4. Understand the codes of ethics of the public accounting and internal auditing professions.
5. Become familiar with the approaches used to improve the quality of public accounting and internal auditing organizations.

Professional Ethics: Maintaining Quality and the Public Trust

Chapter Contents

Chapter Overview

Auditors are frequently faced with ethical dilemmas. It is extremely important that they maintain high ethical standards in such situations. Otherwise, they will lose the respect of users of their services. This chapter provides an overview of basic ethical theory and a framework within which to consider ethical dilemmas. The codes of ethics of the AICPA and IIA are described, and the programs that these two organizations have developed to help ensure ethical behavior of their members are discussed.

A–INTRODUCTION AND OVERVIEW

It has been alleged that the ethical behavior of businesses during the past decade has declined significantly. The financial press is filled with stories, such as the following, of individuals and groups who are involved in unethical behavior.

> **New Fraud Alleged at Army Missile Base.** The General Accounting Office alleged that among several instances of overcharges, favoritism, and phony bills, a company under military contract billed a 45-minute job at 23 hours.
>
> **IRS Focusing on Accounting at Southern Company.** Officials of the Southern Company were improperly accounting for certain spare parts which saved the company several million dollars in income taxes. Key personnel in the audit and tax departments of their audit firm knew of this scheme to defraud the IRS.
>
> **Aftermath of Huge Fraud Prompts Claims of Regret.** A CPA is sentenced to jail after unintentionally getting involved in the perpetuation of a fraud that caused many people to lose their life's savings.

In each of these three situations, an individual or group acted to maximize short-term objectives and ended up in trouble. The individuals apparently did not think about the consequences of their actions or even whether they were making the "right" decisions. The second example seems to be quite common: A mistake is made and then, rather than face the consequences, a cover-up plan is devised only to aggravate the problem.

The long-term success of a profession depends on the ethical behavior of each of its individual members in each professional assignment and in personal conduct. The perception of the profession is influenced by actions of individuals. For audit firms, no amount of audit planning, gathering evidence, or proper reporting will overcome unethical behavior on the part of individuals who represent the profession.

This chapter focuses on the importance of ethical behavior, the *sine quo non* of public accounting, and the codes of ethics of the AICPA and the Institute of Internal Auditors. These codes shape the quality review programs instituted to ensure that auditors, public and internal, carry out their responsibilities.

Professionalism in Public Accounting

A profession holds itself out as having higher standards of conduct than does the society at large. Thus, society looks to a profession to protect its interest. The "P" in CPA stands for public; that is, the accountant who is so licensed is a certified *public* accountant. Public accounting exists to perform unbiased services such as rendering an opinion on a company's financial statements so that third parties can rely on such statements. In fact, the opinion of the auditor has value only if third parties believe that the auditor is *objective* in gathering and evaluating the evidence and is *independent* of client pressures when rendering that opinion. The profession's ethical standards are designed to ensure the public that its trust is merited and to provide the necessary guidelines for the profession to guide its conduct.

The commitment to act in the public's interest is mandated in today's highly competitive environment. When auditors aggressively seek new clients, however, the public interest could become subordinate to individual priorities. The potential loss of commitment to the *public* worries many leading professionals. Arthur R. Wyatt, a former member of the Financial Accounting Standards Board, recently reemphasized this public responsibility:

> Practicing professionals should place the public interest above the interests of clients, particularly when participating in a process designed to develop standards expected to achieve fair presentation. . . . Unfortunately, the auditor today is often a participant in aggressively seeking loopholes.[1]

This concept of professionalism extends beyond an accountant's career in public accounting to include a career as a preparer of an organization's financial statements. At a time when some accountants look on their role as "financial engineering" (that is, using accounting principles to make the financial statements, or the results of a potential deal, look good), the sense of professionalism calls out for accountants and auditors to go back to fundamental accounting concepts to determine *not* whether GAAP can be stretched to meet the client's wishes, *but* rather whether the transaction accurately portrays the economic substance of the financial event. The professional should be asking questions such as these: Is the transaction unbiased with respect to the users? Although it complies with GAAP, does the recording accurately reflect the substance, rather than just the form, of the transaction? The court dockets are replete with cases involving situations in which auditors did not ask such questions. The auditors may have believed that their responsibility could be abdicated by "hiding behind GAAP." Although the courts frequently find that adherence to GAAP is a sufficient defense, they deviate from that position when it becomes evident that financial events may have been portrayed in a manner that does not reflect their underlying substance.

Professionalism should always be the byword for the development of the standards of ethical conduct for all accountants. Preparation for a career in accounting implies preparation for entering a profession. "The profession is no better than what it can do in the future, not what it has done in the past."[2]

Importance of Ethical Conduct

The profession has worked hard to gain the public trust. For that trust to be maintained, professional integrity based on personal moral standards and reinforced by codes of conduct is essential. Whenever a "scandal" surfaces, the profession is diminished and the auditors are personally ruined. An example of such a scandal involved Jose L. Gomez, external auditor for E.S.M. Government Securities. In a lengthy interview reported in *The Wall Street Journal,* Gomez described his weakness in being pulled into a fraud that cost investors millions of dollars:

> The aftershocks from the collapse of E.S.M. Government Securities stunned municipalities and thrifts across the country that had invested with the firm. The scheme that Jose L. Gomez helped perpetrate initially cost investors about $320 million. But perhaps nowhere was the damage greater than in Ohio. "When in March '85 I saw the tragedy of the Ohio depositors, that really hurt," Mr. Gomez says. "This is something I had never looked at—whose money is being played with here. That caused me a great deal of pain and sorrow."
>
> In a recent interview, Mr. Gomez talked of his rise and fall. He says he never intended to do anything wrong. But in August 1979, just days after being told of his promotion to partner, two officers of E.S.M. told him of a crude accounting ruse that was hiding millions of dollars in losses: they had to bring Mr. Gomez in on the scheme to keep it from unraveling.
>
> Mr. Gomez says he had missed the ruse in two previous annual audits, signing off on bogus financial statements showing E.S.M. to be in robust condition. He says one of the E.S.M. officers used that error to draw him into the fraud.
>
> **Gomez**: He must have said it four or five times: "How's it going to look. It's going to look terrible for you, and you just got promoted to partner. Just give us a chance. It just takes time. We're not going to have those losses."
>
> **WSJ**: Do you think he was trying to intimidate you?
>
> **Gomez**: No question about it. And it worked. I was 31 years old. I felt I had a terrific career path in front of me and a lot of ambition.. . . And I agreed just to think about it. And a day or two later, I felt I already had gone too far. I also didn't want to face it. I didn't want to face walking in [to his superiors] and saying this is what happened.[3]

Gomez pleaded guilty to charges that he knowingly approved E.S.M.'s false financial statements for five years, thus allowing the massive fraud to continue. He was sentenced to 12 years in prison and must serve at least four of them. Had Gomez thought carefully about the consequences of his actions, he would probably have taken the problem to his superiors, who had surely faced ethically compromising situations themselves. Gomez's behavior is not typical. Most accountants are highly ethical and would never accept "saving face" as a reason for abhorrent behavior.

It is not difficult to find oneself in ethically compromising situations without realizing it! During the course of an audit, for example, an auditor may become aware of a client's plans that will likely double the market value of its stock. Another client has a significant investment in this stock and is planning to sell these shares. Should the auditor provide "extra-value" services and tell the second client to hold the stock? Can the auditor purchase shares of the stock? Can the auditor advise friends to purchase the stock? These may be simple problems. But the profession has developed guidance to assist auditors in ensuring that the actions they take will not be violating a public or client trust.

Many ethical problems can be resolved by following the code of conduct established by professional association(s): the AICPA, the state societies of CPAs, the state boards of accountancy, and the Institute of Internal Auditors. These codes and their rules of conduct are based in large measure on fundamental ethical concepts as they apply to the profession. When ethical problems are not specifically covered by these codes, the auditor must utilize common sense, moral values, and the general ethical framework of the codes to resolve these ethical problems.

Ethical Theories

An **ethical problem** occurs when an individual is morally or ethically required to do something that conflicts with his or her immediate self-interest. An **ethical dilemma** occurs when there are conflicting moral duties or obligations, such as paying a debt to one person when there is equal indebtedness to another person and sufficient funds do not exist to repay both. Ethical theories present frameworks to assist individuals in dealing with both ethical problems and ethical dilemmas. Two such frameworks—the *utilitarian theory* and the *rights theory*—provide references that have influenced the development of codes of conduct and can be used by professionals in dealing with ethical problems and dilemmas.

Utilitarian Theory

Utilitarian theory holds that what is ethical is the action that achieves the greatest good for the greatest number of people. Actions are considered ethical if they are useful for providing results that bring the greatest overall benefit to the greatest number of people. Those actions that result in outcomes that fall short of the greatest good for the greatest number and those that represent inefficient means to accomplish such ends are less desirable. Utilitarianism requires the following:

- An identification of the potential problem and courses of action.
- The potential direct or indirect impact of actions on each party, (often referred to as **stakeholders**) that may somehow have a vested interest in the outcome of actions taken.
- An assessment of the desirability (goodness) of each action.
- An overall assessment of the greatest good for the greatest number as constrained by minimum definitions of defined "good" outcomes.

Utilitarianism requires that individuals not advocate or choose alternatives that favor narrow interests or that serve the greatest good in an inefficient manner. There can be honest disagreements about the likely impact of actions or the relative efficiency of different actions in attaining desired ends. There are also potential problems in measuring what constitutes "the greatest good" in a particular circumstance. Just how can the "greatest good" be measured when an auditor tells one client to hold shares of stock in the other client?

One cultural problem with the utilitarian theory is the implicit assumption that the "ends achieved" justify the means. Unfortunately, we have often found that such an approach can lead to disastrous, or at least very unpopular, courses of actions when those making the decisions fail to adequately measure or assess the potential costs and benefits. Thus, ethicists generally argue that some other approach ought to mitigate the utilitarian approach. The rights approach presents such a framework.

Rights Theory

Rights theory focuses on evaluating actions in terms of the fundamental rights of the parties involved. But not all rights are equal. In the hierarchy of rights, higher-order rights take precedence over lower-order rights. The *highest-order rights* include the right to life, to autonomy, and to human dignity. *Second-order rights* include rights granted by the government, such as civil rights, legal rights, rights to own property, and license privileges. *Third-order rights* are social rights, such as the right to higher education, to good health care, and to earn a living. The lowest level, *fourth-order rights*, are related to one's nonessential interests or one's tastes, such as the right to get rich, to play golf, or to be attractively dressed.

Rights theory requires that the "rights" of affected parties ought to be examined as a constraint on ethical decision making. In the E.S.M. securities fraud, for example, had Mr. Gomez considered the rights of the retired people who had their life's savings in the Ohio savings bank that went bankrupt because of his actions, he might have worried less about "losing face" and more about the consequences for everyone involved. Rights theory may not be inconsistent with the results obtained from utilitarianism. For example, the same answer is obtained in the Gomez case applying utilitarianism as is obtained applying the rights approach. However, the rights approach is most effective in identifying outcomes that ought to be automatically eliminated, such as the Robin Hood approach of robbing from the rich to give to the poor.

An Ethical Framework: Utilitarianism Constrained by Rights Considerations

Complex ethical decisions cannot be made simply by an individual concluding that one action is "better" or more ethically "correct." Rather, a defined methodology is needed whereby a person can identify ethical issues as they arise, consider the parties involved, and analyze the range of consequences of alternative available actions in terms of the rights of those affected. The following framework is derived from the utilitarianism and rights theories and indicates the specific steps a person needs to utilize in addressing ethical problems or dilemmas:

- Identify the ethical issue(s).
- Determine the affected parties and identify their rights.
- Determine the most important rights.
- Develop alternative courses of action.
- Determine the likely consequences of each proposed course of action.
- Assess the possible consequences, including an estimation of the greatest good for the greatest number. Determine whether the rights framework would cause any courses of action to be eliminated.
- Decide on the appropriate course of action.

The following case, based on an actual situation, is presented to show how to apply this framework to auditing situations. The discussion assumes that some audit firms are willing to become client advocates to gain an audit, that is, some public accounting firms aggressively seek loopholes or take accounting rules to their limit in order to gain a client. Absent this assumption, made for illustrative purposes, the issue is not very controversial: All public accounting firms would come up with the same result.

Apply the Ethical Framework: Potential Client Proposal

You are the managing partner of a local CPA firm. Your firm, three other local CPA firms, and one national firm have been asked to submit a written proposal and bid for the audit of a very attractive growth enterprise, American Company, which is dominated by two owners and is undercapitalized. Through some related-party sale and repurchase transactions over a two-year period, the company has effectively written up its property, plant, and equipment to replacement value.

Management is very careful to spell out all the details of these transactions; it does not try to hide any of them. The owners believe that the balance sheet should show the true market value of the company because the bank seems willing to make a needed, sizable loan if the company's net assets are of sufficient value to collateralize the loan. In fact, the bank has told the company that it will grant the loan if the balance sheet reflects the market value of the assets. Management expects that its new auditors may require some disclosure of the related-party transaction but realizes that some forms of the disclosure may be less likely to jeopardize the potential loan than others. As a required part of each proposal, management asks each firm explicitly to indicate how these transactions should be shown in the financial statements and related notes.

Identify the Ethical Issue(s)

The major issue is whether you should respond to the request for a proposal by including a description of how the transactions should be handled and providing the necessary disclosure wording. Alternatively, should the profession, in the aggregate, be precluded from making such a response?

Determine the Affected Parties and Identify Their Rights

The relevant parties to the issue include the following:

- Company management.
- The bank considering a loan.
- An alternative bank, should management decide to expand negotiations for the loan.
- Your CPA firm.
- Other CPA firms that may submit audit proposals.
- The public accounting profession.
- Other company management.
- Creditors and equity investors, current and prospective.

Listing those potentially affected by the decision on the proposal is a little easier than identifying their rights. The following, however, indicates some of the rights involved.

- Company management would seem to have the *right to request information that would be useful in judging the competence of the auditor* and in obtaining audit services at the lowest cost. To preclude management from gathering this information might restrict its right of free choice. Management would seem to have the right to define the criteria by which it judges the competence of the auditor, in this case, the auditor's ability to account for these related-party transactions.

- Banks have a *right to receive fairly presented financial statements prepared in accordance with generally accepted accounting principles*, including full footnote description of non-arm's-length transactions between the organization and related parties. The banks have the right to receive unbiased opinions from auditors who are hired to perform the attest function on the financial statements.
- Your CPA firm has the *right to compete for new business and to appropriate compensation for its services*. Other CPA firms have the right to expect that competition between the firms will be professional and will not jeopardize fundamental principles of the profession, for example, the integrity of the audit function and the fundamental need to maintain independence in audit engagements.
- The public accounting profession has the *right to expect all its members to uphold the Code of Professional Conduct* and to take actions that enhance the general reputation and perception of the integrity of the profession.
- Other company managements have the *right to receive the benefits of competition within the public accounting profession*.
- Finally, current and prospective creditors and equity investors have a *right to receive fairly presented financial statements* to help them make investment decisions.

Determine the Most Important Rights

The auditing profession exists to provide independent and unbiased opinions to users. Therefore, it would seem that the most important right would be that of the users to independent, professional assessments.

Develop Alternative Courses of Action

Three courses of action seem to be available: (1) have each firm decide whether or not to comment on the proposed accounting treatment, (2) encourage all firms to comment on the proposed accounting treatment, and (3) develop a professionwide rule that would prohibit accounting firms from commenting, in advance, on the proposed treatment of the accounting issue.

Determine the Likely Consequences

If collectively or individually, firms provide the accounting treatment and necessary disclosures as requested by American's management, the following undesirable effects for the firm and the profession could result:

- Decrease in auditor independence.
- Decrease in adherence to the spirit of audit and accounting standards in order to compete and attract a client.
- Perception of a "contingent fee" arrangement in that the fees to be earned essentially depend on the course of action outlined by the auditing firms.

- Loss of an engagement by not complying with management's request, especially if some of the other firms do comply with the request.

On the other hand, if the profession prohibited responses to management's requests of this kind, the following consequences may occur:

- Violation of management's right to know and judge how auditors would handle specific accounting concerns.
- Restriction of competition, which may violate federal antitrust laws.
- Potential abrogation of constitutional rights of free speech.
- Potential addition to the rules that accountants must follow, increasing an already heavy load of professional standards.

Prohibiting this type of bidding should ensure users that American's financial statements are likely to be unbiased and the integrity of the financial reporting process will be maintained. On the other hand, the profession must consider whether other standards are in place, which will allow such bidding to take place without impairing the integrity of the audit function.

Assess the Possible Consequences, Determine the Greatest Good for the Greatest Number, and Determine Whether the Rights Framework Would Cause Any Courses of Action to be Eliminated

Assessing the consequences depends importantly on whether there is confidence that the auditing profession has other safeguards to mitigate the potential compromise of accounting and auditing standards. Independence is considered to be the most important characteristic of the audit profession and individual auditors. If a position is taken on an important issue prior to accepting an audit engagement, the auditor may feel obligated to continue with that position even if it appears not to be consistent with the spirit of GAAP. The auditor might improperly report on American's financial statements. Inaccurate reports could lead to bad investment decisions by the bank and a loss of faith in the value of the independent audit. Once the value of the audit is in doubt, investors will lose faith in the financial reporting system. This result undermines the very core of our capital market system.*

Most CPAs argue that the consequences identified above are not likely. The profession's Code of Professional Conduct requires the auditor to give an unqualified opinion only if the client has followed GAAP; otherwise, the CPA could be found in violation of the Code of Professional Conduct, lose the right to practice as a CPA, and be subject to potential lawsuits filed by those who relied on the misleading financial statements and lost money.

The Constitution grants the right of free speech. It is a higher-order right than the right to get rich. Any action that violates free speech would seem to be unethical unless it involves the right to life, to autonomy, or to human dignity. The right to autonomy refers to each person's right to be the best judge of his or her own interests. If the profession prohibited CPA firms from responding to the management

*It could also be argued that the market value reporting might lead to a loan by the bank that helps the company expand and add new jobs to the economy. Thus, the loan might be good for a greater number of individuals. However, most people would argue that the need for a bank lending officer to show higher market values in the balance sheet to justify the loan should not lead the profession to compromise its principles and potentially affect the integrity of the overall financial reporting process. If the bank wanted market values, it could seek an independent appraisal of such values.

request, the right to autonomy and free speech would be violated, as would the right of the company management to be informed before choosing its auditor.

Decide on the Appropriate Course of Action

The case reflects an ethical dilemma. If the profession prohibits CPAs from providing this type of information, the rights of the client and the CPA are violated, but the statement users' rights are fully protected. If the profession does not prohibit the action, the opposite can result. Because the rules of conduct require auditors to report departures from GAAP, no new rule appears to be necessary to prohibit giving the requested information.

The public accounting profession has assessed the situation and has concluded that, given the strength of existing rules and the overall integrity of the members practicing within the profession, the potential negative effects of allowing CPAs to respond to management's request are not significant enough to prohibit such responses. Therefore, the profession allows CPAs to submit such proposals. If, at some later time, the profession reassesses this situation and determines that the consequences of such proposals would significantly compromise the integrity of the financial reporting system, it would consider developing an auditing standard to provide greater safeguards to the public when auditors bid for new clients.

B–CODES OF CONDUCT

Codes of conduct have been developed by various professional groups to serve as guides (and, in many cases, as rules for their members to follow) and to instill public confidence in their professions. The AICPA, the state societies of CPAs, the state boards of accountancy, and the IIA all have codes of conduct. Many of the state societies of CPAs and the state boards of accountancy have adopted the AICPA's code.

AICPA Code of Professional Conduct

The AICPA Code of Professional Conduct (the Code) consists of two sections: the *principles* and the *rules*. In addition, the AICPA has established the Division of Professional Ethics to issue *interpretations* of the rules and provide further guidelines on the scope and application of the rules. The division also issues *rulings* in response to questions about the applicability of the rules to specific situations that practitioners encounter. The AICPA Council has the authority under its bylaws to identify those bodies authorized to establish technical standards under the rules (such as the Auditing Standards Board). The bylaws require that all members adhere to those rules and standards.

The Principles

The **principles of the Code of Professional Conduct** are analogous to the concept statements of the FASB, which provide the conceptual foundations for the technical financial accounting standards. The principles provide the ethical concepts on which the rules are based as well as the present standards for meeting the public trust. The guiding principles are presented in Exhibit 3.1.

Exhibit 3.1

AICPA PRINCIPLES OF PROFESSIONAL CONDUCT

Responsibilities—In carrying out their responsibilities as professionals, members should exercise sensitive professional and moral judgments in all their activities.

Public interest—Members should accept the obligation to act in a way that will serve the public interest, honor the public trust, and demonstrate commitment to professionalism.

Integrity—To maintain and broaden public confidence, members should perform all professional responsibilities with the highest sense of integrity.

Objectivity and independence—A member should maintain objectivity and be free of conflicts in discharging professional responsibilities. A member in public practice should be independent in fact and appearance when providing auditing and other attestation services.

Due care—A member should observe the profession's technical and ethical standards, strive continually to improve competence and the quality of services, and discharge professional responsibility to the best of the member's ability.

Scope and nature of services—A member in public practice should observe the principles of the Code of Professional Conduct in determining the scope and nature of services to be provided.

Rules of Professional Conduct

The **rules of professional conduct** govern the performance of CPAs in carrying out the practice of public accounting. The rules are specifically enforceable under the bylaws of the AICPA. Although most rules apply to all CPAs, even if not in public practice, some rules apply only to members who practice public accounting. The practice of public accounting is defined in the code as "holding out to be a CPA or public accountant and at the same time performing for a client one or more types of services rendered by public accountants."[4] Examples of the types of services rendered by public accountants are auditing, accounting services, tax services, and management consulting services.*

The rules of professional conduct are intended to be specific enough to guide auditors in most situations likely to be encountered by a practicing CPA. Additionally, the profession has generated a body of specific knowledge through professional interpretations of the rules that provide additional guidance. The rules cover the broad areas of independence, integrity, adherence to professional pronouncements, and responsibilities to the public and colleagues. Independence is often referred to as the "cornerstone of auditing," and the rules begin with that cornerstone.

Rule 101 Independence. *A member in public practice shall be independent in the performance of professional services as required by standards promulgated by bodies designated by Council.*

*AICPA, *Professional Standards*, (New York: AICPA, 1993), MS Section 11.04. Management consulting services include counseling management in analyzing, planning, organizing, operating, and controlling functions; conducting special studies; reviewing and suggesting improvement of policies, procedures, systems, methods, and organization relationships; and introducing new ideas, concepts, and methods to management.

Rule 101 is applicable to audits and other attestation services, such as reviews of historical financial statements and examinations of financial projections. Independence is one concept but is addressed in the professional rules as consisting of two elements, *independence in fact* and *independence in appearance.* To be independent in fact, an auditor must be unbiased and objective. Independence in appearance means that knowledgeable third parties must consider him or her to be independent. An auditor, for example, might own 10 shares of common stock of a client corporation and still be unbiased and objective, but a knowledgeable third party might doubt the auditor's independence because of the stock ownership.

Independence has received more attention than any other rule because the auditor can potentially become involved with a client in a significant number of ways. For example, the auditor's spouse may have a financial relationship in a client through an inheritance. Would the inherited relationship impair the auditor's independence? An overview of the profession's interpretation of independence is given in Exhibit 3.2.

The examples included in Exhibit 3.2 are not intended to be all inclusive but to specify in more detail the independence requirements in relationship to an audit client. The interpretation prohibits any *direct or material indirect financial interest* in

Exhibit 3.2

IMPAIRMENT OF INDEPENDENCE: PROFESSIONAL INTERPRETATIONS

Interpretation 101–1. Independence shall be considered to be impaired if, for example, a member had any of the following transactions, interests, or relationships:

A. During the period of a professional engagement or at the time of expressing an opinion, a member or a member's firm

1. Had or was committed to acquire any *direct or material indirect financial interest in the enterprise.*
2. Was a trustee of any trust or executor or administrator of any estate if such trust or estate had or was committed to acquire any direct or material indirect financial interest in the enterprise.
3. Had any joint, closely held business investment with the enterprise or with any officer, director, or principal stockholders thereof that was material in relation to the member's net worth or to the net worth of the member's firm.
4. Had any loan to or from the enterprise or any officer, director, or principal stockholder of the enterprise except as specifically permitted in interpretation 101-5.

B. During the period covered by the financial statements, during the period of the professional engagement, or at the time of expressing an opinion, a member or a member's firm

1. Was connected with the enterprise as a promoter, underwriter, or voting trustee, as a director or officer, or in *any capacity equivalent to that of a member of management or of an employee.*
2. Was a trustee for any pension or profit-sharing trust of the enterprise. [Emphasis added]

the client. Direct ownership of just one share of common stock is a violation of the rule. Direct ownership includes shares owned not only by the member but also by the member's spouse and dependents living in the same household or any partnerships to which the member belongs. Materiality applies only to indirect ownership, such as through a material investment in a mutual fund that has a significant investment in a client.

The prohibition of a financial interest also applies to a member's firm. Thus, none of the partners or shareholders of a CPA firm can have financial interests in any of the firm's audit clients because they share in the profits of the whole firm. Nor can full- or part-time professional employees of a CPA firm have a financial interest if they work on the audit of that client. Individuals with a managerial position who are located in an office participating in a significant portion of the engagement are also prohibited from having such financial interests, even if they do not work on the audit of that client. Individuals who have responsibilities for the overall planning and supervision of engagements for clients or for client relationships, for example, are considered to be in a managerial position. Other professional employees may have a financial interest in clients of the firm as long as they do not work on the audit. Many CPA firms prohibit all of their professional employees, whether they are staff accountants or partners, from having any financial interests in any of the firm's audit clients to avoid any question about independence.

There are limits on the types and amounts of loans auditors may obtain from a financial institution that is also an audit client. Auditors are, for example, permitted to obtain only automobile loans or leases and credit-card and cash-advance balances that do not exceed $5,000 in the aggregate. They may not obtain a home mortgage or other secured loan from a financial client after 1991.

Independence can also be impacted by having a *relative work for an audit client* in a position that

- Allows significant influence over operating, financial, or accounting policies.
- Involves an element of, or is subject to, significant internal accounting controls, such as cashier, internal auditor, purchasing agent, or warehouse supervisor.

The closeness of the relationship and the importance of the relative's position in the audit client are the key factors to consider. If the auditor's father, for example, is in a key position with the client, such as controller, chief financial officer, or chief executive officer, the auditor would lack independence. However, the audit firm would not necessarily be precluded from performing the audit if other personnel in the audit firm were assigned to the engagement.

Even though the code does not prohibit the auditor from *performing other services such as bookkeeping* for their client, the auditor must take care to ensure that the appearance of independence is not compromised by working too closely with the client. If, for example, the auditor also does bookkeeping, prepares tax returns, performs several management consulting services, plays golf with members of the client's management on a regular basis, or goes on vacations with client personnel, the appearance, if not the fact, of independence has disappeared. Therefore, the members of a CPA firm need to assess all of their relationships with every client to ensure that independence has not been compromised.

The AICPA has held that *performing consulting services* for an audit client is acceptable as long as the CPA only gives advice and refrains from making decisions for management. Critics of the public accounting profession have asserted that performance of management consulting services by a CPA firm might impair auditor independence or, at a minimum, the perception of auditor independence. The basis for the argument against the performance of consulting services normally proceeds as follows:

- Performance of some services may put auditors in situations in which they could be auditing their own work. The auditor would thus not be independent with respect to evaluating the work previously performed.
- Nonaudit services may become so lucrative that the auditor would be tempted to compromise an audit opinion in order to retain the client.

Early research on auditor independence and management consulting focused on situations in which auditors might be *auditing their own work*. It was argued, for example, that auditors should not become involved in information systems design because they would be biased in assessing control risk related to the implemented system. Over time, firms have taken steps to assign different personnel to the audit than those who participated in designing the system. Although there still might be a threat to the auditor's independence, most CPAs no longer believe that this situation represents a real threat to audit independence. The SEC permits the audit firm to design the client's computerized accounting system and even write the computer program for that system, but it prohibits the firm from "auditing financial statements if" the auditor "has participated closely, either manually or through its computer services, in maintenance of the basic accounting records and preparation of the financial statements, or if the firm performs other accounting services through which it participates with management in operational decisions."* Under such circumstances, the SEC believes that the auditors would be auditing their own work. The AICPA, however, disagrees with this position. It believes that auditors have the competence to do the recording, posting, and other bookkeeping activities and that so long as they do not enter into transactions for the client, handle the related assets, or make management decisions, independence is not compromised.

Many public accounting firms have taken other steps to maintain independence, such as not performing management recruitment services for executive-level positions because of the perception that such services could impair audit independence. The fear is that the accountant might be more willing to accommodate "client-preferred" accounting treatments if such an accounting treatment would make the executive look better. For example, it has been argued that a CPA firm might be more willing to "write down" existing assets (sometimes referred to as the *Big Bath Theory*) because the write-off in the current period would result in higher reported future earnings for the new management. Firms that are members of the AICPA's SEC Practice Section are prohibited from performing certain services for audit clients, such as executive recruitment, public opinion polls, and merger and acquisition assistance for a finder's fee.[5]

The potential impact of consulting fees on auditor independence is receiving increased attention.[6] The National Commission on Fraudulent Financial Reporting recommended that public accounting firms report the extent of consulting services

---

*SEC Accounting Guide, Financial Reporting Releases (Chicago: Commerce Clearing House, 1988), par. 3863. One major CPA firm has begun to provide "facilities management" services through its consulting division whereby it manages the data processing facilities, including systems development and maintenance, for a consulting client. The SEC has not ruled on whether such an arrangement by the independent consulting division would constitute "the accounting recording process."

to the client's audit committee. The SEC and the Auditing Standards Board have suggested that audit committees report on whether or not they considered the potential effect of management consulting services on the independence of the auditor. In some countries, such as Japan, France, and Italy, an auditing firm is prohibited from providing other services, such as tax or management consulting, for that same client.

Interpretations of the independence rule are frequently issued to reflect current developments. Recent interpretations have addressed the effect of actual or threatened litigation between the client and the auditor, loans from financial institutions, and greater guidance on *material financial interest.*

Complete independence may not be possible in today's business environment. The client usually pays for the audit. Some argue that complete independence can be attained only when the fees are paid by a body other than management. Audits could be performed under the direction of the SEC or another governmental agency that would collect funds from the audited companies and pay the auditors. Most authorities, including the SEC, agree that the private sector is in the best position to perform effective and efficient audits.

An effective audit committee, a subgroup of the board of directors, composed of directors who are not a part of the day-to-day management of the company, enhances the independence of both internal and external auditors. A strong audit committee can provide oversight of the audit functions and provide a direct communication link between the auditors and the members of the board who are independent of the client's management. Problems the auditor encounters—suspected management fraud, for instance—can be discussed directly with the audit committee, which then has a responsibility to take appropriate action, such as overseeing an investigation of the suspected fraud and disciplining those involved. Audit committees are discussed more thoroughly in Chapter 6.

Rule 102 Integrity and Objectivity. *In the performance of any professional service, a member shall maintain objectivity and integrity, shall be free of conflicts of interest, and shall not knowingly misrepresent facts or subordinate his or her judgment to others.*

Integrity and objectivity can be achieved only if the auditor is free of conflicts and has the individual competence to ensure that his or her judgment is not subordinated to others. The AICPA has ruled that a member not in public practice would knowingly misrepresent facts if the member used the CPA designation to allow an inference as to the reliability of the financial statements that the member had been associated with preparing. Conflicts of interest could occur when a member in the practice of public accounting serves in an officer position with a client or performs other services such as legal services, which could place the auditor in the role of being a client advocate.

Rule 201 General Standards. *A member shall comply with the following standards and with any interpretations thereof by bodies designated by Council.*

A. *Professional Competence. Undertake only those professional services that the member or the member's firm can reasonably expect to be completed with professional competence.*

B. *Due Professional Care. Exercise due professional care in the performance of professional services.*

C. *Planning and Supervision. Adequately plan and supervise the performance of professional services.*

D. *Sufficient Relevant Data. Obtain sufficient relevant data to afford a reasonable basis for conclusions or recommendations in relation to any professional services performed.*

The general standards *apply to all services* performed by public accountants and should not be confused with the general standards, which are the first three generally accepted auditing standards (dealing with proficiency and training, independence, and due professional care) and apply only to audits. Rule 201 applies to the competence of the accountant for *all* services rendered and the adequacy of those services.

Rule 202 Compliance with Standards. *A member who performs auditing, review, compilation, consulting, tax or other professional services shall comply with standards promulgated by bodies designated by Council.*

Rule 202 requires AICPA members to follow appropriate standards when performing public accounting services.

Rule 203 Accounting Principles. *A member shall not (1) express an opinion or state affirmatively that the financial statements or other financial data of any entity are presented in conformity with generally accepted accounting principles or (2) state that he or she is not aware of any material modifications that should be made to such statements or data in order for them to be in conformity with generally accepted accounting principles, if such statements or data contain any departure from an accounting principle promulgated by bodies designated by Council to establish such principles that has a material effect on the statements or data taken as a whole. If, however, the statements or data contain such a departure and the member can demonstrate that due to unusual circumstances the financial statements or data would otherwise have been misleading, the member can comply with the rule by describing the departure, its approximate effects, if practicable, and the reasons why compliance with the principle would result in a misleading statement.*

Rule 203 prohibits a member from issuing an unqualified audit opinion or any other form of assurance if the financial statements or other financial data contain a material departure from GAAP unless the member is convinced that following GAAP would be misleading and reports the existence and effects of such departure. Such situations are very rare, and the burden would be on the auditor to present convincing arguments that departing from GAAP would be necessary to make the financial statements fairly presented. Such a justification would most likely take place only in a situation in which the client's application of GAAP did not present the economic substance of a client's transactions or financial position.

Rules 201, 202, and 203 require the member to comply with technical standards established by various bodies designated by the Council of the AICPA. These bodies and the related standards at the time of publication are shown in Exhibit 3.3.

Rule 301 Confidential Client Informati[illegible] *A member in public practice shall not disclose any confidential client information without the specific consent of the client.*

Exhibit 3.3

AICPA RECOGNITION OF STANDARD-SETTING BODIES

Standard-Setting Body	Area of Standards Responsibilities
Financial Accounting Standards Board (FASB) and its predecessors the Accounting Principles Board (APB) and Committee on Accounting Procedures (CAP)	Accounting standards (Rule 203) and standards on disclosure of financial information outside financial statements (Rule 202)
Governmental Accounting Standards Board (GASB)	Financial accounting principles for state and local governmental entities (Rule 203) and standards on disclosure of financial information for such entities outside financial statements (Rule 202)
Auditing Standards Board (ASB), AICPA	Auditing and attestation standards and procedures and the responsibilities of members with respect to standards for disclosure of financial information outside financial statements in published financial reports containing financial statements (Rules 201 and 202)
Accounting and Review Services Committee, AICPA	Standards with respect to unaudited (primarily compiled or reviewed) financial statements or other unaudited financial information of a nonpublic company (Rules 201 and 202)
Management Consulting Services Executive Committee, AICPA	Standards with respect to the offering of consulting services (Rules 201 and 202)
Auditing Standards Board, Accounting and Review Services Committee, and Management Advisory Services Executive Committee, AICPA	Attestation standards in their respective areas of responsibility (Rules 201 and 202)

During the course of an audit, the auditor develops a complete understanding of the client and obtains **confidential information** such as its operating strengths, weaknesses, and plans for financing or expanding into new markets. To ensure a free flow and sharing of information between the client and the auditor, the client must be assured that the auditor will not communicate confidential information to outside parties. This rule shall not be construed (1) to relieve members of their professional obligations to make disclosures required by GAAP or GAAS, (2) to affect members' obligation to comply with a validly issued and enforceable subpoena or summons, (3) to prohibit review of a member's professional practice under AICPA or state CPA society authorization, or (4) to preclude members from initiating a complaint with or responding to any inquiry made by a recognized investigative or disciplinary body.

Privileged communication means that confidential information obtained about a client cannot be subpoenaed by a court of law to be used against that client. Most states allow privileged communication for lawyers but not for auditors. Therefore, in those states where such privilege does not exist, confidential information obtained by the auditor must be made available when a valid subpoena or summons is issued.

Questions about confidentiality can arise in two different types of circumstances. In programs of quality review sponsored by the AICPA and many state CPA societies, experienced professionals from outside the firm evaluate the quality of the firm's practice. In that process, the reviewers examine audit working papers that contain confidential information. Rule 301 permits this type of "outside" scrutiny of confidential information but prohibits the reviewers from using that information to their own advantage or from disclosing that information to others.

Much more troublesome for accountants is confidential information obtained in one engagement that may be applicable to another. In the case of *Fund of Funds, Ltd. v. Arthur Andersen & Co.* (AA&Co.), a federal court jury found the auditors guilty of fraud because they had failed to use information from one audit client to protect the interests of another audit client. *The Wall Street Journal* reported:

> According to court papers in the suit, John M. King, a Denver oil and gas fund promoter, convinced Fund of Funds to purchase natural resource assets from two concerns he controlled. Fund of Funds eventually paid about $120 million for over 400 natural resource assets, the court papers said.
>
> Fund of Funds alleged that many of the assets were sold at "unrealistically high and fraudulent prices" and that AA&Co. had "knowledge of or recklessly disregarded" the fraudulent activities, the court papers said. AA&Co. for a time also was auditor for the King concern.[7]

AA&Co. audited both Fund of Funds and King Resources, the concern that sold the assets to Fund of Funds. According to the court proceedings, the plaintiffs alleged that the same key audit personnel were involved in both audits and knew, or should have known, that the assets in question were sold at a price that generated profits much higher than comparable sales to other customers of King Resources. AA&Co. admitted knowledge of these overcharges but stated that it had a responsibility under the Code of Conduct to keep the information confidential. The jury was convinced that information obtained while auditing King Resources should have been used during the audit of Fund of Funds. AA&Co. was ordered to pay $80 million to Fund of Funds, the largest judgment ever made against a CPA firm at that time. The damages were later reduced to an undisclosed amount by the judge.[8]

In another case, *Consolidata Services v. Alexander Grant*, the court found the CPA firm guilty of providing confidential information to other clients. Alexander Grant did tax work for Consolidata Services, a company that provided payroll services to other companies. On learning that Consolidata was in financial trouble, Grant warned various clients, who were also Consolidata customers. Consolidata sued Grant charging that the accounting firm's disclosures effectively put it out of business. The jury found for Consolidata.

These types of situations create true ethical dilemmas for auditors. Should they use knowledge obtained during the audit of one client when reporting on the statements of another client, as the *Fund of Funds* decision seems to indicate, or should they follow the Code of Professional Conduct and keep the information confidential? The rules do not address this issue, which the profession needs to clarify for its members. Two principles, however, seem to evolve from the cases. First, the auditor was common for the two audit engagements with Fund of Funds (at least as perceived by the judge) and therefore there was no question of obtaining and applying the information. Second, in the Consolidata case, the jury believed that the auditor had selectively used confidential information, thus violating the public trust. Moreover, although the courts generally uphold the confidentiality standard, they have not been reluctant to appeal to a higher standard of public trust when they perceive a conflict between confidentiality and the public trust. It is the author's expectation that this area will continue to evolve. Auditors facing a potential conflict may be advised to consult legal counsel.

Rule 302 Contingent Fees. *A member in public practice shall not:*

(1) *perform for a contingent fee any professional services for, or receive such a fee from a client for whom the member or the member's firm also performs:*

   (a) *an audit or review of a financial statement, or*

   (b) *a compilation of a financial statement when the member expects, or reasonably might expect, that a third party will use the financial statement and the member's compilation report does not describe a lack of independence, or*

   (c) *an examination of prospective financial information, or*

(2) *prepare an original or amended tax return or claim for a tax refund for a contingent fee for any client.*

This prohibition applies during the period in which the member or the member's firm is engaged to perform any of the services listed above and the period covered by any historical financial statements involved in any such listed services.

A **contingent fee** is defined as a fee established for the performance of any service in which no fee will be charged unless a specified finding or result is attained or in which the amount of the fee otherwise depends on the finding or results of such services. An example of a contingent fee is a consulting firm that agrees to perform an information systems project for a fee to be measured by 50 percent of the defined cost savings attributable to the system for a period of three years. This rule allows the consulting divisions of major public accounting firms to compete with other consulting companies who regularly bid on a contingent fee basis.

Contingent fees are prohibited for any client in which the auditor performs attestation services. To allow a fee to be contingent on the outcome of an audit would destroy the public's confidence in the public accounting firm and its reputation for independence. An auditor's fees, however, may vary, depending, for example, on the complexity of services rendered or the time taken to perform the services.

A related but unresolved issue is whether a CPA firm might enter into a joint consulting contract with an audit client to provide services for a third client. An example of this latter approach would be a joint project performed by the consulting division of Price Waterhouse & Co. and IBM (an audit client) to design and install a computer-based information system for a third entity. To date, such efforts have been prohibited by the SEC, but there is considerable pressure to allow such joint ventures.

Does the complexity of businesses operating in the 1990s mitigate previous concerns about consulting and management services? Alternatively, does the perceived need on the part of an audit partner to serve as the professional business adviser to a client impair independence? How far should firms be allowed to go in developing joint ventures when the projects become too large for one firm to handle? Recent experimental research has shown that the dollars associated with keeping a client may influence the auditor's willingness to go along with a proposed accounting for a transaction even if the accounting does not represent the substance of the transaction.[9] It can be expected that specific adjustments to the Rules of Conduct will continue to take place as these situations mature.

Rule 501 Acts Discreditable. *A member shall not commit an act discreditable to the profession.*

Rule 501 has led to the suspension or revocation of membership in the AICPA for members' infractions such as bribing IRS officials, failing to file their own tax returns, murdering their mother-in-law, and embezzling money from their employers. The suspension or revocation of membership including the disciplined member's name and address is published in the AICPA's *CPA Letter,* a bimonthly publication distributed to all members, thus affecting his or her reputation.

Actions considered discreditable according to the interpretations of the rules of conduct include these:

- Retaining a client's records because the accountant's fees have not been paid even though the client has asked for those records to be returned.
- Discriminating on the basis of race, color, religion, sex, age, or national origin.
- Failing to follow standards required in governmental audits.

Rule 502 Advertising and Other Forms of Solicitation. *A member in public practice shall not seek to obtain clients by advertising or other forms of solicitation in a manner that is false, misleading, or deceptive. Solicitation by the use of coercion, over-reaching, or harassing conduct is prohibited.*

Rule 502 allows the CPA to advertise and solicit potential clients in any way that is not coercive or harassing. In other words, all advertising must be done in good taste. Potential clients can be solicited in person or by mail even if they are currently served by another CPA. (However, see the section on Conflicting Codes later in this chapter.)

Rule 503 Commissions and Referral Fees.

A. Prohibited Commissions.

A member in public practice shall not for a commission recommend or refer to a client any product or service, or for a commission recommend or refer any product or service to be supplied by a client, or receive a commission, when the member or the member's firm also performs . . . [attestation services] for the client.*

This prohibition applies during the period in which the member is engaged to perform any of the services listed above and the period covered by any historical financial statements involved in such listed services.

B. Disclosure of permitted commissions.

A member in public practice who is not prohibited by this rule from performing services for or receiving a commission and who is paid or expects to be paid a commission shall

* As noted earlier, attestation services include audits, reviews, certain compilations, and examinations of prospective financial statements.

disclose that fact to any person or entity to whom the member recommends or refers a product or service to which the commission relates.

C. *Referral Fees.*

Any member who accepts a referral fee for recommending or referring any service of a CPA to any person or entity or who pays a referral fee to obtain a client shall disclose such acceptance or payment to the client.

Rule 503 prohibits a CPA from receiving a **commission** from a person or organization for recommending its products or services to an attestation client. The objective is the same as that for contingent fees: to ensure objectivity on the part of the CPA when performing an attestation service. For example, if a CPA recommends a software package to a client and receives a commission from the vendor, some doubt may be raised as to whether the recommendation may have been influenced by the commission. Thus, even in situations in which commissions are permitted, the code requires disclosure of the nature of the commissions so that a user can assess the potential influence of the commission. Many auditors choose not to accept commissions—even when allowed—to ensure their integrity in recommending the best products to their clients.

Rule 505 Form of Practice and Name. *A member may practice public accounting only in the form of a proprietorship, a partnership, or a professional corporation whose characteristics conform to resolutions of Council.*

A member shall not practice public accounting under a firm name that is misleading. Names of one or more past partners or shareholders may be included in the firm name of a successor partnership or corporation. The firm name should not indicate a partnership when it is a proprietorship.

A firm may not designate itself as "Members of the American Institute of Certified Public Accountants" unless all of its partners or shareholders are members of the Institute.

The primary purposes of Rule 505 are to assure the public that individual public accountants who provide professional services are personally responsible for their actions and that the name of the firm does not mislead the public as to its type of organization. For example, the profession has very explicit rules to ensure that the name of a firm is not misleading. When one of the partners of a firm with a two-member partnership dies, the surviving partner may continue to practice as an individual under the existing firm name for a period of time not to exceed two years.

Public accounting is practiced in the United States under two dominant organizational forms: the partnership and the professional corporation. In both instances, the form of practice is such that the legal liabilities of the organization flow through to the partners/owners. A *professional corporation* differs from most corporations in that the owners must be engaged in the practice of public accounting and any shareholders who cease to remain eligible shareholders are required to dispose of the shares they own within a reasonable period to others qualified to be shareholders or to the corporation. Each partner/owner then is responsible for the actions taken by the whole firm. Thus, in the example discussed earlier in the chapter, the partners of Grant Thornton were responsible for the damages caused the firm by Jose Gomez. Each firm needs to take care in admitting individuals to the partnership/ownership of the firm and must constantly strive to implement quality control practices to ensure adherence by members to the profession's standards of excellence.

Antitrust Concerns

Several years ago, the code prohibited most forms of contingent fees (Rule 302), advertising and solicitation (Rule 502), and commissions and referral fees (Rule 503). As a result of federal antitrust actions taken against the legal profession, however, which require the bar associations to permit advertising and solicitation, and because of **Federal Trade Commission** concerns about the anticompetitive prohibitions in the AICPA's code, the AICPA—on the recommendation of its legal counsel—changed the code.

Previously, it had been a violation of the Code even to be listed in the Yellow Pages of the telephone directory in a manner different from that of other CPAs. Display advertisements and even large or bold type were prohibited. Now you can find not only display advertisements for CPA firms in the Yellow Pages but even full-page advertisements for larger firms in business periodicals.

Some public accounting firms have individuals who specialize in practice development, that is, obtaining new clients. Practice development activities may now include seeking clients who are currently being served by another CPA firm through general institutional advertising, mailings, or even uninvited personal contact. Many in the profession regard such activities as unprofessional; they believe that clients should seek the services of a CPA firm because of its reputation, not because of the size of its advertising budget. Others, including federal antitrust officials, believe that prohibiting most forms of contingent fees, advertising, solicitation, and commissions is a restraint of trade and thus a violation of federal antitrust laws.

Enforcement of the Code

Compliance with the code depends primarily on the voluntary cooperation of AICPA members and secondarily on public opinion, reinforcement by peers, and, ultimately, on disciplinary proceedings by the Joint Ethics Enforcement Program (JEEP), sponsored by the AICPA and state CPA societies. Disciplinary proceedings are initiated by complaints received by the AICPA's Professional Ethics Division. Members found to be in violation of the code may be required to undergo specified educational, remedial, or corrective activities or have their membership in the AICPA suspended or terminated. Membership in the AICPA is not required for a CPA to practice public accounting.

The member's CPA certificate may be suspended or revoked by the state board of accountancy if the member is found to be in violation of the state board's code of ethics. The state board may also require additional continuing education to retain or reinstate the CPA certificate. Each state board of accountancy, however, has the authority to grant, suspend, or revoke a person's CPA certificate and, in some states, a separate license to practice public accounting. Without that certificate or license, a person is legally prohibited from issuing an audit opinion or a review report on financial statements.

Conflicting Codes

CPAs may find that they are subject to different, and sometimes conflicting, codes of conduct. Each state board of accountancy has a code of conduct that should be followed by those to whom they have granted a CPA certificate. A CPA may belong to their state society of CPAs and the AICPA, each of which has its own code. The various codes are usually similar if not identical. Sometimes, however, there are differences. A survey conducted in 1987 found that eight state boards of accountancy had codes of conduct that prohibited direct, uninvited solicitation of potential clients who are currently served by other CPAs.[10] Such solicitation is not prohibited by the AICPA, however. Because of possible conflicts, all CPAs must be aware of the codes of conduct for which they are responsible and adhere to those that are the most restrictive.

The Institute of Internal Auditor's Code of Conduct

Company management relies on internal auditors to assist in fulfilling its management stewardship function. As stated in the IIA's Statement of Responsibilities of Internal Auditors, their audits should cover such areas as the reliability and integrity of information, compliance with policies and laws, safeguarding assets, and economical and efficient use of resources.

It is important to the profession, management, stockholders, and the general public that internal auditors maintain high standards of professional conduct in the performance of their work. In recognition of this need, the Board of Directors of the Institute of Internal Auditors adopted the Standards of Conduct (Exhibit 3.4) as a part of its 1988 revision of the Code of Ethics. The standards apply to all members of the IIA and to certified internal auditors (CIAs), some of whom are not members of the IIA.

Internal Auditing: Reporting Company Fraud

The internal auditor often faces difficult *practical* and *ethical* situations when there may be a conflict between loyalty to the company and the need to disassociate themselves from undesirable or even potentially illegal activities. The potential problem faced by an internal auditor upon the discovery of a corporate fraud that materially affects the reported profit of a Fortune 500 company is illustrated in the Ethical Issues in Auditing box on page 105.

C–QUALITY REVIEW PROGRAMS

The public accounting profession has developed programs to help assure the public that its members are performing quality services. These programs include continuing education, peer review, and practice-monitoring requirements. In addition, some firms have established their own means of quality assurance, such as having a public review board composed of nonpracticing CPAs to provide an outside perspective on the nontechnical aspects of their operations. Many larger firms have also established an interoffice review program to ensure that all of the firm's practice offices adhere to its quality control standards and procedures and auditing standards.

AICPA Program

The AICPA has taken several steps to help improve the practice of public accounting. These steps include establishing requirements for firms and individuals that become members of the AICPA and the establishment of **quality control standards** that are used to monitor the quality of individual public accounting firms.

Exhibit 3.4

IIA STANDARDS OF CONDUCT

I. Members and CIAs shall exercise honesty, objectivity, and diligence in the performance of their duties and responsibilities.

II. Members and CIAs shall exhibit loyalty in all matters pertaining to the affairs of their organization or to whomever they may be rendering a service. However, members and CIAs shall not knowingly be a party to any illegal or improper activity.

III. Members and CIAs shall not knowingly engage in acts or activities which are discreditable to the profession of internal auditing or their organization.

IV. Members and CIAs shall refrain from entering into any activity which may be in conflict with the interest of their organization or which would prejudice their ability to carry out objectively their duties and responsibilities.

V. Members and CIAs shall not accept anything of value from an employee, client, customer, supplier, or business associate of their organization which would impair or be presumed to impair their professional judgment.

VI. Members and CIAs shall undertake only those services which they can reasonably expect to complete with professional competence.

VII. Members and CIAs shall adopt suitable means to comply with the Standards for the Professional Practice of Internal Auditing.

VIII. Members and CIAs shall be prudent in the use of information acquired in the course of their duties. They shall not use confidential information for any personal gain nor in a manner which would be contrary to law or detrimental to the welfare of their organization.

IX. Members and CIAs, when reporting on the results of their work, shall reveal all material facts known to them which, if not revealed, could either distort the reports of operations under review or conceal unlawful practices.

X. Members and CIAs shall continually strive for improvement in their proficiency, and in the effectiveness and quality of their service.

XI. Members and CIAs, in the practice of their profession, shall be ever mindful of their obligation to maintain the high standards of competence, morality, and dignity promulgated by The Institute. Members shall abide by the bylaws and uphold the objectives of The Institute.

Source: Institute of Internal Auditors, *Code of Ethics*, (Altamonte Springs, FL, 1988)

Membership Requirements for Public Accounting Firms

The AICPA has established the **Division of Firms** to help improve the quality of public accounting firms' practice. It has two sections, the SEC Practice Section and the Private Companies Practice Section. Members of the SEC Practice Section usually have, or plan to have, clients who are subject to SEC regulation. Some firms belong to both sections. Membership is voluntary and open to all CPA firms. The division publishes an annual directory of the member firms. To be a member of the SEC Practice Section, a firm must:

- Adhere to the AICPA quality control standards.
- Participate in a peer review of the firm's accounting and audit practice every three years.
- Ensure that all professionals in the firm meet the continuing professional education requirements, currently 120 hours every three years.
- Rotate the partner in charge of each audit every seven years.
- Have a partner who did not participate on the audit review the audit and concur with the audit report before it is issued.
- Refrain from performing certain management consulting services for SEC audit clients, such as psychological testing, public opinion polls, merger and acquisition assistance for a finder's fee, executive recruitment, and certain actuarial services for insurance companies.
- Report to the audit committee or board of directors

  The total fees received from the client for management consulting services rendered during the year and the types of such services.

  The nature of disagreements with the management of the client on accounting and reporting matters and auditing procedures that, if not satisfactorily resolved, would have prevented the issuance of an unqualified opinion.

Only the first three of these membership requirements apply to members of the Private Companies Practice Section.

Peer reviews by internal professionals (sometimes referred to as interoffice reviews) are needed to ensure that the policies and procedures established by the firm are being followed by all offices and professionals. The SEC Practice Section requires that each audit undergo a *concurring partner review* or a *cold review*. The intent is to have someone not involved in the day-to-day activities of the audit, as well as not directly concerned with pressures to retain a client, perform an independent review of the audit and the appropriateness of the audit opinion rendered.

Peer reviews by external professionals can provide a fresh, and perhaps a more objective, assessment of the appropriateness of those policies and procedures as well as of the degree of compliance with them. The SEC Practice Section requires a peer review at least every three years. Peer review reports are issued to the firm and become public documents available from the AICPA.* The peer review reports are also utilized by the SEC in its oversight of the accounting profession. Several states require CPA firms to undergo a peer review every three years in order to practice in those states.

The Public Oversight Board of the SEC Practice Section monitors and evaluates the section's self-regulatory program. It is authorized to report any information based on its oversight activities to the SEC, congressional committees, or the public at large.

Continuing Education Requirements for Individual Members

The AICPA requires all of its members, whether in public practice or not, to meet continuing education requirements to enhance their ability to provide quality

*The peer review reports represent a good source of information about the reputation of firms with which a student might be interviewing.

Ethical Issues in Auditing

CORPORATE FRAUD, CONFIDENTIALITY AND THE INTERNAL AUDITOR

During a recent audit, the internal auditor became aware of "some previously hidden code in a computer program that manipulated cost data to inflate cost-plus billings sent to the Defense Department. Upon further investigation, the internal auditor became convinced that this programming was done with the knowledge of the company's top marketing director and was apparently known by only a very select few top people in the organization and a couple of data processing people who helped implement the program. The auditor was also convinced that the amount of error generated was large and represented a significant portion of the company's profit during the past year."*

Should the auditor tell top management and the audit committee? If they are told but they do nothing about it, is the auditor then a knowing party to the conspiracy? Should the "whistle be blown" and this situation reported to the authorities outside of the company? If the auditor blows the whistle, the auditor may lose the job, and other companies may be hesitant to hire a "tattletale." If the fraud is not reported, the auditor may be accused of aiding and abetting the crime.

The IIA Standards of Conduct make it clear that an internal auditor should "not knowingly be a party to any illegal or improper activity." Nor should an internal auditor "use confidential information for any personal gain nor in a manner which would be contrary to law or detrimental to the welfare" of the auditor's employer. After studying the legal implications of the case, two scholars concluded that "the auditors should:

- Document the findings and include the findings in an audit report.
- Report the findings to the board of directors, the audit committee, and appropriate members of top management.
- Consult with an attorney on appropriate actions as they fit the particular circumstances of the case.
- Consider the need for any further positive action to disassociate oneself from the potentially alleged conspiracy."†

What should you do if you are the company's independent external auditor and you become aware of this situation? This is an irregularity often referred to as *management fraud.* Statement on Auditing Standards, No. 53: *The Auditor's Responsibility to Detect and Report Errors and Irregularities,* makes it clear that you should be sure that the audit committee is properly informed about it. In addition, it says

> Disclosure of irregularities to parties other than the client's senior management and its audit committee or board of directors is not ordinarily part of the auditor's responsibility, and would be precluded by the auditor's ethical or legal obligation of confidentiality unless the matter affects his opinion on the financial statements. The auditor should recognize, however, that in the following circumstances a duty to disclose outside the client may exist . . .
>
> d. To a funding agency or other specified agency in accordance with requirements for the audit of entities that receive financial assistance from a government agency. [AU 316.29]

Thus, the auditor should report this to the Defense Department if the audit is required to conform to Government Auditing Standards (covered in Chapter 24).

* Michael E. Meier and Larry E. Rittenberg, "Dealing with Known Corporate Wrongdoing," *The Internal Auditor* (April 1986), 37.

† Meier and Rittenberg, 41.

Source: Michael E. Meier and Larry E. Rittenberg, "Dealing with Known Corporate Wrongdoing," The Internal Auditor, (April 1986).

service, no matter what their current job responsibilities may be. Members in public practice are required to complete 120 hours of acceptable continuing education every three years. Members who are not in public practice are required to complete 90 hours of acceptable continuing education every three years.[11]

Each member has complete discretion in selecting continuing education suitable to his or her professional activities as long as they conform to the guidelines established by council. For example, members can get credit for taking college courses, continuing professional education courses sponsored by various professional organizations, monitored self-study courses, and firm training programs.

Practice-Monitoring Program

All public accounting firms that have members in the AICPA are required to enroll in an approved quality review program. The goal of quality is sought primarily through education and remedial or corrective actions. This program, which is supervised by the Quality Review Division of the AICPA, is conducted in cooperation with state CPA societies.

To enroll in the program, a firm must agree, among other things, to adhere to the applicable quality control standards; undergo a quality review of its accounting and auditing practice every three years; require its eligible proprietor, partners, or shareholders to be AICPA members; and ensure that its AICPA members meet their continuing professional education requirements.[12]

Quality Control Standards. The AICPA has developed a set of elements of quality control to assist organizations in developing programs to maintain high standards of quality. The standards also serve as criteria when conducting peer reviews to measure the quality of a firm's practice. Firms should consider each of the following elements of quality control in establishing quality control policies and procedures:

- Independence.
- Assigning personnel to engagements.
- Consultation.
- Supervision.
- Hiring.
- Professional development.
- Advancement.
- Acceptance and continuance of clients.
- Inspection.[13]

Those performing a quality review of a firm determine whether the firm has established, and follows, appropriate policies and procedures for each of these elements. For example, the reviewer determines whether the firm has policies and procedures that encourage personnel to seek assistance from persons having the knowledge, competence, judgment, and authority to help resolve a problem (consultation). The inspection element requires the firm to have policies and procedures to help ensure that the other elements are being effectively applied.

The product of the quality review process is a report containing an opinion on the quality of the firm. An example of a peer review report is shown in Exhibit 3.5.

Exhibit 3.5

PEER REVIEW REPORT

Deloitte Haskins+Sells

Executive Office

1114 Avenue of the Americas
New York, New York 10036
(212) 790-0500
Telex 12267

To the Partners of
Arthur Andersen & Co.

October 7, 1986

We have reviewed the system of quality control for the accounting and auditing practice of Arthur Andersen & Co. (the Firm) in effect for the year ended August 31, 1986. Our review was conducted in conformity with standards for peer reviews promulgated by the peer review committee of the SEC Practice Section of the AICPA Division for CPA Firms (the Section). We tested compliance with the Firm's quality control policies and procedures at the firm's Chicago World Headquarters and at selected practice offices in the United States and with the membership requirements of the Section to the extent we considered appropriate. These tests included the application of the Firm's policies and procedures on selected accounting and auditing engagements. We tested the supervision and control of portions of engagements performed outside the United States.

In performing our review, we have given consideration to the general characteristics of a system of quality control as described in quality control standards issued by the AICPA. Such a system should be appropriately comprehensive and suitably designed in relation to a firm's organizational structure, its policies and the nature of its practice. Variance in individual performance can affect the degree of compliance with a firm's prescribed quality control policies and procedures. Therefore, adherence to all policies and procedures in every case may not be possible. As is customary in a peer review, we are issuing a letter under this date that sets forth comments related to certain policies and procedures or compliance with them. None of these matters were considered to be of sufficient significance to affect the opinion expressed in this report.

In our opinion, the system of quality control for the accounting and auditing practice of Arthur Andersen & Co. in effect for the year ended August 31, 1986, met the objectives of quality control standards established by the AICPA and was being complied with during the year then ended to provide the Firm with reasonable assurance of conforming with professional standards. Also, in our opinion the Firm was in conformity with the membership requirements of the Section in all material respects.

[signed]
Deloitte Haskins & Sells

Institute of Internal Auditor's Program

The Institute of Internal Auditors has developed a continuing education program requirement for Certified Internal Auditors and a quality assurance standard for internal audit departments.

Continuing Professional Development

To retain CIA certification, a person must complete 100 hours of acceptable professional development every three years. Acceptable professional development consists of educational activities, which are basically the same as those for CPAs, publication of articles and books, oral presentations, and participation in professional or industry organizations.

Quality Assurance Standard

Standard 560 of the Standards for the Professional Practice of Internal Auditing states that "The director of internal auditing should establish and maintain a quality assurance program to evaluate the operations of the internal auditing department."[14] The quality assurance program includes internal reviews periodically performed by members of the staff to appraise the quality of the work done and the external reviews performed by qualified persons who are independent of the organization. The external review should be performed every three years and include a formal report that specifically addresses compliance with the Standards for the Professional Practice of Internal Auditing. These external reviews are performed primarily by internal auditors from other companies.

Summary

A professional's behavior must be above reproach. This means acting in an ethical manner and following (or exceeding) the standards of the profession. As a student, you can be assured that, in the long run, following or exceeding the profession's standards will enhance your opportunities for advancement as a professional. The ethical theories and framework, as well as the professional standards discussed in this and the previous chapter, have been developed to help you become a professional.

Public trust is key to the existence of the public accounting profession. Without it, the profession would not survive. With it, the profession remains a vital part not only of our society but also of the societies of the world. Certified public accountants have established high standards but at the same time recognize that the standards must evolve to meet new situations. Auditors encounter situations in which existing standards do not clearly specify the appropriate action. In such cases, they must resort to wide, societal based, ethical frameworks to make decisions that are in society's and the profession's best interests. When you are making important moral decisions, ask "Would the child I was be proud of the adult I am?"

Significant Terms

commission The payment of a fee for selling an item or as a percentage of the fees generated for performing a service, which is generally prohibited by the AICPA but may be allowed in some instances for nonattestation clients; when one is accepted, the CPA must disclose its nature to the user affected by the auditor's service.

confidential information Information obtained during the conduct of an audit related to the client's business or business plans; the auditor is prohibited from communicating confidential information except in very specific instances defined by the code or with the client's specific authorization.

contingent fee A fee established for the performance of any service pursuant to an arrangement in which no fee will be charged unless a specified finding or result is attained or in which the amount of the fee otherwise depends on the finding or results of such services.

Division of Firms A formal division of the AICPA to implement quality control standards for the profession at the firm level; it presently has two divisions: the SEC Practice Section and the Private Companies Practice Section; membership in the former is mandatory for firms with SEC clients. Member firms must adhere to the membership requirements of each division, including those of mandatory peer review.

ethical dilemma A situation in which moral duties or obligations conflict, one action is not necessarily the correct action.

ethical problem A situation in which an individual is morally or ethically required to do something that conflicts with his or her immediate self-interest.

Federal Trade Commission (FTC) A governmental agency charged with responsibility to oversee and monitor the fairness of competition within U.S. industry; it has been a prime agent in forcing the auditing profession to remove elements of the code of professional conduct that it believed constrained trade. FTC pressure has dramatically influenced the amount of competition among CPA firms for audit clients.

peer review An independent review of the quality of a public accounting firm or internal audit organization performed by professionals who are not a part of the firm or organization, or review of an audit report and accompanying work papers by a partner or review function, independent of the engagement personnel, before an audit report is issued.

Principles of the Code of Professional Conduct Express the profession's recognition of its responsibilities to the public, clients, and colleagues, guide members in the performance of their professional responsibilities, and express the basic tenets of ethical and professional conduct; they call for an unswerving commitment to honorable behavior, even at the sacrifice of personal advantage.

privileged communication Information about a client that cannot be subpoenaed by a court of law to be used against a client; it allows no exceptions to confidentiality.

quality control standards Encompasses the firm's organizational structure and the policies adopted and procedures established to provide the CPA firm with reasonable assurance of conforming with professional standards. The system of quality control should be suitably designed in relation to the firm's organizational structure, its policies, and the nature of its practice.

rights theory An approach (framework) for addressing ethical problems by identifying a hierarchy of rights that should be considered in solving ethical problems or dilemmas.

rules of professional conduct Detailed guidance to assist the CPA in applying the broad principles contained in the AICPA's Code of Professional Conduct; they have evolved over time as members of the profession have encountered specific ethical dilemmas in complying with the principles of the code.

stakeholders Those parties that have a vested interest in, or are affected by, the decision resulting from an ethical problem or dilemma.

utilitarian theory An ethical theory (framework) that systematically considers all the potential stakeholders that may be affected by an ethical decision and seeks to measure the effects of the decision on each party; it seeks to assist individuals in making decisions resulting in the greatest amount of good for the greatest amount of people.

Review Questions

A–Introduction and Overview

3–1 What factors may have motivated Jose Gomez to agree to become a knowing party in the E.S.M. fraud?

3–2 Briefly describe the concepts and approaches underlying the utilitarian theory and the rights theory.

3–3 How can the ethical framework developed in this chaper help the auditor solve ethical dilemmas?

B–Codes of Conduct

3–4 Briefly describe the sections of the AICPA Code of Professional Conduct. What are the major purposes of each section? Are any sections more important than others? Explain.

3–5 What is meant by independence (a) in fact and (b) in appearance? Give an example of an auditor being independent in fact but not in appearance.

3–6 How can an audit committee enhance auditor independence? Explain by identifying the composition of an audit committee and the reporting obligations of the auditor to it.

3–7 A CPA owns one share of common stock of an audit client of the CPA firm. In which of the following situations is the CPA in violation of the AICPA rule on independence:

a. The CPA is a partner of the firm but does not participate on the audit?

b. The CPA is a staff auditor who works on the audit?

c. The CPA is a staff auditor who does not work on the audit but is a "managerial employee"?

d. The CPA is a staff auditor who does not work on the audit and is not a "managerial employee"?

3–8 How do the AICPA's and the SEC's independence rules on providing bookkeeping services for an audit client differ?

3–9 When must Rule 201 General Standards be followed? When must the general standards in GAAS be followed?

3–10 Does the AICPA's Code of Professional Conduct require its members to follow standards when performing

a. Audits?

b. Management services?

c. Tax services?

d. Reviews and compilations?

3–11 What standards must be followed for each of the services listed in question 10?

3–12 Under what circumstances is it appropriate for a CPA to disclose confidential information about a client?

3–13 What is meant by "privileged communication"?

3–14 Under what circumstances is it appropriate for a CPA to

a. Provide services on a contingent fee basis?

b. Accept a commission for referring a product or service to the client?

c. Pay a referral fee to another CPA?

3–15 When the AICPA's code permits direct, uninvited solicitation of nonclients but the code of the state board of accountancy of the state in which a CPA is licensed prohibits it, which code should the CPA follow? Why?

3–16 What are some examples of acts discreditable to the profession?

3–17 Under what circumstances is it ethical for a CPA firm operating as a sole proprietorship to use a name indicating a partnership?

3–18 How does the ownership of a professional corporation practicing public accounting differ from a standard corporation?

3–19 In what ways has the Federal Trade Commission affected the AICPA's code?

3–20 How is the AICPA's code enforced?

C–Quality Review Programs

3–21 How are the membership requirements of the SEC Practice Section and the Private Companies Practice Section the same? different?

3–22 What are the AICPA's requirements for individual membership?

3–23 What is meant by practice monitoring or peer review? How are the elements of quality control used in a peer review?

3–24 What are the continuing education requirements for (a) an AICPA member in public practice, (b) an AICPA member not in public practice, and (c) a CIA?

Multiple Choice Questions

3–25 (Independence) Manny Tallents is a CPA and a lawyer. In which of the following situations is Tallents violating the AICPA's Rules of Conduct?

a. He uses his legal training to help determine the legality of an audit client's actions.

b. He researches a tax question to help the client make a management decision.

c. He defends his audit client in a patent infringement suit.

d. He uses his legal training to help determine the accounting implications of a complicated contract of an audit client.

*3–26 (Independence) A CPA in public practice must be independent in fact and appearance when providing which of the following services?

	Preparation of a Tax Return	Compilation of a Financial Forecast	Compilation of Personal Financial Statements
a.	Yes	No	No
b.	No	Yes	No
c.	No	No	Yes
d.	No	No	No

*3–27 (Independence) If requested to perform an audit engagement for a non-public entity in which an auditor has an immaterial direct financial interest, the auditor is

a. Independent because the financial interest is immaterial; therefore, a review report may be issued.

b. Not independent and, therefore, may *not* be associated with the financial statements.

c. Not independent and, therefore, may *not* issue an unqualified audit report.

d. Not independent and, therefore, may issue a review report but may *not* issue an auditor's opinion.

*3–28 (Independence) According to the profession's ethical standards, an auditor would be considered independent in which of the following instances?

a. The auditor's checking account, which is fully insured by a federal agency, is held at a client financial institution.

b. The auditor is also an attorney who advises the client as its general counsel.

c. An employee of the auditor donates service as treasurer of a charitable organization that is a client.

d. The client owes the auditor fees for two consecutive annual audits.

*3–29 (Independence) A violation of the profession's ethical standards would most likely have occurred when a CPA

a. Purchased a bookkeeping firm's practice of monthly write-ups for a percentage of fees received over a three-year period.

b. Made arrangements with a bank to collect notes issued by a client in payment of fees due.

c. Named Smith formed a partnership with two other CPAs and uses Smith & Co. as the firm name.

d. Issued an unqualified opinion on the 1987 financial statements when fees for the 1986 audit were unpaid.

---

*Adapted from the Uniform CPA examination or the Certified Internal Auditor examination.

*3–30 Which of the following statements best explains why the CPA profession has found it essential to promulgate ethical standards and to establish means for ensuring their observance?

a. Vigorous enforcement of an established code of ethics is the best way to prevent unscrupulous acts.

b. Ethical standards that emphasize excellence in performance over material rewards establish a reputation for competence and character.

c. A distinguishing mark of a profession is its acceptance of responsibility to the public.

d. A requirement for a profession is to establish ethical standards that stress primarily a responsibility to clients and colleagues.

*3–31 Quality control for a CPA firm, as referred to in Statements on Quality Control Standards, applies to

a. Auditing services only.

b. Auditing and consulting services.

c. Auditing and tax services.

d. Auditing and accounting and review services.

*3–32 Which of the following are elements of a CPA firm's quality control that should be considered in establishing its quality control policies and procedures?

	Advancement	Inspection	Consultation
a.	Yes	Yes	No
b.	Yes	Yes	Yes
c.	No	Yes	Yes
d.	Yes	No	Yes

3–33 CPA firms performing management consulting services can accept contingent fee contracts when

a. The amounts are not material in relationship to the audit billings.

b. The consulting services are for clients for whom the auditor does not provide any form of attestation services related to a company's financial statements.

c. The consulting services are nonattestation services for a client.

d. The consulting services are derived from a joint contract with an audit client to perform consulting services for an independent third party.

e. All of the above.

3–34 Applying utilitarianism as a concept in addressing ethical situations requires the auditor to perform all of the following *except*:

a. Identify the potential stakeholders that will be affected by the alternative outcomes.

b. Determine the effect of the potential alternative courses of action on the affected parties.

c. Choose the alternative that provides either the greatest good for the greatest number or the lowest cost (from a societal view) for the greatest number.

d. Examine the potential outcomes to see whether the results are inconsistent with the rights or justice theories.

*3–35 Pursuant to the AICPA rules of conduct, if a partner in a two-member partnership dies, the surviving partner may continue to practice as an individual under the existing firm title that includes the deceased partner's name:

a. For a period of time not to exceed five years.

b. For a period of time not to exceed two years.

c. Indefinitely since any partnership can contain the names of current or past partners.

d. Until the partnership pay-out to the deceased partner's estate is terminated.

*3–36 (Internal Audit Code of Ethics) A certified internal auditor, working for a chemical manufacturer, believed that toxic waste was being dumped in violation of the law. Out of loyalty to the company, no evidence regarding the dumping was collected. The auditor

a. Violated the Code of Ethics by knowingly becoming a party to an illegal act.

b. Violated the Code of Ethics by failing to protect the well-being of the general public.

c. Did not violate the Code of Ethics. Loyalty to the employer in all matters is required.

d. Did not violate the Code of Ethics. Conclusive evidence of wrongdoing was not gathered.

3–37 (Internal Audit Code of Ethics) In their reporting, certified internal auditors are required by the Code of Ethics to

a. Present sufficient factual evidence without revealing confidential information that could be detrimental to the organization.

b. Disclose all material evidence obtained by the auditor as of the date of the audit report.

c. Obtain factual evidence within the established time and budget parameters.

d. Reveal material facts known to the auditor that could distort the report if not revealed.

Discussion and Research Questions

3–38 (Purpose of Codes of Conduct) Various professions have developed various forms of codes of conduct. The public accounting profession has developed detailed guidance in its code.

Required:

a. Why have the AICPA, state boards of accountancy, state societies of CPAs, and the IIA seen fit to enact and enforce codes of conduct?

b. What are the potential sanctions if a CPA is found to have violated the Professional Code of Conduct?

3–39 (Potential Violations of Ethical Standards) Following is a list of potential violations of the AICPA's Code of Professional Conduct.

Auditor Situation

1. T.O. Busy is unable to perform a service requested by a client. Therefore, Busy refers the client to Able, who pays Busy $200 for referring the business. Neither Busy nor Able tells the client about the referral fee.
2. M.R. Big's wife owns 10 shares of common stock in an audit client of Big's CPA firm, in which he is a partner.
3. I.M. Aggressive personally visits potential clients without invitation for the purpose of obtaining business from them.
4. C.P. Lawyer, a sole practitioner, serves as an audit client's legal counsel.
5. A public accounting firm places a full-page, four-color advertisement in *Business Week* that describes some of the services it provides.

Required:

For each of the preceding situations, indicate

a. Whether the CPA is in violation of the AICPA's Code.

b. The specific rule or principle that is violated.

3–40 (Commissions and Contingent Fees) Two CPAs visiting at a recent meeting of the state CPA society were talking about accepting commissions and performing work on a contingent fee basis. The first one said he did not accept commissions for services provided to any client because it was unethical. The second one said she did accept commissions for work done for any of her clients and that it was ethical.

Required:

a. Under what circumstances would each be correct? Under which situations could commissions for services be accepted?

b. What are contingent fees and why might a client be interested in bids for services on a contingent fee basis?

c. What other professions allow contingent fee work? What is the rationale for contingent fees in the professions?

d. What was the most likely rationale for the AICPA to prohibit the performance of any contingent fee services for attestation clients? Why do you believe that the AICPA didn't allow contingent fees as long as they are not for attestation services?

3–41 (Auditor Independence) Independence is often hailed as the "cornerstone of auditing" and recognized as the most important characteristic of an auditor.

Required:

a. What is meant by independence as it is applied to the CPA?
b. Compare independence of an auditor with that of a
   1. Judge.
   2. Lawyer.
c. Describe the difference between the independence of an external and internal auditor.
d. For each of the following situations, indicate whether the auditor is in violation of the AICPA's Code. Explain your answers.
   1. The auditor's father works for an audit client as
      (a). A custodial engineer.
      (b). The treasurer.
   2. The auditor's third uncle is treasurer of an audit client.
   3. The auditor of a charitable organization is also its treasurer.

3–42 (Comparability of AICPA and IIA Standards) The external auditor has a "special function" as indicated in Chapter 1 to meet the public's expectations and maintain the public trust. Increasingly, the internal audit profession is recognized as fulfilling an important role in monitoring the integrity, as well as efficiency, of organizational actions. Additionally, the internal auditor is required to report information to audit committees that might have been considered confidential.

Required:

a. How might the confidentiality rule for the internal audit profession differ from that of the AICPA developed for external auditors?
b. For each of the IIA Standards of Conduct, identify a similar rule in the AICPA's Code.
c. What are the major differences between the AICPA's and IIA's Codes of Professional Conduct?

3–43 (Ethical Scenarios and Standards) Following are a number of scenarios that might constitute a violation of the Code of Professional Conduct.

Required:

For each of the situations described below, identify whether the situation involves a violation of the ethical standards of the profession and indicate which principle or rule would be violated.

Ethical Situation Facing the Auditor

a. Tom Hart, CPA, does the bookkeeping, prepares the tax returns, and performs various management services for Sanders, Inc. One management service involved the assessment of the microcomputer needs and identification of equipment to meet those needs. Hart recommended a product sold by Compter Co., which has agreed to pay Hart a 10 percent commission if Sanders buys its product.
b. Irma Stone, CPA, was scheduled to be extremely busy for the next few months. When a prospective client asked if Stone would do its next

year's audit, she declined but referred them to Joe Rock, CPA. Rock paid Stone $200 for the referral.

c. Nancy Heck, CPA, has agreed to perform an inventory control study and recommend a new inventory control system for Ettes, Inc., a new client. At the present time, Ettes engages another CPA firm to audit its financial statements. The financial arrangement is that Ettes, Inc., will pay Heck 50 percent of the savings in inventory costs over the two-year period following implementation of the new system.

d. Brad Gage, CPA, has served Hi-Dee Co. as auditor for several years. In addition, Gage has performed other services for it. This year, the financial vice president has asked Gage to perform a major computer system evaluation.

e. Due to the death of its controller, an audit client had its external auditor, Gail Klate, CPA, perform the controller's job for a month until a replacement was found.

f. Chris Holt, CPA, conducted an audit and issued a report on the 19X1 financial statements of Tree, Inc. Tree has not yet paid the audit fees for that audit prior to issuing the audit report on 19X2 statements.

3–44 (Application of Ethical Framework) As the auditor for XYZ Company, you discover that a material sale ($500,000 sale, cost of goods of $300,000) was made to a customer this year. Due to poor internal accounting controls, the sale was never recorded. Your client makes a management decision not to bill the customer because such a long time has passed since the shipment was made. You determine, to the best of your ability, that the sale was not fraudulent.

Required:

a. Do GAAP require disclosure of this nontransaction? Cite specific applicable standards.

b. Regardless of your answer to part a, utilize the ethical framework developed in the chapter to determine whether or not the auditor should require either a recording or disclosure of the transaction. If you conclude that the transaction should be disclosed or recorded, indicate the nature of disclosure and your rationale for it.

3–45 (Application of Ethical Framework) Your audit client, Germane Industries, has developed a new financial instrument, the major purpose of which is to boost earnings and to keep a significant amount of debt off the balance sheet. Its investment banker tells the firm that the instrument is structured explicitly to keep it off the balance sheet and that she has discussed the treatment with three other Big 6 firms that have indicated some support for the client's position. The transaction is not covered by any current authoritative pronouncement.

Your initial reaction is that the item, when viewed in its substance as opposed to its form, is debt. The client reacts that GAAP do not prohibit the treatment of the item it advocates and that the financial statements are those of management. The client notes further, and you corroborate this, that some other firms would account for the item in the manner suggested by management, although it is not clear that a majority of other firms would accept such accounting.

Required:

a. What is the ethical dilemma?

b. Does competition lead to a lower ethical standard in the profession?

c. What safeguards are built into the profession's standards (Chapter 2) and its Code of Professional Conduct that would mitigate the potential effect of competition on the quality of the profession's work?

3–46 (Independence and Consulting Services) Most public accounting firms perform consulting services for their clients. Additionally, many CPA firms have now developed software products that they sell to clients. In some cases, CPA firms have even become selling agents for particular brands of software. In at least one case, a CPA firm practicing as a professional corporation owned a Computerland store.

Required:

a. In what ways might the performance of consulting services affect the independence of the auditor? What actions might be taken by the profession and the individual CPA firm to mitigate potential problems affecting audit independence when a firm provides consulting services?

b. Would selling software products be the same as receiving a commission on a product? Explain.

c. Does owning a Computerland store constitute a conflict of duties for a public accounting firm? Explain. How does the public accounting profession determine which types of activities would constitute a conflict of interest for a public accounting firm?

3–47 (Confidentiality) Rule 301 on confidentiality recognizes a fundamental public trust between the client and the auditor and is reflective of the manner in which all professionals conduct themselves. However, in certain instances the auditor may be required to communicate confidential information.

Required:

a. Briefly explain the purpose of the confidentiality rule. Why is it important to ensure the client of confidentiality of information?

b. Under what circumstances is the CPA allowed to communicate confidential information, and who are the parties to which the information can be communicated?

c. Assume that an auditor is the partner in charge of two separate engagements, but during the conduct of the audit of Client A, the auditor learns of information that will materially affect the audit of Client B. Client B is not aware of the information (the inability of Client A to pay its debts). What alternative courses of action are available to the auditor? Would communication of the information to Client B be considered a violation of confidentiality? What guidance might the auditor seek other than Rule 301 in developing an answer to this ethical dilemma?

d. Is the auditor's report considered a confidential communication? Explain.

3–48 (Independence) Under what circumstances would independence *not* be impaired if Mate Cooney, CPA, had a direct financial interest in an audit client of the public accounting firm for which she works?

3–49 (Internal Audit Code of Ethics) Certified internal auditors are often faced with situations that may involve ethical considerations.

Required:
Consider the following cases. For each of the cases, identify the relevant standard and state whether the condition is a violation of the IIA's Code of Ethics.

Ethical Scenarios for Certified Internal Auditors

a. Auditor A has not participated in any type of professional development activity since the company stopped paying his IIA dues three years ago.
b. Auditor B participates in the activities of a religious organization that provides sanctuary to undocumented political refugees. The refugees are then hired, with Auditor B's assistance, to work for substandard wages by the company that also employs Auditor B.
c. Auditor C is assigned to supervise the auditor of a cost-type subcontract. The auditor's spouse is a silent partner in the company to be audited.
d. Auditor D uses vacation time to prepare and present an in-house session for the audit staff of the company's major customer. The agreed-upon gratuity is a videocassette recorder.
e. Auditor E discovers evidence that the company has been disposing of toxic waste in a manner contrary to contractual provisions and public policy. The responsible department manager insists that what it is doing is in the company's best interest and requests that the auditor not mention this matter in the report.
f. Auditor F has been assigned to work with the company's acquisition team. The auditor's father has been dealing speculatively in the securities of a firm with which the company is negotiating for an acquisition merger.
g. Auditor G receives the following message from the company's CEO, to whom the auditor reports administratively: "The controller informs me that you have discovered a number of questionable account classifications involving the capitalization of research and development expense. You are directed to discontinue any further investigation of this matter until informed by me to proceed. Under no circumstances is this matter to be discussed with the outside auditors."

3–50 (Ethics Scenarios) Although professional guidance is provided to assist CPAs in making judgments about the appropriate response to individual situations, many situations tend to be in a "grey" area. Following are a number of scenarios that CPAs periodically encounter.

Required:
For each situation, identify the potential ethical issue involved, the appropriate action per the professional standards, and the rationale for the suggested actions.

a. The CPA is considering obtaining a loan from a major bank in the city. The bank is an audit client of the CPA's firm.
   1. The CPA is the partner in charge of the bank's audit and wants to obtain a mortgage to build a home.
   2. The CPA is a partner who does not work on the audit and wants to obtain a mortgage to build a home.
   3. The CPA is a partner on the audit but the bank is the only one that provides home mortgages in the city in which the audit firm is located.
   4. The partner on the audit engagement seeks a $14,000 car loan.
   5. The CPA is a staff auditor seeking a home mortgage. She does not work on the audit of the bank.
   6. The loan will assist the audit partner in a real estate development with a number of other partners. The other partnership has been successful and its track record is good. The loans are not material to the bank but are material in relationship to the partner's total assets.

b. The CPA suspects that the audit client may be violating current environmental rules, but there is no evidence that the EPA or state authority is aware of it. The client believes it is "stretching" the terms of existing law but that defending a lawsuit is less costly than complying with the existing regulations. The auditor is considering whether or not an ethical duty exists to notify the EPA of the problem. The auditor is environmentally conscious and does not believe in social policy that would tolerate stretching environmental laws.

c. The client of a publicly-held company has hired a number of relatives at extravagant salaries. The relatives do not perform any work. The cost is buried in salaries expense and no separate disclosure is presented.

d. An internal auditor discovers that a divisional manager has been systematically overcharging the government for goods sold to it on a cost-plus basis. The external auditors have not found the misstatement. The internal auditor is personally convinced that the activities are material and fraudulent and reports this to the president of the company, who assures the auditor that the problem will be addressed by management and that appropriate action will be taken.

3–51 **(Research Ethics)** Obtain a copy of your state board of accountancy's code of conduct or ethics and identify any differences between that code and the AICPA's code.

3–52 **(Research—LEXIS Data Base)** Perform a key word search of the LEXIS (Mead Data Central) data base of court cases to identify any involving accounting, auditing, or public accounting firms and the issue of *confidentiality* of information or *confidential* information. Select three to five cases and summarize the court's concern with confidential information, the issue of concern, and the court's ruling regarding the confidential information.

Alternative Research
Use the same approach identified above, but address the issue of *audit independence* as addressed by the courts.

Cases

3–53 You have been engaged to examine the balance sheet of Hi-Sail Company, which provides services to financial institutions. Its revenue source comes from fees for performing these services. Its primary expenses are related to selling and general and administrative costs. The company has assets and liabilities of approximately $1 million. Operating losses in recent years have resulted in a retained earnings deficit and stockholder's equity close to zero. The assets consist primarily of restricted cash and accounts receivable. Its liabilities consist of accounts payable, accrued expenses, and reserves for potential losses on services previously provided.

Your preliminary audit work indicated that the company generates a high volume of transactions. The internal control system surrounding these transactions is weak. It is also apparent that management is involved only moderately in day-to-day activities and spends most of its time dealing with nonroutine transactions and events.

You expended a significant amount of time and cost to complete your examination of the balance sheet. The client understood the extended efforts and stated a willingness to pay whatever cost to complete this engagement. However, monthly progress billings have not been paid.

On completion of the audit fieldwork, you reviewed a draft of the balance sheet and related notes with the company's president and chief financial officer/controller. With minor wording modification, they agreed with the draft. They requested that you issue this report as soon as possible. You committed to the issuance of your opinion, subject to a review of the draft with the company's chairperson of the board.

After the chairperson reviewed the draft, she requested a special meeting outside the company's office. At the subsequent meeting, she stated that the drafted balance sheet and notes are severely in error. Included in her comments are the following:

1. The previous year's tax returns have not been filed and the company has extensive potential tax liabilities.
2. The company has guaranteed significant amounts of debt related to joint ventures. These ventures have failed, and the company's partners are insolvent.
3. Significant notes payable to the chairperson have not been recorded.
4. Amounts payable to the chairperson and other officers related to reimbursement of monies expended by these individuals personally for travel, entertainment, and related expenses on the company's behalf have also not been recorded.

The chairperson surmised that the president and the chief financial officer/controller did not disclose these items because of their detrimental impact on the company. She believed that those officers were trying to stage a shareholder dispute to unseat her.

You continued to have separate meetings with these individuals. It became clear that the parties are in dispute, and you found it increasingly difficult to understand what is fact and what is not. The two officers, in particular, requested urgent conclusion of the audit and delivery of your opinion. They claimed the chairperson's position is self-serving and not representative of the company's financial position.

You discover that the reason the two officers are anxious for the opinion and balance sheet is that they are attempting to sell the company. You also learn from the company and from another of your clients that the second client is interested in purchasing the company. This second client has asked you why you have not yet issued your report on Hi-Sail.

Discussion Issues:

a. Refer to the ethical framework in the chapter and write a report describing what course of action you would take concerning the audit and how you decided on that course of action.
b. Indicate what you will do in response to the second client's inquiry and why.

End Notes

1. Arthur R. Wyatt, "Professionalism in Standard-Setting," *CPA Journal* (July 1988), 24.
2. Louis Harris and Associates, "A Survey of Perceptions, Knowledge, and Attitudes towards CPAs and the Accounting Profession" (New York: Louis Harris and Associates, 1986), 11.
3. *The Wall Street Journal*, March 4, 1987.
4. AICPA, *Professional Standards* (New York: AICPA, 1993), ET Section 92.09.
5. SEC Practice Section, Division for CPA Firms, *Peer Review Manual*, rev. ed. (New York: AICPA, 1981), 1–9.
6. For a more complete discussion of some of these issues, see Abraham Briloff, "Do Management Advisory Services Endanger Independence and Objectivity," *CPA Journal* (August, 1987), 22–29.
7. *The Wall Street Journal*, November 6, 1981, 24.

8. *Fund of Funds, Ltd. v. Arthur Andersen & Co.*, 545 F Supp. 1314 (S.D.N.Y. 1982).
9. Timothy Farmer, Larry Rittenberg, and Greg Trompeter, "An Investigation of Economic and Organizational Factors on Auditor Independence," *Auditing: A Journal of Practice and Theory* (Fall 1987), 1–14.
10. Bradley J. Schwieger, Wayne R. Wells, and Ronald E. Carlson, "Solicitation—Where Do We Stand Today?" *The CPA Journal* (November, 1988).
11. AICPA Professional Standards, (New York: AICPA, 1993), BL Section 230R.04-06.
12. AICPA, *Plan to Restructure Professional Standards*, (New York: AICPA, 1987), 24.
13. AICPA, *Professional Standards*, QC Section 10.07 (New York: AICPA, 1993).
14. The Institute of Internal Auditors, Inc., *Standards for the Professional Practice of Internal Auditing*, (Altamonte Springs, FL: IIA, 1978), 4.

CHAPTER

4

Learning Objectives

Through studying this chapter, you will be able to:

1. Become aware of the liability environment of public accountants.
2. Understand auditor responsibilities to clients and third parties under common law and statutory law.
3. Know the types of defenses auditors may use when sued by clients or third parties.
4. Identify approaches to minimize exposure to liability suits.

Auditor Liability and Exposures

Chapter Contents

Chapter Overview

Even though most audits are properly performed, a significant percentage of the gross revenues of CPA firms is currently being spent on professional liability insurance and litigation costs. Litigation costs and settlements recently caused Laventhol, Horwath, and Horwath, one of the largest CPA firms in the United States, to declare bankruptcy. In today's litigious environment, it is extremely important that auditors use due professional care to minimize such costs. Even when due professional care is used, the government, investors, and clients sue auditors. This chapter discusses the legal environment and concepts related to audits. We will look at several key court cases and their impact on the profession and discuss approaches to minimizing exposure to liability.

A–INTRODUCTION TO THE LEGAL ENVIRONMENT

The following headlines from the financial press reflect the litigious nature of our society:

> "PW Verdict Rocks Profession: Arizona Jury Levies $338 Million Penalty in Audit Case"
>
> "Award Claiming Negligent Audit Is Thrown Out—Price Waterhouse Is Told It Doesn't Have to Pay Standard Chartered PLC"
>
> "Coopers & Lybrand Agrees to Payment of $95 Million in the Miniscribe Case"
>
> "Ernst Agrees to Pay U.S. $400 Million—Pact Settles Charges Firm Inadequately Audited 4 Thrifts That Failed"
>
> "Legal-Liability Awards Are Frightening Smaller CPA Firms Away from Audits"
>
> "Big Six Beg State Boards for Help"
>
> "Liability Crisis Goes Global"
>
> "Accounting Firms Face More Than 3,000 Suits Seeking up to $13 Billion"

These headlines represent just a sampling of the coverage the financial press has devoted to legal action against auditors in recent years. Public accounting firms are being sued for the conduct of audits of both large and small firms. The diverse group of litigants includes class action suits by small investors and suits by the U.S. Justice Department. Legal liability cases are expensive, win or lose. It has been estimated that about $30 billion in damage claims are currently facing the profession. In 1991, total expenditures for settling and defending lawsuits were $477 million, nine percent of auditing and accounting revenues in the United States.[1] These costs do not include indirect costs, such as the time of the partners and other personnel devoted to defending the firms.

The responsibility of public accountants to safeguard the public's interest has increased as the number of investors has increased, as the relationship between corporate managers and stockholders has become more impersonal, and as government increasingly relies on accounting information. When auditors agree to perform audits, they purport to be experts in assessing the fairness of financial statements on which the public relies. In a substantial majority of audits, auditors use great care, perform professionally, and issue appropriate opinions, thus serving the interests of the public. Even when an audit is properly performed, however, the public accounting firm may be sued and incur substantial legal costs. Even if the CPA firm wins the litigation, its reputation and that of those involved may be unfairly tarnished.

Occasionally, auditors do not use due professional care and issue wrong opinions on the fairness of the financial statements—usually an unqualified opinion on financial statements that are not fairly presented. The client or third-party users may suffer financial loss, due at least in part to reliance on those financial statements. Auditors should be, and are, held liable to their clients and third parties who can show that they relied on audited financial statements for important decisions and suffered losses due to substandard work by the auditors. That liability rests on a variety of legal theories that are explored more thoroughly in this chapter. These theories include the following:

Contract law under which liability is based on the breach of contract. The contract is usually between the auditor and the client for the conduct of an audit in accordance with generally accepted auditing standards.

Common law by which liability concepts are developed through court decisions based on negligence or fraud as applied to users of a company's financial statements.

Statutory law by which liability is based on state statutes, or more likely, federal securities laws. The most important of these statutes to the auditing profession are the Securities Act of 1933 (1933 act) and the Securities Exchange Act of 1934 (1934 act).

Most newspapers report a lawsuit of some kind. Students sue teachers, customers sue manufacturers, patients sue their doctors, and clients sue their lawyers and accountants. The trend and the societal costs related to lawsuits is illustrated in the Legal Environment box.

Factors Affecting Extent of Litigation against Auditors

Auditing firms are not unique in being the targets of litigation. A number of factors that lead to increased litigation against the auditor are at work in our society. Some of these factors include the following:

- User awareness of the possibilities and rewards of litigation.
- Joint and several liability statutes that permit a plaintiff to recover the full amount of a settlement from a public accounting firm even though that firm

Legal Environment

EVERYBODY PAYS: THE HARSH TRENDS OF CIVIL SUITS

Evidence of the trend toward excessive compensation of plaintiffs is all around us. Both the number of lawsuits and the dollar amounts of awards and out-of-court settlements are climbing:

- The number of lawsuits filed annually in federal courts jumped from 86,000 in 1962 to 239,000 in 1982.
- By 1985, 8 million lawsuits were pending in state and local courts—about one suit for every 20 adult Americans.
- A 1987 Rand Corporation analysis of civil jury awards shows staggering increases over the last 25 years. The average malpractice jury award in Cook County, Illinois, for example, increased by 2,167 percent between 1960 and 1984.

These trends have been severely affecting accountants. The personal assets of those who practice in a partnership, as well as their investments in the partnership, are at risk. And this is no mere theoretical matter:

- More suits have been filed against accountants in the past 15 years than in the entire previous history of the profession.
- The number of lawsuits reported to the special investigations committee of the AICPA's SEC Practice Section has increased in each of the last several years.
- According to available data, the largest accounting firms collectively have paid more than $250 million in settlements of mostly audit-related lawsuits since 1980. Some large firms have suggested that their annual practice protection expenditures may be over $60,000 per partner, an amount that approaches practice protection of medical doctors.

Inevitably, the ground swell of litigation and the quantum leap in awards to plaintiffs have made it nearly impossible for CPA firms and their insurers to predict the future standards to which the courts will hold the profession, and this uncertainty has destabilized the market for professional liability insurance. Premiums are escalating, coverage is shrinking, and many carriers have ceased to offer any such insurance. The following are some telling examples:

- Insurance premiums for the largest CPA firms have multiplied by a factor of five since 1984; at the same time, available commercial coverage has been cut in half, and deductibles have increased many times over.
- The AICPA liability insurance plan's 1980 premium for firms with 25 professionals was about $64 a person for $1 million in coverage. By 1986 the premium had risen to about $1,160 a person, and the deductible had doubled.
- One of five firms responding to a recent Wisconsin Institute of CPAs survey of its members indicated that it had been forced to drop its professional insurance coverage.

But there is fallout for the public, too. Consumers will pay, through increased costs of goods and services and ever-higher insurance premiums. And let's not forget the transaction costs associated with civil suits. The Rand Corporation has estimated that, of the $29 billion to $36 billion spent on general litigation terminated in 1985, plaintiffs received only half. Legal fees and other litigation-related costs ate up the rest.

Source: Robert Mednick, "Accountants' Liability: Coping with the Stampede to the Courtroom," *Journal of Accountancy* (September 1987), 119.

is found to be only partially responsible for the loss (often referred to as the *deep pocket theory:* sue those who can pay).

- Increased complexity of audits caused by computerization of businesses, new types of business transactions and operations, more international business, and more complicated accounting standards.
- More demanding auditing standards for detection of errors and irregularities, including fraud and
- pressures to reduce audit time and improve audit efficiency in the face of increased competition among public accounting firms.
- A potential misunderstanding by users that an unqualified opinion is an insurance policy against investment losses.
- The advent of contingent fee-based compensation for law firms, especially in class action suits and
- class action suits.
- Punitive damages and the Racketeer Influenced and Corrupt Organizations Act.

Joint and Several Liability

Joint and several liability concepts are designed to protect users who suffer major losses due to misplaced reliance on a company and its assertions about financial health. For example, depositors in an Ohio savings and loan were damaged by the fraudulent activities and misstated financial statements of E.S.M. Corporation as described in Chapter 3. Most of the damage was due to the fraudulent scheme of the management of E.S.M. However, the CPA firm knowingly allowed this scheme to go undisclosed. Society has a dilemma in determining the compensation for damages in such cases. **Joint and several liability** states that the damages ought to be paid by each party identified in the suit in the proportion of the damages that the judge or jury determines are applicable to each party. For example, if a jury decided that management was 80 percent at fault and the auditor was 20 percent at fault, the damages would be apportioned 80 percent to management and 20 percent to auditors. Unfortunately, in most lawsuits involving auditors, the client is in bankruptcy, management has no assets, and the auditor is the only one left with adequate resources to pay the damages. Joint and several liability is then implemented by apportioning the damages over the remaining defendants in proportion to the relative damages. If management has no resources, 100 percent of the damages is then apportioned to the auditing firm.

Audit Time and Fee Pressures

Auditors operate in a difficult environment. Most audits do not result in litigation and most auditors will never be involved in litigation during their professional career. On the other hand, most auditors feel intense pressure to make their audits more efficient and competitive. One study showed that more than 50 percent of staff auditors at one time during their career had admitted to signing off on performing procedures (without doing the procedures) when they thought such procedures were not necessary, even though they were required as part of the audit. The perception of the *"it-can-never-happen-to-me"* attitude can create a false sense of security. Auditors will not normally lose lawsuits when the working papers show that generally accepted auditing standards were followed. Many of the best audits come in "over budget" because the auditor identified a potential problem and pursued it to its conclusion. Public accounting firms have built in quality review procedures to mitigate the time and fee pressures on an actual engagement.* Finally, the auditor should remember that the client exerting the most time and fee pressure may be the client who is attempting to hide something from the auditor and is thus the client whose pressure should be most resisted.

Audits Viewed as an Insurance Policy

Auditors perform a significant role in our free market economy, but an audit accompanying a financial statement is not a guarantee that an investment in the audited company is free of risk. Unfortunately, some investors mistakenly view the unqualified audit report as an insurance policy against any and all losses from a risky investment. When they do suffer losses, these investors believe that they should be able to recover their losses from the auditor. This view, coupled with joint and several liability, encourages large lawsuits against auditors even in cases in which the plaintiffs are aware in advance that the auditor is only partially at fault.

Contingent Fee Compensation for Lawyers

Contingent fees for lawyers have evolved in our society to allow individuals who cannot afford high-priced lawyers to seek compensation for their damages. Lawyers take **contingent fee cases** with an understanding that a client who loses a case owes the lawyer nothing; however, if the case is won, the lawyer receives an agreed-upon percentage (usually one-third) of the damages awarded. This arrangement protects the underprivileged and encourages lawsuits by a wide variety of parties. The plaintiffs have little to lose and the lawyers have a large incentive to successfully pursue the case.

Class Action Suits

Class action suits are designed to prevent multiple suits that might result in inconsistent judgments and to encourage litigation when no individual plaintiff has a claim large enough to justify the expense of litigation. One example of a class action suit was recently brought against a pharmaceutical company on behalf of all women who had used one of their products. Newspaper ads were taken out to notify all potential members of the class—the women—of their right to join the class action suit and how to do so. The lawyers were collecting a large contingent fee on the case and wanted to identify every potential member of the class. Damages in such cases, and thus fees for the lawyers, can be extremely large.

Punitive Damages and RICO Provisions

Many lawsuits ask for punitive damages against the defendants on the grounds that the defendant's performance was so poorly or recklessly performed that punitive damages ought to be assessed to teach the defendant a lesson. For example, many of

*The pressure to get jobs done within budget often leads a staff auditor to (1) accept the first reasonable explanation given by management to explain a significant deviation in an account, (2) short-cut the documentation of audit work performed, and (3) perform procedures, such as reviewing documents, with less than reasonable care, potentially causing the auditor to fail to identify material misstatements in a company's financial statement. None of these short-cuts are acceptable.

the lawsuits filed against Exxon resulting from the *Exxon Valdez* oil tanker spill sought punitive damages. Such damages often far exceed the actual damages sought in the lawsuit, generally, double or triple the actual damages sought.

The **Racketeer Influenced and Corrupt Organizations Act (RICO)** has increased the likelihood of punitive damages on many lawsuits. RICO was designed to assist the U.S. government in prosecuting organized crime, which had spread into legitimate businesses. To encourage prosecution of organized crime, the act allows any injured person to sue and recover triple the damages incurred *plus* the cost of the suit, including a reasonable attorney's fee. Except for RICO, lawyer fees, which often run 50 percent or more of damages, are not usually awarded in addition to actual damages. Not surprisingly, a study conducted in 1985 showed that more than 77 percent of the lawsuits brought to trial under RICO provisions involved either securities fraud or common law fraud in a commercial setting. Indeed, one of the major complaints is that RICO is like a wild child brought into the world with good intentions but with no control. Thus, a large number of legitimate businesses, including accounting firms, have found themselves the victims of lawsuits based on RICO provisions. One scholar responded to the plight of these legitimate businesses by expressing the plaintiff's view: "Victims care little that their life savings are stolen by mobsters in black shirts and white ties or by accountants in white shirts and black ties."[2]

In a 1993 decision in the case of *Reves v. Ernst & Young,* the U.S. Supreme Court said "outside professionals who don't help run corrupt businesses can't be sued under" RICO, thus limiting triple damages under RICO to professionals that "participate in the management or operation of the corrupt business."[3]

The actions to extend legal redress to persons who might otherwise not have the ability to sue have contributed substantially to the increased exposure to legal liability that accountants now face. Many public accounting firms face lawsuits, potentially under RICO and class action provisions, for problems associated with the savings and loan industry. The joint and several liability provisions of most jurisdictions create potential large damages for any firms that lose such suits. Although various state societies of CPAs have lobbied their legislatures to cut back on the liability facing auditors, it is important to understand that the public interest concept that underlies the above legal concepts make it difficult to make significant changes that benefit one profession without providing adequate protection for damaged parties. Auditors need to be innovative in developing new plans that will appeal to legislators as being fair to all parties.

B–SPECIFIC LEGAL CONCEPTS AFFECTING THE AUDITING PROFESSION

The legal environment facing the practicing auditor is extremely complex and diversified, much as its client's base is diversified. To understand the potential liability, the auditor must understand three important dimensions of liability:

- Concepts of *negligence and breach of contract* as they may affect the auditor.
- *Parties* who may bring suit against the auditor.

- *Legal precedence and statutes* that may be used as a standard against which to judge the auditor's performance.

These concepts are illustrated in Exhibit 4.1 and are discussed in more detail below.

A complex interplay exists between the three major factors affecting liability in Exhibit 4.1. The parties that sue may be either audit clients or third-party users. They may accuse the auditor of breach of contract, negligence, constructive fraud, or actual fraud. The party bringing the suit may choose between statutory law or common law as a basis for the suit.

Concepts of Negligence and Breach of Contract

Parties that bring suit against auditors usually allege that the auditors did not meet the standard of "due care" in performing the audit or other professional services utilized by a client. The concept of due care is defined in tort law by *Cooley on Torts*:

> Every man who offers his service to another and is employed assumes the duty to exercise in the employment such skill as he possesses with reasonable care and diligence. In all these employments where peculiar skill is prerequisite, if one offers his service, he is understood as holding himself out to the public as possessing the degree of skill commonly possessed by others in the same employment, and, if his pretensions are unfounded, he commits a species of fraud upon every man who employs him in reliance on his public profession. But no man, whether skilled or unskilled, undertakes that the task he assumes shall be performed successfully, and without fault or error. He undertakes for good faith and

Exhibit 4.1

OVERVIEW OF LIABILITY ISSUES AND RELATIONSHIPS

Auditors may be sued by
- Clients
- Third parties
  - Investors
  - Government agencies

Suit may be brought under
- Contract law
- Common law
- Statutory law

Auditors may be sued for
- Breach of contract
- Negligence
- Constructive fraud (gross negligence)
- Fraud

Courts differ as to which third parties may be successful in common lawsuits for auditor negligence
- Identified users
- Foreseen users
- Foreseeable users

integrity, but not for infallibility, and he is liable to his employer for negligence, bad faith, or dishonesty, but not for losses consequent upon pure errors of judgment.[4]

The third general auditing standard (due professional care) reflects this same concept. Auditors are responsible for due care, but that doesn't necessarily mean that auditors are infallible. This broad concept of due care is implemented by the courts through the concepts of breach of contract, negligence, gross negligence, and fraud.

Breach of contract occurs when a person fails to perform a contractual duty that has not been excused. An example is an auditor's failure to finish an audit by an agreed-upon date because of the auditor's own procrastination. If the client was damaged by the auditor's failure to live up to the terms of the contract, the client would have a basis to sue the auditor for the damages incurred. Had the audit not been finished on a timely basis because of some mitigating circumstance beyond the auditor's control, such as the client's failure to provide agreed-upon help, the auditor would not be considered to be in breach of contract.

Negligence is the failure to exercise reasonable care, thereby causing harm to another or to property. It is defined as "the omission" of something that "a reasonable person, guided by those considerations which ordinarily regulate human affairs, would do," or, conversely, "doing something which a prudent and reasonable person would not do."[5] If an auditor, for example, did not detect an embezzlement scheme because of a failure to follow up on evidence that would have brought it to light, but a prudent auditor would have performed such follow-up, the auditor is negligent. The profession's standards require that audits be conducted in accordance with generally accepted auditing standards; thus, a failure to meet GAAS requirements could be construed as an act of negligence on the part of the auditor.

Gross negligence (also referred to as **constructive fraud**) is the failure to use even minimal care but without intending to deceive or cause damage to someone. "Reckless disregard for the truth" or "reckless behavior" are phrases often used to characterize gross negligence. Expressing an opinion on a set of financial statements with careless disregard of GAAS is an example of gross negligence.

Fraud is an *intentional concealment* or *misrepresentation* of a material fact that causes damage to those deceived. In an action for fraud, scienter must generally be proved. **Scienter** means knowledge on the part of the person making the representations, at the time they are made, that they are false. An auditor has perpetrated a fraud on investors, for example, by expressing an unqualified opinion on financial statements that the auditor knows are, in reality, not fairly presented. The purpose of the fraud is to deceive. Thus, **fraudulent financial reporting** is producing fraudulent financial statements to boost stock market prices and derive benefit for current holders of the stock.

The development of case and statutory law shows a fine balance between protecting users and avoiding an unreasonable standard of care on the part of the auditors. In viewing the preceding concepts, it is obviously much more difficult to prove that the auditor was fraudulent in issuing an audit opinion than it is to prove that the auditor was negligent in the conduct of the audit. Should, for example, the auditor be held liable for any act of negligence against any potential—even if unforeseen—user of a company's financial statements? These issues have been carefully considered by the courts over the decades and provide guidance. First, it is necessary to understand the potential population of users who may bring suit against an auditor.

Parties That May Bring Suit against the Auditor

In most cases, *anyone who can support a claim that damages were incurred based on reliance on misleading financial statements that were attested to by the auditor is in a position to bring a claim against the auditor.* For ease of discussion, these parties are typically labeled as *the client* and *third-party users.* Note, however, that third-party users can potentially be any of the third-party users identified in Chapter 1.

Liability to Clients

Auditors are expected to fulfill their responsibilities to clients in accordance with their contracts, which usually take the form of engagement letters. Auditors can be held liable to clients under contract law for breach of contract and can also be sued under the concepts of negligence, gross negligence, and fraud. In most audit engagements, the client contracts with the auditor to perform specific services, such as to conduct an audit in accordance with generally accepted auditing standards and to complete the audit within 45 days after the company's year-end. The contract with the client may identify a specific third-party who will receive the audited financial statements, such as the local banker. If this party is specifically identified, the party becomes a part of the contract and is described as a **third-party beneficiary.** The specific liability of the contract then extends directly to this party.

Liability to a Client for Negligence. A client seeking to recover damages from an auditor in an action based on negligence must meet four requirements: duty, breach of that duty, causal relationship, and actual damages. The client must show that the auditor *had a duty* not to be negligent. In determining this duty, courts use as criteria the standards and principles of the profession, including GAAS and GAAP. Liability may be imposed for lack of due care either in performing the audit or in presenting financial information. The auditor must have *breached that duty* by not exercising due professional care. An audit usually includes verification of cash, confirmation of receivables, and observation of inventory. Failure to perform these procedures properly may constitute negligence. The client must show there was a *causal relationship* between the negligence and damage. The client must prove *actual damages:* The amount of damages must be established with reasonable certainty and must demonstrate that the auditor's acts or omissions were the cause of the loss.

Liability to a Client for Fraud. Auditors are liable to clients for fraud when they misrepresent facts to clients and act with scienter. For example, an auditor might fail to tell the board of directors about the treasurer's ongoing embezzlement of cash because the revelation would embarrass the auditor, who may have recommended hiring the treasurer. Such misconduct by the auditor constitutes *fraud.* Five conditions must be present for an auditor to be liable for fraud. First, the auditor must have acted with *scienter* and with the intent to induce the client to act or refrain from acting. Second, the misrepresentation must be *material.* Third, the client must have *justifiably relied on and acted on the misrepresentation.* Fourth, the client must have *suffered damages* as a result of the reliance. Fifth, there must be a *causal connection* between the misrepresentation and damages suffered.

Breach of Contract. **Breach of contract** may occur when there is nonperformance of a contractual duty. Causes for action against the auditor for breach of contract include the following:

- Violating client confidentiality.
- Failing to provide the audit report on time.
- Failing to discover a material error or employee irregularity.
- Withdrawing from an audit engagement without justification.

Remedies for breach of contract include (1) requiring specific performance of the audit agreement, (2) granting an injunction to prohibit the auditor from doing certain acts, such as disclosing confidential information, and (3) providing for recovery of amounts lost as a result of the breach. When specific performance or an injunction is not appropriate, the client is entitled to recover **compensatory damages.** In determining the amount of compensation, courts try to put the client in the position in which it would have been had the contract been performed as promised.

The auditor can use the following as defenses against a breach of contract suit:

- Generally accepted auditing standards were followed.
- The client was contributorily negligent.
- The client's losses were not caused by the breach.

Misleading Financial Statements. Although management is responsible for the preparation of financial statements, it is possible that they contain material errors that should have been discovered by the auditor during the course of the audit. If the client was unaware of the errors and has suffered losses due to them, the client may attempt to recover the damages from the auditor. For example, the auditor may have failed to discover a fraud that was being perpetrated against the management of the company. The auditor will usually argue that the client was contributorily negligent (the damage was at least in part caused by management's carelessness). Nonetheless, successful cases have been brought against auditors by a client when financial statements were misleading or frauds were not detected (see Court Application box).

Common Law Liability to Third Parties

In most engagements, the auditor does not know explicitly who will be using the financial statements but is aware that third parties will be using them. Generally, the courts have held that the auditor's liability does not extend to all potential groups or individuals that might casually look at the financial statements, but that somehow the *user*, or at least the *use* to which the financial statements might be put, must be known to the auditor if the auditor's liability is extended to these groups. Potential users of the auditor's report can be categorized as follows:

- An **identified user,** including third-party beneficiaries and other users when the auditor has specific knowledge that known users will be utilizing the financial statements in making specific economic decisions.
- A **foreseen user,** individually unknown third parties who are members of a known or intended class of third-party users, but whom the auditor through knowledge gained from interactions with the client, can foresee. Thus, although not identified in the engagement letter, the auditor may have first-hand knowledge that the financial statements will be used to obtain a loan from some bank, for example.

Court Application

1136 TENANTS' CORP.

One of the most publicized lawsuits against a public accountant by a client is *1136 Tenants' Corp. v. Max Rothenberg & Co.* The principal issue in this case centers on the scope of service agreed to between the plaintiff and defendant. Rothenberg claimed to have been hired to perform bookkeeping services, prepare (compile) financial statements without verification, solely from information furnished by the managing agent on the client's behalf, and some tax work. The plaintiff (a cooperative apartment corporation) contended that it had engaged Rothenberg as an auditor, not as a bookkeeper. This work was done under an *oral retainer agreement* providing for payment of $600 per annum.

Rothenberg failed to discover the embezzlement of funds from the cooperative by its managing agent. The financial statements were accompanied by letters of transmittal that began "pursuant to our engagement, we have reviewed and summarized the statements of your managing agent and other data submitted to us by Riker & Co., Inc., pertaining to 1136 Tenants' Corporation . . ." [and concluded:] "The following statements (i.e., the financial statements and appended schedules) were prepared from the books and records of the Corporation. No independent verifications were undertaken thereon."

On each page of the financial statements was the following: "Subject to comments in letter of transmittal." Through apparent carelessness, however, the defendant used the word *audit* in the financial statements and on the bills. The trial court held that the defendant undertook to perform an audit and was negligent in its performance. The judge awarded over $200,000 to the plaintiff but allowed the auditor a counterclaim of $1,349, which represented the additional fee for an audit![6]

- A **foreseeable user,** who the auditor may not know specifically will be using the financial statements but knows that current and potential creditors and investors will use them.

Each of these user concepts has specific legal implications for the auditor, especially in the degree of due care which may serve as a defense in a lawsuit. The courts have generally moved to expand the auditor's responsibilities to users, but there are differences among courts and states as discussed below. For example, early lawsuits against auditors found that it was not reasonable to hold auditors liable to all potential users for mere negligence in the conduct of the audit. That standard was essentially eroded over a period of time so that auditors now have greater responsibility to foreseeable users for negligently performed audits.

Civil Liability to Third Parties. Civil liability is based on common law that relies on precedents of court cases in shaping responsibilities and obligations of auditors to specific third parties. To win a claim against the auditor, plaintiffs must prove that

- The auditor failed to meet the usual professional standards.
- The plaintiffs sustained a loss due to decisions based on reliance on the misleading financial statements.
- The auditor's actions caused the plaintiff's loss.

The auditor's major defense is to prove that the above allegations are not correct. Another defense, if the plaintiff is the client, is to prove that the client was partly responsible for the loss **(contributory negligence)**. Courts are often reluctant to allow the defense of contributory negligence because the auditor has special skills that most clients do not have. The auditor is expected to discover things such as material employee embezzlement, legitimate tax deductions, and other matters for which they were hired. However, when the client failed to follow its auditor's advice or when the client has information that makes its reliance on the auditor unwarranted, courts will usually allow the contributory negligence defense.

Court Case Precedence under Common Law. Common law is based on court decisions. Perhaps the major issue facing the courts over the past 60 years has been deciding the standard of negligence to which auditors ought to be accountable to various types of third-party users. The courts have almost always held the auditor responsible for damages when the plaintiffs successfully prove fraud or gross negligence on the part of the auditor. The more perplexing situation faced by the courts has been the extent to which auditors should be held responsible for ordinary negligence to an unknown group of users. As explained below, the concept started very narrowly, limiting the auditor's responsibility for ordinary negligence to those who are in privity of contract, but the concepts of foreseeable users has been utilized by some courts to expand the auditor's liability for negligence.

Limited Liability: The* Ultramares *Case. The landmark case that set the precedent for an auditor's liability to third parties for *negligence* is *Ultramares Corporation v. Touche,* which was decided by the New York Court of Appeals in 1931.[7] The details of the case are provided in the Court Case box. *Ultramares* established the precedent that an auditor can be held liable to third parties for fraud and gross negligence, but auditor *liability for ordinary negligence is limited to those who are in privity of contract.* **Privity of contract** means that a party must be one of the signers of the contract, such as the client, or be named in the contract as the primary beneficiary of the audit (a third-party beneficiary). If a bank is named in the engagement letter as a primary recipient of the audited financial statements as part of a loan application, the auditor would be held liable for ordinary negligence under the *Ultramares* precedent. If the bank had not been named in the engagement letter, such liability would not exist. The *Ultramares* precedent dominated judicial thinking for many years and is still followed in many jurisdictions. Other courts, however, have expanded the classes of persons who may sue an auditor for negligence.

Expansion of* Ultramares*: The Identified User Test. The *Ultramares* court adopted a narrow version of the **identified user test** for imposing liability for auditor negligence by requiring privity of contract. In *Credit Alliance Corp. v. Arthur Andersen & Co.,*[8] a 1985 case, the New York Court of Appeals reaffirmed the *Ultramares* precedent but extended it to those third parties who the auditors specifically knew would use the audited financial statements. To implement the concept, the court established two criteria that the plaintiffs must meet to be successful in suing under a simple negligence standard: (1) the auditors must know that the audited financial statements will be used for a *particular purpose* by a *known party* and (2) the auditors must, through their conduct or actions, acknowledge that third party and demonstrate the auditors' understanding of that party's reliance. Under this identified user test, therefore, the auditor has a liability for ordinary negligence only to those third parties for whose primary benefit the auditor conducts the audit and prepares the report.

Court Case

ULTRAMARES CORPORATION V. TOUCHE

Fred Stern and Co., a firm importing and selling rubber, required the extensive use of loans to finance its operations. Stern hired Touche, Niven & Co. to audit the balance sheet as of December 31, 1923. The auditors knew their report and the balance sheet would be used by Stern to obtain credit and issued an unqualified opinion even though the client was insolvent and had more than $700,000 of fictitious accounts receivable on the books that the auditors failed to discover. Ultramares Corporation, relying on the auditor's report, loaned money to Stern. Shortly thereafter, Stern went bankrupt and Ultramares sued the auditors, claiming negligence and fraud.

Judge Benjamin Cardozo, writing the unanimous decision for the New York Court of Appeals, found negligence on the part of the auditors. But he held that they had no liability to third parties for ordinary negligence even though liability to third parties could be imposed for fraud or gross negligence. Cardozo expressed concern about expansive auditor liability to third parties:

> If liability for negligence exists [between the auditor and unknown third parties], a thoughtless slip or blunder, the failure to detect a theft or forgery beneath the cover of deceptive entries, may expose accountants to a liability in an *indeterminate* amount for an *indeterminate* time to an *indeterminate* class. . . . Our holding does not emancipate accountants from the consequences of fraud. It does not relieve them if their audit has been so negligent as to justify a finding that they had no genuine belief in its adequacy, for this again is fraud. It does no more than say that, if less than this is proved, if there has been neither reckless misstatement nor insincere profession of an opinion, but only honest blunder, the ensuing liability for negligence is one that is bounded by the contract, and is to be enforced between the parties by whom the contract has been made.

Source: *Ultramares v. Touche*, 174 N.E. 441 (N.Y. 1931).

Foreseen Users and Class of Users Test. The 1965 *Restatement (Second) of Torts** expanded auditors' liability for negligence to intended or known third-party users and *to any individually unknown third parties who are members of a known or intended class of third-party users.* Under this test, the client must have informed the auditor that a third party or class of third parties intends to use the financial statements. The *Restatement* extends liability beyond **identified users** in that the auditor need not know the third party's identity. For example, an auditor who knows that the audit report and financial statements are to be included in a loan application would be liable to the particular bank to whom the client delivers the application, even though the auditor did not know the name of the bank when the audit report was given to the client.

The "foreseen users" test was used by a Rhode Island court in *Rusch Factors, Inc. v. Levin.* The audit was performed specifically for Rusch Factors, Inc. Even though

*The *Restatement (Second) of Torts* is published by the American Law Institute. Courts may refer to this treatise when considering an issue of outdated precedent. It provides a unique perspective on the law because its purpose is to state the law as it would be decided today by the majority of courts. It does not necessarily reflect the rules of the common law as they have been adopted by the courts. Rather, it represents principles of common law that the American Law Institute believes would be adopted if the courts reexamined their common law rules.

the plaintiff was a primary beneficiary, the court's opinion extended liability for negligence by stating that "the accountant should be liable in negligence for careless financial misrepresentation relied upon by actually foreseen and limited classes of persons."[9] Under these first two tests—the identified user test and the foreseen users test—most third parties are precluded from suing negligent auditors under common law. Shareholders, creditors, and other third parties are, in most cases, merely "reasonably foreseeable" third parties.

Foreseeable Users Test. Some courts have extended auditors' liability to foreseeable users of audit reports. In some cases, foreseeable users were potential creditors but not prospective purchasers of the corporation's stock.[10] In *Citizens State Bank v. Timm, Schmidt & Co.*, the Wisconsin Supreme Court argued that auditor liability should extend to creditors who could *foreseeably* use the audited financial statements. The court stated that the auditor could be held "fully liable for all foreseeable consequences of his act except as those consequences are limited by policy factors. The Restatement's statement of limiting liability to certain third parties is too restrictive a statement of policy factors for this Court to adopt."[11] The New Jersey Supreme Court has taken a similar position in *Rosenblum, Inc. vs. Adler* (see Court Case box). The lower courts had dismissed the case on the grounds that Touche Ross was unaware that the plaintiffs would use and rely on the audited financial statements. The Supreme Court recognized that the nature of the economy had changed since the *Ultramares* case of 1931 and that auditors are indeed acting as if a number of potential users will be relying on their audit opinion.

Current Status. Courts since *Ultramares* have upheld auditors' liability for negligence to those third parties who are in privity of contract or who are acknowledged primary beneficiaries of the audited statements. Depending on the jurisdiction and the circumstances, however, courts have in the past 60 years extended that liability to both foreseen and foreseeable users who might reasonably rely on the auditor's work. In 1992, the California Supreme Court sharply limited the legal liability of auditors in that state by ruling that only the actual clients of accounting firms can sue for alleged professional negligence in the course of a financial audit. All others are barred from filing suit unless they can allege fraud or deceit.[12] Exhibit 4.2 summarizes this historical evolution of the auditor's common law liability to third parties.

The primary benefit defense of the *Ultramares* and *Credit Alliance* decisions has been eroded over time by the *Restatement* and by recent case law in jurisdictions such as Wisconsin (*Citizens State Bank*) and New Jersey (*Rosenblum*). The precedent, however, was reaffirmed in 1988 in *William Iselin & Co. Inc. v. Mann Judd Landau*. The New York State Court of Appeals, the same jurisdiction that had heard both the *Ultramares* and *Credit Alliance Corp.* cases, extended its own identified user precedents to review engagements.[13] It was also reaffirmed in an Idaho Supreme Court ruling in the case of *Idaho Bank and Trust v. KMG Main Hurdman*, which stated that "CPAs can be held liable only when they know a specific noncontractual party is relying on their audit."[14]

The status of auditor liability to third parties for ordinary negligence is clearly uncertain. The liability to which the accountant is exposed depends on the court involved and the precedent that the court chooses to use. The best defense against being held liable is, as always, to perform every audit without negligence.

Court Case

ROSENBLUM, INC. V. ADLER

The Rosenblum brothers acquired shares of common stock of Giant Stores Corporation, which subsequently became worthless. Adler was a partner in Touche Ross & Co., Giant's auditors. The auditors had issued an unqualified opinion on Giant's financial statements, which turned out to be fraudulent. The Rosenblums claimed that the auditors were negligent and that their negligence caused the loss. The defendants claimed the Rosenblums were not in privity of contract and thus did not constitute a foreseen party. The New Jersey Supreme Court clearly rejected the narrow plea of the auditor stating:

> When the independent auditor furnishes an opinion with no limitation in the certificate as to whom the company may disseminate the financial statements, he has a duty to all those whom that auditor should reasonably foresee as recipients from the company of the statements for its proper business purposes, provided that the recipients rely on the statements pursuant to those business purposes. The principle that we have adopted applies by its terms only to those foreseeable users who receive the audited statements from the business entity for a proper business purpose to influence a business decision or the user, the audit having been made for that business entity. . . .
>
> *Certified financial statements have become the benchmark for various reasonably foreseeable business purposes and accountants have been engaged to satisfy those ends. In those circumstances accounting firms should no longer be permitted to hide within the citadel of privity and avoid liability for their malpractice. The public interest will be served by the rule we promulgate this day. . . .* (*Emphasis added.*)

Source: *H. Rosenblum, Inc. v. Adler*, 461 A.2d 138 (N.J. 1983).

Exhibit 4.2

TESTS USED IN COMMON LAW COURT DECISIONS CONCERNING AUDITOR NEGLIGENCE

		Test			
Source	Date	Client Only	Identified User	Foreseen User	Foreseeable User
Ultramares (NY)	1931		X		
Restatement (2d) of Torts	1965			X	
Rusch Factors (RI)	1968			X	
Milliner (Utah)	1974				X
Citizens State Bank (Wisc)	1983				X
Rosenblum (NJ)	1983				X
Credit Alliance (NY)	1985		X		
William Iselin (NY)	1988		X		
Idaho Bank (Idaho)	1989		X		
Osborne Computer Corp. (Calif)	1992	X			

Liability for Foreign Audits

As business has become increasingly multinational, audit risks have grown. Foreign nationals and foreign states have even been granted standing to sue in U.S. courts under certain circumstances. In a $260 million lawsuit brought by the British government against Arthur Andersen & Co. for its allegedly negligent audits of De Lorean Motor Co.'s Irish units between 1978 and 1981, a federal judge ruled that U.S.–based CPA firms can be sued in U.S. courts for allegedly substandard audits in other nations. In this case, the British government lost $80 million by buying De Lorean securities, which subsequently became worthless. They are seeking triple damages under U.S. antiracketeering laws, plus punitive damages. The judge ruled that the plaintiff had shown that the auditor's reports were a direct cause of the British government's losses. The plaintiffs also convinced the judge of a high degree of symbiosis between De Lorean's U.S. and Irish operations, providing "justification for our exercise of jurisdiction." This extension of jurisdiction creates new legal exposures for accounting firms, particularly those doing audits of foreign operations of U.S. companies: not only do U.S. courts tend to be "far tougher on accountants than English and European courts"[15] but also multinational audits can be far more complex to manage and carry out.

Statutory Liability to Third Parties

Auditor liability under statutory law is primarily established by the Securities Act of 1933 and the Securities Exchange Act of 1934. These laws were enacted to ensure that investors are provided full and accurate disclosure of relevant information. They require audited financial statements to be included in information provided to current and prospective investors and impose substantial responsibilities and potential liabilities on auditors of companies subject to regulation by the Securities and Exchange Commission (SEC).*

Auditors found to be unqualified, unethical, or in willful violation of any provision of the federal securities laws are disciplined by the SEC, which can impose administrative sanctions. These sanctions include

- Prohibiting, for some specified period of time, the firm or one of its offices from accepting new clients that are subject to SEC regulation.
- Requiring special continuing education of firm personnel.
- Denying, temporarily or permanently, the right to practice before the SEC (meaning that the SEC will not accept its audit reports).
- Requiring extensive peer review of its auditing practice by other professionals.

Auditors may also be held liable to third parties for damages under the various civil liability provisions of the securities laws. These provisions are described in the next two sections.

Securities Act of 1933. The Securities Act of 1933 requires companies to file registration statements with the SEC before they may issue new securities to the public. A registration statement contains, among other things, information about the com-

*Companies subject to SEC regulation are called *public companies,* which are companies whose securities are traded on the stock exchanges and in the over-the-counter market.

pany itself, its officers and major stockholders, and its plans for using the proceeds from the new securities issue. Part of the registration statement, called the **prospectus,** must be provided to prospective investors. The prospectus includes audited financial statements.

The most important liability section of the 1933 act is Section 11, which imposes penalties for misstatements contained in registration statements. For purposes of Section 11, the accuracy of the registration statement is determined at its effective date, which is the date the company can begin to sell the new securities. Because the effective date may be several months after the end of the normal audit fieldwork, the auditors must perform certain audit procedures covering events between the end of the normal fieldwork and the effective date.

In understanding the liability provisions of the 1933 act, it is important to know that the intent of the SEC is to ensure full and fair disclosure of public financial information. Thus, the standard of care is unusually high. Anyone receiving the prospectus may sue the auditor based on damages due to alleged misleading financial statements or inadequate audits. The burden of proof shifts from the plaintiff to the defendant in proving that the financial statements were fair or that the auditor had reason to believe the financial statements were fair based on the audit, or that the damage incurred by the plaintiff was due to other causes. Liability under the 1933 act presents a standard in which the auditor exerts a high degree of due care because the auditor is aware of the potential legal obligations.

The courts have shown a willingness to accept a **due diligence** standard in the conduct of audits under the 1933 act. Due diligence basically means lack of negligence. The need for experienced auditors who are alert for danger signals in an audit is best illustrated in the *Escott v. Bar Chris Construction Corporation* case brought under the 1933 act and described in the Court Case box. As described below, the court is also willing to identify situations when it believes the auditor deviates from the substance of a transaction to record it according to a form that masquerades the difficulty of the client's financial position.

Under the 1933 act, an auditor may be held liable to purchasers of securities for negligence, as well as fraud and gross negligence. Purchasers need to prove only that they incurred a loss and that the financial statements were materially misleading or not fairly stated. They do not need to prove reliance on the financial statements, that such statements had been read or even seen, or that the auditors were grossly negligent.

To avoid liability under Section 11, auditors must prove that (1) their audit was not negligent or fraudulent, (2) the statements were not materially misstated, or (3) the purchaser did not incur a loss caused by the misleading financial statements.

Securities Exchange Act of 1934. The 1934 act regulates the trading of securities after their initial issuance, that is, in the secondary market. Regulated companies are required to file periodic reports with the SEC and stockholders. These are the most common periodic reports:

- ***Annual reports*** to shareholders and ***10-Ks,*** which are annual reports filed with the SEC, both of which contain audited financial statements.
- ***Quarterly financial reports*** to shareholders and ***10-Qs,*** which are quarterly reports filed with the SEC. 10-Qs must be filed within 45 days of the end of each of the first three quarters.

Court Case

ESCOTT V. BARCHRIS CONSTRUCTION CORP.

BarChris constructed bowling centers and wished to sell debenture bonds to finance its growth. According to the prospectus, net sales had increased from $800,000 in 1956 to more than $9,000,000 in 1960. The company filed a registration statement that became effective in May 1961 and sold the debentures in less than two weeks. In October 1962, however, BarChris filed a bankruptcy petition, and one month later, it defaulted on the interest payments due on the debentures. Escott and other bond purchasers brought suit against the BarChris directors who had signed the registration statement and against the auditors, Peat, Marwick, Mitchell & Co. (PMM), alleging that the registration statement contained material false statements and omissions. PMM used the due diligence defense.

Most of the audit was performed by Bernardi, a senior accountant who was not yet a CPA, and junior assistants. This was his first job as a senior. He had no previous experience with the bowling industry. As part of the audit of the 1960 financial statements, Bernardi performed S-1* procedures to determine whether any material changes had occurred between the balance sheet date and the effective date of the registration statement that should be disclosed to prevent the balance sheet from being misleading.

Bernardi failed to discover that a material sale recorded in 1960 was actually a sale and leaseback. GAAP at that time required disclosure only of material obligations under long-term leases and the principal details of any important sale-and-lease transaction.† GAAP did not require the deferral of the profit from the sale and BarChris recognized the profit in 1960. The court determined that this was improper accounting. It held the auditor liable for allowing the client to record the transaction according to its form rather than its substance, producing materially misleading financial statements, regardless of the absence of specific accounting rules. Bernardi also failed to discover that there had been a material change for the worse in BarChris' financial position by April 30, 1962.

The court held as follows:

> There had been a material change for the worse in BarChris's financial position. That change was sufficiently serious so that the failure to disclose it made the 1960 figures misleading. Bernardi did not discover it. As far as results were concerned, his S-1 review was useless.
>
> Accountants should not be held to a standard higher than that recognized in their profession. I do not do so here. Bernardi's review did not come up to that standard. He did not take some of the steps which Peat, Marwick's written program prescribed. He did not spend an adequate amount of time on a task of this magnitude. Most important of all, he was too easily satisfied with glib answers to his inquiries.
>
> This is not to say that he should have made a complete audit. But there were enough danger signals in the materials which he did examine to require some further investigation on his part. Generally accepted auditing standards require such further investigation under these circumstances. It is not always sufficient merely to ask questions.
>
> Here again, the burden of proof is on Peat, Marwick. I find that burden has not been satisfied. I conclude that Peat, Marwick has not established its due diligence defense.‡

*S–1 is the registration statement form that BarChris filed with the SEC.

†*Accounting Research and Terminology Bulletins: Final Edition,* Bulletin No. 43 (New York: AICPA, 1961), 126.

‡*Escott v. BarChris Construction Corp.,* 283 F.Supp. 643 (S.D.N.Y. 1968).

- ***8-Ks,*** which are reports to be filed with the SEC upon the occurrence of specific events that provide current information about material items with the registrant, including a change in auditors.

Under the 1934 act, an auditor may be held liable for fraud in the purchase or sale of any security. The liability provisions are similar to common law. The act explicitly makes it unlawful to make any untrue statement of a material fact or to omit to state a material fact that is necessary for understanding the financial statements.

In *Herzfeld v. Laventhol, Kreckstein, Horwath & Horwath* (1974), the auditors were found liable under the 1934 act for failure to fully disclose the facts and circumstances underlying their qualified opinion. Judge Friendly stated that the auditor cannot be content merely to see that the financial statements meet minimum requirements of GAAP, but that the auditor has a duty to inform the public that the adherence to GAAP does not fairly portray the economic results of the company being audited. More specifically, the trial court judge stated:

> The policy underlying the securities laws of providing investors with all the facts needed to make intelligent investment decisions can only be accomplished if financial statements fully and fairly portray the actual financial condition of the company. In those cases where application of generally accepted accounting principles fulfills the duty of full and fair disclosure, the accountant need go no further. But if application of accounting principles alone will not adequately inform investors, accountants, as well as insiders, must take pains to lay bare all the facts needed by investors to interpret the financial statements accurately.[16]

Generally, showing compliance with GAAP is an acceptable defense by the auditor. However, as shown here, the auditor must take care to ensure that GAAP are not being manipulated to achieve a specific financial presentation result that is not in accord with the substance of the transaction.

Federal courts have struggled with the negligence standard implied by the 1934 act. The standard of holding auditors responsible for gross negligence or constructive fraud had essentially eroded to a standard of negligence. In 1976, a case reached the U.S. Supreme Court that provided greater guidance in its review of *Ernst & Ernst v. Hochfelder.* The court held that Congress had intended that the plaintiff prove that the defendant auditor acted with *scienter* to hold the auditor liable under the 1934 act. The court reserved judgment as to whether reckless disregard for the truth (gross negligence) would be sufficient to impose liability. Ordinary negligence is not sufficient to hold the auditor liable under the court's interpretation of the 1934 act.

Although it would appear that the *Hochfelder* ruling ought to provide a great deal of comfort for the auditor, a number of cases that have followed *Hochfelder* indicate that it is not difficult for a judge or jury to infer "reckless conduct" by the auditor and hold the auditors to that standard. Additionally, depending on the jurisdiction, a plaintiff also has the option to bring the case under common law.

Exhibit 4.3 illustrates the factors plaintiffs must prove in a lawsuit brought under the 1934 Act or common law against auditors and possible defenses the auditors might use.

Criminal Liability to Third Parties

Both the 1933 and 1934 acts provide for criminal actions against auditors who willfully violate provisions of either act and related rules or regulations or who know

Exhibit 4.3

LITIGATION OVERVIEW

Situation

Plaintiffs purchased stock in the stock market. The market price subsequently went up and plaintiffs purchased more stock. Company profits, the economy, and general stock market prices then declined. Plaintiffs sold the stock at a loss. Plaintiffs sued the company's management and auditors for damages measured by the difference between the highest market price and the sales price. Defendants other than the auditors do not carry professional liability insurance and do not have very much personal wealth. Proofs required of the plaintiffs and possible defenses the auditors might use are summarized in the following table.

Proof	Auditor Defenses
Damage is the difference between the highest market price and the sales price.	Damage should be the difference between cost and sales price.
Statements were false and misleading.	Statements were in accordance with GAAP or not materially misstated.
Reliance on financial statements when making investment decisions.	Plaintiffs relied on a personal guarantee of the president and/or on separate inquiry before buying the stock.
Damage was due to false/misleading financial statements.	Damage was due to the decline in general stock market prices, the downturn in the economy, and reduced company profitability subsequent to the time the plaintiff purchased the stock.
Auditor knowledge of false/misleading financial statements 1. Knew—fraud/scienter. 2. Should have known—negligence, lack of due professional care.	Auditor 1. Did not know. 2. Used due professional care and followed GAAS, was misled by management.
Judgment—joint and several liability Auditors are 30 percent responsible for the losses. However, they are required to pay 100 percent of the damages because the other defendants cannot pay.	Proposal—change state law to proportionate liability and to allow incorporation of CPA firms with limited liability for stockholders.

that financial statements are false and misleading, and who issue inappropriate opinions on such statements. Guilty persons can be fined or imprisoned for up to five years. John Burton, a former chief accountant of the SEC, stated the SEC's position on criminal action against auditors:

> While virtually all Commission cases are civil in character, on rare occasions it is concluded that a case is sufficiently serious that it should be referred to the Department of Justice for consideration of criminal prosecution. Referrals in regard to accountants have only been made when the Commission and the staff believed that the evidence indicated that a professional accountant certified

financial statements that he knew to be false when he reported on them. The commission does not make criminal references in cases that it believes are simply matters of professional judgment even if the judgments appear to be bad ones.[17]

Among the most publicized criminal actions against auditors are *United States v. Simon* (Continental Vending) and *Equity Funding.* These cases resulted in the criminal conviction of several auditors. Details of *Continental Vending* are in Appendix A and of *Equity Funding* in Appendix B.

Continental Vending. In the *United States v. Simon* (*Continental Vending*) action, the jury found two partners and a senior associate of the public accounting firm of Lybrand, Ross Bros. & Montgomery guilty of a conspiracy involving the preparation of, and giving an unqualified opinion on, misleading financial statements of Continental Vending Machine Corporation for the year ending September 30, 1962. The case represented the first criminal action against auditors who were found guilty even though they did not personally gain from this conspiracy.[18] Additionally, the judge charged the jury to determine whether the financial statements were fairly presented; following GAAP does not automatically lead to fairness, he said.

Equity Funding. In *Equity Funding,* the senior partner of Wolfson Weiner, Equity's auditors, and the in-charge auditor were convicted of criminal violations of the federal securities laws and their right to practice before the SEC was automatically suspended. The SEC found that the auditors engaged in acts and practices in flagrant violation of its rules and standards of the accounting profession relating to independence. In those statements, approximately two-thirds of the life insurance reported to be in force, as well as certain investments, were fictitious, and the audit failed to discover any of the bogus transactions.

C–APPROACHES TO MITIGATING LIABILITY EXPOSURE

Public accountants can mitigate their exposure to lawsuits by clients and third parties by improving the quality of their practice. Practice improvement is based on two major programs: (1) implementing sound quality control procedures and submitting to a peer review and adopting the resulting recommendations (described in Chapter 3). In addition, public accountants can practice defensive auditing.

Peer Review

An effective peer review program conducted by internal and external professionals (described in Chapter 3) will help a firm maximize the quality of its practice.

Defensive Auditing

Defensive auditing[19] means taking special actions to avoid lawsuits. These actions include establishing good quality control and submitting the firm to peer reviews. There are, however, other actions that firms can take.

Engagement Letters

The cornerstone of any defensive practice program is the engagement letter. The engagement letter should clearly state the scope of the work to be done so there can be no doubt in the mind of the client, public accountant, or courts. Care should be taken, however, when describing the degree of responsibility the auditor takes with respect to discovering fraud and misstatements. If the client wants its auditors to go beyond the requirements of the auditing standards, the auditors should have their attorneys review the wording to make sure that it says not only what is intended but what is possible.

Client Screening

One of the quality control elements deals with accepting and retaining clients. This decision should involve more than just a consideration of management's integrity. Strict client acceptance guidelines should be established to screen out the following:[20]

- *Clients that are in financial and/or organizational difficulty*, for example, with poor internal accounting controls and sloppy records.
- *Clients that constitute a disproportionate percentage of the firm's total practice.* They may attempt to influence the firm into allowing unacceptable accounting practices or issuing inappropriate opinions.
- *Disreputable clients.* Most public accounting firms cannot afford to have its good reputation tarnished by serving a disreputable client.
- *Clients that offer an unreasonably low fee for the accountant's services.* The auditor may attempt to cut corners imprudently or lose money on the engagement. Conversely, auditors may bid for audits at unreasonably low prices. Thirty-one states now have what are called *antilowball* laws, generally part of commercial rather than accountancy law, which prohibit predatory pricing.[21]
- *Clients that refuse to sign engagement or management representation letters.* Allowing clients to waive this requirement increases the probability that the scope of services will be expanded by the court.

Evaluation of the Firm's Limitations

A firm should not undertake an engagement that it is unqualified to handle. This prohibition is especially important for the smaller, growing firms. Statistics show that firms covered by an AICPA professional liability insurance plan that are most susceptible to litigation are those with staffs of 11 to 25 accountants. They appear to become overzealous and undertake engagements that they are not qualified to perform.

Maintenance of Accurate and Complete Working Papers

Working papers should document everything done on the audit. It is difficult to persuade a jury that anything was done that is not documented in them. The working papers should be initialed by reviewers, particularly in those areas with the greatest potential for improprieties, such as inventories, sales cutoffs, and loan reserves. These areas should be identified for special emphasis in the audit program. The working papers should clearly reflect the identification and investigation of related-party transactions, which are ripe for abuse. The investigation of unusual transactions, such as debt swaps and other barter transactions, should be carefully documented. These often lend themselves to inflation of income and avoidance of loss recognition.

Role of Insurance

Many public accounting firms protect themselves from the financial impact of lawsuits by carrying professional liability insurance. In recent years, however, insurance premiums have soared because of the size and frequency of settlements paid by the insurance companies. In just one year, one firm's premium tripled. With massive in-court and out-of-court settlements of major accounting firms, the desire of insurance companies to insure accountants is waning. Professional liability coverage has become harder to find as fewer insurance companies offer it.

The largest CPA firms are insured by an underwriting syndicate at the Lloyd's of London Insurance Exchange. In 1985, the annual insurance premium for the largest CPA firms ran as high as $10 million. These insurance policies have deductibles that now exceed $25 million for a first loss and upper limits on the amount of damages covered. Damages exceeding the upper limits have to be paid from the personal assets of the CPA firm's partners. Some partners have filed for personal bankruptcy as a result of paying such damages.

Support Changes in State Laws to Limit Auditor Liability

Many states have laws that include joint and several liability for professionals (described earlier in this chapter) and that prohibit professionals from limiting their personal liability by incorporating. CPAs should strongly support changes in these laws to provide for proportionate liability, to allow CPA firms to form limited liability corporations, and to require plaintiffs to pay for defendant's legal fees if the court determines that the suit was meritless. The Big Six CPA firms have joined with the AICPA and concerned businesses in calling for federal securities and state liability law reform to curb unwarranted litigation.[22] Recent courtroom victories and legislative advances may bring some reality to auditor liability (see Current Events box).

D–EFFECT OF COURT CASES ON AUDITING STANDARDS AND PRACTICE

Our court system serves as a check on the integrity of the financial reporting system, that is, it acts (albeit imperfectly) as the ultimate representative of third-party users. There is a clear linkage between certain court cases and the emergence of new auditing standards and practices.

Engagement Letters

The *1136 Tenants Corp.* case, discussed earlier in this chapter, led to the good professional practice of confirming the terms of each engagement in an engagement letter. Having the nature of each engagement in writing avoids disagreements about

Current Events

TURNING THE TIDE ON LIABILITY

A series of hard-fought courtroom victories, a few small legislative advances and an emerging boldness to adopt innovative and aggressive offensive strategies are dramatically reshaping the accounting profession's battle against excessive liability and abusive litigation.

From Coopers & Lybrand's decision to take the extraordinary step of counter-suing a client, to an Ernst & Young victory in California on third-party liability, the profession is savoring a string of new breakthroughs.

So far this year, the Big Six have been hit with about $1 billion in court judgments. Litigation costs are topping 10 percent of audit income.

In Youngstown, Ohio, for instance, Coopers broke new and largely untested ground for the profession by counter-suing Phar-Mor Inc., a client that went bankrupt in a $350 million embezzling scandal. "Suing a client just isn't done," gasped an official at another firm.

Part of Coopers' legal strategy may depend on an auditing standard, SAS 19, which obligates management to provide fair and accurate financial records. Legal advisors to the profession are said to be following the tactic very closely.

In California, the state Supreme Court, ruling in the closely followed Osborne Computer case, imposed new and welcome limits on third-party liability claims. "An auditor is a watchdog, not a bloodhound," said the chief justice in language so strong that it startled even officials at the California Society of CPAs, which had filed briefs in support of the profession.

In New York, Price Waterhouse was celebrating a landmark victory against the Securities and Exchange Commission over the 1980 audit of former Addressograph owner AM International. U.S. District Judge John T. Sprizzo in New York dismissed the SEC suit because the auditor "acted in good faith and made reasonable professional judgments."

In yet another recent victory for the profession, the Fifth Circuit U.S. Court of Appeals upheld a 1991 decision by a U.S. District Court Judge Barefoot Sanders in Dallas which threw out a suit by the Federal Deposit Insurance Corp. against Ernst & Young in the failure of Western Savings.

Judge Sanders had spared Ernst $560 million in penalties by ruling that the firm's audit could not be responsible for the thrift's failure, considering that the thrift's management was so thoroughly corrupted.

In Washington, the Coalition to Eliminate Abusive Securities Suits, a Big Six–led group of 150 public companies, has succeeded in getting legislation introduced in Congress to curb liability penalties and to shift some legal fees to the losing side in a lawsuit.

Source: Excerpts from "Turning the Tide on Liability," *Accounting Today*, September 7, 1992, 1.

whether the accountant should have done an audit or another level of service. Obtaining an understanding with the client regarding the services to be performed, preferably in writing, is required for compilation and review services [AR 100.08].

Audit Procedures

In the 1930s, the president of McKesson & Robbins, a drug company, had a history of aliases, fraud, and imprisonment. He had perpetrated a management fraud by reporting material amounts of nonexistent inventory and accounts receivable. At that time, general auditing procedures did not include observing inventory or confirming receivables unless requested to by the client. The fictitious assets were accidentally discovered by one of the audit partners, who, while on vacation near one of the warehouse sites, decided to visit the location only to find that it was an empty lot. The SEC questioned the adequacy of then-existing standard auditing practices. As a result, the members of the AICPA voted to require the observation of inventory and confirmation of accounts receivable.

Subsequent Events

The auditors for Yale Express had rendered an unqualified opinion on its financial statements. During the following year, while performing a special management service engagement, the auditors found that the manner of revenue and expense recognition was improper. Had Yale Express used proper accounting, its prior year profit of over $1 million should have been a loss of over $1 million. This error was not reported to the public until the subsequent year's audited financial statements were distributed. When the public learned that the auditors knew of this error much earlier than it was reported, they sued the auditors for failing to notify them on a timely basis. A new standard, *Statements on Auditing Procedure 41*, "Subsequent Discovery of Facts Existing at the Date of the Auditor's Report,"* was issued in 1969 and is now incorporated in *SAS 1* [AU 561]. This standard prescribes the procedures to be followed by the auditor in such situations and is discussed in Chapter 20.

Related-Party Transactions

U.S. Financial was a publicly held company that traded in real estate. In an effort to boost earnings, its management engaged in a scheme to sell and repurchase real estate to a number of obscure, affiliated companies. The transactions had special terms that the SEC believed should have caught the attention of the auditors. The SEC required the CPA firm to develop an audit strategy for identifying and disclosing related-party transactions and prohibited its San Diego office from adding any new SEC clients for a six-month period. The profession subsequently developed *SAS 6*, "Related Parties [AU 334]." *SAS 6* is interesting in that the auditing standard prescribed the appropriate accounting. The concepts in *SAS 6* were subsequently adopted by the FASB in its *Statement No. 57*, "Related Party Disclosures."

Summary

The most important lesson of this chapter is that the old concept of "it can't happen to me" is dangerous for auditors to believe. Clients can sue for an auditor's breach of contract, negligence, or fraud. Third parties can sue under common or statutory law for an auditor's negligence, constructive fraud, or fraud. Auditors are clearly more susceptible to liability in cases brought against them under the 1933 act than under the 1934 act or common law. Auditors can be found liable for ordinary negligence under the 1933 act but not under the 1934 act. Auditors have the burden of proving their innocence under the 1933 act. However, plaintiffs have the burden of proving the auditor's guilt under common law and the 1934 act.

Although audits aren't necessarily conducted with an eye toward potential litigation, the concepts included in this chapter should be instilled in the minds of every

---

Statements on Auditing Procedure were predecessors of *Statements on Auditing Standards* and were codified as *SAS 1* in 1972.

practicing auditor. Performance of engagements with due professional care does not necessarily guarantee that the auditor will avoid lawsuits. CPAs must practice defensive auditing and work for changes in state laws to limit liability exposures.

Significant Terms

breach of contract Failure to perform a contractual duty that has not been excused; for public accounting firms, the parties to a contract normally include clients and designated "third-party beneficiaries."

class action suits Brought on behalf of a large group of plaintiffs to consolidate suits and to encourage consistent judgments and minimize litigation costs; plaintiff shareholders may bring suit for themselves and all others in a similar situation, that is, all other shareholders of record at a specific date.

common law Developed through court decisions, custom, and usage without written legislation and operating on court precedence; may differ from state to state or by jurisdictions.

compensatory damages Awarded to clients or third parties to compensate them for losses incurred as a result of reliance on misleading financial statements or breach of contract.

contingent fee cases Lawsuits brought by plaintiffs with compensation for their attorneys contingent on the outcome of the litigation, usually one-third of the damages awarded (including punitive damages), but could be for any amount negotiated between plaintiff party and the lawyer.

contributory negligence A finding that part of the damages incurred were due to the negligence of the party bringing the lawsuit; presents an important defense for the auditor.

constructive fraud See *gross negligence*.

due diligence defense Proving that reasonable procedures were used, there was reason to believe the financial statements were fairly presented, and that the auditor planned and conducted the audit with "due professional care," can prove that the financial statements were fairly presented, or had a justifiable reason (evidence) to believe the financial statements were fairly presented.

foreseen user Individually unknown third parties who are members of a known or intended class of third-party users who the auditor, through knowledge gained from interactions with the client, can foresee will use the statements. Although not identified in the engagement letter, the auditor may have first-hand knowledge that the financial statements will be used to obtain a loan from some bank, for example.

foreseeable user Those not known specifically by the auditor to be using the financial statements, but recognized by general knowledge as current and potential creditors and investors who will use them.

fraudulent financial reporting Preparing and disseminating intentionally misleading financial statements by management as a basis for stock gains or other rewards for management.

fraud Intentional concealment or misrepresentation of a material fact with the intent to deceive another person, causing damage to the deceived person.

gross negligence Failure to use even minimal care, or evidence of activities that show a "recklessness or careless disregard for the truth"; evidence may not be present but may be inferred by a judge or jury because of the carelessness of the defendant's conduct.

identified user Third-party beneficiaries and other users when the auditor has specific knowledge that known users will be utilizing the financial statements in making specific economic decisions.

identified user test A legal concept requiring the auditor to know of the third party who would primarily benefit from the audited financial statements in order to be held liable to that party for ordinary negligence; established in the *Ultramares* case.

joint and several liability Individual responsibility for an entire judgment against all, when one defendant cannot pay the damages awarded to a plaintiff. Apportions losses among all defendants who have an ability to pay for the damages.

negligence Failure to exercise reasonable care, thereby causing harm to another or to property.

privity of contract A mutual relationship between parties to a contract.

prospectus The first part of a registration statement filed with the SEC issued as part of a public offering of debt or equity and used to solicit prospective investors in a new security issue containing, among other items, audited financial statements. Liability for misstatements in a prospectus is imposed by the Securities Act of 1933.

Racketeer Influenced and Corrupt Organizations Act (RICO) A federal law passed by Congress to enable the Justice Department and others to bring suits against organized crime that had moved into ostensibly legitimate businesses; provides for treble damages, plus reasonable lawyer fees, as compensation to victims.

scienter An intent to deceive.

statutory law Developed through legislation, such as the Securities Act of 1933 and the Securities Exchange Act of 1934.

third-party beneficiary A person who was not a party to a contract but to whom the contracting parties intended benefits be given.

Appendix A: *United States v. Simon*

This case* revolves around loans by Continental Vending Machine Corporation (Continental) to its affiliated company, Valley Commercial Corporation (Valley), most of which was subsequently loaned to Harold Roth. Roth was president of

*Three auditors were found guilty of issuing an unqualified opinion on financial statements that omitted material information causing the statements to lack fairness by a jury in the District Court for the Southern District of New York; the auditors appealed the verdict. In this case, Judge Friendly affirmed the guilty verdict, writing for the U.S. Court of Appeals for the Second Circuit.

Continental, supervised the day-to-day operations of Valley, and owned about 25 percent of the stock of each company. He used the money to speculate in the stock market. These loans amounted to about $3.5 million on September 30, 1962, the balance sheet date, and $3.9 million by February 15, 1963, the audit report date. By this date, the auditors learned that Valley was not in a position to repay its debt, and it was accordingly arranged that collateral would be posted. Roth and his family transferred their equity in certain securities to a trustee to secure Roth's debt to Valley and Valley's debt to Continental. About 80 percent of the value of these securities consisted of Continental stock and convertible debentures. The second footnote to the financial statements, which concerned these loans, stated:

> The amount receivable from Valley Commercial Corp. (an affiliated company of which Mr. Harold Roth is an officer, director, and stockholder) bears interest at 12 percent a year. Such amount, less the balance of the notes payable to that company, is secured by the assignment to the Company of Valley's equity in certain marketable securities. As of February 15, 1963, the amount of such equity at current market quotations exceeded the net amount receivable.

The notes payable to Valley could not legally be offset against the receivable from Valley because the notes payable were discounted at various banks. The government claimed the footnote *should have* said:

> The amount receivable from Valley Commercial . . . , which bears interest at 12 percent a year, was uncollectible at September 30, 1962, since Valley had loaned approximately the same amount to Mr. Roth who was unable to pay. Since that date Mr. Roth and others have pledged as security for the repayment of his obligation to Valley and its obligation to Continental (now $3,900,000, against which Continental's liability to Valley cannot be offset) securities which, as of February 15, 1963, had a market value of $2,978,000. Approximately 80 percent of such securities are stock and convertible debentures of the Company.

The financial statements were mailed on February 20. By February 25, the collateral was worth only $395,000. The same day a Continental check to the Internal Revenue Service bounced. Two days later, the government padlocked the plant and the American Stock Exchange suspended trading of Continental stock. Continental filed for bankruptcy, and the SEC began its investigations. The SEC charged three auditors with filing false statements with a government agency and violation of the 1934 act.

The defendants used eight expert witnesses who were leaders of the profession. With the exception of the error of netting the payables and receivables, they testified that Note 2 did not violate generally accepted accounting principles or generally accepted auditing standards. They testified that the standards did not require disclosure of the makeup of the collateral or of Roth's borrowings from Valley. Seven of the eight went so far as to say that disclosure of Roth's borrowings would be inappropriate.

The defendants asked that the jury be told that a defendant could be found guilty only if, according to GAAP, the financial statements, as a whole, did not fairly present the financial condition of Continental at September 30, 1962, and then only if the departure from accepted standards was due to willful disregard of those standards with knowledge of the falsity of the statements and an intent to deceive. The judge declined to give these instructions. He said that the critical test was whether the financial statements, as a whole, "fairly presented the financial position of Continental as of September 30, 1962, and whether it accurately reported the operations for fiscal 1962." If they did not, the basic issue became whether defendants acted in good faith. He went on to say that proof of compliance with generally accepted standards was evidence that may be very persuasive but not necessarily conclusive as to acting in good faith, and that the facts as certified were not materially false or misleading.

The judge also stated:

> it simply cannot be true that an accountant is under no duty to disclose what he knows when he has reason to believe that, to a material extent, a corporation is being operated not to carry out its business in the interest of all the stockholders but for the private benefit of its president.

He continued by saying that GAAP instruct

> an accountant what to do in the usual case where he has no reason to doubt that the affairs of the corporation are being honestly conducted. Once he has reason to believe that this basic assumption is false, an entirely different situation confronts him.

It was proven that the auditors knew of Roth's use of Continental's money for several years and closed their eyes to what was plainly to be seen. The judge said:

> The jury could reasonably have wondered how accountants who were really seeking to tell the truth could have constructed a footnote so well designed to conceal the shocking facts. This was not simply by the lack of affirmative disclosure but by the failure to describe the securities under circumstances crying for a disclosure and the failure to press Roth for a mortgage on his house and furnishings, description of which in the footnote would necessarily have indicated the source of the collateral and thus evoke inquiry where the money advanced to Valley had gone.

Concerning the failure to describe the collateral, the judge said:

> As men experienced in financial matters, they must have known that the one kind of property ideally unsuitable to collateralize a receivable whose collectibility was essential to avoiding an excess of current liabilities over current assets and a two-thirds reduction in capital . . . would be securities of the very corporation whose solvency was at issue—particularly when the 1962 report revealed a serious operating loss. Failure to disclose that 80 percent of the "marketable securities" by which the Valley receivable was said to be "secured" were securities of Continental was thus altogether unlike a failure to state how much collateral were bonds or stocks of General Motors and how much of U.S. Steel. . . .
>
> We are likewise unimpressed with the argument that defendants cannot be charged with criminality for failure to disclose the known increase in the Valley receivable from $3.4 to $3.9 million. Here again the claim that generally accepted accounting practices do not require accountants to investigate and report on developments since the date of the statements being certified has little relevance. Note 2 stated, "As of February 15, 1963, the amount of such equity at current market quotations exceeded the net amount receivable." This means the net amount receivable as of February 15.

The jury could find that failure to reveal the known increase in the Valley receivable, rather than being motivated by adherence to accepted accounting principles, was due to fear that revelation of the increase would arouse inquiry why a company in the desperate condition of Continental would go on advancing money to an affiliate and thus lead to discovery of Roth's looting.

Concerning the auditors intent, the judge said:

We think the Government produced sufficient evidence of criminal intent. Its burden was not to show that defendants were wicked men with designs on anyone's purse, which they obviously were not, but rather that they had certified a statement knowing it to be false.*

Appendix B: *Equity Funding*

The Equity Funding scandal broke on April 2, 1973, in a *Wall Street Journal* article, parts of which follow:

A Scandal Unfolds

One of the biggest scandals in the history of the insurance industry is beginning to break around Equity Funding Corp. of America, a financial-services concern with a go-go growth record in insurance sales.

The scandal centers in Equity Funding Life Insurance Co. (EFLIC), a key subsidiary. The parent company, which has four life insurance subsidiaries, reported total life insurance in force of $6.5 billion at the end of 1972; Equity Funding Life accounted for about half of that.

An unknown but sizable hunk of this "insurance," however, doesn't exist, sources allege. It is apparently bogus business, pulled out of thin air, put on the books, and then sold for cash to reinsurers. It has long been known around the company as "the 'y' business" or as "department 99," according to present and past employees.

Their stories, pieced together with information from other sources, outline a complex scheme allegedly conceived and operated by several managers and executives of the subsidiary and the parent company—and widely talked about in offices and corridors. "It even became a joke, a game," says one former official. "People laughed and laughed about it."

Fooling the Auditors The alleged bogus business, however, required extensive coverups. Special treatment of the "y" business in data processing was imperative, for example, lest the wrong statements be sent to the wrong people. Auditors had to be hoodwinked, and regularly were. Teams of employees worked after hours forging policy files that the auditors had reviewed, and others posed as policyholders when the auditors tried to confirm the existence of business that was bogus. . . .

On occasion, a nonexistent policyholder was sent to his last reward via a forged death claim dispatched to the reinsurer holding his policy. The trusting reinsurer would then forward the money to Equity Funding Life. The latter, having no

**United States v. Simon,* op.cit.

widow to pay, kept it. (When a policy written by one firm is sold to another, the reinsurer bears the risk and the company that sold the policy continues to handle all the paperwork, including claims processing. Both, however, get to count the same policy on their books as insurance in force.)

The Genesis Sources believe the idea of the "y" business had its genesis in a questionable deal that Equity Funding Life urged on its employees for a year or so before making up bogus policies. This was so-called "special class" or "employee franchise" insurance policies offered to employees and their families with free premiums the first year. It was often represented, in fact, as "free insurance for a year."

At first glance, this would seem an expensive benefit. Actually, it helped in a small way to ease Equity Funding's cash flow problems, which were chronic. It takes several years for an ordinary insurer to start making money on a life-insurance policy, largely because heavy sales commissions exceeding the annual premium must be paid off early in the policy's life. In Equity Funding's case, the profit must wait for 10 years, but the expenses are still incurred right away.

Equity Funding needed cash because it had pioneered in the sale of combined insurance-mutual fund packages, in which a purchaser agrees to invest a certain amount of money in a mutual fund; the shares he gets are then used as collateral for a loan from Equity Funding that is used to pay his insurance premium. The next year he buys fund shares again, and another premium payment loan is made. This goes on for 10 years, at which time he cashes in enough of his fund shares to pay off his total debt—leaving him, it is hoped, with some fund stock remaining and a policy with a tidy cash value in it.

The idea intrigued Wall Street, and Equity Funding became a hot company. But the very package plan that was so appealing to the Street also left the company perennially hungry for cash; the remedy was heavy coinsurance of its new business. . . .

For every $1 in premium the seller turns over, he gets $1.80 back from the buyer. The price takes into account the heavy first-year commissions the seller has paid, and affords him a small profit besides. The buyer is gambling that not too much of the insurance he has bought will lapse quickly, or he will lose money on the deal. In succeeding years, he may get 90 cents of every premium dollar, allowing 10 cents to the seller who is still handling all the policy accounts and claims.

With coinsurance in mind, Equity Funding thus "really applied the pressure on us to buy the special class," according to one former executive. A lot of people did, loading up on as much as $50,000 each for themselves and their wives and $25,000 on each of their children, premium-free the first year. As might be anticipated, in the second year much of this insurance was canceled or sharply reduced. By then, however, Equity Funding Life had sold it to reinsurers, scattering the dubious "special class" business in among good policies in order to keep the overall lapse rate reasonable.

The EFLIC executives involved were jubilant. "They thought it was hilarious," says one former officer. "They thought it was funny as hell to jab another company that way."

In late summer or early fall of 1970, this former officer says, he was informed that "we are going into the 'y' business." According to his account, this was described to him as the creation of bogus policies for sale to coinsurers. The cash-flow advantage was obvious; with no commission to pay an agent, since no agent had written the policy, the company could keep even more money.

The "new" policyholders, he says, were slightly altered versions of existing real ones, with minor variations in name spelling, different types and amounts of insurance, slight changes in birth date and, of course, different policy numbers. They were assigned to certain policy number blocks and scattered through them, in seemingly random fashion.

Inflated Earnings While these fictitious policyholders were being invented, the parent company was demanding more and more earnings from the life insurance subsidiary. Sources say an Equity Funding Life official would come down from a visit at the parent company, bearing a piece of paper with an earnings target for the current quarter on it. At the end of the quarter, these sources say, the accountants would work up the figures based on what the books really showed. But when the unaudited quarterly reports came out in final form, the earnings were inflated, the sources say. The figures grew more inflated as the year advanced, according to a source who saw both sets of figures. . . .

When the company reported its sales for all 1970, however, he was staggered to see that it had posted sales of ordinary life insurance totaling 18,650 policies with a face amount of $828.6 million. "That means they wrote more in the last six weeks of the year than they did in the previous 46," he says. "Some salesmen."

The Forgery Party The year was salvaged, and profit projections apparently met, by opening the books again after December 31 and plugging into the general ledger (kept on magnetic tape for running through the computer) big blocks of business heavily larded with bogus policies and sold to coinsurers after the year-end. According to data-processing workers, these tape files of reinsurance business are specially handled. Under some computer runs of the company's master file—a record on tape of all its in-force policies and all salient information about them—the programming is so arranged that they don't show up at all.

In all but a handful of cases, the bogus insurance policies have no policy files, either. These are physical records, containing applications for insurance, doctors' reports, underwriters' work sheets, credit checks, and the like, and there is supposed to be one for every policy the company lists in force. Given the apparently high volume of bogus business at EFLIC, it would be physically impossible to dummy up enough of them to cover all the fictitious policies. Nevertheless, EFLIC had managed to keep the auditors at bay with an in-house institution—the forgery party.

Rifling a Black Bag Auditors will customarily ask for a sampling of policy files, checking the contents and then cross-checking with premium receipts and policy reserve information. At EFLIC, however, there were often many files temporarily unavailable; that night a half-dozen to a dozen employees would sit down to forge the missing ones so they could be ready the next day. "It takes a long time, and you have to be careful about date stamps and other details," says one participant, who says he did it once to find out what was going on. "But I had fun being the doctor, giving the guy's blood pressure and all that."

Another time, a forgetful auditor left his black bag unlocked overnight. An auditor's bag may contain his audit plan among other things. An EFLIC executive, in full sight of others, filched the audit plan and was able to anticipate the

> accountant's moves. Another time, an auditor wanted to send out policy confirmation letters to a sampling of policyholders. EFLIC officials, eager to help, did some of his clerical chores for him. The letters would end up addressed to branch sales managers and agents, who dutifully filled out the forms themselves.
>
> Team after team of auditors has come and gone at EFLIC over the past few years without uncovering the "y" business. These include men from Haskins & Sells, Peat, Marwick & Mitchell, and Seidman & Seidman. Given the general audit procedures used on an insurance company, says one state regulator, it isn't that surprising that an ingenious, complex plan like EFLIC's could confound them. "We are just going to have to overhaul our methods," he remarks.*

It turns out that about two-thirds of the insurance on the books was bogus. In addition, $25 million of negotiable bonds were also bogus. Following are excerpts from the May 4, 1973, *Wall Street Journal* article entitled "Why Didn't Auditors Find Something Wrong with Equity Funding?"

> The man who was in day-to-day charge of the Equity Funding audit for Wolfson Weiner is Solomon Block, 44. He was in charge of it for about four years. . . .
>
> During all that time, Mr. Block wasn't a certified public accountant. He just became one the other day, on April 27. Ironically the State Board of Accountancy, at the same meeting at which it made Mr. Block a CPA, asked its staff to collect all the information it could about the licensed accountants involved in the Equity Funding scandal.
>
> There are three schools of thought as to whether outside auditors with their eyes open shouldn't after all, have noticed something amiss at Equity Funding. The first school stresses that routine auditing procedures aren't designed to detect fraud, and especially not a scheme involving what appears to have been wholesale collusion at the top of a client company. [It turns out that over 130 employees participated in this fraud, spearheaded by top management.]
>
> The second school of thought accepts this general rationale but contends that when fraud becomes massive, the argument is inoperative. A leading expert on audits puts it this way—*"If one of the factories is missing, the auditors should notice."* [emphasis added]
>
> The third school suggests that the question about outside auditors with their eyes open may not really apply in this case, that the relationship between Equity Funding and Wolfson Weiner was so comfortable for both of them, before and after Wolfson Weiner merged with Seidman & Seidman, that they both began thinking of Wolfson Weiner as inside rather than outside auditors.

It seems that Julian Weiner, the head of the CPA firm, created the basic Equity Funding investment/insurance concept. The Equity Funding audit accounted for 60 percent of the total billings of Wolfson Weiner, which had been trying for at least three years to merge with a larger firm and probably feared losing Equity Funding as a client. Equity Funding insisted that Block remain in charge of the audit after Wolfson Weiner merged with Seidman & Seidman. Block had attempted to pass the CPA Exam for over 11 years and was finally successful in 1972.

People who worked in Equity Funding's computer room say the auditors hardly ever talked to them and never attempted to run a computer test tape. At one time,

**The Wall Street Journal*, March 2, 1973, 1.

when Block indicated he wanted to bring in "a computer type" to learn the operation, the client rejected the idea and it was dropped.

Employees at one of Equity Funding's life-insurance subsidiaries have come up with their own candidate for a corporate song, which would be sung to the tune of "Mother":

E is for the earnings overstated.
Q is for the questions never asked.
U is for the usual faked expenses.
I is for investments disappeared.
T is for the tapes which were created.
Y is for the business reinsured.
Put them all together, they spell EQUITY,
*The company that gypped us all.**

Review Questions

A–Introduction to the Legal Environment

4–1 Distinguish between common law and statutory law. What companies can be sued under statutory law?

4–2 The chapter describes societal and judicial factors that have served to increase the number of lawsuits, in general, and the number of lawsuits against auditors in particular. Identify the major factors that have led to increases in lawsuits and briefly describe their contribution to the increased number of suits.

B–Specific Legal Concepts Affecting the Auditing Profession

4–3 Briefly describe each of the following legal terms.

a. Prudent person concept.
b. Breach of contract.
c. Negligence.
d. Gross Negligence.
e. Fraud.
f. Privity of contract.
g. Third-party beneficiary.
h. Scienter.
i. Joint and several liability.

4–4 What are the potential causes of action against an auditor under a breach of contract lawsuit?

4–5 In what significant ways might settlements brought against an auditor under a breach of contract suit differ from those when a client wins a lawsuit under common law?

**The Wall Street Journal*, May 24, 1973.

4–6 When a client sues the auditor under common law, is the client or the auditor required to furnish the burden of proof? What must be proven in order for the client to receive damages?

4–7 What defenses might an auditor use in successfully defending a

a. Breach of contract suit?

b. Suit brought under common law?

4–8 What precedent was set by the *Ultramares* case? What was the primary argument used by Judge Cardozo in setting the precedent?

4–9 Three tests have been used by various courts in common law decisions to determine which third-party users can successfully bring a suit against the auditor for negligence. Identify each of these tests and describe the parties that are defined in each of these tests.

4–10 Briefly explain the primary purpose of the

a. Securities Act of 1933.

b. Securities Exchange Act of 1934.

To what extent do the legal liability concepts differ under the 1933 and 1934 acts?

4–11 What are the administrative sanctions the SEC can bring against auditors? What is the major purpose of giving the SEC power to implement administrative sanctions against auditors without a court hearing?

4–12 What is meant by the effective date of a registration statement? How does this affect the auditor's responsibility for reviewing subsequent events?

4–13 How does the auditor's liability to third parties differ under the 1933 act and the 1934 act?

4–14 What is meant by the due diligence standard? What factors might an auditor cite in using due diligence as a defense in a court case?

4–15 What is

a. A 10-K?

b. A 10-Q?

c. An 8-K?

4–16 Must scienter be proven in a case brought under the

a. 1933 act?

b. 1934 act?

4–17 RICO was intended to stimulate costly actions against organized crime, but research shows that actions are taken more often against legitimate businesses, and many auditors have suffered damages due to RICO provisions. Why might auditors be sued under RICO when there is no connection to organized crime?

4–18 Under what circumstances is the SEC likely to bring criminal action against an auditor?

4–19 What is meant by *defensive auditing*? What are some of the actions a public accounting firm can take to minimize the likelihood of lawsuits?

4–20 What are the negative effects on a public accounting firm of

a. Losing a lawsuit?

b. Winning a lawsuit?

4–21 Is there a conceptual difference between an "error" on the part of the auditor and "ordinary negligence"? Explain.

4–22 What was the main defense used by the auditor in the *Escott v. BarChris* case described in the chapter? Why did the judge apparently not find the defense to be very compelling?

4–23 What precedent was set in the *Hochfelder* case described in the chapter? What actions would be necessary to change the precedent?

4–24 A CPA firm gives an unqualified opinion on financial statements that the auditor knows is materially misstated, and additionally, knows the financial statements will be given to a bank for the purposes of obtaining a loan. Assuming the auditor does not know which bank the client will take the financial statements to, can the auditor be held liable? What level of negligence would the plaintiff likely be able to establish?

4–25 Why is the *Rosenblum* case a particularly important case in auditor liability?

Multiple Choice Questions

*4–26 Nast Corp. orally engaged Baker & Co., CPAs, to audit its financial statements. Nast management informed Baker that it suspected the accounts receivable were materially overstated. Although the financial statements audited by Baker did, in fact, include a materially overstated accounts receivable balance, Baker issued an unqualified opinion. Nast relied on the financial statements in deciding to obtain a loan from Century Bank to expand its operations. Nast has defaulted on the loan and has incurred a substantial loss.

If Nast sues Baker for negligence in failing to discover the overstatement, Baker's best defense would be that

a. Baker did *not* perform the audit recklessly or with an intent to deceive.

b. Baker was *not* in privity of contract with Nast.

c. The audit was performed by Baker in accordance with generally accepted auditing standards.

d. No engagement letter had been signed by Baker.

*4–27 If a stockholder sues a CPA for common law fraud based on false statements contained in the financial statements audited by the CPA, which of the following, if present, would be the CPA's best defense?

a. The stockholder lacks privity to sue.

b. The false statements were immaterial.

c. The CPA did *not* financially benefit from the alleged fraud.

d. The client was guilty of contributory negligence.

*Adapted from the Uniform CPA examination or the Certified Internal Auditor examination.

*4–28 One of the elements necessary to hold a CPA liable to a client for conducting an audit negligently is that the CPA

a. Acted with scienter.
b. Was a fiduciary of the client.
c. Failed to exercise due care.
d. Executed an engagement letter.

*4–29 Which of the following, if present, would support a finding of constructive fraud on the part of a CPA?

a. Privity of contract.
b. Intent to deceive.
c. Reckless disregard.
d. Ordinary negligence.

*4–30 A CPA who recklessly departs from the standards of due care when conducting an audit, will be liable to third parties who were unknown to the CPA, based on

a. Strict liability.
b. Gross negligence.
c. Negligence.
d. Breach of contract.

4–31 In establishing a negligence standard against an auditor, a *foreseen user* would best be defined as

a. Someone in privity of contract.
b. Someone acknowledged by the client and the auditor who will receive the audited financial statements.
c. A class of users acknowledged by the client and the auditor who will receive the audited financial statements.
d. Someone who had used the audit report in previous years—even if there is no direct evidence that the party will use the report this year.

4–32 In a suit for damages, the jury awards the plaintiffs $1 million. The jury also determines that management is 80 percent at fault, the auditors are 15 percent at fault, and management's counsel is 5 percent at fault. Assume that management is unable to pay any damages. Under the joint and several liability provisions, the auditor would be responsible for damages of

a. $1 million.
b. $750,000.
c. $270,000.
d. $150,000.

4–33 During the course of an audit of Pero Wholesale Company, the auditors failed to uncover a fraud by divisional management that resulted in a large overstatement of bonuses awarded to those managers. Which of the following defenses (if true) would be *least likely* to support the auditor's position?

a. The client contributed to the fraud by failing to improve the internal control structure of the organization.

b. The audit was conducted with due professional care.

c. The auditor had expanded procedures due to suspicions of error, but the fraud was cleverly devised, involved collusion, and was not detectable by the application of auditing procedures that would normally be utilized.

d. The fraud was not material to the company's financial statements.

4–34 An auditor may be subject to criminal liability if he or she

a. Refuses to provide confidential information to a plaintiff in a lawsuit brought against the client.

b. Refuses to turn over the working papers to the client.

c. Failed to perform the audit of receivables with reasonable professional care.

d. Willfully omits a material fact required to be stated in the registration statement filed with the SEC.

4–35 Class action suits and joint and several liability provisions encourage lawsuits against auditors because

a. Potential damage awards are greater.

b. Contingent fees by lawyers will be larger.

c. The auditing profession carries good insurance and thus will be able to pay damages, even if the auditor is found to be only partially responsible for damages.

d. A combination of all of the above work to encourage lawsuits against auditors.

Discussion and Research Questions

4–36 (Liability for Negligence) An auditor is being sued for negligence.

Required:
For each of the following situations, indicate the likelihood the plaintiff would win if the plaintiff is

a. A financial institution that was known to the auditor as the primary beneficiary of the audit, suing under common law.

b. A stockholder suing under common law.

c. A financial institution that loaned money to the client based on the audit financial statements but the auditor knew only that the client would use the statements to obtain a loan from some financial institution. (The plaintiff is suing under common law.)

d. An investor suing under the 1934 act.

e. An investor suing under the 1933 act.

4–37 (Evolution of Negligence and Foreseeability Standards) Compare an auditor's liability to third parties for negligence under the *Ultramares* precedent, the *Restatement*, and *Rosenblum*. Which approach do you think auditors prefer? Why?

4–38 (Recoverability of Damages) An auditor issued an unqualified opinion on financial statements that failed to disclose that a significant portion of the accounts receivable were probably uncollectible. The auditor also failed to follow generally accepted auditing standards with respect to inventory. The auditor knew that the financial statements would be used to obtain a loan. The client subsequently declared bankruptcy.

Required:
Under what concepts might a creditor who loaned money to the client on the basis of the financial statements recover from the auditor?

4–39 (Defense against an Investor) An investor is suing an auditor for issuing an unqualified opinion on the financial statements of Duluth Industries that contained a material error. The auditor was negligent in performing the audit. The investor had reason to believe the statements were wrong prior to purchasing stock in the company. In the subsequent period, Duluth Industries sustained operating losses, the stock price went down by 20 percent, and the investor sold the stock at a loss. During the period that the investor held this stock, the Dow Jones Industrial Average declined 10 percent.

Required:
What defenses might the auditor use?

4–40 (Primary Beneficiary Test) A client applied for a bank loan from First Bank. In connection with the loan application, the client engaged an auditor to audit its financial statements, and the auditor issued an unqualified opinion. On the basis of those statements, First Bank loaned money to the client. Shortly thereafter, the client filed for bankruptcy and First Bank sued the auditor for damages. The auditor's work papers showed negligence and possible other misconduct in performing the audit.

Required:
a. Under what circumstances is First Bank a primary beneficiary?
b. What exceptions to the primary beneficiary test might First Bank argue?

4–41 (Interpreting the Negligence Standard) It is often difficult for courts to interpret the negligence standard in deciding whether or not an act or omission by the auditor constitutes a simple error, negligence, or gross negligence. Often the courts look to the standards of prudent professionals in the conduct of auditing to provide guidance.

Required:
For each situation listed below, briefly describe whether you think the act or omission constitutes negligence, gross negligence, or neither. Support your answer with a brief rationale. Assume that each of the situations led to material errors in the financial statement and to a lawsuit against the auditors.

a. The auditor failed to note that a confirmation signature was a forgery.
b. The auditor had the client mail out the accounts receivable confirmations in order to expedite the completion of the audit and to save audit

fees. The client and auditor had agreed, in advance, to this procedure as a basis to reduce audit fees.

c. The auditor failed to recognize that the client's warranty accrual was understated. The understatement was due to a new product introduction with which the client had no experience.

d. The client's loan loss reserve (allowance for uncollectible loans) was materially understated. Many of the client's loans were not documented and were not properly collateralized.

e. The auditor failed to discover a material misstatement of sales and accounts receivable. The auditor had noted a large increase in year-end sales and receivables but did not plan any special procedures because previous audits had not indicated any errors. Most of the year-end sales were fictitious.

f. The client had inappropriately charged a material amount of new capital equipment to repairs and maintenance expense. The client did so in order to minimize its tax liability. The auditor did not perform a detailed review of repairs and maintenance but did note that the account had risen only 15 percent above the previous year and that sales had increased 5 percent.

g. Same situation as part f, except that the auditor assigned an inexperienced auditor to the audit of maintenance. It was the auditor's first time on the job, and she failed to recognize that items should have been capitalized because she was not familiar with the industry or the client's capitalization policy.

4–42 (1933 Securities Act) The Solid Gold Co. engaged the accounting firm of Gasner & Gasner to audit the financial statements to be used in connection with a public offering of securities. Solid Gold's stock is regularly traded on the American Stock Exchange. The audit was completed and an unqualified opinion was expressed on the financial statements that were submitted to the SEC along with the registration statement. Three hundred thousand shares of Solid Gold common stock were sold to the public at $13.50 per share. Eight months later, the stock fell to $2 per share when it was disclosed that several large loans to two "paper" companies owned by one of the directors were worthless. The loans were secured by the stock of the borrowing corporation and by stock of Solid Gold that was owned by the director. These facts were not disclosed in the financial statements. The director and the two corporations are insolvent.

Required:
Indicate whether each of the following statements is true or false and briefly explain the rationale for your choice.

a. The Securities Act of 1933 applies to the preceding public offering of securities.

b. The accounting firm has potential liability to any person who acquired the stock described in connection with the public offering.

c. An investor who bought shares in Solid Gold would make a prima facia case if he or she alleged that the failure to explain the nature of the loans in question constituted a false statement or misleading omission in the financial statements.

d. The accountants could avoid liability if they could show that they were not fraudulent in the conduct of the audit.

e. The accountants could avoid, or reduce, the damages asserted against them if they could establish that the drop in price was due in whole or in part to other causes.

f. The SEC would establish contributory negligence as a partial defense for the auditor because the SEC approved the registration statement.

g. The auditor could reduce the liability if the auditor could prove that the loans were a fraud perpetrated by management to inflate the stock price.

4–43 (Negligence for a Small Audit) The public accounting firm of Gasner & Guzzler audit a number of local bars in northern Wisconsin. According to their financial statements, the bars are not profitable, yet they seem to be doing well each year and the bank has always been willing to make loans, although the owners seem hardly able to pay minimum wages.

The public accountant is aware that most bars have poor internal controls and that the owners are most likely making a comfortable living by simply underreporting revenues. This could be done by not ringing up all the sales on the cash register or throwing away cash receipts. In fact, the public accountant is certain that such activities are occurring with some clients. The primary reason for the understatement of income is to avoid income taxes.

Required:

a. Assume that an audit is performed and the auditor was aware that an understatement of income was taking place, but there was no evidence to support the understatement because records are so poor. Do you believe the auditor would be held responsible for gross negligence, negligence, or fraud if the IRS brought a suit against the auditor? Assume that the auditor also uses the financial statements to prepare the client's tax return.

b. Assume the public accountant is simply compiling the financial statements from the client's records and is issuing a disclaimer of opinion.

4–44 (Court Influence on Auditing Standards) It has been generally asserted that a standard of "due care" was sufficient to meet the negligence standard. Yet the chapter also indicated that the court system has been an influence on the development of auditing standards in such areas as related-party transactions, discovery of events subsequent to the balance sheet date, and development of specific procedures required on all audits.

Required:

a. If adherence to GAAS is generally considered a sufficient defense, why might the courts decide that the auditors were negligent in the examples given? What standard of negligence might the courts be utilizing?

b. The chapter also talks about the *Herzfeld v. Laventhol et al* case where the judge decided that adherence to a literal interpretation of GAAP was not sufficient for fair presentation. What was the court's rationale? What are the specific implications of the *Herzfeld* case for auditors?

c. What do these court cases imply regarding a literal interpretation of GAAP and GAAS versus a "substance" interpretation of the accounting and auditing standards?

4–45 (Peer Review) It was indicated that peer review could occur in two ways: (1) an internal peer review of each audit engagement before a report is issued to the public and (2) an outside peer review of the overall quality standards and quality of audits of a public accounting firm by another firm.

Required:

a. Explain how an internal peer review might work on an audit engagement for a SEC client. What material would be reviewed as part of the peer review process?
b. Briefly explain how an external peer review would differ from an internal peer review. What are the objectives of the external peer review? Are such reviews mandatory?
c. To whom are external review peer reports issued?

4–46 **(Research)** Using the resources of your library, such as *The Wall Street Journal Index*, the *Accountants Index*, *ABI Inform*, and the *Business Periodicals Index*, prepare briefs of recent common law cases brought against auditors, including the tests used by the courts to decide the cases. This can be done in groups that can then give oral presentations to the class.

4–47 **(Research)** The SEC plays a significant role in setting accounting and auditing standards. Sometimes the SEC can set precedence through its *Accounting Series Releases*, now issued in the form of *Financial Reporting Releases* and *Auditing Enforcement Releases*.

Required:

a. Select a sample of either the *Financial Reporting Releases* or the *Auditing Enforcement Releases*, or their predecessor, the *Accounting Series Releases* and summarize the findings and describe any accounting or auditing precedent that is set in the release.
b. Alternatively, select *Accounting Series Release No. 177* or *No. 150* dealing with audit deficiencies. Describe the nature of the deficiencies found and the recommendations of the SEC.

Cases

*4–48 (SEC Statutes) To expand its operations, Dark Corp. raised $4 million by making a private interstate offering of $2 million in common stock and negotiating a $2 million loan from Safe Bank. The common stock was properly offered pursuant to Rule 505 of Regulation D, which exempts the offering from the 1933 act, but not the antifraud provisions of the Federal Securities Acts.

In connection with this financing, Dark engaged Crea & Co., CPAs, to audit Dark's financial statements. Crea knew that the sole purpose for the audit was so that Dark would have audited financial statements to provide to Safe and the purchasers of the common stock. Although Crea conducted the audit in conformity with its audit program, Crea failed to detect material acts of embezzlement committed by Dark's president. Crea did not detect the embezzlement because of its inadvertent failure to exercise due care in designing its audit program for this engagement.

After completing the audit, Crea rendered an unqualified opinion on Dark's financial statements. The financial statements were relied on by the purchasers of the common stock in deciding to purchase the shares. In addition, Safe approved the loan to Dark based on the audited financial statements.

Within 60 days after selling the common stock and obtaining the loan from Safe, Dark was involuntarily petitioned into bankruptcy. Because of the president's embezzlement, Dark became insolvent and defaulted on its loan to Safe. Its common stock became virtually worthless. Actions have been commenced against Crea by

- The purchasers of the common stock who have asserted that Crea is liable for damages under the Securities Exchange Act of 1934.
- Safe, based on Crea's negligence.

Required:

a. In separate paragraphs, discuss the merits of the actions commenced against Crea by the purchasers of the common stock and by Safe, indicating the likely outcomes and the reasons therefor.

b. How would your answer be different if the client filed a registration statement and the purchasers of the common stock were able to bring suit under the 1933 act?

c. If Dark sued Crea under common law, indicate the likely outcome and the reasons therefor.

*4–49 (Federal Securities Laws)

Part A

The common stock of Wilson, Inc., is owned by 20 stockholders who live in several states. Wilson's financial statements as of December 31, 1982, were audited by Doe & Co., CPAs, who rendered an unqualified opinion on the financial statements.

In reliance on Wilson's financial statements, which showed net income for 1982 of $1,500,000, Peters on April 10, 1983, purchased 10,000 shares of Wilson stock for $200,000. The purchase was from a shareholder who lived in another state. Wilson's financial statements contained material misstatements. Because Doe did not carefully follow GAAS, it did not discover that the statements failed to reflect unrecorded expenses, which reduced Wilson's actual net income to $800,000. After disclosure of the corrected financial statements, Peters sold his shares for $100,000, which was the highest price he could obtain.

Peters has brought an action against Doe under federal securities law and state common law.

Required:

Answer the following, setting forth reasons for any conclusions stated.

a. Will Peters prevail on his federal securities law claims?

b. Will Peters prevail on his state common law claims?

Part B

Able Corporation decided to make a public offering of bonds to raise needed capital. On June 30, 1982, it publicly sold $2,500,000 of 12 percent debentures in accordance with the registration requirements of the Securities Act of 1933.

The financial statements filed with the registration statement contained the unqualified opinion of Baker & Co., CPAs. The statements overstated Able's net income and net worth. Through negligence, Baker did not detect the overstatements. As a result, the bonds, which originally sold for $1,000 per bond, have dropped in value to $700.

Ira is an investor who purchased $10,000 of the bonds. He promptly brought an action against Baker under the Securities Act of 1933.

Required:

Answer the following, setting forth reasons for any conclusions stated.

a. Will Ira likely prevail on his claim under the Securities Act of 1933?

b. Identify the primary issues that will determine the likelihood of Ira prevailing on the claim.

End Notes

1. Arthur Andersen & Co., Coopers & Lybrand, Deloitte & Touche, Ernst & Young, KPMG Peat Marwick, and Price Waterhouse, "The Liability Crisis in the United States: Impact on the Accounting Profession," a statement of position, August 6, 1992, 2–3.
2. G. Robert Blakely, *RICO Is Working,* Brief, Summer 1985, at 18.
3. Barrett, Paul M., "High Court Gives Accountants a Shield Against Civil Racketeering Lawsuits," *The Wall Street Journal,* 3/4/93, p. A3.
4. D. Haggard, *Cooley on Torts,* 472 (4th ed. 1932), 472.
5. *Blyth v. Birmingham Waterworks Co.,* 11 Ex. 781, 784, 156 Eng. Rep. 1047, 1049 (Ex. 1856).
6. Emanuel Saxe, "Accountants' Responsibility for Unaudited Financial Statements," *The New York Certified Public Accountant* (June 1971), 419–423.
7. *Ultramares v. Touche,* 174 N.E. 441 (N.Y. 1931).
8. *Credit Alliance v. Arthur Andersen & Co.,* 483, N.E.2d 110 (N.Y. 1985).
9. *Rusch Factors, Inc. v. Levin,* 284 F.Supp. 85 (D.C.R.I. 1968).
10. *Milliner v. Elmer Fox & Co.,* 529 P.2d 806 (Utah Sup. Ct. '4).
11. *Citizens State Bank v. Timm, Schmidt & Co.,* 335 N.W.2d 361 (Wis. Sup. Ct. 1983).
12. "California Court Limits Liability of Auditors," *The Wall Street Journal,* August 28, 1992, A3.
13. "CPAs Not Liable for Third-Party Loss in Review Engagement," *Journal of Accountancy* (June 1988), 14.
14. "Idaho Supreme Court Rules on Privity Issue," *Journal of Accountancy* (July 1989), 17.

Similar decisions were given in *Law Offices of L.J. Stockler P.C. v. Rose*, 436 N.W. 2d 70, Michigan Court of Appeals (1989) and *First Florida Bank v. Max Mitchell & Company*, P.A. 541 So, 2d 155 (1989).

15. "Accounting Firms Can Be Sued in U.S. over Audits Done Abroad, Judge Rules," *The Wall Street Journal*, March 10, 1988, 10.
16. *Herzfeld v. Laventhol, Krekstein, Horwath & Horwath* [1973-1974 Transfer Binder] CCH FED. Sec. Law Reporter # 94,574, at 95,999 (S.D.N.Y. May 29, 1974).
17. John C. Burton, "SEC Enforcement and Professional Accountants: Philosophy, Objectives and Approach," *Vanderbilt Law Review* (January 1975), 28.
18. *United States v. Simon*, 425 F 2d 796 (2d Cir. 1969).
19. Many of the ideas in this section come from Stephen H. Miller, "Avoiding Lawsuits," *The Journal of Accountancy* (September 1988), 57–65.
20. Miller, "Avoiding Lawsuits," 57–65.
21. "Anti-Lowball Law in Effect in Texas," *Accounting Today*, October 9, 1989, 5.
22. Arthur Andersen & Co. et al., "The Liability Crisis in the United States: Impact on the Accounting Profession," 1992, 6–7.

CHAPTER

5

Learning Objectives

Through studying this chapter, you will be able to:

1. Understand the need for accounting firm growth.
2. Develop an understanding of the risks associated with the acceptance of new audit clients and the approaches an audit firm can take to minimize those risks.
3. Understand the various types of fraud and the auditor's responsibility for detecting fraud.
4. Develop an audit approach to identify fraud situations and adjusting the audit approach to detect material fraud.
5. Understand the role of audit committees in promoting the independence and effectiveness of the audit function.

Obtaining Clients: Opportunities and Auditor Responsibilities

Chapter Contents

The Commission's review of significant cases involving auditors and of other evidence makes it amply clear that when management is untrustworthy, there is a significant chance that a valid independent audit cannot be performed. A dishonest management group that is determined and innovative has the ability, under the right circumstances, to perpetrate fraud and avoid detection by an auditor for a significant period of time.

Thus, if at any point serious doubts arise concerning the honesty, integrity, or good faith of management, the auditor should take all reasonable actions to resolve the doubts to his satisfaction. If the auditor is unable to satisfactorily resolve his doubts, he should consider resignation or other appropriate responses.[1]

The auditor should assess the risk that errors and irregularities may cause the financial statements to contain a material misstatement. Based on that assessment, the auditor should design the audit to provide reasonable assurance of detecting errors and irregularities that are material to the financial statements. [AU 316.04]

Chapter Overview

This chapter has three main messages. First, public accounting firms must grow and adapt to a changing economy and competitive environment. The various ways in which public accounting firms acquire new clients are explored. But not all potential clients should be pursued. The auditor must address the risks associated with a potential client. Those risk factors and the approach the auditor should follow to identify them and to incorporate them into an audit are discussed. Second, a "high-risk" client may be more likely than other companies to commit fraud. The auditor's responsibility for detecting and reporting fraud is discussed and an approach is recommended for identifying high-risk clients that are more likely to commit fraudulent financial transactions. Third, the role of the audit committee in the financial reporting process and the auditor's required communication to them are discussed.

A–GROWTH AND MARKETING OF AUDITING SERVICES

Public accounting firms are constantly seeking new clients or looking for ways to expand services to existing clients. Firms that do not seek to change or expand are often caught in a downward spiral that will cause them to lose business or even to fail. This chapter discusses the need for public accounting firms to grow and the manner in which they seek new clients. However, a CPA firm must be cautious in determining which potential new clients to accept. Therefore, we also discuss factors that a public accounting firm should evaluate before accepting a new client. Finally, the acceptance of a client implies acceptance of responsibilities to those clients and to third-party users. Two of the most important auditor responsibilities include meeting the public's expectations regarding detection of fraud and communicating information (beyond an opinion on the fairness of a company's financial statement presentation) to audit committees. These responsibilities are also discussed in this chapter. Once the auditor accepts and understands these responsibilities, the audit can be planned. Chapter 6 begins the coverage of the audit planning process.

Professionalism and Competition

A constant of business life is that organizations must grow and adapt to an ever-changing environment or risk failure. The same is true for the public accounting profession. CPA firms can achieve that growth either by acquiring new clients or by expanding their services to existing clients. Both approaches to expansion represent potential threats to "professionalism." Competition, for example, is generally considered beneficial to both the public and the profession, but excessive competition can encourage substandard work that can, in turn, result in lawsuits and loss of reputation.* Offering new services may lead a public accounting firm into practices that regulatory agencies or the public may view as incompatible with the attest function. Thus, CPA firms must continue to seek new clients and offer expanding services to growing clients, but that growth must never stand in the way of maintaining the public's confidence that the profession can ensure the "fair" presentation of an entity's financial statements.

The Need for Growth in Public Accounting

The need for growth comes from (1) the expansion and growth of existing clients, (2) the desire for new challenges, (3) competition from other CPA firms, and (4) the necessity of maintaining competitive partner and employee compensation levels.

1. *The expansion and growth of existing clients.* As clients grow, they face an increasingly complex world of competition and regulation. They often need assistance in such specialized areas as tax planning, regulatory reporting, and information system design and implementation. Because one individual rarely has all the expertise any given client requires, accountants who want to meet the increased needs of their clients' organizations will have to add specialists to provide the range of services necessary.
2. *The desire for new challenges.* Most professionals relish the challenges of serving growing clients, solving their problems, and contributing to their success. By facing new challenges, the individual auditor grows professionally.
3. *Competition from other CPA firms.* If a CPA firm does not grow, it frequently stagnates as other firms aggressively seek new clients. Firms that have in the past failed to expand have often lost their competitive edge, and many of them have not survived. Regulatory activity has contributed to the increase in competition among firms. During the 1970s, the Federal Trade Commission (FTC) began an active campaign to promote greater competition in the auditing profession. As noted in Chapter 3, the profession responded by removing or rewriting those provisions of the Code of Professional Ethics that the FTC viewed as anticompetitive. Subsequently, the profession entered a period of extremely intense competition—especially price competition—for clients.
4. *The necessity of maintaining competitive partner and employee compensation levels.* One effect of price competition has been to reduce the auditor's "real" (constant dollar) income. During the past 15 or so years, public accounting went from one of the highest-paid entry-level professions to one of the lower

*In a study of public accounting, the AICPA's *Commission on Auditors' Responsibilities* issued a report in the late 1970s that cited "excessive competition" as one of the major threats facing the profession. The commission feared that, if competition were not controlled, there would be a tendency to perform all services at the lowest common denominator.

paid. Now, as the challenges of the profession demand "the best and the brightest" college graduates, it must keep its compensation competitive to attract and then retain these highly qualified individuals.

The Business of Public Accounting Firms

Although auditing is the core business of most large public accounting firms, many CPA firms do much more than auditing. The services that CPA firms perform have traditionally included tax assistance and consulting in addition to accounting and auditing services. But the nonaccounting, nonauditing services have expanded so dramatically in recent years that some public accounting firms no longer refer to themselves as CPA firms but instead as "international accounting, auditing, and consulting firms." Now CPA firms* routinely provide such diverse consulting services as actuarial planning, manufacturing scheduling and layout, compensation and employee benefit analysis, merger and acquisition analysis and assistance, information system design and implementation support, marketing research and retailing strategy, and much more (see Exhibit 5.1).

Some public accounting firms have expanded by acquiring previously independent management consulting firms. For example, Price Waterhouse & Co. acquired a firm that specialized in strategic retail management, and KPMG Peat Marwick acquired an information systems consulting firm, which now operates as a separate subsidiary of KPMG. Other firms have acquired businesses in such areas as information systems consulting and employee compensation and benefit analysis. More and more, CPA firms view themselves as providers of "professional services" to their clients.† As a partner in one large firm commented, "we see our job as helping clients wrestle with problems."[2] Many public accounting firms derive 50 percent or more of their fees in consulting and tax services, with some of the smaller firms also deriving the majority of their fees from nonaudit services. Many auditors believe that the skills they can offer beyond a traditional audit can be instrumental in attracting new audit clients.

Attracting Audit Clients

As discussed in Chapter 3, the 1970s revision of the Code of Professional Ethics allowed the auditing profession to use marketing tools that had previously been prohibited. CPA firms began to advertise, make unsolicited bids for potential clients to provide auditing services, and used price as a "weapon" to obtain clients. In the past 20 years, competition among firms has increasingly shifted from the country club to the free market. Businesses that had never before considered changing auditors became interested in other CPA firms that offered to perform the audit at a fraction of the cost charged by its continuing firm or to provide additional audit-related services for essentially the same fee.

These changes in the competitive environment dictate that every public accounting firm consider how best to market its professional services. The marketing tools now available include both institutional and targeted advertising, surveys of client

*For our purposes, we will continue to refer to the firms that practice public accounting as CPA firms even if they choose to emphasize other services they perform.

†The services provided by most CPA firms represent areas in which the clients, because of economies of scale, normally would not have available in-house. Like other consulting firms, CPA firms have the advantage of developing the special expertise that they can share with a number of clients and therefore provide services at lower cost than their clients can provide for themselves.

Exhibit 5.1

CONSULTING SERVICES PROVIDED BY PUBLIC ACCOUNTING FIRMS

Information Systems Consulting

- Systems analysis and design, ranging from large mainframe to microcomputer applications
- Database management system installations
- CASE–developed systems: Systems developed by computer-assisted systems engineering (CASE) of new client applications
- Data security and control
- Control of access to computer systems
- Data communications
- Development of application systems

Manufacturing

- Just-in-time production and inventory management systems
- Integrated manufacturing software
- Cost accounting systems

Management Planning and Advice

- Strategic management analysis
- Marketing studies
- Overview of personnel needs
- Organization structure analysis

needs, and the identification of targeted industries and companies for unsolicited preliminary proposals. New clients are often obtained as a result of the following:

1. Referrals from existing clients.
2. Professional and social contacts with key executives.
3. References from other professionals, especially lawyers or bankers.
4. Client mergers, acquisitions, or management buy-outs of existing operations.
5. Requests for an audit proposal from other organizations.
6. Direct proposals by the firm to "targeted companies" or companies in "targeted industries."
7. Growth by an "other services" client to the extent that such a client needs an audit.
8. Referrals by other public accounting firms.

Personnel Policies

- Management compensation
- Employee benefits and compensation
- Employee/personnel handbooks

Financial Related

- Merger and acquisition analysis
- Financial accounting advice
- Cash and cash flow management
- Capital structure analysis
- Leveraged buy-out analysis
- Prospective financial analysis
- Cost accounting
- Management decision support systems
- Make or buy decisions

Other

- Actuarial consulting
- Retail or other industry specialty analysis

9. Other professional contacts with, for example, the firm's "alumni" or professional friends.

Referrals from Existing Clients

One of the best sources of new clients is a recommendation from an existing client. Although not a major source of new clients, the unsolicited referral from an existing client is welcome not only because it attests to the firm's quality of service but also because such a recommendation increases the probability that the CPA firm will obtain the referred client.

Professional and Social Contacts with Key Executives

Because most auditing and consulting engagements are under the supervision of a specific partner in charge, most clients are interested in the services rendered by a specific auditor or consultant, and the team of experts that individual can bring to the engagement. Thus, CPAs need to become acquainted with key executives in the business community to develop the necessary personal contacts. Business relationships fostered in voluntary organizations, in community activities, or at a country club often expand the CPA's potential client base.*

References from Other Professionals in the Business Community

Every business community develops its own network of professional contacts. CPAs frequently work closely with banks and lawyers in providing comprehensive services to mutual clients. The quality of that working relationship can lead to valuable future references.

Mergers, Acquisitions, and Buy-Outs

Mergers, acquisitions, or buy-outs generally lead to the expansion of some CPA firms' work base while other firms lose clients in the process. A CPA firm serving as the auditor of an acquisitive firm will likely generate increased business, although the audit fees associated with the acquired organization will normally be far less than the fees that were previously generated when the company was independent. As a part of a much larger entity, the acquired business has a different materiality dimension and generally requires less continuing audit work.

Some audit firms have established merger and acquisition consulting services to assist their clients in finding merger and acquisition partners.

Requests for Proposals

Many organizations periodically reevaluate their current level of audit services and audit fees. In the past, few clients changed auditing firms because the cost involved was thought to be very high. A new CPA firm would have to learn about the company and perhaps even the industry. New auditors would need to rely on the previous auditors to establish the basis for beginning balance sheet accounts. Within a competitive environment, however, clients have found that many auditors are willing to absorb these additional costs and still perform an audit for less than the continuing auditors charge. Management and audit committees of the board of directors now find it prudent occasionally to test the market to determine whether significant cost savings can be achieved by changing auditors.

Thus, CPA firms today are frequently asked to submit proposals for potential new clients. The auditor must be able to write a coherent proposal that explains the services the firm can provide and that demonstrates a keen knowledge of the client's business, its problems, and its industry. The written proposal typically includes an overview of the CPA firm and its particular areas of expertise, a description of the engagement team and its qualifications, the potential services available beyond the audit, and the fee structure and billing requirements for the engagement. (For a more detailed description of the contents of a proposal package, see Exhibit 5.2.) The written proposal package also includes a cover letter that stresses the CPA firm's perspective and unique advantages. Because most audit clients are not publicly traded companies, the proposals often emphasize the business advising expertise the audit firm can bring to the auditor-client relationship rather than SEC-client experience. Most businesses expect the written proposal to be followed by an oral presentation to the audit committee of the board of directors or to management before employing the CPA firm.

---

*Because a major part of many firms' compensation packages for audit partners is based on their ability to bring in and retain profitable audit clients, a Chamber of Commerce banquet or a golf match at the country club, while enjoyable, may also serve very necessary business purposes.

Exhibit 5.2

PROPOSAL PACKAGE FOR A NEW CLIENT

Cover Letter

This document explains the nature of the proposal and emphasizes the "unique" manner in which the audit firm can add value to the audit. The cover letter often describes nonaudit services the firm believes it will be able to provide to assist the client.

Executive Summary

This part of the proposal, usually two to six pages in length, provides an overview of the audit firm as a whole and of the local office in particular, and it identifies the engagement team and its expertise. The summary also discusses other services the firm has to offer, with an emphasis on what the audit firm can do to contribute to the client's success. Finally, the summary includes a description of the fee structure for the audit, the basis for billing, and the number of years of fee commitment contained in the bid.

Service Capabilities of the Audit Firm

This section normally emphasizes the CPA firm's ability to audit the client's organization efficiently and effectively. Included are descriptions of the unique approaches or capabilities of the firm to audit the client's computer system, understand the client's industry, or work with the client's personnel in the audit. The audit-specific proposals are generally supplemented by a description of other services the CPA firm has to offer—merger and acquisition experience, personal financial planning for executives, tax planning, cash management, environmental engineering, distribution analysis, and the like.

Audit Approach

This section describes the CPA firm's overall audit approach. Because many organizations are heavily computerized, the audit firm often uses this opportunity to extol its computerized audit capabilities (including auditing with and through the client's mainframe computer) and the extent to which it can bring microcomputer support to the audit. Generally, the firm also includes a description of how the transition from the previous auditors will be handled to minimize duplication of effort and staff disruption in the client's organization. The section normally concludes with a discussion of the cooperative relationship the firm hopes to foster between the client's audit committee or management and the auditor and of the planned interaction between the internal auditors for the organization and the external auditors on the engagement team.

Timing and Fees

This section contains a more detailed description of the audit fee structure than appears in the executive summary. The basis of billing is generally outlined and fees allocated among audit, tax, and any consulting services to be performed. In some cases, the auditor offers a specified number of hours of free consulting work as part of the bid process. The section also includes the preliminary audit schedule, including any plans for preaudit interim work, and a target date for completion of the audit.

Qualifications and Resumes of the Audit Engagement Team

This section contains a more detailed discussion of the qualifications of the members of the audit team: their education, experience, and unique expertise in relation to auditing in the client's industry. All personnel whose talents may be used on the client's behalf are included, from the audit engagement partner and staff to tax and consulting personnel. The narrative description is followed by formal resumes of all personnel mentioned.

Client List and References

This section normally includes a list of all local office clients and selected individual references from that client list (particularly those served by the engagement partner). In addition, any industry references on a regional or national basis are also included to emphasize the firm's overall qualifications for auditing in that industry. Local offices of national firms often also list "selected" national clients to indicate its association with "prestige" or highly visible organizations.

Auditing firms prefer to charge their clients based on hours worked. In most bidding situations, however, the auditor needs to estimate the number of hours the audit will require and make a one- to three-year commitment on the approximate cost of the annual audit.* That fee commitment assumes that no major unforeseen problems arise during the course of the engagement; the written proposal, therefore, also includes the specification of charges for any substantial additional work either in extending audit procedures or in providing services not contained in the audit proposal.

Advertising

CPA firms rushed to experiment with advertising as soon as it was allowed. Firms developed themes to create images of their quality and their commitment to service. Deloitte & Touche suggested that its approach went "Beyond the Bottom Line"; while Ernst & Whinney (predecessor to Ernst & Young) announced that "Ernst & Whinney and Results . . . They Go Together." Local firms often highlighted the tax aspects of their practice or even their expertise in the area of personal financial planning. Occasionally, an audit firm advertised the development of new technology, such as KPMG Peat Marwick's approach to evaluating system controls. Much of the advertising, however, has evolved toward developing a positive image of, and positive recognition for, the firm rather than selling specific services, and advertising is now seen as only one element in a total marketing plan. The success of advertising in procuring new clients, moreover, is open to question. Some firms believe that it has had little or no effect; others believe it has created a subtle positive image that has had an impact on client acquisition.

Direct Proposals to a Targeted Industry or Company

Many CPA firms develop strategies to target an industry or a specific company. For example, an audit firm wishing to become known as a health care specialist might target the university hospital system in the state as a potential audit client. The targeted approach includes building key contacts with the important decision makers in the organization, developing an understanding of the business and industry, and promoting a positive image.

Growth through the Performance of Other Services

Quite often an auditing relationship begins with nonauditing client services. A small business, for example, may initially require only compilation or review and tax services. As the business grows, the client then requires audit services. Growing as clients grow is a major strategy for most firms, one that has led many of the national CPA firms to establish small business or emerging business divisions to serve such clients. These small business divisions emphasize accounting assistance, business advising, and tax services. Much of the consulting is accounting oriented because many small businesses have not yet established good internal control or cost accounting systems for sound financial management.

Referrals by Other Public Accounting Firms

A surprise! Why would a CPA firm refer clients to another CPA firm? The answer is fairly straightforward. A number of very high-quality, small CPA firms serve

*The cooperation and scope of the work of the internal auditors can significantly affect the amount of work the external auditors perform, and, therefore, the cost of the proposed audit.

growing businesses, and the needs of these clients may come to exceed the ability of the local firms to serve them effectively. In such cases, local firms recommend a larger firm. In similar fashion, a national firm might refer a potential client to a local firm, although this latter type of reference is becoming rarer.

Other Professional Contacts

CPAs are members of an elite professional community. Contacts established as early as college may lead to client referrals. All professionals are eventually selling the unique quality of the individuals associated with their firm. In the long run, the quality of the services each member of the firm brings to each client will sell the firm's services.

B–ACCEPTING A CLIENT

Although "selling" auditing services is important, CPA firms do not want to accept all potential clients. Association with the wrong audit client can be costly to a CPA firm in time, money, and reputation. Lack of specific client or industry knowledge, for example, may require substantial staff training before an auditor can serve a particular client effectively. Or a company close to bankruptcy may be unable to pay for the services the auditors provide or may have complex, hard-to-audit transactions as it struggles to stay afloat. Whenever questions of management integrity arise, the auditors face severe risks.

Determining the Reason for Changing Auditors

Before it accepts a client changing audit firms, the prospective firm should learn what motivated the potential client to make a change. On many occasions, the motivation may be simply that management or the audit committee wants a change, either from dissatisfaction with the level of service from the current auditors or in the hope to lower the cost of the audit. Other reasons for change include standard company policy for rotating auditing firms to gain fresh perspectives or disagreements about how complex transactions should be treated. For their own protection, auditors need to understand fully what lies behind the potential client's desire to engage a different CPA firm. If, for example, the previous auditors were fired or resigned because they discovered fraud or disagreed significantly with the client on a proposed accounting treatment, the prospective auditors need to know this. Therefore, existing auditing standards require that prospective auditors attempt to discuss the reasons for the change with the predecessor auditor.

The Auditing Standards on Accounting Firm Changes

To gain an understanding of the reason for the change in CPA firm, a successor auditor is required by AU 315 to initiate discussions with the **predecessor auditor**. The auditor is particularly interested in determining whether the previous auditor discovered anything prejudicial to the client or disagreed with the client on auditing or accounting procedures—anything substantive that would have led to the auditor's dismissal or resignation. Because of the confidentiality required of all auditors, the potential successor auditor must obtain the client's permission to talk with the predecessor auditor. The standard urges the auditor to make certain inquiries to assist in deciding whether to accept the potential client. These inquiries include the following:

> specific questions regarding, among other things, facts that might bear on the *integrity of management*; on *disagreements with management* as to accounting principles, auditing procedures, or other similarly significant matters; and on the predecessor's understanding as to the reasons for the change of auditors. AU 315.06 [Emphasis Added]

Should the successor auditor, during the conduct of the audit, discover information that suggests that the financial statements reported on by the predecessor auditor contain material errors, the auditor has the responsibility to arrange a meeting of all three parties—the client, the predecessor auditor, and the successor auditor—to attempt to correct any prior misstatements. If the client refuses or the successor auditor is not satisfied with the result, the auditor should seek legal counsel to determine the most appropriate course of action.

The Securities and Exchange Regulations Regarding Auditor Changes

For all SEC–registered companies, third parties can obtain information about the reasons for a change in auditors. Registrants are required to report any change in auditing firm and the reasons for that change within five business days of the change on Form 8-K. The registrant must specifically comment on whether the company had any significant disagreements with its auditors over accounting principles, auditing procedures, or other financial reporting matters and must indicate the new CPA firm of record. A copy of the form is sent to the dismissed auditors, who must send a letter to the client, addressed to the SEC, stating whether the auditor agrees with the information in the 8-K, and the client must file the auditor's letter with the SEC within 10 business days. The Reporting in Action box illustrates that such a requirement can be effective in protecting the public. It is likely that the SEC will scrutinize any substandard reporting by auditors regarding changes.

Considerations for Accepting or Continuing an Audit Client

Most audit firms follow formal procedures before accepting a new client. In addition to learning about any disagreements between management and the predecessor auditor over accounting and auditing matters, CPA firms also want to make preliminary assessments of the following:

1. Management's integrity and reputation.
2. Any legal proceedings involving the company.
3. The overall financial position of the company.
4. The existence of related-party transactions.

All, to some extent, are interrelated. Legal proceedings, for example, can include not only regulatory proceedings but also civil and criminal actions, each of which can have bearing on management integrity and reputation. Of course, **management integrity**—management's honesty and trustworthiness—has direct bearing on

Reporting in Action

COOPERS BLOWS WHISTLE ON FORMER CLIENT'S 8-K

Coopers & Lybrand blew the whistle on a former client, warning the Securities and Exchange Commission that the company failed to report potentially serious cash flow problems that the accounting firm had identified. The warning was issued after Coopers & Lybrand's dismissal by the client, a group of real estate investment partnerships headed by Roger J. Clifton of Tucson, Arizona.

Clifton's companies—Clifton Income Fund Limited Partnership I and II and the Morgan Clifton Fund Limited Partnership—reported the change of accountants to the SEC late last year, noting in an 8-K filing that "after consideration of all relevant factors, it is in the best interest of the partnership to replace" Coopers with Henry and Horne. In that statement, Clifton told the SEC that the partnership had experienced no disagreements with Coopers and that the firm's reports on the funds' financial statements were unqualified.

Not so, Coopers replied in a filing with the commission. In a letter sent to Clifton on November 22, 1988, the accounting firm said that the SEC should have been informed that "the Fund has provided an $800,000 allowance for potential losses" on some of its holding due to real estate market conditions in Arizona. "In addition," the auditors said, "due to apparent cash flow difficulties experienced by the general partner (Roger Clifton) and its affiliates, the Fund has provided a $369,784 allowance for potential losses on its receivables from affiliates." Coopers further noted that "permanent financing from an unrelated party" has not yet been secured for one of the company's apartment investment projects. "If this financing cannot be obtained," the accountants warned, "the net realizable value of the Fund's ADC arrangement, amounting to $3,106,192, may become further impaired."

Source: *Accounting Today*, March 6, 1989, 3.

related-party transactions—transactions between management/owners and the corporate entity. Such transactions, not in the normal course of business, could adversely affect a small company's financial position as well. There are several sources of information regarding management integrity available to the auditor, including correspondence with predecessor auditors and other professionals, information in regulatory filings and various news media, and interviews with audit committee members. The auditor should be prepared to pursue many of the sources of information shown in Exhibit 5.3 if there are preliminary indications that management integrity issues may be important in accepting a potential client.

Many CPA firms have developed a checklist to assist them in determining whether to accept or continue an audit client. Some CPA firms, moreover, require in-depth evaluations of potential clients from certain "high-risk" industries—those that, because of the very nature of the business, may have fewer controls or greater liability exposure. Auditors do not always exclude all companies in high-risk industries as clients, but they do insist on taking additional precautions before accepting such clients and often increase their audit work to minimize the potential risk associated with the clients. At least one national firm requires the concurrence of the regional office before an individual audit partner can accept new clients in the high-risk industries the firm has identified. Exhibit 5.4 presents examples of high-risk

Exhibit 5.3

SOURCES OF INFORMATION REGARDING MANAGEMENT INTEGRITY

1. *Predecessor auditor*. Information obtained directly through inquiries as required by AU 315. The predecessor is required to respond to the auditor unless such data are under a court order or if the client will not approve communicating confidential information.
2. *Other professionals in the business community*. Examples include lawyers and bankers, with whom the auditor will normally have good working relationships and will make inquiries of them as part of the process of getting to know the client.
3. *Other auditors within the audit firm*. Other auditors within the firm may have dealt with current management in connection with other engagements or with other clients.
4. *News media*. Information about the company and its management may be available in financial journals or magazines or industry trade magazines.
5. *Public databases*. Computerized databases, such as the NAARS database (periodical index) can be searched on a keyword basis for any public documents dealing with management or any articles on the company. Similarly, public databases such as LEXIS can be searched for the existence of legal proceedings against the company or key members of management.
6. *Preliminary interviews with management*. Such interviews can be helpful in understanding the amount, extent, and reasons for corporate turnover in key positions. Personal interviews can also be helpful in analyzing the "frankness" or "evasiveness" of management in dealing with important company issues affecting the audit.
7. *Audit committee members*. Members of the audit committee may have been involved in disputes between the previous auditors and management and may be able to provide additional insight.
8. *Inquiries of federal regulatory agencies*. Although this is not a primary source of information, the auditor may have reason to make inquiries of specific regulatory agencies regarding pending actions against the company or the history of regulatory actions taken with respect to the company and its management.
9. *Private investigation firms*. Use of such firms is rare but would be taken if the auditor becomes aware of issues that seriously question the integrity of management or management's involvement in potential illegal activities.

industries.* A more detailed examination of risk and its implications for an audit is provided in Chapter 6.

Pricing Audit Services

CPA firms must price their services to attract and retain excellent personnel as well as to attract and retain audit clients. Competition, then, demands that services be reasonably priced. Competition has led to advances in auditing technology, including computerized audit techniques that help reduce labor costs. But extreme client sensitivity to price can signal potential problems for the client-auditor relationship. Prospective clients who have in the past regularly changed CPA firms primarily

*Each year, the AICPA issues a general and several industry-specific audit risk alerts that identify risks to which auditors should be especially alert during current year audits.

Exhibit 5.4

EXAMPLES OF HIGH-RISK INDUSTRIES AS IDENTIFIED BY ONE CPA FIRM

Brokerage Firms and Tax Shelter Advisers
Many brokerage firms have severe capital shortages. Tax shelter–advising businesses tend to be risky because of the nature of the investments and because significant funds are often entrusted to the advisers without any review or regulation.

Casino, Gaming, Wagering (Racetrack, Dog Track) Enterprises
There may be questions about the background of individuals running the businesses. Additionally, such businesses create many opportunities for fraud because they involve the handling of large quantities of cash.

Construction Contractors
Construction is risky because one badly bid job can cause a company to face bankruptcy. Some contractors have difficulties dealing with organized labor.

Financial Institutions (Banks and Savings and Loans)
The woes of these industries have been adequately chronicled in the financial press. It is difficult to audit the value and collectibility of loans as well as the collateral associated with the loans.

Real Estate and Land Development
Unfortunately, some real estate and land development companies have operated without sufficient capital aiming to make "quick deals" and leave. There have been many abuses in this industry; therefore, an auditor must be sure of the type of client activities before accepting an engagement.

Waste Management and Trash Handling
This industry has been characterized by rapid growth and competitive activities to acquire new contracts or disposal areas. Some of the activities have been found to be illegal. Additionally, many of the companies have engaged in "border-line" accounting to make their operating results appear to be better than they actually were.

because of price will likely continue to do so in the future. A CPA firm can, on occasion, cut prices to obtain a key client in an important industry, but it cannot routinely price its services at unprofitable levels. Discounted pricing overall will not allow a CPA firm to keep compensation at levels that will attract and retain talented individuals.

Importance of the Engagement Letter

By the time an audit engagement is accepted, the auditor and client should have a mutual understanding of the nature of the audit services to be performed, the timing of those services, the expected fees and the basis on which they will be billed, the responsibilities of the auditor in searching for fraud, the client's responsibilities for preparing information for the audit, and the need for other services to be performed by the CPA firm. The CPA firm should prepare an **engagement letter** summarizing and documenting this understanding between the auditor and the client. The engagement letter clarifies the responsibilities and expectations of each party

Exhibit 5.5

EXAMPLE OF AN ENGAGEMENT LETTER

Rittenberg & Schwieger
5823 Monticello Court
Madison, WI 53711
June 1, 1995

Mr. Fred S. Jacobs, President
Rhinelander Equipment Co., Inc.
700 East Main Street
Rhinelander, WI 56002

Dear Mr. Jacobs:

Thank you for meeting with us to discuss the requirements of our forthcoming engagement.

We will audit the consolidated balance sheet of Rhinelander Equipment Co., and its subsidiaries, Black Warehouse Co., Inc., and Green Machinery Corporation, as of December 31, 1995, and the related consolidated statements of earnings, retained earnings, and cash flows for the year then ended. Our audit will be made in accordance with generally accepted auditing standards and will include our examining, on a test basis, evidence supporting the amounts and disclosures in the financial statements, assessing the accounting principles used and significant estimates made by management, as well as evaluating the overall financial statement presentation.

The objective of our engagement is the completion of the foregoing audit and, upon its completion and subject to its findings, the rendering of our report. As you know, the financial statements are the responsibility of the management (and Board of Directors where pertinent) of your company who are primarily responsible for the data and information set forth therein as well as for the maintenance of an appropriate internal control structure (which includes adequate accounting records and procedures to safeguard the company's assets). Accordingly, as required by generally accepted auditing standards, our procedures will include obtaining written confirmation from management concerning important representations on which we will rely.

Also as required by generally accepted auditing standards, we will plan and perform our audit to obtain reasonable, but not absolute, assurance about whether the financial statements are free of material misstatement. Accordingly, any such audit is not a guarantee of the accuracy of the financial statements and is subject to the inherent risk that errors and irregularities (or illegal acts), if they exist, might not be detected. If we become aware of any such matters during the course of our audit, we will bring them to your attention. Should you then wish us to expand our normal auditing procedures, we would be pleased to work with you to develop a separate engagement for that purpose.

Our engagement will also include preparation of federal income tax returns for the three corporations for the year ended December 31, 1995, and a review of state income tax returns for the same period prepared by your accounting staff.

and is acknowledged by the client (see Exhibit 5.5). Also, as noted in Chapter 4, it can serve as a basis for a breach of contract suit by a client. Notice the degree to which a good engagement letter parallels and expands on the description of the responsibilities of both management and the auditor as well as the nature of an audit

Our billings for the services set forth in this letter will be based upon our per diem rates for this type of work plus out-of-pocket expenses; billings will be rendered at the beginning of each month on an estimated basis and are payable upon receipt. This engagement includes only those services specifically described in this letter, and appearances before judicial proceedings or government organizations, such as the Internal Revenue Service, the Securities and Exchange Commission, or other regulatory bodies, arising out of this engagement will be billed to you separately.

We are enclosing an explanation of certain of our Firm's Client Service Concepts. We have found that such explanation helps to avoid misunderstandings and enhances our ability to work more closely with our clients.

We look forward to providing the services described in this letter, as well as other accounting services agreeable to us both. In the unlikely event that any differences concerning our services or fees should arise that are not resolved by mutual agreement, we both recognize that the matter will probably involve complex business or accounting issues that would be decided most equitably to both parties by a judge hearing the evidence without a jury. Accordingly, you and we agree to waive any right to a trial by jury in any action, proceeding, or counterclaim arising out of or relating to our services and fees.

If you are in agreement with the terms of this letter, please sign one copy and return it for our files. We appreciate the opportunity to (continue to) work with you.

Very truly yours,

Larry E. Rittenberg

RITTENBERG & SCHWIEGER

Larry E. Rittenberg
Engagement Partner

LER:lk
Enc.

The foregoing letter fully describes our understanding and is accepted by us.

RHINELANDER EQUIPMENT CO., INC.

June 1, 1995 — *Fred S. Jacobs*

Date — Fred S. Jacobs, President

as described in a standard audit report. Note also that the auditor has requested that any disputes that may end in litigation be tried before a judge and that the client waive the right of a jury. Many clients will not agree to such a stipulation, but that should not serve as a basis for rejecting such a client.

Practical Illustration

COMPENSATION AND THE STAFF AUDITOR

As new staff auditors, many college graduates quickly become aware of the expectation to generate "billable time," that is, hours that can be charged directly to the client. Staff auditors also become aware of the relatively large difference between billings to the client for their services and their current salary. Staff auditors must not only cover their own costs but also contribute to cover the overhead of the auditing firm and the salaries of partners.

To understand the difference between salary and billing rates, consider the following:

1. *Fringe benefits.* Fringe benefits—health insurance, life insurance, vacation pay, employer contributions to social security, and so forth—must be built into the firm's billing rates.
2. *Firm overhead.* All firms have a number of indirect costs: office support staff, office furnishings, administrative overhead (telephone, supplies, rent, etc.), national research and development staff support, staff training, and microcomputer and other technological equipment, to name only a few of the overhead costs associated with running a successful CPA firm. In addition, all the expenditures made as part of the employee recruiting process or in sponsoring Beta Alpha Psi or accounting club meetings must be paid for out of fees that are eventually billed to clients.
3. *Non–per diem rates.* All CPA firms prefer to bill and collect fees at regular **per diem** (standard billable) **rates.** Occasionally, however, partners conclude that some clients cannot be billed at such rates and become or remain clients. Often a CPA firm will bid for engagements with guaranteed charges below the firm's standard billing rates. The firm may also cut rates for "off-season" clients—those who have a fiscal year end other than December 31.
4. *Partner compensation.* Partners leverage their earnings from the work of the staff and other support personnel. Although partners have high billing rates, they generally have fewer chargeable hours than do staff auditors. This difference does not mean that their work is nonproductive; rather, the differential in billable time reflects most partners' focus on practice development for future firm productivity.

C–AUDITOR RESPONSIBILITIES FOR DETECTING ERRORS, IRREGULARITIES, AND ILLEGAL ACTS

Auditors are engaged to determine whether an organization's financial statements as represented by management contain material misstatements. The primary responsibility of an auditor, therefore, is to determine the fairness of the client's financial presentation. The auditor has a direct responsibility to the client to conduct the audit on the client's behalf in accordance with the understanding reached by the client and auditor and outlined in the engagement letter.

Beyond the auditor's direct responsibility to the client, however, is the auditor's overall professional responsibility. This special responsibility encompasses but is not limited to the obligation to the client: The auditor must conduct the audit in full accordance with professional standards so that all users can have a basis on which to rely on the audited financial statements.

Fair financial presentation means that no misstatements or **illegal acts** materially affect the organization's reports of its operating results, cash flows, or financial position. The auditor, therefore, needs to approach each audit with a sufficient degree of professional skepticism to be alert to any signals of misstatement—especially of fraud—and to expand audit procedures accordingly whenever such signals are present.*

Responsibilities for Detecting Errors

Auditors provide assurances that financial statements are free from material misstatements. The most common type of misstatement occurs in the form of errors. These may be caused by poor judgment of employees who process data, carelessness, problems associated with the design of the client's accounting system, or failure to apply accounting standards properly. Errors are distinguished from other misstatements, for example, irregularities or illegal acts, because they are unintentional; they are not introduced with a specific purpose to cause the financial statements to be misleading, even though that could be the result. They are no less important to consider as the auditor designs an audit program. Indeed, most audit procedures are planned around the auditor's assessment of the potential that errors are likely to exist in the underlying accounting records used in developing the financial statements.

Responsibilities for Detecting and Reporting Irregularities

Fraud, the most common irregularity, can take one of two forms: defalcations and fraudulent financial reporting. A common denominator in all fraud is the intent to deceive for personal benefit. A **defalcation** is defined as a type of fraud in which an employee takes assets from an organization for personal gain. Examples include theft of assets such as cash (embezzlement) or inventory or the manipulation of wire (money) transfers. Many organizations have developed strong systems of internal accounting controls to prevent defalcations and to detect those that do occur. Companies often insist on segregation of duties, for example, so that an employee cannot both perpetrate and cover up a fraud without the assistance of at least one other employee. Auditors have traditionally been alert for defalcations, but detection of all such theft, especially in amounts that are considered immaterial, would be unduly expensive. **Fraudulent financial reporting** is the intentional manipulation of reported financial results to portray a misstated economic picture of the firm. The perpetrator of such a fraud seeks gain through the rise in stock price and the commensurate increase in personal wealth. High-risk, "high-flyer" companies can be especially prone to fraud of this type. The first such major fraud involved Equity Funding (see Chapter 4). Other frauds on a grand scale have included Barry Minkow's ZZZZ Best with its totally fictitious sales and MiniScribe's pressure-cooker environment with grossly inflated operating results reported at every management level. The "pressure cooker" environment of MiniScribe is described in the Practical Illustration "Cooking The Books."

*"The auditor neither assumes that management is dishonest nor assumes unquestioned honesty. Rather, the auditor recognizes that conditions observed and evidential matter obtained . . . need to be objectively evaluated to determine whether the financial statements are free of material misstatement." [AU 316.16]

Practical Illustration

COOKING THE BOOKS: HOW PRESSURE TO RAISE SALES LED MINISCRIBE TO FALSIFY NUMBERS

As other computer-disk-drive companies were laying off hundreds of employees, MiniScribe Corp. announced its 13th consecutive record-breaking quarter. This time, however, the surge in sales sent a shiver of apprehension through MiniScribe's board.

"The balance sheet was scary," says William Hambrecht, one of the directors.

What worried Mr. Hambrecht was a sudden, three-month run-up in receivables to $173 million from $109 million, a 59 percent increase. Inventories were similarly bloated, swelling to $141 million from $93 million—a dangerous development because disk drives can become obsolete from one quarter to the next.

Seven months later, the portents that had worried Mr. Hambrecht generated grim headlines. MiniScribe's spectacular sales gain had been fabricated. In fact, the company acknowledged, it didn't know whether it could produce accurate financial statements for the prior three years.

MiniScribe was under the direction of Q.T. Wiles, a respected manager known as "Dr. Fix-It." Mr. Wiles clearly wanted everyone to know he was in charge. Four times a year, he would summon as many as a hundred employees to Palm Springs for several days of intense "dash meetings," at which participants were force-fed his idiosyncratic management philosophy. At one of the first such meetings he attended, says a former division manager, Mr. Wiles demanded that two controllers stand, "and then he fired them on the spot, saying to everyone, 'That's just to show everyone I'm in control of the company.' "

Mr. Wiles wanted to be remembered as the man who made MiniScribe a billion dollar company. Sales objectives became the company's driving force—the sole determinant of whether bonuses were awarded.

Accounting Maneuvers

1. Hitting the number became a company-wide obsession. Although many high-tech manufacturers accelerate shipments at the end of a quarter to boost sales, MiniScribe shipped more than twice as many disk drives to a computer manufacturer as had been ordered (about $9 million).
2. Shipments were normally made from Singapore by air-freight, but when shipments had to go by cargo ships, a division manager would change purchase orders to make it look like title changed hands in Singapore.
3. The problem of inadequate reserves became so great that private analysts began noticing it in 1988. Despite $177 million in receivables, MiniScribe was booking less than 1 percent in allowances, while the rest of the industry was booking allowances ranging from 4 percent to 10 percent.
4. Returned merchandise was shipped as new merchandise.
5. The company developed warehouses around the country to store its products under just-in-time inventory agreements with major customers. Of course, the customers were not billed until they actually used the goods. However, MiniScribe recorded the sales as soon as the goods were shipped to the warehouses. The number of disk drives shipped were totally at MiniScribe's discretion.

Investors say they, too, have been cheated, having seen the value of their stockholdings tumble from a high of $14 a share to less than $3. A dozen shareholder lawsuits have been filed in federal court in Denver charging that MiniScribe "engineered phony sales to artificially inflate its stock to benefit insiders. In 1988, MiniScribe officers and directors sold 350,000 shares of company stock. The suits also charge that the company's auditors 'participated in the conspiracy' by 'falsely' certifying the company's financial statements."

Source: Excerpted from "Cooking the Books: How Pressure to Raise Sales Led MiniScribe to Falsify Numbers," *The Wall Street Journal*, September 11, 1989, 1.

In these and similar cases, users who depended on independent audit reports suffered damages. In the late 1980s, a Congressional oversight committee (often referred to as the *Dingell Committee,* after its chair) became concerned and urged the SEC and the profession to develop a more responsive program for detecting fraud and protecting the public.

Responsibilities for Discovering Fraud

The public generally expects the auditor to detect and report fraud. In the 1986 Lou Harris poll of individuals knowledgeable about public accounting practice, respondents were asked to comment on the following statement: "The most important function of an independent auditing firm is to detect management fraud and dishonesty." Almost all* of the third-party users strongly agreed.[3] In essence, the public believes that too many companies have failed because management manipulated transactions to misstate financial results. Income and assets have been overstated with hopes of higher stock market valuations, and operating performance has been inflated so that executives have been awarded unwarranted stock options, bonuses, or outright shares of company stock. Because management compensation has become so linked to company earnings, unscrupulous executives have found that fraudulent financial reporting is a quick way to achieve personal financial success at shareholder expense. In such cases, users rightly ask, "Where were the auditors?"

The profession responded first by sponsoring a major study of fraudulent financial reporting and then by issuing an auditing standard clarifying auditor responsibilities for identifying and reporting on fraud. Auditors must assess the likelihood that errors or irregularities may occur. Based on that assessment, the auditor must "design the audit to provide reasonable assurance of detecting errors and irregularities that are material to the financial statements" [AU 316.05]. The standard emphasizes the need for the auditor to exhibit "professional skepticism" in conducting the audit so that signals of the possibility of fraud will not be overlooked.

Fraud Risk Assessment

Studies of fraud and fraudulent financial reporting have shown that specific individual and organizational characteristics are often associated with entities or executives that have committed fraud, whether defalcations or fraudulent financial reporting. These range from personal traits of the individual (for example, a strong financial need or a grievance against the organization) to company conditions (poor internal accounting controls, for example). The "white-collar criminal" is often portrayed as an educated individual who occupies a position of trust but is subject to weak oversight. Often such frauds start out small and grow over a period of time as the perpetrator assesses the risk of being caught as low.

These characteristics of fraud are referred to as **red flags.** Current auditing standards identify some of these red flags, as shown in Exhibit 5.6. The auditor needs to look at fraud indicators in the three broad categories of management characteristics (decision-making dominated by a single individual, for example), operating and industry characteristics (such as declining profitability or excessively high stock market expectations for the firm), and characteristics specific to the engagement (for example, significant, complex, or convoluted transactions) in assessing the potential for fraud. The alert reader will note that many of the "red flags" described in Exhibit 5.6 were present in the MiniScribe case previously described.

*Only a few special groups—audit committee members, attorneys, and creditors—tended to disagree with the statement.

Exhibit 5.6

CHARACTERISTICS OF AUDIT CLIENTS THAT RAISE THE ISSUE OF FRAUD

Management Characteristics

- Operating, investing, and financing decisions are dominated by a single person.
- Attitude toward financial reporting is unduly aggressive.
- Management (particularly senior accounting personnel) turnover is high.
- Undue emphasis is placed on meeting earnings projections.
- Reputation in the business community is poor.

Operating and Industry Characteristics

- Profitability of entity relative to its industry is inadequate or inconsistent.
- Operating results are highly sensitive to outside economic conditions (inflation, interest rates, unemployment, etc.).
- Direction of change in entity's industry is declining with many business failures.
- Organization is decentralized without adequate monitoring.
- Internal or external matters that raise substantial doubt about the entity's ability to continue as a going concern are present.

Engagement Characteristics

- Many contentious or difficult accounting issues are present.
- Significant difficult-to-audit transactions or balances are present.
- Significant and unusual related-party transactions are present.
- Nature, cause (if known), or the amount of known and likely misstatements detected in the audit of prior period financial statements is significant.
- Client is new with no prior audit history.

Source: AU 316.10

A more comprehensive model of fraud risk assessment was recently developed by Loebbecke, Eining, and Willingham.[4] Their model was based on a comprehensive study of frauds uncovered by KPMG Peat Marwick auditors and thus represents real-world factors. The categories in their fraud model differ somewhat from that in the professional standards, but the overall red flag characteristics are very similar. The companies most likely to perpetrate fraud were characterized by five dominant factors: management domination by a few (84 percent), weak control environment (53 percent), heavy emphasis on meeting earnings objectives (36 percent), frequent disputes with the auditor (36 percent), and an overly aggressive management attitude toward financial reporting (33 percent). Over one-half of the detected frauds resulted in material asset overstatements.

Detecting Fraud: Changes in Auditing Procedures

Once the risk of fraud has been assessed as more than minimal, the auditor faces three major tasks: (1) assigning experienced personnel to the audit engagement, (2) determining the most likely way in which a fraud might have taken place, and (3) developing specific audit procedures to determine whether fraud indeed exists.

Appropriate audit procedures and applicable organizational control analysis differ, depending on the type of fraud most likely to have occurred. With fraudulent financial reporting, the auditor generally looks for fictitious transactions, accounting which is not in accord with the substance of transactions, incorrect valuation of assets, or omission of liabilities. For defalcations, the auditor focuses on the inadequate segregation of duties or other control deficiencies that can allow a fraud to take place. When control weaknesses exist the auditor should develop specific procedures aimed at determining whether the control weaknesses led to specific instances of errors or irregularities. If, for example, a control deficiency allows an individual to perform an inventory-based defalcation, the auditor needs to expand audit procedures to ensure the correctness of recorded ending inventory.*

When planning the audit, the auditor should view the red flags as *warning signals*. The auditor should develop information regarding the potential existence of the fraud characteristics on each engagement as a basis for identifying a high-risk fraud profile. The auditor must plan the audit with an appropriate degree of skepticism. The modification of the audit approach may include (1) extending audit procedures beyond those normally required for similar type audits, (2) assigning more experienced personnel to the audit, (3) relying less on management representations as part of the evidentiary-gathering process, and (4) being especially alert for unusual ratios or account balance changes that are difficult to verify. The red flags do not necessarily indicate that a fraud has taken place, but the auditor should plan and conduct the audit with an awareness that fraud is more likely to exist when the red flags are present than in an audit where the red flags are not present.

Reporting on Detected Defalcation

If a material defalcation has occurred but is not separately disclosed, the financial statements are misstated. Defalcation is not an expense; thus, the financial statements must show, at minimum, a reclassification of the amount from an expense to a loss. The auditor will have to determine the appropriate account title and classification for the loss. Because material defalcation would normally be both unusual and nonrecurring, it can reasonably be argued that the amount should be classified as an extraordinary item and proper footnote disclosure given to explain its nature. If there is a high probability of full or partial restitution, the probability and the amount of restitution should be considered in determining the amount of loss to book.

Two things should become apparent from this discussion. First, fair financial presentation is not attained unless material defalcation is fully disclosed as a loss because a loss from defalcation does not meet the definition of expense. Second, if the financial statements are appropriately adjusted and have full footnote disclosure, the auditor's report can contain an unqualified opinion. In some instances, however, the auditor might not be able to determine the amount of the loss; if the amount is not susceptible to reasonable estimation, the auditor may have to qualify the audit opinion because of a lack of evidence.

Other Reporting Responsibilities

Traditionally, the auditor has not been required to report the existence of fraud beyond the company, its audit committee, and board of directors. Present governmental audit standards require the auditor to report instances of illegal acts, including fraud, to the director of the governmental entity. The auditor should also consider reporting the acts to the appropriate oversight committee. However, recent

*Chapter 16 presents more detailed discussion of the particular procedures the auditor would perform in auditing inventory. Some of those additional procedures might include requiring a complete count of existing inventory or a more extensive examination of supporting documentation for purchases and sales of inventory.

lawsuits and public pressure have induced Congress to consider stricter reporting requirements.

The new legislation would require the auditor of SEC-registered companies to report material instances of fraud to management, which would, in turn, be required to report the fraud to the SEC. If management does not report the fraud within ten working days, the auditor must report the existence of the fraud to the SEC. The auditor is always obligated to communicate the existence and details of the fraud to the audit committee of the board of directors or its equivalent, and to management at least one level above that where the fraud occurred. If it is truly management fraud, in the sense that top management was involved, it should be reported to the audit committee and to the board of directors as a whole.

Responsibilities for Detecting and Reporting Illegal Acts

Illegal acts are defined as "violations of laws or governmental regulations . . . by management or employees acting on behalf of the entity" [AU 317.02].* A company that violates tax laws or pays bribes to government officials (foreign or domestic), for example, would be committing an illegal act. Some illegal activities may result in fines against the company as well as the individuals involved; others may not carry fines but still need to be disclosed. Illegal acts often have direct financial statement ramifications. The auditor must therefore design the audit to identify illegal acts that have a direct, material effect on the financial statements.

Few audit procedures are designed specifically to test for the existence of illegal acts. A number of procedures can, however, provide information that could lead to the discovery of such acts if they exist. Some of these procedures include reading corporate minutes, making inquiries of management and legal counsel, and performing various tests of details to support specific transactions or balances. In reviewing such information, the auditor should be especially alert to large payments for unspecified services to consultants or employees, excessively large sales commissions, unexplained governmental payments, and unauthorized or unnecessarily complex transactions.

If such acts are discovered, the auditor is advised to consult the client's legal counsel about the application of relevant laws because determining whether something is indeed illegal is generally beyond an auditor's professional competence. If illegal acts do impact the financial statements, the auditor should take steps to ensure fair presentation, including both necessary account adjustments and proper disclosure. Finally, the auditor should communicate the nature of these acts to the audit committee of the board of directors or its equivalent.

D–AUDIT COMMITTEES

All companies listed on the New York Stock Exchange and those whose stock is traded in the over-the-counter market are *required* to have audit committees. In addition, the American Stock Exchange *recommends* the use of audit committees.

* Note that the definition excludes "personal misconduct" by company personnel that is "unrelated" to the business activities of the entity. [AU 317.02]

Finally, both the Report of the National Commission on Fraudulent Financial Reporting and recent auditing standards recommend the institution of, and expanded roles for, corporate audit committees.

Audit Committee Defined

An **audit committee** is a subcommittee of the board of directors; thus, all members of the audit committee sit on the board. Preferably, the audit committee is composed of "outside" members of the board—that is, those members who do not hold company management appointments. Although the selection of the external auditors is subject to shareholder vote, the CPA firm is essentially hired by management and the board. In such circumstances, the audit committee can act as a direct surrogate of the nonmanagement shareholders and third-party interests as the highest level of board oversight of the audit function. The audit committee should serve as a proactive voice in promoting the independence of both the internal and external auditors.

Responsibilities of the Audit Committee

An audit committee should bring a user's perspective to the board's review of the annual audit and any special investigations that may be required. As an integral part of the corporate financial reporting process, the audit committee should have the knowledge to make inquiries of the auditor as to the appropriateness of accounting principles used by the company and its presentation of the economic substance of important transactions. Remember, the audit committee, in theory, is not a management or auditor advocate but is an advocate for fair financial reporting from the perspective of the organization's major constituencies: shareholders, creditors, and employees. There have been increased calls for even greater responsibility by audit committees in corporate governance areas such as determining compliance with laws and regulations and determining the integrity with which management conducts the organization's activities. Thus, audit committees often engage either internal or external auditors to perform special investigations on their behalf.

The audit committee meets periodically with both the internal and external auditors, usually two to four times per year. At a minimum, the audit committee and the external auditors meet just prior to the annual audit to discuss issues of accounting principles and audit timing and procedures. The committee also meets with the external auditors at the conclusion of the audit to review the annual audit report and to learn of any significant adjustments needed as a result of the audit or any disagreements with management that may have occurred. The audit committee is available for special meetings at the request of the auditors. Many audit committees meet quarterly to review the audit work plan and the reports of the company's internal auditors. If the audit committee has major disagreements with management, those disagreements need to be discussed at the board of directors level to determine the proper action to be taken. The SEC has called for public reporting by the audit committee on the scope of their activities and any disagreements with management or the auditors.

Required Communication to Audit Committees

Recent auditing standards have expanded and clarified the external auditors' responsibilities for communicating with audit committees. Auditors should review their planned work schedule with the audit committee and should report on changes in major accounting policies and estimates, scope limitations imposed by management, audit recommendations that have not been implemented, and significant difficulties encountered in conducting the audit. (For a summary of the required communication, see Exhibit 5.7). The required communication is intended to "dampen" potential problems when it is perceived that management might have leverage power over the auditor. The presumption underlying the communication to audit committees is that the committee members are truly independent of management and will operate in the best interests of the broad group of third-party users they represent. Unfortunately, in some companies, audit committees are not truly independent of management so that many of the advantages of the audit committee embodied in the auditing standards are not attained.

Summary

The auditing firm that has just accepted a new audit client looks forward to a long and mutually prosperous relationship with that client. As the client's business grows, the auditing firm will likely grow with it and provide advice on more complex issues and rise to the challenges of auditing a larger and more complex organization. The auditor also, however, faces significant immediate challenges: carefully evaluating the risks associated with every potential client.

In their quest for growth through accepting new clients, some CPA firms have taken on high-risk clients without correspondingly extending their auditing procedures or have short-cut those procedures to complete an audit at lower cost. Inevitably, most of these situations hurt the auditing firm. Broader damage to the profession results from Congressional inquiries in the wake of business failures, such as those in the savings and loan industry. Thus, the public accounting firm is faced with trade-offs between pursuing growth and minimizing "excessive competition" that could potentially destroy it. Fortunately, the profession has adopted guidelines to help individual firms address such trade-offs.

With sound judgment and good planning, the preliminary assessment of risk associated with the initial acceptance of each audit client will have heightened the auditor's awareness of all significant issues likely to be encountered in the first year's audit. But risk analysis and audit planning must take place each year.

Significant Terms

audit committee A subcommittee of the board of directors responsible for monitoring audit activities and serving as a surrogate for the interests of shareholders; should preferably be composed of outside members of the board—that is, members who do not hold company management positions.

defalcation A type of fraud in which the perpetrator takes assets from the organization for personal gain; the theft of cash is a well-known form of embezzlement.

engagement letter Specifies the understanding between the client and the auditor as to the nature of audit services to be conducted and, in the absence of any other formal contract, is viewed by the courts as a contract between the auditor and the client; generally covers items such as client responsibilities, auditor responsibilities, billing procedures, and the timing and target completion date of the audit.

Exhibit 5.7

REQUIRED COMMUNICATION WITH AUDIT COMMITTEES

Auditor's Responsibility under Generally Accepted Auditing Standards

This includes a communication of the auditor's responsibility to assess the fairness of the financial statements, to communicate the auditor's assessment of the entity's control structure, and to design the audit to detect material misstatements.

Significant Accounting Policies

The auditor should ensure that the audit committee is informed about the initial selection of, and changes in, significant accounting policies or their application.

Management Judgments and Accounting Estimates

Some of the major corporate failures have been coupled with inadequate estimates of key accounting balances such as loan loss reserves. The auditor should ensure that the audit committee is aware of the processes used by management in making sensitive accounting estimates.

Significant Audit Adjustments

Significant audit adjustments may reflect on the stewardship and accountability of management. The audit committee should be made aware of such adjustments, even if management readily agrees to make them.

Other Information in Annual Reports

The auditor should briefly describe the auditor's responsibility to review other information contained in an annual report and ascertain that such information is consistent with the audited financial statements.

Disagreements with Management

All major accounting disagreements with management, even if eventually resolved, should be discussed with the audit committee. This requirement is intended to insulate the auditors from management pressure to change or bend accounting treatments to suit management and should remove any subtle hints that the auditing firm may be replaced because it disagrees with management's proposed accounting treatments.

Consultations with Other Accountants

On occasion, management may seek the views of other public accounting firms regarding the treatment of potentially controversial accounting issues. If the auditor is aware of such consultation, it should be communicated to the audit committee.

Major Issues Discussed with Management Prior to Retention

This requirement is intended to dampen potential "shopping around" for accounting principles. The audit committee needs to know if the auditors had committed to specific accounting treatments or other items prior to accepting the engagement.

Difficulties Encountered in Performing the Audit

An efficient audit requires cooperation between the auditor, management, and the internal auditors. Management may subtly hinder an audit in a number of ways: by providing incomplete information, employing delaying tactics by misstating or omitting facts, or making key personnel unavailable during part of the audit process. Often such problems indicate deeper problems within the organization, including the possibility of management fraud.

Source: AU 380.06–.14

fraud Intentional misrepresentation for personal or corporate gain; can occur through the distortion of financial statements (fraudulent reporting) or the theft of assets (defalcation).

fraudulent financial reporting The intentional manipulation of reported financial results to misportray the results of operations or the financial position of the entity; intent is to inflate earnings or assets and thereby realize economic gain through higher stock prices or additional lines of credit.

illegal acts Acts that violate statute or regulatory law and may subject the company to fines or other penalties.

management integrity The honesty and trustworthiness of management as exemplified by past and current actions; auditors' assessment of management integrity reflects the extent to which the auditors believe they can trust management and its representations to be honest and forthright.

per diem billing rates Standard hourly billing rates that CPA firms establish as the reference billing rate to charge their clients; they vary by responsibility (partner rates are higher than manager rates, which are higher than staff rates).

predecessor auditor The immediately previous auditor of the client for which the new auditor is proposing or beginning to serve.

red flags Characteristics that research has shown are often associated with fraud, including personal characteristics of top management, organization structure, and economic or financial conditions that provide both the motivation for and the opportunity to commit fraud.

Appendix A: *How Barry Minkow Fooled the Auditors*

By Daniel Akst

Larry Gray may well be the world's unluckiest accountant. Overweight and affable, he was the Ernst & Whinney partner in charge of auditing Barry Minkow's ZZZZ Best, and although he isn't necessarily the sharpest guy in the world, the truth is that what happened wasn't really his fault.

"It could have happened to any of us," says a senior partner at a rival Big Eight firm who is known around Los Angeles as a very savvy guy. "Any of us," he says over and over, shaking his head sadly as if considering a healthy colleague felled by lightning on a Palm Springs golf course.

Gray, who ran the San Fernando Valley office of what is now Ernst & Young, was in the strange position of having a client who was too young to buy a drink. Barry Minkow was a remarkable combination of innocence and sophistication, genius and illiteracy, youth and maturity. Most of his victims were investors and lenders, who lost more than $100 million as the result of Barry's handiwork and the unwitting complicity of so many lawyers, accountants and investment professionals. Theirs is a cautionary tale for all of us.

In 1986 Larry Gray noticed that ZZZZ Best had a $7 million contract to restore a damaged building in Sacramento. Sensibly enough for the independent auditor of a company about to sell stock to the public, Gray demanded to see it.

Source: Daniel Akst, "How Barry Minkow Fooled the Auditors," *Forbes*, October 2, 1989, 126–132.

Barry responded characteristically. He stalled and he lied, claiming that his contracts restricted access to the jobs for liability reasons. But stockbroker Rooney Pace was threatening to hold up its planned ZZZZ Best stock offering, and Ernst & Whinney wasn't going to certify the company's financial statements. Reluctantly, Barry agreed to let them visit the Sacramento job.

Of course there was no Sacramento job. But if ZZZZ Best needed one to show its auditors, it would just have to be found. Barry dispatched two of his chief lieutenants, Tom Padgett and Mark Roddy, to scope out a likely building. They made a good team. Padgett is an avowed white separatist, and no one could be whiter than Roddy, a 6-foot-1-inch, 275-pound albino with a conviction on a cocaine charge. Padgett called him the UWM—the Ultimate White Man—to distinguish him from another Minkow aide named Mark.

Once in Sacramento, Padgett and Roddy quickly discovered there was only one building big enough to harbor $7 million worth of damage: the towering 300 Capital Mall building.

Padgett and Roddy took a deep breath and told the building managers they needed to lease a considerable amount of space, "but our investors can't come except on a weekend."

In fact, Gray's visit was scheduled for Nov. 23, a Sunday. ZZZZ Best told Gray this was in order to avoid interfering with ongoing work, but actually it was to avoid chance encounters, since even a casual washroom conversation could torpedo their plan. To Padgett's and Roddy's relief, they got the keys.

On Nov. 17, a Monday, they went with Minkow's right-hand man, Mark Morze, to one of those instant-office places, where they plunked down $2,000 in cash. Overnight something called Assured Property Management sprang into being, complete with office, furniture, phones and copying privileges. Assured existed only on paper, of course, but it was supposedly in the business of looking after the interests of the insured party in various restoration jobs. It enabled Roddy plausibly to stand in for the building's owners, managers and insurers, who could prove troublesome if contacted directly by the auditors.

Roddy and company put up a big map with pins in it, signifying all the jobs Assured was, uh, assuring, and the instant office suddenly looked convincing.

Things were coming together, but before Gray and a Harvard-trained securities lawyer named Mark Moskowitz headed for Sacramento, they acceded to Barry's demand for secrecy. Both pledged in writing not to disclose the site to anyone, even at their own firms: "We will not make any follow-up telephone calls to any contractors, insurance companies, the building owner or other individuals (other than suppliers whose names have been provided to this firm by the Company) involved in the restoration project. . . . " In short, they promised not to make the slightest independent effort to determine what was going on.

On Saturday, Nov. 22, Morze flew up to check things out. All seemed well; Barry's men even had the foresight to memorize the route between the airport, Assured's offices and the Capital Mall building, because they knew they'd have to seem as if they'd made the drive many times before.

Barry called frequently. "This is the Super Bowl," he told Padgett. "It's like a field goal with no time left on the clock."

"Barry," Padgett said, "I'm going to center it, and Morze is going to kick it."

On Sunday morning it was time to put their plan into action. At 10:20 a.m. Roddy approached security guard Tom Myers at the Capital Mall building.

"Listen, would you like to make an extra $50 for yourself?"

"What do I have to do?"

"Just be nice to some people I've got coming through here later on, guys named Mark Morze, Larry Gray and Mark Moskowitz."

"Well," said Myers, accepting a $50 bill, "being nice is part of the job."

Roddy explained that there was a "big deal" going on, and he wanted his guests treated like important people. An honest man, Meyers nodded and then filed an incident report with his employer, Burns International. He also turned in the $50.

Upstairs, Roddy and Padgett posted ZZZZ Best signs wherever they could, left a ZZZZ Best T shirt in one of the empty rooms and swiped a set of blueprints to carry around like some sort of magic wand. Then it was only a matter of time. Roddy sat down in the conference room of his fake offices and watched a football game on television.

Back in Los Angeles, Gray, Moskowitz and Morze caught a flight north. In Sacramento, they visited the supposed office of Assured Property. Then they drove over to the 300 Capital Mall building. It was Sunday, and the place was deserted. Moskowitz and Gray were wearing idiotic little ZZZZ Best badges with their pictures on them.

"Every time I talk to accountants and lawyers, I get into trouble," Roddy joked.

"Hey, we're on your side," they replied jovially. Roddy, free on bail after his drug arrest in New Mexico, laughed.

In the lobby, security guard Myers dutifully exchanged pleasantries with Roddy and Morze, who seemed completely at home. Roddy signed in at 1:15 p.m. Gray wrote in a memo to the ZZZZ Best file the next day that the tour first went up to the 17th floor, which was occupied by a law firm; he later told police that they also visited five lower floors chosen at random.

"ZZZZ Best's work is substantially complete and has passed final inspection," he wrote. "Final sign-off is expected shortly, with final payment due to ZZZZ Best in early December."

Gray added that "The tour was beneficial in gaining insight as to the scope of the damage that had occurred and the type of work that the Company can do."

Roddy and Padgett couldn't believe it. Gray and Moskowitz had walked through a building that had absolutely nothing to do with ZZZZ Best, and they were completely fooled. Like Catherine the Great, they had toured a Potemkin village, one of the phony fronts set up to make the Russian countryside look prosperous for the tsarina.

Such successes made it possible for Barry to raise more and more money, which he needed to keep his Ponzi scheme going.

On Nov. 28 he met with executives from Union Bank of Los Angeles. As in so many of his relationships, the balance of power in this one had subtly shifted; now the bankers were coming to him. Barry told them he wanted to borrow more cash. They lent him another $300,000.

Barry knew he was about to hand the bankers an enormous deposit from the upcoming stock offering, and he intended to get a lot out of them in exchange. He also knew enough not to ask for it all at once, but rather to proceed in increments. He had already borrowed $900,000.

On Dec. 4, a Thursday, Barry and the bankers met again. He was in fine fettle, and told them ZZZZ Best had just been awarded an $8.2 million restoration job in San Diego, as well as several other insurance jobs. He went on to say that publicity surrounding his stock offering had brought in "more business than I know what to do with," and that he needed more money to capture these opportunities. He asked to borrow $1.3 million—plus a $7 million line of credit.

On Dec. 9—not a minute too soon for Barry's ravenous money-eating enterprise—the SEC declared the ZZZZ Best offering effective. Union Bank soon granted the $1.3 million loan.

Finally, on Dec. 16, the glorious moment had arrived: Barry was handed a check for $11,550,000, the net proceeds from the stock offering. He got the $7 million credit line from Union Bank later the same day. Thus ZZZZ Best hauled in more than $21 million in a single day. Grown-ups weren't just taking Barry seriously. Now they were treating him with respect.

On Saturday night, he celebrated. ZZZZ Best held a Christmas party for between 500 and 1,000 guests at the slick Bonaventure Hotel in downtown Los Angeles. The event was a combination revival meeting, sales rally and Academy Awards ceremony. As usual, no expense was spared. Barry was in a snow-white tuxedo, white shoes and black tie. His hair was cut razor sharp, and there wasn't the slightest trace of nerves about him.

When the crowd chanted in unison, "Bar-ry . . . Bar-ry . . . Bar-ry . . ." he seemed once again at the center of some sinister personality cult, and his exalted position before the adoration of his minions sent him into ecstasies.

Alas, the accountants remained curious. Ernst & Whinney's Larry Gray was demanding to see another big job, this time the one in San Diego, and so in January of 1987, Padgett and Roddy sallied forth once again.

"It was like watching Laurel and Hardy," says one man who dealt with them. "Roddy would do all the talking while Padgett would walk around looking at a gun catalog, looking at machine guns and bazookas. He had the thing highlighted in yellow ink."

The trouble was, Barry for some reason had told the lawyers and accountants that the $8.2 million restoration job in question was in National City, just outside San Diego. When Padgett and Roddy got there, there weren't any buildings that could even remotely pass for a structure in the midst of an $8 million face-lift.

The two partners in crime were undaunted. They checked into the swank old Hotel del Coronado, across the bay from San Diego, found themselves a commercial real estate broker and then laid out $22,560 for a year's lease on a small office and industrial space by the Miramar Naval Air Station near the city. As for the little discrepancy about where the job actually was, they'd just say, "Well the *supplies* are in National City, but see, the *job*, that's actually in San Diego." To fill the warehouse, they ordered in $168,000 worth of the cheapest carpet they could get.

By now it was early February, and time was getting short. This warehouse was to be the local outpost of Roddy's phony Assured Property Management. They put up a map and circled all the supposed San Diego–area jobs. They threw popcorn all over the floor, to make the place look lived-in. Then they went over to see Christopher M. Penrose, who figured they were nuts but who still had a building to lease.

Penrose is a handsome, cheerful, sandy-haired guy who was in training for a triathlon when Roddy and Padgett stumbled into his life. He was working for Merrill Lynch Realty at the time, representing the Federal Savings & Loan Insurance Corp. in its sullen receivership of the brand-new eight-story structure at 1551 Fourth Avenue in San Diego. For FSLIC, the building was just another headache in the ongoing collapse of the nation's savings and loan industry. For ZZZZ Best, it was a godsend.

But there was no time to waste; Larry Gray had signed another confidentiality letter, and would soon be on his way. Roddy and Padgett went to work, claiming they were set to lease much of the Fourth Avenue building.

"Our investors are coming in this weekend," they said, remembering their lines from Sacramento. All they needed was the keys, so they could show their backers around. As expected, they got them.

Events moved fast. On Friday, Feb. 6, Gray and his family arrived in San Diego, combining his visit to the job with a family outing. Early the next morning, the ZZZZ Best gang went into the building and put up ZZZZ Best signs and phony contractors' permits, just as they had in Sacramento. They took down any "For Rent" signs.

"Poor Larry Gray," one of the conspirators said later. "They'll ask him, 'How do you know this is a courtroom, Larry? How do you know you were working for an accounting firm? How do you know you're you?'"

Soon Mark Morze collected Gray and drove him over to the Assured office, where a ZZZZ Best truck had been carefully parked out front. Gray sees rolls and rolls of carpet and padding; Morze explains that the broadloom is intended for a building damaged by both fire and water, which they will visit next. Gray takes notes so he won't forget anything. Then he and Morze drive over to Fourth Avenue, where they are greeted by Roddy.

"How're you doing, Larry?" Roddy asks jovially. "Gee, looks like you're following me all over the state."

At that very moment, Roddy must have experienced the scrotum-tightening sensation which James Joyce associated with the sea, because suddenly some *real* contractors drove up to the building, threatening to ruin everything by their mere unthinking presence.

Now, Mark Roddy is not perfect. He has a criminal record, he eats too much and he can have a nasty temper. But at that particular moment he was impeccable. He immediately ran over and told the contractors that he and his party were buying the place. He even found out what floors they were working on and made sure to avoid them. Then everybody went inside.

To Gray's uncritical eye, the work looked satisfactory, and no wonder. ZZZZ Best hadn't done a thing to it. Apparently Gray saw some finished space—he was told this was done for prized tenants who got first priority—and lots of unfinished space, which ZZZZ Best was supposedly still working on. He also saw various ZZZZ Best signs and permits on the walls.

"It was a very clean job site," he wrote for the files.

But Gray was nothing if not tenacious. When ZZZZ Best later claimed to have finished the San Diego job, he demanded to see it again.

This was a crisis. It was one thing to walk some people through a little empty office space, but now Barry and his friends would somehow have to get control of the same building and finish its interior in time to show the place. It would cost a fortune, but it had to be done.

So after declining to lease the building the first time around, Roddy was sent to try to make a deal weeks later.

"Don't get too attached to that beach house," he told Padgett on the phone.

"What do you mean?"

"We're having trouble down here. That building is in receivership. They just won't lease it to us."

Actually, the main problem was that the building's prospective owner, Broe Co. of Denver, found the whole thing so suspicious it wanted no part of it.

The more Roddy pleaded, the more adamantly Broe turned him down. The stakes were higher now, too. By the spring of 1987, ZZZZ Best had climbed to more than $18 per share. Drexel Burnham Lambert was planning to raise $40 million for it to buy the company that had the coveted nationwide concession to clean carpets under the Sears banner. (The deal later fell through.) With Gray's new demand, it seemed, the jig was at last up. Everyone was frantic. The world was about to end.

Brian Morze saved the day. Brian is Mark's older brother. Both brothers are physically powerful, but where Mark is huge above the waist, Brian is gigantic at it. He is fat, bald and diabetic, with a scraggly red beard and piercing eyes set halfway back into his head. He is also something of an intellectual, the only person involved with ZZZZ Best who can use the word "cognitive" in a sentence. He can tell you what Jainism is, too, and about the weak force in physics. He never finished high school, but can speak subtly of Schopenhauer, Nietzsche and Goethe, as well as Melville, Einstein and God. "*Tha-tt* is writing," he will say of a favorite author, giving "that" two syllables, the last a delicate explosion of tongue and palate that gives him the air of a grizzly bear eating with his pinky raised.

Brian arrived from Pittsburgh in time to help his brother solve the San Diego crisis. Barry and his cohorts were bickering over how to proceed. Roddy had already offered to rent the entire building either for one year or just several months, meeting the asking price and doing all interior construction at or above the local building code. His pleas were unavailing.

But Barry would not hear of failure. Finally Brian Morze flew to Denver and basically told the Broe people, "Okay, guys, you win. The truth is, Padgett and Roddy work for ZZZZ Best, and ZZZZ Best is the party that really wants the building. We wanted to keep the whole thing secret because of some unusual activity in our stock lately." And so on.

Barry confirmed all this, and a lease was negotiated. ZZZZ Best had to take the place for seven years, put down $500,000 as a security deposit and pay a month's rent in advance. It hurt, but Larry Gray, in his plodding but insistent way, had made it unavoidable.

Now that they had the building, Barry's men faced another hurdle: getting the interior finished in time for Gray's May 11 visit. ZZZZ Best took possession around May 1, so it had just ten days to wire, drywall, paint, carpet and otherwise complete six floors of office space (two were already done).

Because ZZZZ Best was incapable of changing a light bulb on its own, much less renovating an entire building overnight, it had already promised a building contractor unlimited access to a bank account across the street from the work site.

Time was of the essence. Roddy, Padgett and Brian Morze set up a command post at what was then the Inter-Continental Hotel, looking out across the water, and immediately sent out for some gorgeous $200-an-hour call girls. "Look, I'm under a lot of tension," Padgett told one. "Let's start with the massage and go from there."

Working round the clock, the construction crews attacked the unfinished building with a passion. Everybody was worried—Barry had already been hospitalized twice for ulcers and exhaustion—but also excited; they couldn't believe things had come this far. At one point Barry himself came down to see how the work was going, touring the facility like Churchill visiting his men at the front.

The place was a madhouse, but there were signs of progress. Thinking ahead, Roddy handed out some ZZZZ Best T shirts and got the workers to pose momentarily for pictures.

On the afternoon of May 10, less than 24 hours before Larry Gray was scheduled to visit, the job was basically done. It had cost $1 million, but Barry always understood that you have to spend money to steal money. "ZZZZ Best magic," Padgett called it, touring the building in awe. "This is a miracle."

The following morning, at the appointed hour, the Morze brothers walked Larry Gray through the building.

"Job looks very good," Gray wrote later in a memo to the file, not noticing that some ceilings apparently were dropped so low that the closet doors wouldn't open. "Per Morse [sic] they expect full acceptance on the job later this week."

That same day, Gray was flown out to a warehouse in Dallas, where he looked at a bunch of carpet—the same stuff he'd seen in San Diego months before. While he was there, Mark Morze staged a phone call that supposedly brought news of $10.1 million in new jobs for ZZZZ Best.

As for the actual work in Dallas, Gray wrote, "I was informed that the contracts are in hard-hat stage and outside spectators were not allowed." Morze was taking a huge chance with this, because no other arrangement had been made in Dallas. But time was short anyway, and Gray, who was accustomed to things being in order at ZZZZ Best, said this was fine.

Everybody flew back to Los Angeles. Barry and his friends had done it again.

Appendix B: *How Don Sheelen Made a Mess That Regina Couldn't Clean Up*

By John A. Byrne

The letter G has broken apart in the huge sign atop the Regina Co. corporate headquarters in Rahway, N. J. A tattered flag flaps above the squat concrete building on the street named for the vacuum-cleaner company.

Within a month, the few remaining employees at the huge complex that once employed hundreds will bolt the door on another symbol of failure in American business. This was not, however, a company whose fatal flaw was an inability to compete. This was a company whose entrepreneurial CEO turned out to be a con man.

Overzealous. Donald D. Sheelen had taken over the single-product company in 1984 at the age of 38 and, everyone thought, transformed it into a marketing powerhouse, with a host of new products. By 1988, he had more than tripled reported sales in a string of four years of record profits and sales. He talked about setting off "consumer hot buttons" and of achieving his "dream of entrepreneurship." What he didn't say was that he cooked the books, plunging Regina into a morass of lawsuits and, finally, bankruptcy. Sheelen, who pleaded guilty to fraud, is serving time in a work-release correction center.

What happened to the company is a tale of the '80s, the story of an overzealous MBA entrepreneur, cheerleading Wall Street analysts, and independent auditors who failed to uncover a less-than-subtle fraud. "The story of Don Sheelen," his lawyers contend with hyperbole, "is similar to the great fictional Shakespearean and Greek tragedies."

Sheelen, who declines comment, seemed more suited to the role of Shakespeare's conniving Iago than the tragic hero Othello. It depends on whose story you believe. His wife, Louise, a former Franciscan nun, described him in a presentencing appeal to the judge as a "good, honest, sincere, and loving" man. She related how he

Source: John A. Byrne, "How Don Sheelen Made a Mess That Regina Couldn't Clean Up," *Business Week*, February 12, 1990, 46–50.

helped his eldest son set up a business selling flowers on Mother's Day at the local supermarket.

Sheelan's business colleagues saw a different side of him. They saw him as a tough, aggressive boss. Some associates found him so abrasive that even when he was a marketing vice-president, they discouraged him from making calls for fear he would offend customers. And once Sheelen become CEO, he committed fraud rather than accept failure.

Son of a Gulf Oil Co. salesman, Sheelen was born into a middle-class family in Middletown, N.Y. The boy with rugged good looks was an overachiever from the start, playing varsity football and basketball in high school and emerging as a Big Man on Campus at the University of Dayton. He was senior-class president and graduated with a business degree in 1968. Armed with an MBA from Syracuse University, he joined Bache & Co. as a stockbroker in 1970. Three years later, he landed an accounting job with Johnson & Johnson, ending up at a small subsidiary called Jelco, which made catheters and syringes. In 1980, he joined Regina, where he became head of marketing. The company, founded in Rahway in 1892 as a maker of music boxes, virtually owned the market for electric brooms, but growth was slowing.

'Envious.' What his colleagues quickly noticed about Sheelen was his ambition. He put in long hours, and he talked about the success of others in his family, particularly his sister, a real estate broker. "He was envious that his sister had done so well," recalls Ronald Nolan, then vice-president of sales. "And he said he didn't feel like being last in the foot race with them."

They noticed something else: Sheelen's drive to succeed alienated people. Turnover in his department was high. "When you reported to him, you faced a good grilling," says John Borowiec, a former sales manager. "He would just intimidate people."

Still, Sheelen brought good ideas with him. He moved Regina, then owned by conglomerate General Signal Corp., into higher-margin accessories, such as vacuum bags. He also promoted a new product, a carpet shampooer. He climbed the ladder, becoming CEO in 1984, the same year he led Regina in a $31.4 million leveraged buyout. Sheelen anted up $750,000 for nearly a 54 percent stake in the company. Little more than 17 months later, he brought Regina public.

The shareholders who attended his first annual meeting in 1986 at The Landmark Inn in Woodbridge, N. J., were treated to their first glimpse of his showmanship. A woman clad in a bathing suit sat in a see-through bathtub to demonstrate one of his newest products, the Homespa. It used the exhaust side of a vacuum motor to blow bubbles in water and create, for less than $100, the effect of a whirlpool. He also launched the Housekeeper, his bid to compete in the upright vacuum-cleaner market. Huge ad spending helped 1987 sales surge 68 percent, to $128 million. Earnings grew 74 percent, to $7.1 million.

'Sexy Story.' Wall Street, eager to feed investors' frenzy for hot growth companies, began to take notice. "If you listened to Don and looked at the company's numbers, it was a very sexy story," says James M. Meyer of Janney Montgomery. His firm jumped on the bandwagon, and so did many other brokerage houses, including Shearson Lehman Hutton, Inc. Shearson promoted Regina on its emerging growth-stock list, informing investors on June 16, 1988, that the company's stock could appreciate by 50 percent in the next year. Meyer was one of the first to remove

Regina from his "aggressive buy" list, but Shearson, which declined comment, didn't advise investors to retreat until the stock began dropping like a stone.

Analysts liked Sheelen's combative, no-frills approach to business. A tall, stocky man with dark, curly hair, he showed up at analysts' meetings in rumpled suits with his shirttails untucked. He was going to "bomb" industry leader Hoover Co. And at the entrance to his office, Sheelen placed a Hoover doormat on the orange shag carpet so that people could "walk over" his rival. Once inside, analysts couldn't help but notice the mousetrap with cheese under the radiator.

Yet, nothing fired Sheelen's emotions like the company's stock price. Even a temporary flutter would cause him to rush to the phone to drum up support. "He would pick up the phone himself and say, 'Why don't you write something to get the stock up?' " says Meyer.

No wonder. By July, 1988, it had soared to a peak of $27.50 from the equivalent of $5.25 a share when the company went public in 1985—making Sheelen's stake worth more than $99 million. His 1988 compensation, amounting to $577,500 in salary and bonus, enabled him to live in a spacious 12-room house on 1.8 acres on Sycamore Lane in tony Rumson, N. J.

Trouble was brewing, though. Sheelen's secretary tried out one of the first Housekeeper vacuums and quickly reported to Sheelen that when she lifted the vacuum, its handle fell off and the belt often slipped off the motor. "There were so many things wrong with it," recalls Barbara Drozdowski, "but he didn't want to hear it. He said, 'Well, we'll fix it on the next go-round, but we've got to get it out of here.' "

So anxious was he to ramp up the company's revenues that he skipped proper testing, says David A. Jones, who has headed Regina since its purchase by Electrolux Corp. in June. Product returns swamped the company, beginning as early as the spring of 1987. An internal memo showed that customers returned more than 40,000 Housekeeper vacuums in the quarter ended on Sept. 30, a daunting 16 percent of sales.

Defective. Sheelen became "desperate." In December, 1987, he ordered his chief financial officer, Vincent P. Golden, not to record the company's returned products. Golden, who declined to be interviewed for this story, initially protested but obliged by having his staff alter Regina's computer systems. He went along, his lawyer would later say, "to protect his job." The returns, meanwhile, kept piling up. The problem became so severe that Sheelen leased a building to store the defective products.

Even as brokers advised their clients to buy Regina stock in mid-1988, Sheelen was making his deceit more elaborate. As detailed in stipulations entered as part of their guilty pleas, Sheelen told Golden to come up with sales of about $180 million and per-share earnings of $1.20. The solution: By booking a sale when Regina received an order, rather than when it shipped the goods, Golden put $6 million worth of extra sales into Regina's fourth quarter. By understating expenses, he squeezed $3 million in profits from the income statement. Golden then rigged the computer systems to generate about 200 fake invoices worth $5.4 million on the last three business days of the fiscal year ended on June 30.

These machinations enabled Sheelen to fool Wall Street one last time. On Sept. 15, Sheelen and his secretary met the analysts in New York. He was buoyant, showing the superiority of a Housekeeper over a Hoover by sprinkling corn flakes on the carpet and vacuuming them up. The impressed analysts didn't know that the Regina model was rigged by engineers to have greater suction and could not be purchased in stores, says Drozdowski.

If Sheelen worried that he would be discovered, he didn't show it. At board meetings, he played the cool, confident CEO, recalls Malcolm L. Sherman, former head of Zayre Stores, Inc., who joined Regina's board earlier in 1988. But the board sessions were largely consumed by product and marketing plans.

"At the first board meeting, the fact that I didn't get any numbers didn't bother me," says Sherman. "By the third meeting, I was extremely concerned. 'If we don't start seeing something specific, this isn't the right board for me,' I told him. He said, 'Don't worry. From here on, you'll get numbers.' "

Sherman did not realize how shocking those numbers would be. On September 20 Sheelen called his two outside directors separately to read a press release saying that Regina would post substantially lower sales and a loss for the September quarter because of a slowdown in orders and product returns. Sheelen assigned most of the blame to a computer snafu. "He seemed very upset, extremely upset," remembers board director Richard Skelly. "He started to cry."

The news sent Regina's stock tumbling. On Sept. 21, a Wednesday, shares fell from 17 to 7-1/8. Shearson finally yanked the stock from its growth list. Sheelen closeted himself in his office, refusing to take all but a few of the 100 calls being logged in daily from angry investors and analysts.

Country Club Prison? Over the weekend, according to his lawyers, Sheelen confessed to his wife and then to his priest. On Monday, he resigned. A week later, Sheelen would make a full confession to the U.S. attorney in Newark and he eventually would plead guilty to one count of mail and securities fraud.

Sheelen is now serving a one-year sentence in the Goodwill Industries Community Correction Center in St. Petersburg, Fla. It is not a hard life. There are no bars on the windows nor locks on the doors. With its brightly painted beds and lockers, the building has the feel of a college dorm. Sheelen, his lawyer says, leaves the center every weekday to work at an undisclosed business. Sheelen also was fined $25,000. (Golden's sentence and fine were exactly half of Sheelen's.) The court ultimately reunded the fine from Sheelen's Regina stock that had been turned over to the court as restitution to the shareholders in April. The stock is now virtually worthless.

Sheelen hasn't given up hope of resuming his business career. Prior to his sentencing, he asked Sherman—then interim chairman—if he could return to Regina. "When his attorney asked me what I thought," says Sherman, "I said, 'You could tell him it's a straight no. Or you could say to him, Are you f——— crazy? Pick whichever one you want.' "

Why Didn't Peat Marwick Smell the Books Cooking?

It was the kind of article that executives would pay to get into print. It praised the CEO and told how he brought "disciplined management planning" and "measured risks" to an ailing company and turned it around.

The problem was that the "masterful practitioner" was Regina Co. Chief Executive Donald D. Sheelen. And only months after the 1987 profile appeared in *World* magazine, a slick quarterly published by auditors KPMG Peat Marwick, Sheelen began to falsify Regina's financial statements. Worse, as Regina's auditors, Peat withdrew its unqualified opinion only after Sheelen publicly reported his company would have an unexpected loss in the quarter ended in September, 1988.

Why couldn't the accountant spot it? "This is a case where the CEO and chief financial officer pleaded guilty to fraud," says a Peat spokesman. "If you're a good book-cooker, it's almost impossible to detect."

Regina is one of three recent New York area cases, along with Coated Sales and Crazy Eddie, in which the firm has been named a defendant in lawsuits alleging a failure to detect flawed bookkeeping. Peat says the cases have nothing in common.

Regina's interim chairman, Malcolm L. Sherman, launched an investigation after Sheelen resigned. But one month into the probe, Sherman, an outside director, was unsatisfied. "I think that Peat was doing nothing more or less than a full-scale 'How do you cover your ass?' " he says.

Hot Seat. Sherman was particularly frustrated with William J. Murray, the Peat partner on the Regina account. "I'd ask one question and get an answer to a different question," he says. It wasn't Murray's first time on the hot seat. In 1975, Peat entered a consent decree with the Securities & Exchange Commission over its accounting work for bankrupt homebuilder Stirling Homex Corp. Murray was a consulting partner on the Stirling assignment. Sherman fired Peat in April. Murray, 58, retired in July as he had previously planned, according to a Peat spokesman, who added: "Murray conducted himself in an appropriate and professional manner."

Eventually, Sherman called in Coopers & Lybrand. When the books were sorted out, the supposedly profitable Regina showed a $16.8 million loss for the 15 months that ended on Sept. 30, 1988.

Review Questions

A–Growth and Marketing of Auditing Services

5–1 Why is growth important to CPA firms? Why is CPA firm growth important to you as you enter the profession?

5–2 The chapter refers to the *business of public accounting firms*. What is meant by that phrase? Why is it important to view public accounting firms as a business?

5–3 In what ways might managing a public accounting firm as a business negatively affect the professionalism of the public accounting profession? Explain.

5–4 What are the positive and negative aspects to "competition" within the public accounting profession?

5–5 What are the advantages and disadvantages to public accounting firms having large management consulting divisions?

5–6 Why might the acquisition of new clients through the merger and acquisition activities of an existing client result in the loss of overall audit work for the public accounting profession as a whole?

5–7 Marketing CPA services includes utilizing all avenues to obtain new audit clients. Identify the major sources of new clients. Which of these methods have traditionally been used?

5–8 Has advertising been effective for CPA firms? Explain.

5–9 To what extent is the nature of advertising limited by the standards of the public accounting profession?

5–10 "Excessive competition has been harmful to the public accounting profession." This comment was made in a 1978 study of the public accounting profession. How might this be true?

B–Accepting a Client

5–11 What are the principal factors an auditing firm ought to consider before accepting a new client?

5–12 What information should be contained in a proposal for a new client? Are auditors prohibited from seeking new clients through sending unsolicited proposals to companies that are audited by other CPA firms? If so, under which circumstances might unsolicited proposals be prohibited?

5–13 When making a proposal to a potential new audit client, what responsibility does the auditor have to contact the previous auditor? What information, if any, should be gathered from the previous auditor prior to accepting a new audit engagement?

5–14 What is a related party? How might the existence of significant related parties affect the auditor's approach either to accept an audit engagement or to conduct the audit?

5–15 Why is a staff auditor's annual salary significantly less than the per diem annual billing rates for that position?

5–16 Why is an engagement letter of crucial importance to the auditor? What information is contained in an engagement letter?

C–Auditor Responsibilities

5–17 What is *fraud?* What is the auditor's responsibility for detecting fraud?

5–18 What is the difference between a *defalcation* and *fraudulent financial reporting?*

5–19 What are *red flags?* How might an auditor use them in planning an audit to ensure a reasonable possibility of detecting material fraud if it exists?

5–20 How does an illegal act differ from fraud? To what extent do the audit approach and audit responsibilities differ for illegal acts than for fraud?

5–21 "Auditors should not be held responsible for detecting financial fraud directed by management because management has the ability to cover up transactions and also coerce other employees to misstate transactions." To what extent, or under what circumstances, might you agree with this statement?

5–22 The auditing standards have identified major characteristics often associated with fraud. Briefly indicate how an auditor might use the fraud characteristics to plan audits that will have a good chance of detecting material fraud.

D–Audit Committees

5–23 What is an audit committee? What are the major responsibilities of an audit committee?

5–24 What information should the external auditor communicate to an audit committee each year?

5–25 "An audit committee should be the group with the power to recommend the hiring and firing of auditors to the company's shareholders." Do you agree or disagree with this statement? Briefly indicate the rationale for your answer.

Multiple Choice Questions

5–26 Which of the following is the *least likely* consequence of competition in the public accounting profession?

a. Increased efficiency of audits as CPA firms work to implement new technology aimed at improving audit efficiency.
b. Lower audit fees for most audit clients.
c. An increase in the number of substandard audits conducted.
d. An increase in audit compensation and starting salaries because of the increase in audit technology.

5–27 Which of the following is the *least valid* rationale explaining the need for growth of a CPA firm?

a. Expansion and growth of existing clients.
b. Provision of a larger basis over which to allocate training costs.
c. Need to provide expanded services to clients that face increasingly complex environments.
d. Provision of growth opportunities for outstanding professionals who join the firm.

5–28 An auditor proposing to conduct the audit of an organization should contact the predecessor auditor to inquire about

a. The integrity of management and the existence of any accounting dispute with the client.
b. The integrity of management and the amount of unpaid audit fees.
c. The beginning accounting balances and the use of the auditor's prior year's working papers.
d. The number of hours that the previous auditor took in performing the previous year's audit.

5–29 Which of the following factors would constitute an improper basis on which to base the auditor's billing to the client for services rendered in conjunction with the audit?

a. The number of hours spent on the audit with hours categorized by staff level.
b. The number of hours spent plus a percentage of client savings directly attributable to auditor recommendations made during the audit.
c. A flat fee based on a proposal at the beginning of the year that considered the amount of time the audit should take.
d. A flat fee based on a proposal plus an additional fee because of work that was unanticipated but necessary to complete the audit.

5–30 An engagement letter should be written before the start of an audit because

a. It limits the auditor's legal liability by specifying the auditor's responsibilities.
b. It specifies the client's responsibility for preparing schedules and making the records available to the auditor.
c. It specifies the cost of the audit for the upcoming year.
d. All of the above.

5–31 Which of the following would constitute a *defalcation*?

a. Company management manipulates reported profit by recording January's sales as December sales of the previous year.
b. Company management overstates loans receivable by developing and recording fictitious loans to nonexistent customers.
c. The divisional controller, in conjunction with the inventory warehouse supervisor, develops a scheme to ship electronics equipment to their personal warehouse and account for the shipments as inventory shortages.
d. The divisional controller and the warehouse director develop a scheme to overstate inventory by adding fictitious tags to the ending physical inventory count and then counting the tags as if they represented real merchandise.

5–32 Which of the following statements best represents the auditor's responsibility for fraud detection?

a. The auditor should assess the risk of fraud by identifying any red flags and then include design specific audit procedures that would detect any fraud that would be material to the financial statements.
b. The auditor should assess the risk of fraud by identifying any red flags, but if such identification indicates that fraud is not likely, the auditor is not responsible for detecting fraud.
c. The auditor is responsible for carrying out planned auditing procedures with due professional care and for detecting fraud only if such procedures are ordinarily capable of detecting the type of fraud encountered.
d. All of the above.

5–33 If a material financial fraud is detected, it should be reported

a. To management at least one level above where it occurred.
b. To the audit committee.
c. As a separate line item and adequately footnote disclosed in the financial statements.
d. All of the above.

5–34 The risk of financial fraud increases in the presence of

a. Incentive-based compensation systems based on operating income.
b. Substantial increases in sales.
c. Improved computerized control systems.
d. Frequent changes in suppliers.

5–35 An audit committee should do all of the following except

a. Recommend the retention or dismissal of the outside auditors.

b. Determine whether material financial fraud ought to be reported in a company's financial statements.

c. Consult with the auditor prior to the audit to convey any special concerns they have and to request any special investigations.

d. Review the audit fees for reasonableness and investigate the reasons why audit fees may be higher than proposed.

5–36 If the auditor has concerns about the integrity of management, which of the following would *not* be an appropriate action?

a. Refuse to accept the engagement because a client does not have an inalienable right to an audit.

b. Expand audit procedures in areas where management representations are normally important by requesting outside verifiable evidence.

c. Raise the audit fees to compensate for the risk inherent in the audit.

d. Plan the audit with a higher degree of skepticism including specific procedures that should be effective in uncovering management fraud.

5–37 Which of the following would *not* be required to be communicated to the audit committee by the outside auditor?

a. Significant audit adjustments made during the course of the audit.

b. Significant disagreements with management regarding accounting principles even if the disagreements were eventually resolved to the auditor's satisfaction.

c. The auditor's knowledge of management's consultation with other public accounting firms regarding the proposed treatment of a controversial accounting item.

d. The extent to which the internal auditors assisted in the conduct of the audit and the specific areas in which the internal auditors assumed major responsibility for the audit.

5–38 Which of the following would represent the most rational response by the auditor to an assessment of higher than average risk of fraud in an upcoming audit engagement?

a. Assign more experienced auditors to the engagement.

b. Increase the audit fee to compensate for the added risk and potential insurance cost associated with the high risk environment.

c. Assign more auditors to the engagement.

d. Increase the amount of control testing performed.

Discussion and Research Questions

5–39 (Effects of Competition) CPA firms must increasingly compete with each other to obtain audit clients. It has been argued that competition may both benefit and harm the profession through an increase in the amount of substandard work performed.

Required:

a. Identify the main ways in which a CPA firm may distinguish itself from other CPA firms and thus give itself a competitive advantage in the audit marketplace.

b. Briefly indicate how the profession protects itself against substandard work that may possibly be performed by some CPA firms.

5–40 (Audit Committees) Audit committees have been proposed as an important group to support the independence of the external auditor. The New York Stock Exchange has made it mandatory for all companies listed on it to have an audit committee composed solely of outside directors. The AICPA and the Institute of Internal Auditors have recommended the formation of audit committees.

Required:

a. Define the term *audit committee*. Indicate its composition.

b. What is the basis for the requirement by the NYSE to require that audit committees be composed solely of outside directors?

c. What are the responsibilities of the external auditor to communicate information to the audit committee? Identify all required information that must be communicated to the audit committee and briefly indicate the likely rationale for requiring the communication.

5–41 (Red Flag Literature and Fraud) Studies of fraudulent financial reporting indicate that most frauds are associated with either organizational or personal factors that often are readily apparent to outsiders who are able to take a skeptical view of an organization and its management. It has been suggested that auditors identify such red flags prior to planning an audit to assess the extent of fraud risk that may be apparent in a client.

Required:

a. Briefly describe some of the findings of research done to identify red flags and their implications for the audit.

b. Identify the major components of a comprehensive red flag or fraud model and indicate how the auditor would implement such a model during the conduct of an audit.

5–42 (Auditing for Fraud) During the planning of the audit, the auditor becomes aware of the following separate situations:

1. Divisional management is compensated with a base salary plus a year-end bonus. The bonus applies to operational management and the controller of the division. The bonus often exceeds 100 percent of the base salary and is calculated solely on reported divisional income. If managers are successful, they often receive promotions to larger divisions.

2. The company is dominated by a charismatic top manager who seems to be able to convince everyone that he can sell more products, even though financial results seem to be deteriorating and the company's products seem to be falling behind the industry leaders in technology. Management, however, is confident that the company has achieved a technological breakthrough and will be offering a new product in the

fourth quarter. Everyone at the company believes the new product will solve most of the company's problems.

3. The company has not experienced major financial problems, but it has always been reluctant to fix significant control weaknesses. Management believes that controls are just overhead and are not important but that selling products is important. During the planning for the engagement, the auditor notices that the number and amount of related-party transactions have appeared to increase, particularly in the sales area.
4. The company is suffering from severe solvency problems. Company management has asked the auditor for advice on structuring transactions so that more of the company's financing is "off the balance sheet." The "off the balance sheet" treatment appears to be acceptable, albeit not necessarily very good accounting.
5. The company is experiencing rapid growth and is continually introducing new products. The accounting system seems to be lagging behind the growth of the rest of the company. Although the auditor recommended that the company start an internal audit department last year, it decided it could not afford to do so.
6. The company has an outside audit committee, but it is dominated by the president of the company. The auditor has not had major problems with the company in the past, but discussions about accounts that are material to the financial statements are increasing. Most involve judgments, such as allowance for doubtful accounts or warranty expense estimates. Disagreements between the auditor and management regarding these accounts are increasing.
7. The company has been acquired as part of a hostile takeover and is now being run by a management that has earned its reputation in finance rather than in operations. Current management has handled similar acquisitions by selling off assets, slashing payroll, increasing reported profits through manipulation of accounting principles, and then selling the entity to another party in a relatively short period of time. Management is very aggressive in its financial accounting posturing and places a great deal of emphasis on quarterly financial results. Although the auditor has not dealt directly with this management team previously, she is aware that it does not have a good reputation in the business community but is unaware of any record of management dishonesty.

Required:

For each situation identified

a. Briefly indicate how the auditor would have discovered the information.
b. Indicate whether the situation indicates a higher than average risk of fraud, all other things being equal.
c. Briefly indicate the implications of the finding to the conduct of the audit. Indicate specifically whether the scenario suggests that the auditor needs to implement specific audit tests in a particular area.

5–43 (Detecting Fraud) Two major frauds that occurred in 1989 involved Regina Vacuum Cleaner and MiniScribe. Both frauds were characterized by weaknesses in internal controls.

Required:

a. Assume that at both Regina and MiniScribe, the client did not record returned merchandise in inventory until a credit had been issued to the returning company, but that merchandise would often be shipped to another customer before the credit was issued. What financial statement distortions would occur because of this practice? Identify specific accounts.

b. Identify *two* audit procedures that would be most effective in discovering the financial statement errors indicated in part a.

5–44 (Auditor Responsibilities) The following comments have been made by a number of students regarding prospective careers in the public accounting profession. The comments are presented for discussion purposes and do not necessarily contain a defined "right" or "wrong" answer.

Comments:

1. "Competition has been harmful to the public accounting profession because it has encouraged many firms to perform substandard work in order to attract clients for which audit fees are bid on a 'price' basis. The profession may require more regulation to deal with the detrimental effects of price competition."
2. "Salaries for partners in public accounting firms (such as a national firm partner salary of $250,000) are too high in proportion to the benefits that society receives from the public accounting profession."
3. "Audits should be viewed as a commodity. An audit is an audit. It is difficult, if not impossible, to differentiate the services provided by CPA firms unless the CPA firms provide nonaudit services (for example, providing management business advice or executive personal financial planning)."
4. "The most effective way to obtain new audit clients is to provide high-quality service at reasonable professional prices to existing clients."
5. "The most effective way to obtain new clients is to aggressively market all professional services. This means that firms should advertise and that partners should spend approximately 40 to 50 percent of their time working on practice development (attracting new clients)."
6. "The mergers that have recently taken place in the public accounting profession are good for it."
7. "Auditors have done a poor job of detecting and reporting on financial fraud because they have been more interested in pleasing and retaining clients than in approaching each audit with a high degree of professional skepticism."
8. "Although the profession has not been perfect in detecting and reporting on fraud, its performance has been exemplary."
9. "Although audits could be designed to provide an extremely high probability that all material fraud would be detected, the cost of performing such audits would outweigh the benefits to society."
10. "Audit committees can be effective but only if both the audit committee and management want CPA firms that are primarily responsible to third-party users rather than to the company management."

Required:

a. Indicate whether you agree or disagree with each of the comments.

b. For each comment with which you disagree, indicate the reason for your disagreement and any misconceptions your colleague may have regarding the subject.

c. For each comment with which you agree with your colleague, provide support for that position.

5–45 (Fraud and Defalcations) The following represents a list of defalcations that have taken place within various organizations. You may assume that the amounts involved are material.

1. The treasurer of a small city also managed the city's pension fund. Over a period of a few years, the treasurer diverted a substantial amount of the earnings of the fund to his personal use. Most of the funds were invested in money market funds and certificates of deposit. To cover the diversion, the treasurer systematically underrecorded income earned on the funds.
2. The purchasing agent of a company set up a fictitious vendor and periodically sent purchase orders to the fictitious vendor. The agent then created bogus receiving reports and sent the receiving reports, vendor invoices, and purchase orders to accounts payable for processing. The fraud amounted to $125,000 a year for a company with approximately $12,000,000 of annual sales.
3. The social services workers of a state agency set up fictitious files for welfare recipients and paid them monthly support. Of course, because the recipients were fictitious, the social services workers collected the checks and deposited them into an intermediate bank account and then transferred the amount to the account of the fraud perpetrators. All of the records are kept on computerized files.
4. A purchasing agent systematically paid higher than market prices for goods received from an important vendor. In turn, the purchasing agent received various perks from the vendor and kickbacks that amounted to more than half of the purchasing agent's regular annual salary.
5. The supervisor of a small manufacturing company and the payroll clerk colluded to add an extra person to the payroll. Time cards were approved by the supervisor, who split the nonemployee paychecks with the payroll clerk.
6. The branch manager of a bank manipulated the dormant accounts (of inactive depositors) and transferred amounts from those accounts to a fictitious account from which he eventually withdrew the cash. All of the accounts were computerized. Monthly statements were sent to the customers, but all the bank personnel were instructed to refer questions about account balances directly to the manager so he could show personal interest in the customers. He would then correct the accounts of any customers who complained.
7. The accounts receivable bookkeeper opens the cash and makes the cash deposit. Over a period of time, she diverted significant funds to herself and covered up the diversion either by misstating the accounts receivable totals by misfooting of the accounts, recording debits to discounts

or returns for the amount of money diverted, or writing off as uncollectible the accounts of customers whose payments had been diverted.

Required:

For each defalcation, briefly indicate

a. How the defalcation would likely have been detected.
b. Whether you believe that the auditor should have detected it.
c. The types of controls that might have been effective in preventing or detecting it.

5–46 (Illegal Acts) An audit client of the Peninsula CPA firm is extensively involved in defense contracting. During the past year, the Defense Department has conducted an ongoing investigation of the client for possible overbillings on governmental contracts. Most of these overbillings would be considered illegal. After an extensive investigation, it is determined that, in fact, some of the billings were illegal. The client reached an agreement with the Defense Department whereby the client did not admit guilt but agreed to make restitution to the government of $1.2 million, to pay a fine of $300,000, and to establish procedures to ensure that the government will not be overbilled in the future.

The client cooperates with the auditor and discloses the details of the investigation and settlement during the course of the audit. The auditor verifies the nature of the act and is convinced that the client's characterization is correct. The auditor discusses the need to disclose the nature of these transactions—the restitution and the fine—either as a line item or in a footnote to the financial statements. Management replies that it has adequately dealt with the situation by classifying the transactions as part of the cost of doing business with the government, that is as marketing and administrative costs associated with governmental clients. Besides, management states, "The agreement reached with the Defense Department does not require the admission of guilt on our part. Therefore, classifying the costs as losses from illegal acts would be totally improper because there is no allegation or proof of illegality."

Required:

a. How should the auditor respond to the client? Indicate explicitly your opinion on the necessary disclosure, if any, in the company's financial statements.
b. Should the nature of the situation be discussed with the auditor's attorney or the client's legal counsel (or both) before determining whether an illegal act that should be disclosed has occurred?
c. Should the nature of the settlement be discussed with the audit committee prior to determining the proper treatment on the financial statements? What should your response be if the audit committee believes these transactions do not require separate disclosure because the client did not admit guilt?
d. Would any of your answers change if the client admitted guilt and paid a smaller fine?

5–47 (Fraud and Red Flags) The following quote is from "Six Common Myths about Fraud," *The Journal of Accountancy* (February 1990, 82–88) by Joseph Wells:

Opportunity almost always relates to position. Managers are no more or less honest than employees—they just have more opportunity to commit bigger thefts. In McKinley's case, it was a common pattern: excessive leverage, marital problems, too much control. Yet had the internal auditor not fallen for the first myth (most people will not commit fraud), he might have at least known whom to look at, if not where to look. Considering there are almost countless ways to defeat internal controls, knowing whom to suspect of fraud is critical to its detection.

Required:

a. Is it possible to conduct an audit efficiently if the auditor suspects that everyone, particularly management, may be capable of conducting a fraud? Explain.

b. How would knowledge of the red flags discussed in the chapter assist the auditor in dealing with the myth that most people will not commit fraud?

c. How would the auditor go about gathering information on the "common pattern" the author refers to in the excerpt, that is, excessive leverage, marital problems, too much control? How should such information, if gathered, be documented in the audit work papers?

5–48 (Fraud and Auditor Responsibility) In an article in *The Wall Street Journal*, "Battle of the Books: Audit Firms Are Hit by More Investor Suits for Not Finding Fraud" (January 24, 1989), the following comments appear:

> (Comment 1): John Shank, an accounting professor at Dartmouth College, . . . says, "The very time an auditor should be the most cynical about a company is when his client is applying the most pressure."
>
> (Comment 2): An attorney representing shareholders against Peat Marwick says, "Auditors can close their eyes to danger signs." Mr. Grossman adds that in some of his lawsuits, he has found that lower-level accountants had discovered signs of fraud or impropriety but were ignored by their superiors. "The higher-ups at accounting firms usually seem to be willing to give management a chance to get its house in order," he says.
>
> (Comment 3): Arthur Young's Mr. Liggio says accounting firms check out suspicions of lower-level staffers even if the partner in charge of the audit doesn't agree. "But more often than not, these suspicions don't prove to be true." Mr. Liggio says, "In one instance, we even spent $40,000 of our own money for a second review, and no problem was found."
>
> (Comment 4): However, Mr. Liggio concedes that auditors sometimes can be guiled if they don't take "that extra step needed when they suspect fraud." He cites the chief executive of one company who insisted that he paid for spare parts in cash—a practice apparently common in his industry. In reality, the cash was used to bribe the buying agents of several large customers. "But the auditor didn't check to see that the spare-part inventory was increasing during that period," Mr. Liggio says.

Required:

a. To what extent can the first three comments be reconciled strictly by the position of the speaker and the vested interests of each speaker?

b. How does a public accounting firm in a competitive environment walk the fine line between developing a skeptical attitude toward the possibility of fraud and working with the client's management to help the firm grow—and as it grows help the CPA firm's fees grow? Support your answer.

c. In response to the comment by Professor Shank, what kinds of pressure might management apply to a CPA firm to lead the auditors to be less skeptical?

d. How does an auditor decide that a situation merits special investigation? For example, comments 3 and 4 by Mr. Liggio indicate that many additional investigations are dead ends, but he cites a case in which the auditor should have performed further investigation.

5–49 **(Research Question—Fraud)** The existence of fraudulent financial reporting has been of great concern to both the accounting profession and the regulatory agencies such as the SEC. It has been asserted that companies in trouble frequently go bankrupt shortly after receiving unqualified opinions from auditors. The auditing profession argues that such cases are rare and that the cases that appear in the press give the impression that the profession is doing a poorer job than it actually is.

Required:

a. Distinguish between an "audit failure" and a "business failure." Explain why the press may have a difficulty in distinguishing between the two.

b. Review *The Wall Street Journal* or other financial publications and identify two or three business failures in which fraud may have been present. Analyze the reported fraud in terms of the red flags discussed in the chapter.

c. Review recent literature on the auditor's responsibility for detecting fraud. Should the auditor's responsibility for detecting fraud be increased or decreased? Explain.

d. To what extent will the increased computerization of major companies either inhibit or encourage the development of fraudulent financial reporting? Explain.

5–50 **(Research Question—High-Risk Industries)** Auditors consider some industries to be high risk because of their nature. Classification as high risk is not meant to imply that the auditor should not accept clients in the industry; rather, the auditor needs to be aware of all the issues that might make the client high risk and decide whether or not to accept that risk.

Required:

a. Select one of the high-risk industries listed in Exhibit 5.4 and perform a background analysis of the industry by reading industry analysis reports from brokerage firms, trade magazines, or business articles. Identify the "general" risks that are associated with all companies competing in that industry.

b. Select one company within the same industry and perform a background review to determine the ways in which the risks associated with that company may differ from the risks associated with the industry as a whole.

5–51 **(Research Question—Audit Committees)** An audit committee's effectiveness in promoting the independence of the auditing firm supposedly comes from acting as a surrogate for the shareholders. Their effectiveness, in part, is attributed to their outsider status on the board of directors (i.e., they are members who do not hold company management positions). There is increasing concern, however, that audit committees may not be as effective as initially envisioned because, although they are technically outsiders, they are colleagues and friends of management and have been recommended for their positions on the board of directors by management.

Required:

a. To what extent are audit committees effective in achieving the goals that are implied in AU 380, "Communication with Audit Committees"? Review the current articles on audit committee effectiveness to address this question.

b. To what extent are many of the recommended audit committee communications a reflection of the failure of the public accounting profession, as a whole, to act independently in a competitive environment? Explain and support your answer.

c. The Report of the National Commission on Fraudulent Financial Reporting (October 1987) recommends that "all public companies should be required by SEC rule to include in their annual reports to stockholders a letter signed by the chairman of the audit committee describing the committee's responsibilities and activities during the year."

   Do you agree with the recommendation? What would be the primary advantages associated with implementing the recommendation?

5–52 **(Research Question—Marketing Audit Services)** Marketing audit services may differ markedly between local firms, regional firms, and large national firms. Each firm may have a different strategy for seeking or developing new clients.

Required:

Perform one of the following.

a. Interview practitioners in your area to determine their major approaches to marketing auditing services and obtaining new clients.

b. Request Beta Alpha Psi or your accounting club to sponsor a meeting and invite a practitioner from each of the three types of firms to present a discussion of marketing and obtaining new clients. Compare and contrast their marketing strategies.

5–53 **(Research Question—Competition in Auditing)** There has been considerable research regarding competition in the auditing profession. Some of the work has focused on whether significant economies of scale can be realized either through consolidation of CPA firms (thereby making large firms larger) or by specializing in certain industries. For example, some CPA firms seem to dominate certain industries such as public utilities or banking.

Required:

Review the audit literature to obtain a basis for addressing the question of whether significant economies of scale seem to be associated with the size and specialization of CPA firms.

a. To what extent can a small local firm address the economies of scale issue and remain competitive in the marketplace? Identify strategies that have been taken by small CPA firms to remain competitive.

Cases

5–54 (ZZZZ Best) It is often difficult to envision the auditor's difficulty in discovering fraud unless one can visualize the actual procedures the auditor went through and the potential red flags that should have alerted the auditor to potential difficulties during the conduct of the audit. One of the major frauds in recent times was that of the ZZZZ Best Company, a company that had been referred to as the "General Motors of Carpet-Cleaning" but, unfortunately for the auditors, was one big scam instead.

Required:

Read the article in Appendix A. After reading it, address the following questions.

a. To what extent do you believe "any auditor" would have been fooled by the scheme developed by Barry Minkow?

b. What were the key red flags that the auditor probably missed while conducting the audit of ZZZZ Best?

c. Does it appear, judging just from the article, that the fraud could have been detected by following generally accepted auditing standards? Explain.

5–55 (Regina Vacuum) Read the article in Appendix B describing the failure of Regina Vacuum cleaner. It is alleged that the auditor attested to financial statements that were full of promise at a time when the prospects for the company were actually quite dim.

Required:

a. Identify the red flags that the auditor should have noted during the conduct of the audit.

b. Briefly discuss the role of analytical review—the detailed financial analysis of a company's operations much as a critical financial analyst might perform—in auditing a client like Regina. What information could the auditor generate from such a review? To what extent could such a review be automated as part of every audit? Explain.

End Notes

1. AICPA, *The Commission on Auditor's Responsibilities: Report, Conclusions, and Recommendations* (New York: AICPA, 1978), 38.
2. Stanley Slom, "Large or Small, Firms Are Marketing," *Accounting Today*, March 6, 1989, 3.
3. Lou Harris & Associates, Inc., *A Survey of Perceptions, Knowledge, and Attitudes towards CPAs and the Accounting Profession* (New York, 1986), 9.
4. James Loebbecke, Martha Eining, and John Willingham, "Auditors' Experience with Material Irregularities: Frequency, Nature, and Detectability," *Auditing: A Journal of Practice and Theory* (Fall 1989), 1–28.

CHAPTER

6

Learning Objectives

Through studying this chapter, you will be able to:

1. Understand the user perspective of materiality and how it affects the planning of audits.
2. Develop an understanding of the risk-based approach to auditing.
3. Differentiate between engagement risk and audit risk.
4. Understand the audit risk model and how it affects the planning and implementation of audit programs.
5. Understand the process used to identify risk factors and analyze their impact on planning the audit.
6. Apply the audit risk model to the planning of an audit.

Audit Planning: Materiality and Audit Risk

Chapter Contents

Chapter Overview

The two most important factors affecting the planning and conduct of an audit are (1) the auditor's assessment of materiality and (2) the risk that the auditor's report may be questioned. An audit report states an opinion that the financial statements are presented fairly *"in all material respects."* But who judges what is material? This chapter develops the materiality concept as it affects the design, conduct, and reporting of an audit. Unfortunately, this is a difficult concept because the auditor must use professional judgment in reflecting the perspective of an informed **user.** The process of making materiality judgments is discussed in this chapter.

The auditor needs to consider two different types of client-associated risk in order to plan and conduct an audit. This chapter defines these risks as (1) engagement risk, the risk of being associated with the client, and (2) audit risk, the risk that the auditor may inappropriately issue an audit opinion. Factors affecting each type of risk are identified and applied to the conduct of an audit.

Audit risk and materiality, among other matters, need to be considered together in determining the nature, timing, and extent of auditing procedures and in evaluating the results of those procedures. The existence of audit risk is implicit in the phrase "in our opinion." [AU 312.02-.03]

The standard audit report states: "We *planned and performed* the audit to obtain *reasonable assurance* about whether the financial statements are free of *material misstatement."* This sentence in the audit report reflects the underlying process of auditing. The auditor conducts the audit to provide reasonable, *but not absolute,* assurance that the financial statements are free of material misstatements. Audit risk is the risk that such misstatements are not detected. To effectively plan and conduct the audit, the auditor must understand the concepts of materiality and audit risk. An understanding of materiality is essential to determine whether sufficient audit work is planned. An understanding of audit risk is necessary to focus audit attention on areas in which material misstatements are likely to occur.

A–OVERVIEW OF THE AUDIT PROCESS

Exhibit 6.1 provides an overview of the audit process. *Audit planning* involves obtaining an understanding of the client and its industry to determine how to perform the audit. This includes establishing an appropriate materiality threshold and audit risk for the client (discussed later in this chapter).

The auditor must then obtain an understanding of the policies and procedures used by the client to help ensure that the financial information is accurately recorded in the accounting records. This involves *assessing control risk,* that is, the risk that these policies and procedures will fail to prevent or detect material misstatements. In many audits, this includes testing certain control procedures to determine their effectiveness. Based on the auditor's assessment of control risk, the auditor then determines what audit evidence to obtain through *substantive tests of transactions, direct tests of account balances, and analytical procedures*. Near the end of the audit, the auditor makes a *final assessment* of the evidence obtained to be sure that it is adequate and evaluates the client's financial statement presentation. The auditor then decides on the appropriate *opinion* to express on those financial statements.

B–MATERIALITY: THE BASIS FOR AUDIT PLANNING

Materiality is an elusive, but fundamental, concept to accounting and auditing. Authoritative pronouncements are expected to be applied to all *material* transactions. The auditor is expected to design and conduct an audit that provides reasonable assurance that *material* errors or irregularities will be detected. As used in auditing, materiality is meant to convey a sense of significance or importance of an item. But significant to whom? And how important? The auditor and management can, and often do, disagree on whether a transaction or misstatement is *material.* Further, a dollar amount that may be significant to one person may not be significant to the president of General Motors. Or the misrecording of a complex transaction may be significant to one group of users but not to others. The concept of materiality is pervasive but elusive to the practicing auditor who may be called on to defend a financial statement a particular user believes contains a material misstatement but that the auditor did not believe was material when the audit report was issued.

Although it is difficult to think of materiality without a dollar amount associated with it, the auditor's judgment of materiality does not have to be quantified during the planning process. Most firms do, however, quantify materiality for planning the audit and for evaluating misstatements uncovered during the audit.

Materiality Defined

Clearly, the concept of materiality embodies multiple dimensions. As such, the concept can be elusive to the auditor trying to plan and conduct an audit. In *Concepts Statement No. 2,* the FASB defines **materiality** as the

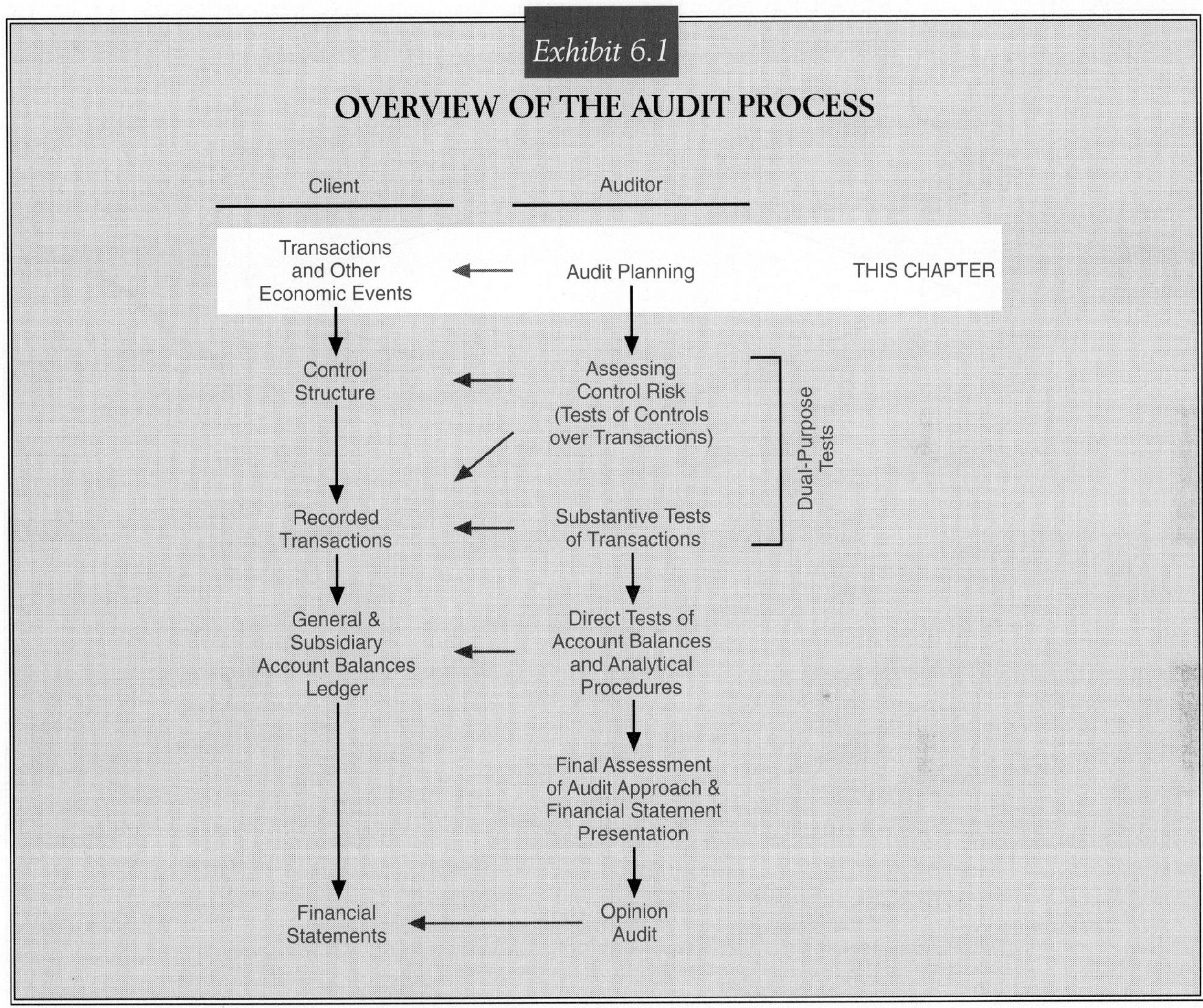

magnitude of an omission or misstatement of accounting information that, in the light of surrounding circumstances, makes it probable that the judgment of a reasonable person relying on the information would have been changed or influenced by the omission or misstatement.

This definition helps identify three important dimensions of materiality:

1. The dollar magnitude of the item.
2. The nature of the item under consideration.
3. The perspective of a particular user.

These dimensions are captured in Exhibit 6.2.

For any given client, materiality is not simply a function of specific dollar amounts in the organization's financial statements. Some transactions, by their very nature, are likely to be more controversial than others and thus may affect a user's decision to invest in or to make a loan to the company. An auditor must understand who the potential users are and the type of judgments made by those users when relying on

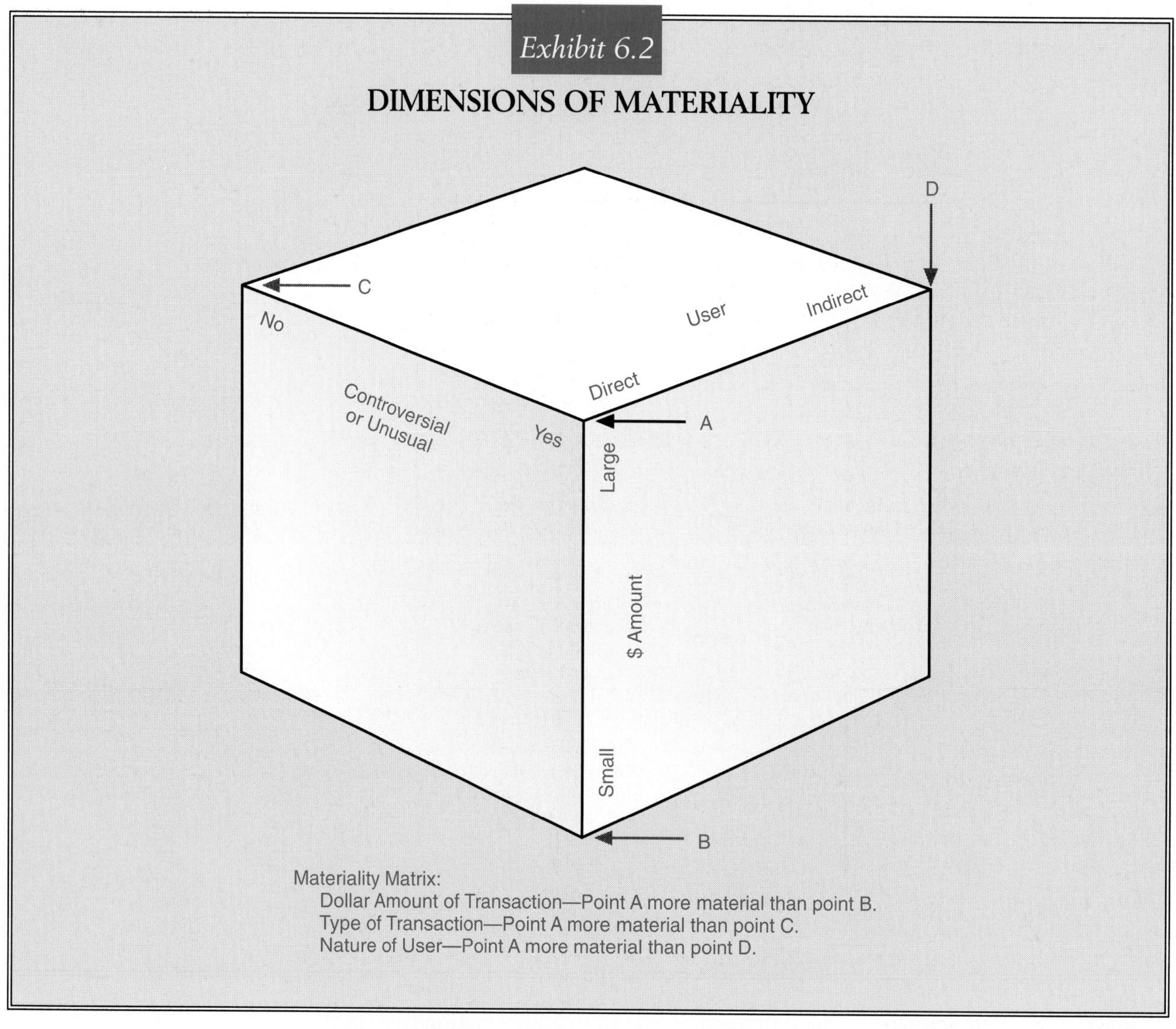

financial statements. The auditor considers the matrix of potential materiality portrayed in Exhibit 6.2; that matrix may differ for each client.

Dollar Amount of Transactions

Planning for materiality usually begins with some assessment of the dollar magnitude of a misstatement that would affect the judgment of an informed user. Although the concept seems clear, there are practical difficulties in developing criteria to judge materiality based on dollar amounts alone. Accounting and psychological research during the past two decades has attempted to measure minimum amounts of "noticeable differences" that could be related to the concept of materiality. Both the psychological-based research and the accounting research show that five percent of an item represents a "noticeable difference." But, just because five percent is noticeable, it still may not be "material" to a user's judgment.

Even after determining that some percentage of misstatement is material, the auditor must decide on the base to which to apply that percentage. A given account balance may be misstated by 15 percent, for example, but result in only a 3 percent misstatement in net income. Are the financial statements free from material misstatement? Obviously, the answer depends on the nature of the item(s) misstated and the decision-making criteria of users. Auditors sometimes use net income as a basis and preliminarily establish overall materiality as a percentage of that income. But net income may vary considerably from year to year or may even include losses in some years. In such situations, auditors can use normalized income over a period of time. More frequently, auditors use a percentage of revenues or total assets as a basis because they are more stable from year to year.

Dollar misstatements of relatively small amounts may also affect trends in reported performance. For example, an older company in a stable industry may operate a subsidiary in an area unrelated to the company's main business. Investors seem optimistic about the potential of the subsidiary's new product line, and a significant portion of the stock's value appears to be tied to the prospects of this subsidiary, even though it accounts for only a small portion of the entity's consolidated income. The subsidiary's past growth rate and projections for that growth rate in the future are important to investors. Significant changes in the subsidiary's financial performance will affect the market's evaluation of the company's prospects. The auditor must consider dollar misstatements that would significantly change the reported growth rate of the subsidiary even if the dollar amount of the misstatement is less than some percentage threshold of the reported net income, revenues, or assets of the consolidated entity.

Nature of the Item Being Misstated

In some situations, a misstatement in an account may affect net income by a relatively small amount, but the account balance may be misstated by a material amount. The auditor must consider the nature of the transaction and the account balance affected along the continuum depicted in Exhibit 6.2 ranging from routine or insignificant to controversial or inherently important transactions. Controversial transactions include those with related parties, potentially fraudulent or unethical transactions, unusual transactions for the entity, or misstatements in particular account balances that might signal a change in direction or risk exposure for the organization. In the *Continental Vending* case discussed in Chapter 4, the judge ruled that a misstatement of accounts receivable from a related party was material even though reported net income was unaffected.

Types of Users

Materiality is a user-driven concept. Thus, the auditor is given the unenviable task of trying to determine what is important to *specific users* of a client's financial statements. In planning an audit, the auditor must identify financial statement users and the nature of their decisions. These decisions normally deal with making loans to the entity, buying or selling the entity's stock, granting trade credit to the entity, or determining whether regulatory action is needed.

The user dimension of Exhibit 6.2 is depicted as falling along a line from direct to indirect users. Direct users include creditors, investors, potential shareholders, and potential lenders. Indirect users may include regulatory agencies or other governmental institutions, employees, or customers of the entity.

Overall Materiality versus Individual Materiality

An audit must be designed to detect material misstatements. Therefore, a **planning materiality** must be developed as a basis for determining the *amount* of work to be performed. Generally, planning materiality decisions apply to the financial statements taken as a whole. Auditors then allocate that amount to individual account balances. But the overall level of misstatement possible must be determined, as part of audit planning, and be periodically reassessed during the course of the audit.

Materiality Approaches

Because of the difficulty in making materiality judgments, most public accounting firms attempt to provide decision-making guidance to their staff auditors to promote consistent judgments across the firm. The guidelines usually involve applying percentages to some base, such as total assets, total revenue, or pre-tax income. In choosing a base, the auditor considers the stability of the base from year to year so that overall materiality does not fluctuate significantly between annual audits. Income is often more volatile than total assets or revenue. A simple guideline for small business audits could be, for example, to set overall materiality at one percent of the higher of total assets or revenue. The percentage may be smaller for large clients. Other CPA firms have more complicated guidance that may be based on the nature of the industry or a composite of materiality decisions made by experts in the firm. But any guidance is just that. The auditor may use it as a starting point that should be adjusted for the qualitative conditions of the particular audit. There may be restrictive covenants in the client's bond indenture, for example, requiring it to maintain a current ratio of at least 2 to 1. If that ratio per book figures is near to the requirement, a smaller overall materiality may be required.

To illustrate the implementation of materiality, we will use LeFlam Company, which is discussed in depth in Chapter 11. LeFlam manufactures and distributes outdoor camping products. It is a publicly held company with good growth and high management integrity. The auditor considers the assets and net sales as a preliminary basis for establishing materiality. Current year unaudited amounts and prior year amounts are as follows:

	(In thousands) 1994	1993
Total assets	21,070	14,306
Net sales	29,500	24,900
Pre-tax income	4,032	2,964

If the guideline of one percent of the higher of total assets or revenue is used, the starting point for planning materiality would be $295,000. The $295,000 would then have to be allocated across different accounts in developing materiality for audits of individual accounts. Although not illustrated here, one of the Big Six firms has a guideline that would have generated a $180,000 figure as the auditor's first estimate of materiality, far lower than the $295,000 suggested by our rule. Is one more right than the other? That is where professional judgment is required. The auditor considers the various types of users, the financial health of the company, the likelihood that the audit might be questioned, and so forth to adjust to a planning materiality. But, the initial determination of planning materiality will have a major effect on the amount of audit work performed.

When planning the audit of a particular account, such as Accounts Receivable, the auditor may allocate a smaller amount, such as $75,000 as the maximum tolerable error in that account. Does this mean that a $75,000 misstatement in Accounts Receivable is material? Or would a $75,000 misstatement make the financial statements misleading? Not necessarily. The potential misstatement in Accounts Receivable must be considered in conjunction with other errors in other accounts to determine whether errors, in the aggregate, may be material to the financial statements as a whole. But the auditor also needs to consider that a misstatement of $75,000 in Accounts Receivable might be material to a particular group of users (such as lenders) even though it would take a larger misstatement to make the income statement misleading. Thus, the auditor needs to consider materiality at both the individual level and the aggregate level.

C–RISK APPROACH TO AUDITING

Risk Concepts

Many auditors talk about a **risk-based** approach to **auditing** or about the need to minimize audit risk. This kind of discussion can be confusing because the auditor often uses the term *risk* to mean many different things, all of which affect the approach to the audit. To understand the concepts of risk as they apply to auditing, we must first define the two ways in which the concepts are often used. They are engagement risk* and audit risk.

> **Engagement risk** refers to the risk the audit firm encounters because it is associated with a particular client. The risk may manifest itself in lawsuits, a loss of professional reputation, or a loss of clients. Engagement risk may be higher when there is a concern about the integrity of the client's management and may result in increased costs of doing an audit. It may exist even if there are no misstatements in the financial statements and the audit is conducted in accordance with professional standards. For example, the auditor may incur unforseen costs simply because a client is going bankrupt.
>
> **Audit risk** refers to the risk that the auditor may unknowingly fail to appropriately modify the opinion on financial statements that are materially misstated. Audit risk occurs when an unqualified opinion is issued on financial statements that are materially misstated. Audit risk may lead to lawsuits or other action that may be costly to the auditor.

The auditor assesses engagement risk as a basis for establishing audit risk as part of the process of planning the audit. That is, if the auditor perceives that the risk of being associated with the client is high, either because of issues associated with management integrity or other factors that may affect the economic success of the client, the auditor should plan lower levels of audit risk. More succinctly, audit risk should be set at a lower level to protect the auditing firm from economic losses. Conversely, if the risks of being associated with a client are low (e.g. the company is healthy and management has high integrity), the auditor can plan the audit with a higher amount of audit risk because there are fewer factors that might lead to the auditor's report

*Engagement risk is sometimes referred to as *business risk*.

being questioned. In such cases, the auditor can set audit risk higher as long as the level set is still within the maximum allowed by the professional standards in achieving its objective of protecting the public. Thus, a high engagement risk requires the auditor to conduct the audit with low audit risk (more audit work). In contrast, a low level of engagement risk allows the auditor to conduct the audit with higher audit risk (less audit work).

The auditor can control the amount of audit risk incurred but can only assess, not control, engagement risk. Understanding engagement risk helps the auditor assess materiality and the potential losses that may come through association with the client.

Engagement Risk

Engagement risk is present even if a proper audit is performed and an appropriate opinion is issued. Auditors are often named as defendants in lawsuits when they are associated with businesses that fail or businesses in which management has performed frauds. *By accepting particular clients*, auditors, in other words, subject themselves to a higher than normal risk of being sued. Thus, auditors need to assess the risk associated with each client. Many auditing firms have developed systematic procedures to assist in making the decision to accept a new client or to continue an existing client. One international accounting firm requires the following factors be assessed in determining client acceptance and planning the extent and timing of audit procedures.

- The presence of domineering senior executives with little real limit to their authority.
- The existence of financial problems, such as declining earnings, inadequate working capital, or relatively inflexible debt covenants.
- The presence of breakdowns in the organization's control systems.
- The existence of high turnover in key financial positions.
- Previous records of unusually large payments to business advisers in relation to services provided.
- The existence of a complex corporate structure that does not appear warranted.
- A pattern of premature announcement of operating results.

In some instances, CPA firms may even require an independent investigation of management integrity before accepting a new client. The point is that the auditor must carefully examine a number of factors to assess the engagement risk associated with a potential client.

Audit Risk

An incorrect audit opinion occurs when an auditor issues (1) a qualified or adverse audit opinion when the financial statements are free from material misstatement or (2) an unqualified audit opinion when the financial statements contain material misstatements. *Audit risk refers only to the latter situation.*

The two alternatives appear to be equally risky, but they are not. If the auditor plans to issue a qualified or adverse opinion when, in fact, the statements are free of material misstatement, management has a built in bias that will cause the auditor to do more work before such an opinion could be issued. This is reasonable when one considers that audits are conducted using sampling techniques. If projected errors from sampling indicate that material errors *may be present*, audit tests will be expanded to gather more evidence on the potential existence of errors. Because management does not believe the statements are misstated (because they prepared them), they will normally insist that the auditor do more work to develop persuasive evidence before adjusting the statements.

If the auditor issues an unqualified opinion when, in fact, the statements contain a material misstatement, management will not likely object. Therefore, an unqualified opinion will be issued because the auditor has not gathered evidence contrary to that opinion. There is a chance that users who rely on the auditor's opinion and the materially misstated financial statements will suffer damages and bring suit against the auditor to recover those damages. Thus, it is most important to control against this risk.

Inseparability of Audit Risk and Materiality

Audit risk and engagement risk relate to factors that would likely encourage someone to challenge the auditor's work. If a company is on the brink of bankruptcy, transactions that might not be material to a "healthy" company of similar size may be material to the users of the potentially bankrupt company's financial statements. The following factors are important in integrating concepts of risk and materiality in the conduct of an audit:

1. *All audits involve testing* and thus cannot provide 100 percent assurance of the absolute correctness of a company's financial statements without inordinately driving up the cost of audits.
2. Auditing firms must *compete in an active marketplace* for clients who choose auditors on the basis of such factors as fees, service, personal rapport, industry knowledge, and the ability to assist the client.
3. Auditors need to *understand society's expectations* of financial reporting to minimize audit risk and formulate reasonable materiality judgments.
4. Auditors must *identify the risky areas of a business* to determine which account balances are more susceptible to misstatement, how the misstatements might occur, and how a client might be able to cover them up.
5. Auditors need to develop methodologies to *allocate overall assessments of materiality* to individual account balances because some account balances may be more important to *some users*.

The Profession's Audit Risk Model: Practice Implications

The Auditing Standards Board issued *SAS No. 47*, "Audit Risk and Materiality in Conducting an Audit" [AU 312] to provide a conceptual model of audit risk to guide the practice of auditing. The model leaves room for individual implementation differences among CPA firms and for different clients. For example, some firms implement the model quantitatively; other firms use qualitative terminology to implement the model.

Components of the Audit Risk Model

The auditor faces audit risk only when two independent events happen. First, a material misstatement occurs in the financial recording process. Second, the misstatement is not discovered by the auditor. The possibility of misstatement leads to the following general observations applicable to audit risk.

1. Complex or unusual transactions are more likely to be recorded in error than are recurring or routine transactions.
2. If misstatements are likely to occur in the recording process, the auditor should develop procedures to detect the misstatements.
3. Some managers may be more motivated to misstate earnings or assets to achieve personal goals than others may be.
4. The better the organization's control structure, the less likely it is that material misstatements will be present in the accounts.
5. The amount of audit work performed should vary directly with the likelihood of material misstatements existing in the accounting records, that is, the higher likelihood of misstatements means more audit work.

These general premises have been incorporated into an audit risk (*AR*) model with three components: inherent risk (*IR*), control risk (*CR*), and detection risk (*DR*) as follows:

$$AR = f(IR, CR, DR)$$

Audit risk is a function of inherent risk (likelihood that a material misstatement will occur), control risk (failure of the control system to prevent or detect the misstatement), and detection risk (failure of audit procedures to detect the misstatements). Although the model often is viewed as a multiplicative model, it is intended that the auditor consider each component and combine them in an overall audit risk model. We will treat the model as a multiplicative model below *for illustrative purposes only* to explain the basic relationships among the components.

Inherent Risk. **Inherent risk** is the susceptibility of transactions to be recorded in error. More formally, it is defined as "the susceptibility of an assertion [related to an account balance] to a material misstatement, assuming that there are no related internal control structure policies or procedures" [AU 312.20a]. For example, an error is more likely to occur in calculating foreign currency translations amounts or in making deferred income tax projections than in recording a normal sale. As the auditor identifies accounts that are more susceptible to material misstatement, the audit plan should be adjusted to reflect the increased risk.

As stated previously, the auditor must understand the business being audited. For example, consider the possibility of auditing a brokerage firm without knowing the nature of processing that takes place when stocks are bought or sold or the terms of settlement. Or auditing an electronics company without knowing the status of competitors' products and how they might affect the realizability of the client's inventory. Knowledge of the business environment—and its risks—allows the auditor to anticipate the accounts that are most likely to contain misstatements and concentrate audit work on those accounts.

Control Risk. **Control risk** is the risk that a material misstatement that could occur in a transaction or adjusting entries will not be prevented or detected on a timely basis by the entity's internal control structure [AU 312.20b]. In other words, control risk reflects the possibility that the client's system of controls over the processing of transactions will allow erroneous items in material amounts to be recorded.

A number of important elements in the concept of control risk guide the development of an audit approach for a particular organization. First, some organizations may implement outstanding control procedures. Second, those control procedures may vary with classes of transactions: Control procedures over the recording of receivables, for example, may be strong, but those for recording foreign currency transactions may be much weaker. Third, the amount of audit work designed to directly test for errors in an account balance should vary directly with the auditor's assessment of control risk, that is, a high control risk should lead to more extensive testing of account balances. Because of the inherent limitations associated with all internal control structures, the professional standards recognize that some control risk is present in every audit engagement.

Environmental Risk. The combination of inherent risk and control risk is often referred to as the **environmental risk.** This is the risk that a material misstatement occurred, went undetected by the internal control structure, and exists in the accounting records prior to the audit. Environmental risk exists independently of the audit; auditors can assess it but have no ability to change it. Therefore, they must adjust their audit work accordingly.

Detection Risk. **Detection risk** is the risk that the auditor will not detect a material misstatement that exists in an account balance [AU 312.20c].

Three important concepts are directly related to this definition. First, detection risk is inversely related to environmental risk. The more likely it is that errors exist in an account balance, the more the auditor will directly test the account balance. Second, audit effectiveness in minimizing detection risk depends directly on (1) the selection of the *right* audit procedures for the types of misstatements likely to occur, (2) the *timing* of these procedures, (3) the *extent* of the procedures, and (4) the *proper application* of these procedures by the auditor. Third, when sampling is used to gather evidence, there is a risk that the sample results will cause the auditor to conclude that the related account balance is not materially misstated when, in fact, it is. This is referred to as the *risk of incorrect acceptance*, and is covered in detail in Chapters 12 and 14.

Illustration of the Audit Risk Model

The audit risk model may be implemented using a quantitative approach with probability assessments applied to each of the model's components. Although useful, a strictly quantitative approach tends to give the appearance that each individual component can be precisely measured when in fact none can be without a 100 percent testing of the account balances. Therefore, many public accounting firms apply subjective, qualitative assessments to each model component; control risk, for example, is identified as high, medium, or low. All of the examples below assume that the firm has a policy of setting planned audit risk at 0.05.

Example: Environmental Risk Assessed as Maximum. Assume an audit of an organization that has many complex transactions and does not have strong control procedures. The auditor assesses both inherent risk and control risk at their maximum. The effect on detection risk and, thus, the extent of audit procedures are as follows:

$$AR = IR \times CR \times DR \text{, therefore, } DR = AR / (IR \times CR)$$

$$DR = 0.05 / (1.00 \times 1.00) = 0.05 \text{, or 5 percent}$$

Detection risk at five percent implies that the audit must be conducted with extensive direct tests of the company's financial statement accounts and related transactions because the auditor cannot rely on the client's control system to detect and correct the misstatements. Auditing with a detection risk of 5 percent is the same as taking statistical samples utilizing a 95 percent confidence level (only a 5 percent chance of being in error). The illustration yields the intuitive result: poor controls and a high likelihood of misstatement lead to extended audit work to maintain audit risk at an acceptable level and to minimize the possibility the auditor will fail to find material misstatements.

Example: Environmental Risk Assessed as Low. Assume that the client has simple transactions, well-trained accounting personnel, and an effective control structure. The auditor's previous experience with the client and the results of preliminary testing this year indicate a low risk of material misstatement existing in the accounting records. The auditor assesses environmental risk as low: inherent risk is 50 percent and control risk is 20 percent. The auditor's determination of detection risk for this engagement would be

$$DR = AR / (IR \times CR)$$

$$DR = 0.05 / (0.50 \times 0.20) = 0.50, \text{ or } 50 \text{ percent}$$

In other words, the auditor could design tests of the accounting records with a lower detection risk, in this case 50 percent, because the direct tests of account balances are needed only to provide corroborating evidence on the auditor's expectations that the control environment will minimize misstatements. This is equivalent to designing a statistical test using a 50 percent confidence level rather than a 95 percent confidence level. The amount and type of direct tests of the client's accounts will be considerably less than that in the previous example. If, however, the auditor's tests show more errors than expected, the auditor would reassess environmental risk and adjust the audit work accordingly.

Limitations of the Audit Risk Model

The *SAS No. 47* model has a number of limitations that make its actual implementation difficult. In addition to the danger that the auditors will look at the model too mechanically, the following limitations have been considered by CPA firms in determining their approach to implementing the model:

1. *Inherent risk is difficult to formally assess.* Auditors therefore apply the concept at the individual transaction or account balance level but not at the financial statement level. In overall audit planning, inherent risk is often established conservatively at 100 percent.
2. *Audit risk is subjectively determined.* It is important to remember that most auditors set audit risk at some nominal level, such as 0.05, but no firm could survive if 5 percent of their audits were in error. Audit risk on most engagements is much lower than the 0.05 level because of conservative assumptions that take place when inherent risk is set at 1.00 (at the maximum). Setting inherent risk at 1.00 implies that every transaction is initially recorded in error. It is very rare that every transaction would be in error. Because such a conservative assessment leads to more audit work, the real level of audit risk will be less than 0.05.

3. The model *treats each risk component as separate and independent* when in fact the components are not independent. The strength of an organization's control system, for example, often depends on inherent risk and vice versa.
4. *Audit technology is not so precisely developed that each component of the model can be accurately assessed.* Auditing is based on testing; precise estimates of the model's components are not possible. Auditors can, however, make relatively subjective assessments and use the audit risk model as a guide.

Adjusting Audit Risk

A risk-driven approach to auditing suggests that the auditor is capable of identifying specific areas of a client that are more susceptible to misstatement and then allocating sufficient audit resources to those areas to determine whether material misstatements exist. Given that the auditor does not control the risk of material misstatement occurring, is it appropriate to talk in terms of the auditor setting audit risk for each engagement? Fortunately, the answer is yes! The auditor can control the risk that the audit team will fail to uncover material misstatements during the course of an audit. Thus, by setting audit risk, the auditor is designing the audit to minimize the possibility that the audit team will fail to detect material misstatements.

Overall audit risk is set at the beginning of each audit by the engagement partner or manager. This risk judgment is influenced by the

- Auditor's assessment of engagement risk.
- Audit firm's policies and guidelines.
- Individual risk attitudes of auditors.

Auditor's Assessment of Engagement Risk. Engagement risk plays a major role in determining audit risk. More specifically, the elements of engagement risk that most affect the determination of audit risk are (1) the extent to which the financial statements are relied on by the users and (2) the economic health of the client.

Creditors and investors are likely to place more reliance on the financial statements of publicly owned companies than privately owned companies. Users of the financial statements of privately owned companies are more likely to have direct contact with management and more direct knowledge of the financial condition and activities of such companies.

Users of financial statements of economically healthy companies are much less likely to be financially injured than are financial statement users of companies that are in financial trouble. Operating losses and bankruptcies of clients often lead to lawsuits against auditors.

Given the effect of engagement risk in determining audit risk, one might ask whether it is appropriate to modify (raise) audit risk if the auditor encounters a situation in which little engagement risk is perceived. Say, for example, the client is a privately owned, small insurance company. There are no outside users of the financial statements. Could audit risk be set at a very high level, such as 50 percent? The answer is an unequivocal no! GAAS imply that a maximum level of audit risk is specified for all engagements and is implied in the concept of reasonable assurance. In other words, the auditor's recognition of engagement risk can serve only to lower the auditor's planned audit risk level; it can never be used to raise it.

Audit Firm's Policies and Guidelines. As noted earlier, the auditor normally sets audit risk at a very low level. Some firms have defined policies setting audit risk at five percent for most audits and one percent for engagements that are characterized by higher than average engagement risk. Setting audit risk at five percent might not seem conservative because that level implies that the auditor would issue, on average, an incorrect audit opinion on 5 of every 100 audit reports. Experience has shown, however, that the incurred level of audit risk for the profession, as measured by lawsuits and defined audit failures, is substantially less than one-half of one percent (that is, less than .005). Why would actual experience be so much less than the auditor's initial risk settings? The answer is fairly simple. The guidelines of many firms that set audit risk at five percent also, by policy, assess inherent risk at 100 percent. To assume that there are material misstatements in the accounting records of every client is extremely conservative.* Setting inherent risk at 100 percent has the effect of making the actual level of audit risk substantially less than the five percent contained in the firm guidelines. For example, if inherent risk is assessed by the auditor as only 10 percent (or at a minimum level) but the auditor uses a higher assessment of inherent risk in the audit model, such as 100 percent (or at the maximum), the net effect of this conservative use of inherent risk in the audit model is to require more audit work, reducing the actual level of audit risk to an amount lower than the nominal level set by the auditor. In the preceding example, the actual level of audit risk incurred would be one-tenth of that set by the auditor because the auditor used an inherent risk factor that is ten times as high as the initially assessed level.

Individual Risk Attitudes of Auditors. Some individual auditors are willing to take more risk than are others. Additionally, in a given audit situation, auditors may have different perceptions of the engagement risk and may set audit risk at a different level than would another auditor. Others may simply be more risk averse. Finally, the litigious environment may cause all auditors to be more risk averse and set audit risk at lower levels.

Relating Audit Risk to Significant Components of the Financial Statements. Audit risk is set at the financial statement level. In addition, the auditor needs to consider audit risk at the individual account balance or class of transactions level in such a way that at the completion of the audit, an opinion can be expressed on the fairness of the financial statements at an appropriately low level of audit risk. This means that the auditor must consider inherent risk, control risk, and detection risk for each significant component of the financial statements.

D–OBTAINING AN UNDERSTANDING OF THE CLIENT

The auditor must assess the *potential engagement risk* and the likelihood of material errors prior to accepting a new audit client. However, the process is continuous. It occurs for continuing clients as the auditor examines changes in the nature of the client and its business, the regulatory environment, and management changes as a basis for planning the audit. The auditor attempts to assess the risk that the client's

*An item that is omitted or never recorded is also considered a recording error; that is, failure to record a transaction is a recording error.

accounts may contain misstatements and where those misstatements are most likely to occur. The auditor is also trying to understand whether there are factors associated with a client that would suggest a higher likelihood of misstatements in the financial statements. For example, the auditor is interested in knowing whether there are outside pressures that might lead management to misstate the financial statements. An overview of the factors affecting the auditor's assessment of engagement risk is shown in Exhibit 6.3.

The determination of the *riskiness* of a client failing and of potential misstatements in account balances is referred to as a *risk approach* to auditing. Many public accounting firms have specific risk assessment questionnaires that incorporate many of the factors in Exhibit 6.3. The auditor's assessments of these factors should be documented along with the implications for planning the audit.

Individual Risk Factors Affecting the Planning of the Audit

Management Integrity

Assessing **management integrity** is one of the most crucial aspects in determining whether to accept (or retain) an audit client and the nature and extent of audit work to be performed. Engagements in which management integrity is low are more susceptible to undetected fraud, unavailability of critical audit evidence, management

Exhibit 6.3

ENGAGEMENT RISK FACTORS AFFECTING AUDIT PLANNING

- Management integrity
- Financial trends and current financial position
- Existence of related-party transactions
- Changes in auditors
- SEC investigations of client
- Nature of the industry
- Nature of the company's products—Dependence on few key products or short-lived products with intense competition
- Concerns about default on loans or restructured debt
- New financial deals such as restructuring or leveraged buy outs affecting the company
- Turnover in key executive positions
- Companies that are potential takeover targets
- Company operating environment susceptibility to fraudulent transactions
- High stock market expectations of financial performance
- Problems encountered during prior year's audit
- Role of financial statements in decision making by users
- Industry that is politically visible or receives a great amount of public attention
- Product introductions: a large number of them, or too few; company lags behind others in the industry.
- Company subject to a high level of governmental regulation
- Auditor familiarity with specialized industry

misstatements about management intent or the details of important transactions, management disagreement on the proper accounting for transactions, and misstated financial statements.

If the auditor has reason to believe that management integrity is low, the following should be considered:

- The extent the auditor can rely on management's representations.
- The likelihood that management might materially misstate the financial statements to accomplish personal goals (fraudulent financial reporting).
- The likelihood the company (and thus potentially the auditor) might end up in court because of the auditor's role in attesting to the company's financial statements.

If the auditor's assessment of these factors indicates management integrity is low, the auditor should seriously consider whether the client is "too risky" to continue as an audit client or initially to accept it as a client.

Most audit firms have developed systematic approaches to assess management integrity. These procedures include the following:

- Inquiry of persons within the professional community in which the client operates, such as bankers and lawyers.
- Review of recent regulatory or court cases against the client, including recent SEC filings.
- Review of the financial press for articles about the company and its management.
- Inquiry of predecessor auditors as to management integrity, existence of disagreements on the audit, or management's motivation to manipulate accounting principles.
- Thorough review of previous financial reports to uncover financial problems and the quality of financial reporting utilized.

In some—albeit rare—situations, auditors have actually hired private investigators to gather information on management's integrity.

Financial Trends and Current Financial Position

A client with a poor financial position can pose a significant risk to the auditor. First, corporate failures result in losses, sometimes significant, to some parties. And the injured parties are likely to seek redress through the courts to gain partial compensation for their losses. Second, poor financial results may force the company to violate important debt covenants. Dollar amounts that otherwise might not be considered material may become so when the company fails to meet mandatory debt covenant limits. Lower levels of materiality mean more audit work for which the additional fees are not likely to be collectible.* Third, poor financial results may provide motivation to stretch the limits of accounting to record transactions in a way

*As part of most loan agreements for either debentures or short-term loans, specific covenants protect the lender against the potential default by the borrower. These covenants typically contain language on the maintenance of a specified current ratio, a limitation on the payment of dividends, and other restrictions specific to the situation. If the organization violates any of these covenants, the entire amount of the loan immediately becomes due. The organization will then seek a waiver of the loan covenant, or the debtor will have the ability to demand immediate payment and may, in some instances, have the ability literally to shut down the organization and seize assets to collect the debt.

that does not accurately portray their economic substance. Fourth, poor financial results may lead management to focus its attention on *financing or finance-type solutions* to problems to the detriment of company operations.

A CPA firm will conduct a thorough analysis of a client's unaudited financial statements as a basis for identifying accounts that are more likely to be misstated. For example, if the company's gross margin increases from 35 percent to 45 percent with no discernible changes in operation, it is likely that either the cost of goods sold or sales are misstated. The most common approach to assist the auditor in identifying potential misstatements is to perform financial statement analysis using ratio and trend techniques. The auditor must be able to analyze significant changes in account balances or ratios and assess the likely cause of the changes, including the likelihood that an account balance is misstated. An example of such an approach is shown in the Financial Statement Analysis Illustration. Often the auditor will compare the client's results with those of other companies in the same industry to uncover potential problems. The auditors will also read industry trade journals to find out more about the company's products and the economic outlook for them.

Existence of Related-Party Transactions

A related party is an entity that is owned or controlled by a client. Many organizations, particularly small, closely held companies, engage in **related-party transactions.** Such transactions are *not* per se illegal or undesirable, but they can be used to portray a financial result that could be misleading to outside users if not separately disclosed. Common examples of related-party transactions include these:

1. The sole owner of a corporation sets up a leasing partnership (owner and spouse) and leases all equipment to the corporation.
2. One controlled entity sells its partially finished products to another separate, but commonly controlled, entity that finishes the products and sells them back to the first entity.
3. A corporation controlled by one individual sells its receivables to a separate corporation controlled by the same individual.
4. A corporation transfers its debt to a partnership with the same owners of the corporation and in return receives an equity investment from the partnership.

These, and similar, related-party transactions abound. Some are motivated by tax planning considerations. Related-party transactions can be risky because (1) without management's cooperation, they can be difficult to identify; (2) they can be manipulated to produce misleading financial statements; and (3) the business purpose of such transactions can be easily obscured.

The auditor must plan the audit to detect all material related-party transactions to ensure that the financial statements contain disclosures describing the nature of the transactions, the parties and dollar amounts involved, and any significant terms such as interest rates substantially below market rates, buy-back, or other contingency provisions. Auditors use a variety of procedures to learn of the existence of significant related-party transactions. One approach focuses on identifying related parties and documenting transactions with them. A second approach involves examining large, potentially unusual transactions to determine whether related parties are involved. Selected auditing procedures* would include the following:

*AU 334 contains a detailed list of potential auditing procedures.

Illustration

EXAMPLES OF FINANCIAL STATEMENT ANALYSIS TO IDENTIFY RISK AREAS

The auditor often performs an overview financial analysis of a company, similar to one that might be performed by a financial analyst at a bank, to understand the risks associated with a client or potential client. Often this analysis is fairly simple and utilizes ratio and trend analysis to assist in identifying risks. Most of this analysis can be incorporated within spreadsheets and will be routinely performed on most audit engagements.

This ratio and trend analysis is generally carried out at three levels:

1. Comparison of client data with industry data.
2. Comparison of client data with similar prior period data.
3. Comparison of preliminary client data with expectations developed from industry trends, client budgets, other account balances, or other bases of expectations.

Comparison with Industry Data

A comparison of client data with industry data may identify potential problems. For example, if the average collection period for accounts receivable in an industry is 43 days but the client's average collection period is 65 days, this might indicate problems with product quality or credit risk. Or a bank's concentration of loans in a particular industry may indicate greater problems if that industry is encountering economic problems.

Financial service companies such as Dun and Bradstreet, Dow Jones Information Services, and Robert Morris Associates accumulate financial information for thousands of companies and compile the data for different lines of businesses. Many CPA firms purchase these publications as a basis for making industry comparisons. In some instances, a CPA firm may develop its own database based on its clients.

One potential limitation to utilizing industry data is that such data might not be directly comparable to the client. Companies may be quite different but still classified within one broad industry. Also, other companies in the industry may use dif-

- Making inquiries of management regarding the existence of such transactions and the company's approach to identifying related-party transactions.
- Reviewing prior year audit work papers for agreements entered into with related parties and existence of related-party transactions identified earlier.
- Making inquiries of the predecessor auditors about previous related-party transactions and management's treatment of such transactions, especially any attempts to conceal them or prevent their disclosure.
- Reviewing previous financial statements and, when appropriate, reports filed with the SEC.
- Reviewing stockholder lists for identification of related parties.
- Making inquiries within the business and professional community in which the client operates.
- Reviewing minutes of board of director meetings for evidence of authorization for agreements with related parties.
- Reviewing unusual transactions, particularly those near year-end or the end of quarters to determine whether they are related-party transactions.

ferent accounting principles than the client (for example, LIFO versus FIFO).

Comparison with Previous Year Data

Simple ratio analysis prepared as a routine part of planning an audit can highlight potential problems as well. The auditor often develops ratios on asset turnover, liquidity, and product line profitability to search for potential signals of risk. For example, an inventory turnover ratio might indicate that a particular product line had a turnover of 8.2 for the past three years but only 3.1 this year. The change may indicate potential obsolescence, realizability problems, or errors in the accounting records.

Comparison with Expectations

The development of informed expectations and a critical appraisal of client performance in relationship to those expectations is fundamental to a risk analysis approach to auditing. The auditor needs to understand developments in the client's industry, general economic factors, and the client's strategic development plans to generate informed expectations about client results. Critical analysis based on these expectations could lead the auditor to detect many material misstatements. Fundamental questions arising from expectations might be as simple as these:

- Why is this company experiencing such a rapid growth in insurance sales when its product depends on an ever-rising stock market, and the stock market has been declining for the past three years? (See the reference to Equity Funding in Chapter 4.)
- Why is this company experiencing rapid sales growth when the rest of the industry is showing a downturn?
- Why is a bank client's loan repayments on a more current basis than are similar banks operating in the same region with the same type of customers?

Much of this analysis is conducted prior to beginning the audit. However, it is important to understand that *risk analysis continues throughout the audit engagement*. The auditor incorporates new information to revise previous risk assessments continuously as the audit progresses.

- Providing all of the audit staff with a list of known related parties so they can be alert to any transactions between such parties.

Change in Auditors

As discussed in Chapter 5, an organization might change auditing firms for many good reasons. These range from dissatisfaction with the services of the previous firm, lower audit fees offered by the new firm, inability of the previous firm to provide services needed as the company grows, or a company policy to rotate auditors every so many years.* On the other hand, a change in auditors could signal potential problems. For example, there might be disagreements on the proper accounting for a controversial transaction. Or the previous auditor might have discovered a material misstatement or even a fraud.

SEC or Other Regulatory Investigation of the Organization

The auditor *must* understand the regulatory environment in which the client functions to determine the potential effects of regulation on the firm and its accounting

*Some U.S. companies have adopted a policy to rotate their CPA firms every few years. They believe this helps (1) to lower audit fees, (2) to ensure auditor independence, and (3) to bring a fresh business approach to the audit. The Canadian banking industry mandates that auditors be rotated on banks every few years.

system. For example, the approach taken by the Environmental Protection Agency in cleaning up hazardous waste material disposals could dramatically affect the adequacy of the client's accrual for hazardous waste clean-up costs.

Nature of the Industry

Each industry is subject to risks that the auditor needs to understand. Some industries, such as the savings and loan industry, might be the subject of political and financial attention. Some industries are characterized by rapid product changes or significant competitive threats. Others may be subject to stringent governmental regulation. The auditor must have sufficient industry expertise to assess risks and efficiently and effectively conduct the audit. If the auditor does not have such expertise, the CPA firm must be committed to develop such expertise as part of accepting the audit engagement.

Other Issues Unique to the Client

A number of other issues unique to the client should be assessed as part of every audit engagement. These include company dependence on one or two key products, the introduction of new products, the involvement of the company in highly suspect *financial deals*, or a high amount of turnover in key executive positions. The client may be the subject of a corporate "takeover" that focuses increased attention on the integrity of the company's financial statements. An acquiring company will be critical of potential overstatement of inventories or understatement of liabilities. Companies have sometimes manipulated the financial statements to meet stock market expectations, such as published forecasts of earnings. Significant problems encountered in prior year audits may continue during the current audit.

Gathering Information on Client and Engagement Risk

Knowledge of the client and industry should be obtained prior to beginning each audit. Some of the approaches utilized by auditors in obtaining such information include these:

- Reviewing financial filings with regulatory agencies.
- Reviewing the financial press and industry trade magazines to understand significant developments affecting the industry and the recording of financial statement items.
- Reviewing prior year audit working papers or discussing the previous engagement with predecessor auditors.
- Discussing significant developments with management and the audit committee, including their plans for the upcoming year.
- Reviewing the client's budget for the next year.
- Touring the client's production and operational facilities.
- Reviewing important debt covenant agreements.
- Reviewing pertinent government regulations.

Review of Financial Filings

Public corporations whose securities are traded on a stock exchange or on the over-the-counter market must file annual reports with the Securities and Exchange Commission. In addition to the annual financial statements, these reports contain other information useful to planning an audit, such as a list of large shareholders, a discussion of management compensation programs, and detailed information on operations. In addition, whenever the company files registration statements for offering new debt or equity to the public, it must file a prospectus with the SEC containing similar information as well as an assessment of company and industry risks and prospects.

Review of Financial Press and Industry Trade Magazines

Auditors often subscribe to industry trade magazines such as *Automotive Weekly*, *Retail Management*, or *Advertising Age*, which contain in-depth articles on the industry. Most auditing firms regularly clip financial press articles about their clients. In addition, many public accounting firms subscribe to computerized data retrieval services such as the National Automated Accounting Research System (NAARS) service operated by Mead Data Central.

Review of Prior Year Audit Working Papers

Prior year working papers identify important issues that were addressed during previous audits and normally highlight the areas that the auditor should investigate in the current year. For example, determining the actual obsolescence or realizable value of some products is often difficult. The engagement team on the previous audit may have raised concerns about the valuation of particular inventory items that should be reevaluated during the current audit. Issues related to the accrual of liabilities and estimates of the allowance for doubtful accounts or other loss reserves should also be reviewed.

Review of Significant Developments with Management

Senior management is a primary source of information on most audit engagements. Executives deal with the problems of the business and develop plans for its future. They are familiar with new product developments, problems with product introductions, financing arrangements, and major contingencies facing the organization. Even if no question of management integrity has arisen, the auditor cannot rely solely on the information represented by management. The auditor will need to corroborate management representations throughout the course of the audit.

Review of Client's Budget

The budget represents management's plan of activities for the forthcoming year. As such, it provides insight on management's approach to operations and to the risks the organization may face. The auditor looks for significant deviations from budgets such as planned disposition of a line of business, significant research or promotion costs associated with a new product introduction, new financing or capital requirements, changes in compensation or product costs due to union agreements, and significant additions to property, plant, and equipment. The budget, then, can be a very useful tool for analyzing organizational directions and potential areas of concern for the viability of the business.

Tour of Client's Plant and Operations Facilities

A tour of the client's production and distribution facilities provides good insight on potential audit issues. Cost centers can be visualized. Shipping and receiving procedures, inventory controls, potentially obsolete production, and possible inefficiencies can all be observed. Although the information from such a tour is not considered persuasive audit evidence, it serves to heighten the auditor's awareness of company procedures, to increase the auditor's understanding of operations, and to make concrete items that are otherwise only seen as financial exhibits.

Similarly, the auditor should tour the data processing center and meet with the center's director to understand the computerization of company operations. The role of the computer system is likely to extend significantly beyond that of the accounting system, and the auditor will need to assess that role in planning for the accumulation of audit evidence and in determining whether the organization is subject to unusual or uninsured risks should the computer system fail.

Review Important Debt Covenants and Board of Director Minutes

Most bond issues and other debt agreements contain covenants, often referred to as *debt covenants*, that the organization must adhere to or risk default on the debt. Common forms of debt covenants will often include restrictions on the payment of dividends, requirements for maintaining minimum current ratios, or requiring annual audits. For a continuing audit client, such information will normally be included in a **permanent file,** an audit working paper file containing a summary of items of continuing audit significance. In addition to **debt covenants,** the permanent file contains highlights from board of director meetings, banking information, standing company policies, corporate charter and bylaws, and other information of a relatively permanent nature.

Review Relevant Governmental Regulations and Client's Legal Obligations

Few industries are unaffected by governmental regulation, and much of that regulation affects the audit. An example is the need to determine potential liabilities associated with clean-up costs defined by the Environmental Protection Agency.

Both the auditor's engagement risk and audit risk may be affected by the nature of the client's current legal problems, if any. The auditor normally seeks information on litigation risks through an inquiry of management but follows up that inquiry with an analysis of litigation prepared by the client's in-house counsel. In addition, the auditor monitors press reports of litigation involving the client to determine whether contingent liabilities ought to be recognized.

Risk Analysis and Audit Planning

Audits are planned to minimize audit risk. Risk analysis provides an opportunity for the auditor to pinpoint account balances more susceptible to misstatement. The risk assessment initially affects the decision on whether to accept or retain an audit client. Beyond the basic question of accepting the audit engagement, risk assessment influences the following:

1. *Assigning personnel to the audit.* Relatively speaking, a more risky audit engagement should have more experienced personnel assigned to it than a less risky engagement.

Practical Application

SMALL BUSINESSES

The approach to gathering information on audit risk for small, non public clients is similar to that described in this chapter, but some significant differences exist. Because these companies do not file reports with the SEC, that source of information is not available. It is unlikely that there will be national press coverage about these clients. But equivalent local sources as well as contacts with community or regional business leaders can provide valuable information. These sources include the local press, organizations such as service clubs and the Chamber of Commerce, and bankers, lawyers, and other businesspeople. Small clients may or may not use budgets; for those that do not, management can provide qualitative information on items generally quantified in a budget.

Management often owns all, or a significant portion, of these companies. The owner/manager may be motivated to understate income to reduce tax liability rather than overstate income to improve the "market price" of its stock. Therefore, audits of small businesses often must focus on tax considerations.

In establishing audit risk, several considerations are unique to small businesses:

- The degree to which owners are active in its management.
- The size and diversity of the ownership group.
- The existence of significant disagreements among owners.
- The degree of expertise management brings to operating the business.

When the owners are not active in management, when they have significant disagreements, or when they lack business experience, audit risk should be set lower than normal.

2. *Searching for fraud.* A preliminary assessment of the environmental risk and fraud potential influence the auditor in planning effective procedures in uncovering material fraud.
3. *Determining nature, timing, and extent of audit tests.* The actual procedures employed during the audit and the timing of those procedures will be influenced by the audit risk established by the auditor. For audits in which the audit risk is set lower than normal, the auditor concentrates more of the audit work at the year-end rather at interim dates. The auditor pinpoints the procedures for high-risk areas and allocates materiality accordingly.

Other Factors Assessed in Planning an Audit

The analysis thus far has focused on identifying risk factors that may significantly affect the nature and timing of the audit process. Most likely, though, other features of the client may affect the amount of audit work performed, both positively and negatively. Before finalizing the overall plan, the auditor will consider the following factors:

- The audit committee's special concerns or its requests for special investigations.
- The existence and effectiveness of the client's internal audit department.
- The number and diversity of locations where significant assets are used or where significant accounting takes place.

Illustration

APPLICATION OF AUDIT PLANNING AND AUDIT RISK

As a manager, you are given the task to develop a preliminary audit plan for a potential client. The client is a fast-growing electronics components manufacturer whose stock is listed on the American Stock Exchange. The partner has told you that she believes the client may be viewed as one for which audit risk should be set low and that the potential for future growth and success with the company is good.

Your preliminary investigation of audit risk and client knowledge yields the following information:

Communication with Predecessor Auditor

The predecessor auditors and the client disagreed on the accounting for stock compensation, which the auditors believed should have been accounted for as salary expense. The client took the position that without any ruling by the FASB, it was not required to be accounted for as an expense. Additionally, the client had identified inventory by product classes and had managed LIFO layers to smooth reported earnings. The client had also capitalized a large amount of expenditures associated with the promotion of a new product.

A review of prior year working papers indicates that a number of adjustments were made to the financial statements. Additionally, the auditor had identified a number of control weaknesses for the past three years, none of which seem to have been addressed.

Review of Industry Trade Journals

The company has been recognized as a pioneer but is currently at a crossroads with its product mix. It had been built through its domination with a leading state-of-the-art product. However, manufacturers have brought out clones at lower prices, and other, larger competitors have more advanced products in the market place. The company has rushed a new product to market, but initial product reviews indicate performance problems. The client warrants its products for one year.

Review of Filings with the SEC

The SEC filings describe the company's products and its marketplace risk. Additionally, the filings indicate that a significant amount of management compensation is tied to stock options and reported earnings. Management is dominated by J. Don Kloetzke, who owns 20 percent of the outstanding stock. Additionally, two senior management positions are filled by Kloetzke's brother and daughter.

Interviews with Management

Management is optimistic about its prospects. However, the interview with the controller raises suspicions about the quality of the accounting staff. There seems to be a heavy emphasis on producing results, but little attention is being paid to addressing the control problems identified by the predecessor auditors. Management believes that problems reported in the press are overblown and will be solved by increasing sales of its new products.

Your review of the minutes of audit committee meetings yields very little useful information. The committee seldom meets, and there is no indication it has addressed the control weaknesses identified by the previous auditors. The audit manager raises this issue with the predecessor auditors, who share their view that the audit committee is weak and is essentially an extension of management even though members are outside directors.

The client is heavily computerized but controls appear weak. The staff seems overworked and is constantly being challenged to develop new reports for management to present to financial groups.

Analysis of Previous Financial Statements and Debt Covenants

The company financed its growth with a significant amount of convertible debt. The debt restricts the company's ability to pay dividends and requires certain debt/equity and current ratios. Current cash does not appear to be sufficient to meet the company's needs.

Identification of Risk Factors and Affect on Audit

A number of risk factors are identified by the manager for this engagement. These include the following:

- Disagreements with the predecessor auditors on accounting principles.
- Manipulation of accounting by management to increase reported earnings (manipulating LIFO layers).
- Company reliance on a new product and increased competitive pressure.
- Significant control weaknesses that are not addressed by a weak accounting staff.
- An ineffective audit committee.
- Management compensation tied to stock market performance of the company's stock.
- Increased competition.
- Potential financial problems associated with cash flow needs and debt covenants.

Effect on Audit Planning

The audit manager concludes that the client is "high risk," meaning that there is a high engagement risk associated with the client. The manager determines that the audit engagement, if accepted, should be conducted using the lowest level of audit risk specified in the firm's manuals and assesses environmental risk as high.

In addition, the manager makes the following recommendations to the audit partner:

1. The engagement should be staffed with experienced auditors who have either had experience in this industry or experience with other high risk, first-time audits.
2. Materiality levels for planning the audit should be set low.
3. The audit approach should concentrate on direct tests of the account balances rather than relying on management integrity or the control system.
4. The audit team should monitor the marketplace and product reports of the client's industry for any new outside objective evidence concerning the client's products.
5. The audit team should develop a comprehensive plan to ensure that product returns are recorded appropriately and in a timely manner and that the client has sufficient procedures to repair goods before shipping them back to customers.
6. Detailed analytical review (comparison of trends in sales, etc.) should be performed to search for any unusual trends.
7. A significant portion of the audit time budget should be assigned to inventories and accounts receivable because of the problems with manipulation of the LIFO inventory, potential inventory obsolescence, and potential product quality problems.
8. A computer audit specialist should perform an in-depth analysis of data processing controls and in the development of audit procedures.
9. The client should be billed monthly for all work to date. Any significant problems with payment should be addressed immediately by the partner, including potential withdrawal from the audit. The engagement letter should be expanded to address this latter point specifically.
10. The audit should be performed with a heightened awareness of the necessity to review complex contracts or potential related-party transactions.
11. The audit team should meet prior to the engagement to discuss the nature of audit risks and should meet regularly during the audit to ensure that appropriate follow-up is given to any unusual transactions.

- Previous audit coverage, such as number of locations visited, last time visited, and audit problems encountered at each location.

Audit Committee Requests

As noted, the auditor should meet with the audit committee prior to beginning the audit to determine whether it has any special requests or special concerns it wishes to have addressed during the audit. The auditor can determine whether such requests can be met by the application of already planned auditing procedures or whether audit procedures need to be extended.

Existence and Effectiveness of the Internal Audit Department

Many audit clients have effective internal auditing departments. Recent research shows that many internal audit departments are doing sophisticated computer and operational auditing across all aspects of an organization. In addition, the internal auditor's work may complement that planned by the external auditor. If the internal auditing department has sufficient independence from management to be objective and is evaluated by the external auditor as highly competent, the external auditor can benefit by coordinating the work with the internal auditor. The external auditor may be able to rely on the work performed by the internal auditor in some areas and complement that work by performing similar tests. Further, the internal audit department may provide direct assistance in carrying out the external auditor's audit program. In such cases, the external auditor must review and supervise the audit work as if it were performed by the external audit team. On many engagements, the fees bid to conduct the audit assume a significant amount of coordination with the internal audit function.

Number and Diversity of Locations

Frequently, audits must be coordinated with other offices of the auditing firm, sometimes on a national basis, and in many cases, on a global basis. The auditor must assess risk associated with various locations and the potential risk of not auditing all locations or of having the internal audit group perform limited audits at some locations. Additionally, the auditor must consider the risk of misstatement that could be introduced by auditing only selected accounts at selected locations. In essence, the auditor is assessing risk and materiality across locations and account balances in making such a judgment.

Previous Audit Coverage and Audit Working Papers

Analysis of previous audits, including audit coverage at various locations, is helpful in identifying areas in which misstatements have routinely occurred. Additionally, many auditors rotate locations visited if the company's environmental risk is assessed as being low. This information needs to be evaluated while planning the audit to ensure that risk areas are appropriately identified. A review of previous audit working papers can yield important information such as the following:

- The nature of previous audit adjustments (cause and account balances).
- The auditor's assessment of control risk by classes of transactions based on previous tests of the client's system and the nature of misstatements found.
- The allocation of time to audit areas and any problems associated with the audit area, including lack of client cooperation.

- Existence of related-party transactions.
- Other items of continuing audit significance found in the permanent file maintained for the client.

Summary

Proper audit planning is the key to a successful audit approach. During the planning phase, the auditor must establish audit risk. In addition, the auditor must also assess the engagement risk related to the acceptance of a particular audit engagement. That planning begins with an assessment of materiality for a client, which is directly tied to the financial decisions of important users; thus, the auditor must fully understand the types of decisions that important users will be relying on the financial statements in making.

The auditor must be thoroughly knowledgeable about the company, its industry, its products, its financing, and its plans to assess the risks associated with the client and to plan an effective and efficient audit. Automated news services can assist the auditors in keeping up to date with changes in the industry. However, the auditor must still gather key elements of information from company's management on plans and assessments of risk affecting the organization and then plan the audit to corroborate management's representations during the course of the audit.

Significant Terms

audit risk The risk that the auditors may unknowingly fail to qualify their opinion on financial statements that are materially misstated; audit risk refers to the likelihood that the auditor will issue an unqualified opinion on financial statements that are materially misstated.

control risk The risk that a material misstatement could occur but would not be prevented or detected on a timely basis by the organization's control structure, including specific control procedures applied to the recording of financial statement items.

debt covenant An agreement between an entity and its lender that places limitations on the organization; usually associated with debentures or large credit lines, common limitations include restrictions on dividend payments, requirements for a specified working capital or debt/equity ratio, and annual audits of company's financial statements to be furnished to the lender. Failure to satisfy may result in loans or bonds becoming immediately due and payable or redeemable.

detection risk The risk that an auditor's direct test of account balances will lead to the conclusion that the financial statements are free from material misstatement when in fact the statements contain material misstatements.

engagement risk The risk, beyond audit risk, associated with a particular audit client such that the association with the audit client may result in financial losses to the auditing firm; aspects include the likelihood that the client may fail or that the client's senior management lacks integrity.

environmental risk The combination of inherent risk and control risk, referred to thus because it is a risk that the auditor cannot control but can only assess.

inherent risk The susceptibility of transactions to be recorded in error, assuming there were no related internal accounting controls.

management integrity The general honesty of management and motivation for truthfulness (or lack thereof) in financial reporting.

materiality The magnitude of an omission or misstatement of accounting information that, in the light of surrounding circumstances, makes it probable that the judgment of a reasonable person relying on the information would have been changed or influenced by the omission or misstatement.

permanent file A working paper file that contains information that will be of continuing interest to the audit. The file generally contains information such as debt covenants, corporate charters, and highlights of board of director's meetings.

planning materiality The assessment of materiality by the auditor on the financial statements as a basis for planning the nature, extent, and timing of audit procedures.

related-party transaction A transaction with a commonly controlled entity such that the transaction cannot be viewed as an "arm's-length" transaction.

risk-based auditing An overall audit approach whereby the auditing firm assesses key factors of risk that may affect a particular audit client and then adjusts the auditing procedures to emphasize these areas. In some cases, the risk-based analysis leads an auditor not to accept a particular client.

Review Questions

B–Materiality: The Basis for Audit Planning

6–1 Define the accounting concept of *materiality*. How does the concept of the reasonable person affect the auditor's determination of materiality?

6–2 Identify four major classes of financial statement users. For each group identified, (1) indicate how differences between the groups might affect materiality and (2) how those differences might affect the importance of the presentation of individual items included in financial statements. How does the auditor reconcile potential differences between groups in determining planning materiality for an audit engagement?

6–3 What are the three critical dimensions of materiality? What criteria does the auditor utilize in evaluating the materiality of an item within each dimension?

6–4 Given the following potential errors by the auditor, explain why one is more important than the other:

a. The auditor issues an unqualified audit opinion on financial statements that are materially misstated.

b. The audit evidence gathered on the audit supports a conclusion that the financial statements are materially in error, when in fact, they are not materially in error.

C–The Profession's Audit Risk Model

6–5 Why are audit planning and gaining an understanding of the specific risks associated with a client crucial to the audit function?

6–6 How are client acceptance and engagement risk related? What are the primary factors the auditor should review in determining whether to accept a potential audit client?

6–7 How does engagement risk for an audit client differ from audit risk for that same client? How are the two concepts related?

6–8 Define the following terms and briefly indicate their importance to planning an audit engagement: *audit risk, inherent risk, control risk, environmental risk,* and *detection risk.*

6–9 A recent graduate of an accounting program went to work for a large international accounting firm and noted that the firm sets audit risk at 0.05 for all major engagements. What does a literal interpretation of setting audit risk at 0.05 mean? How could an audit firm set audit risk at 0.05 (i.e., what assumptions must the auditor make in the audit risk model to set audit risk at 0.05)?

6–10 What is inherent risk? How can the auditor measure it? What are the implications for the audit risk model if the auditor assesses inherent risk at less than 1.0?

6–11 What is control risk? How does the auditor assess control risk on an engagement? How are the concepts of inherent risk and control risk related?

6–12 What are the major limitations of the audit risk model? How should those limitations affect the auditor's implementation of the audit risk model?

D–Implementing Audit Risk Concepts

6–13 This chapter, as well as previous chapters, stated that management integrity is one of the crucial factors the auditor must evaluate when planning and conducting an audit. What is management integrity? How does an auditor go about assessing it?

6–14 Janice Johnson is an experienced auditor in charge of a number of clients. Her approach to an audit is to plan the audit without referring to previous year's working papers to ensure that a fresh approach will be taken in the audit. Explain why Johnson may want to examine the permanent file, as well as other selected audit working papers, as part of her risk analysis and audit planning.

6–15 Explain how ratio analysis and industry comparisons can be useful to the auditor in identifying potential risk on an audit engagement. How can such analysis also help the auditor plan the audit?

6–16 In preparing the audit for a new client, the manager has asked the auditor to read the revolving loan contract with the First National Bank and the bond indenture. Identify the information that can be obtained from these sources and how the information will be utilized in the audit.

6–17 What background information might be useful to the auditor in planning the audit to assist in determining whether the client has potential obsolescence or receivables problems? Identify the various sources the auditor would utilize to develop this background information.

6–18 On accepting a new manufacturing client, the auditor usually arranges to take a tour of the manufacturing plant. Assuming that the client has one major manufacturing plant, identify the information the auditor might obtain during the tour that will help in planning and conducting the audit.

6–19 What is a related-party transaction? How does the accounting for such transactions differ from other transactions? For most organizations, are there legitimate business purposes for related-party transactions? Explain.

6–20 What two primary approaches does the auditor use to identify related-party transactions? Are both necessary, or can the auditor choose between them? Explain.

6–21 Explain how computerized technology can assist the auditor in identifying risk areas for a specific audit client. Identify three or four types that might be utilized and indicate how that technology might assist the auditor.

6–22 How might the auditor's approach to setting audit risk in a small business differ from the auditor's approach in a large business whose stock is publicly traded?

6–23 How does the auditor's assessment of audit risk affect (1) the assignment of personnel to an engagement and (2) the auditor's responsibility for conducting the audit to search for material fraud?

6–24 The audit firm has just obtained a new privately held client. The client has no debt outstanding, and the audit report is to be distributed only to the sole shareholder. The audit, however, was obtained through a competitive bid process, and the firm will not be able to realize standard billings unless the audit is budgeted for fewer hours than normally required for a client of its size. The firm's policy is that audit risk should be set at 0.05 for all engagements unless the partner believes that sufficient engagement risk exists to lower it below 0.05. Clearly, in the manager's view, there is very little engagement risk associated with the client. Consequently, he has proposed that the audit be planned with an audit risk of 0.10. Explain whether such a proposal is acceptable.

6–25 Is audit risk something that is "evaluated" as part of the audit planning process or is it something that is "established" at the conclusion of the audit planning process? Explain.

Multiple Choice Questions

6–26 Audit risk is associated with

a. Issuing an unqualified opinion on materially misstated financial statements even if the auditor does not get sued because of the misstatement.

b. Issuing an unqualified opinion on materially misstated financial statements when the auditor incurs a loss because of a lawsuit brought against the firm.

c. Incurring a loss related to the attestation function performed for an audit client.
d. Incurring extra, and costly, work on an audit engagement because the initial work performed indicated a potential misstatement even though such a misstatement did not exist.

6–27 Materiality of an item for financial statement presentation can be assessed only when the auditor considers
a. The potential impact of a misstatement of the item on important user groups.
b. The dollar magnitude of the potential misstatement or omission of the item.
c. The qualitative nature of the item.
d. All of the above.

6–28 Dollar misstatements of a relatively small magnitude, such as one percent of net income, can be material because
a. Psychological research shows that individuals are sensitive to changes as small as one percent and that such changes can affect their judgments.
b. The misstatement may indicate a trend in a subsidiary or may affect a qualitatively important item.
c. The auditor is responsible for detecting fraud as long as it represents more than one percent of net income.
d. All errors are material to some users.
e. All of the above.

6–29 If the auditor knows that there may be a lack of management integrity, the auditor should
a. Increase planning materiality for the audit engagement.
b. Leave planning materiality unchanged but lower audit risk.
c. Decrease planning materiality and consider lowering audit risk.
d. Leave planning materiality the same but consider steps to decrease engagement risk.

6–30 Which of the following combinations of engagement risk, audit risk, and materiality would lead to the most audit work?

	Engagement Risk	*Audit Risk*	*Materiality*
a.	Low	High	High
b.	Moderate	Lowest	Lowest
c.	Low	Moderate	Lowest
d.	High	High	High

6–31 Which of the following would *not* be considered a limitation of the audit risk model?
a. The model treats each risk component as a separate and independent factor when some of the factors are actually related.

b. Inherent risk is difficult, if not impossible, to formally assess.

c. It is difficult, if not impossible, to formally assess either control or detection risk.

d. The model provides an overall framework for determining the allocation of audit work to risk areas.

*6–32 Which of the following models expresses the general relationship of risks associated with the auditor's evaluation of control risk (*CR*), inherent risk (*IR*), and audit risk (*AR*) that would lead the auditor to conclude that additional substantive tests of details of an account balance are *not* necessary?

	IR	*CR*	*AR*
a.	20%	40%	10%
b.	20%	60%	5%
c.	10%	70%	4.5%
d.	30%	40%	5.5%

*6–33 Analytical procedures used in planning an audit should focus on identifying

a. Material weakness in the internal control structure.

b. The predictability of financial data from individual transactions.

c. The various assertions embodied in the financial statements.

d. Areas that may represent specific risks relevant to the audit.

6–34 Comparing client data with industry data and with its own data for the previous year, the auditor finds that the number of days' sales in accounts receivable for this year is 66 for the client, 42 for the industry average, and 38 for the previous year. The increase in this ratio could indicate all of the following *except:*

a. Fictitious sales during the current year.

b. A policy to promote sales through less strenuous credit policies.

c. Potential problems with product quality and the ability of the client to warrant the products.

d. Increased production of products for expected increases in demand.

6–35 Before accepting a new client, the auditor decides to communicate with the predecessor auditor. Which of the following items would normally *not* be covered in the communication with the predecessor auditor?

a. Any concerns the predecessor auditor might have about the integrity of management.

b. Any disagreements on accounting principles between the predecessor and management.

c. The predecessor's assessment of audit risk for the client.

d. The existence of scope limitations on the predecessor's audit and the rationale for them.

*Adapted from the Uniform CPA examination or the Certified Internal Auditor examination.

Discussion and Research Questions

6–36 (Audit Assessment of Materiality) The audit report provides reasonable assurance that the financial statements are free from material misstatements. The auditor is put in a difficult situation because materiality is defined from a user viewpoint, but the auditor must assess materiality in planning the audit to ensure that sufficient audit work is performed to detect material misstatements.

Required:

a. Define *materiality* as used in accounting and auditing.

b. Identify the three major dimensions of materiality and discuss their interaction. Give an example of an item at each end of the continuum for each of the three dimensions.

c. Once the auditor develops an assessment of materiality, can it change during the course of the audit? Explain. If it does change, what is the implication of a change for audit work that has already been completed? Explain.

*6–37 (Sources of Information for Audit Planning) In early summer, an auditor is advised of a new assignment as the senior auditor for Lancer Company, a major client for the past five years. She is given the engagement letter for the audit covering the current calendar year and a list of personnel assigned to the engagement. It is her responsibility to plan and supervise the field work for the engagement.

Required:

Discuss the necessary preparation and planning for the Lancer Company annual audit *prior* to beginning fieldwork at the client's office. In your discussion, include the sources that should be consulted, the type of information that should be sought, the preliminary plans and preparation that should be made for the fieldwork, and any actions that should be taken relative to the staff assigned to the engagement.

6–38 (Audit Risk and Materiality) Audit risk and materiality should be considered when planning and performing an examination of financial statements in accordance with generally accepted auditing standards. Audit risk and materiality should also be considered in determining the nature, timing, and extent of auditing procedures and in evaluating the results of those procedures.

Required:

a. 1. Define *audit risk.*

   2. Describe the components of inherent risk, control risk, and detection risk.

   3. Explain how these components are interrelated.

b. 1. Define *materiality.*

   2. Describe the relationship between materiality for planning purposes and audit risk.

6–39 (Related-Party Transactions) Fitzpatrick & Roberts, CPAs, are auditing the financial statements of Lots of Lumber, Inc., a chain of lumberyards whose stock is traded over the counter. The company went public three years ago and, according to management, is changing auditors because it believes that it needs better service. Approximately 25 percent of the company's stock is held by the Clark family, who dominate senior management positions. This is the first-year audit of the company by Fitzpatrick & Roberts. Because the Clark family is prominent in the business community, the auditor is aware that they also own a number of other companies separately, some of which he believes do significant amounts of business with Lots of Lumber.

Required:

a. Define *related-party transactions* as used in accounting and explain the disclosure standards required for them and the rationale for such disclosures.
b. How do related-party transactions differ from parent-subsidiary type transactions? Why is the distinction important?
c. Identify several types of related-party transactions that could take place in the environment described here.
d. Describe the audit procedures that Fitzpatrick & Roberts should use to identify related-party relationships and transactions.
e. Assume that on identifying the scope of related-party transactions, management asserts that the transactions took place at the same terms that would have prevailed if they were with nonrelated parties, and therefore it does not want separate disclosure. What actions should the auditor take?

*6–40 (Analytical Review in Planning an Audit) Analytical review can be an extremely powerful tool in identifying potential problem areas on an audit. Analytical review can consist of trend and ratio analysis and can be performed by comparisons within the same company or comparisons across industry. The following information shows the past two periods of results for a company and a comparison with industry data for the same period.

Analytical Data for Jones Manufacturing

	Prior Period (000 omitted)	Percent of Sales	Current Period (000 omitted)	Percent of Sales	Percent Change	Industry Average as of Percent of Sales
Sales	$10,000	100%	$11,000	100%	10%	100%
Inventory	$2,000	20%	$3,250	29.5%	57.5%	22.5%
Cost of goods sold	$6,000	60%	$6,050	55%	0.83%	59.5%
Accounts payable	$1,200	12%	$1,980	18%	65%	14.5%
Sales commissions	$500	5%	$550	5%	10%	Not available
Inventory turnover	6.3	—	4.2	—	(33%)	5.85
Average number of days to collect	39	—	48	—	23%	36
Employee turnover	5%	—	8%	—	60%	4%
Return on investment	14%	—	14.3%	—		13.8%
Debt/Equity	35%	—	60%	—	71%	30%

Required:

a. What are the advantages and limitations of comparing company data with industry data during the planning portion of an audit?

b. From the preceding data, identify potential risk areas and explain why they represent potential risk. Briefly indicate how the risk analysis should affect the planning of the audit engagement.

6–41 (Analytical Review and Planning the Audit) Following are the calculations of several key ratios for Indianola Pharmaceutical Company, a maker of proprietary and prescription drugs. The company is publicly held and is considered a small- to medium-size pharmaceutical company. Approximately 80 percent of its sales have been in prescription drugs; the remaining 20 percent are in medical supplies normally found in a drugstore. The primary purpose of the auditor's calculations is to identify potential risk areas for the upcoming audit. The auditor recognizes that some of the data may signal the need to gather other industry or company-specific data.

A number of the company's drugs are patented. Its number one selling drug, Anecillin, which will come off of patent in two years, has accounted for approximately 20 percent of the company's sales during the past five years.

Indianola Pharmaceutical Ratio Analysis

Ratio	Current Year	One Year Previous	Two Years Previous	Three Years Previous	Current Industry
Current ratio	1.85	1.89	2.28	2.51	2.13
Quick ratio	0.85	0.93	1.32	1.76	1.40
Interest coverage:					
Times interest earned	1.30	1.45	5.89	6.3	4.50
Days' sales in receivables	109	96	100	72	69
Inventory turnover	2.40	2.21	3.96	5.31	4.33
Days' sales in inventory	152	165	92	69	84
Research & development as a percent of sales	1.3	1.4	1.94	2.03	4.26
Cost of goods sold as percent of sales	38.5	40.2	41.2	43.8	44.5
Debt/Equity ratio	4.85	4.88	1.25	1.13	1.25
Earnings per share	$1.12	$2.50	$4.32	$4.26	n/a
Sales/tangible assets	.68	.64	.89	.87	.99
Sales/total assets	.33	.35	.89	.87	.78
Sales growth over past year	3%	15%	2%	4%	6%

Required:

a. What major conclusions regarding risk can be drawn from the preceding information? State how that risk analysis will be used in planning the audit.

b. Based on the preceding information, what other critical background information might you want to obtain as part of the planning of the audit or would you gather during the conduct of the audit? Briefly indicate the probable sources of the information.

c. Based on the information, what actions likely took place during the immediately preceding year? Explain.

d. Based on the above information and your knowledge of the pharmaceutical industry, identify three potentially important accounting issues the auditor will likely address during the conduct of this audit.

6–42 (Utilizing Financial and Operating Ratios) Ratio analysis often is employed to gain insight into the financial risks associated with an audit client. The calculation of ratios can lead to a better understanding of a firm's financial position and performance. A specific ratio or a number of selected ratios can be calculated and used to measure or evaluate a specific financial or operating characteristic of an audit client.

Required:
For the five financial ratios and four operating ratios listed below

1. Describe how the ratio is calculated.
2. Identify a financial characteristic of a firm that would be measured by an analysis of the ratio.
3. Identify how the auditor would use the information to potentially identify risk areas.
4. Identify a trend in the ratio that would indicate an increase in risk and then indicate the specific effect that such a trend would have on the conduct of the audit. For example, indicate additional audit evidence that should be acquired during the audit, whether planning materiality ought to be changed, or whether any risk factors ought to be changed.

Financial Position Ratios:

a. Current ratio.
b. Quick ratio.
c. Number of days' sales in receivables.
d. Number of days' sales in inventory.
e. Debt/Equity ratio.

Operating Ratios:

f. Gross margin.
g. Net operating margin.
h. Earnings before interest and taxes.
i. Number of times interest earned.

6–43 (Management Integrity and Audit Risk) The auditor needs to assess management integrity as a potential indicator of risk, including the likelihood of management fraud. Although the assessment of management integrity takes place on every audit engagement, it is difficult to do and is not often well documented.

Required:

a. Define *management integrity* and discuss its importance to the auditor in determining the *type* of evidence to be gathered on an audit and the *evaluation* of it.

b. Identify the types of evidence the auditor would gather in making an assessment of the integrity of management. What are sources of each type of evidence?

c. For each of the following situations listed

   1. Indicate whether you believe that the scenario reflects negatively on management integrity and state why.
   2. Indicate how the assessment would affect the auditor's planning of the audit.

Management Scenarios:

a. The owner/manager of a privately held company also owns three other companies. The entities could all be run as one entity, but they engage extensively in related-party transactions to minimize the overall tax burden for the owner/manager.

b. The president of a publicly held company has a reputation as being a "hard nose" with a violent temper. He has been known to fire a divisional manager on the spot if the manager did not achieve profit goals.

c. The financial vice president of a publicly held company has worked her way to the top by gaining a reputation as a great accounting manipulator. She has earned the reputation by being very creative in finding ways to circumvent FASB pronouncements to keep debt off the balance sheet and to manipulate accounting to achieve short-term earnings. After each short-term success, she has moved on to another company to utilize her skills.

d. The president of a small publicly held firm was indicted on tax evasion charges seven years ago. He settled with the IRS and served time doing community service. Since then, he has been considered a pillar of the community and has made significant contributions to local charities. Inquiries of local bankers yield information that he is the partial or controlling owner of a number of corporations that may serve as shells to assist the manager in moving income around to avoid taxes.

e. James J. James is the president of a privately held company that has a community reputation for having dirty facilities. The company also has been accused of illegally dumping waste and failing to meet government standards for worker safety. James responds that his attitude is to meet the minimum requirements of the law and if the government deems that he has not, he will clean up. "Besides," he asserts, "it is good business; it is less costly to clean up only when I have to, even if small fines are involved, than it is to take leadership positions and exceed government standards."

f. Carla C. Charles is the young, dynamic chairman of Golden-Glow Enterprises, a rapidly growing company that makes ceramic specialty items, such as Christmas villages for in-house decorations. Golden-Glow recently went public after five years of 20 percent per year growth. Carla has a reputation for being a fast-living, party-animal type, and the society pages have been full of "extravagant" parties at her home. However, she is well respected as an astute businessperson.

6–44 (Audit Planning: Review of Prior Year Working Papers) It is important that the planning for the current year's audit not be a repeat of "just following last year's program." However, an important part of audit planning is to review the previous year's audit working papers.

Required:
For each of the audit working papers listed below

a. Indicate the type of information the auditor might expect to find that would be useful in identifying various components of audit risk.
b. Indicate how the information would be used by the auditor in planning the audit.

Type of Audit Working Papers:

1. Permanent file.
2. Audit time: Actual and budget.
3. Manager or senior summary memos for each significant audit area.

6–45 (Tour of Manufacturing Plant and Distribution Center) As part of the audit of a new client, you arrange to take a tour of the manufacturing plant and the distribution center. The client is a manufacturer of heavy machinery and is located in the eastern part of the United States. Its distribution center is located in a building adjacent to the manufacturing facility.

Required:
Following is a list of observations the auditor made during the tour of the plant and distribution center. For each observation, indicate

a. The potential audit risk associated with the observation.
b. How the audit should be adjusted for the knowledge of the risk.

Tour of Plant Observations:

1. The auditor notes three separate lines of production for three distinct product lines. Two seem to be quite well automated, but one is seemingly antique.
2. The auditor notes that a large number of production machines are sitting idly outside and that a second line of one of the company's main products is not in operation.
3. The client utilizes a large amount of chemicals. The waste chemicals are stored in vats and barrels in the yard before being shipped for disposal to an independent disposal firm.
4. The distribution center seems busy and messy. Although there appear to be defined procedures, the supervisor indicates that during peak times when orders must be shipped, the priority is to get them shipped. They "catch up" on paper work during slack time.
5. One area of the distribution center contains a number of products that seem to have been there for a long time. They are dusty, and the packaging looks old.
6. A number of products are sitting in a transition room outside the receiving area. The supervisor indicates that the products either have not been

inspected yet, or that they have failed inspection and he is waiting orders on what to do.

7. The receiving area is fairly automated. Many products come packaged in cartons or boxes. The receiving department uses computer scanners to read the contents on a bar code and when bar codes are used, the boxes or containers are moved immediately to the production area in which they will be used.
8. One production line uses just-in-time inventory for its major component products. These goods are received in rail cars that sit just outside the production area. When production begins, the rail cars are moved directly into production. There is no receiving function for these goods.
9. The company uses minimum security procedures at the warehouse. There is a fence around the facilities, but employees and others seem to be able to come and go at ease.

6–46 (Related-Party Transactions) Following is a list of transactions, some of which may require separate disclosure.

Required:

a. For each situation, indicate whether the transaction would be classified as a related-party transaction.
b. If the transaction were not brought to the auditor's attention by management, indicate the type of evidence the auditor would have reviewed to identify the transaction.

Transaction Scenario:

1. Company A sells $5 million of goods to a subsidiary that uses the material in production and sells the finished goods back to Company A.
2. A shoe company has excess shoes. The company's distribution manager and divisional production manager have established a separate company as a factory outlet of the excess. The shoe company sells excess inventory and returned items to this company at heavy discount prices, either at original cost or, in the case of damaged goods, at less than cost.
3. The same shoe company buys leather from a number of different suppliers. The second largest supplier is a company that is owned by the president of the company and his niece.
4. Company A is publicly held but management holds approximately 20 percent of its stock. Company A sells approximately 15 percent of its annual sales to Company B, which acts as a conduit and sells the goods immediately to Company C. Company C is owned by the president of the company.
5. Company ZZ purchased major equipment from a supplier who has agreed to sell the company the land next to the plant that is badly needed for expansion.
6. The Carthage Construction Co. is privately held. It does highway construction. A second company, 50 percent owned by the company, 25 percent owned by management, and 25 percent owned by an independent investor, owns all the equipment the company uses. The construction company uses only equipment from the equipment company and

pays for its use based on the actual number of hours worked. The hourly rental rate is the same as is charged by an independent company in the same region.

7. Company A and Company B are both publicly held. An investor, R.J. Wilson owns approximately 10 percent of each company. After Wilson's investment in the stock of Company B, Company A now purchases approximately one-third of its raw material from Company B. Company A has signed a long-term agreement to acquire the goods from Company B at normal market prices.

6–47 (Coordination with Internal Audit Department) An effective internal audit department enhances an organization's overall control structure and provides opportunities for the external auditor to coordinate some of the annual audit with the internal auditing department. That coordination may take place by having the external auditor review the reports of the internal auditor or by having the internal auditor carry out part of the audit program under the overall review of the external auditor.

Required:

a. The profession's auditing standards require that the auditor evaluate the independence and competence of the internal audit function as a basis for determining potential reliance on the function. What factors might the auditor examine to determine the
   - *Independence* of the internal audit function?
   - *Competence* of the internal audit function?

b. Most large internal audit departments have separate computer audit groups (often referred to as *EDP auditors*). Why may the existence of a computer audit group be significant to the external auditor? How might the external auditor benefit from the work performed by the internal EDP auditors?

c. In planning to observe the client's inventory, which is held at 13 locations, the CPA firm is considering having the internal audit department observe inventory being taken at six locations, including performing test counts and gathering other audit information. Would this approach likely be acceptable? If so, under what conditions would it be acceptable?

6–48 (Factors Affecting the Auditor's Materiality Determination) You have been assigned to plan the audit for the Brenner Manufacturing Company, a maker of electronic goods used in a wide array of sporting goods ranging from exercise equipment to racing bicycles. Some of its better-known products include an electronic pulse meter that monitors an athlete's pulse during a workout, an electronic speedometer for bicycles, and an electronic workout module showing calories burned, and so on that is used on products such as the Nordic Trak and exercise bicycles often found in health clubs. The company has been active and tries to maintain state-of-the-art equipment but is faced with increasing competition from larger companies such as Casio and Aerodyne. Although the total market is not large, it is growing and is very competitive. The company is constantly looking for new product ideas and areas in which to expand its market.

The company's unaudited balance sheet, statement of changes in retained earnings, and income statement for the current year are as follows:

Brenner Manufacturing Co.
Balance Sheet
December 31, 1995 and 1994

	Current Year (Unaudited)	Previous Year (Audited)
Assets		
Cash	$ 77,982	$ 85,000
Accounts receivable	1,051,622	964,328
Inventory	1,790,408	1,356,978
Total current assets	2,920,012	2,396,306
Land	365,000	365,000
Equipment, net of depreciation	1,987,000	1,630,000
Building, net of depreciation	1,350,000	1,425,000
Prepaid assets	53,565	63,500
Total assets	$6,675,577	$5,879,806
Liabilities and Owners' Equity		
Accounts payable	$ 953,000	$ 815,000
Short-term bank note	1,500,000	1,250,000
Accrued payroll	27,500	20,000
Other accrued expenses	165,000	128,770
Total current liabilities	2,645,500	2,213,770
Long-term debt	1,500,000	1,250,000
Total liabilities	4,145,500	3,463,770
Stockholders' Equity		
Common stock: $10 par value, issued and outstanding, 100,000 shares	1,000,000	1,000,000
Additional paid-in capital	500,000	500,000
Retained earnings	1,030,077	916,136
Total stockholders' equity	2,530,077	2,416,136
Total liabilities and equity	$6,675,577	$5,879,806

Brenner Manufacturing Company
Statement of Changes in Retained Earnings
Year Ended December 31, 1995

Balance, December 31, 1994	$ 916,136
Add: Net income for the year	393,941
	1,310,077
Less: Dividends declared	280,000
Retained earnings, December 31, 1995	$1,030,077

Brenner Manufacturing Company
Income Statement
Years Ended 1995 and 1994

	Current Year (Unaudited)	Previous Year (Audited)
Sales	$11,753,027	$10,357,876
Less returns & allowance	921,320	359,000
Net sales	10,831,707	9,998,876
Cost of goods sold	6,228,231	5,949,331
Gross margin	4,603,476	4,049,545
Administrative expense	1,631,000	1,497,000
Selling commissions	541,550	499,500
Research & development	965,000	825,000
Warranty expense	575,000	475,000
Interest expense	270,000	225,000
Total selling & administrative	3,982,550	3,521,500
Income before taxes	620,926	528,045
Income tax	226,985	190,096
Net income	$ 393,941	$ 337,949

Required:

a. Using the guidance provided in the text and the limited knowledge about the company, prepare an estimate of materiality for the audit client. On a judgment basis, allocate the materiality to the individual asset accounts. Assume that you will be auditing some of the accounts on a statistical basis and as a rough rule of thumb, the amount of materiality that should be allocated to the individual asset accounts should equal 150 percent of overall planned materiality. Briefly justify your decisions.

b. For each of the following situations, indicate how the information would affect the auditor's judgment of (1) overall materiality and (2) the amount of materiality assigned to a particular account (if noted in the problem). Also indicate whether the scenario would cause the auditor to adjust materiality or audit risk, or both. Each item should be considered independently of the other items.

1. Instead of a profit, the company incurred a loss of $379,000, and retained earnings dropped to a negative $325,000. There is some indication that the company may have to declare some form of bankruptcy during the year.
2. The company has been profitable, but there have been allegations in the press that much of the profit has been attained through "accounting tricks" such as recognizing revenue early or through other activities such as postponing research and development. Assume that the profit for the company was the same as that reported in the three financial statements but that it was all obtained by cutting research and development expenditures this year to $50,000.
3. The company's gross margin has increased this year so that it is at a historical high and a full five percentage points above that of the

industry. Assume also that the company's returns and allowance account would have decreased from the previous year rather than increase with the corresponding amount going directly to profit.

4. The company has been privately held but is planning a public offering of stock next year.
5. This is the first year of the audit engagement. The company changed auditors because of significant disagreements with the previous auditors. There is some question about the integrity of the manager, Frances Palmer, but not enough to preclude your firm from accepting the audit.
6. Assume the same situation as in part 5 but that you have taken over the audit from another firm. Your discussion with predecessor auditors tells you that they suspected fraud in receivables and inventory but were precluded from doing sufficient work to corroborate their suspicions.
7. The company is a long-standing privately owned client with high management integrity. The only users of the financial statements are members of management and the local bank. There are no plans to sell the company, and it has a very good relationship with the local bank. This is the tenth consecutive year of earnings. You believe that the company is soundly and conservatively managed.

6–49 **(Research—Industry Analysis)** Auditors cannot effectively audit clients unless they fully understand the client's industry and the risks inherent in it that may affect their client. Therefore, an important part of every audit plan is to understand how current developments in the industry may be affecting an audit client.

Required:

a. Perform a background analysis of the following industries:
   1. Banks.
   2. Property and casualty insurance companies.
b. Perform a risk analysis of the industries, identifying the following:
   - Potential problems within them as identified in the financial press.
   - Current economic trends within them as described in industry publications.
   - The regulatory environment affecting them, including pending legislation.
   - Components of the balance sheets of companies in each industry that would represent high risk.

In performing the analysis, consult the periodical index in your library for news articles and trade statistics. See, for example, Robert Morris statistics for banks or *Best's Review* for insurance companies. Additionally, if your school has the NEXIS service (part of LEXIS, NAARS), consult with your instructor about using it to search for the industry information.

6–50 **(Research—Company Analysis)** With the consent of your instructor, identify a company and perform a background review of it to identify high-risk areas for an upcoming audit. Consult industry trade data and other information available in the library. If the company is publicly traded, obtain a copy of its latest 10-K report to the SEC. If a local company is chosen, consider arranging an interview with the controller to find out more about its operations.

Required:
Prepare an analysis of risk areas for the company selected and discuss the implications of the risk areas for the audit of that company.

Case

6–51 (Lincoln Federal Savings & Loan) The following is a description of a number of factors that affected the operations of Lincoln Federal Savings & Loan, a California savings and loan (S&L) that was a subsidiary of American Continental Company, a real estate development company run by Charles Keating.

Required:

a. After reading the discussion of Lincoln Federal Savings & Loan, identify the high-risk areas that should be planned for in an audit of it.
b. The auditor would often see independent appraisals in folders for loans indicating the market value of the real estate. How convincing would you find such appraisals? What characteristics would have to exist in the appraisal to convince you that they represented the underlying values of the property?

Lincoln Federal Savings & Loan

Savings and Loan Industry Background. The S&L industry was developed in the early part of the century in response to a perceived need to provide low-cost financing to encourage home ownership. As such, legislation by Congress made the S&L industry the primary financial group allowed to make low-cost home ownership loans (mortgages). For many years, the industry operated by accepting relatively long-term deposits from customers and making 25- to 30-year loans at fixed rates on home mortgages. The industry was generally considered to be safe. Most of the S&Ls (also known as *thrifts*) were small, federally chartered institutions with deposits insured by the FSLIC. "Get your deposits in, make loans, sit back, and earn your returns. Get to work by 9 AM and out to the golf course by noon" seemed to be the motto of many S&L managers.

Changing Economic Environment. During the 1970s, two major economic events hit the S&L industry. First, the rate of inflation had reached an all-time high. Prime interest rates had gone as high as 19.5 percent. Second, deposits were being drawn away from the S&L by new competitors that offered short-term variable rates substantially higher than current passbook savings rates for most S&L depositors. The S&Ls responded by increasing the rates on certificates of deposit to extraordinary levels (e.g., 15 or 16 percent) while servicing mortgages with 20- to 30-year maturities made at old rates of 7 to 8 percent. The S&Ls attempted to mitigate the problem by offering variable rate mortgages or selling off some of their mortgages (at substantial losses) to other firms. However, following regulatory accounting principles, the S&Ls were not required to recognize market values of loans that were not sold. Thus, even if loan values were substantially less than the book value, they would continue to be carried at book value as long as the mortgage holder was not in default.

Changing Regulatory Environment. Congress moved to deregulate the S&L industry. During the first half of 1982, the S&L industry lost a record $3.3 billion (even without marking loans down to real value). In August 1982, President Reagan signed the Garn–St Germain Depository Institutions Act of 1982 hailing it as "the most important legislation for financial institutions in 50 years."[1] The bill had two key elements:

- S&Ls would be allowed to offer money market funds free from withdrawal penalties or interest rate regulation.
- S&Ls could invest up to 40 percent of their assets in nonresidential real estate lending.

Commercial lending was much riskier than home lending, but the potential returns were greater. In addition, the regulators helped the deregulatory fever by

- Removing a regulation which had required a thrift to have 400 stockholders with no one owning more than 25 percent to allowing a single shareholder to own a thrift.
- Making it easier for an entrepreneur to purchase a thrift. Regulators allowed buyers to start (capitalize) their thrift with land or other "noncash" assets rather than money.
- Allowing thrifts to stop requiring traditional down payments and to provide 100 percent financing with the borrower not required to invest a dime of personal money in the deal.
- Permitting thrifts to make real estate loans anywhere. They had previously been required to make loans on property located only in their own geographic area.[2]

Accounting. In addition to these revolutionary changes, owners of troubled thrifts began stretching already liberal accounting rules—with regulators' blessings—to squeeze their balance sheets into [regulatory] compliance. For example, goodwill, defined as customer loyalty, market share, and other intangible "warm fuzzies," accounted for over 40 percent of the thrift industry's net worth by 1986.

Lincoln Federal S&L. Lincoln Federal S&L was purchased by American Continental Corporation, a land development company run by Charles Keating and headquartered in Phoenix. Immediately, Keating expanded the lending activity of Lincoln to assist in the development of American Continental projects, including the Phoenician Resort in Scottsdale.* Additionally, Keating sought higher returns by purchasing junk bonds marketed

---

*The Phoenician was so lavishly constructed that a regulator estimated that just to break even, the resort would have to charge $500 per room per night at a 70 percent occupancy rate. Similar resort rooms in the area were available at $125 a night.

by Drexel Burnham and Michael Millken. Nine of Keating's relatives were on the Lincoln payroll at salaries ranging from over $500,000 to over $1 million.

Keating came up with novel ideas to raise capital. Rather than raising funds through deposits, he had commissioned agents working in the Lincoln offices who sold special bonds of American Continental Corp. The investors were assured that their investments would be safe. Unfortunately, many elderly individuals put their life savings into these bonds thinking they were backed by the FSLIC because they were sold at an S&L, but they were not.

Keating continued investments in real estate deals, such as a planned mega community in the desert outside of Phoenix. He relied on appraisals, some obviously of dubious value, to serve as a basis for the loan valuation.

End Notes

1. Stephen Pizzo, Mary Fricker, and Paul Mulolo, *Inside Job: The Looting of America's Savings and Loans* (New York: McGraw-Hill, 1990), 1.
2. Ibid, 12–13.

CHAPTER

7

Learning Objectives

Through studying this chapter, you will be able to:

1. Understand and apply the assertions approach to developing audit programs.
2. Understand the impact of fundamental concepts that affect the development of audit programs.
3. Understand the concepts of transactions testing, direct testing, and directional testing.
4. Identify the factors affecting the reliability of audit evidence.
5. Understand the nine basic approaches to gathering audit evidence.
6. Understand the requirements for documenting audit evidence.
7. Understand how audit working papers are designed and organized, and how they are changed by the electronic environment.

Audit Evidence

Chapter Contents

Chapter Overview

Auditing is a process of objectively gathering and evaluating evidence pertaining to assertions. This chapter discusses the assertions contained in financial statements and relates those assertions to evidence. All audit programs, no matter what their size, whether standardized or customized, are based on the financial statement assertions and the auditor's assessment of evidence needed to provide reasonable assurance on the correctness of the assertions. Different types of evidence are identified along with characteristics that impact the persuasiveness of audit evidence. The auditor's process of gathering and assessing the evidence must be documented in working papers, which should explain the evidence and the auditor's reasoning process and the conclusions reached.

Obtaining and evaluating evidence is particularly complex in the auditing environment, for three main reasons. First, the audit is a complex, sequential, and hierarchical process with many potential evidence sources. Second, the audit is characterized by an interplay between experience and evidence, both of which can provide assurance for propositions. Subjective judgment will, therefore, always be an important part of the audit. . . . Finally, the audit environment is probabilistic—the auditor's task is not so simple as observing E and concluding P in an "if-then" causal chain. . . . it is usually the case that a particular piece of evidence may be consistent with more than one proposition.[1]

Most of the auditor's work in forming his opinion on financial statements consists of obtaining and evaluating evidential matter concerning the assertions in such financial statements. [AU 326.02]

A–INTRODUCTION: AUDIT EVIDENCE FRAMEWORK

The evidence-gathering process is the heart of an audit. As the first quote describes, it is an extremely complex process. Often there are no right or wrong answers as to the best evidence to gather. Rather, the auditor considers the risk associated with an account balance assertion, the types of evidence available, and the reliability of alternative sources of evidence and then develops an audit approach that will lead to persuasive evidence with the maximum audit efficiency. This chapter develops a framework for the evidence-gathering process.

Auditing is a process of gathering evidence to test assertions. Regardless of the variety of audit settings, all audits involve testing management's assertions contained in written communications to another party and independently gathering **evidence** for that testing to determine the correctness of those assertions. Management makes assertions about a number of different things: earnings and financial conditions, the organization's internal control structure and its operations, compliance with governmental regulations. Auditors may be called on to perform audits of any of these kinds of assertions. In fact, the type of audit that could be performed is limited only by the demands for reliable information and an auditable information system by which assertions could be tested.

No two audits are exactly the same. Some organizations are large and heavily computerized; others are small and still use manual or semiautomated systems. Organizations as diverse as insurance companies, public utilities, state and local governments, churches and charities, retailers, manufacturers, and service providers all require audits. Different audit procedures apply, and different evidence is appropriate to each of these audits. Thus, no general audit program suits the needs for all situations.*

Although the audits themselves differ, they can all be approached in a similar fashion. This chapter develops an overall framework for audit evidence that serves as a basis for developing audit programs for a variety of audit engagements.†

Development of an Assertions Framework

Management's account balance assertions are the focal point of the approach to every audit engagement. They become linked with evidence in persuading the auditor of the fairness of the financial statements.

The opinion paragraph of the auditor's standard report contains the primary account balance assertion that auditors address:

> In our opinion, the financial statements referred to above present fairly, in all material respects, the financial position of XYZ Company as of December 31, 1995 and 1994, and the results of its operations and its cash flows for the years then ended *in conformity with generally accepted accounting principles*. [AU 508.08. Emphasis added.]

Just what audit implications are apparent in an entity's financial statements as judged by the auditor's opinion?

To take a specific example, review the current asset section of the consolidated balance sheets and inventory footnotes for Coca-Cola Company (see Exhibit 7.1). Inventory for 1991 is valued at $988 million, and the auditor states that the balance is fairly presented in relation to the financial statements taken as a whole. And because the footnotes are an integral part of the financial statements, "fairly presented" also applies to appropriate and adequate footnote disclosure—in this instance, for inventory, the note on inventory composition, and costing. Coca-Cola's auditor, in other words, must thoroughly understand generally accepted accounting principles (GAAP) as they might apply to the company.

The financial statements, therefore, form the basis of the assertions the auditor tests. To continue using inventory at $988 million as an example, the financial statements convey the following assertions:

- The various inventories actually *exist* and are controlled by Coca-Cola Company.
- The inventories are *owned* by Coca-Cola, and the account balances (both the footnote-listed subtotals and in aggregate) reflect only those items Coca-Cola owned at the end of 1991.

*Many CPA firms have general audit programs for the conduct of financial statement audits. These programs contain auditing procedures for specific accounts. But the auditor on the engagement is expected to modify the general audit program to whatever degree necessary according to the specific circumstances of the organization and risks associated with the account balance or transaction class under examination.

†Although the assertions tested, and therefore the evidence gathered, are somewhat different for an operational audit, the approach is still very similar. Audit programs appropriate to operational auditing are further developed in Chapter 24.

Exhibit 7.1

THE COCA-COLA COMPANY AND SUBSIDIARIES
CONSOLIDATED BALANCE SHEETS

(In thousands except share data)	December 31 1991	1990
Assets—Current		
Cash and cash equivalents	**$1,058,250**	$1,429,555
Marketable securities, at cost (approximates market)	**58,946**	62,569
	1,117,196	1,492,124
Trade accounts receivable, less allowances of $34,567 in 1991 and $29,510 in 1990	**933,448**	913,541
Finance subsidiary—receivables	**36,172**	38,199
Inventories	**987,764**	982,313
Prepaid expenses and other assets	**1,069,664**	716,601
Total current assets	**4,144,244**	4,142,778

1. Accounting Policies

Inventories

Inventories are valued at the lower of cost or market. In general, inventories are valued on the basis of average cost or first-in, first-out methods. However, certain soft drink and citrus inventories are valued on the last-in, first-out (LIFO) method. The excess of current costs over LIFO stated values amount to approximately $27 million and $42 million at December 31, 1991 and 1990, respectively.

2. Inventories

Inventories consist of the following (in thousands):	December 31 1991	1990
Raw materials and supplies	**$615,459**	$567,694
Work in process	**23,475**	18,451
Finished goods	**348,830**	396,168
	$987,764	$982,313

- Inventories are *properly valued* according to acceptable inventory cost flow assumptions.
- *Calculations* leading to the $988 million were all made correctly.
- *No obsolete* inventory items are included in that figure, and items not readily marketable have been written down to their approximate net realizable value.
- Footnote *disclosures* related to inventory pricing, major consignments, composition, and the like are complete and adequate.

Similar assertions are implied in the other financial statement accounts whether assets, liabilities, equity, revenue, or expenses. The major difference in audit approach between assets and liabilities—as well as between sales and expenses and between gains and losses—lies in the auditor's normal concern about potential overstatement of assets, revenues, and gains as well as potential understatement of liabilities, expenses, and losses. Management is not generally motivated to understate assets or income or to overstate liabilities.[*]

Account Balance Assertions

Developing a checklist of the assertions associated with each account balance can be difficult without an overarching framework to identify them and to specify the focus of evidence necessary to satisfy them. Moreover, the auditor must assess the environment in which evidence is formulated to determine its reliability and competence for testing each assertion. The Auditing Standards Board has provided a framework for the specific assertions addressed in an audit program:

- Existence or occurrence.
- Completeness.
- Rights and obligations.
- Valuation or allocation.
- Presentation and disclosure.[†]

The **assertions** subsumed under these five headings form the major categories for assessing the reliability and competence of the evidence the auditor gathers to test the account balances of the financial statements. Auditors also gather evidence regarding the integrity of the recording and reporting process. That process embodies its own assertions, which is the subject of Chapter 8.[‡]

Existence or Occurrence. Management asserts that all of the assets and liabilities shown on the balance sheet *exist* at the balance sheet date and that all of the transactions reflected in the financial statements occurred during the period covered by those statements. Thus, the assertion implies that all events recognized in the statements represent *bona fide transactions*. Existence or occurrence also covers questions of overstatement: Management asserts that nothing is overstated in the financial statements or that nothing extraneous has been recorded and reported to inflate any

---

[*] The difference in emphasis is also reflected in that most lawsuits involving auditors deal with overstatement of assets and income and understatement of liabilities. As with everything, there are some exceptions. Small, privately held businesses might be motivated to minimize taxes and therefore understate income and assets. Such a business might, for example, be more likely to expense rather than capitalize some equipment, which overstates expenses and understates both income and assets.

[†] It should be noted that assertions addressed by auditors are not limited to this framework. For example, the internal audit professional standards recognize organizational assertions that internal auditors regularly test including:

- Reliability and integrity of information.
- Compliance with policies, plans, procedures, laws, and regulations.
- Safeguarding assets.
- Economical and efficient use of resources.
- Accomplishment of established objectives and goals for operations or programs.

The General Accounting Office recognizes similar standards for governmental audits. The alert reader will quickly note that internal auditing is much broader than financial statement audits.

[‡] As Chapter 8 discusses at greater length, the stronger the integrity of the recording process, the less the auditor needs to test individual account balances directly.

account balances. The financial statements, therefore, include only events of the period and no more.

Completeness. Management asserts that all of the transactions and balances that should be presented in the financial statements are included in them. Thus, the assertion implies that no events have been overlooked. Thus, completeness also covers questions of understatement: Management asserts that nothing is understated in the financial statements.

Rights and Obligations. The balance sheet represents an accumulation of the organization's rights and obligations. Management asserts that the assets and liabilities reported actually represent those rights and obligations. Implied in rights is *ownership* or noncancelable use of assets. An item listed as an account receivable, for example, represents the *right* of the organization to the future cash due the organization from a past transaction. The right also exists in the legal sense because the organization can sue to collect the receivable or can sell it to a third party (called *factoring*). Management asserts that the liabilities are *obligations* of the reporting entity—not the personal obligation of one of its officers, for example. Others can legitimately look to the entity for redress if the obligation is not met.

Valuation or Allocation. Management's valuation assertion is complex. Determining value involves much more than simply following GAAP. The auditor must analyze complex transactions to determine the entity's responsibilities and the value of either rights or obligations. The auditor analyzes assets such as accounts or loans receivable to determine whether a sufficient allowance for uncollectible accounts is recorded. Also implied in valuation is the rational allocation of costs and revenues over time. Systematic, consistent allocation of historical costs thus underlies—and even indirectly determines—asset valuations.

Presentation and Disclosure. Management asserts that all transactions and balances are properly classified, that all necessary parenthetical notations appear on the face of the financial statements, and that the footnote disclosures are appropriate and adequate. Classification refers to the categories used and the subtotals presented. If marketable securities, for example, are classified as a current asset, a reader can infer that it is management's intent to sell those securities in the relatively near future as cash needs dictate. Guidelines for minimum disclosures appear in FASB statements, APB opinions, and other technical pronouncements. All financial statements should have, for example, a footnote that summarizes significant accounting policies.*

Examples of Assertions. The assertions to be tested by the auditor can be seen in Exhibit 7.2, which details these assertions for the inventory balance in Coca-Cola Company's financial statements. To give an unqualified opinion on the balance sheet of Coca-Cola Company, the auditors had to determine (1) *what evidence* is needed to address each assertion, (2) *which audit procedures* will provide persuasive

---

*The AICPA, many public accounting firms, and some private publishers have developed **disclosure checklists** to assist auditors in reviewing disclosure requirements as a normal part of reviewing the adequacy of financial statement disclosures.

Exhibit 7.2

FINANCIAL ASSERTIONS FOR INVENTORY

Inventory valued at $988 million represents:

Existence or occurrence. The account balance consists of physical inventory owned and controlled by Coca-Cola Company as of the balance sheet date. All inventory transactions entered into during the year have been recognized in the account balance. The account balance does not include any transactions that were not completed during the period covered by the financial statements. Inventory stored at other locations on consignment is recorded as inventory, not as sales.

Completeness. All inventory transactions have been appropriately recorded within the correct time period. All items recorded as sales represent bona fide revenue transactions, and the company is not contingently liable to reassume title to the inventory.

Rights and obligations. Coca-Cola has clear title to the inventory and can control its use. For example, it can sell or otherwise dispose of or use the inventory reflected in the account balance entirely at its own discretion.

Valuation or allocation. The inventory is properly valued according to a generally accepted cost flow assumption (FIFO, LIFO, or average cost) at the *lower of historical cost or market*. Items that are difficult to sell have been reduced to their net realizable value. Obsolete goods have been written off or reduced to their expected realizable value. The computation of the inventory cost is mathematically correct; that is, price times quantity equals extended cost, and that amount is summed (footed) and agrees with the amount contained in the account balance.

Presentation and disclosure. All required disclosures—such as the valuation method, any changes in that method, the division of products among finished goods, work in process, raw material, and the existence of any pledges of the inventory—are adequately disclosed. In addition, the accounting principles identified in the disclosures are consistent with those that Coca-Cola used in prior periods reported, or any changes in principles have been properly accounted for in the financial statements and disclosed in the notes.

evidence for each of the assertions, (3) *how much* evidence is needed to reach a conclusion (i.e., gain satisfaction as to the correctness of the assertion), and (4) the *most efficient* means to gather that evidence. The *type* of audit evidence to be gathered is covered in this chapter. The discussion of the *amount* of evidence to be gathered is deferred to Chapters 12 and 14 on audit sampling.

There are alternative sources of audit evidence for many of the assertions. For example, the existence assertion might be evaluated by (1) observing the taking of Coca-Cola's year-end physical inventory or (2) testing Coca-Cola's perpetual inventory system by selecting items from the perpetual inventory records and counting the physical items to determine whether the inventory records are accurate. The auditor must determine which evidence meets minimum levels of persuasiveness at the least cost consistent with the auditor's planned level of audit risk.*

*The minimum needs for persuasiveness depends on the level of audit risk following the framework established in Chapter 6. The amount of evidence to be gathered depends on the auditor's relative assessment of inherent risk and control risk as it applies to a *particular* account balance.

Nature of Audit Testing

Audit programs are designed by determining the most efficient manner in which to gather sufficient evidence to satisfy the auditor as to the correctness of the assertions. This task is summarized in the third standard of fieldwork:

> Sufficient competent evidential matter is to be obtained through inspection, observation, inquiries, and confirmations to afford a *reasonable basis* for an opinion regarding the financial statements under audit. [AU 150.02. Emphasis added.]

The auditor has many choices in determining the most efficient approach to gather persuasive evidence.

Tests of Transactions versus Direct Test of Account Balances

The auditor can choose to test either the *transactions* that build up account balances, test the *account balance* directly, or some combination of both. The Inventory account will reflect a number of transactions during the year:

Inventory	
Beginning balance	
Purchases	Cost of goods sold
Miscellaneous adjustments	Write down of obsolete items
Returns of goods sold	Market value adjustments
Ending balance	

Evidence on the correctness of the inventory account (and the underlying management assertions) can be obtained by either *directly testing* the final account balance or by testing the accounting transactions that have been recorded during the year. Evidence on the correctness of the cost of goods sold, however, can be obtained only by testing transactions during the year **or** by inferring the correctness of the account through evidence gathered on the beginning and ending inventory balances and the related purchases accounts. When considering evidence regarding inventory and cost of goods sold, two points should be kept in mind:

1. The better the client's control structure and the better the controls implemented in the accounting system, the less likely it is that the account balance contains material misstatements. Thus, any tests that substantiate the effectiveness of the client's control structure provide indirect evidence of the correctness of the account balance.
2. Audit procedures that independently establish the correctness of the ending inventory account balance (a direct test of the account balance) *also* provide evidence of the accuracy of the transactions that have been recorded. The audit evidence obtained in evaluating the correctness of the inventory balance provides corroborative evidence on the correctness of cost of goods sold.

Although the auditor performs both **tests of transactions** and **direct tests of account balances,** the auditing profession has traditionally focused most of its audit procedures on the direct tests of account balances (particularly the asset and liability accounts) because

1. There are usually *fewer* items in the ending balance than are contained in the transactions that have taken place during the year. Most companies, for example, have fewer items in ending inventory than the number of purchase and sales transactions recorded during the year.
2. *Reliable evidence*, which can be gathered efficiently, usually exists for ending balance items more so than for transactions. Ending inventory can be physically observed, but goods sold are gone and cannot be observed. The auditor testing cost of goods sold would have to rely on the client's documentation and records more heavily than when concentrating the testing on the intervening transactions.

These observations have held true historically and are expected to continue to hold true in many environments, but the current trend is toward highly integrated computerized systems. Auditors operating in environments with highly computerized systems may find it both more effective and more efficient to directly test the correctness of processing through detailed testing of a client's computer system than to follow the traditional audit approach.

Directional Testing

Many audit program guidelines are based on directional testing concepts. **Directional testing** involves testing transactions or balances primarily for one type of error, either over- or understatement, but not for both at the same time. Directional testing can lead to audit efficiency because testing one account for an over- or understatement provides indirect evidence on other accounts. The concept of directional testing is derived from the double-entry form of accounting and the auditor's risk analysis. As an example, an audit test of Accounts Receivable for overstatement also tests Sales for overstatement. Directional testing leads to audit efficiency for these reasons:

1. Misstatements of some accounts are more likely to occur in one direction than the other. For example, management may be compensated on reported profits and, therefore, may be more motivated to overstate sales transactions for the year than to understate them. Alternatively, if a company is experiencing credit problems, it is more likely to understate liabilities than to overstate them.
2. Directional testing of an account balance provides evidence on a complementary set of accounts. For example, testing Accounts Receivable for overstatement indirectly provides evidence on the possible overstatement of Sales or understatement of Cash.
3. Specific assertions are normally tested directionally. Existence assertions are most often tested for overstatement; completeness assertions are tested for understatement; and valuation assertions are tested for both under- and overstatement.

The use of directional testing depends on the availability of evidential matter and the time and cost of testing. Efficiency requires the auditor to consider the effects of

Exhibit 7.3

DIRECTIONAL TESTS AND RELATED INDIRECT EVIDENCE

Account Balance	Direct Test	Indirect Evidence on Related Accounts			
		Assets	Liabilities	Revenues	Expenses
Asset	Over	Under	Over	Over	Under
Liability	Under	Under	Over	Over	Under
Revenue*	Under	Under	Over	Over	N/A
Expense	Over	Under	Over	N/A	Under

*Although it seems that the auditor would primarily test revenues for overstatement, it must be remembered that the directional tests on the balance sheet accounts provide considerable evidence on the overstatement of revenue.

directional testing of a particular account and its relationship to other accounts. Exhibit 7.3 summarizes the relationship of directional testing and audit planning.

Assets are most often tested for overstatement and provide indirect evidence on the overstatement of revenue and liabilities and on understatements of other asset and expense accounts. If accounts receivable are overstated, for example, revenue may be overstated because of incorrectly recording revenue early, or cash may be understated if a receivable has been paid. If inventory is overstated, accounts payable is overstated if title has not yet transferred for goods in transit, or cost of goods sold (an expense) is understated.

Similarly, tests of liabilities for understatements provide indirect evidence on understatement of expenses and assets and on overstatement of revenue and other liabilities. If there are unrecorded liabilities, for example, the related expenses or inventory may also be understated. If unearned subscription revenue is understated because too much of it is recognized as earned, subscription revenue is overstated.

Testing revenue for understatement also tests accounts receivable for understatement. Testing maintenance and repairs expense for overstatement also tests property, plant, and equipment for understatement due to expensing items that should be capitalized.

Analytical Procedures

Analytical procedures provide a third type of evidence about the correctness of assertions. These procedures take several forms.

Testing of Linked Account Relationships. The double-entry bookkeeping system dictates that a number of accounts have direct ties to each other. An example is the relationship of Interest Expense to Bonds Payable. Once the bonds have been issued, the periodic interest expense is easy to estimate. The relationship of the liability and expense account makes interest expense easier to audit. If, for example, the auditor were to test individual interest transactions, the auditor would have to review the following (assuming the bond was issued at discount):

Bond Interest Expense		
Semi annual interest payment		
Bond discount amortization		
Semi annual interest payment		
Bond discount amortization		
Year-end accrual		
Total	$ XXX	

However, instead of directly testing individual transactions making up the interest expense balance, the auditor could estimate the bond interest expense for the year by multiplying the face amount of the bond by the stated interest rate and adjusting for the discount amortization. More likely, the auditor will set up a spreadsheet on a microcomputer to make such estimates each year. If the client's recorded transactions either equal or approximate the amount computed by the auditor, the auditor would not need to test the individual transactions unless there were other compelling reasons to do so.

Examples of other accounts for which such relationships exist are shown in Exhibit 7.4.

The account balances and relationships shown in Exhibit 7.4 are not meant to be inclusive but to be illustrative of many accounting relationships. Typically, for many

Exhibit 7.4

DIRECT ACCOUNT RELATIONSHIPS

Assets	**Related Expenses**
Prepaid Insurance	Insurance Expense
Marketable Securities	Investment Income (short-term)
Investment in Equity-Based Affiliate	Equity Investment Income
Property Plant and Equipment	Depreciation Expense
Goodwill	Amortization Expense
Notes Receivable	Interest Income
Capitalized Leases/Assets	Lease Amortization Expenses
Liabilities	**Related Expense or Income**
Magazine Subscription Advanced Receipts	Subscription Revenue
Notes Payable	Interest Expense
Capitalized Lease Obligations	Lease Amortization and Interest
Equity	**Related Equity Transactions**
Preferred Stock	Preferred Dividends
Common Stock	Common Stock Dividends
Income Statement Items	**Related Accounts**
Sales	Royalty Expense
Wage Expense	Unemployment Insurance Taxes

of these accounts, the auditor can efficiently accumulate audit evidence by directly testing the balance sheet account and estimating the related expense or revenue account.

Account Relationships to Other Independent Factors. The auditor is normally aware of a number of relationships of *particular* account balances to other outside factors. The term *outside factors* refers to information that is not formally recorded in the company's accounts but may be available in other forms within the organization or from sources outside the organization, such as trade organizations. Examples of relationships include the number of individuals employed and payroll expense, revenue reports from other companies and royalty income, or the number of cable company subscribers and basic cable income.

If the validity of the independent data and the stability of the relationship can be established, the auditor may be able to directly estimate the account balance to be tested by utilizing the independent data. For example, knowledge that the basic cable rate is $20 per month and that a cable company had an average of 40,000 customers each month should give the auditor a good idea of whether the recorded cable income of $9,850,000 is correct. Note that the assessment depends on the quality of the independent data and the auditor's *line of reasoning* or overall reasoning ability. The estimate of cable revenue is valid only if it is reasonable that revenue should be directly related to the number of customers.

B–SOURCES OF AUDIT EVIDENCE

Auditors must choose among sources of evidence on the basis of the relevance to the assertion to be tested, its persuasiveness with respect to that assertion, and the cost of gathering it. Audit evidence can be classified in a number of ways for easier identification and discrimination: external versus internal evidence, computer-generated versus manually generated evidence, or documentary versus testimonial evidence. One classification that has proven to be useful first divides evidence into types—for example, testimonial—and subdivides those types by the nature and source—internal versus external, for example.

This framework helps the auditor recognize the degree of reliability likely to be associated with the evidence and integrate the assertions to be tested with the evidence.

- **Documentary evidence** may be generated by the client (inventory receiving reports) or by third parties (vendor invoices).
- **Testimonial evidence** may involve either client personnel or third parties and may be either oral or written.
- **Auditor-generated evidence** entails independent procedures performed by the auditor including recomputations of client computations, vouching of client transactions, and application of the auditor's line of reasoning to determine the appropriateness of account balances.

In choosing among alternative sources, the auditor must evaluate their potential reliability. (For a summary of evidence types and examples, see Exhibit 7.5.)

Exhibit 7.5

EVIDENCE TYPES AND EXAMPLES

Documentary Evidence

Client documentation:
Copies of sales invoices, client-prepared bank reconciliations, and receiving reports

Outside documentation:
Vendor invoices, correspondence from customers, and legal contracts

Testimonial Evidence

From client personnel:
Inquiries, management analyses, and internal reports

From outside parties:
Confirmations of accounts receivable from customers, bank statements, and assessments of pending litigation by outside legal counsel

Auditor-generated evidence

Recomputations:
Recalculations and mathematical tests of client records and reports

Auditor analysis and reasoning:
Auditor analysis of account relationships and outside factors on recorded account balances

Reprocessing of transactions:
Tracing transactions through the recording process to ensure complete and accurate processing

Reliability of Evidence

To test a particular client assertion, the auditor must often choose between the following:

- Evidence obtained *directly* or gained *indirectly* through third parties.
- Evidence obtained from *examining documents* or from hearing *testimonials*.
- Evidence generated by computer systems under *good accounting controls* or by manual systems that are potentially *subject to management override*.
- Independent evidence from *outside* the organization or the clients' *internal documentation*.
- Evidence that is *persuasive by itself* or that depends on the auditor's *line of reasoning* to establish appropriate relationships.

In each example, the first source listed is generally considered more reliable.

The Auditing Standards Board (AU 326) has established the following guidelines to assist auditors in evaluating the **reliability of audit evidence:**

More Reliable	**Less Reliable**
Directly observable evidence	Indirectly observable evidence
Evidence derived from a client's strong internal control structure	Evidence derived from a client's weak internal control structure
External documentation	Internal documentation

Notice that third-party evidence is preferable to client evidence, direct evidence is preferable to indirect evidence, and a client's good control structure provides better internal evidence than a client's weak control structure.

Internal Documentation

Internal documentation ranges from legal agreements (leases, sales contracts, and royalty arrangements) to business documents (purchase orders and canceled checks) to accounting documents (depreciation schedules and standard cost system standards) to planning, and control documents (original source documents such as time cards, inventory scrap reports, and market research surveys). See Exhibit 7.6 for examples of internal documents. The scope of such evidence is therefore very broad.

The reliability of internal documentation varies according to the following:

1. The quality of the client's internal control structure.
2. The potential motivation of management to misstate individual accounts (fraud potential).
3. The formality of the documentation such as acknowledgement of its validity by parties outside the organization or independent of the accounting function.

One internal document common to all organizations is a personnel record (for an example, see Exhibit 7.7). A personnel record shows the employee's date of hire, job classification, wage rate, number of dependents, membership in voluntary health plans or pension plans, and any extra withholdings (charitable contributions, for example) the employee requests. The information contained in the personnel record is instrumental in determining the correct employee pay, the employer's payroll tax liability, and the related wage expense. Although it is an internal document, it is generally prepared by a department other than accounting and is accompanied by additional documents such as signed employee withholding authorizations. Both of these elements contribute to the reliability of the document as compared to one prepared solely by the accounting department and not subject to review by anyone outside the department.

External Documentation

External documentation is generally considered to be highly reliable, particularly when the auditor receives it directly so that it is not subject to client manipulation or alteration. Most external documentation, however, is directed to the client. Therefore, when auditors have reason to suspect the validity of the external documentation, and that documentation is important to the audit, they should confirm such third-party information with that outside party.

Exhibit 7.6

INTERNAL DOCUMENTATION

Legal Documents	Labor and fringe benefit agreements Sales contracts Lease agreements Royalty agreements Maintenance contracts
Business Documents	Sales invoice Purchase orders Canceled checks Payment vouchers
Accounting Documents	Estimated warranty liability schedules Depreciation or amortization schedules Standard cost computations and schedules
Other Planning, and Control Documents	Employee time cards Shipping and receiving reports Inventory movement documents such as scrap reports and transfer receipts Market research surveys Pending litigation reports Variance reports

Note: Many of the planning and control documents have analyses attached. Market research survey data usually appear as part of the marketing department's opinion of new product potential; variance reports are accompanied by explanations of the causes of the variances and recommendations with respect to them. These analyses are generally considered to be testimonial rather than documentary evidence.

External documentation can vary in content even more than internal documentation because it ranges from business documents normally found in the client's possession (vendor invoices and monthly statements) to confirmations generally sent directly to the client's legal counsel, banker, or customer, to trade and credit information (U.S. government statistics and bond quality ratings). External documentation varies broadly in reliability as well, according to the formality and objectivity of the document and its source and to the degree of separation between the documentation and the client. See Exhibit 7.8 for a list of external documentation.

One standard business document normally in the client's possession is a vendor invoice (see Exhibit 7.9), which contains a wealth of information. A vendor's invoice shows the purchase price (cost) of items in the client's inventory, date of invoice and of shipment, payment and ownership terms, shipping address (inventory location), purchase order reference, purchasing agent (evidence of authorization), and amount due (liability as well as asset valuation evidence). Because a vendor invoice is quite formal, it is generally not subject to client alteration, even though it is in the client's

Exhibit 7.7

EXAMPLE OF EMPLOYEE PERSONNEL RECORD

Name	Johnson, Johanna J.
Date of Hire	08/23/82
Job Classification	Administrative Supervisor I
Wage Rate	$8.93 / hr.
W-2 Withholdings	M-2
Health Plan Coverage	Company—Standard
Pension Plan Coverage	Company—Standard
Other Withholdings	$25 per paycheck to Christmas Savings Plan

Exhibit 7.8

EXTERNAL DOCUMENTATION

Business Documents	Vendor invoices and monthly statements Customer orders Sales or purchase contracts Loan agreements Other contracts
Third-Party Documents	Confirmation letters from legal counsel Confirmation statements from banks Confirmation replies from customers Vendor statements requested by auditors
General Business Information	Industry trade statistics Credit rating reports (Moody's bond ratings or Dun and Bradstreet credit reports) Data from computer service bureaus such as LEXIS, NEXIS, or NAARS

Exhibit 7.9

VENDOR INVOICE

LeFlam Manufacturing Company
200 Pine Way
Kirkville, WI 53800
Phone (607) 255-3311 Fax (607) 256-1109

Sold To:
Bain's Sporting Goods
123 Lock Avenue
Cedar Rapids, Iowa 52404

Ship To:
Bain's Sporting Goods
123 Lock Avenue
Cedar Rapids, Iowa 52404

Invoice # 44779
Invoice Date 8/30/94
PO # 32348

Quantity

Shipped Via
Roadway 8/30/94

Terms:
Net 30

Account # 127000

Ordered	Shipped	Back Ordered	Item Number & Description	Unit Price	U/M	Extension
125	125	0	T-332B 2-person tents	34.99	Each	4,373.75
50	50	0	T-500Y Umbrella tents	55.75	Each	2,787.50
Freight Collect			Comments: Finance Charge of 1 1/2% per month on overdue invoices.		Sale	7,361.25
					Tax	
					Total	7,361.25

possession, and is therefore considered reliable except in situations in which the auditor questions management's integrity and has assessed the client as being high risk.

The extent of outside documentation gathered during an audit varies *inversely* with the quality of the client's control structure and the established audit risk; it varies *directly* with the auditor's assessment of the fraud environment (likelihood of fraud).

Approaches Utilized in Gathering Audit Evidence

An **audit program** specifies the procedures to be used, as well as the amount and types of audit evidence to be gathered. Procedures for gathering audit evidence include the following:

- ***Observing*** client personnel and procedures.
- ***Physically examining*** client assets.
- ***Examining documents,*** both internally and externally generated.
- ***Making inquiries*** of client personnel.
- ***Confirming*** data with outside parties.
- ***Recalculating*** client computations.
- ***Reprocessing*** client transactions such as simulating a client's processing system.
- ***Vouching the processing*** of client transactions.
- ***Using analytical procedures***, such as comparing the client's data with financial data or nonfinancial data from both within and outside the organization.

Many of these procedures overlap. Physical examination often focuses on documentary evidence (as in verifying investment balances by examining stock certificates). Thus, these procedures are not necessarily independent but may be used in conjunction with each other in gathering sufficient competent audit evidence.

Observation

Observation involves watching the client's employees process transactions or performing other activities. Observation is often used to help the auditor assess the quality of the performance of a client's accounting function and its internal control structure. But observation is rarely unobtrusive. Individuals who know they are being observed typically react differently than do those who are not being observed.*

Observation is often limited by the difficulty the auditor has in generalizing from the evidence gathered. Observation of the processing of transactions on one day does not necessarily indicate the manner in which the transaction might have been processed six months—or even six days—earlier. For these reasons, observation is usually limited to gaining an understanding of an accounting system.

Physical Examination

A variation of observation, physical examination generally involves physically examining assets. The auditor might physically inspect assets to verify their existence or for signs of obsolescence or wear and tear. It is a reliable audit procedure but is appropriate only for certain types of assertions or in specific situations. Observation of physical inventory, for example, is generally a highly reliable and convincing source of evidence regarding the existence of inventory. Establishing existence, however, does not establish either ownership or proper valuation. An auditor's observation may not uncover problems of obsolescence or quality control.

Examination of Documentation

Much of the audit process depends on examining *documents*. Documents exist in forms such as client invoices, payroll time cards, and other forms described in

*As a test of this observation, reflect on your actions at a party or an outing when you become aware that you are the subject of the roving eye of someone's video camera. Your actions for that period of time are probably not the same or as natural as they would have been had you not noticed the camera. To a certain extent, the same problem applies if the auditor attempts to utilize observation extensively as a source of audit evidence.

Exhibits 7.6 and 7.8. Historically, such documentation has existed on paper and has often constituted much of the audit evidence reviewed on most audit engagements.

Auditors will face increasing challenges in the next decade because much of this traditional paper-based documentation will no longer be used. Instead, many client records and supporting materials will exist only in computer databases. In essence, the types of documents that have been so prevalent on many audits *may not exist in the future*. In such cases, the auditor must necessarily focus on the evaluation of the controls and correctness of processing in computerized information systems.

Inquiry

Inquiry is used extensively to gather internal client information essential to formulating an overall opinion. Inquiry is used to gain an understanding of (1) the client's accounting system; (2) management's plans for new products, disposal of lines of business, new investments, and the like; (3) pending or actual litigation against the organization; (4) changes in accounting procedures or accounting principles; (5) management's assessment of the valuation of key accounts, such as the collectibility of accounts receivable or the salability of inventory; and (6) management's or the controller's assessment of potential problems related to the audit. Inquiry is a strong source of evidence, but such evidence is generally not persuasive by itself. Auditors need to corroborate the understanding they gain through inquiry with other forms of audit evidence, when available.

Confirmation

Confirmation consists of sending a letter to an outside party to *confirm or corroborate* an assertion represented in the financial statements. Confirmations typically ask outside parties to substantiate information derived from the client's records using their own independent records and other documentation. The outside parties address their response directly to the auditor, indicating whether they agree with the client's information. If the third parties disagree, they are asked to itemize the differences between their records or assessment of the item under inquiry. Confirmations may include inquiries such as a request from legal counsel for an assessment of current litigation and the client's potential liability. They are commonly used to verify the existence of accounts receivable. The debtor is provided with an itemization of the current receivable balance and is asked to confirm the correctness of the information.

Although confirmations can be a strong source of evidence, auditors must not rely on them unduly. All too often customers ignore the request or respond affirmatively without thoroughly checking for and investigating any discrepancies. To provide persuasive evidence, the auditor must gain assurance as to the following:

- The recipient is independent of the client and has sufficient knowledge to respond meaningfully.
- The recipient is likely to respond conscientiously and appropriately.
- The recipient can respond in a meaningful fashion without an inordinate time delay.
- The recipient is unlikely to be biased toward a particular kind of a response (a bank customer, for example, may have a bias toward confirming all balances that are higher than actual and challenging only those balances that are lower than actual).

In the past, auditors have relied on confirmations without fully investigating these underlying assumptions. Confirmations are efficient because they are a low-cost auditing procedure.* At one time, the professional standards required confirmation of accounts receivable on all audits. Today, however, many other sources of evidence may exist, such as the customer's subsequent payment of the outstanding balance that may be both more reliable and efficient.

Recalculation

Auditors often find it useful to *recalculate* a number of client computations. Recalculations include the following:

- *Footing:* Adding a column of figures to verify the correctness of the client's totals.
- *Cross-footing:* Checking the agreement of the cross-addition of a number of columns of figures that sum to a grand total. (The sum of net sales and sales discounts should, for example, equal total sales.)
- *Tests of extensions:* Recomputing items involving multiplication (for example, multiplying historical cost by quantity to arrive at cost per inventory item).
- *Recomputations:* Recalculating estimated accounts or allowances (recomputing the allowance for doubtful accounts based on a formula related to the age of accounts receivable ending balances).

Although it may seem trite in today's computerized environment to perform recalculations, skeptical auditors realize that many major frauds have been covered up by mathematical mistakes. Moreover, many of the client's estimated figures are derived from calculations made using microcomputer spreadsheets; common examples include goodwill amortization, bond discount or premium amortization, and capitalized lease amortization. Auditors can test the accuracy of the estimates either by recalculating them (often in an auditor-developed spreadsheet) or by evaluating the logic incorporated in the client's spreadsheet.

Reprocessing

Reprocessing can be viewed as an extended form of recalculation. Reprocessing is broader, however, because it includes reviewing the journalizing of and posting transactions to accounts as well as verifying the accuracy of mathematical calculations. Reprocessing involves selecting a sample from a population of source documents, such as bills of lading, and reprocessing them to be sure they have been properly recorded. In heavily computerized environments, reprocessing might include processing auditor-submitted sets of test transactions to determine whether all calculations and postings to the intermediate records are performed properly.

Vouching Recorded Transactions

Vouching is complementary to reprocessing. It takes a sample of already recorded transactions and traces them back to their original source, usually a source document. For example, vouching would take a sample of items recorded in the sales

*Although low in cost to the client, the procedure assumes that nonclients (the recipients of the confirmation) have the time, knowledge, and willingness to conscientiously respond to all the confirmations received during the time period in which a number of audits are taking place.

journal and trace them back to shipping documents. Reprocessing, on the other hand, traces transactions from their origination to their final recording in the accounting records. Vouching helps establish that all *recorded transactions are valid* (occurrence); reprocessing helps establish that all *valid items have been recorded* (completeness).

Analytical Procedures

Analytical procedures are defined as studies of plausible relationships among both financial and nonfinancial data (AU 329.02):

> A basic premise underlying the application of analytical procedures is that plausible relationships among data may reasonably be expected to exist and continue in the absence of known conditions to the contrary.

Analytical procedures involve comparing recorded amounts or ratios of recorded amounts to expectations developed by the auditor. Analytical procedures represent an efficient alternative to traditional transaction testing. Such a technique requires the auditor to understand the business and to exercise a business approach to analyzing potential problem areas. Typical approaches to analytical procedures include ratio analysis, trend analysis, and overall reasonableness tests including regression and time-series statistical analysis.

The expectations may include informal trend analysis, formal mathematical analysis such as regression analysis, or simple comparisons of interrelationships among the data such as basic ratio analysis. Typical examples of relationships and sources of data commonly used in an audit process include the following:

- *Financial information for equivalent prior periods*, such as comparing the trend of fourth-quarter sales for the past three years.
- *Expected or planned results* developed from budgets or other forecasts, such as comparing actual division performance with budgeted divisional performance.
- *Ratios of financial information within the period*, such as examining the relationship between sales and cost of goods sold.
- Company and *industry trends*, such as comparing gross margin percentages of product lines or inventory turnover with industry averages.
- Financial information in terms of relevant *nonfinancial information*, such as analyzing the relationship between the number of items shipped to royalty expense or number of employees with payroll expense.

When plausible relationships exist, analytical procedures can be used if the underlying data are considered reliable. The evidence-reasoning approach for analytical procedures, however, differs from that for other tests. Most audit tests reason from the details in the account balance to the total; that is, if all tested details are correct, the accumulation of that detail in the account balance is inferred to be correct. Analytical procedures function in an opposite manner. If the total balance is reasonably correct, the detail contained in the account is deduced to be correct.

An example of the differences in approach helps make the difference in the reasoning process clearer. (See Exhibit 7.10.) Detailed transactions testing of Supplies Expense might consist of sampling individual transactions and reviewing documents or other evidence to form an opinion about the correctness of the recorded account

Exhibit 7.10

COMPARISON OF DETAILED TESTING AND ANALYTICAL REVIEW APPROACHES

Detailed Test of an Account—Supplies Expense

* = Randomly Sampled Items

Presumption: If sampled transactions are recorded correctly *and* individual items foot to account balance, the account balance (Y) is correct.

Reasoning: From detail to total.

Supplies Expense	
xxx	
*xxxx	
xx	
x	
xxx	
xx	
*xxx	
xxxx	
xxx	
*xxx	
xx	
xxxx	
xx	
*xxx	
Total Y	

Analytical Approach to Account Evaluation

Determine the historical relationship between supplies expense and sales. If internal controls are good, the relationship is stable, *and* conditions have not changed, then predict the current balance of supplies expense.

Presumption: If the predicted balance is within an acceptable range of the recorded balance (Y), the recorded balance is reasonable and the underlying transactions have been correctly recorded.

Reasoning: From total to detail.

Supplies Expense	
xxx	
xxxx	
xx	
x	
Y	

Sales	
	Z

balance. An analytical procedure, in contrast, involves comparing the recorded amount with other already audited or independent data in which a stable relationship has been established for prior periods and is expected to continue in the current period. The auditor can use the historical relationships to predict the currently recorded balance. If the recorded balance falls within a reasonable level of the predicted range, the auditor may assume that the account balance is not materially misstated. For example, assume that Sales is $29,500,000 and Supplies Expense is $150,400. If Supplies Expense has averaged 0.5 percent of Sales over the past three years, the auditor would predict that the current Supplies Expense should be about

$147,500. Because the predicted total is within an acceptable range of the recorded total, the auditor concludes that the recorded total is reasonable and, therefore, that the underlying transactions have been correctly recorded. The analytical approach takes much less time than the detailed testing of transactions approach.

Of course, if the recorded balance does not fall within an acceptable range of the predicted balance, the auditor must gather additional evidence to determine whether the account may contain a material error. The additional evidence may include sampling the transactions making up the account and vouching them to supporting invoices.

Analytical procedures require auditors to understand the business and to exercise a business approach to analyzing potential misstatements. Although an efficient approach, the use of analytical procedures to gather evidence is not considered as persuasive as is performing detailed tests of transactions. Use of analytical techniques might be good to indicate whether material errors exist in an account, but they do not provide details as to how the account should be adjusted. Finally, auditors using analytical procedures must establish the validity of the assumptions underlying the analytical model.

Analytical procedures are *required* to be performed as part of the audit planning process discussed in Chapter 6 to identify potential risk areas such as account balances that are likely to be misstated. They are also highly recommended for assessing the reasonableness of the conclusions reached during the audit. In both instances, microcomputer programs, such as spreadsheets or the AICPA's *Accountant's Trial Balance*, provide an excellent support for performing analytical procedures.

C–DOCUMENTING AUDIT EVIDENCE

Auditors would like to assume that their work will never be questioned, especially by a plaintiff in a lawsuit or by a partner evaluating job performance. We live in a litigious society, however, and the auditor's work is often challenged in court. Some lawsuits seem frivolous, but a bright lawyer often uses the power of "discovery" to hire expert witnesses to review the auditor's work to search for any "holes" in the audit. It is extremely important that the audit process of gathering evidence, evaluating it, and reaching a conclusion to support the auditor's opinion on the financial statements be carefully planned and documented. The documented audit work needs to stand on its own, that is, the evidence should be able to be evaluated independently of the individuals who performed the audit.

The process of gathering and evaluating evidence is documented in various forms, including these:

- Audit planning documents.
- The audit program.
- Copies of client documents and external documents.
- Memos describing the auditor's approach to the audit and reasoning process in support of account balances.
- Computer printouts of analysis and tests of client records.
- Auditor-generated analysis of account balances.

Together, these items form the auditor's working papers and serve as the primary evidence in support of audit conclusions. Working papers have traditionally been prepared manually. Today, they are often prepared using a microcomputer.

Audit Planning Documentation

The planning process, as discussed in Chapter 6, lays the foundation for the audit and should be carefully documented. Interviews with key executives should be summarized in a memo placed in the file (with implications clearly drawn for the conduct of the audit). Analytical procedures should be documented in spreadsheets or similar documents with a clear identification of accounts identified for special audit attention. The auditor's assessment of materiality and overall audit approach should be summarized. The documentation serves an important planning function for the audit; it also serves as evidence that the auditors took their responsibilities seriously in evaluating potential problems or special circumstances involved in, or related to, the audit.

The Audit Program

An audit program specifies the *actual procedures* to be performed in gathering the required audit evidence about the assertions embodied in the client's financial statements. The auditor performing each procedure should indicate the successful completion of each step in an audit program by initialing the step when finished. This initialing of an audit step when finished is often referred to as *signing off* on the audit step. Because the audit program guides the overall conduct of the audit, *it is the single most important piece of documentation in an audit engagement.* In addition, an audit program provides an effective means for the following:

- Organizing and distributing audit work.
- Monitoring the audit process and progress.
- Reviewing for possible omission of material areas from the audit.
- Recording the audit work performed.
- Reviewing the completeness and persuasiveness of procedures performed.

Many audit firms have developed standardized audit programs that can be modified to correspond to an individual client's unique features. For example, the audit of accounts receivable in many commercial enterprises is approximately the same but may differ depending on the customer mix and credit terms available and may affect the selection of *some* specific procedures and sample sizes to be taken. The standardized audit programs are designed to address the assertions embodied within each particular account. An example of a standardized audit program for accounts receivable is contained in Exhibit 7.11. Note that the audit program develops specific procedures that address the assertions embodied in the financial statements.

Copies of Documents

Some documents received by the auditor are deemed important enough that a copy is included in the working papers. These include both internal and external evidence. Copies of lease agreements, bond covenant agreements, significant portions of the board of director minutes, official governmental correspondence regarding

Exhibit 7.11

STANDARDIZED AUDIT PROGRAM FOR ACCOUNTS RECEIVABLE

Audit Objectives

Determine that accounts receivable are authentic obligations owed to the company at the balance sheet date (existence, rights).

Verify that accounts receivable include all amounts owed to the company at the balance sheet date (completeness).

Determine that the allowance for doubtful accounts is adequate but not excessive. If the direct write-off method is used, determine that all significant doubtful accounts have been written off, and the bad debt exposure in the remaining accounts is insignificant (valuation).

Verify that pledged, discounted, or assigned accounts receivable are properly disclosed. Related-party receivables are properly disclosed (presentation and disclosure).

Determine that accounts receivable are appropriately classified in the balance sheet (presentation).

Audit Procedures	Performed by	Working Paper Index
1. Test the mechanical accuracy of the underlying accounting records.		
2. Take a sample of recorded accounts receivable balances, and confirm the balance with the customers (existence, valuation, rights).		
3. Vouch aging details to supporting documents, discuss collectibility of receivables with responsible officials, and review correspondence (valuation).		
4. Take a sample of recorded receivables and prepare a list of subsequent cash receipts to determine if they are fully paid before the end of the audit (existence, valuation, rights).		
5. Verify cutoff for sales, cash receipts, and returns by examining transactions near the end of the year (completeness, existence).		
6. For a sample of items shipped, reprocess sales from shipping records to sales invoices, sales register, and accounts receivable subsidiary ledger (completeness, valuation, rights).		
7. Take a sample of recorded sales and vouch from sales register back to shipping records (existence).		
8. For sales invoices selected, examine inventory prices by tracing to authorized sales price lists (valuation).		
9. Determine sequential numbering of sales invoices for a period of time to determine if all items are accounted for (completeness, existence).		
10. Determine adequacy of disclosure of related-party, pledged, discounted, or assigned receivables (presentations).		

client investigations, and loan agreements are normally copied and maintained in the audit working papers. Responses to the auditor's confirmation requests for accounts receivable, pending litigation, or bank loans are examples of documents from parties outside the organization. Finally, management representations are formally documented in a *management representation letter*.

Auditor-Generated Memos

Effective auditors do more than trace items through the records and examine documents. They piece evidence together and reach an opinion as to whether a particular account balance is misstated. They independently assess the likelihood that a contingent liability might result in a loss to the company that can be estimated and should be booked. Auditors need to document the reasoning process related to accounts such as accounts receivable or inventory to support the conclusions reached on the adequacy of the account balance. For example, the senior might draft a memo describing the adequacy of the client's physical inventory procedures. The partner may summarize the adequacy of the work and the conclusions reached based on all the work performed on the account balance.

Computer Printouts

Most of today's accounting systems are highly computerized, and the auditor is either directly testing the output of the computer or testing the computer process itself. Often the auditor works with copies of the client's computer output. For example, the client might print two copies of a final inventory listing, one for the auditor and one for the company. If the auditor performs tests on the printout, it is saved as part of the audit documentation.

Audit Working Papers

Audit working papers serve as the primary documentation of an audit. A well-developed audit working paper contains the following:

- A heading that includes the name of the audit client, an explanatory title, and the balance sheet date.
- The initials of the auditor performing the audit test and the date the test was completed.
- The initials of the senior, manager, or partner who reviewed the working paper and the date the review was completed.
- A description of the nature of the test performed and the findings.
- An assessment of whether the test indicates the possibility of material misstatement in an account.
- Tick marks and legend indicating the nature of the work performed by the auditor.
- An index to identify the location of papers.
- A cross-reference to related working papers, when applicable.

An example of a working paper used as the basis to document the performance of a price test on a client's inventory is shown in Exhibit 7.12. The working paper indicates the tests performed, the source of evidence the auditor examined, and the conclusion of the audit tests. It also indicates the dollar amounts tested and those not tested. In the working paper shown in Exhibit 7.12, the auditor did not find any exceptions. If exceptions had been noted, the auditor would have documented them and would have projected the potential misstatement to the total account balance to determine whether the work might indicate material misstatements in the account balance.

Working Paper Organization

Audit working papers are typically organized around the phases of the audit, such as the planning phase, the control evaluation phase, the detailed testing, and the audit wrap-up. In the detailed testing phase, the working papers are organized according

Exhibit 7.12

WORKING PAPER FOR INVENTORY PRICE TEST

C-1/3

CMI Manufacturing Company
Inventory Price Test
Year Ended December 31, 1994

Prepared by: ______
Date: ______
Reviewed by: ______

Item No.	Item Name	Quantity	Cost Per Unit	Extended Cost
4287	Advanced Micro stamping machine	22*	$5,128†	112,816.00‡
5203	1/4 HP electric motor	10*	$ 39†	390.00‡
2208	Assembly kit for motor housing	25*	$ 12†	300.00‡
1513	Micro stamping machine, Model 25	200*	$2,100†	420,000.00‡
0068	Rack & Pinion component	300*	$ 42†	12,600.00‡
8890	Repair kits for stamping machines	1,000*	$ 48†	48,000.00‡
	Total value of items tested			594,106.00
	Items not tested			1,802,000.00
	Balance per general ledger			2,396,106.00§
				F T/B

Sampled items were selected utilizing a dollar unit sampling technique with materiality set at $50,000, and internal control judged to be good.

Tick Mark Legend:
* Quantities agree with client physical inventory tested earlier
† Traced to client's standard cost system which was independently tested. Amount agrees with client's standard cost.
‡ Tested Extension, no exceptions
§ Footed, no exceptions; agrees with trial balance

Conclusion: In my opinion, the pricing and clerical accuracy of inventory is proper.

to classes of transaction, such as specific revenue or expenses, or types of accounts, such as specific assets or liabilities. The extent of working papers varies with the size of the client, with many small- or medium-size audits containing only the basic components identified below.

Permanent file. Information of continuing importance to the on-going audit over a period of years. Items would include abstracts of the board of director's minutes and copies of important documents, such as bond covenants or major leases.

Planning file. All evidence related to the planning of the audit.

Control risk file. The documentation of the auditor's knowledge of the client's control structure, tests of the client's control procedures, and an assessment of the client's control risk.

Other audit risk areas. Information on related-party transactions or on other areas, such as potential liabilities associated with environmental protection.

Trial balance and audit adjustments. The client's trial balance, adjusted trial balance, and a summary of proposed adjustments that were not made by the client.

Asset file. Items related to tests of assets.

Liabilities file. Items related to tests of liabilities.

Equities. Audit work on the equity section.

Working Trial Balance and Lead Schedules

One of the main working papers is a trial balance of the client's general ledger. It may be automatically prepared by the client's computer, entered into a microcomputer software program by the client or auditor, or prepared manually by the client or auditor. Any working paper prepared by the client should be clearly marked as such and verified (footed, traced into the ledger, etc.) to be sure it is correct. One way to indicate that it was prepared by the client is to write "PBC" in an obvious place on the working paper.

When there are a large number of accounts in the general ledger, they are often grouped into **lead schedules,** the totals of which are then put in what is called a **working trial balance.** The latter shows the information much as it will appear on the financial statements: all cash accounts are totaled and shown as cash, all general expenses are combined into one total and so on. Exhibit 7.13 shows a partial working trial balance, lead schedule for cash, and a supporting bank reconciliation.

Indexing and Cross-Referencing

Each working paper should have a unique index to facilitate locating it when it is filed with the other working papers. The index allows cross-referencing information between working papers. Most CPA firms have their own scheme for indexing the working papers. Exhibit 7.13 shows three working papers. Notice that the cash line on the working trial balance is referenced to the cash lead schedule **A** and the total line on the cash lead schedule is referenced back to the trial balance, **TB.** Similarly, the general checking line on the cash lead schedule is referenced to the bank reconciliation **A-1,** which is referenced back to the lead schedule **A.** This is called *cross-referencing.* Numbers appearing on different working papers are referenced by

Exhibit 7.13

INDEXED AND CROSS-REFERENCED WORKING PAPERS

T/B

LeFlam Manufacturing Co.
Working Trial Balance
12/31/94

Account	Ref	12/31/93	12/31/94 Balance per Books	Adjustments/ Reclassifications Debits	Adjustments/ Reclassifications Credits	12/31/94 Final Balance
Cash	A	673,229	100,291		AJE#1 500	99,791
Accts Receivable (net)	B	2,790,150	5,444,115			
Inventory	C	8,892,774	13,385,227			
Other current assets	F	652,330	798,694			
Total current assets		13,008,483	19,728,327			

A

LeFlam Manufacturing Co.
Cash Lead Schedule
12/31/94

Account	Ref	12/31/93	12/31/94 Balance per Books	Adjustments/ Reclassifications Debits	Adjustments/ Reclassifications Credits	12/31/94 Final Balance
General Checking—NB Milwaukee 101	A-1	644,343	95,248		AJE#1 500	94,748
Check Clearing—NB Oconomowoc 102	A–2	1,000	1,000			1,000
Payroll—First Local Bank 103	A–3	26,385	2,543			2,543
Petty Cash 104	A–4	1,500	1,500			1,500
Total	T/B	673,229	100,291		500	99,791

Exhibit 7.13

A-1

LeFlam Manufacturing Co.
Bank Reconciliation—General Checking—NB Milwaukee
12/31/94

PBC Done by ________
Date ________
Reviewed by ________
Date ________

Balance per bank	$149,867.40	
Deposits in transit	0.00	
Outstanding checks	(55,119.58)	
Adjusted balance	$ 94,747.82	
Balance per books	$ 95,247.72	
Bank service charge	(500.10)	AJE #1
Adjusted balance	$ 94,747.82	
	A	

placing the index of the other working paper next to the numbers. Indexing and cross-referencing help those who review the working papers to find the information by providing an organized structure and a trail of the important numbers.

The Development of an Audit Program: An Example

An audit consists of gathering evidence to assist the auditor in judging the reasonableness of management assertions. We now turn our attention to the current assets for Coca-Cola Company in Exhibit 7.1 and focus on the inventory account. The account labeled Inventory in the balance sheet represents a number of assertions implied by management as to the existence, completeness, ownership, valuation, and presentation of the account balance. The audit program links assertions and audit evidence as follows:

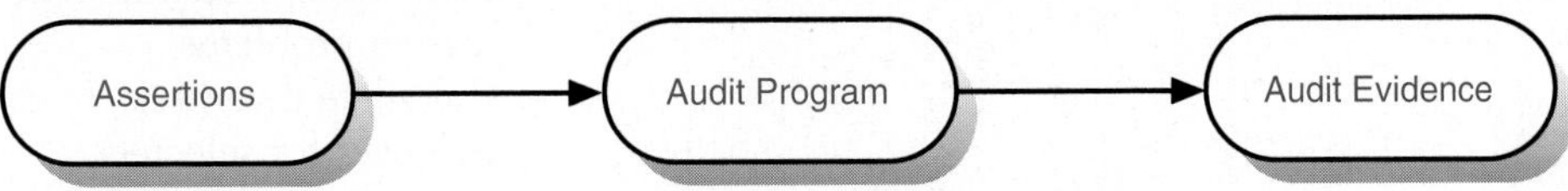

The development of an audit program could begin by simply aligning the assertions with alternative types of audit evidence. For the Inventory account, we might proceed as follows:

Assertion	Objective	Potential Audit Evidence
Existence	Determine that recorded inventory exists.	1. Physically observe the client's count of existing inventory. 2. Confirm with warehouse the existence of inventory held at outside warehouse. 3. Test client's perpetual inventory records.
Completeness	All inventory and related transactions are recorded and are recorded in the correct time period.	1. Review documentation evidencing purchase transactions to determine the completeness of recording. Review documents for title terms such as FOB shipping point or destination. 2. Review sales contracts for important terms to determine whether recognition of revenue is appropriate.
Rights and obligations	All inventory represented on the financial statement is owned by Coca-Cola Company.	1. Review selected purchases for documentation of ownership.
Valuation	The inventory is properly valued at the lower of historical cost or market. All obsolete goods have been written down to net realizable value.	1. Test accuracy of purchase price (cost) by examining selected purchase documents. 2. Test the standard cost system for accuracy and completeness of costing methods. 3. Review current sales of inventory and compare with existing levels for evidence of potential realization problems. 4. Calculate inventory turnover for selected items for evidence of obsolescence. 5. Recalculate extensions and footings.

Presentation and disclosure	Inventory footnote disclosures and financial statement presentation conform with GAAP.	1. Review working papers for evidence of special disclosure needs, paying particular attention to contracts commiting the company to the sale or purchase of significant amounts of inventory at nonmarket or fixed prices. 2. Review draft of financial statements for adequacy and completeness.

An example of a potential audit program for the audit of inventory is shown in Exhibit 7.14. The audit program is based on the assumptions that (1) the company has good controls, (2) the inventory is relatively homogenous and is valued according to the FIFO cost assumption, and (3) the client's records are highly computerized. We also assume that the auditor has previously tested purchase and sales transactions and has determined that they have been appropriately recorded in the related inventory accounts.

Exhibit 7.14

COCA-COLA COMPANY
AUDIT OF INVENTORY
YEAR ENDED DECEMBER 31, 19X1

Audit Procedures	Performed by	Working Paper Index
1. General		
a. Review industry trends and determine the potential implications for the realizability of Coca-Cola's inventory.	______	______
b. Inquire of management regarding any changes in lines of business or product mix that may affect inventory *and* whether there are any pending actions against the company resulting from the handling or disposal of inventory or related material used in producing inventory.	______	______
c. Review prior year working papers to identify any problem areas identified in last year's inventory audit and determine the potential effect on this year's audit.	______	______

(Continued)

Exhibit 7.14

COCA-COLA COMPANY
AUDIT OF INVENTORY
YEAR ENDED DECEMBER 31, 19X1

Audit Procedures	Performed by	Working Paper Index
2. Planning		
a. Perform an analytical review of inventory by product line and by location to determine whether there are any significant changes from the prior period.	________	________
b. Inquire of management as to whether any inventory lines have been disposed of or added.	________	________
c. Inquire of management as to whether there have been any significant pricing or other changes the auditor should be aware of in determining the valuation of inventory.	________	________
d. Determine the location of computer records and the computer applications and file structures on which inventory data are located.	________	________
e. Determine the need for specialized personnel, either computer audit experts or inventory specialists, in performing the audit.	________	________
3. Audit Procedures		
a. Take a statistical sample (based on a PPS sampling approach) of items from the client's perpetual inventory records and do the following:		
(1). Identify the location of the items, observe their existence, and count them. Statistically analyze any exceptions and determine whether the exceptions could lead to a material error in the inventory account balance.	________	________
(2). For items selected, observe their condition and determine whether they appear to be in saleable condition.	________	________
b. Using a computerized audit technique (such as generalized audit software), do the following:		
(1). Foot the inventory file and verify that it agrees with the trial balance.	________	________
(2). Select a statistical sample for performing price tests.	________	________
(3). Compute inventory turnover by product lines and prepare a printout of any product whose turnover is 25 percent less than the previous year.	________	________

Exhibit 7.14

COCA-COLA COMPANY
AUDIT OF INVENTORY
YEAR ENDED DECEMBER 31, 19X1

Audit Procedures	Performed by	Working Paper Index
(4). Based on previous tests, which show net realizable value to be 88 percent of sales price, compute net realizable value by multiplying sales price by 0.88 and prepare a printout of all items for which net realizable value is less than cost.	______	______
(5). Test extensions by multiplying price by cost for the items selected in the sample taken in b (1).	______	______
c. For the items selected in b (1), perform price tests by tracing the product FIFO cost per the printout to the latest purchases from an outside vendor or to the company's standard cost prices, which have been independently tested in audit program F-12.	______	______
Note: This illustrative program deals only with the FIFO portion of inventory. Additional steps would need to be developed for the inventory priced according to LIFO.		
(1). Note and statistically analyze any exceptions and project the results to the population as a whole.	______	______
(2). Based on the exceptions, determine whether there is any pattern to the errors such that they might be isolated to a particular time period, product, or location.	______	______
(3). Based on the exceptions and any pattern to the errors found, determine whether there is an unacceptable risk of material error existing in the account balance. If such a risk exists, consult with the partner in charge regarding the expansion of audit tests.	______	______
(4). Determine the ownership of the items by inspecting relevant sales documents, shipping documents, and other related documentation.	______	______
d. Observe the shipping and receiving cut-off procedures of the client to determine that all goods are recorded in the proper period. Obtain the		

(Continued)

Exhibit 7.14

COCA-COLA COMPANY
AUDIT OF INVENTORY
YEAR ENDED DECEMBER 31, 19X1

Audit Procedures	Performed by	Working Paper Index
last number of relevant shipping and receiving documents. Review the December and January sales journal to determine that all items have been recorded in the proper time period.	______	______
e. Scan the sales journal for large or unusual sales made near the end of the year. If such sales exist, examine the sales contract to determine the likelihood that all or part of the inventory might have been returned to the client.	______	______
f. Review the client's presentation of the balance sheet inventory items and all related footnotes for completeness and accuracy of presentation.	______	______
4. Completion		
a. Perform an analytical review of inventory by comparing current year inventory by product line with previous inventory levels in relation to sales. Determine whether there are any large or unusual increases in inventory that have not been adequately explained. If not adequately explained, determine the extent to which our investigation ought to be extended.	______	______
b. Formulate an opinion on the fairness of the financial statement presentation. Document that conclusion and the adequacy of the testing performed on inventory in a memo to be included in the inventory file.	______	______

Summary

Each audit is unique, but the approach to all audits is essentially the same. Implicit assumptions exist in accounting entries. These assumptions are embodied in the form of assertions that are directly tested during an audit. The strength of any particular audit depends on the relevance and reliability of the evidence gathered. *Relevance* is determined by the assertions tested, that is, some evidence will be relevant to an existence assertion but only tangentially relevant to a valuation assertion. *Reliability* relates to the quality of the evidence gathered and is affected by the independence of the evidence from the influence of the client or by the quality of the client's overall control structure. The auditor uses the risk assessments discussed in the previous chapter to assist in determining the potential reliance on internally generated audit evidence. An efficient audit combines relevant and persuasive audit evidence to provide reasonable assurance that the financial statements are free of material misstatement when the auditor renders an opinion on the financial statements.

Significant Terms

assertions Management's representations that are embodied in the financial statements reflecting generally accepted accounting principles as applied to the preparation of financial statements. Account balance assertions are classified in five broad categories: existence or occurrence, completeness, rights and obligations, valuation or allocation, and presentation and disclosure. Assertions present a framework for audit testing of account balances and classes of transactions.

analytical procedure A study of plausible relationships among both financial and nonfinancial data as a basis for identifying potential misstatements in account balances or providing corroborative evidence on the assessment that an account does not contain material misstatements; often uses ratio or trend analysis to identify potential misstatements.

auditor-generated evidence Evidence generated by the auditor, including through the auditor's reasoning process, to substantiate the correctness of account balances. Examples include recomputations, estimates, and analytical analysis.

audit program An auditor-generated document that specifies the actual evidence-gathering procedures to be performed in an audit; identifies the individual performing the procedures, the date completed, and the review of the audit procedures by supervisory audit personnel.

audit working papers The primary documentation of the work performed by the auditor; documents the items sampled, the work done, the conclusions reached, the auditor performing the tests, the date completed, and the auditor's assessment of potential misstatements in the account balance tested.

directional testing An approach to testing account balances that considers the type of misstatement likely to occur in the account balance and the corresponding evidence provided by other accounts that have been tested. The auditor normally tests assets and expenses for overstatement and liabilities and revenues for understatement because (1) the major risks of misstatements on those accounts are in those directions or (2) tests of other accounts provide evidence of possible misstatements in the other direction.

direct tests of account balances An audit approach to testing that focuses on independent evidence to substantiate the year-end balance as opposed to testing the transactions affecting the account balance throughout the year.

documentary evidence Evidence obtained through the examination of internally or externally generated documents; includes legal contracts or other evidence supporting the recording of transactions.

evidence The underlying accounting data and all corroborating information utilized by the auditor to gain reasonable assurance as to the fairness of an entity's financial statements. Evidence must be relevant, reliable, and persuasive before an audit can be completed.

lead schedules Working papers that combine similar accounts from the client's general ledger, such as all of the cash accounts; the totals from them appear on a working trial balance.

linked account relationships The effect of the double-entry bookkeeping method whereby specific accounts are directly related; an example is bond interest expense and bond liability. The auditor can gather evidence regarding both accounts by testing one account and estimating the effect on the other account. Most often the auditor tests the asset or liability account balance and uses it as a basis for determining the related expense or revenue account.

reliability of audit evidence A key characteristic of the evidence that must be evaluated by the auditor in determining the persuasiveness of the evidence-gathering procedures.

testimonial evidence Evidence based on the written or oral representations of individuals from either inside or outside the organization, often in the form of confirmations; reliability depends heavily on the independence, competence, and care used by the individual furnishing the evidence.

test of transactions Detailed procedures applied to account balances to determine the validity of the processing of individual transactions throughout the year by tracing the origination of the transaction to its subsequent recording in the accounts and vice versa and to determine the correctness and timeliness of the recording process.

working trial balance A trial balance of the client's general ledger accounts that has similar accounts combined into one total, such as all cash accounts; the individual account detail appears on lead schedules.

Review Questions

A–Introduction: Audit Evidence Framework

7–1 Explain the importance of audit assertions. Then define each of the following types of assertions:

- *Existence or occurrence.*
- *Completeness.*
- *Rights and obligations.*
- *Valuation or allocation.*
- *Presentation and disclosure.*

7–2 Auditing is described as a process of gathering and evaluating evidence to test assertions. Are the financial assertions tested by auditors necessarily limited to account balance assertions? If not, what are the boundaries of financial assertions that can be tested by auditors?

7–3 What is directional testing? How can the concept of directional testing assist the auditor in attaining audit efficiency?

7–4 The valuation assertion is usually the most difficult to detail. Identify all the components of the valuation assertion for short-term investments in marketable securities.

7–5 Explain how the concept of double-entry bookkeeping and linked accounts can be used by the auditor to achieve audit efficiency. Give two examples.

7–6 What is meant by *testing transactions*? Give an example of how the auditor would test transactions as a major source of audit evidence.

B–Sources of Audit Evidence

7–7 What factors determine the reliability of audit evidence? Give an example of two types of evidence, one that is more reliable and one that is less reliable.

7–8 Explain how testing an asset account for overstatement provides evidence on potential overstatements of revenue and understatement of expenses. Illustrate using Accounts Receivable and Inventory as examples.

7–9 What is testimonial evidence? Identify the types of testimonial evidence the auditor obtains during an audit. For each type listed, identify the factors that affect its perceived reliability and persuasiveness.

7–10 The third standard of fieldwork provides that the auditor should gather sufficient competent evidential matter to afford *a reasonable basis* for an opinion regarding the financial statements under audit. Explain how the concept of reasonable basis identified in the standard relates to audit risk. Does the auditor do sufficient work to be absolutely convinced that the financial statements are correct?

7–11 Consider the concepts of reliability of evidence discussed in this chapter and audit risk discussed in the previous chapter. Are the two concepts interrelated or are they two separate concepts? For example, could the auditor accept less reliable audit evidence for an engagement in which audit risk has been set for a normal audit than for an engagement in which audit risk has been set lower than normal? Explain.

7–12 Distinguish between internal and external documentation as a form of audit evidence. Give two examples of each.

7–13 Over a coffee break, a senior auditor stated that he found external documentation always to be more reliable and persuasive than internal documentation. As a matter of policy, he plans audits to minimize the use of internal documentation and always relies on external documentation whenever it is available. Do you agree or disagree with the auditor's assessment of the relative value of internal and external documentation? Explain by discussing the relative reliability and usefulness of the two forms of documentation.

7–14 Explain why the auditor is more likely to perform direct tests of account balances than to perform detailed tests of all the transactions that affected the account balance during the year under audit.

7–15 What is the difference between reprocessing a transaction and vouching a transaction? What underlying processing assertions does each process address?

7–16 Assuming that the client has external documentation on hand, such as correspondence with its lawyers or payments from its customers, why is sending confirmations to those same parties considered necessary?

7–17 Confirmations at times may be unreliable even if they involve external documentation. What assumptions should the auditor address concerning confirmations before concluding that utilizing confirmations will result in reliable audit evidence?

7–18 Explain the difference in reasoning between performing tests of details and making an inference about the correctness of an account balance and performing analytical procedures to make similar inferences.

7–19 Analytical procedures can be performed using accounting data or nonfinancial data (including data generated outside of the organization) as a predictor. Would using accounting data be considered more reliable than using nonfinancial data? What determines the reliability of analytical procedures? Explain.

7–20 What decisions regarding audit evidence must be made on every audit engagement? For each decision, identify the major factors affecting an auditor's decision.

C–Documenting Audit Evidence

7–21 What is an audit working paper? What are the key components that each working paper should contain?

7–22 Is a memo explaining the rationale for an auditor's conclusion as to the adequacy of the audit work performed and the correctness of an account balance a working paper? Explain. Should such memos be filed with the working papers and made available for peer reviews?

7–23 Many organizations are consciously eliminating paper documents by integrating their computer system with those of their suppliers and customers. Paper documents, such as purchase orders, are being replaced by machine-generated purchase orders. How will this change in documentation likely affect the audit approach for such clients? Explain and give an example.

7–24 Define *permanent file working paper*. Identify several types of information typically included in such a file. What is the relevance of that information to the current year audit? Is the permanent file considered to be a part of the current year audit working papers? Explain.

7–25 What is meant by the phrase, "The audit working papers ought to stand on their own"? What is the importance of this concept to the documentation included in working papers?

Multiple Choice Questions

7–26 A test of an asset for overstatement provides corresponding evidence on expenses, revenues, and liabilities as follows:

a. Expense overstatement, revenue overstatement, and liability understatement.

b. Expense understatement, revenue overstatement, and liability overstatement.
c. Expense understatement, revenue understatement, and liability understatement.
d. Expense overstatement, revenue overstatement, and liability overstatement.

7–27 Observation is considered a reliable audit procedure but one that is limited in its usefulness. Which of the following does *not* represent a limitation of the use of observation as an audit technique?
a. Individuals may react differently when being observed than they do otherwise.
b. It is rarely sufficient to satisfy any assertion other than existence.
c. It can provide an overview of the nature of the client's processing, but that processing may be different than the client's procedures specify.
d. It is difficult to generalize from one observation to the correctness of processing throughout the period under audit.

*7–28 Confirmation is most likely to be a relevant form of evidence with regard to assertions about accounts receivable when the auditor has concern about the receivables'
a. Valuation.
b. Classification.
c. Existence.
d. Completeness.

7–29 The permanent file section of the working papers that is kept for each audit client most likely contains
a. Review notes pertaining to questions and comments regarding the audit work performed.
b. A schedule of time spent on the engagement by each individual auditor.
c. Correspondence with the client's legal counsel concerning existing and pending litigation.
d. Narrative descriptions of major adjustments made during the course of the previous audit.

*7–30 Audit evidence can come in different forms with different degrees of persuasiveness. Which of the following is the *least* persuasive type of evidence?
a. Bank statement obtained from the client.
b. Computations made by the auditor.
c. Prenumbered client sales invoices.
d. Vendor's invoice.

*Adapted from the Uniform CPA examination or the Certified Internal Auditor examination.

*7–31 The auditor most likely performs extensive tests for possible understatement of

a. Revenues.

b. Assets.

c. Capital.

d. Liabilities.

*7–32 An auditor would most likely verify the interest earned on short-term bond investments by

a. Examining the receipt and deposit of interest checks.

b. Confirming the bond interest rate with the issuer of the bonds.

c. Recomputing the interest earned on the basis of face amount, interest rate, and period held.

d. Recomputing interest according to the face of the bond and adjusting by a bond discount or premium amortization.

*7–33 Which of the following is the *least* persuasive documentation in support of an auditor's opinion?

a. Schedules of details of physical inventory counts conducted by the client.

b. Notation of inferences drawn from ratios and trends.

c. Notation of appraisers' conclusions documented in the auditor's working papers.

d. Lists of confirmations and the nature of responses received from the client's customers.

7–34 The auditor wishes to gather evidence to test the assertion that the client's capitalization of leased equipment assets are properly valued. Which of the following sources of evidence will the auditor find to be the most persuasive (most reliable and relevant)?

a. Direct observation of the leased equipment.

b. Examination of the lease contract and recomputation of capitalized amount and current amortization.

c. Confirmation of the current purchase price for similar equipment with vendors.

d. Confirmation of the original cost of the equipment with the lessor

7–35 Which of the following statements is *not* true concerning the auditor's work documentation contained in working papers?

a. The auditor should document the reasoning process and conclusions reached for significant account balances even if audit tests show no exceptions.

b. Working paper review is facilitated if a standard working paper format is utilized.

c. Individual working papers should cross-reference other working papers if the other papers contain work that affects the auditor's overall assessment of an account balance contained in the work paper.

d. The client should not prepare working paper schedules even if they are independently tested by the auditor.

Discussion and Research Questions

7–36 (Classification and Reliability of Audit Evidence) Following are examples of documentation typically obtained by auditors. For each example:

a. Classify the documentation as internal or external evidence.
b. Classify the documentation as to its relative reliability (high, moderate, or low).
c. Identify an account balance and assertion for which the auditor might use the documentation.

Documentary Evidence Utilized in an Audit

1. Vendor invoices.
2. Vendor monthly statements.
3. Sales invoices.
4. Shipping documents for sales.
5. Bank statements.
6. Employee payroll time cards.
7. Receiving reports for goods received from vendors.
8. Sales contracts.
9. Purchase commitment contracts.
10. Lease agreements.
11. Estimated warranty schedules.
12. Loan agreements.
13. Credit rating reports.
14. Canceled checks.

7–37 (Audit Assertions, Evidence, and Program Development) Johnson Company is a medium-size manufacturing client that has expanded its operations over the past few years by acquiring smaller companies that had complementary products or that manufactured products that could be used in its primary products. The auditor believes that some of the acquisitions were made because the client had not invested in its own research and development sufficiently to maintain a competitive edge and therefore some of the acquisitions seem to have been needed to keep up with technological change. The client has been relatively, but not spectacularly, profitable over the past decade.

You have been assigned to audit the Goodwill account. The senior tells you that goodwill existed in previous years and that if the beginning balance agrees with last year's balance, you can assume that there is support for that balance. Before beginning your detailed audit work, you perform some background review and note that five acquisitions were made over the past five years. Three have worked out well, but two others (on whom a large amount of goodwill was recorded) were not successful. Both of the subsidiaries have continued to incur large losses, and company management is now considering disposing of both.

The Goodwill account balance for the year is as follows:

Goodwill	
Beginning balance	$475,000
Acquisition	300,000
Amortization (beginning balance)	(25,000)
Amortization (Acquisition)	(7,500)
Ending balance	$742,500

The senior on the engagement indicates that it is the client's policy to take a full year's amortization during the year of acquisition; your firm has agreed that this is an appropriate policy followed consistently by the client.

Required:

a. Identify the assertions that will be addressed by the auditor in auditing the Goodwill account. Identify the assertions in detail; for example, identify the appropriate GAAP basis that would serve as a reference for valuing goodwill.

b. What other account will be examined at the same time the Goodwill account is audited? Explain.

c. Starting with the beginning goodwill, identify audit evidence that would address each of the assertions. Briefly identify the audit procedures that would be utilized to gather the audit evidence.

d. For the newly acquired goodwill, identify the audit evidence that would address each of the assertions. Briefly identify the audit procedures that would be utilized to gather the audit evidence.

7–38 (Types of Audit Procedures) Nine major types of audit procedures were identified as part of the audit evidence-gathering process. These procedures included

Observation	Physical examination
Examination of documentation	Inquiry
Confirmations	Recalculations
Reprocessing	Vouching
Analytical procedures	

Required:

Following is a list of audit procedures performed. For each procedure, classify the evidence procedure gathered according to one (or more, if applicable) of the nine audit procedure types.

Auditing Procedures Performed

a. Calculate the ratio of Cost of Goods Sold to Sales as a test of overall reasonableness of the Cost of Goods Sold balance.

b. Trace a sales transaction from the origination of an incoming sales order to the shipment of merchandise to the generation of an invoice to the proper recording in the sales journal.

c. Test the accuracy of the sales invoice by multiplying the number of items shipped by the authorized price list to determine extended cost. Foot the total and make sure that it agrees with the total invoiced.

d. Select a recorded sales invoice and search through the records for shipping documents to verify the existence of goods shipped.

e. Examine canceled checks returned with the client's January bank statement as support of outstanding checks listed on the client's December year-end bank reconciliation.

f. Perform test counts of the client's marketable securities held in a safe deposit box.

g. Tour the plant to determine that a major equipment acquisition was received and is in working condition.

h. Review a lease contract to determine the items covered and its major provisions.

i. Request a statement from a major customer as to its agreement or disagreement with a year-end receivable balance shown to be due to the audit client.

j. Develop a microcomputer spreadsheet to calculate an independent estimate of the client's warranty liability (reserve) based on production data and current warranty repair expenditures.

k. Develop a microcomputer spreadsheet to independently test the calculations made by the client in computing a warranty liability (reserve).

l. Meet with the client's internal legal department to determine its assessment of the potential outcome of pending litigation regarding a patent infringement suit against the company.

m. Review all major past due accounts receivable with the credit manager to help determine whether the client's allowance for doubtful accounts is adequate.

n. Make test counts of inventory items and record the items in the audit working papers for subsequent testing.

o. Obtain information about the client's processing system and associated controls by asking the client's personnel to fill out a questionnaire.

p. Examine board of directors minutes for the approval of a major bond issued during the year.

q. Have the client's outside law firm send a letter directly to the auditor providing a description of any differences between the lawyer's assessment of litigation and that of the client.

7–39 (Evaluation of Testimonial Evidence) One of the major tasks of an auditor is to evaluate the reliability of testimonial evidence, which may come in the form of oral representations from management or in written form from parties outside the organization.

Required:

a. In the course of an audit, the auditor asks many questions of client officers and employees. Describe the factors the auditor should consider in evaluating oral evidence provided by client officers and employees.

b. For each of the following examples of testimonial evidence, identify either (1) an alternative source of evidence or (2) corroborative evidence the auditor might seek.

Examples of Testimonial Evidence

1. Confirmations received from customers as to the balance of accounts receivable shown by the client.
2. Management is very optimistic that all items in a product line will be sold at normal prices in spite of a temporary downturn in sales.
3. Management intends to hold investments in marketable securities with an intent to convert into cash within the next operating period as cash needs dictate.
4. Management tells the auditor that the Food and Drug Administration has approved its new drug for commercial sale.
5. The auditor interviews the production manager, who candidly identifies quality control problems and points out substantial pieces of inventory that should be reworked before shipment.

7–40 (Persuasiveness of Audit Evidence) The chapter identified several different kinds of audit evidence. The following questions concern the reliability of audit evidence.

a. Explain why confirmations are normally considered more reliable than inquiries of the client. Under what situations might the opposite hold true?

b. Give three examples of reliable documentation and three examples of less reliable documentation. What characteristics distinguish them?

c. Explain why observation is considered strong, but limited, evidence. Under what circumstances would the auditor's observation of inventory be considered of limited use?

d. Identify characteristics of internal evidence that would lead the auditor to assess its reliability as high.

e. Explain why tests of details may be more reliable than analytical procedures.

f. Explain how analytical procedures might lead to insight about the correctness of an account balance that might not be obtained through tests of details.

g. Identify three instances in which an auditor would likely use recomputations as audit evidence. Why is it important that recomputations take place? Is an auditor-prepared spreadsheet a recomputation or an independent estimate of an account balance? Explain.

7–41 (Alternative Sources of Evidence) The following situations present the auditor with alternative sources of evidence regarding a particular assertion.

Required:

a. For each situation listed below, identify the assertion the auditor is most likely testing with the procedure.

b. For each situation, identify which of the two sources presents the most persuasive evidence, and briefly indicate the rationale for your answer.

Sources of Audit Evidence

1. Confirming accounts receivable with business organizations versus confirming receivables with consumers.
2. Visually inspecting an inventory of electronics components versus performing an inventory turnover and sales analysis by products and product lines.
3. Observe the counting of a client's year-end physical inventory versus confirming the inventory held at an independent warehouse by requesting a confirmation from the owner of the warehouse.
4. Confirming a year-end bank balance with the client's banking institution versus reviewing the client's year-end bank statement versus having a cut-off bank statement as of January 20 for all activity from December 31 to January 20 sent to the auditor.
5. Observing the client's inventory composed primarily of sophisticated radar detectors and similar electronics equipment versus observing the client's inventory composed primarily of sheet metal.
6. Confirming the client's year-end bank balance with the bank versus confirming the potential loss due to a lawsuit with the client's outside legal counsel.
7. Testing the client's estimate of warranty liability by obtaining a copy of the client's spreadsheet used for calculating the liability and determining the accuracy of the spreadsheet's logic by entering new data into the spreadsheet and independently calculating the result versus developing an independent spreadsheet and using regression analysis to develop an independent estimate of the warranty liability using client sales and warranty return data.
8. Reviewing all payments made to vendors and suppliers after year-end to determine if they were properly recorded as accounts payable versus requesting vendor statements at year-end for all significant vendors from which the client made purchases during the year.
9. For a financial institution, test the organization's controls for recording customer savings deposits, including the existence of an independent department to explore any inquiries by customers versus confirming year-end savings account balances with customers.
10. For a financial institution, test the organization's controls for making and recording loans versus confirming year-end loan balances directly with customers.

7–42 (Audit Program and Assertions) You have been assigned to audit the notes receivable of a medium-size audit client, Eagle River Distributing. The Notes Receivable account is new this year and per discussion with the controller, it came about because three major customers were experiencing payment difficulties. The three customers account for approximately 15 percent of the client's annual sales. The account was first used in July with a $300,000 balance and now has a year-end balance of $2.5 million (this compares to an accounts receivable year-end balance of $6.0 million).

On further investigation, you determine that the year-end balance is composed of the following notes:

J.P. McCarthur Printing, 10%, due July 1 of next year	$1.2 million
Stevens Point Newspaper, 11%, due Sept. 30 of next year	$0.8 million
Orbison Enterprises, 12%, due in 18 months	$0.5 million

You further discover the following:

1. Orbison Enterprises is a company wholly owned by the president of Eagle River Distributing and is backed by the personal guarantee of the president (including the pledging of personal assets).
2. The company continues to make sales to each of these companies. The notes represent a consolidation of previous outstanding receivables. All three companies are current in their payments of existing receivables.

Required:

a. Identify any special risk concerns that you might have regarding the audit of this new account.

b. Identify the major assertions to be tested by the auditor in auditing this account. For each assertion listed, identify one or two auditing procedures the auditor might use to gather audit evidence in determining the correct financial statement presentation of the account.

7–43 (Audit Working Papers) The audit working papers represent the auditor's accumulation of evidence and conclusions reached on an audit engagement. Prior year audit working papers can provide insight into an audit engagement that will be useful in planning the current year audit.

Required:

a. What are the purposes or primary functions of audit working papers?

b. Who owns the working papers, the auditor or the client?

c. What important planning information might an auditor learn when reviewing the prior year audit working papers of a client?

d. The auditor often requests the client to prepare a lead schedule, such as a schedule listing all repair and maintenance expenses over $5,000 for the past year. The client asks for a copy of the previous year's working paper to serve as a guide. The auditor is reluctant to furnish the working paper to the client.

   1. Is it permissible to provide the client copies of the auditor's previous working papers? If so, are there any particular conditions the auditor should examine before furnishing the working paper to the client?
   2. What procedures should the auditor use to ensure that the client has properly prepared the requested working paper?

7–44 (Audit Working Papers) The following equipment working paper schedule was prepared by the client and audited by Sam Staff, an audit assistant, during the calendar-year 1994 audit of Roberta Enterprises, a continuing audit client. As engagement supervisor, you are reviewing the working paper.

Roberta Enterprises
12/31/94

		Cost				Accumulated Depreciation			
Description	Date Purchased	Beginning Balance	Additions	Disposals	Ending Balance	Beginning Balance	Depreciation Expense	Disposals	Ending Balance
1020 Press	10/25/89	15,250		15,250	0	10,500†	1,575‡	12,075§	0
40" Lathe	10/30/89	9,852		9,852	0	7,444†	1,250‡	8,694§	0
505 Router	10/15/89	4,635			4,635	3,395†	875		4,270
MP Welder	9/10/89	1,222			1,222	850†	215		1,065
1040 Press	3/25/94		18,956§		18,956	0	3,566		3,566
IBM 400AS Computer	7/16/91	12,547			12,547	7,662†	3,065†		10,727
60" Lathe	5/29/94		13,903		13,903	0	950		950
Fork Lift	6/2/89	7,881			7,881	3,578†	810		4,388
Totals		51,387	32,859	25,102	59,144	33,429†	12,306	20,769	24,966
		II		II			II	II	II**

†–Traced to 12/31/93 working papers
‡–Recalculated
§–Verified
II–Footed/crossfooted
**–Traced to trial balance

Required:
Identify the deficiencies in the working paper.

*7–45 (Audit Evidence) The procedures followed and the selected results of an audit of the regional sales division of a discount department store chain are listed below.

Required:

a. Classify each item in the audit as *fact* or *opinion*. Briefly distinguish between the two.
b. Classify each item as to the type of evidence gathered using the categories of observation, testimonial, documentary, or analytical. More than one category of evidence may be appropriate in each situation. Use the format shown below.

Fact or Opinion			Type of Evidence			
Item	Fact	Opinion	Observation	Testimonial	Documentary	Analytical
1.						
2.						
etc.						

Procedures Followed and Selected Results

1. The auditor observed the receipt of product on a test basis.
2. The receipt of a product was traced to a purchase order on a test basis.
3. The auditor tallied employee inventory tags on a test basis.
4. The auditor test counted inventory represented by a sample of tags.
5. The auditor observed that ordering and receiving functions were performed independent of each other.
6. The auditor concluded that internal control was adequate in the ordering and receiving area.
7. The auditor confirmed that cash receipts were counted immediately on opening of envelopes containing checks.
8. The audit concluded that the credit policy was appropriate to maximize net income.

7–46 (Persuasiveness of Evidence) During the investigation of the Building and Land accounts, the internal auditor notices that one of the buildings was sold last year for a very large profit as authorized by the board of directors. The director of internal auditing did not understand why the profit was so large.

The director instructs you to determine which one or more of the land or building properties were sold during the year. In addition, if the property was sold, she wants you to verify the amount of profit recognized.

The auditor is considering the following procedures:

1. Checking the depreciation schedule to determine which properties are still being depreciated.
2. Reviewing the property ledger to determine which properties had been deleted during the year.
3. Physically inspecting and photographing all properties.
4. Inspecting the tax receipts for each property.
5. Inspecting the taxing authority records for title to the properties.
6. Inspecting the property insurance policies.

Required:

a. Identify the one best procedure listed above as evidence as to which property or properties were sold. Defend the choice by identifying its major strengths and the major weaknesses in the other procedures.
b. Identify the best procedure (or combination of procedures) to determine whether the proper amount of profit was recognized on the sale.

7–47 (Account Relationships and Audit Efficiency) One way in which the auditor might achieve audit efficiency is to recognize the interrelationship between accounts. In many situations, evidence gathered in auditing a balance sheet account (asset, liability, or equity) can be easily expanded to audit a related income statement account.

Required:

a. For each of the accounts listed below,

1. Identify one or more related accounts that could be audited efficiently by expanding on the audit evidence gathered during the audit of the account.
2. Identify how the evidence gathered from auditing the balance sheet account could be used in auditing the income or equity account.

b. Explain why auditors generally consider it to be more efficient to directly test a year-end balance sheet account rather than testing transactions during the year. Does this mean that auditors do not need to test the transactions that make up an account balance, that is, they need to test only the year-end balance? Explain your answer in terms of the reliability and persuasiveness of audit evidence.

Account Balances Audited:

(1). Marketable Equity Securities.
(2). Bond Payable.
(3). Property, Plant, and Equipment.
(4). Goodwill.
(5). Capitalized Leases.
(6). Capitalized Lease Obligations.
(7). Notes Payable.
(8). Estimated Warranty Liability (Reserve).
(9). Preferred Stock.
(10). Equity Method Investments.

*7–48 (Use of Confirmations) As the auditor of Star Manufacturing Company, you have obtained the following data:

- There are no inventories consigned either in or out.
- All notes receivable are due from outsiders and are held by Star.
- The following trial balance taken from the books of Star one month prior to year-end.

	Dr. (Cr.)
Cash in Bank	87,000
Trade Accounts Receivable	345,000
Notes Receivable	125,000
Inventories	317,000
Land	66,000
Building, Net	350,000
Furniture, Fixtures, and Equipment (net)	325,000
Trade Accounts Payable	(235,000)
Mortgages Payable	(400,000)
Common Stock	(300,000)
Retained Earnings	(510,000)
Sales	(3,130,000)
Cost of Goods Sold	2,300,000
General and Administrative Expenses	622,000
Legal and Professional Fees	3,000
Interest Expense	35,000

Required:
What accounts should be confirmed with outside sources? Briefly describe by whom they should be confirmed and the information that should be confirmed. Organize your answer in the following format:

Account Title	From Whom Confirmed	Information to be Confirmed

7–49 (Audit Assertions for a Liability Account) Accounts Payable is generally one of the larger, and most volatile, liability accounts to audit. However, the auditor can use the assertion approach developed in this chapter to develop an overall audit program for accounts payable.

Assume that you are auditing the accounts payable for Appleton Electronics, a wholesaler of hardware equipment. You may assume that the company has a good control structure and is not designated as a high risk audit client. You are the continuing auditor. There have been adjustments made during the previous audit regarding Accounts Payable, but none of them was considered material.

Required:
a. Identify, in significant detail, the audit assertions that would apply to the audit of Accounts Payable.
b. For each assertion identified, list two or three types of audit evidence that would address the assertion and the procedures used to gather the audit evidence. Organize your answer as follows:

Audit Assertion	Audit Evidence and Procedures

c. How would the evidence-gathering procedures be affected if you had assessed the client as a high-risk client because (1) there are questions of management integrity, (2) the company is in a perilous financial situation, and (3) the company has an inadequate control structure. Be specific in your answer as to what additional evidence, or alternative types of evidence, you would gather.

7–50 (Use of Analytical Procedures Techniques) Use of analytical procedures is an alternative that may lead to audit efficiency in situations when the client has good control, and reliable data may be utilized in making estimates of an account balance.

Required:
a. What is the underlying reasoning process used in analytical procedures? What are the major assumptions that should be reviewed before relying on analytical procedures.
b. Drawing on your knowledge of financial analysis covered in your intermediate accounting class, indicate how ratio or trend analysis could be used in estimating the correctness of the following account balances. Identify the independent data that would be used in estimating it. Briefly explain whether you believe the account could be reliably estimated using analytical procedures.

Accounts to Be Estimated Using Analytical Procedures Techniques
1. Interest Expense.
2. Revenue for a natural gas utility located in the Midwest.

3. Cost of Goods Sold for a manufacturing company.
4. Selling Expense for a distributor that compensates its salespeople on a commission basis.
5. Allowance for Uncollectible Accounts.
6. Warranty Expense.
7. Legal Expense.
8. Distribution Expense for a manufacturer that ships all its goods to five different wholesalers.

7–51 (Complementary Effect of Audit Tests) Testing one account balance produces audit evidence concerning another account balance or class of transactions due to the double-entry accounting system. For example, testing for overstatement of current marketable securities may uncover an understatement of long-term investments due to a missclassification (presentation and disclosure).

Required:
For each of the following tests of account balances, indicate at least two other account balances or classes of transactions for which evidence is also provided, as well as the related assertions.

1. Testing Inventory for overstatement (existence and valuation).
2. Testing Revenue for understatement (completeness).
3. Testing Accounts Receivable for overstatement (existence).
4. Testing Accrued Salaries for understatement (completeness).
5. Testing Repairs and Maintenance Expense for overstatement (existence).
6. Testing the adequacy of the Allowance for Doubtful Accounts (valuation).

7–52 **(Research Question)** A major development of computer processing during the 1990s is referred to as *image processing.* It is the process of making copies of paper documents and storing them in computerized form.

Required:
Review periodicals to determine the nature of image processing as it has developed to date. After gaining an understanding of the nature of image processing, prepare a two- to three-page overview of the potential audit implications. At this point, you do not have to go into detail on computer auditing; you need only to consider the implications as they pertain to the auditor's use of documentary evidence. For example, what would need to be added to maintain the major attributes of documentary evidence used by auditors today?

7–53 **(Research Question—Audit Program Generators)** If your school has copies of the AICPA's software *Audit Program Generator,* obtain a copy of it. Use the software to develop an audit program for Notes Receivable. Compare the program with that developed in response to Question 7–42. Identify the assertions addressed by each auditing procedure generated by the program.

7–54 **(Research Question)** Two of the classic essays on audit evidence are contained in the *Philosophy of Auditing* (1961) by Mautz and Sharaf and by the

Statement of Basic Auditing Concepts (1972) both published by the American Accounting Association.

Required:
Read either the AAA *Statement of Basic Auditing Concepts* or Chapter 6 of the Mautz and Sharaf monograph (as directed by your instructor). Compare and contrast the assertions approach developed in those readings with the assertions approach contained in this chapter and in AU 326. What is a "warranted belief"? How does the concept of a "warranted belief" affect the type and extent of audit evidence gathered?

Case

7–55 (MiniScribe—Audit Evidence for Sales, Accounts Receivable, and Inventory)

As reported in *The Wall Street Journal* (September 11, 1989), MiniScribe, Inc., inflated its reported profits and inventory through a number of schemes designed to fool the auditors. At that time, MiniScribe was one of the major producers of disk drives for personal computers. The article reported that MiniScribe used the following techniques to meet its profit objectives:

- An extra shipment of $9 million of disks was sent to a customer near year-end and booked as a sale. The customer had not ordered the goods and ultimately returned them, but the sale was not reversed in the year recorded.
- Shipments were made from a factory in Singapore, usually by air freight. Toward the end of the year, some of the goods were shipped by cargo ships. The purchase orders were changed to show that the customer took title when the goods were loaded on the ship. However, title did not pass to the customer until the goods were received in the United States.
- Returned goods were recorded as usable inventory. Some were shipped without any repair work performed.
- MiniScribe developed a number of just-in-time warehouses and shipped goods to them from where they were delivered to customers. The shipments were billed as sales as soon as they reached the warehouse.

Required:
For each of the items identified above, identify the following:

a. The assertion the auditor might be testing in relationship to the account balance and the transaction.

b. The audit evidence that should be gathered to assist in addressing the assertion.

End Notes

1. Abraham Akresh, James Loebbecke, and William Scott, "Audit Approaches and Techniques," in *Research Opportunities in Auditing: The Second Decade*, ed. A. Rashad Abdel-khalik and Ira Solomon (Sarasota, Fla.: American Accounting Association, 1988), 52.

CHAPTER

8

Learning Objectives

Through studying this chapter, you will be able to:

1. Understand the elements of an entity's internal control structure.
2. Perform a control risk assessment.
3. Identify the key elements of an entity's control environment and the audit approach to assessing each component.
4. Identify approaches taken to obtain information about an organization's accounting system and control procedures.
5. Understand the relationship between the auditor's control risk assessment and the development of substantive tests of account balances.

Assessing Control Risk: An Overview

Chapter Contents

Chapter Overview

The quality of an entity's control structure affects the likelihood that misstatements will occur in the financial reporting process. Thus, the auditor needs to assess the organization's control structure as part of the process of controlling audit risk and designing an efficient audit. The organization's control structure is multifaceted, consisting of the overall control environment, the accounting system, and specific control procedures implemented to ensure the correctness and completeness of processing. The chapter identifies methods auditors frequently use to assess control risk, test the effectiveness of control procedures, and integrate the understanding of control risk into the design of detailed tests of account balances.

The development of reliable internal control systems by auditees has allowed the auditor to perform financial-statement audits that are both efficient and effective. . . . Internal control must be recognized as rapidly changing (because information systems and data processing methods are rapidly changing). Auditors must remain current with respect to systems developments because as information systems change, so do the needs and techniques of internal control.[1]

In all audits, the auditor should obtain a sufficient understanding of each of the three elements [of the internal control structure] to plan the audit by performing procedures to understand the design of policies and procedures relevant to audit planning and whether they have been placed in operation. [AU 319.02]

A–INTRODUCTION

The auditor's understanding of an organization's control structure and the related assessment of control risk is essential to the planning of an efficient audit (see Exhibit 8.1). Most of today's organizations would cease to function if they did not have a strong control structure. By the same token, the lack of a strong control structure allows the abuses and incorrect financial reporting that occurred in many organizations during the 1980s.

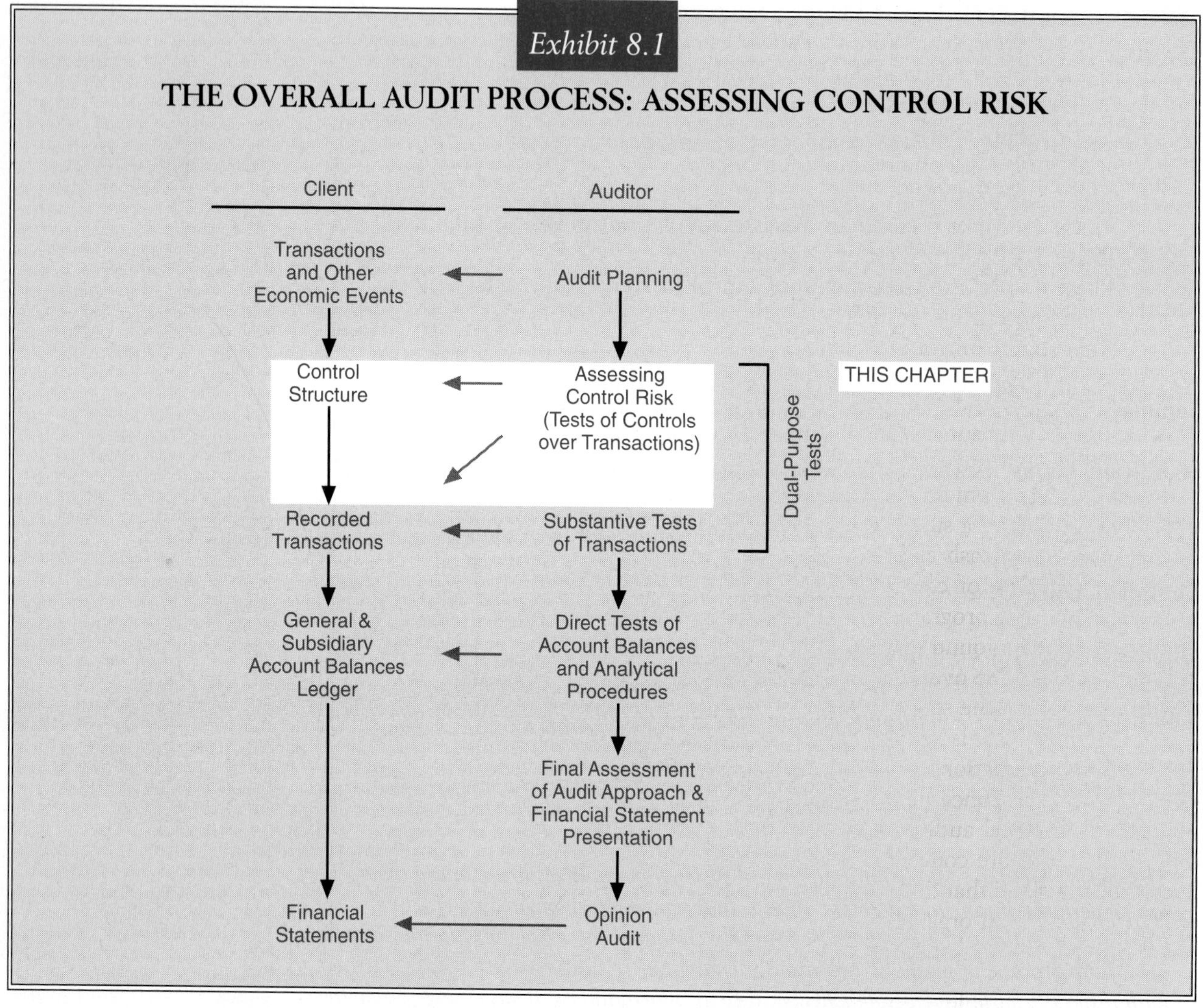

A recent study of insurance company failures in Wisconsin found that the characteristic the failed companies shared was the lack of good internal controls. The companies' senior managers ignored both accounting controls and financial planning; instead they operated under a philosophy that any problem could be solved by selling more insurance policies. Public accounting firms routinely deal with clients that lack good controls. Auditors who fail to recognize and compensate for an organization's poor control structure can find themselves in court. For example, the failure of Crazy Eddie's, a fast-growing electronics retailer in the late 1980s, was partially attributable to a poor control system that failed to warn managers and others of nonexistent inventory that was recorded in the company's books.

As these examples illustrate, the quality of controls in an organization affects the quality of performance of the organization and can, in turn, have a significant effect on the conduct of an audit. This chapter examines internal controls and an organization's control structure as it affects the auditor's assessment of **control risk** and the determination of audit procedures.

Internal Control Structure: Definition and Relation to Audit

An entity's **internal control structure** is defined as:

> the policies and procedures established to provide reasonable assurance that specific objectives will be achieved. Although the internal control structure may include a wide variety of objectives and related policies and procedures, only some of these may be relevant to an audit of an entity's financial statements. Generally, the policies and procedures that are relevant to an audit pertain to the entity's ability to record, process, summarize, and report financial data consistent with the assertions embodied in the financial statements. [AU 319.06]

Controls, then, are methods, procedures, and policies designed to achieve specific objectives such as ensuring that all transactions are properly authorized, all transactions are recorded, and assets are adequately safeguarded. Controls can be found in many forms. Management that sets a tone for the organization by quickly disciplining a wrongdoing by a subordinate is exhibiting a form of control. Segregating the duties of receiving cash and of recording accounts receivable is another, probably more familiar, type of control. Controls may be found over individual processes, such as a computer program, or over a process for accepting and filling sales orders; or controls may be found in broad policies set by management to guide overall corporate activities. The overall design and implementation of controls in an organization to accomplish the specific organizational objectives is referred to as the *control structure*. The auditor is interested in evaluating the control structure as it affects the recording of transactions and presentation in the financial statements. Thus, the external auditor is concerned primarily with controls related to the financial recording process. Internal auditors, or external auditors performing other than financial statement audits, are concerned with a wider variety of control policies and procedures such as those that deal with operational effectiveness and efficiency.

The quality of an organization's control structure affects an audit in six crucial ways:

1. Some *minimum* level of control is necessary for an entity to be *auditable*. Without a minimal set of controls to ensure that transactions are recorded and documentation exists, an audit would not be possible.

2. The overall structure of controls can significantly affect the operations of the organization and may have an impact on the ability of the organization to remain a *going concern*. Many failing businesses have had an inadequate control structure. The problems the savings and loan industry faced in the past decade, for example, were accentuated by a poor or nonexistent overall control structure for the organization to ensure that authorized loans were consistent with the risk levels the organization was willing to accept.

3. The quality of an organization's control structure significantly affects both the audit approach and the amount of testing needed on any given audit engagement.

4. An analysis of deficiencies (control risk) in specific accounting processes is helpful to the auditor in identifying the types of misstatements that might

occur in the financial statements. Because the audit is designed to search for material misstatements, knowledge of *how misstatements might occur* is useful in developing specific tests to determine whether such misstatements do in fact exist.

5. An inadequate control structure may place an organization in violation of federal laws. The Foreign Corrupt Practices Act of 1977 requires all businesses registered with the SEC to "establish and maintain a system of internal accounting controls" sufficient to meet specific control objectives related to authorizing transactions, safeguarding assets, maintaining accountability, and limiting access to assets.
6. The auditor is often called on to issue a formal report to third-party users assessing the organization's control structure. The FDIC Improvement Act of 1991 requires the management of large financial institutions to report publicly on the status of its control structure and to have its independent auditors attest to that report. Similar requirements now exist for government audits, and the SEC has been considering mandating such reports for all public companies.

An understanding of a client's control structure—what it is, how it operates, its effectiveness, any changes in it since the last audit, the extent of its reliance on computerization—is essential to the efficient conduct of every audit.

A Framework for Evaluating Controls

Many of you have had some experience working for a business organization. You did not need an accounting job to sense whether the organization was control conscious. You perhaps noted a lackadaisical attitude on the shipping dock or perhaps a less than conscientious approach to filling out documents. Or you might have been involved in a small business owned and run by the manager who perhaps set a tone that clearly indicated that theft, carelessness, or lack of documentation would not be tolerated.

Such traits are part of an organization's control structure. In essence, management sets a tone that influences the level of control consciousness in the organization and of employees in carrying out their duties. Within the framework of a company's broad control guidelines and policies, specific control procedures are developed for accounting functions, such as shipping customer orders and recording sales. Specific controls are developed and implemented, such as using and accounting for prenumbered documents to ensure accurate, complete, and timely recording of shipments.

Elements of an Organization's Control Structure

The three major elements of an organization's control structure [AU 319.08] are the following:

1. The control environment.
2. The accounting system.
3. Specific control procedures to accomplish control objectives.

The **control environment** represents the collective effect of various factors on establishing and implementing controls to accomplish organizational objectives. As such, it reflects the overall attitude, awareness, and actions of the board of directors, management, and others concerning the importance of control and its emphasis in the entity. The **accounting system** consists of the methods and records established to account for and report an entity's transactions and maintain accountability for the related assets and liabilities. We will sometimes refer to an **accounting subsystem or cycle,** which is a subset of the overall accounting system. For example, an accounting subsystem might be the subset of accounting that includes all of the activities involved in recording sales and collections, processing payroll, or recording changes in inventory. Each accounting subsystem is composed of one or more **accounting applications.** For example, the sales/collection subsystem is composed of the following accounting applications: processing customer orders and recording sales transactions, cash collections, sales returns and allowances, and write-offs of doubtful accounts. **Control procedures** are additional policies and procedures that management has established to provide reasonable assurance that specific entity objectives will be achieved. Although auditors tend to look at specific control procedures such as prenumbered documents, reconciliation of subsidiary ledgers to the general ledger, or segregation of duties, the adequacy of the overall design of the controls can be assessed only in conjunction with the specific processing objectives.

The relationship among the three elements can be seen in Exhibit 8.2. The control environment is pervasive and affects the design of the accounting system and the implementation of specific controls. The accounting system is not one system but contains a number of separate accounting subsystems, often referred to as *cycles*, such as sales and collections, payroll, and purchases and payments. Some of these accounting subsystems are heavily integrated in a computer system; others operate autonomously. Processing and recording objectives are established for the accuracy, completeness, and timing of transaction processing within each of these subsystems. Specific controls are designed within each accounting subsystem to accomplish the overall objectives.

B–CONTROL STRUCTURE ELEMENTS

Control Environment

An organization's control environment is established by management, owners, and the board of directors and is exemplified by the overall attitude, awareness, and actions taken in achieving and conveying the commitment to a well-controlled organization. Do not, however, confuse the concept of a well-controlled organization with that of a bureaucracy consisting of hundreds of tightly defined policies and procedures with individuals who are willing only to follow specific rules. The control environment must fit the organization. Some organizations (such as many governmental agencies and large corporations) are bureaucratic in nature and function through rules and regulations which are developed over time to address problems the organization has encountered. Unfortunately, some of these organizations fail to recognize the need to continue to change as the outside environment changes.

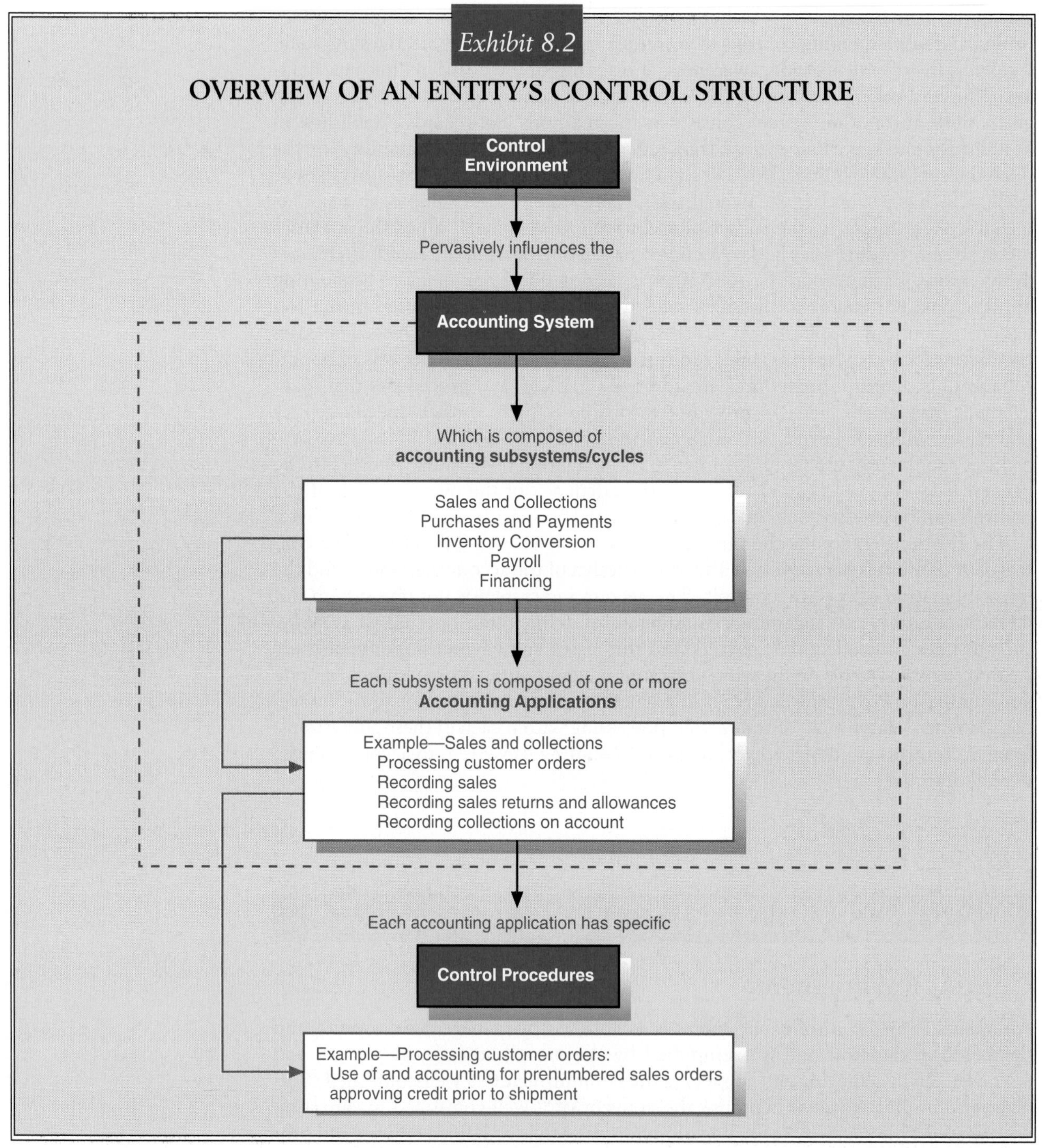

Other organizations are more open in their management approach and are not bureaucratic in nature. For example, the original organization structure of Apple Computer was not bureaucratic. The organization wanted to foster creativity and believed that too many rules stifle creativity. However, it still needed controls, which were implemented in a different form than we expect to find in large, stable environments. They matched their control structure to the organization environment. The organization grew as a result of creativity and wanted to remain creative, however, it could not achieve that creative growth unless it implemented sufficient controls to ensure that all its sales were billed and collected and that its cash was managed properly. Too often, companies with great ideas forget to pay attention to the detail required for adequate accounting and fail because of financial, not creative, problems.

The factors of an organization's control environment that should be considered by the auditor as part of the process of assessing control risk [AU 319.09] include these:

- Management's philosophy and operating style.
- The entity's organization structure.
- The functioning of the board of directors and its committees, particularly the audit committee.
- Methods of assigning authority and responsibility.
- Management's control methods for monitoring and following up on performance, including internal auditing.
- Personnel policies and practices.
- Various external influences that affect an entity's operations and practices, such as examinations by bank regulatory agencies.

Together, these factors (which are explained after the following example) provide the overall guidance to the organization in implementing specific controls. Because it is the broadest manifestation of the organization's control philosophy, the auditor needs to gain an understanding of its control environment.

Control Environment Example

A number of years ago, *The Wall Street Journal* reported a fraud that had taken place at the divisional manager level of a Fortune 500 company. The company had a number of divisions and an apparently sound control structure. Control policies were developed at the corporate level and divisional managers were expected to act consistently with the policies. The external auditors had confidence in the client's controls and assessed control risk as low. Consequently, they did not perform detailed audit work at each division each year. Some divisions were audited on a three-year rotating basis.

Management's major control over divisional management was in the form of bonuses based on division profitability. Managers who performed well were given frequent promotions to become vice presidents at larger divisions. Divisional management set the tone for controls at their respective division. Some divisional managers quickly learned that enhanced profits could be reported by keeping the books open after year-end; that is, they could record subsequent year's sales as current year's sales. Because all members of the division's top management reaped the benefits, resistance to overstating sales was minimal. In addition, because success led to promotions, the divisional manager was likely to be transferred to another location before the end of the following year and therefore would not suffer from the shorter time period to measure the subsequent year's results. In fact, the promoted manager would look even better because the successor would have only 11 months to match the performance the previous manager attained in 13 months.

Although the organization had an apparently good control structure, there was no direct follow-up by central management; indeed, management rewarded manipulative behavior by compensating managers for results based on an accounting measure that was subject to manipulation. Moreover, the company's organization structure and methods of assigning responsibility only compounded the problem. An organization code of ethics was insufficient to overcome the motivation of large year-end bonuses and neither the internal nor external auditors carefully examined the recording of year-end sales because they did not perceive a high control risk. The company quickly corrected the problem when it became apparent to the board of directors and central management. At that point, however, it had been allowed to exist—even indirectly encouraged—for a number of years.

Control Environment: Assessing the Factors

Control is a management function that influences human behavior to make things happen in a certain way to achieve specific organizational objectives. The key is human behavior. The owner-manager of a small business, for example, who immediately fires an employee for a minor theft of inventory influences the behavior of all other employees. Likewise, because individuals develop computer systems or submit transactions for processing, the human element retains its paramount importance even in highly computerized environments.

Management Philosophy and Operating Style. The Fortune 500 example reveals much about management style and philosophy. For example, does top management have a "hands-off" approach? Are division actions reviewed? Are detailed divisional or functional plans prepared and then used to evaluate performance? Is the management style consistent with the nature of the organization and the competitive environment in which it operates? For example, is management too conservative for the competitive environment or vice versa? Is management aggressive on accounting matters? These are the types of questions that partners on audit engagements must answer as they look at the impact of the management style on organization controls.

Organization Structure. Well-controlled organizations have clearly defined lines of responsibility, authority, and accountability. The auditor must assess the compatibility of the organization structure with the nature of the organization's operations. The auditor must anticipate problems that are likely to occur when an organization structure is inconsistent with the nature of the client's business and its competitive environment.

Board of Directors and Audit Committees. The members of the board of directors are the elected representatives of shareholders and have the major responsibility for management oversight, including evaluating and approving the basic direction of the organization. Auditors are concerned that the board of directors performs its oversight function and reviews and approves major corporate initiatives to ensure that such initiatives are in the best interest of the organization, not just in the best interest of corporate management.* For example, the board of directors should approve the following:

- Major new financing, either new debt or equity offerings.
- Acquisitions of other companies.
- Major divestitures and corporate realignments.
- Appointment of, and compensations for, top officers.

Two committees of the board of directors are of special importance: (1) the audit committee (whose role was discussed in Chapter 5) and (2) the personnel and compensation committee. The personnel and compensation committee is responsible for recommending the appointment of top officers and compensation packages for senior management. Because most stock compensation or stock option plans have tax implications, many of the recommendations by this committee may have financial implications.

Most not-for-profit organizations have a governing body similar to a board of directors. Sometimes these groups are referred to as *boards of trustees, boards of regents, advisory boards,* or *councils.* Members of these boards often are elected, although on occasion they are composed of volunteer members. Auditors need to determine whether such boards have the ability to carry out the oversight functions required by the organization. These functions are often specified in legal documents that the auditor needs to review as part of the background for the audit.

Methods of Assigning Authority and Responsibility. The auditor must understand the formal mechanisms by which the organization assigns responsibility and apportions authority and then must follow up to see that the functions are properly carried out. Pertinent questions include: How much autonomy is present in the purchasing department? Does anyone review its work? Who approves major new product line expenditures? Who has the authority to commit the organization to plans of operation that will require substantial long-term financial resources? Who decides what major systems should be developed for the computer?

Management Control Methods. Organizations use diverse control methods. Controls exist in the form of internal audit activities, operating budgets, capital budgets, monthly variance reports and review, and product development plans. The auditor needs to determine whether management's control methods are effective or whether they exist primarily in form, not in substance. An *internal audit function* can be one of the *key elements* of a management control system.

Personnel Policies and Procedures. Personnel policies and procedures are designed to ensure that the organization hire the *right people,* that hiring and retention decisions *comply* with applicable federal and state laws and regulations, that employees are properly trained and supervised, and that the organization respect employee

*As noted in Chapter 4, the board of directors includes members of top management as well as outside directors (not members of management). The auditor needs to determine whether the outside directors actually act as if they are autonomous and independent of management. If the board of directors does not act in the best interests of shareholders, it may be subjected to shareholder suits.

rights and delineate employee responsibilities. Some organizations have formal personnel policies and procedures and may even require special investigations before hiring for high-security jobs. The auditor's review of personnel policies is designed to provide an understanding of the overall control philosophy embodied within those policies and whether they are effectively implemented. Employing competent, trustworthy personnel is the cornerstone of a sound internal control structure. Further, personnel policies may contain information of importance to financial statement accounts such as payroll expense and associated liabilities.

Influences of Regulatory Agencies. Regulatory agencies significantly influence the operations of some companies. Regulatory banking agencies, for example, perform periodic audits of financial institutions as a basis for determining the need for regulatory action. These agencies often issue findings aimed at affecting the manner in which some transactions are handled or the valuation of its balance sheet accounts, especially in the loan area. Auditors need to be familiar with the regulatory influences on a client and should correspond with the agency to determine whether specific findings affect the audit client. Moreover, the audit firm should continually monitor regulatory activity for potential implications for all clients in a particular industry.

Control Environment: Implications for Control Risk Assessment

A client's control environment evolves over time as the organization changes to meet its competitive forces. Therefore, an organization with a strong control environment in one year may be significantly different in the next year under new management. Thus, auditors must guard against overfamiliarity with a client, as the Fortune 500 example illustrated. Some auditing firms require that a partner or manager complete a checklist to evaluate each of the control environment factors specified in the standards. Other firms require only a memo summarizing the auditor's assessment of the control environment and detailing the implications for the rest of the audit.

Understanding and Evaluating Accounting Systems

Accounting systems capture, record, summarize, and report financial data and supporting information. All but the smallest of organizations have multiple accounting subsystems, most of which are semi-independent of each other. The trend, however, is toward integrating major accounting subsystems within computerized data processing.

Exhibit 8.3 presents a list of typical accounting systems found in most medium- to large-size organizations. The actual form of a client's accounting system, of course, depends on the nature of its operations and management's overall control environment. The accounts receivable system for a retailer with substantial credit card sales, for example, differs markedly from that of a manufacturing organization that sells multimillion dollar machines to other manufacturers.

Several items are worthy of note with respect to accounting subsystems (Exhibit 8.3). First, although each subsystem functions within the overall control environment, each is unique and may vary in the strength of control procedures built into the application. Second, no matter how heavily computerized accounting systems are today, *all* depend on *key personnel*. Individuals remain responsible for transaction processing either through the design of the data processing system or through the

Exhibit 8.3

OVERVIEW OF ACCOUNTING SUBSYSTEMS

Sales	Records sales and updates inventory and accounts receivable.
Accounts receivable	Records changes in customer's accounts receivable balances and provides analysis of account collectibility.
Accounts payable	Records accrual of purchases on account. Computerized systems set up pay dates and automatically schedule items for payment.
Cash disbursements	Records cash payments and resulting debits to appropriate accounts.
Cash management	Records and manages cash transactions, including temporary investments in short-term securities.
Payroll	Accumulates payroll data and generates paychecks for employees and accounting data for inventory costing and wage and salary expenses.
Fixed assets	Provides detailed accounting for all fixed asset holdings, including cost, accumulated depreciation, yearly depreciation expenses, and differences between financial reporting and tax.
Inventory	Records and classifies inventory information through subsystems including Perpetual inventory control. Inventory costing. Inventory analysis.
Loan accounting	Controls and accounts for a financial institution's loan portfolios.
Securities accounting	Provides accounting and control over marketable securities.
General ledger	Overall accounting system accepts data from many of the other accounting subsystems.
Insurance policy accounting	Provides detailed accounting of insurance policies in force for insurance companies. Information normally captured in the system includes detailed listing of policies in force, payment due dates, face amount of policies, and other relevant information needed for managing and servicing the portfolio.

authorization of transactions submitted for processing. Third, many of the systems depend on the quality of information received from other (nonaccounting) parts of the organization. Payroll, for example, depends on information received from the personnel function. Accounts payable depends on the receiving function to carefully count goods and fill out receiving reports. Auditors do not necessarily perform detailed analyses of all accounting subsystems within an organization, but are primarily interested in the accounting applications that produce transactions that may have a material effect on the financial statements.

Overview of a Typical Accounting System

Payroll accounting is a typical accounting system that is necessary to all organizations. Payroll accounting is often computerized, but requires an interdependence of computer and people controls. (See Exhibit 8.4.) Key components of the payroll system include authorization for hiring a new employee and adding that individual to payroll; authorization of employee wage rates; verification of employee hours worked and jobs worked on; the computer generation of payroll checks; job costing reports; and an update of the employee master file data (such as year-to-date earnings, withholdings, etc.). The accounting data generated from payroll also update the client's general ledger.

Exhibit 8.4 illustrates other important control features that a trained auditor would notice:

1. *The personnel, payroll, and timekeeping departments are all separate.* Authorization for adding employees comes from the personnel department, but only the payroll department can generate paychecks based on data from the automated timekeeping function located on the factory floor.

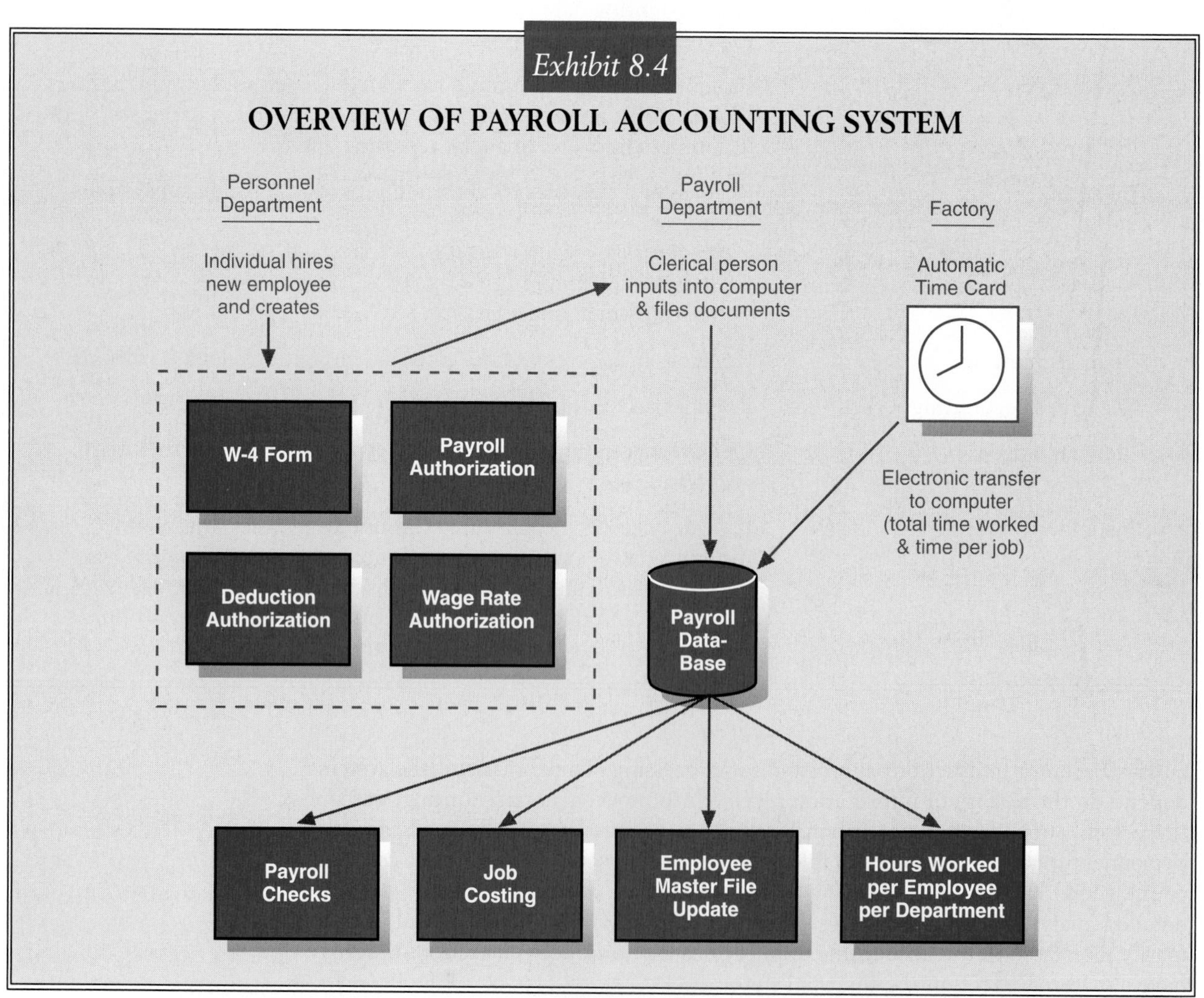

2. *The system contains a mixture of manual processing and computerized processing.* The timekeeping system is automated and connected directly to the computer or the timekeeping in many small organizations might be performed solely by the supervisor on a job. In either case, organizations need to ensure that reported employee time corresponds to time actually worked on the job.
3. *An "outside" control exists within the system.* The employee receiving the payroll check provides an independent check on the system's performance. The employee will know whether the payroll check is incorrect.
4. *The auditor is concerned with the integrity of the payroll system as it affects the recording of financial information.* The auditor is concerned that the pay is for bona fide employees, is correctly calculated, is allocated to the correct accounts, is recorded in the correct accounts (and includes all payroll tax liabilities), and that all files are correctly updated.
5. *The payroll systems contain documentary evidence on the working of the subsystem.* A transaction trail exists such that the auditor can review basic documents to verify that recorded transactions are appropriate. Most of the transaction trail exists in paper form, but some computerized systems are mostly paperless. For example, the payroll subsystem shown in Exhibit 8.4 has no time cards evidencing the hours worked, but an attendance report is prepared by the computer program for the factory supervisor to use to verify the presence of employees during the work period. In some payroll systems, pay is deposited directly by electronic funds transfer to the employee's bank account, thus bypassing the creation of a paper check.

The payroll system is but one of several accounting systems that affect the financial statements. Once an auditor gains an overall understanding of the system, as with payroll above, the next step is to analyze the effectiveness of specific controls designed in the system to prevent or detect misstatement.

An Approach to Assessing Control Procedures

Each accounting subsystem must be designed to meet specific control objectives in order to accomplish its processing tasks. Public accounting firms may formulate these control objectives differently, but most differ only in their details. The basic control objectives are derived from the account balance assertions developed in Chapter 7. For example, specific control procedures ought to be developed to ensure that the existence assertion will be met and that transactions are properly valued. The relationship between assertions embodied in the financial statements and control objectives is shown in Exhibit 8.5. The relationship can be seen by examining the existence/occurrence assertion. To ensure that existing transactions are recorded, there must be proper authorization of the transaction and a proper recording of the transaction on a timely basis. Thus, three specific processing objectives related to the existence assertion are noted in Exhibit 8.5:

1. Recorded transactions are valid.
2. Recorded transactions are properly authorized.
3. Transactions are recorded on a timely basis and in the time period in which the transactions take place.

Similar processing objectives relate to each of the other assertions.

Exhibit 8.5

ACCOUNT BALANCE ASSERTIONS AND RELATED CONTROL OBJECTIVES

Existence/Occurrence

1. Recorded transactions are valid.
2. Recorded transactions are properly authorized.
3. Transactions are recorded on a timely basis and in the time period in which the transactions take place.

Completeness

4. All transactions are recorded.

Rights/Obligations

5. Recorded transactions or accruals properly reflect transfer of ownership or obligation.

Valuation

6. All transactions are recorded at their proper amount and all calculations related to the recording of the transactions are carried out correctly.
7. All transactions and adjustments to account balances are recorded in accordance with generally accepted accounting principles.

Presentation and Disclosure

8. All transactions are correctly classified.

The audit approach utilizing the objectives approach is to identify the eight control objectives enumerated in Exhibit 8.5 and gather evidence to determine whether sufficient controls appear to be in place to accomplish the objectives. For example, the auditor considers various types of controls that will satisfy each of the control objectives related to existence/occurrence as shown in Exhibit 8.6.

Note that in Exhibit 8.6 the control procedures are specific to each situation. Although auditors tend to refer to control procedures in such terms as authorization, segregation of duties, or prenumbered documents, the control procedures are more specific and refer to those procedures along with *specific actions to be taken by employees* in accomplishing the control objectives. Some controls (such as those to reject the processing of incomplete data) are embodied in a computer application, but they require followup by personnel to ensure that the transaction is recorded correctly.

The control objectives approach is the most systematic approach for gathering information and evaluating the control risk for an audit client.

To implement the control objectives approach, the auditor needs to understand the operations of the accounting application and identify control procedures designed to satisfy each control objective. If sufficient control procedures are not in place to accomplish a control objective, the auditor will note the following:

1. Lack of control procedures in the accounting sub-systems.
2. Potential consequence of control deficiencies, that is, the types of misstatements that might take place and not be detected because sufficient control procedures are not in place.
3. Implications for the conduct of the audit, that is how direct tests of account balances should be modified to test for the potential misstatements because desired control procedures are not in place.

Exhibit 8.6

EXAMPLES OF CONTROL PROCEDURES TO ACCOMPLISH POTENTIAL EXISTENCE OBJECTIVES

Processing Assertions	Control Procedures to Accomplish Objectives
1. Recorded transactions are valid.	Receipts of merchandise are recorded only when accompanied by a receiving slip filled out by someone in the receiving function.
	Paychecks can be generated only when a valid employee time card for a valid employee has been submitted to payroll for processing.
2. Recorded transactions are properly authorized.	Merchandise is received only if a valid purchase order signed by an authorized purchasing agent exists for the order.
	Purchase orders for merchandise are issued only on a valid requisition by authorized personnel.
	All time cards are approved by supervisors or authorized personnel for the hours worked.
	Time cards are accepted only for employees who have been added to the master list of employees by the personnel function (segregation of duties between payroll and personnel).
3. Transactions are recorded on a timely basis in the time period in which they occur.	Receiving documents are prenumbered and accounted for. Any missing transactions not accounted for in a minimum period of time are properly investigated.
	Payroll transactions are batched and immediately processed on determination of validity. Any missing transactions are identified through reconciliation of items processed versus items received and then processed on a timely basis.
	A master file of current employees is maintained and matched against the current period's payroll checks. Any missing items are brought to the attention of a supervisor in the payroll function and are promptly investigated.
	Supervisory payroll personnel promptly handle all inquiries or complaints by employees regarding the correct computation of pay.

An example of how an auditor might analyze and document the existence/occurrence control procedures over payroll transactions is shown in Exhibit 8.7.

Accounting Application Controls

An *accounting application* refers to all the processes relevant to accomplish a particular accounting task, such as recording a sales transaction. An application includes the computerized processes and all the attendant manual procedures related to every aspect of processing the transaction from its origination (such as taking a sales order) to its final recording in the general ledger. The processes involved in a payroll application are shown in Exhibit 8.3. After assessing the impact of the control

Exhibit 8.7

ANALYSIS OF EXISTENCE/OCCURRENCE CONTROL PROCEDURES FOR PAYROLL

Objectives	Existence of Control	Evaluation and Effect on Audit
Recorded transactions are valid.	Paycheck cannot be issued unless employee is added to master list through update form W-99 from personnel and hours are received from automated timekeeping. A summary of time by department is prepared at the end of each day and sent to each supervisor for review and approval.	Controls, if operating effectively, provide assurance that objective is met.
Recorded transactions are authorized.	See controls above.	Controls, if operating effectively, provide assurance that objective is met.
Transactions are recorded on a timely basis and in the time period for which the transaction takes place.	See controls above. Hours worked per payroll is reconciled with hours approved by supervisors. Payroll is generated every Thursday.	Controls, if operating effectively, provide assurance that objective is met.

environment on an organization, the auditor identifies important accounting applications (based on financial statement impact), develops an understanding of the application transaction processing, and develops a preliminary understanding of the controls contained in the application and thus a preliminary assessment of control risk associated with the application.

Pervasive Accounting Controls

As noted previously, the adequacy of an organization's control structure can be evaluated only in relationship to specific control objectives. Additionally, many controls involve some form of human action, either identification of problems or follow up to problems. However, a few application control procedures are implemented (in various forms) across almost all accounting applications and organizations. These control types include the following:

- Adequate segregation of duties.
- Authorization procedures.
- Adequate documentation to form a transaction trail.
- Physical controls to safeguard assets.

- Reconciliations of control accounts with subsidiary ledgers and of transactions recorded with transactions submitted for processing.
- Competent, trustworthy employees.

Segregation of Duties. Adequate segregation of duties is perhaps the most fundamental of all accounting controls. The need for segregation of duties arises because accounting and financial records are vulnerable to manipulation and potential fraudulent activity. In addition, the potential for human error in transaction processing can be mitigated by a separate check on performance. The concept underlying **segregation of duties** is that individuals should not be put in situations in which they could both perpetrate and cover up fraudulent activity by manipulating the accounting records. Proper segregation of duties requires that at least two employees be involved in processing a transaction so that one employee provides an independent check on the performance of the other.

The functions of *authorizing* a transaction, *recording* the transaction, and *taking physical custody* of assets related to a transaction should be kept separate. Separating these three functions prevents someone from authorizing a fictitious or illegal transaction and then covering it up through the accounting process. Separating record keeping and physical custody of assets is designed to prevent someone with custodial responsibilities such as the person in charge of a retail electronics inventory from taking such inventory and covering it up by making fictitious entries to the accounting records. In addition, there should be independent checks on the assets and records whereby one department reconciles or otherwise acts as a double check on another department.

The auditor is concerned that users of data processing services adequately exercise responsibilities separately from data processing operations. User departments such as accounts receivable need to provide an independent check on data processing activities. Data processing personnel, for example, should not be able to *originate* transactions or unilaterally change accounting applications. Users need to maintain responsibility for the integrity of the operations even though most of the processing is automated. Users are responsible for designing authorization policies and accounting applications and testing to see that such designs are correctly implemented.

Some of the more common examples of segregation of duties in accounting systems include the following:

- The personnel department can add employees and set wage rates, but the payroll department must independently process the payroll transactions. The payroll department cannot add employees and the personnel department cannot process payroll checks.
- The data processing department processes transactions, but the user departments remain responsible for initiating the transactions and reconciling the data processing reports with the number of transactions submitted for processing.
- The accounts payable department can authorize payment for vendor invoices *only* after obtaining a receiving slip that provides independent evidence of receipt of the goods and a purchase order from the purchasing department that authorizes the items, quantity, and the price of the purchase.

An auditor concerned about whether there is a proper segregation of duties should ask these crucial questions:

- What kinds of errors and/or irregularities could take place if these functions are not separated?
- Could the errors or irregularities be covered up because incompatible duties were present in one person or function?

If the answers indicate that errors could occur and be easily covered up, segregation of duties is inadequate.

Authorization Policies. Another fundamental control concept involves procedures that ensure that only authorized transactions take place and that unauthorized personnel do not have access to, or the ability to change, already recorded transactions. Organizations should ensure that someone does not commit them to the purchase of large quantities of inventory unless that person is authorized to do so. Likewise, organizations do not want individuals to have access to computer records that are not relevant for the performance of their job duties and, more important, do not want those unauthorized to do so to have the ability to change records. The specific implementation of authorization policies varies among businesses and in part depends on the size and relative centralization or decentralization of the organization. However implemented, the following authorization guidelines are pertinent:

- The *authorization* to enter into transactions should be consistent with the responsibility associated with the job or management function.
- The ability to *commit* the organization to any long-range plans with substantial financial impact should be reserved for the highest functional level in the organization.
- Authorization policies should be clearly spelled out, documented, and communicated to all affected parties within the organization.
- *Blanket authorizations,* if used, should be periodically reviewed by the functional area responsible for such authorizations to determine compliance with them and to determine whether changes should be made to the policy. An example of a blanket authorization is the purchase order generation process embedded in a computer program to purchase new inventory automatically when existing inventory reaches a predetermined minimum level. The purchase order may be sent directly to the vendor or may be reviewed by a purchasing agent before being sent to the vendor.
- Only departmental supervisors should have the ability to authorize transactions for that area. Data processing personnel, for example, should not authorize transactions or changes to programs. Similarly, the sales force should not have the authority to extend credit to customers.

Adequate Documentation. A significant portion of every audit involves reviews of documentation. The documentation provides evidence of the authorization of transactions, the existence of transactions, the support for journal entries, and the financial commitments made by the organization. The broad classes of documentation likely to be reviewed on every audit were discussed in Chapter 7. Guidelines for developing reliable documentation and ensuring adequate control are identified below.

Organizational Guidelines for Developing Documentation. The following broad guidelines for developing documentation generally improve the organization's control:

- *Prenumbered documents* facilitate the control of and accountability for transactions and are crucial to the completeness assertion. Prenumbered shipping documents, for example, provide evidence of shipments and assist in ensuring that all sales transactions are billed and recorded.
- *Timely preparation* of documents improves the creditability and accountability of the documents and decreases the rate of errors on all documents. It is often difficult to remember specific information without writing it down as soon as it is available. For example, do you remember what you paid for dinner last Wednesday?
- *Authorization* for the transaction should be clearly evident on the document.
- Sufficient information should be captured to facilitate the development of a *transaction trail,* to provide information to respond to customer inquiries and identify and correct errors. Information facilitating the development of a transaction trail includes the date of the transaction, location, outside parties (ship to or receive from), products shipped or received, terms, and dollar amounts involved.
- *Simplified designs* (including computer screens) should facilitate ease and completeness of entry and checks on acceptable entries to minimize the possibility of errors.

Many accounting systems are no longer paper based. For example, a computer might be programmed to reorder merchandise. Rather than filling out prenumbered receiving slips, the receiving department passes the merchandise received across a scanner which enters receiving information directly into the computer system. The computer application compares the receipts with the purchase order to determine whether the receipt is authorized. Vendor invoices are entered when received and the computer searches to see whether the purchase order, receipts, and invoice match. If everything matches, checks could be sent to vendors without creating paper documentation for any of the steps in the process.* Controls need to be designed into these **paperless systems** to ensure that invoices are paid only when matched with actual receipt of goods, invoices are not paid more than once, and receipts are accepted only if a valid purchase order preceded the receipt.† A similar control problem can be seen in the automatic deposit the Social Security Administration uses to pay beneficiaries. The risk with automatic deposit is obvious and significant: The recipient might move or die, but the deposits continue to be made to the same bank account. Supplementary controls need to be designed into the system to mitigate such risks.

---

*In addition, many organizations do not send checks but electronically transfer funds to authorized vendors.

†There is always a concern that computerized media can be more easily modified or destroyed than paper-based media. Unless an organization and the auditor pay close attention to the controls over the general operations of the data processing department, such a vulnerability will always exist. *The New York Times* reported that a data processing employee of Exxon "inadvertently" destroyed all the data the company had retained on the *Exxon Valdez* oil spill off the coast of Alaska. The data existed only in a computerized form.

Physical Controls to Safeguard Assets. Physical controls are necessary to protect and safeguard assets from accidental or intentional destruction and thus constitute an important element of any organization's control structure. Examples of physical controls include the following:

- Security locks to limit access to computer facilities.
- Inventory warehouses with fences, careful key distribution, and environmental (climate) control.
- Vaults, safes, and similar items to limit access to cash and other liquid assets.
- Procedures such as physical segregation and custody to limit access to records and documents to those authorized.

The auditor needs to determine whether the level of physical controls implemented is commensurate with the potential risk the organization faces through destruction or manipulation of the assets. In addition, the auditor assesses the adequacy of insurance for the assets.

Reconciliations. **Reconciliation** controls operate by checking for agreement between submitted transactions and processed transactions or between detailed accounts and the corresponding control account. Reconciliations are important to *all* accounting systems but take on added importance with heavily computerized accounting systems such as those for financial institutions. Reconciliations can also be very effective in maintaining accountability for functions. A bank teller, for example, must reconcile the balance in the cash drawer at the end of the day with the posted transactions entered at the computer terminal by that employee (see Exhibit 8.8). The sum of cash, checks, money orders counted at the end of the day, and other cash equivalents recorded and paid out should agree with the transactions recorded for the day, for example:

Beginning balance
+ Cash deposits (including checks and other liquid assets)
- Cash withdrawals (including cash-like items)
+ Miscellaneous adjustments (journal entries or other documented entries)
= Ending balance.*

Some financial institutions do not let employees complete their shifts until their reconciliations are complete and any differences are reconciled, explained, and corrected. Some institutions also require employees to reimburse the organization for any cash shortages uncovered in the reconciliation. Such a policy reinforces employee awareness that control is important and carelessness will not be tolerated.

Competent, Trustworthy Employees. Errors are made by humans either in processing transactions or in designing and implementing the computer-based accounting applications. The auditor gains a sense of employee competence throughout the course of the audit. The auditor can observe the conscientiousness of client person-

*The reconciliation will likely be even more detailed than shown in the example. For example, it is likely that there will be a reconciliation by employee and employee records and then a summarized reconciliation across all employees for all transactions submitted and processed during a specific period of time.

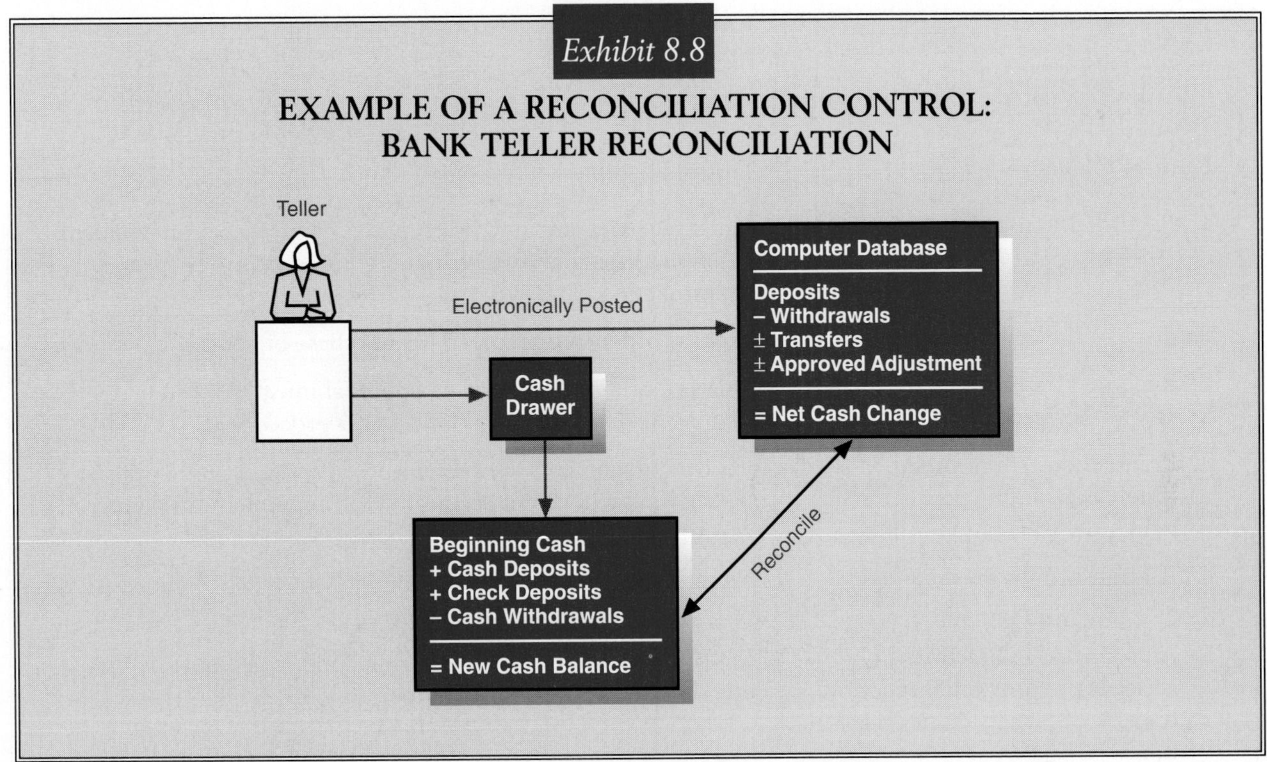

nel in carrying out their functions or sense whether employees are dissatisfied and believe that they occasionally deserve unauthorized "benefits" from their employer because they are not adequately compensated or recognized for their work. Most public accounting firms do not formally document their assessment of employee competence or trustworthiness, but they still make the assessment and it influences the auditor's overall evaluation of control risk.

Other Application Controls

Each organization chooses to implement specific controls from a number of control alternatives. Some controls effectively address more than one control objective. Examples of controls that address each control objective in the process of purchasing merchandise are shown in Exhibit 8.9. Note that many of the controls are applicable to both manual and computerized environments.

Evaluating Adequacy of Application Controls

The auditor faces two questions when evaluating the application controls for any important accounting application:

1. Are adequate controls built into the application to ensure that it is well controlled; that is, does the design of the application include sufficient controls to provide reasonable assurance that the application's processing objectives will be achieved?
2. If adequate controls are designed into the application, are the controls functioning as planned?

Exhibit 8.9

EXAMPLES OF CONTROL PROCEDURES FOR MAJOR ASSERTIONS

Control Objective	Control Examples
1. Recorded transactions are valid.	Signed receiving documents prepared by someone independent of the purchasing department are required before processing the transaction.
	Purchase orders are prepared for purchase of goods.
2. Recorded transactions are properly authorized.	Signature or initials exhibiting approval must be on the vendor's invoice or voucher submitted for processing.
3. Transactions are recorded on a timely basis in the period for which the transaction occurs.	Receiving documents are prenumbered and accounted for. Any missing transactions not accounted for in a minimum period of time are promptly investigated.
4. All transactions are recorded.	Prenumbered documents and independent reconciliations are used to account for all documents.
5. All recorded transactions or accruals properly reflect the transfer of ownership or obligation.	Formal documents such as receiving documents must be prepared before transactions are processed.
6. All transactions are recorded at their proper amount and all calculations related to the recording of the transactions are carried out correctly.	Vendor invoices are compared with receiving reports and purchase orders as to quantities received and total dollars billed.
7. All transactions and adjustments to account balances are recorded in accordance with GAAP.	Accounting policy and procedures manual specify appropriate accounting for transactions.
	Complex transactions are reviewed by the controller.
8. All transactions are correctly classified.	Accounting policy and procedures manual specify proper accounting and disclosure.

If the auditor determines that control procedures are not adequate to achieve processing objectives, that is, material misstatements would not be prevented or detected by the control procedures, the auditor must design specific audit procedures to test for potential misstatements. In other words, if it is determined that control procedures are not sufficient to prevent or detect and correct the recording of unauthorized or invalid transactions, the auditor needs to consider how such transactions could be misstated and then develop specific tests of details to determine whether the account balance is materially misstated.

C–CONTROL RISK ASSESSMENT

Control risk assessment is a complex and important task in every audit. That assessment follows directly from the audit risk model. The auditor's control risk assessment influences the planned level of detection risk (type and amount of direct tests of account balances, analytical procedures, and/or substantive tests of transactions). Control risk can be evaluated on a scale from high to low. Most firms find it convenient to assess control risk within broad categories: maximum, slightly below the maximum, moderate, or low.

Assessment of control risk at its *maximum* implies that the auditor cannot rely on the control structure to prevent or detect material misstatements. When control risk is assessed at the maximum, the emphasis of the audit is placed on substantive testing of the account balance. Assessment at the *minimum*, conversely, implies that the auditor can count on the control structure to prevent and/or detect material misstatements and therefore the amount of substantive audit testing can be decreased to an amount sufficient to corroborate the assessment that material misstatements are not occurring. In other words, the substantive tests of the account balances can be performed at a minimum level, resulting in a less costly audit for the client.*

It is helpful to think of the approach to control risk assessment as a series of sequential phases, even though these phases are often not performed as separate activities (see Exhibit 8.10). For example, while obtaining an understanding of the internal control structure, the auditor may also perform a test of controls, such as noting that monthly bank reconciliations are independently prepared on a timely basis. The approach to assessing control risk can be divided into four logical phases:

Phase 1	Obtain an understanding of the internal control structure.
Phase 2	Make a preliminary evaluation of control risk and decide whether to test control procedures.
Phase 3	If appropriate, perform tests of control procedures.
Phase 4	Reconsider the preliminary assessment of control risk and approach to substantive testing and revise as necessary.

These phases are described in the following sections.

Phase 1—Obtain an Understanding

The auditor begins by *obtaining an understanding* of the three elements of the internal control structure: the control environment, the key accounting systems, and the specific control procedures associated with each accounting system. For a continuing client, this understanding is based on the knowledge obtained during the prior year audit updated for changes in the system and personnel that have occurred during the current year. The assessment of the control environment should include an analysis of the control environment and its impact on the design and functioning of important accounting applications.

*It is important for organizations to realize that investment in sound controls pays many dividends. Besides contributing to the effective operation of the organization, it also has a side effect of reducing costs such as the annual audit.

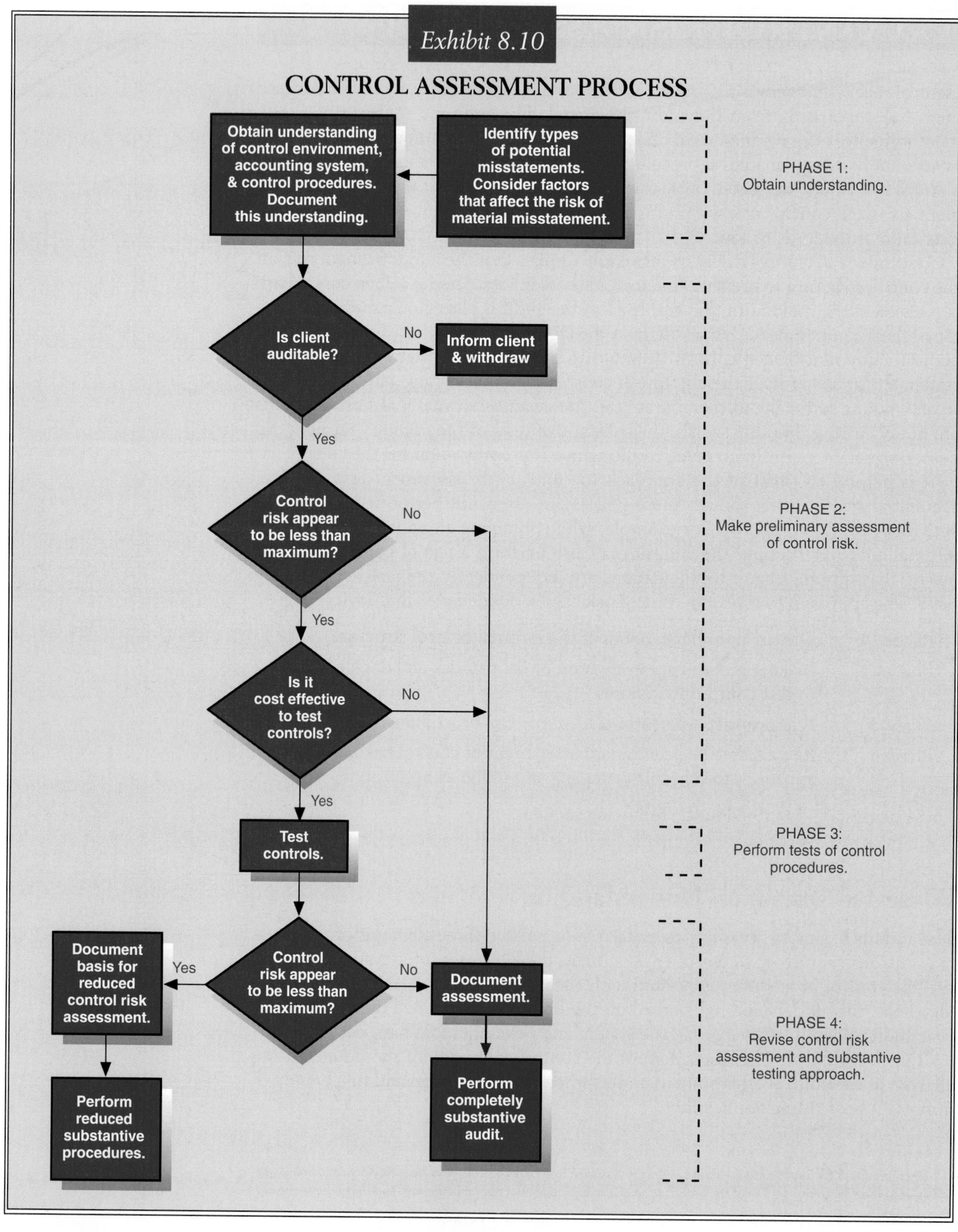
Exhibit 8.10
CONTROL ASSESSMENT PROCESS
Obtain understanding of control environment, accounting system, & control procedures. Document this understanding.
Identify types of potential misstatements. Consider factors that affect the risk of material misstatement.
PHASE 1: Obtain understanding.
Is client auditable?
No
Inform client & withdraw
Yes
Control risk appear to be less than maximum?
No
Yes
Is it cost effective to test controls?
No
PHASE 2: Make preliminary assessment of control risk.
Yes
Test controls.
PHASE 3: Perform tests of control procedures.
Document basis for reduced control risk assessment.
Yes
Control risk appear to be less than maximum?
No
Document assessment.
PHASE 4: Revise control risk assessment and substantive testing approach.
Perform reduced substantive procedures.
Perform completely substantive audit.

Key accounting applications should be identified and the auditor should obtain an understanding of these applications even if control risk has been assessed at the maximum. This understanding is necessary to gain knowledge of the existence of documentation, the flow of the documents within the organization, where and how the documents are stored, the types of accounting records used, the extent to which computers are used, and the types of misstatements that might result from the lack of sufficient controls.

While obtaining an understanding of the control environment and the key accounting subsystems, the auditor is likely to obtain an understanding of at least some of the control procedures the client has designed into the subsystems. For example, the auditor probably notices certain segregation of duties and whether assets are physically safeguarded. It may not be necessary to devote additional attention to this step. Ordinarily, audit planning does not require detailed knowledge of the control procedures for each account balance, each class of transactions, or every related assertion. If, on the other hand, when deciding that it may be possible to assess control risk at less than the maximum, the auditor needs to gain a thorough understanding of the control procedures designed into important applications.

Obtaining Information about the Accounting System and Control Procedures

The auditor needs to obtain evidence of the functioning of the accounting system, the documentation it generates, and the control procedures implemented to accomplish the basic processing objectives. The auditor gathers this information in the following ways:

- Performing walk-throughs of the accounting system and its processing procedures.
- Making inquiries of accounting and operational personnel (including asking client personnel to fill out a control questionnaire).
- Reviewing accounting manuals and job descriptions.
- Taking plant and operational tours.
- Reviewing client-prepared documentation including program and systems descriptions and flowcharts.
- Reviewing prior year or predecessor auditor working papers.

Walk-Throughs. A **walk-through** of transactions provides an understanding of the nature of processing in important accounting applications. After obtaining an overview of *how* the accounting system operates, the auditor takes a document that evidences the initiation of a transaction and walks it through the system to determine how the system actually operates. The auditor inquires of employees regarding the processing that takes place, to whom the results of the transactions are sent, how long the document stays in their possession, how new documentation is created, and to whom new and old documentation is sent. Walk-throughs, combined with good interviewing skills, are very effective in gaining an understanding of how the system *actually operates*. The auditor normally documents the understanding gained through the walk-through in a narrative or a flowchart.

Inquiries. Inquiries play an important role in understanding the operation of an entity's accounting system and control procedures. The auditor interviews key employees (usually the department head) in important accounting applications to learn about segregation of duties within the department, the extent of computer usage, the documents the application generates, the implementation and operation of important controls, and the overall nature of the transaction processing in the department. When reviewing the accounts receivable and credit function, for example, the auditor asks about the procedures and personnel involved in writing off old accounts. The auditor also asks about procedures for authorizing credit and billing a transaction.

Review of Accounting Manuals and Job Descriptions. Larger organizations usually have detailed accounting manuals that contain a wealth of information. Such manuals normally contain a description of the accounting policies adopted by the organization, a detailed chart of accounts, and an outline of procedures for processing all of the various types of accounting transactions.

Plant and Operational Tours. Many control procedures depend on the integrity of control information developed in nonaccounting areas. For example, important information on the receipt of goods is generated at the receiving dock. Information regarding the transfer of goods from work-in-process to finished goods is generated by inventory or production personnel. The auditor should attempt to assess the conscientiousness with which these operational employees carry out these "office-type" procedures. Part of this assessment is made by examining documentary evidence, but part of it can be obtained from a plant tour and brief interviews with personnel. The auditor can observe whether the receiving dock is orderly, whether employees fill out receiving reports when the shipment is received (as opposed to filling it out at their convenience), and whether goods are being independently counted and evaluated for quality.

Client-Prepared Documentation. Many clients have prepared documentation to describe *how* the organization's accounting systems are supposed to operate. Such information can be gathered conveniently and serves as an initial understanding of procedures. But the auditor needs to make inquiries and perform other tests to determine whether transactions are processed as the accounting or data processing system's manual says they should be processed. Unfortunately, many organizations do not keep their system documentation up-to-date and the descriptions of the systems do not reflect actual processes.

Prior Year Working Papers. The evaluation of an organization's control structure is an on-going process. In many cases, the auditor has, in the working papers for previous years, a fairly complete description of key accounting applications and processing procedures. The auditor can use the previous work as a basis for review and update when necessary. The auditor's work in the current year audit can then focus on understanding changes that have taken place in key applications during the year and determining how such changes may affect the current audit.

Documentation of Auditor's Understanding of an Organization's Control Structure

Auditing standards and good common sense require the auditor to document the understanding and evaluation of the organization's control structure. The documentation methods used should clearly identify each important accounting application and the key controls thought to exist in the application. In addition, the documentation of the auditor's assessment of **control risk** should clearly delineate implications for the substantive testing of accounts. For example, if the auditor uncovers a control weakness that leads to a conclusion that errors are likely to be made in the timely recording of credit memos, the implications for year-end testing of credit memos should be clearly specified.

The auditor's assessment of control risk needs to be documented on every audit even if the auditor has decided to assess control risk at a maximum. When risk is assessed at less than the maximum, the auditor needs to document an understanding of the systems and how this effectively address the control objectives. The three major alternative methodologies for documenting the auditor's understanding of controls are flowcharts, questionnaires, and written narratives. The approaches are not necessarily alternatives but are complementary. A firm could use one, two, or a combination of all three approaches to document their understanding of controls and control implications.

Flowcharts. **Flowcharts** provide a graphic description of an application or process. They can be highly detailed or prepared on a more global level, depicting a broad overview of an application. Auditors routinely develop their own flowcharts but may also use those prepared by the client. The auditor, for example, reviews the client's *systems flowchart* to obtain an overview of how documents flow into and out of a computerized application. To a lesser extent, the auditor may review a client's *program flowchart* to understand the processing and controls built into the client's computer program.

Flowcharts prepared for audit analysis do not have to be as detailed as those typically found in a client's information systems department. The auditor's purpose in preparing a flowchart is threefold:

1. To gain an understanding of, and document, control procedures present in the system.
2. To communicate an understanding of how the system operates to all members of the audit team.
3. To identify key processes involved with the application and its interaction with any other important accounting applications.

Flowcharts are usually complemented by a description of control objectives and the auditor's identification of key control procedures that address each objective. If sufficient control procedures are not present, the auditor normally includes comments on the implications of the control deficiencies on the design of substantive audit tests. An example of an overview flowchart identifying major processes and controls is shown in Exhibit 8.11. Items numbered (1) through (8) represent control features

1. The supervisor periodically observes employees punching time cards to ensure that they do not punch in or out for someone else.
2. The supervisor reviews time cards and approves them for payment to ensure that employees are paid for appropriate hours worked.
3. The payroll clerk develops batch totals to compare with those developed by the computer while processing the payroll.
4. The computer is programmed to detect various types of errors such as hours in excess of a reasonable limit and wrong employee numbers.

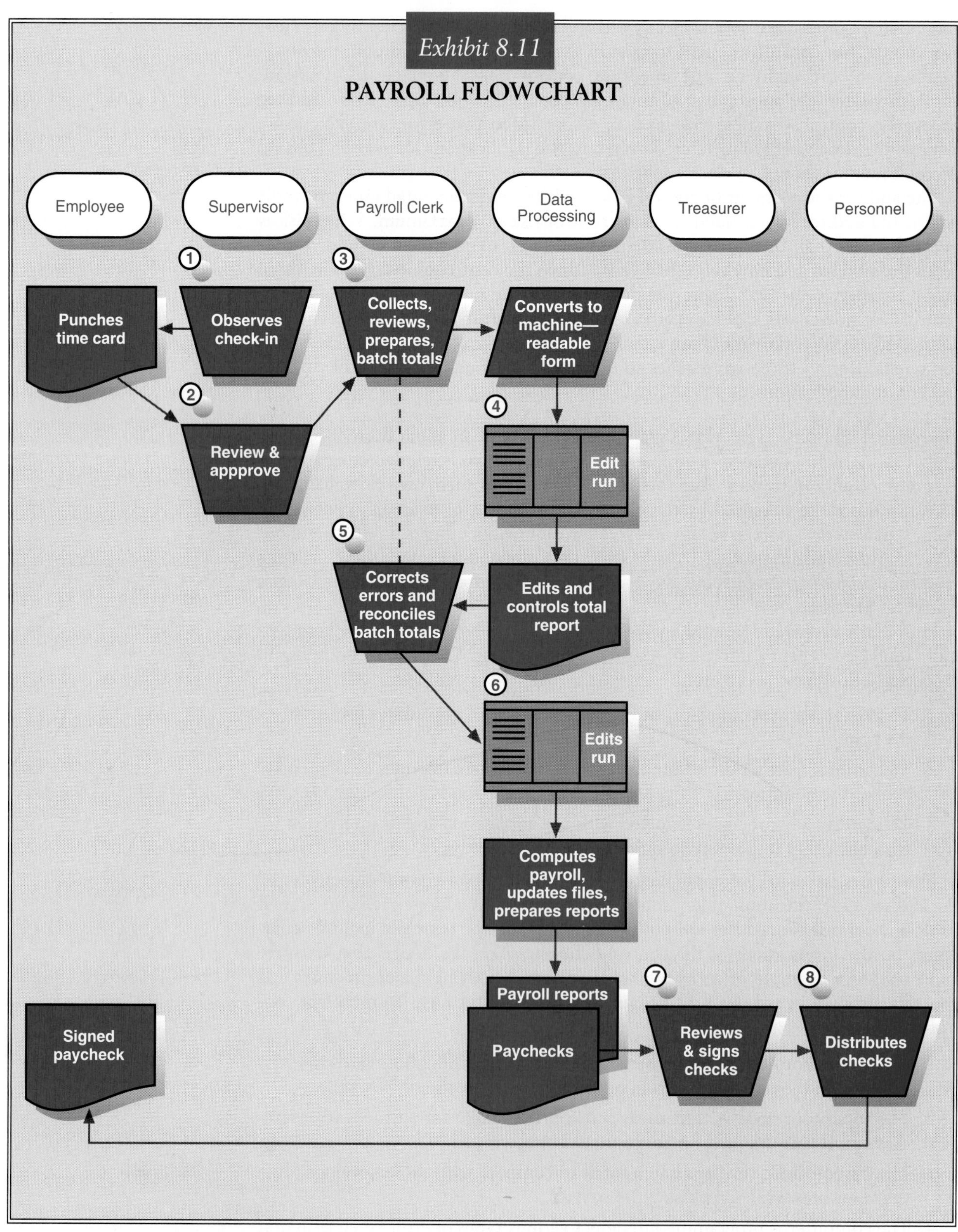
Exhibit 8.11
PAYROLL FLOWCHART
Employee
Supervisor
Payroll Clerk
Data Processing
Treasurer
Personnel
1
Punches time card
Observes check-in
3
Collects, reviews, prepares, batch totals
Converts to machine—readable form
2
Review & appprove
4
Edit run
5
Corrects errors and reconciles batch totals
Edits and controls total report
6
Edits run
Computes payroll, updates files, prepares reports
Payroll reports
Paychecks
7
Reviews & signs checks
8
Distributes checks
Signed paycheck

5. The supervisor prepares a reconciliation of items processed with those submitted for processing.
6. Corrections resubmitted by payroll are run through the edit routine again to ensure that there are no other apparent errors.
7. The treasurer, who is not otherwise involved with payroll processing, reviews the payroll records before signing the paychecks.
8. A clerk in the personnel office, who is not otherwise involved with payroll processing, distributes the paychecks to prevent someone from having a fictitious employee paid.

Because a flowchart can cover all aspects of an accounting application, it has the advantage of identifying any compensating controls.

Questionnaires. **Questionnaires** present an efficient alternative, or complementary approach, to document an organization's control structure. A questionnaire, which is normally supplemented by a brief narrative describing the system, is designed to gather information by functional area such as accounts receivable, credit analysis, accounts payable, fixed asset accounting, payroll, and other important accounting applications. Questionnaires are designed so that a negative answer indicates the absence of a key control procedure or an inadequate segregation of duties. Combinations of negative answers can be analyzed to determine the possibility of misstatements that could occur without being prevented or detected. An example of a questionnaire for accounts payable is shown in Exhibit 8.12.

Questionnaires have the advantage of being comprehensive yet fairly simple to use. Perhaps most important, they can be computerized and, with the power of microcomputers and expert systems, can assist the auditor in identifying types of errors that could occur in the accounting records.

Questionnaires have two disadvantages, however. First, they tend to be standardized and thus are perceived to be less flexible than flowcharts. Most auditors therefore recognize the need to customize their questionnaire for each client. Some firms have developed separate questionnaires for small businesses and for specialty industries such as insurance, banking, and public utilities and then make appropriate changes for specific client situations. Second, questionnaires can be completed with little thinking about the implications of the various negative answers. Many firms address this second problem by (1) supervision and review and (2) utilization of microcomputer support systems to assist in the evaluation of questionnaire responses.

Narratives. **Narratives** are used to describe accounting applications and often are prepared as supplements to flowcharts or questionnaires. They can be used to describe the client's processing in more detail and identify key client personnel. Narrative memoranda are often used to provide the complete documentation of relatively simple applications or for small business applications.

Phase 2—Make Preliminary Assessment of Control Risk

After having gained an understanding of the control environment, the accounting system, and applicable control procedures, the auditor is in a position to make a preliminary assessment of control risk. The preliminary assessment is crucial because it determines the audit planning for the remainder of the audit. If the auditor assesses

Exhibit 8.12

CONTROL PROCEDURES QUESTIONNAIRE—ACCOUNTS PAYABLE

	Yes	No	N/A
Purchases Authorized			
1. Purchase requests are signed by the department supervisor.	____	____	____
2. Approval of a purchase request is noted by the initials or signature of the purchasing manager.	____	____	____
3. An approved vendor listing is readily available to all department supervisors requesting goods or services.	____	____	____
Valid Recorded Purchases/Payables			
1. Receiving reports are independently signed and dated.	____	____	____
2. Receiving reports are prenumbered, controlled, and accounted for.	____	____	____
3. The purchase order, receiving report, and vendor invoice are agreed before recording the payable.	____	____	____
4. Vendor invoices and supporting documents are defaced (e.g., stamped when paid) to prevent duplicate recording.	____	____	____
Proper Account Distribution			
1. The account distribution is authorized by the department supervisor requesting the goods or services.	____	____	____
2. Computer-generated account distribution reports are approved by an appropriate person signing or initialing the report.	____	____	____
All Liabilities for Goods or Services Recorded			
1. Prenumbered purchase orders are accounted for.	____	____	____
2. Computer batch control tickets are reconciled to edit reports.	____	____	____
3. Edit reports identify invalid vendor numbers and part numbers.	____	____	____
4. On-line entry includes the input of vendor invoice control totals.	____	____	____
All Payments Properly Supported			
1. Supporting documents are reviewed before the check is signed.	____	____	____
2. Vendor invoice approval for payment is noted by the initials of the department supervisor authorizing the account distribution.	____	____	____
Payments for Nonroutine Purchases			
1. Approved check request forms and/or billing statements accompany the check and are reviewed before the check is signed.	____	____	____
All Returns Accounted for Properly			
1. Debit memos are prenumbered, controlled, and accounted for.	____	____	____
2. Debit memos are approved by appropriate purchasing managers.	____	____	____

control risk at the maximum, all remaining audit testing must be planned so that no reliance is placed on the client's internal control structure. The following shows a linkage of audit tests to control weaknesses.

Scenario. The auditor finds that the client neither uses prenumbered receiving slips to record the return of sales merchandise nor has procedures to ensure prompt recording of returns. Finally, the auditor is concerned that the overall control environment exhibits a lack of control consciousness by top management; rather, top management seems obsessed with increasing earnings.

Linkage to Audit Tests. The auditor expands the tests for sales returns by (1) arranging to be on hand at the end of the year to observe the taking of physical inventory and observing items received and the client's procedures for documenting receipts, (2) tracing receipts for items received back to credit memos to determine if they are issued in the correct time period, (3) reviewing all credit memos issued shortly after year-end to determine whether they are recorded in the correct time period, and (4) determining whether any credit memos issued before year-end are properly recorded. More accounts receivable confirmations may also be sent.

An assessment of control risk as low means that the auditor places a great deal of confidence in the design of the client's accounting system and believes that the likelihood of material misstatements occurring in the account balances is relatively remote. Remember, however, that an auditor's assessment of control risk can vary across accounting subsystems. For example, the auditor might assess the control risk for the payroll subsystem as low, but the control risk for accounts payable at the maximum.

Phase 3—Perform Test of Controls

The auditor's preliminary assessment of control risk is based on an understanding of the control system as it *has operated in the past* and *how it is designed to operate.* Experienced auditors know, however, that many accounting systems do not operate throughout the year in the manner they are supposed to operate. Personnel may change. Some control procedures may be omitted when employees are pressured to process a large backlog of transactions. Or the divisional manager may override controls to obtain special processing for a customer. If the auditor is going to reduce substantive audit procedures because control risk is considered low, assurance must be obtained that the controls *are operating effectively.*

When control risk is assessed below the maximum, the auditor must gain assurance as to the operation of controls and therefore designs audit tests to determine the effectiveness of controls that led to the control risk assessment. For example, assume that the auditor believes that the credit approval function is important in minimizing uncollectible accounts. The credit function is designed so that predefined poor credit risks are rejected by the computer system and are subject to credit department review and approval before processing. In addition, all credit sales over a certain dollar limit must be approved by the credit function. When such sales are approved, the credit function requires additional documentation such as an outside credit rating or a past payment history. The auditor must gather a sufficient amount of evidence to determine that controls are operating effectively. One approach would be to design an audit test in which the auditor randomly samples sales orders and traces them through the credit approval process to determine whether they were handled according to the documented procedures.* If the controls are operating as designed, the auditor is justified in assessing the control risk at an amount less than the maximum.

An example of an audit program to test the effectiveness of control procedures is shown in Exhibit 8.13. The auditor has identified specific control procedures that are important to assessing control risk below the maximum over the shipment of items and recording of sales transactions. Those important control procedures are (1) use of prenumbered shipping documents, which are periodically accounted for, (2) review of sales order forms by supervisory personnel for completeness, (3) requirement that all shipments have specific supervisory authorization, (4) requirement that sales have credit approval before shipment, and (5) the proper recording of all transactions and the reconciliation of the total number of items recorded with the number of items shipped. In reviewing Exhibit 8.13, note that the auditor has designed specific procedures that will be effective in determining whether each important control is operating effectively. However, the auditor may do more than that. For example, the auditor also traces selected transactions through the system and into the general ledger, thus providing information about the correctness of the recorded balance as well. Although it may not seem like much, the auditor is developing evidence about the correctness of the processing (thus testing specific assertions) as well as the effectiveness of controls. The auditing profession uses the term **dual-purpose tests** to describe tests of transactions that incorporate both the **testing of controls** and the **substantive testing** of the recording of the items in the accounts. Dual-purpose tests help increase audit efficiency.

The auditor may also believe that control risk is less than the maximum but decides that the cost of gathering evidence on the operation of the controls will be higher than the savings obtained by reducing the substantive audit tests. In such cases, the auditor designs the substantive audit tests as if the control risk assessment was at the maximum or at least at a moderate level because no evidence is gathered on how controls are operating. Auditors should assess risk at the moderate level without testing controls only if (1) the organization audited is a continuing client, (2) past year audit results indicate that the system was operating effectively, and (3) the preliminary analysis of the system does not indicate any significant changes since last year.

Phase 4—Revise Assessment of Control Risk and Approach to Substantive Testing

The auditor's work in gaining an understanding of the operation of a client's control structure is not an end in itself. It is part of the process designed to conduct the most efficient audit possible while minimizing overall audit risk. If control risk is assessed at the maximum, both the extent and amount of substantive audit tests must be high. In addition, the auditor may need to rely more extensively on outside audit evidence as opposed to internally generated audit evidence.

Alternatively, if control risk is assessed as low, the auditor can rely more heavily on internally generated documentation and can reduce the amount of substantive

*The number of items the auditor would have to examine is covered in the Chapter 11 discussion of attribute sampling.

Exhibit 8.13

AUDIT PROGRAM FOR TESTING THE EFFECTIVENESS OF CONTROL PROCEDURES

Procedure	Performed by
1. Review shipping procedures and determine the shipping department's procedures for filing copies of shipping documents. Select two blocks of 50 shipping documents and review to determine that all items are accounted for either by a sales invoice or voided. Investigate the disposition of any missing document numbers. [Completeness]	______
2. Select a sample of sales orders and perform the following for each:	
a. Review sales order form for completeness and approval by an authorized agent of the company. [Authorization]	______
b. Determine whether sales order requires additional credit approval. If so, determine whether such approval has been granted and documented. [Authorization]	______
c. Trace sales order to the generation of a shipping document and determine that appropriate items have been shipped. [Occurrence]	______
d. Trace shipping document to sales invoice noting that all items have been completely and correctly billed. [Completeness and Valuation]	______
3. Review the daily error report generated by the computer run to process sales transactions and note the type of transactions identified for correction. Take a sample of such transactions and trace them to resubmitted transactions noting	
a. Approval of the resubmitted transactions. [Authorization]	______
b. Correctness of the resubmitted transaction. [Valuation]	______
c. Proper update of the resubmitted transaction in the sales account. [Completeness]	______

tests while maintaining overall audit risk at the amount originally specified. The amount of audit evidence that would be gathered in performing substantive audit procedures is covered in more detail in subsequent chapters.

Reporting Control Deficiencies

The auditor has an obligation to report significant deficiencies in the organization's control structure discovered during the course of the audit engagement to the audit committee or its equivalent, such as the board of directors, board of trustees, or similar body, and to senior management. The quality of the organization's control structure is considered important information for those parties who exercise oversight responsibilities for the organization. The auditor may become aware of matters relating to the internal control structure that may be of interest to the audit committee. These matters are referred to as **reportable conditions** and are defined in the professional standards [AU 325.02] as follows:

> Specifically, these are matters coming to the auditor's attention that, in his judgment, should be communicated to the audit committee because they represent

Applications to Small Organizations

ASSESSING CONTROL RISK IN SMALL ORGANIZATIONS

Many small organizations do not have the economic resources to add sufficient staff necessary to attain an adequate segregation of duties. For example, one individual who has access to a microcomputer accounting system could make changes to any account balance without supervisory review by anyone else in the organization. Because adequate segregation is a pervasive control concept, the auditor will most likely assess control risk as high for many of these small organizations. Remember that assessing control risk as high does not imply that the client's system contains numerous errors or that the employees are not trustworthy. It simply means that the risk is present that material misstatements *could occur* and *would not be detected* by the normal function of the accounting system.

Owner/manager controls become very important in small organizations. The owner can create better segregation of duties by performing a detailed overview of functions and setting the tone for employee operations. The auditor should assess whether the owner-manager controls are seriously applied throughout the year under audit or if they are implemented only occasionally when the owner is not too busy with other things.

significant deficiencies in the design or operation of the internal control structure, which could adversely affect the organization's ability to record, process, summarize, and report financial data consistent with the assertions of management in the financial statements.

Reportable conditions could reflect deficiencies in the internal control structure design (such as absence of a procedure to ensure appropriate reviews and approvals of transactions) or failures in the operation of the internal control structure (such as evidence of failure to safeguard assets from loss or misappropriation) or other problems (such as absence of a sufficient level of control consciousness within the organization). Examples of reportable conditions are shown in Exhibit 8.14.

Reportable conditions may be identified while obtaining an understanding of the internal control structure or while performing tests of controls or substantive procedures.

The report on control deficiencies is not intended as a comprehensive report on the overall quality of the organization's control structure. The audit, by necessity of efficiency, does not examine or test all components of an organization's control structure. Thus, the report is limited to items that have come to the auditor's attention during the audit and is thus more limited than a full report on the organization's internal control structure. The required report does not provide any assurance that *all significant deficiencies have been identified.* The SEC and other parties have been advocates of expanding the auditor's responsibilities to include comprehensive reports on an organization's internal control structure—for the reasons discussed at the beginning of this chapter, including the fact that significant business failures have been highly correlated with an inadequate control structure. The profession has developed a report model for comprehensive reports on internal control. The reporting is covered more thoroughly in Chapter 22.

Exhibit 8.14

REPORTABLE CONDITIONS

Deficiencies in Internal Control Structure Design

Inadequate overall internal control structure design.

Absence of appropriate segregation of duties consistent with appropriate control objectives.

Absence of appropriate reviews and approvals of transactions, accounting entries, or systems output.

Inadequate procedures for appropriately assessing and applying accounting principles.

Inadequate provisions for safeguarding assets.

Absence of other control techniques considered appropriate for the type and level of transaction activity.

Evidence that a system fails to provide complete and accurate output that is consistent with objectives and current needs because of design flaws.

Failures in the Operation of the Internal Control Structure

Evidence of failure of identified controls to prevent or detect misstatements of accounting information.

Evidence that a system fails to provide complete and accurate output consistent with the entity's control objectives because of the misapplication of control procedures.

Evidence of failure to safeguard assets from loss, damage, or misappropriation.

Evidence of intentional override of the internal control structure by those in authority to the detriment of the overall objectives of the system.

Evidence of failure to perform tests that are part of the internal control structure, such as reconciliations not prepared or not timely prepared.

Evidence of willful wrongdoing by employees or management.

Evidence of manipulation, falsification, or alteration of accounting records or supporting documents.

Evidence of intentional misapplication of accounting principles.

Evidence of misrepresentation by client personnel to the auditor.

Evidence that employees or management lacks the qualifications and training to fulfill their assigned functions.

Others

Absence of a sufficient level of control consciousness within the organization.

Failure to follow up and correct previously identified internal control structure deficiencies.

Evidence of significant or extensive undisclosed related-party transactions.

Evidence of undue bias or lack of objectivity by those responsible for accounting decisions.

*Source: AU 325.21

The auditor's documentation of the organization's control structure should be sufficient to identify reportable conditions as required by AU 325. A reportable condition may be of such magnitude as to be considered a **material weakness in internal accounting control,** which is a "condition in which the specific control procedures or the degree of compliance with them do not reduce to a relatively low level the risk that errors or irregularities in amounts that would be material in relation to the financial statements being audited may occur and not be detected within a timely period by employees in the normal course of performing their assigned functions" [AU 325.15]. The auditor may, but is not required to, separately identify any material weaknesses when communicating reportable conditions. The auditor may choose also to communicate deficiencies in the control structure that are not significant enough to meet the criteria of a "reportable condition." Such items should be separately identified in the auditor's communication as other items that have come to the auditor's attention.

Summary

Control risk assessments take place on every audit. The knowledge the auditor gains from the control risk assessment facilitates the development of an efficient audit program for the client. The process of performing the control risk assessment enables the auditor to understand the nature of the client's processing and thus determine the account balances that are most susceptible to misstatement. This knowledge allows the auditor to develop the remainder of the audit with the full knowledge of potential for misstatements and to implement the audit procedures most appropriate to address such misstatements.

There is no one best approach to assess control risk. Firms combine a wide variety of techniques including questionnaires, flowcharts, walk-throughs, and inquiries of client personnel. Many firms have computerized decision aids that link the control risk assessment to the design of specific substantive audit tests.

Most accounting applications are computerized. Even in these environments, the control concepts and principles addressed in this chapter will be applicable. Some detailed control concepts, however, are specifically applicable to computerized systems. We turn our attention to those systems in Chapter 9.

Significant Terms

accounting application All programs and procedures involved in processing a particular class of transactions, such as the procedures and computer programs involved to process a sales order and to record sales transactions; most accounting applications include both manual and computerized procedures.

accounting subsystem or cycle Often referred to as accounting cycles such as sales/collection, acquisition/payment, payroll, inventory, and financing cycles; each subsystem is composed of one or more accounting applications.

accounting system The methods and records established to identify, assemble, analyze, classify, record, and report an entity's transactions and to maintain accountability for the related assets and liabilities; made up of several accounting subsystems.

control environment The overall tone of operations of an organization that collectively serves to enhance or mitigate the functioning of specific control policies and procedures; reflects the overall attitude, awareness, and actions of those in control of the organization in creating an atmosphere of control.

control procedures Those policies and procedures that management has established to provide reasonable assurance that specific entity objectives will be achieved.

control risk The risk that material misstatements that occur will not be prevented, detected, or corrected by the control procedures in place.

control risk assessment The auditor's assessment of the control risk that is present for each significant account balance and class of transactions and related assertions; assessment is based on the auditor's knowledge of the entity's control environment, accounting system, and control procedures, including the effectiveness of specific controls in operation.

dual-purpose tests An auditor's test of transaction processing whereby the auditor is evaluating both the operation and effectiveness of controls *and* the correctness and completeness of processing and posting to the appropriate account balance. Thus, both tests of controls and substantive tests of account balances are performed at the same time with the same transactions.

flowchart A graphic representation of an accounting application that normally identifies key controls that are effective in achieving specific control objectives as part of the auditor's preliminary assessment of control risk.

internal control structure The elements that operate within an organization to promote adherence to management's control policies and procedures; consisting of three elements: (1) the control environment, (2) the accounting system, and (3) the control procedures.

material weakness in internal accounting control A condition in which the specific control procedures or the degree of compliance with them does not reduce to a relatively low level the risk that the financial statements being audited may contain errors or irregularities in material amounts that will not be detected within a timely period by employees in the normal course of performing their assigned functions.

narrative A written description of an accounting application and the controls within the application.

owner/manager controls Controls that operate in small businesses in which the owner-manager provides detailed review and oversight of accounting transactions and performs many of the review procedures that could be attained only through segregation of duties in large organizations.

paperless systems Accounting applications in which key records and documentation are created and stored only in electronic form within computer systems.

questionnaire An approach to understanding and documenting a client's control structure through answers to prestructured questions designed to depict the client's processing and potential exposures in the client's application system under investigation.

reconciliations Controls that operate by checking for agreement between submitted transactions and processed transactions or between detailed accounts and corresponding control accounts.

reportable conditions Matters coming to the auditor's attention that represent significant deficiencies in the design or operation of the internal control structure which could adversely affect the organization's ability to record, process, summarize, and report financial data consistent with the assertions of management in the financial statements and therefore that, in the auditor's judgment, should be communicated to the audit committee.

segregation of duties The separation of functions across individuals so that one individual is not put in a situation to both *perpetrate* and *conceal* a fraud or error through the manipulation of accounting records.

substantive tests Tests of transactions to ensure that they are properly recorded and direct tests of account balances either by performing tests of details making up an account balance or through analytical review techniques to estimate the overall correctness of account balances.

tests of controls Specific audit evidence gathered to determine whether control procedures are operating the way in which they have been described and documented in the auditor's preliminary understanding of controls; the auditor must determine whether they are operating as posited if the auditor wishes to assess control risk below the maximum.

walk-through An audit approach designed to gain an understanding of the processing that takes place in the accounting system; the auditor "walks" a transaction through its process and inquires of client personnel about the nature of the processing that takes place.

Review Questions

A–Introduction

8–1 What is a control risk assessment? What is the importance of a control risk assessment in an audit engagement?

8–2 Define the term *control structure* as used in an auditing context. What are the three main elements of an organization's control structure?

B–Control Structure Elements

8–3 What is an organization's control environment? What are the major elements of a control environment?

8–4 Define an *accounting application*. Explain the relationships among accounting applications, accounting subsystems, and the accounting system. Must an accounting application be completely computerized? Explain.

8–5 What function does an organization's board of directors and the audit committee of the board of directors play in promoting a strong control environment? Explain.

8–6 What is segregation of duties? What kinds of segregation of duties are important in accounting applications? Give an example of each type of segregation of duties that an auditor might look for in evaluating the controls in a given accounting application.

8–7 Describe how the objectives approach to evaluating the adequacy of controls in an accounting application is implemented.

8–8 Identify the major objectives associated with the valuation control objective. Briefly identify one or two controls that an organization might adopt to achieve the valuation objective.

8–9 Define the term *accounting control procedure*. Identify how the auditor determines whether a particular control is a *key control*, that is, a control procedure that is critical to the proper processing of a transaction.

8–10 What types of controls might a large-scale organization use to ensure that its divisional management is conducting business in a manner that will best achieve the overall objectives of the business? What control risks might be associated with a compensation system that places a heavy emphasis on year-end bonuses based on divisional profit performance?

8–11 What are the control objectives related to the *completeness* assertion? Identify two or three key controls an organization might implement to assist the organization in accomplishing the completeness objectives.

8–12 Identify controls the auditor might find to achieve the objective that "all valid transactions are recorded." For each control identified, briefly indicate how the auditor would go about testing whether the control operated effectively.

8–13 Identify the major control objectives related to the *existence* assertion. How is the existence assertion related to the valuation assertion? Identify two or three key controls an organization might implement to achieve the existence objectives.

C–Control Risk Assessment

8–14 What are the implications to the conduct of an audit if the auditor concludes that an organization's control environment does not promote a strong control conscientiousness on the part of employees? Give an example in your answer.

8–15 What are the advantages and disadvantages of a questionnaire over a flowchart as a basis for documenting and assessing control risk? What are the relative advantages of a flowchart over a questionnaire as a basis for documenting and assessing control risk?

8–16 Explain how a walk-through would serve as a basis for understanding and documenting the adequacy of controls in an accounting application.

8–17 How does an auditor gather information on an organization's control environment? How is the information on the client's control environment documented?

8–18 What information does an auditor expect to find when reviewing a company's personnel policies and procedures? How would the information gathered potentially affect the conduct of the audit?

8–19 Are auditors required to evaluate an organization's control structure and the attendant control risk on every audit? What documentation is required if the auditor evaluates control risk at the maximum and chooses to plan the audit assuming maximum control risk?

8–20 Describe a *dual-purpose test.* What is the purpose of such a test? Give an example of such a test.

8–21 How should an auditor use previous year working papers in performing the control risk assessment for the current year? What are the advantages and disadvantages of using previous year working papers in performing this year's control risk assessment?

8–22 How could a tour of the plant assist the auditor in gaining an understanding of the controls in place for important accounting applications?

8–23 What is a reportable condition as defined in conjunction with the auditor's responsibilities to communicate deficiencies in the internal control structure to the audit committee? How does the auditor identify reportable conditions?

Multiple Choice Questions

8–24 Which of the following would *not* be considered an advantage of using an internal control questionnaire in understanding and documenting the controls in an important accounting application?

a. The questionnaire can be computerized to provide linkages of weaknesses to particular types of errors that might occur in the account balances.

b. Questionnaires can be used for many years without updating.

c. Questionnaires can be easily understood and provide easy identification of potential control deficiencies through "no" responses to questions.

d. Questionnaires can be adapted to both large and small businesses as well as to different industries and still provide an assessment of overall controls.

8–25 Which of the following is a correct statement regarding the auditor's assessment of an organization's control environment?

a. The control environment ought to be assessed by the auditor even though the auditor cannot make a direct linkage from the control environment assessment to specific audit tests.

b. Most deficiencies in a company's control environment can be effectively mitigated by a proactive and effective audit committee.

c. Management compensation schemes are personal in nature and should not affect the auditor's assessment of an organization's control structure.

d. The board of directors is ultimately responsible for developing an overall control environment for the organization; management only implements the control structure designed by the board of directors.

8–26 Which of the following controls would be most effective in assisting the organization in achieving the completeness objective?

a. All employee time cards should be collected by the supervisor and transmitted directly to the payroll department for processing.

b. All shipments must be approved by the credit manager to ensure that the total amount of the invoice does not exceed approved limits.

c. All receipts of merchandise must be independently counted or weighed by someone in the receiving department who also reviews the goods for potential quality control deficiencies.

d. All shipments must be recorded on prenumbered shipping documents that are independently accounted for.

8–27 Proper implementation of reconciliation controls would be effective in detecting all of the following errors *except*

a. Transactions were appropriately posted to individual subsidiary accounts, but because of a computer malfunction, some of the transactions were not posted to the master account.

b. The client has experienced inventory shrinkage, which has caused the perpetual inventory records to be overstated.

c. Three shipments were never invoiced because employees in the shipping room colluded with a shipper to deliver goods to their own private company for resale and never recorded the shipments on any documents.

d. A bank teller properly recorded all transactions involving checks but pocketed all cash receipts even though customers were given a receipt as evidence of the deposit to their accounts.

8–28 Which of the following statements would *not* be correct regarding the authorization function as implemented in an organization?

a. Blanket authorizations can be implemented in computer systems on the approval of the user area. All changes to the authorization parameters embodied in the computer should be made only on written documented requests by the user area responsible for the authorization.

b. General authorizations may be delegated by top management in the form of company policies.

c. The auditor can rely on an authorization control only when there is documentary evidence of the authorization in the form of a signature or an authorizer's initials somewhere in the system.

d. Effective implementation of a "password" scheme to limit access to computer records is a form of an authorization control.

8–29 Which of the following items, if omitted, would constitute an important weakness in the preparation of an auditor developed flowchart to document the control structure of an important accounting application?

a. The document numbers used in recording the transactions during the current year.

b. Key controls within the system that effectively meet important control objectives for transaction processing.

c. The names of client personnel that handle the processing of the transaction.

d. The distribution of copies of documents to personnel outside of the accounting area.

8–30 Segregation of duties is best accomplished when the auditor can determine that

a. Employees perform only one job; for example, someone working on accounts payable does not have access to other accounting records such as the detail in property, plant, and equipment.

b. The internal audit department performs an independent test of transactions throughout the year and reports any errors to departmental managers.

c. The person responsible for reconciling the bank account is responsible for cash disbursements, not cash receipts.

d. The payroll department cannot add employees to the payroll or change pay rates without the explicit authorization of the personnel department.

8–31 Authorization of transactions in a computerized, mostly paperless, processing environment can take place in the form of

a. Computerized authorization in the form of user-approved blanket authorizations.

b. Electronic authorization of specific transactions carefully controlled through the use of a password system.

c. User-approved (and tested) program to automatically compute economic order quantities and reorder when stock levels fall below a specified limit.

d. All of the above.

e. None of the above.

*8–32 During the review of a small business client's internal control structure, the auditor discovered that the accounts receivable clerk approves credit memos and has access to cash. Which of the following controls would be most effective in offsetting the weakness?

a. The owner reviews errors in billings to customers and postings to the subsidiary ledger.

b. The controller receives the monthly bank statement directly and reconciles the checking accounts.

c. The owner reviews credit memos after they are recorded.

d. The controller reconciles the total of the detail accounts receivable accounts to the amount shown in the ledger.

*8–33 The accounts payable department receives the purchase order form to accomplish all of the following *except*

a. Compare invoice price to purchase order price.

b. Ensure that the purchase had been properly authorized.

---

*Adapted from the Uniform CPA examination or the Certified Internal Auditor examination.

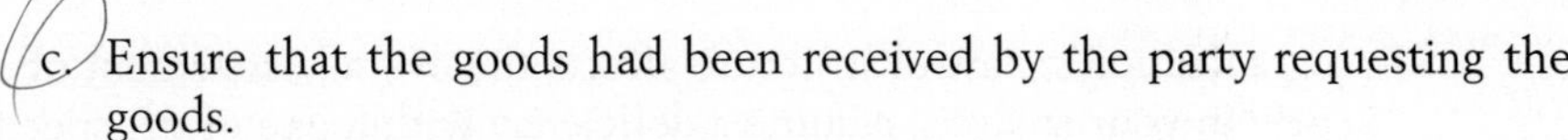

c. Ensure that the goods had been received by the party requesting the goods.

d. Compare quantity ordered to the quantity purchased.

Discussion and Research Questions

8–34 (Components of Control Risk Assessments) A review of corporate failures as described in the financial press such as *The Wall Street Journal* often describes the "tone at the top" as one of the major contributors to the failure. Often this tone at the top reflects a disdain for controls and an emphasis on accomplishing specific objectives perceived to be important by top management.

Required:

a. Identify the key components an auditor will evaluate in assessing the control environment of an organization and indicate how the auditor's assessment of the overall control environment of an organization should affect the design and conduct of an audit.

b. For each component of the control environment identified above, indicate the information (and the sources of the information) the auditor would gather in evaluating the factor.

c. Briefly describe how the auditor should go about documenting the assessment of the client's control environment. Does the auditor's evaluation of the control environment need to be documented in a memo or could it be documented in some other way? Explain.

8–35 (Authorization Controls) Authorization of transactions is considered to be an important accounting control. The movement to computerized and paperless accounting systems poses new problems for management in implementing authorization techniques as well as for the auditor in evaluating the authorization controls.

Required:

a. Why is the authorization control so important to the auditor? What is the implication to the audit if important transactions do not meet the organization's criteria for authorization?

b. What should the auditor do upon discovering important unauthorized transactions?

c. How can authorization controls be incorporated into computerized, paperless accounting systems?

8–36 (Elements of a Control Structure) The auditing standards describe an organization's control structure in terms of three elements: a control environment, the accounting system, and control procedures.

Required:

a. Briefly describe the relationship among the three elements of an organization's control structure.

b. Briefly explain how a deficiency in any one of the elements of an organization's control structure affects the overall assessment of control risk. In your analysis, assume a deficiency within one of the specific elements and no serious deficiencies in the other two elements.

c. Is a control risk assessment made for the overall organization or for specific subsystems of the organization's transaction processing systems? Explain.

8–37 (Operation of Controls) The auditing standards indicate that if the control risk assessment is reduced below the maximum level, the auditor must gain some assurance that the controls are operating effectively.

Required:

a. What is meant by testing the effectiveness of control procedures? How does an auditor decide which controls to test?

b. Do all control procedures need to be tested? Explain.

c. How is the auditor's assessment of control risk affected if a documented control procedure is not operating effectively?

8–38 (Segregation of Duties) For each of the following situations, evaluate the segregation of duties described and indicate the following:

a. Any deficiency in the segregation of duties described (indicate *None* if no deficiency is present).

b. The potential errors or irregularities that might occur because of the inadequate segregation of duties.

c. Compensating, or additional, controls that might be added to the process to mitigate potential misstatements.

d. A specific audit test that ought to be performed to determine whether the potential misstatement had occurred.

Situations:

1. The company's payroll is computerized and is handled by one person in charge of payroll who is responsible for keying all weekly time reports into the computer system. The payroll system is password protected so that only the payroll person can change pay rates or add/delete company personnel to the payroll file. Payroll checks are prepared weekly and the payroll person batches the checks by supervisor or department head for subsequent distribution to employees.

2. XYZ is a relatively small organization but has segregated the duties of cash receipts and cash disbursements. However, the employee responsible for handling cash receipts also reconciles the monthly bank account.

3. Nick's is a small family-owned restaurant in a northern resort area whose employees are trusted. When the restaurant is very busy, any of the waitresses has the ability to operate the cash register and collect the tab. All orders are tabulated on "tickets." Although there is a place to indicate the waiter or waitress on each ticket, most do not bother to do so.

4. Bredford Manufacturing is an audit client with approximately $15 million in annual sales. All of its accounting is performed on a high-end microcomputer located in a separate office area in the accounting

department. The microcomputer has three terminals, one in the controller's department (used mostly for analysis purposes), one in the assistant accountant's area (individual is responsible for all accounting except cash receipts and sales billing), and one in the office of the individual responsible for billing and cash receipts. The office housing the microcomputer is locked each night when the controller leaves, but if the office is behind in processing, she often leaves it open for the sales clerk to work overtime and catch up on processing.

5. Bass Pro Shops takes all customer orders over a toll free phone number. The order taker sits at a terminal and has complete access to the customer's previous credit history and a list of inventory available for sale. The order clerk has the ability to input all the customer's requests and then generate a sales invoice and shipment without any additional supervisory review or approval.

6. The purchasing department of Big Dutch is organized around three purchasing agents. The first is responsible for ordering electrical gear and motors, the second orders fabrication material, and the third orders nuts and bolts and other smaller supplies that go into the assembly process. To improve the accountability of vendors, all receiving slips and vendor invoices are sent directly to the purchasing agent placing the order. This allows the purchasing agent to better monitor the performance of vendors. When approved by the purchasing agent for payment, the purchasing agent must forward (a) a copy of the purchase order, (b) a copy of the receiving slip, and (c) a copy of the vendor invoice to accounts payable for payment. Accounts payable will not pay an invoice unless all three items are present and match as to quantities, prices, and so forth. The receiving department reports to the purchasing department.

7. The employees of Americana TV and Appliance are paid based on their performance in generating profitable sales for the company. Each salesperson has the ability to determine a sales price (within specified but very broad parameters). Once a sales price has been negotiated with the customer, an invoice is prepared. At the close of the day, the salesperson looks up the cost of the merchandise on a master price list. The salesperson then enters the cost of the merchandise on to the copy of the invoice and submits it to accounting for data entry and processing. The salesperson's commission is determined by the gross margin realized on sales.

8–39 (Documentation of Control Structure) The auditor might document the preliminary analysis of an organization's control structure in a number of ways. Three of the most common methods are (1) a flowchart, (2) an internal control questionnaire, and (3) a written narrative.

Required:

a. For each of the three approaches identified,
   1. Identify the relative strengths and weaknesses of the approach.
   2. Indicate how important control procedures are identified and documented.

b. For each approach, explain how the auditor might use a microcomputer to assist in documenting, updating, and evaluating the control structure of an organization and then determining the impact of the control structure on the conduct of the audit.

8–40 (Tests of Controls) If a company's control risk is assessed at less than the maximum, the auditor needs to gather evidence on the operation of the controls. The effective operation of control procedures is thus needed to support a control risk assessment at other than the maximum.

Required:

a. For each of the following control procedures indicate the audit procedure the auditor would use to determine its operating effectiveness.
b. Briefly indicate the audit implication, that is, how direct tests of account balances would need to be modified if the auditor finds that the control procedure is not working as planned.

Controls

1. Credit approval by the credit department is required before salespersons accept orders of more than $5,000 and for all customers who have a past due balance higher than $3,000.
2. All merchandise receipts are recorded on prenumbered receiving slips. The numerical sequence of the receiving slips is periodically accounted for by the controller's department.
3. Payments for goods received are made only by the accounts payable department on receipt of a vendor invoice, which is then matched for prices and quantities with approved purchase orders and receiving slips.
4. The accounts receivable bookkeeper is not allowed to issue credit memos or to approve the write-off of accounts.
5. Cash receipts are opened by a mail clerk who prepares remittances to send to accounts receivable for recording. The clerk prepares a daily deposit slip, which is sent to the controller. Deposits are made daily by the controller.
6. Employees are added to the payroll master file by the payroll department only after receiving a written authorization from the personnel department.
7. The only individuals who have access to the payroll master file are the payroll department head and the payroll clerk responsible for maintaining the payroll file. Access to the file is controlled by computer passwords.
8. Edit tests built into the computerized payroll program prohibit the processing of weekly payroll hours in excess of 55 and the payment to an employee for more than three different job classifications during a one week period.
9. Credit memos are issued to customers only on the receipt of merchandise or the approval of the sales department for adjustments.
10. A salesperson cannot approve sales return or price adjustment for an individual customer that exceeds five percent of the cumulative sales

for the year for the customer. Any subsequent approvals of adjustments for such a customer must be approved by the divisional sales manager.

8–41 (Authorization) Authorization of transactions is considered a key control in most organizations. It is important that the organization not be committed to transactions not in their best interest. It is also important that individuals who have incompatible functions not be allowed to commit organizations to transactions that could result in fraudulent gains for the employee.

Required:
Indicate the individual or function (for example, the head of a particular department) that should have the ability to authorize each of the following transactions. Briefly indicate the rationale for your answer.

Transactions
1. Writing-off old accounts receivable.
2. Committing the organization to acquire another company that is one-half the size of the existing company.
3. Paying an employee for overtime.
4. Shipping goods on account to a new customer.
5. Purchasing goods from a new vendor.
6. Temporarily investing funds in common stock investments instead of money market funds.
7. Purchasing a new line of manufacturing equipment to remodel a production line at one of the company's major divisions. The purchase represents a major new investment for the organization.
8. Replacing an older machine at one of the company's major divisions.
9. Rewriting the company's major computer program for processing purchase orders and accounts payable. The cost of rewriting the program will represent one-quarter of the organization's computer development budget for the year.

*8–42 (Developing an Internal Control Questionnaire for Shipments) Taylor, CPA, has been engaged to audit the financial statements of Johnson's Coat Outlet, Inc., a medium-size mail-order retail store that sells a wide variety of coats to the public.

Required:
Prepare the shipment segment of Taylor's internal control questionnaire. Each question should elicit either a yes or no response. Do *not* prepare questions relating to the cash receipts, sales returns and allowances, billing, inventory control, or other segments.

Use the following format:

Question	Yes	No

*8–43 (Internal Control Questionnaire: Purchases) Green, CPA, has been engaged to audit the financial statements of Star Manufacturing, Inc., a medium-size entity that produces a wide variety of household goods. All acquisitions of materials are processed through the purchasing, receiving, accounts payable, and treasury functions.

Required:
Prepare the purchases segment of the internal control questionnaire to be used in the evaluation of Star's internal control structure. Each question should elicit either a yes or no response. Do not prepare the receiving, accounts payable, or treasury segments of the internal control questionnaire. Do not discuss the internal controls over purchases.

Use the following format:

Question	Yes	No

8–44 (Reportable Conditions) *Statement on Auditing Standards No. 60* [AU 325] requires the auditor to communicate reportable conditions in an organization's internal control structure to the audit committee or its equivalent.

Required:

a. Define the term *reportable condition* and give three specific examples of items you would consider to be a reportable condition if found during the conduct of an audit engagement.
b. If the auditor's preliminary assessment of control risk was low but during the test of account balances, the auditor discovered a number of material errors in the accounts, does the discovery of the errors indicate that significant deficiencies exist in the controls structure that the auditor should include in a report to the audit committee? Explain.
c. How would the auditor normally identify reportable conditions during the course of an audit engagement?
d. Should the audit be expected to identify all significant weaknesses in an organization's control structure? Explain, taking into consideration that the auditor must design the audit report to provide reasonable assurance that all material misstatements will be identified.

*8–45 (Internal Controls: Office Service Client) Brown Company provides office support services for more than 100 small clients. These services consist of the following:

1. Supplying temporary personnel.
2. Providing monthly bookkeeping services.
3. Designing and printing small brochures.
4. Copying and reproduction services.
5. Preparing tax reports.

Some clients pay for these services on a cash basis, some use 30-day charge accounts, and some others operate on a contractual basis with quarterly payments. Brown's new office manager was concerned about the effectiveness of control procedures over sales and cash flow. At the manager's request, the process was reviewed and disclosed the following:

a. Contracts were written by account executives and then passed to the accounts receivable department where they were filed. Contracts had a limitation (ceiling) as to the types of services and the amount of work covered. Contracts were payable quarterly in advance.

b. Client periodic payments on contracts were identified on the contract and a payment receipt was placed in the contract file. Accounting records showed Credit Revenue; Debit Cash.

c. Periodically a clerk reviewed the contract files to determine their status.

d. Work orders relating to contract services were placed in the contract file. Accounting records showed Debit Cost of Services; Credit Cash or Accounts Payable or Accrued Payroll.

e. Monthly bookkeeping services were usually paid for when the work was complete. If not paid in cash, a copy of the financial statement marked "Unpaid $________________" was put into a cash-pending file. It was removed when cash was received and accounting records showed Debit Cash; Credit Revenue.

f. Design and printing work was handled like bookkeeping's work. However, a design and printing order form was used to accumulate costs and to compute the charge to be made to the client. A copy of the order form served as a billing to the client and when cash was received as a remittance advice.

g. Reproduction (copy) work was generally a cash transaction that was rung up on a cash register and balanced at the end of the day. Some reproduction work was charged to open accounts. A billing form was given to the client with the work and a copy was put in an open file. It was removed when paid. In both cases, when cash was received, the accounting entry was Debit Cash; Credit Revenue.

h. Tax work was handled like the bookkeeping services.

i. Cash from cash sales was deposited daily. Cash from receipts on account or quarterly payments on contracts was deposited after being matched with evidence of the receivable.

j. Bank reconciliations were performed using the deposit slips as original data for the deposits on the bank statements.

k. A cash log of all cash received in the mail was maintained and used for reference purposes when payment was disputed.

l. Monthly comparisons were made of the costs and revenues of printing, design, bookkeeping, and tax service. Unusual variations between revenues and costs were investigated. However, the handling of deferred payments made this analysis difficult.

Required:

a. List the eight elements of poor internal control that are evident.

b. List six elements of good internal control that are in effect.

*8–46 (Internal Controls: Payroll Flowchart) A CPA's audit working papers contain a narrative description of a *segment* of Croyden Factory, Inc., payroll system and an accompanying flowchart as follows:

- The internal control structure with respect to the personnel department functions well and is *not* included in the accompanying flowchart.

- At the beginning of each work week, payroll clerk 1 reviews the payroll department files to determine the employment status of factory employees and then prepares time cards and distributes them as each individual arrives at work. This payroll clerk, who is also responsible for custody of the signature stamp machine, verifies the identity of each payee before delivering signed checks to the supervisor.
- At the end of each work week, the supervisor distributes payroll checks for the preceding work week. Concurrent with this activity, the supervisor reviews the current week's employee time cards, notes the regular and overtime hours worked on a summary form, and initials the aforementioned time cards. The supervisor then delivers all time cards and unclaimed payroll checks to payroll clerk 2.

Required:

a. Based on the narrative and accompanying flowchart, what are the weaknesses in the internal control structure?

b. Based on the narrative and accompanying flowchart, what inquiries should be made with respect to clarifying the existence of possible additional weaknesses in the internal control structure?

c. Must the auditor's working papers state the assessed level of control risk for each financial assertion in the client's financial statements, or is it acceptable to establish one overall control risk assessment for the client? Explain.

8–47 (Documentation of Control Risk Assessment) Shelley Romano is explaining the procedures used to document control risk to a new staff assistant. There is considerable discussion about the nature of documentation required for various levels of control risk assessment, especially when the auditor chooses to assess control risk at a maximum (no reliance on the controls).

Required:

a. What is the auditor required to document when control risk is assessed at the maximum for an assertion?

b. Explain the documentation requirements when the level of control risk is assessed as low for an assertion.

c. Must the auditor's working papers state the assessed level of control risk for each financial assertion in the client's financial statements, or is it acceptable to establish one overall control risk assessment for the client? Explain.

8–48 (Understanding an Organization's Control Environment) During a discussion, a new auditor stated that "an assessment of the organization's control environment is not very meaningful because it does not directly affect the processing of individual transactions. And it is the transactions that make up the account balance. As long as the auditor can test the details making up the account balances, the assessment of the control environment is unnecessary."

Required:

a. Do you agree or disagree with the above statement? Justify your answer.

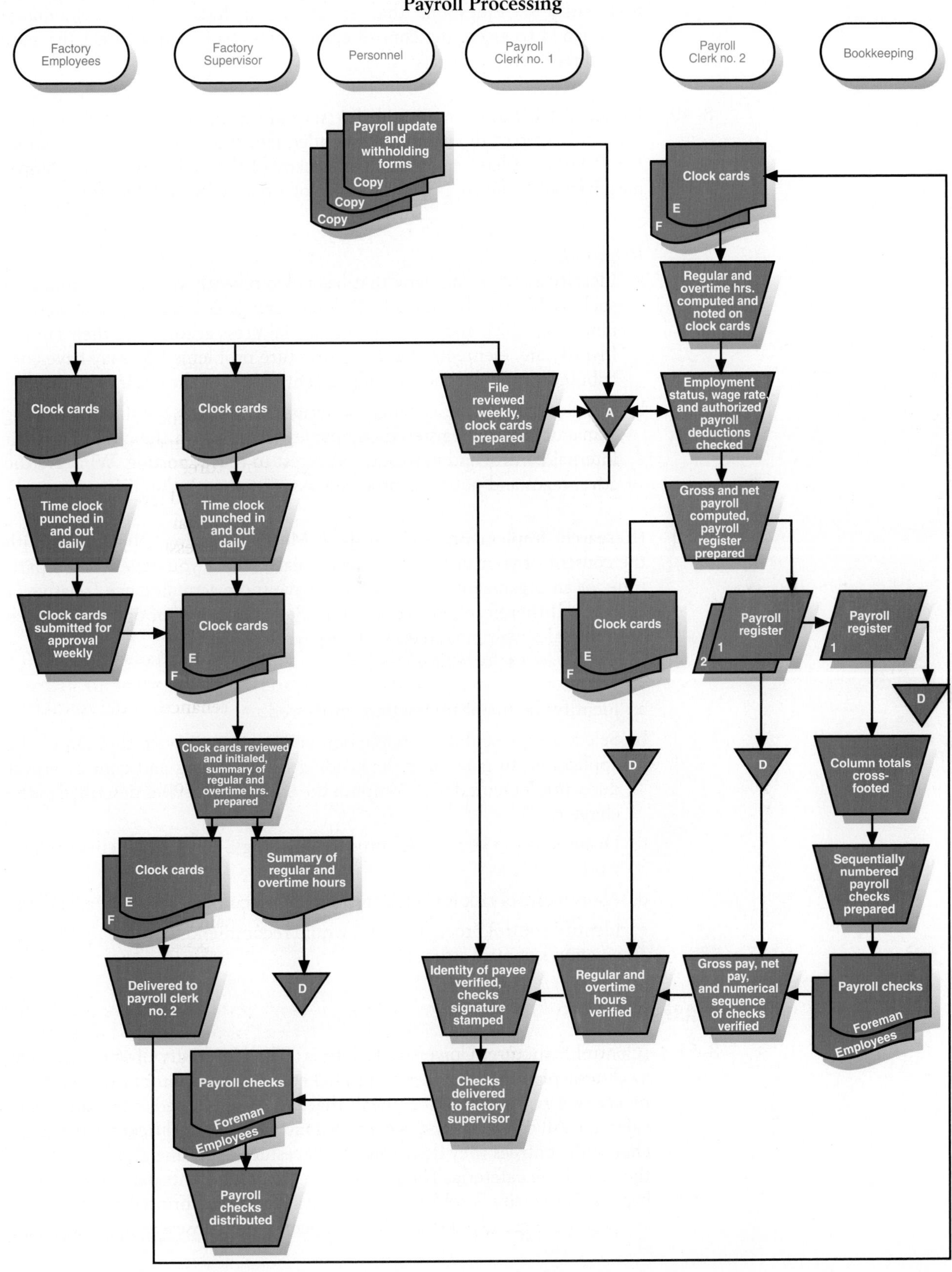

Problem 8-46
Crayden Factory, Inc.
Payroll Processing
Factory Employees
Factory Supervisor
Personnel
Payroll Clerk no. 1
Payroll Clerk no. 2
Bookkeeping
Payroll update and withholding forms
Copy
Copy
Copy
Clock cards
E
F
Regular and overtime hrs. computed and noted on clock cards
Clock cards
Clock cards
File reviewed weekly, clock cards prepared
A
Employment status, wage rate, and authorized payroll deductions checked
Time clock punched in and out daily
Time clock punched in and out daily
Gross and net payroll computed, payroll register prepared
Clock cards submitted for approval weekly
Clock cards
E
F
Clock cards
E
F
Payroll register
1
2
Payroll register
1
D
Clock cards reviewed and initialed, summary of regular and overtime hrs. prepared
D
D
Column totals cross-footed
Clock cards
E
F
Summary of regular and overtime hours
Sequentially numbered payroll checks prepared
Delivered to payroll clerk no. 2
D
Identity of payee verified, checks signature stamped
Regular and overtime hours verified
Gross pay, net pay, and numerical sequence of checks verified
Payroll checks
Foreman
Employees
Payroll checks
Foreman
Employees
Checks delivered to factory supervisor
Payroll checks distributed

b. Identify six questions that should be included in a questionnaire designed to assess the control environment as it would affect the sales and receivable cycle.

8–49 **(Research)** It has been alleged that several recent corporate failures have been in large part due to the lack of adequate controls in the organization. For example, it has been alleged that many of the savings and loan companies that failed did so, in part, because of a poor control structure.

Required:

a. Identify a major company that has failed recently or choose a company such as MiniScribe, Lincoln Federal Savings & Loan, Great American Financial, ESM, and review the financial press accounts of their failure. Identify any elements of control structure problems that may have contributed to the decline and subsequent failure of the organization.

b. The Securities and Exchange Commission has been considering making it mandatory for registered companies to report on the quality of their internal control and have auditors attest to that reporting. What are the advantages and potential problems associated with the SEC's proposal?

8–50 **(Research: Implementing Controls to Meet Processing Objectives)** With the consent of your instructor, select a place where you have worked part-time, or an organization in which you have some acquaintance (relative or friend) and therefore have access to it. Select one area of operations (cash receipts, sales, shipping, receiving, or payroll) for review.

For the area selected for review:

a. Identify the major transactions processed.

b. Select a representative transaction and perform a walk-through of the application to gain an understanding of processing and control procedures implemented to accomplish the control objectives described in the chapter.

c. Document the key control procedures using a control objectives framework.

d. Assess control risk for the assertions and document that understanding.

e. Identify control procedures you would recommend to improve the organization's control structure.

Cases

8–51 (Control Structure: University Cafeteria) The University of Wisconsin has a cafeteria plan that provides a meal ticket to each dormitory resident. Each meal ticket represents $20 of meals that can be purchased in any university cafeteria. All cafeterias also accept cash instead of a meal ticket. Customers choose the entrees they desire and pay a cashier operating a cash register at the exit of the cafeteria. The cashiers are mostly students paid on an hourly basis by University Food Service. The meal tickets are printed on blank card stock and are readily transferable. Students who subscribe to a meal plan level that is more than they need often sell their excess meal tickets to other students or faculty members. Each cafeteria is open only at specified times, such as lunch from 11:15 A.M. to 1:00 P.M.

Required:
Identify the controls the University should implement to ensure that all purchases of meal tickets are recorded, the meal tickets are properly deducted for the amount of purchase, and all cash is promptly and correctly deposited. Also consider the controls needed to protect against fictitious meal tickets.

*8–52 (Internal Controls in a Credit Department) You have been assigned to review the internal controls of the credit department of a recently acquired subsidiary. The subsidiary imports several lines of microcomputers and sells them to retail stores throughout the country. The department consists of the credit manager hired six months ago to replace the previous manager who retired, a clerk, and a part-time secretary.

Sales are made by 15 sales representatives, 5 at headquarters who handle large accounts with retail chains and the local area and 10 located throughout the country. Sales representatives visit current and prospective customers and, if a sale is made, prepare a customer order form consisting of the original and three copies. One copy is retained by the customer, one by the sales representative, one is sent to the warehouse, and the original is sent to headquarters. For new customers with orders of more than $5,000, a credit application is also completed and sent along with the order to headquarters. The credit application includes a bank reference and three credit references along with financial statements.

The sales order sent to headquarters goes first to the credit department for approval. The credit department looks up the customer's credit in a card file that is maintained for customers with "good credit." If the customer is found, the clerk examines a monthly report listing all accounts that have not been paid in 60 days. If the customer's account is not listed in the report, the clerk initials the order as approved and sends it to accounting for recording and billing. Orders from new customers or from customers listed on the 60-day report are held for review by the credit manager.

For orders of more than $5,000 from new customers, the credit manager reviews the credit application along with the financial statements and calls at least one of the credit references. If approved, the manager initials the order and gives it to the secretary to prepare a card for the clerk's card file and to file the credit application. If denied, the manager adds the customer's name to a list of past rejected credit applications and canceled accounts. For new customers with orders for less than the $5,000 limit, the credit manager reviews the order and checks it against the list of past rejections. If the customer's name is not on this list, the order is initialed as approved and sent to accounting. For orders from customers with accounts 60 days past due, the manager reviews the details of the accounts and the original credit application. If approved, the order is initialed and sent to accounting.

If orders are not approved, the credit manager calls the warehouse to stop shipment. The order is marked "Credit Not Approved" and given to the secretary, who notifies the sales representative and the customer. The order and the credit application are then thrown away. Once each quarter, the credit manager requests that the accounting department provide a list of all accounts more than 90 days old with supporting detail of account activity for the past 12 months. The credit manager reviews the information and determines whether action should be taken. Action consists of the following:

- Calling the sales representative and asking him or her to contact the client about payment.
- If payment is not made in three weeks, the credit manager calls the customer and requests payment. The customer's card is also pulled from the customer card file.
- If payment is not made within two additional weeks, the account is turned over to a collection agency.

When an account has been with a collection agency for two months without receiving payment, it is written off. The necessary adjusting entries are prepared by the credit manager.

Required:

a. Identify the deficiencies associated with the credit function as described above. Use the following format:

Deficiency	Associated Risk	Recommended Control

b. Identify control improvements that could be made by computerizing more of the process.

*8–53 (Segregation of Duties) As the internal auditor for a large savings and loan association, you are concerned about segregation of duties for a wholly owned real estate investment subsidiary. The subsidiary, despite its tens of million dollars in assets, operates from the main office of the parent. The parent company administers all purchasing, payroll, and personnel functions. The subsidiary's board of directors consists entirely of selected officers of the parent.

The real estate investment subsidiary's activities consist primarily of buying, developing, and selling real estate, with some development projects involving joint ventures with contractors. Day-to-day operations are handled by the president and two vice presidents. The president also acts as a liaison with the parent. Each vice president has his or her own projects to manage.

All invoices and itemized statements requiring direct payment or reimbursement to contractors or vendors are delivered to one of the two vice presidents for review and approval. After they are approved, the staff accountant prepares checks and then has one of the vice presidents sign them. After they are signed, the checks are returned to the staff accountant for mailing and filing of the supporting documentation. All blank checks are kept by the staff accountant.

All customer payments on notes and accounts receivable originating from the sale of real estate are remitted to one of the two vice presidents and then forwarded to the staff accountant, who records the payment and prepares the deposit slip. The deposit may be given to the parent's accounting department or to a teller of the parent.

If the subsidiary experiences a cash shortage, a promissory note is prepared by the staff accountant and signed by the president or one of the vice presidents. The staff accountant submits the promissory note to the parent and awaits receipt of the funds. The staff accountant is responsible for billing customers and advising management when payments are due. The staff accountant reconciles the bank statement once a month.

The staff accountant prepares monthly financial statements, including the accrual of interest receivable and the capitalization of certain interest charges. The financial statements are prepared to reflect the substance of both joint ventures and subsidiary operations. The board of directors reviews the financial statements.

Required:

a. Identify specific areas in which segregation of duties is inadequate and suggest ways in which segregation could be improved.
b. If segregation were adequate, how would the auditor gather evidence to test the actual segregation of duties during normal operation?

End Notes

1. Abraham Akresh, James Loebbecke, and William Scott, "Audit Approaches and Techniques," in *Research Opportunities in Auditing: The Second Decade*, ed. A. Rashad Abdel-khalik and Ira Solomon (Sarasota, Fla.: American Accounting Association, 1988), 26.

CHAPTER

9

Learning Objectives

Through studying this chapter, you will be able to:

1. Understand the nature of computer systems and their impact on auditing.
2. Identify major computer processing technology and applicable controls.
3. Assess control risk in computer applications.
4. Understand computer technology trends and paperless information systems.
5. Identify audit approaches to test the effectiveness of controls.
6. Design an audit approach for a client with sophisticated computerized processing.

Assessing Control Risk in Computerized Applications

Chapter Contents

The nature of auditing will undoubtedly continue to undergo substantial changes as the level of technology improves. Experts are forecasting continued improvement in the power and flexibility of computers and communications devices, while costs are expected to continue to decrease. A proliferation in the number of computers and terminals also is expected in the next decade; this will in turn lead to more widespread end-user computing.[1]

Control procedures in a computerized environment generally comprise a combination of user control procedures, computer application control procedures (programmed control procedures and manual follow-up procedures), and computer general control procedures. When planning a lower assessed level of control risk, the auditor should consider the extent of the understanding of control procedures that, when considered in conjunction with the understanding of the control environment and accounting system, is needed. . . . If computer general control procedures operate effectively, there is greater assurance that programmed control procedures are properly designed and function consistently throughout the period. Tests of computer general control procedures, combined with tests of manual follow-up procedures, often provide the evidential matter sufficient to plan a lower level of control risk.[2]

Chapter Overview

Most companies find that they must use computer technology effectively to remain competitive. The nature of that technology, however, continues to change rapidly. Clients continue to integrate their accounting systems and operations. Diverse operating units are becoming computerized, and end-user computing is growing rapidly. Today's auditor must be able to identify the important computer controls and determine the impact of those controls on the overall control structure. In addition, the auditor must understand the design of the client's computer system to audit efficiently. This chapter identifies the basic elements of computerized accounting systems, the important controls built into computer applications, and alternative approaches to testing those controls.

A–INTRODUCTION

The complexity of today's business organizations dictates that successful organizations utilize highly complex computer processing to account for and control the millions of transactions affecting their organization. For example, today's financial institutions transact monetary transfers in billions of dollars per day—all controlled by highly sophisticated computer systems. Many organizations, not just businesses, depend totally on the accuracy and integrity of their computer systems. A recent Massachusetts Institute of Technology study predicted that the organizations that did not plan computer integration for strategic and business planning for the 1990s would most certainly fail.[3]

The past decade has only accentuated the dependency of organizations and organization growth on effective computer systems. Database systems and distributed processing now spread computing across organizational units and global boundaries. On-line computerized systems have dramatically increased the speed with which transactions are processed. Finally, paperless processing has begun to replace traditional paper-based systems. And, as noted above, further technological change is expected in the next decade and will affect the nature of processing in virtually every organization.

The auditor facing these environments has little choice but to thoroughly understand the control risk associated with the client's computerized environment. In assessing control risk in these environments, two points are important: (1) although computerized accounting systems and the control procedures found therein are changing rapidly, management must find effective ways to control those systems or the organization will not be able to compete effectively in its marketplace or even to survive and (2) the auditor's objective for assessing control risk in computerized environments does not change from that used in less sophisticated systems, but the technology for implementing and testing the effectiveness of the controls in those systems may differ. But the impact of computers is not limited to understanding the client's control risk. The auditor must use computer-based audit techniques to improve the efficiency and effectiveness of the audit.

Overview of Computerized Accounting Systems

Computer systems might be described in a number of ways. For example, they could be characterized by size, but technology moves so quickly that characteristics associated with the large mainframe computers a few years ago are now incorporated in small stand-alone desktop microcomputers.

Today's computer systems are highly integrated and networked. The computing environment includes hardware, software, telecommunications, data and mass data storage, and people who manage the computing environment and support end users. Today's computer systems may be integrated across functional lines, for example, entering the completion of a production process into the system may update accounting records, such as inventory and payroll, and may also update the production management system. The auditor needs to understand this environment and the security features designed to ensure that only authorized users access the system for approved processes.

Components of the Computer Environment

Mainframe Computer. The heart of most computer systems is the mainframe computer (also referred to in some environments as the info-server), which has the capability to perform multitasking (processing more than one transaction or more than one program at once), has large memory capabilities, has access to large amounts of data storage, and can process data at phenomenal speeds.

As noted in Exhibit 9.1, the mainframe computer may be connected to a number of other computers. In some instances, the processing of one computer may be shifted to another computer within the company's system. This is referred to as

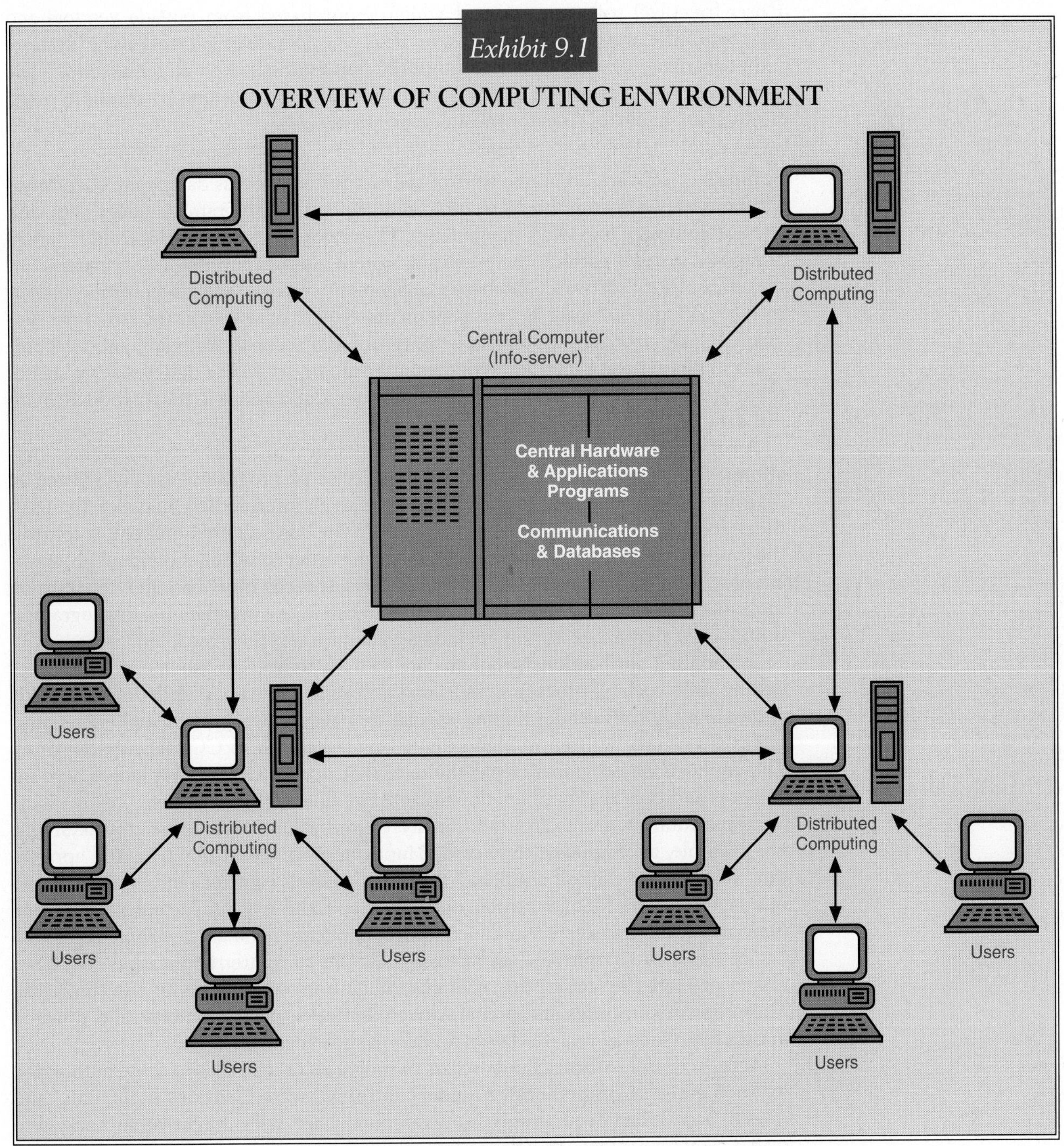

distributed processing. In addition, the mainframe computer may be connected with other organizations' mainframe computers to enable transferring and sharing data. As an example, students in a university may use their computer terminal to access data located on another computer as part of an assigned research project.

Small organizations may use a microcomputer instead of a mainframe system. The microcomputer is distinguished from other computers almost solely by its ability to sit on a desktop. Typically, the microcomputer is accompanied by easy-to-use ("user-friendly") software, most of which is purchased from outside vendors and adapted to the organization and has the ability to operate as a "stand-alone" system, although many of today's microcomputers are connected to larger systems. The microcomputer's powerful ability, combined with ease of access by multiple users, poses unique control risks for most organizations.

Software. Software programs control the computer, process data, control communications between computers, restrict access to data or programs, manage data, and prepare complete logs of all transactions. The major types of software found in most computer systems include the operating system, application programs, access control and security software, database management systems, and telecommunications software. Some software is pervasive in its effects on the control structure. For example, the operating system, access control and security software, and telecommunications software interact with most user programs. Major deficiencies in any of these programs may directly affect the computer applications used to produce financial data.

A computer's **operating system** controls all aspects of a computer's internal operations. The operating system consists of a series of programs, usually written in machine code or assembly language, that acts as an intermediary between the user, the processor, and the applications software. In the business environment, it controls the processing of user programs, determines the order in which individual programs are processed, and provides logs of transactions. It is the most complex software on most machines. Because the operating system can access any data file or program, it is important that access to the operating system be severely restricted.

Accounting **applications programs** are written to accomplish specific data processing tasks such as processing sales and accounts receivable, updating inventory, computing payroll, or developing special management reports. Application programs are usually written in higher-level languages such as COBOL, Pascal, or C. The applications programs create the data that update the general ledger account balances and thus the numbers flowing into the financial statements.

Application programs are traditionally viewed as input-process-output systems. For example, an employee time card is input, then processed by a payroll application to generate a payroll check and a job cost analysis (output) and to update various payroll master files (electronic output). (See Exhibit 9.2.) The employee's time is automatically transferred to the computer application via an electronic collection device when the employee logs in for a job. The computer application accesses a master pay rate file (table) that contains the authorized pay rate for the employee. The program computes and prepares payroll checks, payroll reports, and updated master files (such as year-to-date pay and withholdings).

Access control software limits access to programs or data files to those authorized for such access. Comprehensive access control software identifies users, data, and rules to access data or programs. For example, a bank teller might be authorized to read a customer's account balance but might not be allowed to make a transfer to another account without supervisory approval. Some access control software controls the access to all items within the computing environment; others are built into individual applications or databases.

A *database* is a planned and controlled collection of data. A **database management system** refers to the software to organize the collection of data into logically similar records and files. Database systems separate the data from application programs, thus creating data independence and allowing greater flexibility in meeting

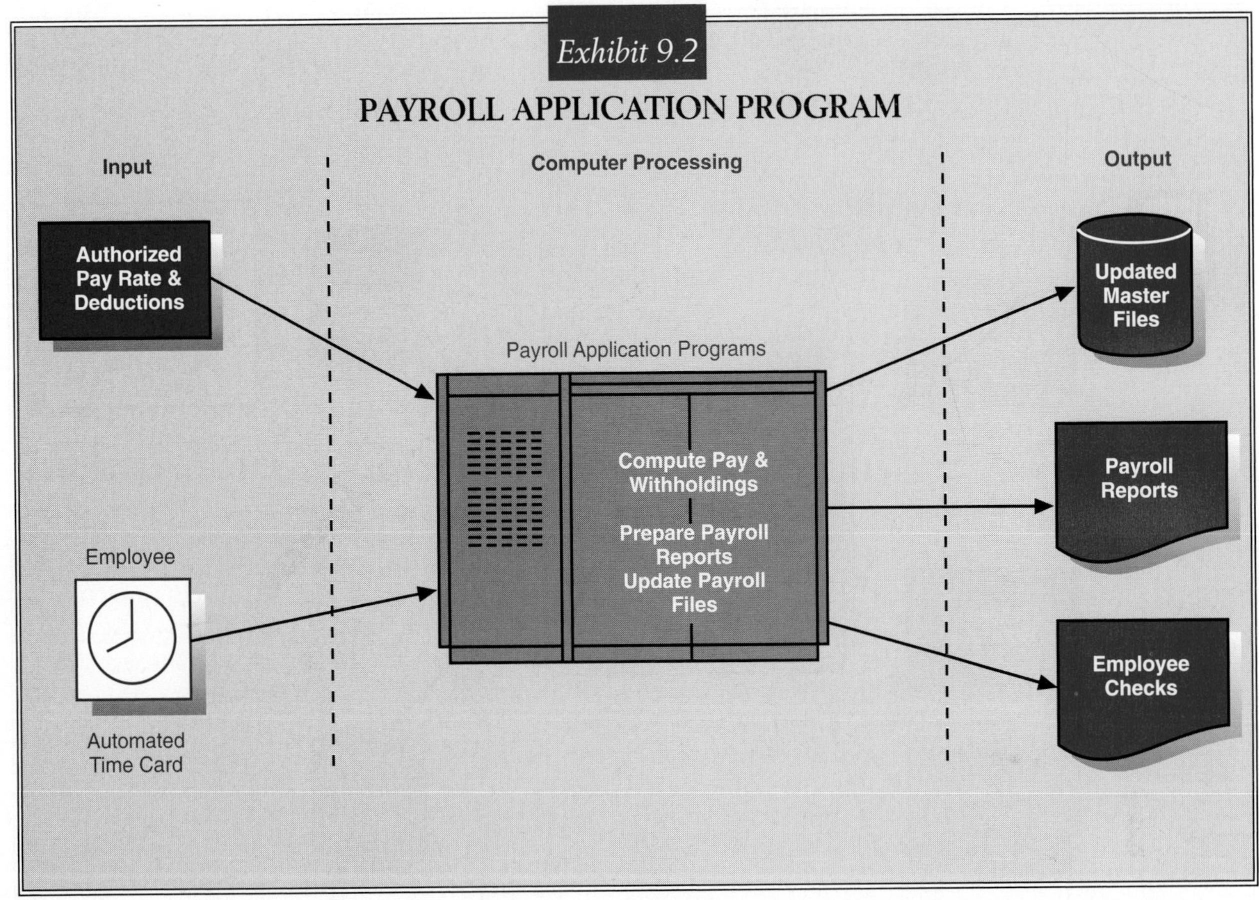

organizational data needs. A user can use database management systems to create special reports on an as needed basis.

Database management systems differ from traditional application programs in that transactions are processed against a master database. The database system maps out relationships among data elements. The identification of the data relationships facilitate inquiries and generation of reports. Access to information and the ability to generate needed reports are not dependent on existing application programs. Users can query the entire database to generate a report. For example, a student might query a database to find all published articles regarding environmental issues for a particular company. Or a personnel manager may query a personnel database to develop a list of all employees with more than 10 years of experience in a particular job category. In addition, the personnel manager may want to know the year-to-date wages and a list of all jobs these employees worked on during the current year. The user, sitting at a PC connected to the network, can access a database (see Exhibit 9.3) and, with an inquiry through the query language, develop a list of all employees with more than ten years of service in the job category environmental engineer. The user provides a suggested report format; database system searches the database and prepares the report.

Today's computer systems are connected to other computer systems both within an organization and outside it. **Telecommunications software** must ensure that all data are properly transmitted to the correct parties and are completely received. The management of telecommunications must consider the method of communication, the

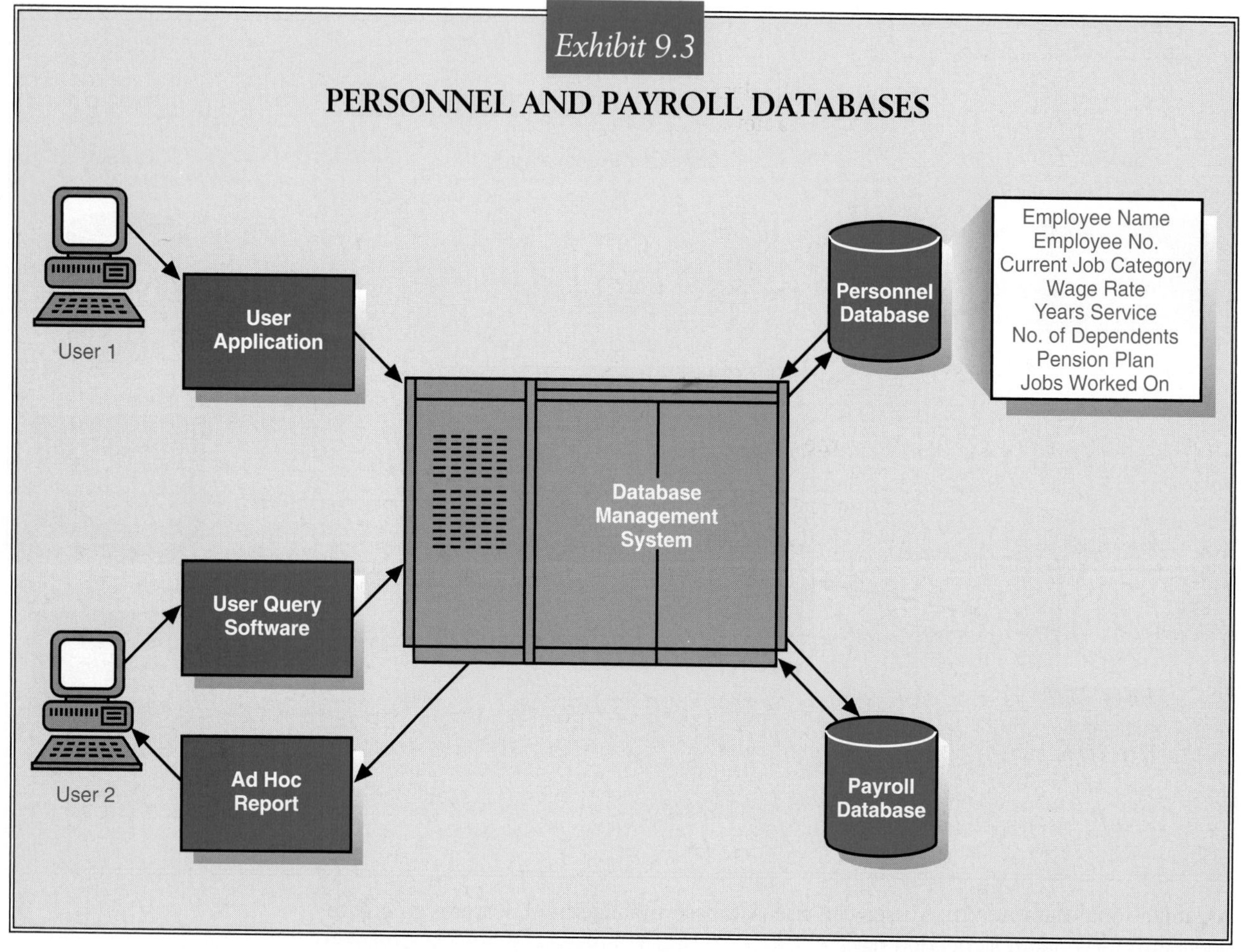

medium of communication (laser, fiber optics, microwave), the points within the system that can transmit or receive data, and whether the data should be encrypted. Most telecommunications software has controls built in to test for lost or added data.

Personnel. The organization of the information systems function and its relationship to users is an integral part of the overall control structure of an organization. In some organizations, such as small companies using microcomputers, the users are also the operators of the system. In most large organizations, more control (and efficiency) is obtained by separating the information systems and user functions. It is imperative that the organization clarify the responsibilities of each party. For example, the relative roles of information systems personnel, user personnel, and internal auditors in establishing and maintaining controls built into applications should clearly be established. Otherwise, each group will claim that responsibility for adequacy of controls rests with some other group.

Depending on the size of the organization, the *information systems function* is organized to promote both control and efficiency. Some of the more typical organization personnel include the following:

- *Systems programmers*—usually a very small, elite group—are responsible for maintaining the operating system.

- *Application programmers* develop the coding for major computer applications and maintain existing computer programs.
- *Systems analysts* are responsible for analyzing the current system, information flows and user needs and designing a new application.
- *Operators* are responsible for operating the computer system. Their duties typically include mounting reels of tape, running scheduled jobs, monitoring systems output, and notifying management of any problems.
- *Librarians* are responsible for the maintenance and security of programs and data files.
- *Database administrators* are responsible for the design, maintenance, control, and accessibility to the organization's databases.

In many organizations, some of the roles are combined. For example, it is quite common for the analyst and programming functions to be combined. However, better control is achieved when the operating, programming, librarian, and database functions are separated because each of these functions provides an independent check on the others.

Computer systems are developed to serve the needs of the organization; therefore the primary responsibility for the types of computer applications developed, the integrity of those applications, and the control of those applications rest with the *users*. The auditor is interested in understanding the manual follow-up procedures employed by users to determine whether all data were completely and correctly processed.

B–GENERAL AND APPLICATION CONTROLS

The process by which the auditor evaluates control risk in computerized environments begins by determining that computerized processing may significantly affect financial statement balances. The evaluation proceeds within the framework established by the auditor's assessment of the overall control environment for the organization. The control risk assessment within computerized environments is at the accounting system and control procedures level. Once the auditor has determined that computerized applications are important to the accounting process, the control risk evaluation begins with an assessment of the overall control structure and organization of data processing.

Identifying Important Computerized Applications

A *computer application* is defined as a *computer program*, or a *set of programs, and all the attendant manual procedures* involved in processing data from their origination to the update of computer files and the generation of reports. Typical computerized accounting systems include sales, receivables, inventory, payroll, and accounts payable applications. Once the important accounting applications are identified, the auditor evaluates the general control environment and application control procedures which influence the control risk associated with the application.

General Control Concepts

General controls are pervasive control procedures that affect all computerized applications. These controls address the following:

- Planning and controlling the data processing functions.*
- Controlling applications development and changes to programs and/or data files and records.
- Controlling access to equipment, data, and programs.
- Maintaining hardware to ensure that failures do not affect data or programs.

The control risk in any one application is affected by the combination of general controls and application control procedures as they affect that particular application. The auditor often begins the risk assessment process by obtaining an understanding of the general controls because pervasive weaknesses in general controls may preclude the auditor from assessing control risk in the environment at anything less than the maximum or at least moderate. Some auditors, however, choose to concentrate their general control review on only control procedures for those applications with a direct impact on important financial application programs.

Planning and Controlling the Data Processing Function

According to the previously mentioned study by Massachusetts Institute of Technology, the major ingredient for success in the worldwide competitive environment of the 1990s is the innovative use of information technology.[4] The auditor must be able to assess the impact of important strategic decisions made by the organization, including the strategic plan for information technology. The information management resource is no longer designed around the accounting system; rather, the accounting system is but one component of a strategic information system. Accounting data either may drive other applications or may be generated as a by-product of other processing.

Research in management information systems has shown that there is no single best way to organize the data processing function. Some companies encourage more user development of applications; others centralize all development within a specific development group. Therefore, the auditor must focus on seven fundamental control concepts in evaluating the organization of data processing:

1. The *authorization* for all transactions should originate outside the data processing department. This authorization includes the review and approval of program logic that automatically originate transactions in accordance with the user's overall directions.
2. The users, not data processing, are responsible for authorization, review, and testing of all application developments and changes in computer programs. Data processing is a service function to the rest of the organization. Based on these two premises, there is a fundamental *segregation of duties between users and data processing.* Users provide an independent check on the integrity of data processing.

*The terms *information systems department, data processing department,* and *DP function* are used synonymously in the text. Some organizations refer to these functions as the management information systems (MIS) department or information services (IS) department to better recognize information as a strategic resource.

3. *Access to data* is provided only to authorized users as determined by the owner of the data and consistent with organization policies and guidelines for information privacy.
4. The data processing department is responsible for all *custodial functions* associated with data, data files, software, and related documentation. This responsibility includes limiting access to authorized users, building integrity checks into programs and systems, and maintaining adequate back-up and security of all applications, data files, and documentation.
5. Users, jointly with data processing, are responsible for the adequacy of *application controls* built into computer applications or database systems. Organizations should develop *control guidelines* that specify minimum control objectives for every application, alternative controls that could be implemented, and responsibility for the controls.
6. Management should periodically evaluate the information systems function for operational efficiency, integrity, security, and consistency with organizational objectives for information technology. This evaluation may be performed by the internal audit department or by the external auditors as an additional nonaudit service.
7. The *internal audit staff* should be adequately trained in computer auditing and should periodically audit applications and operations.

Segregation of Duties within Data Processing. Organizations need to protect themselves from unauthorized and undetected access to programs and/or data. Two important concepts to help implement proper segregation are that (1) data processing personnel should not have access to programs or data except when authorized to make changes and (2) users should review and test all significant computer program changes.

Other important duties that should be segregated include these:

- *Computer operator and programming functions.* If not segregated, the operator (because of the access to the logs of the system) could make both unauthorized and undetected changes to computer programs or data.
- *Librarian and other functions.* Access to programs and data should be restricted to authorized users for specifically authorized purposes.
- *Database administrative and data input functions.* The database administrator should set up and maintain the integrity of the database, but users should be responsible for the completeness and integrity of data input into the database.

Adequate Documentation–A Key Control. Adequate documentation is critical to the effectiveness and continuity of the operation of a data processing department. The auditor reviews the adequacy of the client's documentation to (1) assess the risk to the organization, such as maintaining the continuity of operations; (2) assess the adequacy of controls built into important applications; and (3) understand the operation of computer applications in determining the most efficient way to audit the application. As an example of the latter, the auditor reviews documentation to gain an understanding of the file structure to develop computer audit techniques to extract data for audit analysis.

Controlling Applications Development and Program Changes

Organizations that write their own computer applications generally develop a *systems development life cycle methodology* that specifies the stages through which all developments must proceed. The methodology usually delineates the responsibility of users in identifying needs and of systems analysts in creating a conceptual overview of the system and in performing detailed tests of the application before implementation. The auditor's major concern with the systems development process is that the applications are adequately tested by the users before implementation, that control standards specifying the adequacy of controls built into the applications exist, and that the applications are properly documented.

As organizations become more dependent on computer processing, adequate control over changes to computer programs becomes even more critical. It is not unusual for more than one-half of all computer programming efforts to be dedicated to the program maintenance function. User needs change over time, and the organization must establish mechanisms (1) to determine which changes should be made and (2) to ensure that changes are implemented as authorized.

Most organizations with even moderately sized computer systems have purchased automated program libraries that control the storage and access to computer programs. An organization normally has two program libraries: (1) a *production library* containing the compiled program in a form ready to be executed by the computer and (2) a *source code library* containing the application program written in its original language (such as COBOL or PASCAL). The production code library is ultimately the most important because all applications are executed from it. Access to these libraries should be limited to the computer operator and a librarian supervisor. To make changes to an application, the librarian supervisor, acting on approval of the program maintenance steering committee, moves a copy of the source code program to a third library, the *programmer's test library*. Access to the test library is limited to the programmer and the librarian supervisor.

Exhibit 9.4 illustrates a number of important control elements associated with the program change process. First, changes are made only on the approved request of a user and a program maintenance committee. Second, only the programmer has access to a copy of the source code in the programmer's test library. Third, the programmer is required by company policies and guidelines to document and independently test all changes. Fourth, users are required to test the changed program to determine that all changes have been made as authorized and that no unauthorized changes have been made. Fifth, the librarian supervisor must review the changes to determine whether they are in accordance with company policies, that is, that testing has been done and that documentation has been appropriately updated. Sixth, only the librarian supervisor has the ability to move the changed program back to the source library, compile the program, and move the compiled version into production.

In evaluating the control structure over program changes, the auditor should determine that control procedures are sufficient to ensure that

- Only authorized changes are made to computer applications.
- All authorized changes are made to computer applications.
- All changes are adequately tested, reviewed, and documented before being implemented.
- Only the authorized version of the computer program is run.

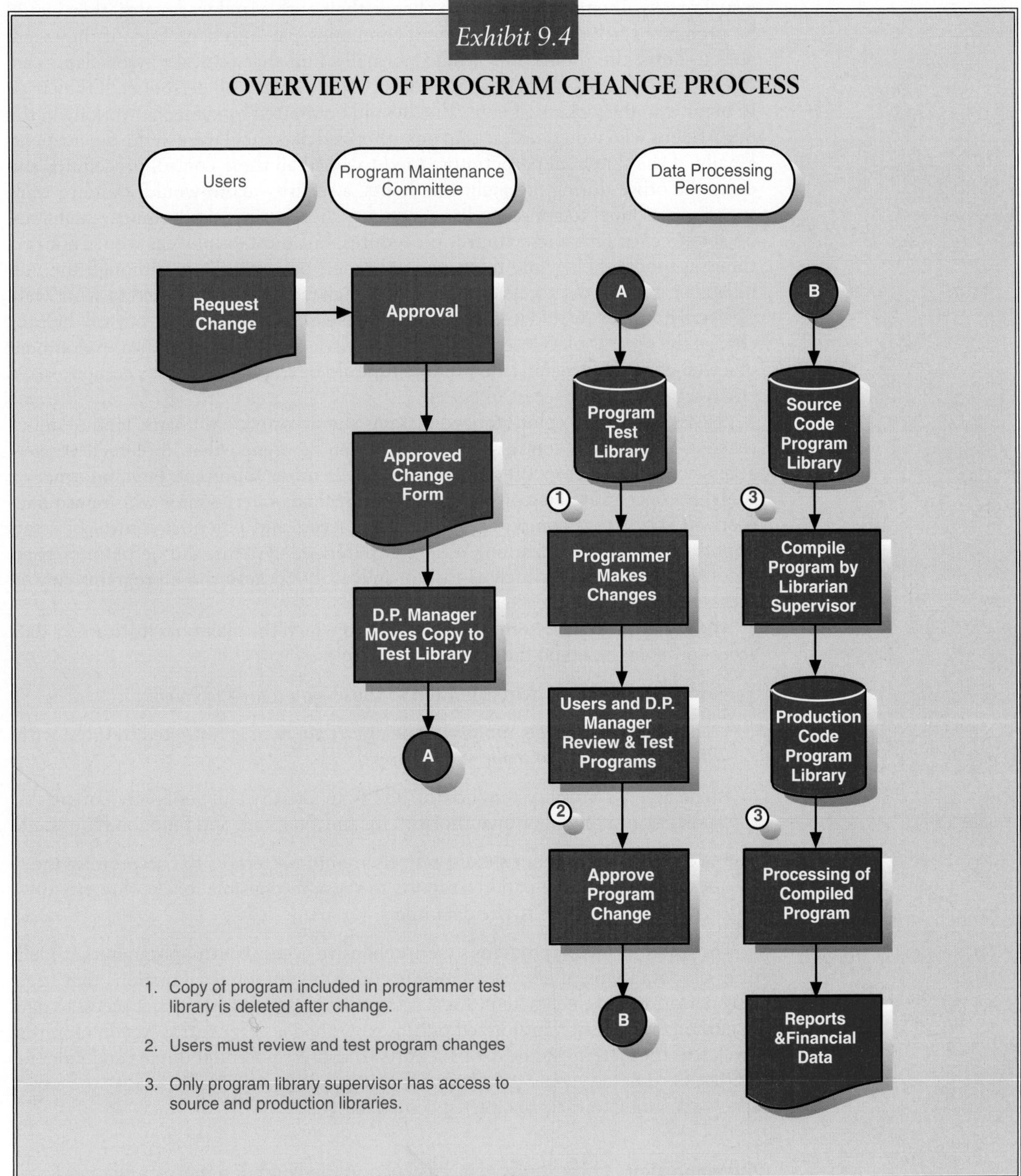

Controlling Access to Equipment, Data, and Programs

Restricting access to assets to authorized users for authorized processes is a fundamental internal control concept. In traditional manual systems, access to confidential data was physically restricted by walls between offices, security clearances, and visual review. If employees tried to change their authorized wage rates, they would be prohibited from entering the room containing pay rate data. Even if they were able to enter the room, they would normally find that critical payroll data were safely locked in storage devices and accessible only by payroll personnel. If they tried to break into the locked cabinets, they would be spotted by someone working in the department who would realize that unauthorized personnel were in the department. Finally, if the potential perpetrators tried to avoid all these control procedures and enter the office during the nighttime hours, a security alarm would sound to warn security personnel to apprehend any intruders. The really smart criminal might still be able to overcome these control procedures, but most employees would not find the risks worth their while to change only their pay rate. Thus, although the vulnerability existed, the access controls over the manual systems tended to work well. Generally, frauds would require collusion, such as someone in payroll helping change the records of a close friend. The same concepts that led to the development of a well-controlled manual environment should be implemented in a computerized environment to limit access to assets.

Access controls in computerized systems should provide the same kind of deterrence as the manual controls. However, it can be argued that implementation of access controls in a computerized system is even more important. First, information is highly concentrated in computer systems. Second, a perpetrator who gains unauthorized access to a computer system gains access and potential control of assets important to the organization. With computerized systems, the perpetrator gains access to physical assets such as cash or inventory because those programs control access to actual physical assets.

The auditor should determine the extent to which the client has instituted a data access program based on the following principles:

- Access to any data item is limited to those *with a need to know.*
- The ability to change, modify, or delete a data item is restricted to those with the authorization to make such changes.
- The access control system has the ability to identify and verify any potential users as authorized or unauthorized for the data item and function requested.
- A security department should actively monitor attempts to compromise the system and prepare periodic reports to those responsible for the integrity of data items or access to the data items.

These four principles require a comprehensive access control program that identifies all data items, users, user functions, and the authorized functions that users may perform on each data item. An access control system must restrict access to data to authorized users for authorized purposes. A good access control system monitors threats to the system and develops reports to address potential threats and vulnerabilities. Fortunately, some excellent software products provide the ability to restrict access according to the principles specified above.

Authentication. Once the system has been implemented, a means must be developed for the system to **authenticate** users, that is, to determine that the individual requesting the access privilege is the individual he or she claims to be. Three methods to identify users are available:

- *What they know,* such as a password or something that should be known only to them.

- *Something they possess,* such as a card with a magnetic strip.
- *Something about themselves,* such as a fingerprint, a voice print, or some other type of physical identification.

A *password* system is most widely used, but it is subject to problems associated with lost, stolen, or easily guessed passwords. To be effective, passwords must be changed frequently and should be difficult to guess. *Something possessed* is most often implemented in the form of a plastic card with a magnetic strip to identify the user to the system. The card is often combined with passwords to provide a higher level of security than could be obtained if only one of the methods were used by itself. For example, an individual wishing to use an automated teller machine (ATM) must identify himself or herself to the computer terminal by something possessed (the ATM or bank card) and by a password. The user is allowed access to the ATM network only if the two match each other and a list of authorized users for the identification used. Identification of users on the basis of *physical characteristics* continues to be the least widely used of the three authentication methods because of cost and reliability concerns. Continuing developments could cause this situation to change over the next decade.

Security and Backup. Every heavily computerized organization needs a good security and backup plan to protect both physical assets (hardware and computer documentation) and magnetic media (programs and data files). A security plan should be developed to minimize the organization's risk to both man-made and natural threats and should include monitoring and contingency plans. The auditor needs to consider the potential effect of a loss of computing facilities on the ability of an organization to remain in business. Consider many of the companies with which you personally interact and ask yourself how long they might be in business should their computer system be destroyed. If an audit client does not have adequate backup and recovery procedures, the auditor needs to discuss the risks with management and the audit committee to determine whether any disclosure of the risks is required. Minimum elements in a backup and recovery plan include these:

1. Standardized procedures for backup and disaster recovery. Most items such as master files and transaction tapes should be backed up on a daily basis. Other items such as documentation manuals should be backed up as changes are made, and duplicates of source code and documentation should be stored off site.
2. Plans for reconstruction in the event of a full or partial destruction of the data processing center including the following:
   a. Agreements with vendors to replace hardware.
   b. Agreements with independent companies or provisions within the organization for facilities to which hardware, employees, and support could be moved to continue operations.
   c. Agreements with telephone companies or other providers for continued telecommunication facilities.
   d. Formal plans in divisions or departments to continue operations in the event of a loss of current computing facilities.
3. Periodic review and testing of the backup and recovery plans and procedures by the data processing department and internal audit.

Auditing in Practice

UNDERSTANDING THE IMPACT OF GENERAL CONTROLS IN A STAND-ALONE MICROCOMPUTER ENVIRONMENT

The computerization of accounting in small organizations with microcomputer stand-alone systems often places all the computing power in the hands of one individual. Accounting records are concentrated in one place and often on one medium (floppy disk or hard disk). Today's microcomputer systems allow concurrent access by multiple users and on-line processing. In many ways, today's microcomputer is very similar to the mainframe computers of a decade ago. Microcomputers can operate many applications, and multiple users can, and do, use them to run their applications. Many end users develop their own applications using spreadsheets or database packages.

Without thoroughly exploring the nature of control procedures, the auditor should be alert to particular risks associated with the microcomputer environment:

- Loss of data and programs through an actual theft of the computer or of disks.
- Risk of *unauthorized* changes made to data and/or programs because formal access control methods are not implemented. The risk is further compounded by the ease of access by multiple users.

A more systematic review of the general control environment often leads the auditor to the following analysis.

Planning and Controlling the Data Processing Functions

Many firms do no formal planning as to the control of data processing. The control lies in the authority of the user to acquire software currently available from vendors to meet the firm's processing needs or to develop spreadsheets. Although the planning is not formalized, the organization is small enough that the users are also the long-term planners of the organization. There is a tendency to focus on current processing needs and to avoid strategic information planning for the future. Although this latter problem does not affect the audit, it is worthy of periodic monitoring and discussion with the client as a basis for value-added services.

Controlling the Development, Documentation, and Changes to Programs and/or Data Files

Most of the applications are purchased and contain adequate documentation. There is a general percep-

Hardware Controls

Most systems today have features built into the hardware to detect electronic failures such as dropping bits of data or altering data during transmission. The auditor's major concern is that the company has a policy to monitor and follow up on hardware failures and that it actively engages in supervised preventive maintenance.

Application Control Procedures

Application control procedures are those specific control procedures (manual and computerized) designed into the computer program to ensure that processing objectives are attained. The application control procedures should match the complexity

tion that because the programs are purchased, the client cannot change them, which is fallacious. But the more serious concern is that multiple users can make changes to programs or data files and records without creating evidence of the change or identifying its perpetrator.

User-developed applications are not reviewed or tested as thoroughly for accuracy or completeness as are more formally developed programs. The auditor will most likely want to test the operation of the program during the year, trace the processing of transactions into the records and recompute the correctness of the processing. The auditor will also want to review steps taken by the organization to physically safeguard the computer and related files and documentation.

Controls over Access to Equipment, Data, and Programs

Physical access to the computer is usually not restricted, nor is it guarded during the off-hours. Anyone from the custodian to the assistant controller can probably access the computer. Some vendor-supplied programs provide the user the option to implement password controls. However, the password system is a function of the desire of the owner of the application. Access is not often monitored.

Programs are stored on-site because the user has little fear of loss since they can be replaced by vendors. In some situations, the users formally back up files to disks or tape cartridges. However, backed-up files are usually stored in the same area as the computer, which provides the client no protection against the loss from fire or by destruction of the physical facilities.

Hardware Controls

Technology has improved to the extent that most microcomputers have sufficient hardware controls built into them. However, the user may not know when the hardware controls are malfunctioning except when reconciling the processing results with input items. Some users perform such reconciliations, but others ignore this important control procedure because they believe that failures or errors will not happen to them.

General Control Review Implications

The auditor most likely will find that the pervasive weaknesses in the general controls in a microcomputer environment requires that control risk be assessed as high even if the organization has a positive attitude toward data processing integrity. The auditor needs to test the actual processing of important applications and to concentrate the audit on designing year-end tests of account balances.

of the applications. The control procedures are often referred to as *input, processing,* and *output control procedures*. We will adapt a broader framework categorizing application control procedures as *boundary, input, communication, processing,* and *output control procedures*. To better understand the nature of the control procedures, an overview of alternative processing modes is first discussed.

Approaches to Processing Transactions

Three major approaches dominate data processing: (1) batch processing, (2) on-line processing, and (3) database processing. These three approaches are further complicated by the advent of distributed processing and networking, which integrates all three types of processing across multiple locations, often occurring at the same time.

There are a number of permutations of these three approaches. For example, there can be on-line input with batch update. Database management systems represent a unique and prevalently used alternative to traditional file-oriented processing.

Batch-Processing Applications. Early computerized accounting applications grouped transactions into batches for processing, such as a group of 50 cash receipts to update the accounts receivable file. Batch processing applications were used because (1) they were more efficient (and thus less costly) and (2) they provided an effective control to ensure that all transactions were processed. **Batch processing** was efficient because early computer systems relied on keypunched cards for input and magnetic tape for file storage which could only be accessed sequentially. To make even a single change or to update a transaction, the whole file, such as an accounts receivable file, would have to be processed. When transactions could be grouped and sorted in the same order as the master file, processing efficiency was attained.

Computer batch processing is similar to traditional processing in manual systems in that both have a specifically defined input/output relationship. In the accounts receivable example, the input consisted of cash receipts and the output included updated computer files and the printed cash receipts journal. Rapid changes in technology, however, have made magnetic tape–oriented systems practically obsolete, except for backup purposes. Virtually all computer systems now use disk or other randomly accessible storage media. However, many accounting applications continue to be processed in a batch mode because the controls embodied in batch processing are important in ensuring both the accuracy and the completeness of processing.

The control totals used to ensure the completeness of processing in a batch processing environment include the following:

Record count. A count of the number of transactions included in the batch.

Control total. The total of some field that will be processed such as the total amount of cash submitted for processing.

Hash totals. The sum of a field that will be processed, the summation of which does not necessarily make any sense, such as the summation of customer account numbers. Hash totals complement control totals and record counts because its totals are most useful in identifying a specific transaction that has not been processed.

An example of the process of using batch control totals is shown in Exhibit 9.5.

On-Line Processing. With the advent of larger and more efficient storage media, the ever-increasing speed of processing by computers, and the development of more sophisticated software, most computer applications now process transactions "on-line and real time (almost instantaneously)." On-line applications often obtain significant cost and operational advantages over batch processing applications. Consider, for example, the on-line order entry system of a major catalog operation. A customer's order can be immediately entered into the system and the order taker can access the inventory files to determine product availability, the approximate shipping date, and the customer's credit history.

In many ways, the on-line system presents more opportunities for control than does a batch application. For example, the customer's credit history can be viewed to determine whether credit should be granted. On-line processing is frequently complemented by database management systems to facilitate data inquiries.

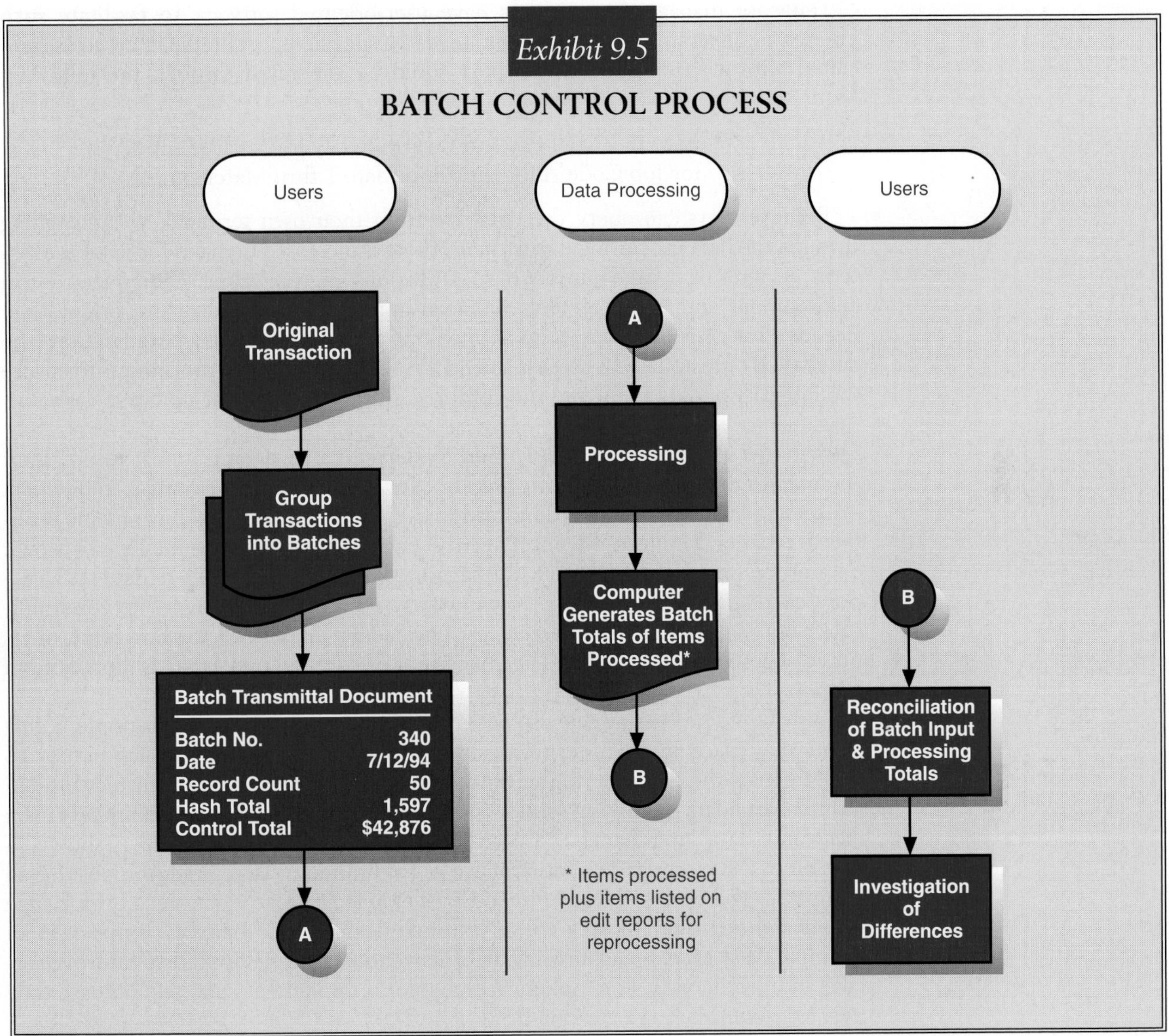

Database Management Systems. Many accounting applications have been file oriented, that is, a specific transaction updates a file or files such as sales transactions updating a sales master file, an accounts receivable master file, a sales commission master file, perpetual inventory master records, and a product sales master file. File-oriented applications suffer from two major defects. First, data incompatibility may occur if a transaction updates some, but not all, of the files. Second, reports can be generated only from existing files and file structures that limit the flexibility of the system in meeting user needs.

Database management systems differ from traditional applications in that all transactions of a particular type are processed against a master data set (database). The data elements and relationships among pieces of data are specified. These relationships are specified for data not only within a given data set but also among data sets. Information access and report generation, therefore, do not depend on predefined patterns. Users can query the entire database for analysis and reporting purposes.

Database management systems have user-oriented software to facilitate such queries. For example, if management needed a special report on the labor costs associated with a specific job, the report could be generated through the following request:

Compute the Total Pay and Overtime Pay in Department XY
for Job Code *A* for the Period Jan. 1 thru March 31.

Because users can query the database from their own terminal, without going through the data processing department, there is increased demand for database systems. As a result, a large number of organizations are converting their entire control environment and many of their financial applications to a database orientation. Because, for example, there is no defined output from processing a transaction (the database is only updated), there is a need for even more control procedures to ensure the integrity of data input and the completeness of the database updates.

Distributed Processing or Networked Systems. Large organizations do not limit themselves to one manufacturing facility. Nor do they limit themselves to one data processing facility. A corporation headquartered in Chicago may have major facilities in Atlanta, Minneapolis, and Phoenix. Each of these facilities may have its own data processing department, but the organization may need to share data on a corporatewide basis. Therefore, the computer systems must be designed to communicate with each other. In emergencies, one facility may need to shift some of its processing to another facility. The concept of distributed processing is illustrated in Exhibit 9.6.

Distributed processing can also occur between organizations. For example, a customer may place an order electronically to a vendor. The data transmission may go directly from the customer to the vendor or more likely will be transmitted through a third-party data processing service (often referred to as a *value-added vendor*) in an **electronic data interchange (EDI)** environment. Such a relationship is shown in Exhibit 9.7. Electronic data interchange is not limited to large organizations. Small companies will be increasingly forced to develop facilities to electronically exchange orders and other data if they are to continue dealing with major customers. As an example, Wal-Mart is encouraging all of its vendors to develop EDI to improve service and profitability. If suppliers are unable to implement such technology, they may lose Wal-Mart as a customer.

Audit Trail Provisions

The term **audit trail** is frequently used to indicate an organization's ability to trace a transaction from its origination to its final disposition or vice versa. In fact, a better term would be to refer to it as a *management trail* because every organization needs records to ensure the correctness and completeness of its recording as well as to respond to customer and vendor inquiries. But the traditional paper-based audit trail has ceased to exist in some organizations, and the trend toward a paper-reduced, if not paperless, audit environment is growing.

The auditor has traditionally been able to follow a trail documenting the origination of a transaction to its final disposition in the general ledger or vice versa. The audit trail provided significant evidence in most audits concerning the authorization of a transaction, its contract or sale terms, and its shipping or receiving information and served as evidence that transactions were recorded accurately in the correct time period.

Exhibit 9.6

DISTRIBUTED PROCESSING

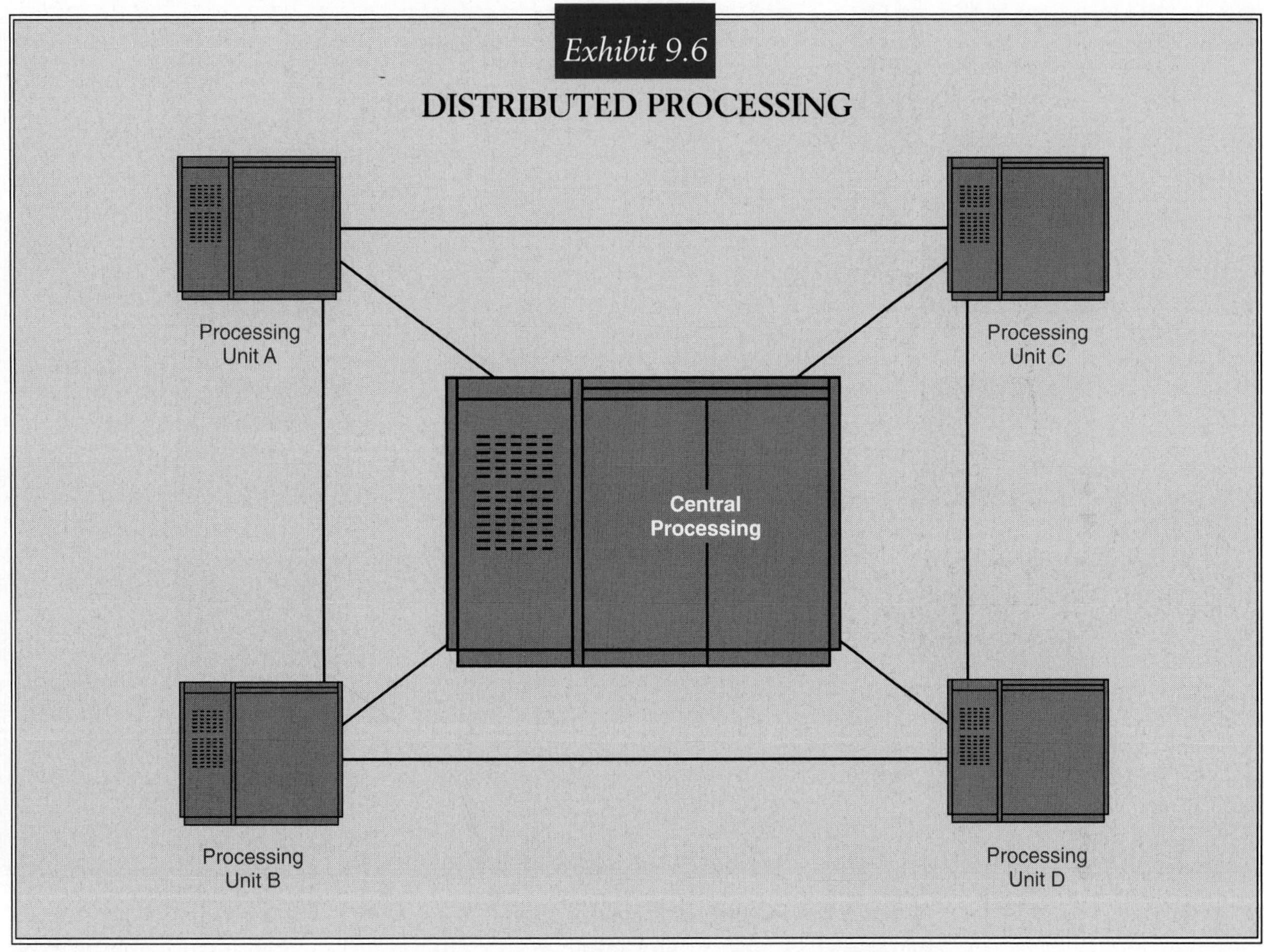

When a paper document is not produced, the evidence of authorization for a transaction might exist only in the form of an authorized sign-on and identification recorded in a computer system. Receiving slips for the acceptance of goods might not be generated, but the receipts might be read into the computer system and a **computer log** (or item listing) created to be matched with open purchase orders. The computerized audit trail must capture data to allow a unique identification of each transaction, the party responsible for it, and any cross-referencing to other transactions. Items that should be included in an electronic audit trail are listed in Exhibit 9.8. The fundamental elements of the audit trail may not have changed, but the media have, and the auditor needs to adapt audit procedures to the new media.

Boundary Control Procedures

The control procedures designed to ensure that the organization fully captures all the transactions between itself and another entity are referred to as **boundary control procedures,** which are designed to establish initial control and responsibility for the completeness of transactions. Boundary control procedures include the use of (and accounting for) prenumbered documents and the following:

A *unique transaction identifier established by the computer* along with all the audit trail information contained in Exhibit 9.8.

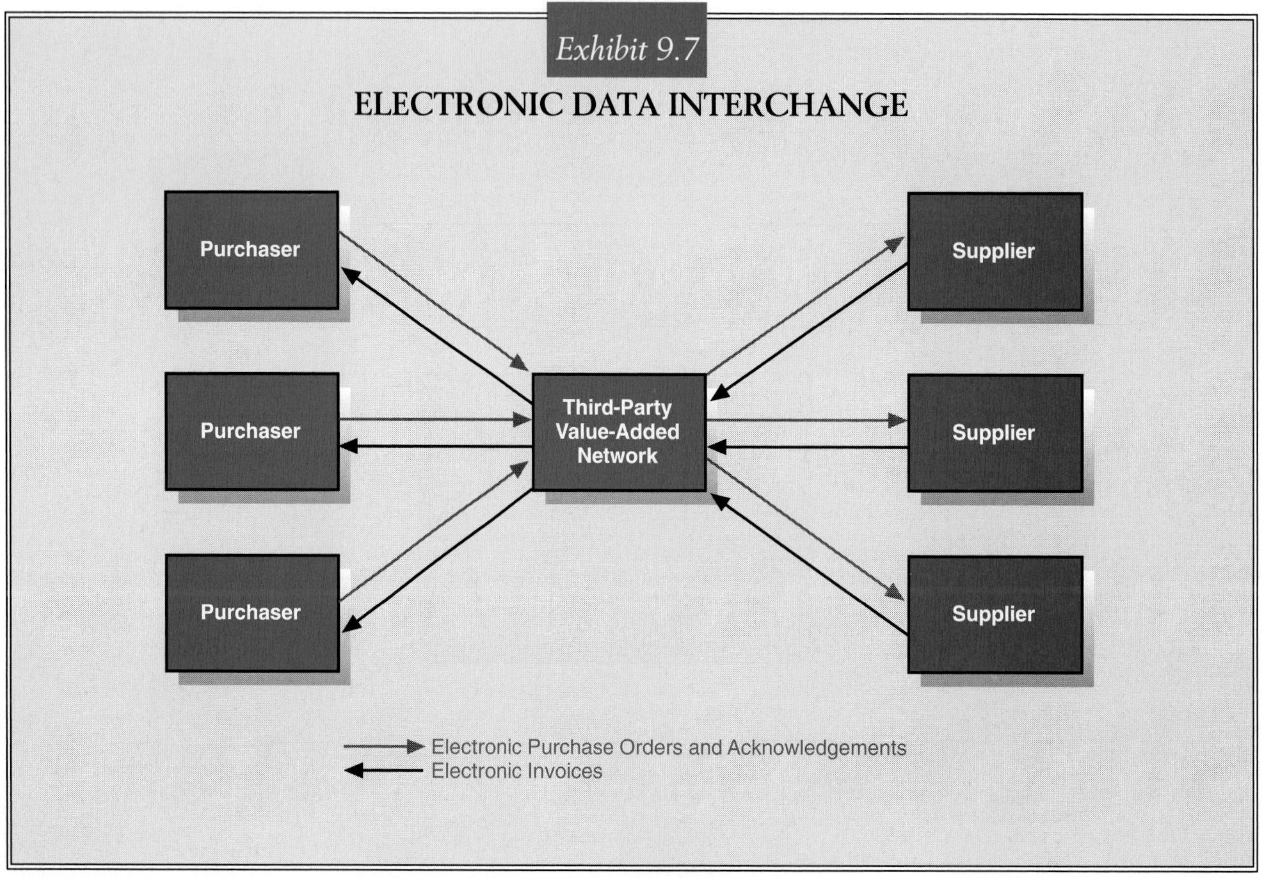

Batch control and batch control totals.

Procedures to limit access to the transactions in accordance with management's specific policies.

Since boundary controls establish initial accountability for all transactions, deficiencies in boundary controls may lead the auditor to conclude that an entity cannot be audited.

Input and Validation Control Procedures

Input controls are designed to ensure that authorized transactions are correct, complete, and recorded in a timely fashion and that only authorized transactions exist. The major control procedures of audit interest include these:

- Computerized input validation procedures (often referred to as *edit tests*).
- Batch control procedures.
- Self-checking digits.
- Use of stored data reference items (often referred to as table values).
- On-screen input verification techniques.

Input validation tests are often referred to as *edit tests* because they are control tests built into the application to examine input data for obvious errors. Edit tests are

Exhibit 9.8

ELECTRONIC AUDIT TRAIL—ELEMENTS OF A COMPUTER LOG

Unique identification of transaction. Examples include the assignment of a number by the computer. The unique identifier could be assigned sequentially or could consist of a location identifier and unique number within a location. Sales invoices, for example, are sequentially numbered by the computer application.

Date and time of transaction. These could be assigned automatically by the computer application.

Individual responsible for the transaction. The log on to the computer terminal provides evidence of the party authorizing or initiating the transaction.

Location from which the transaction originated. The log on to the computer can identify the source of the transaction.

Details of the transaction. These should be noted in a computer log. Essentially, all the details normally found in a paper document, such as the quantities ordered, back-order provisions, and so forth, should also be captured and saved for the electronic audit trail.

Cross-reference to other transactions. When applicable, all cross-referencing to other transactions should be captured. For example, if a payment cross-references a specific invoice, the information needed to complete the cross-reference should be captured.

Authorization or approval of the transaction. If the transaction requires authorization by a party other than the one initiating the transaction, the proper electronic authorization should be captured.

Other information. As required, should also be recorded as part of the electronic audit trail.

The organization should make provisions to retain the electronic audit trail for a period of time as would be required for a paper audit trail.

designed to review transactions much like experienced personnel do in manual systems in which an employee would know, for example, that no one worked more than 55 hours in the past week. The following types of edit controls are found in most computer applications:

- Alphanumeric field.
- Reasonableness of data (within prespecified ranges or in relationship to other data).
- Limits (data must be under specified limits).
- Validity (data must take on valid values).
- Missing data.
- Sequence (items are in sequence and are not duplicated).
- Invalid combinations of items.
- Other relations expected to exist in the data.

Exhibit 9.9 contains a detailed description of each of these edit controls. If an item entered on-line does not meet the edit criteria, the operator is notified and a correction is made or a decision is made as to whether the transaction should be processed or reviewed further before processing. When transactions are entered in a

Exhibit 9.9

EXAMPLES OF INPUT VALIDATION TESTS

Alphanumeric	Each data field is compared with a prespecified type to determine whether the field contains appropriate alpha or numeric characters.
Reasonableness	Reasonable ranges for an item are prespecified based on past history and current expectations. For example, a company that trades commodities on the Chicago Mercantile Exchange can develop a reasonableness range for an exchange price because the exchange prohibits trades that differ by more than a specific percentage from the previous day's closing price.
Limits	Limit tests are specified for items that require supervisory review before processing. A limit test, for example, might be placed on the number of hours factory personnel work during a one-week period. If it is highly unlikely that anyone would work more than 55 hours in a week, a limit test of 55 hours could be incorporated into the edit test.
Validity	A specific set of values could be programmed into the application and the identified fields could be tested to determine whether they contain one of the valid values. For example, a company may have only five jobs in progress during a particular time period. The validity test could determine whether a job accounting entry contains one of the job classifications currently in progress.
Missing data	Fields could be reviewed to see whether data were missing. If fields crucial to processing were incomplete, the edit tests would reject the transaction.
Sequence	If some transactions should be processed in a specific sequence, that sequence could be programmed as a validation test. Further, the system may be programmed to determine whether any items in a specified sequence are missing, such as prenumbered documents, or to search for potential duplicates. An example of the latter would be a retailer's accounts payable program that searches to determine whether a vendor had previously been paid for an invoice that has been submitted for processing.
Invalid Combinations of Items	If data items must logically be consistent, the computer application should test for that consistency. For example, if it is not possible for an employee to have a job code as janitor and machinist during the same time period, the program should test for the invalid combination.
Other	The designer of the computer application should build into the application any other test that would have been manually reviewed before the application was automated and that has the ability to be computerized.

batch, a transaction not passing the edit test is written to an edit report and returned to the users for correction and resubmission. Further processing of a transaction rejected because of an edit test requires supervisory approval.

Batch control totals, including record counts, control totals, and hash totals are designed to ensure that data are not lost or duplicated in the processing. However, as noted earlier, most organizations are moving away from batch processing, but the need to develop control procedures to ensure the completeness of processing remains. Fortunately, batch control procedures can be used in on-line environments by capturing control total data on a *logical batch* basis, such as the number of transactions entered per terminal per hour. This control total information can be captured at the data-entry terminal and reconciled with the computer-generated control totals for data processed during that same time period to ensure that all data input were processed.

Patterns of data input errors are common. For example, individuals often transpose (reverse the order of) two numbers such as recording the digits on a MasterCard account number as 52494807 instead of the valid number of 52944807. Many computer applications are designed to process transactions according to their account number because numbers are more likely than names to be unique. Examples of numeric identification for processing include accounts such as credit card, bank account, or inventory, accounts receivable customers, or employee's payroll.

Self-checking digit algorithms have been developed to test for transposition errors and other common input errors associated with the input of identification numbers. Self-checking digits operate by computing an extra digit, or several digits, that are added (or inserted) into a numeric identifier. The algorithms are designed to detect the common types of mistakes. Whenever the identifier is entered into the system, the application recalculates the self-checking digit to determine whether the identifier is correct. An example of the use of a self-checking digit is shown in Exhibit 9.10, using a simple algorithm. Most organizations have much more sophisticated algorithms, and some even have the ability to diagnose and identify the most probable cause of the error.

Many computer applications are designed to use reference data, most often referred to as *table values* to minimize the number of items required for entry. If common data are required and those data are related to some other value, it should be unnecessary to reenter those data and risk a data-entry error. A common example is wage rates for employees under a union contract. Rather than entering an employee's wage rate each time payroll is computed, the application can be programmed to search a wage rate file for the current pay of an employee with a specific job classification. These files are often referred to as **tables** because they are designed as *tables of values* (job classification by wage rate). Additional control is afforded because access to the tables can be limited to those in the personnel department authorized to change the rates. Because of the potential manipulation of data, the auditor is usually very interested in testing the controls over access to these computerized tables.

Because data are commonly entered on-line, the computer application should be developed to facilitate correct and complete input into the system. A solution is to develop *screen validation techniques* that combine good screen design with procedures such as oral confirmation with customers to verify the data input. Some on-screen validation concepts include these:

- *Use of stored data to minimize data input.* For example, a customer calling a catalog retailer may be asked for information such as last name and zip code.

Exhibit 9.10

EXAMPLE OF A SELF-CHECKING DIGIT (MODULUS 11 APPROACH)

1. Original number: 52940587
2. Calculation of a self-checking digit:
   a. Multiply each digit in the number by a predetermined algorithm and sum the products. The algorithm used below multiplies each digit by a descending number beginning with 9:

5	2	**9**	**4**	0	5	8	7		
×	×	×	×	×	×	×	×		
9	8	7	6	5	4	3	2		
45 +	16 +	**63** +	**24** +	0 +	20 +	24 +	14	=	206

   b. Divide the sum by 11. The remainder is the check digit:

$$\frac{206}{11} = 18 \textit{ with a remainder of } 8$$

   In this illustration, the check digit (8) becomes the last digit of the account number, but could be added anywhere in the number. Thus the account number on your MasterCard, for example, would have the digit 8 included in the number embossed on your card.

3. Detection of a transposition error:

   Correct account number: 529405878

   Transposed number: 524905878

   The computer calculates a self-checking digit on the transposed number:

5	2	**4**	**9**	0	5	8	7		
×	×	×	×	×	×	×	×		
9	8	7	6	5	4	3	2		
45 +	16 +	**28** +	**54** +	0 +	20 +	24 +	14	=	201

$$\frac{201}{11} = 18 \textit{ with a remainder of } 3$$

The computed check digit is 3, but the self-checking digit keyed into the system is 8. Therefore, there must be either a transposition error or the check digit was keyed in incorrectly.

Upon entering the data, the system automatically generates a complete name, shipping and billing addresses, and phone number. These data can be verified orally with the customer.

- *Screen layout that logically follows the order in which data are gathered.* The screen format should be uncluttered and request data in a form that is consistent with the manner in which they are normally gathered.
- *Edit errors are noted automatically so that the data can be immediately investigated and corrected.* Timely identification of errors allows the data-entry person to investigate the potential error while all the data are available and information can be easily verified with a third party (when applicable).

- *Authorization for the input is noted and verified.* The specific individual entering the data and any other authorizations should be clearly noted on the screen and captured on a transaction log.
- *Unique identifiers are automatically added to the transaction.* For example, the data should be entered automatically by the system and a unique sequential identifier should be calculated by the application and added to the transaction to help ensure that all transactions are recorded.

Communication Controls

Communication controls are those specific controls implemented by data processing to ensure the completeness and correctness of data transmitted between a computer application and another remote device such as a terminal or another computer system. The specific controls are beyond the scope of this text but include hardware controls to detect a malfunction or loss of data through transmission. These controls also include specific procedures to minimize the risk of data alteration or addition of data by an unauthorized intruder. Some common control procedures include the following:

- *Call back.* The receiving computer application disconnects the line of the sender and calls back the identified sender, which protects against someone masquerading as a valid user. However, it also requires that the system specifically identify all valid data-entry sources.
- *Echo check.* The receiving unit echoes back the message to the sender for verification.
- *Encryption of highly sensitive data.* Encryption transforms data via an algorithm into a form that is difficult to read by anyone intercepting the data transmission but can be easily decrypted by the authorized receiving party.
- *Bit reconciliation.* Some data are transmitted through modems, which change the electronic signal. Messages can be developed to carry control counts to determine whether bits of data are added or deleted.
- *Feedback.* The unit receiving the message communicates the message back to the sending unit (electronic terminal) to verify whether the message received was the same as the message transmitted. This is often used with ATM cards to verify all elements of the transaction before it is processed.
- *Private lines.* Sensitive data are not sent over public communication lines but are restricted to lines that are owned, secured, and operated by the organization.

The method chosen to communicate data is an important consideration. Most electronic data are currently transmitted over public lines, including fiber optics, radio wave, or other common message-carrying services. If data are extremely sensitive, the company may choose to transmit them only over private or leased lines to further prevent the possibility of an intruder eavesdropping and capturing the output.

Processing Controls

Processing controls are designed to ensure that the correct program is used for processing, all transactions are processed, and the correct master file and transaction files are updated. Batch control totals help determine the completeness of processing. Other control procedures include the use of file labels for transaction and data identification, access controls over programs, and run-to-run control totals to calculate intermediate results when transactions update multiple files.

Output Controls

Output controls are designed to ensure that all data were completely processed and that output is distributed only to authorized recipients. Typical controls include reconciliation of control totals, output distribution schedules and procedures, and output reviews. For critical data, the user may perform a detailed review of the output contents with input to determine the completeness of a crucial process. The organization should also develop policies regarding the protection of privacy and the retention of records.

C–OVERVIEW OF CONTROL RISK ASSESSMENT PROCESS

The approach for assessing control risk in a computerized environment is not conceptually different than the approach taken in a manual environment. The auditor begins by identifying critical accounting applications. There is one major difference: The existence of heavily computerized, mostly paperless accounting applications may leave the auditor no choice but to thoroughly understand the control risk associated with the processing. Because of the level of auditor expertise often needed, many public accounting firms have developed computer audit specialists to deal with the most complex situations, but the firms expect all their auditors to be able to assess control risk in all but the most complex environments.

Many internal audit departments also have computer audit sections which perform detailed audits of controls over program changes, controls built into new applications, and the integrity of data communications. They are also more likely to implement advanced audit techniques to evaluate the operation of controls and the correctness of processing.* The external auditor works closely with the internal auditor in planning audits of the client's data processing operations and may either rely on the internal auditor's work in some areas or jointly perform some control evaluations.

Gaining an Understanding of the Control Structure

An understanding of the control structure is normally gained through inquiry and observation. The auditor also examines client documentation to understand the nature of processing and the file layout of important computer records to be used in developing computer-assisted audit techniques. The process of assessing control risk in a computerized environment proceeds as follows:

*These techniques are often referred to as *concurrent audit techniques* because audit transactions are processed concurrently with the organization's regular transactions. Examples of these concurrent audit techniques include the integrated test facility and the snapshot and are discussed in more detail in Chapter 10.

1. Identify important accounting applications and the extent of computerization within those applications.
2. Develop an understanding of the general controls within data processing, such as program change control and access controls, to determine how those controls may affect the integrity of important applications.
3. Develop an understanding of the flow of transactions in important accounting applications and identify and document control procedures that address important processing objectives.
4. Develop a preliminary assessment of the control risk for the application including the *types* of misstatements that are likely to occur and *how* those misstatements might occur.
5. If preliminary control risk is assessed at other than the maximum, test the controls in operation.
6. Develop an updated assessment of control risk based on a complete understanding of the design of the application and the tests of the controls in operation.

Testing the Effectiveness of Control Procedures

The audit firm must decide on the most efficient approach to test the integration of general and application controls. Some firms choose to test general controls as a whole for heavily computerized clients because these controls affect all accounting applications. Other firms may test the general control procedures *only as they affect the important applications;* for example, they may test control over program changes only as the program change control affects a financial reporting application, but not over other applications. Often the external auditor relies on the work performed by the internal auditor in testing the general controls and then tests only the general controls applicable to the most important applications.

Many control procedures result in the creation of documentary evidence of their operation. That evidence will serve as a basis to develop specific audit procedures to test the effectiveness of the controls. For example, if the auditor wanted to test control procedures over program changes, he or she would look for evidence of a change request form, a feasibility proposal, test results, documentation of a review and sign-off by a user, updated program documentation, a data processing supervisor review, and evidence of a new program loaded into the production library. An auditor could test controls over program changes by taking a random sample of change request forms and examine them to determine whether the changes followed prescribed procedures and were implemented as authorized.

Many application control procedures leave physical evidence of their performance. There should be batch control reconciliations, authorization of input on forms originating transactions, exception reports for unprocessed data or transactions, and logs of accesses made to a transaction file. Other control procedures may not create documentary evidence, however. Input edit controls, for example, do not leave any paper evidence except in a printout of items that were rejected. Examining such a printout does *not* provide evidence that only valid items were processed, but that at least some invalid ones were not processed. If the actual operation of the edit control procedures is important to the auditor, it could be tested with computer audit techniques such as submitting auditor-developed test data for processing and

Audit Illustrations

TESTING THE OPERATION OF ACCESS CONTROL PROCEDURES

A large client processes most of its data on-line. The auditor is interested in the overall operation of data access control procedures and the specific access control procedures over payroll, especially the following:

- The ability to change the authorized pay rates for each job classification or individual.
- The ability to add or delete an employee from the authorized employee list.

All hourly employees check in using automated time cards which record time in and time out and transmit the data electronically to the company's main computer for processing. Each employee is identified to the system through the use of a plastic card that has a magnetic strip.

Gaining an Understanding

The auditor determines that an understanding of the control procedures must be gained at two levels: (1) the overall implementation of access control procedures for all of data processing and (2) the specific control procedures implemented by the personnel and payroll function to ensure that the control procedures are working properly. The auditor uses interviews and reviews documentation to determine the following related to the *overall access control procedures:*

- The company uses a popular and well-regarded access control software product that allows data items to be identified at the field level (such as an address within an individual's payroll record) and further allows the company to specify individual access in terms of specific functions (such as READ ONLY, NO ACCESS, CHANGE). The access system has been implemented for payroll and other important applications.
- Access is controlled through passwords. An individual can choose his or her own password (up to eight digits or alphabetic characters), which must be changed quarterly. Although there is a software feature that will test for ease of guessing the passwords, the feature has not been implemented.
- The company has a data security office that has developed policies for adding or deleting employees on a timely basis. Based on an interview with personnel in that office, it appears that employees are added on a timely basis, but processing the changes to terminate employees may not be done on a timely basis.

The auditor supplements the overall understanding through interviews with the personnel and payroll department and documents the following understanding of *specific procedures within each department:*

- Only the personnel department has the ability to add or delete employees or change wage rates.
- Access to the table (file) of authorized wage rates is limited to a senior person in the personnel department. When a change is made, the computer generates a report showing previous and current wage rates. The report goes to the individual making the change and to the manager of the department, who reviews the changes on a one-by-one basis to ensure that only authorized changes were made.
- Each employee has an identification number. When employees are added or deleted, the computer generates a hash total of the employee file based on employee identification numbers. The personnel department reconciles the computer hash total with its independently compiled hash total of employee identification numbers.
- The access control software develops a weekly report of all accesses (successful and unsuccessful) made to the wage rate file. The report goes to the personnel director for review and follow-up. The supervisor determines that a reconciliation report has been generated and reviewed for each reported access. There have

been no reported discrepancies, and the manager indicates that he would seriously follow up any discrepancies.

- Division management monitors labor costs by department. Variance reports are prepared on a weekly and monthly basis for management analysis.
- The computer prepares a report of all employees and hours worked on a daily basis that is sent to the applicable departmental supervisor for review and approval. The supervisors must sign off indicating approval and that all employees were working during the logged in time.
- All paychecks are directly deposited in a financial institution designated by the employee.

Preliminary Risk Assessment

The auditor has identified a number of strengths and weaknesses in the access control procedures. Potential *weaknesses* include the following:

- Passwords may be easy to guess because the software to detect easily compromised ones is not implemented and the employee can choose the passwords.
- Passwords are not changed on a frequent basis.
- The data security department may be slow in deleting terminated employees. This is considered very important because a disgruntled terminated employee could seriously compromise the system. (However, the auditor notes that there has not been any turnover in the payroll or personnel department in the past year.)
- The access control system has not been fully implemented across all applications.
- Employees log in using only plastic cards. This is considered a weakness because the plastic cards can be easily loaned to other individuals.

The auditor has also noted a number of compensating controls that are considered to be *strengths* in the access control over payroll, including the following:

- There is separation of duties between payroll, personnel, and factory supervisors.
- There is a reconciliation of all changes made to the wage rate file by both the supervisor submitting the changes and the personnel department manager.
- Access to the wage rate file is limited and a report is generated on all unauthorized attempts to access the file. There is supervisory follow-up.
- The number of hours worked on a daily basis is verified by the supervisors, thus limiting the opportunities for employees to pass their identification cards among each other.
- All payroll deposits go directly to a designated financial institution. This, coupled with personnel department authority to add individuals, prevents the generation of fictitious employee paychecks.
- There is timely management review of labor costs.

Based on the strength of compensating controls, the auditor assesses the control risk for payroll access to be low.

Tests of Effectiveness of Control Procedures

The auditor chooses to test the effectiveness of the control procedures because (1) the payroll application is a primary interest and (2) the control procedures leave documentary evidence of their performance. If the overall access controls had been determined to be important to a number of other applications, the auditor might have decided also to test the operation of the overall access control procedures.

The auditor chooses the following procedures to test the effectiveness of the access control procedures:

1. Review a selected number of wage rate changes. Verify the wage rate changes by

Continued

comparing the rates to authorized approval, such as labor contracts. Determine that a reconciliation of all changes was performed by the supervisor and the personnel department manager.

2. Review procedures with the personnel department manager for following up discrepancies. Obtain a list of changes to the wage rate file and determine that the manager performed a reconciliation for each change.
3. Select the list of the number of hours worked for a few days and determine whether a report was generated and signed by the supervisor.
4. Observe the activities and conscientiousness of employees. Determine whether software exists to shut down a terminal or a networked personal computer that is left idle. Determine that the supervisor who makes changes does so from a restricted terminal (in her own office, not accessible by other employees, etc.).
5. Determine that labor cost reports are prepared on a timely basis and reviewed by management. This can be done in conjunction with other work with management through an interview and a review of selected reports.

Control Risk Assessment

Assuming that no problems in performing the audit procedures were identified, the auditor can assess control risk as low. The assessment implies that the auditor has confidence that employees are paid at correct wage rates for actual hours worked. The control risk assessment indicates that it is unlikely that the payroll expense will be misstated. Thus, the auditor's direct tests of the account balance can be performed at a minimum level. Alternatively, the auditor may be able to gain satisfaction of the correctness of the account through analytical procedures. The control procedures and audit procedures to test them would be appropriately documented and become part of the auditor's working papers.

determining whether the expected result was obtained. This is referred to as the *test data method* and is discussed further in the next chapter.

Client's Use of a Service Bureau

Some clients, particularly small ones, find it easier to use an independent data processing service bureau to process their transactions than to develop their own in-house systems. For example, many small, independent banks use the processing services of larger banks to process all their transactions. These service bureaus might serve hundreds or even thousands of different customers.

If important accounting applications are processed at a service bureau, the auditor must evaluate the bureau's control procedures to determine whether they are adequate to ensure the completeness and correctness of processing. In planning the audit approach, the auditor needs first to determine the extent to which the service bureau can initiate transactions on behalf of the client and the control procedures that the client has instituted to ensure completeness of processing. The following options exist:

1. *The service bureau's services are limited to receiving and processing client transactions.* In such an instance, the auditor should determine whether the client's control procedures are sufficient to ensure the completeness and correctness of processing. If such control procedures are effective, the auditor may not need to investigate the control structure of the service bureau.

2. *The service bureau executes the client's transactions and maintains accountability for the transactions.* In such circumstances, the auditor needs to understand the service bureau's control structure. An independent report by an outside auditor that describes the policies and control procedures of the service bureau can be obtained. The client's auditor should be alert that many of the reports on service bureau processing may not cover tests of the effectiveness of control procedures implemented at the service bureau. Consequently, that auditor should find it difficult to reduce the control risk assessment to a minimum unless the auditor tests controls at the service bureau.

The auditor may also find it useful to have the service bureau's auditor assist in developing computer audit techniques at the service bureau to perform substantive tests of the client's records. For example, the service bureau auditor may have a program to sample a client's accounts receivable file and generate confirmations.

D–COMPREHENSIVE ILLUSTRATION: CONTROLS IN A PAPERLESS SYSTEM

Dreyfet is a retail chain of department stores located in the Southwest. The company currently has 42 stores and is expanding at the rate of about 5 per year. Sales last year were approximately $600 million. Dreyfet, which has been an audit client for the past three years, has just finished a major revision of its purchase, receiving, inventory, and accounts payable systems.

Purchase Order Subsystem

Buyers (purchase order agents) have a great deal of responsibility and authority in retail institutions. They are responsible for ordering goods in their product category, determining quantities and delivery dates, negotiating purchase prices, setting selling prices, and authorizing markdowns or sales of their products. The overall guidance for all purchase and promotion activities is directed by the marketing manager.

Company management approved the development of a comprehensive purchase order/inventory/vendor/accounts payable database that was completed this year. The database shows inventory on hand (by store), items on order, and the buyer's current authorization to buy (in dollars for product line). The setting of a buyer's limit, or authorization to buy, is made by the marketing manager. Orders cannot exceed this authorization to buy without the marketing manager's approval.

The data processing manager has just implemented two enhancements of the database. A complete vendor file was developed that includes only authorized vendors and other relevant data such as negotiated discount and trade terms. To eliminate written purchase orders for separate batch input, an on-line purchase order facility has been developed. Purchase orders are sent electronically to vendors using EDI. A significant amount of purchasing is negotiated during the annual fall and spring fashion shows. On a limited basis, the company has acquired portable microcomputers that can be taken to the trade shows and used to communicate directly with the main computer system to generate purchase orders. However, orders can only be placed with authorized vendors. Dreyfet believes that purchase errors will decrease and timely delivery will increase. The buyers at Dreyfet initially resisted training and the implementation of the control procedures. However, it appears that they see the advantage of having up-to-date inventory and vendor status databases and have cooperated to make the system successful.

Goods are received in a company warehouse and are directed to stores according to the purchase order. Buyers would like more flexibility in directing goods to specific stores. They want to be able to wait until they receive notice that the goods have been shipped before designating to which store the goods should be directed.

Preliminary Analysis of Control Structure

The partner in charge of the audit engagement has determined that the purchase order system is a critical application and has noted that the client is moving rapidly to a paperless accounting system. A preliminary understanding of the general controls indicates that the company is very control conscious. But two potential weaknesses were noted:

1. A comprehensive access control program has not been fully implemented. A password system is in place, but not all data items are covered by the security system. Further, buyers, unwilling to get bogged down in clerical activities, share their passwords with secretaries so they could enter the necessary data to generate the purchase orders.
2. Because Dreyfet needed to implement the system quickly, users performed minimal testing. The data processing manager, however, has confidence in the integrity of the programmers and shows the auditor comprehensive tests that were performed before the system was implemented.

Application Control Procedures

The control risk assessment is built around the control objectives identified in Chapter 8. For illustration purposes, only the objectives related to authorization, completeness, valuation, and timeliness of recording are discussed. *Note that the preliminary assessment of control risk proceeds by assessing the risk of errors or misstatements related to each assertion. That assessment, at the objectives level, also assists the auditor in determining the types of direct tests of account balances that should be performed if control risk is assessed at other than the minimum.*

Authorization

The auditor is interested in three elements of authorization: (1) only authorized individuals are allowed access to the purchase order database, (2) all purchases comply with the authorization to buy limits set forth by the marketing manager, and (3) all purchases are made from vendors on the authorized vendors file.

Analysis. The auditor needs to gather evidence that only authorized buyers can gain access to the purchase order database and that each buyer is limited to only that part of the database for which he or she is responsible. The auditor determines that the controls to log on to the system ensure that this objective is met. Further, the auditor determines that passwords are generated randomly and are changed on a monthly basis. The auditor tests the operation of the control procedures by interviewing buyers as to procedures and reviewing records of password changes within data processing. The auditor then attempted to use currently valid passwords to determine whether access to components of the database is restricted as stated. The auditor finds that control procedures are operating as stated.

Second, the auditor tests the authorization to buy by obtaining a printout of the current authorization to buy on a sample of product lines and compares the list with the authorized approval maintained by the marketing manager. Only two exceptions were noted, and the marketing manager indicates that he had directly authorized the additional purchase. The auditor concludes that the control is operating as stated and is an effective control.

Finally, the auditor discusses the sharing of passwords with the buyers. The buyers believe that sufficient control is maintained because they review all purchase orders generated during a day with a list they maintain. As a compensating test, the auditor selects a random sample of purchase orders and reconciles it with buyer activity reports, which are prepared on a weekly basis and reviewed by each buyer. The auditor is satisfied that the weekly activity report summarizes all purchase activities for that week and the buyer thoroughly reviews the reports and would notice the existence of any unauthorized reports.

Conclusion. Sufficient documentary evidence exists that the authorization control objective is being attained. The auditor concludes that control risk related to authorization can be assessed at the minimum.

Completeness

The auditor is concerned that all valid purchase orders are properly generated and all related accounts are properly updated.

Analysis. Each purchase order is assigned a unique reference number. Each purchasing agent receives a daily report of all purchase orders and reviews it for validity. Additionally, each purchasing agent receives a biweekly report of all unfilled purchase orders.

Tests of Operation and Conclusion. The auditor reviews a sample of daily reports and makes inquiries of selected purchasing agents as to the detail of their review. The auditor also accounts for a block of transactions to determine that the sequential numbering is used. The auditor concludes that the review is performed conscientiously and the risk of incomplete items is small and assesses control risk for this assertion as low.

Valuation

The issuance of the purchase order directly affects the valuation assertion because all purchase prices are determined by the purchase order. One audit concern is that the buyer might issue purchase orders at inflated prices and receive private kickbacks from the vendors. Another concern is that the client might not be taking advantage of its purchasing power to receive the best available price.

Analysis. Through interviews, the auditor learns that buyers are rewarded on their overall profitability performance measured by sales volume and gross margins realized. Edit controls are in place so that any ordered product is compared with past purchases to determine whether the purchase price is within a predetermined price range. Other edit tests include identifying a product SKU (identification code) and performing a self-checking digit test. Selling price is initially set by the buyer at the time the purchase order is created. (Setting the retail price is necessary because all goods are marked with the retail price at the warehouse on receipt.) The auditor reviews edit test reports and determines that the control procedures are functioning as stated. Further, the auditor concludes that the performance reports are motivators for correct input.

Tests of Controls and Conclusion. The auditor inputs a sample of test purchase orders and determines that all edit tests are working as stated. In addition, because the exception reports and performance analysis reports work as stated, the auditor determines that the risk of incorrect prices is small and is compensated for by management review.

Timeliness

The purchase orders do not lead directly to the recording of accounting data. However, the auditor wishes to determine that all purchase orders are recorded on a timely basis because failures might affect inventory and accounts payable.

Analysis and Tests of Controls. The auditor selects a sample of purchase order input lists and compares that with the date of the recorded purchase order on the purchase order database and concludes that the database is updated concurrently with the submission of the transaction. The auditor makes a decision that any other errors would show up as problems with either receipt of merchandise (only goods that have outstanding purchase orders can be received) or payment of the goods (vendor invoice must match the outstanding purchase order). Further testing is deferred to the analysis of those applications. Based on the existing evidence, the auditor determines that the control risk is low.

Conclusion: Application Controls

Based on the controls identified above, the auditor has determined that the risk of incorrect purchase orders is low. Based on the tests performed, the auditor determines that the purchase order database can be relied on as an integral part of the purchase order, inventory, and accounts payable system.

Summary

Today's auditor encounters a wide variety of computer systems that form an integral part of every audit client's accounting system. The trend is to increasing integration of computer data processing systems. Accounting applications will be integrated with order entry and manufacturing applications. An organization's computer facilities will be regularly transferring data from a division to the corporate headquarters and vice versa. Electronic data interchange will become a reality for many audit clients.

The auditor needs to assess computer-based controls in almost every engagement. Most organizations have come to realize that complex systems need to be well controlled. One strong control is the existence of a qualified internal audit department that periodically tests the effectiveness of control procedures implemented in computer applications as well as management's controls over the information systems function.

The auditor's process of assessing control risk for a heavily computerized client does not differ significantly from the assessment of a manual system. A computerized environment can provide opportunities for the implementation of control procedures that contribute not only to the integrity of accounting processing but also to the efficiency of operations. Management often develops control reports that are used to monitor computer operations. Auditors can test the effectiveness of many control procedures by submitting test data for processing. However, the auditor can also determine the extent to which management has set up control procedures to monitor the effectiveness of controls. Because the latter approach often provides documentary evidence of the effectiveness of the control procedures, the auditor is often able to use the evidence in assessing control risk.

Significant Terms

access control software Software designed to limit access to programs or data files to those authorized for such access, comprehensive access control software identifies all users and rules to access data or programs.

applications programs Written to accomplish specific data processing tasks such as processing sales and accounts receivable, updating inventory, computing payroll, or developing special management reports, usually are written in higher-level languages such as COBOL, Pascal, or C.

audit trail A term used to describe the documents and records that allow a user or auditor to trace a transaction from its origination through to its final disposition or vice versa; must have cross-references to documents or other computer records, may be electronic or paper based.

authentication A means developed for a computer application to determine that the individual requesting the access privilege is who he or she claims to be; popular methods include use of passwords and plastic cards with magnetic strips.

batch processing A method of processing transactions that groups similar transactions (such as accounts receivable payments) into batches, which are then run at one time to update the accounts. Batch controls can then be used to provide assurance that all submitted transactions were processed.

boundary control procedures Control procedures designed to establish initial control and responsibility for the completeness of transactions; implemented at the point in which an organization enters into transactions with other organizations.

computer log The electronic record of all information related to a transaction or attempts to access data files; generated automatically by most operating systems for all transactions.

database management systems A centrally planned and controlled collection of data; the management system includes the software to organize the collection of data into logically similar records and files; it separates the data from application programs, thus creating data independence and allowing greater flexibility in meeting the organization's data needs.

distributed processing Shifting the processing of transactions to different computing units within a network of computers, depending on size and processing requirements.

electronic data interchange (EDI) The electronic exchange of documents between organizations, eliminating the development of paper documents and substituting electronic documents for them; prevalent examples include electronic transmission of purchase orders and invoices between customers and vendors.

general controls A term describing computer control procedures that affect more than one application. Examples include control procedures over program changes, access control methods, and application development methodologies.

operating system A complex computer program that controls and coordinates the running of the computer and its many functions.

tables A commonly used computer term to describe computer files that contain data necessary for the processing of common transactions.

telecommunications software Software that controls the paths and completeness of all data communications between a computer system, terminals, or other data processing locations; designed to ensure that all data are properly transmitted through authorized media to correct parties and are completely received.

Review Questions

A–Introduction

9–1 Define and differentiate *operating systems* and *application programs*. Is the auditor primarily interested in the operating system or in application programs? Explain.

B–General and Application Controls

9–2 Explain why there should be a segregation of duties between data processing and users. Should data processing be allowed to initiate transactions (for example, a purchase order is initiated automatically when inventory levels fall to a pre-specified level)?

9–3 What are general controls in computer environments? Do the general controls directly affect computer applications? How does the auditor determine whether general control procedures should be tested?

9–4 What are application control procedures? How do they differ from general controls in a computerized environment?

9–5 Why is the existence of an information technology committee and an information systems steering committee important to an organization? How does the absence of these two committees affect the auditor's assessment of control risk and the approach to an audit engagement?

9–6 Identify the seven fundamental concepts important to evaluating the organization's data processing control structure and briefly indicate the importance of each to the auditor's risk assessment process.

9–7 Explain why it is important for the computer operator and computer programmer function to be segregated but not for the computer programmer and the systems analyst functions to be.

9–8 What is end-user computing? How might the development of end-user computing affect the integrity of control procedures built into accounting applications?

9–9 Developing adequate control over changes to computer programs is one of the most important procedures in computerized environments. Briefly describe the differences between production program libraries, source code libraries, and programmer test libraries and indicate the importance of each to the overall control over program changes.

9–10 One of your colleagues makes the statement that application controls are stronger in on-line systems than they are in batch systems. Do you agree or disagree with the statement? Give the rationale for your answer.

9–11 What are the major principles that should guide the development of a comprehensive access control program for a data processing center? Assume that the organization uses automated access control software to implement the principles.

9–12 Identify the three primary means that might be used to authenticate a user attempting to gain access to a restricted program or file. Briefly identify the major advantages and disadvantages of each method.

9–13 Briefly identify how an internal audit department with a strong computer audit orientation might affect the audit plan for a heavily computerized client.

9–14 Briefly describe the purposes of the following control procedures and how each works: (1) control total, (2) hash total, and (3) record count. Briefly indicate how these control procedures could be implemented in an organization with on-line data processing.

9–15 What is a computer log? How might it be used by a client?

9–16 What is a self-checking digit? Why is its use such an important control procedure? What happens to a transaction if it is rejected from processing because an identifier does not match the self-checking digit?

9–17 Why is it important that the following functions be segregated in a computerized environment:

a. Applications programmer and operator?

b. Systems programmer and applications programmer?

c. Users and data processing personnel?

d. Librarian and applications programmers?

9–18 Briefly describe the application program change process. What major control procedures should be implemented to ensure that only authorized changes are made and that those changes are completely and correctly made?

9–19 What are the major elements of an audit trail? How does an audit trail in a computerized environment differ *conceptually* from an audit trail in a manual environment? How does it differ *physically* from an audit trail in a manual environment?

9–20 What is electronic data interchange (EDI)? What applications are most likely to be converted to EDI?

9–21 What is meant by *boundary control procedures?* Identify three types of boundary control procedures expected to be found in a data processing environment and briefly describe the control objectives accomplished by each.

9–22 Briefly define the following communication controls and describe how they work:

a. Encryption.

b. Callback.

c. Echo check.

9–23 The chapter referred to tables, such as a payroll wage rate table. What are the functions of such tables? What controls should be instituted to ensure the accuracy of the tables?

C–Overview of Control Risk Assessment Process

9–24 During a discussion between two staff auditors, one remarked that the "only way in which computer control procedures can be adequately tested for operation is to actually process some test data through the computer application. Otherwise, there is no effective way to know that the designed control procedures are actually working." Do you agree or disagree with the staff auditor? Explain your rationale.

9–25 What is a compensating control procedure? Can the auditor test the effectiveness of compensating control procedures or is such testing limited to testing the effectiveness of primary control procedures?

Multiple Choice Questions

9–26 A deposit for Julie A. Smith at the local bank was inadvertently recorded as a deposit in the account of June A. Smith. The control that would have most likely detected the error in depositing the amount to the wrong account would be

a. The use of self-checking digits on account numbers.

b. Range tests on accounts in which the deposit is related to the size of the account.

c. Limit tests.

d. Validity tests to determine whether Julie Smith is a valid customer.

9–27 From an audit viewpoint, which of the following represents a potential disadvantage associated with the widespread use of microcomputers?

a. Their portability.

b. Their ease of access by novice users.

c. Their easily developed programs using spreadsheets which do not have to be documented.

d. All of the above.

9–28 In an automated payroll system, all employees in the finishing department were paid at the rate of $7.45 per hour when the authorized rate was $7.15 per hour. Which of the following controls would have been most effective in preventing such an error?

a. Access controls which would restrict the personnel department's access to the payroll master file data.

b. A review of all authorized pay rate changes by the personnel department.

c. The use of batch control totals by department.

d. A limit test that compares the pay rates per department with the maximum rate for all employees.

9–29 Which of the following errors would be detected by batch controls?

a. A fictitious employee was added to the processing of the weekly time cards by the computer operator.

b. An employee who worked only 5 hours in the week was paid for 50 hours.

c. The time card for one employee was not processed because it was lost in transit between the payroll department and the data entry function.

d. All of the above.

9–30 Which of the following is *not* correct concerning the processing of transactions through the on-line input of transactions at a computer terminal:

a. Batch controls cannot be used.

b. Oral verification is an effective control when customers call in to place orders.

c. Control has decreased because transactions are no longer manually reviewed.

d. Each transaction should be assigned a unique, preferably sequential identifier to establish an audit trail.

9–31 Which of the following functions would have the least effect on an audit if it was not properly segregated?

a. The systems analyst and the programmer functions.

b. The computer operator and programmer functions.

c. The computer operator and the user functions.

d. The applications programmer and the systems programmer.

9–32 Which of the following statements is correct regarding the implementation of good controls over the program maintenance function in an organization?

a. Only programmers should have access to the production library.

b. Users should have access to the test library to determine whether all changes are properly made.

c. Only the librarian should be allowed to make changes to the production library.

d. The computer operator should have access to both the production library and the source code library.

*9–33 An auditor who is testing EDP controls in a payroll system would most likely use test data that contain conditions such as

a. Deductions *not* authorized by employees.
b. Overtime *not* approved by supervisors.
c. Time cards with invalid job numbers.
d. Payroll checks with unauthorized signatures.

*9–34 To obtain evidence that user identification and password control procedures are functioning as designed, an auditor would most likely

a. Attempt to sign on to the system using invalid user identifications and passwords.
b. Write a computer program that simulates the logic of the client's access control software.
c. Extract a random sample of processed transactions and ensure that the transactions were appropriately authorized.
d. Examine statements signed by employees stating that they have *not* divulged their user identifications and passwords to any other person.

*9–35 All administrative and professional staff in a corporate legal department prepare documents on terminals connected to a network file server. The best control over unauthorized access to sensitive data is

a. Required entry of passwords for access to the system.
b. Physical security for all disks containing document files.
c. Periodic server back-up and storage in a secure area.
d. Required entry of passwords for access to individual documents.

Discussion Questions

9–36 (Access Control Policies) Many auditors now consider a comprehensive program to control access to the computer equipment, computer programs, and data to be one of the most important control elements in a data processing environment. In evaluating the comprehensiveness of an access policy, the auditor considers both physical and data access (that is, access to data by gaining access to computer files through the computer).

Required:

a. Identify questions the auditor might ask regarding the physical controls over access to the equipment and computer documentation.
b. What are the components of a comprehensive data access program that the auditor should evaluate?
c. Assume that the client has an adequate access control plan and, based on your interviews, the access policies are operating as described. The control procedures identified by the auditor include restricted use of passwords, frequent changes in passwords to keep pace with job changes, and monitoring of repeated attempts at accessing the system by unauthorized users. Write an audit program that would gather evidence to determine the effectiveness of the control procedures in operation.

---

*Adapted from the Uniform CPA examination or the Certified Internal Auditor examination.

9–37 (Controls over Program Changes) Re-Tool Corporation, one of the firm's larger audit clients, has a data processing staff of approximately 75 individuals. Past audits have indicated that the general control environment is effective. During the past year, the client has revised the manner in which changes to existing programs are controlled. The client believes that the changes in procedures represent an overall improvement in controls. This is your first year on the audit and the partner assigns you the task of gathering information about the revisions in procedures regarding program changes, evaluating the control risk apparent in the changes, and, if merited, testing the operations of the control process.

Required:

a. What are the major control objectives over the application program change process?

b. What are the major elements that the client should have implemented to control the program change process?

c. Identify the audit procedures the auditor might use to test the effectiveness of the operation of the control process over application program changes.

9–38 (Evaluation of Computer Operations) You have been assigned to the audit of MidState Electronics Corporation, a medium-size distributor of electronics equipment serving a geographic area within a radius of 150 miles. MidState has installed a state-of-the-art microcomputer. The client primarily uses it for inventory control and accounting functions, such as billing, sales, accounts receivable, inventory, and payroll. All of the software has been purchased from a major software vendor and has not been modified for MidState. The software has the ability to implement password controls.

During the audit planning process, the auditor has identified the accounting applications as important. The partner has asked you to assess control risk in the computer environment and expects you to make a recommendation on the nature of substantive testing that might be required.

Required:

a. Develop a control questionnaire that might be used to capture information about *general controls* and *application controls* in the computer environment at MidState Electronics.

b. Assume that during the course of your inquiry, you discover that the client does not have a systematic process to back up data or programs. The client does not see the need to back up programs because they can be replaced by directly contacting the software vendor and are available within a very short period of time. Data files are backed up, but not on a scheduled basis, and are stored in a file cabinet maintained in the controller's office. What are the implications of these findings to the conduct of the audit?

9–39 (Application Controls) Bass Pro Shops is a catalog retailer concentrating on fishing and hunting equipment. It prints an annual catalog containing over 200 pages of products as well as approximately six special sale catalogs during the year. Products range from fishing lures retailing for $1.29 to boat packages for over $15,000. Purchases can be paid for by personal check, MasterCard, or Visa. Customers can send in their order (with check or credit card information included) or may place it by calling the company's toll-free number.

The company has recently implemented an on-line order entry system by which computer operators take the customer order, check the availability of items for shipment, and confirm the invoice amount with the customer. Once an order is taken, the system generates a shipping and packing document, places a hold on the inventory, and prepares an invoice (and recording of sales), when items are shipped.

Required:

a. Identify the application control procedures (including edit controls) you would recommend to control the on-line order-taking process.
b. Briefly indicate how control procedures might differ for the orders that are sent in by the customer compared with those placed directly over the phone.
c. For each control procedure identified, briefly indicate the implication on the audit if a deficiency in the control procedure is found:
   1. Indicate the potential types of errors or irregularities that could occur because the control is not operative.
   2. Identify the audit steps the auditor might take to test the year-end account balances.

9–40 (Application Controls) The following represent errors that could occur in a computerized environment. For each error, identify a control procedure that would have been effective in either preventing or detecting the error.

Errors Found:

a. The selling price for all products handled by company salespersons was consistently reduced by 25 to 40 percent by a salesperson who was paid commission on gross sales made. The marketing department did not authorize the salesperson (or any other salesperson) to discount price from authorized price lists unless the marketing manager or the district sales manager provided specific approval.
b. Duplicate paychecks were prepared for all employees in the company's warehouse for the week ended July 31. This occurred because the employee time cards were processed twice by the data processing department.
c. An employee in the sales order department who was upset about an inadequate pay raise copied the client's product master file and sold it to a competitor. The master file contained information on the cost and sales price of each product as well as special discounts given to customers.
d. An individual in the customer relations department gained access to the product master file and, in an attempt to change prices for a customer, inadvertently changed prices for the products identified for all customers.
e. A nonexistent part number was included in the description of goods on a shipping document. Fortunately, the individual packing the item for shipment was able to identify the product by its description and included it in the order. The item was not billed, however, because it was not correctly identified in the system.

f. A customer number was transposed during the order-taking process. Consequently, the shipment was billed to another customer. By the time the error was identified, the original customer was out of business.

g. The accounts receivable clerk, who also operated the company's microcomputer, took cash remittances and recorded the credit to the customer's account as discounts.

h. An employee consistently misstated his time card by returning at night and punching out then rather than when his shift was over at 3:30. Instead of being paid for 40 hours per week, he was paid, on average, for over 60 hours per week for almost one year. When accused of the error, he denied any wrongdoing and quit.

i. A customer order was filled and shipped to a former customer that had already declared bankruptcy. The company's standard billing terms are 2 percent, 10 days or net 30.

9–41 (Concentration of Risks in Computerized Systems) The concentration of data within computer systems, coupled with the increased data communications abilities across computer systems, has combined to create risks that did not occur in the same magnitude in manual systems.

Required:
Identify the additional risks that have developed because of the concentration of data within computer systems and the increased data communication abilities of systems.

*9–42 (Control Procedure Analysis) Ajax, Inc., an audit client, recently installed a new computer system to process its shipping, billing, and accounts receivable records more efficiently. During interim work, an assistant reviewed the accounting system and the internal controls. The assistant determined the following information concerning the new computer system and the processing and control of shipping notices and customer invoices.

Each major computerized function (i.e., shipping, billing, accounts receivable, etc.) is permanently assigned to a specific computer operator who is responsible for making program changes, running the program, and reconciling the computer log. Responsibility for the custody and control over the magnetic tapes and system documentation is randomly rotated among the computer operators on a monthly basis to prevent one person from having access to the tapes and documentation at all times. Each computer programmer and computer operator has access to the computer room via a magnetic card and a digital code that is different for each card. The systems analyst and the supervisor of the computer operators do not have access to the computer room.

The computer system documentation consists of the following items: program listing, error listing, logs, and record layout. To increase efficiency, batch totals and processing controls are omitted from the system.

Ajax ships its products directly from two warehouses that forward shipping notices to general accounting, where the billing clerk enters the price of the item and accounts for the numerical sequence of the shipping notices. The billing clerk also prepares daily adding machine tapes of the units shipped and the sales amount. Shipping notices and adding machine tapes are forwarded to the computer department for processing. The computer output consists of (1) a three-copy invoice that is forwarded to the billing clerk and (2) a daily sales register showing the aggregate totals of units shipped and sales amounts that the computer operator compares to the adding machine tapes. The billing clerk mails two copies of each invoice to the customer and retains the third copy in an open invoice file that serves as a detail accounts receivable record.

Required:
Make one specific recommendation to correct each condition in which internal control procedures are not considered adequate in the new computer system and are not efficient for processing and control.

*9–43 (Control Considerations: Banking Environment) A bank uses an automated human resource system to facilitate management of bank personnel assigned to its 12 regional offices as well as to its operations center. Operating in a database environment, the human resource system supports traditional personnel functions, such as master payroll data, promotions, terminations, and retirements. In addition, it supports management's affirmative action and equal employment opportunity goals and staff development policies.

Managers at each of the 12 regional offices and functional managers at the bank's operations center are authorized to initiate human resource actions. Multiple-copy documents initiated by regional managers are delivered to the human resource manager for approval prior to data conversion and batch-mode data entry via terminals at the bank operations center. Functional activities at the operations center are authorized to update selected on-line applications systems within the database without hard copy input. Input documents are filed after data entry. The database is updated during processing, and output reports are generated for managers who initiated actions as well as for the manager of human resources.

Required:
The internal auditor's review of the processing described above identified six areas where specific control objectives should be addressed.

a. Based on the description above and your understanding of the nature of processing, briefly identify the control objective for each area of audit concern, using the following format:

Areas of Management Concern	**Control Objectives**
1. Initial data capture.	
2. Transaction authorization.	
3. Transaction processing.	
4. Reporting and use of output.	
5. Security.	
6. Systems responsiveness/performance.	

b. For each audit objective listed, describe two audit procedures that might be utilized to gather audit evidence on the effectiveness of control procedures and operating procedures related to the area.

9–44 (Backup Plans for Data Processing) The auditor should evaluate the ability of an organization to continue to operate should the data processing center be destroyed. Most organizations have reacted to the risk by developing comprehensive backup plans.

Required:

a. Identify the major elements that should be included in a comprehensive data processing backup plan.

b. Contrast the potential roles of the external auditor and internal auditor in evaluating the effectiveness of the organization's backup plan for computer processing capabilities.

c. What is the impact on the auditor's report if the auditor concludes that an audit client has concentrated all its data processing in one location and does not have any backup plans, and its data processing center has moderate security provisions?

9–45 (Computer Fraud)

Required:

For each of the following situations involving computer fraud, briefly describe

a. A control procedure that would have been effective in preventing or detecting the fraud.

b. An audit procedure that would have detected the fraud.

Computer Frauds:

1. A computer programmer added a module to the payroll program that started with an "IF" statement to identify his employee number. If it were his record, the program was instructed to multiply computed pay by 1.5, thus increasing the programmer's pay by 50 percent.
2. A state health and social services department made support payments to needy residents. A resident could be input into the system only on the recommendation of a supervising caseworker. Some caseworkers entered fictitious residents on the system and had support payments sent to authorized addresses. The caseworkers then cashed the support payments and eventually transferred the cash to their own accounts.
3. A student posed as a newspaper reporter doing a story on a phone company's data processing center. After leaving the center, he noticed a data processing manual that had been discarded. He took the manual home and learned the access code to the company's parts repair system. He could then log on and have repair parts delivered to a specific location. Later he picked up the parts, which he sold back to the company and to other customers.
4. A manufacturing company required all its hourly workers to sign in by passing their personal identification cards across an automated time clock that captured the data and transmitted it to the computer for subsequent processing. An employee who worked the first shift arranged with her brother who worked the second shift to use her card to sign out when her brother completed his work shift. The employee thus generated pay for 16 hours per day, one-half at overtime rates. The employee and her brother split the additional pay.
5. A disgruntled programmer often came to the office in the evenings to

copy confidential client data such as customer lists, discounts, and so forth onto magnetic tapes, which he sold to competitors at handsome prices.

9–46 **(Research Question)** The chapter discusses the importance of internal audit departments with separate computer audit functions. Indeed, the computer audit profession has emerged in the past decade with its own professional certification program (The Certified Information Systems Auditor) and its own set of auditing standards.

Required:

a. Review the *EDP Auditor* journal and *The Internal Auditor* for the past two years and prepare a list of computer audit topics addressed in each journal. Prepare a summary of topics covered. Classify the topics and use the classification as a basis for determining an aspect of the scope of computer audit activities.
b. Interview an computer auditor and inquire about the nature of audit work performed. Review his or her audit plan for a year.
c. To what extent, and under what conditions, might the external auditor utilize the work of an internal computer auditor in either performing substantive testing or in assessing control risk associated with a client's computerized environment?
d. List 5 to 10 audit activities pertaining to a computerized environment in which an internal computer audit function might have a competitive advantage in performing detailed analysis over the external auditor. Briefly indicate why you believe the competitive advantage might exist with the internal computer audit function.

9–47 **(Research Practice Question)** Interview the controller and director of data processing at a company that you have worked for, or with which you have contact, to determine the company's access control policies. Determine how the policies are implemented and report any potential deficiencies in them. Determine whether the company may have any compensating control procedures that might be effective in offsetting any deficiencies in its access control procedures.

Cases

9–48 Dreyfet department store maintains on-line prices on minicomputers in stores connected to the automatic cash registers. For most products, the product and price are read into the cash register by scanning devices that read the bar codes on the merchandise. The product name (abbreviated) and the prices are printed on the customer's cash receipt and are also captured internally as part of the sales recording process. The process also updates the perpetual inventory record at the store.

Prices for all products are set by the buyers and are entered on to the client's mainframe computer system and downloaded to the stores. Only the store manager can override the price on the store's minicomputer. All overrides are supposed to be reported to the buyer and the general merchandise manager for the department store division. The dollar amounts of sales of products for which price changes were made are used to develop a special report showing sales volume by product, average retail price, product cost, and loss (profit) per product.

Required:

a. Identify the key control procedures the auditor would expect to find in the environment described.

b. Develop an audit program to determine whether the control procedures are working as described.

c. What are the implications to the audit if the control procedures are not working as described, especially if the store manager is making a wide variety of product price markdowns, but the price changes are not generating any exception reports?

d. What are the implications to the audit if the auditor tests prices in 6 of 42 stores and finds that on 10 percent of the items tested, the price in the store's cash register differs from the price on the master sales file? Assume for the present that most of the changes result in a lower price being charged.

9–49 Hastings Manufacturing Company makes special-order equipment to be used by other manufacturers. The company has three major product lines and approximately 10 variations of each product line. The company uses a job cost accounting system in which all labor and materials are directly charged to the cost of building each stamping machine. (Each machine retails, on average, for about $500,000.)

All direct labor hours are captured by automated time capture machines when each employee punches in the job order number and the start and finish times worked on the job each day. All raw materials are also assigned the same job order number and are entered into the system on work order requisitions received by inventory control.

Required:

a. Identify the controls the company should implement to ensure that only authorized employees are paid, that they are paid at the authorized rate for hours actually worked, and that the labor cost is recorded to the correct job.

b. Develop an audit program to test the labor part of the system identified in part a above.

End Notes

1. Gary Holstrum, Theodore Mock, and Robert West, *The Impact of Technology on Auditing—Moving into the 21st Century* (Altamonte Springs, Fla.: Institute of Internal Auditors, 1988), 1.
2. AICPA, *Audit Guide: Consideration of the Internal Control Structure in a Financial Statement Audit* (New York: AICPA, 1990), Sec. 2.72 and 2.75.
3. Arthur Young, *The Landmark MIT Study: Management in the 1990s* (New York: Arthur Young, 1989).
4. Arthur Young, *The Landmark MIT Study: Management in the 1990s.*

CHAPTER

10

Learning Objectives

Through studying this chapter, you will be able to:

1. Identify audit situations and determine the most appropriate computer audit techniques.
2. Identify situations in which generalized audit software can be used to achieve audit efficiency.
3. Understand the differences between various types of computer audit techniques and the efficiencies of each.
4. Utilize the microcomputer to achieve audit efficiency.
5. Identify major changes in computer processing and their effect on the conduct of an audit.
6. Apply computer audit techniques to the design of an audit.

Computer-Assisted Auditing: Today's Environment for Efficient Auditing

Chapter Contents

Chapter Overview

Today's auditor must be equipped with an understanding of alternative tools and approaches to test the operation of computerized accounting systems and to gather and analyze data contained in computerized files. Audit tools are available to (1) test the effectiveness of computer processing and the operation of computer-based control procedures and (2) gather data to analyze the correctness of details contained in recorded account balances. These approaches are discussed in the chapter. Then the role of microcomputer technology in achieving audit efficiency is discussed and examples are presented. The nature of changes in the computing environment is identified and audit implications are discussed.

Computer technology has become an integral part of most organizations. Organizational needs for efficient storage, processing, and retrieval of data have engendered widespread acceptance of new hardware and software. In addition, competitive factors have made it necessary for both auditors and clients to apply new technological developments. The pervasiveness of computer applications as well as the rapid growth of technological abilities to the point of absorbing entire functions (such as database systems) has fostered systems that are complex enough to limit the effectiveness of traditional approaches to control and audit.[1]

Evidential matter about the effectiveness of design or operation [of control policies and procedures] may be obtained through . . . the use of computer-assisted audit techniques. [AU 319.49]

The audit environment is constantly changing, with many clients today using complex computer systems, and tomorrow's auditors will audit clients with even more complex systems. To be effective and efficient, tomorrow's auditors must understand computer technology and must be able to use that technology to both (1) gain competent evidence to satisfy financial statement assertions and (2) perform the audit efficiently. This chapter discusses computer technology developments, the effects of such developments on the audit engagement, and the types of computer audit procedures that can be utilized to improve the efficiency of the audit.

Today's auditors work constantly with computerized records. It is likely that many audit clients either have eliminated, or will eliminate a substantial portion of their paper documents and replace them with electronic documents filed only in a computerized form. As noted previously, purchase orders may exist only on computerized files. Similarly, invoices, shipping documents, records of payroll disbursements, and so forth may exist only in computerized files. An auditor who is unable to use computerized audit tools effectively will be at a tremendous disadvantage. This chapter reviews automated tools that assist the auditor in conducting audits in computerized environments, regardless of the size and complexity of the client's computer environment.

Computerized audit tools can be useful in *testing the effectiveness of control procedures* and in *directly testing the validity of account balances.* This chapter covers computer audit approaches that might be utilized to both test control procedures and to directly test assertions relating to the ending account balances (substantive tests). Computer audit tools have been widely used in performing direct tests of account balances, and they are beginning to be used to test the control procedures over the processing of transactions and to assist in planning, administering, documenting, and conducting the audit.

A–COMPUTER AUDIT TOOLS TO TEST COMPUTER PROCESSING

The computer can be used to gather audit evidence about controls designed to ensure the correctness of input and processing of the client's system. Although such approaches are just starting to become widely used, their use is expected to increase dramatically during the next decade as computer systems become more integrated and as the elimination of paper documents continues.

Approaches to testing the computer processing fall into three major categories:

1. *Test data* or *integrated test facility*—transactions entered into the system by the auditor to verify correctness and completeness of processing.
2. *Parallel simulation*—developing a computer program to emulate the processing of client transactions to be compared with processing by the client's computer application.
3. *Concurrent processing*—transaction selection and/or tracing methodologies whereby the auditor submits or identifies transactions to be processed concurrently with the client's regular processing.

Each of the approaches accomplishes slightly different objectives, and the auditor should know the advantages of each method. In addition, it is likely that many of these approaches will be implemented by internal audit departments so the external auditor should consider potential reliance on the internal auditor's work when that is the case.

Test Data: Auditing through the Computer

The **test data approach** involves developing and submitting fictitious transactions to be processed by important computer applications. Test data are developed to determine whether

1. *Control procedures* that are supposed to be built into the application *are functioning as documented* and can be considered effective.

2. The computer application is *processing transactions correctly.*
3. All transaction and master *files are fully and correctly updated.*

An overview of the test data approach is shown in Exhibit 10.1. The auditor develops a specific set of test data (fictitious data) to test important controls and important aspects of applications processing. Note, however, that the auditor does not necessarily test *every* control or every aspect of processing but only those that the auditor has predetermined as being important to evaluating the particular application.

To avoid contaminating the client's existing files with test data, the auditor develops a fictitious master file against which to run the "test" transactions. Alternatively, the auditor could run the test data against a copy of the client's master files if there were reason to suspect that errors were occurring on specific accounts. The auditor precomputes the outcome and then compares the processed outcome with the auditor's computed outcome and investigates any differences. The auditor attempts to

Exhibit 10.1

OVERVIEW OF TEST DATA APPROACH

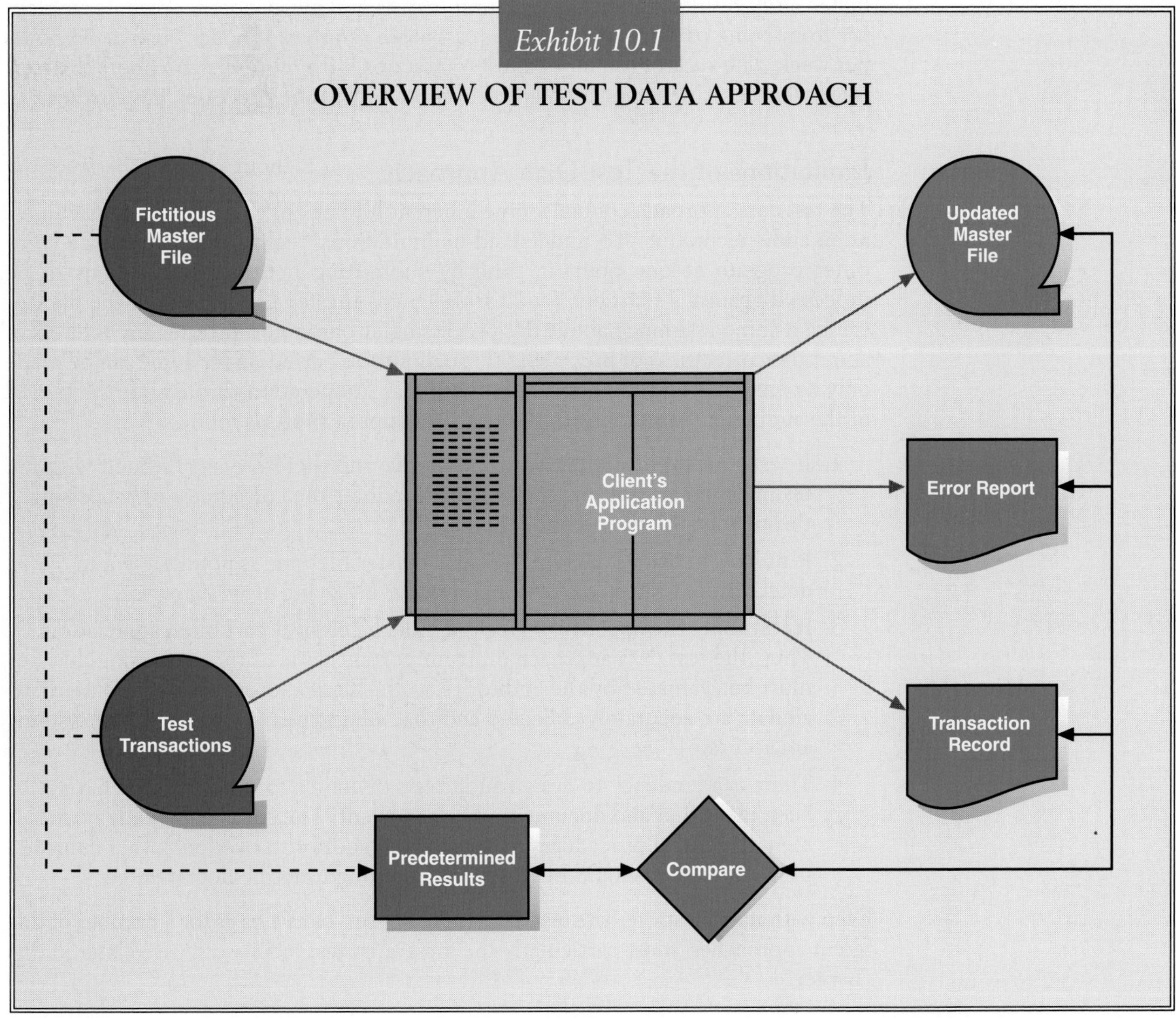

determine the potential audit impact of any differences and the extent to which processing errors or control failures affected the accounting for transactions throughout the year.

Example of Controls to be Tested Using the Test Data Approach

The auditor considers using the test data approach for applications that process high volumes of transactions throughout the year and in which computerized edit controls are considered important. A typical application meeting such criteria is payroll. Often the payroll system contains numerous edit tests and processes relatively noncomplex transactions that update a number of important files.

The test data approach begins with the identification of *key* control procedures that affect the integrity of the application. Examples of control procedures and potential test data are shown in Exhibit 10.2. For each control or calculation identified, the auditor designs specific tests by submitting test data to the application for processing. The actual results from the processing are then compared with the predicted audit results. For example, a limit test, as previously noted, prevents employees from being paid for more than a reasonable number of hours, such as 55 hours per week. The auditor can input a test transaction with more than 55 hours to determine whether it will appear on an edit report and not be processed any further.

Limitations of the Test Data Approach

The test data approach contains some inherent limitations that restrict its usefulness as an audit technique. To understand its limitations, realize that it tests the computer program at one point in time by submitting fictitious transactions to be processed against a fictitious (auditor-designed) master file. Although the auditor can gain some assurance about the processing at one point in time, any inferences about the correctness of processing throughout the period under audit can be made only by ensuring that the application used was in operation throughout the period of the audit. The limitations to the test data approach are as follows:

1. It tests the application at *one point in time* and therefore it is difficult without testing controls over program changes to infer the correctness of processing throughout the period under audit.
2. It utilizes fictitious data on fictitious master files and is not designed to detect processing errors that might occur involving *active employees.*
3. It tests only the *application program,* not the clerical part of an application. Thus, the test data approach omits important parts of the processing that must be evaluated by the auditor (e.g., the clerical processing to ensure that all data are accurately collected and that all updates to "tables" in the system are accurate).
4. There is a tendency to design audit tests of control procedures that have been identified and documented by the client. The focus on already documented control procedures may cause the auditor to overlook other control procedures that should be tested but that might not be documented.

Even with its limitations, the test data approach serves as a basis for a number of different approaches, most particularly the integrated test facility discussed later in this chapter.

Exhibit 10.2

USING TEST DATA IN A PAYROLL APPLICATION

Type of Control	Example of Control	Potential Test Data
Limit test	Weekly hourly payroll for an individual employee should not exceed 55 hours.	Input transactions for hours less than 55 and greater than 55 to determine if processed correctly.
Logical relationships	Social Security withholding to date should not exceed gross pay to date times the rate (up to the maximum amount of withholding).	Input errors in the master file and current payroll that would cause the relationship to be in error and determine whether controls detect the errors.
	Gross pay to date does not exceed the maximum hours worked to date times the employee's wage rate for the employee's job class.	Submit data both above and below the stated amounts to determine correctness of control operation.
Validity tests	All time data must be numeric, and all employee name and address fields, etc., must be alpha characters.	Develop test data that input alpha characters for numeric fields and vice versa.
	All employee numbers are valid and include appropriate check digits.	Develop set of data to test company's criteria for valid employee numbers and test correct calculation of check digits.
	Wage rate applied in calculating pay is consistent with employee job category.	Submit test data for employees with diverse labor categories and determine whether the correct wage rate is applied.
Calculations	All calculations are made correctly including gross pay, authorized deductions, and net pay.	Develop test data that cover a wide variety of job classifications, wage rates (e.g., labor contracts), various withholding provisions, etc., and determine that calculations are correct.

Fraud Analysis: A Good Application for Test Data

A common computer fraud is to add a code to a computer program to be executed only on encountering specific criteria. For example, a bank fraud may be implemented by a programmer inserting a code that says, "If it is my account, do not print any overdraft messages." From a programming view, the coding looks like this:

```
IF ACCOUNT-NO. EQUAL 8075EMP GO TO EMP-MODULE ELSE
CONTINUE
```

The programmer has implemented a module that is executed only if a transaction affects his or her account. Because test data normally do not use live data, it is reasonable to ask how test data might detect such a fraud. Fortunately, other software, often referred to as *process tracing software*, can complement the use of test data. The process tracing software identifies computer program modules that *were not executed* by the test data. The auditor then reviews the computer code of the nonexecuted modules to determine whether the modules and the flow of the program might be fraudulent.

Integrated Test Facility

The **integrated test facility (ITF)** is a logical extension of the test data approach and is designed to overcome a major limitation of test data that confines test results to one point in time. In utilizing an ITF approach, the auditor (usually an internal auditor) develops a "dummy company" against which transactions are submitted for processing concurrently with normal processing of other transactions by the application. The testing is transparent, that is, data processing does not know when the computer application is being tested. Audit objectives are similar to those for test data: to determine whether (1) controls are working properly, (2) processing is performed correctly, and (3) all files are correctly and completely updated. An ITF also has the ability to detect misstatements that might have been caused by changes made to the program during the year. For example, the data processing department might have changed the payroll program for calculating fringe benefits but omitted a related change to charge the increased expense to departments. If the auditor tests the application shortly after the change, the error in logic will likely be discovered because the computer-generated output will differ from the auditor's expectations.

ITFs are particularly well suited to environments in which applications process data for numerous departments or divisions at the same time. For example, the payroll application for a major insurance company may do the processing for over 100 departments. The auditor can utilize the ITF by establishing a division against which the transaction data can be processed. Normally, such a process is developed with the full knowledge and assistance of data processing and is aimed at testing the continuing integrity of the application, not for detecting computer programmer fraud. Most errors in accounting applications occur because of inadvertent errors rather than fraudulent transactions; thus, the ITF can be very effective in many environments.

Because the transactions are run against the "live" program, there is a potential problem that the fictitious data could update the general ledger accounts. Auditors generally have two choices in dealing with such a problem. One solution is to submit reversing journal entries to the controller to back out the transactions recorded as a result of the ITF processing. A more common solution is to design the ITF so that the transactions for the "dummy entity" are "peeled off" and not used to update the accounting records. An overview of the ITF in which the transactions are split off before updating is shown in Exhibit 10.3.

To summarize, the ITF concurrently tests computer applications as the application normally processes other transactions. It is ideally suited for environments in which the application processes data for numerous departments or divisions. The

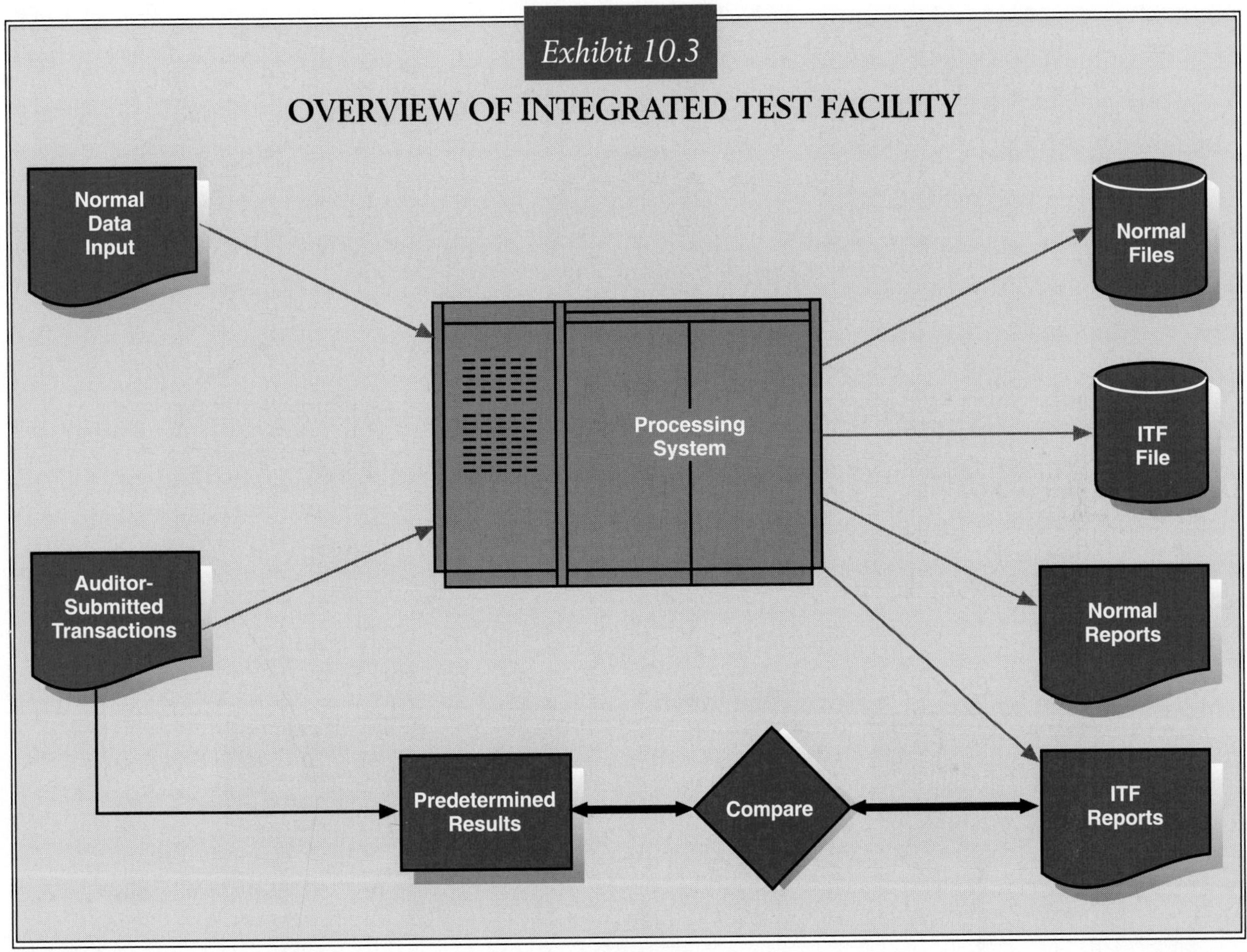

ITF provides assurance about the correctness of processing and operation of controls but depends on the test data developed by the auditor. The ITF processes data against a live program, but normally does not process data against "live files," (although such an approach has occasionally been utilized by auditors). Because of its development cost, it is most often implemented by internal auditors.

Parallel Simulation

Parallel simulation is an alternative approach used to evaluate the correctness of current processing. Instead of submitting test data to be processed by the computer application, a portion of the application program is simulated using generalized audit software (GAS) or an auditor-prepared program against which actual transactions are processed, such as processing yesterday's transactions and comparing the output with the output obtained from the client's program. An overview of the parallel simulation approach is shown in Exhibit 10.4.

The auditor utilizes parallel simulation to address concerns about problems encountered in the processing of "actual" transactions (including the possibility of fraud) by a client. For example, the auditor may be concerned that a program used to compute daily interest may have been modified so that calculations for selected

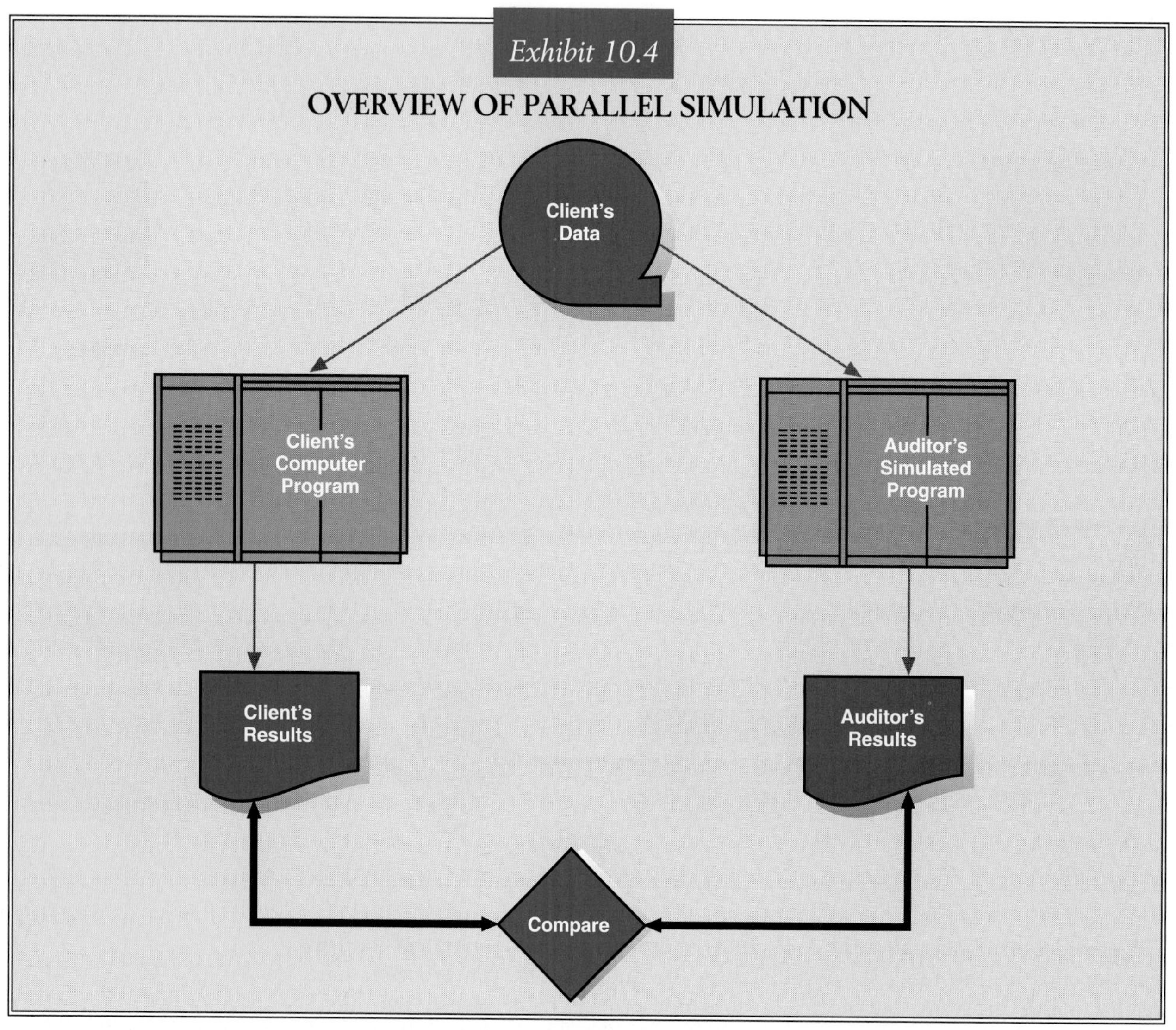

employees might be in error. The error may be caused by the insertion of a code that causes the daily interest to be truncated at the second digit even though it calculates daily interest to four digits. The truncated digits (the one-hundredths of a cent) may be added to a programmer's or employee's account. Such fraud would not be easily detectable by test data unless fraud were suspected and process tracing were used, or the auditor were particularly alert to errors occurring at the one cent level due to inappropriate rounding.

To use parallel simulation the auditor in the preceding example would develop and test a simulated program for the part of the application that computes the daily interest.* Once developed, the auditor would process the same data through the

*Parallel simulation does *not* simulate the complete accounting application because many of the accounting applications were developed at considerable cost and may include many years of developmental time. Rather, parallel simulation focuses on the development of a particular portion of the application that is crucial to the auditor and then uses that portion to compare with the client's processing.

simulated program that was processed by the client's "live" program and then perform a detailed comparison of the output of the two processes. If there are no differences, the auditor would be confident that the program is processing data correctly. If differences are noted, the auditor would investigate to determine their cause and extent.

Concurrent Transaction Selection and/or Tracing Methodologies

Concurrent audit techniques consist of audit modules or other programming code built by the auditor and implemented directly into important computer applications to select and monitor the processing of data. As such, concurrent audit techniques are likely to receive increased use in complex and interconnected computer applications. Two of the most promising of these methods are referred to as the snapshot approach and the systems control audit review file approach.

The Snapshot Approach

The **snapshot approach** creates a "snapshot" of a preselected transaction as it is processed through key points in the computer application. It is not really a snapshot in the literal sense, but usually consists of a printout or electronic record of the status of the transaction at various points in a process, and might include the value of the transaction, the date, the point in the process at which the snapshot is taken, the value of a record before and after its update, and any other information prespecified by the auditor. A snapshot might take a transaction submitted by a remote terminal in Phoenix, trace its processing through a communications system in Denver, and its updating of files in Chicago. An example of the process and the snapshot data that might be generated is shown in Exhibit 10.5.

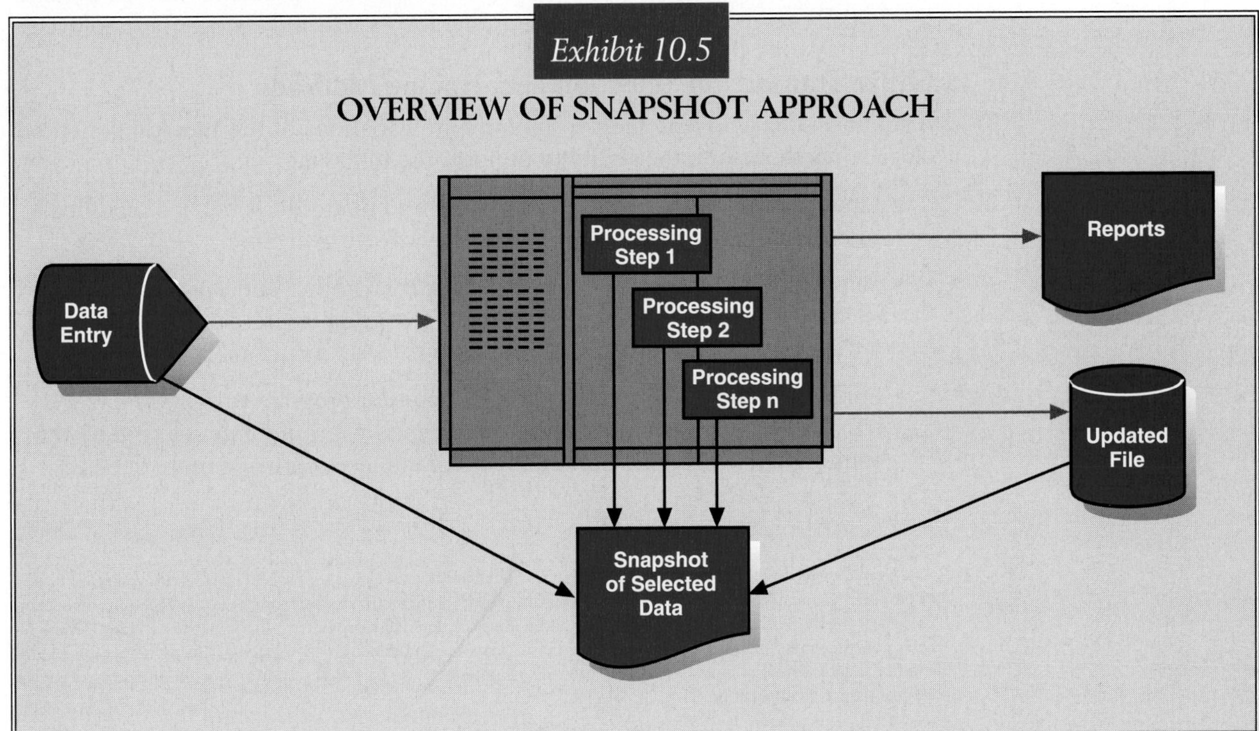

An important advantage of the snapshot approach is that it works concurrently with the client's processing of regular transactions. The auditor selects transactions to be marked to generate the snapshot later in processing. The transactions can be randomly selected at various input points or judgmentally selected by the implementation of specific criteria (e.g., dollar size of the transaction), which would be programmed into the application. It allows the auditor to effectively trace transactions through complex computer systems and ensure the correctness and completeness of its processing.

The ability to randomly choose transactions at a point early in the processing cycle* provides evidence on the accuracy, completeness, and timeliness of processing in complex computer networks. As such, it is well suited for gathering evidence in EDI or similar networked environments.

The SCARF Approach

The **systems control and audit review facility (SCARF)** approach differs from the snapshot in that SCARF requires the auditor to install code into the computer application to select transactions that meet specified audit criteria for subsequent audit review. The auditor codes selection criteria so that all selected transactions are written out to a file for subsequent audit review (hence the name system control audit review file) to be examined for the completeness and accuracy of the processing, as well as the operating effectiveness of selected control procedures.

A common use of SCARF is to select for review all transactions that are processed by overriding edit controls. An example would be selecting for review all bank transfers over $5 million to determine whether supervisory approval had been obtained. Often these resubmitted transactions are correct, but the auditor wants to know if the authorization system is breaking down. The auditor may use SCARF to select transactions that had violated edit criteria to determine whether there is a pattern to them. Routinely overridden edit controls may indicate a problem with the parameters initially set for the edit or a pattern that favors selected vendors or employees.

Other Transaction Selection and Tracing Methods

A number of concurrent audit techniques are variations of the preceding methodologies. These include the ability to perform the following:

- Input transaction selection criteria on-line so that criteria may be modified to suit audit objectives and concerns as they evolve over time.
- Select transactions as a precursor to performing other audit procedures. For example, transactions could be selected according to pre-defined criteria and once selected, a confirmation could be written to a customer.
- Implement "hooks" (modules) in the computer program to provide data on transactions that have been either judgmentally or randomly selected by the auditor. These modules are usually programmed to provide more detailed

*Even though the example given suggests that the data have been selected for processing when they were input into a computer terminal, it is also possible for the auditor to mark a transaction for selection before it encounters any manual processing by clerical employees. Thus, the audit approach could also provide feedback on the accuracy, completeness, and timeliness of transaction processing before data are entered into the system. The accumulation of this additional data would, of course, require greater development on the part of the auditor in gathering data during the manual part of an application.

Practice Observation

INTERNAL AUDITING AND INFORMATION SYSTEMS AUDIT TECHNIQUES

The need to provide greater assurance to management as to the integrity and risks associated with advanced computer systems has led to the development of a subset of auditing commonly referred to as *information systems auditing.* As of 1993, one organization (the Information Systems Auditor's Association) is solely devoted to meeting the needs of information systems auditors. These needs are often met by sharing experiences on implementing concurrent audit techniques.

Many of the concurrent audit techniques have been implemented by internal auditors. The internal auditor's information systems audit work can affect the external auditor's work in four important ways. First, it may act as an important control element that improves the integrity of computerized applications. Second, the internal auditor may evaluate the control structure of data processing. Those evaluations—when made by an objective, competent, and independent internal audit department—can serve as important input to the external auditor's own control evaluations. Third, the internal auditor's proper use of concurrent audit techniques can provide the external auditor with substantial evidence about the integrity of important computer applications. Fourth, the external auditor may find it efficient to work with the internal audit department to submit test data or select transactions for testing. Alternatively, the external auditor may find it highly efficient to utilize concurrent audit techniques developed by internal auditors.

Internal auditors often participate in evaluating the adequacy of control procedures designed for new application developments. In many cases, internal auditors represent the most knowledgeable source of information about the strengths and weaknesses of a client's computer system and its major applications.

There will be increasing cooperation between internal and external auditors in planning and conducting the audit of a company's financial statements. The external auditor should assess the competence and objectivity of internal auditors when deciding how much to utilize work done by them. As organizations become more aware of their vulnerability to computer systems, the work of the internal "information systems" auditors will take on increasing importance.

printout of information than is normally obtained through the snapshot approach.

Research shows that these methods are beginning to be used increasingly by internal auditors in the financial services and insurance industries. These industries are involved with integrated data processing and provide a barometer of future audit needs in other organizations.

Concurrent Audit Techniques, Internal Auditors, and Systems Development

The alert reader will note that virtually all of the concurrent audit techniques require considerable audit development as well as computer program development. Although programming can be retrofitted to existing applications, it is much less costly and more efficient if auditability is designed into the application during its development. The majority of concurrent audit techniques have been implemented by internal auditors. External auditors need to work closely with internal auditors to determine that the latter are actively building "auditability" into important applications and performing *systems design audits* of new application developments to ensure that adequate controls are built into the application. The external auditor will increasingly work with the internal auditor in planning audit requirements for new applications.

Audits of Tables (File Data)

An audit of a computer application is much more than an audit of the computerized processing. As noted earlier, the auditor must evaluate controls to ensure that all data are properly and accurately input into the computer. In evaluating complex software, the auditor is aware that data are often stored in tables (small files) that are regularly accessed by a computer application when the program is processed. For example, a payroll application accesses a wage rate file to determine the current wage rate and withholding data for employees. The auditor should ensure that access to these tables and the ability to change data in them are limited.

An accounting application's components can be depicted as shown in Exhibit 10.6. The auditor's view of an application focuses on the important components of the process, that is, the input, processing, stored data (tables), and output. The auditor can use this schematic to identify key inputs and outputs of the system. Input of

Exhibit 10.6

AUDITOR VIEW OF COMPUTER APPLICATIONS

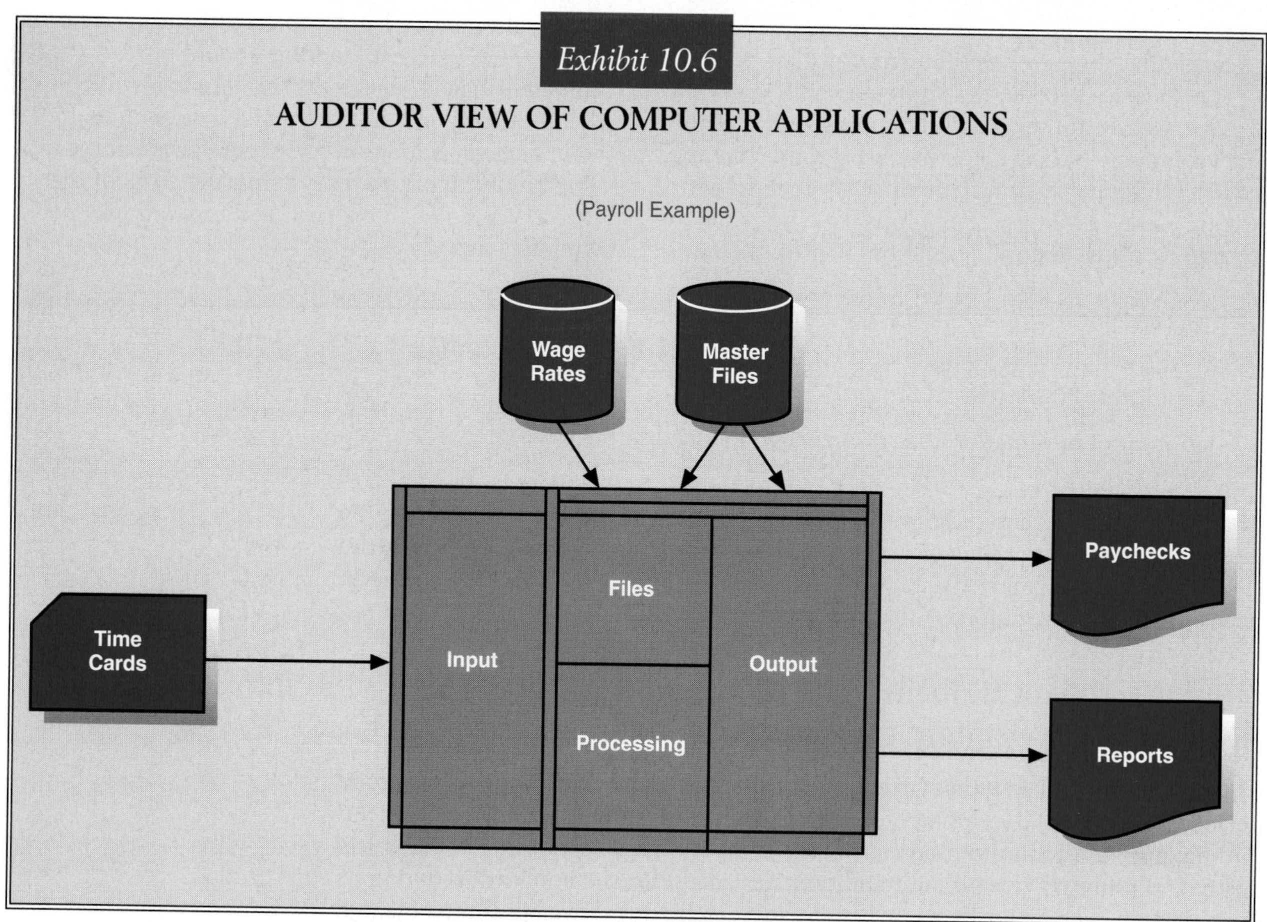

the payroll application normally includes current hours worked, and outputs include employee checks, payroll register, withholding files, and so forth. The processing involves the computation of gross and net pay. Files accessed include existing master files and data contained in tables.

The auditor should determine the quality of control procedures for the stored data. Control procedures include limiting access to the tables to supervisory personnel and preparing printouts of all changes and the contents of the file before and after changes are made and independent reconciliation by supervisory personnel.

B–USING THE COMPUTER TO HELP TEST ACCOUNTING RECORDS

Much of an auditor's work involves gathering evidence on the correctness of an account balance through the examination of the details making up the balance. For example, the auditor tests accounts receivable by gathering evidence on the existence and accuracy of receivables from individual customers through the types of procedures shown in Exhibit 10.7. Fortunately, the auditor can use computer audit tools to increase the efficiency of many of these audit procedures.

Visualize an auditor sitting in the chair in Exhibit 10.8 with a 10-inch-thick printout of the year-end accounts receivable list. Then note the general nature of the procedures performed in Exhibit 10.7: foot, test the aging, select individual items for further audit tests, print confirmations, statistically evaluate the results, and make a judgment on the need for an audit adjustment. Now visualize how long it would take for the auditor to perform those procedures accurately while working with the paper document (printout) and a calculator; adding up all the individual accounts and determining whether they agree with the amount in the general ledger or statistically selecting a sample and manually preparing the confirmation requests and verifying their accuracy.

Alternatively, an auditor with good programming skills could write a program to read the computer subsidiary ledger file and utilize the computer to perform all of the tests listed. If the auditor had verified that the correct computer file was used, a substantial amount of time could be saved. However, it takes a significant amount of time to develop such *custom programs*. Fortunately, CPA firms and software companies have developed *generalized audit software programs* to aid in performing direct tests of account balances maintained on computer files. Some of these programs are designed to run in a mainframe environment, while others work with microcomputers and can interact with data files that were created on mainframe, mini-, or microcomputers (see Exhibit 10.9).

Generalized Audit Software

Generalized audit software (GAS) is a set of computer programs designed to run on multiple computers to perform common audit tasks on a variety of data files. The GAS packages developed to date vary considerably in complexity, ability to read different file structures, and ease of use. Although the software is generalized, it is likely that a CPA firm might utilize more than one package to meet the demands of

Exhibit 10.7

SELECTED AUDIT PROCEDURES PERFORMED ON DETAILED ACCOUNTS RECEIVABLE RECORDS

1. *Obtain* an aged trial balance of individual customer balances from the client.
2. *Foot* the trial balance and check to see if it agrees with the general ledger year-end balance.
3. *Test* the client's **aging** of the customer balances to determine that individual account balances are correctly classified as current, 1 to 30 days overdue, etc. This test can be done by (1) *selecting* some individual account balances and tracing the balances to the subsidiary ledger to determine their appropriate aging or (2) *recomputing* the client's aging process for selected transactions.
4. *Confirm* individual account balances directly with customers by selecting
   a. All customer balances in excess of $50,000.
   b. All customer balances that are overdue and higher than $25,000.
   c. A random statistical sample of the remaining customer balances.
5. *Print* the confirmation requests and send to the customers selected in step 4.
6. Investigate all nonresponses to the confirmations and those indicating a disagreement with the client balance by examining underlying supporting documents such as contracts, shipping notices, correspondence with the customer and by searching for evidence of subsequent payments by the customer.
7. *Statistically evaluate* the sample and make a projection of the potential misstatement in the account balance. *Combine* the statistical projection with the known misstatements found through other audit procedures.
8. *Evaluate* the sample results and make a judgment on whether the account balance needs to be adjusted.

Note: These steps represent only selected procedures that would be performed and should not be viewed as a full audit program.

audit clients with widely varying computer environments. An auditor will most likely learn how to use the primary audit software utilized by the audit firm and a computer audit specialist will learn the capabilities of one or more complex software packages.

GAS that runs on client mainframe computers is used primarily to audit the very largest clients that do not make frequent or significant changes to their computer hardware. Installing generalized audit software on mainframe computers is time-consuming. Therefore, microcomputers are being used with increasing frequency to access client data. Microcomputer-based audit software (1) can now interact with or download data files created on other computer systems and (2) are more user friendly and have sufficient file capacity and processing speed to meet the auditor's needs for all but a handful of the largest audit clients.

Interactive GAS provides the auditor with access to client data files which may be imported data into spreadsheet, database, word processing, and other microcom-

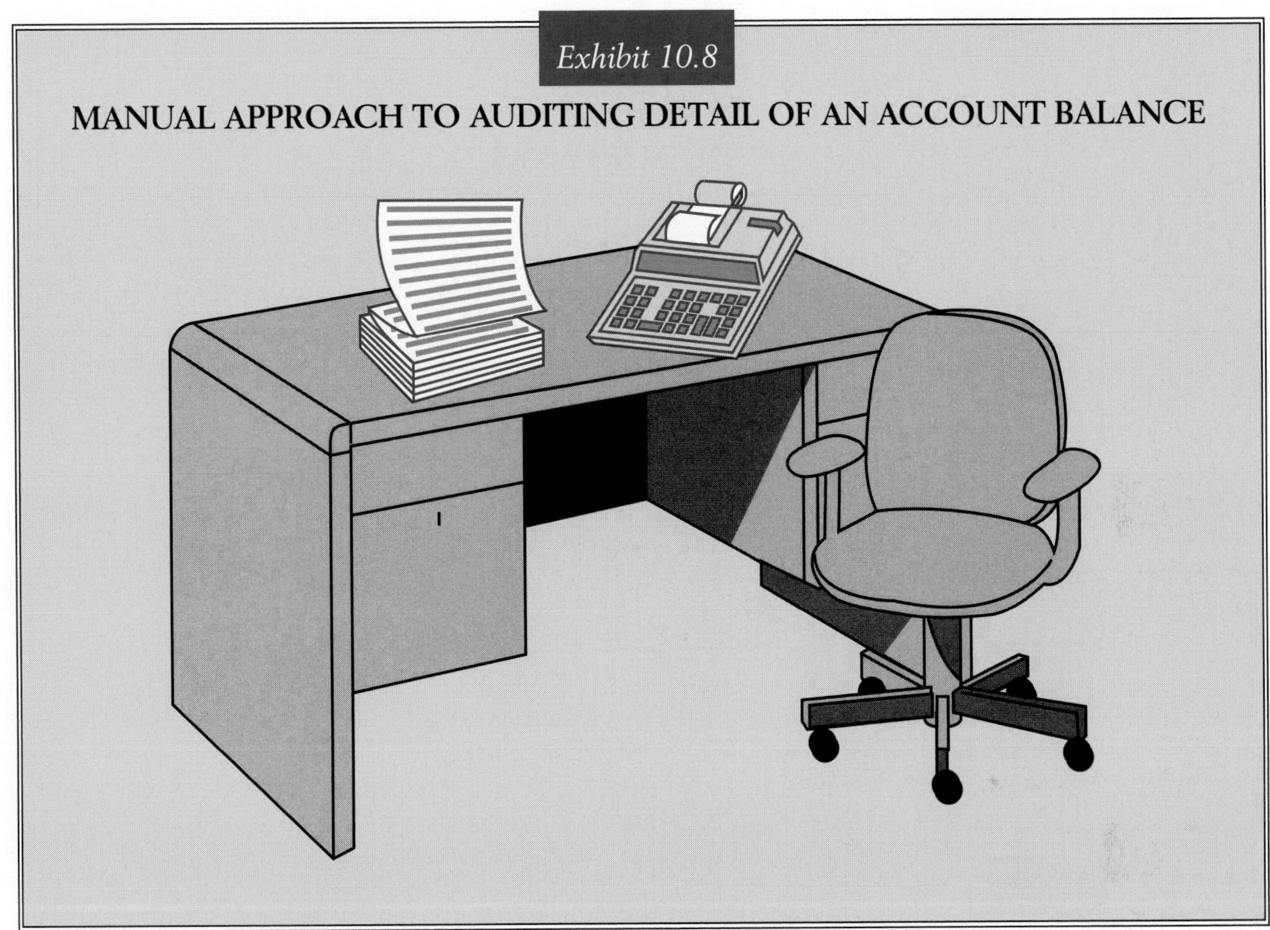

Exhibit 10.8

MANUAL APPROACH TO AUDITING DETAIL OF AN ACCOUNT BALANCE

puter programs for additional analysis. Most GAS allows auditors to download data to their microcomputer based on specified criteria. Historically, public accounting firms developed their own audit software. Today, however, there are several good commercial software packages including *APPLAUD; Audit Command Language (ACL); FOCAUDIT,* which works with a fourth-generation language called FOCUS; and *Paradox.* The Canadian Institute of Chartered Accountants has developed the program *Interactive Data Extraction and Analysis (IDEA),* which is available from the AICPA. Several public accounting firms have similar programs.

Tasks Performed by Generalized Audit Software

GAS can be used to read existing computer files and perform such functions as footing a file; selecting a sample; extracting, sorting, and summarizing data; obtaining file statistics (totals, minimum/maximum/average values); finding how many transactions or population items meet specified criteria; checking for gaps and duplicates; doing arithmetic calculations; and preparing custom reports.

The designers of GAS anticipated the need for auditors to select items from accounts, scan accounts for unusual entries, project errors based on samples, perform basic mechanical tests such as testing extensions, and perform basic and advanced mathematical functions. Based on the auditor's description of the file to be examined and proper coding of the software, GAS examines the file, selects

Exhibit 10.9

APPROACHES TO ACCESS COMPUTERIZED DATA FILES WITH GENERALIZED AUDIT SOFTWARE

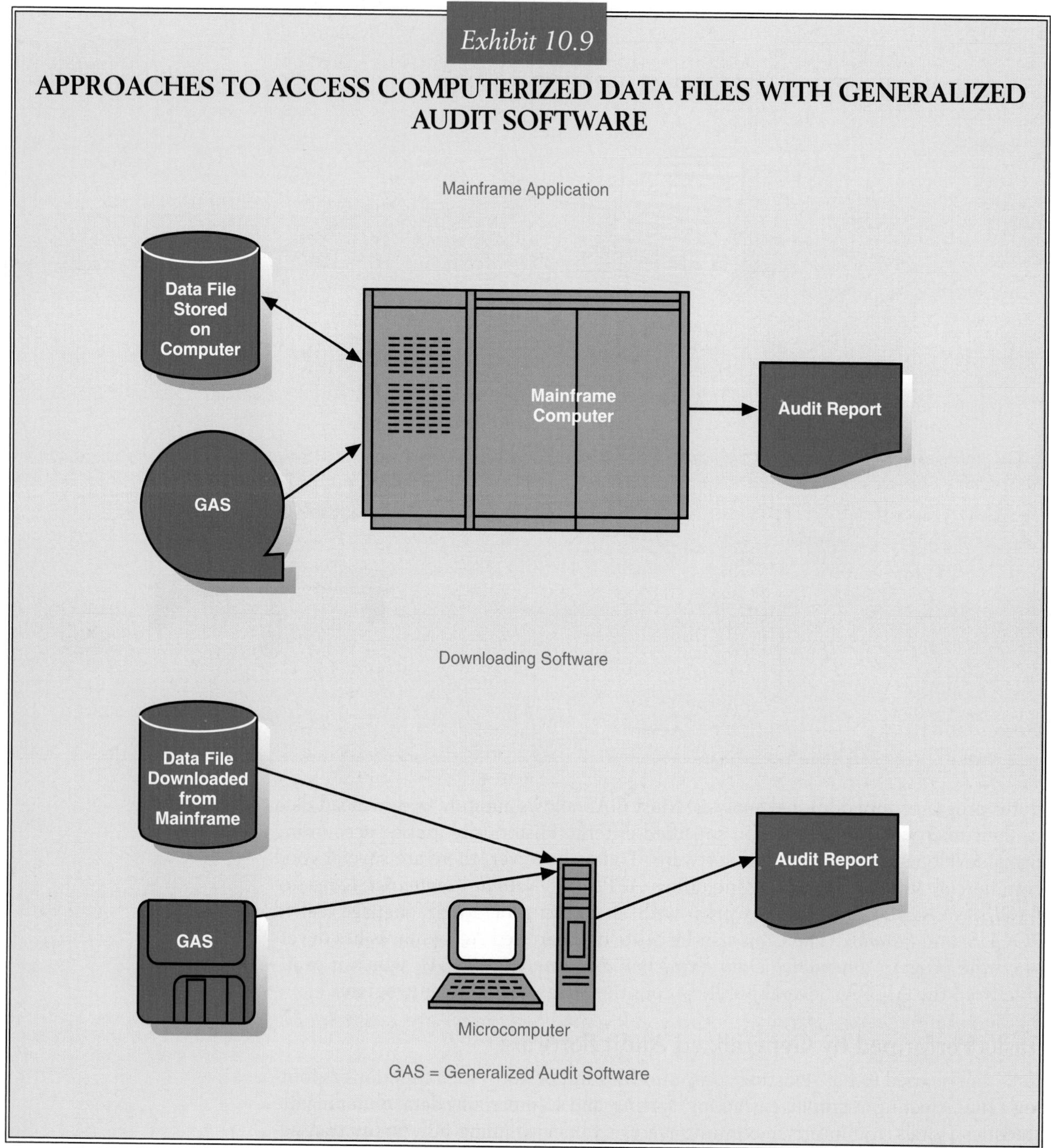

GAS = Generalized Audit Software

certain records, and creates the reports prespecified by the auditor. Although each GAS package contains unique features, most have modules to assist the auditor in performing the tasks described in the following sections.

Select Transactions Based on Logical Identifiers. Auditors often need to review transactions or subsidiary accounts that meet *specific criteria* for audit testing. For example, the auditor may want to confirm all transactions above a specific dollar limit and all those in excess of a lower dollar limit that are a specific period of time past due. Most GAS allows the auditor to select transactions based on the Boolean operators of the logical IF, GREATER THAN, LESS THAN, EQUAL TO, OR, and AND. This combination of operatives allows the auditor great flexibility in selecting transactions. For example,

> SELECT ALL TRANSACTIONS GREATER THAN $50,000 OR 30 DAYS PAST DUE IN PAYMENT

would result in the selection of *all* transactions that met *either* of these criteria. On the other hand, the following statement:

> SELECT ALL TRANSACTIONS GREATER THAN $50,000 AND 30 DAYS PAST DUE IN PAYMENT

would result in the selection of only items that met *both* conditions.

Select Statistical Samples. The auditor often needs to select samples from computerized files utilizing the statistical sampling approach most suitable for the audit objectives and population characteristics. Virtually all audit software products contain a wide variety of statistical sampling routines, as well as modules for random or systematic sampling selection. Once an auditor chooses a sampling methodology, the system then prompts the auditor to input the appropriate parameters, such as tolerable error and detection risk.

Evaluate Samples. GAS saves the sample population in both a computerized form and paper form to facilitate sample evaluation. The auditor needs only to input the exceptions for statistical evaluation and projection. The audited data can be statistically evaluated at the risk levels and tolerable error limits prespecified by the auditor. Most audit software packages have the ability to suggest additional sample sizes if the existing sample does not achieve the auditor's desired precision levels. GAS can also be programmed to make projections based on nonstatistical samples.

Print Confirmations. Audit software can be used to select account balances for independent confirmation by outsiders. Most GAS packages have the ability to print a confirmation request and attach it directly to a monthly statement sent to customers. The approach is efficient because the auditor does not have to spend additional time attaching such requests manually. In addition, the software provides a detailed list of the accounts selected for confirmation and the type of confirmation (positive, negative, or open) attached to the statement.

Analyze Overall File Validity. Most computer applications contain edit controls to detect and prevent transactions from being recorded in error. Although the auditor can test the correct functioning of these controls by other means, GAS can be used to verify the effectiveness of the controls by reading the computer file and comparing individual items with control parameters to determine whether edit controls were overridden during the year. Such an approach can be especially useful in circumstances in which the auditor may be suspicious of fraudulent activity.

Assume, for example, that the auditor has tested a control procedure that limits credit to individual customers in accordance with the credit department's rating of the customer. For example, the credit department might rate each customer on a 1 to 5 scale with a 5 representing the least credit risk. A 1 rating might indicate that shipments can be made only on a prepayment basis and a 2 rating might indicate total credit cannot exceed $5,000. The auditor could devise audit software logic to compare the current receivable balance with the maximum specified by the credit policy and generate a printout of any instances in which the receivables exceeded the specified credit limit. The auditor could then determine the extent of deviations and investigate, when necessary, the potential causes for such deviations.

Generate Control Totals. Most software is designed to assist the auditor in verifying that the correct file is being used. For example, assume that the auditor wishes to query the December 31, 1995, accounts receivable file containing 13,000 individual records and a balance of $75,482,919. The audit software can be programmed to develop control totals such as a record count and a footing of the balance. The software can also print out all the information utilized to identify the file to the operating system, which the auditor can then employ to verify that the correct file has been used.

Other Specialized Functions. Some software packages contain other specialized features that may be valuable to the auditor. These other features often include the ability to perform regression analysis of account balances or to read complex database files.

Implementing Generalized Audit Software in an Audit Situation

The implementation process in an audit situation begins with meetings with the client's data processing personnel to gain access to the system, obtain copies of the data files at the testing date, or to arrange processing. The planning begins during the auditor's interim work and continues through the year-end work. Once arrangements have been made to facilitate audit software use, the auditor performs the following steps:

1. Identify the client's computerized files to be read by audit software or to be downloaded to a microcomputer to be read by the audit software. Develop a description of the file characteristics to facilitate audit software use including
   a. *Type* and *location* of the file (e.g., indexed—sequential file contained on disk or sequential file contained on tape).
   b. Description of the file including specification of each field
      1. Length of records and individual data fields.
      2. Type of field such as alpha or numeric.
2. Determine the computer configuration and operating system on which the file is contained.
3. Determine whether to run the software on the client's computer system or to download the data to a microcomputer.
4. Develop the job control language (commands that tell the operating system the specific files and programs to be utilized), if run on a mainframe system.
5. If run on a mainframe system, monitor operating system messages that might indicate difficulties in running the program or addressing the correct file.

Because some aspects of utilizing GAS tend to be more technical, they are often carried out under the supervision of a **computer audit specialist** within the firm. However, the trend is to move more of the processing to auditor-owned microcomputers run by audit seniors rather than specialists.

Example of Coding of Audit Software

Most software is designed for easy use by knowledgeable persons. After design, the auditor's coding is interpreted by a compiler and is used to generate a program that describes the file to be read and the procedures to be performed. An example of the number of commands needed by the auditor to foot an account balance and to select account balances over $50,000 or over 30 days old and to select remaining items on a statistical basis is shown in Exhibit 10.10. Similar coding techniques are finding their way to microcomputers with more user-friendly menu-oriented processing.

Custom-Designed Software

An alternative to GAS is to use **custom-designed software** where needed for individual clients. Although referred to as custom designed, this software normally contains a number of utilities that might be used in different environments and often

Exhibit 10.10

PROGRAMMING FOR GENERALIZED AUDIT SOFTWARE

Note: Software coding is designed to select all current balances (less than 30 days old) over $50,000 and any noncurrent balance (over 30 days old) over $25,000. The remaining items are selected using a statistical sampling approach. The specific field identifiers have not been input into the example.

```
001  FOOT        [A/R BALANCE]   DETAIL-TOTAL
002  COMMENTS    SELECT INVOICES FOR CONFIRMATION AND PUT TO TAPE AND
                 PRINT A REPORT ITEMS SELECTED.
003  INCLUDE     [A/R BALANCE]   50,000       GRT
004  INCLUDE     [DATES]         30           LES
005  EXIT
006  INCLUDE     [A/R BALANCE]   25,000       GRT
007  INCLUDE     [DATES]         30           GRT
008  EXIT
009  PRINTDTL
010  TAPE        PUT REMAINING ITEMS IN TAPE FOR STAT SAMPLE.
010  STATSAMPL   [A/R BALANCE]   PARAMETERS TO BE SPECIFIED.
011  EXIT
```

assists the auditor in developing evidence in more complex computerized environments. For example, consider the technology used in telephone systems such as those at AT&T or MCI that controls the management of phone calls and gathers information for accounting and billing purposes. GAS is not normally designed to interface with such a complex computer environment. The auditor may choose to develop specific data extraction programs that can be efficiently used with several telephone companies or clients within several divisions of a larger company. Examples of customized audit software and tasks that can be accomplished by the software are shown in Exhibit 10.11.

Exhibit 10.11

OVERVIEW OF CUSTOMIZED AUDIT SOFTWARE

Audit Tool	Use	Advantages	Disadvantages
Customized extract programs	Performing specialized functions not performed by GAS. Commonly used in banks and telephone and insurance companies where file sizes are extremely large and processing efficiency is important.	Efficient processing. Interface with complex client applications.	Requires specialized knowledge and computer audit support on the engagement. Might not contain standard GAS modules such as statistical sampling and may still require GAS as a supplement.
Report writers and other query utilities	Helping nontechnical users query complex databases. Some packages contain sampling techniques and many come standard with database management systems.	Very efficient alternative to query databases or other complex data structures.	May require auditor to learn a number of query packages. The packages belong to the clients, are not controlled by the auditor, and may or may not contain all needed modules.
Systems utility packages	Performing standard tasks such as sorting or analyzing files.	Powerful and conveniently located and installed on client's hardware.	Requires expertise to use efficiently, functions performed are limited.
Code comparison software	Reading two versions of a client's computer program and comparing the code to identify changes made in the programs.	Effective in gaining assurance about changes made in application programs.	Requires the auditor to maintain a copy of the client's application program against which changes are to be measured.

C–USE OF THE MICROCOMPUTER IN PERFORMING THE AUDIT

Advances in microcomputer technology have made it possible to pack the power of a mainframe computer of a decade ago into a small box that can be carried to the audit engagement. Today's microcomputer has significant power and data storage capacities that allow the auditor to utilize them on virtually all audits. Although the microcomputer will continue as an individual audit tool with spreadsheet and word processing capabilities, public accounting firms are taking advantage of their data processing and storage capabilities to accomplish tasks that had formerly been reserved for only large-scale computers. This section introduces microcomputer technologies as they might be utilized on an audit.

Traditional Uses of Microcomputers: Word Processing and Spreadsheets

The use of microcomputers for word processing and spreadsheet applications has greatly increased audit efficiency. Word processing provides the ability to document and update major memos related to the audit, footnotes to the client's financial statements, audit programs, planning documents, and a host of other functions. Advances in word processing software now make it possible to incorporate spreadsheet functions such as time management within the context of the word processing program.

The microcomputer spreadsheet has significantly affected auditing practice. **Spreadsheets** can be utilized by clients and auditors to routinely carry out tasks such as performing consolidations, ratio and trend analysis; developing prospective financial statements; summarizing audit tests for particular accounts; and posting adjustments to trial balances. Audit firms will assume that an auditor is competent in utilizing one or more spreadsheet packages and has the ability not only to perform math functions using a spreadsheet but also to download data from a mainframe for analysis or to incorporate a spreadsheet analysis into a printed document developing graphical presentations to assist in understanding financial trends. Current uses of spreadsheets are listed in Exhibit 10.12.

Expanded Uses of Microcomputer Software

Documenting and Evaluating Control Structure

Many public accounting firms have developed microcomputer programs to assist the auditor in documenting and evaluating a client's control structure. The software is necessarily based on the firm's overall audit methodology for evaluating control structure. Some provide automated flowcharting capabilities while others are designed around the firm's internal control questionnaires.

Utilizing software for control evaluations has two distinct advantages. First, it is relatively easy to update for changes in the control structure. Second, most control evaluation software has built-in decision support aids to assist the auditor in linking potential control deficiencies to substantive audit procedures. For example, if it

Exhibit 10.12

SPREADSHEET APPLICATIONS ON AUDIT ENGAGEMENTS

Audit Application	Description
Financial statement analysis	Audited financial statement data for the past five years are stored on a spreadsheet. The auditor inputs this year's unaudited financial data. Financial analysis procedures such as ratio or trend analysis are performed as a basis for directing the auditor's planning to potential problem areas.
Consolidations	A spreadsheet containing macros for recurring consolidation entries is developed. Audited financial data are either input into the spreadsheet or are imported to the spreadsheet from other spreadsheets and the consolidation is performed.
Regression analysis	Data compiled from previous year audits can be used as a database for predicting the current balance in the account being audited within specified precision ranges.
Graphical analysis	Financial ratios or other information can be generated from spreadsheets and printed in a graphical form to show relationships among data that might not be apparent from just viewing the data themselves. The graphical presentations may also be useful in analyzing and presenting data to client management to assist in their understanding of trends affecting the organization.
Statistical evaluation	Templates can be evaluated to assist the auditor in evaluating samples on either a judgmental basis or calculating statistical parameters from a PPS sample or other sampling methodology.
Detailed analysis of account balance	Spreadsheets can be highly useful in performing detailed analysis of an account. The analysis may include regression or trend analysis on an individual account or may summarize the extent of work performed on it.

appears that controls are deficient, the software will suggest substantive tests to address potential financial statement errors that may be caused by the control deficiency. This is an important advantage because it can raise the auditor's awareness of possible errors or irregularities that might occur in the financial statements and how they might occur.

Access to Database Information

Laser disk technology has made it possible to store and access large amounts of data on a small disk. Copies of substantial databases can now be made on laser disk for a relatively nominal amount. Given the complexity of today's accounting standards, some CPA firms provide their auditors with instant access to the firm's internal accounting and auditing documents as well as authoritative accounting and auditing pronouncements, all on a laser disk the size of a compact disk. The laser disks are updated on a frequent basis.

The AICPA and some accounting firms provide microcomputer linkages to mainframe computer systems such as Mead Data Central to provide similar access to audit teams. The AICPA linkage, called Total On-Line Tax and Accounting Library (TOTAL), provides access to tax laws, regulations, IRS materials, and tax analysis literature. A library of over 4,000 corporate annual reports, authoritative accounting and auditing literature, government regulations, company analyses, and business and legal publications are all available. These services allow the auditor to perform a computer search of all authoritative information on a particular issue without going to a library or leaving the office. Valuable information about clients and their industries is at the auditor's fingertips.

Auditors can search these databases through keyword searches or by identifying an authoritative pronouncement to be reviewed. For example, assume that the auditor wishes to review notes of other companies to determine how redeemable preferred stock was disclosed. The auditor could search the National Automated Accounting Research Service (NAARS) database for all instances in which the phrase "redeemable preferred stock" was utilized in a note to the financial statements. Alternatively, the auditor could search the CPA firm's disk for internal and professional references on accounting for redeemable preferred stock.

Expert Systems

Expert systems are computer programs designed to emulate expert human judgment. The basic premise behind expert systems is that some decision makers (presumably those who have risen to the top ranks in a firm and have shown insight in making key decisions in the past) are better at analyzing some situations and making judgments than is the traditional staff person. For example, some CPAs may exhibit more expertise in tax issues, in evaluating a bank's loan portfolio for potential loan loss reserves, in evaluating a client's computer data processing for potential control deficiencies, or in analyzing accounts receivable for potential losses. Researchers working in the expert systems area (sometimes referred to as *artificial intelligence*) believe that experts have developed systematic approaches to evaluating problems and that these systematic approaches can be emulated through the development of computerized expert systems.

Expert systems have been developed by CPA firms for the areas identified above: preparing tax returns (EXPERT-TAX), evaluating loan loss reserves in financial institutions (LOAN-PROBE), evaluating EDP internal control, estimating accounts receivable losses, judging materiality, and identifying financial institutions for investigation by a federal agency. The expert systems in use today are designed to supplement, not to replace, the auditor's judgment. The expert systems identify areas that should be considered and develop tentative conclusions and the support for those conclusions. When choosing to deviate from the solution suggested by the system, the auditor should document the decision and the rationale for it. The state of development of such systems is presently such that the CPA firms cannot afford to have auditors simply acquiesce to the decisions suggested by the system. However, the discipline inherent in the systems can impose a structure on the auditors in a worldwide or national firm that ensures that all important factors in a decision are recognized and evaluated by the auditor. A more detailed description of expert systems and their development is covered in Chapter 23.

Audit Program Generation

The AICPA and a number of public accounting firms have developed audit program generators that utilize microcomputers. For example, an auditor can select the account balance area and the program will generate a number of different audit procedures, depending on the adequacy of the client's control structure for the area under audit investigation. The auditor can then select procedures and thereby generate a printout of an audit program tailored to the particular client. Some of the software assists the auditor in choosing particular audit procedures by providing a decision aid that evaluates the effectiveness of alternative procedures.

Statistical Sampling and Evaluation

Virtually all the sampling techniques normally used by auditors have been implemented in microcomputer software. These software packages calculate sample size, generate random numbers, select samples, and statistically evaluate sampling results. Some software allows the auditor to perform financial analysis of accounts and use regression analysis.

Audit Planning

Many firms have developed microcomputer capabilities to consolidate and summarize large amounts of data needed to effectively plan, and document the planning of, an audit engagement. Software can efficiently analyze current year financial results and compare them with previous year results or industry data. The software can utilize decisions made by the auditor on such areas as materiality and control risk and incorporate those judgments into audit programs.

Audit Working Paper Software

The AICPA and many firms have developed microcomputer software to facilitate the preparation of audit working papers and to perform certain analytical procedures. The AICPA's software, *Accountant's Trial Balance,* can enter adjusting and reclassifying entries that are automatically posted to lead schedules and the trial balance, creating new totals. Trial balances for prior years can be retained. Analytical routines calculate basic ratios and provide dollar and percent changes from the prior year for each account. If industry or budget data are entered, the software provides comparative information. Some of the software packages assist in the preparation of income tax returns. Some CPA firms have implemented "paper-less" audits on selected clients and are expected to continue to do even more in the near future.

Automatic Generation of Documents

Software has been developed to allow the auditor to create tailored documents for each client by modifying standard documents through word processing capabilities. The software is often used to create engagement, confirmation, and management representation letters; audit, review, and compilation reports; audit programs; standard working papers, and other documents routinely used on a particular engagement.

D–AUDITING COMPUTERIZED APPLICATIONS: NEW CHALLENGES

The computer environment has been characterized by rapid change throughout its short history. The speed at which rapid advances in technology are being implemented ensures that the audit environment 10 years from now will be increasingly computerized and interconnected. Four major changes seem certain to be implemented and will have an audit impact this decade:

1. Electronic data interchange (EDI).
2. End-user computing.
3. Distributed processing.
4. Database management systems.

Electronic Data Interchange

The use of EDI is dramatically increasing because of the size of today's organizations and because the volume of paper associated with existing transactions dictates that organizations find a more efficient way to handle the large volumes of transactions with its clients, vendors, and banking institutions. Most companies and most banks have already implemented electronic funds transfer capabilities. Most of an organization's assets (as well as our own assets) exist only in the form of electronic media stored on a computer system. Auditors will consider the concurrent audit techniques discussed in this chapter to continuously monitor the integrity of these systems. An annual review will not be sufficient because the risks of failure in such systems are so large that failure could put some organizations out of business.

End-User Computing

One of the more significant developments in the past five years has been the improvement of fourth-generation languages (4GLs), which bring the user friendliness of the microcomputer to large-scale (mainframe) computing. With a 4GL, an end user can interact with organizational databases and develop applications, many of which will directly or indirectly affect the financial statements. For example, an actuarial department of an insurance company might develop an application to estimate the reserves for its lines of insurance products. The data developed from end-user applications will directly affect the financial statements. The risk, however, is that the applications may not be subjected to the control and documentation requirements that have become typical of mainframe computing developments. There may be a higher control risk when end user computing begins to significantly affect financial statement balances because end users, who believe that they do not make mistakes, often bypass traditional controls.

The most widely used form of **end-user computing** is the development of electronic spreadsheets for such areas as consolidations, foreign exchange transactions, allocation of production overhead, and calculation of reserve or allowance balances. The auditor is faced with auditing data that are generated by these spreadsheets. The spreadsheets are not often tested independently of the developer and may not have sophisticated controls built into them. Thus, the auditor will most likely consider some method to test the output of the spreadsheet directly. Three approaches exist for the auditor to consider:

1. *Parallel simulation approach.* The auditor creates a spreadsheet to perform the critical functions included in the client's spreadsheet. The auditor then verifies the accuracy of the input data and runs them through the auditor's spreadsheet and the client's spreadsheet to determine that the same results are obtained.
2. *Test data approach.* The auditor prepares some test data and inputs them into the client's spreadsheet to determine that all critical computations are carried out correctly.
3. *Manual audit approach.* The auditor manually recomputes key calculations based on the data input into the client's spreadsheet to determine the accuracy and completeness of the spreadsheet's calculations.

Distributed Processing

Networking and *distributed processing* are rapidly becoming watchwords of computer processing. Most computer systems are, or will be, networked across divisions of large organizations. In addition, most computer systems will either be linked, directly or indirectly through third-party service centers, to other organization's computer systems. An example of such linking is the commonly used debit cards most often seen as bank ATM cards.

A bank debit card holder may take the bank card to the local grocery store and use it to pay for the weekly groceries. When the card is run through the grocery store's electronic reader, it sets into motion communication messages that will, in a very short time frame, transfer funds from the user's account at the bank to the grocery store's account at its financial institution. Shortly, the user will be able to take the card on a vacation and use it at local retailers to make purchases. Retailers like the cards because they instantaneously transfer cash to their accounts and decrease the risk of bad debts. But the transfer has to be routed through data communication lines that include an intermediate data center, which communicates between the user's bank and the retailer. The extensiveness of the required communication creates opportunities for errors or irregularities. The auditor must devote considerable effort to understanding and evaluating data communication controls as they affect these types of applications.

The point in the preceding example is not that bank debit cards will be the mode of conducting business, although it may become so in the next decade, but that networking and data communication will affect virtually every business. The auditor must be prepared to assess the risks of such communication on the audit.

Database Management Systems

Database management systems represent a different way of looking at and processing data in an organization. Rather than developing multiple files to update master records as a result of transaction processing, the organization's data are organized in a database file structure. An advantage is that data are processed only once.

Most database management systems have query languages attached to the software which contain many of the selection techniques found in audit software. Some auditing firms, as well as internal auditors, use such software extensively. Alternatively, many auditing firms have developed generalized audit software capable of making inquiries to database management systems. Finally, the auditor will place a large part of the audit emphasis on the evaluation of controls associated with the database system.

Summary

It is difficult to conceive of many audit engagements in which the auditor is not heavily involved in either auditing or utilizing computer technology. As organizations become increasingly computerized—and paperless—auditors will need to reevaluate their computer audit approaches. The most likely affect of such a reassessment will be the increasing emergence of the computer audit tools discussed in this chapter as a major part of most audits. Additionally, many of these tools will be developed and implemented by sophisticated internal audit departments, and the external auditor will likely be working closely with the internal audit departments in developing approaches to auditing these systems. Quite often, the audit approach to the system will be designed at the same time that the computer application is designed. In other words, the challenges of auditing during the next decade will be to *design auditability into the application.*

Many of the approaches discussed in this chapter have been rightly identified as activities that would be implemented by the information systems audit specialists. However, we must all remember that the work performed by the computer audit specialists of 10 years ago are regularly performed by staff auditors today. Other changes will occur in the next 10 years. Today's auditor must view the computer environment as an opportunity, not as something to be avoided.

Significant Terms

computer audit specialist An individual within a CPA who has detailed knowledge in computer auditing, including the ability to implement sophisticated computer audit approaches; most firms support them with advanced training in computer auditing.

concurrent audit techniques Computer audit tools implemented within the client's applications to assist the auditor in testing transactions as they are being regularly processed by the client.

custom-designed software A computer program developed by the auditing firm for use in a particular client's operating environment; most often used on highly sophisticated computer applications.

end-user computing An alternative to traditional systems development methodology whereby the end users use advanced program languages and databases to develop their own applications independent of the data processing assistance.

generalized audit software (GAS) A computer program that contains general modules to read existing computer files and perform manipulations of the data contained on the files to accomplish audit tasks; designed to build an easy user interface that then translates the user instructions into program code to carry out the desired audit tests by reading the client's file and performing the necessary program steps.

integrated test facility (ITF) A concurrent audit technique by which auditor-submitted transactions are processed concurrently with regular processing to determine whether controls are working properly and processing is correct.

parallel simulation A static computer audit approach whereby the auditor develops a computer program intended to simulate an important part of a client's computer program to process live client data, the results of which are compared with the results obtained when the same data were processed by the client's application program.

systems control and audit review facility (SCARF) A concurrent audit technique by which transactions identified by the auditor (either specifically or by preset criteria) are written to a data file for subsequent review by the auditor to determine their completeness, correctness, and authority related to their processing.

spreadsheet Software developed initially for microcomputers that allows auditors to emulate manually prepared spreadsheets containing sophisticated mathematical functions; can be used effectively in performing "what-if" analysis and financial statement analysis and in developing significant accounting entries.

snapshot approach A concurrent audit technique whereby transactions are selected and "tagged" for future identification by the client's application program. When they are processed, specific output is generated to describe the processing to date for the transactions and the files, computations, and so on, that have been made as a function of these data being processed by the application.

test data approach A static testing approach whereby the auditor develops fictitious transactions to submit for processing by an application of interest to the auditor, the objectives of which are to determine whether (1) computerized controls are operating effectively and (2) computer processing is carried out correctly and completely.

Review Questions

A–Computer Audit Tools to Test Computer Processing

10–1 Identify the major objectives for which an auditor might utilize computer-assisted audit approaches. To what extent can one computer audit approach satisfy each objective? Identify approaches that might satisfy both objectives.

10–2 What objectives are addressed by the auditor's use of test data?

10–3 What are the significant differences between the test data approach and the integrated test facility (ITF) approach? What deficiencies of the test data approach does the ITF overcome?

10–4 Contrast the test data and the parallel simulation approaches. What are the advantages of parallel simulation over the test data approach? Identify when each approach would most likely be used.

10–5 A staff auditor was discussing the use of concurrent audit techniques with a partner during the course of an audit engagement on a client with a relatively unsophisticated computer system. The partner responded as follows:

"Concurrent audit techniques have not been utilized in the past because they are simply not efficient. Further, concurrent audit techniques accomplish only limited objectives. For the most part, auditors can satisfy themselves on most audits by using GAS on the balance sheet accounts." Do you agree or disagree with the partner's comment? How would you respond to the partner?

10–6 How do concurrent audit techniques differ from the more static audit techniques such as test data, parallel simulation, or GAS? What audit objectives are accomplished by the concurrent audit techniques that might not be accomplished by the other techniques?

10–7 To what extent can an external auditor rely on the work of the internal auditor in evaluating and testing a client's internal control structure in a data processing environment? To what extent can the external auditor rely on internal audit–implemented concurrent audit techniques in evaluating the correctness of financial statement account balances?

10–8 Briefly explain how code comparison software works and how the auditor might utilize it.

10–9 Briefly explain how the snapshot audit approach works and the objectives it addresses.

10–10 Briefly explain how the SCARF audit approach works and the objectives it addresses. Compare and contrast the SCARF approach with the snapshot approach.

10–11 Why is it important that the auditor evaluate controls over internally stored data (often referred to as *tables*)? What controls should be implemented by an organization to ensure the integrity of data contained in these files (tables)?

B–Using the Computer to Help Test Accounting Records

10–12 What is generalized audit software? What are the major audit tasks for which an auditor would use it? What are its major advantages?

10–13 A practicing auditor recently said that GAS can be used only on mainframe systems because microcomputers are not sufficient to handle the records that would be associated with clients like Ford Motor Company, Pillsbury, and Apple Computer. Do you agree? Explain.

10–14 Why might some CPA firms develop customized audit software rather than using GAS? Compare and contrast the relative advantages of GAS and customized audit software. Indicate the type of client environment in which each type of software may have a competitive advantage.

10–15 What are the major tasks generally performed by GAS?

10–16 How might an auditor perform an "overall file validity analysis" using GAS? What does the auditor expect to learn from such an analysis? How would such information be utilized in conducting the audit?

10–17 When deciding to utilize GAS on a client's computer, how can the auditor be sure that the client is actually running the software against the file the auditor wishes to examine? How does the auditor determine that the client has not modified any of the control statements that would cause the computer to modify the running of the GAS? Are these concerns any different when an auditor uses audit software on a microcomputer?

10–18 What are the major steps that must be performed in developing a GAS application? Should GAS applications be developed by staff auditors or computer audit specialists? Explain.

10–19 Identify one task, or one computer environment, in which the auditor would most likely prefer to use customized audit software as opposed to GAS.

10–20 How can auditors use GAS on different computerized files, such as accounts receivable and inventory files, that have different record formats?

C–Using the Microcomputer to Assist in Performing the Audit

10–21 An audit manager who is a computer audit specialist recently returned from a major conference on "Computer Audit, Control, and Security" and was fuming mad. He stated: "I'm tired of hearing that the most sophisticated computer auditing is being performed by internal auditors. Some of them are good, but I don't believe that statement. We have more expert systems and customized audit software than any internal audit department." In what ways might internal auditors claim to utilize more sophisticated computer audit techniques? How does one judge the "sophistication" of computer audit techniques?

10–22 What is an expert system? How might one be utilized in an audit engagement? What are the relative advantages and disadvantages of expert systems?

10–23 Identify three documents that an auditor could prepare utilizing microcomputer software in planning an audit.

10–24 It has been asserted that the microcomputer has dramatically increased the efficiency of audits. Identify five ways in which a microcomputer can be utilized to improve both the efficiency and the effectiveness of an audit.

10–25 Can an auditor ever utilize a program that was written by the client to make queries of a file or a database? If you believe the answer is yes, indicate the procedures the auditor would have to perform before utilizing such a program.

10–26 Identify five ways in which an auditor might utilize a spreadsheet in conducting an audit.

10–27 What is end-user computing? How might the increased development of end-user computing affect the audit?

10–28 How does a database management system differ from a conventional file structure? What are the implications to the audit of the client's use of database management systems for significant accounting data?

Multiple Choice Questions

10–29 A significant advantage of the integrated test facility over the test data approach is that the ITF

a. Tests the operation of manual controls that are contained in an accounting application.

b. Tests transactions throughout the time period under audit investigation.

c. Tests the correctness of processing of transactions that would not regularly be processed by the test data method.

d. Tests all of the above.

10–30 Which of the following would not be an appropriate use of GAS?

a. Developing a parallel simulation routine.

b. Reading a complete master file for an overall integrity review.

c. Reading a file to select accounts receivable transactions over $5,000 and over 30 days past due for subsequent audit analysis.

d. Generating transactions for submission to an integrated test facility.

10–31 An auditor would most likely develop customized software rather than using GAS in which of the following situations?

a. The client utilizes a database management system for inventory.

b. The client's master file is relatively small.

c. The client's processing is complex and many intermediate files are developed as part of the process of gathering data and recording a transaction.

d. The client has installed an integrated test facility and the auditor wishes to further evaluate its processing of transactions.

10–32 Electronic data interchange refers to

a. The electronic transfer of documents between organizations (e.g., sending invoices electronically between organizations).

b. The transfer of files between a division of a company and the company's centralized computer system.

c. Distributed data processing in which processing can be shifted from one of an organization's computer systems to another computer system.

d. The electronic interchange of confidential information between the client's computer system and an independent service bureau.

10–33 Which of the following would *not* be considered a limitation of the test data approach?

a. It tests data at only one point in time.

b. It can be utilized only on a specific application.

c. It tests only the processing of controls built into the application.

d. There is a tendency to design audit tests for controls that have been previously documented by the client.

10–34 Process tracing software can be utilized with test data to investigate an application for fraud because process tracing software

a. Can be utilized to trace a transaction from its origination through to the final recording of the transaction by the client's application.

b. Can compare two versions of a computer program to identify, and then trace to their sources, any changes made in the software.

c. Can trace transactions processed by the software and identify any modules of the program that were not executed.

d. Can perform all of the above activities.

10–35 The snapshot audit approach would most likely be considered for implementation when

a. The auditor is concerned with complex processing and wants detailed printouts of transactions as they are being processed.

b. The client utilizes a significant portion of batch processing and the auditor wishes to automate the reconciling of input with output.

c. The auditor wishes to select transactions to be printed out to an audit file for subsequent audit review and testing.

d. The auditor is concerned that significant edit controls are being overridden by supervisory personnel.

10–36 Public accounting firms are likely to utilize expert systems to

a. Supplement the auditor's judgment in areas where defined answers are not clear-cut.

b. Ensure that all major aspects of a judgment are identified and appropriate factors affecting such a judgment are considered.

c. Train staff auditors regarding factors affecting significant audit adjustments.

d. Perform all of the above.

10–37 Database management systems differ from traditional accounting file structures in that

a. A database organizes data and their relationships into one file structure rather than in multiple files as is traditional.

b. All input transactions must be subjected to edit tests before processing.

c. Database files cannot be accessed through audit software or similar query languages.

d. Most database systems are on-line.

10–38 Which of the following procedures is least likely to be performed by an auditor using GAS?

a. Selection and printing of accounts receivable confirmations from a client's master file.

b. Evaluation of the audit results based on a statistical sample of inventory.

c. Identification and selection of inventory items that have characteristics that the auditor believes indicate obsolete inventory.

d. Create a detailed printout of a file so that an auditor can read the complete file and select items for audit verification.

10–39 Detailed testing of controls in a computer system through the use of test data or an integrated test facility

a. Can be performed using either real or simulated transactions.
b. Is not convincing because many of the computer controls leave no visible evidence of operation.
c. Is likely to contaminate the client's master files and thus should be used only as a last resort.
d. Is insufficient unless all controls and elements of processing are identified and tested.

10–40 A primary advantage of using generalized audit software is that it enables the auditor to

a. Utilize the speed and the comprehensiveness of a computer to perform routine audit tasks.
b. Verify the performance of operations that leave no visible evidence of occurrence.
c. Omit manual procedures such as confirmations or observing inventory and replace them by more comprehensive computerized procedures.
d. Test the operations of controls on a real-time basis.

Discussion and Research Questions

*10–41 (Use of Microcomputers) Microcomputer software has been developed to improve the efficiency and effectiveness of the audit. Electronic spreadsheets and other software packages are available to aid in the performance of audit procedures otherwise performed manually.

Required:
Describe the potential benefits to an auditor of using microcomputer software in an audit as compared to performing an audit without the use of a microcomputer.

*10–42 (Generalized Audit Software) A CPA's client, Boos & Baumkirchner, Inc., is a medium-size manufacturer of products for the leisure-time activities market (camping equipment, scuba gear, bows and arrows, and so forth). During the past year, a computer system was installed, and inventory records of finished goods and parts were converted to computer processing. The inventory master file is maintained on a disk. Each record of the file contains the following information:

- Item or part number.
- Description.
- Size.
- Unit-of-measure code.

*Adapted from the Uniform CPA examination or the Certified Internal Auditor examination.

- Quantity on hand.
- Cost per unit.
- Total value of inventory on hand at cost.
- Date of last sale or use.
- Quantity used or sold this year.
- Economic order quantity.
- Code number of major vendor.
- Code number of secondary vendor.

In preparation for year-end inventory, the client has two identical sets of preprinted inventory count cards. One set is for the client's inventory counts and the other is for the CPA to use in making audit test counts. The following information has been keyed into the client's system:

- Item or part number.
- Description.
- Size.
- Unit-of-measure code.

When all counts are complete, the counted quantity will be entered into the system. The data will be processed against the disk file and quantity-on-hand figures will be adjusted to reflect the actual count. A computer list will be prepared to show any missing inventory count cards and all quantity adjustments of more than $100 in value. These items will be investigated by client personnel and all required adjustments will be made. When adjustments have been completed, the final year-end balances will be computed and posted to the general ledger.

The CPA has available generalized audit software that will run on the client's computer and can process both inventory card and disk files.

Required:

a. In general and without regard to the facts in this case, discuss the nature of generalized audit software and list the various types and uses.

b. List and describe at least five ways generalized audit software can be used to assist in all aspects of the audit of the inventory of Boos & Baumkirchner, Inc. (For example, the software can be used to read the disk inventory master file and list items and parts with a high unit cost or total value. Such items can be included in the test counts to increase the dollar coverage of the audit verification.)

10–43 (Automated Cash Registers—Retailer) Woodman's Grocery is a small chain of grocery retailers with four megasize stores. Each store has a minicomputer that runs the automated cash registers. All price changes are approved by the merchandising manager on the recommendation of the section managers. The authorized prices are maintained in a sales price table (file) maintained on the central computer and downloaded to the store's minicomputers on a daily basis. No other applications are run on the store's minicomputers.

The auditor has identified the following control procedures in ensuring the correct prices:

- Only the merchandising manager and one assistant have authority to change the prices.
- Access to the sales price table is limited by passwords.
- The system creates a printout of all changes, which is sent to the merchandising manager for review and reconciliation.

Required:

a. Explain how the auditor might use reports from access control software in performing an audit related to the valuation of revenue for the grocery chain.

b. Would this situation be a good place to implement an integrated test facility? Explain.

10–44 (Use of Advanced Audit Techniques) IDS Corporation processes payroll for its numerous employees through one major payroll application program, which is changed frequently. Because there are a number of divisions and job categories, the applicable edit tests for a particular division or department are stored in a table utilized as part of a general validation routine before transactions are processed. Authorized wage rates are kept in another table and are called by the application program according to identified job codes.

Required:

a. Explain how the auditor might use the test data approach in auditing the payroll application described above.

b. What are the major limitations of using the test data approach in this situation?

c. Explain how the client might use the integrated test facility in this application.

d. If the auditor uses the integrated test facility, what alternatives are available to ensure that nonauthorized data do not update the client's general ledger?

e. Assume that the auditor is concerned with the operation of the edit controls and is especially concerned that the control procedures either are not functioning effectively or are overridden by management. What concurrent audit technique might you suggest the auditor utilize?

*10–45 (Alternative Computer Audit Techniques—Payroll) A medium-size company purchased a mainframe-based payroll software package to service 2 plants, 5 distribution centers, and 10 sales offices. The old system was completely manual and was reviewed by the internal auditing department last year. The audit included the following steps:

1. A system walk-through to identify control points and to verify proper segregation of duties.
2. Performing a pay delivery (i.e., taking a sample of employee checks and actually delivering them to the employees to determine that each employee exists).
3. Verifying the gross-to-net payroll calculation.
4. Reviewing payroll files.
5. Checking signatures.
6. Verifying completeness of documentation, including completeness of governmental reports and reconciliation of reports to personnel and payroll files.
7. Footing and cross-footing departmental totals.
8. Verifying the labor distribution system journal entry to both the cost system and the general ledger.
9. Testing additions, deletions, and changes to the master payroll based on data gathered from the payroll supervisor's files.

Required:
Contrast the required audit steps performed to audit the new automated system versus the audit steps performed last year for each appropriate control objective in a payroll system. Maximize the use of computer audit–assisted techniques and consider the information systems environment. Presume that a microcomputer is available and that an appropriate audit software or a report writer is available with the package. Use the following format for your answer:

Control Objective	Manual Test	Automated Test

*10–46 (Advanced Computer Audit Techniques) Auditors have various EDP audit techniques available to aid in testing computer-based systems. Included in these audit techniques are (1) test data, (2) parallel simulation, (3) integrated test facility (ITF), (4) snapshot, and (5) system control audit review file (SCARF or embedded audit data collection).

Required:
Describe each of the five identified audit techniques and list two situations in which they are most appropriately used.

10–47 (Information Systems Auditing and Internal Auditors) It has been stated that internal auditors have developed some computer audit approaches that should be considered by the external auditor in planning the conduct of an audit of a client that has a highly sophisticated information system.

Required:
a. Without specific regard to computer auditing, what are the major guidelines the external auditor should consider in planning an audit in conjunction with audit work completed by the internal auditor?

b. What is systems development auditing? How might the performance of systems development auditing by internal auditors enhance the auditability of computer applications? Explain.

c. In what ways might an internal auditor have a competitive advantage in developing and implementing concurrent audit techniques? Explain.

d. Briefly identify some of the major concurrent audit techniques used by internal auditors and explain why they might be used.

10–48 (Electronic Data Interchange) The past two chapters have described EDI as a major data processing development that will increase in scope over the next decade. Assume that your audit client has implemented EDI for the purchasing and payment processes.

Required:

a. Explain how the snapshot approach might be used in an EDI environment.

b. Explain how test data or the integrated test facility might be used in the EDI environment.

c. Explain how generalized audit software might be used in the EDI environment.

d. Briefly identify the relative advantages of each method in the context of the purchasing and payment process.

10–49 (Computer Audit Techniques and Fraud Investigation) The use of computer-assisted audit techniques can assist the auditor in investigating alleged fraud.

Required:

Following is a list of scenarios in which fraud is suspected. Briefly indicate how the auditor might use some of the computer audit techniques discussed in this chapter to assist in the fraud investigation. Use the following format:

Computer Audit Technique	Description of Use
a.	
b.	

Note: More than one technique might be used in each situation. If more than one approach is applicable, identify all the approaches and briefly indicate which approach you believe is preferable, along with the rationale for your choice.

Potential Fraud Scenarios:

a. The operator is processing sales transactions with an unauthorized version of the sales program. The unauthorized version was changed by a programmer who agreed to split one-half of the profits with the computer operator. The unauthorized program invoices products to three customers (all owned by or affiliated with the programmer) at approximately one-third of normal sales prices. The programmer's companies resell the goods at normal price and make a substantial profit on the sales.

b. A social service worker has processed fictitious recipients and generates checks to them which she then picks up and cashes.

c. A bank programmer has programmed the interest rate application to add daily interest to her account at the rate of .5 percent each day. This amounts to an interest rate of over 200 percent per year. The error apparently occurs only on the programmer's account.

d. An unauthorized individual in accounts payable has gained access to the pricing table that controls the prices for all merchandise processed by the automated cash register at the retailer. The individual changes prices for selected goods, goes to the store and purchases the goods, and changes the prices back the next morning.

e. The payroll manager has implemented an unauthorized wage increase for all employees in the paint department of a manufacturer. The manager's brother, sister-in-law, and two friends work in the six-member department. The increase is approximately 25 percent of the authorized wage rate.

f. An unauthorized individual has gained access to the computer program of a telephone company. The program is used to order repair parts to be delivered to specific locations on the following day to be used in repairs. The amount of goods requested has increased sharply over time.

10–50 (Auditing a Spreadsheet) The use of electronic spreadsheets is becoming increasingly common. Many accounting entries are now based on electronic spreadsheets. Examples include computation of foreign currency translations, consolidations, computation of warranty expenses, and goodwill amortization.

Required:
Identify the alternative approaches an auditor might utilize in auditing the entries that are developed on a client's electronic spreadsheet. In developing your answer, consider the two extremes of sophistication in the spreadsheets: (1) a relatively noncomplex spreadsheet that calculates goodwill amortization for a client that has only one purchased goodwill account and (2) a very complex spreadsheet that calculates foreign currency translations for a company with operations in over 45 different countries.

10–51 (Testing the Operation of Controls) The auditor has identified each of the following control procedures as important in reducing control risk in major accounting applications.

Required:
For each control procedure identified, indicate how the auditor would test the control. Assume that all controls pertain to the input, processing, and maintenance of file data over sales transactions.

Control Procedures:

a. All sales orders are received by the order department from the sales staff. Each order is prenumbered. The orders are opened, visually reviewed for completeness and authorization, and then are batched for data input and processing. Control totals are established for record count, number of items purchased, and a hash total of number of product numbers. The control totals per batch are reconciled with the control totals developed by the computer processing.

b. Self-checking digits are used for all product numbers.

c. The master price file (table) is accessible only by two people in the marketing department (the manager and a clerk). Access is controlled by password. The manager receives a detailed printout of all authorized price changes and compares the input changes with the authorized changes for completeness and accuracy of the input.

d. Passwords are issued to authorized users only after the user department (supervisor) has submitted a document listing all authorized users. Passwords are changed every six weeks. They must not be easily guessable (a computer program tests each one for ease of use).

e. Only authorized sales orders are entered. Authorization is indicated by the salesperson's signature on a sales order form and the salesperson's ID number, which is tested against a master file of valid ID numbers.

f. The sales price on the sales order is equal to the master sales price unless the marketing manager explicitly approves the change. The approval is on a document authorizing the change.

g. Same as part f except that the authorization is done on-line to a field in the salesperson's record that is accessible only by the marketing manager or the manager's designee.

h. Authorized credit limits are established by the credit department. The limit is entered into a credit file and is updated two ways: (1) an automatic update based on the volume of transactions and the customer's credit history (allowed to increase to only 150 percent of the original credit limit set by the credit department) and (2) authorized update submitted to data processing by the credit department. The credit department reviews all changes.

i. On three competitive products (accounting for 20 percent of the company's sales), the salesperson is allowed to discount the master sales price by up to 10 percent without any additional approval. The discount price is allowed only if the order of the product exceeds $35,000. The salesperson's commission on discounted sales is changed from 5 percent to 4 percent.

10–52 **(Research)** Review recent articles and interview auditors to determine the changes that have taken place in the use of generalized audit software during the past few years. Review descriptions of microcomputer audit software such as ACL (Audit Command Language) and compare the software characteristics with other audit software that runs on mainframe systems.

10–53 **(Research—EDI)** Review published research and write a report on the development of EDI. Interview at least one company in your area that has implemented EDI to determine the types of applications used, the control procedures implemented in the application, the audit approach, and any problems encountered.

10–54 **(Research—Concurrent Audit Techniques)** Review recent reports on the use of concurrent audit techniques. Identify the trends in use and the rationale for the specific use or nonuse of the concurrent audit techniques identified in the chapter.

Case

10–55 (Computer Fraud: The Equity Funding Example)

In the mid-1970s, the Equity Funding case (see Appendix to Chapter 4 for more details) was often cited as the first major case of computer fraud. It was alleged that the computer played an instrumental role in allowing the fraud to exist. For example, the computer records truncated the first two digits of all insurance policies so that repeat numbers occurred frequently. Thus, a policy number of 4580293 was listed as 80293. If items were selected for auditor review, the auditor frequently gave the client one or two days to find all the files, preventing the auditor from detecting the fraud.

In addition to the changes to policy numbers, it was alleged that the computer was used to generate revenue statistics so that the revenue and number of fictitious policies were kept consistent. When the auditor requested detailed printouts of items, the computer operator cited a system overload so that preparation of such reports was not possible. Other problems existed as well. For example, confirmations were sent to post office box numbers where Equity Funding employees picked them up and returned them.

Required:

a. Review the Equity Funding case in Chapter 4. Should it be considered a computer fraud? Explain.
b. Explain how generalized audit software might have been used in the Equity Funding audit. Confine your answer to the problem of fictitious loan policies described above.
c. What is the relationship to the fraud of the duplicate policy numbers and the delay in retrieving the supporting documents?

End Note

1. Andrew D. Bailey, Lynford E. Graham, and James V. Hansen, "Technological Development and EDP," in *Research Opportunities in Auditing: The*

Second Decade, ed. A. Rashad Abdel-khalik and Ira Solomon (Sarasota, Fla.: American Accounting Association, 1988), 50.

CHAPTER

11

Learning Objectives

Through studying this chapter, you will be able to:

1. Understand the revenue accounting cycle.
2. Identify inherent risk factors and their impact on audits of revenue cycle accounts.
3. Identify the factors affecting the assessment of inherent and control risk in the revenue cycle.
4. Identify important control procedures in the revenue cycle.
5. Understand and apply manual and computer-assisted approaches to test the effectiveness of revenue cycle control procedures.

Assessing Control Risk: Revenue Cycle

Chapter Contents

Chapter Overview

This chapter illustrates the audit testing concepts developed in Chapters 6 through 10 by applying them to the revenue cycle. Sales transactions are always material to a company's financial statements and often are subject to manipulation. Many audit failures have been characterized by alleged misstatement of sales. This chapter describes the basic sales recording process, identifies the major documents and control procedures present in that process, and identifies approaches to testing the control procedures. Because sales are often subject to misstatement, special attention is paid to the control environment and to management's motivation to "stretch" accounting principles to achieve desired revenue reporting.

Eighty-seven percent of the cases against public companies involved manipulation of the financial disclosures. . . . Frequently used techniques were improper revenue recognition methods (47 percent). . . . In 45 percent of the cases against public companies, the SEC alleged that the fraud had occurred because of a breakdown of the company's internal controls.[1]

The auditor uses the knowledge provided by the understanding of the internal control structure and the assessed level of control risk in determining the nature, timing, and extent of substantive tests for financial statement assertions. [AU 319.05]

A–AN OVERVIEW OF CONTROL RISK IN THE REVENUE CYCLE

The methodology for assessing control risk discussed in Chapters 8 and 9 and the use of computer audit techniques discussed in Chapter 10 are illustrated in this chapter through the discussion of control risk assessments for revenue-related accounts. We refer to a group of transactions and the accounts related to a particular activity as a **cycle.** The approach provides a convenient way to look at the interrelationship of account balances. Financial transaction processing in most organizations can be classified into the following cycles:

- Revenue.
- Acquisition/payment.
- Payroll.
- Financing.

In addition, a manufacturing company has an inventory cycle that tracks inventory costs through work in process to finished goods and finally to cost of goods sold.

The **revenue cycle** addresses the process of receiving a customer's order, approving credit for the sale, determining whether the goods are available for shipment, shipping the goods, billing the customer, collecting cash, and recognizing the effect of this process on related accounts such as Accounts Receivable and Inventory. The audit emphasis for assessing control risk is on (1) understanding the control structure and risks associated with processing revenue transactions and (2) developing tests of the effectiveness of control procedures. This phase of the overall audit process is identified in Exhibit 11.1.

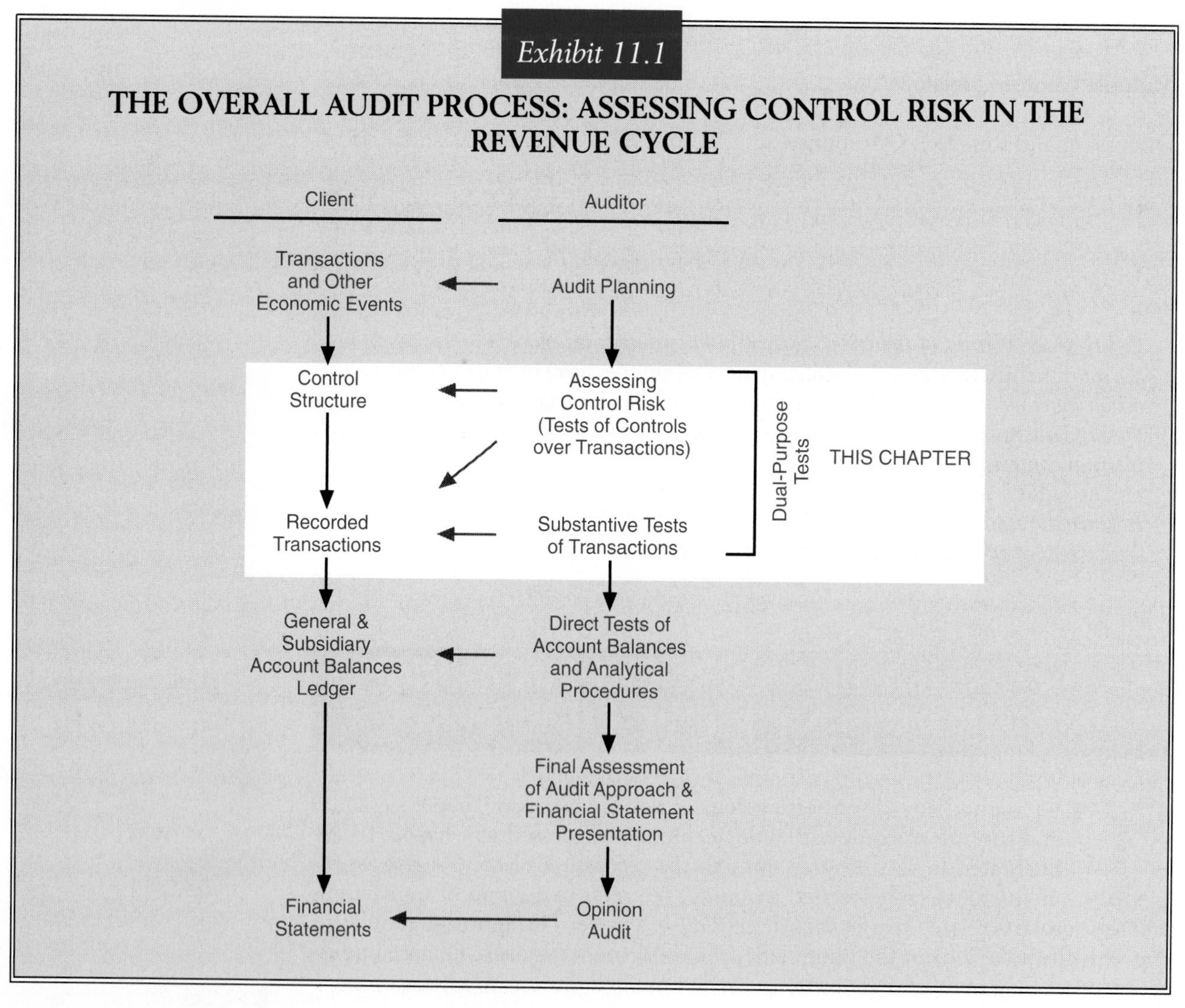

Assessment of Control Risk: Audit Steps

The audit steps taken to assess control risk include the following:

1. Develop an understanding of the client's control structure including the overall control environment, accounting systems, and specific control procedures developed to accomplish the basic processing objectives. This understanding includes the identification of specific documents and procedures used in processing transactions.
2. Document the operation of specific accounting systems, such as revenue-related accounting applications, and the important control procedures that contribute to an assessment of control risk at less than the maximum.
3. Develop a preliminary assessment of control risk for the account balances affected by the processing and determine whether it is cost beneficial to develop tests of the effectiveness of the control procedures. If control risk is assessed at a maximum, consider the manner in which misstatements are most likely to occur and document that understanding as a basis for developing substantive tests of the related account balances.
4. Develop audit procedures, including the specification of relevant sample sizes, to test the effectiveness of control procedures deemed important in the previous steps.
5. Perform the audit tests, determine the implications of such tests for the conduct of the remainder of the audit, and document the testing.
6. Determine whether the preliminary control risk assessment should be modified based on the testing results and document the implications for the remainder of the audit program.

Except for the determination of the appropriate sample size for testing control procedures, these steps are illustrated in this chapter. Audit sampling concepts for testing control procedures are discussed in Chapter 12.

Overview of Revenue Cycle

The cycle concept serves as a convenient framework for viewing the interrelationship between accounts affected by the same transaction or business activity. The revenue cycle can be visualized as all the procedures involved in generating a sales order, shipping the required products, recording the transaction, and collecting the related accounts receivable. Audit evidence verifying the existence and proper valuation of accounts receivable also provides evidence of the existence and valuation of sales and vice versa. When examining sales transactions, the auditor also gathers evidence on proper credit authorization and the proper valuation of the recorded transactions. Further, a review of sales contracts provides evidence to analyze the adequacy of the client's warranty expenses and related liability.

Sales transactions often serve as a basis for computing commissions for sales staff. Sales information is used for strategic long-term decision making and marketing analysis. Thus, the accuracy of the accounting in the revenue cycle is important for management decisions as well as for the preparation of financial statements.

The accounts typically affected by a sales transaction are shown in Exhibit 11.2. The sales process differs with each client, but the commonalities of the revenue cycle can be used to develop audit programs for most organizations. For example, a

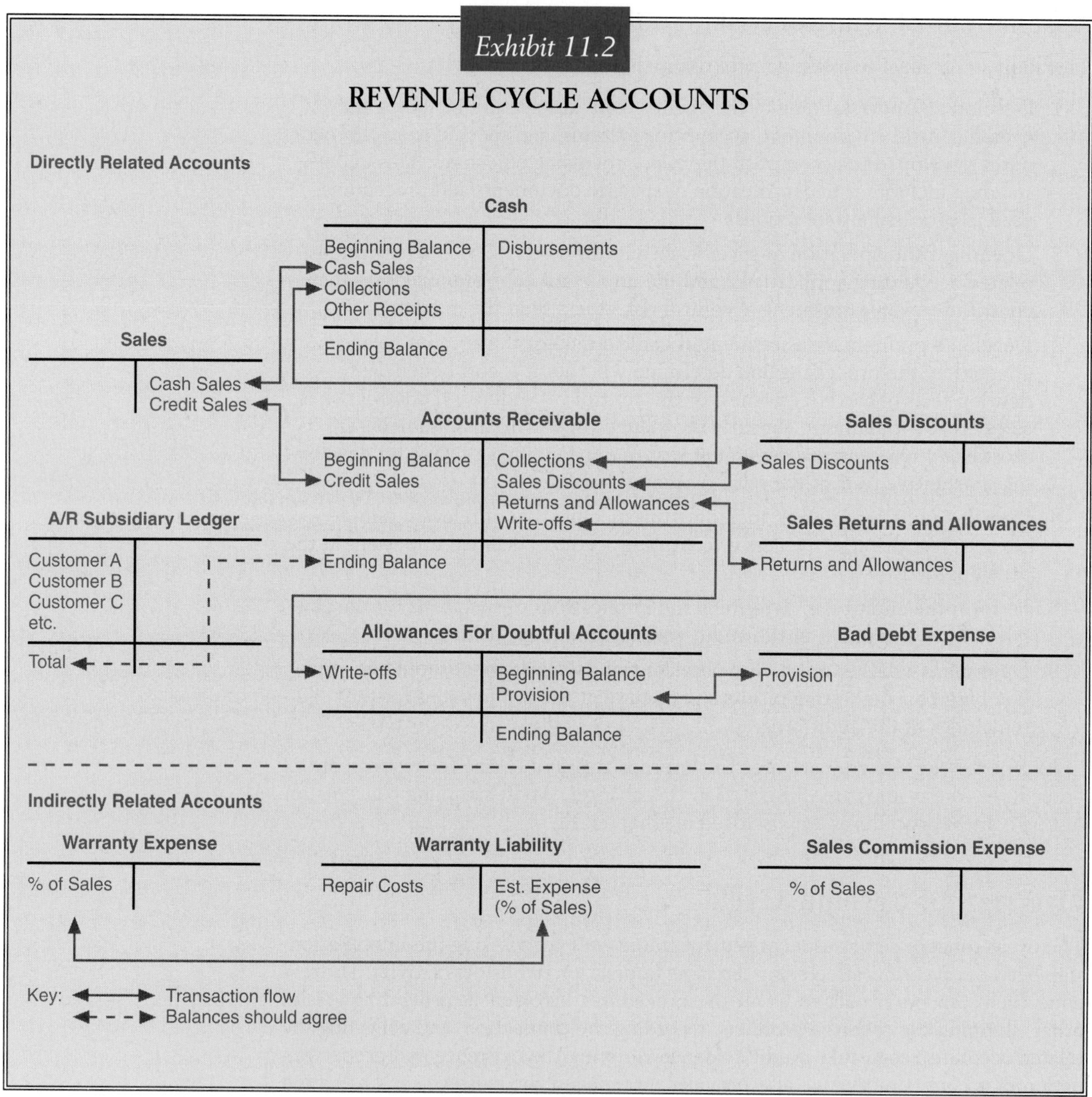

sales transaction for a briefcase in a department store differs from a sale of construction equipment, and both of these differ from a catalog sale for a lamp taken over the phone. Some organizations generate detailed paper for sales documentation; others maintain an audit trail only in computerized form. The control concepts are similar, but the means to implement them differ.

Internal Control Objectives

The control objectives in the revenue cycle are the same as those developed in Chapter 8. The auditor should determine that the design of the system and the control procedures implemented ensure the recording of the *occurrence* of the transactions, the *completeness* of the recording process, the proper *valuation* of the recorded transactions, and the rights *existing* in the assets generated. Audits of revenue transactions are primarily oriented toward identifying the potential overstatement of revenue and the related asset accounts. Although sales transactions may be omitted, most intentional misstatements overstate sales.

The Revenue Accounting System

Most sales transactions include the procedures and related documents shown in Exhibit 11.3. In many computerized organizations, a number of these procedures are combined into one step. Note that a number of documents may be prepared either manually or electronically. Many of the documents are prepared internally and are less reliable than external documents unless the auditor has confidence that the client's control risk is low. The customer's purchase order, the bill of lading (signed by a representative of the common carrier), and the turnaround document (on which the customer writes the amount of payment) are at least in part prepared externally. The auditor also needs to know where the documents are filed (manually or electronically) because many of the tests performed to evaluate the effectiveness of control procedures or to determine that all transactions have been correctly processed require reprocessing or vouching of documents.

Receive a Customer Purchase Order. Processing begins with the receipt of a purchase order from a customer or the preparation of a sales order by a salesperson. The order might be taken by (1) a clerk at a checkout counter at a clothing store, (2) a salesperson making a call on a client, (3) a customer service agent of a catalog sales company answering a toll-free number, (4) a computer receiving purchase order information electronically from the customer's computer (*electronic data interchange, EDI*—discussed in Chapter 10), or (5) received directly by the sales department in the form of a purchase order. The nature and extent of documentation vary considerably. For example, of the order takers identified above, it is likely that only the salesperson making a call on a client will generate a hard copy document. The check-out clerk in a retail store records the order and sale on the cash register and the catalog order taker enters the order directly into a computer terminal.

The sales order document, if created on paper, should contain elements that provide a basis for determining that all transactions are properly authorized and completely recorded. These control procedures include requiring the use of prenumbered sales orders, requiring an authorized signature of the salesperson and customer, requiring formal approval (by the credit department) for credit requested, requiring a description of part number, sales price, and shipping terms of the products ordered, and requiring an authorized billing address before a shipment can be made. Purchase orders received from customers contain the same information, but the client cannot account for the prenumbering of these documents and therefore needs to implement other control procedures to ensure that all orders received are promptly processed.

Even if a sales order is not physically generated, the same information is recorded, usually in computerized form. Consider a customer service agent for a catalog merchandiser taking an order over the phone. The information is keyed into a computer file and each transaction is uniquely identified. The computer file (often referred to as a *log of transactions*) contains all the information for sales orders taken for a period of time and can be used for control and reconciliation purposes.

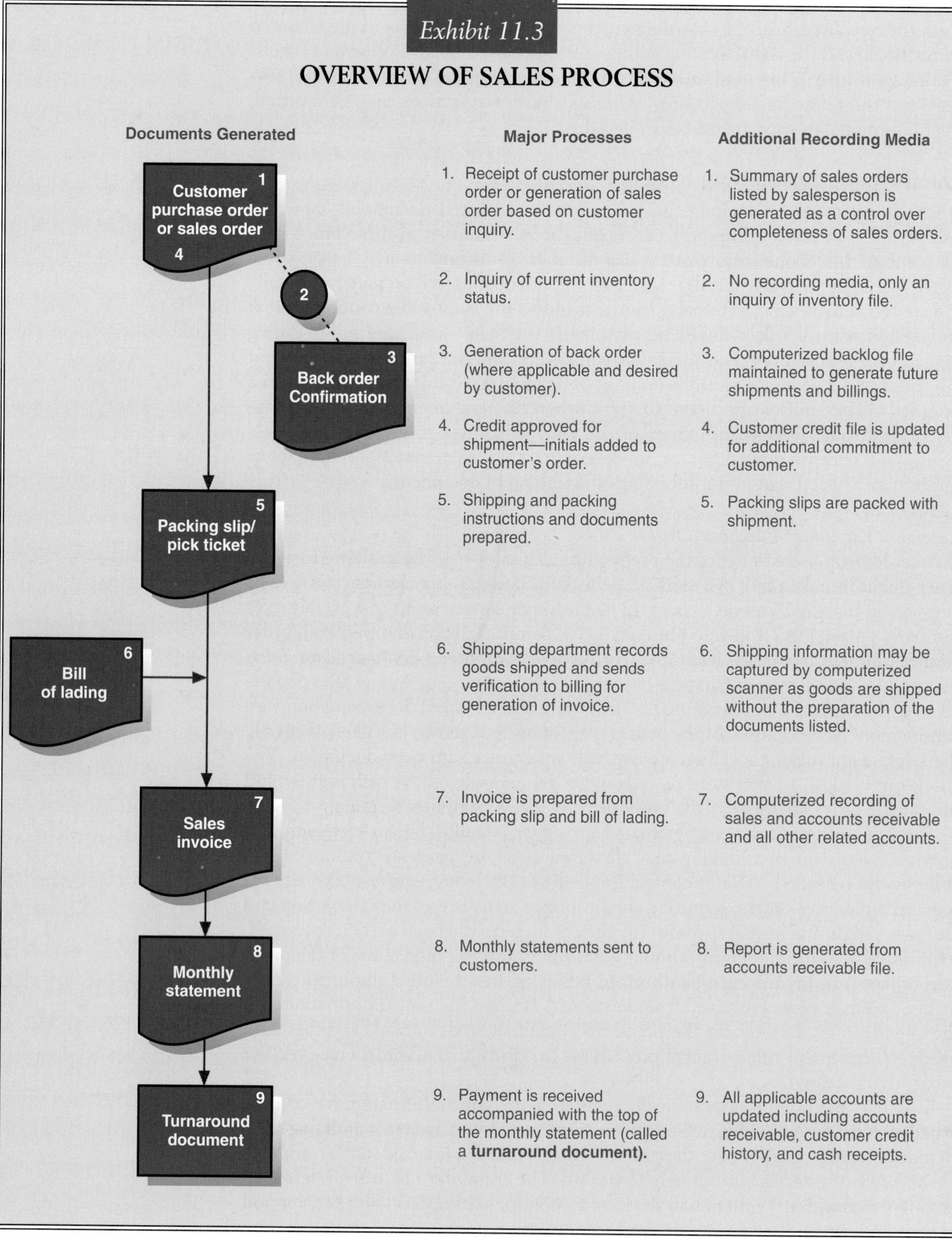
Exhibit 11.3
OVERVIEW OF SALES PROCESS
Documents Generated
Major Processes
Additional Recording Media
1 Customer purchase order or sales order 4
2
3 Back order Confirmation
5 Packing slip/ pick ticket
6 Bill of lading
7 Sales invoice
8 Monthly statement
9 Turnaround document
1. Receipt of customer purchase order or generation of sales order based on customer inquiry.
2. Inquiry of current inventory status.
3. Generation of back order (where applicable and desired by customer).
4. Credit approved for shipment—initials added to customer's order.
5. Shipping and packing instructions and documents prepared.
6. Shipping department records goods shipped and sends verification to billing for generation of invoice.
7. Invoice is prepared from packing slip and bill of lading.
8. Monthly statements sent to customers.
9. Payment is received accompanied with the top of the monthly statement (called a turnaround document).
1. Summary of sales orders listed by salesperson is generated as a control over completeness of sales orders.
2. No recording media, only an inquiry of inventory file.
3. Computerized backlog file maintained to generate future shipments and billings.
4. Customer credit file is updated for additional commitment to customer.
5. Packing slips are packed with shipment.
6. Shipping information may be captured by computerized scanner as goods are shipped without the preparation of the documents listed.
7. Computerized recording of sales and accounts receivable and all other related accounts.
8. Report is generated from accounts receivable file.
9. All applicable accounts are updated including accounts receivable, customer credit history, and cash receipts.

Check Inventory Stock Status. Many organizations have computer systems capable of informing a customer of current inventory status and likely delivery date. Usually no formal documents are created, but the customer is informed of potential back-ordered items as well as expected delivery date. Control procedures to ensure the accuracy of the inventory file assists the organization in meeting customer needs as well as ensuring that sales orders can be completed.

Generate Back Order. If an item is to be back ordered for later shipment to the customer, a confirmation of the back order is prepared and sent to the customer. If the back order is not filled within a specified time, the customer is often given the option of canceling the order. An accurate list of back-ordered items must be maintained to meet current customer demand and future inventory needs. This is usually done by appending a separate field to the individual inventory records to show back-ordered items. Back orders are filled before new orders.

Obtain Credit Approval. Formal credit approval policies are implemented by organizations to minimize credit losses. Many mail-order companies eliminate credit risk by requiring payment through a credit card, such as MasterCard or Visa, or requiring that a check accompany the order. The company generally delays a shipment for the period of time it takes a check to clear through the banking system to ensure that the payment is collectible. Companies taking a credit card for payment eliminate credit risk but incur a cost levied by the credit card company for the services. An overview of the way a typical retail organization handles the recording of a credit card sale is shown in the Sidelights on Auditing which follows.

The credit approval process typically includes a review of sales orders and customer credit information by a credit manager to determine whether credit should be extended to the customer for the amount of the current sale. Although this process was accurate 20 years ago, it does not typify today's environment in which an organization must provide quick feedback to customers, nor does it reflect the extent to which major businesses have utilized the computer to develop credit information and credit approvals. Most medium- to large-size companies have computerized credit histories for their major customers and provide preapproved credit up to certain limits. The computer file is regularly accessed to determine whether a sales order exceeds preapproved credit limits. If it does exceed the preauthorized limit, credit is either denied or is formally reviewed by the credit department.

Prepare Shipping and Packing Documents. Many organizations have computerized the distribution process for shipping items from a warehouse. *Picking tickets* (documents that tell the warehouse personnel the most efficient order to pick items for shipment and the location of all items to be shipped) are generated from the sales order or from the customer's purchase order. Some organizations also automate the picking of items for shipment. Separate packing slips are prepared to insert with the shipment and to verify that all items have been shipped.

Ship and Verify Shipment of Goods. Most goods are shipped to customers via common carriers such as independent trucking lines, railroads, or air freight companies. The shipper prepares a bill of lading describing the packages to be conveyed to the common carrier, the shipping terms, and the delivery address. The **bill of lading** is a formal legal document that conveys responsibility to the shipper. A signed bill of

Sidelights on Auditing

MINIMIZING CREDIT RISK: USE OF BANK CARD SALES

The credit card business is actually three separate businesses: (1) the credit card franchisor such as Visa or MasterCard, (2) the credit card issuer such as Bank One or Citicorp, and (3) the merchant bank that accepts credit card receipts from retail businesses. The credit card franchisor is responsible for developing a network to process (clear) transactions between banks and identifying card holders who have poor credit histories and to communicate that information to retailers accepting the card. The card issuer (bank or other financial institution) issues the credit cards to individuals and can be associated with franchises such as Visa or MasterCard or can be a wholly owned company such as American Express or Discover. The credit card issuers assume the responsibility for customer credit default and earn income through credit card annual fees and interest on past-due accounts. Recent history in the U.S. indicates that 60 to 65 percent of credit card holders do not pay off their account each month and are assessed interest.

The merchant banker in the transaction acts as the regular banker for the retailers that accept credit card receipts. The issuer of the credit card often requires the business accepting the card to verify the credit for all transactions over a specific dollar limit. If the credit is not good and the retailer did not receive an authorization for the credit, the retailer is responsible for amounts not collected. Credit card sales may be documented by paper or electronically.

Paper Documentation of Credit Card Purchases

Under this process, a credit card imprint is made and the receipts are deposited in the retailer's bank account much as cash would be deposited. If individual amounts exceed a specific dollar limit, however, the retailer may have to receive proper authorization before the bank will accept the credit card receipts and treat them as cash. This is done to minimize the bank's potential losses for invalid cards.

Authorization of a Credit Card Purchase

The franchisor prepares a weekly bulletin, referred to as the *combined warning bulletin,* which is essentially a list of card numbers that should not be honored. Retailers that do not have on-line access to the merchant bank should have procedures in place to require a review of the list before processing a sale. For many retailers, the authorization begins with the retailer's direct line to the merchant bank. The merchant bank switches the transaction to the appropriate credit card service provider. If the card service is the issuer (such as Discover and American Express), the transaction will be approved (or disapproved) by the service provider. If the service provider is Visa or MasterCard, the transaction is switched (electronically) to the issuing institution (assuming that it exceeds the limits set by that institution). If the transaction does not exceed the preset parameters, the transaction is processed against a negative file containing a list of lost, stolen, or fraudulent cardholder accounts. If the sale is approved following this step, the retailer continues the preparation of the credit card document and obtains the cardholder's signature.

Further Processing

At the end of the business day, the retailer batches the credit card sales transactions and puts a total on the batch control sheet. The credit card transactions are listed on a bank deposit slip that is delivered to

lading provides evidence of conveyance to the common carrier for shipment. An example of a bill of lading is shown in Exhibit 11.4.

The shipping department confirms the shipment by (1) completing the packing slip and returning it to the billing department, or (2) electronically recording every-

the bank. The franchisor of the credit card (Visa, MasterCard, etc.) charges a specific processing fee, which is negotiated directly with the business. The fee can range from as little as 1.25 percent for major customers such as Kmart and as high as 2.5 percent for some catalog operations. The merchandising bank charges an additional fee, which generally runs from 1 percent to 3 percent, resulting in a total charge to the business accepting the credit card from 1.5 percent to 6 percent or more.

Electronic Deposits of Credit Card Sales

The most widely used method to record credit card sales today is the electronic hookups between the retailer and the merchant bank. The sales amount is entered directly into an electronic device (electronic cash register or a data capture terminal) and the authorization request is transmitted directly to the merchant bank. The authorization process is similar to that described for paper-based credit card sales.

Some devices work in conjunction with a printer capable of printing a receipt for the cardholder to sign. If a printer is not present, the retailer prepares a credit card document similar to that used for paper-based sales.

At the end of the business day, the retailer presses a button on the data capture device to indicate to the bank that a settlement should occur. The merchant bank maintains a file for each retail customer and prints the totals received from the retailer during the day. If the total agrees with the retailer's totals, the deposits are electronically added to the retailer's account. The processing fee may be assessed immediately or may be charged against the retailer on a periodic basis, depending on the agreement reached with the retailer. If the retailer is considered to be a high risk customer by the banking institution, the fee is charged at the front end.

Chargebacks

Chargebacks occur when goods are returned to the store or when there is a dispute between a customer and the retailer. Consumer legislation generally has given the cardholder a great deal of leverage in settling such disputes. A cardholder has 60 days after receipt of a statement containing a questionable transaction to dispute the transaction. If a chargeback is allowed, it goes against the merchant bank and the retailer. Normally, it is deducted from the retailer's checking account, but some banks net the chargeback against a current deposit.

Control Overview

The use of credit cards may minimize credit risk for the retailer, but it does have a cost. First, the merchant bank charges a fee. Second, there is cost associated with the electronic equipment and the control procedures implemented to ensure that all transactions transmitted to the bank have been captured on the retailer's media so that proper reconciliation with the bank can be made. Most electronic cash registers have the ability to separately label and total credit card sales to assist in reconciling with the bank's totals. These control procedure costs may be offset by lower bad debt costs. The types of control procedures for processing credit card transactions are the same as those that a retailer would perform for cash transactions, complemented by batch to control totals to ensure that all transactions are recorded.

thing shipped and transmitting the shipping information via computer to the billing department, or (3) preparing independent shipping documents, a copy of which is sent to the billing department. The most common approach for verifying the shipment of goods and ensuring that they will be billed properly is completing the

Exhibit 11.4

BILL OF LADING

LeFlam Manufacturing Co. 200 Pine Way, Kirkville, WI 53800			Date 1-17-94
Send to: Ace Hardware 12345 Mars Blvd. East Fishville, VA 22222		Shipper's No. C441456	LeFlam Mfg. Co. ________ (Signature of Consignor)
		C.O.D. Charges to be paid by consignee	Collect on Delivery $________ Remit to Shipper
Customer's P.O. Number V28753J			
Routing		Car No.	
No. Pkgs.	Kind of Packages, Description of Articles, Special Marks, Exceptions	Weight	Class or Rate
17	Item RCML - Rain Coats - Men's Large	340	
Name of Carrier AZY Trucking Company	Agent's Signature		
CARRIER'S COPY			

packing slip and sending a copy to the billing department, but companies are increasingly entering shipping information on a computer screen which updates a billing database.

Prepare the Invoice. Invoices are normally prepared when confirmation is received that goods were shipped. Some companies, however, find it efficient to prepare invoices in advance as long as records show that sufficient levels of inventory are on hand. These companies need to implement control procedures to ensure that the invoices are not processed until there is evidence of shipment. Invoices can be transmitted to the customer by preparing hard-copy documents and sending one to the customer or electronically transmitting the invoice to the customer.* At the time the invoice is generated, the Sales account and the related asset account (Accounts Receivable, Credit Card Receivables, or Cash) are updated, as are Inventory and Cost of Goods Sold. The invoice should correspond with the sales order as to terms of sale, payment terms, and prices for merchandise shipped.

Send Monthly Statements to Customers. Many companies prepare monthly statements of open items and mail these statements to customers. The *monthly statement* provides a detailed list of the customer's activity for the previous month and a statement of all open items. The volume of transactions in many organizations dictates that open account statements be prepared on a cycle basis. For example, if you have a MasterCard or Visa account, you may receive a statement around the 5th of the month with a due date of the 16th of the month; one of your classmates may receive her statement around the 20th of the month with a payment due date around the 29th of the month. If the auditor chooses to confirm the correctness of the accounts receivable by direct correspondence with the customer, information as to when and how the client prepares monthly statements will be important.

Receive Payments. The control over cash receipts is often addressed separately as part of the cash receipts and cash management cycle. However, the proper recording of all receipts is crucial to the ultimate valuation of both cash and accounts receivable. Thus, as part of the control structure over accounts receivables, control procedures to ensure the completeness and accuracy of cash receipt recording are important.

B–INHERENT AND CONTROL RISK CONSIDERATIONS

Inherent Risk in Revenue Cycle Transactions

Sales transactions are highly routine for most organizations and do not represent an abnormally high risk. The sales at retail organizations such as Wal-Mart or Kmart, for example, are routine and are controlled through computerized cash registers and detailed procedures reconciling daily sales recorded by the cash registers with deposits at the bank. On the other hand, for many organizations, sales may not be routine and management may override the normal processing of the transactions to achieve a particular sales or profitability goal. A large number of court cases against auditors have revolved around alleged improper recognition of sales transactions.

*The term *transmitted to the customer* is used here instead of the more common term *mailed to the customer* to recognize that changes in data communications and computer networking are continually occurring. Many organizations will be transmitting documents to their customers via electronic media by the middle of the 1990s. However, we expect that paper sales invoices will continue to dominate most of these transactions because of their role in conveying title to merchandise.

Overview of Inherent Risks: Sales Transactions

Some sales transactions are quite complex, often making it difficult to determine when a sale has actually taken place. The auditor must be aware of issues addressed by the Financial Accounting Standards Board to determine whether a client is affected by recent pronouncements. Some of the difficult issues concerning sales transactions include the determination of the following:

- The point in time when revenue should be recognized.
- The impact of unusual terms on the recording of the transaction and whether title has passed to the other party.
- All goods that have been recorded as sales have been shipped.
- The proper treatment of sales transactions made with recourse or that have an abnormal amount of returns.

Many of these risks can be identified by the auditor when developing an understanding of the control environment and the types of transactions entered into by the company.

Sales Recognition: Normal Situation. Most sales transactions are recognized when title transfers and all parties to the transaction have completed their obligations or have formally recognized their obligations, usually when goods or services are delivered. There is not much question as to when a sale should be recognized at Wal-Mart. But some industries, such as construction, recognize sales on a percentage of completion basis. Other companies have inappropriately attempted to apply percentage of completion concepts to recognize revenue prior to an exchange.

Sales Recognition: Existence of Unusual Terms. Some sales transactions contain unusual terms that should lead the auditor to question whether a sale has actually taken place. For example, a sales agreement may have been signed but the goods will not be shipped until an unspecified future date and the customer has the right to return the goods. Should revenue be recognized? The client will argue that a bona fide sales agreement has been signed. The auditor must be able to read the sales agreement and determine whether a significant risk exists that the sale may never be realized.

Determination of Shipment or Cut-Off Date. Most sales follow regular procedures and are recognized when the goods are shipped. However, some organizations may attempt to inflate current period sales by shipping more goods than were ordered near the end of the year or may actually record next year's transactions on this year's books. The auditor must assess the likelihood that management might be motivated to override the accounting system to record inappropriate sales in the current year.

Sales with Abnormal Returns. Companies that suddenly show an abnormal amount of merchandise returns most likely have problems that should lead the auditor to further evaluate the control structure for sales. One example of such a problem is MiniScribe, a manufacturer of disk drives for personal computers.* The

*For a fuller description of the MiniScribe case, see the case material in Chapter 6.

company had a very aggressive, sales-oriented chairman who communicated specific sales goals to the financial press. The goals were set assuming that MiniScribe could continue to grow at a rate that had been obtained in the past even when the computer industry was changing dramatically. Poor quality control led to a high rate of returns by vendors. Rather than reworking the returns, MiniScribe shipped the returned disk drives as new orders. When the auditors discovered the situation, the company had to write down assets more than $200 million.

Summary: Inherent Risk in Sales Transactions. Inherent risk may increase due to the complexity of the transactions and the difficulty in determining when revenue is earned. This risk may be accentuated by management's desire to recognize revenue prematurely, or even inappropriately. In assessing inherent risk, the auditor normally considers the following:

- The nature and terms of the sales transactions to determine whether any unusual risk remains with the client, such as the purchaser's ability to return the merchandise without prior approval.
- The existence of authoritative pronouncements, such as FASB pronouncements on similar types of transactions, or whether the client's proposed accounting treatment is under discussion by the Emerging Issues Task Force of the FASB or by the SEC.
- The existence of litigation or financial press allegations asserting improper treatment of sales transactions by the client or other companies in the same industry.

Sales transactions that have inherent risk and have caused problems for auditors are reported in Exhibit 11.5.

Overview of Inherent Risks: Receivables

The primary risk associated with receivables is that the net amount shown is not collectible either because the receivables recorded do not represent bona fide claims or there is an insufficient allowance or reserve for uncollectible accounts. If a valid sales transaction does not exist, a valid receivable does not exist.

Potential additional risks associated with receivables include the following:

- Sales of receivables made with recourse and recorded as sales transactions rather than financing transactions.
- Receivables pledged as collateral against specific loans with restricted use. Disclosures of such restrictions are required.
- Receivables incorrectly classified as current when the likelihood of collection during the next year is low.
- Collection of a receivable that is contingent on specific events, which cannot be presently estimated.

The Control Environment: Effect on Sales

The impact of an organization's overall control environment as it affects revenue-related transactions focuses on the integrity of management, the financial condition

Exhibit 11.5

INHERENT RISK IN COMPLEX SALES TRANSACTIONS

Confirmed Sales of High-Tech Products, but Shipment Held in Local Warehouse

Company XYZ produced and marketed a highly complex biological product that segregates and grows new blood cells outside the human body. The financial press was optimistic about the prospects for the company. In addition, local governments were falling over each other to entice the company to build facilities in local research parks developed by the municipalities. Initial sales were promising, but the company began experiencing product difficulties. Over one-half of its sales were to overseas customers. Under a complex agreement with a Japanese company with apparent high name recognition (but actually only a shell company with seven employees), the audit client arranged for significant sales near the end of the year to the overseas company. However, actual shipment of the products overseas was to be made later. At year-end, however, the products were shipped from the client's facilities to a public warehouse in the same city. The overseas company confirmed the terms and existence of the sale and the local warehouse also confirmed that it was holding the merchandise for the overseas client. The sales and the related effect on profits were crucial to the company in obtaining new financing to expand production and develop new products.

Did a sale occur?

Selling Receivables

Company ABC decides to improve its financing by selling receivables. It does so by establishing a wholly owned subsidiary under the name of ABC Credit Corporation. ABC Credit Corporation buys all the receivables from ABC Company and in turn sells a 95 percent interest in the receivables to a major bank syndicate at a discount. An agreement is established whereby all future receivables will be sold in the same manner. The bank syndicate has complete recourse to ABC Credit Corporation, but not to ABC, for uncollectible receivables. ABC Credit Corporation, in turn, has recourse only to the parent.

Is this a transaction that should be recorded as a sale of receivables or as a borrowing with the receivables serving as major collateral?

Future Performance Guarantees

CCC Car Company sells cars with a rebate of $1,000 and a guarantee that if any higher rebate should be offered during the next year, the difference between the $1,000 and the higher rebate will be refunded to all customers who initially purchase a car with the $1,000 rebate. Although the guarantee is for the calendar year, the client's fiscal year ends on June 30. There is a high probability that the rebate will be increased to $1,500, but as of the date of the audit, no official decision has been made by the company and the best assessment is that it is a 50–50 proposition as to whether such a rebate will be given.

How much revenue was generated from the original sale and should be recorded as sales revenue during the year under audit?

of the organization, the financial pressures facing the organization, and possible management behavior caused by the company's management compensation system. Some companies create high budget expectations and reward divisional management handsomely for achieving the goals. The organization might not pay much attention as to *how* the goals are achieved but rather whether they are achieved. Such an approach may encourage manipulation of accounting figures to attain budgeted results. Representations regarding performance expectations by the company to the financial press are important as well. Once expectations are made public, companies and their management are motivated to meet the expectations.

An understanding of the control environment is intended to focus the auditor's attention on the *nature* of potentially troublesome transactions. Generally, a high degree of concern with the control environment leads to detailed examination of material transactions near the end of the year. An example of the typical questions in a revenue cycle control environment risk questionnaire is shown in Exhibit 11.6.

Exhibit 11.6

CONTROL ENVIRONMENT QUESTIONS: REVENUE CYCLE

1. What is the nature of financial projections given to the press regarding the current year and next year's operations? Do the projections reflect a high degree of optimism on the part of the company? Are the financial projections reasonably achievable without major new financing or other inputs into the organization?
2. What is the nature of competition for the company's products? How is the industry changing? What is the potential effect of such changes on the company's products and the ability of the company to realize projected revenue without incurring significant additional costs?
3. What has been the history of the company with respect to revenue recognition? Has it been aggressive in recognizing income? Has the auditor had previous disputes with the company regarding revenue recognition or has the company been the subject of any SEC or financial press investigations regarding the nature of its revenue recognition policies?
4. Does the company engage in any complex sales transactions, that is, transactions without normal shipment and billing terms? If so, can the auditor determine the economic substance of such transactions? Has the proper accounting for such transactions been addressed by the FASB or the SEC in any of its formal or informal communications?
5. To what extent is the compensation of top management and divisional management affected by achievement of specific sales goals or stock performance? Describe the relationship.
6. Do any future developments, such as expansion or obtaining needed financing, depend on the achievement of a certain level of sales and profitability for the organization? To what extent might these needs affect the company in changing its accounting approaches or accelerating the recognition of sales transactions?
7. Have there been any significant changes in the key accounting personnel during the past year? Have there been any significant management changes in the past year that might affect the company's desire to change its revenue recognition procedures? If so, what is the potential impact?
8. Does the internal audit function regularly review revenue cycle transactions? Do its reports go to the audit committee? Does the auditor have copies of its reports?
9. Does it appear that the audit committee provides effective overview of the company's transactions? Are controversial or aggressive accounting approaches discussed with the audit committee?
10. Has the company reached any agreements, or is it contemplating any agreements, that have the effect of selling receivables and recognizing financing income as a part of the transactions to sell the receivables? If so, what is the nature of the agreements and what is the potential impact on the accounting for both the sales and the receivables?

The questions are designed to obtain information about the nature of revenue transactions, the pressure the company faces in achieving particular levels of financial performance, and the effectiveness of environmental controls, such as effective audit committees and internal auditors.

Identifying Important Control Procedures

The auditor normally performs a walk-through of the transaction processing to determine how they are processed and the key control procedures that affect processing. Generally, the auditor documents the basic accounting system function (in this case, revenue-related applications) and the important control procedures at the same time. The auditor documents that understanding through the use of a narrative description, a flowchart, or a questionnaire as described in Chapter 8.

Existence/Occurrence

Validity of Recorded Transactions. Sales transactions should be recorded only when title has passed and the company has a valid claim on the assets (a receivable) from another organization. Control procedures should (see Exhibit 11.3) ensure that a sale is recorded only when shipment has been made, such as evidence of shipment obtained from the shipping department.

The occurrence of transactions can also be corroborated by customer monthly statements that are prepared and mailed independently of the department initially processing the transaction. Further control is accomplished by routing all customer questions to a separate section of the accounts receivable department to determine potential errors in the recording process. Because the accounts receivable department is a significant user of the computerized application, it should be actively involved in the conceptual design of application programs to ensure audit trail adequacy and to facilitate rapid investigation of customer inquiries.

Authorization. Specific managerial authorization should be required for all sales transactions involving very large amounts, unusual sales or credit terms, or that are otherwise considered out of the norm for the company. Such transactions should be authorized by someone at the executive level of the company. Other transactions may be authorized by sales managers or divisional managers. Authorization should be noted on all sales orders as part of an audit trail. The authorization function should not be performed by the same person who records the transactions.

Authorization of credit is normally determined by checking the client's computerized credit file. Transactions below a certain dollar limit can generally be authorized by obtaining verification from the computerized file. Transactions that are rejected by the automated system should be completed only on the explicit authorization of the credit manager or some executive responsible for sales and credit.

The credit policies should fit the organization. For example, clients that sell large special-order products, such as computerized manufacturing equipment, should develop credit policies that require (1) information on past customer payments, (2) current credit rating information from companies such as Dun & Bradstreet, and, in some cases, (3) a customer's annual report and/or current interim financial information. Some small businesses often extend credit to a number of customers on the approval of the owner-manager.

Timeliness of Recording. Most of the control procedures applicable to the validity of the transaction should ensure the timeliness of the recording. Each transaction should be specifically identified and control procedures set up to determine that all transactions are recorded on a timely basis. A control procedure could involve the accounting for, and follow-up of, prenumbered shipping documents to determine that all shipments have been recorded in a timely manner. Many organizations introduce extra control procedures near year-end to ensure that all transactions are recorded in the correct period. Timely identification of the last shipping document used and a prompt reconcilement of recorded sales with shipping documents are two examples of such control procedures.

Completeness

Completeness control procedures ensure that all valid transactions are recorded and correctly summarized in subsidiary ledgers such as the sales journal or the accounts receivable subsidiary ledger. Control procedures should be in place to uniquely identify a transaction, record it, and ensure that all transactions are captured and not lost. Control procedures that assist in accomplishing the objective include these:

- Use of *prenumbered* documents and subsequent accounting for all numbers.
- Immediate *on-line entry* into the computer system and immediate assignment of unique identification by the computer application.
- Reconciliation of shipping records with billing records.

Rights/Obligations

Control procedures should exist to ensure that the recorded assets resulting from revenue transactions belong to the client. Such procedures are primarily the same as those to accomplish the existence/occurrence objectives. Sales should not be recognized before the client has a legitimate claim to the assets of the customer or a transfer of assets has taken place.

Valuation

The valuation of most sales transactions is relatively easy. Sales are frequently made from authorized price lists, which may be contained in a computer file accessed through a cash register or by a sales representative. Or the price list may be carried by a salesperson making calls on customers. Valuation at retail stores is often accomplished by accessing a price list contained in the automatic cash register. Control procedures need to be designed to ensure the correct *input of authorized price changes* for products. Control procedures include the following:

- Limiting access to the files to authorized individuals.
- Printing a list of changed prices for review by the department authorizing them.
- Developing computer control procedures to reconcile input and output to ensure that all changes were made and no unauthorized ones were added.
- Limiting authorization privileges to the marketing manager or some other individual with the responsibility for pricing.

Valuation issues most often arise in connection with unusual or uncertain sales terms. Examples include sales on credit with the customer having recourse to the selling company, franchise sales, and contracts based on cost-plus billings or contracts covering long periods with provisions for partial payments. Complex contracts should be reviewed to determine the nature of the client's responsibilities and the economic substance of the contract.

Presentation and Disclosure

The major control procedures designed to achieve these objectives include (1) a comprehensive chart of accounts for classifying transactions, (2) training of employees, (3) review of complex or unusual transactions by supervisory personnel, and (4) computerization of standard transactions to ensure consistency of classification and processing.

Maintaining Accounting Integrity

Once a transaction has been initiated and captured, it is essential that the accounting system contain adequate control procedures to verify that the integrity of the transaction is maintained: no transactions are lost, added, or modified during the recording process. Control procedures include periodic reconciliation of input with output and procedures designed to generate prompt follow-up of missing or unusual transactions.

Control Procedures: An Overview

It is important to realize that the *specific control procedures* implemented by an audit client vary with the nature of the client's processing. But the basic control objectives and types of control procedures do not vary dramatically across similar accounting systems in different types of organizations. An overview of various control procedures to satisfy the specific control objectives in the sales recording function is shown in Exhibit 11.7 on pages 488–489.

Control Structure Regarding Returns, Allowances, and Warranties

Abnormal returns or allowances may be the first sign that a company has problems. Thus, it is crucial that an organization develop control procedures to ensure prompt and timely recording of all returns. As an example, the problems with MiniScribe described earlier were first evidenced by unusually high rates of returns. In many other cases, companies booked large amounts of sales in the fourth quarter only to be followed by large amounts of returns subsequent to the end of the year.

Key control procedures for identifying and promptly recording returned goods or allowances against existing accounts include the following:

1. Contractual return policy and warranty provisions provided in the sales contract.
2. Formal procedures for approving acceptance of returns that are beyond the warranty period.
3. Formal procedures for approving and identifying all returned merchandise.

Auditing in Practice

CREDIT RETURNS: FOOTWEAR MANUFACTURER

During the annual audit of a major U.S. footwear manufacturer, the auditors conducted a test of the client's perpetual inventory of finished goods. Contrary to previous experiences, the auditor noted many instances in which the actual inventory counts of shoes exceeded the amounts recorded on the perpetual inventory records. Previous experience with the client had indicated that the perpetual inventory records were accurate and that any adjustments for inventory write-downs were for shrinkage. The pattern of slightly higher or substantially higher counts for some product lines began to worry the auditor.

Tests of processing of entries into the perpetual inventory records revealed no patterns of error. The records were debited when production was completed and credited when sales were made. Tests of original transactions (tracing from source documents into the perpetual records) revealed very few errors and certainly none that could explain the differences on the test counts.

The merchandise return process had received little prior attention because the previous amounts were not considered material. However, because all other entries into the records were made on a timely basis, the auditor decided to investigate the processing for merchandise returns. Procedures for handling and recording returned merchandise were sloppy. Credit memos for merchandise returned often were not issued until six weeks or longer after the goods were received. Perpetual inventory records were updated when the credit memos were issued. When reviewing the six- to eight-week backlog of returned merchandise that was not recorded, the auditor noted that a preponderance of returns represented a new style of shoe. Subsequent investigation led to the identification of significant quality control problems on this new line. The alert investigation resulting from observing minor, but unexpected, differences on inventory counts led the auditor to discover the need to make major adjustments to the financial statements for obsolete inventory and for credits to sales and receivables.

In this case, the problem with returned merchandise was discovered through tests of the perpetual inventory records. But the case exemplifies the need for the auditor to understand the interrelationship between account balances and potential causes of misstatements in the accounts. In many cases for which there is audit concern as to the company's financial viability or a review of trade journals identifies product quality concerns, the auditor directly tests the control process to record returned merchandise.

4. Formal procedures for granting credit or performing warranty work related to returned merchandise.
5. Formal procedures for accounting for goods returned, such as recording the return of merchandise on prenumbered documents that are accounted for to be sure they are all recorded on a timely basis (see Auditing in Practice on credit returns).
6. Formal procedures for identifying whether credit should be given or whether the goods will be repaired and shipped back to the customer.
7. Prescribed accounting procedures for items returned for which full credit has been granted. Controls should include formal procedures to determine the potential obsolescence or defects in the goods and whether a reasonable

Exhibit 11.7

OVERVIEW OF KEY CONTROL PROCEDURES IN SALES TRANSACTIONS

Control Objectives	Control Procedures
Existence/Occurrence	
1. Recorded transactions are valid.	1. Sales transactions are processed only upon receipt of valid purchase order (or sales order) and evidence of shipment. a. Sales invoices must be accompanied by related shipping and purchase documents. b. The shipping function and the recording function are properly segregated.
2. Transactions are authorized.	2. a. Authorized signature is required before a sales order can be processed and shipped. b. Credit authorization must be obtained before shipment. (1). Authorized signature if system is manual or if special authorization is required. (2). Computer authorization (including verification number) required before shipment. If authorization field is not complete, the computer will not generate a packing or shipping slip. c. Authorization procedures are implemented to ensure appropriate segregation of duties.
3. Transactions are recorded on a timely basis.	3. The computer creates an invoice and updates related records based on receipt of shipping notice. Goods shipped and goods billed are periodically reconciled.
Completeness	
4. All transactions are recorded.	4. a. Prenumbered shipping and invoice documents are used and periodically accounted for. b. On-line computer input of all transactions and independent logging of the transactions are created for subsequent use in performing reconciliations. c. Recorded transactions are periodically reviewed, compared with budgets, and variances investigated.

value exists at which the returned items could be recorded in regular or scrap inventory.

Returned goods might be scrapped, sold through a company factory outlet store, reworked and sold as repaired products, or reworked according to warranty provisions and returned to the customer. Control procedures are necessary to identify and classify all merchandise returned promptly and accurately.

Exhibit 11.7

d. Monthly statements are mailed regularly to customers.
e. Subsidiary ledgers are periodically reconciled to the general ledger and differences investigated.
f. A separate department investigates all customer accounts receivable inquiries.

Rights/Obligations	
5. Recorded transactions and accruals properly reflect the transfer of ownership or obligation.	5. a. Sales invoices or contracts clearly specify ownership terms and transfer of ownership. b. Sales are recognized only when verification of shipment is received from shipping department or as specified in the contract.
Valuation	
6. and 7. Transactions are recorded accurately and are properly valued in accordance with GAAP.	6.&7. a. Sales orders are filled by authorized personnel following an authorized price catalog. b. Sales prices are maintained on the computer and access to the computer file is restricted to those authorized to change it. c. The internal audit department periodically performs tests of sales invoices to see if the terms agree with authorized price lists. d. Executive approval is required of all large, unusual, or complex sales transactions. e. Oral or written verification of prices with customer is required for all nonstandard sales. f. Products shipped and billed must correspond to existing product list.
Presentation and Disclosure	
8. Transactions are correctly classified.	8. a. A chart of accounts is maintained. b. Comprehensive user testing of computer program is performed to ensure that accounts are properly identified and updated.

Importance of Credit Policies Authorizing Sales

Accounts receivable balances arise primarily from credit sales and cash collection transactions. The proper recording of sales thus directly affects the valuation of accounts receivable, especially the procedures to ensure that proper credit authorization procedures are followed before credit is extended. Control procedures should ensure that only acceptable credit risks are taken by the organization. The following control procedures assist this objective:

1. A formal credit policy, which may be automated for most transactions and require special approval for large and/or unusual transactions.
2. A periodic review of the credit policy by key executives to determine whether changes are dictated either by current economic events or by the deterioration of the receivables.
3. Continuous monitoring of receivables for evidence of increased risk such as increased number of days past due of significant portions of receivables or an unusually high concentration in a few key customers whose financial prospects are declining.
4. Adequate segregation of duties in the credit department with specific authorization to write off receivables segregated from individuals who handle cash transactions with the customer.

In some industries, such as financial institutions, statutory rules are intended to minimize the financial credit risk to an organization. For example, banks and savings and loans often have limits as to how much they can lend to a specific organization. In such cases, the auditor must be particularly alert to procedures the client uses to identify all borrowers that are related to each other so that the aggregate amount of loans does not exceed statutory regulations.* Financial institutions normally have specific procedures to collateralize major loans. Unfortunately, reviews by outside agencies have indicated that many financial institutions have not done a good job of developing control procedures to ensure that loans remain fully collateralized, that the collateral's value is greater than that of the loan, and that the lender has the first claim on the collateral. A more detailed discussion of issues specifically related to financial institutions is presented in Chapter 19.

C–ASSESSING AND DOCUMENTING CONTROL RISK

The assessment of control risk begins with the understanding of the control environment and is followed by understanding and documenting control procedures in important accounting systems. The accounting control procedures can be documented in a flowchart, narrative, and/or questionnaire. An example of an internal control questionnaire for sales and accounts receivable is shown in Exhibit 11.8 on pages 492–493.

Each negative answer in the questionnaire represents a potential control procedure deficiency. When a negative answer is appropriate, the auditor should consider the impact of the response on potential misstatements in the account. For example, a negative response to the question regarding the existence of a segregation of duties between those receiving cash and those authorizing write-offs or adjustments of

*In fact, one of the problems that occurred during the savings and loan crisis is that the loans made to an entity, *and all the related parties to that entity* that were directly or indirectly controlled by the entity, often exceeded the legal limits of loans to the entity.

accounts indicates that a *risk* exists that an individual could take cash receipts and cover up the theft by writing off a customer's balance. Unless another control compensates for this weakness, the auditor should consider the risk of that specific misstatement in designing the audit program for direct tests of the account balance.

An alternative approach is the development of a flowchart and control objective narrative for the accounting system. Usually, a high-level flowchart is prepared depicting the flow of transactions to the general ledger.* The flowchart documents control procedures that address specific control objectives. The control procedures may be manual or computerized. For example, the valuation objective may be accomplished by limiting invoice prices to those contained in a master file on the computer system.

When the understanding and documentation of the accounting system and control procedures are completed, the auditor develops a preliminary assessment of control risk present in the account(s). If the auditor determines that the assessment of control risk would be reduced to some reasonably low amount if the control procedures function as described (as noted earlier, most firms find it difficult to assign specific values to control risk and use broad descriptions such as low, moderate, or high), the auditor determines whether overall audit costs can be reduced by testing to see that control procedures are operating as described. In some cases, the auditor finds it cost beneficial to test the control procedures in operation. In other cases, the auditor determines that it is less costly to directly test the account balance with a planned low level of detection risk rather than to test the control procedures.

Testing for the Operating Effectiveness of Control Procedures

If an auditor preliminarily assesses control risk as low and concludes that substantive tests can be reduced cost-effectively, the auditor must gain assurance that the control procedures are operating effectively. For example, in the preceding section, valuation control procedures, as described, were assessed to be effective in reducing control risk. But the auditor must determine that those control procedures are operating effectively, that is, (1) all invoice prices do come from the authorized price list and (2) only authorized price changes are made to the master file. Without assurance that the control procedures are operating effectively, the auditor would have to perform direct tests to determine that invoices are properly valued.

The auditor tests the effectiveness of control procedures through (1) observation, (2) selecting and tracing transactions through the accounting system, or (3) testing computer controls using test data or an integrated test facility as described in Chapter 10. The auditor might be able to *observe* the processing of transactions and the conscientiousness with which employees perform their work. More likely, the auditor selects a representative sample of invoices and traces the selling price to the authorized master price list (assuming a hard copy exists; otherwise, the auditor needs to address the computer master file directly). The auditor reviews procedures used to limit changes to the price list to those authorized and tests the computer system's effectiveness in limiting access to the files.

*The auditor normally needs to focus only on the flow of transactions to the general ledger because all other flows of documents are not germane to the recording process. A common mistake of students is to assume that all aspects of a system must be flowcharted to be meaningful. Generally, the cost to develop and maintain a detailed flowchart is more than the benefit that it can provide.

Exhibit 11.8

CONTROL RISK ASSESSMENT QUESTIONNAIRE: SALES AND RECEIVABLES

Sales Orders:

Check (x) which
Yes No

Sales authorized by: (Describe the source and scope of authority, and the documentation or other means of indicating authorizations. Include explicitly the authorization of prices for customers.

____
____
____

Sales orders prepared by, or entered into the system by:

____
____
____

Individuals authorized to change price tables: (Indicate specific individuals and their authority to change prices on the system and the methods utilized to verify the correctness of changes.)

____
____
____

Existence of major contracts with customers that might merit special attention during the course of the audit: (Describe any major contracts and their terms.)

____
____
____

Restrictions on access to computer files for entering or changing orders: (Describe access control systems and indicate whether we have tested it in conjunction with our review of data processing general controls.)

____
____
____

	Yes	No
1. Are orders entered by individuals who do not have access to the goods being shipped?	______	______
2. Are orders authorized by individuals who do not have access to the goods being shipped?	______	______
3. Are batch and edit controls used effectively on this application? If so, describe the controls.	______	______

____
____

(Continued)

Exhibit 11.8

	Yes	No
4. Are sales invoices prenumbered? Are the sequence of prenumbered documents independently accounted for?	______	______
5. Are control totals and reconciliations used effectively to ensure that all items are recorded and that subsidiary files are updated at the same time invoices are generated? If so, describe the controls. ______________________ ______________________	______	______
6. Do procedures exist to ensure that the current credit status of a customer is checked before an order is shipped? If so, describe. ______________________ ______________________	______	______
7. Are price lists stored in the computer independently reconciled to authorized prices by the marketing manager or someone in the marketing manager's office?	______	______

Dual-Purpose Tests

Note that some of the tests, especially those involved with selecting invoices and tracing to the master price list, can be viewed as **dual-purpose tests,** that is, the test is effective in determining that (1) the control procedures are operating as described and (2) the recording transactions are complete, properly valued, and accurate (a substantive test of the account balance). Most audit programs require the auditor to select documents evidencing a transaction and then trace the transaction through the system to address the *completeness* objective. The auditor may select shipping documents or bills of lading as evidence of shipment and trace the transaction through the system to determine that all goods were properly billed in a timely fashion. Such a test provides evidence as to the correctness of the account balance and therefore is considered a substantive audit procedure. Moreover, the auditor may find it convenient to test for the effectiveness of various control procedures while tracing the transaction through the system. For example, the auditor may be able to determine whether credit approval was obtained or that there is evidence of reconciliation of all goods shipped on that day with goods invoiced. By properly planning dual-purpose tests, the auditor can gain efficiency.

The auditor can test the effectiveness of the control procedures relating to the *existence/occurrence* assertion by selecting a sample of already recorded sales and vouching to evidence of shipment. The auditor determines whether all recorded sales are valid by looking at evidence that verifies that a shipment of goods took place. The auditor also notes the effectiveness of control procedures.

The difference between testing for completeness and existence/occurrence is shown in Exhibit 11.9. Invoice 101 is selected from the sales journal and vouched back through documents to determine the occurrence of a shipment and the validity of the recorded sale. The item selected from the file of shipping documents is reprocessed through the system and the related invoice, to the sales journal, noting that all goods shipped were billed in a timely fashion at the appropriate prices. The two distinct procedures, together, address the existence and completeness assertions. An example of an abbreviated audit program for testing control procedures and the substantive assertions is shown in Exhibit 11.10.

Reassessment of Control Risk

Evidence gained by testing control procedures is used to reassess control risk. In most cases, control procedures are operating effectively and provide support for the reduced level of control risk. In some cases, however, control procedures are not operating effectively. Moreover, because the control procedures are not operating effectively, misstatements may exist in the general ledger. Given the nature of the potential misstatements, there is a need to adjust the audit program to specifically recognize the types of misstatements that may have occurred and to develop audit procedures to determine the extent of such misstatements.

Linking Control Risk Assessment and Substantive Testing

Recall that the basic framework for controlling audit risk is that audit risk is a function of inherent risk, control risk, and detection risk. If control risk is assessed low, the auditor can conduct substantive testing with a higher level of detection risk (less

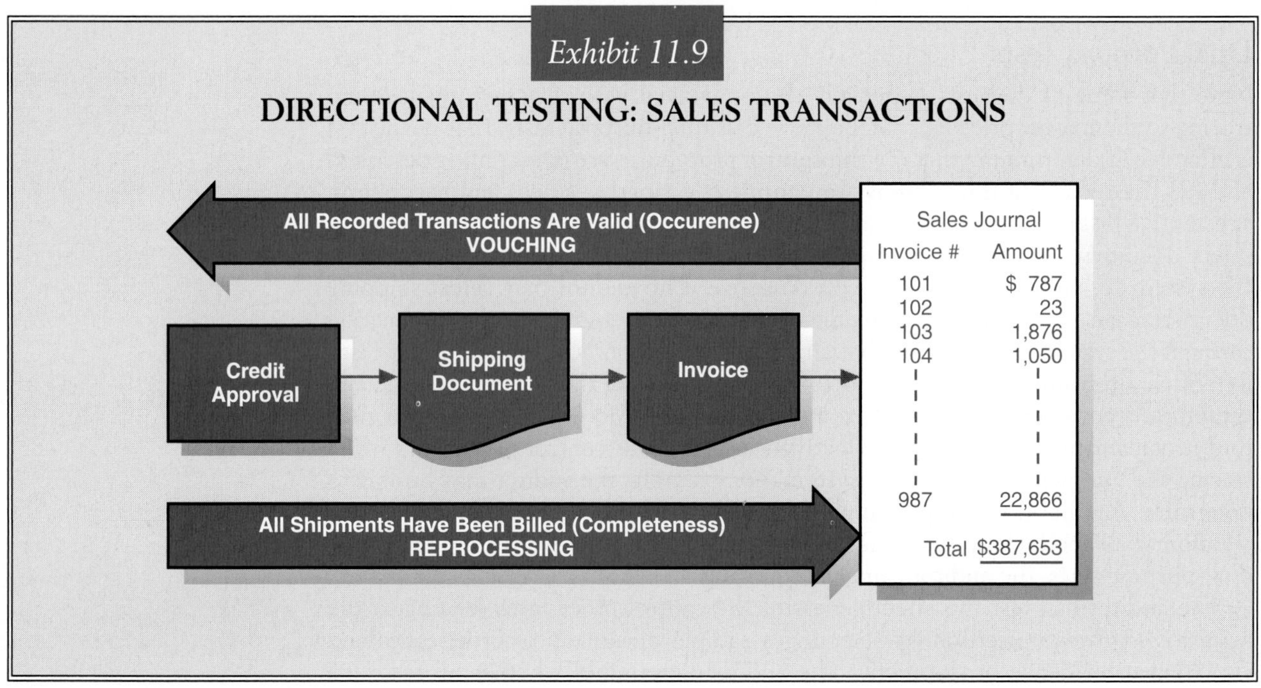

Exhibit 11.10

TESTS OF CONTROL PROCEDURES AND EXISTENCE AND COMPLETENESS ASSERTIONS

1. Select a representative sample of sales orders and perform the following procedures:
   a. Review for evidence of proper authorization.
   b. Review for evidence of credit approval.
   c. Reprocess from the shipping document to the generation of an invoice and determine that
      (1). All goods shipped were billed.
      (2). Goods were shipped within a reasonable period of time after the order was taken.
      (3). Goods were billed in accordance with authorized prices.
      (4). Invoice was properly computed and recorded in the sales journal.
      (5). The sales journal is accurately posted to the general ledger.
2. Select a representative sample of entries from the sales account and by subsampling, vouch selected entries back to the source document (shipping notice) noting:
   a. Invoice is for actual goods shipped.
   b. Proper credit approval was obtained prior to shipment.
   c. Invoice was properly computed (correct price and computation).

extensive audit procedures than would otherwise be needed) than if control risk is assessed at the maximum.

The auditor learns two things during the control risk assessment that directly affect the design of substantive audit procedures:

1. The nature of the accounting system, the control procedures utilized, and the validity of documents generated in the client's processing.
2. The effectiveness of control procedures in preventing or detecting errors and, if not effective, the types of misstatements that are likely to occur.

The first allows the auditor to consider sources of evidence and the relative reliability of evidence to conduct a cost efficient audit. The auditor obtains information about the validity of sales invoices and their relative reliability, for example, based on the effectiveness of control procedures utilized. The second provides information that helps the auditor to determine the nature of misstatements and to tailor the audit program to search for specific types of misstatements. If, for example, the auditor finds situations in which invoices are prepared, but goods are shipped at a later date, the auditor can use that knowledge to expand audit procedures to test specifically for transactions being recorded in the wrong period. Based on the assessment of those two factors, the auditor then needs to determine *what additional procedures* are necessary to corroborate the initial assessment of the correctness of the account balance and *how much additional evidence is needed* for each of the audit procedures selected.

D–ILLUSTRATIVE EXAMPLE: LEFLAM MANUFACTURING COMPANY

The background material in the following case illustrates an audit approach to a medium-size manufacturing company for the major accounting cycles and subsequent chapters. The company uses a mixture of manual and computerized processing.

Background

LeFlam Manufacturing Company is a medium-size audit client located in the Midwest. The company has been a client for the past 10 years, during which its annual sales volume increased from $14 million to $29.8 million. A summary of recent financial information is shown in Exhibit 11.11.

The company expanded rapidly during the latter part of the 1980s. The expansion took place shortly after the founder died in 1986 and new management assumed a much more aggressive posture toward expanding the company's product lines and promoting them to discount chains and other outlets. The company's stock is traded on the over-the-counter exchange. Approximately 28 percent of the company's shares are closely held. Prior to 1987, approximately 47 percent of the company's shares were closely held, and maintaining a high dividend was a high priority of previous management.

Company Products

LeFlam Manufacturing Company manufactures and distributes outdoor camping and sporting goods. Its primary lines of business include the following:

- Fiberglass canoes (approximately 25 percent of sales).
- Tents and other canvas-based merchandise (30 percent of sales).
- Rain gear and other outdoor clothing, including garments worn by fishermen and related accessories (45 percent of sales).

The company was founded by James Lubouy in the 1950s to take advantage of a patent he developed for breathable canvas material that would retain its water repellency. Over the years, the company's products have come to stand for high quality and have been recognized as the premier products on the market. The company expanded into rain gear and other outdoor "hearty" clothing in the 1960s and gained a reputation for quality products. It uses "folksy charm" in promoting its products, such as rugged fishermen talking about the durability and comfort of its products. The canvas-based materials, such as tents, are advertised in specialty magazines. The company has also worked with its sales force to sell products to intermediate brokers, who in turn sell to specialty retailers.

The company continued with its two primary product lines until 1987, shortly after the death of its founder. New management aggressively sought to increase market share and product lines. It acquired the canoe division of a conglomerate in 1987, and the company now produces a line of fiberglass canoes. The products are durable but heavier (approximately 6 to 8 pounds) than competing aluminum

Exhibit 11.11

LEFLAM MANUFACTURING COMPANY
SELECTED FINANCIAL HIGHLIGHTS
(IN THOUSANDS OF DOLLARS)

Sales and Income Figures	Date	Sales	Cost of Products Sold	Income before Income Taxes	Net Income
	1984	14.2	10.3	1.56	0.86
	1985	14.1	10.2	1.44	0.82
	1986	13.7	10.0	1.21	0.67
	1987	13.7	10.4	1.12	0.53
	1988	14.4	10.5	1.61	0.92
	1989	16.6	11.8	1.78	0.97
	1990	17.6	12.6	1.92	1.12
	1991	21.7	15.6	2.25	1.44
	1992	23.9	17.2	2.33	1.38
	1993	24.5	17.8	2.06	1.11
	1994	28.9	21.2	2.98	1.79

Selected Other Financial Data	1984	1987	1990	1992	1994
Cash	0.444	0.562	0.234	0.673	0.100
Receivables	1.336	1.590	3.022	2.890	5.643
Inventory	2.208	2.560	5.234	8.893	13.385
Property, plant, and equipment	0.897	0.931	1.286	1.864	1.997
Total assets	5.285	6.060	10.276	14.870	21.725
Current liabilities	1.620	2.080	2.580	6.310	6.459
Long-term debt	0.500	0.500	3.500	3.500	9.000
Deferred taxes	0.250	0.450	0.860	1.450	1.590
Stockholders' equity	2.915	3.030	3.336	3.610	4.676

canoes. However, they also sell for less than aluminum canoes, are quieter in the water, and appeal to groups such as YMCA camps and individuals who value the quiet over the extra weight. The firm has also developed a specialty niche with a wide-bodied canoe that can be propelled by a small outboard motor.

In addition to the acquisition of the canoe line, new company management made some other major changes. Realizing that it had approximately 35 percent of a mature market, it sought new outlets for its material and developed major accounts with Wal-Mart, Kmart, Sam's Wholesale Club, Target department stores, and Ace Hardware stores. Shipments are made by common carrier directly to the distribution centers of all but Kmart, which prefers shipments by UPS to individual stores. In addition to these major accounts, which now represent 63 percent of the business, the company has approximately 2,000 customers, mostly small retail stores. The company believes it maintains the following competitive advantage over its three major competitors:

1. Its central location, which allows easy access to most distribution points. Its major competitors are located on either the east or west coast.
2. Its reputation for high quality and willingness to stand behind its products. Many long-time users closely identify with its Northern Highland, Scenic, and Raingo product brands. (It should be noted, however, that approximately one-half of the sales to Kmart and Ace are under their retail labels.)
3. Competitive pricing facilitated by integrated manufacturing and a premium reputation.

Marketing Philosophy

Management's philosophy has remained unchanged over the company's 30 years: "Make the best-quality product, make products that people will use (or wear), make the products attractive and responsive to life-style changes, and increase market share." Although new management has been more aggressive toward increasing sales, it retains the long-term business philosophy of its predecessors and is not willing to sacrifice long-term market share for short-term profits. However, the auditor is aware that the top seven executives have a formal bonus program based on profitability. In addition, management is always aware of the threat of being taken over through a hostile offer because the company is publicly traded. However, the 28 percent ownership that is closely held prevents, to some extent, the likelihood of a takeover. The company is control conscious and previous assessments of control risk have been low.

The company is expanding its marketing program overseas. It has made some strong inroads in Spain and has had moderate success in Japan, and somewhat surprising results in Russia. International sales accounts for only eight percent of its current sales, but with the opportunities available in the European Community, it is expanding its efforts in the international area and hopes to attain approximately one-quarter of its sales internationally by the late 1990s. Presently, it is working through brokers to establish an international market but has not made a decision regarding physical expansion overseas.

Accounting Functions

The company's headquarters and major plants are located in southeast Wisconsin except for the canoe factory, which is located in central Missouri. All of the corporate accounting is done in the Wisconsin headquarters. The company has a small accounting function at the canoe factory, which mainly captures data such as shipping and order information, payroll, and purchases, which are transmitted electronically to corporate headquarters.

The company's controller is also its treasurer. Most of the accounting function is supervised by the assistant controller and a total staff of nine people. Data processing is centralized with a relatively small staff. Many of the accounting packages, such as those used with electronic data interchange, are purchased packages. Data processing is staffed by a manager, two operators, and four programmer/managers. Segregation within data processing seems minimal, but there is apparently good segregation between data processing and user groups. Personnel seem to be conscientious, and the company has implemented a control system to restrict access to files to authorized personnel for authorized purposes. An overview of the organization chart for the accounting function is shown in Exhibit 11.12.

Overview of the Revenue Cycle

Customer purchase orders are received by mail, telephone, fax, or EDI. Mail, phone, and fax orders from preapproved customers are batched in groups of approximately 50 items for entry into the computerized order file by a clerk in the order-processing function. Data are entered into the system through a standardized entry interface, which requests all the key information contained on a purchase order. An overview of the process is shown in Exhibit 11.13.

Data Processing

The client utilizes a state-of-the-art minicomputer that has two tape drives and four disk drives. Although the computer is referred to as a *minicomputer*, the data processing manager jokes that the system has one and a half times the storage and computing power of the mainframe computers utilized only one decade ago. The system is connected to six terminals used for order entry and are capable of generating batch total information for subsequent reconcilement. In addition, all of the accounting staff and some of the marketing staff have PCs that stand alone or can be connected

Exhibit 11.12

ORGANIZATION OF ACCOUNTING FUNCTION

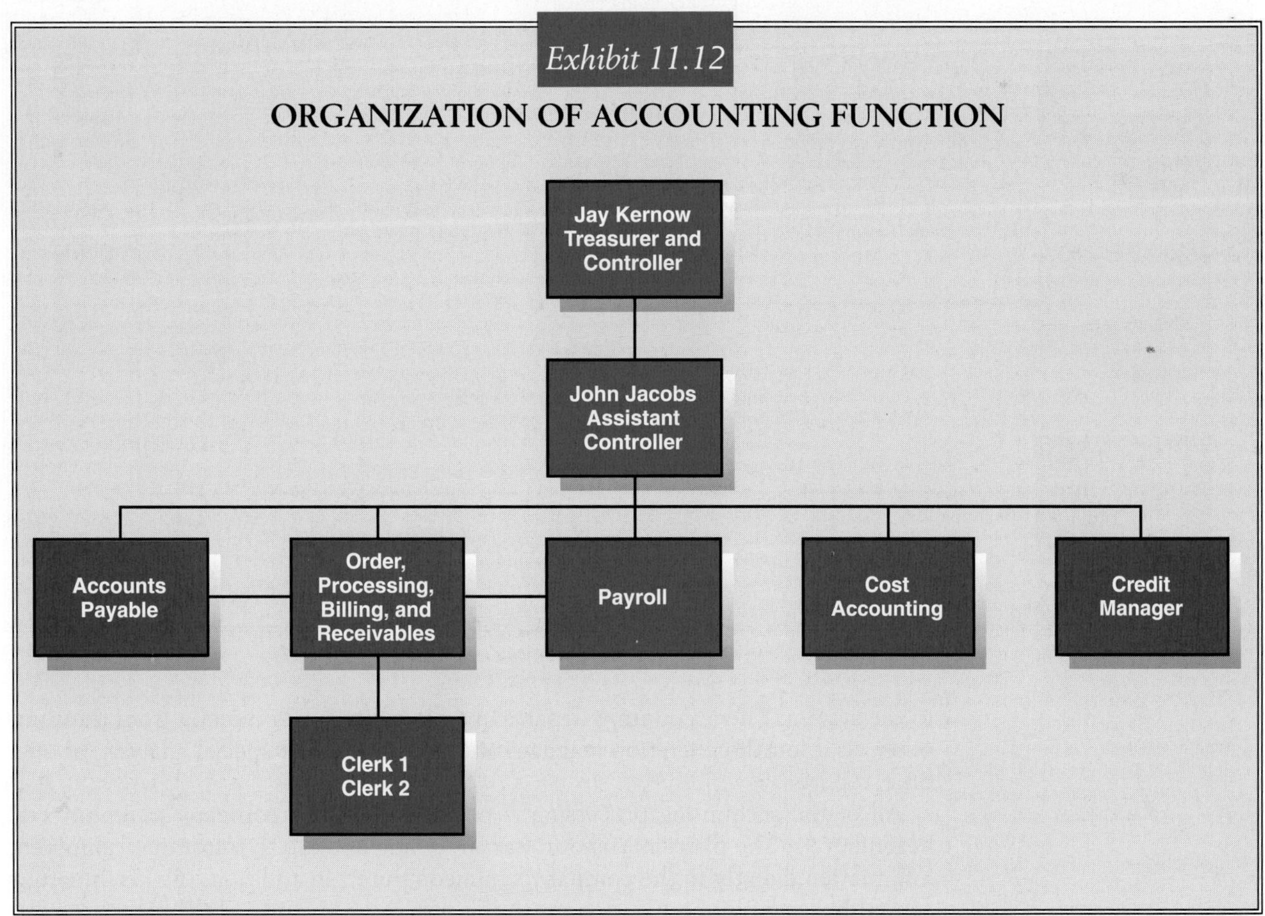

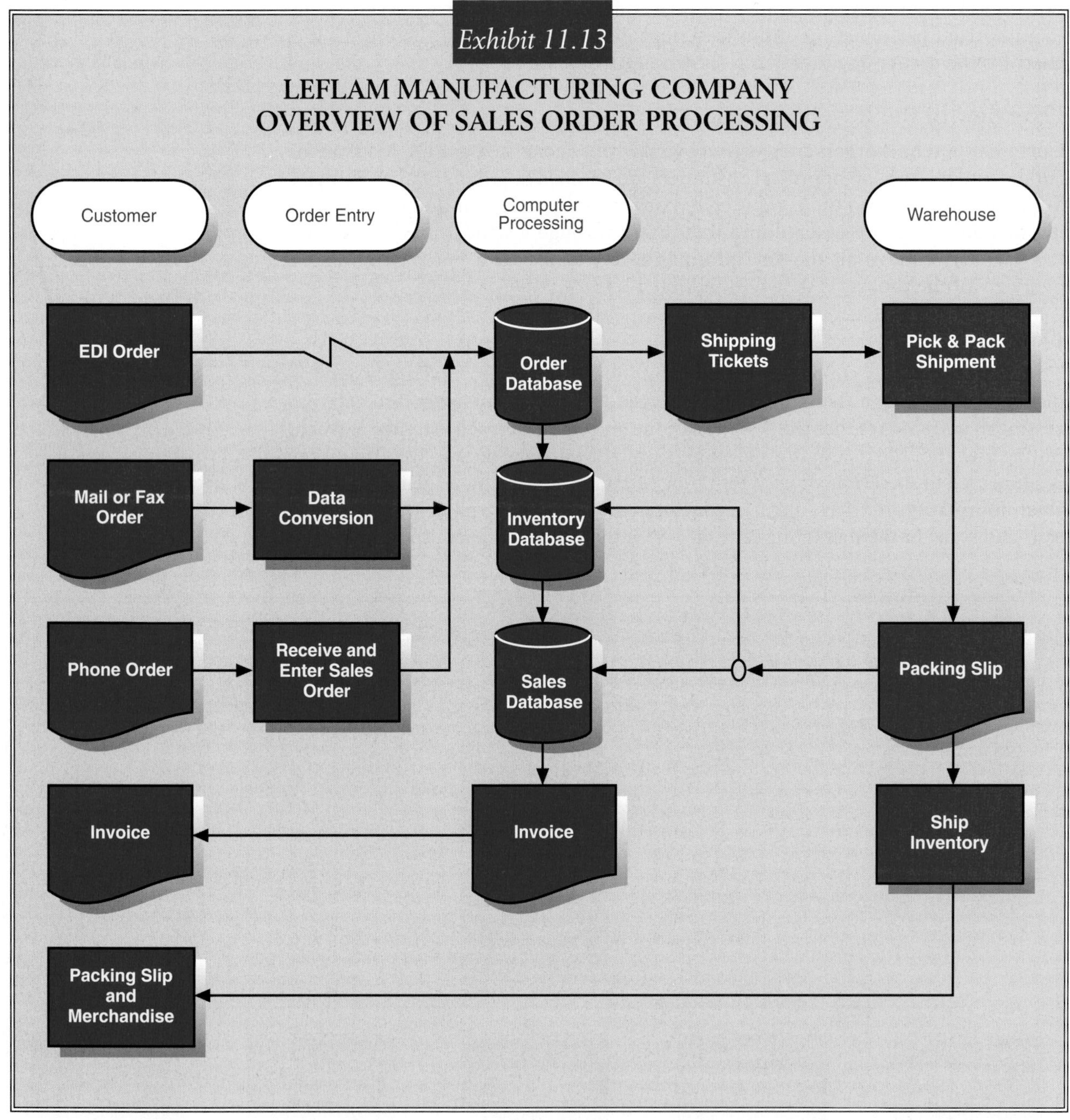

to the system. The accounting department can extract data directly from the computer via a fourth-generation language and generates some special analysis, or one-time, reports.

All of the accounting processing is performed on the company's computer at headquarters. The plant in Missouri has an on-line hookup to transmit all shipment information directly to the company's minicomputer. In addition, the headquarters computer sends shipping directions to the system in Missouri. The major accounting applications in the revenue cycle are the sales and order entry, receivables, inventory, and credit history. The primary files affected by these applications are the following:

1. *Sales,* including sales by product line, geographic region, and various sales analysis, such as responses to special promotions, and so forth.
2. *Salesperson commissions* based on the sales analysis.
3. *Accounts receivable* listed by customer and customer identification.
4. *Back order,* a list of all orders for which the company is out of stock and the customer has been notified.
5. *Shipping order file,* a temporary file of all orders to date organized and scheduled by the automated inventory control system for shipment in a timely fashion and by most economic carrier.
6. *Inventory and cost of goods sold,* both of which are updated by sales transactions.
7. *Credit analysis* is updated by all aspects of customer history but posted monthly with a summary of new credit sales to the customer and payments.

Accounting System and Control Procedures

Orders received by mail usually come in the form of a customer purchase order. If an order is taken by telephone, the order taker generates an order form with features essentially the same as a customer purchase order but prenumbered. Although the company plans to move to on-line order entry, it has not done so because it believes the customer wants to talk with a marketing manager or customer representative who is knowledgeable about the company's products and might be able to offer discounts for larger purchases or may be able to recommend additional products. The large nationwide retailers have encouraged all their suppliers to implement electronic data interchange, and LeFlam has worked with a third-party server to establish EDI with its five major customers. EDI for LeFlam means direct input of sales orders, matching orders with inventory for prompt shipment, and electronically invoicing the customers for the merchandise as shipments are made. A standardized sales order and invoice form are utilized across the industry, which LeFlam uses. An invoice is electronically generated when evidence of shipment matches the customer purchase order. The invoice is recorded and updates sales and accounts receivable (as does the recording of other invoices). However, the invoice is not printed—even for internal usage—thus, the audit trail is in the computer system.

Mail, phone, and fax orders from preapproved customers are batched in groups of approximately 50 items for entry into the computerized order file by a clerk in the order-processing function. Data are entered into the system through a standardized entry interface, which requests all the key information contained on a customer's order. All original orders are filed by customer. All logged orders are given a unique sequential identification number. EDI orders are also assigned a unique sequence number, but with a prefix of E, such as E1027. Additionally, all orders are date stamped either manually or by the computer.

Most of the system files are on-line, and many applications access more than one file. For example, the sales order application accesses the credit file and the inventory file to determine whether credit is authorized and goods are on hand. Even though most of the processing is on-line, the company logs all transactions by terminal and reconciles the total input per day by terminal with the sales order list generated for the day. Any differences are promptly investigated.

The auditor's previous review of control procedures indicated that the company used extensive computer edit tests to flag unusual transactions, that employees seemed to be well trained and conscientious, and that there was prompt follow-up by user departments to correct any transactions that failed the edit tests. The strength of the control procedures had led the previous audit team to assess control risk as low. However, this is the first year the company has utilized EDI very extensively. Although the test results of the company on EDI yielded very few problems last year, the audit partner is concerned about potential problems that may be associated with the increased EDI volume this year and wants specific documentation of control procedures related to EDI and a test of the effectiveness of those control procedures.

A review of the previous year working papers indicates that the following control procedures are implemented at this point:

1. *Batch control totals* are established for all transactions entered into the system. Record counts are computed and control totals developed for the number of products ordered. The control totals are reconciled by terminal by time of day by the order entry department. Any missing items are immediately investigated.
2. For customer orders received in the mail and by phone, the clerk enters the product number first and the system automatically prints its selling price. Special prices are entered for the five major customers. If the customer's order price differs from the price list, the order clerk enters the customer's order price to override the system price. However, this override establishes a hold on the order. A computerized list of all discrepancies is routed electronically to a file used by the product line marketing manager to review and, when appropriate, approve the customer's order price. The file shows the order price and the approved price. The order must have the *authorization* of the marketing manager before it can be processed. The approval can be made electronically by the marketing manager sitting at the desk and reading a list of all price variances for the day.
3. Extensive *computer edit checks* are used in the system. For example, computer checks determine that all fields are complete, that data are entered properly as alpha or numeric characters, that data entered fall within an acceptable range, and that data are within limits established for the product or customer. In addition, all inventory part numbers contain a *self-checking digit* and prices are matched with part number as described above.
4. Any input items failing the computer edit tests are immediately reviewed by a supervisor in the order entry area who compares the computer input with the original source document. If the error cannot be located immediately by this procedure, the document is returned to the originator for follow-up with the customer. A suspense file is maintained for all rejected items. Any items not corrected within four days are flagged and a report is sent to all parties responsible for correction. This procedure is intended to ensure that all items are recorded and that none are lost during this correction process.
5. Upon order entry, the system generates a total for the order and compares that total with the customer's outstanding accounts receivable balance and credit limit. If the total of the order plus outstanding amounts due would put the customer over the credit limit, the transaction is written out on a

special credit report, which is transmitted twice a day to the credit department for review. Each transaction is logged and must be cleared within two days by the credit department, indicating either that the transaction should be processed or that it should be canceled. If canceled, a report is written to the originator of the order and to the customer. If the item is not cleared in two days, a reminder notice of all outstanding items is sent to the credit department.

6. Many orders are associated with a salesperson whose compensation is based on the number and profitability of orders generated. Each salesperson is supposed to maintain a log of all orders submitted each day, and the accounting system also develops such a list. The list is sent to each salesperson for reconciliation and follow-up. Discrepancies are generally noted and corrections are made by the submission of a specific form to a special section of the order-entry department.

As orders are received, the order-entry application accesses the inventory file to determine whether the goods are on hand. If they are on hand, the system requests the quantity ordered, thus restricting the items from being shipped to another customer. If they are not available for shipment, the back-order file is accessed to determine when the goods will be available. The salesperson is immediately notified of the out-of-stock condition for possible follow-up with the customer. However, the accounting system continues with the back-order process. If the goods will be available within three days, the system notes the back order and notifies the customer and salesperson of the intended shipping date. If the back order requires more than three days, this is noted and a notice is sent to the customer and salesperson with an option to cancel the order if the shipment cannot be made on a timely basis. This latter situation is rare because the company prides itself on maintaining next-day shipment on 98 percent of its orders as part of its commitment to customer service. A salesperson may cancel the back-order process.

If goods are available for shipment, the system generates a picking ticket with a preprinted and prenumbered packing slip. Items are packed in the warehouse for shipment according to the specified shipping date. The application develops a preinvoice at the same time the packing slip is generated. The invoice is not printed or recorded until the shipping department acknowledges the shipment of the order by entering the packing slip number into a terminal located at the shipping dock and making any adjustments to items actually shipped. Differences between the packing slip and actual orders are rare because shortages should occur only when the perpetual inventory record is inaccurate. Differences are immediately reported to the warehouse manager for follow-up. In addition, the internal audit department receives a copy of the difference reports for potential follow-up by internal audit.

Prior audit work with this client has shown the inventory records to be highly accurate. The major concern is that goods might actually be shipped without proper notification to the system, potentially leading to a failure to invoice the sale. The following control procedures appear to be in place:

1. Packing slips are prenumbered and developed in triplicate. The shipping department removes one copy before actual shipment, which must be signed by a supervisor who must note any discrepancies between actual shipments and orders. These documents are forwarded to the shipping office for input. The documents are periodically sorted and a computer printout of all

missing items is produced for investigation. The remaining two copies are sent with the order to the customer.

2. The accounting system identifies the expected shipment date for all orders when they are entered into the system. Actual shipment dates are entered by the shipping department. If the system does not receive notice of the shipment by the planned shipping date, an exception report of all open items is prepared and is sent to the shipping department for investigation. If the discrepancies are not resolved within two days, a copy of all open items is sent to the warehouse manager for investigation.
3. The shipment and preparation of an invoice also update the accounts receivable file. A daily report of all invoices is prepared and reconciled with a control total for changes to accounts receivable.

The control procedures established for data processing appear to be adequate for this size installation. A comprehensive access control program has been implemented to effectively prevent unauthorized access to computer files. The access control procedures have been extensively reviewed in previous years and were found to be effective. The company has installed an automated program library, which restricts the ability to make changes to programs to the data processing manager (after the programs have been tested by users). Previous tests indicate that users take their responsibility seriously and regularly reconcile input with output and follow up on discrepancies.

Control Risk Assessment and Control Procedures Testing

The audit approach utilized is built around the control objectives. Important control procedures are identified within each application to address the control objectives. The linkage of control objectives with control testing procedures for sales transactions is shown in Exhibit 11.14. A number of important control procedures have been identified, including these:

1. Control procedures effectively limit access to important computer files.
2. Comprehensive computer edit checks are used to identify incorrect input data.
3. Automated price lists are utilized, with limited access to changing authorized prices.
4. Control procedures are utilized to reconcile input with output to ensure all submitted transactions were processed.
5. All accounts are processed and updated concurrently.

Exhibit 11.14 identifies audit procedures that could be used to test the effectiveness of the control procedures. The auditor should choose among the alternative audit procedures to provide evidence on the existence of the control procedures in an efficient and persuasive manner. One approach that might be utilized in the LeFlam case is the audit program shown in Exhibit 11.15 on pages 508–509, which is derived directly from the testing linkages developed in Exhibit 11.14. But note that the procedures in Exhibit 11.15 are combined into steps to achieve audit efficiency. For example, the first test involves developing test transactions to be processed using the client's computer program. These transactions are used to test (1) the effectiveness of the edit procedures built into the client's computer program, (2) the accu-

Exhibit 11.14

LEFLAM MANUFACTURING COMPANY
LINKAGE OF CONTROL OBJECTIVES AND TESTING PROCEDURES

Control	Testing Procedures
Existence/Occurrence	Existence/Occurrence
1. *Recorded transactions are valid.*	1. *Recorded transactions are valid.*
a. Orders are entered only upon the receipt of an EDI, mail, phone, or fax order from a customer.	a. Select a sample of invoices and trace to purchase order or sales order form, noting date and completeness of the data entered into the computer.
b. Recorded transactions are reconciled with original items of entry on a timely basis.	b. Select a sample of invoices and vouch to shipping documents evidencing shipment of goods.
c. Sales are automatically recorded when shipments are made and confirmation of shipment is received from shipping department. Customary industry terms are FOB shipping point.	
2. *Authorization*	2. *Authorization*
a. Orders are authorized by sales personnel who either take an order over the phone or review the purchase order sent by the customer.	a. Observe order entry process to note its orderliness and restrictions to authorized personnel.
b. EDI orders are negotiated on a blanket purchase order. Quantities and prices are input in a file for EDI orders on the authorized signature of the marketing manager for each product line.	b. Review the blanket purchase order contracts for major customers utilizing EDI. Trace the terms to a printout of prices maintained on the system.
c. Authorized price lists are maintained on the client's system. Changes are entered only on the authorization of the marketing manager. A detailed list is printed after changes for reconciliation by an assistant to the marketing manager.	c. Test and review the marketing manager's reconciliation of price changes with printout of new price lists. Determine accuracy and completeness of changes.
d. Edit checks flag any prices different than the authorized price list. Transactions can be processed only after receiving the approval of the marketing manager.	d. Select one or two days' transactions and review exception reports for items not processed and determine the edit tests that caused the item not to be processed.
e. Credit limits are established by the credit department and are monitored by the system on each order. Any order not qualifying for credit is referred to the credit department for subsequent review. The transaction cannot be processed without credit department approval.	e. Overall: Test access control system by reviewing procedures for authorization, interview personnel regarding access, and review procedures used by data processing for changing access for individuals.

(Continued)

Exhibit 11.14

3. *Transactions are recorded on a timely basis.* Sales are automatically recorded when shipments are made.

4. *Completeness: All transactions are recorded.*
   a. All transactions are assigned a unique sequential number, which is reviewed and all original orders independently accounted for to ensure complete input.
   b. Batch control totals are utilized for input. Batch controls are reconciled with input on a timely basis and discrepancies are immediately followed up.
   c. The same process that enters data also updates the other accounts.
   d. All items are initially time dated with prompt follow-up on all items not recorded on a timely basis.

Rights/Obligations

5. *Recorded transactions and accruals properly reflect the transfer of ownership or obligation.*
   a. All recorded transactions are accompanied by the issuance of a sales invoice transferring title.
   b. Sales are automatically classified by product line by the application.
   c. The subsidiary ledgers are updated at the same time that the original transaction is recorded.

3. *Transactions are recorded on a timely basis.* Review selected invoices and match with shipping documentation to determine whether sales were recorded on a prompt basis.

4. *Completeness*
   a. Determine who accounts for the sequential number of orders. Select a reconciliation and review for completeness and follow up for missing items.
   b. Review reconciliations of batch control totals. Determine whether appropriate follow-up action is taken for all nonreconciling items. Determine that reconciliations are performed on a timely basis.
   c. Review exception reports for all items identified by the system needing follow-up action because of not clearing within a specified date. Determine extent of follow-up action needed.
   d. Consider the use of a test data approach to test the update of all files.
   e. Test file updates through an analysis of control totals for each file to be reconciled with batched input items.

Rights/Obligations

   a. Test of proper invoicing is made in conjunction with completeness test. For a random sample of shipping documents, reprocess to the issuance of an invoice noting proper accounting for all terms.
   b. Review selected invoices to determine the proper timing of recording and classification. Determine that classification is correct.
   c. Review client's procedures for timely reconciling detailed subsidiary accounts with the control accounts.

Exhibit 11.14

Valuation 6. *All transactions are recorded at their proper amount and all calculations are carried out correctly.* 7. *All transactions are recorded in accordance with GAAP.* a. Transactions are recorded according to authorized price lists. b. The ability to change items on the authorized price list is restricted to the marketing manager. c. Access controls are successfully implemented and monitored. d. All prices at other than the original price list must be approved by authorized personnel. The application will not process an item unless authorization is obtained. e. All sales are made on customary terms for the industry. The sale is not recorded until the shipment takes place.	6 & 7. *Valuation* a. Randomly select invoices and compare prices with authorized price list or separate authorization by the marketing manager. b. Test access control system. See step 2. c. Review reconciliation of price list with authorized lists. d. For the invoices selected in step 1, review shipping document noting date of shipment and date of invoicing. Determine whether there is any significant delay between shipment and sales recording.
Presentation/Disclosure 8. *Transactions are correctly classified.*	8. *Presentation/Disclosure* Test invoices selected above to note that they are properly classified.

racy of the computer processing steps, and (3) the accuracy of the file up-dating procedures. Likewise, the second procedure implements the fifth test under completeness in Exhibit 11.14. Note that many of the audit procedures shown in Exhibit 11.15 are dual purpose: The procedures test both the effectiveness of the control and the correctness of the corresponding account balance (a substantive test).

Summary

Although most businesses have developed highly sophisticated automated control structures for recording transactions in the revenue cycle, misstatements can occur because of (1) the sheer volume of transactions that must be recorded and (2) the complexity of some sales transactions. Some sales transactions are further complicated by the difficulty in determining the economic substance of the transaction. The auditor must be able to both understand and test the strength of the client's

Exhibit 11.15

LEFLAM MANUFACTURING COMPANY
AUDIT PROGRAM FOR TESTING CONTROLS—ORDER ENTRY AND INVOICING
DECEMBER 31, 1994

Audit Procedures	Performed by
1. Develop a comprehensive set of test data to test edit controls, correctness of processing, and updating of all related files. Run the test data at the beginning of every audit unless the client indicates there are no major changes in the application during the year and our evaluation remains that the program change process is well controlled.	________
2. Randomly select X batches of input during the year and determine that the client properly reconciles batch input and output *and* that any discrepancies are immediately noted and followed up.	________
3. Observe the order entry process to note its orderliness and restrictions to authorized personnel.	________
4. Review the blanket purchase order contracts from major customers utilizing EDI. Trace selected contract terms to a printout of prices maintained on the system.	________
5. In connection with our general work on data processing controls, perform a comprehensive test of the client's implementation of access control software. Determine that the system includes restricted passwords and that it is monitored on a timely basis by data security. Interview personnel to determine their perception of the access control system.	________
6. Review the marketing manager's reconciliations of price changes with the printout of new price lists. Determine accuracy and completeness of changes.	________
7. Select transaction exception reports for X days. Review the reports to determine	________
a. The type of errors that are causing the transactions not to be processed.	
b. The timeliness with which errors are followed up and corrected.	
c. All items are corrected.	
8. Select a sample of sequentially numbered orders and determine that all items are accounted for and are recorded in a timely fashion.	________
9. Review client's procedures to reconcile initial input of data to updates in the master file and all the related subsidiary files. Determine that reconciliation is performed on a timely basis.	________
10. Randomly select X invoices and	________
a. Compare invoice price with authorized price list or with separate authorization from marketing manager.	

Exhibit 11.15

	Performed by
b. Review for shipping document noting the date of shipment and determine whether there is any significant time delay between shipment and invoicing.	
c. Compare the shipping document and invoice to determine that all items shipped have been billed.	
d. Note that back-ordered items are not billed.	
e. Note that customer had approved credit by determining whether the customer had a credit file established and that the amount of invoice was less than the credit authorized. [The credit authorization system is more fully tested with the test data approach, which compares a new sale with the existing balance and authorized credit limit.]	
f. Note proper classification of sales items.	
11. Select a sample of orders for selected clients and determine that the orders had been completely entered into the system on a timely basis.	________

recording process and the business purpose of transactions in order to assess the control risk in the revenue cycle. Some tests of controls are most efficiently performed by selecting a sample of transactions. Several sampling methods and approaches to sample selection are introduced in Chapter 12.

Significant Terms

bill of lading A shipping document that describes items being shipped, the shipping terms, and delivery address; a formal legal document that conveys responsibility for the safety and shipment of items to the shipper.

cycle A group of accounts related to a particular processing task; represents a convenient way to look at the interrelationship of account balances. Normally, but not always, a transaction cycle encompasses all aspects of a transaction from its initiation to final disposition.

dual-purpose tests Tests of transactions designed to test both the effectiveness of control procedures and the correctness and completeness of the transaction recording process; it is both a test of controls and a direct test of the account balance.

revenue cycle The process of receiving a customer's order, approving credit for a sale, determining whether the goods are available for shipment, shipping the goods, billing the customers, collecting cash, and recognizing the effect of this process on other related accounts such as Accounts Receivable and Inventory.

Review Questions

A–An Overview of Control Risk in the Revenue Cycle

11–1 What are the major accounts in the revenue cycle? Briefly identify the relationships between them.

11–2 What are the major processes involved in generating and recording a sales transaction? What are the major documents generated during each process?

11–3 Automated cash registers can contribute effectively to the control structure of a retail organization. Briefly indicate the control procedures the auditor would expect to find in an automated cash register and how the auditor would gain assurance as to the effectiveness of the control procedures.

11–4 What are the key pieces of control information captured on a sales order? How would the gathering and use of such control information change when a sales order is captured immediately into a computer application?

11–5 We normally think about invoices being transmitted to customers through the mail. How else might invoices by transmitted to customers? What are the implications of these alternative means of transmitting invoices to customers?

11–6 Briefly identify the information the auditor might obtain by examining each of the following documents:

a. Sales order.

b. Bill of lading.

c. Invoice.

d. Customer purchase order.

11–7 Briefly describe the difference between the roles played by the (1) credit card issuer and (2) the merchant bank in processing credit card transactions such as Visa or MasterCard. Address specific issues such as credit authorization, fees charged and earned, and responsibility for uncollectible accounts.

11–8 Why might a retailer choose to sign an agreement with a merchant bank to accept credit cards such as Visa or MasterCard? What advantages might the retailer obtain over the direct issuance of a retail credit card in the retailer's name?

11–9 Briefly identify the key control procedures a retail organization should implement to determine that all credit card receipts are properly credited to its account at the banking institution. Briefly describe how each control works.

11–10 What is a bill of lading? What audit evidence does it provide?

B–Inherent and Control Risk Considerations

11–11 Explain the factors that would tend to cause some sales transactions to have higher risk than other transactions.

11–12 Why is it important for an auditor to carefully analyze the control structure over sales returns and allowances? What evidence about potential accounting problems can be ascertained by a review of the returns and allowances function?

11–13 What key documents are created in a manual (paper-based) accounting system in the process of generating and recording a sale? How would such documentation differ in

a. A retail environment?

b. A firm selling specialized climate control machinery?

11–14 What factors are most likely to affect the inherent risk of a sales transaction? How would a high level of inherent risk affect the development of an audit of sales? Explain using a specific example.

11–15 What are the major factors that most likely determine the auditor's assessment of the control environment affecting the recording of sales? How does the auditor normally gather information on the factors identified?

11–16 Evaluate the following statement: "There is very little need to test for the accuracy of the sales recording process or its attendant control procedures because the auditor can easily verify the correctness of the Accounts Receivable and Cash accounts. If those accounts are fairly stated, it is impossible for sales to be materially misstated." State whether you agree or disagree and justify your position.

11–17 What are the primary risks associated with recording an accounts receivable transaction?

11–18 Explain how electronic date stamping can be an effective control in maintaining the integrity of processing. What follow-up is needed to make date stamping an effective control?

11–19 What important control functions are served by mailing monthly statements to customers? Why is it important that a separate section of the accounts receivable department be set up to handle customer inquiries and complaints?

11–20 What two methods are utilized for granting credit approval? What are the advantages and disadvantages of each method?

11–21 If sales orders are entered on-line to the computer system, prenumbered paper-based documents will not be prepared. What control procedures should be designed into the computer application to accomplish the same objective as the prenumbered documents? Briefly explain how the control procedures should work.

C–Assessing and Documenting Control Risk

11–22 What is a dual-purpose test?

11–23 In assessing whether the control procedures are operating effectively, is it necessary for the auditor to reperform the work of the control itself? For example, if someone tests for the correctness of computations and initials the bottom of a document to indicate that such a control procedure has been performed, is it necessary for the auditor to reperform? Explain the rationale for your response.

11–24 All invoicing for a company is done on a computer system from a price list table incorporated into the system. The prices can be changed only by the sales department on the approval of the department manager. One copy of the up-to-date price list is printed monthly for verification purposes and is maintained in the sales department. A list of all changes is kept by the sales department. The master price printouts are maintained for three months. The quarterly printouts, however, are maintained for one year. Identify two ways in which the auditor might gain assurance that sales transactions are properly valued.

11–25 An auditor discussing the nature of complex sales transactions said, "It's not possible to build control procedures to handle complex, one-of-a-kind sales transactions. The integrity of the recording of such transactions varies with the integrity of senior management and their objectives. The auditor will always need to review such transactions." Do you agree or disagree with the comment? Explain.

Multiple Choice Questions

11–26 Subsequent to the end of the client's fiscal year, the client revealed in a press release that it had encountered significant problems with one of its major products and an unusually high number of those products had been returned for credit. The auditor would most likely have learned of the problem through:

a. Inquiries of the customer service department, which monitors and responds to customer inquiries regarding their current account balance.

b. A review and observation of procedures regarding the authorization of returns and allowances.

c. The physical count of inventory on hand at the end of the client's fiscal year.

d. A review of customer remittances for payments on accounts indicating dissatisfaction with the client's current level of service.

11–27 The auditor is concerned that fictitious sales have been recorded. The *best* audit procedure to identify the existence of the fictitious sales would be to

a. Select a sample of recorded invoices and trace to shipping documents (bills of lading and packing slips) to verify shipment of goods.

b. Select a random sample of shipping documents (bills of lading) and trace to the invoice to determine whether the invoice was properly recorded.

c. Select a sample of customer purchase orders and trace through to the generation of a sales invoice.

d. Select a sample of invoices and trace to a customer purchase order to determine whether a valid customer actually exists.

11–28 Which of the following would not represent a factor the auditor would consider when assessing the inherent risk associated with a sales transaction?

a. The existence of terms that specify the right of return or the right to modify the purchase agreement.

b. Billing for invoices but agreed-upon shipments of goods at a later date.

c. Goods billed according to a percentage-of-completion methodology.

d. The nature of the credit authorization process.

11–29 The auditor generally makes a decision *not* to test the effectiveness of controls in operation when

a. The preliminary assessment of control risk is at the maximum.

b. It is more cost efficient to directly test ending account balances than to test control procedures.

c. The auditor believes that control procedures are not functioning as described.

d. All of the above.

*11–30 At which point in an ordinary sales transaction of a wholesaling business would a lack of specific authorization *least* concern the auditor conducting an audit?

a. Determining discounts.

b. Selling goods for cash.

c. Granting credit.

d. Shipping goods.

*11–31 An auditor selects a sample from the file of shipping documents to determine whether invoices were prepared. This test is performed to satisfy the audit objective of

a. Accuracy.

b. Control.

c. Completeness.

d. Existence.

11–32 To determine whether the internal control structure operated effectively to minimize errors of failure to invoice a shipment, the auditor would select a sample of transactions from the population represented by the

a. Customer order file.

b. Open invoice file.

c. Bill of lading file.

d. Sales invoice file.

*11–33 Sound internal control procedures dictate that defective merchandise returned by customers should be presented to the

a. Inventory control clerk for inspection and determination of appropriate inventory classification.

b. Sales clerk or other individual who authorized the sale.

c. Purchasing clerk responsible for billing the item.

d. Receiving clerk or receiving department.

11–34 A manufacturing client received a substantial amount of goods returned during the last month of the fiscal year and the first month after year-end.

*Adapted from the Uniform CPA examination or the Certified Internal Auditor examination.

The client recorded the returns when credit memos were issued (usually six to eight weeks after receipt of the goods). The control procedure that would have led to more timely recording of the goods would include

a. Prenumbering receiving reports, which are separately identified for goods returned and serve as a control for issuance of credit memos.
b. Aging schedules of accounts receivable prepared at year-end by individuals separate from the billing process.
c. A reconciliation of the detailed accounts receivable with the general ledger accounts receivable account.
d. Prenumbering credit memorandum for which all numbers are periodically accounted.

*11–35 An internal auditor noted that several shipments were not billed. To prevent recurrence of such nonbilling, the organization should

a. Numerically sequence and independently account for all controlling documents (such as packing slips and shipping orders) when sales journal entries are recorded.
b. Undertake a validity check with customers as to orders placed.
c. Release product for shipment only on the basis of credit approval by the credit manager or other authorized person.
d. Undertake periodic tests of gross margin rates by product line and obtain explanations of significant departures from planned gross margin rates.

Discussion and Research Questions

11–36 (Audit Procedures and Objectives) Following is a list of procedures performed in the audit of the revenue cycle. For each procedure, indicate the objective that is accomplished.

a. Select a random sample of sales orders and trace to the shipment and billing for goods shipped.
b. Review the general access controls to the computer application and the authorized ability to make changes to computer price files.
c. Recompute the invoice total and individual line items on a sample of sales invoices.
d. Review client documentation to determine policy for credit authorization.
e. Select a sample of shipping notices and trace to invoices.
f. Randomly sample entries into the sales journal and trace back to sales orders and shipping documents.
g. Take a block of shipping orders and account for the invoicing of all items in the block and account for the prenumbering of the documents.

*11–37 (Weaknesses in Billing Physicians' Services)

A CPA's audit working papers include the narrative description of the cash receipts and billing portions of the internal control structure of Parktown Medical Center, Inc. Parktown is a small health care provider owned by a publicly held corporation. It employs 7 salaried physicians, 10 nurses, 3 support staff in a common laboratory, and 3 clerical workers. The clerical workers perform such tasks as reception, correspondence, cash receipts, billing, and appointment scheduling and are adequately bonded. They are referred to as office manager, clerk 1, and clerk 2 in the narrative.

Narrative

Most patients pay for services by cash or check at the time services are rendered. Credit is not approved by the clerical staff but by the physician who is to perform the respective services, based on an interview. When credit is approved, the physician files a memo with the billing clerk (clerk 2) to set up the receivable from data generated by the physician.

The servicing physician prepares a charge slip that is given to clerk 1 for pricing and preparation of the patient's bill. Clerk 1 transmits a copy of the bill to clerk 2 for preparation of the revenue summary and for posting in the accounts receivable subsidiary ledger.

The cash receipts functions are performed by clerk 1, who receives cash and checks directly from patients and gives each patient a prenumbered cash receipt. Clerk 1 opens the mail and immediately stamps all checks "For Deposit Only" and lists cash and checks for deposit. The cash and checks are deposited daily by the office manager. The list of cash and checks together with the related remittance advices are forwarded by clerk 1 to clerk 2. Clerk 1 also serves as receptionist and performs general correspondence duties.

Clerk 2 prepares and sends monthly statements to patients with unpaid balances and prepares the cash receipts journal and the accounts receivable subsidiary ledger. No other clerical employees are permitted access to the accounts receivable subsidiary ledger. Uncollectible accounts are written off by clerk 2 only after the physician who performed the respective services believes the account to be uncollectible and communicates the write-off approval to the office manager. The office manager then issues a write-off memo that clerk 2 processes.

The office manager supervises the clerks, issues write-off memos, schedules appointments for the doctors, makes bank deposits, reconciles bank statements, and performs general correspondence duties.

Additional services are performed monthly by a local accountant who posts summaries prepared by the clerks to the general ledger, prepares income statements, and files the appropriate payroll forms and tax returns. The accountant reports directly to the parent corporation.

Required:

Based only on the information described in the narrative, identify any apparent weaknesses in the processing and control procedures related to the cash receipts and billing function. For each deficiency, identify the potential financial misstatement that could result from it.

11–38 (Inherent Risks) Drea Tech Company has been growing rapidly and has recently engaged your firm as its auditors. It is actively traded on the OTC and believes it has outgrown the service capabilities of its previous auditor. However, on contacting the previous auditor, you learn that a dispute led to their dismissal. The client wanted to recognize income on contracts for

Growing Rapidly

items produced but not shipped. The client believed the contracts were firm and that all the principal revenue-producing activities were performed. The change in accounting principle would have increased net income by 33 percent during the last year.

Drea is 32 percent owned by Anthony Dreason, who has a reputation as a turnaround artist. He bought out the previous owner of Drea Tech (formerly named Johnstone Industries) three years ago. The company's primary products are in the materials handling business, such as automated conveyors for warehouses and production lines. Dreason has increased profits by slashing operating expenses, most notably personnel and research and development. In addition, he has outsourced a significant part of component part production. Approximately 10 percent of the company's product is now obtained from Materials Movement, Inc., a privately held company 50 percent owned by Dreason and his brother.

A brief analysis of previous financial statements shows that sales have been increasing by approximately 20 percent per year since Dreason assumed control. Profitability has increased even more. However, a tour of the plant gives the impression that it is somewhat old and not kept up-to-date. Additionally, a large amount of inventory is sitting near the receiving dock awaiting final disposition.

Required:

a. Identify the elements of inherent risk associated with the revenue cycle that the auditor should consider.

b. For each element of inherent risk identified, briefly indicate the audit concern and suggest audit procedures to address the risks.

11–39 (Credit Authorization) Verona Shoe Company is considering automating its credit approval function. It manufactures a brushed pigskin shoe and acts as a wholesaler by buying closeouts of other brands and selling them to approximately 3,000 retail customers. The company has moved into new lines by recently acquiring the U.S. distribution rights to an important European brand of ski equipment and ski wear. The ski line will be sold to approximately 750 different retail outlets, but three major chains will constitute over 50 percent of the sales.

Required:

a. What factors should the company consider in setting its credit policies? How could data normally contained in the client's computer system assist the company in setting its overall credit policies?

b. Assume that the company chooses to automate much of its credit approval process. Outline the control procedures the company should consider utilizing to ensure that credit is granted only in accordance with company credit policies.

c. For each control procedure identified in part b, briefly indicate how the auditor might go about testing the effectiveness of its operation.

11–40 (Testing Control Procedures)

Required:

Following is a list of control procedures typically implemented in the processing of sales transactions.

a. For each control procedure identified, briefly indicate the potential financial misstatement that could occur if the control procedure is not implemented effectively.

b. Identify an audit procedure to test for the effectiveness of the control procedure in operation.

Control Procedures Typically Found in Sales Processes

1. Authorization: All transactions under $10,000 may be approved by computer authorization program. All transactions over $10,000 must be approved by the credit manager.
2. All invoices are priced according to the authorized price list maintained on the computer. Any exceptions must be approved by either the regional or divisional sales manager.
3. All shipping documents are prenumbered and periodically accounted for. Shipping document references are noted on all sales invoices.
4. Customer complaints regarding receipt of goods are routed to a customer service representative. Any discrepancies are immediately followed up to determine the cause of the discrepancy.
5. All merchandise returns must be received by the receiving department and recorded on prenumbered documents for receipts. A document is created for each item (or batches of like items). Returns are sent to quality control for testing and a recommendation for ultimate disposition is made (scrap, rework and sell as a second, or closeout as is), noted, and sent to accounting for proper inventorying.
6. The quantity of items invoiced is reconciled with the packing document developed on receipt of the order and the shipping notice by a computer program as the goods are marked for shipment. If discrepancies appear, the shipping document prevails. A discrepancy report is prepared on a daily basis and sent to the warehouse manager for follow-up.
7. The company pays all freight charges, but the customer is charged a freight fee based on a minimum amount and a sliding scale as a percentage of the total invoice. The policy is documented and the charge is automatically added by the computer.

11–41 (Credit Card Sales) Jason Co. accepts Visa and MasterCard for any sales transaction exceeding $50. The company has not yet implemented on-line recording of the credit card transaction but does have a toll-free number to call for authorization for all sales over $50. The company has two cash registers but three clerks work during peak times. The company processes credit card sales as described below.

Blank credit card slips are maintained near the cash register along with two card imprinters. The card imprinter imprints the company's account identification and takes an imprint of the customer's credit card. During most times, credit card sales are rung up on the cash register as would be done with a cash sale. The credit card receipts are kept in a separate location in the cash register. During peak times, however, such as a clearance sale, a special line is set up for credit card customers. The totals are calculated on a regular calculator and a credit slip is prepared and run through the imprinter. The credit card slips are stored in a convenient location and are recorded on a cash register later in the day. At periodic intervals during the day, the store manager collects all credit card receipts, separates the two copies into one for the store and one for the bank, batches all the slips, and prepares an entry to later record the sales. The batches for the day are collected for a deposit. The controller then reconciles the deposits made on a daily basis with the credit card sales recorded.

Required:

a. Identify the strengths and weaknesses of the control procedures for credit card sales identified above.

b. For each deficiency in control procedures noted, identify the potential effect on the company's financial statements.

11–42 (Directional Testing and Dual-Purpose Tests) During a discussion, one auditor noted that her approach to testing sales transactions was to select a random sample of recorded sales and trace back through the system to supporting documents noting that all items billed were shipped and were invoiced at correct prices. She stated that she then had good confidence about the correctness of the sales account and thus having performed a dual-purpose test, the remaining work on sales (assuming the procedures also evidenced the working of control procedures) could be limited.

A second auditor disagreed. Her approach was to select evidence of shipments, such as prenumbered shipping documents, and then trace forward through the system to the actual invoice, noting the existence of control procedures and the correctness of the invoice processing. If no exceptions were noted, however, she agreed with the first auditor that the remaining audit work on the sales account could be limited.

Required:

a. Which auditor is right, or are both right? Explain.

b. What assertion is tested by the second auditor?

c. What is a dual-purpose test? Explain why the tests performed by both of the auditors would or would not be considered dual-purpose tests.

11–43 (Exception Reports) Today's computer systems have the ability to generate exception reports that immediately identify control procedure failures or transactions that are out of the norm so that management can determine whether any special action is needed.

Required:

a. Identify how the auditor might use each type of exception report noted below in assessing the effectiveness of control procedures.

b. If the exceptions are properly followed up and corrected, would the fact that many exceptions occurred affect the auditor's judgment of control risk? Explain.

Types of Exception Reports: Sales Processing

1. A list of all invoices over $5,000 for which credit was not preauthorized by the credit manager (the computer program is designed so that if the authorization is not provided within 24 hours of the original notice to the credit manager, the shipment is made as if it were authorized). This exception report goes to the credit manager.

2. A report of any sales volume to one customer exceeding $2 million in a month is sent to the sales manager with a copy to the credit manager.
3. A report of exceptions for which shipping documents and packing slips did not reconcile.
4. A report noting that goods ordered were not shipped (or back ordered) within five days of receipt of the order as is required per company policy.

11–44 (Implementation of Control Procedures) Hilda is the owner of Hilda's Family Restaurant located in the rustic Ozarks. The restaurant employs only 10 servers. Food and soft drinks are served to patrons; no carry-out orders are filled. All orders are filled by the use of handwritten restaurant checks. The restaurant has one cash register, which is operated during busy hours by Hilda and by other servers when she is busy. All cash register tapes are saved. Hilda makes a daily deposit of all receipts, and she maintains a record of daily sales, cash receipts, and the general ledger.

Required:

a. Identify the control procedures Hilda should consider employing to ensure that all food orders are properly billed and recorded.
b. Briefly explain the important control procedures contained in a cash register that enhances control in an organization such as this one.

11–45 (Internal Control Questionnaire) Finneran Electronics is a manufacturer specializing in various electronic equipment such as telephones, radios, and electronic office equipment. Approximately 50 percent of its sales are made directly to other organizations; the other 50 percent is distributed through wholesalers. The company has a standard 90-day return policy for all direct sales and a 90-day from date of purchase return policy (if registered) for all sales made through the wholesaler. The company may, at its option, repair the item, replace it, or issue a credit for it.

Required:

a. Develop an internal control questionnaire for merchandise returns.
b. Develop an audit program (assuming all control procedures identified in part a are implemented) to test the effectiveness of the control procedures considered important.

11–46 (Documentation of Control Risk Assessment) The auditor is required to document the control risk assessment affecting sales transactions.

Required:

a. Describe the meaning of "assessing control risk at the maximum" for sales transactions and the implications for the conduct of the audit.
b. Describe the meaning of "assessing control risk as moderate" for sales transactions and discuss the implications of such an assessment for the conduct of the audit. Be specific in your discussion as to the meaning of the potential misstatements occurring in the company's financial statement.

11–47 (Control Procedures: Automated Cash Registers) Woodman's is a grocery store chain with seven stores operating in the Southwest. It has automated the customer check-out process by installing electronic cash registers that read the bar codes on most products. The price for each product is approved by the marketing manager or her assistant. The prices are maintained on a large central file on the company's main computer and are transmitted to a minicomputer located at each store. The automated cash register reads the bar code and charges the customer the price currently listed on the store's price file.

Required:

a. What control procedures should Woodman's consider implementing to ensure that only authorized prices are charged the customer and that all customers are charged the correct price for the products purchased?

b. Identify the audit procedures that an auditor should consider to test the operating effectiveness of the control procedures described in part a above.

11–48 **(Research)** A major change that will affect accounting systems in the next decade is the movement to electronic transmission of a standard set of documents such as purchase orders, sales invoices, funds transfers, and so forth. The interchange of electronic documents is referred to as electronic data interchange or EDI. Most often the transfers take place through a third-party computer vendor such as GE Computer Services or IBM network services.

Required:

a. Review recent publications on EDI to determine the development of common documents for EDI and how the transmission of documents is handled through third parties.

b. Interview a company in your area that uses EDI and report back to the class the success and problems associated with its implementation of EDI.

11–49 **(Research: Recognizing Sales Transactions)** The Securities and Exchange Commission has issued a number of pronouncements dealing with problems with the method that registrants use to recognize sales.

Required:

a. Review current *Financial Reporting Releases* and the predecessor *Accounting Series Releases* issued by the SEC. Summarize the types of revenue recognition problems identified.

b. Discuss the audit implications of each revenue recognition problem identified by the SEC.

Case

*11–50 (Control Risk Assessment: Retail Organization)

You are the internal auditor for a company that started over 40 years ago as a local retailer of major home appliances. The company has now grown to include 55 retail stores in 12 metropolitan areas. Because of rapid growth in the number of stores opened in the last three years (46), a professional management team was hired to replace the previous management team, which was composed of members of the owning family. To encourage continued growth, a sales incentive bonus plan was instituted. Under the plan, managers of individual stores receive a bonus based on inventory turnover.

A retail point-of-sale system is used to aid inventory management. Each store is a node with terminals, a local processor, and a storewide data base. The nodes communicate with a central systemwide database located at corporate offices. Retail prices for all merchandise are updated once a month to the storewide database, using a master price list provided by corporate offices.

Because the desired margin is achieved for each product sold at the established master price, inventory turnover is viewed as the critical determinant of profitability for each store. Accordingly, sales volume, by product class, is reported weekly to corporate offices. Revenue is also reported weekly, but only in the aggregate. Detailed sales and inventory data, including unit revenue, product class revenue, revenue generated at discount prices, inventory movement, and inventory levels, are produced daily by each store for use by the store manager.

Selling prices are frequently discounted in widely advertised sales. For sale items, sales clerks in each store must override the master price and input the advertised price. Sales at wholesale prices, such as contractor sales, are prohibited by company policy. Damaged goods can be sold at any time at heavily discounted prices at the discretion of the store manager, who assesses damage and sets the sale price.

Over a two-year period, a store manager inflated unit sales by the following acts:

1. Fictitious credit sales were recorded in the last month of the year, with subsequent return of the goods recorded in the first month of the new year. No goods actually changed hands.
2. Undamaged goods were declared to be damaged and sold at prices significantly less than master prices.
3. Sales were completed at wholesale prices.
4. "Sale" priced merchandise was frequently sold at prices above its advertised sale price.

Acting alone, the store manager also sold selected merchandise for cash with no record made of the sale. Although a register receipt is required for customer pickup, the store manager verbally instructed the warehouse to load the merchandise without a receipt.

Required:

a. Identify six control weaknesses or management deficiencies that permitted the fraud.
b. Identify four indicators that may have signaled the presence of the fraud.
c. Identify four controls needed to detect the fraud.
d. Describe the responsibilities of the internal auditing department in the situation described above.

End Note

1. *Report of the National Commission on Fraudulent Financial Reporting* (New York: National Commission on Fraudulent Financial Reporting, 1987), 112.

CHAPTER

12

Learning Objectives

Through studying this chapter, you will be able to:

1. Understand the meaning of audit sampling.
2. Identify the differences between nonstatistical sampling and statistical sampling.
3. Identify the different sampling methods that can be used to test controls.
4. Describe the different sample selection techniques and when each technique is appropriate.
5. Understand the circumstances in which each of the sampling methods is most appropriate for testing controls.
6. Learn how sampling can be used to test controls.

Introduction to Audit Sampling

Chapter Contents

Chapter Overview

The efficiency of many audit procedures can be enhanced by using some form of sampling. Although the statistics involved in some of the sampling methods are very complex, help is available in the form of tables and computer programs. This chapter provides an introduction to the use of sampling in audits and then discusses the sampling methods appropriate for *testing transactions* for control procedures and accuracy of recording. Chapter 14 covers the sampling methods that are used for *testing the details of account balances.*

Authoritative pronouncements require auditors to select samples that they expect to be representative of the population. Further, these pronouncements permit sample selection to be made either on a statistical or non-statistical basis. Common sense and experience suggest that non-statistical sample sizes and evaluations should be comparable to statistical sampling.[1]

The auditor often is aware of account balances and transactions that may be more likely to contain misstatements. He considers this knowledge in planning his procedures, including audit sampling. The auditor usually will have no special knowledge about other account balances and transactions that . . . will need to be tested to fulfill his audit objectives. Audit sampling is especially useful in these cases. [AU 350.18]

A–INTRODUCTION

Assume that you have been assigned the task of testing the control procedures for granting credit to customers before merchandise is shipped. Credit department approval of each customer's order before shipment is a key procedure; it is evidenced by the initials of an authorized credit department employee on the order, without which no order should be filled. During the year, more than 10,000 orders have been processed.

Why is it important that this control be tested? What are the potential effects of a control failure on the financial statements? Does the auditor need to become satisfied that this control procedure was working all year, or is it sufficient that it was working effectively near and at the end of the year? How can the auditor obtain sufficient evidence to ensure that the control functioned satisfactorily without examining every order placed during the time period being examined?

Audit sampling is used to obtain evidence about (1) the effectiveness of control procedures and (2) the dollar accuracy of account balances and classes of transactions without examining every item in the population. The **population** is defined as the group of transactions or the items that make up an account balance for which the auditor wants to estimate some characteristic, such as the effectiveness of control procedures or the dollar accuracy of an account balance. When audit sampling is used, the sample results are projected to the population as a whole. Assume, for example, that the initials indicating credit approval by authorized personnel do not appear on one order in a sample of 50 orders. The sample is only a part of the population; it is the tip of the iceberg. More than one sales order in the population is likely to be without credit approval. Based on the sample, it is reasonable for the auditor to estimate that approximately two percent of the entire population of 10,000 sales orders show no evidence of credit authorization. But sample results are rarely identical to those that would be obtained by auditing all of the items in the population. How do we know that the sample provides the best estimate of the rate of control failure?

This chapter addresses these and related questions concerning the risks inherent in the sampling process to gather audit evidence. Audit sampling is used not only to test controls but also to make direct tests of transactions and account balances.

Audit Sampling Overview

The auditor constantly faces the challenge of gathering sufficient competent evidence as efficiently as possible. Rarely is it cost effective to examine all transactions, such as all 10,000 sales orders that were processed during the year. Auditors, therefore, routinely examine a sample of the items that make up the class of transactions or the details of an account balance.

Audit sampling [AU 350.01] is

> the application of an audit procedure to less than 100 percent of the items within an account balance or class of transactions for the purpose of evaluating some characteristic of the balance or class.

Audit sampling implies gathering evidence to use as a basis for making valid inferences about the characteristics of the population as a whole. The characteristics most often of interest in an audit are the effectiveness of control procedures and the dollar accuracy of account balances and recorded transactions.

When assessing the effectiveness of control procedures, the audit challenge is to gather sufficient reliable evidence on the degree to which the client's internal control structure prevents or detects misstatements for any given class of transactions. Those transactions form the population to be tested. A population, for sampling purposes, is a collection of individual elements called *sampling units*, such as the sales orders processed during the year. The sampling units selected for testing *must be representative* of the population to control the likelihood that a correct evaluation of the effectiveness of the control procedures will be made. The auditor needs to make four important decisions in sampling:

- Which population should be tested and for what characteristics *(population)?* When testing for credit approval, the population is credit sales, and the sampling units are those documents on which the credit department notes its approval, such as the customers' orders or internally prepared sales orders.

- How many items should be included in the sample *(sample size)*?
- Which items should be included *(selection)*?
- What does the sample information tell about the population as a whole *(evaluation)*?

Although auditors use sampling extensively, it does not apply to all situations in which the auditor examines less than 100 percent of the items within a population, for example,

- Tracing several transactions through the accounting system to *gain an understanding* of the nature of the entity's operations or the design of the internal control structure, referred to previously as a *walk-through*.
- *Examining all items exceeding some dollar amount* and/or testing the remaining items by analytical procedures; in some cases, none are examined because they are immaterial.
- *Observing employees* who are performing a control procedure that does not leave an audit trail, such as observing the physical inventory count [AU 9350.02].

Nonsampling and Sampling Risk

Auditors can use procedures that lead to an incorrect assessment of the population and, potentially, an incorrect audit conclusion. The incorrect assessment can occur because the auditor (1) made an improper assessment of inherent and/or control risk or failed to apply audit procedures carefully (nonsampling risk), or (2) made error projections, based on the sample results, that led to the wrong conclusion about the population (sampling risk).

The auditor must understand and control for these risks on every audit.

Nonsampling Risk

It is generally assumed that auditors *carefully* audit all items in the sample and thoughtfully assess inherent and control risk. If, however, auditors are improperly trained, are careless, are inadequately supervised, use the wrong audit procedures, or misinterpret information, they are likely to reach wrong conclusions about the population based on the sample. **Nonsampling risk** includes all the aspects of audit risk that are not due to sampling. It cannot be quantified but can only be guarded against. Public accounting firms attempt to minimize nonsampling risk by implementing good quality control practices of hiring, training, and supervising competent personnel, carefully designing audit program procedures, and assigning appropriately qualified auditors to each audit.

Sampling Risk

No matter how hard the auditor tries to make the sample representative of the population, sample characteristics rarely match population characteristics exactly. Sample results, however, are projected to the population and are used to make an inference about that population. **Sampling risk** is the risk that such an inference will be incorrect. In testing the control procedure of approving credit for customer orders, for example, a careful audit of all customer orders for credit approval provides 100 percent certainty of the extent of the failure of this control procedure. A sample, however, likely contains proportionately more or fewer instances of control failure than occur in the population. In performing a substantive test of the inventory pricing, careful audit of all inventory costs would provide 100 percent knowledge of all pricing errors in the population. But it is not feasible to audit every item in a population. Thus, the auditor must take a sample, which may contain proportionately more or fewer misstatements than occur in the total population. Sample results are projected to the population as a whole, but *the accuracy of the projection depends on how representative the sample is of the population.*

Sampling Risks Related to Tests of Control Procedures. The auditor can use sampling to assess the effectiveness of specific control procedures. By sampling, however, the auditor risks making an incorrect assessment of the effectiveness of those control procedures because the sample may not accurately reflect the population. Given a nonrepresentative sample, the auditor takes the **risk of assessing control risk too high** or the **risk of assessing control risk too low.** Assessing control risk higher than the effectiveness of the control procedures warrants means that the auditor places less reliance on control procedures and therefore performs more substantive testing than would otherwise be necessary. Thus, assessing control risk *too high* leads to audit inefficiency; the audit is more expensive than it should optimally be.*

Assessing control risk *too low* means that the auditor relies on ineffective control procedures, which increases detection risk because

- The auditor assumes fewer misstatements have occurred in processing transactions than have actually taken place.
- The auditor reduces the amount of substantive testing designed to detect misstatements in the related account balances.
- The auditor faces a greater risk that any existing material misstatements will remain undetected during the audit (detection risk).

The sampling risk of assessing control risk lower than is in fact the case, then, leads to increased detection risk, which in turn increases the probability that an incorrect audit opinion will be issued (audit risk). The sampling risks associated with assessing control risk are presented in Exhibit 12.1.

Although the auditor could control for both risks (assessing control risk either too high or too low), the required sample size to control for both risks becomes relatively large and very expensive. Assessing control risk too low bears directly on audit risk and thus the *effectiveness* of the audit; that is, it increases the probability that the auditor will issue an unqualified opinion on materially misstated financial statements. For this reason, auditors usually design control tests to minimize the risk of assessing control risk too low and discount, for sampling purposes, the risk of assessing control risk too high. Auditors, in other words, emphasize audit effectiveness.

Sampling Risks Related to Substantive Testing. Sampling can also be used to estimate the amount of error in an account balance. The auditor can, for example, select a sample of inventory items and perform a price test. If the sample contains pricing errors, the auditor projects those errors to the population to determine whether the

*However, as noted earlier, the auditor always plans to perform a minimal amount of substantive audit procedures on every audit engagement. Thus, a minor error in assessing control risk too high is not likely to add substantively to overall audit costs. Conservative auditors generally prefer to err with slightly higher audit costs than to err by not finding material misstatements.

Exhibit 12.1

SAMPLING RISKS FOR TESTS OF CONTROL PROCEDURES

Auditor's Assessment of Control Risk	Actual State of Controls: Effective	Actual State of Controls: Not Effective
Less than maximum	Correct conclusion	Risk of assessing control risk too low (Leads to audit ineffectiveness)
Maximum	Risk of assessing control risk too high (Leads to audit inefficiency)	Correct conclusion

population is materially misstated. Because sampling is used, there is always a risk that the sample may not accurately reflect the population. The auditor must consider two potential risks: (1) concluding that the book value is correct when it actually is materially misstated **(risk of incorrect acceptance)** or (2) concluding that the book value is materially misstated when it is not **(risk of incorrect rejection).** (See Exhibit 12.2.)

The auditor's main concern is with the risk of incorrect acceptance. In some statistical sampling methods, the auditor explicitly controls the risk of incorrect acceptance but not the risk of incorrect rejection; in other statistical sampling methods, the auditor explicitly controls for both. Both would obviously result in auditor errors. The auditor considers the dynamics of the client-auditor relationship in making the decision as to what risk to emphasize. When auditors incur the risk of incorrect rejection, they conclude that book value is materially misstated when in fact it is not. For example, the auditor may take a sample of 100 of the 10,000 inventory items, find misstatements of $5,000 (all overstatements), project the result to the inventory account, and recommend that the client write down inventory by

Exhibit 12.2

SAMPLING RISKS FOR DIRECT TESTS OF ACCOUNT BALANCES

Auditor's Assessment	Condition of the Book Value: Does not contain a material misstatement	Condition of the Book Value: Contains a material misstatement
Book value does not contain a material misstatement	Correct conclusion	Risk of incorrect acceptance (Leads to audit ineffectiveness)
Book value may contain a material misstatement	Risk of incorrect rejection (Leads to audit inefficiency)	Correct conclusion

$500,000 (extrapolating the misstatements to the population as a whole). In this situation, the auditor is likely to perform more extensive or additional audit procedures before suggesting that the client adjust the inventory. The additional work should lead to a conclusion that no material adjustments are needed if the account is, in fact, not materially misstated. This is not to say that misstatements do not exist in the account balance. Rather, the misstatements are not material and the account balance does not require adjustment for an unqualified audit opinion to be issued. Most clients will, however, adjust the statements as a result of most misstatements identified by the auditor. The risk of incorrect rejection thus affects the *efficiency* of the audit, but, because of the additional audit work performed, it does not affect the overall correctness of the audited financial statements.

The risk of incorrect acceptance, however, does not have a built-in bias to change the auditor's initial assessment. The client believes the book value does not contain any material misstatement and is in no position to refute any evidence the auditor generates in support of that conclusion. Therefore, when concluding that the book value is correct when in fact it is incorrect, the auditor gives an unqualified audit opinion on materially misstated financial statements (audit risk). Thus, the risk of incorrect acceptance can lead to legal damages, loss of reputation, and loss of clients. Incorrect acceptance is directly related to the *effectiveness* of the audit. Because of the potential costs associated with such risk, auditors normally control for the risk of incorrect acceptance.*

Selecting a Sampling Approach

Auditors can use nonstatistical or statistical sampling. When properly used, either sampling approach can be effective in providing reliable audit evidence. Some firms, however, restrict the use of nonstatistical sampling because it relies on the auditor's judgment and experience to determine the sample size, select the sample items, and evaluate the sample results and is, therefore, less objective than statistical sampling. **Statistical sampling** combines the theory of probability and statistical inference with audit judgment and experience. A statistical approach helps the auditor to:

- Design an *efficient* sample.
- Measure the *sufficiency* of the evidential matter obtained.
- *Evaluate* the sample results.

Statistical sampling techniques are especially *efficient* for testing large populations. Statistical sampling achieves most of its efficiencies because the validity of the sample is based on the absolute size of the sample itself rather than the percent of the population being examined. National samples predicting election results, for example, are quite accurate using samples of 600 to 3,000 of 80 million voters. This same kind of efficiency is applicable to auditing.

Auditors often choose to sample a certain percentage or proportion of a population when using nonstatistical sampling. The sample may be just right in a few cases or too large or too small in others. The audit will not be efficient if the sample is too large; it will not be effective if the sample is too small.

*There is a direct trade-off between the risk of incorrect acceptance and the risk of incorrect rejection: accepting more of one automatically lowers the other.

Determining how much evidence is enough is a difficult audit decision. Statistical sampling helps auditors know whether they have obtained *sufficient* evidence to support their audit conclusion at the chosen level of sampling risk for the client and the particular population examined. Statistical sampling helps the auditor *evaluate* the sample by providing a quantitative measure of:

- The most likely and maximum failure rate of a control procedure that is being evaluated for effectiveness.
- The most likely and maximum amount of error in the recorded account balance or class of transactions.
- The amount of sampling risk present in the sample (for the type of risk the auditor has chosen to minimize).

Combining statistical sampling with good audit judgment generally produces a higher-quality audit conclusion than using audit judgment alone.

In choosing between statistical and nonstatistical sampling, auditors need to consider (1) the need to control sampling risk, and (2) the costs of training auditors properly to use statistical sampling, to design statistical samples, and to obtain randomly selected sample items. The Auditing Standards Board views making trade-offs in these considerations as a cost/benefit decision best made by each public accounting firm [AU 350.44-.45].*

B–SAMPLING TO TEST CONTROL PROCEDURES AND TRANSACTION PROCESSING

Several statistical methods can be used to test the effectiveness of the client's control procedures over transactions and to test the accuracy of recording transactions. The most commonly used methods, derived from **attribute sampling** techniques, are called *attribute estimation, discovery sampling,* and *sequential (stop-or-go) sampling.* An **attribute** is defined as a characteristic of the population of interest to the auditor. An attribute might be, for example, the existence of authorized credit approval on a customer's order. Although nonstatistical sampling can be used for testing control procedures, many public accounting firms require the use of statistical sampling because the results can be measured and evaluated more precisely and objectively.

Planning Factors

Whether nonstatistical or statistical sampling is used, the following issues need to be addressed when planning an audit sample to test control procedures:

- The *audit objective* of the test, the population from which to select the sample, and the sampling unit.

*The advantages and disadvantages of using nonstatistical sampling are more fully discussed later in this chapter under the heading Nonstatistical Sampling.

- The maximum rate of control procedure failure *(tolerable failure rate*)* that can occur and still permit the auditor to assess control risk at the planned level (e.g., moderate or low).
- The *expected rate* of control procedure failure.
- The auditor's *allowable risk of assessing control risk too low* (that is, concluding that the control is effective in preventing or detecting and correcting material misstatements when it is not).

The tolerable failure rate, expected failure rate, and allowable risk of assessing control risk too low affect the sample size.

Audit Objective

The auditor tests control procedures to corroborate an initial assessment that the control procedures are effective in preventing misstatements and that recorded transactions are authorized, complete, accurate, valid, properly valued and classified, and recorded in the proper time period. Control procedures, however, can be implemented in many different forms, and the nature of the implementation affects the auditor's approach to gathering evidence on the effectiveness of the procedure. Consider the credit approval procedure. The auditor generally examines documentation to determine whether credit was properly approved before the goods are shipped (authorization) based on a sample of customer orders that should contain initials signifying an authorized credit approval. But in many computerized systems, credit authorization is embedded in the logic of the client's computer program. For example, the credit department may set a credit limit for each customer, and the computer calculates whether a customer's credit limit is higher than the customer's current balance plus the value of the new order. Alternatively, the organization may build logic into the computer program to dynamically change credit limits based on such factors as volume of purchases, payment history, and current credit ratings. In such cases, the auditor cannot examine a sales order for credit approval but must consider instead how to audit the computer program to determine that appropriate logic is properly designed and consistently applied. The auditor might test the control procedures relating to the establishment of, and changes in, credit limits and test the program logic for proper approval under a wide variety of different circumstances.

Some control procedures may not provide documentary evidence. Proper segregation of duties is an important part of the control structure, and the auditor may have to rely on observation to determine whether adequate segregation is used.[†]

Tolerable Failure Rate

The **tolerable failure rate** is the maximum rate of control procedure failure that, in the auditor's judgment, can occur and still support the preliminary assessment of control risk. For example, the auditor would consider the maximum percentage of sales orders lacking proper credit approval that could be processed without materi-

*The term *tolerable failure rate* is referred to as *tolerable deviation rate* in the auditing standards.

†There may be some situations in which segregation is documented by signatures on documents and the auditor may be able to examine such documents for evidence of the effectiveness of the control structure. But in most cases, the auditor is limited to inquiry and observation to test such controls.

ally increasing the risk that poor quality credit sales are made and impact the collectibility of accounts receivable.

Control procedure failures do not necessarily lead to dollar misstatements in the financial records. For example, a sale to a customer for whom credit was not properly approved may result in an uncollectible receivable. But if the control procedure had been applied correctly, the customer's credit may have been approved anyway. A detection control makes a difference only on a transaction that would have been rejected. The control procedure failure just increases the risk that misstatements could occur. And, if the increased risk is beyond what the auditor believes is tolerable, the amount and types of substantive procedures to be performed will be reassessed.

The determination of tolerable failure rate is related to the planned control risk assessment for the classes of transactions to which the specific control procedure is relevant. If the control procedure is considered a key control procedure in achieving processing objectives and the control risk has been preliminarily assessed as *low*, the tolerable failure rate should be relatively low, perhaps five percent or less. The tolerable rate can never be zero, however, because then the auditor would have to audit every transaction and not find any control failures, a highly unlikely situation. If the planned control risk assessment is *moderate*, a higher rate could be used, perhaps up to 10 percent. In other words, if a 10 percent tolerable rate is acceptable, the auditor is willing to place some reliance on the control even if the procedure, at its worst, is not followed 1 of 10 times. For example, if the credit logic is properly embedded in a computer program and that program does not change during the year, the auditor would expect that it would be uniformly applied throughout the year and would thus expect a zero error rate. (For the relationship between control risk and tolerable failure rate, see Exhibit 12.3.) Note that the determination of the tolerable

Exhibit 12.3

RELATIONSHIP BETWEEN PLANNED CONTROL RISK AND TOLERABLE FAILURE RATE

Potential Guidelines*

Planned Control Risk Assessment	Maximum Tolerable Failure Rate (Percent)
Low	5%
Moderate	10
Slightly below maximum	20
Maximum	The auditor would not test the control procedures.

*The table presents guidelines, or parameters, that the auditor may use as an initial starting point and that should be adjusted up or down, depending on the importance of an individual control procedure. The table presents only guidelines to assist auditor judgment; it should not be used to replace auditor judgment.

failure rate is an *audit judgment* based on the auditor's assessment of the importance of the control procedure in preventing or detecting material misstatements. Thus, the auditor's determination of the tolerable failure rate may vary widely, depending on the significance of a particular control.

Expected Failure Rate

The **expected failure rate** is the auditor's best estimate of the percentage of transactions processed for which the control procedure is not effectively applied. The auditor often bases this rate on prior year results and adjusts for any known changes in personnel or the accounting system. In many cases, this rate is low because few failures are expected, and in some cases may even be set at zero. If prior information is not known, the auditor may take a preliminary sample to estimate the rate.

The expected failure rate should always be lower than the tolerable rate. If the expected failure rate exceeds the tolerable rate, no testing is necessary. The auditor already believes the control procedures are not working satisfactorily and should set control risk at the maximum.

Allowance for Sampling Error (Precision)

Sampling risk is minimized by (1) conservatively estimating the cushion between the control procedure's expected failure rate and the auditor's judgment of tolerable failure rate and (2) selecting a sample that is as representative of the population as possible. A conservative estimate would be estimating expected error rate higher than expected and setting tolerable failure rate at an amount lower than the auditor believes is necessary. The **allowance for sampling error** (often referred to as **precision**) is the spread between the expected and tolerable failure rates. It allows for some difference between the failure rates in a sample and in the population without affecting the auditor's final assessment of control risk. It has a significant effect on the sample size. A smaller desired precision requires a larger sample size. Exhibit 12.4 shows the relationship between precision and sample size using five percent risk of assessing control risk too low and five percent tolerable failure rate. If the auditor expects no error, the precision is 5 percent (5 percent − 0 percent), resulting in a sample size of 58. If the expected rate is 3 percent, the precision is 2 percent (5 percent − 3 percent), resulting in a sample size of 361. And with an expected error rate of four percent, the sample size rises to 722. As the precision narrows, the sample sizes become so large that the auditor should reconsider the assessment of control risk and determine whether a substantive audit approach would be more cost effective.

Allowable Risk of Assessing Control Risk Too Low

The auditor must determine the level at which to set the risk of assessing control risk too low. Normally, that risk should be set fairly low (e.g., 5 or 10 percent) because the auditor's assessment of control risk directly affects the determination of detection risk and, thus, the nature, timing, and extent of the subsequent auditing procedures. Some CPA firms have a policy of setting this risk at the same level as the overall audit risk. If overall audit risk is set at five percent, the allowable risk of assessing control risk too low would also be set at five percent. The reasoning of this approach is analogous to the weak link in the chain. If the auditor wants to hold audit risk to a five-percent level, testing the control procedures using a higher risk level would be inconsistent. However, it is only a guideline; there are no hard-and-

Exhibit 12.4

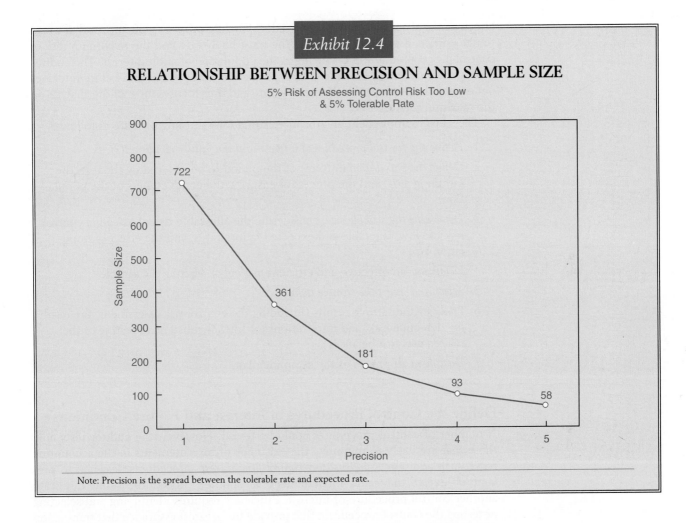

RELATIONSHIP BETWEEN PRECISION AND SAMPLE SIZE

5% Risk of Assessing Control Risk Too Low
& 5% Tolerable Rate

Sample Size
900
800
700
600
500
400
300
200
100
0

722
361
181
93
58

1 2 3 4 5
Precision

Note: Precision is the spread between the tolerable rate and expected rate.

fast rules. As noted earlier, the auditor normally does not control for the risk of assessing control risk too high.*

If the auditor chooses to utilize nonstatistical sampling procedures to test the effectiveness of control procedures, the planning factors are not quantified. Instead, the auditor addresses tolerable and expected error rates through the more global concepts of *none, few,* and *many.* The risk of assessing control risk too low is addressed as *low, moderate,* and *high.* But by making such judgments, the auditor cannot quantitatively assess the risk of making an incorrect inference based on the sample results. For this reason, many auditors who use nonstatistical sampling review the factors and select a sample size consistent with a statistically determined sample.

Attribute Estimation Sampling

The most commonly used statistical method to test control procedures is **attribute estimation sampling.** For control-testing purposes, an attribute is evidence of the

*To some extent, the auditor also ignores the risk of assessing control risk too high because most audit programs will specify a *minimum* set of substantive audit procedures, even if the assessment of control risk is such that substantive audit procedures would not theoretically be required.

effectiveness of a specific control procedure, such as proper credit approval of a customer's order. It is used to estimate the most likely rate and the maximum rate of control procedure failures occurring in the population of audit interest. The auditor is primarily concerned that the sample projection of the maximum failure rate does not exceed the predetermined tolerable rate and thus focuses most of the analysis on the maximum failure rate.

The steps to implement an attribute estimation sampling plan are as follows:

1. *Define the control procedure of interest and the failure condition(s).*
2. *Define the population* in terms of the period to be covered by the test, the sampling unit, and the process of ensuring the completeness of the population.
3. *Determine the sample size,* considering the allowable risk of assessing control risk too low, tolerable and expected failure rates, and the effect of population size.
4. *Determine* an effective and efficient *method of selecting* the sample.
5. *Select and audit the sample items.*
6. *Evaluate* the sample results (including the control risk assessment, the resulting detection risk, and implications for further substantive testing of the related account balances).
7. *Document* all phases of the sampling plan.

Define the Control Procedures of Interest and Failure Conditions

A number of control procedures could be tested. However, the auditor tests only those that are likely to minimize the existence of misstatements in the accounting records. In addition, *compensating control procedures*—procedures designed to prevent or detect the same misstatement as another procedure—often duplicate another control procedure of interest. Efficiency requires identifying and selecting or testing the control procedures that provide the greatest assurance that transaction processing objectives are accomplished. Normally, an auditor does not need to test a compensating control unless the first control tested does not seem to be effective.

Control procedure failure conditions should be precisely stated in advance to ensure that the staff auditor clearly understands the audit procedure to be performed. The specification of a control procedure failure condition reduces nonsampling risk. For example, a typical audit objective might be to determine whether documents supporting a cash disbursement are properly canceled. Without proper cancellation, they might be used to support a duplicate payment. A client's procedure might call for stamping the invoice "Paid" but does not require the cancellation of the other supporting documents, such as the purchase order, receiving report, and voucher. A control procedure failure condition would be defined as "the lack of cancellation of the invoice" because the payment is based on the invoice.

The preceding example is an interesting case of the relationship between defining a control procedure failure condition and the auditor's assessment of the importance of the control procedure. In this case, a failure could not be defined as "lack of cancellation of supporting documents" because failure to cancel the purchase order, receiving report, and voucher is not a violation of the control procedure. But because the purchase order and receiving report are not canceled, the control procedure is not as effective in preventing duplicate payments; if the vendor sends a duplicate or a second invoice, the same bill could be paid twice. Therefore, the auditor should not rely on a control procedure that requires only invoice cancellation as much as on one that calls for the cancellation of all supporting documents. The auditor should reassess whether the control procedure, as it exists, is worth testing.

Define the Population

The following factors need to be addressed in defining the population and selecting sampling procedures: the *period* to be covered by the test, the *sampling unit*, and the process of assuring the *completeness* of the population.

Period Covered by the Tests. The period covered by the audit sample depends directly on the audit objective. In most instances, the *period* is the time period covered by the audited financial statements. The auditor develops tests to determine the effectiveness of the control procedure during the period covered by the financial statements. As a practical matter, tests of controls are often performed prior to the balance sheet date and may cover the first 10 or 11 months of the year. If such control procedures are found to be effective, the auditor should take additional steps to ensure that they continue to be effective during the remainder of the year. The additional steps may include making inquiries, further testing of the control procedures, or gathering evidence of control effectiveness from substantive tests performed later in the audit [AU 319.55].

In some situations, the audit objective and time period may be more limited. If the audit objective is to determine that the allowance for doubtful accounts is adequate, for example, the auditor might focus on credit approvals for the time period applicable to the generation of the unpaid receivables. The auditor is not normally concerned with credit approval for sales that have already been collected by the balance sheet date. Often, however, a number of attributes are tested at the same time using the same source documents. For efficiency, the auditor may then test credit approval for the entire period when that control is most efficiently tested in conjunction with other attributes on the same documents at the same time.

Sampling Unit. The **sampling unit** is the item identified in the population as the basis for testing. It could be a document, an entry or a line item on a document, or a computer-"logged" entry, depending on the audit objective and the control procedure (attribute) being tested. For example, proper authorization of disbursements could be implemented in a number of ways. One company may require supervisory approval with initials on a voucher, which may authorize payment of several invoices; the sampling unit would be the voucher. Another company may require written approval of each invoice; the sampling unit would be the individual invoices processed for payment.

The sample is selected from a physical representation of the population that identifies the sampling units. These are some examples of physical representations:

- A check register that lists all of the checks written for some period of time.
- A computer list of fixed asset additions.
- A computer file of unpaid balances of accounts receivable.

The auditor must make sure that the population used in sampling is a *complete representation* of the total population of interest. The audit conclusion is valid only for the population from which the sample was selected. If that population is not correctly defined, or is incomplete, the audit conclusion may be wrong. The auditor normally performs some procedures, such as footing the file and reconciling the balance to the general ledger, to ensure that the population is complete and consistent with the audit objective.

Determine the Sample Size

An optimally determined sample size will minimize the risk of assessing control risk too low and promote audit efficiency. The following items affect the sample size: (1) the allowable risk of assessing control risk too low, (2) the tolerable failure rate, (3) the expected failure rate, and (4) the population size.

Exhibit 12.5 provides the sample sizes for several combinations of the first three factors. The exhibit shows sample sizes for both 5 percent and 10 percent allowable risk of assessing control risk too low. The risk of assessing control risk too low is the complement of what is sometimes called the *confidence* or *reliability level.* For example, a 5 percent risk corresponds to a 95 percent confidence or reliability level.

An example will clarify the use of these tables. The auditor plans to test credit department approval of customer orders. Audit risk has been set at 10 percent. Therefore, a 10 percent risk of assessing control risk too low will be used for this test. In other words, the auditor is using a 90 percent confidence level (100 percent – 10

Exhibit 12.5

ATTRIBUTE SAMPLE SIZE TABLES

Table 1: 5% *Risk* of Assessing Control Risk Too Low

Expected Population Deviation Rate	Tolerable Rate										
	2%	3%	4%	5%	6%	7%	8%	9%	10%	15%	20%
0.00%	149(0)	99(0)	74(0)	59(0)	49(0)	42(0)	36(0)	32(0)	29(0)	19(0)	14(0)
.25	236(1)	157(1)	117(1)	93(1)	78(1)	66(1)	58(1)	51(1)	46(1)	30(1)	22(1)
.50	*	157(1)	117(1)	93(1)	78(1)	66(1)	58(1)	51(1)	46(1)	30(1)	22(1)
.75	*	208(2)	117(1)	93(1)	78(1)	66(1)	58(1)	51(1)	46(1)	30(1)	22(1)
1.00	*	*	156(2)	93(1)	78(1)	66(1)	58(1)	51(1)	46(1)	30(1)	22(1)
1.25	*	*	156(2)	124(2)	78(1)	66(1)	58(1)	51(1)	46(1)	30(1)	22(1)
1.50	*	*	192(3)	124(2)	103(2)	66(1)	58(1)	51(1)	46(1)	30(1)	22(1)
1.75	*	*	227(4)	153(3)	103(2)	88(2)	77(2)	51(1)	46(1)	30(1)	22(1)
2.00	*	*	*	181(4)	127(3)	88(2)	77(2)	68(2)	46(1)	30(1)	22(1)
2.25	*	*	*	208(5)	127(3)	88(2)	77(2)	68(2)	61(2)	30(1)	22(1)
2.50	*	*	*	*	150(4)	109(3)	77(2)	68(2)	61(2)	30(1)	22(1)
2.75	*	*	*	*	173(5)	109(3)	95(3)	68(2)	61(2)	30(1)	22(1)
3.00	*	*	*	*	195(6)	129(4)	95(3)	84(3)	61(2)	30(1)	22(1)
3.25	*	*	*	*	*	148(5)	112(4)	84(3)	61(2)	30(1)	22(1)
3.50	*	*	*	*	*	167(6)	112(4)	84(3)	76(3)	40(2)	22(1)
3.75	*	*	*	*	*	185(7)	129(5)	100(4)	76(3)	40(2)	22(1)
4.00	*	*	*	*	*	*	146(6)	100(4)	89(4)	40(2)	22(1)
5.00	*	*	*	*	*	*	*	158(8)	116(6)	40(2)	30(2)
6.00	*	*	*	*	*	*	*	*	179(11)	50(3)	30(2)
7.00	*	*	*	*	*	*	*	*	*	68(5)	37(3)

percent) that the actual failure rate in the population will not exceed the tolerable failure rate. Credit approval is seen as an important control on which the auditor wishes to place significant reliance. Therefore, a tolerable failure rate of five percent is chosen. Based on prior year experience and knowledge of changes in personnel and the system, the auditor estimates that the failure rate will not exceed one percent. Using Exhibit 12.5, the auditor determines that the sample size should be at least 77 items. The number in parentheses next to each sample size is the maximum number of misstatements the auditor expects in that sample if the population's error rate is the same as the expected error rate. For example, the auditor would expect to find no more than one error in the sample of 77 items given that the expected error rate is no more than one percent.

Multiple Attributes. Auditors frequently test several control procedures or attributes using the same set of source documents. The allowable risk of assessing control risk too low is the same for all tests of controls. But the tolerable and expected failure rates for these attributes are likely to be different, resulting in different sample sizes. For example, the auditor may want to test the presentation, valuation, and validity assertions concerning sales transactions using tolerable failure rates of five percent, three percent, and three percent and expected failure rates of two percent, one percent, and 0 percent, respectively. If the auditor sets the allowable risk of

Exhibit 12.5

Table 2: *10% Risk* of Assessing Control Risk Too Low

Expected Population Deviation Rate	Tolerable Rate										
	2%	3%	4%	5%	6%	7%	8%	9%	10%	15%	20%
0.00%	114(0)	76(0)	57(0)	45(0)	38(0)	32(0)	28(0)	25(0)	22(0)	15(0)	11(0)
.25	194(1)	129(1)	96(1)	77(1)	64(1)	55(1)	48(1)	42(1)	38(1)	25(1)	18(1)
.50	194(1)	129(1)	96(1)	77(1)	64(1)	55(1)	48(1)	42(1)	38(1)	25(1)	18(1)
.75	265(2)	129(1)	96(1)	77(1)	64(1)	55(1)	48(1)	42(1)	38(1)	25(1)	18(1)
1.00	*	176(2)	96(1)	77(1)	64(1)	55(1)	48(1)	42(1)	38(1)	25(1)	18(1)
1.25	*	221(3)	132(2)	77(1)	64(1)	55(1)	48(1)	42(1)	38(1)	25(1)	18(1)
1.50	*	*	132(2)	105(2)	64(1)	55(1)	48(1)	42(1)	38(1)	25(1)	18(1)
1.75	*	*	166(3)	105(2)	88(2)	55(1)	48(1)	42(1)	38(1)	25(1)	18(1)
2.00	*	*	198(4)	132(3)	88(2)	75(2)	48(2)	42(1)	38(1)	25(1)	18(1)
2.25	*	*	*	132(3)	88(2)	75(2)	65(2)	42(1)	38(1)	25(1)	18(1)
2.50	*	*	*	158(4)	110(3)	75(2)	65(2)	58(2)	38(1)	25(1)	18(1)
2.75	*	*	*	209(6)	132(4)	94(3)	65(2)	58(2)	52(2)	25(1)	18(1)
3.00	*	*	*	*	132(4)	94(3)	65(2)	58(2)	52(2)	25(1)	18(1)
3.25	*	*	*	*	153(5)	113(4)	82(3)	58(2)	52(2)	25(1)	18(1)
3.50	*	*	*	*	194(7)	113(4)	82(3)	73(3)	52(2)	25(1)	18(1)
3.75	*	*	*	*	*	131(5)	98(4)	73(3)	52(2)	25(1)	18(1)
4.00	*	*	*	*	*	149(6)	98(4)	73(3)	65(3)	25(1)	18(1)
5.00	*	*	*	*	*	*	160(8)	115(6)	78(4)	34(2)	18(1)
6.00	*	*	*	*	*	*	*	182(11)	116(7)	43(3)	25(2)
7.00	*	*	*	*	*	*	*	*	199(14)	52(4)	25(2)

Note: The number of expected misstatements appears in parentheses. These tables assume a large population.
* = Sample size is too large to be cost effective for most audit applications.
Source: *Audit Sampling,* (New York: AICPA, 1983), 106–107.

assessing control risk too low at 10 percent, the sample sizes range from a high of 176 for valuation to a low of 76 for validity:

Attribute	Tolerable Failure Rate (Percent)	Expected Failure Rate (Percent)	Sample Size
1. Evidence of independent review of account distribution (presentation)	5%	2%	132
2. Evidence of comparison of description, quantity, and price between the customer's order and sales invoice (valuation)	3	1	176
3. Evidence of proper review and approval for credit (validity and valuation)	3	0	76

If there is an effective review of account distributions, the auditor can assess that control risk below the maximum and limit the extent of substantive testing for proper presentation in the financial statements. If there appears to be effective comparison of information on customers' orders and sales invoices, the auditor can limit the tests of the valuation of sales transactions. If there is good control over credit approval, the auditor is less concerned about the adequacy of the allowance for doubtful accounts (valuation) and the existence of unauthorized sales (validity).

The auditor could use several approaches to select the items for these tests. First, three separate samples could be selected using the three sample sizes. This approach, however, would be inefficient. Second, the auditor could select 176 sales transactions (the largest sample size) and audit all of them for attribute 2, three of four for attribute 1, and every other one for attribute 3. This process, however, is quite cumbersome. Or, third, the auditor could examine the first 76 randomly selected documents for all three attributes and documents 77–132 for attributes 1 and 2, and the remainder only for attribute 2. This process is also quite cumbersome. Often the most efficient approach is to test the 176 items for all three attributes. Attributes 1 and 3 will be in some sense "overaudited," but the overauditing may take less time than keeping track of which sample items should be tested for which attribute. Testing for attributes 1 and 3 does not take very long once the auditor has selected the documents in the sample. The auditor's evaluation of the control is based on the 176 items examined and improves the effectiveness of the control risk assessment.

Sensitivity of Sample Size. The efficiency of the audit depends on using a proper risk of assessing control risk too low and appropriate tolerable and expected rates. These relationships and the resultant effect on sample size can be seen in Exhibit 12.5 and are summarized as follows:

Change	Effect on Sample Size
Reduce the allowable risk of assessing control risk too low	Increase
Reduce the tolerable failure rate	Increase
Reduce the expected failure rate	Decrease

Sample size thus varies inversely with the tolerable failure rate and the allowable risk of assessing control risk too low but varies directly with the expected failure rate.

Finite Adjustment Factor. Sample size tables assume that the population is very large. A **finite adjustment factor** can be used to determine the appropriate sample size when the sample size from the table is a significant part of the population. Some CPA firms recommend making this adjustment if the sample size is more than 10 percent of the population.* The formula for determining the sample size for these smaller populations is:

$$n = n'/[1 + (n'/N)]$$

where:

n' = The sample size from the table

N = The population size.

For example, if the sample size from Exhibit 12.5 is 93 and the population is 800, the adjusted sample size would be 83:

$$83 = 93/[1 + (93/800)].$$

The effect of the finite correction factor is to reduce sample sizes in smaller populations and is thus useful in improving audit efficiency and decreasing audit cost. If the population contained 20,000 items, the adjusted sample size would be 92.57, or 93 for all practical purposes. Exhibit 12.6 illustrates the relationship between sample size and population size using five percent risk of assessing control risk too low, five percent tolerable rate, and one percent expected rate. There is a point (*C*) above which an increase in population size does not affect the sample size. For this set of parameters, that point is a population of around 20,000 (point *C*). The sample sizes in Exhibit 12.5 are based on these large populations.

A careful review of Exhibit 12.6 helps explain why auditing firms can achieve substantial economies of scale when auditing large clients. After a certain point, sample size is insensitive to the population size. Thus, a small client with only 800 transactions (point *B*) requires the auditor to look at about 83 documents (10.375 percent of the population), whereas a client with 20,000 documents (point *C*) would require the auditor to look at only 93 documents (0.465 percent of the population) for the same audit test. For this reason, sampling tends to be used extensively on large clients but not as extensively in audits of small clients. For the latter, the auditor often chooses not to test control procedures but assesses control risk at or near the maximum and achieves audit efficiencies by directly testing the account balances.

Determine the Method of Selecting the Sample

Once the sample size has been determined, the auditor must decide how to select a representative sample. Random-based methods ensure that each item in the population has an equal chance to be included in the sample. Statistical sampling requires **random-based selection** because it eliminates the possibility of unintentional bias in

*Most computer programs that auditors use in sampling applications make this adjustment automatically.

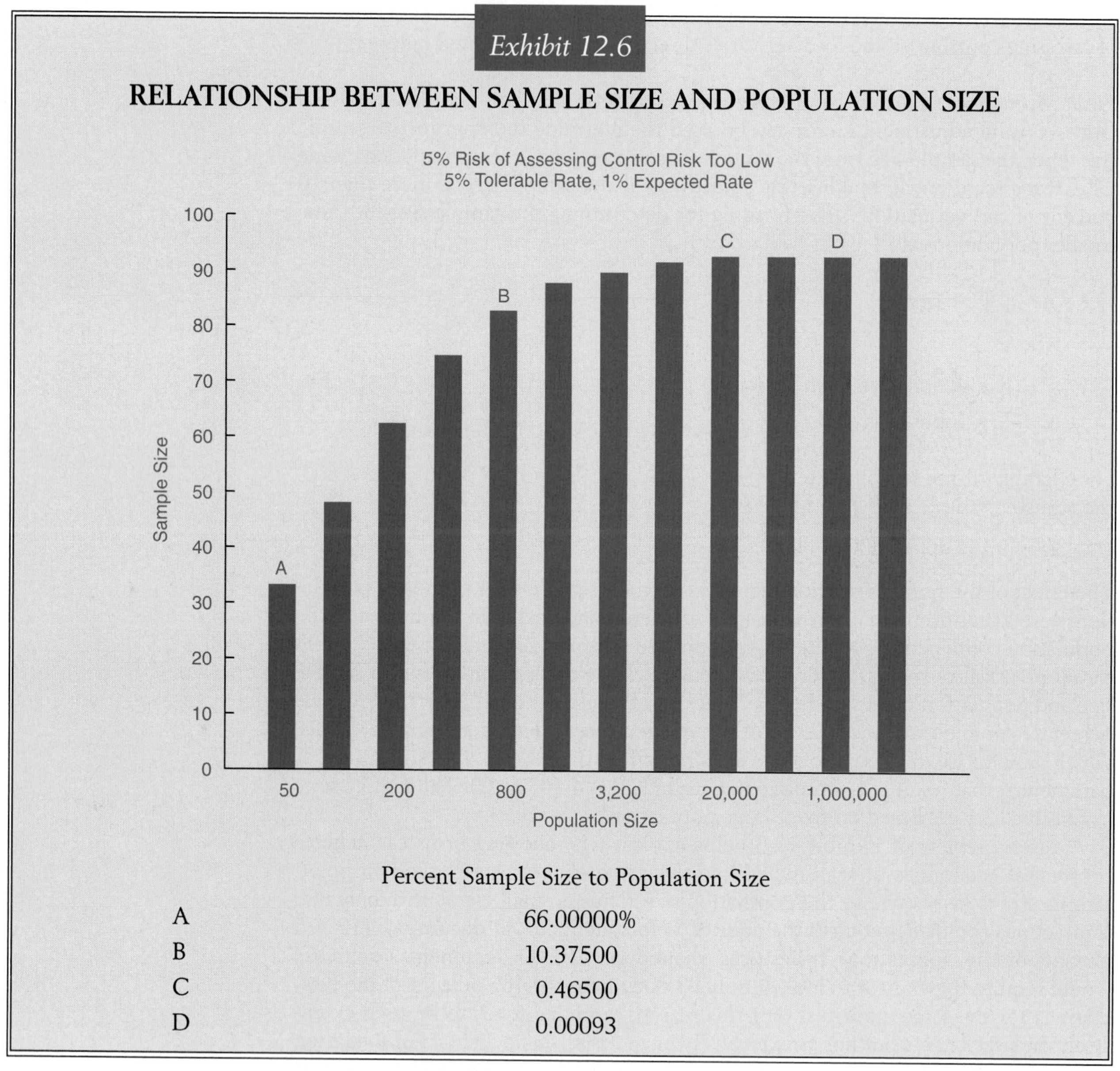

the selection process and helps ensure that the sample is representative. For nonstatistical sampling, any selection method can be used, including random-based selection, that the auditor believes will result in a representative sample. A flowchart for choosing among several selection methods is illustrated in Exhibit 12.7.

Random Numbers. Random number selection is an efficient sample selection method if there is an easy way to relate the random numbers to the population. For example, a random selection of sales invoices could be based on sales invoice numbers. Most CPA firms and internal audit organizations have micro- or mainframe computer programs that generate and sort random numbers and provide the neces-

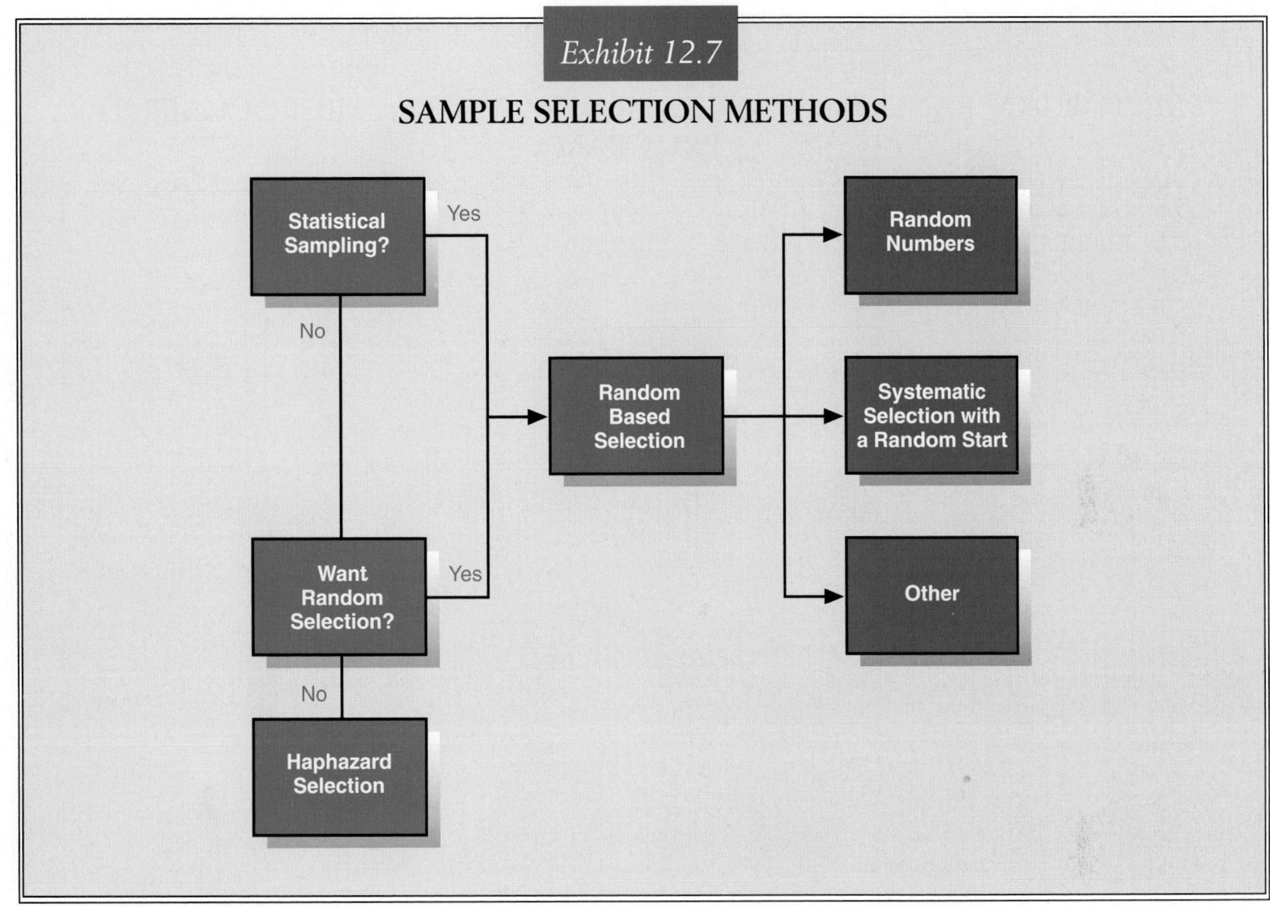

sary printout to document the random number selection process. Exhibit 12.8 is a printout of a *Lotus 1-2-3* template that generated 26* random numbers for a sample of sales invoices issued during the audit period that were numbered from 65,400 through 143,900. Because there may be some voided documents in that series, most programs generate several extra random numbers to replace any voided sales invoices. The order number shows the order in which the random numbers were generated.

If computer support is not available, tables of random numbers can be used. In addition to identifying the necessary numbers in the tables, the auditor needs to sort the numbers and document the selection process in the working papers. These mechanical steps can usually be done more efficiently using a computer.

Systematic Selection. Several **systematic selection** methods meet the requirement of randomness and improve audit efficiency when documents are not numbered in a consecutive sequence or when selecting and locating items in a numbered sequence are difficult. Inventory items are frequently listed by stock numbers that include both letters and numbers.

Systematic selection involves the determination of an interval (n) and the selection of every nth item to be tested. The sampling interval is determined by dividing

*The sample size of 26 is used here for illustration purposes only. Sample sizes are normally larger than this.

Exhibit 12.8

PRINTOUT OF RANDOM NUMBERS GENERATED BY A MICROCOMPUTER PROGRAM

```
LOW NUMBER IN SERIES        }      65400        { INPUT
HIGH NUMBER IN SERIES       }     143900        { INPUT
SAMPLE SIZE DESIRED         }         26        { INPUT
EXTRA UNSORTED NUMBERS      }          5        { INPUT
```

ORDER NUMBER	RANDOM NUMBER
10	68295
1	68714
8	68839
17	74353
23	78832
15	86196
12	86445
9	87095
21	89102
4	91878
6	95053
3	98538
25	99112
16	101220
13	106657
18	110902
5	111051
14	111627
22	113999
11	114677
19	115742
26	122666
7	127922
24	130001
2	131170
20	131767
EXTRA NUMBERS	
27	99736
28	70709
29	136463
30	93646
31	68457

the population size by the desired sample size. A random start between 1 and *n* is chosen to identify the first sample item. As a result, every item in the population has an equal chance of being tested. Payroll transactions in a payroll journal, for example, may be listed in employee number order. These numbers are not in consecutive sequence because of employee turnover. There are 1,300 payroll transactions, and the auditor has determined a sample size of 26. Every 50th transaction (1,300/26 = 50) should be selected for testing. To randomize the selection process, a random number from 1 to 50 should be used to identify the first sample item. This could be done, for example, by using the last two digits of a serial number on a dollar bill. If those digits were 87, subtract 50, leaving 37 as the first sample item. Every 50th transaction thereafter would also be included in the sample.

The validity of a systematic sample is based on the assumption that the items in the population are randomly distributed. The auditor must be knowledgeable about the nature of the population to be sure that no repeating or coinciding pattern in the population would cause the sample not to be representative. Many auditors try to ensure that the systematically selected samples are representative of the population by using multiple random starts.

Implementation of Other Random Methods. The auditor can use the *terminal digits* of serially numbered documents to identify sample items. For example, a separate series of payroll checks is used. Checks numbered from 34,650 to 36,000 were used this year, and the auditor wishes to select every 50th check. This represents two percent of the population. The auditor could select two random numbers from 0 to 99—such as 35 and 60—and select every check ending in either of those two numbers (34660, 34735, 34760, etc.).

Another systematic approach is to randomly select a *specific line* and test every item that is listed on that line on each page, every other page, or every *n*th page, depending on the desired sample size and the number of pages in the listing. For example, if the desired sample size is 26 of the 1,300 transactions and the payroll journal consists of 26 pages with 50 items on each page, a random number from 1 to 50, such as 19, could be selected, and the 19th item on each page would be tested. Another approach is to generate *random pages and lines* to identify the sample items. This approach avoids the coinciding pattern problem.

Auditor-Directed Judgment Sample. The auditor may utilize judgmental criteria to develop a representative sample. That judgment is based on the auditor's experience with a client. Selection criteria may include the size of the transaction, the time period in which it was initiated, or the source of its origination.

Many audit programs encourage the auditor to choose a **block sample** (such as 50 consecutively numbered items) from a specific day. The problem is attempting to generalize the processing results of those 50 items to the full set of transactions processed during the year. The accounting system or control procedures may change; personnel may change; or volume of transactions processed in a day (and thus susceptibility of control procedure failure) may change. The auditor should know that such factors are not present if such a sampling choice is chosen.

Haphazard Selection. **Haphazard selection** involves the arbitrary selection of sample items without any conscious bias but without using a random base. It is often used in nonstatistical sampling applications. Because it is not random based, such a sample cannot be statistically evaluated.

Select and Audit the Sample Items

When selecting the sample, the auditor should decide how to handle inapplicable, voided, or unused documents. An example of an inapplicable document would be a telephone bill when testing for an error defined as "cash disbursement transactions not supported by a receiving report." If the inapplicable or voided document does not represent a failure of a prescribed control procedure, such as not being properly voided, it should be replaced by another randomly selected item. When a selected item cannot be located, it is unlikely that the audit test can be performed on that item because there would not be any evidence of the control procedure having been performed. The auditor should assume the worst—that the control procedure was not followed—and count it as a failure. The auditor may find so many failures before finishing the audit of a sample that, even if the rest of the sample contained no misstatements, the auditor concludes that no reliance could be placed on the tested control procedure. In such a situation, the auditor should terminate the test to avoid wasting any more time.

Evaluate the Sample Results

Evaluation of sample results requires the auditor to project those results to the population before drawing an audit conclusion. If the sample failure rate is no greater than the expected failure rate, the auditor can conclude that the control is at least as effective as expected and can assess the control risk below the maximum according to the original audit plan.

Quantitative Evaluation. If the sample failure rate exceeds the expected failure rate, the auditor should determine whether the projected maximum failure rate is likely to exceed the tolerable rate previously set. To make such an assessment, the auditor should consider the allowance for sampling error. Tables such as those in Exhibit 12.9 help the auditor determine the upper limit of the failure rate in the population based on the sample results. If the achieved upper limit exceeds the tolerable rate, the auditor should either (1) test a compensating control or (2) adjust the nature, timing, and/or the extent of the related substantive testing. Before doing either, the auditor should consider the nature of control procedure failures (pattern of error) and determine the potential effect of such failures on potential misstatement in the financial statements.

To illustrate the use of the tables, assume that the auditor tested credit department approval using a risk of assessing control risk too low of five percent, a tolerable failure rate of five percent, and an expected failure rate of one percent. A sample of 100 orders was selected from a population of 100,000. If one control procedure failure was found in the sample, the sample failure rate of one percent equals the expected rate, and the auditor can assess the control risk below the maximum as planned.

If, however, three control procedure failures were found, the auditor should not conclude that there are only three control procedure failures in the population. Rather, the sample results should be considered to be representative of the population. Because the sample failure rate is three percent, the auditor can project that there are approximately 3,000 of these failures in the population (3 percent × 100,000). Only the tip of the iceberg has been audited. The sample failure rate of three percent exceeds the expected rate of one percent. In addition, Exhibit 12.9 shows that, using a 5 percent risk of assessing control risk too low and a sample size

Exhibit 12.9

ATTRIBUTE ESTIMATION SAMPLE EVALUATION TABLES

Table 1: 5% *Risk* of Assessing Control Risk Too Low

Sample Size	Actual Number of Control Procedure Failures Found 0	1	2	3	4	5	6	7	8	9	10
25	11.3	17.6	*	*	*	*	*	*	*	*	*
30	9.5	14.9	19.6	*	*	*	*	*	*	*	*
35	8.3	12.9	17.0	*	*	*	*	*	*	*	*
40	7.3	11.4	15.0	18.3	*	*	*	*	*	*	*
45	6.5	10.2	13.4	16.4	19.2	*	*	*	*	*	*
50	5.9	9.2	12.1	14.8	17.4	19.9	*	*	*	*	*
55	5.4	8.4	11.1	13.5	15.9	18.2	*	*	*	*	*
60	4.9	7.7	10.2	12.5	14.7	16.8	18.8	*	*	*	*
65	4.6	7.1	9.4	11.5	13.6	15.5	17.4	19.3	*	*	*
70	4.2	6.6	8.8	10.8	12.6	14.5	16.3	18.0	19.7	*	*
75	4.0	6.2	8.2	10.1	11.8	13.6	15.2	16.9	18.5	20.0	*
80	3.7	5.8	7.7	9.5	11.1	12.7	14.3	15.9	17.4	18.9	*
90	3.3	5.2	6.9	8.4	9.9	11.4	12.8	14.2	15.5	16.8	18.2
100	3.0	4.7	6.2	7.6	9.0	10.3	11.5	12.8	14.0	15.2	16.4
120	2.5	3.9	5.2	6.4	7.5	8.6	9.7	10.7	11.7	12.8	13.8
140	2.2	3.4	4.5	5.5	6.5	7.4	8.3	9.2	10.1	11.0	11.9
160	1.9	3.0	3.9	4.8	5.7	6.5	7.3	8.1	8.9	9.7	10.4
200	1.5	2.4	3.2	3.9	4.6	5.2	5.9	6.5	7.1	7.8	8.4

Table 2: 10% *Risk* of Assessing Control Risk Too Low

Sample Size	0	1	2	3	4	5	6	7	8	9	10
25	8.8	14.7	19.9	*	*	*	*	*	*	*	*
30	7.4	12.4	16.8	*	*	*	*	*	*	*	*
35	6.4	10.7	14.5	18.1	*	*	*	*	*	*	*
40	5.6	9.4	12.8	16.0	19.0	*	*	*	*	*	*
45	5.0	8.4	11.4	14.3	17.0	19.7	*	*	*	*	*
50	4.6	7.6	10.3	12.9	15.4	17.8	*	*	*	*	*
55	4.1	6.9	9.4	11.8	14.1	16.3	18.4	*	*	*	*
60	3.8	6.4	8.7	10.8	12.9	15.0	16.9	18.9	*	*	*
70	3.3	5.5	7.5	9.3	11.1	12.9	14.6	16.3	17.9	19.6	*
80	2.9	4.8	6.6	8.2	9.8	11.3	12.8	14.3	15.8	17.2	18.6
90	2.6	4.3	5.9	7.3	8.7	10.1	11.5	12.8	14.1	15.4	16.6
100	2.3	3.9	5.3	6.6	7.9	9.1	10.3	11.5	12.7	13.9	15.0
120	2.0	3.3	4.4	5.5	6.6	7.6	8.7	9.7	10.7	11.6	12.6
140	1.7	2.8	3.8	4.8	5.7	6.6	7.4	8.3	9.2	10.0	10.8
160	1.5	2.5	3.3	4.2	5.0	5.8	6.5	7.3	8.0	8.8	9.5
200	1.2	2.0	2.7	3.4	4.0	4.6	5.3	5.9	6.5	7.1	7.6

Note: These tables present upper limits as percentages assuming a large population.
* Over 20%.

Source: *Audit Sampling* (New York: AICPA, 1983), 108–109.

of 100, the achieved upper limit of the failure rate is 7.6 percent. The auditor can be 95 percent confident (100 percent − 5 percent risk of assessing control risk too low) that the failure rate is no greater than 7.6 percent. The auditor had previously set the tolerable rate of failure at five percent. This sample result is unexpected and indicates that the control cannot be relied on as originally planned. The auditor can consider the following alternative courses of action: (1) test a compensating control or (2) assess control risk at a higher level and revise the remainder of the audit accordingly.

If control risk is assessed at a higher level, detection risk needs to be set lower. This adjustment causes the nature, timing, and/or extent of substantive testing to be changed to a more effective approach for finding misstatements that may have occurred because of this control weakness. For example, inadequate approval of customer orders indicates a higher potential for the understatement of the allowance for doubtful accounts and bad debt expense. The auditor might choose to use a stronger test, such as reviewing details of subsequent payments or reviewing credit ratings of open accounts rather than analytical procedures in testing the adequacy of the allowance account.

Qualitative Evaluation. When misstatements are found, they should be analyzed *qualitatively* as well as quantitatively. The auditor should try to determine whether the misstatements (1) were intentional or unintentional, (2) were random or systematic, and/or (3) had a direct dollar effect.

The auditor is much more concerned if the misstatements appear to be *intentional.* This reflects on the integrity of the individual involved and might cause the auditor to suspect fraud. If the misstatements are *systematic,* the auditor may be able to isolate the problem and reduce the need to change the nature, timing, or extent of the related substantive testing. For example, if all of the misstatements were caused by just 1 of the 50 clerks in the department, the auditor could more carefully review the financial records affected by that person's work to determine the extent of any dollar misstatements that might have occurred.

Many control procedure failures do not lead directly to dollar misstatements in the accounting records. Lack of proper approval for payment of a vendor's invoice, for example, does not necessarily mean that the invoice should not have been paid. If, however, the auditor determines that there are *dollar misstatements* caused by failures uncovered in the sample, the misstatements should not be ignored. They should be projected to the population of dollars being tested, documented in the working papers, and tracked along with the misstatements uncovered through substantive tests.

Document the Procedures

All audit work should be documented in the working papers. For sampling applications, this documentation might include the following:

- The objective(s) of the test.
- The population, the sampling unit, and the way completeness was determined.
- The definition of failure(s).
- The underlying reasons for selecting the level of risk of assessing control risk too low and the tolerable and expected failure rates.

- How the sample size was determined.
- How the sample was selected.
- A description of the procedures performed and the failures found, if any.
- The evaluation of the sample and an overall conclusion.

An example of such a working paper appears in Exhibit 12.15 in conjunction with the LeFlam illustrative example.

Sequential (Stop-or-Go) Sampling

Attribute estimation sampling is a single-step process. One sample is audited and a conclusion is reached based on that sample. **Sequential sampling,** sometimes referred to as **stop-or-go sampling,** is a multistep process involving the selection of the smallest possible sample so that if no failures are discovered, the auditor can conclude that the control procedures are working satisfactorily. If one or more failures are discovered, a decision must be made about whether to expand the sample. Sequential sampling can be used when it is relatively easy to expand the sample if necessary and few failures are expected.

Exhibit 12.10 is an example of a table that can be used for sequential sampling. It is based on a 10 percent risk of assessing control risk too low, a 5 percent tolerable failure rate, and a 0.5 percent expected failure rate. The first step is to select and audit a sample of 50 items (group 1). If no failures are found, the auditor can accept the planned reliance on the control. If one, two, or three failures are found in this first group, additional items in the next group of 51 items are audited. If no more failures are found, the auditor can accept the planned reliance. When four or more failures are found, sampling is stopped and the auditor should reduce the planned reliance on the control.

These sample sizes are different from those for attribute estimation sampling. For example, the sample size for attribute estimation sampling would be 77 for the set

Exhibit 12.10

SEQUENTIAL SAMPLE SIZE TABLE

			Accumulated Failures		
Group	Number of Sampling Units	Accumulated Sample Size	Accept Planned Reliance	Sample More	Reduce Planned Reliance
1	50	50	0	1, 2, or 3	4
2	51	101	1	2 or 3	4
3	51	152	2	3	4
4	51	203	3	NA	4

Source: *Audit Sampling* (New York: AICPA, 1983), 112.

of parameters used in Exhibit 12.10. If no more than one failure is found in that sample, the auditor can use the planned degree of reliance on the control. If more than one failure is found, the auditor reduces the planned degree of reliance. Using sequential sampling, a sample of only 50 items would be required to reach this same conclusion if no failures are found. A sample of 101 would be required if one failure is found. The reason for this difference is that the population is given a "second chance" if failures are found.

In the long term, sample sizes using sequential sampling will be smaller than for attribute estimation sampling if the auditor does not overstate the expected population failure rate. The opposite is true if the expected failure rate is overstated. The auditor needs to weigh these factors and consider how easy it is to expand the sample when deciding which sampling approach to use.

Discovery Sampling

Discovery sampling is used to uncover evidence of fraud or potential control failures considered to be critical if they exist at more than a very low occurrence rate. The purpose of such testing is to uncover at least one incident for investigation rather than to estimate the maximum likely failure rate. Discovery sampling is a special case of attribute estimation sampling using a zero percent expected failure rate and a low tolerable failure rate.

Internal auditors often use discovery sampling to monitor the effectiveness of control procedures over transaction processing. For example, a discovery sampling routine can be imbedded in a computer program to capture a sample of transactions on a separate audit file as they are processed. The auditor can then audit these transactions at a later date. If a control problem is discovered, the internal auditor can bring it to management's attention so corrective action can be taken.

Exhibit 12.11 shows the discovery sample sizes for populations of 10,000 and 50,000.* The sample sizes are somewhat sensitive to changes in the population size, particularly for the lower tolerable rates and risks of assessing control risk too low. For example, the sample sizes for a 0.1 percent tolerable rate are significantly larger for a population of 50,000 than for one of 10,000. For a two percent tolerable rate, however, there is very little, if any, difference. Sample sizes for populations larger than 50,000 will be very close to those for 50,000. The sample sizes tend to be large because of the relatively low tolerable rates. If no failures are uncovered in the sample, the auditor can conclude that such events are within tolerable limits. If just one failure is uncovered, even early in the testing, the auditor will likely stop testing and investigate the cause.

Nonstatistical Sampling

The auditor may believe that a nonstatistical sample is more efficient or may have some idea where to look for problems and wish to direct the sampling toward these items (referred to as **directed sampling**). For example, one or two locations may have new people or a newly installed accounting subsystem, and the auditor should direct attention to a specific set of transactions at these locations.

*These sample sizes are based on the hypergeometric probability distribution.

Exhibit 12.11

DISCOVERY SAMPLE SIZE TABLE

	N = 10,000					N = 50,000				
	Tolerable Rate					Tolerable Rate				
Risk*	.1%	.3%	.5%	1%	2%	.1%	.3%	.5%	1%	2%
1%	3,689	1,421	989	448	226	4,398	1,510	911	457	228
5%	2,588	949	581	294	148	2,907	988	595	298	149
10%	2,056	738	449	227	114	2,250	761	458	229	114
20%	1,486	522	316	159	80	1,584	533	321	160	80

*Risk of assessing control risk too low.

Sample Size

The auditor uses judgment to determine the sample size in a nonstatistical approach. In making this decision, auditing standards require the auditor to consider the importance of the test, the reliance on control procedures and other tests, the tolerable rate of failure, the expected failure rate, the size of the population being tested, and prior experience. Quite often, the auditor simply feels comfortable with a particular sample size for a given purpose; this is particularly true for experienced auditors.

Selection

Auditors frequently use a random-based selection method for nonstatistical sampling applications. In other cases, however, it may take less time to select a haphazard sample, which is appropriate as long as the auditor believes the sample is representative of the population.

Evaluation

In nonstatistical sampling, it is not possible to statistically determine the achieved upper limit of the control failure rate, the allowance for sampling risk, or the risk of assessing control risk too low. The auditor can, however, compare the control failure rate in the sample with the expected rate and, after considering the sampling risk, decide whether to assess the control risk as planned. If there are no failures in the sample, the auditor can assume that the sample results support the planned reliance on the control. When control failures are detected in the sample, the sample failure rate can be calculated by dividing the number of control failures in the sample by the sample size. If the sample failure rate exceeds the expected rate, the auditor should assume that the sample results do not support the planned reliance and do more substantive testing.

If the control failure rate is less than the expected rate, the auditor must still consider whether such a result might be obtained even if the failure rate for the population exceeds the tolerable rate. As noted previously, this is called *sampling risk.*

Exhibit 12.12

NONSTATISTICAL VERSUS STATISTICAL SAMPLING

	Nonstatistical	Statistical
Sample size	Judgment	Judgment and probability theory
Selection	Haphazard or random based	Random based
Evaluation	Judgment	Statistical inference and judgment

Because sampling risk cannot be quantified in a nonstatistical sample, the auditor must rely on judgment in making this determination. The size of the spread between the sample failure rate and the tolerable rate is a major decision factor. Some firms provide guidance based on statistical techniques for their auditors in making these evaluations. Exhibit 12.12 summarizes the differences between statistical and nonstatistical sampling.

C–ILLUSTRATIVE EXAMPLE–LEFLAM MANUFACTURING COMPANY

The audit program developed in the previous chapter to test the operation of control procedures over order-entry and invoicing for LeFlam (see Exhibit 12.13) contains several audit procedures requiring the use of sampling. During the audit year, 12,750 fax, phone, and mail sales orders were processed in 265 batches of about 50 orders per batch. In addition, 3,500 EDI orders were processed. The sales orders and batches are sequentially numbered beginning with the number one each year. The overall audit risk has been set at five percent for this audit because LeFlam's stock is actively traded in the over-the-counter market. Therefore, the risk of assessing control risk too low is also set at five percent.

Nonstatistical Tests

For step 2 (reconciliation of sales order batches), the auditor decides to use nonstatistical sampling because of the relatively small number of batches. Then 20 random numbers from 1 to 265 are selected using a microcomputer random number generator. The auditor locates the 20 batch control sheets and notes that the input and output control totals are properly reconciled. Three of these contained discrepancies. For each of these discrepancies, the reconciliation clerk had initialed and dated the form on which was noted the cause of the discrepancies. The auditor determined

Exhibit 12.13

LEFLAM MANUFACTURING COMPANY
AUDIT PROCEDURES
TESTS OF SALES ORDER PROCESSING
FOR THE YEAR ENDED 12/31/94

(Those for which sampling is used are highlighted in bold type)

Audit Procedures	Performed by
1. Develop a comprehensive set of test data to test edit controls, correctness of processing, and updating of related files. Run the test data at the beginning of every audit unless the client indicates there are no major changes in the application during the year and our evaluation remains that the program change process is well controlled. (Valuation)	________
2. Randomly select *X* batches of input during the year and determine that the client properly reconciles batch input and output and any discrepancies are immediately noted and followed up. (Completeness)	________
3. Observe the order entry process to note its orderliness and restrictions to authorized personnel. (Authorization)	________
4. Review the blanket purchase order contracts from major customers utilizing EDI. Trace selected contract terms to a print-out of prices maintained on the system. (Authorization)	________
5. In connection with our general work on data processing controls, perform a comprehensive test of the client's implementation of an access control software. Determine that the system includes restricted passwords and that the system is monitored on a timely basis by data security. Interview personnel to determine their perception of the access control system. (Authorization)	________
6. Review the marketing manager's reconciliations of price changes with the print-out of new price lists. Determine accuracy and completeness of changes. (Valuation)	________
7. Select *X* days of transaction exception reports. Review the reports to determine:	
a. The type of errors that are causing the transactions to not be processed.	
b. The timeliness to which errors are followed up and corrected. (Completeness)	
c. That all items are corrected. (Completeness)	________
8. Select a sample of sequentially numbered orders and determine that all items are accounted for and are recorded on a timely basis. (Completeness)	________
9. Review clients' procedures to reconcile initial input of data to updates in the master file and all the related subsidiary files. Determine that reconciliation is performed on a timely basis. (Completeness)	________

(Continued)

Exhibit 12.13

(continued)

10. Randomly select *X* invoices and:

   a. Compare invoice price with authorized price list or with separate authorization from marketing manager. (Valuation)

   b. Review for shipping document noting the date of shipment and determine whether there is any significant time delay between shipment and invoicing. (Occurrence)

   c. Compare the shipping document and invoice to determine that all items shipped have been billed. (Completeness)

   d. Note any items labeled as back-ordered and that back-ordered items are not billed. (Occurrence)

   e. Note that customer had approved credit, that the customer had a credit file established, and that the amount of invoice was less than the credit authorized. (The credit authorization system is more fully tested with the test data approach which compares the credit with the existing balance and authorized credit.) (Authorization)

   f. Note proper classification of sales items. (Presentation) ____________

11. Select a sample of orders for selected clients and determine that the orders had been completely entered into the system on a timely basis. (Completeness) ____________

that the causes were properly resolved within one business day. Based on this test, the auditor concludes that this control is working satisfactorily.

For step 7 (test of transaction exception reports), the auditor decides to use the transaction exception reports for the days on which the batches tested for step 2 were processed. A worksheet, part of which is shown in Exhibit 12.14, is created. The test results show that the following edit checks are working and all detected misstatements are corrected on a timely basis: completeness of fields, alpha-numeric check, limit check, self-checking digits on customer numbers, and valid catalog number check.

For steps 8 and 11 (test of sequentially numbered orders and timeliness of order entry), the auditor accounted for the sequence of sales order numbers covered by each exception report tested in step 7. In addition, each of these sales orders received by mail or fax was traced to the customer's order, and the auditor noted that all were entered within one day of receipt, except for five orders from new customers for which credit applications were required. These orders were processed within one day of credit approval by the credit manager.

Statistical Tests

For step 10 (test of sales invoices), the auditor decides to use attribute estimation sampling. Because the sales invoices are not printed for internal use, a computer program is used to select and print a sample of the sales invoices stored in machine-readable form. Exhibit 12.15 is a working paper documenting this application.

Exhibit 12.14

LEFLAM MANUFACTURING COMPANY
TEST OF SALES ORDER TRANSACTION EXCEPTION REPORTS
DECEMBER 31, 1994

Done by ______________

Reviewed ______________

Exception Report Date	Order Number	Error	Date Reprocessed
1/16	E-498	Missing color code	1/17
1/16	505	Missing P.O. number and P.O. date	1/17
3/2	No exceptions		
3/18	3010	Quantity exceeds limit	3/19
4/17	5272	Self-checking digit/customer number do not agree	4/20
5/29	No exceptions		
6/9	E-7467	Missing size	6/10
6/9	7501	Missing shipping address	6/10
7/1	8430	Non-numeric value in quantity field	7/2
7/1	E-8459	Missing P.O. number	7/3
7/24	No exceptions		
8/12	10922	Invalid catalog number	8/15
etc.			

Conclusion: Edit checks appear to be working for these conditions and all detected misstatements have been corrected on a timely basis.

Plan the Sample

Expected deviation rates are based on the results of prior year audits. A three percent tolerable failure rate is used for control procedures over proper price and quantity (attributes 1 and 3) because these are extremely important. If the prices or quantities are wrong, the client will have over- or undercharged customers and the related sales, accounts receivable, cost of goods sold, and inventory records are wrong. A five percent tolerable failure rate is used for timely invoicing (attribute 2) and credit approval (attribute 4). Timely invoicing is most important to the auditor near year-end for cut-off purposes. This attribute is tested here to help determine how much cut-off work needs to be done at year-end. The credit limit test will help determine the effectiveness of the client's credit approval process and the extent of substantive testing of the allowance for doubtful accounts. A 10 percent tolerable failure rate is used for the classification test (attribute 5). Sales recorded in the wrong sales category does not affect net income. Sales recorded as other revenue could affect the gross margin. These are not considered to be critical misstatements. Recall

Exhibit 12.15

LEFLAM MANUFACTURING COMPANY
DOCUMENTATION OF ATTRIBUTE SAMPLE APPLICATION

10-5

Audit Area: Sales Invoices Period: Year ended 12/31/94

Audit Objective: Test processing of sales invoices

Define Population: Sales invoices processed during 1994

Sampling Unit: Sales invoices numbered 359,310 to 375, 760

Selection Method: Random number generator to select random invoices

Population Size 16,250 Risk of assessing control risk too low 5%

	Planning			Sample Results			
Description of Attributes	Expected Failure Rate	Tolerable Failure Rate	Initial Sample Size	Actual Sample Size	Number of Failures	Sample Failure Rate	Achieved Upper Limit
1. Invoiced prices agree with price list or marketing manager authorization.	0.00%	3.00%	99	100	0	0.00%	3.00%
2. Invoice dated the same day as the shipping document.	1.00%	5.00%	93	100	1	1.00%	4.70%
3. Items shipped and quantities agree with shipping document.	0.00%	3.00%	99	100	0	0.00%	3.00%
4. Credit approved and previous balance plus invoice less than credit limit.	0.50%	5.00%	93	100	1	1.00%	4.70%
5. Sales were properly classified.	1.00%	10.00%	46	100	2	2.00%	6.20%
6.	%	%				%	%
7.	%	%				%	%
8.	%	%				%	%

Conclusion: Sales invoices are properly priced, recorded on a timely basis, reflect the quantities and products shipped, are properly approved for credit, and are properly classified.

Done by BJS Date 1/15/95

Reviewed by ______ Date ______

that attributes 1, 2, and 3 test the accuracy/valuation control objective and attributes 4 and 5 test the accounting integrity objective.

These planning factors result in sample sizes slightly less than 100 except for the classification test, for which the sample size is 46. The auditor decides to select and test a sample of 100 invoices for all of the attributes.

Select and Audit the Sample

All sales invoices are sequentially numbered by the computer program. Sales invoice numbers 359310 to 375560 were used during the audit year. The auditor uses a random number generator to select the sample items. Ten extra numbers were generated to replace any invoice numbers that were voided. The client pulled the selected invoices and supporting documents and then the auditor performed the audit procedures on the selected invoices by checking for each attribute as listed in Exhibit 12.15.

Evaluate the Sample

The auditor found three invoices that were not dated and recorded on the date of shipment. In each of these cases, the sale was recorded on the next business day. The auditor also found one order that was approved for credit but exceeded the credit limit. Two invoices were recorded in the wrong sales account. The achieved upper limits on control failures are determined using the evaluation tables in Exhibit 12.9. The achieved upper limits are less than or equal to the tolerable failure rates for all attributes except for dating and recording invoices on the date of shipment. Based on (1) these statistical sample results, (2) the results of the nonstatistical sample results, and (3) the other work done on the control procedures in the revenue cycle that did not involve sampling, the auditor assesses the control risks as low for existence and valuation. However, there is a moderate risk that sales near year-end may have been recorded early in the next year and are not complete. This assessment allows the auditor to do minimal substantive testing of the related account balances—sales, accounts receivable, and the allowance for doubtful accounts—with the exception of expanding the cut-off test of sales recorded early in the subsequent period.

Summary

Sampling can be used to select transactions to test for the effectiveness of controls, the correctness of their recording, or both (a dual-purpose test). Sampling can also be used to select details from an account balance for testing purposes. Both nonstatistical and statistical methods are acceptable when used properly.

Several statistical methods can be used to test control procedures. The auditor needs to choose the method that will best achieve the audit objectives and be most efficient:

- *Attribute estimation sampling.* Use when the objective is to estimate the control failure rate and expansion of the sample is difficult.
- *Sequential sampling.* Use when the objective is to estimate the control failure rate and expansion of the sample is relatively easy.
- *Discovery sampling.* Use when the objective is to uncover at least one instance of fraud or a critical control failure if it exists at more than a relatively low tolerable rate.

Samples should be as representative of populations as possible; random-based selection methods help ensure this. The results of the sample should be projected to the population before drawing an audit conclusion. The results of the tests of controls help the auditor decide what kind of substantive tests to perform, when to do

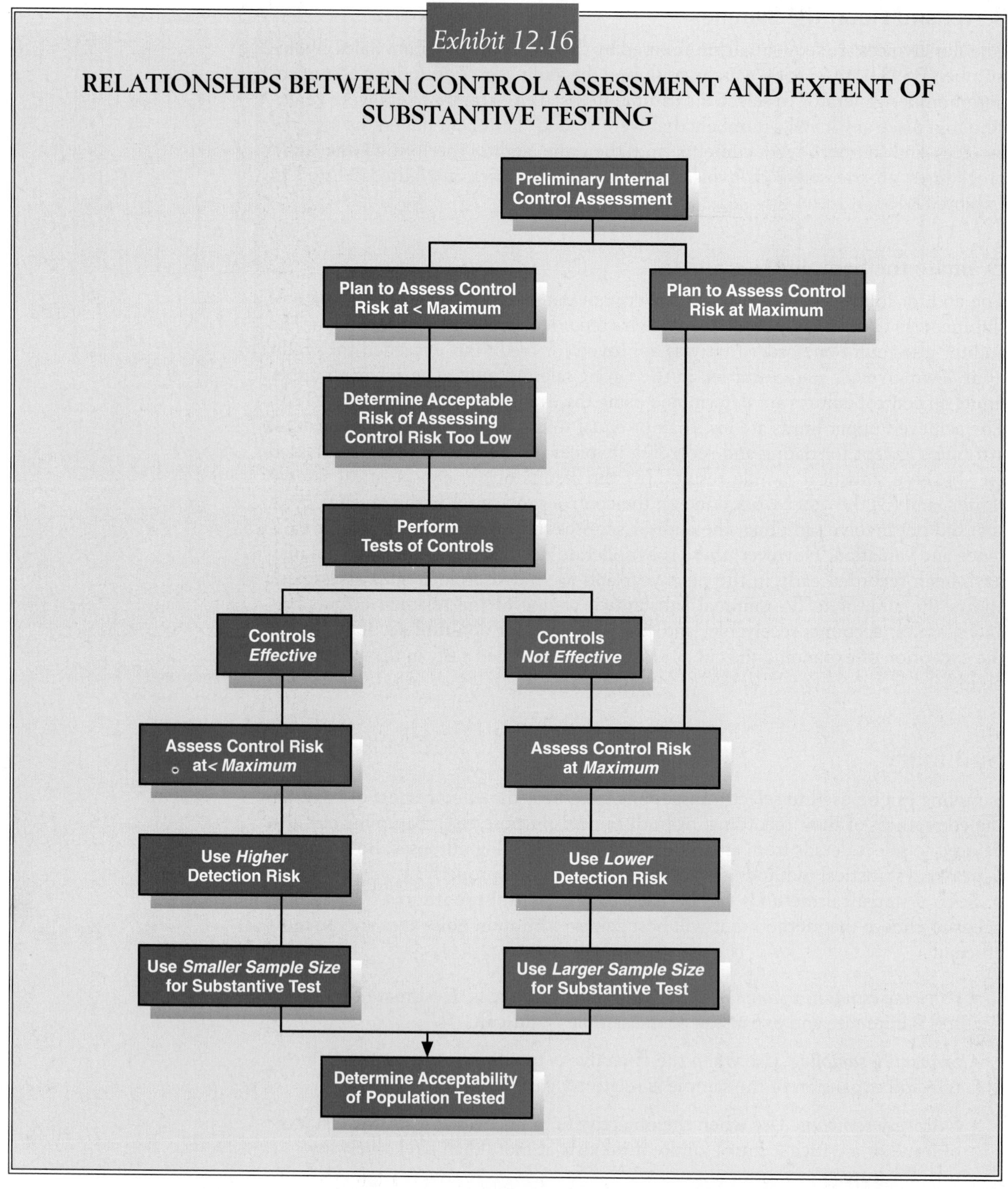

them, and how much to do. Exhibit 12.16 shows the relationships between preliminary internal control assessment, using an acceptable risk of assessing control risk too low for tests of controls, and using the sample results from tests of controls to establish a detection risk that affects the size of related substantive samples.

The auditor plans to assess control risk below the maximum only when there is reason to believe that the necessary control procedures have been designed into the system and that the time spent in testing control procedures will be cost/beneficial. Testing controls may allow the auditor to reduce the assessed level of control risk resulting in reduced substantive testing.

If the control procedures are effective, the auditor assesses control risk below the maximum. This assessment may be quantified at 20 percent or 35 percent, for example, or it may be assessed using such terms as "low" or "moderate." The relationships in the audit risk model mean that a lower control risk allows for a higher acceptable detection risk, which in turn leads to a smaller sample size for substantive testing. Sampling may be the most efficient approach to testing some of the control procedures. Sample results, along with the other related tests of controls, are used to assess control risk.

When the auditor decides to assess control risk at the maximum, the conclusion about the fairness of the related accounting population is based solely on substantive evidence.

Significant Terms

achieved upper limit The maximum likely control procedure failure rate in the population based on an attribute estimation sample.

allowance for sampling error The spread, or difference, between the tolerable and expected control procedure failure rates.

attribute A characteristic of the population of interest to the auditor.

attribute estimation sampling A statistical sampling method used to estimate the most likely and maximum rate of control procedure failures based on selecting and auditing one sample.

attribute sampling A family of statistical sampling methods used to estimate the control procedure failure rate in a population; the family of methods includes attribute estimation sampling, discovery sampling, and sequential (stop-or-go) sampling.

audit sampling The application of an audit procedure to less than 100 percent of the items within an account balance or class of transactions for the purpose of evaluating some characteristic of the balance or class [AU 350.01].

block sampling Selecting a group of adjacent items for testing; not an acceptable method unless several small blocks are randomly chosen because one or a few blocks are not likely to be representative of the entire population.

directed sampling A nonstatistical sampling application in which the auditor has some idea where to look for problems and wishes to direct the sampling toward those items.

discovery sampling An attribute sampling method used to uncover evidence of fraud or potential control failures considered to be critical if they exist at more than a very low occurrence rate; the purpose is to uncover at least one incident for investigation if the attribute exists at more than a relatively low tolerable rate rather than to estimate the maximum likely failure rate.

expected failure rate The auditor's best estimate of the percentage of transactions processed for which the examined control procedure is not operating effectively.

finite adjustment factor A formula used to convert sample sizes based on infinitely large populations to those applicable to relatively small populations.

haphazard selection Selection of sample items without any conscious bias; not random based and, therefore, cannot be used for statistical sampling.

nonsampling risk The risk of improperly auditing sampled items or misjudging inherent or control risk.

population The group of transactions or the items that make up an account balance for which the auditor wants to estimate some characteristic, such as the effectiveness of control procedures.

precision The spread, or difference, between the tolerable and expected control procedure failure rates.

random-based selection Sample selection methods in which each item in the population has an equal chance of being selected; only random-based samples can be statistically evaluated.

risk of assessing control risk too high The risk that the assessed level of control risk based on the sample is greater than the true operating effectiveness of the control structure policy or procedure.

risk of assessing control risk too low The risk that the assessed level of control risk based on the sample is less than the true operating effectiveness of the control structure policy or procedures.

risk of incorrect acceptance The risk of concluding from a sample that the book value is not materially misstated when in fact it is; sometimes referred to as a *Type II statistical error* or the *beta (β) risk.*

risk of incorrect rejection The risk of concluding from a sample that the book value is materially misstated when in fact it is not; sometimes referred to as a *Type I statistical error* or the *alpha (α) risk.*

sampling risk The probability that a sample is not representative of the population, which can lead the auditor to the wrong conclusion about the population; composed of the four immediately preceding risks.

sampling units The individual items (unit) defined by the auditor to be important because they contain evidence of an attribute of importance; the sum of sampling units equals the population total.

sequential (stop-or-go) sampling A multistep process attribute sampling method involving the selection of the smallest possible sample so that the absence of failures allows the auditor to conclude that the tested control procedures are working satisfactorily. If the sample reveals one or more control failures, the auditor must decide whether to expand the sample. Sequential sampling is appropriate for those situations in which it is relatively easy to expand the sample when necessary and few failures are expected.

statistical sampling The application of probability theory and statistical inference in a sample application to assist the auditor in determining an appropriate sample size and in evaluating the sample results.

systematic selection Selecting every *n*th item in a population with a random start, where *n* is the number of items in the population divided by the desired sample size.

tolerable failure rate The auditor's assessment of the maximum rate of control procedure failure that can occur and still allow the auditor to rely on the control.

Review Questions

A–Introduction

12–1 When should an auditor consider using audit sampling?

12–2 What are the basic differences between a nonstatistical sample and a statistical sample?

12–3 Distinguish between nonsampling risk and sampling risk. How can the auditor minimize nonsampling risk?

12–4 Define the following terms. Indicate which affect the efficiency of the audit and which affect the effectiveness of the audit and why.

a. *Risk of assessing control risk too high.*

b. *Risk of assessing control risk too low.*

c. *Risk of incorrect rejection.*

d. *Risk of incorrect acceptance.*

12–5 Which of the risks in Question 12–4 are of the greatest concern to the auditor? Why?

12–6 How can the auditor reduce sampling risk?

12–7 What are the advantages of using

a. Statistical sampling over nonstatistical sampling?

b. Nonstatistical sampling over statistical sampling?

B–Sampling to Test Transactions

12–8 When using sampling to test control procedures, what factors should the auditor consider in setting the

a. Tolerable failure rate?

b. Expected failure rate?

c. Allowable risk of assessing control risk too low?

12–9 When planning a sample, what is meant by the precision of a statistical sample? How does precision affect the sample size?

12–10 What are the three basic statistical sampling plans that can be used to test control procedures? In what circumstances is each of these most appropriate?

12–11 What is the effect of increasing each of the following on an attribute estimation sample size?

a. The allowable risk of assessing control risk too low.

b. The tolerable failure rate.

c. The expected failure rate.

d. Population size.

12–12 How does random number sample selection differ from systematic selection? What precaution(s) must the auditor take when using systematic selection?

12–13 What is meant by haphazard sample selection? Can it be used for statistical sampling? Explain why or why not.

12–14 Differentiate between haphazard sample selection and auditor-directed sample selection.

12–15 An auditor audited a random sample of 60 cash disbursements and found one improperly authorized disbursement (error). The achieved upper limit of control failures is 7.7 percent at a 5 percent risk of assessing control risk too low. What does this achieved upper limit mean? How does the auditor decide whether this result indicates that the control is working as expected?

12–16 Describe how sequential sampling works. When would an auditor choose to use sequential sampling as opposed to attribute estimation sampling?

12–17 An auditor is using discovery sampling to test for payroll fraud using a tolerable rate of 0.5 percent.

a. If no evidence of fraud is uncovered in the sample, what conclusion can the auditor draw?

b. If one incident of fraud is uncovered prior to completing the audit of the sample, what should the auditor do?

12–18 In any sampling application, why is it important

a. To select a sample that is representative of the population?

b. To project the sample results to the population before drawing a conclusion about the population?

12–19 When control procedure failures are discovered in a sample, why is it important for the auditor to evaluate the nature of the failures?

12–20 How does an auditor determine which control procedures should be tested in the revenue cycle? Explain.

12–21 Why is it important for an auditor to determine that a population is complete? How does an auditor determine the completeness of a population?

12–22 Why is it important that the auditor define a *control procedure failure* in advance of beginning the audit procedure? Is it necessary to define such a failure in advance if the auditor uses nonstatistical sampling, or is it necessary only for statistical sampling?

12–23 What is meant by a "pattern of misstatements" in the auditor's analysis of control procedure failures? Why is it important that the auditor analyze any "pattern of misstatements" before considering the possible effect of the control procedure failures on the design of substantive audit procedures?

12–24 What factors might cause the auditor to use a different estimate of the expected rate of control procedure failure than was used in the previous audit?

12–25 Is it necessary for the auditor to test control procedures on every audit engagement? Explain.

Multiple Choice Questions

*12–26 A principal advantage of statistical methods of attribute sampling over nonstatistical methods is that they provide a scientific basis for planning the

a. Risk of assessing control risk too low.
b. Tolerable rate.
c. Expected population deviation rate.
d. Sample size.

*12–27 An advantage of using statistical sampling techniques is that such techniques

a. Mathematically measure risk.
b. Eliminate the need for judgmental decisions.
c. Define the values of precision and reliability required to provide audit satisfaction.
d. Have been established in the courts to be superior to judgmental sampling.

*12–28 When performing a test of control procedures with respect to control over cash receipts, an auditor may use a systematic sampling technique with a start at any randomly selected item. The biggest disadvantage of this type of sampling is that the items in the population

a. Must be systematically replaced in the population after sampling.
b. May systematically occur more than once in the sample.
c. Must be recorded in a systematic pattern before the sample can be drawn.
d. May occur in a systematic pattern, thus destroying the sample randomness.

*12–29 Which of the following combinations results in a decrease in sample size in a sample for attributes?

	Risk of Assessing Control Risk Too Low	Tolerable Rate	Expected Population Deviation Rate
a	Increase	Decrease	Increase
b	Decrease	Increase	Decrease
c	Increase	Increase	Decrease
d	Increase	Increase	Increase

*12–30 Which of the following factors is generally *not* considered in determining the sample size for a test of control procedures?

a. Population size.
b. Tolerable rate.

*Adapted from the Uniform CPA examination or the Certified Internal Auditor examination.

c. Risk of assessing control risk too low.
d. Expected population deviation rate.

*12–31 Given random selection, the same sample size, and the same precision requirement for the testing of two unequal populations, the risk of assessing control risk too low on the smaller population is
a. The same as assessing control risk too low for the larger population.
b. Higher than assessing control risk too low for the larger population.
c. Lower than assessing control risk too low for the larger population.
d. Indeterminate relative to assessing control risk too low for the larger population.

*12–32 The risk of incorrect acceptance and the risk of assessing control risk too low relate to the
a. Preliminary estimates of materiality levels.
b. Allowable risk of tolerable misstatement.
c. Efficiency of the audit.
d. Effectiveness of the audit.

*12–33 A CPA examining inventory may appropriately apply sampling for attributes to estimate the
a. Average price of inventory items.
b. Percentage of slow-moving inventory items.
c. Dollar value of inventory.
d. Physical quantity of inventory items.

*12–34 An internal auditor is testing purchase orders to detect possible instances of fraudulent activity by an employee. Believing the occurrence rate of the fraudulent purchase orders to be quite low, the internal auditor would like to specify the probability of observing at least one irregularity if its true rate of occurrence is greater than expected. The most appropriate sampling technique for this situation is
a. Sequential sampling.
b. Attribute estimation sampling.
c. Variables estimation sampling.
d. Discovery sampling.

*12–35 What is the chief advantage of stop-or-go sampling?
a. The error rate in the population can be projected to within certain precision limits.
b. It may reduce the size of the sample that needs to be taken from a population, thus reducing sampling costs.
c. It allows sampling analysis to be performed on nonhomogeneous populations.
d. It allows the sampler to increase the confidence limits of the analysis without sacrificing precision.

*12–36 An internal auditor plans to test the accuracy of transactions recorded in a payroll journal. Under which of the following conditions would the use of an auditor-directed sample rather than a random sample be appropriate?

a. Every item in the population to be sampled has a known probability of selection.
b. The auditor wishes the sample to represent, as closely as possible, the population from which it is drawn.
c. The auditor plans to perform a mathematical evaluation of the sample results.
d. The auditor suspects recurring payroll defalcations and wishes to find as much evidence of this as possible.

Discussion and Research Questions

12–37 (Audit Procedures) Following is a list of audit procedures related to the revenue cycle.

1. Examine copies of sales invoices for supporting bills of lading and customers' orders.
2. Observe whether monthly statements are mailed and examine customer correspondence files.
3. Examine customers' orders for proper approval of credit.
4. Examine evidence of independent accounting for prenumbered shipping documents.
5. Examine internal verification of quantities, prices, and clerical accuracy of sales invoices.

Required:

a. Identify those procedures for which sampling would normally be appropriate.
b. Explain why sampling would not be appropriate for the items not identified.

12–38 (Audit Procedures and Sampling) Following is a list of audit procedures related to the acquisition/payment cycle.

1. Examine indication of approval for payment.
2. Examine indication of internal verification of quantities, prices, and clerical accuracy of vendors' invoices.
3. Examine evidence of independent accounting for prenumbered vouchers.
4. Examine bank reconciliations and observe their preparation.
5. Observe personnel to determine whether there is proper separation of duties between record keeping, authorization, and check signing.

Required:

a. Identify those procedures for which sampling would normally be appropriate.

b. Explain why sampling would not be appropriate for the items not identified.

12–39 (Sample Size Determination and Implementation)

Required:

a. The risk of assessing control risk too low is 10 percent. Determine the sample size for each of the following controls.

Control	Tolerable Rate (Percent)	Expected Rate (Percent)	Sample Size	Number of Deviations	Achieved Upper Limit
1	5%	0%		0	
2	5	1		3	
3	10	0		1	
4	5	0.5		1	
5	10	3		2	

b. Explain why the sample sizes for controls 2 and 3 are different from those for control 1.

c. What is the general effect on sample size of using a 10 percent risk of assessing control risk too low rather than 5 percent? Explain.

d. How would the auditor decide whether to use the individual sample sizes in part a or to use the largest for all five controls?

e. Assume a sample size of 80 is used for all five controls. Determine the achieved upper limit of failures in the population for each control and complete the table in part a.

f. Based on the answers to part e, on which of the controls can the auditor place the planned degree of reliance? Why?

g. What sample size should be used for control 1 in part a if there were only 500 sales transactions?

12–40 (Sample Selection Methods) The auditor is about to select a sample of 60 items to test controls. For each of the following independent situations, describe the most efficient and effective selection method to identify the sample items.

a. A sample is taken from the cash disbursements journal. The check numbers used during the audit period were 65,300 to 143,890. There are 1,966 pages with 40 checks on most pages. A new page is started each month. There are some voided checks.

b. A sample taken from the payroll journal does not list the check numbers. The same checking account is used for payroll and regular disbursements. There are 140 employees who have worked for the client all year and are listed in the payroll journal in social security number order. There are a maximum of 50 lines per page in the journal; a new page is started each pay period. The employees are paid every two weeks.

12–41 (Evaluation of Sample Results) If the achieved upper limit of control failures exceeds the tolerable rate in an attribute sampling application, what alternative courses of action are open to the auditor?

*12–42 (Attribute Sampling Plan) Carl Jiblum, CPA, is planning to use attribute sampling to determine the degree of reliance he can place on an audit client's system of internal accounting control over sales. He has begun to develop an outline of the main steps in the sampling plan as follows:

1. State of objective(s) of the audit test (e.g., to test the reliability of internal accounting controls over sales).
2. Define the population (define the period covered by the test; consider the completeness of the population).
3. Define the sampling unit (e.g., client copies of sales invoices).

Required:

a. What are the remaining steps in the above outline that Jiblum should include in the statistical test of sales invoices? *Do not present a detailed analysis of tasks that must be performed to carry out the objectives of each step. Parenthetical examples need not be provided.*
b. How does statistical methodology help the auditor to develop a satisfactory sampling plan?

12–43 (Auditor Judgment in Statistical Sampling) You are discussing the use of nonstatistical and statistical sampling with your colleague, Kevin, who believes that the use of statistical sampling eliminates judgment.

Required:

a. Explain to Kevin how judgment is required in a statistical sampling application.
b. Explain briefly how the auditor makes each judgment, specifically commenting on the source or types of information that influence the judgment.

12–44 (Selection of Sampling Procedure)

Required:

For each of the following situations, indicate which sampling method should be used and explain your choice. The following are independent sampling situations.

a. The auditor wants to estimate the maximum rate of control failures in the population. It is difficult to expand the sample.
b. Management has asked the internal auditor to determine whether there is any evidence of employee embezzlement in the cash-receiving function.
c. The auditor wants to audit the smallest sample that will provide evidence that certain control procedures are working satisfactorily. It is relatively easy to expand the sample, if necessary.

12–45 (Judgment and Statistical Evaluation) If a sample size is determined judgmentally and the sample is selected on a random basis, is it proper to evaluate the sample statistically? Identify and briefly explain the potential dangers to this approach.

12–46 (Audit Evaluation of Sample Results) The auditor designed an audit procedure to test the following control procedures in the revenue cycle of a company that makes large-size factory equipment:

1. Credit approval.
2. Sale price taken from authorized sales price list unless specifically approved by the divisional sales manager.
3. A shipping document exists for each invoice.

A random sample of 100 items was selected from the total population of invoices. The following results were obtained:

Attribute	Failures	Description of Failures
1. Credit approval	3	Three credit approvals were bypassed for sales of equipment to new customers. Each of the new customer sales was the result of efforts by the divisional sales manager.
2. Sales price	6	Five of the price deviations were attributable to a senior salesperson (Bonnie James) and represented price discounts ranging from 10 to 18 percent. The other deviation was a five percent reduction of a sale by a different salesperson that took place while the divisional sales manager was on vacation.
3. Shipping document exists	2	Both of the deviations occurred in the last month of the year. The shipping document was later located for one, but not for the other.

In considering your answers to parts a and b, the following information is available to the auditors from the preliminary assessment of the organization's control environment:

1. The company is experiencing some financial difficulty; earnings have been down. Management is optimistic about this year and hopes to position the company to increase its stock value or to participate in a merger.
2. J.P. Maxwell is in his second year as the divisional sales manager. A significant portion of his yearly earnings will be based on reported sales and profits.
3. The auditor expected a low failure rate for all three attributes but considers them important.

Required:

a. Identify the audit steps the auditor should use to follow up in evaluating the sample findings. Be specific as to each attribute.

b. Assume that the audit follow-up in part a reveals the continuance of the same pattern of control procedure failures. Identify the implications for the design of substantive audit procedures and briefly indicate the rationale for your answer.

12–47 (Attribute Sampling and Testing Control Procedures)

The auditor decides to use attribute sampling to assist in the audit of the effectiveness of control procedures. For all the following items, the auditor decides to use the following parameters:

Risk of assessing control risk too low	5%
Tolerable failure rate	4%
Expected failure rate	1%

Required:

a. What is the appropriate sample size?

b. Assume that the auditor chose the next highest number (to the nearest 10) as the sample size. The auditor then used the audit program and found the following misstatements. For each attribute

1. Calculate the best estimate of the population's error rate.
2. Determine whether the tests indicate the control procedure is working effectively (providing underlying statistical support for your conclusion).
3. Indicate the potential misstatements that could be occurring in the account balance.
4. Identify the audit procedures that the auditor should consider implementing if you believe the control is not operating effectively.

Use the blank table on page 568 for your answers.

Audit Program	Results
Randomly select ______ invoices and	
a. Compare invoice with authorized price list or with separate authorization from marketing manager.	6 failures, all at substantial discount to two clients.
b. Compare the shipping document and invoice to determine that all items shipped been billed.	7 failures, 3 had minor discrepancies; the shipping document could not be located for 4 items.
c. Note that customer had approved credit.	4 failures, the same for which that shipping document could not be located.
d. Review shipping document to determine if there is any significant delay between shipment and invoicing.	7 failures; 4 shipping document could not be located. On the other three, invoicing took place before shipment.

Attribute	Estimate the population error rate.	Is control procedure working correctly? Support your answer.	What are some types of errors that could be occurring if the control is not working effectively?	Recommend audit procedures.
(a) Authorized prices				
(b) Shipping document				
(c) Credit approval				
(d) Shipping delay				

*12–48 (Interpreting Attribute Sampling Results) An internal auditor has employed attribute sampling in a test to determine whether sales invoices are adequately supported by shipping documentation. Based on previous experience, the auditor expects a one percent error rate and has set four percent as the tolerable failure rate with a risk of assessing control risk too low at five percent. A sample of 200 sales invoices was randomly drawn and audited. Six misstatements (shipping documents could not be located) were discovered.

Required:

a. What sample size should the auditor have used in conducting this test?

b. Based on the sample results, compute the expected rate of control procedure failures existing in the population.

c. Determine the achieved upper limit of the failure rate at the five percent risk of assessing control risk too low. Assume that the auditor used the sample size computed in part a rounded up to the nearest ten.

d. Interpret the meaning of your answer to part c. If the results are not satisfactory, identify (1) the possible misstatements that could be occurring in the account balance and (2) the potential rationale management might provide for the missing documents.

e. Outline additional procedures that the auditor might follow assuming that the sample results were unsatisfactory.

*12–49 (Discovery Sampling) The internal auditor for a company has been advised of a possible fraud involving the accounts payable section of contract accounting. The alleged fraud involves payments to fictitious contractors. Because of the large dollar amount of the typical contractor payment, an irregularity could involve well in excess of thousands of dollars. An average of 1,100 payments is made each month by the accounts payable section.

The internal auditor has decided to use discovery sampling to test for the existence of fraudulent transactions and has specified a desired sampling risk of 5 percent and a tolerable failure rate of 0.3 percent.

Required:

a. Determine the appropriate sample size and explain how you made the determination.

b. Assume that the sample taken was adequate.

   1. If the auditor found no fraudulent payments in the sample examined, what conclusion is appropriate? What action should the auditor take with respect to the sampling plan?
   2. If the auditor found two instances of fraudulent payments in the sample examined, what conclusion is appropriate? What action should the auditor take with respect to the sampling plan?
   3. If the auditor found 10 instances of fraudulent payments in the sample examined, what conclusion is appropriate? What action should the auditor take with respect to the sampling plan?

c. When testing the sample of payment documents, if one document in the physical sample representing the population was missing, what would be the appropriate auditor's action?

12–50 **(Research)** Different firms have differing philosophies regarding the use of the alternative types of attribute sampling, particularly the use of attribute estimation versus sequential sampling. Review research published on the use of statistical sampling in auditing to determine the extent that attribute sampling techniques are used and the audit areas most frequently addressed.

Cases

12–51 (Sampling Plan) Sally Warner, CPA, used attribute estimation sampling to test the 8,700 cash disbursements processed during the audit period. She used a risk of assessing control risk too low of 5 percent, a tolerable failure rate of 10 percent, and an expected failure rate of 3 percent for each of the five control procedures to be tested. She selected the last 52 disbursements processed during the period as her sample because those documents were easier to find. She found a total of five failures of the various control procedures tested. Warner concluded that the maximum number of control failures in the population was 261.

Required:

Describe the deficiencies in this sampling application and explain why they are deficiencies.

12–52 (Defining Control Procedure Failures) An internal auditor of an insurance company wishes to investigate the procedures used to process claims. The auditor wishes to investigate two particular policies:

1. All claims submitted for processing must be initially processed and the appropriate status determined within 48 hours of receipt. All claims must be cleared within one month or put on an exception report monitored by the supervisor of the claims department.

2. All payments of claims must be accompanied by a document supporting the claim (such as a car repair invoice), a customer signature requesting the claim, a review and validity check by a claims clerk to determine that the claim is within the parameters of the individual's policy (noted by a signature), and approval by the claims supervisor for that type of claim (again noted by initials). All paid claims are filed in numerical order and cross-referenced to each customer. All incoming claims are received by a claims agent and are converted to a prenumbered claims form for follow-up. The status of the claims appears on a daily claims status report.

Required:

a. For each audit objective, define a control procedure failure and give an example of such a failure.
b. For each audit objective, define the sampling unit.
c. For each audit objective, write an audit procedure to describe the sampling process and the evidence to be gathered from each sample item.

Computer-Assisted Problems

Attribute sampling problems for this chapter using the computer audit software called adVenture are in the appendix at the end of the book. You should read the introduction and instructions before working the problems. These problems are:

C–1 Using Attribute Sampling to Test the Processing of Shipping Documents.

C–2 Using Attribute Sampling to Perform a Dual-Purpose Test of Sales Transactions.

End Notes

1. Abraham Akresh, James Loebbecke, and William Scott, "Audit Approaches and Techniques," in *Research Opportunities in Auditing: The Second Decade*, ed. A. Rashad Abdel-khalik and Ira Solomon (Sarasota, Fla.: American Accounting Association, 1988), 37.

CHAPTER

13

Learning Objectives

Through studying this chapter, you will be able to:

1. Understand the factors that influence the effectiveness and efficiency of audits of account balances.
2. State the objectives of auditing the account balances in the revenue cycle.
3. Discuss the effect of control risk assessment on substantive tests of accounts in the revenue cycle.
4. Describe the nature, usefulness, and limitations of the different types of accounts receivable confirmations.
5. Identify and apply approaches to auditing accounting estimates.
6. Describe analytical procedures that can be used as substantive evidence in the revenue cycle.

Substantive Testing in the Revenue Cycle

Chapter Contents

Chapter Overview

Once the auditor has assessed control risk for each significant account balance and related assertions, the audit program for testing account balances is finalized. At this stage of the audit, the auditor should have a good idea where and what types of misstatements might exist in the account balances. The auditor must decide which audit procedures to perform, how extensively those procedures should be performed, and which accounts and account items should be tested. This chapter discusses the substantive audit procedures relevant to revenue cycle accounts. Chapter 14 covers the sampling methods that help answer the questions of how extensive those procedures should be and which items in an account balance should be tested.

Manufactured Homes, via aggressive accounting, front-end loads profits by using assumptions that may prove false. It has issued misleading press releases and made SEC filings that appear to be inaccurate. Last-minute transactions at the end of a quarter frequently provide a fillip to profits.[1]

Generally accepted accounting principles recognize the importance of recording transactions in accordance with their substance. The auditor should consider whether the substance of transactions differs materially from their form. [AU 411.06]

A–INTRODUCTION TO SUBSTANTIVE TESTING

As noted in these quotes, the accounting for sales can be contentious, even though it is often routine for many audit clients. The Sales account is generally the single largest account in a company's financial statements. Furthermore, the balances in many accounts are directly related to the

Sales account. Cost of Goods Sold and Sales Commission Expense, for example, should be directly related to Sales. Accounts Receivable similarly constitutes one of the largest assets in the balance sheet of many companies. The volume of transactions and the complexity of structured transactions make these accounts highly susceptible to error. Thus, the audit of the revenue cycle receives a great deal of attention on many audit engagements.

This chapter builds on the revenue cycle control concepts discussed in Chapter 11 and develops a framework for conducting direct tests of account balances in the revenue cycle. The types of tests performed should reflect the auditor's understanding of the control risk present in the related accounts. If control procedures are not sufficient to reduce control risk to a minimum level, the auditor should consider the types of misstatements that may occur and design specific direct tests of the account balances to determine whether material misstatements may exist in the accounts. Many of the dual-purpose tests covered in Chapter 11 (tests of control procedures and correctness of recorded transactions) are especially important in gaining assurance about the correctness of revenue transactions. Following the integrative illustration in Exhibit 13.1, this chapter discusses the major phase of most audits: direct tests of material account balances. The chapter covers sales and sales-related expenses (warranty expense, sales commissions) and accounts receivable and the related allowance for uncollectible accounts.

Auditor Risk Concerns: Sales Transactions

Revenue recognition has been a pervasive accounting issue since the double-entry method of accounting was invented. The English trading companies waited until the ship returned to recognize revenue. Today, however, the basic revenue recognition principle is to recognize revenue when "(1) the earning process is complete or virtually complete, and (2) an exchange has taken place."[2] Although the concept seems simple, it is often difficult to implement. The difficulty is exacerbated by management's desire to maximize the recognition of revenue and recorded earnings. Revenue recognition varies among industries and circumstances. Most manufacturers, wholesalers, and retailers recognize revenue when title to the product is transferred to the customer. Most often the transfer involves the physical transfer of goods to the customers. A number of industries use different procedures. Airlines recognize revenue when the transportation is provided, not when the ticket is sold. Construction companies usually recognize revenue for long-term projects as progress is made toward completion of the project. No one rule governs all sales transactions.

A study by the National Commission on Fraudulent Financial Reporting found that 47 percent of the fraudulent financial reporting cases brought by the SEC against public companies were the result of management's improperly recognizing revenue.[3] Examples of questionable revenue recognition for which the SEC has asserted that the substance of the transaction was not in accord with the form of the accounting include the following:

- Recording sales in the wrong period (improper sales cutoffs).
- Recording sales under "bill-and-hold agreements" (recording a sale but not shipping the goods or shipping them at a later date, pending customer approval).

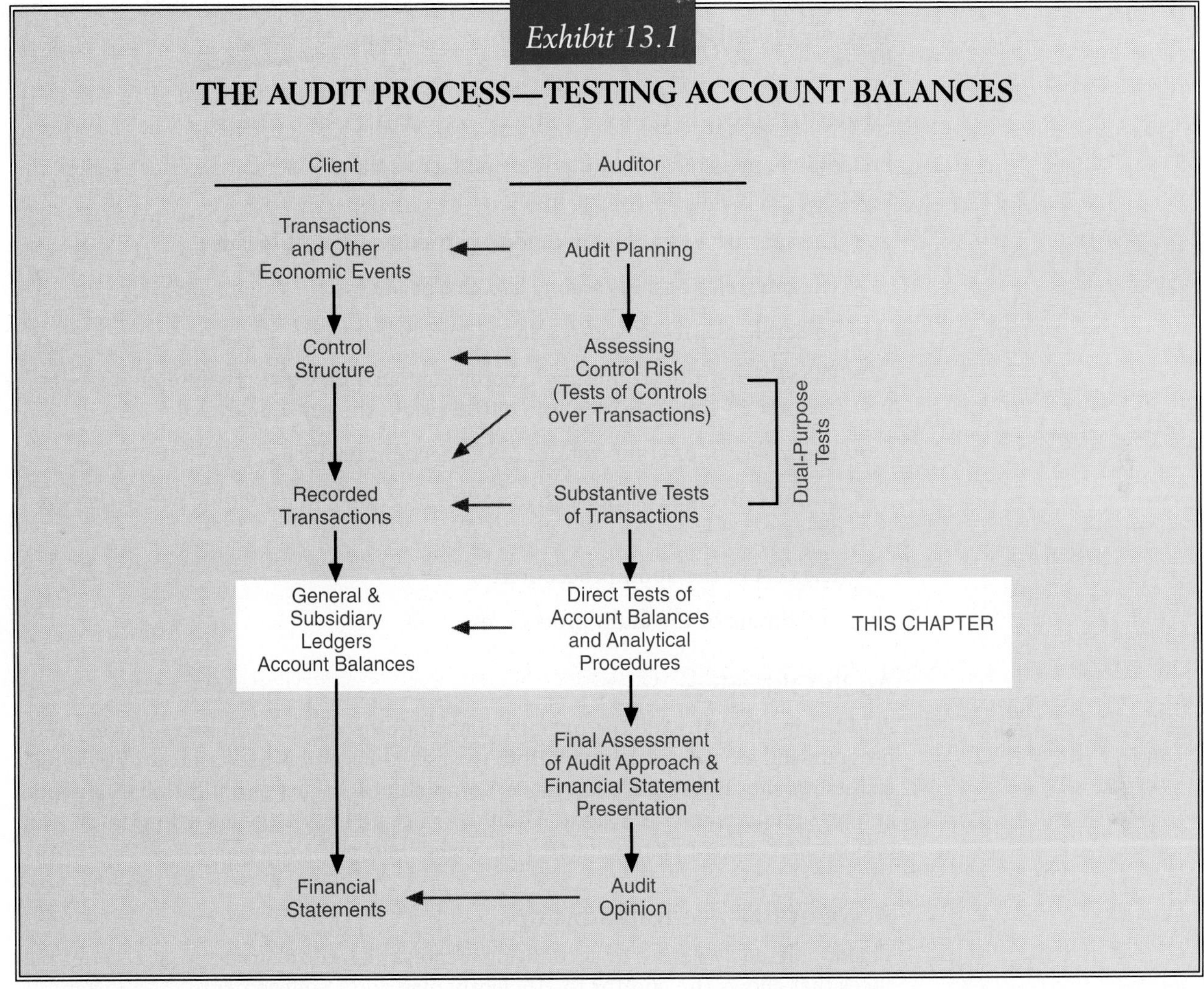

- Recording as sales shipments to third parties "authorized" to accept goods on behalf of buyers, but the goods were never delivered to the buyers.
- Recording sales with rights of return when the likelihood of return is high.
- Recording transactions involving operating leases as sales transactions.
- Failing to record sales returns in a timely fashion (and in some cases failing to record them at all).
- Applying the percentage of completion method improperly.[4]

Actual examples abound. During 1987 and 1988, the senior management of MiniScribe, a computer disk drive manufacturer, perpetrated a massive fraud by recording fictitious sales.* Another high-tech company, Datapoint Corp., almost went out of business several years earlier when its practice of booking sales prematurely got out of hand. DSC Communications Corp., of Dallas, signed a consent

*The details of this situation are presented in the case at the end of the chapter.

agreement with the SEC in which it agreed to restate 1984 and 1985 results that allegedly recognized sales prematurely.

Planning for Direct Tests of Account Balances

Previous chapters have identified several factors that influence the effectiveness and efficiency of audits, including these:

- The specific audit objectives for a particular account balance.
- The interrelationships among account balances.
- Tolerable misstatements for an account balance.
- The risk that the accounting records contain a material misstatement (see Chapter 11 for assessment of control risk in the revenue cycle).
- The makeup, or composition, of the account balances.
- The effectiveness of alternative audit procedures in providing persuasive evidence.
- The cost of the audit procedures.
- The timing of the audit procedures.

Audit Objectives

Audit objectives provide the overall framework for the development of every audit program and are derived directly from the assertions embodied in the audited financial statements: existence/occurrence, completeness, rights or obligations, valuation, and presentation and disclosure. Audit evidence addresses the assertions in the context of the general planning factors discussed below.

Account Balance Relationships

The double-entry nature of accounting creates the interrelationship of account balances that allows the auditor to efficiently plan audit engagements. As an example, Exhibit 13.2 shows the important interrelationships found in the revenue cycle. Audit evidence gathered on one account balance provides evidence about related accounts.

Given the interrelationships among the accounts, the auditor must determine an audit approach that will maximize the persuasiveness of audit evidence for all related accounts at the least audit cost. Normally, the auditor focuses a considerable amount of the audit effort on the Accounts Receivable account because (1) it is relatively easy to audit (it is easier to audit a balance than to audit the accumulation of transactions making up the Sales account), (2) overstatements of sales (usually the greatest risk in the revenue accounts) manifest themselves in the receivables accounts, and (3) more independent evidence is generally available on accounts receivables than on the related accounts.

Accounts receivable balances are normally considered easier to audit using direct tests than are the related Sales account because usually fewer items make up the accounts receivable balance. Independent sources of evidence exist regarding the correctness of accounts receivable, such as confirmations and subsequent collections, whereas less independent evidence is available for sales transactions. The

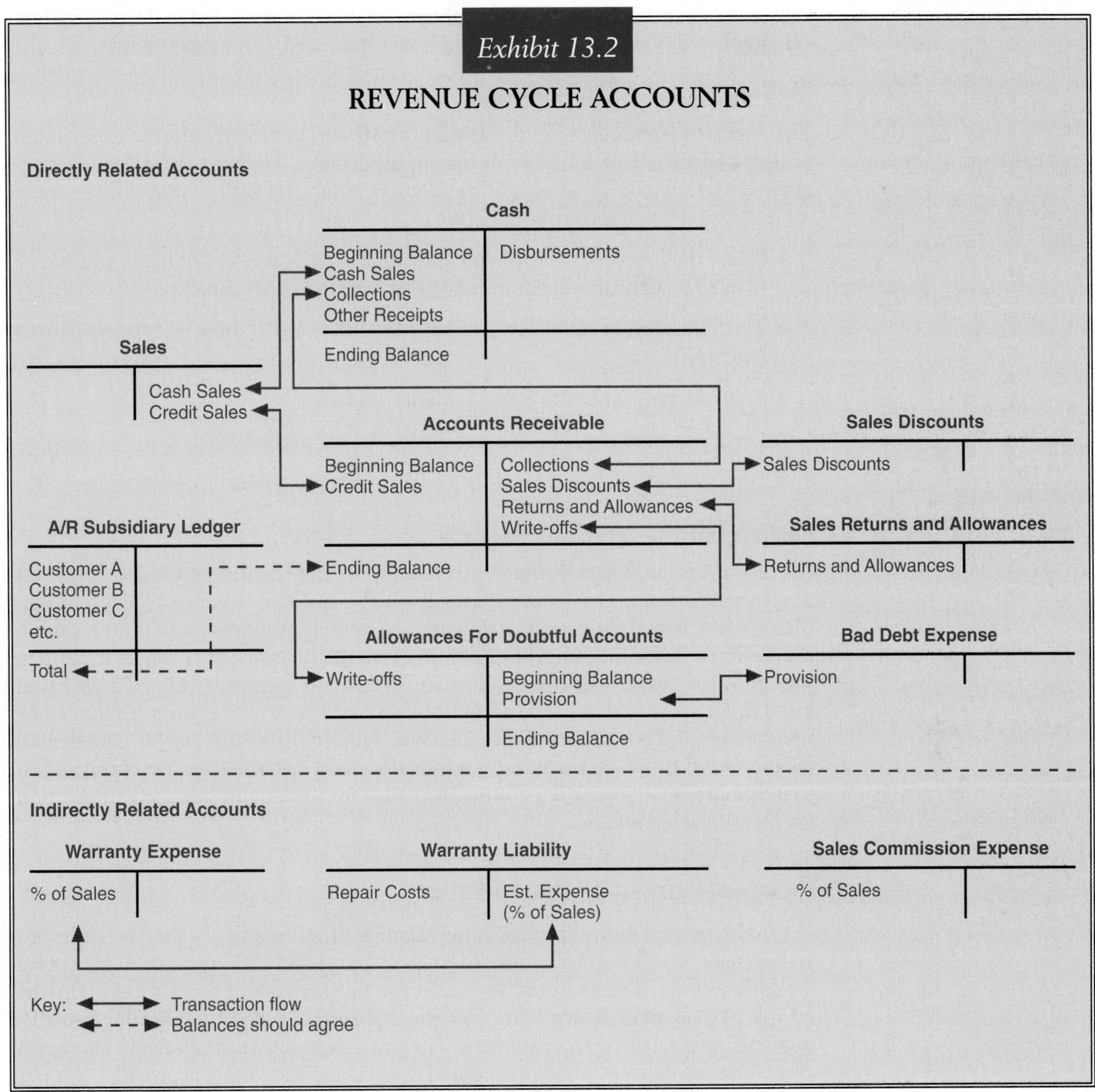

underlying documents for sales transactions, for example, are sales orders, shipping records, and sales invoices. All of these documents are internally created. But confirmations come from customers, and evidence of collection can be traced to deposits on the bank statement, both of which provide external evidence.

Tolerable Misstatement

Tolerable misstatement is a planning concept that relates planning materiality to individual account balances and classes of transactions. Neither planning materiality nor tolerable misstatement is required to be quantified. Most CPA firms, however, do quantify both to help in planning the audit and evaluating the results of the audit evidence. The quantification of tolerable misstatement is needed to develop statistical samples of evidence to be gathered and is discussed in the next chapter.

Risk of Material Misstatement

The auditor's assessment of inherent and control risks directly affect the selection, timing, and extent of substantive testing procedures. Higher control risk leads to lower detection risk. To achieve lower detection risk, the auditor may choose one or more of the following courses of action:

- Select the most persuasive type of evidence, such as a test of details, rather than an analytical procedure (nature of selected procedures).
- Test transactions and balances as of year-end rather than at an interim date (timing).
- Test a larger number of items (extent).
- Use more experienced auditors to perform the audit tests.
- Perform more detailed levels of review and supervision.

Makeup of the Account Balance

An account balance such as Accounts Receivable may consist of thousands of relatively small customer balances or just a few large customer balances. Sales may consist of a few large transactions involving one or two products (such as the sales of multimillion dollar machines) or millions of transactions of either single or multiple products (such as the sales by J.C. Penney). The audit approach utilized must be tailored to the composition of the account balances. If there are very few but large sales transactions and customer balances, each of these transactions and/or balances can be audited. If there are many sales transactions and customer balances, the auditor spends more time testing the control structure over sales and sampling transactions for more detailed review.

Persuasiveness of Procedures

Given the interrelationship of account balances, it follows that a specific audit procedure may provide evidence on different accounts and different assertions regarding each account. The audit task is to select an optimal mix of procedures to provide overall persuasive evidence. Consider the audit procedure of confirming recorded accounts receivables with customers. The procedure provides relatively strong evidence* on the existence of the recorded receivables. However, it provides less persuasive (weak) evidence on the completeness of the recording of sales and accounts receivable because the auditor does not select an unrecorded accounts receivable for confirmation.

As a general rule, tests of the details of a balance are more effective (and thus more persuasive) in detecting overstatements than understatements. If an account balance is *overstated*, it contains an item that is overstated or that does not exist: it is there to be selected for testing. If, on the other hand, an account balance is *understated*, some item that should have been included in the account balance is missing

*The term *strong evidence* is used here to reflect the persuasiveness of the evidence in relationship to the specific audit assertion being addressed. Strong evidence directly addresses the assertion (it is relevant) and is persuasive. Other evidence may be more *limited* either because it does not directly address the assertion or because it is less persuasive.

or is stated at a smaller amount than it should be. If a sale were not recorded, confirmations selected from the trial balance of recorded transactions do not detect the understatement. The auditor needs to identify some other procedure that will test for the completeness of the recorded amounts, such as vouching transactions from shipping documents into the sales and accounts receivable records.

Cost of Procedures

Audit cost is a major constraining variable. Audits must generate sufficient quantities of persuasive evidence at a cost that will prevent the auditor from losing the client to another competitive firm. Although auditors do not specifically price out the cost of each procedure, it is generally agreed that the relative cost of audit procedures ranks from low to high as follows:

1. Analytical procedures (comparisons of relationships with expected relationships).
2. Detailed tests of transaction processing.
3. Direct tests of account balances.

An analytical procedure such as comparing current year balances and relationships with those of prior years or industry statistics is not very time-consuming, but, it has limited persuasiveness, depending on the specific client circumstances. A substantive audit procedure such as confirming customer balances, however, can take substantially more time to complete (audit steps include selecting account balances to be confirmed, reviewing each confirmation letter to be sure that the information is correct, mailing the letters, recording customer responses, and following up on any differences reported by the customers). This process can, on average, take from 15 minutes to one-half hour per confirmation, in some cases even longer. But cost is not the primary factor in determining the procedures; it is only a constraint to be considered.

Timing of Procedures

Determining the timing of audit procedures is an important audit management task. It is not physically possible to perform all the audit work for important client engagements at year-end. The auditor must consider cost-effective means to keep the audit staff busy throughout the year. Performing some or all of them prior to year-end, called *interim work*, has certain advantages:

- Early consideration can be given to significant matters affecting the year-end financial statements, such as related-party transactions or the accounting for complex transactions.
- The audit may be completed at an earlier date.
- The audit staff may work less overtime after year-end.

But testing prior to year-end also entails certain disadvantages:

- An increased risk of failing to detect material misstatements in the year-end balances because less audit work is performed at year-end.
- The audit may be less efficient because the total audit time may be longer due to the additional work needed to reduce that risk to an acceptable level.

Tests of transaction processing, such as reprocessing and vouching sales transactions, can be started prior to year-end and finished after year-end without significantly increasing the time spent on those procedures. However, if a test of details is performed prior to year-end, such as confirming accounts receivable, additional assurance will need to be obtained that the year-end balances are not materially misstated. Some factors to consider in deciding how much additional work to perform include these:

- The strength of the internal control structure (unless the auditor believes control risk is low, there is a need to directly test material account balances at year-end).
- The results of interim testing (for example, the extent of misstatements discovered from confirmation replies).
- The length of time between the interim work and year-end (the longer the time period, the more audit work will have to be performed at year-end).
- The likelihood of a significant change in the account balance by year-end.
- The ability of the auditor to test the account balance effectively for the interim period with a minimum amount of work.

Determining Optimal Mix of Audit Procedures

Determining the optimal mix of audit procedures is a difficult task. No two audits are exactly the same, and although many public accounting firms have standardized audit programs that can be used as guides to individual audits, the programs must be tailored to the specific circumstances applicable to each client. The overriding consideration is reducing audit risk to an acceptable level. The complexity of the judgment process the auditor faces is illustrated in Exhibit 13.3. The auditor must weigh the effect of the various factors in determining an optimal audit approach. In addition, there may be one additional constraint not shown in Exhibit 13.3: the need to train new auditors; thus, the experience and competence of the staff assigned to the audit may also be a consideration. No one approach is necessarily "right"; the auditor must balance a number of different considerations in determining the optimal approach for the audit engagement.

B–DEVELOPING AUDIT PROCEDURES

The audit program for revenue accounts is developed in connection with the program for accounts receivable. Many of the risks associated with sales also affect accounts receivable. A significant portion of the assertions related to sales are addressed in the dual-purpose tests described in Chapter 11. This chapter covers the additional tests of accounts in the revenue cycle that reflect the auditor's assessment of control risk.

Audit Objectives and Assertions

The audit objectives, related assertions, and audit tests for sales and accounts receivable are shown in Exhibit 13.4. Two themes need to be examined in reviewing

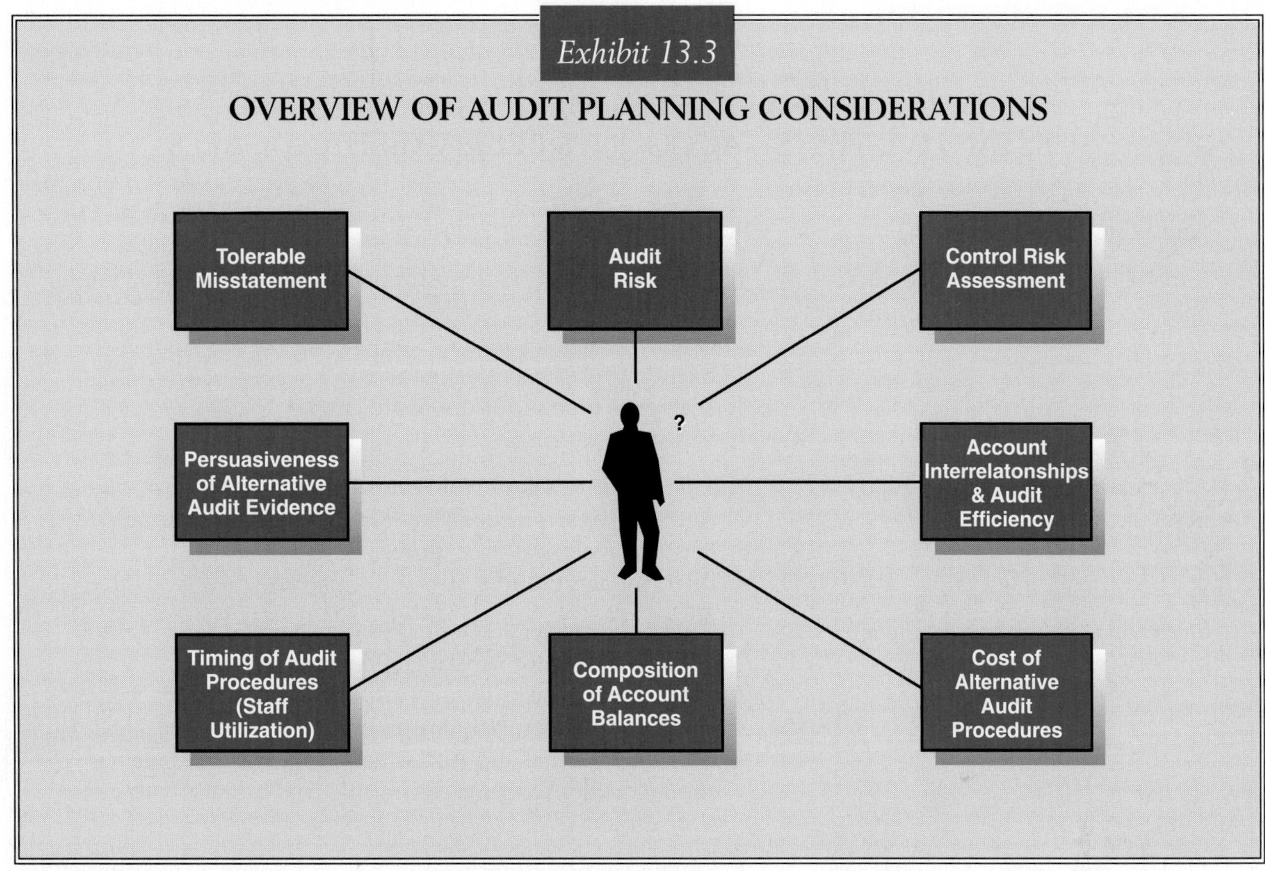

Exhibit 13.4. First, the audit objectives are directly derived from the assertions framework first developed in Chapter 7. However, the assertions are worded very specifically to address sales and receivables. Second, the audit procedures show an integration of tests of transaction processing, direct tests of the sales and receivables balances, and an integration of evidence derived from related accounts (accounts receivable evidence is applicable to sales assertions and vice versa). Third, the specific audit procedures to be selected (including the timing and extent of the procedures) depend on evidence the auditor has obtained regarding control risk.

Accounts Receivable represents the primary balance sheet account in the revenue cycle. Overstatements of sales will cause accounts receivable to be overstated. Because balance sheet accounts are normally easier to test and provide persuasive evidence, a significant portion of the auditor's assurance that revenue cycle accounts do not contain material misstatements is obtained through the audit of accounts receivable. Normally, the most time-consuming objectives relate to the existence and to the valuation of the receivables. It is important to realize that existence is necessary for correct valuation of the receivable, but persuasive audit evidence on the existence of receivables does not necessarily indicate that receivables are reported at net realizable value. For example, a customer might acknowledge the existence of the debt but not have sufficient resources to pay it.

An overview of the auditor's approach is described in the next section and is followed by the discussion of more specific audit procedures for accounts receivable audits.

Exhibit 13.4

RELATIONSHIPS BETWEEN AUDIT OBJECTIVES AND SUBSTANTIVE TESTS—ACCOUNTS RECEIVABLE AND SALES

Audit Objective (Assertion)	Substantive Test
Recorded sales and accounts receivable are valid (existence/occurrence).	1. Trace sales invoices to customer orders and bills of lading (BOL).* 2. Confirm balances with customers. 3. Examine subsequent collections. 4. Scan sales journal for duplicate entries. 5. Perform sales cutoff test.
All sales are recorded (completeness).	1. Trace BOL to sales invoice and sales journal.* 2. Account for sequence of sales invoices in sales journal.* 3. Perform analytical procedures. 4. Perform sales cutoff test.
Sales and accounts receivable are properly valued (valuation).	1. Verify clerical accuracy of sales invoices and agreement of sales invoices with supporting documents.* 2. Trace sales invoices to sales journal and customer's ledger.* 3. Confirm balances with customers. 4. Foot sales journal and Accounts Receivable trial balance and reconcile Accounts Receivable trial balance with control account.
Pledged, discounted, assigned, and related-party accounts receivable are properly disclosed (rights and presentation and disclosure).	1. Obtain confirmations from banks and financial institutions. 2. Review loan agreements and board of directors' minutes. 3. Inquire of management. 4. Review work performed in other audit areas. 5. Review trial balance of accounts receivable for related parties.
Revenue has been properly recognized in accordance with GAAP (presentation and disclosure).	Review the revenue recognition policies for appropriateness and consistency.

* = These procedures are often performed as part of a dual-purpose test as described in Chapter 11.

Existence and Occurrence

The timing and nature of audit tests depend directly on the auditor's assessment of control risk for this assertion. If there is low control risk (the auditor has gained confidence that transactions are recorded correctly in a timely fashion), the auditor may reduce the number of items tested on a substantive basis, perform the substantive tests at an interim date, and/or use less persuasive substantive tests. On the other hand, if control risk is assessed at the maximum for this client, the auditor will select substantive procedures that provide a high degree of assurance of detecting material misstatements, will likely assign more experienced staff to the engagement, and will perform more of the procedures on year-end balances rather than on interim balances. The most widely used auditing procedure is to send confirmations to customers asking them to acknowledge the existence and amount of their indebtedness to the customer. Confirmation of receivables is required by GAAS [AU 330] under most circumstances.

Completeness

Testing for the completeness of sales and accounts receivable is difficult unless the client has effective control procedures to ensure that all transactions are recorded. Without control procedures such as use of prenumbered shipping and billing documents, there is a high probability that some sales transactions go unrecorded. If, for example, prenumbered documents are not used, the auditor must consider alternative audit tests, such as the following, to gain insight into the possibility that there may be material amounts of unrecorded sales:

- Extensive analytical procedures, such as regression analysis using the historical relationship between sales and cost of sales, or comparing recorded sales with production records for a manufacturer or occupancy rates for a hotel.
- Performing detailed cutoff tests with emphasis on transactions recorded in the next fiscal year to determine whether they should have been recorded in the current year.

If the auditor does not believe that adequate evidence can be gathered to satisfy the completeness assertion, the client should be notified and the possibility of a disclaimer of opinion discussed. Because completeness controls are so essential, most organizations take the auditor's advice and install sufficient control procedures.

Valuation

Two valuation questions directly concern the auditor. First, are the sales and receivables transactions initially recorded at their correct value? Second, given that the transactions are initially recorded properly, is it likely that the client will collect the outstanding receivables in a timely fashion? The first concern is addressed during the auditor's tests of transactions processing, which includes verifying the clerical accuracy of sales invoices and agreement of the invoices with supporting documents, tracing sales invoices to the sales journal and customers' ledger, and confirming customer balances. The second concern is more difficult and is addressed in the following discussion related to determining the reasonableness of the allowance for doubtful accounts.

Rights and Obligations

Many companies choose to sell their receivables to banks or other financial institutions. Often the company retains some responsibility for collecting the receivables and may be liable if the percentage of collection falls below a specified minimum in the sales contract. The auditor should review all such contracts and consider obtaining confirmations from the client's banks about any contingent liabilities, including discounted receivables. In addition, the auditor should make appropriate inquiries of the client and review the minutes of the board of directors' meetings for any indication of discounted receivables.

Presentation and Disclosure

Any material amounts of pledged, discounted, or assigned receivables or related-party receivables and sales should be disclosed in the financial statements. Substantive procedures that provide evidence about the need for such disclosures include confirmations from banks and financial institutions; review of loan agreements, board of directors' minutes, and the receivables trial balance; and inquiry of management.

Standard Accounts Receivable Audit Procedures

Although each audit is unique, the auditor most likely performs some standardized audit procedures such as obtaining and evaluating an aged accounts receivable trial balance or sending confirmations to customers.

Aged Accounts Receivable Trial Balance

An **aged receivables trial balance** of the accounts receivable subsidiary ledger lists each customer's balance with columns to show the age of the unpaid invoices. The information is vital in testing the existence and valuation assertions and represents the starting point for most direct testing of the client's receivable balance. The auditor either obtains a copy of the trial balance from the client or uses audit software to assist in performing the procedures described.

Exhibit 13.5 represents an abbreviated trial balance. This document should be tested for mathematical and aging accuracy to be sure that it is a complete representation of the recorded accounts receivable balance that will appear on the balance sheet. It should be footed and checked for agreement with the general ledger, and the aging should be tested to be sure that the client's personnel or computer program that prepared it did it correctly. Many companies have serious algorithm difficulties in determining how to apply partial payments, or applying round payment amounts to account balances when specific invoices are not noted in the customer's remittance.

The aged trial balance can be used to select customer balances for confirmation; to identify amounts due from officers, employees, or other related parties or any nontrade receivables that need to be separately disclosed in the financial statements (presentation and disclosure); and to estimate the allowance for doubtful accounts by identifying past-due balances. Credit balances can also be identified and, if significant, reclassified as a liability (presentation). The auditor also finds it convenient to note collections of balances subsequent to year-end on the trial balance (existence and valuation).

Confirming Balances with Customers

Confirmation of customer balances can provide reliable external evidence on the existence of recorded accounts receivable and should be considered as an audit procedure on every engagement. The requirement for confirming receivables relates to a 1938 landmark case, *McKesson and Robbins*, in which the SEC found a massive fraud involving material amounts of fictitious receivables. The misstatements would have been discovered had the auditors confirmed the receivables. Current standards thus require the use of confirmations unless one of the following conditions exists:

Exhibit 13.5

AGED ACCOUNTS RECEIVABLE TRIAL BALANCE

CUSTOMER NUMBER	NAME	BALANCE	CURRENT	30–60 DAYS	61–90 DAYS	91–120 DAYS	OVER 120 DAYS
1	Alvies	1,327.35	1,327.35	0.00	0.00	0.00	0.00
2	Basch	1,952.81	1,952.81	0.00	0.00	0.00	0.00
3	Carlson	1,283.59	669.59	0.00	0.00	0.00	614.00
4	Draper	32,012.38	32,012.38	0.00	0.00	0.00	0.00
5	Ernst	4,317.71	4,317.71	0.00	0.00	0.00	0.00
6	Faust	1,436.49	1,436.49	0.00	0.00	0.00	0.00
7	Gerber	3,844.54	3,789.54	0.00	0.00	55.00	0.00
8	Hal	(713.78)	(713.78)	0.00	0.00	0.00	0.00
9	Harvs	9,081.03	6,702.03	2,379.00	0.00	0.00	0.00
10	Kaas	3,582.09	2,243.09	1,339.00	0.00	0.00	0.00
11	Kruze	1,255.78	1,066.78	189.00	0.00	0.00	0.00
12	Lere	3,434.66	2,833.66	601.00	0.00	0.00	0.00
13	Misty	1,772.07	1,731.07	0.00	41.00	0.00	0.00
14	Mooney	3,893.00	3,893.00	0.00	0.00	0.00	0.00
15	Otto	1,668.82	668.82	0.00	0.00	0.00	0.00
16	Paggen	874.80	874.80	0.00	0.00	0.00	0.00
17	Quast	3,632.44	3,632.44	0.00	0.00	0.00	0.00
18	Rauch	1,270.94	1,270.94	0.00	0.00	0.00	0.00
19	Sundby	7.36	7.36	0.00	0.00	0.00	0.00
20	Towler	2,694.13	2,694.13	0.00	0.00	0.00	0.00
.		.	.	.	.	.	.
.		.	.	.	.	.	.
N	Nough	3,548.89	3,548.89	0.00	0.00	0.00	0.00
Totals		807,906.00	739,183.00	56,879.00	5,573.00	221.00	6,050.00

- Accounts receivable are not material.
- The use of confirmations would be ineffective. An auditor might determine that confirmations are ineffective if customers have previously refused to confirm their balances and there is no reason to believe that they will do so this year. Or the auditor has reason to believe that the customers might not have a good basis on which to respond to the confirmation.
- The auditor's combined assessment of inherent risk and control risk is low, and that assessment, in conjunction with the evidence expected to be provided by other substantive tests, is sufficient to reduce audit risk to an acceptably low level [AU 330.34].

Information requested in confirmation letters must be objective and independently verifiable by the customers from their own records.

Types of Confirmations. The three basic types of confirmations are positive, negative, and open. **Positive confirmations** are letters sent to selected customers asking them to review the current balance due the client as shown on the client's statement and return the letters directly to the auditor indicating *whether they agree* with the indicated balance. If the customer does not return a signed confirmation, existing auditing standards require follow-up audit procedures to verify the existence of the customer's balance. An example of a positive confirmation is shown in Exhibit 13.6. Notice that it is printed on the client's letterhead, is addressed to the customer, and is signed by the client and that it indicates the balance as of a particular date—

Exhibit 13.6

POSITIVE CONFIRMATION

LeFlam Manufacturing Company
200 Pine Way, Kirkville, WI 53800
January 10, 1995

A.J. Draper Co.
215 Kilian Avenue
Justice, WI 53622

Our auditors, Rittenberg & Schwieger, CPAs, are making an annual audit of our financial statements. Please confirm the balance due our company as of December 31, 1994, which is shown on our records as $32,012.38.

Please indicate in the space provided below if the amount is in agreement with your records. If there are differences, please provide any information that will assist our auditors in reconciling the difference.

Please mail your reply directly to Rittenberg & Schwieger, CPAs, 5823 Monticello Business Park, Madison WI 53711, in the enclosed return envelope. PLEASE DO NOT MAIL PAYMENTS ON THIS BALANCE TO OUR AUDITORS.

Very truly yours,

Joleen Soyka

Joleen Soyka
Controller
LeFlam Manufacturing Company

To: Rittenberg & Schwieger, CPAs

The balance due LeFlam Manufacturing Company of $32,012.38 as of 12/31/94 is correct with the following exceptions, (if any):

Signature: ______________________________
Title: ______________________________
Date: ______________________________

referred to as the *confirmation date*—and tells the customer to respond directly to the auditor in an enclosed self-addressed, postage-paid envelope.

A **negative confirmation** is similar in that it asks the customer to review the client's balance but requests the customer to respond directly to the auditor *only if the customer disagrees* with the indicated balance. Exhibit 13.7 is an example of a negative confirmation in the form of a letter. There are several other negative confirmation forms, such as postcards or stickers attached to selected customers' monthly statements. A negative confirmation is less expensive to administer than a positive confirmation because there are no follow-up procedures when a customer does not return the confirmation. The auditor assumes that a nonresponse has occurred because the customer agrees with the stated balance.

Note that to adequately respond to the positive or negative confirmation request, customers must reconcile any differences between their records and the client's records (such as payments already mailed or invoices not yet received). Sometimes this may involve considerable effort on the part of the customers and, because of the

Exhibit 13.7

NEGATIVE CONFIRMATION

LeFlam Manufacturing Company
200 Pine Way, Kirkville, WI, 53800
January 10, 1995

B. D. Kruze
8163 Pleasant Way
Lucas, TX 77677

Our auditors are making an annual audit of our financial statements. Our records show an amount of $1,255.78 due from you as of 12/31/94. If the amount is not correct, please report any differences directly to our auditors, Rittenberg & Schwieger, CPAs, using the space below and the enclosed return envelope. NO REPLY IS NECESSARY IF THIS AMOUNT AGREES WITH YOUR RECORDS. PLEASE DO NOT MAIL PAYMENTS ON ACCOUNT TO OUR AUDITORS.

Very truly yours,

Joleen Soyka

Joleen Soyka
Controller
LeFlam Manufacturing Company

Differences Noted (If Any)

The balance due LeFlam Manufacturing Company of $1,255.78 at 12/31/94 does not agree with our records because (No reply is necessary if your records agree):

Date: ______________________ By: ______________________
[Individual or Company]

effort, many of them do not take the time to respond. An alternative is an **open confirmation** form on which the client asks the customer to provide the auditor with a detailed itemization of its accounts payable balance. The burden of reconciling the differences between the amount owed shown by the customer and the amount due shown by the client shifts from the customer to the auditor or client. Because of the difficulty in making such a reconciliation and because many customers do not have their accounts payable organized in a form to easily print a detail of balances owed, the open confirmation form is not used very often for accounts receivable. However, it is frequently used in conjunction with audits of accounts payable because, in that case, the auditor is simply requesting a listing of the vendor's accounts receivable.

Confirmations as Audit Evidence. Confirmations may provide evidence on a number of assertions in the revenue cycle, as illustrated in Exhibit 13.8. The persuasiveness of some forms of confirmations, however, is open to question, and the auditor must be aware of potential impairments that jeopardize the integrity of confirmation responses. (See the Auditing Research Results box.) Confirmations are generally considered to provide *strong* evidence about the *existence* of receivables and the *completeness* of collections, sales discounts, and sales returns and allowances. If, for example, a payment had been made, or an invoice was recorded for which there was no shipment, the customer would likely report the discrepancy on the confirmation. It is particularly important to note that a confirmation can be a very effective procedure to address the existence of fictitious sales. The presumption is that if the fictitious sales are recorded to the account of a valid customer, the customer will note that some of the recorded sales are not correct. If the customer is fictitious, the auditor must take care to ensure that it will not be delivered to a location where the client can act as a surrogate and confirm an inappropriate receivable (see Auditing Research Results box discussion).

Exhibit 13.8

STRENGTH OF CONFIRMATIONS OF RECEIVABLES AS A FORM OF EVIDENCE

	Existence/ Occurrence	Completeness	Valuation	Rights
Accounts receivable	Strong	Weak	Strong/ limited	Strong/ limited
Sales	Strong/ limited	Weak	Strong/ limited	(NA)
Returns and allowances	Weak	Strong	Strong/ limited	(NA)
Allowance for doubtful accounts	(NA)	(NA)	Weak	(NA)

Auditing Research Results

RELIABILITY OF CONFIRMATION RESPONSES

Several research studies have shown that confirmations are not as reliable as auditors would like to believe. In one study, installment loan customers of a large bank were sent confirmations with balances that were *known to be incorrect*. Negative confirmations were sent to some customers and positive confirmations to others. In each case, there were equal numbers of small and large understatements and overstatements.

If negative confirmations were a reliable source of evidence, the auditor could expect a response from most of the customers objecting to the balance. On average, however, fewer than 20 percent of the customers with known errors actually responded to the request to indicate differences to the auditor. The auditor ordinarily assumes that the other 80 percent represents correct balances—an erroneous conclusion. Less than 50 percent of those replying to the positive confirmations responded to the auditor indicating that the balance as shown by the bank was incorrect. The majority returned signed statements agreeing with balances that the auditor knew to be incorrect!

Why were the responses so unreliable? Several explanations are possible. First, the borrowers may have compared the confirmation with their records, detected a discrepancy, and declined to inform the auditor because:

- The misstatement was in the borrower's favor, so correcting the bank's books would not be advantageous; borrowers were less likely to respond when their balances were understated.
- The misstatement was perceived as small and not worth informing the auditor.
- The borrowers concluded that their own records were wrong.

The positive confirmation results were also disturbing. Borrowers may fail to compare the confirmation with their records or assume that the balance is correct. In some instances, customers admitted to simply signing and returning the confirmation request to avoid being bothered by further requests.

Source: Horton Lee Sorkin, *The Expanded Field Confirmation*, Research Report No. 21 (The Institute of Internal Auditors, 1978).

Confirmations provide *strong, but more limited*, evidence about the *valuation* of receivables, sales, collections, cash discounts, and sales returns and allowances. It is limited because the customer is more likely to report errors that overstate the receivable balance than those that understate it. Further, a confirmation acknowledges the debt but does not necessarily mean that the customer has the resources to pay it.

A company may discount some of its receivables without notifying its customers. As a result, confirmations provide *strong but limited* assurance about the *right* of the company to show receivables as assets.

Confirmations provide *weak* or *no* evidence about the *completeness* of receivables and sales. Confirming individual unpaid invoices does not detect an unrecorded invoice. Confirmations provide *weak* evidence about the *existence* of sales discounts and sales returns and allowances. Such evidence is better obtained through analytical procedures and tests of transaction processing.

Confirmations provide either *weak* or *limited* evidence about the *valuation* of the allowance for doubtful accounts. An undelivered confirmation may indicate difficulty in pursuing collection efforts or merely a postal service problem. Confirmations provide *no* evidence about *presentation* and *disclosure*.

Accuracy and Security of Confirmation Process. Confirmations may be prepared manually but are more frequently prepared by computer with audit software. If the confirmation is prepared by the client, the auditor should ensure that the information in each letter is correct and should control the mailing of the confirmation requests so that the client cannot modify them. Customers are requested to return the confirmations directly to the auditor's office in an enclosed self-addressed, postage-paid envelope. Similarly, the mailing should show the auditor's address as the return address in the event that the confirmation is not deliverable. A large number of undeliverable confirmations should raise the auditor's suspicion regarding the validity of the recorded receivable.

Sampling Unit. The auditor has a choice in identifying the sampling unit by confirming a customer's entire balance or selecting one or more of the unpaid invoices that make up that balance. When a balance is composed of several unpaid invoices, it will help the customer if a list of those invoices is attached to the confirmation. Some customers may use a voucher system* and not maintain a detailed accounts payable subsidiary ledger. To determine whether their records agree with that of the client, they would have to go through the vouchers payable journal or computer records, try to find all of the related invoices, and determine whether each of those invoices was unpaid as of the confirmation date. As a result, the customer may not return the confirmation or may return it and note that it could not be confirmed. As an alternative to confirming the whole balance, the auditor can confirm one or more selected unpaid invoices to improve the useful response rate.

Undeliverable Confirmations. The auditor should determine the cause of confirmation letters returned as undeliverable. If the wrong address was used, the correct address should be obtained and another letter sent. It is possible that the customer does not exist. Every effort should be made to determine the customer's existence. For example, the customer's name and address could be looked up in the telephone directory or in the publication of a credit rating service.

Follow Up to Nonresponses: Positive Confirmations. Follow-up procedures are required for positive confirmation letters that are not returned within a reasonable time after being mailed, such as two weeks. Second, and sometimes third, requests are mailed. If the amount being confirmed is relatively large, the auditor may consider calling the customer to encourage a reply.

When customers do not respond to the positive confirmation requests, the auditor should consider alternative procedures to verify the existence and validity of the receivable. Remember that mailed confirmations represent only a sampled few of the many account balances shown in the client's records. The results of the sample are intended to represent the total population; thus, it is important that the auditor develop sufficient follow-up procedures to gain satisfaction as to the correctness of the balances selected for confirmation. **Alternative procedures** that can be considered as providing persuasive evidence on the existence of the receivable as of the balance sheet date include the following:

*A voucher system is one in which each individual invoice is set up as a voucher for payment. The accounting unit is the voucher. In many such systems, the organization does not have the ability to readily identify all the amounts owed to an individual supplier or vendor. Thus, a company using a voucher system may have no practical method of responding to a confirmation form. In such a situation, the customer might be able to respond only to individual open invoices.

- Subsequent collection of the balance after year-end. Care should be taken to make sure that these subsequent receipts relate to the balance as of the confirmation date, not to subsequent sales.
- Examination of independent supporting documents. If all, or a portion, of the balance has not been collected, documents supporting the uncollected invoices should be examined. These documents include customer orders, sales orders, shipping documents, and sales invoices. Evidence obtained from such documents is not as persuasive, however, as that obtained from subsequent receipts or confirmations because such documents are not external to the client.

Follow Up to Nonresponses: Negative Confirmations. The basic premise underlying negative confirmations is that if no response is received, the auditor may assume that the customer agrees with the balance and no follow-up procedures are required. This is not always the correct assumption. The customer may not respond even though the balance is wrong because (1) the letter was lost, misplaced, or sent to the wrong address; (2) the customer did not understand the request; or (3) the request was simply ignored and thrown away. The auditor must have some understanding that the reliability of the negative confirmation process is not compromised because of any of the above factors. For example, a large number of negative confirmations that are returned is unexpected and will cause the auditor to perform alternative procedures, such as reviewing subsequent cash collections and investigating the pattern and causes of the misstatements. Negative confirmations are considered less expensive than positive confirmations, but it must also be recognized that the evidence provided is less persuasive.

Follow-Up Procedures: Exceptions Noted. Customers are asked to provide details of any known differences between their own records and the amount shown on the confirmation. Differences are often referred to as **exceptions.** Exceptions should be carefully investigated by the auditor, the client's internal auditors, or other client personnel. No matter who does the investigation, the auditor must be sure that the cause of any difference is properly identified as a customer error, a client error, an irregularity, a timing difference, or an item in dispute. Misstatements need to be projected to the entire population of receivables before determining whether there may be a material misstatement in the account balance.* If the projected amount of misstatement appears to have a material effect on the financial statements, the magnitude and cause of such misstatement should be discussed with the client to decide the appropriate follow-up procedures and whether a client investigation should precede further audit work. If subsequent work supports the conclusion of material misstatement, an adjustment will be required, and the client should adjust both the detailed and general ledger records to reflect that adjustment.

Some indicated exceptions by customers are strictly **timing differences** caused by transactions that are in process at the confirmation date, such as in-transit shipments or payments. They do not represent misstatements in the account balance.

Because irregularities are intentional acts, they have implications beyond their direct monetary effect. They should be discussed with the client and carefully investigated to determine who is involved and what their direct effect is on the financial

*Sample projections are covered in Chapter 14.

statements and other aspects of the audit. Lapping is an irregularity that may be detected by confirmations as described in the Auditing Focus box.

Type of Confirmation to Use. Positive confirmations are considered to be more persuasive than negative confirmations because they result in either (1) the receipt of a response from the customer or (2) the use of alternative procedures. The negative form should be limited to situations in which all three of the following factors are applicable:

- There are a large number of relatively small customer balances.
- The assessed level of control risk for receivables and related revenue transactions is low.
- The auditor has sound reason to believe that the customers are likely to give proper attention to the requests; that is, the customers have independent records on which to make an evaluation, will take the time to do so, and will return the confirmation to the auditor if there are significant discrepancies.

If the negative form is used, the number of requests sent or the extent of other procedures applied to the accounts receivable balance should normally be increased to obtain the same degree of assurance as would have been obtained using the positive form. Therefore, the auditor has a cost/benefit decision to make in choosing between the two forms. More time per confirmation letter is spent on the positive form, but, because it is more reliable, fewer need to be sent and/or the extent of other procedures can be reduced.

Procedures when Accounts Are Confirmed at an Interim Date. If the auditor has chosen to confirm receivables at a date prior to the balance sheet date, additional evidence must be gathered to ensure that no material misstatements have occurred between the confirmation date and year-end (the **roll-forward period**). The procedures used in gathering the additional evidence are often referred to as **roll-forward procedures** and include the following:

- Updating the auditor's assessment of control risk through year-end.
- Comparing individual customer balances at the interim confirmation date with year-end balances and confirming any that have substantially increased.
- Comparing monthly sales, collections, sales discounts, and sales returns and allowances during the roll-forward period with those for prior months and prior years to see if they appear out of line; if they do, obtaining an explanation from management and acquiring corroborative evidence to determine if that explanation is valid.
- Reconciling receivable subsidiary records to the general ledger at both the confirmation date and year-end.
- Testing the cutoff of sales, cash collections, and credit memos for returns and allowances at year-end.
- Scanning journals to identify receivables postings from unusual sources and investigating unusual items.

Auditing Focus

LAPPING: AN ACCOUNTS RECEIVABLE IRREGULARITY

Lapping is a technique used to cover up the embezzlement of cash. Lapping is most likely to occur when there is an inadequate segregation of duties—an employee has access to cash or incoming checks and to the accounting records. The employee steals a collection from a customer. However, that customer does not receive credit for the payment. If no other action is taken, that customer will detect the absence of the credit for payment on the next monthly statement. To prevent detection, the employee covers the defalcation by posting another customer's payment to the first customer. Then the second customer's account is missing credit which is covered up later when a subsequent collection from a third customer is posted to the second customer's account (hence the term *lapping*). At no time will any customer's account be very far behind in the posting of the credit. Of course, there will always be at least one customer whose balance is overstated unless the employee repays the stolen cash.

The defalcation can take place even if all incoming receipts are in the form of checks. The employee can either restrictively endorse it to another company or can go to another bank and establish an account with a similar name. If the lapping scheme is sophisticated, very few accounts will be misstated at any one point in time. Because the auditor selects only a sample for confirmation purposes, it is important that all differences be investigated and the cause for any exceptions determined rather than rationalizing the exception away as an isolated instance. Detailed entries in the cash receipts journal related to credits posted to that customer's account should be traced to the details on the related deposit slips and remittance advices. If the amount the customer paid exceeds the amount of the credit to the account, the detail in the cash receipts journal will not agree with the detail on the deposit slip or with the remittance advice. The pattern of the error should be noted for further investigation.

- Computing the number of days sales in receivables at both the confirmation date and year-end and comparing these data with each other and with data from prior periods.
- Computing the gross profit percentage during the roll-forward period and comparing that to the percentage for the year and for prior periods.

The purpose of performing these procedures is to search for evidence contrary to the auditor's tentative conclusion that control risk is low and that the accounts do not contain material misstatements. Note, however, that if the auditor's confirmation work at the interim date shows the existence of material misstatements, the auditor would perform year-end detailed testing rather than just performing the roll-forward procedures.

Summarizing Confirmation Work. The confirmation work should be summarized to show the extent of dollars and items confirmed, the confirmation response rate, the number and dollar amount of exceptions that were not misstatements, and the number and amount of exceptions that were misstatements (cross-referenced to the detailed explanation and disposition thereof). Such a summary helps the reviewers quickly grasp the extent and results of this work. The following is an example of such a summary:

	Items	Amount
Population	3,810	5,643,200.00
Positive confirmations	29	193,038.71
Percent	.76%	3.42%
Responses	27	180,100.11
Percent	93.1%	93.3%
Exceptions:	5	32,061.50
Cleared	4	19,105.82
Misstatements—B-4	1	971.68
Projected to population		30,446.31

Vouching Subsequent Receipts

Some auditors believe that evidence obtained from testing subsequent collections is a stronger indicator of the validity of the customer's balance than is obtained from confirmations. If a significant amount of the year-end receivables balance is normally collected before the end of the audit, the auditor may choose to emphasize tests of subsequent collections and minimize confirmation work. The auditor should verify that the cash collected subsequent to year-end is applicable to the year-end account balances, not to collections of sales made subsequent to year-end. In a computerized environment, the subsequent receipts may be identified using special computer programs. Testing subsequent collections provides strong evidence about both the existence and collectibility of the related receivables.

Analyzing Customer Correspondence Files

Many companies send their customers monthly statements that show the balance at the beginning of the month, all sales, collections, and return activity during the month, the ending balance due, and the payment due date. Customers who disagree with the detail on their statements can call or write the company. The employee who takes customer calls records the information in a computer file or on a form that is later placed in a correspondence file. Complaints received in the mail are also filed after being answered. These files contain information that the auditor can use to verify the existence, valuation, and collectibility of customer balances. They can also be used to clear up exceptions noted on receivable confirmations.

Related-Party Receivables

Amounts due from officers, employees, affiliated companies, or other related parties should be separately disclosed. As noted previously, audit procedures directed toward the identification of related-party transactions include (1) reviewing the accounts receivable trial balance for names of related parties, (2) inquiring of management, and (3) communicating the names of related parties so that the audit team members can be alert to such transactions in other parts of the audit.

Cutoff Tests

Cutoff tests are procedures applied to sales, sales returns, and/or cash receipts transactions selected from those recorded during the cutoff period to provide evidence as to whether the transactions have been recorded in the proper period. The cutoff period is usually the few days just before and just after the balance sheet date.

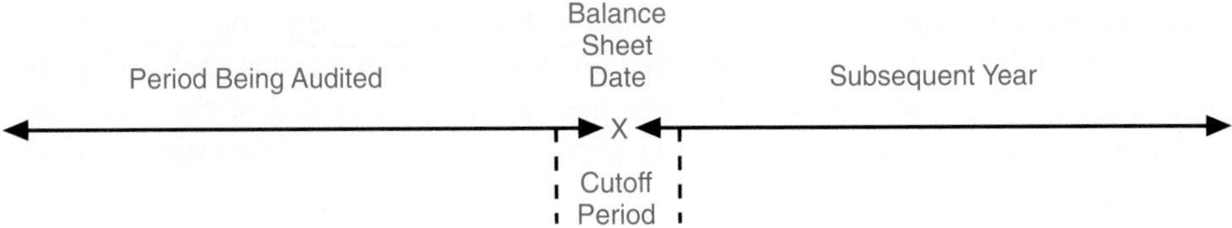

The greatest risk of recording transactions in the wrong period occurs during the cutoff period. The extent of cutoff tests depends on the auditor's assessment of the effectiveness of the client's cutoff control procedures. If the client has strong control procedures to ensure that transactions are recorded in the correct period, the auditor can minimize such testing.* However, it should be emphasized that control procedures can be overridden and that auditors have historically found a high degree of risk related to recording sales transactions in the correct time period.

The following items can be examined to determine whether a proper cutoff has been achieved:

Cutoff Test of	Items to Examine
Sales	Shipping documents and related recorded sales
Sales returns	Receiving reports and related credits to customer accounts
Cash receipts	Deposits per books and per bank Cash on hand at year-end

Sales Cutoff. A sample of sales transactions can be selected from those recorded during a period shortly before and after year-end (normally referred to as the **cutoff period**) to determine the correct time period of recording. The auditor can determine whether the sales were recorded in the correct period by looking at the shipping terms and shipment dates. The auditor may also want to examine the sales contracts to determine the existence of terms that might indicate that the recording of the sale should be postponed. Such terms might include the customer's right of return (and a high probability of return), the existence of additional performance by the seller, the probability of collection based on some future event (contingency), or the existence of an unusually low probability of collection.

Sales Returns Cutoff. Merchandise returned by customers is processed through the receiving department that prepares receiving reports showing the date, description, condition, and quantity of the merchandise. If the auditor is at the client's location on the last business day, the last receiving report issued can be noted in the working papers. At a later date, the auditor can select some of the receiving reports issued during the cutoff period and determine whether the credit was recorded in the correct period. This procedure may be done at the same time as a cutoff test of merchandise purchases and accounts payable. If the client has strong internal control procedures over sales returns and the amount of such returns during the cutoff period is insignificant, the auditor may choose not to perform this test.

*During a first-time audit, the auditor should test the cutoff of transactions at the end of last year as well. If the client has never been audited before, the auditor should perform cutoff tests of transactions recorded during the cutoff period at the beginning of the year similar to those performed at year-end. If the client was audited by a predecessor auditor, the successor auditor can review the predecessor's working papers to ensure that proper cutoff tests were performed.

Cash Receipts Cutoff. The auditor should obtain evidence that only the cash on hand at the balance sheet date is reflected on the balance sheet, that cash collections of accounts receivable by that date have been properly credited to the customers, and that no cash collections in the next period are recorded in the current period. This evidence is covered in Chapter 15.

Noncurrent Receivables

Receivables that are not due within the normal operating cycle or one year (whichever is longer) should be listed as a noncurrent asset. For example, a receivable arising from the sale of a fixed asset and due three years hence or due in installments over a three-year period should be classified wholly or in part as a noncurrent asset. Audit procedures to identify misclassified receivables include making inquiries of management, reading the board of directors' minutes, and scanning the subsidiary ledger to identify unusually large receivable balances, particularly those that resulted from a single transaction that was posted from an unusual source.

Sold, Discounted, and Pledged Receivables

Receivables that have been sold with recourse, discounted, or pledged as collateral on loans should be disclosed. Audit procedures that would reveal these ownership and disclosure items include:

- Inquiring of management.
- Scanning the cash receipts journal for relatively large inflows of cash that are posted from unusual sources.
- Obtaining bank confirmations, which include information on obligations to the bank and loan collateral.
- Reviewing the board of directors' minutes, which generally contain approval for these items.

Adjusting Audit Program to the Environment

The selection of audit procedures to test revenue cycle assertions varies considerably by the nature of the client's business. Testing revenues of a casino is entirely different than testing sales of a manufacturer, and both differ from testing interest revenue of a bank. The implementation and effectiveness of control procedures vary significantly from client to client. The selection of direct tests must reflect the auditor's assessment of control risk inherent in the client's processing and the availability of persuasive evidence.

Large Volume of Cash Transactions: Control Procedure Integration

Consider the audit of a grocery store chain for which all sales are recorded by electronically scanning bar codes on products and recording the result in an automated cash register. Or consider a casino in Las Vegas or Reno where millions of dollars change hands in a short period of time at the blackjack or craps tables or slot machines. How can the auditor be sure that all revenue transactions are properly recorded in these environments? How does the auditor integrate the control risk assessment with direct tests of the account balances in these situations?

The strength of control procedures is of utmost importance to the auditor in these kinds of environments. For example, the auditor is very concerned with procedures for making changes in the authorized price lists contained in the computer system running the grocery store checkout system. Likewise, the auditor is interested in the procedures used by the casino to collect cash from the tables, establish accountability, and reconcile cash received with cash deposited. The audit approach relies heavily on an analysis of the effectiveness of the client's control procedures and the use of management's monitoring controls to signal operations that appear to be out of line. For example, a casino will develop reports that compare actual revenue with expected revenue based on the number of guests staying at the casino and casino traffic volume. A grocery store manager will reconcile sales with expected sales and with inventory and cost of goods sold adjustments.

Once accountability for cash receipts is established, the auditor can test the completeness of the recording process by comparing recorded cash receipts with bank deposits and individual reports from cash registers or from table counts at a casino. However, without the establishment of a sound control structure to establish individual accountability and an audit trail, there is no good way to audit for the underrecording of sales transactions—and if such a control structure is not present, the auditor may seriously consider whether the entity is auditable.

Few but Large Sales—Confirmation of Sales

In some businesses, the balance in the Sales account is made up of relatively few transactions, but each transaction is for a large dollar amount. For example, a company selling supercomputers, such as Cray Research, may sell only 10 or 20 computers during the year. In such situations, the auditor should review sales contracts for questionable sales, being careful to review sales recorded just prior to year-end or reviewing sales returns posted just after year-end. In some situations, the auditor may even choose to confirm recorded sales with major customers. The auditor must be careful, however, to ensure that the customer is legitimate and has a reasonable basis on which to respond to the auditor's inquiry. For an example of potential problems the auditor might face, see the Practical Focus box on the Endotronics case.

Allowance for Doubtful Accounts

Accounts receivable should be valued at its net realizable value, that is, the amount that will be collected on the outstanding receivables. Estimating the allowance for doubtful accounts is one of the more difficult audit tasks because, at the time of the audit, there is not necessarily a correct answer. The estimate, however, must reflect the economic status of the client's customers, current economic conditions, and an informed expectation about default on payment. The method for developing an estimate of the appropriate allowance will vary from client to client. It will be affected by the strength of the client's credit policies and the nature of its business operating environment. In many companies, the appropriate allowance will have a substantial effect on the organization's profitability—and potentially on its viability. In every audit in which accounts receivable is material, the auditor must obtain an understanding of management's approach to estimating and writing off uncollectible accounts.

Practical Focus

ENDOTRONICS: AUDIT OF LARGE SALES TRANSACTIONS

Endotronics, Inc., a Minneapolis-based publicly held company, reportedly recorded $3.7 million in machine sales to a Japanese company, its largest customer. The Japanese company had a common name (like Yamaha, Inc.), but was in fact a small shell company with few financial resources. Endotronics was under pressure to show increasing sales and profitability to obtain larger contracts and municipal financing of expanded plant capacity.

The company engaged in "bill-and-hold" sales whereby a sales transaction for goods was recorded but the equipment was stored in a warehouse near the Minneapolis-St. Paul International airport rather than shipping it to Japan. The auditors obtained confirmation of the sales from the customer and obtained a legal opinion from an independent law firm that the sales contract was valid. The explanation the auditors received for the customer warehousing near a U.S. airport seemed reasonable: The customer could obtain its inventory within 24 hours, and storage costs in Japan are very high. The public warehouse company also confirmed its storage of these machines. However, a warehouse spokesperson was very explicit in noting that they responded only to specific questions asked by the auditor. In other words, the spokesperson seemed to indicate that the auditor failed to ask the critical question and therefore failed to understand the nature of the agreement with the client:

> A spokesman for [the public warehouse company] said the information it supplied merely confirmed that it was holding some Endotronics machines that had been sold, or were being sold, to Japan. [The operations manager] conceded, however, that the information should have made it clear that Endotronics, not the customer, was still in control of the equipment. "We couldn't ship it without getting word from Endotronics."

The machines were, it turned out, still under Endotronic's control. The customer reneged on the contract, and the client was forced into bankruptcy. In spite of all their efforts, the auditors, among others, were sued by—and paid damages to—shareholders. The auditors were also the subject of considerable negative press.

Source: "Firm That Did Endotronics Audit Says It Received Misinformation," *Minneapolis Star and Tribune*, July 28, 1987, 1D.

Estimate of the Allowance for Doubtful Accounts

The recording of the Allowance for Doubtful Accounts and the determination of Bad Debts Expense for the year is the result of an accounting estimate. The allowance should reflect management's best estimate of year-end accounts receivable that will not be collected. The auditor can approach the audit of the allowance account and the related bad debts expense in one of two ways:

1. Determine management's method for making the estimate and perform audit procedures to determine the basis for management's estimate and its likely accuracy.
2. Develop an independent model to estimate the accounts and update the model each year based on past experience and current economic conditions.

The auditor often uses the second approach for small clients whose management does not have sufficient accounting expertise to develop the estimates. Some auditing firms are developing expert systems to assist in making these judgments, and auditors often use a combination of the two approaches in auditing the estimate.

The auditor can track the history of annual write-offs and provisions for bad debts. If they are approximately equal over a period of years for stable credit sales or approximately the same percentage of credit sales or receivables from year to year, these estimates would appear to be reasonable. Such estimates are useful but should be modified for changes in economic conditions, customer demographics, credit policies, or products. Blindly following old approaches often results in substantially underestimating a client's collection problems.

The auditor should ask management about the collectibility of customer balances that have not yet been collected in the subsequent period, particularly those that are long overdue or are relatively large. The auditor can also review credit reports from outside credit bureaus, such as Dun & Bradstreet, to help determine the likelihood of collection and can check customer correspondence files to provide additional insight into the collectibility of specific accounts. In some cases in which material amounts are due from customers whose balance is past due or unusually large, the auditor may want to request a copy of the customer's latest financial statements to perform an independent analysis of collectibility. As noted earlier, many large firms have access to computerized databases where they can also review current articles or other business reports on large customers.

Receivables should be reported on the balance sheet at their realizable value. The auditor and the client can legitimately disagree about the adequacy of the Allowance for Doubtful Accounts. Because the allowance is based on judgment, the auditor cannot expect a precise answer as to what this balance should be, but if the auditor believes the balance is unreasonable, the client should be asked to adjust it.

Write-Offs

Accounts should be written off as soon as they are determined to be uncollectible. The accounts receivable balance should not contain amounts that are known to be uncollectible. The auditor should inquire about the client's procedures for deciding when to write off an account and determine whether the procedures are reasonable and are being followed. If adequate control procedures are not established, it is possible that the accounts are written off, but an employee may be collecting subsequent payments. All write-offs should be approved, and, in most instances, companies turn over the uncollectible amounts to a credit agency for collection. The account should be monitored for subsequent collection for a period of time.

Auditing Other Accounting Estimates

The auditor's responsibilities for accounting estimates include obtaining evidence to provide reasonable assurance that

- All material accounting estimates have been developed.
- Those estimates are reasonable.
- They are presented in conformity with GAAP [AU 342.07].

In addition to the estimates inherent in the allowance for doubtful accounts and long-term construction contracts, there are other accounting estimates related to the revenue cycle, including loan loss reserves of financial institutions, and product warranty liability.

Accounting estimates are based on both judgment and transaction data. Management must use its knowledge and experience of past and current events to make assumptions about future conditions. The auditor is responsible for evaluating the reasonableness of the accounting estimates in relationship to the financial statements taken as a whole. Management is generally predisposed to minimize estimates that reduce revenues. Therefore, the auditor should consider, with an attitude of professional skepticism, both the judgment factors used in making such estimates and the definition of the transactions or balances on which such estimates are based.

After obtaining an understanding of how management developed an estimate, auditors should use one or more of the following approaches to evaluate the reasonableness of the estimate: (1) review and test the process management used to develop the estimate, (2) develop their own expectation of the estimate, or (3) review subsequent events or transactions occurring prior to the end of the fieldwork for evidence of an estimate's appropriateness.

Product Warranty Costs is a typical account for which estimates must be made. Such costs should be matched with the revenue from the sale of the warranted product. Because many of these costs are not known until years later when the product is serviced or replaced, they must be estimated. The auditor may use analytical procedures to provide the necessary evidence about the reasonableness of the estimates.

In the case of new car warranties, for example, the client should have an accounting system to record warranty expenditures, match the expenditures with the vehicle model, and then use that information to make an estimate. The auditor may choose to review and test the client's system for developing these estimates. In testing the system, the auditor determines the procedures for tracking warranty repair costs and relating it to model numbers and model years. For example, some of Chrysler's minivans in 1989 and 1990 had a particular problem with transmissions that caused higher than average warranty repairs. Sophisticated manufacturers such as Chrysler have developed systems in which early warranty repairs can be used to estimate future warranty problems and can adjust the data by model and year. In some cases, the auditor may choose to make an independent estimate to compare with the client's estimate. Then the auditor may review the history of warranty costs and adjust the experience-based estimate for any known changes in the warranty policy or quality of the products. In rare cases, the auditor may use a statistical sampling approach to this estimate.*

Analytical Procedures for Revenue Cycle Accounts

In some situations, analytical procedures can provide strong evidence more efficiently than tests of details. Analytical procedures can be effective in signaling potential misstatements or corroborating other evidence on the correctness of a particular account balance. When considering the use of analytical procedures, the auditor should determine whether other supporting (corroborating) evidence is available for potential management explanations of unexpected findings.

Ratio analysis, trend analysis, and reasonableness tests are three standard analytical procedure types that are often used on revenue cycle accounts. Ratio analysis, for example, often includes consideration of trends. Both trend analysis and reasonableness tests involve estimates of what an amount should be. Some of the analytical

*The only statistical method that can be used for this is called the *mean-per-unit method,* which is described in Chapter 14.

procedures that may be useful for the revenue cycle are described in the following three sections.

Ratio Analysis

Ratios that may provide evidence about the valuation of receivables and the allowance for doubtful accounts include the following:

- Turnover of receivables (ratio of credit sales to average net receivables) or the number of days' sales in accounts receivable.
- Average balance per customer.
- Ratio of receivables to current assets.
- Aging of receivables.
- Ratio of bad debts expense to credit sales.

To understand how ratio analysis might be used in evaluating the correctness of sales and receivables, consider the following example taken from a court case:

- The number of days' sales in accounts receivable increased in one year from 44.2 to 65.
- The gross margin increased from 16.7 percent to 18.3 percent.
- The amount of accounts receivable increased 35 percent from $9 million to $12 million while sales remained virtually unchanged.

An auditor reviewing these ratios should take a hard business look at the changes and ask these questions: (1) Is there a business reason why these ratios changed? (2) What alternatives could potentially explain these changes? and (3) What corroborating evidence is available for potential explanations? The auditor cannot stop at the first reasonable, or palatable, explanation. Rather, the auditor should determine the explanation that is most likely and gather independent corroborating evidence that will either support or contradict the explanation. In the example given, one potential explanation (and the one that actually was used) is that the company was engaged in a complicated scheme of recording fictitious sales. Credit memos were issued for the fictitious sales, but only after the auditor had completed the year-end audit. A judge found that the auditor should have been able to analyze the situation and determine that a fraud had taken place. The point is that ratio analysis, if used properly, can provide insight about potential misstatements. The auditor needs to consider interrelationships among a number of different ratios. This analysis can be meaningfully performed only if the auditor understands the business and can piece the ratio analysis puzzle together.

Ratio analysis can also provide insight into the completeness, existence, and valuation of transactions related to receivables. Some examples include the following:

- Sales in the last month to total sales.
- Ratio of sales discounts to credit sales.
- Ratio of returns and allowances to sales.
- Ratio of interest income to interest-bearing receivables.

Auditing in Practice

REGRESSION ANALYSIS IMPLEMENTATION BY INTERNATIONAL PUBLIC ACCOUNTING FIRM

The firm of Deloitte & Touche has developed a regression program for microcomputers called *Statistical Techniques for Analytical Review (STAR)*. For this illustration, the authors used a data file containing monthly sales and cost of sales by product line and selling expenses for the 36 months preceding the current audit year (the regression base) and for the 12 months of the current year. To help auditors evaluate the evidence of the regression analysis, the program asks for a value for tolerable misstatement, an indicator of the risk of incorrect acceptance (called *monetary precision* and *reliability factor*, respectively, in STAR). The program also needs to know whether the auditor wants to test for overstatement or understatement. In this illustration, the audit objective was to test for potential understatement of sales based on either cost of sales or selling expenses singly or in combination.

The program performed several tests, including a test of the correlation between the dependent variable—sales—and the independent variables—cost of sales and selling expenses—for the regression base period. It dropped selling expenses because they did not make a statistically significant contribution to the regression function. The program developed a regression formula using the 36-month regression base and used the formula to project monthly sales for the current year, based on the current year cost of sales. The program then compared the projected sales with recorded sales for the current year (months 37 to 48) and identified month 48 (the last month in the current year) on the following printout as appearing to be significantly understated. If the auditor does not already have evidence that explains the lower than projected sales for month 48, additional audit evidence should be obtained. Note that the program's printout also provides sample selection information should the auditor decide to use sampling to obtain the additional evidence.*

*The sampling information relates to probability proportional to size sampling described in the next chapter.

Auditors often compare current year ratios to those of prior years and to industry averages to see whether any have changed significantly during the current year of if any are substantially different from industry norms. Unusual results require follow-up inquiry of management.

Trend Analysis

A comparative analysis of monthly sales for the current and preceding period (and of budgeted sales and current sales, if available) can highlight any changes. The auditor should obtain explanations for significant or unusual fluctuations. In making such comparisons, the auditor is interested not only in gross sales but also in discounts granted, returns, credits allowed, and net sales. If the analysis is separated by product line, division, or some other subclassification, the value of the information is enhanced. Such an analysis may also provide corroborating evidence about the

STAR PRINTOUT OF REGRESSION PROJECTION

AUDIT OF PROJECTION DATA
MONETARY PRECISION = 100 (SAME UNITS AS DEPENDENT VARIABLE)
RELIABILITY FACTOR = 3
DIRECTION OF TEST IS UNDERSTATEMENT

REGRESSION PROJECTIONS

OBS NO	RECORDED AMOUNT	REGRESSION ESTIMATE	RESIDUAL	EXCESS TO BE INVESTIGATED	OPTIONAL SAMPLE DATA SELECTION INTERVAL	RANDOM START	MAXIMUM ITEMS
37	362	356	6				
38	411	422	-11				
39	476	469	7				
40	526	499	27				
41	521	528	-7				
42	522	516	6				
43	563	563	-0				
44	630	639	-9				
45	604	602	2				
46	469	463	6				
47	474	472	2				
48	400	441	-41	30	33	15	13
	5958	5970	-12	30			13

Regression Estimate [Y'(t)] of sales for observation t:
Y'(t) = -.6048 + 1.2175 * X1(t)

Coefficient of :

Correlation	0.9978
Regression Improvement	0.9328

completeness, existence, and valuation of transactions. The auditor should obtain reliable evidence that either supports or refutes management's explanations whenever possible. Accepting glib answers from management without obtaining evidence from other sources to validate management's claims has resulted in legal problems for auditors.

Regression analysis can be a very useful tool in trend analysis. For example, a regression formula can be developed based on the historical relationship of monthly sales with cost of sales by product line over the past few years. The formula can then be used to estimate what the current year's sales should be based on the recorded cost of sales. If any of the recorded sales appear to be out of line with the regression estimate, additional audit work may be needed. (See the Auditing in Practice box above on regression analysis.) Similarly, regression formulas can be used to evaluate other revenue cycle relationships—credit sales to accounts receivable balances or sales to product warranty estimates.

Reasonableness Tests

The overall reasonableness of an account balance can sometimes be determined with a relatively simple calculation. For example, revenue from room rental for a motel or from number of beds occupied for a hospital can be estimated using the average room rate and average occupancy rate. Similarly, product warranty liability in the second year of sales can be estimated from the second-year liability and the first year of sales.

Notes Receivable

Sometimes, when customers are unable to pay their open account when due, they may be asked to sign a note receivable requiring payment within a specified period, with interest. The auditor can physically examine or confirm notes receivable. For confirmations, the auditor should ask customers to confirm not only the amount due (as for accounts receivable) but also the date of the note, the due date, the interest rate, and, when appropriate, any collateral pledged as security that should be in the client's possession but is not included on the balance sheet.

The auditor should test the related interest income at the same time as the notes receivable themselves. Both analytical procedures and recomputation are useful techniques for evaluating interest income. Multiplying the average notes receivable balance by the average interest rate, for example, often yields a reasonable estimate of interest income. When the amounts are material, interest income and accrued interest receivable can be recalculated for a sample of the notes, or, if there are not very many, for each note. If the note information is maintained on a computer, the auditor can use computer audit software to make these calculations.

C–ILLUSTRATIVE EXAMPLE–LEFLAM MANUFACTURING COMPANY

There are many factors and potential procedures to consider in developing an effective and efficient audit program for the revenue cycle. We continue the integrative illustration to assist in understanding the process of developing such an audit program. Background information about LeFlam Manufacturing Company was provided in Chapter 11.

Exhibit 13.9 presents the working trial balance for LeFlam, with the final (audited) balances for the prior year (1993), the book balances (unaudited) for the current year (1994), columns for any adjustments and reclassifications, and a column for the current year audited balances. Accounts receivable are more than one-fourth of total assets. Sales are payable within 45 days from the invoice date, and no sales discounts are given. Returns and allowances are relatively few because of good quality control prior to shipment.

Selecting Procedures

Exhibit 13.10 is a planning matrix for LeFlam. For illustrative purposes, the process of planning substantive tests is limited to sales, accounts receivable, the allowance

Exhibit 13.9

LEFLAM MANUFACTURING CO.
WORKING TRIAL BALANCE—BALANCE SHEET
DECEMBER 31, 1994

T/B 1 of 2

($000)

Account	Ref	12/31/93	12/31/94 Balance per Books	Adjustments/ Reclassifications Debits	Adjustments/ Reclassifications Credits	12/31/94 Final Balance
Cash	A	673	100			
Accounts receivable (net)	B	2,790	5,444			
Inventory	C	8,892	13,385			
Other current assets	F	117	144			
Total current assets		12,472	19,073			
Property, plant, & equipment (net)	I/J	1,834	1,997			
Total assets		14,306	21,070			
Accounts payable	AA	2,255	1,942			
Notes payable—current	BB	123	755			
Other accrued liabilities	CC	505	343			
Estimated income tax payable	DD	136	306			
Total current liability		3,020	3,346			
Notes payable	M	1,397	10,711			
Deferred tax	OO	60	66			
Advance from affiliate	PP	6,219	2,271			
Total long-term liability		7,676	13,048			
Common stock	SS	500	500			
PIC in excess of par	TT	600	600			
Retained earnings	ZZ	2,510	3,576			
Total equity		3,610	4,676			
Total liability & equity		14,306	21,070			

(Continued)

for doubtful accounts (shown as the valuation assertion under receivables), and collection transactions. Inherent risk has been assessed as moderate, and control risk has been assessed as low for all assertions. Therefore, a high detection risk will be used for all of the selected substantive procedures and assertions. Less audit assurance needs to be obtained through substantive procedures than if the detection risk were moderate or low. The auditor has concluded that sufficient competent evidence can be obtained by performing analytical procedures and the first five substantive tests.

Exhibit 13.9

LEFLAM MANUFACTURING CO.
WORKING TRIAL BALANCE—INCOME STATEMENT
DECEMBER 31, 1994

T/B 2 of 2

($000)

Account	Ref	12/31/93	Balance per Books 12/31/94	Adjustments/ Reclassifications Debits	Credits	Final Balance 12/31/94
Sales	10	24,900	29,500			
Sales returns and allowances	11	400	600			
Net sales		24,500	28,900			
Cost of sales	20	17,800	20,808			
Gross margin		6,700	8,093			
Selling expenses	30	1,742	1,879			
General and administrative expenses	40	1,994	2,181			
Total operating expenses		3,736	4,060			
Net operating income		2,964	4,032			
Income taxes	50	1,097	1,430			
Net income		1,287	1,678			
Retained earnings—Beg.	ZZ	1,693	2,510			
Dividends	ZZ	(470)	(612)			
Retained Earnings—End	ZZ	2,510	3,576			

Auditing standards require that analytical procedures be performed during the planning and wrap-up stages of an audit. In addition, they may be performed during the audit as a form of substantive procedures. In this audit, the auditor has chosen to perform most of the analytical procedures described earlier in this chapter because they do not take much time. The auditor plans to use the procedures primarily as problem identifiers rather than as substantive procedures.

Testing the mechanical accuracy of the underlying accounting records is done to determine that the records are an appropriate basis for further audit testing. (Mechanical accuracy does not provide corroborative evidence about any of the assertions.) The auditor tests the footings of, and postings from, the sales, cash receipts, and other related journals. The accounts receivable trial balance is footed and checked for agreement with the general ledger control account. The auditor performs all these tests using generalized audit software.

Confirming receivables tests all of the assertions in the matrix with varying degrees of persuasiveness. The number of customers' balances selected for confirmation will be relatively small because detection risk has been set high. Positive confirmations will be used. The confirmation work is done as of December 31. For nonresponses,

Exhibit 13.10

PLANNING MATRIX FOR LEFLAM

	Sales			Receivables				Collections		
Assertions	E	C	V	E	C	V	R	E	C	V
Inherent Risk (High, Moderate, Low)	M	M	M	M	M	M	M	M	M	M
Control Risk (H, M, L)	L	L	L	L	L	L	L	L	L	L
Detection Risk (H, M, L)	H	H	H	H	H	H	H	H	H	H
Analytical procedures	X	X	X	X	X	X		X	X	X
Substantive tests:										
1. Test the mechanical accuracy of the underlying accounting records										
2. Confirm recorded receivables	X	X	X	X	X	X	X	X	X	X
3. Vouch aging details to supporting documents, discuss collectibility of receivables with responsible officials and review correspondence						X				
4. Vouch recorded receivables to subsequent cash receipts	X		X	X	X	X	X			
5. Verify cutoff for sales, cash receipts, returns, etc.	X	X		X	X			X	X	
6. Vouch recorded receivables to supporting documents	X		X	X		X	X			
7. Vouch recorded receivables to write-offs of bad debts and other credits to receivables in the subsequent period				X		X	X			
8. Retrace sales from shipping records to sales invoices, sales register, and accounts receivable sub. ledger	X	X			X	X	X			
9. Vouch sales for sales register to shipping records	X		X	X		X	X			
10. Confirm recorded sales transactions by customer	X	X	X	X		X				
11. Review sales contracts for terms, prices		X	X							
12. Reconcile cash receipts to bank statements					X	X		X		X
13. Tests of processing accuracy:										
Test sales invoice prices/terms to authorized lists			X			X				
Test processing to general and subsidiary ledgers			X			X				
Determine sequential numbering of sales invoices	X	X		X	X					
14. Trace cash receipts from bank statement to cash receipts records and to receivables details					X	X		X		X
15. Vouch write-offs of uncollectible receivables to supporting documentation						X				

Key: E = Existence/occurrence; C = Completeness; V = Valuation; R = Rights/obligations

the auditor decides to perform alternative procedures, primarily testing subsequent cash collections.

Vouching the aging details, discussing collectibility, and reviewing correspondence provides strong evidence about the valuation assertion but can be limited to large account balances or large amounts that are significantly overdue. (This test would also have been performed for a moderate or low detection risk level, but more extensively.)

Vouching receivables to subsequent collections provides evidence about several assertions, including the valuation of receivables. Accounts collected during the subsequent period exist and do not need to be included in the allowance for doubtful accounts. If the subsequent period is long enough, any remaining uncollected accounts become more likely to be uncollectible and a better estimate of the allowance can be made.

Cutoff tests are performed because of the potential for errors at year-end. These tests focus on sales and cash collection cutoff. Sales are made on an FOB shipping point basis. The auditor selects several sales invoices recorded in the sales register for several days before and after year-end and examines shipping records to be sure the sales are recorded in the proper period.

The cash collection cutoff is tested along with the audit of cash, discussed in Chapter 15. The controls over cash are very strong because of the use of a lock box system in which the bank controls the cash collections. Therefore, very little cash collection cutoff work is needed.

Exhibit 13.11 is the audit program resulting from the planning matrix in Exhibit 13.10. Several items should be noted while reviewing this program:

- The audit objectives are related to the account balance assertions.
- The audit procedures are keyed to the audit objectives.
- The program provides fairly detailed instructions to assist the auditor in performing the procedures.
- The planning matrix does not address the presentation and disclosure assertion for which step 7 provides the appropriate procedures.
- Lines are furnished for indicating who did each step, the date of performance, and the working paper reference.

Exhibit 13.11

LEFLAM MANUFACTURING CO.
AUDIT PROGRAM FOR ACCOUNTS RECEIVABLE
DECEMBER 31, 1994

Account balance assertions:

1. Existence or occurrence.
2. Completeness.
3. Rights and obligations.
4. Valuation or allocation.
5. Presentation and disclosure.

Exhibit 13.11

Objectives:

A. Existence and valuation of accounts receivable—To determine that the receivables that exist are authentic obligations owed to the entity and contain no significant amounts that should be written off and that allowances for doubtful accounts are adequate and not excessive. (Assertions 1, 3, and 4)

B. Proper disclosure—To determine that proper disclosure is made of any pledged, discounted, or assigned receivables. (Assertions 3 and 5)

C. GAAP conformity—To determine that presentation and disclosure of receivables is in conformity with generally accepted accounting principles consistently applied. (Assertion 5)

D. Completeness of accounts receivable and sales— To determine that all receivables and sales that should be recorded are recorded. (Assertion 2)

OBJ.	PROCEDURES	Done By	Date	W/P Ref.
	A. Substantive test procedures			
	1. Based on the assessed level of risk, decide on the following:			
	a. Extent of confirmation procedures.	______	______	______
	b. Form of confirmation (positive, negative, or a combination of both).	______	______	______
	c. Timing of confirmation procedures (as of the balance sheet date or some other date).	______	______	______
	d. Anticipated scope of alternative procedures.	______	______	______
	e. Approach for reviewing and evaluating adequacy of allowances.	______	______	______
	f. Sampling method to use (see Chapter 14).			
[A]	2. Review activity in the general ledger control accounts for trade accounts receivable for the period being audited and	______	______	______
	a. Note and investigate any significant entries that appear unusual in amount or source.	______	______	______
	b. Compare the opening balance for the period with the final closing balances per the working papers and reports for the preceding period.	______	______	______
[A]	3. Analyze the relationship of receivables and sales (day's sales in accounts receivable) and compare with relationships for the preceding period(s) (*SAS No. 56;* AU 329).	______	______	______

(Continued)

Exhibit 13.11

OBJ.	PROCEDURES	Done By	Date	W/P Ref.
[A]	4. Obtain or prepare an aged trial balance of trade receivables as of the date selected for confirmation procedures. Perform the following:			
	a. Cross-foot the totals and refoot the total column and (selected or all) analysis columns.	______	______	______
	b. Trace total to the general ledger control account and to the lead schedule or working trial balance.	______	______	______
	c. On a test basis, trace entries for individual customers on the aging analysis (totals and aging detail) to the individual accounts in the accounts receivable subsidiary ledger and select individual accounts from the subsidiary ledger and trace totals and aging detail to the aged trial balance to determine if aging is correct. Test footings of individual customer accounts in the subsidiary ledger.	______	______	______
[A]	5. Select individual customer accounts for confirmation procedures from the aged trial balance (or trial balance) and arrange for the preparation of confirmation requests to be mailed under the auditor's control and tested as follows:	______	______	______
	a. Trace individual confirmation requests as to balances and addresses to the subsidiary accounts receivable records. Send confirmations (using envelopes with the auditor's return address) and prepare confirmation statistics.	______	______	______
	b. Trace confirmation replies to the trial balance and investigate replies with differences.	______	______	______
	Note: The auditor may prepare a control list of exceptions and arrange for the client's staff to investigate the differences and accumulate supporting documentation for the auditor's review.			
	c. Obtain new addresses for all confirmations returned by the post office and remail.	______	______	______
	d. Send second requests for all unanswered positive confirmation requests. Consider sending third requests by registered or certified mail and performing alternative auditing procedures.	______	______	______

Exhibit 13.11

OBJ.	PROCEDURES	Done By	Date	W/P Ref.
[A]	6. For positive confirmation requests to which no reply was received, accounts that declined to provide confirmation information and accounts which the client requested not be confirmed:			
	a. Test items subsequently paid to remittance advices that identify the specific invoices paid.			
	b. Examine customer's purchase orders, related invoices and shipping documents for amounts that are not supported by remittance advices that identify the specific invoices paid.			
	c. Establish the existence of the customer by reference to such sources as Dun & Bradstreet *Reference Book.*			
	7. Summarize the results of the confirmation procedures and project misstatements to the population.			
[A, B] [C]	8. Ascertain whether any accounts or notes have been assigned, pledged, or discounted by reference to minutes, review of agreements, confirmation with banks, etc.			
[A, B] [C]	9. Obtain or prepare an analysis of the allowance for doubtful accounts for the period and:			
	a. Review adequacy of the allowance and related provision by *SAS No. 57* (AU 342):			
	(1). Review the aged trial balance as of the balance sheet date with the client's credit manager or other responsible individual to identify accounts of a doubtful nature and allowances required; review correspondence files and other relevant data in support of client's representations. Items reviewed should include past-due amounts and significant amounts whether past due.			
	(2). Examine credit reports for delinquent and large accounts.			
	(3). Review confirmation exceptions for indication of amounts in dispute.			
	(4). Consider requesting audited financial statements for large accounts that are past due and appear doubtful.			

(Continued)

Exhibit 13.11

OBJ.	PROCEDURES	Done By	Date	W/P Ref.
[D]	10. Perform cutoff tests for sales and returns:			
	a. Select sales invoices for testing from the sales register for several days before and after year-end and examine shipping records and determine that they were recorded in the proper period.			
	b. Select credit memos issued after year-end and examine underlying documentation (for example, record of receipt of returned goods) to determine period to which credit memo isapplicable and whether it was recorded in the proper period.			
	B. Analytical procedures			
	1. Analyze and review trends for the following relationships (*SAS No. 56;* AU 329):			
	a. Accounts receivable to credit sales.			
	b. Allowance for doubtful accounts to accounts receivable (in total and in relation to past-due categories per aging analysis).			
	c. Sales to returns and allowances.			
	d. Expense provisions for doubtful accounts to net credit sales.			
	e. Expense provisions for doubtful accounts to write-offs.			
	f. Moving average relationship of write-offs to trade receivables.			
	g. Average balance per customer.			
	h. Ratio of account receivable to current assets.			

Source: AICPA, *Audit Program Generator,* Version 2.0.

Summary

Knowledge of the interrelationships among transactions, account balances, assertions, tolerable misstatement, persuasiveness of alternative procedures, and the various risk factors allows the auditor to develop an effective and efficient audit program. When detection risk is relatively low, the auditor should choose strong procedures, perform them as of year-end, and test relatively large samples. When detection risk is moderate or high, the auditor may use procedures with less strength, perform some or all of them at an interim date, and/or use smaller sample sizes.

Developing an appropriate audit program requires considerable judgment and experience. Tracking all of the interrelationships is difficult. Many firms use a "standard" program or matrix (such as the one in Exhibit 13.10), which contains a list of possible procedures and which should be tailored to each individual client. Once the procedures have been identified, the auditor needs to determine the extent of testing.

Significant Terms

aged receivables trial balance A list of each customer's balance distributed among columns to show the age (time outstanding) of the unpaid invoices.

alternative procedures Procedures used to obtain evidence about the existence and valuation of accounts receivable when a positive confirmation is not returned, including examining cash collected after the confirmation date and vouching unpaid invoices to customer's orders, sales orders, shipping documents, and sales invoices.

cutoff period The few days just before and just after the balance sheet date, the number of days is chosen by the auditor, depending on the assessment of potential errors made in recording items in the incorrect period (especially sales and receivables).

cutoff tests Procedures applied to transactions selected from those recorded during the cutoff period to provide evidence as to whether the transactions have been recorded in the proper period.

exceptions Differences between a customer's records and the client's records reported on positive or negative confirmations.

lapping A technique used to cover up the embezzlement of cash whereby a cash collection from one customer is stolen by an employee who takes another customer's payment and credits the first customer. This process continues and at any point in time, at least one customer's account is overstated.

negative confirmation A request to customers asking them to respond directly to the auditor only if they disagree with the indicated balance.

open confirmation A request to customers asking them to provide a list of amounts they owe the client; the auditor or client reconciles the customer's output with the client's accounts receivable as a basis for determining the correctness of recorded accounts receivable.

positive confirmation A request to customers asking them to respond directly to the auditor if they agree or disagree with the indicated balance.

roll-forward period The period between an interim date, when a substantive procedure was performed, and the balance sheet date.

roll-forward procedures Procedures performed at or after the balance sheet date to update substantive evidence obtained at an interim date.

timing difference Confirmation exceptions caused by transactions that are in process at the confirmation date, such as in-transit shipments or payments. These are not misstatements.

tolerable misstatement The maximum misstatement in an account balance or class of transactions that the auditor is willing to accept and still conclude that the test results have achieved the audit objective.

Review Questions

A–Introduction to Substantive Testing

13–1 What is the relationship between audit objectives, account balance assertions, and audit procedures?

13–2 Distinguish between planning materiality and tolerable misstatement. How are the two concepts related?

13–3 Explain how audit evidence gathered about accounts receivable also provides evidence about sales and vice versa.

13–4 Why is emphasis usually given to direct tests of the accounts receivable balance rather than the transactions that created that balance?

13–5 Are direct tests of account balances generally more effective in detecting overstatements or understatements? Explain.

13–6 If environmental risk is assessed as low, the auditor obtains less persuasive substantive evidence than if it is assessed as high. Explain this relationship.

13–7 What is the effect on the nature, timing, and extent of substantive tests of accounts receivable when the environmental (inherent and control) risk is assessed as being low instead of high?

13–8 What are the advantages and disadvantages of performing direct tests of account balances prior to the balance sheet date?

B–Developing Audit Procedures

13–9 Identify one substantive test of revenue relating to each of the following assertions:

a. Completeness.

b. Existence.

c. Valuation.

13–10 How can the audit of revenue provide a good opportunity to test the completeness assertion for both sales and accounts receivable?

13–11 From what population should a sample be selected to test the completeness of recorded sales? Explain your choice.

13–12 Explain why a sample should be selected from the sales journal to test the occurrence of the recorded sales.

13–13 Under what circumstances should an auditor consider confirming individual unpaid invoices as opposed to confirming the customer's total balance?

13–14 When should revenue normally be recognized for

a. A construction contractor?

b. An appliance dealer using the installment plan for its receivables?

c. An airline?

d. A manufacturer?

e. A mail-order retailer?

13–15 What is an aged trial balance of accounts receivable? For what purposes does an auditor use it? How does an auditor determine that it is correctly aged?

13–16 Distinguish between the positive, negative, and open forms of accounts receivable confirmation.

13–17 Which confirmation form, the positive or the negative, is considered the more reliable? Why?

13–18 If a confirmation is not returned by a customer, what follow-up work should the auditor perform if it is a

a. Positive confirmation?

b. Negative confirmation?

13–19 Under what circumstances can a customer's confirmation be considered reliable?

13–20 When might an auditor consider using negative confirmations? What factors must be present in the client-customer environment to justify the use of the negative confirmation form?

13–21 Explain why confirmations provide strong evidence about the existence of accounts receivable but only weak evidence about the existence of cash collections.

13–22 What is a confirmation exception? Why is it important to investigate confirmation exceptions?

13–23 What evidence is provided by vouching cash collections after the balance sheet date?

13–24 What are cutoff tests? What assertion(s) do they test?

13–25 What assumptions should a user of financial statements be able to make about the items that make up the balance shown as accounts receivable on the balance sheet?

13–26 What alternative methods might an auditor use to evaluate the reasonableness of accounting estimates?

13–27 How can the auditor determine whether estimated bad debts expense is reasonable?

13–28 Identify and describe the three types of analytical procedures an auditor might use for the revenue cycle.

13–29 How can regression analysis help the auditor determine the reasonableness of recorded sales?

Multiple Choice Questions

*13–30 To test for unsupported entries in the ledger, the direction of audit testing should be from the

a. Journal entries.

b. Ledger entries.

*Adapted from the Uniform CPA examination or the Certified Internal Auditor examination.

c. Original source documents.

d. Externally generated documents.

*13–31 Confirmation is most likely to be a relevant form of evidence with regard to assertions about accounts receivable when the auditor has concerns about the receivables'

a. Valuation.

b. Classification.

c. Existence.

d. Completeness.

*13–32 An auditor should perform alternative procedures to substantiate the existence of accounts receivable when

a. No reply to a positive confirmation request is received.

b. No reply to a negative confirmation request is received.

c. Collectibility of the receivables is in doubt.

d. Pledging of the receivables is probable.

*13–33 Negative confirmation of accounts receivable is less effective than positive confirmation of accounts receivable because

a. A majority of recipients usually lacks the willingness to respond objectively.

b. Some recipients may report incorrect balances that require extensive followup.

c. The auditor can *not* infer that all nonrespondents have verified their account information.

d. Negative confirmations do *not* produce evidential matter that is statistically quantifiable.

*13–34 Which of the following most likely would be detected by an auditor's review of a client's sales cutoff?

a. Unrecorded sales for the year.

b. Lapping of year-end accounts receivable.

c. Excessive sales discounts.

d. Unauthorized goods returned for credit.

*13–35 Tracing bills of lading to sales invoices provides evidence that

a. Shipments to customers were invoiced.

b. Shipments to customers were recorded as sales.

c. Recorded sales were shipped.

d. Invoiced sales were shipped.

*13–36 Which of the following circumstances would most likely cause an auditor to suspect that material irregularities exist in a client's financial statements?

a. Property and equipment are usually sold at a loss before being fully depreciated.

b. Significantly fewer responses to confirmation requests are received than expected.

c. Monthly bank reconciliations usually include several in-transit items.

d. Clerical errors are listed on a computer-generated exception report.

Discussion and Research Questions

*13–37 (Audit of Rent Revenue) Bert Finney, CPA, was engaged to conduct an audit of the financial statements of Clayton Realty Corporation for the month ending January 31, 1994. The examination of monthly rent reconciliations is a vital portion of the audit engagement.

The following rent reconciliation was prepared by the controller of Clayton Realty Corporation and was presented to Finney, who subjected it to various audit procedures:

CLAYTON REALTY CORPORATION
RENT RECONCILIATION
FOR THE MONTH ENDED
JANUARY 31, 1994

Gross apartment rents (Schedule A)	$1,600,800†
Less vacancies (Schedule B)	20,500†
Net apartment rentals	1,580,300
Less unpaid January rents (Schedule C)	7,800†
Total	1,572,500
Add prepaid rent collected (Apartment 116)	500†
Total cash collected	$1,573,00†

Schedules A, B, and C are available to Finney but are not presented here. Finney has conducted a study and evaluation of the system of internal control and found that it could be relied on to produce reliable accounting information. Cash receipts from rental operations are deposited in a special bank account.

Required:
What substantive audit procedures should Finney employ during the audit to substantiate the validity of each of the dollar amounts marked by the †?

*13–38 (Audit of Service Revenue) You are engaged in your first audit of the Licitra Pest Control Company for the year ended December 31, 1994. The company began doing business in January 1994 and provides pest control services for industrial enterprises.

Additional Information:

1. The office staff consists of a bookkeeper, a typist, and the president, Angela Licitra. In addition, the Company employs 20 pest controllers on an hourly basis who are assigned to individual territories to make both monthly and emergency visits to customers' premises. The pest controllers submit weekly time reports that include each customer's name and the time devoted. Time charges for emergency visits are shown separately from regular monthly visits on the report.
2. Customers are required to sign annual contracts, which are prenumbered and prepared in duplicate. The original is filed in numerical order

by contract anniversary date and the copy is given to the customer. The contract entitles the customer to pest control services once each month. Emergency visits are billed separately.

3. Fees for monthly services are payable in advance—quarterly, semiannually, or annually—and are recorded on the books as "income from services" when the cash is received. All payments are by checks received by mail.
4. Prenumbered invoices for contract renewals are prepared in triplicate from information in the contract file. The original invoice is sent to the customer 20 days prior to the due date of payment, the duplicate copy is filed chronologically by due date, and the triplicate copy is filed alphabetically by customer. If payment is not received by 15 days after the due date, a cancellation notice is sent to the customer and a copy of the notice is attached to the customer's contract. The bookkeeper notifies the pest controllers of all contract cancellations and reinstatements and requires written acknowledgment of receipt of such notices. Licitra approves all cancellations and reinstatements of contracts.
5. Prenumbered invoices for emergency services are prepared weekly from information shown on pest controllers' time reports. The customer is billed at 200 percent of the pest controller's hourly rate. These invoices, prepared in triplicate and distributed as described, are recorded on the books as "income from services" at the billing date. Payment is due 30 days after the invoice date.
6. All remittances are received by the typist, who prepares a daily list of collections and stamps a restrictive endorsement on the checks. A copy of the list is forwarded with the checks to the bookkeeper, who posts the date and amount received on the copies of the invoice in both the alphabetical and chronological files. After posting, the copy of the invoice is transferred from the chronological file to the daily cash receipts binder, which serves as a subsidiary record for the cash receipts book. The bookkeeper totals the amounts of all remittances received, posts this total to the cash receipts book, and attaches daily remittance tapes to the paid invoices in the daily cash receipts binder.
7. The bookkeeper prepares a daily bank deposit slip and compares the total with the total amount shown on the daily remittance tapes. All remittances are deposited in the bank the day they are received. (Cash receipts from sources other than services need not be considered.)
8. Financial statements are prepared on the accrual basis.

Required:

a. List the audit procedures you would employ in the examination of the Income from Services account for 1994.

b. You are considering using the services of a reputable outside mailing service for the confirmation of accounts receivable balances. The service would prepare and mail the confirmation requests and remove the returned confirmations from the envelopes and give them directly to you.

   What reliance, if any, could you place on the services of the outside mailing service? State the reasons for your answer.

13–39 (Accounts Receivable Assertions and Audit Procedures) You are planning the audit of LeFlam Manufacturing Company's *accounts receivable*. For each of the two independent situations below, indicate the appropriate detection risk for each assertion (E = existence, C = completeness, V = valuation, and R = rights), identify the audit procedures you would select from the matrix of procedures in Exhibit 13.10, and discuss why you believe that those procedures are appropriate.

a. *Assertions*	*E*	C	*V*	*R*
Inherent risk (High, Moderate, Low)	H	H	L	L
Control risk (H, M, L)	H	H	L	L
Detection risk (H, M, L)	?	?	?	?

b. Assertions	*E*	C	*V*	*R*
Inherent risk (High, Moderate, Low)	L	L	H	L
Control risk (H, M, L)	L	L	H	L
Detection risk (H, M, L)	?	?	?	?

13–40 (Sales Assertions and Audit Procedures) You are planning the audit of LeFlam Manufacturing Company's *sales*. For each of the two independent situations below, indicate the appropriate detection risk for each assertion (E = existence, C = completeness, and V = valuation), identify the audit procedures you would select from the matrix of procedures in Exhibit 13.10, and discuss why you believe that those procedures are appropriate.

a. *Assertions*	*E*	C	*V*
Inherent risk (High, Moderate, Low)	L	M	M
Control risk (H, M, L)	L	M	M
Detection risk (H, M, L)	?	?	?

b. Assertions	*E*	C	*V*
Inherent risk (High, Moderate, Low)	H	L	L
Control risk (H, M, L)	H	L	L
Detection risk (H, M, L)	?	?	?

*13–41 (Accounts Receivable Audit Procedures) Sean Edwards, CPA, is engaged to audit the financial statements of Matthews Wholesaling for the year ended December 31, 1988. Edwards obtained and documented an understanding of the internal control structure relating to the accounts receivable and assessed control risk relating to accounts receivable at the maximum level. Edwards requested and obtained from Matthews an aged accounts receivable schedule listing the total amount owed by each customer as of December 31, 1988, and sent positive confirmation requests to a sample of the customers.

Required:
What additional substantive audit procedures should Edwards consider applying in auditing the accounts receivable?

13–42 (Confirmation of Receivables) Confirmation of accounts receivable balances is a generally accepted auditing procedure when it is reasonable and practical.

Required:

a. Describe the conditions that should exist for confirmations of receivables to be a reliable source of evidence.

b. What factors should the auditor consider in deciding whether to use positive or negative confirmations?

c. Under what circumstances might confirmation of receivables not be reasonable and practical?

d. Describe the alternative procedures auditors can use when confirmations are not returned by some customers. Which of these procedures are the most reliable?

13–43 (Cutoff Procedures) Sales cutoff tests are performed to obtain evidence that sales are recorded in the proper period. You are to perform a cutoff test of sales for a manufacturer that uses prenumbered bills of lading and sales invoices. All sales are FOB shipping point.

Required:
How would you perform the cutoff test if the primary audit concern is the

a. Existence of sales?

b. Completeness of sales?

*13–44 (Accounts Receivable Lapping) During the year, Strang Corporation began to encounter cash flow difficulties, and a cursory review by management revealed receivable collection problems. Strang's management engaged Elaine Stanley, CPA, to perform a special investigation. Stanley studied the billing and collection cycle and noted the following.

The accounting department employs one bookkeeper who receives and opens all incoming mail. This bookkeeper is also responsible for depositing receipts, filing remittance advices on a daily basis, recording receipts in the cash receipts journal, and for posting receipts in the individual customer accounts and the general ledger accounts. There are no cash sales. The bookkeeper prepares and controls the mailing of monthly statements to customers.

The concentration of functions and the receivable collection problems caused Stanley to suspect that a systematic defalcation of customers' payments through a delayed posting of remittances (lapping of accounts receivable) is present. Stanley was surprised to find that no customers complained about receiving erroneous monthly statements.

Required:
Identify the procedures that Stanley should perform to determine whether lapping exists. *Do not discuss deficiencies in the system of internal control.*

13–45 (Existence and Completeness) The existence and completeness assertions are complementary but require different audit approaches.

Required:

a. Why is it more difficult to test for the completeness than the existence/occurrence of an account balance or a class of transactions?

b. What procedures can an auditor use to test the completeness of accounts receivable and sales?

13–46 (Using Generalized Audit Software) Your audit client, Daman, Inc., has a fully computerized accounts receivable system. There are two master files, a customer data file and an unpaid invoice file. The customer data file contains the customer's name, billing address, shipping address, identification number, phone number, purchase and cash payment history, and credit limit. For each unpaid invoice, the second file contains the customer's identification number, invoice number and date, date of shipment, method of shipment, credit terms, and gross invoice amount.

Required:
Discuss how generalized audit software could be used to aid in the examination of Daman's accounts receivable.

13–47 (Performing a Cutoff Test) The following sales were selected for a cutoff test of Genius Monitors, Inc., for the December 31, 1994 financial statements. All sales are credit sales and are shipped FOB shipping point. They are recorded on the billing date.

Invoice Number	Sales Price	Date Shipped	Date Billed
36590	2,750	12/28/94	12/29/94
36591	25,390	12/29/94	1/2/95
36592	9,200	1/3/95	12/31/94
36593	570	1/2/95	1/3/95

Required:
a. What adjusting journal entries, if any, would you make for each of these items? (Do not consider the inventory implications of this cutoff.)
b. What complications are created by shipping terms of FOB destination?
c. Under what circumstances might an auditor accept sales that are recorded when shipped even though they are shipped FOB destination?

*13–48 (Audit of Notes Receivable) You are in charge of your second yearly examination of the financial statements of Hillsboro Equipment Corporation, a distributor of construction equipment. Hillsboro's equipment sales are either outright cash sales or a combination of a substantial cash payment and one or two 60- or 90-day nonrenewable interest-bearing notes for the balance. Title to the equipment passes to the customer when the initial cash payment is made. The notes, some of which are secured by the customer, are dated when the cash payment is made (the day the equipment is delivered). If the customer prefers to purchase the equipment under an installment payment plan, Hillsboro arranges for the customer to obtain such financing from a local bank.

You begin your fieldwork to examine the December 31 financial statements on January 5, knowing that you must leave temporarily for another engagement on January 7 after outlining the audit program for your assistant. Before leaving, you inquire about the assistant's progress in his examination of notes receivable. Among other things, he shows you a working paper listing the makers' names, the due dates, the interest rates, and amounts of 17 outstanding notes receivable totaling $100,000. The working paper contains the following notations:

1. Reviewed internal control structure and found it to be satisfactory.
2. Total of $100,000 agrees with general ledger control account.
3. Traced listing of notes to sales journal.

The assistant also informs you that he is preparing to request positive confirmations of the amounts of all outstanding notes receivable and that no other audit work has been performed in the examination of notes receivable and interest arising from equipment sales. There were no outstanding accounts receivable for equipment sales at the end of the year.

Required:

a. What information should he confirm with the customers?
b. State the objectives of auditing the notes receivable and list the additional audit procedures that the assistant should apply in his audit of the account for notes receivable arising from equipment sales (Hillsboro has no other notes). No subsidiary ledger is maintained.
c. You ask your assistant to examine all notes receivable on hand before you leave. He returns in 30 minutes from the office safe where the notes are kept and reports that notes on hand that have dates prior to January 1 total only $75,000.

    List the possible explanations that you would expect from the client for the $25,000 difference. (Eliminate fraud or misappropriation from your consideration.) Indicate beside each explanation the audit procedures you would apply to determine whether it is correct.

13–49 (Audit of Membership Fees) You are auditing the revenue from membership fees of your local chapter of the Institute of Management Accounting, of which you are not a member. The local chapter receives an allocation of national dues.

Required:

Describe some analytical procedures you could use to provide some assurance that such revenue is fairly stated.

13–50 (Analytical Procedures) You are performing analytical procedures on the accounts in the revenue cycle of the LeFlam Manufacturing Company for the year ended December 31, 1994. Comparative balance sheets and income statements are shown in Exhibit 13.9.

Required:

a. Calculate the following for 1994 (the calculations for 1993, obtained from last year's working papers, and the most recent industry averages are shown in parentheses):
    1. Turnover of average receivables (1993 = 8.578, industry = 6.47).
    2. Ratio of receivables to current assets (1993 = .222, industry = .25).
    3. Ratio of sales returns and allowances to sales (1993 = .016, industry = .03).
    4. Gross profit percent (1993 = .273, industry = .25).
    5. Days' sales in ending receivables (use 365 days) (1993 = 43.055, industry = 57.5).

b. Analyze the audit significance of this information in terms of:
   1. Possible causes of variances from prior year or industry data.
   2. The effect on substantive audit procedures. That is, what audit procedures would help you determine whether these variances reflect material misstatements in the current year financial statements.

13–51 (Estimated Warranty Expense) You are auditing the estimated liability for warranty expense of an automobile manufacturer for the year ended December 31, 1994. The automobiles carry a five-year or 50,000 mile warranty (whichever comes first) covering labor and parts on major components. This warranty policy has been in effect since October 1, 1991. Previously, the warranty was for three years or 36,000 miles.

Required:

a. Should you be most concerned about the potential overstatement or understatement of this liability? Explain your answer.

b. What alternative approaches might you use to verify the reasonableness of this estimate? Which approach do you believe will be most effective and efficient?

c. What audit procedures would you perform to verify the reasonableness of this estimated liability?

*13–52 (Summarizing Confirmation Results) The following Accounts Receivable—Confirmation Statistics working paper (indexed B-3) was prepared by an audit assistant during the calendar year 1994 audit of Lewis County Water Co., Inc., a continuing audit client. The engagement supervisor is reviewing the working papers.

Lewis County Water Co., Inc.
Accounts Receivable—Confirmation Statistics
December 31, 1994

Index B-3

	Accounts		Dollars	
Confirmation Requests	**Number**	**Percent**	**Amount**	**Percent**
Positives	54	2.7%	$ 260,000	13.0%
Negatives	140	7.0	20,000	10.0
Total sent	194	9.7	280,000	23.0
Accounts selected/client asked us not to confirm	6	0.3		
Total selected for testing	200	10.0		
Total accounts receivable at 12/31/91, confirm date	2,000	100	$2,000,000 †*	100
Results				
Replies received through 2/25/92				
Positives—no exception	44 C	2.2	180,000	9.0
Negatives—did not reply or replied "no exception"	120 C	6.0	16,000	.8
Total confirmed without exception	164	8.2	196,000	9.8

Results	Accounts		Dollars	
	Number	Percent	Amount	Percent
Differences reported and resolved, no adjustment				
Positives	6	.3	30,000	1.5
Negatives	12	.6	2,000	.1
Total	18	.9	32,000	1.6
Differences found to be potential adjustments				
Positives	2 CX	.1	10,000	.5
Negatives	8 CX	.4	2,000	.1
Total—.6% adjustment, immaterial	10	.5	12,000	.6
Accounts selected/client asked us not to confirm	6	.3		

Tickmark Legend:
†Agreed to accounts receivable subsidiary ledger
*Agreed to general ledger and lead schedule
§Includes one related-party transaction
C Confirmed without exception, W/P B-4
CX Confirmed with exception, W/P B-5

Overall conclusion: The potential adjustment of $12,000 or .6 percent is below materiality threshold; therefore, the accounts receivable balance is fairly stated.

Required:
Describe the deficiencies in the working paper that the engagement supervisor should discover. Assume that the accounts were selected for confirmation on the basis of a sample that was properly planned and documented on working paper B–2.

13–53 (Follow-up Work: Accounts Receivable) You have sent confirmations to approximately 40 customers of Berg-Shovick Express, a long-time audit client experiencing some financial difficulty. The company sells specialized high-technology goods. You have received confirmations from 32 of the 40 positive confirmations sent. There were a small number of errors noted on these accounts, but the projected amount of errors on the 30 items returned is just below tolerable error. The following information is available to you:

Book value of receivables	$7,782,292
Book value of items selected for confirmations	$3,100,110
Book value of items confirmed	$1,464,000
Audit value of items confirmed	$1,335,000

Summary of items selected but confirmations not returned:

Name	Outstanding Amount	Management Comments on Account Balance
Yunkel Specialty Mfg	$ 432,000	Regular sales, but extended credit terms were given on $200,000 of goods. Yunkel has responded that it does not respond to confirmations.

Hi-Tech Combonitics	$ 300,000	No response to either confirmation request. Management indicates the sale was a special-term sale and the goods are being held for the convenience of this company. The company is located in Albuquerque, New Mexico, and recently had a fire in its main production plant and expects to resume production early next month. The goods will be shipped as soon as production begins, but the sale has legally been completed.
Beaver Dam Electronics	$ 275,000	Account balance represents sales of specialty products made in late December. The president of Berg-Shovick has orally confirmed the receivable because Beaver Dam electronics is 50% owned by him.
California Hi-Fi	$ 200,000	Regular sales, but company has renegotiated its account balance due because of defective merchandise. Management has indicated it has issued a credit to the company, but because management had inspected the goods on the customer's property, it did not require the return of the merchandise. It expects the company to pay the $200,000.
Brenner Specialties	$ 175,000	Regular sales. This is a new company. Most of the sales ($100,000) were made in December.
Sprague Electronics	$ 100,000	Regular sales. Customer is negotiating a potential return of defective items.
Williams Pipeline	$ 100,000	Williams is a large company. Prior experience indicates that it does not respond to confirmations.
Long Tom Towers	$ 54,110	Customer is new this year and is located in Medicine Hat, Saskatchewan.

Required:

a. Indicate the audit procedures (and be specific as to what those procedures will be doing) to complete the work on accounts receivable related to the confirmation process. In other words, identify the specific alternative audit procedures that should be performed. (Note: You do not need to specify a particular procedure for each account balance, but you must indicate the necessary procedures that would address all of the open items.)

b. Assuming that all items could not be cleared to the auditor's satisfaction, identify the audit procedures that should be implemented to finish auditing the valuation of accounts receivable.

13–54 **(Research)** Many management frauds involve improper recording of revenue. Using *The Wall Street Journal*, *Business Week*, and similar sources, find two or three articles reporting management fraud involving revenue and do the following:

a. Read the articles and identify the means companies use to misstate revenues.

b. Identify the procedures the auditor could have used to discover the fraud.

13–55 **(Research)** Revenue recognition and related audit procedures differ from industry to industry. Select one of the AICPA *Industry Audit and Accounting Guides* and write a report on the unique aspects of revenue recognition and audit procedures for that industry.

Case

13–56 MiniScribe Case (Based on "Cooking the Books," *The Wall Street Journal*, September 11, 1989 and 'MiniScribe's Investigators Determine That 'Massive Fraud' Was Perpetrated," *The Wall Street Journal*, September 12, 1989).

In October 1988, MiniScribe, a computer disk drive manufacturer, announced its 13th consecutive record-breaking quarter while its competitors were laying off hundreds of employees. Its receivables had increased significantly, and inventories had increased to a dangerous level because disk drives can become obsolete from one quarter to the next. Its stock price had quintupled in just two years. The company had apparently risen from the dead under the leadership of Q. T. Wiles, who had resurrected other companies and was known as "Dr. Fix-It." It looked as if he had done it again.

Seven months later, it was announced that MiniScribe's sales gains had been fabricated. What was supposed to be the crowning achievement of Wiles's career became an epitaph; he resigned and is living in near seclusion. An internal investigation concluded that senior management apparently perpetrated a massive fraud on the company, its directors, its outside auditors, and the investing public. Most of MiniScribe's top management was dismissed, and layoffs shrank its employment by more than 30 percent in one year. MiniScribe might have to write off as much as $200 million in bad inventory and uncollectible receivables.

Wiles's unrealistic sales targets and abusive management style created a pressure cooker that drove managers to cook the books or perish. And cook they did—booking sales prematurely, manipulating reserves, and simply fabricating figures—to maintain the illusion of unbounded growth even after the industry was hit by a severe slump.

When Wiles arrived at MiniScribe in mid-1985, it had just lost its biggest customer, IBM, which decided to make its own drives. With the personal computer industry then slumping, MiniScribe was drowning in red ink.

Dr. Fix-It's prescription was to cut 20 percent of its work force and overhaul the company from top to bottom. As part of the overhaul, several semiautonomous divisions were created. Each division manager set the division's own budget, sales quotas, incentives, and work rules. The company became a chaotic Babel of at least 20 minicompanies that were constantly being changed and reorganized. One employee held 20 different positions in less than seven years.

Wiles turned up the heat under his lieutenants. Four times a year, he would summon as many as a hundred employees for several days of intense meetings at which they were force-fed his idiosyncratic management philosophy. At one of the first such meetings he attended, Wiles demanded that two controllers stand, and he fired them on the spot, saying, "That's just to show everyone I'm in control of the company."

At each of these meetings, division managers had to present and defend their business plans. Invariably, Wiles would find such plans deficient and would berate their authors in front of their peers. A former controller says Wiles would throw, kick, and rip the plan books that displeased him, showering his intimidated audience with paper while yelling, "Why don't you understand this? Why can't you understand how to do this?"

Then something changed. Wiles started saying, "I no longer want to be remembered as a turnaround artist. I want to be remembered as the man who made MiniScribe a billion-dollar company." Sales objectives became the company's driving force and financial results became the sole determinant of whether bonuses were awarded. Wiles said, "This is the number we want to hit first quarter, second quarter, third quarter and so on," and it was amazing to see how close they could get to the number they wanted to hit.

Hitting the number became a companywide obsession. Although many high-tech manufacturers accelerate shipments at the end of a quarter to boost sales—a practice known as "stuffing the channel"—MiniScribe went several steps beyond that. On one occasion, an analyst relates, the company shipped more than twice as many disk drives to a computer manufacturer as had been ordered: a former sales manager says the excess shipment was worth about $9 million. MiniScribe later said it had shipped the excess drives by mistake. The extras were returned—but by then MiniScribe had posted the sale at the higher number. Wiles denied this practice.

Other accounting maneuvers involved shipments of disk drives from MiniScribe's factory in Singapore. Most shipments went by air freight, but a squeeze on air cargo space toward the end of each quarter would force some shipments onto cargo ships, which required up to two weeks for transit. On several occasions, said a former division manager, MiniScribe executives looking to raise sales changed purchase orders to show that a customer took title to a shipment in Singapore when, in fact, title would not change until the drives were delivered in the United States.

MiniScribe executives tried to persuade an audit team that 1986 year-end results should include as sales the cargo on a freighter that they contended had set sail in late December. The audit team declined to do so. Eventually, the cargo and the freighter, which did not exist, were simply forgotten.

MiniScribe executives also found other ways to inflate sales figures. One was to manipulate reserves for returns of defective merchandise and bad debts. The problem of inadequate reserves grew so great that private analysts began noticing it. MiniScribe was booking less than 1 percent reserves: the rest of the industry had reserves ranging from 4 percent to 10 percent.

To avoid booking losses on returns in excess of its skimpy reserves, defective drives would be tossed onto a "dog pile" and booked as inventory. Eventually, the dog-pile drives would be shipped out again to new customers, continuing the cycle. Returns of defective merchandise ran as high as 15 percent.

At a time of strong market demand, such ploys enabled MiniScribe to seem to grow almost exponentially, posting sales of $185 million in 1986 and $362 million in 1987. In early 1988, Wiles was confidently forecasting a $660 million year, and he held fast to his rosy forecast even as disk drive sales started slipping industrywide in late spring and nosedived in the autumn. Meanwhile, Wiles increased the pressure on his managers. Division reports would be doctored as they rose from one bureaucratic level to the next.

Before long, the accounting gimmickry became increasingly brazen. Division managers were told to "force the numbers." Workers whispered that bricks were being shipped just so a division could claim to have met its quota. Others joked that unwanted disk drives were being shipped and returned so often that they had to be repackaged because the boxes wore out.

Employees also joked about shipments to "account BW," an acronym for "big warehouse." But that wasn't just a joke. MiniScribe established several warehouses around the country and in Canada as "just-in-time" suppliers for distributors. Customers weren't invoiced until they received shipments from the warehouses. MiniScribe, however, was booking shipments to the warehouses as sales. The number of disk drives shipped to the warehouses was at MiniScribe's discretion. It is estimated that between $80 million and $100 million worth of unordered disk drives went to the warehouses.

Wall Street began to smell trouble. Analysts could find no significant customers other than Compaq to support MiniScribe's bullish forecasts. Several major anticipated orders from Apple Computer and Digital Equipment Corp. fell through. MiniScribe reported a fourth-quarter loss and a drop in net income for 1988 despite a 66 percent increase in sales—on paper, that is. A week later, Wiles abruptly resigned. The stock price tumbled from a high of $15 to less than $3 per share, a decline that upset many stockholders!

An investigative committee of MiniScribe's outside directors reported that senior company officials

- Apparently broke into locked trunks containing the auditors' working papers during the year-end 1986 audit and changed inventory figures, inflating inventory values by approximately $1 million.
- Packaged bricks and shipped them to distributors as disk drives in 1987, recording $4.3 million in sales, and when the shipments were returned, MiniScribe inflated its inventory by the purported cost of the bricks.
- Packaged approximately 6,300 disk drives that had been contaminated to inflate inventory during 1988's fourth quarter.

Several lawsuits have been filed charging MiniScribe with engineering phony sales artificially to inflate its stock to benefit insiders. The suits also charge that its auditors participated in the conspiracy by falsely certifying the company's financial statements.

Required:

Write an analysis of MiniScribe's rise and fall, identifying the following:

a. How MiniScribe inflated its financial statements.

b. The factors that lead to the inflated financial statements.

c. The red flags that should have raised the auditor's suspicions about phony sales and other attempts by MiniScribe to inflate income.

d. Normal audit procedures that could have uncovered the falsified numbers in the financial statements.

End Notes

1. Abraham Briloff, "Disappearing Act: How Manufactured Homes' Profit Vanished," *Barrons*, May 29, 1989, 14.
2. *APB Statement No. 4*, "Basic Concepts and Accounting Principles Underlying Financial Statements of Business Enterprises" (New York: AICPA, 1970), chap. 6, paragraph 150.
3. National Commission on Fraudulent Financial Reporting, *Report* (New York: NCFFR, 1987), 112.
4. "Audit Risk Alert—1989," Supplement to *The CPA Letter*, December 1989.

CHAPTER

14

Learning Objectives

Through studying this chapter, you will be able to:

1. Understand the factors that should be considered when planning, performing, and evaluating a substantive sample.
2. Describe the different sampling methods that can be used to test account balances and when each is appropriate to use.
3. Determine how statistically valid samples can be selected.
4. Develop the ability to use statistical sampling methods.
5. Understand alternative courses of action to consider when sample results indicate that there may be a material misstatement in an account balance.

Sampling for Substantive Tests of Account Balances

Chapter Contents

Chapter Overview

Many account balances are composed of a large number of individual items, such as customer balances and inventory items. In such cases, it is not practical to audit all of the items. Therefore, the auditor selects a sample of these items on which to perform certain audit procedures. This chapter describes several sampling plans and sample selection methods the auditor might use for this purpose. It also explains the circumstances in which each of these plans and methods is most appropriate.

Statistical sampling helps the auditor (a) to design an efficient sample, (b) to measure the sufficiency of the evidential matter obtained, and (c) to evaluate the sample results. By using statistical theory, the auditor can quantify sampling risk to assist himself in limiting it to a level he considers acceptable. [AU 350.46]

A–INTRODUCTION

When buying a basket of apples, you want to be sure that the number of rotten apples does not exceed some tolerable limit. If you know that the produce manager at the store checks the apples before putting them on the fruit counter (throwing away any that are rotten), places the new apples at the back of the counter so that the older ones are sold first, and checks the old stock to be sure that any that have rotted while on the counter are thrown away, you may feel safe in buying a basket of apples without spending much time checking for rotten apples because the controls are good. If you are unfamiliar with the store or are aware that the produce manager is careless or does not even bother to check the apples, you will want to obtain more assurance that there are not too many rotten apples in the basket. If it is a small basket, you may look at all of the apples. If it is a large basket, you may not have time to check all of them, so you look at only a sample to determine whether to buy the basket. If you have not looked at all of the apples before buying the basket, there is always a risk that there are more rotten ones than you can tolerate.

Many of the substantive procedures the auditor chooses to perform are, similarly, based on sampling. It usually takes too much time to test every transaction or all of the details in an account balance. The rotten apples are analogous to misstatements in accounting populations. The objective of substantive sampling is to estimate the amount of misstatement in a class of transactions or account balance; if the amount is too large, the client should make corrections or the auditor will have to modify the report. When sampling is used, there is always a risk that the sample results, in combination with the evidence obtained from other procedures, will cause the auditor to reach the wrong conclusion about the amount of misstatement in the population tested. The accounting profession, and the legal and business communities generally agree, however, that this risk (audit risk), if held to an appropriately low level, is acceptable.

As with tests of controls, auditors may choose to use either statistical or nonstatistical sampling for substantive testing. Within statistical sampling, several alternative methods are available. You need to understand the conditions for which each method is appropriate and the circumstances for which each method is most effective and efficient.

This chapter discusses the alternative sampling methods the auditor may choose to use, identifies criteria to assist the auditor in determining the number of items to include in the sample, identifies sample selection methodology, and presents alternative methods to evaluate statistical sample results and relates those results to substantive audit procedures.

Substantive Sampling Considerations

An auditor chooses to perform direct tests of many account balances (substantive tests) because it is not possible to gather sufficient evidence to reduce audit risk to an acceptable level without directly examining the composition of account balances. In other words, for many balances, it is not possible to rely on the organization's control structure and substantive tests of transactions to reduce audit risk to an acceptable level. Fortunately, the auditor has a number of sampling methods from which to choose, including nonstatistical sampling and various statistical sampling methodologies to use in gathering sufficient audit evidence on material account balance assertions and related amounts.

The basic steps involved in using sampling for substantive tests of account balances remain the same whether nonstatistical or statistical sampling approaches are used. The implementation of each step, however, varies with the particular sampling methodology used. These are the basic steps for utilizing sampling in a test of details:

- Specify the audit objective for the test.
- Define a misstatement.
- Define the population to which the sampling relates.
- Choose a sampling method appropriate to the audit test.
- Determine the sample size appropriate for the test with appropriate consideration given to the risk of misstatement in the account, sampling risk, and the auditor's assessment of tolerable misstatement.
- Determine and implement an appropriate methodology to select the sample.
- Audit the selected items.
- Evaluate the sample results, including the projection of misstatements to the population and consider the risk that material misstatements may exist in the population.
- Document the sampling procedure and results obtained.[1]

Determine the Audit Objective of the Test

Sampling procedures are appropriate when the auditor chooses to perform direct tests of audit assertions or account balances. Often the auditor performs detailed tests of account balances that satisfy all the important assertions for the account. However, for most accounts, the auditor uses sampling to test some assertions while using other procedures for other assertions applicable to the account balance. Consider inventory, for example. The auditor will likely use sampling to test the valuation assertion by selecting individual inventory items and gathering evidence on the correctness of the recorded cost. However, the auditor may also use analytical procedures, such as turnover analysis, to help analyze the possibility of obsolete inventory (also a valuation assertion). Thus, it is important to keep in mind that the auditor's use of sampling does not necessarily imply that the results by themselves will provide persuasive evidence on the correctness of the account balance. The sample results will likely have to be combined with other audit results before an audit judgment as to the correctness of the account balance can be made.

Sampling is used in auditing account balances in two primary ways: (1) to determine the reasonableness of a class of transactions or an account balance, such as accounts receivable, by performing detailed analysis of items making up the account balance and projecting the results to the account balance as a whole or (2) to estimate some amount, such as the LIFO index to estimate the LIFO value of inventory. In the latter approach, the auditor might take a sample of inventory, calculate a LIFO value, and use the LIFO value in computing an index to adjust inventory to LIFO for financial statement purposes. This chapter covers only the use of sampling to help determine the reasonableness of an account balance.

Define Misstatement

The auditor using a sampling method encounters many situations in which the audited value of an item, or a customer's confirmation of the item, differs from its recorded value. The auditor is required to project misstatements to the population as a whole to determine whether material misstatements may exist in the account. Thus, it is important that the auditor define in advance what constitutes a misstatement. All identifiable differences might not result in misstatements. Some public accounting firms define a **misstatement** as differences in recorded values and audited values that change pre-tax income arising from any nonexcludable misstatement(s) (income effect). Other firms define it as a difference that affects the account total (account misstatement). Auditors have concluded that certain types of differences are **excludable misstatements.** These include misstatements (1) that the client has independently detected and corrected within the normal accounting system before the auditor begins substantive testing and (2) that the auditor will evaluate more fully in some other procedure, such as cutoff errors when there is a separate cutoff test. A customer, for example, may respond to a confirmation stating that the balance did not reflect a payment that had been made. If the auditor determines that payment had been received but not recorded before year-end, the account balance is misstated. This error should not be projected twice to the population—the first time based on the sample results and the second time based on a separate cash receipts cutoff test. Therefore, to avoid double counting, it should be treated as an error for the cutoff test only.

The identification of a misstatement involves audit judgment. For example, an individual account balance may be misstated because a customer's payment has been credited to the wrong customer. Such an error does not constitute a misstatement for the substantive test of the accounts receivable balance because the auditor gives an opinion on the total of the account, not the individual balances in the subsidiary ledger. The auditor should, however, be sure to check this incorrect posting for indication of possible lapping by accounts receivable personnel. This error should also be brought to the client's attention so the customer's records can be corrected.

Define the Population

The population is that group of items that make up a class of transactions or an account balance that the auditor wants to test. The population, as defined for sampling purposes, does not include any items that the auditor has decided to examine 100 percent or items that will be tested separately. Because sample results can be projected to only that group of items from which the sample is selected, it is extremely important to define the population properly. For example, a sample selected from the inventory at one location can be used only to estimate the amount of misstatement at that location, not at other locations.

Some accounts, such as those that are fully paid, or that contain credit balances, may contain zero or negative values. The auditor needs to decide whether these customer balances should be included in the accounts receivable population or tested separately.

Define the Sampling Unit. **Sampling units** are the individual auditable elements, as defined by the auditor, that constitute the population. A sampling unit for confirming accounts receivable could be defined as the individual customer account balances, individual unpaid invoices, or a combination of both. The choice depends on considerations of effectiveness and efficiency. Some customers are more likely to return a confirmation for a specific invoice than for an entire account balance, for example, customers who are on a voucher system. If a customer does not return a positive confirmation, alternative procedures must be performed. These procedures include identifying subsequent payments and/or vouching the sales transactions to supporting documents. If customers typically pay by invoice, it will be more efficient to perform alternative procedures on individual invoices than on total balances.

Completeness of the Population. A sample is selected from a physical representation of the population, such as a list of customer balances. The auditor needs assurance that the list accurately represents the population. A common procedure is to foot the list and reconcile it with the general ledger.

Identify Individually Significant Items. Many accounts and transaction classes are composed of a few relatively large items and many smaller items. For example, inventory is often composed of a small number of very large items (such as finished goods) and a large number of smaller items (usually raw material components). A graphical example of many accounting populations is shown in Exhibit 14.1.

A significant portion of the total value of many accounting populations is concentrated in a small number of items, each with a value in excess of a specific dollar limit. To minimize sampling risk, the auditor constructs a sample to include all large dollar values, such as all items in excess of a dollar limit shown as in Exhibit 14.1 in the line A–A'. The items above the line are examined 100 percent. The examination of these items represents a census of those items and is not considered a sample. Those items are often referred to as the **top stratum.** The remaining items are then sampled using one of the sampling methods described in this chapter. The audit results reflect the census of top stratum items and a sample projection of items sampled.

The designation of the value in which the auditor chooses to look at all items is a matter of audit judgment. The division of the population into two or more subgroups is referred to as **stratification.** For example, the population could be further stratified into subpopulations represented by points B and C in Exhibit 14.1 where the items in each of the subgroups would be more alike (more homogeneous). As will be discussed later, stratification of the population into more homogenous subpopulations generally creates audit efficiency. The stratification process can be enhanced with the use of audit software that has the capability of creating a graph of the population of book values similar to Exhibit 14.1.

Exhibit 14.1

STRATIFICATION OF TYPICAL ACCOUNTING POPULATIONS

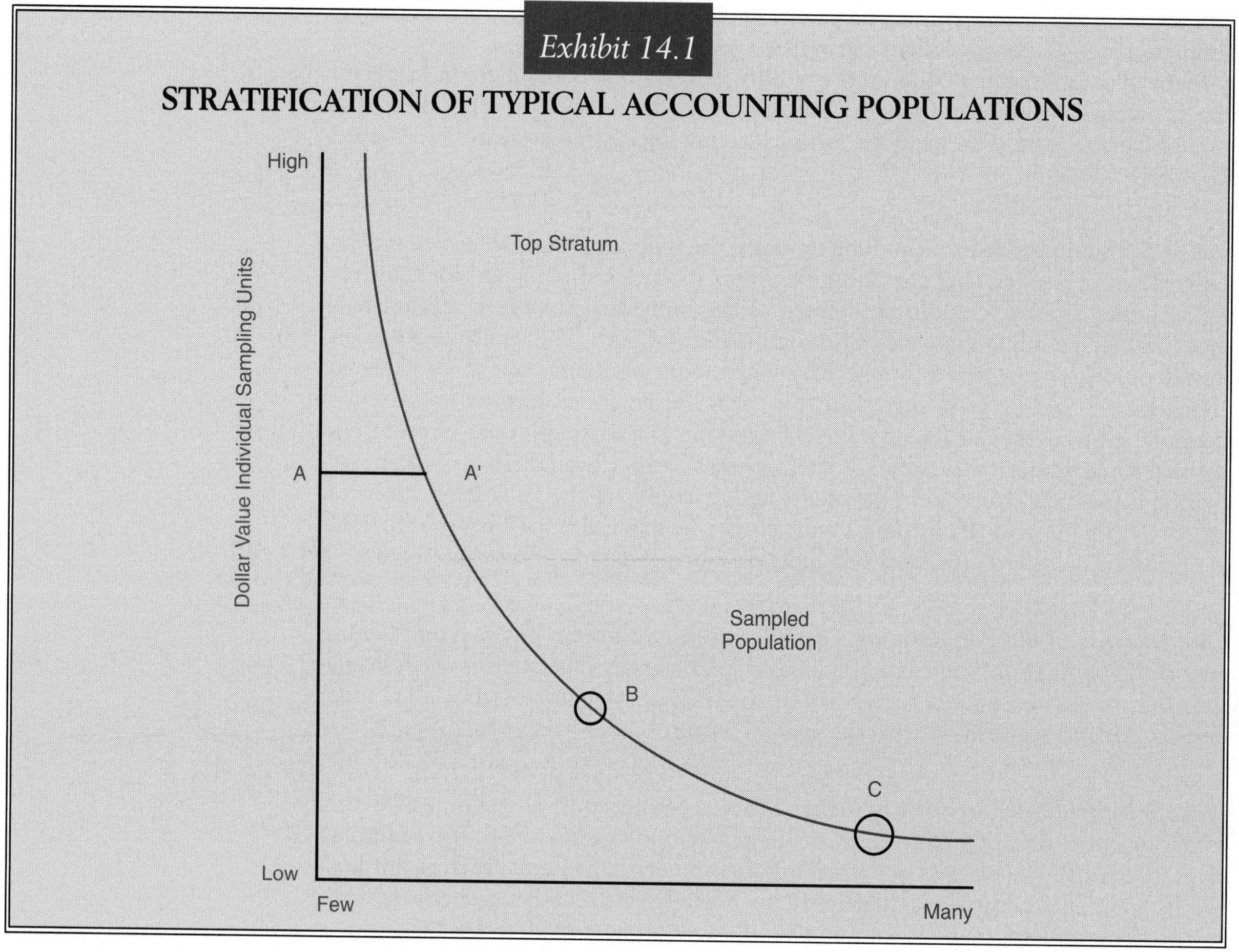

Choose a Sampling Method

The auditor has a choice among a number of different types of sampling techniques, both nonstatistical and statistical sampling. Each method has distinct advantages and possible disadvantages. The methods differ in the following ways:

- *Measure of sampling risk.* The statistical methods provide an objective measure of sampling risk within specified tolerable limits of misstatement. Nonstatistical methodologies cannot provide such measurements.
- *Tests for account balance overstatement.* One statistical method (probability proportional to size sampling) is designed to test whether there is an acceptable risk of account balance overstatement. Other statistical methods are designed to test for both overstatement and understatement.
- *Statistical estimates of account balances.* One set of statistical methods, referred to below as *classical estimation techniques,* is designed to create estimates of account balances within tolerable limits of misstatement and acceptable levels of risk. Another statistical method (probability proportional to size sampling) is designed to provide an estimate of the maximum likely overstatement in the population.

Research studies have identified those circumstances in which alternative statistical methods are most reliable, meaning they provide the best estimate of the amount of misstatement in the population at the desired sampling risk level.[2] The selection of a method depends on

- The audit objective (testing for overstatements, understatements, or both).
- The method of selecting a sample (selecting random dollars or random items).
- Expected misstatement conditions (few or many misstatements).
- Whether the population is based on an estimate (such as product warranty liability) or on individual book values that can be selected for testing (such as individual customer balances).

The conditions in which each method has superiority are discussed below in conjunction with each method.

Audit Objective and Selection Method. When auditing assets, the auditor usually concentrates on the possibility that the account balances are overstated. For an account to be *overstated*, the list of items making up the account balance, such as the list of customers' balances, must contain invalid and/or overstated items. If the sample is selected based on dollars, those items with larger balances are more likely to be included in the sample than those with smaller balances. Well-designed sampling procedures normally detect material amounts of overstatements.

Understatements, on the other hand, are quite a different matter. For an account to be *understated*, either some of the recorded balances are understated or, more likely, material items are simply omitted from the recording process. The auditor could respond by using a sampling methodology that emphasizes selection based on items rather than on dollars to increase the possibility of discovering understatements. No sampling method that samples from items already recorded detect understatements caused by missing items. A complementary population should be tested for understatements. For example, the auditor could employ a cutoff test to detect missing sales and receivables or examine cash disbursements after year-end to see whether there is evidence of accounts payable that should have been recorded as of year-end.

Expected Misstatement Conditions. The number and type of misstatements are an audit consideration in choosing an optimal sampling technique. One technique, probability proportional to size (PPS) sampling, is particularly effective when only a few misstatements are expected. If a large number of smaller misstatements are expected, the auditor must choose another sampling method.

Availability of Individual Book Values. Account balances are often made up of individual items, such as customer balances or inventory items, that can be selected for testing. Other accounts, such as product warranty liability or royalties payable to authors, are usually based on management estimates. Thus, a sampling methodology that would lead to estimates would be appropriate, such as taking a sample of sales transactions from the warranty period, determining the amount of liability remaining at year-end for each of those transactions, and projecting the results to the population of sales for the period covered by the warranty.

Determine the Sample Size, Select the Sample, and Evaluate the Results

Determining the sample size, the method of selecting the sample, and the approach to evaluating the sample results all depend on the sampling method used. The alternatives, probability proportional to size sampling and the three classical variables sampling methods are discussed in the remainder of this chapter.

B–PROBABILITY PROPORTIONAL TO SIZE SAMPLING

Probability proportional to size (PPS) sampling is an adaptation of attribute sampling methods to dollar value testing. It has been developed especially for use in auditing and has been given various names over time, including *dollar-unit sampling, cumulative monetary amount sampling, monetary unit sampling,* and *combined attributes–variables sampling.** PPS sampling was designed to be especially effective when testing for overstatements in situations when few misstatements are expected. Individual book values must be available for testing.

The population for PPS sampling is defined as the number of dollars in the account balance being tested. Each dollar in the population has an equal chance of being chosen, but each dollar chosen is associated with a particular item such as a customer's balance or an inventory item. Thus, a particular account's chance of being chosen is proportional to its size, hence the term *probability proportional to size sampling.* Research has shown that PPS sampling is very efficient in many auditing contexts and has become the most widely used method for substantive audit testing when there are risks of account balance overstatements. It is the only statistical sampling method that has been developed for audit use as described in the Historical Perspective.

Overview of PPS Sample Design

The design of a PPS sample requires the auditor to determine (1) detection risk, (2) tolerable misstatement, and (3) expected misstatement in the account balance. It is important to understand that although statistical sampling is both scientific and quantitative, the design of the sample is based on audit judgments. The nature of those judgments is now described and related to the audit model developed in previous chapters.

Test of Details Risk

To this point, the term *detection risk* has been used to refer to the risk of substantive procedures failing to detect material misstatements. It is now useful to separate this risk into two parts: other substantive procedures risk (OSPR) and the **test of details (TD) risk** as follows:

---

*PPS sampling is based on the Poisson (for manual calculations) or hypergeometric distribution. These distributions are more effective and efficient with low occurrence rates of the characteristic of interest, such as errors, than is the normal distribution, which underlies the classical sampling methods most often seen in introductory sampling courses.

Historical Perspective

THE DEVELOPMENT OF PPS SAMPLING

In the 1960s, an auditor for a firm that is now part of Deloitte and Touche was applying one of the classical sampling methods (described later in this chapter) to test an account balance. For classical sampling, the population is defined as the number of items that make up the account balance, such as customer balances or inventory items. It requires estimating the standard deviation of the population and stratifying the population to obtain a reasonable sample size. The statistical calculations were very complex and computer programs were not readily available for this purpose. He thought that it would make more sense to define the population as the number of dollars in the account balance and randomly select dollars for testing because he was ultimately expressing an opinion on the dollars in the financial statements.

This idea was explored by the firm. A paper written in 1961 by A. van Heerden described the use of a sampling method for testing accounting populations with low error rates.* Kenneth Stringer, a statistician and partner in the firm, used this idea and developed methods for determining sample size, selecting the sample, and evaluating the sample results. His technique was called *cumulative monetary amount (CMA) sampling* and was quite unique. Several others have developed modified versions of his basic results.†

*A. van Heerden, "Statistical Sampling as a Means of Auditing," *Maandblad voor Accountancy en Bedrijfshuish oulkunde* (1961).

†Donald Roberts, *Statistical Auditing* (New York: AICPA, 1978), 119.

$$AR = IR \times CR \times \mathbf{DR}$$

$$AR = IR \times CR \times \mathbf{OSPR} \times \mathbf{TD},$$

therefore:

$$TD = AR/(IR \times CR \times OSPR)$$

The *TD risk* is the risk that the auditor can accept that the inference from a sample will be incorrect. In accordance with the audit model discussed earlier, the auditor wants to control the risk of inferring that the account balance does not contain a material misstatement for the assertion being tested when, in fact, it does contain a material misstatement (risk of incorrect acceptance). PPS sampling is specifically designed to control the TD risk. The TD risk is also referred to as the *allowable risk of incorrect acceptance* and is the complement of the confidence (reliability) level needed from the particular test of details. For example, a 15 percent TD risk is the same as choosing a sample size based on an 85 percent statistical confidence level.

In determining the TD risk, the auditor needs to consider the effectiveness of the other substantive procedures that have been, or will be, performed. Examples of these other substantive procedures are analytical procedures, cutoff tests, and substantive tests of transactions. The risk of these other procedures failing to detect misstatements that could aggregate to more than the tolerable misstatement will be referred to as the **other substantive procedures risk (OSPR).*** The TD risk is determined using an expanded audit risk model and depends on the audit risk (AR), the

*This is referred to as the *analytical procedures (AP) risk* in the professional literature. This name is, however, misleading because it refers to more than just the risk that analytical procedures will fail to detect a material misstatement.

assessment of inherent risk (IR) and control risk (CR), and the other substantive procedures risk (OSPR) for the assertion(s) being tested.

Audit Model Illustrated as a Formula. If AR is 5 percent, IR is 80 percent, CR is 70 percent, and OSPR is 60 percent, the resulting TD risk is determined as follows:

$$TD = \frac{0.05}{0.8 \times 0.7 \times 0.6} = 0.15 = 15\%$$

If inherent risk, control risk, and other substantive procedures risk are all assessed at 100 percent, the test of details risk would be the same as the audit risk (5 percent). This implies that all the evidence needs to be obtained from this sample. A lower test of details risk leads to a larger sample size. In other words, lower risk levels imply that the auditor is relying primarily on the test of details procedures; a high risk level implies that the auditor is relying heavily on other sources of audit evidence in reaching a conclusion about the correctness of the account balance and is using the test of details as a basis for corroborating that evidence. Thus, high risk means that only minor reliance is placed on the procedures (by audit design), and low risk means that the auditor is placing high reliance on the audit procedures underlying the sampling methodology.

Audit Model Treated as a Functional Relationship. A number of firms choose to treat the audit risk model as a functional model rather than a formula. A table like the one shown in Exhibit 14.2 can be used to assist the auditor in converting the risk assessments into a choice of TD risk to be used in determining the sample size. If inherent and control risk are assessed as high, detection risk will be low. If the other substantive procedures are not effective in detecting these potential misstatements, the OSPR is set at high and the test of details risk should be the same as the audit risk. If, however, inherent and control risks are assessed as low, detection risk will be high, meaning that less substantive evidence is needed. The substantive evidence can include a sampling test of the details of the account balance and/or other substantive procedures, such as cutoff tests and analytical procedures. If the other substantive procedures are believed to be effective, the OSPR may be set at moderate or low and no further testing is needed. Some firms set a maximum TD risk for sampling applications, such as 50 percent, as a guide for their auditors. The 50 percent risk is often chosen to be conservative and because conceptually it is hard to argue that any sampling plan would be appropriate when there is less than a 50 percent chance that the sample will detect material misstatements. Exhibit 14.2 conforms to this practice.

Tolerable Misstatement

When planning a test of details using PPS sampling, tolerable misstatement is usually set somewhat lower than planning materiality to allow for estimated or known misstatements in other account balances. Some firms arbitrarily set tolerable misstatement at 75 percent of planning materiality.

Expected Misstatement

Expected misstatement is based on prior year audit results, results of other substantive tests, good audit judgment, and knowledge of changes in personnel and the accounting system. It is usually desirable to be conservative and use a slightly larger

Exhibit 14.2

TEST OF DETAILS (TD) RISK TABLE

Environmental Risk* (Likelihood of Material Misstatement Existing)	Low Audit Risk (5 percent): Other Substantive Procedures Risk			High Audit Risk (10 percent): Other Substantive Procedures Risk		
	Not Effective (High Risk)	Effective (Moderate Risk)	Very Effective (Low Risk)	Not Effective (High Risk)	Moderately Effective (Moderate Risk)	Very Effective (Low Risk)
Low (therefore use a high DR)	TD risk =.50	No detailed tests needed	No detailed tests needed	.50	No detailed tests needed	No detailed tests needed
Moderate (therefore use a moderate DR)	.15	.30	.50	.30	.50	No detailed tests needed
High (must use low DR)	.05	.10	.25	.10	.20	.50

*Environmental risk is the combination of inherent risk and control risk.

expected misstatement than the auditor actually anticipates. This conservative approach may increase the sample size but minimizes the risk of rejecting book value when book value is not materially misstated. The expected amount of misstatement must be less than tolerable misstatement.

Sample Size and Selection

Different sampling units, such as customer balances, contain different numbers of dollars. A sampling unit with more dollars will have a higher probability of selection than will one with fewer dollars. There are two basic approaches to selecting a PPS sample, the fixed interval approach and the random dollar approach. The random dollar approach is seldom used in practice and is not covered in this book. The fixed interval approach involves the calculation of a sampling interval in dollars *(I)*:

$$I = \frac{TM - (EM \times EEF)}{RF},$$

where

TM = Tolerable misstatement

EM = Expected misstatement

EEF = Error expansion factor

RF = Reliability factor.

The **error expansion factor** and **reliability factor** are related to the test of details risk and can be found in Exhibit 14.3. The reliability factor is used to represent the reliability level desired based on a zero-misstatement assumption.

When sampling is used, not all of the items in the population are audited and there is a probability that some misstatements exist in the population even when none are discovered in the sample. Tolerable misstatement represents the maximum amount of misstatement the auditor can accept in the population. When no misstatements are expected in the population, tolerable misstatement represents the maximum amount of sampling error that the auditor can accept at the planned TD risk level.

The maximum sample size is calculated by dividing the book value of the population by the sampling interval:

$$n = \frac{\text{Population Book Value}}{\text{Sampling Interval}}.$$

Exhibit 14.3

PPS SAMPLE DESIGN AND EVALUATION FACTORS

Test of details risk	1%	5%	10%	15%	20%	25%	30%	50%
Error expansion factor	1.90	1.60	1.50	1.40	1.30	1.25	1.20	1.00
Reliability factor	4.61	3.00	2.31	1.90	1.61	1.39	1.21	0.70
Precision gap–widening factors								
Ranked* overstatement errors								
1	1.03	0.75	0.58	0.48	0.39	0.31	0.23	0.00
2	0.77	0.55	0.44	0.34	0.28	0.23	0.18	0.00
3	0.64	0.46	0.36	0.30	0.24	0.18	0.15	0.00
4	0.56	0.40	0.31	0.25	0.21	0.17	0.13	0.00
5	0.50	0.36	0.28	0.23	0.18	0.15	0.11	0.00
6	0.46	0.33	0.26	0.21	0.17	0.13	0.11	0.00
7	0.43	0.30	0.24	0.19	0.16	0.13	0.09	0.00
8	0.41	0.29	0.22	0.18	0.14	0.12	0.10	0.00
9	0.38	0.27	0.21	0.17	0.14	0.11	0.08	0.00
10	0.36	0.26	0.20	0.17	0.14	0.10	0.08	0.00

* Misstatements should be ranked according to their tainting percentages. The largest tainting percentage is multiplied by the largest precision gap-widening factor, the second largest tainting percentage is multiplied by the second largest precision gap-widening factor, and so forth.

Source: A modification of the tables in the AICPA's *Audit Sampling*, Audit and Accounting Guide (see Exhibit 14.15). These factors are based on the Poisson probability distribution.

When misstatements are expected in the population, the auditor cannot accept as much sampling error. The sample must be more precise, which means that a smaller sampling interval is required, resulting in a larger sample size. To accomplish this, tolerable misstatement must be reduced by the amount of misstatement the auditor expects in the population times an error expansion factor. The error expansion factor adjusts for additional sampling error introduced by the expected misstatements resulting in a larger sample size.

The sample is selected using the fixed interval approach—every *I*th dollar—with a random start. Each selected dollar acts as a "hook" for the entire physical unit in which it occurs, such as a customer's account balance or the extended cost of an inventory item. The whole physical unit is audited unless it can be divided into smaller auditable units, such as unpaid invoices making up a customer's balance, in which case, the selected invoice(s) is (are) audited.

Illustration

The auditor is planning to confirm accounts receivable to test the existence and valuation assertions. There are 450 customer balances totaling $807,906. Audit risk has been set as low (five percent), meaning that the auditor cannot accept much risk of failing to detect material misstatements. Detection risk has been determined to be moderate, and the other substantive procedures are not expected to be effective in detecting material misstatements. Following the guidance in Exhibit 14.2, the test of details risk is 15 percent. Tolerable misstatement is set by the auditor at $50,000. No misstatements were found in the past year. However, to be safe, the auditor uses an expected misstatement of $5,000.

The sampling interval is calculated as follows:

$$I = \frac{\$50{,}000 - (\$5{,}000 \times 1.4)}{1.9} = \$22{,}632.$$

The reliability factor of 1.9 and error expansion factor of 1.4 are obtained from Exhibit 14.3 for a 15 percent test of details risk. The maximum sample size will be:

$$n = \frac{\$807{,}906}{\$22{,}632} = 36.$$

If the sample is to be selected manually, it will be easier to select and fewer selection errors will be made if a rounded interval is used, such as $22,000. Rounding the interval *down* ensures that the sample size will be adequate. If computer assistance is available for selecting the sample, rounding the interval down is not necessary.

To make this a random-based selection method, a random start is needed between 1 and the sampling interval (1 to 22,000 in the illustration). This number can be obtained from a variety of sources, including the serial number of a dollar bill, a random number table, a number from a soft drink bottle, or a microcomputer random number generator.

An adding machine or a specially designed computer software program can be used to select the sample. If an adding machine is used, enter the random start, add each book value, and subtotal after each entry, giving a cumulative total for each item. This process is illustrated in Exhibit 14.4 using a random start of $20,000.

The first sample item is the one that first causes the cumulative total to equal or exceed the sampling interval ($22,000). In Exhibit 14.4, that is customer 2.

Exhibit 14.4

FIXED INTERVAL SAMPLE SELECTION

Customer	Book Value	Cumulative Amount	Selection Amount
	Random start	20,000	
1	220	20,220	
2	2,200	22,420	22,000
3	22,000	44,420	44,000
4	880	45,300	
5	6,128	51,428	
6	2,800	54,228	
7	45,023	99,251	66,000 & 88,000
8	10	99,261	
9	8,231	107,492	
10	16,894	124,386	110,000
.	.	.	
.	.	.	
.	.	.	
450	1,900	827,906	

Successive sample items are those first causing the cumulative total to equal or exceed multiples of the interval ($44,000, $66,000, $88,000, and so forth).

The probability of selecting any particular item is relative to the number of dollars in it, thus the name probability proportional to size. For example, the balance for customer 1 has a one percent chance of being included in the sample prior to the selection of the random start (220/22,000). The balance for customer 2, with a book value of $2,200, has a 10 percent chance of being selected. There is a 100 percent chance of including the balance for customer 3 (book value of $22,000) in the sample because it is equal to the interval. All items with a book value equal to or greater than the interval will be included in the sample. As noted, these are sometimes referred to as *top stratum items*. The balance for customer 7 has two selection points. There will be just one sample item resulting in an actual sample size less than that originally calculated. Another sample item does not need to be added in this case because there is adequate dollar coverage with the items identified by this selection process.

The population has effectively been divided into two groups: the top stratum items, which are audited 100 percent, and the lower stratum items from which the sample is selected. The sample selection process used for PPS sampling results in almost infinite stratification because the probability of selecting a particular item from the lower stratum is proportional to the number of dollars in it. This selection method is intuitively appealing to auditors because it provides large dollar coverage with relatively small sample sizes.

This selection method also tests the mathematical accuracy of the population. Note in Exhibit 14.4 that the last cumulative amount is $827,906. This represents the population total of $807,906 plus the random start of $20,000.

The maximum sample size using the rounded interval will be 36 or 37 items ($807,906/$22,000). The actual sample size will be less than this maximum when a population item that exceeds the sampling interval of $22,000 contains two or more of the sample selection points. Each of these items is only one item in the sample unless subsampling (which is described in Appendix C) is used.

Zero and Negative Balances

Population items with zero balances have no chance of being selected using PPS sampling. If evaluation of sampling units with zero balances is necessary to achieve the audit objective of the test, they should be segregated and audited as a different population. Population items with negative balances require special consideration. For example, credit balances in customer accounts represent liabilities; the client owes money, merchandise, or service. Two approaches deal with negative items. One approach is to exclude them from the selection process and treat them as a separate population and test them separately; this should be done when a significant number of such items are included in the population. The second approach is to include them in the selection process and ignore the negative sign associated with the recorded amount; this approach can be used when the dollar amount of the negative items is insignificant. To prove the total of the population, subtract the negative balances twice at the end of the accumulation process.

Sample Evaluation

PPS sampling is designed to compute the likelihood that the account balance may exceed the auditor's tolerable misstatement limit. In other words, if the auditor designs the sample with a 15 percent TD risk level and a tolerable misstatement of $50,000, the auditor is testing the hypothesis that there is no more than a 15 percent probability that the account balance could be overstated by more than $50,000. Recall that the reason the auditor has chosen the 15 percent TD risk level (rather than an even lower level) is that the auditor has some confidence from other audit evidence that the organization's control procedures are somewhat effective in minimizing misstatements and the other substantive procedures were somewhat effective in detecting material misstatements. The auditor's best estimate of the actual amount of misstatement may be much lower, but in using PPS sampling, the auditor is not only estimating the most likely misstatement but also is concentrating on the possibility that the audit evidence would indicate that a material misstatement could exist in the account.

Error Evaluation Terminology

To estimate the potential misstatements in an account balance and to determine whether additional audit work is needed, the auditor will calculate an upper misstatement limit. The **upper misstatement limit** (UML) is defined as the maximum dollar overstatement that could exist in the population at the specified TD risk level. For example, if the auditor calculated a UML of $41,800 using a 15 percent TD risk, this would support a conclusion that there is only a 15 percent chance that the actual amount of overstatement in the population would be greater than $41,800.

The UML is derived from the underlying statistical assumptions made about the population being tested. Fortunately, it is easy to calculate. The UML is computed by adding together three components:

- **Basic precision.** The amount of uncertainty associated with testing only a part of the population. It is equal to the UML if no errors are found in the sample.
- **Most likely misstatement (MLM).** The best estimate of the actual amount of dollar misstatements that exist in the account balance.
- **Precision gap widening.** An increase in upper misstatement estimate caused by the statistical properties of misstatements found.

No Misstatements in the Sample

When no misstatements are found in the sample, the UML is the same as the basic precision, which is the sampling interval used times the reliability factor ($22,000 × 1.9 = $41,800 in the illustration). Basic precision provides an **allowance for sampling error.** Recall that sampling error results from not auditing the entire population. The auditor's best estimate of the total misstatement in the population is zero because no misstatements were discovered in the sample; however, there may be some misstatement in the unaudited items. Basic precision is a measure of the maximum potential misstatement in the unaudited part of the population. Because the basic precision of $41,800 is less than tolerable misstatement ($50,000), the auditor can conclude that there is less than a 15 percent probability that the book value is overstated by a material amount.

Misstatements in the Sample

When misstatements are detected, the evaluation process is more involved. The analysis is separated into two parts: (1) identifying top stratum misstatements and (2) projecting misstatements found in the sample from the lower stratum to the entire lower stratum.

Top stratum	Audited 100%	No projection is made because the total misstatement is known.
Lower stratum	Sampled	Misstatements found in the lower stratum must be projected to the entire lower stratum part of the population.

Recall that the top stratum is audited 100 percent. Thus, the amount of misstatement in that portion of the population is known with certainty; it does not have to be projected. Any misstatements found in the sample from the lower stratum must be projected to the entire lower stratum and combined with the top stratum misstatements to estimate the most likely misstatement and the maximum potential misstatement in the account balance.

Misstatement analysis consists of identifying the percentage that the book value of each misstated sample item is overstated or understated (referred to as the **tainting percentage**). The tainting percentage found in each lower stratum sample item is presumed to be representative of the interval from which it was selected. Thus, a three percent overstatement tainting of a sample item is presumed to represent a three percent overstatement of the interval. These projections are combined with the upper stratum misstatements to calculate the most likely misstatement in the population.

Illustration

Using the sample in Exhibit 14.4, assume the following misstatements are found:

Customer Number	Book Value	Audit Value	Misstatement	Tainting Percent A	Projected Misstatement A × $22,000
2	$ 2,200	$ 2,134	$ 66	3%	$ 660
7	45,023	44,340	683	NA	683
90	8,300	8,217	83	1%	220
			$835		$1,563

The error found in customer 7's balance is a top stratum error because the book value exceeds the sampling interval of $22,000. Because it is the only top stratum error, the auditor knows that the total error in the top stratum is $683.

The other two misstatements are lower stratum misstatements and need to be projected to the lower stratum part of the population. Each lower stratum sample item was selected from an interval of $22,000. The tainting percentage is the error divided by the book value. Customer 2's balance is tainted (overstated) by three percent. Because this item was selected from and thus represents one interval of $22,000, it is assumed that the $22,000 interval from which it was selected is also overstated by three percent, or $660. In the same way, the one percent tainting for customer 90 can be projected to its $22,000 interval as $220. Because none of the other sample items contained a misstatement, the other intervals are assumed to be correct.

It is unlikely that the projected but unknown misstatement exists in the same interval from which the sample item containing a misstatement was selected. However, the sample was randomly selected and, therefore, should be representative of the population. Other misstatements are likely to exist somewhere in the rest of the population. The best estimate of the total misstatement in the lower stratum part of the population is $880 ($660 + $220). Another way to calculate the most likely misstatement in the lower stratum is to multiply the sampling interval by the sum of the tainting percentages (3 percent + 1 percent = 4 percent × $22,000 = $880). The sample evaluation calculations are summarized in Exhibit 14.5.

The most likely misstatement in the population is $1,563 ($683 + $880), the sum of the top stratum misstatement and the most likely misstatement in the lower stratum. Additional allowance for sampling error is necessary because of finding lower stratum misstatements and is calculated by multiplying the tainting percentages by the precision gap widening factors in Exhibit 14.3. The largest tainting percentage is multiplied by the factor in Exhibit 14.3 related to misstatement number 1 (3 percent × 0.48 = 1.44 percent). The second largest tainting percentage is multiplied by the factor related to misstatement number 2 (1 percent × 0.34 = .34 percent), and so forth. The products of these calculations are added, and the sum is multiplied by the sampling interval to obtain the precision gap widening amount. The UML is $43,755 ($41,800 + $1,563 + $392). The statistical conclusion is that the auditor is 85 percent sure that this population is not overstated by more than $43,755. Because the upper misstatement limit is less than the tolerable misstatement ($50,000), the auditor can conclude that, at the prespecified level of risk, the population does not contain a material amount of overstatement misstatement. If the upper misstatement limit had exceeded the tolerable misstatement, additional audit analysis would have been required, as discussed later in this chapter.

Exhibit 14.5

UPPER MISSTATEMENT LIMIT CALCULATIONS

	UML Factor*	Tainting Percent	Sampling Interval	Dollar Conclusion
Basic precision	1.9 ×		22,000 =	41,800
Most likely misstatement:				
Top stratum			683	
Lower stratum				
First largest tainting %		3%		
Second largest tainting %		1%		
		4% ×	22,000 = 880	
Total most likely misstatement				1,563
Precision gap widening				
First largest %	0.48 × 3% =	1.44%		
Second largest %	0.34 × 1% =	.34%		
		1.78% ×	22,000 =	392
Upper misstatement limit (UML)				43,755

A slightly different approach to calculating the UML that is used in the AICPA *Audit Sampling* audit guide is described in Appendix B.

*Upper misstatement limit (UML) factors come from the 15 percent column in Exhibit 14.3.

Understatements

The preceding example assumes that only overstatements were found in the audit sample. However, it is likely that the auditor may encounter situations in which the account balance may be understated. For example, the auditor might discover that an accounts receivable balance may be understated because the client included a freight charge on the invoice that was not recorded in accounts receivable because of a software problem. The misstatement is systematic. Assume, for example, that an account balance of $500 had omitted a $50 freight charge. This is a 10 percent understatement tainting.

When an understatement is encountered, the auditor has two possible courses of action. First, the understatement can be ignored for purposes of this sample evaluation and, if there are other audit tests for understatements, this understatement can be included in that other test. Second, the auditor can perform a separate analysis for understatements following the same format as was used for overstatements in Exhibit 14.5. The auditor would calculate a most likely misstatement of understatement (10% × $22,000 = $2,200). The basic precision level would remain the same ($41,800), the precision gap widening factor would be $1,056 (.48 × .10 × 22,000), and the upper misstatement limit for understatements would be $45,056 ($41,800 + $2,200 + $1,056).

When misstatements are found in both directions, the auditor considers the directional nature of the misstatements in reaching a conclusion about the most likely misstatement (MLM) and net overstatement misstatements. The MLM for the account balance is the net of the over- and understatement misstatements. In this case, a MLM of overstatement is $1,563 and the MLM of understatement is $2,200 yielding a MLM (net) in the account of an understatement of $637. The upper misstatement limit in each direction is computed by taking the upper misstatement limit of one direction and subtracting the most likely misstatement in the other direction. In this example, the UML for overstatements would be $43,755 – $2,200, or $41,555. In a similar manner, the UML for understatements would be $45,056 – $1,563, or $43,493. The auditor would be 85 percent confident that the account balance is not overstated by more than $41,555 or understated by more than $43,493.

Frequent Misstatements Found

When frequent but small misstatements are discovered in the sampled items, the PPS evaluation method described and illustrated often leads to a very conservative (high) estimate of the upper misstatement limit and may lead to an incorrect rejection of the book value tested. The auditor can evaluate such a sample using one of the classical sampling methods described later in this chapter.

Unacceptable Sample Results

When the upper misstatement limit exceeds the tolerable misstatement, the auditor has several possible courses of action available. The auditor can ask the client to correct the known misstatements, determine whether there is a systematic pattern of misstatements in the account balance, expand the sample, or redesign the audit sample.

Correct the Known Misstatement. The client can be asked to correct the known misstatement(s). If this is done, the most likely misstatement and, therefore, the UML can be adjusted for those corrections. In some cases, simply correcting the known misstatement can bring the UML below the auditor's tolerable misstatement level.

Analyze the Pattern of Misstatements. Any time misstatements are discovered, the auditor should look beyond the quantitative aspects of the misstatements to understand the nature and cause of the misstatements. Is there evidence that the misstatements might be systematic, such as the problem on charging freight discussed above? If a systematic pattern of misstatements is found, the client can be asked to investigate and make an estimate of the correction needed, which the auditor can review.

The auditor should also determine whether the misstatements reflect errors or irregularities; the latter signal major audit problems. In addition, the auditor should consider the relationship of the misstatements to other phases of the audit. Problems in recording receivables may also reveal problems in the accuracy of recorded sales. Additional evidence is especially necessary when the evaluation of sample results indicates an irregularity or computer programming error.

Discovering more misstatements than expected in the planning stage of the audit suggests that the planning assumptions may have been in error; perhaps the internal control procedures were not as effective as originally assessed, and the auditor should reconsider that assessment because it affects all aspects of the audit.

Increase the Sample Size. When the most likely misstatement is significantly higher than the expected misstatement, the auditor can calculate the additional sample size needed by substituting the most likely misstatement from the sample for the original expected misstatement in the sample interval/size formula and determine the total sample size based on the new expectations. The number of additional sample items can then be determined by subtracting the original sample size from the new sample size.

A new sampling interval can be calculated and used for selection. Items should be selected that are not already included in the sample.

Design an Alternative Audit Strategy. Another course of action is to design an alternative audit strategy if an analysis of the misstatements identifies a particular problem. For example, when doing an inventory price test, the auditor may find that most of the misstatements were made by one of several employees who did not understand how to price the inventory properly. The auditor might suggest that the client reinstruct that person and have that person reprice that part of the inventory or have another qualified employee redo the pricing. The auditor can then test these prices.

Change Objective to Estimating the Correct Value. In cases in which a significant misstatement appears to exist, it may be necessary to change from an objective of testing details to the objective of helping the client estimate the correct population value, which will lead to an adjustment of the book value. A lower test of details risk and a smaller tolerable misstatement should be used because the auditor is no longer testing the balance but estimating the correct population value from the sample. The auditor will expect the client to adjust the book value to the estimated value. A larger sample size will normally be required; the enlarged sample size can be determined using the revised test of details risk and tolerable misstatement in the PPS sample design approach. Because of the frequency of misstatements underlying the misstated balance, the auditor probably should use one of the classical statistical sampling methods to evaluate the results.

C–CLASSICAL VARIABLES SAMPLING METHODS: OVERVIEW

One of the classical variables sampling methods should be considered for substantive testing if the conditions for effective use of PPS sampling are not met. If the audit objective is to test for possible understatements as well as overstatements, if frequent misstatements are expected, or if the auditor desires to select the sample using random items rather than random dollars, one of the classical sampling methods would be more appropriate.

The three most commonly used **classical variables sampling methods** are mean-per-unit (MPU), difference estimation, and ratio estimation. The classical methods are based on the normal curve distribution and are used to calculate a *best estimate* of a population value and to provide confidence intervals around those estimates. The methods share the same sample size and evaluation formulas but vary in sample size because of differences in the way the standard deviations of the populations are calculated. The **mean-per-unit sampling method** does not depend on book value but is used to make a projection of book value based on the items selected in the sample. In other words, a best estimate is made based on the audit results of the sample items selected. MPU is the only statistical method that can be used to test an account balance that is based on an estimate, that is, an account balance that does not contain individual book values for sample selection. MPU sampling could be used, for example, to test the product warranty liability balance computed as a percentage of sales. The auditor samples sales transactions for which the warranty period has not expired and develops an independent estimate of this liability balance.

Both the **difference estimation sampling method** and the **ratio estimation sampling method** require book values of the individual items making up the account being examined. The auditor calculates either an average difference between book value and audited value (difference method) or a ratio of audited value to book value (ratio method) and projects the calculated difference or ratio to the population as a whole to determine whether book value might be misstated by more than a material amount. The difference and ratio methods generally require smaller sample sizes than the MPU method but are effective only when frequent over- and understatements are expected, such as when the auditor expects small differences between existing inventory and the perpetual records of inventory, and the sample is likely to contain more than 20 misstatements.

An overview of the three methods is presented in Exhibit 14.6. All three methods explicitly control for both the risk of incorrect rejection and the risk of incorrect acceptance. The required sample size for all three methods is highly sensitive to estimates of the variability of the population being tested.

Sample Size

The sample size formula for all three classical methods is

$$n = \left(\frac{N \times U_R \times S_x}{A} \right)^2,$$

where

N = Population size

U_R = Standard normal deviate for the desired risk of incorrect rejection

S_x = Estimated population standard deviation

A = Desired allowance for sampling error.

The population size refers to the number of items in the population, such as the number of customer balances, rather than the number of dollars. The standard normal deviate is the complement of the confidence level used in many sampling applications and is computed from the standard Z table. The most widely used values are shown in Exhibit 14.7.

Note that the risk controlled in classical sampling is the risk of incorrect rejection rather than the risk of incorrect acceptance. The auditor can control for both the risk of incorrect acceptance and the risk of incorrect rejection by adjusting the desired allowance for sampling error.* The risk of incorrect acceptance is the test of details (TD) risk and is based on the audit risk model previously discussed.

*The methodology for controlling such risk is discussed in Appendix A.

Exhibit 14.6

OVERVIEW OF CLASSICAL ESTIMATION TECHNIQUES

Method	Requirements for Use	Advantages/Disadvantages
Mean-per-unit	Few overstatements and understatements are expected.	Can be used when book values for individual items do not exist. May result in very large sample size unless the population is stratified, in which case computer assistance is extremely helpful for calculating sample size and evaluating sample results. Explicitly controls for risk of incorrect rejection and risk of incorrect acceptance. Sample size depends on variability of the population as measured by the standard deviation.
Difference estimation	Book values of individual items are available. Frequent overstatements and understatements are expected. Misstatement pattern is not related to size of book value.	Sample size efficiency when variability of differences is expected to be small. Can be used with stratification techniques.
Ratio estimation	Book values of individual items are available. Frequent overstatements and understatements are expected. Misstatement pattern is related to the size of book value.	Sample size efficiency when variability of differences is expected to be small. Can be used with stratification techniques.

Estimate of Population Standard Deviation

Recall that classical variables estimation operates by selecting a sample of items, determining the audit value of the items, calculating an average of the items, and projecting that average to the population as a whole by multiplying the average by the number of items in the population. Obviously, the more alike the items are to begin, the more accurate such a projection will be because the audit results will be averaged over a relatively homogeneous population. For example, estimating the average age in a large day-care group will require a smaller sample size than would be necessary to estimate the average age of people attending church on a Sunday morning. The children in the day-care group are of similar age. The ages of those in church may range from 1 to more than 100 years. The variability of the items in the population will affect the sample size. Variability is measured by the standard devi-

Exhibit 14.7

STANDARD NORMAL DEVIATE FOR THE DESIRED RISK OF INCORRECT REJECTION (U_R)

Risk of Incorrect Rejection (Percentage)	Standard Normal Deviate (U_R)
5	1.96
10	1.64
20	1.28

The standard normal deviate is the Z value corresponding to the percentage risk of incorrect rejection from a standard normal table.

ation of those items. A larger standard deviation results in a larger sample size. The overall sample size can be reduced by dividing the population into more homogeneous subsections, thus reducing the variability within each subsection. As noted, this division process is referred to as *stratification* and is used by most audit software that calculates MPU samples. Samples are selected from each stratum. The major alternatives for estimating the standard deviation are these:

- Use prior year results; experience is a good guide if the variation in the current population is expected to be about the same as in prior years.
- Select and audit a preliminary sample of 30 to 50 items. The standard deviation of these sample items can be used to estimate the population standard deviation.
- Use the standard deviation of the population book values as an approximation (only for the MPU method).

The standard deviation for difference estimation is based on the differences between the book and audit values of each sample item. For ratio estimation, it is based on the ratio of the audit value to the book value of each item. The standard deviation for MPU sampling is usually much larger than for the other two methods and results in a larger sample size unless stratification methods are used. Details of the calculation of the standard deviation and the desired allowance for sampling error are described in Appendix A.

Desired Allowance for Sampling Error

The desired allowance for sampling error is based on tolerable misstatement and may be modified downward should the auditor wish to control for both the risk of incorrect acceptance and the risk of incorrect rejection. The desired allowance is an estimate of how close the auditor wants the sample estimate to be to the correct, but unknown, population value. For example, if the auditor chooses a desired allowance for sampling error of $50,000 and uses an audit risk level of 5 percent, this essentially says that the auditor wants to be 95 percent confident that the true value is within ± $50,000 of the sample estimate. The desired allowance for sampling error is also referred to as *precision*.

Sample Size Illustration

Assume that the auditor is performing a price test of inventory and expects frequent misstatements because the client purports to be using FIFO but in fact uses only the latest invoice purchase price for each item. There are 15,000 items in inventory with a book value of $27 million. The estimated standard deviation, S_x, based on a preliminary sample of 30 items, is $1,032 for MPU sampling, $118 for difference estimation sampling, and $123 for ratio estimation sampling. The desired allowance for sampling error is $200,000 using a 10 percent risk of incorrect acceptance and a 20 percent risk of incorrect rejection.* The resulting sample sizes, rounded up to the next whole item, for the three classical methods, are

MPU

$$n = \left(\frac{15{,}000 \times 1.28 \times \$1{,}032}{\$200{,}000}\right)^2 = 9{,}816$$

Difference estimation

$$n = \left(\frac{15{,}000 \times 1.28 \times \$118}{\$200{,}000}\right)^2 = 129$$

Ratio estimation

$$n = \left(\frac{15{,}000 \times 1.28 \times \$123}{\$200{,}000}\right)^2 = 140$$

Neither PPS nor MPU sampling is appropriate for this test because frequent misstatements are expected. Also, the sample size for MPU sampling is significantly larger than for the other two classical methods because of the larger estimated standard deviation. If there is not a close correlation between the differences and related book values in the preliminary sample, difference estimation sampling is likely to be more appropriate than ratio estimation sampling. But because the sample sizes are not significantly different, a sample size of 140 could be used in case the full sample shows such a correlation so that ratio estimation sampling is appropriate. The preliminary sample of 30 items can form a part of the sample size of 140 that will be used to evaluate the sample results. Therefore, an additional 110 items need to be selected and audited.

Sample Selection

Samples for the classical methods are selected using random items rather than random dollars. The population should be stratified if the items in the population exhibit significant variability. The formulas for determining the sample sizes for each stratum and evaluating the results are complex and beyond the scope of this text. Computer programs have been developed for this purpose.[3]

If MPU sampling is used, it is helpful to calculate a sample projection of the population value based on book values. If the sample projection based on book values

*The details concerning these standard deviations and the desired allowance for sampling risk are shown in Appendix A.

differs materially (more than the desired allowance for sampling error) from book value, the sample is not representative and should be replaced by a different one.

Sample Evaluation

In evaluating a classical sample, the auditor develops an estimate of the correct value of the population, referred to as the **point estimate.** The **projected misstatement** is the difference between the point estimate and the book value of the population. In making a decision about accepting the book value, the auditor should compare the projected misstatement with the tolerable misstatement and give appropriate consideration to sampling error.

Point Estimate and Projected Misstatement

The calculation of the point estimate depends on the sampling method used. In the inventory price test illustration, there are 15,000 items with a total book value of $27 million. A sample of 140 items was audited to obtain the following totals:

Sample Book Value	Sample Audit Value	Difference AV – BV	Ratio AV/BV
$253,500	$250,937	($2,563)	.99

MPU Sampling. For MPU sampling*, the point estimate (PE) is calculated using the following formula:

$$PE = \frac{\Sigma \text{ Audit Values}}{n} \times N$$

$$PE = \frac{\$250,937}{140} \times 15,000 = \$26,886,107$$

The projected misstatement is a $113,893 overstatement ($27,000,000 – $26,886,107).

Difference Estimation Sampling. The following formula is used to calculate the point estimate for difference estimation sampling:

$$PE = (\frac{\Sigma \text{ Differences}}{n} \times N) + \text{Population Book Value}$$

$$PE = \left(\frac{\$2,563}{140}\right) \times 15,000 + \$27,000,000 = \$26,725,393$$

The projected misstatement is a $274,607 overstatement.

Ratio Estimation Sampling. For ratio estimation sampling, the formula is:

*Even though the proper sample size for MPU sampling would be much larger, 140 is used here to illustrate the calculations needed to evaluate a sample for all three classical methods.

$$PE = \frac{\sum \text{Audit Value}}{\sum \text{Book Value}} \times \text{Population Book Value}$$

$$PE = \frac{\$250,937}{\$253,500} \times \$27,000,000 = \$26,727,018$$

The projected misstatement is a $272,982 overstatement.

Decision Rules

In determining whether to accept the book value, the auditor often uses a decision rule. There are several such rules.* Two of the most commonly used decision rules are the following:

1. Compute the point estimate (PE) and an achieved precision range around the point estimate. Accept the book value if it falls within the computed range.
2. Compute the point estimate. Calculate a decision interval of book value ± the allowance for sampling error. If the point estimate falls within that range, accept book value as not being materially misstated.

For the first alternative, if the population's book value is within the decision interval, the auditor can accept the book value of the population. The **decision interval** is the point estimate (PE) plus and minus the achieved precision (A'). The achieved precision will equal the auditor's planned precision (auditor's allowance for sampling error) unless the sample standard deviation differs from the estimated standard deviation. A smaller standard deviation results in a tighter achieved precision. For example, if the auditor uses the *difference estimation* results in the previous illustration, and if the achieved precision is plus or minus $175,000,† the decision interval is $26,725,393 (PE) plus and minus the achieved precision $175,000 (± A), or $26,550,393 to $26,900,393, as depicted:

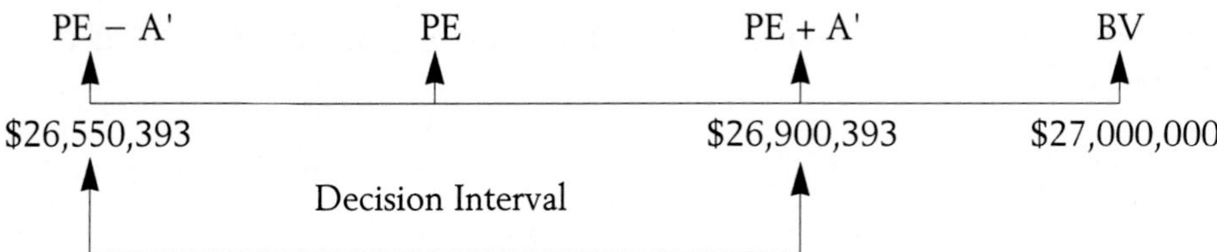

Using the first decision rule, the auditor would not conclude that book value is correct.

The second alternative involves calculating a decision interval of $27,000,000 ± $200,000, or $26,800,000 to $27,200,000. Because the point estimate does not fall within the range, the auditor would also conclude that book value *may be* misstated by more than a tolerable amount. The sample included only 140 of the 15,000 population items. Even though the auditor found only $2,563 in actual misstatements in the sample, the auditor's best estimate is that book value is overstated by in excess of $270,000. This points out the importance of projecting the sample results to the population.

*See *Audit Sampling* 95–99 for a description of these alternatives.

†The details of calculating achieved precision are covered in Appendix A.

Unacceptable Results. Because the auditor's best estimate is that book value may be misstated by more than a tolerable amount, there are several possibilities to consider:

- The account balance may be materially misstated.
- The auditor may be rejecting an acceptable book value when the achieved precision is less than the desired allowance for sampling error.
- The original estimate of the standard deviation may have been too small and a larger sample should have been used.
- The sample may not be representative of the population.

The auditor's best estimate is that the balance may be materially misstated. In evaluating this possibility, the auditor first searches to determine whether a pattern of misstatements may systematically explain the results. If a pattern is identified, the auditor and client can expand their work to fully review all items covered by the pattern to determine the full extent of the adjustment. If no such pattern exists, the client may choose to do an investigation or to book an estimated adjustment to bring book value within the tolerable range (preferably to the auditor's estimate) pending additional work. In any event, the auditor must conduct enough additional work to be satisfied that the audited account balance does not contain any material misstatement.

If the achieved precision is significantly less than that desired, the auditor can calculate an adjusted achieved precision to limit the risk of incorrect rejection to the desired level. This calculation is covered in Appendix A. If the sample was too small, a revised sample size can be determined by substituting the standard deviation from the total sample for the standard deviation based on the preliminary sample in the sample size formula.

Comparison of PPS and Classical Sampling

PPS sampling has become widely used for substantive audit testing because it is designed to explicitly address the most common substantive applications: sampling assets, such as accounts receivable and inventory, for overstatements when few or no misstatements are expected. The major advantages of PPS sampling over other statistical methods include the following:

- Dollar estimates of the likely misstatement and upper misstatement limit are easily obtainable with fairly efficient sample sizes.
- The sample size is based only on the key items of audit interest (tolerable misstatement and test of details risk) and is not influenced by the standard deviation of the population as are classical sampling methods.
- Designing, selecting, and evaluating the sample is relatively simple and can be done without computer assistance.
- Sample selection is relatively easy.
- Testing can begin before the population is complete. (For example, to audit fixed asset additions, the auditor could use the sampling interval and select and audit a sample of additions before year-end and finish the process after year-end.)

- Sample sizes are relatively small when few or no misstatements are expected because of its automatic stratification, which also contributes to audit efficiency.
- It directly controls for the most important sampling risk; the risk of incorrect acceptance.

A major disadvantage of PPS sampling lies in its difficulty in testing for understatements. However, as indicated previously, the problem of testing for understatements generally involves defining an alternative population to test and therefore the problem is not unique to PPS sampling. There is also a second drawback that can occur if there are more than a few misstatements in the sample resulting in a likely rejection of book value; this problem can be overcome by examining the nature of the misstatements and expanding audit testing.

Another disadvantage occurs when frequent misstatements are found in the sample. PPS sampling tends to be ultraconservative and may cause the auditor to conclude that the account balance contains a material misstatement when, in fact, it does not (called the *risk of incorrect rejection*).

Microcomputer Support

Many firms have microcomputer programs to assist in planning, selecting, and evaluating statistical samples; some of these are expert systems. The programs are designed to have the user answer the questions that a statistical expert would ask in deciding what sampling plan to use, what the sample size should be, what approach should be taken to evaluate the sample results, and the conclusion based on those results. Expert systems help eliminate the purely mechanical aspects of sampling and allow the auditor to concentrate on the judgments required. Computer assistance is particularly helpful when using the classical methods because of the complexities of some of the formulas.

D–NONSTATISTICAL SUBSTANTIVE SAMPLING

Both statistical sampling and nonstatistical sampling are acceptable for substantive testing when used properly. Nonstatistical samples should be based on the same audit considerations as those used for statistical sampling.

Tolerable Misstatement

There is no way to mathematically control for sampling risk in a nonstatistical sample; the auditor can only project the detected misstatements and make a judgment as to whether the account is likely to be materially misstated and decide whether more audit work is needed.

Individually Significant Items

Significant items can be identified by scanning the population and can be included in the audit test. The auditor can also select all items over a specific dollar amount.

Determining Sample Size

The auditor should be aware of the effect on sample size of the same factors used in statistical sampling. If test of details risk is low, or if tolerable misstatement is low, the auditor must compensate by using larger sample sizes. Because the approach to projecting the results of a nonstatistical sample is similar to the approach used for classical estimation techniques, the auditor should also consider the effect of the variability of the population in determining sample size.

Selecting the Sample

The auditor must be sure to select a sample that is representative of the population. One way to obtain a representative sample is to use a random-based method, either random dollars or random items, as in statistical sample selection. Another way is to choose items without any conscious bias (haphazard selection) other than intentionally selecting more of the large dollar items.

Evaluating the Sample Results

The misstatements found in the sample must be projected to the population and consideration must be given to sampling error before reaching a conclusion. For example, assume the following:

Items in population	2,000 items
Population book value	$2 million
Sample size	100 items
Book value of sample items	$155,000
Audit value of sample items	$150,000
Overstatement of sample items	($ 5,000)

If the auditor expects that the amount of misstatement is relatively constant per item in the population, it would be best to base the projection on the proportion of items tested:

$$\frac{2{,}000}{100} \times (\$5{,}000) = (\$100{,}000)$$

If the auditor expects the size of misstatements to vary with the book values of the items, the projection should be based on the proportion of the book values in the sample:

$$\frac{\$2{,}000{,}000}{\$155{,}000} \times (\$5{,}000) = (\$64{,}516)$$

The auditor should compare the misstatement projection to tolerable misstatement and consider sampling error. In many cases, tolerable misstatement and an allowance for sampling error are not quantified. Therefore, the auditor must use judgment in deciding whether all of the known and projected misstatements uncovered during the audit are within tolerable limits. There is no objective measure of the risk of incorrect acceptance or of the risk of incorrect rejection when using

Audit Research

CONSIDERATION OF SAMPLING ERROR IN A NONSTATISTICAL SAMPLE

One research study simulated various characteristics of an accounting population, including total book value, the average dollar amount, and the number of items in the population, their variability, and misstatement conditions. One decision rule the researchers considered was if the projected misstatement was less than one-third tolerable misstatement, accept the accounting population; otherwise reject the accounting population as materially misstated. They found that this decision rule was effective in minimizing the risk of incorrect acceptance.

Source: Lucia E. Peek, John Neter, and Carl Warren, "AICPA Non-Statistical Audit Sampling Guidelines: A Simulation," *Auditing: A Journal of Practice & Theory* (Fall 1991), 33-48.

nonstatistical sampling. Consider, however, the results of one research study, shown in the Audit Research box, concerning sampling risk in a nonstatistical sample.

Choosing between Nonstatistical and Statistical Sampling

The auditor should consider the following factors when choosing between nonstatistical and statistical sampling:

- Whether the audit staff is adequately trained to properly use statistical sampling.
- Whether the added costs of designing, selecting, and evaluating a statistical sample are justifiable in terms of the appropriateness of the resulting sample size and the objective measure of sampling risk.
- Whether the auditor wants an objective measure of the risk of drawing a wrong conclusion based on the sample.
- Whether the population lends itself to a random-based selection method.

E–ILLUSTRATIVE EXAMPLE–LEFLAM MANUFACTURING COMPANY

The auditor wishes to confirm accounts receivable of LeFlam as of December 31, 1993. The primary audit objectives are to determine whether

- The recorded receivables exist.
- The receivables are properly valued.
- LeFlam has the right to show the receivables as assets.

Planning the Sample

PPS sampling is chosen because (1) the primary objective is to test for possible overstatement of the account and (2) few misstatements are expected because of strong internal control procedures. A misstatement is defined for this test as any difference that affects pre-tax income. The population is made up of $5,643,200 and 2,090 customers. The individual balances for some of the major customers contain several unpaid invoices. Unpaid invoices are chosen as the sampling units to improve the confirmation responses. The client maintains a computer file of these unpaid invoices in invoice number order. A computer program is utilized to foot the population and select the sample. Positive confirmations are used because they provide the most reliable evidence due to the requirement to follow-up on all nonresponses.

Determining the Sample Size

It was determined in previous chapters that the client has strong controls thereby allowing the auditor to conduct this test with relatively high levels of detection risk. Based on Exhibit 14.2, a test of details risk of 50 percent is chosen. Recall that planning materiality was set at $175,000. Because PPS samples are considered to be drawn from the financial statements as a whole, planning materiality can be used as tolerable misstatement for this sample. Based on similar test results in prior years, you expect no more than $40,000 of net overstatement misstatement. Based on this information and the factors in Exhibit 14.3, the sampling interval and maximum sample size are

$$\text{Interval} = \frac{\$175{,}000 - (\$40{,}000 \times 1.0)}{.7} = \$192{,}857$$

$$\text{Maximum Sample Size} = \frac{\$5{,}643{,}200}{\$192{,}857} = 29$$

The computer program selected 29 sample items with a book value of $193,038.71. None of the unpaid invoices in the population exceeded the sampling interval. The computer program also footed the file and the total ($5,643,200) agreed with the accounting records, indicating that the sample is selected from the complete population that will be reflected in the financial statements.

Evaluation

All but two of the customers return their confirmations. To assure yourself that the addresses were correct and that these two customers do exist, their names and addresses are located in the telephone book and credit reports in their files are reviewed. Second requests are sent but not returned. The auditor turns to alternative procedures to determine the existence and accuracy of the account balances and decides to vouch the two invoices to customer orders, shipping documents, sales orders, and sales invoices. The auditor also reviews subsequent payments and determines that both invoices were subsequently paid.

Five of the confirmations that are returned contain exceptions. Four of these are shipments or payments in transit and represent legitimate timing differences. The remaining exception was a client pricing error. The invoice amount of $12,955.68 should have been $11,984.00, resulting in an overstatement of $971.68 and a tainting percentage of 7.5 percent.

The evaluation of this misstatement (using the factors from Exhibit 14.3) is shown in Exhibit 14.8. The basic precision is $135,000. The most likely misstatement is $14,465, well below the expected misstatement of $40,000. As a result, the auditor is 50 percent confident that accounts receivable are not overstated by more than the upper misstatement limit of $149,465. This is less than the tolerable misstatement of $175,000. Based on the assessed inherent and control risks, this sample result, and the other substantive procedures, the auditor can conclude that accounts receivable are not materially misstated.

Summary of Confirmation Responses

The auditor summarized the confirmation work in the working papers:

	Items	Amount
Population	3,810	5,643,200.00
Confirmed	29	193,038.71
Percent	.76	3.42
Responses	27	180,100.11
Percent	93.1	93.3
Exceptions	5	32,061.50
Cleared	4	19,105.82
Misstatements	1	971.68

Summary

This chapter has described several sampling methods that can be used to test the details of account balances. Auditors should be careful to select the proper method for the circumstances. Exhibit 14.9 summarizes several commonly encountered circumstances and the proper statistical sampling method for each.

Exhibit 14.8

EVALUATION OF LEFLAM MISSTATEMENT

	UML Factor		Tainting Percent	Sampling Interval	Dollar Conclusion
Basic precision	.7	×		192,857 =	135,000
Most likely misstatement					
Top stratum					
Lower stratum					
First largest tainting %			7.5% ×	192,857 =	14,465
Precision gap widening					
First largest %	0	×	7.5% = 0% ×	192,857 =	0
Upper misstatement limit					149,465

Whichever sampling method is used, it is extremely important to select a sample that is representative of the population. Otherwise, the sample results may lead to the wrong conclusion about the population. When evaluating a sample, the auditor must be very careful to identify what are to be considered misstatements and to project them to the whole population before reaching a conclusion about accepting the book value.

The relationships between the factors used in calculating a statistical sample size and the resulting sample size are as follows:

Change	Effect on Sample Size
Increase risk of incorrect acceptance (TD Risk)	Decrease
Increase risk of incorrect rejection*	Increase
Increase variability of the population items*	Increase
Increase tolerable misstatement	Decrease
Increase expected misstatement†	Increase
Increase population size	Increase

* = Used only for the classical methods.

† = Used only for PPS sampling.

Exhibit 14.9

SELECTING A STATISTICAL SAMPLING METHOD

Circumstances	Example	Method
Testing for overstatements, *few or no misstatements* are expected, and selection is based on *dollars.*	Normal confirmation of receivables or price testing inventory.	Probability proportional to size
Testing for over- and understatements, *few or no misstatements* are expected, and selection is based on *items.*	Same as above.	Stratified mean-per-unit
Testing for overstatements, *frequent misstatements* are expected, but the total misstatement is not expected to be material and selection is based on *dollars.*	Price testing inventory when the client claims to use FIFO but you know they only use the latest invoice price for each item.	PPS selection with difference estimation evaluation
Testing for over- and understatements, *frequent misstatements* are expected, selection is based on *items,* and the size of each misstatement is expected to be:		
Correlated with the size of the book value.	Same as above.	Ratio estimation
Not correlated with the size of the book value.	Same as above.	Difference estimation
Recorded *book value* for each population item is *not available.*	Testing adequacy of estimated product warranty liability.	Mean-per-unit

Auditors must look beyond the numbers and consider the qualitative aspects of the discovered misstatements and their impact on other aspects of the audit. The assessment of inherent or control risk may have been too optimistic and the auditor should reassess the effect of this on all aspects of the audit. The auditor should analyze the causes of the misstatements uncovered in a sample: error or irregularity, random or systematic occurrences, human or computer programming error. This analysis will help the auditor decide whether additional audit work is required and if so, what should be done.

Sampling is a useful audit tool, but it is only a tool. The auditor must be sure to understand what the numbers and statistics mean but must look beyond these and use good audit judgment to evaluate the audit findings and their implications on the fairness of the financial statements. Sampling is used in a variety of audit areas in addition to the revenue cycle, and we will return to it in several subsequent chapters of the text.

Significant Terms

achieved precision The precision of an estimate based on the standard deviation of sample items; represents a confidence interval constructed around the point estimate at the confidence level used in constructing the sample. Also referred to as *achieved allowance for sampling error.*

allowance for sampling error A factor used in planning statistical samples that represents the precision required in the sample to keep sampling risk at the desired level; provides "elbow room" for the difference between sample misstatement projections and the actual, but unknown, misstatement in the population.

basic precision The upper misstatement limit when no misstatements are detected in a PPS sample; computed by multiplying the sampling interval by the reliability factor.

classical variables sampling methods The statistical sampling methods that are based on the normal curve and central limit theorem: mean-per-unit, ratio estimation, and difference estimation sampling.

decision interval The range of the point estimate plus and minus the achieved precision.

desired allowance for sampling error The denominator in the sample size formula for the classical methods; determined by multiplying the tolerable misstatement by a factor based on the risk of incorrect acceptance and the risk of incorrect rejection.

difference estimation sampling method A classical sampling method most effective when frequent misstatements are expected and the sizes of misstatements do not have a close correlation with their related book values. An average difference between book value and audit value is calculated and projected to the population as a whole to determine whether book value might be materially misstated.

error expansion factor A factor used in determining the sampling interval/size for PPS sampling to provide for additional sampling error when some misstatement is expected.

excludable misstatements Misstatements the client has independently detected and corrected within the normal accounting system before the auditor begins substantive testing and misstatements that the auditor will evaluate more fully in some other procedure, such as cutoff errors when there is a separate cutoff test.

mean-per-unit sampling method A classical sampling method used when few misstatements are expected and the sample is to be selected based on random items rather than random dollars.

most likely misstatement In PPS sampling, the sum of the top stratum misstatements and the projection of the lower stratum misstatements. It is the auditor's best estimate of the total misstatement in the population and should be posted to the summary of possible adjustments.

misstatement For substantive sampling purposes, the differences in recorded values and audited values resulting in either (1) a misstatement of pre-tax income arising from any nonexcludable misstatement(s) (income effect) or (2) a difference that affects the account total (account misstatement).

other substantive procedures risk (OSPR) The risk that all of the substantive tests, other than the planned sampling test, will fail to detect a material misstatement; professional standards refer to OSPR as *analytical procedures (AP) risk.*

point estimate An estimate of the correct value of the population based on a classical sample result. It is the auditor's best estimate of the population value based on sample results and serves as the basis around which confidence intervals can be constructed.

precision gap widening Provision for additional sampling error when misstatements are detected in a PPS sample. Factors are determined from tables derived from the underlying sampling distribution.

projected misstatement The difference between the point estimate and the book value of the population.

probability proportional to size (PPS) sampling A sampling method based on attribute estimation sampling but involving dollar misstatements rather than failure rates; each item in the population has a probability of being included in the sample proportionate to the dollar value of the item. PPS sampling is most effective when auditing for the overstatement of a population and when no or few misstatements are expected.

ratio estimation sampling method A classical sampling method that is most effective when frequent misstatements are expected and the sizes of misstatements have a high correlation with the related book values.

reliability factors Factors related to the test of details risk used to determine the sample interval/size for PPS sampling.

sampling units The individual auditable elements, as defined by the auditor, that constitute the population, such as customers' balances or individual unpaid invoices.

stratification Dividing the population into relatively homogeneous groups called *strata.* Stratification can be performed judgmentally by the auditor but is most often performed with the assistance of generalized audit software to achieve optimum sampling efficiency.

tainting percentage In PPS sampling, the amount of misstatement as a percent of the sample item's book value. The tainting percentage is calculated individually for each sampled item.

test of details risk A synonym for the risk of incorrect acceptance. It is the part of detection risk related to a sampling application. The other part is the other substantive procedures risk (OSPR).

top stratum Population items whose book values exceed the sampling interval and are, therefore, all included in the test. The top stratum consists of all account balances exceeding a specific dollar amount.

upper misstatement limit The maximum potential amount of misstatement in a population based on sample results at a specified level of test of details risk.

APPENDIX A–CLASSICAL SAMPLING METHODS–ADDITIONAL DETAILS

Sample Design

Estimated Standard Deviation

The estimated standard deviation (S_x) based on a preliminary sample for MPU and difference estimation sampling is calculated using the following formula:

$$S_x = \sqrt{\frac{\Sigma x^2 - n(\bar{x})^2}{n-1}}$$

For *MPU sampling,* x in the formula refers to the book or audit values of the sample items, whichever is available. For *difference estimation sampling,* the x refers to the differences between the book and audited values. The formula for calculating the standard deviation for *ratio estimation* sampling is more complex and beyond the scope of this book.* The estimated standard deviation for all three methods based on a preliminary sample of 30 items is shown in Exhibit 14.10. Note that the standard deviation for MPU sampling is much larger than for the other two methods because it is based on the audit values alone rather than on the relationship between audit and book values.

*See Roberts, *Statistical Auditing,* p. 80.

Exhibit 14.10

COMPARISON OF STANDARD DEVIATIONS AMONG THE CLASSICAL STATISTICAL SAMPLING METHODS

Item	Book Value	Audit Value	Difference	Ratio (AV/BV)
1	107	107	0	100.00%
2	1,792	1,823	(31)	101.73%
3	2,426	2,318	108	95.55%
4	93	93	0	100.00%
5	1,850	1,736	114	93.84%
6	1,242	1,225	17	98.63%
7	1,861	1,861	0	100.00%
8	3,548	3,548	0	100.00%
9	1,840	1,690	150	91.85%
10	1,705	1,680	25	98.53%
11	2,681	2,643	38	98.58%
12	1,781	1,930	(149)	108.37%
13	561	356	205	63.46%
14	2,009	2,009	0	100.00%
15	1,329	1,347	(18)	101.35%
16	2,686	2,686	0	100.00%
17	3,385	3,455	(70)	102.07%
18	1,798	1,798	0	100.00%
19	937	690	247	73.64%
20	3,222	3,017	205	93.64%
21	1,258	1,057	201	84.02%
22	572	688	(116)	120.28%
23	1,832	1,435	397	78.33%
24	300	300	0	100.00%
25	2,449	2,475	(26)	101.06%
26	3,893	3,766	127	96.74%
27	2,097	2,097	0	100.00%
28	3,031	3,031	0	100.00%
29	1,435	1,423	12	99.16%
30	616	419	197	68.02%
	54,336	52,703	1,633	96.99%
Standard deviation		1,032	118	123
Used for		MPU	Difference estimation	Ratio estimation

Note: This presample is a part of the final sample of 140 items.

Desired Allowance for Sampling Error

The **desired allowance for sampling error** is determined by multiplying the tolerable misstatement by a factor that is based on the risk of incorrect acceptance and the risk of incorrect rejection combined (see Exhibit 14.11). For example, assume that tolerable misstatement is $400,000, the risk of incorrect acceptance is set at 10 percent, and the risk of incorrect rejection at 20 percent. The ratio from Exhibit 14.11 (.500) is multiplied by the tolerable misstatement to get the desired allowance for sampling error of $200,000 ($400,000 × .500).

Achieved Precision

The **achieved precision (A')** is calculated using a revision of the sample size formula.

$$A' = N \times U_R \times \frac{S_x}{\sqrt{n}}$$

If the standard deviation of a sample of 140 items is $107.84, there are 15,000 items in the population and the risk of incorrect rejection is 20 percent ($U_R = 1.28$), the achieved precision is

$$A' = 15{,}000 \times 1.28 \times \frac{\$107.84}{\sqrt{140}} = \$174{,}994$$

Exhibit 14.11

RATIO OF DESIRED ALLOWANCE FOR SAMPLING ERROR TO TOLERABLE MISSTATEMENT

Risk of Incorrect Acceptance	Risk of Incorrect Rejection		
	20%	10%	5%
5%	.437	.500	.543
10%	**.500**	.561	.605
15%	.511	.612	.653
20%	.603	.661	.700
25%	.653	.708	.742
39%	.707	.756	.787
40%	.831	.863	.883
50%	1.000	1.000	1.000

Source: Donald M. Roberts, *Statistical Auditing* (New York: AICPA, 1978), 247; see pages 40–48 for the rationale supporting the factors in this table.

Adjusted Achieved Precision

Recall the decision rule that if the population book value lies within the decision interval, which is the point estimate plus and minus the achieved precision, the auditor can accept the book value. When the auditor originally accepts the book value on this basis, a risk of incorrect acceptance remains. To limit this risk to the desired level, the achieved precision must be no greater than the desired allowance for sampling error, which was $200,000 in the illustration. The auditor should calculate an adjusted achieved precision using the formula below.

If the auditor finds that the population book value lies outside the decision interval, a risk of incorrect rejection remains. To limit this risk, the achieved precision should be no less than the desired allowance for sampling error. If the point estimate is $26,725,393 and the achieved precision is $174,994, the decision interval is $26,550,399 to $26,900,387. Because the book value of $27,000,000 lies outside this interval, the auditor should calculate an adjusted achieved precision (A") and related revised decision interval as follows:

$$A'' = A' + \textit{Tolerable Misstatement} \times (1 - \frac{A'}{A})$$

$$A'' = \$174{,}994 + \$400{,}000 \times (1 - \frac{\$174{,}994}{\$200{,}000}) = \$225{,}006$$

Revised decision interval = $26,500,387 to $26,950,399 ($26,725,393 ± $225,006).

Because the book value lies outside this revised interval, the auditor concludes that the book value may contain a material misstatement at a risk of incorrect rejection of 20 percent, which was used to plan the sample.

APPENDIX B–AICPA APPROACH TO EVALUATING MISSTATEMENTS IN A PPS SAMPLING APPLICATION

One approach to evaluating misstatements using PPS sampling was illustrated in the chapter in Exhibit 14.5 for the following misstatements:

Customer Number	Book Value	Audit Value	Misstatement	Tainting Percent
2	$ 2,200	$ 2,154	$ 66	3%
7	45,023	44,340	683	NA
90	8,300	8,217	83	1%
			$832	

Recall that the test of details risk (risk of incorrect acceptance) is 15 percent. The basic precision was $41,800, most likely misstatement was $1,563, and precision gap widening was $392, resulting in an upper misstatement limit of $43,755.

In the AICPA's audit and accounting guide, *Audit Sampling,* another approach is used that achieves the same upper misstatement limit as in the illustration. The results are the same because the factors used in that illustration (from Exhibit 14.3) are derived from the factors used in the AICPA's approach (Exhibit 14.12). The relationships among these factors are as follows (for a 15 percent risk of incorrect acceptance):

	Audit Guide Approach		Used in Exhibit 14.5	
Number of Overstatement Misstatements	Reliability Factor (Exhibit 14.12)	Incremental Change in Reliability Factor	Most Likely Misstatement	Precision Gap Widening Factor*
0	1.90	NA		
1	3.38	3.38 − 1.90 = 1.48	1	.48
2	4.72	4.72 − 3.38 = 1.34	1	.34

*= Factors shown in Exhibit 14.3

The difference between these two approaches is that the AICPA's approach combines the calculations of the most likely misstatement and precision gap widening into what is called *projected misstatement plus incremental allowance for sampling error* as follows:

Exhibit 14.12

PROBABILITY-PROPORTIONAL-TO-SIZE SAMPLING TABLES RELIABILITY FACTORS FOR OVERSTATEMENTS

Number of Overstatements	Risk of Incorrect Acceptance 1%	5%	10%	15%	20%	25%	30%	37%	50%
0	4.61	3.00	2.31	1.90	1.61	1.39	1.21	1.00	0.70
1	6.64	4.75	3.89	3.38	3.00	2.70	2.44	2.14	1.68
2	8.41	6.30	5.33	4.72	4.28	3.93	3.92	3.25	2.68
3	10.05	7.76	6.69	6.02	5.52	5.11	4.77	4.34	3.68
4	11.61	9.16	8.00	7.27	6.73	6.28	5.90	5.43	4.68
5	13.11	10.52	9.28	8.50	7.91	7.43	7.01	6.49	5.68
6	14.57	11.85	10.54	9.71	9.08	8.56	8.12	7.56	6.67
7	16.00	13.15	11.78	10.90	10.24	9.69	9.21	8.63	7.67
8	17.41	14.44	13.00	12.08	11.38	10.81	10.31	9.68	8.67
9	18.79	15.71	14.21	13.25	12.52	11.92	11.39	10.74	9.67
10	20.15	16.97	15.41	14.42	13.66	13.02	12.47	11.79	10.67

This table should be used for the AICPA evaluation approach, not that described in the body of this chapter.

Source: *Audit Sampling* (New York: AICPA, 1983), 117.

Tainting Percent	× Sampling Interval	= Projected Misstatement	× Incremental Change in Reliability Factor	= Projected Misstatement Plus Incremental Allowance for Sampling Error
3%	$22,000	660	1.48	977
1%	$22,000	220	1.34	295
			Total	1,272

The upper misstatement limit is then calculated by adding to this total the basic precision and top stratum misstatement:

Projected Misstatement + Incremental Allowance for Sampling Error	$ 1,272
Basic precision	41,800
Top stratum misstatement	683
Upper misstatement limit	$43,755

Note that this upper misstatement limit is the same as that calculated in Exhibit 14.5.

APPENDIX C–PPS SUBSAMPLING

Items selected using the PPS sample selection method may contain more than one auditable unit. Also, sample items may contain more than one selection point. A customer's balance, for example, may contain several unpaid balances. The auditor may use subsampling to select specific unpaid invoices to confirm rather than confirming the entire balance. This is likely to improve the useable confirmation response rate. Customers are more likely to confirm one or a few unpaid invoices rather than the entire balance because it takes time to go into the accounts payable system, which is often a voucher system, to find the information.

The information from Exhibit 14.4 will be used to illustrate subsampling:

Customer	Book Value	Cumulative Amount	Selection Amount
	Random Start	20,000	
1	220	20,220	
2	2,200	22,420	22,000
3	22,000	44,420	44,000
4	880	45,300	
5	6,128	51,428	
6	2,800	54,228	
7	45,023	99,251	66,000 & 88,000
8	10	99,261	
9	8,231	107,492	
10	16,894	124,386	110,000
.	.	.	
.	.	.	
.	.	.	
450	1,900	827,906	

There are two selection points in customer 7's balance. That balance is made up of the following unpaid invoices:

Unpaid Invoice Number	Book Value	Cumulative Amount	Selection Amount
Previous Cumulative Amount		54,228	
15,239	$10,113	64,341	
16,783	1,500	65,841	
16,922	**15,677**	**81,518**	**66,000**
17,448	**9,391**	**90,909**	**88,000**
19,005	8,342	99,251	
Total	$45,023		

The starting point is the cumulative amount (54,228) that precedes customer 7's book value. The cumulative amounts are then calculated as before. The selection amounts of 66,000 and 88,000 identify invoices numbered 16,922 and 17,448 for confirmation.

Subsampling has other applications. It can be used to select invoices on which to apply an alternative procedure when the customer will not confirm the balance. It can also be used when the auditor has a lengthy computer printout with page totals or cumulative page totals but it is not practical to have the computer select the sample. Page totals can be used instead of customer balances to develop cumulative amounts with a random start in a manner similar to that illustrated in the chapter. The selection points identify the pages with selection items. Subsampling can be used to identify the item(s) on those pages to confirm. To test the footing of the population, those pages with selection items can be footed to ensure that the computer totals are accurate. If cumulative totals are shown on each page, they can be used to identify the pages with selection items. The only difference is that those cumulative page totals do not give a random start. Therefore, the selection amounts begin with a random start, such as the 20,000 in the second preceding table, and subsequent selection amounts are determined by adding the sampling interval (22,000) to the preceding selection amount, such as 42,000, 64,000, 86,000, 108,000, 130,000, etc.

Review Questions

A–Introduction

14–1 Why is it important that misstatements be carefully defined when planning a sample?

14–2 How would the auditor decide whether to confirm customers' balances or individual unpaid invoices?

14–3 Why is it important to determine the completeness of the physical representation of the population (such as a trial balance of accounts receivable) from which a sample is to be selected?

14–4 What factors should be considered when determining which statistical sampling method to use for a substantive test?

14–5 What population should the auditor sample from when testing accounts receivable for

a. Overstatement?
b. Understatement?

B–Probability Proportional to Size Sampling

14–6 In what circumstances is PPS sampling most effective?

14–7 What information is needed to design a PPS sample? Where does the auditor gather such information?

14–8 Explain the relationship between planning materiality and tolerable misstatement when using PPS sampling.

14–9 If the sampling interval for PPS sampling is $30,000, would an item in the population with a book value of $50,000 always be included in the sample using
a. The fixed interval approach? Explain.
b. The random number approach? Explain.

14–10 All else being equal, what is the effect on a PPS sample size of a
a. Larger tolerable misstatement?
b. Larger expected misstatement?
c. Larger allowable risk of incorrect acceptance (TD risk)?
d. Larger population?

14–11 What alternatives are available to the auditor when a population contains a few items with negative balances, such as credit balances in accounts receivable, and the auditor wishes to utilize PPS sampling?

14–12 Would an item with a zero balance be included in a PPS sample? If not, what is the effect of not including the item in the sample?

14–13 What is basic precision, and how is it determined?

14–14 What is the upper misstatement limit, and how is it determined?

14–15 What are the advantages of PPS sampling over other statistical methods?

14–16 Is the risk of incorrect acceptance utilized for both PPS sampling and classical sampling, or for just one of the methods? Explain.

14–17 What is other substantive procedures risk (OSPR)? How does the auditor measure or estimate it?

14–18 What is the relationship among detection risk, OSPR, and test of details risk?

14–19 Why is it important to determine whether the difference between the customer's balance shown in the client's records and the amount confirmed by the customer is the client's error or irregularity, the customer's error, or a timing difference? What are the implications of this determination on the conduct of the audit and further investigation of the account balance?

14–20 What is an excludable error condition? Does such a condition mean that it is not considered in evaluating sampling results?

C–Classical Variables Sampling Methods: Overview

14–21 How does the definition of the population in PPS sampling differ from the definition for classical sampling?

14–22 When should the auditor consider using

a. Mean-per-unit sampling?

b. Ratio estimation sampling?

c. Difference estimation sampling?

14–23 What information is needed to determine the sample size for a classical sampling method that is not required for PPS sampling?

14–24 Why is the estimated standard deviation for mean-per-unit (MPU) sampling usually larger than for ratio or difference estimation sampling? How can it be reduced for MPU sampling?

14–25 What methods can an auditor use in preparing an estimate of the standard deviation to use in a classical statistical sampling application?

14–26 How does the selection of a sample differ between the classical variables sampling and PPS sampling? What are the potential implications of this difference on the detection of understatements in the population?

14–27 How do the decision rules for determining whether an account balance may contain a material misstatement differ between the classical sampling methods and PPS sampling?

14–28 What is the effect on the sample size of an increased standard deviation when using

a. A classical method?

b. PPS sampling?

D–Nonstatistical Substantive Sampling

14–29 Do the professional standards support the use of nonstatistical sampling for substantive testing? Explain the circumstances in which nonstatistical sampling might be used.

14–30 When using nonstatistical sampling, how does the auditor

a. Determine the sample size?

b. Select the sample?

c. Evaluate the sample results?

Multiple Choice Questions

*14–31 The use of probability proportional to size sampling would be inefficient if

a. Bank accounts are being audited.

b. Statistical inferences are to be made.

c. Each account is of equal importance.

d. The number of sampling units is large.

*Adapted from the Uniform CPA examination or the Certified Internal Auditor examination.

*14–32 An internal auditor selects a statistical sample from a large inventory of replacement parts. Which of the following audit objectives would be most appropriate if the sampling method used is probability proportional to size (PPS)?

a. The auditor plans to estimate the total dollar value of the inventory when a recorded book value does not exist.

b. The auditor plans to make a statement concerning the total dollar amount of misstatement in the population from the recorded book value.

c. The auditor wishes to accept or reject the hypothesis that the proportion of defective parts in the population is less than five percent.

d. The auditor wishes to estimate the proportion of defective parts in the population.

*14–33 Which of the following best describes an inherent limitation of the probability proportional to size (PPS) sampling method?

a. It can be used only for substantive testing of asset accounts.

b. It is complicated and always requires the use of a computer system to perform the calculations.

c. Error rates must be large and the misstatements must be overstatements.

d. Error rates must be small and the misstatements must be overstatements.

*14–34 During an audit involving the testing of accounts receivable balances, an internal auditor decides to specify a precision interval of $100,000 instead of the $200,000 precision interval that was called for in the sampling plan contained in the audit program. Which of the following would be a result of the auditor's decision to decrease the precision interval?

a. An increase in the required sample size.

b. A decrease in the required sample size.

c. An increase in the population standard deviation.

d. A decrease in the population standard deviation.

*14–35 In a probability proportional to size sample with a sampling interval of $10,000, an auditor discovered that a selected account receivable with a recorded amount of $5,000 had an audit amount of $2,000. The projected misstatement of this sample was

a. $3,000.

b. $4,000.

c. $6,000.

d. $8,000.

*14–36 In an application of mean-per-unit sampling, the following information has been obtained:

Reported book value	$600,000
Point estimate (estimated total value)	591,000
Allowance for sampling error (precision)	± 22,000
Tolerable misstatement	± 45,000

The appropriate conclusion would be that the reported book value is

a. Acceptable only if the risk of incorrect rejection is at least twice the risk of incorrect acceptance.
b. Acceptable.
c. Not acceptable.
d. Acceptable only if the risk of incorrect acceptance is at least twice the risk of incorrect rejection.

*14–37 In variables estimation sampling, the sample standard deviation is used to calculate the

a. Point estimate of central tendency.
b. Tainting of the sample interval.
c. Reliability or desired confidence level.
d. Attained sample precision.

*14–38 Using statistical sampling to assist in verifying the year-end accounts payable balance, an auditor has accumulated the following data:

	Number of Accounts	Book Balance	Balance Determined by the Auditor
Population	4,100	$5,000,000	?
Sample	200	$ 250,000	$300,000

Using the ratio estimation technique, the auditor's estimate of year-end accounts payable balance would be

a. $6,150,000.
b. $6,000,000.
c. $5,125,000.
d. $5,050,000.

*14–39 Use of the ratio estimation sampling technique to estimate dollar amounts is *inappropriate* when

a. The total book value is known and corresponds to the sum of all the individual book values.
b. A book value for each sample item is unknown.
c. There are some observed differences between audited values and book values.
d. The audited values are nearly proportional to the book values.

*14–40 The major reason that the difference and ratio estimation methods would be expected to produce audit efficiency is that the

a. Number of members of the populations of differences or ratios is smaller than the number of members of the population of book values.
b. Beta risk may be completely ignored.
c. Calculations required in using difference or ratio estimation are less arduous and fewer than those required when using direct estimation.
d. Variability of the populations of differences or ratios is less than that of the populations of book values or audited values.

*14–41 The inventory of a subsidiary consists of 14,980 items valued at $19,625,000. The inventory data are not available in computer-readable form but are contained in 217 pages of printout with 60 lines per page. Each page has a page total. Based on the last audit, the auditor expects there to be few misstatements that are overstated. The most efficient sampling technique to test the reasonableness of the stated value is

a. Stratified mean-per-unit estimation.
b. Dollar unit (PPS) sampling.
c. Difference estimation.
d. Ratio estimation.

*14–42 In conducting a substantive test of an account balance, an auditor hypothesizes that no material misstatement exists. The risk that sample results will support the auditor's hypothesis when a material misstatement actually does exist is the risk of

a. Incorrect rejection.
b. Alpha error.
c. Incorrect acceptance.
d. Type I error.

*14–43 An auditor is performing substantive tests of pricing and extensions of perpetual inventory balances consisting of a large number of items. Past experience indicates numerous pricing and extension misstatements. Which of the following statistical sampling approaches is most appropriate?

a. Unstratified mean per unit.
b. Probability proportional to size.
c. Stop or go.
d. Ratio estimation.

Discussion Problems

14–44 (Risk Factors and Sample Size—PPS sampling) You are designing a PPS sample to determine how many accounts receivable confirmations to send. There are 2,000 customer accounts with a total book value of $5,643,200. You estimate the maximum misstatement to be $40,000 and tolerable misstatement is set at $175,000.

Required:

a. Complete the following table using the audit risk model ($AR = IR \times CR \times OSPR \times TD$):

	Risks (In Percent)						
Case	AR	IR	CR	OSPR	TD	Sampling Interval	Sample Size
1	5 %	100%	100%	100%			
2	10	100	100	100			
3	5	100	50	100			
4	5	50	25	80			
5	5	50	50	20			

b. What is the effect on sample size (increase or decrease) of:
   1. Increasing the audit risk?
   2. Increasing the TD risk?
   3. Increasing the tolerable misstatement?
   4. Increasing the expected misstatement?

14–45 (PPS Sample Design and Selection) You are planning the confirmation of accounts receivable. There are 2,000 customers with a total book value of $5,643,200. Tolerable misstatement is set at $175,000 and expected misstatement is $40,000. The allowable risk of incorrect acceptance (TD risk) is 30 percent.

Required:

a. What is the sampling interval?

b. What is the maximum sample size?

c. What is the largest value you can use for a random start?

d. Using the following list of the first 15 items in your population, a random start of $25,000, and a rounded sample interval of $100,000, identify the items to be included in your sample.

Item	Book Value	Cumulative Amount
	Random Start	
1	3,900	
2	26,000	
3	5,000	
4	130,000	
5	20,000	
6	360,000	
7	100	
8	25,000	
9	190,000	
10	10,000	
11	90,000	
12	2,500	
13	65,000	
14	110,000	
15	8,992	

e. What is the probability of selecting each of the following population items, assuming a $100,000 sampling interval?

Item	Book Value	Probability of Selection
1	3,900	
2	26,000	
4	130,000	
6	360,000	

f. Explain how item 1 in part e ($3,900) would be included in your sample prior to selecting a random start.

g. Why might the final sample size be less than the maximum sample size?

h. (Subsampling—based on Appendix C)

The balance for customer 6 is made up of the following unpaid invoices. Which of these invoices should the auditor confirm when confirming individual unpaid invoices?

Invoice Date	Book Value	Cumulative Amount	Selection Amount
	Previous		
11/25/X1	120,000		
12/10/XI	15,000		
12/18/X1	130,000		
12/23/X1	35,000		
12/28/X1	60,000		

14–46 (Sample Misstatements) In confirming individual accounts receivable balances, your client's customers reported the following exceptions.

Required:
Which of these exceptions should be considered misstatements for evaluation purposes if misstatements are defined as

a. Differences that affect the account balance?

b. Differences that affect pre-tax income?

Explain your reasoning in each instance.

1. The wrong trade discount was used.
2. The client charged sales tax to a tax exempt customer.
3. The client failed to record returned merchandise.
4. The invoice contained a clerical error.
5. The payment was posted to the wrong customer's account.
6. The client failed to record a sale.
7. The payment was in transit at the confirmation date.
8. Freight was charged to the customer when the terms were FOB destination.
9. The customer subtracted a cash discount for a payment made after the discount period.

14–47 (PPS Sample Evaluation) Based on the information in Problem 14–45, assume that your sampling interval is $100,000. Five customers had balances in excess of the $100,000 sampling interval, and their combined balances totaled $800,000.

Required:

a. What is your statistical conclusion if no misstatements are found in the sample? Is this acceptable? Explain.

b. Calculate the most likely misstatement and upper misstatement limit and prepare a summary like the one illustrated in Exhibit 14.5, assuming the following misstatements are found in the sample.

Misstatement Number	Book Value	Audit Value
1	$210,000	$208,000
2	9,000	8,910
3	15,000	14,250

c. Are these results acceptable? Explain.

d. If the results are not acceptable, what courses of action are available to you?

14–48 (PPS Sampling) The auditor is auditing accounts receivable. The company is a long-time client and has a sound control structure. However, because of problems encountered in previous years, the auditor has assessed control risk as moderate and assigns a control risk assessment of 25 percent and a desired audit risk of 5 percent. Other factors considered by the auditor:

1. The auditor will not be performing any other substantive audit procedures.
2. Inherent risk, by firm policy, is assessed at 100 percent.
3. Client book value is $8,425,000.
4. Tolerable misstatement is set at $200,000.
5. Previous audits have shown an expected error of $40,000 overstatement is reasonable.

Required:

a. Calculate test of details risk.

b. Calculate (and show the calculation) of the sample selection interval.

c. Assume that the auditor rounds the sampling interval *down* to the next nearest 10,000. Calculate the approximate largest sample size the auditor would expect.

d. Assume the auditor found the following differences when performing the audit work.

Book Value	Audited Value	Nature of Difference
$25,000	$15,000	Amount was billed to Jason Company, but it should have been billed to Johnson Company. Subsequent follow-up work confirmed that it should be billed to Johnson and Johnson acknowledged the debt.
$40,000	$20,000	Merchandise was returned, but credit was not given in a timely fashion.
$325,000	$250,000	Major dispute on cost overrun charges. Subsequent review supports customer position.
$105,000	$100,000	Another dispute on cost overrun. Again customer position is correct.
$122	$0	A credit memo was supposed to have been issued for defective merchandise but was not.

Note: Show all calculations for the items requested below.

1. Calculate the *most likely error and the upper error limit* for accounts receivable.
2. Discuss the audit implications, that is, whether the audit work supports book value or whether additional audit work should be recommended, and if so, the nature of the audit work.

14–49 (Choosing a Sampling Method) You are deciding which statistical sampling method to use. Indicate which of the methods described in this chapter is most appropriate in each of the following circumstances. Explain your answer.

Required:

a. Your client uses standard cost to approximate FIFO valuation. You expect frequent but not material differences and desire to select random items to test. You expect the sizes of the misstatements to have a high correlation to the related book values.
b. Same as part a except you do not expect there to be a close correlation of the size of misstatements to the related book values.
c. Your audit objective is to determine whether inventory is materially overstated; you do not expect many misstatements, and you desire to select the sample based on dollars.
d. Your audit objective is to determine whether inventory is fairly stated. There is very little variability in the extended values of the inventory items. You do not expect many misstatements and desire to select random items to test.

14–50 (Sample Size Effects—MPU Sampling) You have decided to use unstratified mean-per-unit sampling.

Required:

Indicate the effect on sample size (increase, decrease, no effect, or indeterminate) for each of the following changes and explain your answer.

a. Increase in the population size.
b. Increase the standard deviation.
c. Increase the desired precision from $200,000 to $300,000.
d. Rather than test the population without stratification, you decide to stratify it into three strata: all of the items over $100,000 in one stratum, all of the items between $25,000 and $100,000 in a second stratum, and the items less than $25,000 in a third stratum.

14–51 (PPS Sampling) Winston's raw material inventory is made up of 5,000 items with a total book value of $500,000. You have decided to use PPS sampling for a price test. The audit risk is 5 percent, inherent risk is 75 percent, control risk is 100 percent, the other substantive procedures risk is 70 percent. Tolerable misstatement is $50,000. Expected misstatement is $3,000.

Required:

a. What risk of incorrect acceptance (test of details risk) should be used for this test?

b. What is the computed sampling interval?

c. What is the maximum sample size?

d. Without prejudice to your previous answers, assume the risk of incorrect acceptance is 10 percent and the sampling interval is $20,000. You have selected a random start of $4,500, which is added to begin the selection process. Identify the items that would be included in the sample from the first 10 book values listed below.

Item	Book Value
1	5,000
2	12,500
3	25,000
4	200
5	1,500
6	3,800
7	9,000
8	2,000
9	17,500
10	7,000

e. Assume the following misstatements were found.

Book Value	Audit Value
10,000	9,800
30,000	29,000
5,000	4,750

1. What is the most likely misstatement in the population?
2. What is the upper misstatement limit?
3. Are these results acceptable? Explain.
4. Assume that the results indicate that there may be a material misstatement in the inventory. What are the alternative courses of action you could take?

14–52 (PPS Design and Evaluation of Overstatements and Understatements) You are performing a price test of inventory, which has a book value of $2,750,699 and 3,875 items. Tolerable misstatement is $150,000, expected misstatement is $30,000, and the TD risk is 10 percent.

Required:

a. What sampling interval should be used for this sample?

b. Without prejudice to your answer in part a, assume that the sampling interval was $45,000 and the following misstatements were found. Evaluate these misstatements and determine the most likely net misstatement and separate "upper misstatement limits" for overstatements and understatements.

Book Value	Audit Value	Misstatement
$ 5,000	$ 4,750	$250
10,000	10,300	(300)

14–53 (Effect of Misstatement Analysis) Your evaluation of a statistical sample indicates that there may be a material misstatement in the population. Upon analyzing the detected misstatements, a common cause was discovered: most of the misstatements were caused by the failure to record sales returns on a timely basis. That is, sales were returned prior to December 31 but were recorded as January returns because the person who normally records sales returns was on vacation at year-end.

Required:
How should the auditor proceed to determine whether accounts receivable and sales returns and allowances contain a material misstatement?

14–54 (Classical Sampling Application) You are to sample accounts receivable balances using a classical method. There are 1,500 customers and the book value is $3,000,000. The desired risk of incorrect rejection is 5 percent, risk of incorrect acceptance is 20 percent, and tolerable misstatement is $200,000.

Required:

a. Sample size

Calculate the sample size for each of the classical methods if the desired allowance for sampling error is $140,000, and the estimated standard deviation is

1. $1,531 for mean-per-unit sampling.
2. $397 for ratio estimation sampling.
3. $393 for difference estimation sampling.

b. Point Estimate and Projected Misstatement

Without prejudice to your answers in part a, assume that you confirmed or performed alternative procedures on 64 customer balances having a total book value of $133,000 and a total audit value of $130,000. Calculate the point estimate of the correct value of accounts receivable and projected misstatement using

1. Mean-per-unit sampling.
2. Ratio estimation sampling.
3. Difference estimation sampling.
4. Nonstatistical sampling (sample was selected randomly).

c. In part b, why is the MPU estimate of the difference an understatement and the others an overstatement?

d. Decision interval

You have determined that difference estimation sampling is the most appropriate method to use for evaluation. The achieved precision is $143,325.

1. What is the decision interval?
2. Are these results acceptable? Explain.
3. What is the risk of incorrect rejection? Explain.

e. Allowance for sampling error and precision based on a above (Appendix A). Using difference estimation sampling:

1. Show how the desired allowance for sampling error of $140,000 is determined.
2. Show how the achieved precision of $143,325 is calculated. The standard deviation of the sample differences is $390.
3. The achieved precision ($143,325) exceeds the desired allowance for sampling error ($140,000).
   (a). Calculate the adjusted achieved precision and the related decision interval.
   (b). Are these revised sample results acceptable?
   (c). What is the risk of incorrect acceptance?
   (d). What is the risk of incorrect rejection?

*14–55 (PPS Advantages, Sample Design, and Evaluation Using AICPA Approach—Appendix B) Edwards has decided to use probability proportional to size (PPS) sampling in the audit of a client's accounts receivable balance. Few, if any, misstatements of account balance overstatement are expected. Edwards plans to use the table shown in Exhibit 14.12.

Required:

a. Identify the advantages of using PPS sampling over classical variables sampling.
b. Calculate the sampling interval and the sample size Edwards should use given the following information:

Tolerable misstatement	$15,000
Risk of incorrect acceptance	5%
Number of misstatements allowed	–0–
Recorded amount of accounts receivable	$300,000

c. (*Note:* Requirements b and c are *not* related.) Calculate the total projected misstatement if the following three misstatements were discovered in a PPS sample:

	Recorded Amount	Audit Amount	Sampling Interval
First misstatement	$ 400	$ 320	$1,000
Second misstatement	500	–0–	1,000
Third misstatement	3,000	2,500	1,000

14–56 (PPS Subsampling—Appendix C) To improve the useful confirmation response rate, you have decided to use subsampling to select the unpaid invoices to confirm. One of the customer's balances contains the following unpaid invoices. The selection amounts in this account are 200,000 and 210,000. Identify the unpaid invoices to confirm.

Unpaid Invoice Number	Book Value	Cumulative Amount	Selection Amount
Previous Cumulative Amount		198,655	
48,772	$5,119		
49,319	150		
50,200	3,557		

Unpaid Invoice Number	Book Value	Cumulative Amount	Selection Amount
50,446	8,822		
51,032	2,843		
Total	$12,551		

14–57 **(Research Question)** Review published research studies on the extent to which the various statistical sampling methods are used and for what they are used. Write a report summarizing the results.

14–58 **(Research Question)** Review audit software programs used by public accounting firms or internal audit organizations and determine the sampling capabilities of the software and write a report on your findings. *Note:* Summaries of the capabilities of the audit software packages are frequently published in the professional journals.

Case

14–59 (Cost/Benefit Considerations) The auditor often has alternative approaches that can be taken in auditing the major components of financial statements, particularly when the client has good internal controls.

Required:
Using the information from discussion problem 14–44, discuss the factors, including cost/benefit, that the auditor should consider in choosing among the approaches used in cases 1, 3, and 4.

Computer-Assisted Problems

Problems for this chapter using adVenture are in the Appendix at the end of the book. You should read the introduction and instructions before working the problems. These problems are as follows:

C–3 Using Generalized Audit Software Procedures on Accounts Receivable

C–4 Using PPS Sampling to Confirm Accounts Receivable.

C–5 Accounts Receivable Confirmations: Sampling Sensitivity Analysis

C–6 Using Nonstatistical Sampling to Confirm Accounts Receivable

C–7 Accounts Receivable Confirmations: Sampling and Audit Costs

C–8 Using Sampling to Test Sales Cutoff

End Notes

1. American Institute of Certified Public Accountants, *Audit Sampling,* AICPA Audit and Accounting Guide (New York: AICPA, 1983), 41 and 42.
2. See, for example, John Neter and James K. Loebbecke, *Behavior of Major Statistical Estimators in Sampling Accounting Populations,* Auditing Research Monograph #2 (New York: AICPA, 1975).
3. For a discussion of stratified sampling, see Roberts, *Statistical Sampling,* chapter 6.

CHAPTER

15

Learning Objectives

Through studying this chapter, you will be able to:

1. Understand the risks inherent in audits of cash, marketable securities, and other liquid assets.
2. Understand and evaluate new technological developments that assist organizations in managing cash.
3. Understand the nature of newer marketable securities and the risks that affect the audit approach.
4. Create audit programs and apply the audit programs to audit cash, marketable securities, and other liquid assets.

Audits of Liquid Assets and Marketable Securities

Chapter Contents

Chapter Overview

Cash accounts need to be well controlled for most organizations to function effectively. This chapter examines approaches organizations take to control their cash assets and applies those concepts to the evaluation of control risk over the accounts. Even though a high volume of transactions flow through the Cash account, it usually has a relatively small balance. Because of the vulnerability to error or misappropriation, organizations and auditors usually emphasize the quality of control procedures over the account.

There has been a remarkable increase in new types of marketable securities, which may present new risks to the organization. The auditor must understand the nature of these new financial instruments and the risks associated with them to perform an audit of marketable securities.

There has been a remarkable explosion in the number of new financial instruments in recent years creating an equal number of new accounting issues. Usually these issues arise because the accounting for these new financial instruments are not addressed in the accounting literature, or the literature itself provides conflicting guidance.[1]

Declines in market value [of marketable securities] may be temporary in nature or may reflect conditions that are more persistent. The distinction between temporary and persistent, however, has been largely undefined.. . . The auditor should ascertain management's investment objectives to determine whether the securities are properly classified in the financial statements . . . To corroborate management's representations as to its intent, the auditor should consider whether such classification is feasible in light of the company's financial position, working capital requirements, debt agreements, and any other contractual obligations. The client's needs may be such that it is reasonable to presume that the securities will need to be sold to raise operating capital, and consequently should be classified as current assets. [AU 9332.03 - .04]

A—INTRODUCTION

Each organization's economic health depends on its ability to successfully manage its cash flow and to temporarily invest its excess funds. When an organization's economic health is in question, there will generally be a comment such as the following in the auditor's report: "Company XYZ is experiencing a severe cash shortage and may not be able to survive unless actions are taken to improve the company's cash flow." In addition to assessing the economic health of an organization, the auditor needs to understand the control procedures designed to prohibit unauthorized use of cash. The volume of transactions flowing through these accounts makes them material to the audit—even if the year-end cash balance is immaterial.

This chapter discusses audit approaches to cash and related liquid assets in today's sophisticated cash management environments. Techniques such as electronic transfers of funds, lockboxes, and cash management arrangements with banks are used by organizations to effectively manage cash flow. In some companies, cash management is tied to just-in-time inventory management programs. Some companies have detailed cash budgets; others operate more informally. Most organizations move cash into and out of liquid assets on an almost continuous basis.

Risks Associated with Cash

The volume of cash transactions leads the auditor to place more emphasis on the audit of cash than would normally be justified by its year-end account balance. The specific risks associated with cash that leads to a greater audit emphasis include the following:

- *Susceptibility to error.* The volume of transactions flowing through the account during the year make the account more susceptible to error than most other accounts.
- *Fraud.* Cash and liquid assets are more susceptible to fraud or other irregularities than are other assets.
- *Automated systems.* The electronic transfer of cash and the automated controls over cash are such that if errors are built into computer programs, they will be repeated on a large volume of transactions. There is a risk that poorly developed programs will not provide proper audit trail requirements.

The audit of cash involves the evaluation of the control environment and operation of control procedures throughout the year. In some smaller organizations, audit efforts will concentrate on the substantive testing of these accounts at year-end. Audits of larger organizations often focus on the control structure for processing transactions.

Cash Accounts Affected

An organization may have many different kinds of bank accounts, each for a special purpose and operating under different control structures. The major types of bank balances the auditor will likely encounter include general checking accounts, savings or excess cash management accounts, and imprest payroll accounts.

General Checking Accounts

The general checking account is used to transact the majority of cash transactions. The organization's regular cash receipts and disbursements are processed through this account. In some cases, the receipts are received directly by the bank through a lockbox and are directly deposited in the customer's account by the bank. Most organizations have cash budgets to assist in planning disbursements and have cash management arrangements with the bank to temporarily invest excess funds in interest-bearing securities.

Savings Accounts

Most organizations, particularly small organizations, have a savings account, either a regular savings account or certificates of deposit. The traditional savings accounts are being replaced, however, by investments in short-term securities providing greater flexibility in managing risk and return.

Imprest Payroll Accounts

Organizations cannot afford to leave cash sitting idle; therefore, most of them establish the payroll account on an imprest basis. Cash is deposited in the **imprest bank account** as needed to cover the payroll checks when they are issued. If all payroll checks are cashed by the employees, the bank balance returns to zero. The imprest account provides additional control by restricting access to the general corporate Cash account and facilitating bank account reconciliation because payroll checks usually clear the bank within a relatively short time period. Some state laws require old uncashed payroll checks be transferred to the state (escheatment laws). Therefore, most companies do not write off old checks but search to find the rightful owner of the check. Of course, these problems can be eliminated through electronic direct deposit into the employee's bank account.

Types of Marketable Security Accounts

Marketable securities include a wide variety of **financial instruments.** Some of these securities are quite complex and difficult to understand, and the auditor's inability to understand the risks associated with these financial instruments has led to audit failures.* For ease of discussion, most of the instruments can be classified into the following categories:

- Marketable securities (held as temporary investments).
- Short-term cash management securities, such as U.S. Treasury notes, certificates of deposit, and commercial paper.
- Short-term hybrid-type securities intended to improve the organization's return on temporary investments.

Marketable Securities

Good cash management principles dictate that idle cash be invested. Organizations often develop cash budgets to temporarily invest funds for periods of time ranging

*For example, the audit difficulties associated with the ESM audit failure were due to the company's fraudulent trading in complex government securities referred to as *repos*. They were securities held overnight in a financial institution to generate interest income for the overnight idle period. The SEC alleged that the auditor did not understand the nature of the financial instruments and transactions entered into by the audit client.

from a day to a year. **Marketable securities** may range from short-term commercial paper to investments in common stock. Because some of the securities have a duration of more than one year, the auditor must determine management's intent regarding the holding of securities for a short-term or as a longer-term investment.

Short-Term Cash Management Programs

Most banks can automatically transfer excess cash to short-term interest-bearing accounts—even on an overnight basis. Other programs direct client investments into specific securities for longer periods. An auditor must understand these banking contracts to identify special risks that may be present in the securities.

New Types of Financial Instruments

During the past decade, there has been a literal explosion of new types of financial instruments. Some are referred to by such exotic names such as *collars*, *swaps*, *zebras*, or by other acronyms that reflect the nature of the underlying financial instrument. Many of the instruments reflect a modification of a traditional security in some manner to shift the risks among parties. When such instruments are encountered, the auditor should acquire a thorough understanding of the risks assumed by each party to the financial transaction.

Planning for Audits of Cash and Marketable Securities

The auditor's planning for audits of cash and marketable securities is affected by the auditor's assessment of the materiality, inherent risk, and control risk associated with the accounts.

Materiality Considerations for Cash and Marketable Securities

When cash is managed correctly, it is not a large account balance at the end of the year. Yet the Cash account is generally considered material to the auditor for three reasons:

1. The Cash account is the culmination of a large volume of transactions that occur throughout the year.
2. The Cash account is more susceptible to fraud than are most other accounts because cash is liquid and easily transferable. The increasing computerization of accounts makes the Cash account even more susceptible to fraud and/or errors.
3. Many debt or loan agreements (covenant) may be tied to cash balances or the maintenance of minimum levels of working capital.

Debt covenant agreements specify restrictions on the organization to protect the lender. Typical covenants restrict cash balances, specify the maintenance of minimum working capital levels, and may restrict the ability of the company to pay dividends. The covenants may affect management's actions in its endeavor to present financial statements that do not violate the debt covenants.

Inherent Risk

Inherent risk with Cash and cash-related accounts may be high due to the volume and liquidity of the transactions; the susceptibility to mishandling increases inherent risk. Marketable securities also may have high inherent risk due to the complexity of the financial instruments. Simple investments in short-term commercial paper or certificates of deposit in a bank do not contain significant inherent risk. Other financial instruments such as junk bonds, debt instruments with put options, and payment-in-kind debt instruments, may have high inherent risk, because market valuations may not be readily available, and the risks to the client may not be readily determinable or may be subject to rapid change.

Control Risk

An analysis of the client's control environment over cash and marketable securities should take place during the planning of the audit. In assessing the control environment, the auditor is concerned with questions such as: Does management understand and control the risks inherent in marketable securities? Is the board of directors informed of the organization's investment in risky securities? Does the internal audit department regularly monitor adherence to management's policies? Examples of questions used to assist in the assessment of the control environment are shown in Exhibit 15.1.

New Cash Management Techniques

New cash management techniques have been developed to (1) speed the collection and deposit of cash while minimizing the possibility of error or fraud in the process, (2) reduce the amount of paperwork, and (3) automate the cash management process. Many of the improvements in cash management are directly attributable to recent developments in computer technology and related software. Three of the more important developments affecting cash management are the use of lockboxes, EDI and automated transfers, and cash management agreements with financial institutions.

Lockboxes. **Lockboxes** are used to accelerate the collection of cash and reduce the possibility of fraud. Customers are instructed to send payments directly to the company at a specific post office box number, which is a depository (lockbox) at the organization's banking institution. The bank receives and opens the remittances, prepares a list of cash receipts by customer, credits the client's general Cash account, and notifies the client of the details of the transactions. Notification can either be a document listing customer receipts or an electronic list of the same information. The electronic data sent by the bank are used directly to update Cash and Accounts Receivable without any direct review by the client's personnel.

The processing of the accounts by the financial institution is performed for a fee. The lockbox arrangements have these distinct advantages for the audit client:

- Cash is deposited directly at the bank. There is no delay, and the client immediately earns interest on the deposited funds.
- The manual processing associated with the opening of remittances, maintaining control of the receipts, and developing detail for the posting of the accounts receivable is shifted to the bank.
- The client usually establishes a number of lockboxes geographically to minimize the delay between the time the check leaves the customer's premises and when the client receives the cash. This speeds the receipt of the cash and allows the organization to use the cash to earn a return.

Exhibit 15.1

CONTROL ENVIRONMENT QUESTIONNAIRE: CASH AND MARKETABLE SECURITIES (EXAMPLES OF QUESTIONS TO BE ADDRESSED)

Cash

1. Does the company have significant cash flow problems in meeting its current obligations on a timely basis? If yes, identify and analyze the steps the company is taking to minimize the problem.
2. Does the client use cash budgeting techniques? How effective are the client's cash management budgeting techniques? Explain.
3. Does the company use the cash management services offered by its banker? What is the nature of these arrangements? Have the arrangements been reviewed by management and the board of directors? Are the arrangements monitored on a current basis?
4. Has the client made significant changes in its cash processing during the past year? Have any major changes taken place in the client's computerized cash management applications during the past year? If yes, explain and document the implications for the audit.
5. Does the client have loan or bond covenants that affect the use of cash or the maintenance of working capital ratios? Document the restrictions and cross-reference to the audit program.
6. Do management and the board periodically review the cash management process? Does the cash management organization provide for effective segregation of duties, review, and supervision?
7. Are cash transactions, including electronic cash transfers, properly authorized? What authorization is required to make electronic cash transfers?
8. Are bank reconciliations performed on a timely basis by personnel independent of processing? Is follow-up action taken promptly on all reconciling items?
9. Does the internal audit department conduct timely reviews of the cash management and cash handling process? If yes, review recent internal audit reports.
10. Does there appear to be any reason to suspect that management may desire to misstate the cash balance? If yes, explain and reference to expanded procedures.
11. Does the company use a lockbox to handle the collection of cash receipts? What is the nature of the agreement with the financial institution? Document the organization's control procedures associated with the lockbox agreement.

Sufficient controls must be established to ensure that all customer remittances received by the bank are posted. For example, all remittance advices should be sent to the client to facilitate follow-up should the customer have any questions about the posting of accounts. The client should also reconcile the total of the remittance advices with the cash deposit recorded by the bank.

EDI and Automated Transfers. Many organizations have adopted EDI as an integral part of their business. The full implementation of EDI will occur when

Exhibit 15.1

12. Identify the individuals authorized to make cash transfers, including electronic fund transfers, and the procedures by which that authorization is verified before the transfers take place. Identify the procedures management uses to ensure that the authorization process is monitored.

Marketable Securities

1. Does the client regularly invest in marketable securities?
2. Does the client have written policies and guidelines regarding investments in marketable securities? Are the policies approved by the board of directors? What process is used to authorize investments in marketable securities?
3. Does the client take possession of, or provide any restrictions on, collateral associated with marketable securities?
4. Does the client periodically obtain appraisals or revalue the collateral associated with the underlying securities?
5. Does the client systematically identify the risks associated with its holdings of marketable securities? Has the board of directors approved the risk associated with the investment in nontraditional marketable securities?
6. What is the company's exposure to losses on marketable securities? What impact would the potential default of the securities have on the client?
7. Is there a ready market for the securities classified as marketable securities? If the securities are not traded on a national stock exchange, present evidence on the existence of marketability—including depth and breadth of transactions in the security.
8. Does the company establish limits over the amounts that can be invested in various types of financial instruments, with specific counterparties, or by individual traders? Explain.
9. Does the organization provide for effective segregation of duties among individuals responsible for making investment and credit decisions and those responsible for the custody of the securities?
10. Does the internal audit department conduct regular audits of the organization's controls over marketable securities? If yes, review recent reports.

organizations send electronic messages to their financial institutions indicating the date and amount of cash transfers to other organizations. The cash transfers will be made automatically and instantaneously; checks will no longer exist. The client, the financial institution, and the auditor will be concerned with the control procedures to ensure accurate and complete recording of the electronic transfers. The use of lockboxes and other cash collection approaches will decrease, although they will still be maintained for customers that do not have the capability to make electronic transfers.

Cash Management Agreements with Financial Institutions. Financial institutions provide automated services such as cash management programs for many of their clients. The auditor should determine the procedures for monitoring the risk associated with the investments and the control procedures utilized to ensure that investments are not subject to undue risks.

Compensating Balances

Most companies have short-term loans and lines of credit with their primary financial institution. The line of credit provides the company with a prenegotiated loan available for use when the company needs it. The financial institutions usually require the company to maintain a specified balance in a non-interest-bearing account. The amount available for the loan is the credit line minus the compensating balance. If the amounts are material, the company is required to disclose the compensating account arrangement and its affect on the effective rate of interest.

B–AUDITS OF CASH ACCOUNTS

If errors occur in the Cash account, it is likely that other accounts are also misstated. A failure to properly record a cash receipt affects both Accounts Receivable and Cash. A failure to properly record a disbursement misstates Cash and the corresponding liability. Because Cash represents the largest volume of transactions of any account and is the most susceptible to fraud, the auditor normally performs detailed tests of control procedures and direct tests of balances.

Evaluating Control Risk: Cash Accounts

Fundamental control elements the auditor would expect to find in place for all cash processing systems include the following:

- Separation of duties.
- Restrictive endorsements.
- Independent reconciliation control procedures.
- Computerized control totals and edit tests.
- Authorization of transactions.
- Prenumbered documents and turnaround documents.
- Periodic internal audits.
- Competent, well-trained employees.

Segregation of Duties

The general concept of segregation of duties does not change as processing systems become more automated and integrated. Automation simply provides opportunities for errors or irregularities to occur on a larger scale. For example, for companies like WWW described in the Practical Illustration, it is important that incoming customer

Practical Illustration

AUTOMATING THE CASH RECEIPTS PROCESS

WWW Company is a national wholesaler of merchandise ranging from electric motors to electronic surveillance equipment. It has annual sales of more than $1.5 billion, approximately 855,000 customers, 300 branches, and 6,200 employees. Customers may appear in person at any of the branches to order and pick up merchandise or may call any branch to order the merchandise. The branch's computer is on-line with the central database.

Some customers pay in cash for merchandise received. All cash receipts are deposited by the branch daily in a local financial institution and the records are electronically transferred daily to the corporation's Chicago bank account. Most customer purchases are on credit with payment due within 30 days. All payments are directed to the national accounts receivable department. Approximately 16,000 checks totaling about $6 million are received daily; many of the remittances are for small dollar amounts. The company uses a significant amount of automation in controlling the processing of cash receipts including the following:

1. An optical scanner that reads the following information from the customer's remittance advice:
   a. Customer account number.
   b. Customer invoice number.
   c. Dollar amount of sale.
   d. Invoice date.
   e. Freight and tax on the sale.
2. A magnetic ink character recognition (MICR) machine that reads lines from the check and scans for the check amount.
3. An encoder that endorses the back of the check for deposit only and encodes the dollar amount of the check onto the front of it for efficient processing by the company and its financial institution.

Once initial accountability has been established, the receipts are sorted into batches for computer processing. Checks and remittance advices are separated and differences are reconciled and corrected. Remittance advices are created for cash receipts that do not contain a remittance advice. Most of the processing is handled by computerized equipment with selected manual review and reconciliation to ensure that batches of items are not lost and that the credits to Accounts Receivable do not differ from cash remitted.

Important control procedures that will be reviewed by the auditor include the detailed reconciliation of cash and receivable updates and the use of batch control totals for all postings and edit tests that are built into the computer application.

checks and remittance advices be segregated on receipt and processed by different people. Posting to Accounts Receivable should be based on remittance advices and reconciled to the postings to Cash, which are based on checks received. Segregation of duties is further enhanced if inquiries by customers concerning their account balance are referred to a third party for investigation. Finally, the individuals who perform reconciliations should not handle cash or record cash transactions.

Restrictive Endorsements

Customer checks should be restrictively endorsed for deposit when opened. The restrictive endorsement helps prevent modifications and theft of customer remittances.

Independent Reconciliation Control Procedures

Two types of reconciliations should occur:

1. *Reconciliation of items received with items recorded (control totals).* Reconciliation is made more effective when control procedures exist to establish the initial integrity of the population (for example, for WWW, each remittance opened was given a unique identifier before processing was performed).
2. *Reconciliation of the bank accounts on a periodic basis.* Reconciliation of the balance on the bank statement with the balance on the books indicates misstatements and unusual banking activity.

The auditor normally tests the reconciliation control procedures by reviewing the client's reconciliations to determine that they were independently performed.

Computerized Control Totals and Edit Tests

Computerized control procedures help ensure that all items are uniquely identified and an adequate audit trail exists for transactions. Computerized control procedures include the following:

- *A unique identifier assigned to each item.* The unique identifier establishes the scope of the total population and provides a basis to ensure that no items are added to or dropped from the population.
- *Control totals and reconciliations to ensure the completeness of processing.* In WWW Company, control totals are established for each batch and the computer processing of the transactions are reconciled with the control totals. A control total would also be established to reconcile the debits to cash and the credits to accounts receivable.
- *Edit tests to identify unusual or incorrect items.* Standard edit tests such as reasonableness tests, field checks, self-checking digits on account numbers, and alpha-numeric tests should be implemented as deemed applicable to the particular application.

Authorization of Transactions

Individuals with proper authorization are able to electronically transfer millions of dollars each day. As a result, opportunities for abuse abound. Two authorization controls should be implemented:

1. Authorization privileges should be assigned to individuals based on their level of authority in the organization. Authorization should also follow the principles of "need to know" and "right to know."
2. The authorization process should be implemented so that the privileges can be executed only by appropriately authorized individuals for the specific transactions (authentication). The authentication process may be implemented through electronic verification by the use of elements such as passwords, physical characteristics, cards, encryption, or terminals that are hard-wired to the computer to keep someone from tapping in through a phone line. In a manual system, the authorization controls may involve limiting access to the area where checks are signed and to the prenumbered checks.

Technological Risk: New Challenges

DESKTOP FORGERY—TECHNOLOGY MAKES IT POSSIBLE

As reported in *Forbes* (November 27, 1989), the ability to develop fraudulent checks has been enhanced by the widespread availability of quality graphics packages for microcomputers and the lower prices of equipment used to code checks for processing using magnetic ink character recognition, which is embedded in the checks and used by the bank to process the checks against the customer's account. To develop fraudulent checks against a company, the following are needed:

1. Blank check stock (i.e., the check forms).
2. A high-quality graphics program and printer with the capability of duplicating letterheads, different font styles, and signatures.
3. A copy of a check from the company whose account the check is to be written against so that all important aspects of the check, such as MICR coding, can be duplicated.
4. A machine to perform MICR coding ability.

Forbes found that the equipment needed to carry out such a scam could be obtained at a cost somewhere between $30,000 and $50,000. The equipment is capable of developing a fake check that is virtually indistinguishable from the real check.

Are there any solutions or safeguards against such frauds? Fortunately, basic controls could be implemented. *Forbes* suggests the following:

- Develop organization logos that are embedded in the checks, making them difficult to duplicate.
- Use multiple colored checks.
- Restrict the type of paper used in the blank check stock.
- Use separate accounts for small dollar value checks.
- Implement edit controls over the use of smaller checks, thus treating the small dollar accounts as impress bank accounts.
- Provide timely and thorough independent reconciliations of the account balances.

Prenumbered Documents and Turnaround Documents

As discussed previously, prenumbered documents are important in establishing the completeness of a population. The numbering may occur after the receipt such as in WWW Company, where each remittance is assigned a unique identifier after it is received by the company. Another option is to use **turnaround documents** that customers return with their cash payment. A clerk can quickly review the turnaround document and compare the amount indicated paid with the actual cash remittance. The turnaround document contains other information useful for further processing such as account number, invoice number, date billed, and date received (entered by clerk). Many of these documents are machine readable and eliminate data entry errors. If a turnaround document is not returned, a similar document should be developed for recording purposes.

Periodic Internal Audits

Internal audit departments are effective deterrents when they periodically conduct detailed audits of cash control and cash management. Internal auditors may also review the development of new computerized applications to determine whether adequate control procedures and auditability have been implemented.

Competent, Well-Trained Employees

The auditor normally is aware of the manner in which key employees perform their duties. In some cases, employees have actually sabotaged automated systems that they did not understand. Although the auditor does not normally document the assessment of employee competence in a questionnaire, any concerns should be documented along with an assessment of how the audit should be adjusted.

Understanding and Testing Control Procedures

An understanding of the control structure affecting cash processing is gained through interviews, observations, and review of procedures manuals and other client documentation. A questionnaire, such as the one shown in Exhibit 15.2, is often used to guide the auditor in obtaining this understanding. The questionnaire is designed to elicit information about specific control procedures performed and the extent of documentation that might exist to verify that the control procedure is operating effectively. Usually the questionnaire identifies the specific individual responsible for performing each procedure, which assists the auditor in evaluating the segregation of duties. The auditor develops a preliminary assessment of control risk based on the identification of control procedures evident in the process.

If the auditor assesses control risk as low and believes that it is cost-efficient to test the control procedures, an audit program for testing the controls is developed. An example of such a program is shown in Exhibit 15.3. The first part of the program focuses on gaining an understanding of the control procedures and control risk; the remaining part identifies tests of control procedures. The program is designed around the basic control objectives and is cross-referenced to the audit objectives. The program shown in Exhibit 15.3 does not cover all cash audit procedures; it omits audit procedures of cash disbursements.

Substantive Testing of Cash Balances

When control risk is assessed to be high or concerns about the integrity of processing exist, the auditor performs detailed substantive tests of the cash balance. In determining the type of tests to be performed, the auditor is guided by the general assertion approach developed in Chapter 7 (existence, completeness, rights, valuation, and presentation). The specific risks that the auditor would want to assess in connection with cash transactions include the following:

- Transactions are recorded in the wrong period.
- The account balance is misstated. The misstatement may be covered by a fraudulent scheme such as omitting outstanding checks or underfooting the outstanding checks on the reconciliation.
- The company is manipulating accounts to record cash in two different places at the same time.
- Cash is embezzled and therefore not recorded.
- Cash is overstated for some reason other than those identified.

The primary substantive audit procedures include testing year-end bank reconciliations, year-end cutoffs and bank transfers, as well as performing tests of deposits.

Exhibit 15.2

CONTROL RISK EVALUATION QUESTIONNAIRE: CASH RECEIPTS (PARTIAL EXAMPLE)

	Yes	No	N/A
A. Are all payments received deposted intact on a timely basis? Consider:			
1. Control procedures:			
a. A list of incoming receipts is prepared by the person who opens the remittances and who delivers the list to a person independent of the deposit function.	______	______	______
b. A duplicate deposit slip is prepared by someone other than the person opening the mail.	______	______	______
c. Deposits are made daily.	______	______	______
d. An authorized person compares the deposit slip with the listing prepared in 1.a., noting agreement and completeness of deposit.	______	______	______
2. Documented evidence of performance is noted by:			
a. The listing prepared in 1.a. is initialed by its preparer.	______	______	______
b. The listing is attached to the deposit slip and is initialed by the person in 1.d.	______	______	______
c. Independent reconciliation of bank accounts.	______	______	______
B. Are payments received completely credited to the correct customer accounts? Consider:			
1. Control procedures:			
a. When the posting process is a function of a computerized application, assurance is gained by:			
1. Prenumbered batch control tickets are used and include control totals of number of remittances to be processed and total dollars to be applied.	______	______	______
2. Batch edit reports or on-line edit routines identify invalid customer numbers, invoice numbers, and invoice amounts.	______	______	______
3. On-line entry includes the input of a control total and/or hash total for each payment.	______	______	______
2. Documented evidence of performance is noted by:			
a. Edit reports and/or processing transmittals, which are saved and signed by the person clearing the exceptions.	______	______	______
b. The person performing the independent check initials the remittance, noting agreement of the posting operation.	______	______	______

(Continued)

Exhibit 15.2

c. On-line entry control totals and/or hash totals are noted on the face of the appropriate documents. ______ ______ ______

d. Batch control tickets are agreed to the edit reports and are initialed indicating agreement. ______ ______ ______

C. Are all overdue accounts followed up? Consider:

1. Control procedures:

a. An authorized individual makes regular collection calls on past-due accounts. ______ ______ ______

b. The company systematically sends past-due notices to delinquent customers. ______ ______ ______

c. Past-due accounts are periodically reviewed by senior collection officials to determine alternative collection procedures. ______ ______ ______

2. Documented evidence of performance is noted by:

a. The cash register tape that is balanced to the cash drawer is initialed by the person performing the balancing function. ______ ______ ______

b. The adding machine tape is attached to the deposit slip and is initialed by an authorized person. ______ ______ ______

Conclusion:

Procedural controls appear adequate to justify a preliminary control risk assessment as:

______ Low control risk

______ Moderate control risk

______ High control risk

Independent Bank Reconciliations

An independent reconciliation of the client's major bank accounts provides strong evidence as to the correctness of the year-end cash balance. The reconciliation process starts with the balance per the bank statements and reconciles to the balance per the books. If the client has major misstatements in the cash accounts (perhaps covered by omitting outstanding checks), it is likely that these errors will be detected by the independent bank reconciliation. Although the auditor may test the bank reconciliations on clients with low control risk, in many cases (especially on smaller clients) the auditor performs the reconciliation because there is no one independent in the organization (other than the president) to perform the reconciliation. An example of a working paper for a bank reconciliation is shown in Exhibit 15.4.

Exhibit 15.3

AUDIT PROGRAM FOR CASH RECEIPT AND CASH MANAGEMENT CONTROLS

Control Procedure Objectives

Existence/Occurrence

1. Recorded transactions are valid.
2. Recorded transactions are properly authorized.
3. Transactions are recorded on a timely basis and in the time period in which the transactions take place.

Completeness

4. All transactions are recorded.

Rights/Obligations

5. Recorded transactions or accruals properly reflect transfer of ownership or obligation.

Valuation

6. All transactions are recorded at their proper amount, and all calculations related to the recording of the transactions are carried out correctly.
7. All transactions and adjustments to account balances are recorded in accordance with generally accepted accounting principles.

Presentation and Disclosure

8. All transactions are correctly classified.

UNDERSTANDING	Performed by	W/P Ref.
1. Inquire of management about the existence of lines of credit, special cash management programs, and related fees with the company's primary banking institution. Analyze the arrangements for existence of special risks and for obligations of the client that should be considered in the audit.	________	________
2. Document the control procedures over cash by completing the internal control questionnaire or by flowcharting the process.	________	________
3. Prepare and document a preliminary assessment of control risk. Identify the specific control procedures that need to be tested if control risk is assessed at less than the maximum. *(Note: The following audit steps assume that sufficient control procedures are present in the system. We will also focus on the cash receipts process described in the WWW company illustration.)*	________	________

(Continued)

Exhibit 15.3

General Tests of Controls:

4. Observe the processing of cash collections starting with their receipt through the preparation of documents for processing. Note the conscientiousness with which the work is done, the procedures used in developing batches and performing reconciliations, and the efficiency with which the work is done. Interview supervisory personnel regarding potential problem areas. Determine whether any concerns exist regarding employee conscientiousness that would affect the risk assessment. __________ ________

Testing of Specific Control Procedures

5. Select x number of cash receipts as determined by attribute sampling concepts and determine that the following takes place:
   a. Each remittance is given a unique identifier, which is subsequently entered into the system. __________ ________
   (Objective 4)
   b. The cash received is the same as the amount applied to the update of accounts receivable. Determine how the differences (if any) are handled. Determine that the control procedure is operating effectively. __________ ________
   (Objectives 6 and 7)
   c. Cash and remittances are segregated into batches for processing. __________ ________
   (Objectives 4, 6)
   d. Documents that are prepared when turnaround documents are not returned with the remittances are accurate. __________ ________
   (Objective 6)
   e. Batches are prepared according to company standards. Review the reconciliation of batch controls to determine their accuracy and timeliness. __________ ________
   (Objectives 3, 6)
   f. Exception reports contain all items rejected by the edit controls. The rejected items are properly followed up and recorded correctly. __________ ________
   (Objective 4)
6. Determine who has the authorization to
   a. Make changes in documents or adjustments when cash amounts differ from invoiced amounts. __________ ________
   b. Make deposits. __________ ________
   c. Make withdrawals. __________ ________
   d. Make transfers among the organization's accounts or between the organization and other entities. __________ ________
   (Objective 2)

Exhibit 15.3

UNDERSTANDING	Performed by	W/P Ref.
7. Review reports for unusual cash transactions such as transfer of funds to other accounts, deposits other than through the normal cash receipts process, and disbursements not processed through the regular cash disbursements process. Select a sample of the transactions and review for proper authorization and completeness and correctness of processing.	________	________
(Objectives 1, 9)		
8. Review the procedures for authorizing passwords or other access codes for individuals who are authorized to initiate electronic transfers of cash. Select a limited number of transactions and trace back to the authorization. *(As part of the general controls review of data processing, determine the procedures in existence to ensure that passwords are provided only to those properly authorized and that the passwords are kept secure. Determine through testing and observation that such controls continue to be in existence.)*	________	________
(Objective 2)		
9. Review bank reconciliations for completeness and trace selected items on the reconciliation to the bank statement. Determine that the reconciliations are performed by someone independent of the processing.	________	________
(Objectives 1, 2, 4, 5, 6)		
Potential Substitute Tests		
10. Review any internal audit working papers and audit program for work performed over cash management. Determine whether there is a need to corroborate the internal auditor's work by performing audit tests on similar items.	________	________
11. Determine whether we or the internal audit department have utilized either test data or an integrated test facility to test the accuracy of cash processing and the operation of computerized controls. Consider using test data to determine the comprehensiveness to which computerized controls are being utilized.	________	________
Documenting Work Performed		
12. Document your assessment of control risk—including the types of misstatements that might occur because of any deficiencies in the control procedures. Write a brief memo citing the implications for the remainder of the audit.	________	________

Exhibit 15.4

TEST OF CLIENT'S BANK RECONCILIATION FOR THE YEAR ENDED DECEMBER 31, 1994

Prepared by ________

Reviewed by ________

Date ________

Balance per bank statement:		$1,073,852.65*
Add: Deposits in transit:		
12/28 Deposit	$287,000.00 †	
12/31 Deposit	$300,000.00 †	$ 587,000.00
Bank charges not recorded		$ 25.00‡
NSF checks		
Bailey's Main	$ 12,000.00 §	
Crazy Eddie's	$ 15,000.00 ‖	$ 27,000.00
Less: Outstanding checks		
2809	$ 435.56 #	
3678	$ 67,892.09 #	
3679	$ 75,000.00 #	
3899	$ 700.00 **	
3901	$ 12,500.00 #	
3903	$ 50,000.00	$ 206,527.65
Balance per books		$ 407,497.35 ††

* Confirmed per bank. See WP reference C-1>

† Traced to deposits shown on bank statement on 1/3 and 1/4 contained in bank cutoff statement. The 12/31 deposit was traced to bank transfer WP C-12 and was listed as an outstanding check on the subsidiary account.

‡ Traced to bank cutoff statement. Charge was for service fees, which should have been recorded by the client. Amount is not material and no adjustment is proposed.

§ NSF check was returned with 12/31 bank statement. Examined support showing client redeposited the checks. Traced to deposit in cutoff bank statement and determined that it had not been returned in subsequent statement.

‖ Examined NSF check returned with 12/31 bank statement. Crazy Eddie's is a retail firm that has gone bankrupt. The likelihood of ultimate collection is low. Based on discussion with the client, the amount should be written off. See AJE #35.

\# Outstanding checks were traced to checks returned on 1/20/95 bank cutoff statements. Checks were examined and all were dated 12/31 or prior and were canceled by the bank subsequent to 12/31.

** Check had not cleared as of 1/20/95. Examined supporting document for the check. All appeared proper and no exceptions were noted.

†† Footed, no exceptions noted.

When testing the client's bank reconciliation, the auditor should verify all material items such as the balance per the bank statement, deposits in transit, outstanding checks, and other adjustments. Fortunately, there are two forms of evidence available from the client's bank that facilitates the reconciliation: a cutoff bank statement and a standard bank confirmation.

The Cutoff Bank Statement. A **cutoff bank statement** is a normal bank statement prepared at an interim agreed-upon date which is sent directly to the auditor. The auditor asks the client to make arrangements to have the bank send a cutoff bank statement directly to the auditor for some period after year-end. For example, if the client's year-end is December 31, the auditor may make arrangements for the bank to send a cutoff bank statement as of January 15 directly to the auditor. The auditor can examine canceled checks returned with the bank statement to determine that the checks dated prior to year-end were included as outstanding checks on the reconciliation and can trace deposits in transit into the statement to determine if they were deposited in a timely fashion. The auditor should be alert for groups of checks that do not clear for an unusually long time after year-end. The delay in clearing the bank may indicate the recording of checks but not mailing them until after year-end in an effort to improve the appearance of the balance sheet.*

The Standard Bank Confirmation. The auditor usually sends a standard **bank confirmation** (Exhibits 15.5 and 15.6) to each bank with which the company has transacted business during the year. The confirmations have two parts. The first part, shown in Exhibit 15.5, seeks information on client account balances. The second, shown in Exhibit 15.6, seeks information on the existence of loans, due dates of the loans, interest rates, dates through which interest has been paid, and collateral for all loans outstanding with the bank at year-end.

If loans are outstanding, the auditor usually asks for copies of the loan agreements to identify any restrictions on the ability of the organization to pay dividends or to determine whether the organization will have to maintain specific working capital or debt ratios. These requirements are generally referred to as *covenants;* violation of them will make the loans immediately due and payable unless they are temporarily waived by the financial institution. If covenants are violated and the financial institution will not waive them, the auditor will have to consider whether the client will be able to continue to operate as a going concern. Reservations by the auditor on going concern ability may lead to a modification of the standard audit report as discussed in Chapter 2. Additionally, the auditor normally makes inquiries as to the existence of cash management or other programs that the client has with the financial institution.

Obtaining Year-end Cutoff Information. In many instances of fraud, management has either held open the cash receipts book to record the next period's sales as part of the current period or had mailed checks to vendors but did not record the cash disbursements until the subsequent period. Sometimes these problems occurred because the company was in dire financial straits and needed an improved balance sheet to avoid violation of loan covenants.

*It should be noted that many financial institutions are sending this information to their larger clients in electronic form, many of which have automated much of the bank reconciliation process. The auditor wishing to perform an independent reconciliation on these accounts will likewise have to use automated techniques and should make arrangements with the client and the financial institution in advance.

Exhibit 15.5

STANDARD BANK CONFIRMATION—ACCOUNT BALANCES

Financial Institution's Name and Address

[ ]

[ ]

CUSTOMER NAME

We have provided to our accountants the following information as of the close of business on__________, 19 ____, regarding our deposit and loan balances. Please confirm the accuracy of the information, noting any exceptions to the information provided. If the balances have been left blank, please complete this form by furnishing the balance in the appropriate space below. Although we do not request nor expect you to conduct a comprehensive, detailed search of your records, if during the process of completing this confirmation additional information about other deposit and loan accounts we may have with you comes to your attention, please include such information below. Please use the enclosed envelope to return the form directly to our accountatns.

1. At the close of business on the date listed above, our records indicated the following deposit balance(s):

ACCOUNT NAME	ACCOUNT NO.	INTEREST RATE	BALANCE*

2. We were directly liable to the financial institution for loans at the close of business on the date listed above as follows:

ACCOUNT NO./ DESCRIPTION	BALANCE*	DATE DUE	INTEREST RATE	DATE THROUGH WHICH INTEREST IS PAID	DESCRIPTION OF COLLATERAL

(Customer's Authorized Signature) (Date)

The information presented above by the customer is in agreement with our records. Although we have not conducted a comprehensive, detailed search of our records, no other deposit or loan accounts have come to our attention except as noted below.

(Financial Institution Authorized Signature) (Date)

(Title)

EXCEPTIONS AND/OR COMMENTS

Please return this form directly to our accountants:

*Ordinarily, balances are intentionally left blank if they are not available at the time the form is prepared.

Approved 1990 by American Bankers Association, American Institute of Certified Public Accountants, and Bank Administration Institute.
Additional forms available from: AICPA – Order Department, P.O. Box 1003, NY, NY 10108-1003. D 451 5851

Exhibit 15.6

STANDARD BANK CONFIRMATION—LOAN GUARANTEES

(Date)
Financial Institution Official*
First United Bank
Anytown, U.S.A. 00000

Dear Financial Institution Official:

In connection with an audit of the financial statements of (name of customer) as of (balance-sheet date) and for the (period) then ended, we have advised our independent auditors of the information listed below, which we believe is a complete and accurate description of our contingent liabilities, including oral and written guarantees, with your financial institution. Although we do not request nor expect you to conduct a comprehensive, detailed search of your records, if during the process of completing this confirmation additional information about other contingent liabilities, including oral and written guarantees, between (name of customer) and your financial institution comes to your attention, please include such information below.

Name of Maker	Date of Note	Due Date	Current Balance
Interest Rate	Date Through Which Interest Is Paid	Description of Collateral	Description of Purpose of Note

Information related to oral and written guarantees is as follows:

____

Please confirm whether the information about contingent liabilities presented above is correct by signing below and returning this directly to our independent auditors (name and address of CPA firm).

Sincerely,

(Name of Customer)

____

By: ____________________
(Authorized Signature)

Dear CPA Firm:

The above information listing contingent liabilities, including oral and written guarantees, agrees with the records of this financial institution.** Although we have not conducted a comprehensive, detailed search of our records, no information about other contingent liabilities, including oral and written guarantees, came to our attention. (Note exceptions below or in an attached letter.)

____

____
(Name of Financial Institution)

________________ ________
(Officer and Title) *(Date)*

**This letter should be addressed to a financial institution official who is responsible for the financial institution's relationship with the client or is knowledgeable about the transactions or arrangements. Some financial institutions centralize this function by assigning responsibility for responding to confirmation requests to a separate function. Independent auditors should ascertain the appropriate recipient.*

***If applicable, comments similar to the following may be added to the confirmation reply by the financial institution: This confirmation does not relate to arrangements, if any, with other branches or affiliates of this financial institution. Information should be sought separately from such branches or affiliates with which any such arrangments might exist.*

If the auditor assesses the risk of such misstatement to be high, the following procedures should be considered:

1. Obtain information on the last checks issued for payment for goods and services, such as the last check number, and observe that all previous checks had been mailed. The mailing of the checks can be corroborated by observing whether the checks clear the bank in a timely fashion as evidenced in the bank cutoff statement.
2. Obtain information on the last cash receipts. The auditor usually notes the last few receipts as a basis for determining the recording in the correct

period. The information is traced to the company's bank reconciliation and bank accounts to determine if items are properly recorded.

Proof of Cash Bank Reconciliation

The **proof of cash** is a four-column bank reconciliation that is usually performed only for clients about which the auditor has serious concerns as to the effectiveness of their cash controls. A proof of cash shown in Exhibit 15.7 reconciles the beginning and ending bank balances with the similar balances per the books (same as a regular month-end reconcilement). In addition, the proof of cash reconciles the cash activities of the period by reconciling deposits per the bank with receipts per the books and withdrawals per the bank with disbursements per the books. The audit procedure is useful when there is concern about the proper timing of cash receipts or that recorded checks were not actually disbursed. It may be also used when the auditor suspects fraud.

Exhibit 15.7

XYZ MANUFACTURING COMPANY
PROOF OF CASH
FOR THE YEAR ENDED DECEMBER 31, 1994

	Balance November 30	Deposits/ Receipts	Withdrawals/ Disbursements	Balance December 31
Balance per bank*	$125,000.00	$864,392.48	$798,300.00	$191,092.48 C,CF
Add: Deposits in transit				
11/30	75,000.00‡	(75,000.00)‡		
12/31		100,000.00 ‡		100,000.00‡
Bank charges:				
11/30	25.00§		25.00 §	
12/31			(40.00) §	40.00§
NSF checks returned and redeposited:				
		(4,000.00)‖	(4,000.00)‖	
			(3,000.00)‖	3,000.00‖
Total	$144,025.00F	$885,392.48 F	$822,285.00F	$207,132.48F

* Per the bank statement
CF Cross-footed
C Confirmed with bank, no exceptions
‡ Traced to cash receipts records and bank statement
§ Traced to bank statement
‖ Traced to bank's debit memo
F Footed

Bank Transfer Schedules

A company with many divisions frequently transfers cash from one division to another. Companies wanting to overstate cash often resort to a technique called **kiting** whereby they make transfers from one bank account to another bank account but do not record the disbursement on the first company's (division's) account but record the deposit on the second company's account. For example, a December 31 transfer would show the receipt on one account but not the disbursement on the other, resulting in the recording of the transferred amount twice. The elements of a simple kiting scheme is shown in Exhibit 15.8. A more sophisticated kiting scheme used by the E.F. Hutton Company is illustrated in the Auditing Alert: Practical Example.

The most effective and efficient way to test for the existence of kiting is to prepare a **bank transfer schedule** similar to the one shown in Exhibit 15.9. The bank transfer schedule lists all transfers between the company's bank accounts for a short period of time before and after year-end. All transfers are accounted for to determine if they are recorded in the correct period and the client is not overstating the year-end cash account. Note the transfer of check number 8702 recorded as a deposit on December 30—an example of kiting. The check was recorded as a deposit in the Cleveland account on December 31 but was not recorded as a disbursement in the Rockford account until after year-end.

Cash Trace

A cash trace is another procedure that might be performed when the auditor is concerned that cash receipts are misappropriated or not deposited intact in a timely fashion. The **cash trace** is simply a procedure where the auditor attempts to account for all receipts during a specified time period to determine whether they were

Exhibit 15.8

EXAMPLE OF KITING

Division A	Division B
• Transfers $1,000,000 to Division B near the end of the year but records the transaction in the following year.	• Receives $1,000,000 before year-end and records the deposit in the current period.
• Transfer does not clear the bank in the current year.	• Deposit may or may not be deposited by year-end. If not, the deposit will be shown as a deposit in transit in the division's bank reconciliation.
• Transfer does not decrease the year-end cash balance because it has not been recorded in the current period.	• Transfer increases the year-end cash balance by the amount of the transfer. The net effect is to overstate cash on the consolidated financial statements by the amount of the transfer.

Result: Cash is recorded in both divisions at year-end, resulting in double counting.

Auditing Alert: Practical Example

KITING SCHEMES: THE CASE OF E.F. HUTTON

Kiting can occur without fraudulently misstating financial statements. In the 1980s, the Securities and Exchange Commission accused the brokerage firm of E.F. Hutton of participating in a kiting scheme to earn excess interest at the expense of their customers. Hutton set up an impress account for disbursements at geographic locations far removed from the customer who would receive one of E.F. Hutton's checks. For example, a bank account might be set up in Billings, Montana, for disbursements to customers located on the east coast. The agreement Hutton had with the bank was that the bank would wire Hutton with a message indicating the amount of checks cleared each day and Hutton would wire funds to cover the cleared checks. Meanwhile, Hutton had the use of the cash for the time it took for the checks to clear the remotely located bank. The firm eventually settled with the SEC and agreed to refrain from such practices in the future. As the banking system continues to automate, the likelihood of such schemes in the future will lessen because all checks will clear the banks in even shorter periods of time.

deposited intact in a timely fashion. The auditor selects a period of time (for a small business it might be as much as 15 days) and lists all receipts recorded in the books. For all items selected, the auditor traces the receipts in the books directly to deposits listed in the bank statement. If there are large time lags or differences in amounts, the auditor also examines the detailed deposit slips to determine the nature of the differences and the possibilities of errors or fraudulent activities.

Operational Audits of Cash

It was noted earlier that internal auditors often perform detailed tests of the operating effectiveness of control procedures over the cash accounts. Many internal audit departments perform operational audits of the cash and treasury function to evaluate the efficiency and effectiveness of the treasury function in comparison with standards of excellence found in other companies. Such an audit identifies areas in which cash management might be improved to contribute to the overall profitability and effectiveness of the organization. The internal auditor uses the following procedures on an operational audit:

- Review procedures for handling cash receipts and amount of time it takes to make deposits.
- Review procedures for identifying and investing excess or idle funds.
- Measure and evaluate the effectiveness of cash management and cash budgeting techniques.
- Review financial arrangements made with financial institutions to identify the riskiness of the investments and whether the risks are consistent with the risk levels authorized by the board of directors.
- Determine compliance of treasury activities with company policies.
- Determine the amount of risks inherent in electronic transfers of cash and compliance with company policies and procedures for such transfers.

Exhibit 15.9

BANK TRANSFER SCHEDULE
XYZ COMPANY
FOR THE YEAR ENDED DECEMBER 31, 1994

Transferred from	Check Number	Amount	Date Deposited		Date Withdrawn	
			Per Books	Per Bank	Per Books	Per Bank
Cleveland	15910	45,000	12/26*	12/27 †	12/26 *	12/30 †
Cleveland	15980	100,000	12/28*	12/29 †	12/27 *	12/31 †
Rockford	8702	87,000	12/30*	12/31 †	1/2*‡	1/3 †
Cleveland	16110	25,000	1/3*	1/4 †	1/2 *	1/5 ‡
Rockford	8725	65,000	1/5*	1/7 *	1/4 *	1/8 †

* Traced to cash receipts/disbursement records
† Traced to bank statement
‡ Withdrawal recorded in wrong period. See AJE C-11.

- Determine the effectiveness of control procedures to minimize the risk of loss or misuse of cash or other liquid assets.

The external auditor should review all operational audit reports as a basis for understanding the existing system and potential changes that may be taking place in the system.

C–MARKETABLE SECURITIES AND NEW FINANCIAL INSTRUMENTS

Audits of Marketable Securities

Marketable securities are either debt or equity securities that are readily marketable and that management intends to hold for a short time. The determination of the proper accounting for most marketable securities is usually easy because many marketable securities have short durations such as 60 or 90 days. On some occasions, the organization may also invest in equity securities or other debt instruments that have due dates of longer duration. In such instances, the appropriate classification and accounting for the security depends on management's intent, that is, whether it is to be held for a short time period or is viewed as a longer, more permanent investment. The major classes of marketable securities include commercial paper, marketable equity securities, and marketable debt securities.

Audits of Commercial Paper

The term **commercial paper** refers to notes issued by major corporations, especially finance companies, that generally have good credit ratings. The audit program for commercial paper follows the assertions developed in Chapter 7. An example of an audit program for substantive testing of commercial paper is shown in Exhibit 15.10. Note the specific linkage between assertions and the audit procedures and that the related interest income is tested at the same time.

For large organizations that invest regularly in commercial paper, the auditor tests transactions throughout the year to determine that all transactions were authorized and accounted for. In addition, the amount of interest income is also verified. If control risk is low, the auditor needs only to selectively test the year-end balances.

Exhibit 15.10

ASSERTIONS AND AUDIT PROCEDURES: COMMERCIAL PAPER

Assertions:	Audit Procedures:
Existence or occurrence	1. Request that the client prepare a schedule of all commercial paper held by the organization at year-end. Verify the existence of the securities by either (1) counting and examining selected ones or (2) confirming the existence with trustees holding them.
Completeness	2. Foot the schedule of commercial paper and examine the securities (step 1). Examine selected transactions and brokers' advices near year-end to determine that the transactions are recorded in the correct time period.
Rights	3. Examine selected documents to determine if there are any restrictions on the marketability of the documents. Inquire of management as to existence of any restrictions.
Valuation	4. *(Note: Commercial paper should be valued at year-end market value.)* Determine current market value through reference to a financial reporting service such as *The Wall Street Journal.*
	5. Recompute interest and determine that accrued interest is properly recorded at year-end.
Presentation and disclosure	6. Determine management's intent to hold securities as a short-term investment. Document that intention in a management representation letter. *(Note: This procedure may not be needed for commercial paper because the duration may be very short.)*
	7. Determine whether the securities are classified as a current asset and any restrictions on their use are appropriately disclosed in the notes to the financial statements.

Audits of Other Short-Term Securities

Short-term investments may be in marketable equity securities such as common stocks and corporate bonds. If the intent is to hold them as short-term investments, the securities must be accounted for on the lower of cost or market basis (determined on an aggregate basis). If the securities are held for a longer term, they are valued on either the equity method or the cost method. An example of an audit working paper for the testing of marketable securities is shown in Exhibit 15.11.

A number of points need to be made concerning the review of the audit working paper:

1. The client prepares a schedule of all marketable securities it owns at year-end. The schedule includes all the accrued interest and dividends associated with each security for the period of time held. The auditor is testing both the balance sheet and the related income accounts at the same time.
2. The working paper shows three items related to the value of the security:
   a. Cost.
   b. Year-end market value.
   c. Carrying value for debt instruments.
3. Disposals and resulting gains/losses are shown for all accounts during the year.
4. The auditor verifies the cost or sales price of the assets through examination of broker's advices evidencing either the purchase or the sale of the security. If control risk is low, there is a need to examine only selected items.
5. Current market value is determined by referring to the year-end closing price in *The Wall Street Journal* or other financial source.
6. Income is recomputed for both interest and dividends.
7. The schedule is footed to determine the mechanical accuracy and the correct valuation of the account.
8. The needed adjustment to reduce the securities to market value or to recover previously written down adjustments is calculated and referenced to an adjustment working paper.
9. The audit tests evidenced in the working papers address all of the audit assertions except presentation and disclosure. That assertion is verified directly with management and documented separately.
10. The only remaining work to be done on marketable securities is the auditor's documentation of the conclusion regarding the fairness of presentation of the account balance as adjusted.

The auditor seeks audit evidence from a wide variety of sources. These include the following:

- Confirmation of securities held by trustees in client accounts at the end of the period.
- Observation of securities held by the client.
- Review of investment agreements including specification of **collateral.**

Exhibit 15.11

LEFLAM COMPANY
MARKETABLE SECURITIES
FOR THE YEAR ENDED DECEMBER 31, 1994

Marketable Investments	Beginning Balance	Purchase Date	Purchases	Date	Sale Disposals
Gen. Motors 8% commercial paper	$45,000.00	10/31/93		4/30/92	$45,000.00*
Ford Motor 8.25% comm paper	$100,000.00	12/1/93			
1000 Sh Land's End common stk	$22,367.00	10/31/93			
1000 Sh AMOCO	$48,375.00	12/31/92		7/13/93	$62,375.00*
1000 Sh Consolidated paper	$0.00	7/31/94	$41,250.00*		
2000 Bank America Zero Cpn Bond	$1,378.00	6/30/92			
Totals	$217,120.00		$41,250.00		$107,375.00
	T/B				F

*	Correct, per examination of broker's invoice.
C	Securities held in broker's account, confirmed with broker.
R	Recomputed, no exceptions.
†	Per December 31 stock transaction listing in *The Wall Street Journal*.
‡	Amount should be $1,000. Company failed to accrue dividend declared.
T/B	Per December 31, 1993 trial balance and 12/31 working papers, schedule M-2.
F	Footed.
CF	Cross-footed.
§	Loss not recorded. Trace to AJE #31.
‖	Traced to year-end trial balance.
#	Interest and dividend payments verified through examination of Standard & Poor's *Dividend and Interest Digest* for year-end December 31, 1993.

Exhibit 15.11

Prepared by ____________

Date ____________

Reviewed by ____________

Date ____________

Gain/Loss Disposal	Ending Balance	Market Value (12/31)	Income Accounts		Total
			Interest	Dividends	
$0.00	$0.00		$ 1,800.00 R		$ 1,800.00
	$100,000.00C	$ 100,000.00 †	$ 8,937.50 R		$ 8,937.50
	$ 22,367.00C	$ 16,375.00 †		$1,000.00 R	$ 1,000.00
$14,000.00 R	$0.00C	$ 0.00		$1,000.00 R	$ 1,000.00
	$ 41,250.00C	$ 44,500.00 †		$ 500.00 ‡	$ 500.00
	1,378.00C	$ 1,587.00 †	$ 209.00 R		$ 209.00
$14,000.00	$164,995.00	$ 162,462.00	$10,946.50	$2,500.00	$13,446.50
F	CF F	F	F	F	F
Market value	$162,462.00		#		
Excess cost > Mkt. Value	$ 2,533.00§ F	‖	‖	‖	

- Review of collateral if the auditor determines that the collateral is important to the valuation of the account.
- Review of broker's advices evidencing the cost or sales price of the securities.
- Analytical review for reasonableness of interest and dividend income.
- Review of standard reporting service list of dividend dates and rates for securities.

Standard & Poor's and Moody's, two investment advisory services, publish annual dividend and income guides for stocks listed on major exchanges. Most CPA firms obtain these year-end guides to facilitate the audit.

Development of New Financial Instruments and Marketable Securities

During the past decade, there has been a literal explosion of new financial instruments. Many of these instruments have been created to take advantage of short-term market anomalies, such as differences in interest rates between short- and long-term securities. Others have been developed for the explicit purpose of removing liabilities from a company's balance sheet (see Chapter 18 for a more complete discussion of liabilities). Selected examples of these new kinds of securities are listed in Exhibit 15.12.

In regard to these securities, the following should be noted:

1. The examples are only a few among hundreds of similar instruments existing on the current marketplace.
2. Although there are commonalities among all the instruments, each contains unique features that may shift risks to the investor.
3. Some instruments do not provide recourse to other specific resources in the event of default on the underlying instruments but try to "sweeten the deal" by providing other terms, such as higher interest rates, to entice users to invest in the securities. For example, most debt securities may be collateralized or provide preference in liquidation. Many of the new securities do not carry such privileges.
4. Although many of the instruments are described as marketable securities, the market for them is often very thin. Thus, market quotations may not be an accurate assessment of what the marketable value of the specific securities might be at the balance sheet date.
5. Some of the instruments defer the payment of cash to the future, often in the hope that the instrument will be replaced by another one at that time and thus will not constitute a significant cash flow burden on the issuer.
6. Some of the instruments have specific options, such as the put option that allows the investor to put (sell) the instrument back to the original issuer on the occurrence of a specific event. It would seem that the market value of such instrument would be near par, but it must be remembered that the ability of the holder of the instrument to realize par value depends on the original issuer's ability to pay at the time of the triggering event.

Exhibit 15.12

EXAMPLES OF THE NEW TYPES OF MARKETABLE SECURITIES

Event-risk protected debt. This is a debt covenant associated with bonds that is intended to protect the bondholder in the case of a credit downgrading of the bond, such as might happen in the case of a leveraged buy out (LBO). The covenants generally allow the investors to resell the debt back to the original issuer at par if a stipulated event (such as a change in ownership) were to occur.

Floating rate note. A debt instrument with a variable interest rate. Interest rate adjustments are made periodically, often every six months, and are tied to a money market index such as the Treasury bill rate or London InterBank Organizational Rate (LIBOR).

Junk bond. A term that became popular in the mid to late 1980s to signify a high-yielding bond issued by a borrower with a lower than investment grade credit rating. Many of these bonds were issued in connection with LBOs; others were issued by companies without long records of sales and earnings.

Pay-in-Kind (PIK) debenture. A bond that pays interest during the initial few years in additional PIK debentures rather than in cash. Although the investor gets only more paper, the bonds have a scheduled date in which cash interest will be paid on both the original paper and the paper issued as dividends. Most of these bonds become callable by the issuer when cash payments are scheduled for payment. These bonds have been issued by high-risk companies that have large debt obligations. Many issuing firms need asset sales to pay down debt.

Zero-coupon bond. With no periodic interest payments, these bonds are sold at a deep discount from face value. The holder of the bond receives gradual appreciation in the carrying value of the bond, which is redeemed at face value at maturity. The appreciation in value represents interest income.

Securities sold with a put option. Marketable securities sold by an investor (not the original issuer) together with a put option that entitles the investor to sell the securities back to the seller at a fixed price in the future. These securities often carry low yields.

Collateralized mortgage obligation (CMO). Debt obligation issued as a special-purpose instrument collateralized by a pool of mortgages. The financial instrument is handled as a purchase of a group of mortgages using the proceeds of an offering of bonds collateralized by the mortgages. The new financial instrument uses the underlying cash flows of the collateral to fund the debt service on the bonds. The bonds are priced based on their own maturity and rate of return rather than that of the underlying mortgages. CMOs have created secondary markets in the mortgage industry and have assisted the industry in attaining greater levels of liquidity. However, they are subject to the default risk of the underlying mortgages.

Securitized receivables. Receivables converted into a form that can be sold to investors (similar in concept to CMOs). The issuer of the special financial instrument uses the cash flows of the receivables to fund debt service on the securities. In most cases, investors have no recourse to the sponsor or originator of the financial instrument if the underlying loans go into default.

Financial institutions often have had heavy investments in such instruments. In many cases, there was a ready market for such instruments, and the risk of the instrument could be calculated and controlled, but in other instances, the entity treated the instruments as if they were no different than marketable securities readily traded on a national stock exchange. For example, junk bonds were *the financial instrument of the 1980s*. The quoted market values used for carrying the securities were often illusive and misleading, however, because they were based on quoted sales at volumes significantly lower than the volume of instruments on a company's books. In other words, a security that has the term marketable in its name is not necessarily readily marketable. The risks associated with the new types of financial instruments require the auditor to understand the control procedures a client has implemented to minimize risks. Guidelines for assessing risks and controls are shown in the Practice Illustration which follows.

The management control procedures should be reviewed by the auditor as part of the audit of marketable securities. The auditor should obtain an understanding of the risks associated with the securities and determine whether the risks are accurately reflected in the valuation assigned the particular account balance or adequately disclosed in the notes to the financial statements.

Special Concerns Regarding Liquidity

As the name implies, liquid assets can be moved quickly and can easily be substituted for one another. As an example, cash that may have been counted in the morning could purchase marketable securities in the afternoon. When the auditor believes that the control environment contains high risk and management might be motivated to misstate, it is best to audit all the liquid assets simultaneously (or as close to simultaneous as possible) to preclude the double counting of assets at year-end.

D–ILLUSTRATIVE EXAMPLE–LEFLAM MANUFACTURING COMPANY

LeFlam's cash balance of $100,291 is significantly less than it was last year, $672,874 and, by itself, is not material when compared with total current assets of $19,728,138. However, the flow of cash receipts and disbursements through the checking accounts is material. The company's general checking account is maintained with the Northeast Bank in Milwaukee; it also maintains a checking account at the Northeast Bank in Oconomowoc, on which disbursement checks are written. Daily transfers are made to the Oconomowoc bank from the Milwaukee bank to cover checks clearing each day. The payroll account is maintained in a local bank. There are also three petty cash accounts totaling $1,500, which have relatively little activity. Exhibit 15.13 is the cash lead schedule. The discussion that follows concentrates on the general checking account.

Understanding the System

The auditor begins by obtaining an understanding of the internal control structure over cash receipts and disbursements. The auditor's findings are detailed in the fol-

Practice Illustration

CONTROLLING RISKS ASSOCIATED WITH NEW FINANCIAL INSTRUMENTS

In a *Guide to Financial Instruments*, Coopers & Lybrand offers the following management control considerations for investors to understand and monitor when investing in the new kinds of financial instruments:

1. *Understand the product.* Analyzing the economic effect of a transaction on each party is crucial for gaining insight into potential risk. Transactions are becoming more complex, with a single instrument often divided into a dozen or more instruments with differing yields and maturities.
2. *Understand the accounting and tax ramifications.* The Financial Accounting Standards Board (FASB) has worked on a comprehensive document to clarify the accounting for financial instruments based on risks and obligations. Although the FASB cannot anticipate every kind of instrument that may evolve in the next decade, the general concepts in the guide serve to lead the client and management to proper accounting. Many of the instruments have been motivated by potential tax savings; thus, potential tax law changes may affect the economics of the instruments.
3. *Monitor the transactions.* Procedures should be established to monitor the transaction (instrument) on a regular basis to determine whether the expected benefits fall within the assumed risk levels. If the risk was initially hedged or collateral was obtained, the value of the hedge or collateral should be remeasured. Procedures should be in place to react to risk that has grown greater than the entity wishes to bear.
4. *Understand the credit risk.* Investors should ensure that proper protection exists against default by counter parties. A mechanism is needed for continued monitoring of the counterparty's economic health. Formal credit monitoring procedures—similar to credit policies for accounts receivable—need to be considered (even for counterparties with prominent names).
5. *Control collateral when risk is not acceptable.* Sometimes credit risk becomes higher than anticipated, but the investor allows the counterparty to keep the collateral. In such cases, investors should implement procedures to ensure that they have possession of the collateral.
6. *Develop corporate policies and procedures.* Companies should have explicit policies, preferably in writing, defining the objectives for entering into the new forms of financial transactions. Management should clearly define the nature, risk, and economics of each authorized instrument or type of transaction. The overall corporate policy should be approved by the board of directors.

lowing sections. Exhibit 15.14 is a macro-flowchart of the accounting process for cash receipts and disbursements.

Cash Receipts

Customers mail their checks to a lockbox in Milwaukee that can be accessed only by Northeast Bank. Bank personnel open the mail and prepare an adding machine tape of all the remittances. The bank then credits LeFlam's checking account for the total amount received each day and then sends a copy of the tape and a photocopy of each check to LeFlam. An accounts receivable clerk enters the collection information into the computer from the copies of checks received from the bank. She also enters the

Exhibit 15.13

LEFLAM MANUFACTURING COMPANY
CASH LEAD SCHEDULE
DECEMBER 31, 1994

Account	Ref	12/31/93	12/31/94 Balance Per Books	Adjustments/ Reclassifications Debits	Adjustments/ Reclassifications Credits	12/31/94 Final Balance
General Checking—NB Milwaukee 101	**A-1**	644,343	95,248		AJE#1 500	94,748
Check Clearing—NB Oconomowoc 102	A-2	1,000	1,000			1,000
Payroll—First Local Bank 103	A-3	26,385	2,543			2,543
Petty Cash 104	A-4	1,500	1,500			1,500
Total	**T/B**	673,229	100,291		500	99,791

total cash collected by the bank as shown on the tape. The computer generates a total from the individual collections that were entered and prints a daily cash receipts report showing the detail of each entry, the computer-generated total, the total entered by the clerk, and any difference between those totals. The clerk must balance out before the computer posts the information to the customers' accounts and the accounts receivable and cash accounts in the general ledger. The accounts receivable detail is automatically reconciled daily by the computer with the control account. Monthly statements are mailed only to customers with overdue balances.

Cash Disbursements

Each vendor's invoice is compared with the purchase order and receiving report by clerks in the purchasing department who check for correct price, quantity, extensions, and footings. Prenumbered checks and a check register are automatically prepared by the computer based on the due date. Checks and supporting documents are forwarded to the controller for review and signature. A copy of the check is stapled to the supporting documents and filed by the controller's secretary in vendor files. The secretary also mails the checks. The accounts payable clerk prepares the monthly bank reconciliation.

Checks are paid through Northeast Bank in Oconomowoc, Wisconsin. The bank determines the total of checks to be paid each day and notifies the Milwaukee bank to transfer that amount of cash to cover the checks. The total is charged to LeFlam's account the next business day when the wire transfer is received from the Milwaukee bank. This process provides an extra day of float before the checks are charged against LeFlam's account.

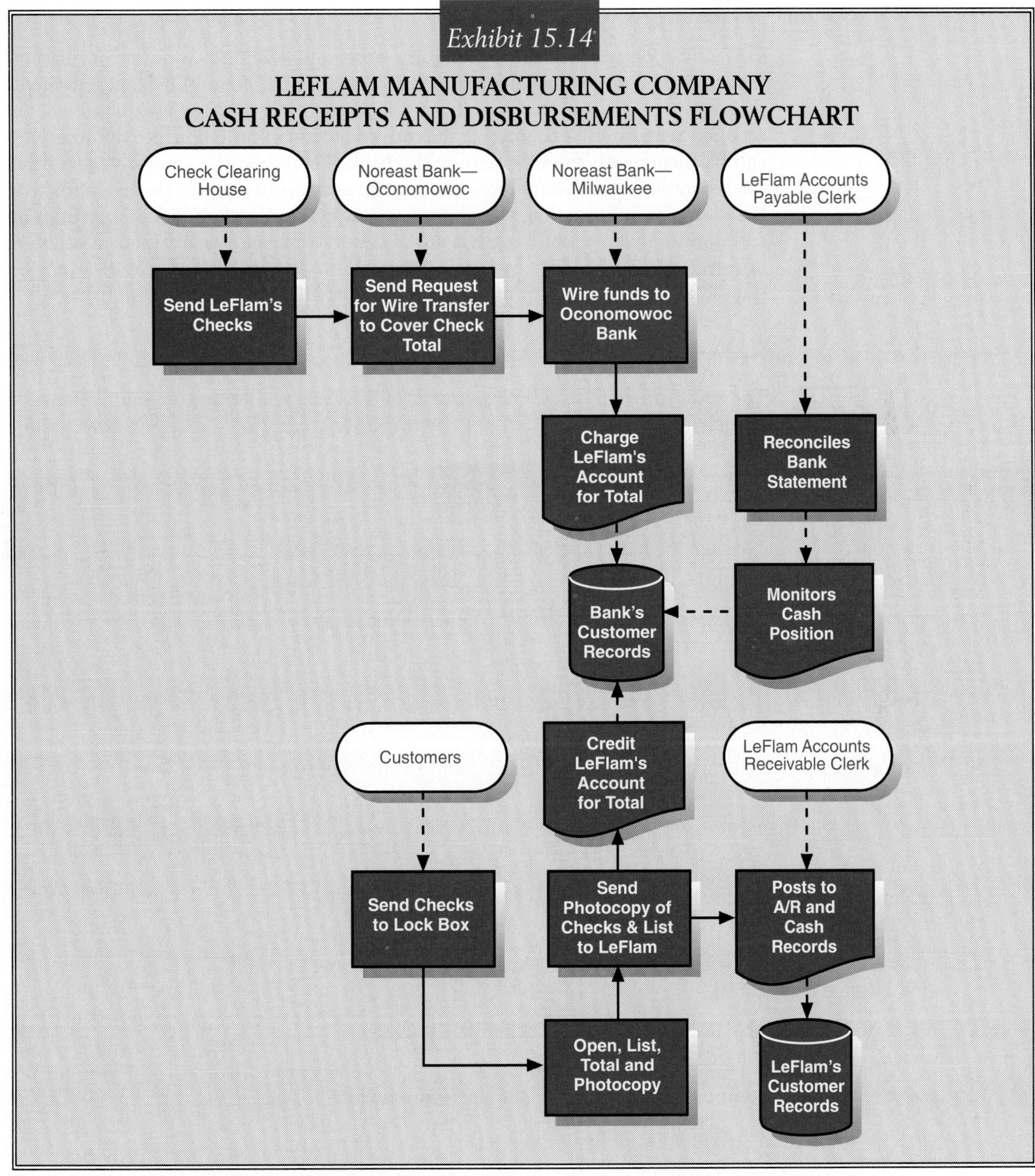

A microcomputer in the accounts payable department is electronically connected to Northeast Bank in Milwaukee, which shows cash collection, wire transfers to the Oconomowoc bank, and cash balance information as reflected in the bank's records. This helps management monitor its cash position.

Assessing Control Risk

The auditor determined through inquiry, observation, and review of reconciliations that the accounts payable clerk does in fact reconcile the monthly bank statements shortly after they are received from the banks. The auditor also observed the accounts receivable clerk entering the cash collection information into the computer and balancing with the tape sent by the bank. Therefore, the auditor believes that the separation of cash handling, authorizing, and record-keeping duties is effective. Based on this information, the auditor assesses control risk at less than maximum and decides that a proof of cash is not necessary. The auditor has made a decision, however, that it would not be efficient to perform detailed tests of controls over cash transactions and therefore concentrates on substantive tests of the cash balance.

Substantive Tests

The audit program for substantive tests of the general checking account is shown in Exhibit 15.15.

Exhibit 15.15

LEFLAM MANUFACTURING COMPANY
SUBSTANTIVE AUDIT PROGRAM—GENERAL CHECKING ACCOUNT
DECEMBER 31, 1994

Audit Objectives

a. Determine that the cash balance represents actual cash items on hand, in transit to the bank, or in the bank.

b. Determine that the cash balance is properly classified and related disclosures are adequate.

	W/P Ref.	Done by
1. Obtain a confirmation of balance directly from the bank and reconcile with amounts recorded per the books.	A-1/2	Auditor
2. Obtain a cutoff statement covering at least 10 business days subsequent to the balance sheet date.	Done	Auditor
3. Verify cutoff for cash received, disbursed, and interbank transfers through the preparation of a bank transfer statement.	A-1&2	Auditor
4. Reconcile bank statement to the confirmation and the lead schedule.	A-1	Auditor
5. Verify the propriety of reconciling items through reference to bank cutoff statement and other investigations.	A-1	Auditor
6. Verify the clerical accuracy of the reconciliation and any supporting schedules.	A-1&2	Auditor
7. Consider the need for noncurrent classification and disclosures.	A-1	Auditor
8. State your conclusion and implications for further audit work.	A-1	Auditor

The auditor had the controller send a letter to the Northeast Bank in Milwaukee and in Oconomowoc, instructing them to send bank confirmations for the Milwaukee bank and cutoff statements as of January 15, 1995, directly to his office. The accounts payable clerk has given him a copy of the bank reconciliation (Exhibit 15.16) for December 31, 1994, adding machine tape of outstanding checks (Exhibit 15.17), the December bank statements, paid checks, wire transfer, and other debit memos. Bank statements from the Oconomowoc bank usually show a $1,000 balance. This is the minimum required balance. The bank does not charge LeFlam's account for checks received from the clearing house until it receives a wire transfer from the Milwaukee bank to cover those checks. Therefore, the charges and credits cancel each other out daily.

Exhibit 15.16

LEFLAM MANUFACTURING COMPANY **A-1**
BANK RECONCILIATION
NORTHEAST BANK—GENERAL CHECKING
DECEMBER 31, 1994

PBC
Performed by LER
Date 1/28/95

		Reference
Balance per bank	$149,867.40*	
Deposits in transit	0.00†	A-1/2
Outstanding checks	(55,119.58)	A-1/1
Adjusted bank balance	$ 94,747.82	
Balance per books	$ 95,247.72‡	
Bank service charge	(499.90)§	
Adjusted bank balance	$ 94,747.82	
	F	

* Agrees with bank confirmation.
† No deposits are in transit. The last credit recorded by the bank is the last cash receipt total recorded on the books at December 31, 1994.
§ Traced to December bank statement and debit memo from bank. Includes charge for lockbox and wire transfer services. Pass adjustment—immaterial.
F Footed.
‡ Agrees with lead schedule.

Conclusion: The cash balance is fairly stated.

Exhibit 15.17

LEFLAM MANUFACTURING COMPANY **A-1/1**
OUTSTANDING CHECKS—GENERAL CHECKING ACCOUNT
DECEMBER 31, 1994

Prepared by Client
Performed by LER
Date 1/31/95

#35,669	$5,478.94*
35,676	512.22*
35,701	18,250.85*
35,720	1,000.00†
35,763	1,500.00*
35,765	25.77*
35,771	710.56*
35,778	6,133.86*
35,780	7,152.81*
35,781	866.50*
35,782	1,112.59*
35,783	1,272.26*
35,784	10.00*
35,785	210.05*
35,786	8,218.44*
35,787	2,488.23*
35,788	176.50*
	55,119.58
	F A-1

* Check cleared during cutoff period per the bank cutoff statement.
† Did not clear; payable to the United Fund. Examined support and concluded amount was proper.
F Footed.
All checks returned with the cutoff bank statement and dated prior to January 1, 1995 appear on the outstanding check list.

The auditor places the letters *PBC* on the face of the reconciliation and outstanding check working papers to indicate that they were prepared by the client. Notice the headings and the use of index numbers, cross-references, tickmarks, and explanations in the working papers. Notice that the auditor indicates work done in the audit program by indicating a working paper reference and initials behind each audit step in the program.

Verify Cutoffs

Receipts. No deposits are in transit because of the use of a lockbox; the receipts are received directly by the bank from LeFlam's customers. You have verified that the cash receipts credited to the LeFlam account by the Milwaukee bank on December 31, 1994 were recorded as a deposit on the books as of the same date and that this was the last cash receipt recorded for the year.

Disbursements. The check register printed by the computer for December 31, 1994 indicates that the last check number used was 35,788. This is the last check shown on the outstanding check list. The checks returned with the cutoff bank statement dated prior to January 1, 1995 were traced to the outstanding check list to be sure that they were all listed; they were. The only outstanding check not clearing during the cutoff period was to the United Fund. The auditor traced the check number and amount to the check register and found the memo from the public relations department authorizing this contribution. The auditor footed the outstanding check list and agreed it to the reconciliation.

Perform Other Procedures

The auditor footed the reconciliation and traced the bank balance to the bank confirmation and the book balance to the trial balance, which was taken from the general ledger. The auditor also traced the bank service charge to the December bank statement and supporting debit memo prepared by the bank. It represented bank charges for lockbox and wire transfer services. It is the client's normal practice to record these charges in the month in which it receives the bank statement. The auditor decides that the amount is immaterial and does not require an adjusting entry by itself. He does not, however, want to forget about it, and so he posts it to a working paper entitled Summary of Possible Adjustments (SPA), which is discussed further in Chapter 20.

A $1,000 balance is required to be maintained in the Oconomowoc bank at all times. Technically, this is a noncurrent asset and should be reclassified as such. However, the auditor determines that it is not material and does not need to be reclassified or disclosed, but he posts it to the SPA.

Document a Conclusion

The auditor should come to an audit conclusion about each significant account or class of transactions tested. He states his conclusion on the working paper containing the reconciliation.

Summary

In today's environment, organizations manage cash and liquid assets to maximize their potential return. Companies develop sophisticated agreements with their bankers to invest excess liquid assets in interest-bearing securities. Many audit clients are significant investors in new forms of marketable securities; some of those investments are unfortunately made without a full understanding of the risks associated with the securities. Audits are more complex because market values of new, and more complex, marketable securities are not readily available. The auditor must use sound business sense to understand and evaluate the risks associated with these new instruments. Likewise, internal auditors are likely be heavily involved in evaluating the completeness of management's policies and monitoring adherence to those policies. A well-informed board of directors is a positive factor in evaluating the potential risk, but an uninformed board may mean that an organization is subject to greater risk than the board or management desire.

As an overall guideline, the audit approach to these assets centers around the following major steps:

1. Identify the assets and management's control structure for safeguarding the assets and maximizing returns within the risk parameters set by the board of directors.
2. Understand the economic purpose of major transactions and/or agreements with financial institutions and the economic impact on the client.
3. Identify the risks associated with the company's financial instruments (assets) and the parties that hold the risks.
4. Confirm agreements and examine contracts associated with the agreements to determine necessary audit steps and accounting and financial statement disclosure.
5. Review and test transactions and related accounting and disclosure for their economic substance and adherence to appropriate accounting and SEC pronouncements.
6. Determine the existence of a market for securities and determine the appropriate accounting for year-end account balances. The accounting for cash and marketable securities has often been assigned to first-year auditors because it was thought that the auditing procedures were mostly mechanical in nature: reconciling bank accounts, examining canceled checks, and so forth. As this chapter has communicated, the audit of cash and liquid assets is far from mechanical and represents a real challenge for a number of audit clients.

Significant Terms

bank confirmation A standard confirmation sent to all banks with whom the client had business during the year to obtain information about the year-end cash balance and additional information about loans outstanding.

bank transfer schedule An audit working paper that lists all transfers between client bank accounts starting a short period before year-end and continuing for a short period after year-end; its purpose is to ensure that cash in transit is not recorded twice.

cash trace An audit procedure by which the auditor lists cash receipts for some period of time and traces the receipts to deposits in the bank statement to determine whether cash receipts are deposited intact on a timely basis.

collateral An asset or a claim on an asset usually held by a borrower or an issuer of a debt instrument to serve as a guarantee for the value of a loan or security. If the borrower fails to pay interest or principal, the collateral is available to the lender as a basis to recover the principal amount of the loan or debt instrument.

commercial paper Note issued by major corporations, usually for short periods of time and at rates approximating prime lending rates, usually with high credit rating; its quality may change if the financial strength of the issuer declines.

cutoff bank statement A bank statement for a period of time determined by the client and the auditor that is shorter than the regular month-end statements; sent directly to the auditor, who uses it to verify reconciling items on the client's year-end bank reconciliation.

financial instruments A broad class of instruments—usually debt securities, but also equity or hedges—that represents financial agreements between a party (usually an issuer) and a counterparty (usually an investor) based on either underlying assets or agreements to incur financial obligations or make payments; they range in complexity from a simple bond to highly complex agreements containing puts or options.

imprest bank account A bank account that normally carries a zero balance and is replenished by the company when checks are to be written against the account; provides additional control over cash. The most widely used imprest bank account is the payroll account to which the company makes a deposit equal to the amount of payroll checks issued.

kiting A fraudulent cash scheme to overstate cash assets at year-end by recording deposits in transit in both the account from which the cash is withdrawn and the account to which it is transferred.

lockbox A cash management arrangement with a bank whereby an organization's customers send payments directly to a post office box number accessible by the client's bank; the bank opens the cash remittances and directly deposits the money in the client's account.

marketable security A security that is readily marketable and held by the company as an investment.

proof of cash An audit technique that reconciles beginning and ending balances per the bank with the books and the month's deposits per the bank with the receipts per the books and the bank's withdrawals for the company for the month with the disbursements per the books.

turnaround document A document sent to the customer to be returned with the customer's remittance; may be machine readable and may contain information to improve the efficiency of receipt processing.

Review Questions

A–Introduction

15–1 Why is it important to coordinate the testing of cash and other liquid asset accounts?

15–2 Explain the purpose and risks associated with each of the following types of bank accounts:

a. General Cash account.

b. Imprest payroll account.

c. Branch accounts.

15–3 Describe how a lockbox arrangement with a bank works. What is its advantage to an organization? What risks are associated with it? What controls should an entity develop to mitigate each of the risks identified?

15–4 What is a compensating balance? How does the auditor become aware of the existence of compensating balances?

B–Audits of Cash Accounts

15–5 How should processing duties be segregated in a cash receipts processing system that is heavily automated such as the WWW example in the chapter? Explain the rationale for the segregation chosen.

15–6 What are the major *authorization* principles the auditor should investigate regarding both cash management and investments in marketable securities?

15–7 Explain how turnaround documents can improve the controls over the cash receipts process. Does the existence of a turnaround document negate the need to assign a unique identification number to each cash receipts transaction? Explain.

15–8 What is the impact on the audit if the client does not perform independent periodic reconciliations of its cash accounts? What audit procedures would be dictated by the lack of the client's independent reconciliations?

15–9 Explain the purpose of the following audit procedures:

a. Sending a bank confirmation to all the banks with which the client does business.

b. Obtaining a bank cutoff statement.

c. Preparing a bank transfer statement.

15–10 What information does an auditor search for in reviewing loan agreements or cash management agreements with the client's bank?

15–11 What types of operational audits should an internal audit department perform in the cash and cash management area?

15–12 Identify the circumstances in which an auditor might utilize a proof of cash as an audit procedure. What information or evidence would the auditor expect to gather from a proof of cash that could not be obtained using other procedures?

15–13 Define and illustrate kiting. What procedures should the client institute to prevent it? What audit procedures should the auditor utilize to detect kiting?

15–14 Why is there a greater emphasis on the possibility of fraud in cash accounts than for other asset accounts of the same size? Identify three types of frauds that would directly affect the Cash account and indicate how the frauds might be detected by the auditor.

15–15 What audit objectives are accomplished by a cash trace? Would an auditor normally perform a cash trace on every engagement? Explain.

C–Marketable Securities and New Financial Instruments

15–16 Under what circumstances might it be acceptable to use an audit procedure other than physically examining marketable securities to verify their existence?

15–17 In what ways do the new types of marketable securities (new financial instruments) differ from traditional financial instruments? What additional risks are associated with such securities?

15–18 What controls should an organization implement if it wishes to become an investor in newer, and more complex, financial instruments? Explain the purpose of each control.

15–19 Evaluate the following statement made by a third-year auditor: "In comparison with other accounts, such as accounts receivable or property, plant, and equipment, it is my assessment that cash and marketable securities contain less inherent risk. There are no significant valuation problems with cash. You count the bills and multiply by one. Marketable securities can be verified by consulting the closing price in *The Wall Street Journal.* There isn't much risk there!" Do you agree or disagree with the auditor's assessment of inherent risk? Explain.

15–20 How does the auditor determine whether marketable securities are properly classified as short-term securities or long-term investments? What are the accounting implications of the classification as short term or long term? What types of evidence does the auditor gather to substantiate management's classification as a short-term security?

15–21 What role should the board of directors have regarding an organization's investment in marketable securities? What documentation would the auditor expect to find regarding the board's oversight role?

15–22 What role does collateral play in valuing marketable securities? Would an audit of marketable securities ever require an audit of the underlying collateral? Explain.

15–23 How would the absence of each of the following factors affect the auditor's assessment of the control environment? Assume that the company's investment in marketable securities is material to the financial statements.

a. The board of directors is not actively involved in monitoring the company's policies regarding marketable securities.

b. The company has an internal audit department, but it does not have any computer audit expertise and has not conducted audits of the cash or marketable securities account during the past three years.

c. Management does not have written guidelines for investments in marketable securities. The financial executive has been successful in procuring good returns on investments in the past, and management does not want to tamper with success.

Multiple Choice Questions

15–24 Which of the following would *not* represent an advantage to using a lockbox arrangement with a bank?

a. It expedites the receipt of cash and provides earlier access to it.
b. It is less costly than processing the cash receipts internally.
c. It provides additional segregation of duties because the bank handles cash.
d. It reduces the organization's susceptibility to fraud caused by diverting cash receipts to personal use.

15–25 XYZ Company concealed a cash shortage by transporting funds from one location to another and by converting negotiable instruments to cash. Which of the following audit procedures would be most effective in discovering the cash cover-up?

a. Periodic review by internal audit.
b. Simultaneous verification of cash and liquid assets.
c. A surprise count of all cash accounts.
d. Verifying all outstanding checks associated with the year-end bank reconciliation.

15–26 The auditor suspects that client personnel may be diverting cash receipts to personal use. The individual who opens the mail also prepares the bank deposit and sends turnaround documents to accounts receivable for posting. Which of the following audit procedures would be the *least* effective in determining whether cash shortages are occurring?

a. Confirmation of accounts receivable.
b. Preparation of a detailed cash trace.
c. Review of all noncash credits to accounts receivable for a selected period of time.
d. Year-end reconciliation of the bank account.

15–27 The auditor obtains a bank cutoff statement for a short period of time subsequent to year-end as a basis for testing the client's year-end bank reconciliation. However, during the testing, the auditor notes that very few of the outstanding checks have cleared the bank. The most likely cause for this is that the client

a. Is engaged in a kiting scheme.
b. Prepared checks to pay vendors but did not mail them until well after year-end.
c. Was involved in a lapping scheme.
d. Needed to overstate the year-end cash balance to increase the working capital ratio.

15–28 New types of financial securities differ from traditional investments in marketable debt securities; the new securities

a. Cannot contain fixed interest rates.
b. May shift more of the risk of default to the investor.
c. Reduce the need for the investor to obtain collateral or other security against default.
d. Are not handled by traditional brokerage firms.

15–29 An audit client has invested heavily in new marketable securities. Which of the following would not constitute an appropriate role for the company's board of directors?

a. Receive and review periodic reports by the internal audit department on compliance with company policies and procedures.
b. Approve all new investments.
c. Review and approve written policies and guidelines for investments in marketable securities.
d. Periodically review the risks inherent in the portfolio of marketable securities to determine whether the risk is within parameters deemed acceptable by the board.

15–30 The auditor would send a bank confirmation to all banks with which the client had business during the year because

a. The confirmation seeks information on indebtedness that may exist even if the bank accounts are closed.
b. Confirmations are essential to detecting kiting schemes.
c. Confirmations provide information about deposits in transit that is useful in proving the client's year-end bank reconciliation.
d. All of the above.

15–31 Which of the following auditing procedures is the most appropriate when internal control over cash is weak or when a client requests an investigation of cash transactions?

a. Proof of cash.
b. Bank reconciliation.
c. Cash confirmation.
d. Evaluation of ratio of cash to current liabilities.

15–32 An unrecorded check issued during the last week of the year would most likely be discovered by the auditor when the

a. Check register for the last month is reviewed.
b. Cutoff bank statement is reviewed as part of the year-end bank reconciliation.
c. Bank confirmation is reviewed.
d. Search for unrecorded liabilities is performed.

15–33 Internal control over cash receipts is weakened when an employee who receives customer mail receipts also

a. Prepares initial cash receipt records.
b. Prepares bank deposit slips for all mail receipts.

c. Maintains a petty cash fund.

d. Records credits to individual accounts receivable.

Discussion and Research Questions

15–34 (Audit Approach: Cash) In a discussion of third-year auditors, one auditor who had been associated primarily with audits of large clients offered the opinion that "substantive testing of cash accounts is obsolete. The primary emphasis on cash audits ought to be on auditing the control procedures over the cash process, assessing the risks associated with the control environment, and selectively testing the client's year-end reconciliation." The second auditor replied, "Unfortunately, you have audited in a very sheltered world. Most of the audit clients I see are small and don't have particularly good control procedures. There is little segregation of duties. Most posting of accounts is to microcomputer systems under the control of the controller's department. Unless we perform a primarily substantive audit, supplemented by a detailed cash trace or some similar procedure, we could not gain sufficient evidence to render an opinion on cash."

Required:

a. What are the primary elements of an organization's overall control structure that the first auditor must be relying on in reaching her conclusion about the needed audit approach to cash?

b. For each item identified in part a, indicate an audit procedure the auditor might utilize to corroborate the initial understanding of the risk or the control.

c. What are the primary substantive audit procedures the second auditor would most likely utilize? Describe the audit objectives accomplished with each procedure.

15–35 (Cash: Audit Evidence) The following items were discovered during the audit of the Cash account. For each item identified,

a. Indicate the *audit procedure* that most likely would have led to the discovery of the error.

b. Identify one or two control procedures that would have prevented or detected the misstatement or irregularity.

Audit Findings:

1. The company had overstated cash by transferring funds at year-end to another account but failed to record the withdrawal until after year-end.
2. On occasion, customers with smaller balances simply send in cash payments. The client has an automated cash receipts process similar to that used by WWW Company. The employee opening the cash pocketed the cash and destroyed other supporting documentation.
3. Same as part 2, but the employee prepared a turnaround document that showed either an additional discount for the customer or a credit to the customer's account.
4. The controller was temporarily taking cash for personal purposes but intended to repay the company (although the repayment never

occurred). The cash shortage was covered up by understating outstanding checks.

5. The company had temporary investments in six-month certificates of deposit at the bank. The CDs were supposed to yield an annual interest rate of 12 percent, but apparently are yielding only 6 percent.
6. Cash remittances are not deposited in a timely fashion and are sometimes lost.
7. Substantial bank service charges have not been recorded by the client prior to year-end.
8. A loan has been negotiated with the bank to provide funds for a subsidiary company. The loan was made by the controller of the division who apparently was not authorized to negotiate the loan.
9. A check written to a vendor had been recorded twice in the cash disbursements journal to cover a cash shortage.

*15–36 (Internal Control Procedures over Cash) Pembrook Company had poor internal control over its cash transactions. The following are facts about its cash position at November 30: The cash books showed a balance of $18,901.62, which included undeposited receipts. A credit of $100 on the bank statement did not appear on the company's books. The balance, according to the bank statement, was $15,550. Outstanding checks were no. 62 for $116.25, no. 183 for $150.00, no. 284 for $253.25, no. 8621 for $190.71, no. 8623 for $206.80, and no. 8632 for $145.28. The only deposit was in the amount of $3,794.41 on December 7.

The cashier handles all incoming cash and makes the bank deposits personally. He also reconciles the monthly bank statement. His November 30 reconciliation follows:

Balance, per books, November 30			$18,901.62
Add:	Outstanding checks:		
	8621	$190.71	
	8623	$206.80	
	8632	$145.28	$ 442.79
			$19,344.41
Less: Undeposited receipts			$ 3,794.41
Balance per bank, November 30			$15,550.00
Deduct: Unrecorded credit			$ 100.00
True cash, November 30			$15,450.00

Required:

a. You suspect that the cashier may have misappropriated some money and are concerned specifically that some of the undeposited receipts of $3,794.41 may have been taken. Prepare a schedule showing your estimate of the loss.
b. How did the cashier attempt to conceal the theft?

*Adapted from the Uniform CPA examination or the Certified Internal Auditor examination.

c. On the basis of this information only, name two specific features of internal control that were apparently missing.

d. If the cashier's October 31 reconciliation is known to be in order and you start your audit on December 10, what specific auditing procedures could you perform to discover the theft?

*15–37 (Audit of Cash: Reconciliations) Toyco, a retail toy chain, honors two bank credit cards and makes daily deposits of credit card sales in two credit card bank accounts (Bank A and Bank B). Each day Toyco batches its credit card sales slips, bank deposit slips, and authorized sales return documents and sends them to data processing for data entry. Each week detailed computer printouts of the general ledger credit card cash accounts are prepared. Credit card banks have been instructed to make an automatic weekly transfer of cash to Toyco's general bank account. The credit card banks charge back deposits that include sales to holders of stolen or expired cards.

The auditor examining the Toyco financial statements has obtained the copies of the detailed general ledger cash account printouts, a summary of the bank statements, and the manually prepared bank reconciliations, all for the week ended December 31, as shown here.

Required:
Review the December 31 bank reconciliation and the related information contained in the following schedules and describe what actions the auditor should take to obtain satisfaction for each item on the bank reconciliation. Assume that all amounts are material and that all computations are accurate. Organize your answer sheet as follows using the code contained on the bank reconciliation:

<u>Code Number</u> <u>Actions to Be Taken by the Auditor to Gain Satisfaction</u>
1. [Audit action or procedures to be taken]

Toyco
Bank Reconciliation
For the Week Ended December 31, 1994

	Bank A	Bank B
Code No.	Add or (Deduct)	
1. Balance per bank statement, December 31	$8,600	$–0–
2. Deposits in transit, December 31	2,200	6,000
3. Redeposit of invalid deposits (deposited in wrong account)	1,000	1,400
4. Difference in deposits of December 29	(2,000)	(100)
5. Unexplained bank charge	400	
6. Bank cash transfer not yet recorded	–0–	22,600
7. Bank service charges	–0–	500
8. Chargebacks not recorded—stolen cards	100	–0–

9. Sales returns recorded but not reported to the bank	(600)	(1,200)
10. Balance per general ledger, December 31	$9,700	$29,200

Toyco
Detailed General Ledger Credit Card Cash Accounts Printouts
For the Week Ended December 31, 1994

	Bank A	Bank B
	Dr. or (Cr.)	
Beginning balance, December 24	$12,100	$ 4,200
Deposits:		
December 27	2,500	5,000
December 28	3,000	7,000
December 29	0	5,400
December 30	1,900	4,000
December 31	2,200	6,000
Cash transfer, December 17	(10,700)	–0–
Chargebacks—expired cards	(300)	(1,600)
Invalid deposits (deposited in wrong account)	(1,400)	(1,000)
Redeposit of invalid deposits	1,000	1,400
Sales returns for week ended December 31	(600)	(1,200)
Ending balance	$ 9,700	$29,200

Toyco
Summary of the Bank Statements
For the Week Ended December 31, 1994

	Bank A	Bank B
	(Charges) or Credits	
Beginning balance, December 24	$10,000	$–0–
Deposits dated:		
December 24	2,100	4,200
December 27	2,500	5,000
December 28	3,000	7,000
December 29	2,000	5,500
December 30	1,900	4,000
Cash transfers to general bank account:		
December 27	(10,700)	–0–
December 31	–0–	(22,600)
Chargebacks:		
Stolen cards	(100)	–0–
Expired cards	(300)	(1,600)

(Continued)

	Bank A	Bank B
	(Charges) or Credits	
Invalid deposits	(1,400)	(1,000)
Bank service charges	-0-	(500)
Bank charge (unexplained)	(400)	-0-
Ending balance	$ 8,600	$-0-

15–38 (Marketable Securities) The client prepared the following worksheet listing all activities in the marketable securities account for the year under audit. For purposes of this question, you may assume that there are no unusual securities except the note from XYNO Corporation (a related party) and a note from Allis-Chalmers Corporation (a customer). Assume also that control risk was assessed as moderate to high and that the auditor decides not to rely on the control structure but concentrates on substantive tests of the account balance. The account balances at the beginning and end of the year per the company's trial balance are as follows:

	Beginning Balance	Ending Balance
Marketable securities	$ 400,000	$ 675,000
Allowance to Reduce Securities to Market	$ 35,000	$ 35,000
Balance per general ledger	$ 365,000	$ 640,000
Interest Income		$ 25,000
Dividend Income		$ 18,000
Net Gain on Disposal of Securities		$ 32,000

Required:
Identify the audit steps needed to complete the audit of marketable securities for year-end. You may assume that the client was audited last year.

15–39 (Bank Confirmations) Generally accepted auditing standards require that auditors send confirmations to all banks with which the client has done business during the year. The AICPA has developed a standard bank confirmation form to ensure consistent communication with the banking community.

Required:

a. Is the auditor required to send a bank confirmation to banks for which the client receives a bank cutoff statement shortly after year-end? Explain.

b. What additional information is gathered through a bank confirmation? Explain how the other information gathered is used on the audit.

c. For each of the scenarios listed below, recommend an audit procedure or additional audit work that should be performed:

   1. The client has one major bank account located in a distant city and the auditor is not familiar with the bank. The auditor has assessed control risk as high on this engagement. The mailing address of the

bank is simply a post office box number, but such a number is not considered unusual.

2. The client has three accounts with its major bank. The confirmation returned by the bank shows different balances for two of the three accounts than what the client shows. The balance per the client for one of the accounts is the same as the bank shows in the cutoff statement received from the bank shortly after year-end. The auditor did not request a cutoff statement on the other account for which the confirmation differs.
3. The returned confirmation shows a loan that the client does not list as a liability.

15–40 (Loan and Debt Covenants) The auditor must be aware of loan and debt covenants that may affect the client. A regular part of each audit should include the examination of these covenants.

Required:

a. What information should the auditor normally obtain while reviewing loan covenant agreements? Where would the auditor obtain the agreements?
b. What action should an auditor take upon discovering that the client might be in violation of a loan agreement? Assume, for example, that the client is required to maintain a working capital ratio of 2.0 to 1.0 or all the bank's short-term and long-term loans are declared in default and currently payable.
c. Do significant loan covenants have to be disclosed in a company's financial statement? Explain, including all circumstances in which you believe the covenants might need to be disclosed.

15–41 (Internal Audit of Investments) The existence of an internal audit department is recognized as a strong element of a company's control environment. Internal auditors can perform financial audits (similar to that of the external audit) or operational audits (audits of the effectiveness of operations and compliance with controls).

Required:

Assume that the client has started investing in the new variety of financial instruments. Develop a comprehensive operational audit program for a board of directors' requested audit of the investment area.

15–42 (Audit of Collateral) Financial institutions usually require collateral as part of a lending agreement. For example, loans to build shopping centers usually require the property to be put up as collateral in case the borrower cannot repay the loan. The bank then takes title to the collateral. However, as reported by the GAO, many financial institutions, especially savings and loans, did not obtain adequate collateral or were overly optimistic on the value of collateral for many loans.

Required:

a. Identify the control procedures an organization might implement to ensure that adequate collateral is obtained for loans.

b. During an audit of a financial institution, the auditor becomes concerned about the collateral that exists for some of the financial instruments in which the company has invested (such as collateralized receivables and mortgages). Develop an audit program to address the auditor's concerns regarding the adequacy of collateral.

c. How would a deficiency in collateral affect the financial presentation of a company's investment account? Explain.

15–43 (Bank Transfer Problem) Eagle River Plastics Company has a major branch located in Phoenix. The branch deposits cash receipts daily and transfers the receipts to the company's home office in Eagle River on a periodic basis. The transfers are accounted for as intercompany entries into the home office and branch office accounts. All accounting, however, is performed at the home office under the direction of the assistant controller. The assistant is also responsible for the transfers. The controller, however, independently reconciles the bank account each month or assigns the reconciliation to someone in the department (which, in some cases, could be the assistant controller). The company is relatively small; thus, the controller is also the financial planner and treasurer for the company. As part of the year-end audit, you are assigned the task of conducting an audit of bank transfers. As part of the process, you prepare the following schedule of transfers:

Date per Branch	Amount	Date per Home Office	Date Deposited per Home Bank	Date Cleared per Branch Bank
12-27	$23,000	12-31	12-31	1-3
12-29	$40,000	12-31	12-31	1-7
12-31	$45,000	1-2	1-3	1-8
1-2	$14,000	12-31	12-31	1-5
1-5	$28,000	1-3	1-7	1-12
1-3	$10,000	1-3	12-31	1-5

Required:

a. Identify the audit procedures that would be used to test the correctness of the client's bank transfers identified.

b. Identify any adjusting journal entries that would be needed on either the home or branch office accounting records as a result of the preceding transactions.

*15–44 (Bank Reconciliation) The following client-prepared bank reconciliation is being examined by Kautz, CPA, during an examination of the financial statements of Concrete Products, Inc.:

Concrete Products, Inc.
Bank Reconciliation
December 31, 1994

Deposits in transit (b):		
December 30	1,471.10	
December 31	2,840.69	4,311.79

Outstanding checks: (c)		
837	6,000.00	
1941	671.80	
1966	320.00	
1984	1,855.42	
1985	3,621.22	
1986	2,576.89	
1991	4,420.88	(19,466.21)
Subtotal		3,221.49
NSF check returned Dec. 29 (d)		200.00
Bank charges		5.50
Error check no. 1932		148.10
Customer note collected by the bank ($2,750 plus $275 interest) (e)		(3,025.00)
Balance per books (f)		$ 550.09

Required:
Identify one or more audit procedures that should be performed by Kautz in gathering evidence in support of each of the items (a) through (f) above.

15–45 (Overview and Objectives of Audit Procedures)

The following represents a critical review of the working papers of a new auditor for the cash and marketable securities audit areas. Several deficiencies are noted; they resulted in significant errors not being initially identified.

Required:
For each item listed below

a. Identify the audit procedure that would have detected the error.
b. Identify the basic financial assertion tested by the audit procedure.

Working Paper Deficiencies and Financial Statement Misstatements

1. Contingent liabilities, considered material for this client, were not discovered and appropriately disclosed in the financial statements.
2. The client was in violation of important loan covenant agreements.
3. The client was engaged in a sophisticated kiting scheme involving transfers through five geographically disbursed branch offices.
4. The December cash register was held open until January 8. All receipts through that date were recorded as December sales and cash receipts. The receipts, however, were deposited on a daily basis.
5. Cash disbursements for December were written but the checks were not mailed until January 10 because of a severe cash flow problem.
6. The client's bank reconciliation included an incorrect amount as balance per the bank.
7. Approximately 25 percent of the cash receipts for December 26 and December 28 were recorded twice.

8. The client's bank reconciliation covered up a clever fraud by the controller by incorrectly footing the outstanding checks and including fictitious checks as outstanding.

15–46 (Authorization Concepts) One of the major controls over cash and cash transfers is to ensure that only authorized personnel are handling cash, making cash transfers, or investing excess cash.

Required:

a. For each of the following situations, indicate the appropriate position of the individual who should be authorized to initiate and implement the transaction.
   1. Electronic transfer of excess cash funds to the organization's major account for cash management and investment.
   2. Regular disbursement of payment for accounts payable.
   3. Transfer of funds to the imprest payroll account.
   4. Investment of excess funds in nontraditional financial instruments.
   5. Endorsement for daily cash deposits.
b. For each type of authorization identified above, indicate the audit evidence the auditor would gather to determine whether transactions were appropriately authorized.

15–47 **(Research Question)** The advent of new financial instruments has dramatically changed the nature of investing during the past decade. Many of these new financial instruments offer potentially greater returns for the investor but at higher levels of risk.

Required:

Review the FASB's discussion on financial instruments to identify the types of financial instruments not discussed in the text. Select five instruments that you consider interesting and prepare a report addressing (1) the nature of the instrument; (2) the underlying business purpose of the instrument for all parties to the instrument, that is, identify the economic purpose of the instrument; and (3) identify any special audit considerations that might be associated with the instrument and any special audit procedures that should be applied during the audit of a client with a significant investment in the instrument.

15–48 **(Research Question)** EDI has been identified as a major method of transferring cash for most organizations within the next few years.

Required:

Complete *one* of the following.

a. Review recent publications on EDI to determine how EDI is being implemented for cash transfers and the controls that an organization should implement over EDI of cash.
b. Interview an organization in your area to determine the problems it may have encountered in implementing EDI and the solutions it implemented.

c. Interview someone in the public accounting or internal audit profession to determine the audit and control approach he or she has taken to address the electronic transfer of cash.

15–49 (Computer Spreadsheet Template) Assume that you have just gone to work for Wipfli, Barber, & Zeitlow, a regional CPA firm with seven offices in your state. Given your recent graduation from a reputable accounting school and your knowledge of microcomputers and spreadsheet software, the partner in charge of training asks you to prepare a spreadsheet template to be used by the firm for auditing marketable securities of their clients.

Required:

Prepare a microcomputer spreadsheet template (spreadsheet with the logic built into it so that all the staff auditors have to do is to input the current securities and the template will calculate expected values) to be used in the audit of marketable securities of clients. In developing the template, assume that the clients invest in a wide range of marketable securities including common stocks, preferred stocks, certificates of deposits, and bonds, as well as non-interest or dividend instruments such as puts or calls. The template should be set up to accomplish the following as a minimum:

- Indicate the preparer of the worksheet.
- Calculate needed cost or market adjustments.
- Estimate expected income including dividend income, interest income, and gain or loss on disposal of securities.
- Project ending balances.
- Establish a standard electronic tickmark legend.

The spreadsheet should be printed in such a manner to show the development of any macros and the logic built into it.

Cases

15–50 (Marketable Securities: Control Environment) Justin Company is a medium-size manufacturing client located in the Southwest producing supplies for the automobile industry. The company is publicly traded on the American Stock Exchange. Joann Sielig took over as chief executive officer three years ago after a successful career working with a New York investment banking firm. The company had been earning minimal returns and Sielig is intent on turning the company around. She has analyzed the situation and determined that the company's main manufacturing arm could be treated as a "cash cow," in other words, although the operations do not generate a lot of profit, they do generate cash flow that could be used for investment purposes. After analyzing the situations, Sielig has decided that the best opportunities for superior returns lie in investments in high-risk marketable securities. When questioned on this strategy during a board meeting, she cited the finance literature that she asserted "shows that greater returns are consistent only with greater risk. However, the risk can be minimized by appropriately diversifying the investment portfolio." Given

Sielig's knowledge of the subject and quick grasp of the company's situation, the board gave her complete control over all aspects of management. She personally manages the investment portfolio. Moreover, the board was so impressed with her analysis that she was given an incentive pay contract with an annual bonus based on a percentage of profits in excess of the previous year's profits. In addition, she received stock options.

The company has an internal audit department that reports directly to the CEO (Sielig). Although an audit committee exists, it exists more in form than substance and meets with the director of internal audit only occasionally. The audit program for the year is determined by the director of internal audit in conjunction with Sielig and is strongly influenced by two factors: (1) Sielig's perception of areas needing review and (2) areas of potential cost savings.

Sielig has let it be known that all units of the company must justify their existence and if the internal audit department expected future budget increases, it must generate recommended cost savings in excess of the current internal audit budget.

Your CPA firm audits Justin Company. During the preliminary planning for the audit, you note the following:

1. The investment account has grown from approximately 7 percent of total assets to approximately 30 percent of total assets.
2. The investment portfolio includes some long-term investments in company stocks; however, most of the stocks appear to be identified by the investment community as "high fliers."
3. The remainder of the investment portfolio consists of a wide variety of new financial instruments including junk bonds, collateralized mortgages, and so forth.
4. Broker fees have increased dramatically. There is also a new line item for investment consulting fees. It appears that most of these fees are to a company that might be somehow related to Sielig.
5. Most of the securities are held by the brokerage firm, but a few are held by the investment consulting company, and a few others are held directly by the company.
6. The company has shown a 25 percent increase in reported net income over the past year.
7. The company's stock value has appreciated more than 20 percent during the past year.

Required:

a. Identify the elements of inherent risk and control environment risk in the above scenario that should be considered in planning the audit. For the control environment issues identified, briefly indicate the potential audit implication.

b. Outline an audit program that could be utilized for auditing the marketable securities account for the current year.

15–51 (Application Controls) Rhinelander Co. is a regional retailer with 45 stores located in the Southeast. The company accepts major credit cards and its own credit card in addition to cash. Approximately 25 percent of the company's sales are made on the firm's own credit cards. The company has decided to process sales and cash receipts itself. Monthly statements are sent out on a cycle basis. The customers are requested to return the upper portion of the statement with their remittance as a turnaround document.

The client has attempted to automate the cash collection process. The turnaround documents are machine readable. The computer program is new this year, but your experience with the client has indicated that it is likely that the system is well designed.

Required:

a. Identify the important application controls that this system would include if the auditor had assessed control risk as low.

b. For each control identified, indicate (1) the sources of evidence the auditor would examine to determine whether the control existed and (2) how the auditor would test to determine that the control is functioning as indicated.

End Notes

1. R. D. Nair, Larry E. Rittenberg, and Jerry J. Weygandt, "Accounting for Interest Rate Swaps—A Critical Evaluation," *Accounting Horizons* (September 1990), 20.

CHAPTER

16

Learning Objectives

Through studying this chapter, you will be able to:

1. Understand the important processes and control procedures present in the acquisition cycle.
2. Understand how computerized processing affects the acquisition cycle.
3. Identify areas where analytical procedures are most efficient in auditing payables and expense accounts.
4. Understand the audit risks associated with inventory, inventory control procedures and alternative methods of auditing year-end inventory.
5. Apply analytical procedures to the audit of inventory and cost of goods sold.

Audit of Acquisition Cycle and Inventory

Chapter Contents

Crazy Eddie's new management alleged that the Antar group had created "phantom" inventory and profits and then destroyed records in a cover-up. Crazy Eddie accused its former management of scheming to "artificially inflate the net worth of the company." For example, the company said its former management inflated the March 1987 inventory count at one warehouse by $10 million by drafting phony count sheets and improperly including merchandise that was being returned to suppliers. . . . The total shortfall [for the company] was later revised to $65 million.[1]

Observation of inventories is a generally accepted auditing procedure. The independent auditor who issues an opinion when he has not observed inventory must bear in mind that he has the burden of justifying the opinion expressed. [AU 331.01]

Chapter Overview

The acquisition cycle is an integral part of the audit of every organization. The cycle includes all the procedures included from identifying products or services to be acquired through the receipt of goods and the payment for goods and services received. In many organizations, the cycle is considered a high-risk area. Major frauds have been conducted in the inventory area. The auditor must be able to assess the risks in the cycle in order to determine the extent of audit work and whether the work should be concentrated at year-end. A number of computerized audit techniques can be used to assist in auditing these areas. This chapter discusses the risks associated with this cycle, identifies the issues that should be considered in deciding the extent and timing of audit procedures, and identifies a number of computerized audit techniques to enhance audit efficiency.

A–AUDITS OF THE ACQUISITION CYCLE

The acquisition cycle turns our attention to liabilities and expenses. The cycle represents a convenient framework for viewing a number of interrelated accounts that may be subject to a common set of control procedures. We also extend the acquisition cycle to discuss inventory, which for many clients represents one of the largest and most difficult accounts to audit. Much of the discussion assumes a manufacturing client because that setting facilitates a wider discussion of issues related to inventory and cost of goods sold.

An overview of the major accounts included in the acquisition cycle is shown in Exhibit 16.1. The process begins with a **requisition** for goods and services (not shown in the exhibit). The receipt of goods or services should cause the recognition of accounts payable with debits to expense accounts, inventory, or other asset accounts. Payroll is handled separately and creates either a payroll expense or a debit to Inventory. The shipment of goods and the recognition of obsolete inventory is recorded as debits to Cost of Goods Sold. Finally, the payment for goods or services received is reflected as cash disbursements or a transfer of cash to the payroll imprest account.

Overview of Control Procedures and Control Risk Assessment

The acquisition and payment process consists of six major phases:

- Authorized requisition (request) for goods or services.
- Authorized purchase of goods or services according to company policies.
- Receipt of goods and services.
- Accounting for receipt of goods and services (accounting classification and valuation).
- Approval of items for payment.
- Cash disbursements.

The specific control procedures used vary with the automation of the process. The following discussion assumes a high degree of computerization.

Requisition of Goods and Services

The acquisition process begins with the recognition of the need for the purchase by either an individual or a computer program. Normally, a requisition form is forwarded to the purchasing department by a departmental supervisor, although some departments may have authority for individual purchases up to a specific dollar limit. Computer-generated purchase orders are often reviewed by the purchasing department, but in newer systems such as just-in-time inventory arrangements with vendors, the purchase order may be electronically communicated to the vendor without any additional review. An overview of the requisition process is shown in Exhibit 16.2.

Exhibit 16.1

OVERVIEW OF MAJOR ACCOUNTS IN ACQUISITION AND PAYMENT CYCLE

Cash	
	Payments

Accounts Payable	
Payments	Purchase of: Raw materials Other goods & services

Inventory	
Purchases	Shipments

Expense Accounts	
Expenses	

Factory Overhead	
Expenses	Applied overhead

Cost of Goods Sold	
Shipments Obsolescence	

Note that the requisition for purchase can exist for specific items or could include the negotiation of a long-term contract. For example, in just-in-time contracts, goods are shipped to meet production plans for the next period. The contracts are very specific and include penalties for failure to meet the contract's terms.

Authorized Purchase of Goods and Services. Many organizations centralize the purchasing function in a separate purchasing department. The rationale for a separate purchasing function is that it

1. Promotes efficiency and effectiveness. One group is responsible for dealing with vendors, monitoring their performance, and shopping around for the best combination of quality, service, and price.
2. Eliminates potential favoritism that could take place if individual department heads were allowed to place orders.
3. Reduces the opportunity for fraud by segregating the authorization to purchase from the custody and recording functions.
4. Centralizes control in one function.

Although there are advantages to centralized purchasing, there have been instances in which purchasing agents have abused their power by entering into kickback arrangements with vendors or accepting services from vendors for favored treatment. Compensating control procedures include requiring competitive bids for large purchases and rotating purchase agents across product lines.

Prenumbered forms are used to establish the completeness of the purchase order population. The purchase order identifies the quantity and prices of goods ordered,

Exhibit 16.2

OVERVIEW OF THE REQUISITION PROCESS

Inventory

Form of requisition

Written requisition for specific products by the production manager or stock room manager.

Computer-generated requisition based on current inventory levels and production plans.

Retail organization (seasonal)

Overall authorization to purchase product lines is given to individual buyers by the marketing manager. The authorization is built into the computer as a control procedure. The limits for individual goods can be exceeded only on specific approval by the marketing manager.

Store managers may be granted authority to purchase a limited number of goods. The store manager's ability to issue a purchase order may be subject to overall corporate limits, usually specified in dollars.

Just-in-Time Manufacturing Process

An agreement is signed with the supplier whereby the supplier agrees to ship merchandise (just in time) according to the production schedule set by the manufacturer. A long-term supply contract is negotiated specifying price, quality of products, estimated quantities, penalties for product shortages or quality problems, and so forth. Specific purchase orders are not issued; rather, the production plan is communicated to the supplier with the specified delivery dates. The production plan serves as the requisition.

Supplies: Manufacturing

Requisitions are issued by production departments and sent to the production manager for approval.

Supplies and Miscellaneous: Other Departments

Formal requisitions are approved by the departmental supervisors.

Each department may be given a budget for supplies and may have the ability to issue purchase orders directly for the needed items or may be able to purchase a limited number of items without a purchase order.

Service Contracts

Contracts are negotiated directly by the department. For example, the data processing department may negotiate a service contract with a vendor for back-up service.

quality specifications, and the delivery date. The receiving department can also use the purchase order to determine whether a shipment of goods should be accepted. The accounting department (accounts payable) uses the purchase order to determine whether a purchase was authorized and whether the vendor's invoice is correct.

Two variations of the traditional purchase order are becoming more common: the computer-generated purchase order and the long-term negotiated contract.

Computer-Generated Purchase Order. These purchase orders are designed to increase both purchasing and warehousing efficiency. Good inventory management identifies levels for inventory reorders. For example, a hardware store may have a reorder tag hung on a rack of items to show when inventory drops to a prespecified level. The same concept is applied in computerized inventory accounting systems whereby the order criteria are programmed into the system. The computer-generated purchase order is sent directly to a prespecified vendor. Two additional control procedures may be desirable: (1) a maximum quantity that can be ordered within a given time period and (2) a required review by a purchasing agent for some accounts or for high dollar levels.

Long-Term Contracts. Integrated production techniques, such as just-in-time inventory control methods, require the negotiation of long-term contracts with vendors. The contracts provide for delivery of goods that have been quality tested and meet the production schedule of the customer. To respond on a timely basis, the supplier needs advanced knowledge of the production schedule and a long-term contract so that it can commit the resources to meet the delivery requirements. These contracts provide audit evidence for costing inventory and identifying potential liabilities for purchase commitments.

Receipt of Goods and Services

Receiving departments should ensure that only authorized goods are received, that the goods received meet order specifications, that an accurate count of the goods received is attained, and that initial accounting is established to assure that all receipts are recorded. Several control procedure options are available, including these:

1. The receiving department manually prepares prenumbered receiving documents to record all receipts.
2. The receiving department electronically scans codes on the goods received to record quantity and vendor and visually inspects the goods for quality. The computer prepares a sequentially numbered receiving record for goods scanned in.
3. Goods, such as supplies, might be received directly by departments which must approve payment for the merchandise.
4. Goods may be received as part of the just-in-time inventory and production process. It is possible that no documentation will be generated on their receipt. The vendor will be paid according to the long-term contract based on the purchaser's actual production during the specified time period.

The traditional receiving process results in the preparation of prenumbered receiving documents. A copy of the purchase order (usually with quantities blanked out) is reviewed to determine whether a shipment is authorized. The receiving department must independently count the merchandise received. Prenumbered receiving documents establish the completeness of the population and are useful in determining that all goods are recorded in the correct period.

Automated scanning can improve both control and efficiency. In some systems, the scanned information is appended to the purchase order instead of generating a separate receiving document. This can create some difficulty because multiple shipments may be required to fill one purchase order, but such contingencies can be built into the system. Control procedures should be designed into the system to ensure that duplicate goods are not received and duplicate payments are not made for goods received.

The auditor of the 1990s will increasingly encounter integrated order, delivery, and payment systems. The major control procedures applicable to the automated receipt of goods include the following:

- A contract specifying terms of delivery, penalties, billing and payment terms, and a defined process for resolving differences.
- Access, edit, and reasonableness controls built into the computerized accounting application.
- Defined procedures for testing the quality of goods received.
- Reconciliation of the purchaser's production data with the vendor's billing.
- Control procedures designed to ensure that the receipt and movement of goods are recorded on a timely basis.

Regardless of the approach taken to implement the receiving function, the auditor must gain assurance that management has a control structure in place to monitor purchases and control costs. If errors occur, they are most likely to show up in Inventory or in an expense account.

Account Classification

Control is enhanced when the purchasing, receiving, and paying functions are all independent of each other. The accounting system ensures proper valuation by matching the invoice, receiving report, and purchase order before making payment. Charts of accounts are useful to properly classify items. Most purchase order systems assign the account classification when the purchase order is issued. If it is not assigned, the accounts payable department assigns the account number. The classification process should be periodically reviewed by someone in the accounting department.

Approval of Items for Payment

Manual Matching. The traditional, document-based acquisition and payment system requires personnel in accounts payable to match the vendor invoice, the purchase order, and the receiving report to determine the validity of the requested payment. If all items properly match, the vendor's invoice is set up as an accounts payable with a scheduled payment date. Discrepancies are reviewed by calling the purchasing agent to determine whether a price change for an item received is approved, to investigate quantity differences, or to issue debit memos for differences between the vendor invoice and the correct billing. The supporting document is presented to accounting supervisory personnel or the treasury department with authorization to pay. The control structure should ensure that all items are recorded in a timely manner as accounts payable, that the authorization process includes a review of documents, and that supporting documentation is canceled on payment to avoid duplicate payments.

Automated Matching. Consider for a moment the volume of paper that even a medium-size department store must deal with in purchasing, receiving, and paying for merchandise. Thousands of items from hundreds of different vendors may be received each day. The merchandise may be received at a central warehouse for later distribution to individual stores. The traditional approach to controlling the receipt of, and payment for, purchases is labor intensive and very error prone. The **automated matching** process represents an efficient alternative. Purchase orders are entered into a purchase order database which is accessed by the receiving department to determine whether an incoming shipment of goods should be accepted. The receiving department electronically records the receipt of goods and cross-references the receipt to the purchase order.

One simple way to program the computer matching process is to match the gross amount of the vendor invoice with the total purchase order price of the goods received. The computerized application matches the three documents (purchase order, receiving document, and vendor invoice), and if the three match within a prespecified tolerance limit, the invoice is approved for payment. A payment date is scheduled, and a check is automatically generated on the scheduled date and is signed using an authorized signature plate. The complete payment is made without any apparent human intervention: There is no authorized reviewer; there is no physical matching; and no individual physically mails the checks. In some systems, the payment may be transferred electronically to the vendor.

The lack of human intervention is compensated by control procedures and authorization concepts built into the system:

- Access must be severely restricted to all databases, in particular to the vendor database and the purchasing database. Anyone with the ability to add a vendor or make unauthorized purchase orders is in a position to set up fictitious vendors and purchases. Therefore, the vendor database (a list of approved vendors) should be maintained by someone outside the purchasing department.

- Although the receiving department has access to the purchase order (read only), the use of automatic scanners and other counting devices lessens the potential counting errors. The designer of the control system has an important dilemma. Providing access to quantities ordered might permit receiving personnel to record the receipt without independently counting items. On the other hand, without such information, the receiving department would not know whether to accept a large shipment. Most organizations believe that other control procedures identify receiving errors. The potential problem can be further mitigated by restricting access to the purchase order to supervisory personnel in receiving.

- Most retailers mark retail prices on the goods at the distribution center when they are received. The retail price tickets for an order can be generated from the purchase order. The actual number of tickets used should be reconciled with the goods received and any leftover tickets should cause an adjustment to be made to the receiving report.

- Vendor invoices are entered into the system by accounts payable personnel, thereby segregating this process from the other two functions. Alternatively, vendor invoices might be received directly through EDI. It is important that purchasing and receiving not have the ability to enter vendor invoice data or access the vendor invoice file.

- Access to the check signature plate is limited.

- Activity reports are prepared on a regular basis for management to review for unusual transactions.

Because most of the control procedures are developed during the system's design process, it is important that users and internal auditors actively participate in reviewing the effectiveness of control procedures during the design phase.

Cash Disbursements

In a manual system, someone in the organization (the president in some small organizations, the treasurer in others) reviews the completeness of the documentation and signs a check for the payment of the goods and services. The supporting documents are immediately canceled to avoid duplicate payments. In most automated systems, the checks are generated automatically according to the scheduled payment date and the supporting documents are canceled when the invoice is set up for payment.

Testing Controls over Accounts Payable and Related Expenses

Attribute sampling is often used to test transactions for accounting classification, timeliness of recording, and the correctness of valuation. A sample can be selected from a population of payments made, and documents can be traced back through the process to test existence, account classification, and timeliness of recording. The completeness assertion can be tested by taking a sample of receiving reports and tracing them through the recording process to a debit to an expense account and a credit to Accounts Payable.

Transaction Testing of Key Control Procedures

Evidence of proper authorization should be available for each purchase and payment. Paper-based systems provide evidence of authorization through signatures. Computerized systems, on the other hand, control authorization through access control procedures and exception reports. The effectiveness of these control procedures should be tested during the auditor's overall review of data processing controls and supplemented by specific tests of the acquisition and payment applications. The auditor might, for example, review access logs to determine whether a pattern of unauthorized access exists.

The financial press has documented many business failures in which the managers were using the business assets as if they were personal property. The auditor should pay particular attention to items such as expense reimbursements or other expenses that do not seem to have a justifiable business purpose.

Transactions should be reviewed for *proper valuation and classification*. The auditor should pay particular attention to the dates items are received, are recognized as a liability, and are paid to verify recording in the proper period. Significant lags in the recording of the liability indicate potential problems that should be addressed in the substantive testing of accounts payable at year-end.

Substantive Tests of Accounts Payable

The auditor's major concern with Accounts Payable is that the account will be understated. Therefore, a great deal of emphasis is placed on testing the completeness assertion.

Testing for Completeness

Two approaches are used for testing completeness and possible understatement of accounts payable. The most common approach is to examine a sample of cash disbursements made after the end of the year to determine whether the disbursements are for goods and services applicable to the previous year, and if so, whether a liability was recorded in the previous year. The disbursements review is followed by an examination of unrecorded vendor invoices and receiving reports to determine whether goods or services received in the previous year was properly set up as a payable.

The second approach involves requesting vendors' monthly statements or sending confirmations to major vendors requesting a statement of open account items. The auditor reconciles the vendor's statement or confirmation with the accounts payable trial balance of the client.

Is one approach better than the other? The review of subsequent disbursements is often used in small businesses that tend to pay their balances on a timely basis. But, the auditor should recognize the following assumptions inherent in the approach:

1. The client pays all disbursements on a timely basis.
2. The client has implemented sufficient control procedures to ensure that vendor invoices are paid on a timely basis and the auditor is able to locate all unpaid invoices.
3. Management is not motivated to understate accounts payable.

Requesting vendor statements is more likely to be used when the auditor has evaluated control risk as high.

Other Accounts Payable Substantive Tests

Year-End Cutoff Tests. Cutoff (correct time period) errors are common. Some of these difficulties occur because year-end is a hectic time and errors can occur, especially with inventory, if precautions are not taken to ensure timely recording. Or management may fraudulently misstate the accounting records to overstate inventory or to understate liabilities. Because year-end transactions are susceptible to error, the auditor normally conducts year-end cutoff tests in conjunction with accounts payable and inventory. The specific procedures to be performed are discussed in the inventory section of this chapter.

Review of Contracts for Purchase Commitments. Organizations increasingly enter into long-term contracts to purchase inventory at fixed prices or at a fixed price plus inflation adjustments. These contracts can extend over a period of years and there is always some risk that economic circumstances can change and the contracts may no longer be economically viable. The contracts should be examined to determine penalties associated with default, and the auditor should gain sufficient knowledge to assess the client's estimate of the probability of contract default or losses. An example is discussed in the Nuclear Power Plant Supply Contract box which follows.

Audits of Expense Accounts

Audits of payables and the cash disbursements system also provide evidence about the correctness of expense accounts. However, some additional analysis of selected expense accounts is usually merited. For example, the Legal Expense account should

Auditing in Practice

THE NUCLEAR POWER PLANT SUPPLY CONTRACT

During the 1970s, Westinghouse Electric was heavily involved in building nuclear power plants. To market its services, it agreed to provide a 15-year supply of uranium to all utilities that purchased a power plant from it. At the time the contracts were written, Westinghouse had only about a one-year supply of uranium, but the market had been stable and the company did not foresee any problem in meeting the contract terms. Unfortunately, Canada and Australia entered into an international cartel to limit the supply, which subsequently raised the price of uranium sevenfold. Westinghouse could not afford to purchase uranium at the new market price and supply it to the utilities at the contract price without going bankrupt. It was forced to break the contract and negotiate a settlement with the utilities. The potential loss to Westinghouse Electric should be disclosed in the financial statements.

be examined as a possible indicator of litigation that may require recording or disclosure. When evaluating evidence regarding expense accounts, the auditor should consider that management is more likely to (1) understate rather than overstate expenses and (2) classify expense items as assets rather than vice versa.*

Detailed Test of Expense Accounts

Some accounts are of intrinsic interest to the auditor simply because of the nature of the account. These include accounts such as Legal Expense, Travel and Entertainment Expense, and Repairs and Maintenance Expense. Underlying documentation should be examined on a sampling basis to determine the nature of the expenditure, its appropriate business use, and the correctness of the recorded item.

Analytical Review of Expense Accounts

Many account balances are directly related to the client's volume of activity. Stable relationships are expected between specific accounts (such as Cost of Goods Sold and Sales) which can be investigated for unusual discrepancies. Examples of expenses that should vary directly with sales include Warranty Expense, Sales Commissions, and Supplies Expense. Analytical review procedures can effectively test these accounts if the auditor has previously assessed control risk as low. The analytical model should be built using either audited data or independently generated data. If the Expense account falls within expected ranges, the auditor can be comfortable in concluding that it is not materially misstated. If the account balance is not within the specified ranges, the auditor develops hypotheses as to why it may differ and systematically investigates the situation. The investigation should include inquiries of client personnel and the development of corroborating evidence (including a detailed examination of the expense accounts where merited). For example, sales commission may have averaged three percent of sales over the past five years. If that ratio drops to one percent this year, the auditor should examine the cause of the change.

*Unless, of course, the company is motivated by tax considerations to minimize income taxes and thus would want to understate income.

B–AUDIT OF INVENTORY AND COST OF GOODS SOLD

Accounting for inventories is a major consideration for many clients because of its significance on both the balance sheet and the income statement. Inventories are defined in *ARB No. 43*, chapter 4 as "those items of tangible personal property which are held for sale in the ordinary course of business, are in the process of production for such sale, or are to be currently consumed in the production of goods or services to be available for sale." Inventory thus includes steel held for future production of an automobile, complex electronic goods in a retail store, drugs on shelves in hospitals or pharmaceutical companies, and petroleum products. Inventory represents a complex accounting and auditing area due to the following:

- Variety (diversity) of items in inventory.
- High volume of activity.
- Various cost flow alternatives that may be chosen to determine the account valuation.
- Potential difficulty in correctly classifying inventory.
- Difficulty in identifying obsolete inventory and applying the lower of cost or market principle to determine valuation.

The difficulties in valuing inventory have been further complicated by new types of transactions, such as product financing arrangements, whereby an entity sells inventory and agrees to repurchase the same inventory at an amount equal to the original sales price plus carrying and financing costs. It is important for the auditor to review the substance of the transaction to determine the appropriate accounting.

But the accounting issues are only one component of the audit task. Inventory audits take on added complexity because:

- Inventory is easily transportable. An inventory consisting of oil held in tanks, for example, could be transported through underground pipes almost as quickly as the auditor could move from one location to another to observe the existence of inventory.
- Inventory often exists at multiple locations with some locations being remote from the company's headquarters.
- Inventory may become obsolete due to technological advances even though there are no visible signs of wear.
- Defective inventory may appear to be good. For example, the case of the Regina vacuum cleaner discussed in Chapter 5 is an example of an inventory item that appeared to be marketable but was not.
- Determining the valuation of a particular item of inventory may be difficult. The physical condition of electronic components, for example, cannot be determined through visual inspections. Similarly, it is difficult, without the aid of a specialist, to identify or value specialized inventory such as jewelry or chemicals.

- Companies often use different cost flow assumptions for different lines of their inventory.
- The company may have a policy to accept returned goods. In many cases, the returns might be expected, such as with a catalog company such as L.L. Bean, but in other cases care must be taken to separately identify returned merchandise and record it at a lower market price.
- The diversity of products held by a client increases the knowledge that the auditor must obtain to address obsolescence and valuation questions.
- Some inventory valuation methods are needlessly complex, such as the link-chain method of estimating a LIFO inventory.

Inventory Flow and Components

The auditor usually begins by developing an understanding of the cost components of inventory and how the inventory valuation is affected by current market prices. We will concentrate on the inventories of a manufacturing client because it is the most complex and normally presents the most difficult audit problems.

Understanding the Control Structure for Inventory

A well-conceived inventory control structure should ensure the following:

- All purchases are authorized.
- The accounting system is sufficient to ensure timely, accurate, and complete recording of inventory transactions.
- Receipt of inventory is properly accounted for and there is independent testing of receipts to verify adherence to the company standards.
- An independent quality control department reviews and tests selected finished inventory and segregates defective products for special processing.
- The cost accounting system is up-to-date, and costs are properly identified and assigned to products, expense items are recorded as inventory, and variances are analyzed, investigated, and properly allocated to inventory and cost of goods sold.
- A perpetual inventory system serves as a basis for management reports and to assist in managing inventory.
- All products are systematically reviewed for obsolescence and appropriate accounting action is taken.
- Management periodically reviews inventory, takes action on excessive inventory, and manages inventory in light of technological advances.
- New products are introduced only after market studies and quality control tests are made.
- Long-term contracts are closely monitored. Excess purchase requirements are monitored and potential losses are recognized.

Automated Purchases and Potential Obsolete Inventory. Many companies have automated the purchasing process to allow the system to automatically generate purchase orders for products when inventory reaches a specific reorder point. But there could be problems with such a system if the perpetual records are not accurate or the system is not updated to reflect new designs of products. The auditor should determine the approach used by the company to minimize such problems.

Accounting System. The accounting system should have the capability to individually identify products and record all transactions in a timely fashion. The control procedures the auditor would expect to find in such a system include the following:

- Self-checking digits incorporated into inventory product identification.
- Edit tests on all transactions, especially limit and reasonableness tests.
- Automated updating of inventory records as transactions take place.
- Periodic testing of the perpetual inventory system through cycle counting or random selection and independent counting of inventory items.
- Periodic management reports on inventory usage, scrap, defects, and reworks.
- Authorization and authentication of transactions, including the automated reorder process.
- Independent user testing in the design and/or maintenance of inventory applications.

Receipt of Inventory. In addition to the control procedures governing the acceptance, identification, and counting of items received, there should be an independent testing of the quality of products received. The new watchword in manufacturing is *quality*. Quality begins with the organization's approach to accepting goods from suppliers. Quality specifications are often built into purchase contracts which may specify the tests to be performed by the supplier and may specify a maximum defect rate.

Accounting for Returned Items. Accounting for customer returns represents a potential problem area. Approved returns should generate a credit memo and a debit to inventory, a special returns account, or an expense account. The auditor must determine the procedures utilized by the company to identify returned merchandise and segregate it from purchased merchandise. Further, the auditor must determine that the returned goods are properly accounted for at net realizable value (which may be scrap).

Quality Control Process. The complement to quality inspection is a total quality process that permeates the production and storage functions. From an accounting standpoint, it is important that the **quality control** system identify defective units and categorize defective items as scrap. Because penalty provisions are built into supplier contracts, the auditor should review quality control reports and consider the implications for unrecorded liabilities.

Cost Accounting System. Most manufacturing companies have implemented standard cost systems to assist in controlling costs, streamlining accounting, and costing inventory. Valuation of ending inventory is directly affected by the quality of the client's cost system. The auditor should make inquiries about the following:

- The method for developing standards, including whether engineering studies of product usage and labor input are used.

- The method for identifying components of overhead and of allocating overhead to products.
- The methods used for identifying variances, following up on their causes, and allocating them to inventory and cost of goods sold.

An overview of the components leading to the cost buildup is illustrated in Exhibit 16.3. The auditor also tests the procedures of assigning raw material costs to products or cost centers. In many modern manufacturing systems, labor is no longer the major conversion cost. Rather, the manufacturing process is highly automated, and allocating overhead costs to products on the basis of direct labor hours is conceptually unrealistic. In such situations, the auditor must determine the reasonableness of the method of allocating capital costs to specific periods or production units.

An audit program to test the standard cost system is shown in Exhibit 16.4. The program is intended to determine the accuracy and reliability of the standard cost system as a basis for valuing a client's year-end inventory. The audit program

Exhibit 16.3

STANDARD COST BUILDUP—PRODUCT A250

Product Description: A250 is the finished product Bicycle Frame Assembly (back unit) with brass customization for the European market.

Product Process: Frame is assembled from raw machine stock in the bent frame assembly unit. Frames are shaped and cut to precision with the two Cougar framing machines. The frames are polished and customized on the smaller Jet frames. Finished products are sent to final assembly to be packaged with other frame components. The costs and the basis for the standard costs are computed as follows:

Description	Products or Costs Used	Rate	Standard Cost
Raw material, 16 ft. 3/8" thick, 1" square, black finished, aluminum tubing	16 ft. used, plus 1 ft. scrap.	49 ft.	8.33
Direct labor for bending and finishing	Bending— 1/30 hr.	$5.50	0.91
	Finishing—1/12 hr.	$7.50	
Factory overhead	Applied at 250% of standard labor cost.	$0.91	$2.28
Total			$11.52

Costs were accumulated 7/1/93 by engineering department based on time study of production and current cost of raw material. Factory overhead rate reviewed by cost accounting manager.

Reviewed and Approved by:

Ken J. Hannes

Ken. J. Hannes
Cost Accounting Manager

Exhibit 16.4

AUDIT PROGRAM FOR STANDARD COST SYSTEM

Audit of Standard Cost System	Prepared by ______	
	Reviewed By ______	
	Performed by	**W/P Reference**
1. Review previous year working papers for a description of the standard cost system used by the client. Inquire as to any major changes made in the system during the current year.	______	______
2. Tour the production facilities and make note of cost centers, the general layout of the plant, the storage of inventory, the functioning of the quality control department, and the process for identifying and accounting for scrap or defective items.	______	______
3. Examine prior year working papers and current year variance accounts as a basis for determining the amount of variances identified by the standard cost accounting system. Determine whether the variances imply the need for significant revisions in the standard cost system.	______	______
Inquire of the process used to update standard costs. Determine the extent to which revisions have been made during the current year.	______	______
4. Inquire whether significant changes have been made in the production process during the current year, whether major manufacturing renovations have taken place, and whether new products have been added.	______	______
5. Randomly select X number of standard cost build-ups for products and for each product build-up selected:		
• Review engineering studies on the cost build-up, noting the items used, the amount of product used, and the standard cost of the product used.	______	______
• Test the reasonableness of the client's costs by randomly sampling components of product cost and tracing back to purchases or contracts with suppliers.	______	______
• Review payroll records to determine that labor costs are specifically identified by product or cost center and used in calculating variances.	______	______
• Review the reasonableness of the method for allocating overhead to products. Determine whether any significant changes have been made in the method of allocation.	______	______

(Continued)

Exhibit 16.4

	Performed by	W/P Reference
6. Select a representative sample of products requisitioned into work-in-process and determine that all entries are properly recorded.	______	______
7. Review the method for identifying overhead costs. Review the list of costs identified and determine whether they are applicable to the production process.	______	______
Select some of the large overhead accounts and have the client prepare a schedule of the expenditures during the year. Select a representative sample of expenditures and trace to the underlying support to determine that the costs are properly classified.	______	______
8. Review variance reports. Determine the extent to which the client has investigated and determined the causes of the variances. Determine whether the causes of the variances signal a need to revise the standard cost system.	______	______
9. Inquire as to the method used by the client to allocate variances to inventory and cost of goods sold at year end. Determine the reasonableness of the method and its consistency with prior years.	______	______
10. Document your conclusion on the accuracy and completeness of the standard cost system used by the client. Indicate whether the standard costs can be relied on in assigning costs to year-end inventory.	______	______

assumes a standard cost system, but the concepts implicit in the program could be modified for other systems such as a job cost system.

Existence of an Accurate Perpetual Inventory System. Most manufacturing (and many retail) companies have implemented perpetual inventory systems to better manage the business. A perpetual inventory system allows an organization to know the current stock of its inventory, to identify products that need to be reordered, products that have not sold for some period of time, or products that might be obsolete.

The auditor normally tests transactions associated with the perpetual inventory record to ensure that all receipts and sales of products are properly recorded. The audit objectives of such tests are to determine that (1) all authorized receipts and sales of inventory are recorded accurately and timely and (2) only authorized receipts and sales of inventory have been recorded. An overview of the testing of the perpetual records can be seen in Exhibit 16.5. Note that the auditor selects transactions from the perpetual record and traces them back to the source documents to determine that only authorized transactions have been recorded. The auditor then

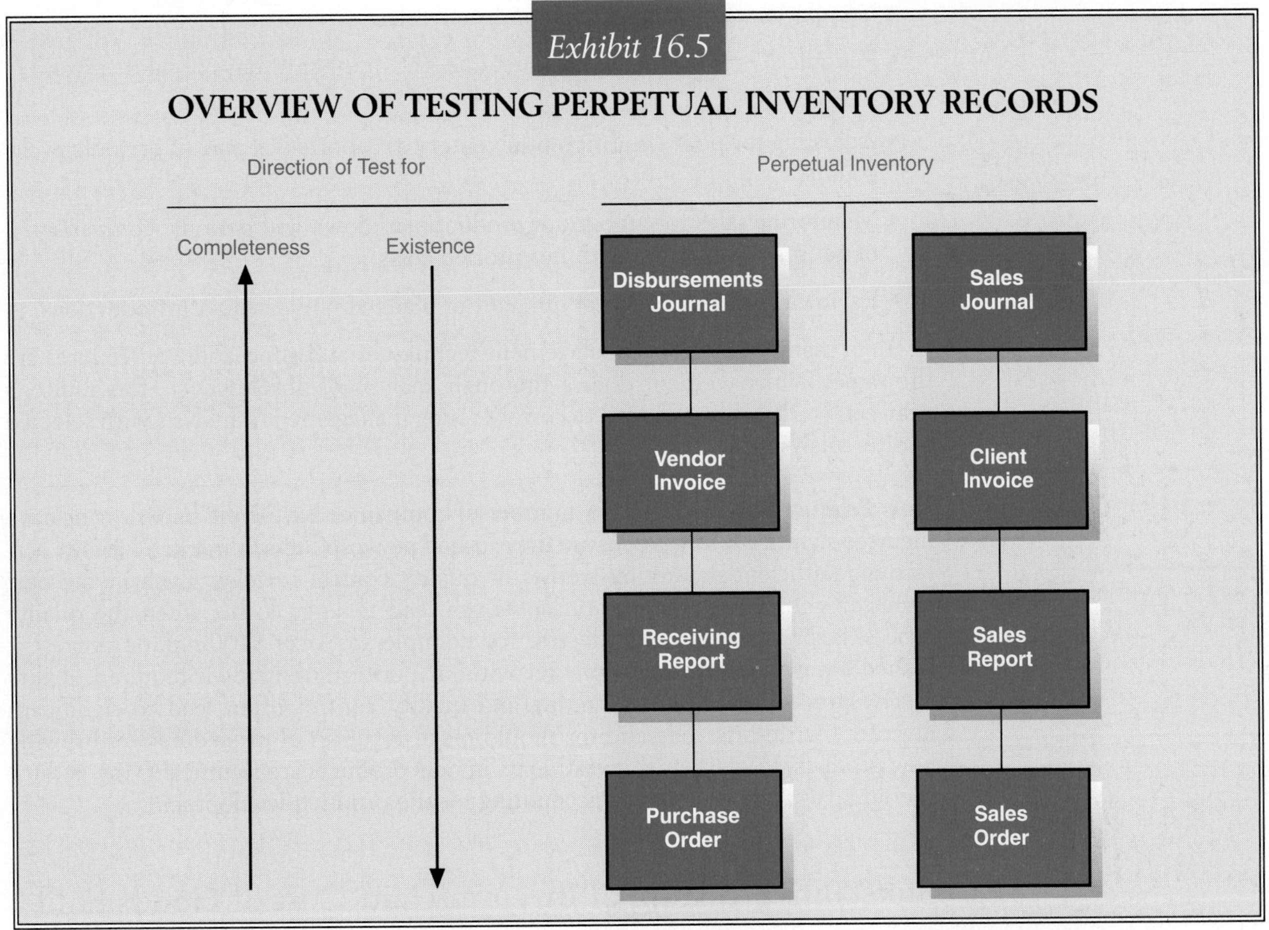

selects items from the source documents and traces them to the perpetual records to determine that all receipts and sales are recorded accurately and on a timely basis. Finally, the auditor examines support for any material adjustments made to the perpetual records.

Another major control procedure is periodic testing, or **cycle counts,** of the perpetual inventory records by internal audit or other personnel to determine their accuracy, the need for adjustments, and the cause of any major inaccuracies. The auditor should determine that such counts are taken and corrections are made to the records.

Systematic Review for Obsolescence. Today's automated systems provide a wealth of information for a company to systematically review its inventory for potential obsolescence. Procedures that are effective in searching for possible obsolescence include these:

- Monitoring turnover by products and product lines and comparing the turnover with past performance and expectations for the current period.
- Monitoring the impact of competitors' new technological introductions on the client's products.

- Comparing current sales with budgeted sales.
- Periodically reviewing, by product line, the number of days of sales currently in inventory.
- Adjusting for poor condition of inventory as reported as part of periodic cycle counts.
- Monitoring sales for amount of product markdown and periodic comparison of net realizable value with inventoried costs.
- Reviewing current inventory in light of planned new product introductions.

As in many cases, good management techniques and good audit procedures are the same. If management does a thorough analysis of obsolescence, the auditor's year-end work can be reduced to corroborating management's analysis with selected auditor analyses.

New Product Introductions. A number of companies have gone bankrupt or have incurred significant losses because they rushed new products to market without performing sufficient marketing studies or quality control reviews. Even in the best managed companies, temporary lapses can lead to large losses when the quality process is short cut. General Electric, for example, lost over $400 million because it rushed a new refrigerator to market without performing its own required quality review procedures. Poor marketing and quality control often lead to significant inventory write-offs. The auditor should make inquiries of procedures for bringing new products to market. If investments in new products are significant, the auditor should investigate the client's accounting for the product development.

Substantive Testing of Inventory and Cost of Goods Sold

The assertions and audit procedures that would be used to gather evidence for the LeFlam Manufacturing Company are presented in Exhibit 16.6 and discussed in more detail below. The audit program is typical of one that would be used for most manufacturing clients.

Existence

Complete Year-End Physical Inventory. Not many years ago, it was standard procedure for most organizations to shut down operations at year-end or near year-end to take a complete physical inventory. The client's book inventory would be adjusted to this physical inventory (often referred to as the *book to physical adjustment*). These procedures are still followed by many small clients that do not use perpetual inventory records or where the records are not deemed reliable. The auditor should (1) observe the client taking inventory to determine the accuracy of the procedures, (2) make selected test counts which can later be traced into the inventory compilation, and (3) test the client's inventory compilation by tracing test counts to the compilation and independently test the client's computation of extended cost.

The auditor should review the client's plan to count inventory and plan to observe the client's count. The overall procedures for observing the conduct of the client's physical inventory are shown in Exhibit 16.7. The process assumes that the client systematically arranges the inventory for ease of counting and attaches prenumbered

Exhibit 16.6

LEFLAM MANUFACTURING COMPANY
ASSERTIONS AND AUDIT PROCEDURES FOR INVENTORY

Assertions	**Audit Procedures**
Existence	Observe and test the completeness of the client's proposed physical inventory procedures and determine whether the client's procedures are likely to result in a complete and correct physical inventory.
	Observe the client's count of the annual physical inventory. Perform test counts of the observations and trace to the client's compilation of inventory.
	(Alternative Procedure) Randomly select items from the client's perpetual inventory record and observe (count) the items on hand. Sample should emphasize high dollar value items.
Completeness	Perform year-end cutoff tests by noting the last shipping and receiving document numbers used before physical inventory is taken. Review the purchase and sales journals for a period of time shortly before and after year-end, noting the shipping and receiving document numbers to determine whether the goods are recorded in the proper time period.
	Make inquiries of the client regarding the potential existence of goods on consignment or located in outside warehouses. For material items, either visit the locations or send a confirmation to the outside warehouse management.
	Make inquiries of the client regarding allowances made for expected returns. Determine client policy for accounting for returned items. Review receipt of transactions for a selected period of time to determine whether significant returns are received and appropriately accounted for.
Rights	Review vendor invoices when testing disbursements to determine that proper title is conveyed.
	Review sales contracts to determine whether the customer has rights to return merchandise and whether the rights are such that recognition of a sale might not be appropriate.
Valuation	Determine whether the valuation method is appropriate for the nature of the client's transactions.
	Inquire of production and warehouse personnel about the existence of obsolete inventory.
	Note potentially obsolete inventory while observing the physical inventory counts. Trace the potentially obsolete items to the client's inventory compilation and determine whether they are properly labeled as obsolete items.
	Test inventory cost by taking a sample of recorded inventory and trace to source documents including
	• Tracing raw material purchases to vendor invoices.
	• Testing standard costs as built up through the standard cost system (see Exhibit 16.4).

(Continued)

Exhibit 16.6

Assertions	Audit Procedures
Valuation (continued)	Test for the possibility of obsolete inventory that should be written down to market value: • Review trade journals for changes in product technology. • Follow up potentially obsolete items noted during the observation of the client's physical inventory counts. • Use generalized audit software to read the inventory file and compute inventory turnover. Investigate products with unusually low turnover. • Use generalized audit software to identify items with slow sales. • Inquire of the client as to sales adjustments (markdowns) that have been offered to sell any products. • Verify sales price by reviewing recent invoices to determine whether the sales price is the same as included on the computer file. Use generalized audit software to compute net realizable value for inventory items and prepare an inventory printout for all items where net realizable value is less than cost. • Analyze sales by product line, noting any significant decreases in product line sales. • Review purchase commitments for potential loss exposures. Determine whether contingent losses are properly disclosed or recorded. • If the client uses indexes, such as for making a LIFO adjustment, verify the correctness of the index. • Use audit software to test extensions and prepare a printout of differences. • Use audit software to foot the inventory compilation. Trace the total to the trial balance.
Disclosure	Review client's financial statement disclosure of • Inventory valuation method used. • FIFO cost figures and LIFO liquidation effects if LIFO is used. • The percentage of inventory valued by each different valuation method. • The classification of inventory as to raw material, work-in-process, and finished goods. • The existence of contingent losses associated with long-term contracts or purchase commitments. • Inventory policy regarding returns and allowances, if expected to be material, for merchandise expected to be returned.

tags to each group of products. After the counts are reviewed by supervisory personnel (usually from the accounting department) and the auditors, the tags are pulled, accounted for, and used to compile the year-end physical inventory. During the counting process, the client makes arrangements not to ship or receive goods or to segregate all goods received during the process to be labeled and counted as "after inventory."

The auditor walks through the inventory areas observing the first and last tag number used and notes these observations on a test count sheet. The auditor also performs the following tasks:

- Makes test counts of selected items and records the test counts for subsequent tracing into the client's inventory compilation.
- Makes notations of all items that appear to be obsolete or are in questionable condition. The auditor follows up on these items with inquiries of client personnel.
- Observes the handling of scrap and other material.
- Observes whether there is any physical movement of goods during the taking of the physical inventory.
- Writes down all large dollar-value items for subsequent tracing into the client's records.

The notation of large dollar-value items is a check against potential client manipulation of inventory by adding new items or adjusting the cost or quantities of existing items after the physical inventory is completed. Because large dollar-value items are noted, the auditor can systematically review support for major items included on the final inventory compilation that were not noted during the physical inventory observation. An example of audit problems that can occur when such procedures are not followed can be seen in the CMH case described in the Real-World Application.

Once the inventory is taken, the auditor's observations and test counts provide an independent source of evidence on the correctness of the client's inventory compilation. If the tag number sequence is noted, such evidence would prohibit the insertion of additional inventory items. Finally, the auditor's record of potentially obsolete items can be used to determine whether the client has properly written the goods down to their net realizable value.

Many organizations that take an *annual physical inventory* find that year-end is not the most convenient time to take inventory. For example, the company may have a natural model changeover and shut down operations during that time. Or it may want to take the physical inventory before year-end to expedite the preparation of year-end financial statements.

It is generally acceptable to have the client take inventory before year-end provided that

- Control risk over the account is not high.
- The auditor can effectively test the year-end balance through a combination of analytical review techniques and selective testing of transactions during the roll-forward period.

The auditor reviews the intervening transactions for evidence of any manipulation or unusual activity.

Exhibit 16.7

PROCEDURES FOR OBSERVING A CLIENT'S PHYSICAL INVENTORY

1. Meet with the client to discuss the procedures, timing, location, and personnel involved in taking the annual physical inventory. Make arrangements to have audit personnel meet the supervisor at each location and gain a familiarity with the plant layout and counting procedures.
2. Review the client's plans for counting and tagging inventory items. Determine whether such procedures are sufficient to ensure an accurate inventory.
3. Review the inventory-taking procedures with all audit personnel. Familiarize them with the nature of the client's inventory, potential problems with the inventory, and any other information that will ensure that the client and audit personnel will properly recognize inventory items, large dollar-value items, and obsolete items, and understand potential problems that might occur in counting the inventory.
4. Determine whether specialists are needed to identify, test, or assist in correctly identifying inventory items.
5. Upon arriving at each site
   a. Meet with client personnel, obtain a map of the area, and obtain a schedule of inventory counts to be made for each area.
   b. Obtain a list of sequential tag numbers to be used in each area.
   c. Observe the procedures the client has implemented to shut down receipt or shipment of goods.
   d. Observe that the client has shut down production.
   e. Obtain document numbers for the last shipment and receipt of goods before the physical inventory is taken. Use the information to perform cutoff tests.
6. Observe the counting of inventory and note the following on inventory count working papers:
   a. The first and last tag number used in the section.
   b. Account for all tag numbers and determine the disposition of all tag numbers in the sequence.
   c. Make selected test counts and note the product identification, product description, units of measure, and number of items on a count sheet.
   d. Items that appear to be obsolete or of questionable value.
   e. All large dollar-value items included in inventory.
   f. Movement of goods into or out of the company during the process of inventory taking. Determine if goods are properly counted or excluded from inventory.
7. Document your conclusion as to the quality of the client's inventory-taking process, noting any problems that could be of audit significance. Determine whether a sufficient inventory count has been taken to properly reflect the goods on hand at year-end.

Real-World Application

INVENTORY OBSERVATION—THE CASE OF CMH

CMH was an SEC–registered company that went bankrupt in 1976 after it had materially misstated its financial statements for a number of years. It inflated the reporting of its physical inventory by 50 percent during both 1973 and 1974. The fraud was perpetrated by "(1) altering the quantities recorded on the prenumbered, two-part inventory tags used in counting the inventory; (2) altering documents reflected on a computer list prepared to record the physical count of inventory; and (3) creating inventory tags to record quantities of nonexistent inventory."

The SEC asserts that the auditors should have detected the fictitious inventory but did not because the audit firm "left the extent of various observation testing to the discretion of auditors, not all of whom were aware of significant audit conclusions which related directly to the extent of such testing. Observation of inventory counts at year end was confined to six locations (representing about 40% of the total CMH inventory) as opposed to nine in the preceding year. The field auditors did not adequately control the inventory tags and Seidman & Seidman did not detect the creation of bogus inventory tags which were inserted in the final inventory computations." The SEC was also critical of the CPA firm for assigning interns to a significant portion of the inventory observation without training them as to the nature of the client's inventory or its counting procedures.

Source: R. W. V. Dickenson, "Why the Fraud Went Undetected," *CA Magazine*, April, 1977, 67–69.

Sample Physical Inventory. Companies with reliable perpetual inventory records either (1) count all inventory at least once during the year on a cycle basis or when items reach their reorder points or (2) use statistical sampling to select items to be physically counted. The exact approach and its timing depend on the control environment and sophistication of the perpetual inventory system of the client. The auditor can take a statistical sample of the perpetual inventory system and observe the existence of the inventory.

Completeness

The auditor normally tests receipts and shipments of inventory at year-end to determine that all items are recorded in the correct time period. The cutoff test is usually accomplished by capturing information on the last items shipped and received at year-end and examining the sales and purchases journals to determine whether all items were recorded in the correct time period. The auditor should pay particular attention to potential cutoff errors occurring during the inventory count because the cutoff errors will affect net income by 100 percent of the error since the books are adjusted to the inventory on hand.

Allowance for Returns. In most situations, the expected amount of returns is not material enough to estimate and record an allowance for returns. However, some companies, such as mail-order companies including Lands' End or L.L. Bean with return guarantees, expect significant returns and can use previous experience to develop estimates of returns. When such returns are material to the overall financial presentation, allowances for returns should be established and the gross profit on the original sale reversed. The allowance is not restricted to mail-order companies but should be considered when a company is experiencing a large volume of returns. An example of the disclosure of such returns for Lands' End is shown in Exhibit 16.8.

Rights

Most of the audit work regarding the rights and ownership to inventory is addressed during the auditor's test of the initial recording of purchases. The auditor should also review long-term contracts to determine obligations to take delivery of merchandise, customer rights to return merchandise, or buy-back obligations.

Valuation

Valuation is the most complex assertion because of the volume of transactions, the diversity of products, the variety of costing methods, and the difficulty in estimating net realizable value of products. A combination of direct tests and analytical procedures is used to estimate inventory valuation.

Direct Tests of Product Costs. Statistical sampling techniques, especially PPS sampling, can be used to select items for testing. As an example, assume that the auditor selected product A250 to test the valuation of the perpetual inventory record as follows:

PRODUCT A250

			Balance	
Transaction	Quantity	Price	Quantity	Dollars
Beginning balance			100	$1,000
3/1 Purchase	50	$ 550	150	1,550
6/1 Purchase	100	1,200	250	2,750
6/1 Sale	150	1,550	100	1,200
9/1 Purchase	50	500	150	1,700
10/1 Sale	25	275	125	1,425
12/1 Sale	50	600	75	825
12/1 Purchase	75	975	150	1,800

Exhibit 16.8

LANDS' END FOOTNOTE
CUSTOMER RETURNS 1990

G. Reserve for losses on customer returns

At the time of sale, the company provides a reserve equal to the gross profit on projected merchandise returns, based on its prior returns experience. The reserve balances at January 31, 1990 and 1989, were $2,575,000 and $2,200,000, respectively. These balances are included in accrued liabilities.

Authors' Note: Sales for the respective years were $545 million and $455 million. The total amount of returns for the year are not disclosed. Reported gross margin for 1990 and 1989 were 42 percent and 43 percent, respectively.

Assume also that the client uses the FIFO inventory valuation method and has a year-end balance of $1,800 with 150 items in inventory. Invoices would be examined for the purchases of the last 150 items 12/1, 9/1, and 6/1 to determine whether $1,800 was the correct cost. (Note: The reader should verify that the recorded cost should have been $1,775.) Differences should be projected to determine whether they might be material. Similar tests should be performed if other valuation methods are utilized, such as average cost or LIFO. If the company uses a standard cost system, the costs are verified by tests of the cost system and tracing the selected items to standard costs.

Tests for Obsolete Inventory. Determining the amount that should be written off because of obsolescence is a difficult and challenging audit task because (1) the client will usually state that most of the goods are still salable at current selling prices and (2) net realizable value is only an estimate (i.e., there is not a specific correct price at which inventory should be valued). Thus, the auditor attempts to gather evidence on potential inventory obsolescence from a number of corroborating sources including the following:

- Noting potential obsolete inventory when observing the client's physical inventory.
- Calculating inventory turnover, number of days' sales in inventory, date of last sale or purchase, and other similar analytic techniques to identify potential obsolescence.
- Calculating net realizable value for products by reference to current selling prices, cost of disposal, and so on.
- Monitoring trade journals for information regarding the introduction of competitive products.
- Inquiring of management as to its approach to identify and classify obsolete items.

The auditor then investigates any item that appears to be obsolete by reviewing sales subsequent to year-end and discussing future sales prospects with management.

Disclosure

The auditor reviews the client's proposed disclosure for compliance with the guidelines established by GAAP. In addition to the normally required inventory disclosures, the auditor must determine whether there are any unusual circumstances regarding sales or purchase contracts that would merit additional disclosure. An example of a typical inventory disclosure, for Textron Industries, is shown in Exhibit 16.9.

Cost of Goods Sold

The audit of cost of goods sold can be directly tied to the audit of inventories. If beginning and ending inventory have been verified and acquisitions have been tested, cost of goods sold can be directly calculated. The auditor does not usually visit every location on many audits to observe inventory or test the perpetual records, however. An alternative approach is to use analytical procedures to test the cost of goods sold.

Exhibit 16.9

TEXTRON INDUSTRIES
INVENTORY FOOTNOTE 1990
(AMOUNTS IN MILLIONS)

	December 29, 1990	December 30, 1989
Finished goods	$ 240.0	$ 245.9
Work in process	1,232.9	1,310.7
Raw materials	184.3	181.5
	1,657.2	1,738.1
Less progress payments	363.0	417.3
	$1,294.2	$1,320.8

Inventories aggregating $504 million at December 29, 1990 and $581 million at December 30, 1989 were valued by the last-in, first-out (LIFO) method. Had such LIFO inventories been valued at current costs, their carrying values would have been approximately $123 million and $106 million higher at those respective dates. The remaining inventories, other than those related to certain long-term contracts and programs, are valued generally by the first-in, first-out method.

Inventories related to long-term contracts and programs, net of progress payments, were $514 million at December 29, 1990 and $499 million at December 30, 1989. Such inventories include unamortized tooling, deferred learning costs and costs related to unnegotiated, customer-directed changes of approximately $121 million at December 29, 1990 and $150 million at December 30, 1989. Textron expects to recover such amounts on the related contracts and programs. As to government contracts, inventory costs also generally include general and administrative expenses ($41 million at December 30, 1990; $48 million at December 30, 1989). Costs attributed to units delivered are based generally upon the estimated average cost per unit at contract or program completion.

Analytical Procedures as a Substantive Test of Cost of Goods Sold

Analytical review procedures can be very effective in estimating account balances when (1) there is an established relationship between the accounts, (2) one of the account balances has already been audited, and (3) the company has low control risk. To illustrate the general approach, assume that the auditor is performing the audit of a small manufacturing company with low control risk and has completed tests of accounts receivable, inventory, and sales. The auditor wishes to use analytical procedures to estimate cost of goods sold to determine whether the amount recorded is likely to contain material misstatements.

Steps in the Process. Analytical procedures require a systematic analysis on the part of the auditor in determining the important relationships and the approach to be utilized. The following are the steps:

1. Establish the relationship between the account to be audited and other audit work already performed.

2. Establish the validity (reliability) of accounts or other data that might serve as an independent variable in performing the procedures.
3. Develop prior expectations of risks for the account balance.
4. Determine an appropriate analytical procedure and establish the stability of the relationship.
5. Develop expectations about the relationship and the values expected for this period.
6. Perform the analytical procedure.
7. If results are within the previously defined acceptable range, document the findings and conclude this portion of audit procedures.
8. If the results are not within the predetermined acceptable range,
   a. Generate a list of alternative explanations of why the account balance might be different than expected.
   b. Investigate through inquiry, subsequent analysis, and detailed testing the correctness of the alternative explanations.

Analytical procedures can be efficient because no additional audit work is needed if the expected relationship is found. If, on the other hand, the expected relationship is not found, the auditor can use directed testing to determine whether the account is materially misstated. The procedures for this assumed company would proceed as follows.

Step 1: Establish Relationship to Other Accounts. Cost of Goods Sold is directly affected by sales and inventory transactions. Cost of Goods Sold should vary directly with Sales.

Step 2. Establish Reliability of Other Accounts. Transactions in the Sales account have been tested and the transaction processing is considered reliable. In addition, the client has production data that are independent of the accounting system and are also considered to be reliable. Inventory has already been tested.

Step 3. Develop Prior Expectations. There is low control risk with no expectation of material error in the account. However, the auditor is concerned about potential understatement of cost of goods sold. The production and shipping process has remained the same throughout the year. The client does not expect that any marked changes in the gross profit realized during the year. Therefore, the auditor expects that cost of goods sold as a percentage of sales should not be materially changed from the past year.

Step 4. Determine Analytical Technique and Relationship. The gross margin percentage captures the major relationship between Sales and Cost of Goods Sold. If the organization is complex, the analysis is performed on a product-line basis. The assumption in this example is less complex. The previous year relationship is reviewed, and it is found that cost of goods sold average about 60 percent of sales and has fluctuated between 59 percent and 61 percent over the past five years. Based on inquiries and analysis of related procedures, the auditor believes that there is no significant change in the sales mix for this year and that pricing policies have remained stable. The data for the past five years are shown in Exhibit 16.10.

Exhibit 16.10

ANALYTICAL DATA FOR SALES AND COST OF GOODS SOLD

	Current	1995	1994	1993	1992	1991
Sales	$110,000	99,450	93,060	87,900	83,850	78,000
Cost of Goods Sold	60,500	58,975	55,900	52,700	49,900	46,600
Cost of Goods Sold as percent of percentage of Sales	55.0	59.3	60.1	60.0	59.5	59.8
Percent increase in:						
Sales	10.6	6.9	5.9	4.8	7.5	
Cost of Goods Sold	2.6	5.5	6.1	5.6	7.1	

Step 5. Develop Expectations about Account Balance. Given the stability of the relationship, the product mix, and the pricing policy, the auditor expects that the ratio of cost of goods sold to sales to remain around 60 percent. Any deviation of more than 2 percent would be considered a material deviation and would warrant further investigation.

Step 6. Perform the Analytical Procedures. As shown in Exhibit 16.10, the ratio of cost of goods sold to sales has decreased to 55 percent. In addition, while the Sales account has increased by 10.6 percent during the last year, the Cost of Goods Sold account increased by only 2.6 percent. The growth in sales is above past averages, the cost of goods sold percentage is below past averages, and the rate of growth in cost of goods sold is not consistent with the rate of growth in sales.

Step 7. Document and Conclude Audit Test if Results Are within Acceptable Limits. Efficiency is attained when the results support existing book value. In Exhibit 16.10, the results do not support the recorded book value. Cost of goods sold has dropped to 55 percent of sales and that result is not expected. More investigation is warranted.

Step 8a. Generate Possible Explanations for the Unexpected Value. Based on previous knowledge and discussions with the client and other members of the audit team, the auditor generates a potential set of alternative explanations for the unexpected decline in the cost of goods sold ratio. The following alternative hypotheses are generated:

1. Although the sales account had been tested, the auditor did not perform a detailed review of the year-end sales and purchase cutoff. A problem with inventory cutoff may be affecting the cost of goods sold calculation.
2. Some inventory purchases may have been misclassified or omitted.

3. There has been a decrease in inventory, causing the company to dip into a LIFO layer, thereby matching older and lower costs against the current revenue.
4. Manufacturing operations have been improved and are more cost effective than in the past. Labor is more efficient and less costly.

Step 8b. Prioritize the Alternative Explanations and Systematically Investigate Them. Any of the preceding explanations (or others) might account for the unexpected change in the gross profit ratio. By deciding which is most likely, the auditor can direct the audit work to gain the greatest efficiency. For example, the auditor might decide that dipping into the LIFO layer is the most likely explanation. The effect can be easily documented. The auditor might find that there was such an effect but that it accounted for only three percent of the decline in the ratio. The auditor then proceeds to identify the next most probable explanation and develops audit procedures to document the validity of the alternative explanation.

C–ILLUSTRATIVE EXAMPLE–LEFLAM MANUFACTURING COMPANY

This part of the illustrative example covers two audit areas, the acquisition cycle and inventory.

Acquisition Cycle

The audit of the acquisition cycle includes the following:

- Obtaining an understanding of the system.
- Assessing control risk by performing a dual-purpose test of purchase and cash disbursement transactions.
- Performing analytical procedures.
- Performing direct tests of the account balances.

Understanding the Control Structure

The company has automated most of the purchasing function. The control procedures provide for separation of duties between authorizing purchases, authorizing payments, controlling the assets, and record keeping. Some important control procedures include the following:

- The company obtains bids for purchases over $10,000. Exceptions to this procedure exist for the major vendors of fiberglass and canvas, with whom the company has long-term purchase contracts.
- Purchase orders are consecutively numbered by the computer. Receiving reports are consecutively numbered via a numbering stamp used by the receiving department.

- Clerks in the purchasing department verify vendors' invoices by comparing the price and quantity with the purchase order, comparing the quantity with the receiving report, and checking the mathematical accuracy of the invoice. They initial an audit stamp placed on each invoice to indicate that these procedures were performed. The senior buyer then approves the invoice for payment. Exhibit 16.11 is an example of an audit stamp filled in and the initials of the buyer approving payment.
- The computer prepares a weekly exception report listing missing receiving report numbers, which is followed up by the accounts payable supervisor.
- The controller reviews the check register, account distribution detail, and supporting documents before signing the checks.
- The controller's secretary mails the signed checks to the vendors, staples the second copy of the check to the supporting documents to show they were paid, and files these documents.

Purchase requisitions for raw materials come from the production department. Most of the company's raw materials are purchased from 12 vendors. The lead time between placing an order and receiving the material is less than five working days for most purchases. There are no automatic reorder points because production needs vary from season to season. Sales are heaviest between September and May. The company tries to level out its manufacturing workload by producing basic, standard products during the months of slow sales and producing special orders when requested by customers.

Exhibit 16.12 is the audit program for the acquisition cycle based on this understanding of the control structure.

Assessing Control Risk

The analysis of the internal control structure leads to a preliminary assessment that there are strong controls in this cycle. If that conclusion is correct, the most efficient way to audit the accounts affected by the acquisition cycle is by performing (1) a dual-purpose test of purchase transactions processed during the year and (2) cutoff

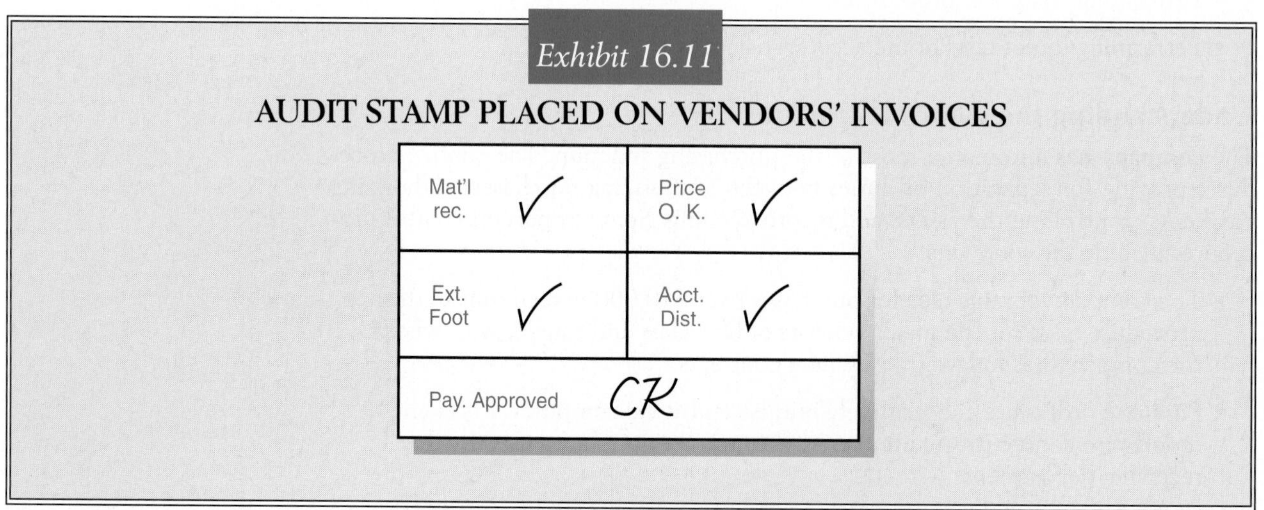
Exhibit 16.11

AUDIT STAMP PLACED ON VENDORS' INVOICES

Mat'l rec. ✓	Price O. K. ✓
Ext. Foot ✓	Acct. Dist. ✓
Pay. Approved CK	

Exhibit 16.12

LEFLAM MANUFACTURING COMPANY
AUDIT PROGRAM—ACCOUNTS PAYABLE AND PURCHASES
DECEMBER 31, 1994

	W/P Ref.	Done by
Audit Objectives		
Assess the control risk over purchase and cash disbursement transactions and determine the completeness, existence, valuation, presentation, and obligations of purchases, operating expenses, and trade accounts payable.		
Dual-Purpose Test of Transactions		
1. Select a sample of cash disbursement transactions and note initials indicating that employees:	________	________
a. Compared prices and quantities with the purchase order and receiving report (existence and valuation).		
b. Verified the mathematical accuracy of the invoice (valuation).		
c. Independently verified the account distribution (presentation).		
d. Approved the invoice for payment (existence).		
e. Attached the copy of the check to the supporting documents to avoid duplicate payment (existence and completeness).		
2. Trace each sample item to the daily purchases journals (completeness and valuation).	________	________
3. For each of the items selected above,	________	________
a. Compare the prices and quantities on the invoice with the purchase order and receiving report (existence and valuation).		
b. Verify the mathematical accuracy of the invoice (valuation).		
c. Determine whether the account distribution is proper (presentation).		
d. Verify that the amount and payee of the check are proper (existence and valuation).		
4. Select some weekly exception reports, including the last one for the year, and note whether there was proper follow up on missing receiving report numbers (completeness).	________	________

(*Continued*)

Exhibit 16.12

	W/P Ref.	Done by
Analytical Procedures		
1. Prepare a common-size income statement and compare to the prior period. Identify and investigate significant differences.	________	________
Tests of Details		
1. Obtain a list of accounts payable as of year-end and verify mathematical accuracy and agree to general ledger (valuation).	________	________
2. Identify the major vendors and obtain monthly statement as of year-end (completeness).	________	________
3. Send confirmation letters to major vendors not providing monthly statements (completeness).	________	________
4. Agree monthly statements and confirmations from major vendors with accounts payable list (existence, completeness, valuation, and obligation).	________	________
5. Review liabilities recorded after year-end and review subsequent cash payments (completeness).	________	________
6. Review long-term purchase commitments and determine whether a loss needs to be accrued (completeness and presentation and disclosure).	________	________
7. State your conclusion as to the correctness of the account balances.	________	________

tests of purchase and cash disbursement transactions around year-end (cash disbursements cutoff was tested in the audit of cash). If these tests confirm the preliminary assessment of control risk, the direct substantive tests of accounts payable, raw material purchases, fixed asset additions, and operating expenses can be minimized.

Test of Purchase and Cash Disbursement Transactions. The dual-purpose *tests of purchase and cash disbursement transactions* are designed to determine whether key internal control procedures are effective (a test of controls) and whether such transactions are recorded in the correct amount, account, and time period (a substantive test). An attribute sampling procedure is chosen to address these objectives. Each of the selected transactions is tested for the following:

Test of control procedures:

- Initials of appropriate purchasing department personnel appear on the vendor's invoice indicating that they

Compared prices and quantities with the purchase order and receiving report.

Verified the mathematical accuracy of the invoice.

Independently verified the account distribution.

Approved the invoice for payment.

- The copy of the check is attached to the supporting documents to avoid duplicate payment.
- Each sample item is traced to the daily purchases journals to test the accuracy of data entry.

Substantive tests:

- Compare the prices and quantities on the invoice with the purchase order and receiving report.
- Verify the mathematical accuracy of the invoice.
- Determine whether the account distribution is proper.
- Verify that the amount and payee of the check are proper.

These tests are documented in Exhibit 16.13. The risk of assessing control risk too low is set equal to the overall audit risk, five percent. The tolerable failure rate is set at 10 percent for the first three attributes. The tolerable failure rate is set at five percent for attributes 4 and 5 because their failure is more likely to result in improper or duplicate payments. The tolerable failure rate for the remaining attributes is set at 10 percent except for errors in recording the information (attribute 6) and in the amount and payee on the checks (attribute 10). Sixty cash disbursements are randomly selected based on the sampling plan and tested for each of the attributes. One control procedure failure each was detected in the sample for attributes 1, 2, and 8. The resulting upper limits (7.7 percent) are less than the tolerable failure rate of 10 percent.

Because this test was performed as of November 30, 1994, the effectiveness of the control procedures for the remainder of the year should be verified. This is done through inquiries of the accounts payable supervisor about any changes in the system or personnel. There were no major changes. Analytical procedures are considered sufficient to identify major misstatements; therefore, no substantive changes in the audit program are made.

One exception report detailing missing receiving documents is selected from each month, including the one for the last week in December. Ten of these reports indicate no missing receiving document numbers. Each report is initialled by the accounts payable supervisor. The two reports with missing document numbers are discussed with the accounts payable supervisor. A follow-up review of documents indicates that the missing receiving documents were processed the following week. There were no missing numbers on the last report for the year.

Based on these procedures, it can be concluded that the controls are effective and purchase transactions are recorded in the proper period. Control risk can appropriately be assessed as low for these transactions.

Exhibit 16.13

LEFLAM MANUFACTURING COMPANY
DOCUMENTATION OF ATTRIBUTE SAMPLE APPLICATION

Audit Area: Purchase and Cash Disbursement Transactions Period: 11 months to 11/30/94

Audit Objective: Test controls over and accuracy of accounting for purchases and cash disbursements

Define Population: Cash disbursements processed during 1994 through 11/30

Sampling Unit: Checks numbered 25,102 to 32,774

Selection Method: Random number generator to select random check numbers

Population Size 7,662 Risk of assessing control risk too low 5%

	Planning			Sample Results			
Description of Attributes	Expected Failure Rate	Tolerable Failure Rate	Initial Sample Size	Actual Sample Size	Number of Failures	Sample Failure Rate	Achieved Upper Limit
1. Initials indicate invoice prices and quantities were compared with purchase order and receiving report.	0.50%	10.00%	46	60	1	1.67%	7.70%
2. Initials indicate invoice was mathematically verified.	0.50	10.00	46	60	1	1.67	7.70
3. Initials indicate independent verification of account distribution.	0.00	10.00	29	60	0	0.00	4.90
4. Evidence of approval for payment exists.	0.00	5.00	59	60	0	0.00	4.90
5. Check copy is stapled to supporting documents.	0.00	5.00	59	60	0	0.00	4.90
6. Vendor, date, account distribution, and amount agree with purchases journals.	0.00	5.00	59	60	0	0.00	4.90
7. Prices and quantities on the invoice agree with purchase order and receiving report.	0.50	10.00	46	60	0	0.00	4.90
8. Extensions and footings on the invoice are accurate.	0.50	10.00	46	60	1	1.67	7.70
9. Account distribution are proper.	0.00	10.00	29	60	0	0.00	4.90
10. Amount and payee on check are proper.	0.00	5.00	59	60	0	0.00	4.90

Conclusion: In my opinion, the internal controls tested above are in operation and being applied effectively and purchase transactions are being properly recorded in the right amount and account.

Done by Auditor Date 12/20/94

Reviewed by ______ Date ______

Analytical Procedures

A common-size income statement is prepared to show each expense as a percent of net sales by year. An expanded version with dollar and percent change between years is shown in Exhibit 16.14.* Any unexpected changes or differences from industry statistics can be identified for investigation. The common-size statement shows that the percent increase of cost of sales and selling and administrative expenses was less than the percent increase in net sales. Management indicates the cost of sales percentage decline is primarily caused by the introduction of a new product that sells at a higher markup than the rest of the product line. This management assertion is verified by a review of sales reports.

A review of the personnel records reveals that the company hired several new salespersons during the last quarter of the previous year and provided extensive training to launch the new product. LeFlam spent a significant amount of money advertising this new product toward the end of 1993. The new salespersons, training, and advertising caused last year's selling expenses to be unusually high in comparison with earlier years and explains why the 1994 selling expenses did not increase as rapidly as sales.

Legal and audit expense declined this year. This decline is due to:

- Audit billings being reduced, resulting from the use of more efficient audit techniques during the interim work and from spending less time updating the permanent files relating to the client's internal control structure. There were fewer changes in that structure this year.
- Legal fees were reduced because of fewer product liability cases in process during the year.

The other administrative expenses appear reasonable. Explanations of the unexpected results should be contained in the working papers and cross-referenced to the common-size statements.

Direct Tests of Account Balances

The extent of direct testing of the accounts payable and expense balances is simplified for two reasons: (1) control risk was assessed as low and (2) 80 percent of all purchases are made from only 12 vendors. The primary audit objective is concerned with accounts payable understatement. Consequently, the audit procedures focus on reviewing vendor monthly statements and directly obtaining confirmations from the 12 major vendors and reconciling them with the recorded accounts payable.

There is a greater risk of the client recording liabilities and cash disbursements in the wrong period shortly after year-end than in later weeks. Therefore, it is proper to review all cash disbursement transactions recorded after year-end for amounts exceeding $5,000 for the first two weeks and for amounts exceeding $20,000 thereafter.

Had controls not been as strong, additional procedures that may have been performed include

- Tracing unmatched receiving reports and vouching unmatched invoices to account payable detail as additional tests of completeness.

*Many CPA firms use microcomputer software for developing audit working papers that automatically prepares statements similar to this common-size income statement.

Exhibit 16.14

LEFLAM MANUFACTURING COMPANY
COMMON-SIZE INCOME STATEMENT ($000)
DECEMBER 31, 1994

20 = 1

Done by JK Date 1/20/95

	December 31, 1994		December 31, 1993			
	Amount	Percent of Net Sales	Amount	Percent of Net Sales	Dollar Change	Percent Change
Net sales	28,900	100.00%	24,500	100.00%	4,400	17.96%
Cost of sales	20,808	72.00	18,000	73.47	2,808	15.60
Gross margin	8,092	28.00	6,500	26.53	1,592	24.49
Sales salaries and commission	811	2.81	737	3.01	74	10.04
Sales payroll tax	170	0.59	155	0.63	15	9.68
Employee benefits	162	0.56	147	0.60	15	10.20
Advertising	347	1.20	325	1.33	22	6.77
Travel and entertainment	175	0.61	160	0.65	15	9.38
Promotional literature	95	0.33	83	0.34	12	14.46
Training	90	0.31	110	0.45	(20)	−18.18
Miscellaneous selling expenses	29	0.10	25	0.10	4	16.00
Total selling expenses	1,879	6.50	1,742	7.11	137	7.86
Exec/Off salaries	796	2.75	711	2.90	85	11.95
Admin payroll tax	210	0.73	191	0.78	19	9.95
Employee benefits	200	0.69	182	0.74	18	9.89
Insurance	33	0.11	30	0.12	3	10.00
Office supplies	15	0.05	13	0.05	2	15.38
Delivery	23	0.08	21	0.09	2	9.52
Telephone	9	0.03	8	0.03	1	12.50
Legal and audit	125	0.43	137	0.56	(12)	−8.76
Bad debts	309	1.07	95	0.39	214	225.26
Electricity	150	0.52	128	0.52	22	17.19
Gas	196	0.68	174	0.71	22	12.64
Travel and entertainment	17	0.06	15	0.06	2	13.33
Postage	28	0.10	20	0.08	8	40.00
Depreciation—	48	0.17	47	0.19	1	2.13

Exhibit 16.14

	December 31, 1994		December 31, 1993			
	Amount	Percent of Net Sales	Amount	Percent of Net Sales	Dollar Change	Percent Change
Office repairs and maintenance	4	0.01	5	0.02	(1)	−20.00
Miscellaneous general expenses	18	0.06	17	0.07	1	5.88
Total administration	2,181	7.55	1,794	7.32	386	21.52
Total selling and administrative	4,060	14.05	3,536	14.43	524	14.82
Income from operations	4,032	13.95	2,964	12.10	1,068	36.03
Other expenses	924	3.20	580	2.37	344	59.31
Income taxes	1,430	4.95	1,097	4.48	333	30.36
Net income	1,678	5.81	1,287	5.25	391	30.38

- Obtaining monthly statements or confirmations from some of the other vendors and reconciling them to the recorded accounts payable.
- Using lower dollar amounts for selecting transactions for review when testing subsequent cash disbursements.
- Vouching the details in expense accounts (some selected expense accounts will always be reviewed, such as repairs and maintenance, travel and entertainment, and legal fees, during the final stages of the audit because the accounts may contain information that affects other parts of the financial statements).

The substantive audit procedures indicate that accounts payable, purchases, and operating expenses have been properly recorded in the correct accounting period. The only error detected was one invoice for $6,500 received after year-end for the Christmas party that was recorded as a liability in 1993. This was posted to the Summary of Possible Adjustments working paper.

Inventory

Inventory is by far the most significant asset (see Exhibit 13.12), comprising over 67 percent of current assets and over 60 percent of total assets. The inventory lead schedule is shown in Exhibit 16.15 and indicates about 1,800 items of raw material and 1,200 items of work in process (WIP) and finished goods. Perpetual inventory records are maintained. Inventory is priced at standard costs that are updated annually. The discussion below, however, covers only the audit work related to the inventory observation.

Exhibit 16.15

LEFLAM MANUFACTURING COMPANY
INVENTORY LEAD SCHEDULE
DECEMBER 31, 1994
(IN THOUSANDS)

Account	Ref	December 31, 1993	December 31, 1994 Balance per Books	Adjustments/ Reclassifications Debits	Adjustments/ Reclassifications Credits	December 31, 1994 Final Balance
Finished goods	C-1 p24	5,484,902	8,256,120			
Work in process	C-1 p13	1,246,940	1,886,444			
Raw materials	C-1 p60	2,065,956	3,125,500			
Factory supplies	C-1 p5	94,352	116,796			
Total	C-1 p60	8,892,150	13,384,860			
			T/B			
			F			

F = Footed

T/B = Traced to Trial Balance

Client's Physical Count Procedures

The inventory is physically counted at the end of each year. The year-end counts are made between December 26 and 31. Any products that need to be shipped during that period are segregated in the shipping room prior to the physical count. There is no production during the count. Jim Weaver, director of Materials and Production Control, has overall responsibility for the physical inventory.

Raw materials are counted by personnel from the warehouse and purchasing department. This takes about one and one-half days. Work in process (WIP) and finished goods are counted by the cost accounting manager and production supervisors. WIP can be counted in about five hours. In addition to counting items in process, the degree of completion must be noted. This requires some judgment and is done by the cost accounting manager and production supervisors. The finished goods count takes about two days.

Prenumbered, three-part inventory tags are used to record the counts (see Exhibit 16.16). There are several two-person count teams, each of which is assigned a set of tags. Different tag colors are used for raw materials, WIP, and finished goods counts. The supervisor logs these tag numbers and accounts for all of the numbers at the end of the count. Every item is independently counted by two teams, and the two counts are compared by the supervisor and any discrepancies are immediately investigated. The supervisor checks each area to be sure that all items have been counted before the teams go to another location.

When the counting is completed and all of the count tags are accounted for, information from them is entered into the computer by cost accounting personnel. The computer program prepares a summary of the tags by product, compares the phys-

Exhibit 16.16

INVENTORY COUNT TAG

Tag No. 296

Description #10 Canvas 36"

Stock # C1036

Stage of Completion (WIP only)

Location Whse A. Second Floor E

Unit of measure Running Feet

Quantity 1,500

Initials BER LJS

Date 12/31/93

ical counts with the perpetual records (Exhibit 16.17), and automatically adjusts the perpetual records to agree with the physical counts. The summary is reviewed by the cost accounting supervisor to determine whether any unusually large adjustments should be investigated. Management wants the inventory records to be as accurate as possible and insists that the records be adjusted to the physical count even though the differences are usually immaterial.

Observation of the Physical Inventory

The audit program for inventory observation is shown in Exhibit 16.7. Prior to the inventory count date, the auditor meets with Jim Weaver to discuss the procedures, timing, locations, and personnel who will be taking the physical counts. The auditor is satisfied that the procedures are adequate to ensure an accurate count and determines that there is no need to obtain the services of a specialist because the inventory items have no unusual characteristics. All the inventory except canoe items is located at company headquarters. Two staff auditors are needed to assist in observing the inventory at the headquarters and one at the canoe factory. The client's procedures and observation responsibilities are reviewed with the other staff auditors. In addition, an interim list of inventory is reviewed to identify the

Exhibit 16.17

SAMPLE COMPUTER PRINTOUT OF INVENTORY DIFFERENCES

C-1
LeFlam Manufacturing Company — Page 60 of 60
Inventory Count Comparison Run as of December 31, 1994 — JMV 1/19/95

Tag Number	Location	Stock Number	Description	Unit of Measure	Quantity per Count	Quantity per Records	Standard Cost	Extended Value per Count	Extended Difference
2996	A2E	C1036	#10 Canvas 36"	Running feet	15,500	15,490	.765	11,857.50	7.65
2997	A2E	C1048	#10 Canvas 48"	Running feet	3,975	3,975	.993	3,947.18	–0–
2998	A2E	C1236	#12 Canvas 36"	Running feet	19,330*	19,333	.812†	15,695.96	(2.44)‡
2999	A2E	C1248	#12 Canvas 48"	Running feet	1,250	1,250	1.088	1,360.00	–0–
3000	A2E	C1260	#12 Canvas 60"	Running feet	22,440	22,425	1.490	33,435.60	22.35
						Total—Raw materials		8,256,120	(1,872.96)
						Total—all inventory		13,384,86	(2,701.00)

* Agrees with test count C-2.

† Agrees with standard cost sheet.

‡ Recalculated.

individually significant items to be given special attention during the count. The following audit procedures were also followed at the canoe factory:

- The process of distributing and recording the count tags given each count team is noted. The actual counting was selectively observed to obtain evidence that established procedures were followed.
- Several test counts are made, recorded (see Exhibit 16.18), and compared with the counts recorded on the client's tags. The test counts include the individually significant items and a sample of other items. One count discrepancy was noted, and the client agreed to recount it. The final quantity agreed with the auditor's count.
- The recorded test counts were traced into the computer report shown in Exhibit 16.18 (prepared after the physical counts were recorded).
- A pile of apparently damaged products was noted and discussed with the supervisor. The goods were considered to be scrap and were not included in the inventory count.
- A review of the accounting for sequentially numbered tags indicates that all were accounted for. The sequencing reconciliation agrees with the auditor's

Exhibit 16.18

LEFLAM MANUFACTURING COMPANY
INVENTORY TEST COUNTS
DECEMBER 31, 1994

Prepared by: JMV 1/30/95

Tag Number	Stock Number	Description	Unit of Measure	Count
2998	C1236	#12 Canvas 36"	Running feet	19,33 * –0–
2154	PH36	Polyester-heavy 36"	Running feet	10,44 * 7
779	RCML	Rain coat—men's large In process through rough sewing	Each	60 *
2190	NT1060	#10 Nylon taffeta 60"	Running feet	8,731 *
2600	PE1036	#10 Polyethylene 36"	Running feet	12,31 * 8
2898	SR548	1/2" Steel Rod 48"	Each	3,784 *
Etc.	Etc.	Etc.	Etc.	Etc.

*Agrees with inventory count comparison run as of December 31, 1994, C-1.

physical observation of first and last tag numbers used. The reconciliation is documented for further audit testing.

Summary

The audits of the acquisition cycle, expense accounts, inventory, and cost of goods sold are highly interrelated. The Inventory and Cost of Goods Sold accounts have been the subject of a variety of manipulation schemes ranging from outright addition of fictitious inventory, movement of inventory from one location to another, recognition of defective items as good items, and failure to recognize decreases in market value due to technological changes. The extent of work the auditor performs depends heavily on the client's control environment. When control risk is assessed as high, the auditor extends the work on inventory. On the other hand, management of many well-managed companies has realized that it must have accurate accounting controls over the inventory and disbursements if the company is to operate profitably. In such situations, the audit work can concentrate on testing the client's control system and corroborating the analysis with analytical procedures of cost of goods sold and selected testing of the perpetual inventory records.

Significant Terms

accounts payable confirmation A confirmation process that seeks a vendor statement as a basis for identifying potential understatement of the accounts payable liability.

automated matching A process by which the computer matches a purchase order, receiving information, and a vendor invoice to determine whether the vendor's invoice is correct and should be paid.

cycle count Periodic testing of the accuracy of the perpetual inventory record by counting all inventory on a cycle basis.

quality control An approach by an organization to ensure that high-quality products are produced and high-quality services are provided. The approach specifies quality requirements for processes and products and integrates those concepts into vendor contracts.

requisition A request for the purchase of goods or services by an authorized department or function within the organization; may be documented on a paper or in a computer system.

Review Questions

A–Audit of the Acquisition Cycle

16–1 Identify the major phases of the acquisition cycle and the control objectives that should be addressed in the design of control procedures for each phase.

16–2 Identify the different ways in which the requisition process might be implemented. For each method, indicate how the requisition is authorized and the evidence the auditor would gather to determine authorization.

16–3 Why should the functions of requisitioning the purchase of goods be segregated from the issuance of purchase orders?

16–4 How does the existence of long-term contracts tied in with just-in-time inventory practices affect the control procedures implemented over the acquisition of the goods and the auditor's approach to auditing transactions in the acquisition cycle?

16–5 How does an automated receiving function differ from a traditional manual receiving function? How do the control procedures differ in the automated function? What control procedures does the auditor normally find most useful in reviewing the control over an automated receiving function?

16–6 Assume that prenumbered receiving documents are not used in an organization that has attempted to automate much of the purchase and receiving function. What control objective is addressed by having prenumbered receiving documents? What compensating controls should the auditor expect to find when prenumbered receiving documents are not used?

16–7 Many organizations use the computer to generate purchase orders. Who is responsible for authorizing a purchase when the purchase order is generated by the computer? How does the responsible individual ensure that computer-generated orders are correct and are generated only for purchases that should be made?

16–8 Explain how an automated matching process works with the processing and payment of accounts payable. What control procedures need to be implemented in the automated matching process to ensure that only authorized payments are made for goods and services actually received and that the payments are made at the authorized prices?

16–9 Explain the alternative approaches that might be utilized in designing a computer program to perform the automatic matching process associated with accounts payable. What approach do you believe is preferable? Explain.

16–10 Why does much of the audit work in the acquisition cycle focus on tests of transactions rather than year-end tests of account balances?

16–11 What are the important control procedures that an auditor would expect to find in an accounts payable environment when payments are automatically scheduled and checks or electronic transfers of cash are generated by the computer program?

16–12 What objectives are addressed by accounts payable confirmations? What form is used for accounts payable confirmations? Explain why accounts payable confirmations are often not used on an audit.

16–13 What assumptions must hold true if the auditor chooses to test the completeness of accounts payable by examining subsequent disbursements and reviewing open accounts payable? What options exist to discover unrecorded accounts payable?

16–14 What information should an auditor gather in reviewing long-term purchase contracts or long-term supply contracts? How might the information affect the audit?

16–15 Some expense accounts, such as legal expenses, are often examined in detail by the auditor even if the account balance is not material. Explain why.

16–16 How might the auditor effectively use analytical procedures in the audit of various expense accounts, such as miscellaneous expenses? Give an example of how analytical procedures might be used in the audit of such accounts.

16–17 An auditor has been assigned to audit the accounts payable of a high-risk audit client. The control environmental risk is assessed as high, management integrity is marginal, and the company is near violation of important loan covenants, particularly one that requires the maintenance of a minimum working capital ratio. Explain how the auditor should approach the year-end audit of accounts payable.

B–Audit of Inventory and Cost of Goods Sold

16–18 What factors contribute to the audit complexity of inventory?

16–19 Why is it important that an auditor audit the standard cost system? How would the auditor test the standard cost system to determine that payroll expenses are appropriately charged to products?

16–20 During the observation of the client's year-end inventory, the auditor notes that shipping document 8702 was the last shipment for the year and that receiving report 10,163 was the last receiving slip for the year. Explain how the information gathered would be used in performing an inventory cut-off test.

16–21 The Northwoods Manufacturing Company has automated its production facilities dramatically during the last five years to the extent that the number of direct labor hours has remained steady while production has increased fivefold. Automated equipment, such as robots, have helped increase productivity. Overhead, which previously had been applied at the rate of $7.50 per direct labor hour, is now being applied at the rate of $23.50 per direct labor hour. Explain how you would evaluate the reasonableness of the application of factory overhead to year-end inventory and cost of goods sold.

16–22 During the observation of a client's physical inventory, you note that the client had undergone a change in the numbering system used to identify inventory products. During your observations, you noted a number of errors on the product number recorded on the inventory tags and brought the errors to the attention of the supervisor who corrected every one that you noted. You also note that the count of inventory items was highly accurate. How would these findings affect the year-end audit of inventory?

16–23 A client with just-in-time inventory does not formally receive goods but unloads supplies from the railroad car directly into the production line. The client has a long-term contract with the supplier specifying delivery terms, quality requirements, and penalties for noncompliance. The vendor is paid based on production during the month plus a small allowance for loss. The auditor is concerned that accounts payable is properly stated at the end of the period. How would the auditor gather evidence to satisfy himself or herself that the accounts payable is properly recognized for vendors that are part of the just-in-time system?

16–24 The auditor has always received good cooperation from a particular client and has been willing to share information about the audit with the controller on a timely basis. The controller has requested copies of the auditor's observations on the physical inventory because she wants to ensure that a good inventory was taken. Should the auditor comply with this request? State your rationale.

16–25 Why is it important that a quality control function be utilized for the receipt of important inventory items? What is the financial statement risk if such a function is not utilized by a manufacturing client?

16–26 The auditor has been assigned to the audit of Marathon Oil Company and will observe the testing of inventory at a major storage area in Ohio. The company has approximately 15 different types of fuel oils stored in various tanks. The value of the fuel varies dramatically according to its grade. Explain how the auditor might use a specialist in auditing the inventory.

16–27 Assume that customers are allowed to return merchandise that is defective or that they simply did not like. What is the proper accounting for the returns? What control procedures should be implemented to ensure that all returned items are properly recorded?

16–28 The auditor is always concerned that slow-moving or potentially obsolete inventory is included in inventory and that the goods should be reduced to a lower market value. Identify five procedures the auditor might utilize to determine the existence of obsolete goods or goods whose market value is less than cost.

16–29 During the audit of inventory, you note that the client had generated substantial cost and material variances. The client explains that many of the variances were due to irregular production schedules, heavy overtime for the summer period, and lighter production during other times of the year. The controller has allocated the variances (all negative) to Finished Goods and Work in Process Inventory based on the relative proportion of each inventory category. Comment on the appropriateness of the allocation method used by the controller.

16–30 Explain the procedures the auditor would utilize to verify the cost of inventory, assuming the client uses the following valuation approaches:

- FIFO valuation on a periodic inventory basis.
- LIFO based on an index of FIFO cost computed each year and then used to adjust the inventory to LIFO.
- Average cost on a perpetual inventory basis.

16–31 Explain the purpose of the test counts and other inventory observations that the auditor notes while a physical inventory is being taken. Explain how each written observation is used in completing the audit of inventory.

16–32 What financial statement disclosures are required for inventory? How does the auditor determine the adequacy of the client's financial statement disclosures?

16–33 Explain why self-checking digits is an important control procedure found in computerized inventory systems. What potential errors are prevented by the use of self-checking digits?

16–34 Identify two audit approaches that might be used to gain assurance about the correctness of the perpetual inventory records.

Multiple Choice Questions

16–35 Auditors try to identify predictable relationships when using analytical procedures. Relationships involving transactions from which of the following accounts and total cost of production for the year most likely would yield the most persuasive evidence?

a. Accounts payable.

b. Advertising expense.

c. Accounts receivable.

d. Payroll expense.

*16–36 The auditor's analytical procedures are facilitated if the client

a. Uses a standard cost system that produces variance reports.
b. Segregates obsolete inventory before the physical inventory count.
c. Corrects reportable conditions in internal control before the beginning of the audit.
d. Reduced inventory balances to the lower of cost or market.

*16–37 After accounting for a sequence of inventory tags, an auditor traces a sample of them to the physical inventory list and reconciles the sequences counted to the inventory list to obtain evidence that all items

a. Included in the list have been counted.
b. Represented by inventory tags are included in the list.
c. Included in the list are represented by inventory tags.
d. Represented by inventory tags are bona fide.

*16–38 Which of the following is *not* one of the independent auditor's objectives regarding the examination of inventories?

a. Verifying that inventory counted is owned by the client.
b. Verifying that the client has used proper inventory pricing.
c. Ascertaining the physical quantities of inventory on hand.
d. Verifying that all inventory owned by the client is on hand at the time of the count.

*16–39 The auditor tests the quantity of materials charged to work-in-process by tracing these quantities from the work-in-process accounts to

a. Cost ledgers.
b. Perpetual inventory records.
c. Receiving reports.
d. Material requisitions.

*16–40 Which of the following audit procedures is best for identifying unrecorded trade accounts payable?

a. Examining unusual relationships between monthly accounts payable balances and recorded cash payments.
b. Reconciling vendors' statements to the file of receiving reports to identify items received just prior to the balance sheet date.
c. Reviewing cash disbursements recorded subsequent to the balance sheet date to determine whether the related payables apply to the prior period.
d. Investigating payables recorded just prior to and just subsequent to the balance sheet date to determine whether they are supported by receiving reports.

16–41 Which of the following controls would be most effective in ensuring that recorded purchases are free of material errors?

*Adapted from the Uniform CPA examination or the Certified Internal Auditor examination.

a. The receiving department compares the quantity ordered on purchase orders with the quantity received indicated on receiving reports.

b. Vendors' invoices are compared with purchase orders by an employee who is independent of the receiving department.

c. Receiving reports require the signature of the individual who authorized the purchase.

d. Purchase orders, receiving reports, and vendors' invoices are independently matched in preparing vouchers.

*16–42 To determine whether accounts payable are complete, an auditor performs a test to verify that all merchandise received is recorded. The population of documents for this test consists of all

a. Vendor's invoices.

b. Purchase orders.

c. Receiving reports.

d. Canceled checks.

*16–43 Which of the following procedures in the cash disbursements cycle should *not* be performed by the accounts payable department?

a. Comparing the vendor's invoice with the receiving report.

b. Canceling supporting documentation after payment.

c. Verifying the mathematical accuracy of the vendor's invoice.

d. Signing the voucher for payment by an authorized person.

*16–44 The accounts payable department receives the purchase order form to accomplish all of the following except to

a. Compare invoice price to purchase order price.

b. Ensure that the purchase had been properly authorized.

c. Ensure that the goods had been received by the party requesting them.

d. Compare quantity ordered to quantity purchased.

Discussion and Research Questions

*16–45 (Accounts Payable) Paul Mincin, CPA, is the auditor of Raleigh Corporation. Mincin is considering the audit work to be performed in the accounts payable area for the current year engagement.

The prior year working papers show that confirmation requests were mailed to 100 of Raleigh's 1,000 suppliers. The selected suppliers were based on Mincin's sample that was designed to select accounts with large dollar balances. Mincin and Raleigh staff spent a substantial number of hours resolving relatively minor differences between the confirmation replies and Raleigh's accounting records. Alternative audit procedures were used for those suppliers who did not respond to the confirmation requests.

Required:

a. Identify the accounts payable audit objectives that Mincin must consider in determining the audit procedures to be followed.

b. Identify situations in which Mincin should use accounts payable confirmations and discuss whether he is required to use them.

c. Discuss why the use of large dollar balances as the basis for selecting accounts payable for confirmation might not be the most effective approach and indicate what more effective procedures could be followed when selecting accounts payable for confirmation.

16–46 (Automated Receiving Function) Hodag Company has automated its receipts as follows:

- A receiving supervisor accesses an open purchase order file listed by vendor to determine whether a shipment should be accepted. If the shipment is not on the open order list, the supervisor must obtain permission from a purchasing agent before the shipment can be accepted.

- Most items are accepted, opened, and counted. The counts are entered on paper documents that are copies of the purchase order with the quantity ordered blocked out. The document is batched in the receiving office, and all items are input by a clerk.

- Selected items are read by an automated scanner, but the boxes are not opened. The computerized scanning count is automatically recorded on the receiving document. If differences are noted between the scanning from the outside of the carton and the actual contents when opened, an adjusting document is prepared and sent to accounts payable and the purchasing agent.

- A quality control department selectively tests goods before they are put into production. Any defective items are noted and a document is sent to accounts payable and the purchasing agent and the goods are marked for return. The goods are not returned to the vendor, however, unless specifically authorized by the purchasing agent.

- The receiving document contains information on who should pay freight. If the shipment comes with freight due, the receiving department is authorized to make the payment. Where applicable, the receiving department prepares a chargeback notice for the freight and forwards it to the purchasing agent and accounts payable.

Required:

a. What additional computerized control procedures would the auditor expect to be implemented in the system described?

b. What risks are present in the system as described? What additional control procedures, or improvements in control procedures might be implemented to lessen the risks?

c. What audit procedures might the auditor use to ensure that goods are accepted and paid for only when authorized for receipt and that the payments are for the correct quantity and correct price?

16–47 (Potential Fraud in Purchasing Function) Assume that the internal auditor has assessed that the potential is high that some purchase agents are involved in a kickback scheme with vendors who have received preferential treatment. The purchasing agents are receiving gifts or cash payments directly from the vendors for steering new contracts their way, or negotiating purchase prices higher than could be obtained elsewhere. The auditor has some limited information that some specific purchasing agents have been living a somewhat lavish lifestyle.

Required:

a. What control procedures would be effective in preventing such kickback schemes?

b. What audit procedures might be used to determine whether the purchase agents might be involved with kickback schemes?

16–48 (Audit Procedures and Objectives) The following audit procedures are found in audit programs addressing the acquisition and payment cycle.

Required: For each audit procedure described

a. Identify the objective of the procedure or the audit assertion being tested.

b. Classify the procedure as primarily a substantive test, a test of control procedures, or both.

Audit Procedures

1. The auditor examines payments to vendors subsequent to year-end and then reviews any open accounts payable files.
2. The auditor reviews computer center records on changes to passwords and the client's procedures to monitor unusual amounts of accesses by password type. The auditor makes inquiries of purchasing agents as to the frequency that passwords are changed and whether assistants are allowed to access computer files in their absence in order to efficiently handle inquiries or process standing orders.
3. The auditor reviews a report of all accounts payable items that are not matched by the automated matching system. A sample of selected items is taken and traced to the vendor payment and supporting documentation.
4. The auditor uses software to prepare a report of all debits to Accounts Payable for other than payments to vendors. A sample of the debits is selected and examined for support.
5. The auditor uses software to access all recorded receipts of merchandise that have not been matched to an open purchase order.
6. The client prepares a report from a database showing inventory write-downs by product line and by purchasing agent. The auditor reviews the report and analyzes the data in relation to sales volume by product.
7. The auditor creates a spreadsheet showing the amount of scrap generated on a monthly basis by product line.
8. The auditor downloads client data to create a report showing sales and inventory level by product line on a monthly basis.

16–49 (Expense Fraud) Each year Susan Riley, president of Bargon Construction, Inc., takes a three-week vacation to Hawaii and signs several checks to pay major bills during the period she is absent. The vacation often occurs near the end of Bargon's fiscal reporting period because it is a slack time for the construction business. Jack Morgan, head bookkeeper for the company, uses this practice to his advantage. He makes out a check to himself for the amount of a large vendor's invoice and records it as a payment to the vendor for the purchase of supplies. He holds the check for several weeks to make sure the auditors will not examine the canceled check. Shortly after the first of the year, Morgan resubmits the invoice to Riley for payment approval and records the check in the cash disbursements journal. At that point, he marks the invoice "paid" and files it with all other paid invoices. Morgan has been following this practice successfully for several years and feels confident that he has developed a foolproof fraud.

Required:

a. What is the auditor's responsibility for discovering this type of embezzlement?

b. What weaknesses exist in the client's internal control structure?

c. What audit procedures are likely to uncover the fraud?

16–50 (Acquisition Controls: Small Business) Because of the small size of the company and the limited number of accounting personnel, Dry Goods Wholesale Company initially records all acquisitions of goods and services at the time cash disbursements are made. At the end of each quarter when financial statements for internal purposes are prepared, accounts payable are recorded by adjusting journal entries. The entries are reversed at the beginning of the subsequent period. Except for the lack of an accounts payable or vouchers journal, the controls over acquisitions are excellent for a small company. (There are adequate prenumbered documents for all acquisitions, proper approvals, and adequate internal verification where appropriate.)

Before the auditor arrives for the year-end audit, the bookkeeper prepares adjusting entries to record the accounts payable as of the balance sheet date. A list of all outstanding balances is prepared by vendor and is given to the auditor. All vendors' invoices supporting the list are retained in a separate file for the auditor's use.

During the current year, the accounts payable balance has increased dramatically because of a severe cash shortage. (The cash shortage apparently arose from expansion of inventory and facilities rather than lack of sales.) Many accounts have remained unpaid for several months, and the client is getting pressure from several vendors to pay the bills. Because the company had a relatively profitable year, management is anxious to complete the audit as early as possible so that the audited statements can be used to obtain a large bank loan.

Required:

a. Explain how the lack of an accounts payable or vouchers journal will affect the auditor's test of transactions for acquisitions and payments.

b. What should the auditor use as a sampling unit in performing tests of expenses and accounts payable?

c. Assuming there are no errors discovered in the auditor's tests of transactions for acquisitions and payments, how will that result affect the verification of accounts payable?

d. Discuss the reasonableness of the client's requests for an early completion of the audit and the implications of the request from the auditor's point of view.

e. List the audit procedures that should be performed in the year-end audit of accounts payable to meet the cutoff objective.

f. State your opinion as to whether it is possible to conduct an adequate audit in these circumstances.

*16–51 (Internal Audit of Accounts Payable) In conjunction with the proposed acquisition of a major competitor in the same industry, the internal audit department of the acquiring company has audited the accounts payable of the company to be acquired. The reported accounts payable balance was $1,750,000 and represented the cost of purchases from outside suppliers for goods and services used in regular operations.

Tests were performed with data gathered as follows:

1. Reviewed internal controls over accounts payable. Auditors read the accounting policy manuals, familiarized themselves with the general ledger system, observed the accounts payable activity, walked several transactions through the accounting system (from purchase requisition through receipt to initial recording), and completed the internal control questionnaire after interviewing management.
2. Selected a sample of entries in accounts payable and vouched the entries to supporting documents (purchase requisition, purchase order, and receiving report).
3. Obtained a schedule of accounts payable by supplier. Footed this schedule and checked its agreement to the general ledger and financial statement balances.
4. Performed a cutoff test. Verified the cutoff for both inventory and accounts payable by tracing receipt of goods to inventory records and the accounts payable subsidiary ledger.
5. Reviewed supporting documentation for selected accounts payable to ascertain whether any items were of special character requiring reclassification. Tests of authorization and valuation were performed.
6. Confirmed accounts payable with small or zero balances. Differences were then investigated and resolved.
7. Prepared an aging schedule of accounts payable.

Required:

a. For each procedure described, identify the type of evidence gathered.

b. Identify the audit objective of each procedure.

*16–52 (Accounts Payable Procedures) Kane, CPA, is auditing Star Wholesaling Company's financial statements and is about to perform substantive audit procedures on Star's trade accounts payable balances. After obtaining an understanding of Star's internal control structure for accounts payable,

Kane assessed control risk at the maximum. Kane requested and received from Star a schedule of the trade accounts payable prepared using the trade accounts payable subsidiary ledger (voucher register).

Required:
Describe the substantive audit procedures Kane should apply to Star's trade accounts payable balances.

16–53 (Sampling of Perpetual Records) Ace Corporation does not conduct a complete annual physical count of purchased parts and supplies in its principal warehouse but uses statistical sampling instead to estimate the year-end inventory. Ace maintains a perpetual inventory record of parts and supplies and believes that statistical sampling is highly effective in determining inventory values and is sufficiently reliable to make a physical count of each item of inventory unnecessary.

Required:

a. Identify the audit procedures that should be used by the independent auditor that change or are in addition to normal required audit procedures when a client utilizes statistical sampling to determine inventory value and does not conduct a 100 percent annual physical count of inventory items.
b. List at least 10 normal audit procedures that should be performed to verify physical quantities when a client conducts a periodic physical count of all or part of its inventory.

16–54 (Acquisition and Payment Cycle Audit Procedures) Following are some of the tests of transactions procedures frequently performed in the acquisition and payment cycle. Each is to be done on a sample basis.

Required:

a. State whether each procedure is primarily a test of control or a substantive test of transactions.
b. State the purpose(s) of each procedure.

Audit Procedures:

1. Trace transactions recorded in the purchase journal to supporting documentation, comparing the vendor's name, total dollar amounts, and authorization for purchase.
2. Account for a sequence of receiving reports and trace selected ones to related vendor's invoices and purchase journal entries.
3. Review supporting documents for clerical accuracy, propriety of account distribution, and reasonableness of expenditure in relation to the nature of the client's operations.
4. Examine documents in support of acquisition transactions to make sure that each transaction has an approved vendor's invoice, receiving report, and purchase order included.
5. Foot the cash disbursements journal, trace postings of the total to the general ledger, and trace postings of individual payments to the accounts payable master file.

6. Account for a numerical sequence of checks in the cash disbursements journal and examine all voided or spoiled checks for proper cancellation.
7. Compare dates on canceled checks with dates on the cash disbursements journal and the bank cancellation date.

16–55 (Analysis of Errors) The following errors or omissions are included in the accounting records of Westgate Manufacturing Company.

Required:

a. For each error, identify the internal control objective that was not met.
b. For each error, identify a control procedure that should have prevented it from occurring on a continuing basis.
c. For each error, identify a substantive audit procedure that could uncover it.

Errors or Omissions Noted:

1. Telephone expense (account 2112) was unintentionally charged to repairs and maintenance (account 2121).
2. Purchases of raw materials are frequently not recorded until several weeks after the goods are received due to the failure of the receiving personnel to forward receiving reports to accounting. When pressure is received from a vendor's credit department, the accounts payable department searches for the receiving report, records the transactions in the accounts payable journal, and pays the bill.
3. The accounts payable clerk prepares a monthly check to Story Supply Company for the amount of an invoice owed and submits the unsigned check to the treasurer for payment along with related supporting documents. When she receives the signed check from the treasurer, she records it as a debit to Accounts Payable and deposits the check in a personal bank account for a company named Story Company. A few days later, she records the invoice in the accounts payable journal, resubmits the documents and a new check to the treasurer, and sends the check to the vendor after it has been signed.
4. The amount of a check in the cash disbursements journal is recorded as $4,612.87 instead of $4,162.87.
5. The accounts payable clerk intentionally excluded from the cash disbursements journal seven large checks written and mailed on December 26 to prevent cash in the bank from having a negative balance on the general ledger. They were recorded on January 2 of the subsequent year.
6. Each month a fictitious receiving report is submitted to accounting by an employee in the receiving department. A few days later, he sends Westgate an invoice for the quantity of goods ordered from a small company he owns and operates. The invoice is paid when the receiving report and the vendor's invoice are matched by the accounts payable clerk.

16–56 (Inventory Observation) The auditor is required by existing auditing standards to observe the client's inventory. That requirement could be met by observing the client's annual physical count of inventory, and, in some circumstances, by observing inventory in connection with tests of the accuracy of a client's perpetual inventory.

Required:

a. What is the major purpose served by requiring the auditor to observe the client's physical inventory count? Why is the rationale behind the profession's decision to require the inventory observation?

b. Identify at least five items related to inventory items that the auditor should be looking for and should note on a working paper prepared during the observation of the client's inventory.

c. How does the nature of the observation process differ when an auditor chooses to observe inventory through testing of the perpetual records as opposed to observing the client's annual count of its physical inventory?

16–57 (Inventory Obsolescence Tests) You have been assigned to the audit of Technotrics, a company specializing in the wholesale of a wide variety of electronic products. Its major product lines are stereo and similar electronic equipment and computers and computer add-ons such as hard disks, memory boards, and so forth. The client has four major warehouses located in Atlanta, Las Vegas, Minneapolis, and Philadelphia. At year-end, the client has approximately $250 million in inventory, an increase of $7 million.

Required:

a. Indicate how the auditor would gain information on major changes in products handled by the client and the effect of competition on the existing products.

b. Indicate how the client could use generalized audit software to search for slow-moving or potentially obsolete goods in the client's year-end inventory.

c. What other procedures might the auditor utilize in determining whether significant portions of the client's year-end inventory has a market value less than cost?

16–58 (Inventory Cutoff Problem) The auditor has gathered shipping cutoff information for Johnny M. Golf Company in conjunction with its December 31 year-end. The auditor has observed the client's year-end physical inventory and is satisfied with the client's inventory procedures. The client has adjusted the year-end book value to the physical inventory compilation (book to physical adjustment) so that the account balance at year-end equals the physical count. For purposes of analysis, you should assume that all items have a gross margin of 30 percent. The last shipping document and bill of lading used during the current year is 4500 and is the primary evidence as to whether the goods were shipped before or after inventory. All shipping documents are sequentially numbered, and the auditor has established that the client uses them in order.

The shipping date listed in the journal is the date recorded on the sales invoice. Cost of goods sold is recorded at the same time the invoice is recorded.

December Sales Journal

Date	Billed to	Shipping Terms	Ship Date	Ship Number	Amount
12/31	Bartifshoski Electric	FOB shipping point	12/31	4498	$ 4,500
12/31	Schlagel Electric	FOB shipping point	12/31	4501	$11,000
12/31	Schenk Comptometer	FOB shipping point	12/31	4502	$20,000
12/31	Schoone Const.	FOB shipping point	1/3	4503	$20,000
12/31	Tomahawk Const.	FOB destination	12/31	4496	$10,000

January Sales Journal

Date	Billed to	Shipping Terms	Ship Date	Ship Number	Amount
1/3	Smith Electric	FOB shipping point	12/31	4504	$10,000
1/3	Lampley Const.	FOB shipping point	1/3	4499	$ 8,000
1/3	Montana Mt. Const.	FOB shipping point	1/3	4505	$12,000

Required:

a. Briefly discuss why the auditor would rely on the shipping document number instead of the recorded shipping date as the primary evidence of whether the goods were shipped before or after inventory.

b. Identify the items that should be adjusted. Prepare a journal entry to record the adjustments to Cost of Goods Sold, Inventory, Accounts Receivable, and Sales based on the preceding data. Prepare the journal entries needed only for the December 31 year-end.

c. Assume that the client took physical inventory on October 31 and adjusted the books to the physical inventory at that time. Given the information from the December and January sales journals above, prepare the necessary year-end adjusting entries. Why are the entries different from those suggested for b?

*16–59 (Organization of Acquisition Function) The organization structure of a manufacturing firm includes the following departments: purchasing, receiving, inspecting, warehousing, and the controllership. An internal auditor is assigned to audit the receiving department. The preliminary survey reveals the following information:

- A copy of each purchase order is routinely sent to the receiving department by the purchasing department. Intracompany mail is used. Each purchase order is filed by purchase order number. In response to a job enrichment program, everyone in receiving is authorized to file the purchase orders. Whoever happens to be available when the company mail is received is expected to file any purchase orders it contains.

- When a shipment of goods is brought to the receiving dock, the shipper's invoice is signed and forwarded to the controller's office, the vendor's packing slip is filed in receiving by vendor name, and the goods are stored in the warehouse by receiving personnel. In response to a job enrichment program, all persons in receiving have been trained to perform all three activities independently and without the notification of anyone else. Whoever happens to be available when a shipment arrives is expected to perform all three of the activities associated with that shipment.

Required:
Based on the information provided, draft a portion of a preliminary internal audit report for discussion with the head of the receiving department. Include only the following headings: (1) purchase order, (2) shipper's invoice, (3) vendor's packing slip, and (4) warehousing. Under each heading, discuss only the following subheadings: (a) criteria for assessing potential weaknesses, (b) facts, (c) cause of potential problems or control deficiencies, (d) potential effect, and (e) recommendations. Use the following format for each major heading:

1. Purchase order
   a. Criteria
   b. Facts
   c. Cause
   d. Potential effect
   e. Recommendations

16–60 (Inventory Valuation and Adjustments) Inshalla Retail Company keeps its inventory on a perpetual FIFO basis for internal reporting but adjusts the year-end FIFO balance to a LIFO basis using a dollar value LIFO index. The auditor is satisfied that the FIFO perpetual inventory is accurate. The LIFO adjustment is made by calculating an index for each of the company's four product lines. The index is applied to determine whether there was an increase or decrease in inventory for the year and the appropriate entry is made.

Required:
Explain how the auditor would audit the LIFO adjustment.

16–61 (Analytical Procedures) One of the firm's largest clients, Ropper Company, makes gas grills, gas stoves, and gas dryers. Its financial position has deteriorated, but its management is confident that the worst has past. Management points to new home starts associated with the current drop in interest rates and notes that it has implemented total quality management in operations and has cut down the number of defects in products. However, the auditor remembers reading *Consumer's Report,* which indicated that Ropper has had a much higher than average incidence of repairs in recent years. The relevant financial information for the past four years is as follows (dollars stated in millions, 1994, is unaudited):

	1994	1993	1992	1991
Sales	$178.4	$162.0	$160.2	$154.3
Sales returns and allowances	2.1	8.3	7.4	6.8
Returns as a percentage of sales	1.17%	5.12%	4.62%	4.40%
Net income	8.3	2.1	2.8	3.1

Required:
a. Suggest reasons for the different level of sales returns in 1994. Prioritize the list based on the information given above.

b. Indicate the inquiries and follow-up audit procedures that might be performed before developing specific audit procedures to test the most likely hypotheses.

16–62 (Analysis of Price Test Results) The auditor for Toron Company, a manufacturer of lawnmowers and snowblowers, has used PPS sampling to draw a sample as a basis to perform a price test of ending inventory. The following information is available for your review and analysis:

Inventory at year-end:	
Materials and work-in-process	$ 8,450,000
Finished goods	9,500,000
Total	$17,950,000
Number of items sampled	132 (62 on raw material and 70 on finished goods)
Number of items in error	15 (11 on raw material and 4 on finished goods)
Dollars sampled—raw materials	$ 1,841,000
Dollars sampled—finished goods	$ 2,345,000
Raw materials:	
Errors of overstatement	$ 85,000
Most likely error	$ 225,000
Upper error limit	$ 475,000
Finished goods:	
Errors of overstatement	$ 3,000
Most likely error	$ 8,000
Upper error limit	$ 28,000
Planning materiality	$ 350,000

Analysis of errors: Ten of the 11 errors related to the raw material inventory involved the failure to record a manufacturing volume rebate on the purchase of a basic component (engines from Briggs and Stratton). The other error was due to a clerical mistake in paying the wrong amount for an invoice. The four errors on finished goods were due to transferring outdated standard costs to the product.

Required:

a. Do the statistical results merit additional audit work? Explain.

b. Assuming that additional audit work is merited, identify the procedures the auditor should utilize to finish the testing of inventory costing. If the auditor should have the client perform additional work, identify the work the client should perform.

16–63 **(Research)** Perform a literature search involving business failures and inventory (key word search through an automated library or through the LEXIS facility of Mead Data). Identify the role that inappropriate accounting for inventory played in disguising the business problems of the organization before it finally went bankrupt. How were inventory misstatements covered up? What audit procedures would have led to the detection of the inventory misstatements?

16–64 **(Research)** Review trade journals for the retail or manufacturing industries to determine the extent that automated purchase and receiving systems have been implemented. Identify the various approaches taken by the organizations in automating the functions.

Case

16–65 (Case—CMH) Could the fraud at CMH (see the Real World Application in the chapter) have been detected if standard audit procedures had been used to observe the client's physical inventory? Explain why it is important that auditors assigned to the observation of a client's inventory be knowledgeable about the client's products and experienced in inventory observations.

16–66 (CMH Case—SEC Alleged Deficiencies) The SEC alleged that many deficiencies occurred during the audit of CMH as discussed in the Real World Application in the chapter. Among the complaints were the following:

- The audit firm "left the extent of various observation testing to the discretion of auditors, not all of whom were aware of significant audit conclusions which related directly to the extent of such testing. Observation of inventory counts at year end was confined to six locations (representing about 40% of the total CMH inventory) as opposed to nine in the preceding year. The field auditors did not adequately control the inventory tags and Seidman & Seidman did not detect the creation of bogus inventory tags which were inserted in the final inventory computations."
- The comparison of recorded test counts to the computer lists in the nine warehouse locations in which the inventory count was observed (in 1973) indicated error rates ranging from .9 percent to 38.3 percent of the test counts, with error rates in excess of 10 percent in several locations. Management attributed the differences to errors made by a keypunch operator. When the auditors asked to see the inventory tags, the CMH official stated that they had been destroyed.
- The Seidman auditor who performed the price testing of the CMH inventory determined that, as in previous years, in numerous instances CMH was unable to produce sufficient vendor invoices to support the purchase by CMH of the quantities being tested. This was true even though Seidman & Seidman ultimately accepted vendor invoices reflecting the purchase of the item by any CMH branch, regardless of the location of the inventory actually being price tested.
- A schedule of comparative inventory balances reflected significant increases from the prior year. A CMH financial officer wrote on this schedule management's explanations for the increases in inventory accounts.
- CMH did not utilize prenumbered purchase orders and shipping documents.

- There were a number of differences between the tags reflected on the computer list for the Miami warehouse and the observation of the same tag numbers by the Seidman & Seidman auditors. The computer list contained a series of almost 1,000 tags, covering about 20 percent of the tags purportedly used and more than 50 percent of the total reported value of the Miami inventory, which were reported as being unused on the tag control document obtained by Seidman & Seidman during its observation work.
- Because CMH management did not provide sufficient invoices as requested, the auditors relied primarily on vendor catalogs, price lists, and vendor invoices to test the accuracy of the CMH inventory pricing representations.

Required:

a. For each of the deficiencies identified above, indicate the appropriate action that should have been taken by the auditor.
b. What inventory information should be communicated to an auditor who is not regularly assigned to the audit of a particular client prior to the observation of a physical inventory count?
c. How do questions of management integrity affect the approach that should be taken in planning the observation of a client's inventory-counting procedures?

Computer Assisted Problems

Problems for this chapter using the adVenture software are in the Appendix at the end of the book. You should read the introduction and instructions before working the problems. These problems are:

C-9. Using Attribute Sampling to Perform a Dual-Purpose Test of Cash Disbursements.

C-10. Using Sampling to Test Subsequent Disbursements.

C-11. Using Attribute Sampling to Perform Dual-Purpose Tests of Receiving Report Processing.

C-12. Using Generalized Audit Software to Test Perpetual Inventory.

C-13. Using Sampling to Test the Perpetual Inventory Account Balance.

End Note

1. "Short Circuit: How Mounting Woes at Crazy Eddie Sank a Turnaround Effort," *The Wall Street Journal*, July 10, 1989, 1.

CHAPTER

17

Learning Objectives

Through studying this chapter, you should be able to:

1. Understand the unique factors associated with employee compensation and related benefits.
2. Understand the magnitude and diversity of employee compensation expenses.
3. Identify and understand the major elements of a control structure for employee compensation and benefits.
4. Develop an audit approach for employee compensation and related benefits.
5. Understand the human resources function and its control implications.

Audit of Employee Compensation and Related Benefits

Chapter Contents

Chapter Overview

Employee compensation has become an increasingly complex and diverse management area. It no longer involves simply providing a paycheck at the end of the work week. Compensation also includes plans for postretirement employee benefits such as pensions and the provision of health care. Government regulations affect most compensation plans and may require that the company comply with specific rules or procedures. The auditor needs to understand the broad control structure for the administration of employee benefits in order to assess the risks of financial misstatements or inadequate disclosure.

Other Post Retirement Employee Benefits (OPEB) plan terms are sometimes not as well defined as those of a pension plan. The promise may be an unwritten but well-established practice of providing benefits; or, the substance of an employer's promise to provide OPEB may extend beyond the written terms of the plan.. . . The open-ended nature of promises to provide health care and the sheer size of the unaccrued obligations present employers with significant accounting and business challenges. The primary business challenge is to provide an appropriate level of retiree benefits at the lowest possible cost. The accounting challenge is to quantify the promises made to provide in-kind benefits. This requires estimates of cost far into the distant future.[1]

Management is responsible for making the accounting estimates included in the financial statements. Estimates are based on subjective as well as objective factors and, as a result, judgment is required to estimate an amount at the date of the financial statements. Management's judgment is normally based on its knowledge and experience about past and current events and its assumptions about conditions it expects to exist and courses of action it expects to take. The auditor is responsible for evaluating the reasonableness of accounting estimates made by management in the context of the financial statements taken as a whole. [AU 342.03 and 342.04]

The quotes point out potential audit problems associated with employee compensation and benefits. Employee compensation and related benefits constitute a major portion of most organizations' total expenditures. Compensation may take the form of hourly payroll, salary payroll, health care benefits, retirement benefits, postretirement health benefits, insurance, payroll taxes, and even day-care services provided for employees. Organizations may encounter other employee-related costs if they fail to file appropriate forms with regulatory agencies on a timely basis or if they fail to design and implement personnel policies that ensure that the organization will not perform discriminatory actions. Most large organizations have established human resource departments and have invested millions of dollars in human resource accounting systems to manage personnel and related expenses and to ensure compliance with applicable state and federal regulations. In today's environment, human resource management involves much more than recruiting and compensation. Today's auditor must understand the human resource functions, the nature of employee compensation, and computerized systems that automatically capture employee time and prepare relevant payroll checks and related financial information.

A–PAYROLL AND RELATED EXPENSES

Payroll includes amounts paid to both salaried and hourly wage earners. It may also include individuals whose compensation is based on piecework commissions, bonuses, and profit-sharing plans. Related expenses include vacation pay, insurance, pensions, other employee benefits, and payroll taxes. Although an audit of payroll is not generally considered complicated, the increased complexity of supplemental compensation and benefit packages creates difficult accounting and audit issues that require additional audit attention.

Payroll usually represents one of the largest expenses in most organizations. The magnitude of the expense makes the proper accounting and control structure important to the auditor. In addition, payroll is of interest to the auditor because it has often been the subject of fraud or misuse. For example, the press reported that Charles Keating had nine relatives on the payroll of Lincoln Savings & Loan (or its parent), each at a salary either approaching or exceeding $1 million. Frauds can easily take place in the payroll area if controls are not sufficient. It might be easy, for example, to insert a fictitious employee on the payroll and send checks directly to a prearranged address.

Payroll is also important because it directly affects the inventory account. Further, many other expenses are directly associated with payroll. The auditor should understand the nature of a client's compensation package as a basis for determining the expense and related liabilities associated with these other types of compensation.

Understanding the Payroll Control Structure

The major control components of payroll processing include the following:

1. A *personnel department* responsible for screening applicants, hiring new personnel, and administering personnel issues.
2. A *human resources department* responsible for negotiating long-term union contracts, setting pay rates, and developing contracts for employee benefits. The human resources department may also be responsible for government compliance reports.
3. A *payroll department* responsible for adding and deleting employees to the payroll based on authorization from the personnel department, receiving input on hours worked, implementing wage rate changes, preparing accounting reports, computing payroll and issuing checks, preparing tax forms, and remitting payroll withholdings to the appropriate agencies.
4. A *computerized data processing function* designed to automate payroll processing and facilitate report preparation.
5. *Employees* who receive paychecks and recalculate their earnings to detect underpayment of earned wages.

Exhibit 17.1 presents an overview of the components of a control structure for payroll. The structure is designed to provide segregation of duties so that one group (or individual) is not in a position to add employees to the payroll, input employee time data, and create paychecks. Departmental management regularly receives labor expense reports to assist in monitoring labor expense. Control is enhanced when

Exhibit 17.1

OVERVIEW OF PAYROLL CONTROL STRUCTURE

Personnel Department	Human Resources	Payroll Department	Data Processing

• Plan personnel needs.
• Develop and administer personnel policies.
• Recruit and screen potential new employees.
• Authorize additions to payroll after offer is made by department managers and acceptance is made by employee.
• Authorize additions to and deletions from payroll.
• Keep relevant personnel records.
	• Negotiate and administer employee contracts.
	• Develop and administer comprehensive employee database capable of preparing management and regulatory reports.
	• Monitor company compliance with regulations, administer legal proceedings involving personnel issues.
		• Develop (with data processing) payroll applications and relevant processing control procedures.
		• Process all payroll data including:
		  • Addition of employees to file or deletion of them on written authorization by personnel department.
		  • Changes in wage rates or job classifications.
		  • Development of paychecks and associated withholdings.
		  • Development of payroll distribution reports and other management reports.
			• Provide computerized data processing of all payroll.
			• Maintain limited access to payroll files and records per the policies set by the payroll and human resources departments.
			• Implement changes to computer application and files as authorized by payroll department and human resources department.
			• Generate paychecks or direct deposit tapes to deposit employee wages into specified bank accounts.
			• Develop control reports to identify potential out-of-control conditions.

exception reports regularly compare actual expense with expectations and timely investigation and corrective action is taken.

The Human Resources and Personnel Departments

The **human resources department** and personnel department are responsible for screening new hires, administering employee compensation policies, and keeping records to ensure that employees are properly compensated in compliance with governmental and company regulations. The departments maintain records of employees and potential benefits due each employee. The benefits may range from accrued vacation and sick leave to pension benefits and other postretirement health plans. In some cases, the human resources department negotiates long-term labor contracts, but most contracts, such as the Ford Motor Company labor agreement with the United Auto Workers, require senior management approval. The personnel and human resource departments are often combined in smaller organizations.

The personnel department should provide a list of all employee changes to the payroll department. Changes include the addition or termination of employees, as well as changes in wage rates, job classifications, withholdings, and benefits. Payroll changes should be summarized and reviewed for completeness and correctness by the initiating (personnel) department.

The personnel and human resources departments should not process employee pay because of the potential for fraud when the functions are combined. Some human resources departments, however, administer employee benefit plans. If it does, there should be segregation of duties within the department and supervisory review, so that an individual is not in a position both to approve someone for the benefits and to generate a payment for the benefits.

Often the human resources department is responsible for administering employee-employer litigation involving discrimination, workers' compensation, or negligence caused by unsafe working conditions. The auditor should inquire of the nature of any such litigation and assess the likelihood that a liability should be recorded.

Many companies must prepare reports to show compliance with federal laws and regulations. A construction contractor, for example, bidding on a federally funded highway project must employ a minimum percentage of disadvantaged work groups to receive the contract. Failure to comply with these requirements can result in forfeiture of existing contracts, the imposition of penalties and/or fines, and losses of contracts.

Human Resources Information Systems

The need to administer the human resource function, maintain compliance with governmental regulations, and process increasingly complex retirement benefits has led to the development of comprehensive database systems to effectively manage requirements. Payroll processing often becomes a by-product of these systems. Other accounting data, such as estimates of the pension liability, may be generated from these systems.

The Payroll Department

The payroll department is responsible for capturing hours worked data, preparing employee paychecks, and accounting for employee services and related benefits. A number of documents are generated in that process, including these:

- Employee paychecks or direct deposits to banks.
- Pension benefit checks or direct deposits to banks.
- Reports on employee withholdings and checks to governmental units (and other organizations) for amounts withheld and for the employer's share of the benefits.
- Labor cost distribution reports.
- Management reports, including, but not limited to (1) reports on employees and hours paid within specific departments, (2) labor variance reports, and

(3) labor efficiency reports. The payroll department also prepares payroll tax returns, develops the year-end payroll liability, and updates each employee's earnings record.

Data Processing and Payroll

In all but the smallest companies, payroll is processed by a computer system. Many small clients contract with service bureaus to process weekly and monthly payroll. As production systems become more automated, the timekeeping process becomes automated as well. Employees may no longer punch time cards but will log in at a data capture machine and record data on jobs worked on to facilitate the preparation of management reports.

The data processing function and its users are responsible for implementing control procedures to ensure the following:

- Access to employee data and master files are restricted to those authorized to review or make changes to them.
- Data transmissions of employee work data are complete and accurate.
- Data have been edited for correctness.
- Distribution of output (paychecks and direct deposit tapes) are limited to authorized parties.
- Changes to applications and file data are made on a timely basis.
- Payroll reports are distributed only to authorized parties.

Gaining an Understanding of the Control Environment

The auditor's understanding of the payroll control environment serves as the basis to determine the most efficient audit approach. The understanding may be obtained through interviews and the use of an internal control questionnaire similar to the one illustrated in Exhibit 17.2. The questionnaire is designed to assist the auditor in understanding the organizational and processing structure of the payroll area and covers all four functions: personnel, human resources, payroll, and data processing. Information is also gathered on the existence of personnel-related litigation and the organization's response to it. Finally, information on computer-based control procedures, the user's role in developing and testing the computer systems, and the use of management exception reports is gathered.

Operational Audits of Personnel Function: A Control Strength

In addition to regular audits of payroll processing, internal audit departments often perform operational audits of the personnel and human resource departments to determine compliance with company and regulatory policies and to determine the effectiveness and efficiency of operations. The audits often address the following:

- The adequacy of personnel policies and the company's adherence to them.
- Compliance with governmental regulations.
- The role of departmental management in selecting employees.
- Adherence to performance bases for promotion.

Exhibit 17.2

CONTROL ENVIRONMENT ASSESSMENT QUESTIONNAIRE—PAYROLL

Control Environment Questions: Payroll	Yes	No	N/A
Personnel			
1. Does a separate personnel department exist?			
2. Does the personnel department act as an independent check on the payroll processing by			
a. Screening and authorizing new employee hires?			
b. Authorizing changes in employee job classification and payrates?			
c. Maintaining independent records of employee performance?			
3. Does the personnel department review all changes made to the major tables (computer reference files) for employee wage rates to ensure that all changes are made as authorized? After changes have been made by payroll, does the personnel department independently receive a printout of the tables and reconcile the changes to the list of authorized changes?			
4. Are terminations processed in a timely fashion to ensure that employees are not paid for services not rendered?			
Human Resources Department			
1. Are major labor contracts reviewed by top management before approval?			
2. Does the department prepare analyses of the future expected costs of benefits negotiated during the labor negotiation process? For example, are estimates prepared on the cost of future health costs when postretirement employee benefits are negotiated?			
3. Does the department administer benefit programs that include the disbursement of funds by the department? If yes, indicate the control procedures implemented to ensure that payments are not made to unauthorized individuals.			
4. Does the department prepare federal compliance reports on a timely basis? If not, is there any potential liability applicable to late filing of the reports?			
5. Are wage contracts sufficiently monitored to ensure compliance with federal privacy act provisions?			
6. Is there any pending litigation against the company alleging employee discrimination or employer misconduct? If yes, obtain a complete description of the status of such litigation.			

- Competitiveness of compensation policies.
- Administration of the functions and the adequacy of the organization's control structure for maintaining the personnel database and administering benefit programs, if applicable.

The auditor should review the internal auditor's report to determine potential implications for the planning of the external audit.

Exhibit 17.2

	Yes	No	N/A
Payroll Department			
1. Is the payroll department sufficiently segregated from the personnel and production functions to ensure that only authorized individuals are added to the payroll and only authorized individuals are paid? Explain.	____	____	____
2. Is there an independent authorization of the hours worked for hourly employees, or does the department provide summary reports to supervisors of all employees and hours worked for the time period for review and approval by the supervisors? Explain the procedures utilized by the entity.	____	____	____
3. Who distributes the paychecks to employees? Are sufficient controls established to help ensure that fictitious employees are not being paid?	____	____	____
4. Are all payroll tax reports and filings filed on a timely basis? If not, might penalty provisions be applicable?	____	____	____
Computer-Based Control Procedures			
1. Are all major user groups (personnel, human resources, payroll, and supervisory management) involved in major changes to the payroll and personnel computer applications? Do the user groups exercise authority over changes to the payroll application? Are controls independently reviewed and tested by both users and the internal audit department?	____	____	____
2. Are access controls over computer tables and applications sufficient to ensure that unauthorized parties do not have the ability to change existing records or to input new records?	____	____	____
Other			
1. Are exception reports prepared and effectively used by supervisory management to ensure that timely action is taken on major labor problems?	____	____	____
2. Is the accounting for labor costs periodically reviewed by the accounting department, especially cost accounting, to ensure that labor is appropriately allocated to inventory costs, overhead, and administrative expense?	____	____	____

Understanding and Testing Application Control Procedures

It is usually efficient to simultaneously test payroll-related transactions and control procedures. The tests should include both manual and computerized controls.

Overview of Computer Control Procedures

The elements of the computer processing of payroll are shown in a simplified fashion in Exhibit 17.3. The processing of payroll can be viewed within a framework of

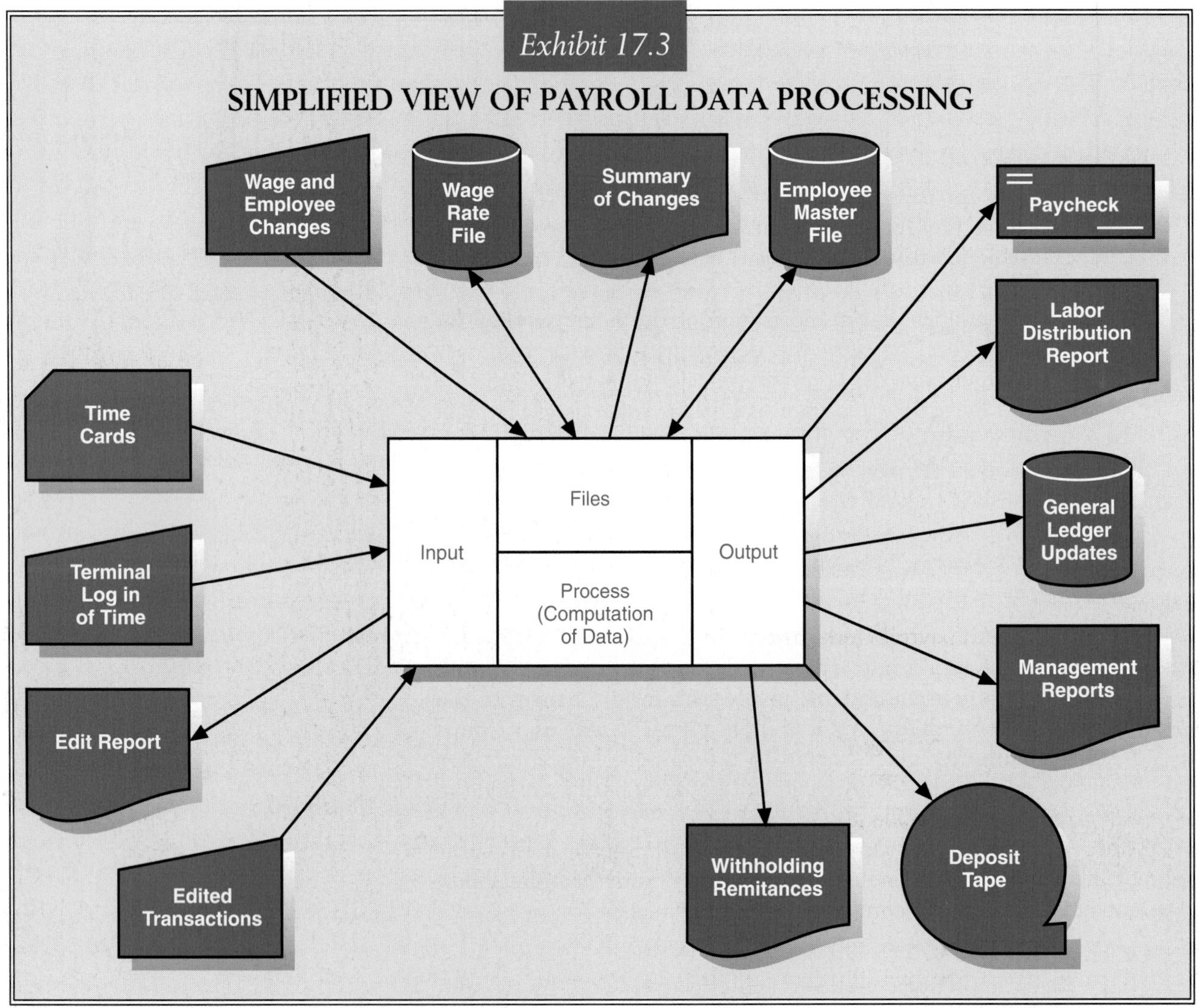

four primary functions: input, output, processing, and files. Also shown are the basic input items into the payroll application and the major outputs. Auditors review the manual and computerized control procedures as well as the management control procedures designed to monitor the effectiveness of processing. An example of the latter is the exception report that management uses to review labor expense by department.

Input. Time cards or computer log in of time provide the major input to the payroll application. The data are edited by the application control program and an edit report is prepared for all items failing the computer edit controls. Typical edit controls were discussed in Chapter 9 and include these:

- Self-checking digits on employee ID number or job code data.
- Limit tests on hours worked.

- Reconciliation of hours worked and hours charged to jobs.
- Valid job codes.
- Valid employee ID numbers.

The edit report is sent to payroll, which investigates and makes necessary changes either to correct the items or to indicate that the input data were valid, for example, that an employee actually worked 75 hours during the previous week. Audit information is gathered on the effectiveness of edit controls implemented, the reliability of the data capture process, and timeliness and completeness of corrections to initially rejected data.

Computer Files (Tables). Payroll applications should reference data that are common to a group of employees but that might change frequently. Common examples include wage rates for each job classification and employee job history. The data are stored in computer files (often referred to as **computer tables**). The payroll program can reference the files for information such as employee wage rate. Changes made to wage rates or other basic data are made to the tables rather than changing the application program or changing the individual employee's records.

Access to the tables should be limited to authorized employees. All changes should be independently reviewed by someone other than the individual making them. For example, a payroll clerk may make changes to the files, but the departmental supervisor should review a printout of the changed master file to ensure that all changes are made as authorized.

Processing. The processing function is relatively simple. The number of hours worked is multiplied by the wage rate to determine gross pay. Calculations are made for overtime hours, withholdings, and net pay. The process also calculates summary figures to apply labor cost to inventory or jobs. The amounts due for withholding remittances are also calculated and used to update master files and generate disbursements.

Output. The major outputs of the payroll application are paychecks, updated employee master files, job cost data, and accounting file updates. Most of these updates prepare paper-based reports. However, the trend is to automate much of this process. Rather than generating paychecks, many organizations now send employee deposits to financial institutions via electronic media. The employee may receive only a printout of the pay stub and a verification of the deposit in the financial institution's monthly statement. Similarly, withholdings of federal tax can be electronically transferred to the IRS. Thus, in many instances, the auditor is not able to examine paper documents but must review the control procedures designed to ensure completeness of processing or perform other substantive tests such as analytical review.

Important Computer Control Procedures

The auditor should gain assurance that computerized control procedures are implemented and are working properly. The following types of control procedures should be reviewed:

- **Access control procedures** to ensure that only authorized employees are allowed to make changes to data files or computerized tables. Control is strengthened if the personnel department conducts an independent review of all changes to the payroll tables.

- **Batch controls** (record counts, control totals, and hash totals) to ensure that all data entered are processed. An effective control procedure for salaried payroll is to reconcile the total number of paychecks issued with the number of currently active employees on the master file.
- **Edit controls** to ensure that unusual data are rejected and reviewed by the payroll department to determine the validity of the input. Edit controls normally include limit tests, self-checking digits on employee or job numbers, overall reasonableness tests, and alpha-numeric tests.
- **Output controls** to ensure that output are distributed to appropriate parties. Control procedures are needed to ensure that payroll checks are delivered to authorized employees and that sensitive data are distributed only to authorized members of management.

Other specific control procedures should be reviewed if they are important to the application. If the client, for example, uses distributed processing, the data transmission control procedures should be tested.

Approach to Testing Control Procedures and Correctness of Processing

The auditor can select either manual or computerized audit approaches to test the adequacy of control procedures and the correctness of payroll processing. Approaches that should be considered by the auditor include the following:

1. Select source documents such as time cards and trace through the recording process to the generation of a paycheck.
2. Select a sample of recorded payroll transactions and trace to source documents such as time cards or other recording media.
3. Use the test data approach or an integrated test facility to process auditor-submitted transactions.

The first two approaches have traditionally been used. The first approach effectively tests completeness, cutoff, and valuation. The second approach tests for existence as well as valuation (validity of employee). As systems have become more automated, many internal auditors and some external auditors use test data or the integrated test facility to test for the completeness and correctness of processing. However, as noted in Chapter 10, such an approach does not ensure that all employees are paid; it tests only for the correctness of processing once an item is entered into the system.

Tracing from Source Document to Payroll Calculation

The auditor selects a sample of source documents such as time cards or personnel department lists of salaried employees, traces the data to the calculation of gross pay, and recomputes applicable deductions to determine that payroll is accurately computed and allocated to the appropriate jobs. The audit test also examines the authorization for payment, wage rates, and withholdings. Correctness of processing—even within a computer environment—is tested through the auditor's recomputations.

Special Considerations When Time Cards Are Not Prepared. Many organizations have implemented automated time collection systems to facilitate the capturing of detailed labor data. Employees use cards and personal identification numbers to log in time worked and jobs worked on. The appropriate audit approach depends on the specific control procedures set up by the organization.

Management controls are important when such systems are used. For example, a potential management control is to print out all employee hours per department (and per job, if applicable) on a daily basis for review by department supervisors. Corrections are noted and investigated. Assuming that supervisors are knowledgeable and conscientious, such a control procedure is effective in determining that employees are paid only for authorized hours worked. Evidence of the effectiveness of such a control procedure may be sufficient to assess control risk as low. Test of controls could include randomly selecting reports and determining that supervisory review took place. Inquiry should be made into the payroll department's perception of the rigor with which the reports are reviewed and problems routinely detected. The control procedure is considered even stronger if labor reports are reviewed by departmental management and unexpected cost increases are investigated.

An alternative approach is to directly test the operation of the system by either observing employees logging in and noting the details of the transaction to subsequently trace into the payroll record. Another alternative represents a modification of an integrated test facility whereby an auditor logs in at various locations to determine the correctness and completeness of processing.

Selecting Transactions from the Payroll Register

Selecting recorded transactions from the payroll register tests the assertion that only valid employees are paid for hours actually worked and that there are no material amounts of fictitious payroll expense. The procedure is performed by tracing the selected transaction to underlying documentation such as a time card or a supervisory report noting approval for payment. Pay rates and withholdings are verified through reference to signed documents in the employee's personnel file. Payroll calculations are tested. A typical payroll audit worksheet details the testing performed and the recomputations made by the auditor. An example of such a worksheet is shown in Exhibit 17.4. Frequently, the auditor will complement these tests with analytical procedures, such as comparing labor expense with production records, to determine whether the payroll expense might be materially overstated.

Integrated Test Facility

Payroll is often an ideal place to implement an integrated test facility (ITF). Transactions for a number of separate departments are often processed by one computer application. Internal audit departments often find it cost beneficial to develop an ITF and test transactions throughout the year. An overview of the implementation of an ITF is shown in Exhibit 17.5. The ITF transactions are shown above the dotted line in the exhibit. A separate dummy entity is established against which test payroll transactions are submitted for processing. Auditor-submitted transactions can test for completeness, correctness of processing, and the effectiveness of application control procedures built into the computer program. Separate edit reports are prepared for the ITF transactions but are processed by the same application program procedures that generate the normal edit report. In the ITF implementation in Exhibit 17.5, a payroll register, not payroll checks, is generated from the transactions. The ITF is designed so that the auditor-submitted transactions do not update the general ledger.

Exhibit 17.4

PAYROLL TEST WORKSHEET

Performed by ___________

Date ___________

					Withholdings				
Employee	Hours Worked	Wage Rate	Gross Pay	Deduct Claim	Fed Tax	State Tax	Soc Sec Tax	Other	Net Pay
Reid, Penny	40*	$7.50†	$300.00‡	M4§	$52.22‡	$28.73‡	$21.45‡	$20.00‖	$177.60‡
Romenesko, Stan	40*	$7.50†	$300.00‡						
	8*	$11.25†	$90.00‡						
Total			$390.00‡	S1§	$76.20‡	$38.90‡	$27.89‡	$20.00‖	$227.02‡
Gauthier, Andy	38*	$6.00†	$228.00‡	S1§	$34.44‡	$18.00‡	$16.30‡	$20.00‖	$139.26‡
Smith, Sammy	40*	$7.50†	$300.00‡	M2§	$51.12‡	$32.33‡	$21.45‡	$20.00‖	$175.10‡
Wendt, Joh	40*	$8.25†	$330.00‡	M2§	$55.00‡	$39.87‡	$23.60‡	$20.00‖	$191.54‡

*Traced to employee time card or supervisory sheet signed by supervisor. No exceptions.

†Traced to authorized wage rate in personnel department. No exceptions noted.

‡Recomputed. No exceptions noted.

§Traced to employee W-2 form. No exceptions noted.

‖ Examined authority for deduction. Represents union dues. No exceptions noted.

Although an ITF is highly efficient, the auditor must be aware of its limitations. It cannot test the effectiveness of access controls over reference files, such as those containing wage rates. Nor can the ITF test that only authorized transactions are submitted to the payroll application. But when supplemented by other procedures, such as analytical review of payroll expense accounts, it can provide persuasive evidence on the correctness of payroll processing.

Testing of Labor Distribution

The distribution of labor to the proper accounts should be tested in conjunction with the other payroll tests. The auditor must understand the client's cost accounting system and the process for assigning direct cost and allocating indirect costs to products. An effective audit procedure is to trace transactions selected in the payroll worksheet tests to the labor distribution report.

Other Substantive Tests of Payroll

The tests of payroll transactions described in the preceding section provide evidence about the correctness of processing. Depending on specific circumstances, the audi-

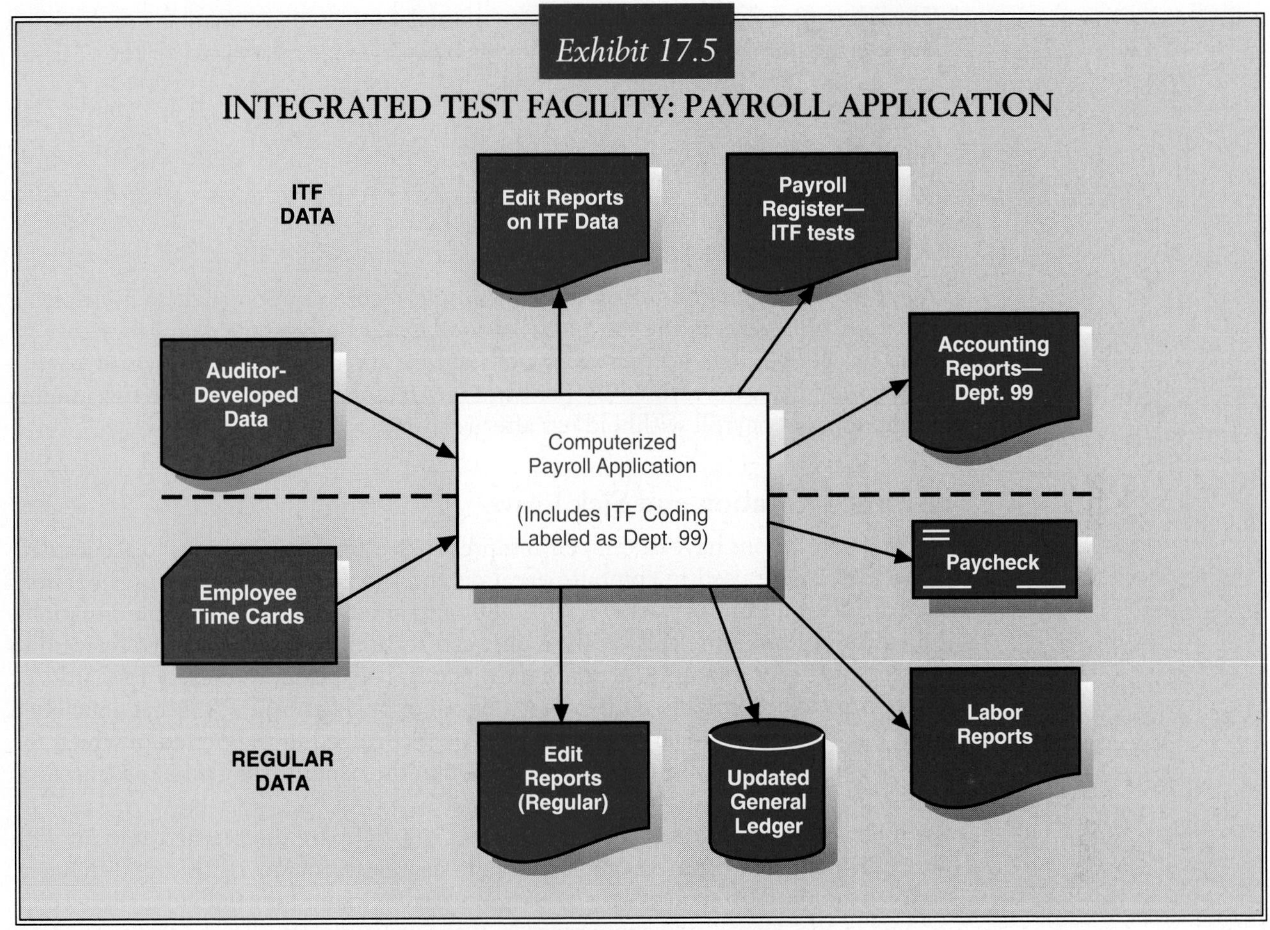

tor may choose to perform direct tests of salary or wage expense or of the related year-end liabilities. Associated liabilities include accrued payroll, sick leave, vacation pay, and payroll taxes due.

Ratio or Trend Analysis

Ratio or trend analysis may be used as an overall substantive audit procedure when independent reliable bases exist on which to make projections. Examples of ratio analysis applied to payroll expense include the following:

- Ratio of direct labor to material used or some other relevant basis such as production volume or number of employees.
- Ratio of payroll-related costs to total payroll expense.
- Ratio of sales commissions to sales or sales by product lines when commissions vary by product line.

Trend or reasonableness tests could include these:

- Comparison of labor costs to those in prior periods and/or budgets.
- Comparison of payroll expense and payroll-related costs with relevant data obtained from reliable sources.

The last approach includes a calculation of total salary expense made by multiplying the average number of salaried employees by an average salary rate for the year.

Tests of Accrued Liabilities

Accrued Payroll and Payroll Taxes

Accrued payroll can be tested through simple recomputation such as multiplying the number of days in the last payroll period times the average daily labor cost for that pay period. The accrual of payroll taxes is directly related to overall payroll expense and can be verified by performing a reasonableness test or by examining remittances of payroll withholdings after year-end.

Accrued Vacation and Sick Leave

Most organizations have developed comprehensive personnel systems to accumulate data that can be used to compute vacation and sick leave pay. Many organizations provide for a number of sick days in addition to annual vacation. In some situations, unused sick leave time and vacation time can accumulate and be carried forward to future years. For example, at some universities, it is possible to carry forward sick leave time to accumulate up to a year's worth of benefits. The FASB has concluded that the expense for such benefits should be recognized in the period in which the services are performed and the accumulation of the benefits should be recognized as a liability.

If benefits do not accumulate, the auditor can compare the accrued amount with the previous year's estimates and investigate the reason for any significant difference. Explanations of differences may be corroborated by examining individual detail contained in the client's personnel records. If the amounts are allowed to accumulate, the auditor should perform some detailed testing of the client's personnel records to ensure their accuracy and use the data either to independently test the client's accrual or to make a separate estimate of the accrual. For first-time audits, the auditor may send out confirmations to a sample of employees to verify the accuracy of the client's database.

Accrued Commissions and Bonuses

Many organizations partially compensate sales personnel on a commission based on recorded sales. The sales commission expense can be tested when testing revenue transactions or can be addressed through overall reasonableness tests.

Year-end bonuses represent a significant portion of executive compensation for some companies. The bonuses are generally tied to reported profits and failure to accrue these bonuses could result in a material understatement of expenses. Some companies have developed specific formulas for bonuses; others base the bonuses on the judgment by management or the board of directors' assessment of accomplishments (including profitability). A board of directors may be reluctant to declare the bonus until all information about audit adjustments are known, and the approval may not take place until well after year-end. The auditor normally reviews the formulas, if available, as a basis for testing the calculation of bonuses, as well as the minutes of the board of directors' meetings for approval.

Tests of Payroll Payments

This procedure involves observing the distribution of payroll checks to employees on a surprise basis. It is not utilized often but is used in special instances when the auditor suspects fictitious personnel are on the payroll. The auditor requires verification of each employee's identification, such as driver's license or an employee identification card, to ensure the validity of the individual receiving the check.

Many organizations now deposit employee paychecks electronically in the employee's bank account. The employee receives a copy of the check stub, showing gross pay, withholdings, and net pay. If the auditor believes that fictitious employees are set up to receive the electronic deposits and wants to directly test the possibility (as opposed to testing the personnel department controls), few options are available. The auditor could take a sample of payroll records and trace to the authorization of employment by the personnel department.

Tests of Officers' Compensation

Each officer's compensation, including that obtained through stock bonuses, is required to be reported to the Securities and Exchange Commission for all companies registered with it. The data are normally reviewed and verified by comparing the earnings records of the officers with amounts authorized by the board of directors. The auditor also reviews compensation agreements such as "golden parachutes" whereby management is given special bonuses if a company is taken over.

Review of Unusual Amounts of Compensation

The public has become concerned with situations in which management is perceived as using corporation resources as if they were their own resources. Charles Keating, with nine relatives on the payroll at more than a million dollars a year, is but one example of such abuses. The public has been appalled that such a lack of stewardship took place and was not reported. Thus, many audit committees will request auditors to review the payroll records for unusual or unauthorized forms of management compensation.

Travel and Entertainment Expense Reimbursements

Travel and entertainment expense is often examined in connection with compensation because such expenditures may be considered a form of compensation by the Internal Revenue Service or the SEC. Although travel and entertainment expenditures may not be material to the financial statements, there is an increasing expectation that auditors will examine sensitive areas to determine whether management is misusing organizational funds or using the funds for personal purposes. There is one other reason to look at travel and entertainment expenses—its abuse is usually a strong red flag indicative of other problems, even fraud, within the organization. It shows management's attitude toward the overall control structure of the organization.

Auditors often use the following guidelines to analyze travel and entertainment expense. The approach is applicable to both large and small organizations, public as well as private.

- Determine whether the organization has a stated policy on travel and entertainment reimbursements and, if so, whether it has been approved by the board of directors.
- Perform analytical review of the relevant expense accounts to determine whether the amounts have increased significantly in comparison with past years.
- If the increases are significant, or the account balances constitute a large sum, take a PPS–based sample of expense reimbursements and examine supporting documents to determine that (1) there is evidence that the request is consistent with stated policies, (2) there is adequate documentation and a business purpose for the reimbursement, and (3) the reimbursement is properly classified.
- Review correspondence with the Internal Revenue Service to determine whether items were questioned during their last audit. Determine the disposition of the items.
- If discrepancies are noted, discuss them with senior management and the audit committee.
- Determine the need either to reclassify the expenditures or to disclose the expenditures in the notes to the financial statements.

The company's approach to travel and expense reimbursements can serve as a barometer to the integrity of management. One experienced auditor put it this way:

> It has been said the best measure of how serious a company is about its internal control is the strictness of its expense reporting policies—from top to bottom. While that may be an oversimplification, it is certainly a warning to auditors if they find executives who have difficulty distinguishing between a company's interests and their own. There is no requirement for auditors to continue a client relationship if they feel uncomfortable with management's ethics, whether or not there have been any illegal acts.[2]

B–AUDITING EMPLOYEE BENEFITS

Many employee benefits are directly related to payroll and are not difficult to audit. For example, the organization may provide health insurance to all employees or life insurance based on the amount of salary. Most often these benefits are provided through arrangements with an insurance company. The client negotiates a contract (usually for one to three years) with an insurance company to provide specific benefits. The insurance company administers the contract and the client pays a contracted fee to the insurance company for the benefits provided. Management usually monitors benefit costs and makes adjustments to contracts over time. In some instances, the benefits are negotiated as part of a union contract and the entity agrees to contribute a specific amount per hour worked to a union-administered fund to provide health and similar benefits.

The auditor's main task in auditing these benefits is to understand the contract and to verify that the expenses have been properly recognized and any liability or asset has been accrued. The auditor normally requests the client to prepare a schedule of payments and expenses as a basis for verifying the expense and estimating the accrual.

Two types of employee benefits are difficult to audit and account for: pension expense and its related liability, and other postretirement employee benefits (mainly health benefits). To audit both of these areas, the auditor uses the services of an outside specialist to assist in estimating the expenses and liabilities.

Pension Expense and Liabilities

Most entities provide some form of pension benefits for their employees. Most of the plans require a vesting period, a required period for which the employee must work for the entity before becoming eligible for pension benefits. The FASB requires that pension expense be recognized during the time period in which services are rendered and that a pension liability be established. Organizations cannot treat pension expense on a "pay-as-you-go" basis. Some companies manage their pension funds but most often they engage a third party such as an insurance company to manage the fund assets and administer the benefits. We will assume this arrangement in our subsequent discussion.

The pension expense and related liability or asset are based on a number of contract specific items and assumptions about the future. These include the following:

- Vesting terms.
- Benefit basis and projected benefits.
- Inflation adjustments expected over the life of the projected benefits.
- Expected return on invested assets.
- Anticipated, or known, future changes to the pension plan.

The client must have a comprehensive personnel database to support the computation of pension obligations and to ensure that correct payments are made to retired employees. Federal laws mandate specific controls over the management of pension assets to protect employees from losing their pension should management decide to sell the firm.

The client and auditor normally work with an actuary in determining pension expense and the related liability or asset. The auditor is responsible for understanding the approach used by the actuary and the effect of the actuary's estimates on the fairness of the financial statement presentations. When evaluating the work of the actuary, the auditor should address the following:

- The personnel data (a complete description of the population of current and retired employees) and the plan asset data given to the consulting actuary are reasonably accurate and complete.
- The actuary is independent of the client and is considered competent by the actuarial profession.
- The financial statements fairly present the actuarially determined pension data.

Working with a specialist does not mitigate the auditor's responsibility for the fairness of the financial statement presentation. Thus, the auditor has a responsibility to ensure that the specialist is independent of the client, has high professional standards and a good reputation, and understands the nature of the engagement and the possible effect of his or her estimates on the financial statements. The understanding should be documented in a working paper. The auditor is responsible for understanding the nature of the actuary's work and the effect of changes in actuarial assumptions on the financial statements. For example, a change in the interest rate assumption from seven percent to eight percent can have a dramatic effect on the pension liability or asset and reported expense. The auditor must understand the basis for such an adjustment and find out why it was made this period. It could represent a manipulation of reported income for this period.

An example of an audit program for auditing the pension expense and liability or asset is shown in Exhibit 17.6.

The audit program reiterates the auditor's responsibility for determining that the data used by the actuary are reasonably correct. Thus, even though the system generating the information used by the actuary may be a personnel system rather than an accounting system, the auditor should evaluate the accuracy of the data used in estimating the pension liability. Also, the disclosure requirement for pensions requires a thorough understanding of the nature of the pension agreement with an entity's employees. An example of the extent of disclosure required is shown in Exhibit 17.7.

The detail contained in the AMOCO footnote in Exhibit 17.7 illustrates the complexity of the pension and other retirement benefits audit. Are the assumptions reasonable? What caused the decline in the fair market value of the plan assets in 1990? The auditor addresses such questions during the audit. Clearly, a small change in assumptions results in a large change in the amount recognized in the financial statements.

Other Postretirement Employee Benefits

Many organizations have informally guaranteed executives and, in some cases all employees, a continuation of health insurance after retirement. Some organizations also provide **other postretirement employee benefits (OPEB).** Even when such plans are not formally documented, the courts have held that the existence of the informal plan may create employee expectations and barring a formal plan, employees have a right to expect the continuation of the plan. Many companies have responded by formally adopting plans.

The FASB has been studying the issue and has determined that accounting for OPEB does not differ conceptually from the accounting treatment for pensions. The cost of the benefits should be attributed to the time period in which the individual works for the organization and a liability should be accrued for the net present value of expected benefits at the conclusion of the employee's career. Applying this overall concept to these other benefits is difficult because of the following complicating factors:

1. Many companies have not developed comprehensive information systems to be used in projecting the expected future costs of such benefits.
2. It is more difficult to project future medical expenses than it is to project retirement benefits that are accumulated according to a specific plan. For

Exhibit 17.6

AUDIT PROGRAM FOR PENSION EXPENSE AND LIABILITY

Overall assertions: Determine that the currently earned, actuarially computed pension expense and related liability or asset are properly estimated and recorded. Determine that any adjustments in assumptions are properly reflected in the computation of the pension liability or asset.

Audit Procedures	Done by	Date	W/P Ref.
1. Obtain copies of the following documents: • Latest actuarial valuation report. • Pension plan documents. • Permanent file containing information on actuary's reputation and previous experiences with client's designated actuary. • Trustee's statement of plan assets for the most recent period and the preceding year. • Census (complete description of covered employees) and plan asset data given to consulting actuary. • Correspondence of client with the consulting actuary.	_____	_____	_____
2. Reconcile aggregate data (such as number of employees, covered compensation, etc.) to amounts shown in the actuarial valuation report of the consulting actuary's letter.	_____	_____	_____
3. Compare selected census data to payroll records including such data as current pay, years of employment, current age, and plan benefit coverage.	_____	_____	_____
4. Based on the pension plan document, make appropriate tests to determine whether all eligible employees are included in the data given to the consulting actuary.	_____	_____	_____
5. Reconcile plan assets per the trustee's report to amount shown in the actuarial valuation report.	_____	_____	_____
6. Review the client's procedures for determining employee eligibility to receive pension payments. Select a sample of employees and determine plan eligibility for each employee. Determine whether company procedures comply with plan.	_____	_____	_____
7. Obtain an understanding of the control structure governing the disbursement of pension payments. Test selected transactions to determine whether control procedures are operating effectively.	_____	_____	_____
8. Select a sample of pension payments and trace to underlying supporting documentation to determine whether payments are made in accordance with pension plan provisions and the employee is eligible for the payments.	_____	_____	_____
9. Perform an analytical review of overall pension expenditures for the period under audit. Compare pension expenditures with previous years, accounting for changes in retirements and changes in the pension plans. Determine whether unusual fluctuations exist and should be investigated further.	_____	_____	_____

(Continued)

Exhibit 17.6

	Done by	Date	W/P Ref.
10. Determine whether the consulting actuary appears to be professionally qualified using the guidelines established in *SAS No. 11* (AU Sec 336).	______	______	______
11. Inquire as to any relationship between the consulting actuary and the client that would impair the independence of the actuary.	______	______	______
12. Review the latest pension plan document and compare pertinent plan provisions with those summarized in the actuarial valuation report. If the report does not include a description of the plan provisions, confirm with the actuary his or her understanding of such provisions.	______	______	______
13. Inquire as to the most recent plan amendment considered in making the actuarial valuation.	______	______	______
14. Inquire of the client whether there is any intent to terminate, or significantly modify, the plan.	______	______	______
15. Review the actuary's most recent report and determine whether there are any qualifications given, and if so, the reasons for the qualifications.	______	______	______
16. Discuss with the client and actuary the basis and rationale for any significant changes in assumptions affecting the computation of pension expense and liability. Evaluate the reasonableness of important assumptions made in terms of current economic conditions.	______	______	______
17. Update all firm worksheets on the pension expense and liability or asset account.	______	______	______
18. Determine whether information contained in the actuary's report might merit a qualified audit opinion. If yes, consult with the actuary on the potential nature of the qualification and the reference to be made to the actuary's report.	______	______	______
19. Determine the adjustments needed to make the financial statements fairly presented. Review the client's recording of the transactions. Discuss with the client any adjustments that are not made to determine whether there could be a material effect on the financial statements.	______	______	______
20. Review the financial statement disclosure of pension-related expense and liability or asset for conformance with generally accepted accounting standards, particularly *SFAS No. 87*.			
21. Document your conclusion on the fairness of the financial statement presentation.	______	______	______

example, many projections of medical expense, if extrapolated at the current rate of cost increase for medical care, would cause medical expenses to equal our gross national product within the next 20 to 30 years.

3. Because many of the plans are not formalized, companies may change or modify the informal plan at any time.

Exhibit 17.7

AMOCO CORPORATION ANNUAL REPORT, 1990
RETIREMENT PLAN AND PENSION DISCLOSURE

18. Retirement Plans

The corporation and its subsidiaries have a number of defined pension plans covering most employees. Plan benefits are generally based on employee's years of service and average final compensation. Essentially all of the cost of these plans is borne by the corporation. The corporation makes contributions to the plans in amounts that are intended to provide for the cost of pension benefits over the service lives of employees.

Millions of Dollars	1990	1989
Fair value of plan assets, principally equity and fixed income securities	**$2,473**	**$2,804**
Actuarial present value of benefit obligations:		
Vested benefits	**$1,973**	1,910
Nonvested benefits	**19**	15
Accumulated benefit obligation	**1,992**	1,925
Additional benefits based on estimated future salary levels	**535**	475
Projected benefit obligation	**2,527**	2,400
Plan assets over (under) projected benefit obligation	**(54)**	404
Unrecognized gains at date of adoption of Statement No. 87	**(109)**	(116)
Other unrecognized net losses/(gains)	**91**	(308)
Unrecognized prior service cost	**135**	130
Prepaid pension cost (included in other assets)	**$ 63**	$ 110

The components of net pension cost for the past three years were as follows:

Millions of Dollars	1990	1989	1988
Service costs—benefits earned during the period	**$ 82**	$ 74	$ 56
Interest cost on projected benefit obligation	**202**	184	170
Actual loss (return) on assets	**103**	(548)	(103)
Less: Unrecognized (loss) gain	**(340)**	322	94
	(237)	(226)	(210)
Amortization of unrecognized amounts	**9**	(3)	(9)
Net pension cost	**$ 56**	$ 29	$ 7

The assumptions used for the corporation's principal pension plans for 1990 and 1989 were as follows:

	1990	1989
Discount rate for service and interest cost	**8.0%**	8.5%
Discount rate for the projected benefit obligation	**8.0%**	8.0%
Rate of increase in compensation levels	**6.0%**	6.0%
Long-term rate of return on assets	**9.5%**	9.5%

The corporation also has an unfunded excess benefit plan that provides for payments of amounts in excess of limits imposed by federal tax law on benefit payments under the principal plans. The projected benefit obligation of this unfunded plan was $69 million at December 31, 1990, and $62 million at December 31, 1989, of which $36 million and $35 million, respectively, had been recognized as a liability in the Consolidated Statement of Financial Position at year-end 1990 and 1989.

Most employees are also eligible to participate in defined contribution plans by contributing a portion of their compensation. The corporation matches contributions up to specified percentages of each employee's compensation. Matching contributions charged to income were $76 million in 1990, $72 million in 1989, and $60 million in 1988.

Exhibit 17.8 summarizes the difficult estimates that must be made in auditing OPEB.

Few third parties, such as insurance companies, have been willing to manage OPEB plans. However, as more companies gain experience with the costs of alternative plans, it is likely that more plans will be developed with specifically defined benefits rather than open-ended medical coverage as organizations presently offer. The audit approach to such benefits will be very similar to the audit program for pension expense and the pension liability presented in Exhibit 17.6. An example of the disclosure of other postretirement employee benefits for a company that utilizes a separate insurance company is shown in Exhibit 17.9.

Summary

The audit of payroll is usually not complex because many controls are developed to ensure that employees are correctly paid and the appropriate governmental agencies receive their share of tax withholdings. The auditor should gain an understanding of the nature of payroll processing and the impact of automated time capture and data processing on the overall process.

Many companies have developed comprehensive human resource systems to capture data and manage their human resource requirements. In many situations, the

Exhibit 17.8

ESTIMATES NEEDED TO COMPUTE THE OBLIGATION FOR OTHER POSTRETIREMENT EMPLOYEE BENEFITS

The audit of other postretirement employee benefit plans is difficult because a number of crucial areas are difficult to estimate. These areas include the following:

- Average retirement age and the number of years that an employee can be expected to live beyond retirement.
- Nature of health benefits presently promised in either an implied (promised, but not formalized) plan or in a defined benefit plan.
- Current cost of providing such benefits.
- Expected costs of future benefits based on plan specifications, wage rates, and future cost of medical care.
- Changes in technology affecting the delivery of health care, which may further affect the cost of health care.
- Other estimates similar to those for pension plans:
    - Percentage of employees who will drop out and not retire with the organization.
    - Income earned on invested assets (if the plan is funded).
    - Recognition and amortization of prior service cost.
    - Benefit plan amendments.

Exhibit 17.9

DISCLOSURE OF OTHER POSTRETIREMENT BENEFITS FORD MOTOR CO. 1992 ANNUAL REPORT

Note 2. Employee Retirement Benefits

Postretirement Health Care and Life Insurance Benefits. The company and certain of its subsidiaries sponsor unfunded plans to provide selected health care and life insurance benefits for retired employees. The company's U.S. and Canadian employees may become eligible for those benefits if they retire while working for the company. However, benefits and eligibility rules may be modified from time to time. Prior to 1992, the expense recognized for postretirement health care benefits was based on actual expenditures for the year. Beginning in 1992, the estimated cost for postretirement health care benefits has been accrued on an actuarially determined basis, in accordance with the requirements of the Statement of Financial Accounting Standards No. 106, "Employers' Accounting for Postretirement Benefits Other Than Pensions." Implementation of the standard will not increase the company's cash expenditures for postretirement benefits. The company has elected to recognize immediately the prior-year unaccrued accumulated postretirement benefit obligation of this accounting change, resulting in an adverse effect on income of $7,540 million in the first quarter of 1992. The change reflects an unaccrued retiree benefit obligation liability of approximately $12 billion, partially offset by projected tax benefits of $4.5 billion. In addition, the loss was increased by $455 million ($723 million before tax) for 1992 accruals.

The following sets forth the plans' status, reconciled with the amounts recognized in the company's balance sheet as of December 31, 1992 (in millions):

Accumulated Postretirement Benefit Obligation	
Retirees	$ 7,035.0
Active employees eligible to retire	2,269.6
Other active employees	5,090.6
Total accumulated obligation	$14,395.2
Unamortized net (loss)	(807.0)
Accrued liability recognized in balance sheet	$13,588.2
Assumptions:	
Discount rate	8.5%
Health care cost trend rate	10.3
Ultimate trend rate in ten years	5.5
Weighted average trend rate	6.9

The net postretirement benefit cost for 1992 included the following components (in millions):

Benefits attributed to employees' service	$ 235.7
Interest on accumulated benefit obligation	1,128.7
Net postretirement benefit expense	$ 1,364.4

Retiree benefit payments were as follows (in millions): 1992—$641; 1991—$628; 1990—$582. Changing the assumed health care cost trend rates by one percentage point in each year would change the accumulated postretirement benefit obligation as of December 31, 1992 by approximately $1.7 billion, and the aggregate service and interest cost components of net periodic postretirement benefit cost for 1992 by approximately $190 million.

accounting data are increasingly becoming a by-product of these other systems, and the auditor spends more time understanding management controls over these systems. In addition, there are increasing requirements for governmental reports on compliance with specific federal regulations. These comprehensive systems also form the basis for estimates of pension liabilities and other postretirement employee benefits.

Significant Terms

computer tables (files) A computer file that contains information needed to process transactions and may change frequently; common examples include wage rates for each job classification and employee job history. The tables are efficient because the application program can reference the data to determine current information for processing the transactions without changing the computer program.

human resources department A separate department responsible for negotiating long-term union contracts or developing contracts for employee benefits; may also be responsible for developing reports on compliance with applicable government laws and regulations.

other postretirement employee benefits Benefits, other than pensions, paid by an organization to its retirees, the most common of which is health insurance. The plans may be formal or informal and may involve a third party such as an insurance company that administers the benefits. The FASB has determined that the cost of providing such benefits should be recognized over the period in which the employee provides productive services for the organization. An expense and liability should be accrued during the period of employment.

Review Questions

A–Payroll and Related Expenses

17–1 What functions are performed by the personnel department? Why are the functions of the personnel department important to the auditor in evaluating the control risk associated with payroll processing?

17–2 What account balances are either directly or indirectly affected by payroll processing?

17–3 The auditor wishes to test the assertion that payments are made only to authorized employees for actual hours worked. Assuming that the company utilizes time cards for collecting hours worked, identify the audit procedure that would best test the assertion.

17–4 Explain how segregation of duties is enhanced if an organization has a separate payroll department, personnel department, and human resources department.

17–5 Many companies have automated the time collection function whereby employees log on at data capture machines located in the production area. How does the elimination of time cards affect the audit of payroll? Explain.

17–6 Computerized tables are important components in processing payroll. Identify the function of these tables and three control procedures an organization should implement to ensure their integrity.

17–7 What audit procedures might be utilized to ensure the auditor that data contained in computerized tables are correct and up-to-date?

17–8 What are the advantages of segregating the payroll function into hourly and salaried sections?

17–9 Explain how an integrated test facility might be used in an audit of payroll. What are the advantages and limitations of using an integrated test facility to test payroll processing?

17–10 The integrated test facility was discussed primarily as an audit approach to test payroll processing. Explain how an integrated test facility might be utilized for testing pension-related costs and liabilities.

17–11 What function is served by furnishing the personnel department a detailed printout of all changes made to the file containing wage rates for each job classification?

17–12 How does the auditor determine that the appropriate amount of direct labor cost is capitalized into the Inventory account?

17–13 What underlying documentation would the auditor examine to determine whether employees are paid correctly and withholdings are properly calculated? Assume that withholdings include state and federal withholding taxes, union dues, and vacation pay, which are remitted to the employee (plus interest) at the end of the year.

17–14 Is it necessary to separately examine executive salaries? Where would the auditor find the authorized rate for executive salaries?

17–15 Identify five computer-based control procedures that should be evaluated during an audit of payroll. Explain the purpose of each control procedure.

17–16 Explain how analytical procedures could be used in testing sales commission expense and administrative salary expense. Identify two or three bases the auditor might use in developing a model to perform analytical review of these two accounts.

17–17 Identify the audit objectives addressed by the following procedures:

a. Select a sample of time cards and trace to the payroll register, verifying the proper calculation of payroll expense, employee withholdings, and net pay. Determine that the expense is charged to the correct accounts.

b. Select a sample of items from the payroll register and trace to the underlying time cards, if available, for the pay period. Verify the proper calculation of payroll expense, withholdings, and net pay. Determine that the expense is charged to the correct accounts.

17–18 The internal auditor may be called on to perform a fraud investigation involving payroll. Identify two procedures the auditor might use to test for the existence of fictitious employees on the payroll and for employees compensated at inflated wages.

17–19 How might the auditor test the accrual of vacation pay?

17–20 Distinguish between an employee's earnings record, a W-4 form, and a payroll tax return. Explain the purpose of each.

17–21 During an audit, the auditor discovers that the client has a provision whereby executive bonuses are paid in the amount of 40 percent of pre-tax, audited income. The client states that it cannot determine the bonus until the audit is done, but at the same time the auditor believes that the audit cannot be completed until the board of directors declares the bonus. How should the auditor proceed to get out of this "catch-22" situation?

17–22 A staff auditor recently stated that she doesn't believe that an auditor needs to thoroughly understand the client's human resources system or the manner in which that department carries out its function. After all, she asserts, "Payroll is what is of interest to us—something that affects an account balance—not what the personnel or human resource people do." Explain to the auditor why the statement is in error. Present a detailed rationale for your response.

17–23 How could either attributes sampling or PPS sampling be utilized in the audit of payroll? Identify the audit procedures for which each is best suited.

B–Auditing Employee Benefits

17–24 Why might an audit of other postretirement employee benefits be more complicated than an audit of pension expense and the pension liability?

17–25 Assume that a client independently engages an actuarial firm to estimate the pension expense and pension liability or asset. The client records the amounts suggested by the actuary. What are the auditor's responsibilities for auditing the pension expense and pension liability or asset?

Multiple Choice Questions

17–26 If the auditor is concerned that employees are being paid for hours not actually worked, the best audit procedure would be to

a. Select a sample of employees from the personnel database and trace to the current payroll to verify existence of employees on payroll.

b. Select a sample of employees on the payroll register and trace to the underlying time cards to verify hours worked.

c. Select a sample of time cards and trace to the payroll register to determine that pay was computed for actual hours worked.

d. Select a sample of employees from the payroll register and trace to the personnel file to determine the validity of the employee listing on the payroll.

*17–27 A common audit procedure in the audit of payroll transactions involves tracing selected items from the payroll journal to employee time cards that have been approved by supervisory personnel. This procedure is designed to provide evidence in support of the audit proposition that

*Adapted from the Uniform CPA examination or the Certified Internal Auditor examination.

a. Only bona fide employees worked and their pay was properly computed.

b. Jobs on which employees worked were charged with the appropriate labor cost.

c. Internal controls relating to payroll disbursements are operating effectively.

d. All employees worked the number of hours for which their pay was computed.

*17–28 During 1994, a bookkeeper perpetrated a theft by preparing erroneous W-2 forms. The bookkeeper's FICA withheld was overstated by $500, and the FICA withheld from all other employees was understated. Which of the following is an audit procedure that would detect such a fraud?

a. Multiplication of the applicable rate by the individual gross taxable earnings.

b. Utilizing form W-4 and withholding charts to determine whether deductions authorized per pay period agree with amounts deducted per pay period.

c. Footing and cross-footing of the payroll register followed by tracing postings to the general ledger.

d. Vouching canceled checks to federal tax form 941.

17–29 The department that is authorized to add employees to the payroll and to change pay rates is the

a. Personnel department.

b. Payroll department.

c. Data processing department.

d. The executive supervisor of payroll.

17–30 An employee with a job classification of 4 with an hourly rate of $8.50 per hour was inadvertently and incorrectly paid at a job classification of 6 at an hourly rate of $11.50 per hour. The employee did not complain about the error in pay. The most effective control to prevent or detect such an error would be

a. The use of self-checking digits on employee I.D.s to ensure that the employee is correctly identified to the application.

b. Supervisory approval for the hours worked.

c. Validity test in which job classification is compared with department.

d. A limit test on gross pay.

17–31 A salaried employee in the payroll department changed his salary to $2,200 per month rather than the authorized rate of $1,500 per month. Which of the following controls would have been effective in preventing or detecting the unauthorized change in pay?

a. Restricted access to the files containing authorized pay rates.

b. Limit tests built into the application on pay rates per job classifications.

c. Review of a detailed printout of all changes made to authorized pay rates by the personnel department and restricted access to the pay rate file.
d. Rotation of payroll duties within the payroll department on a six-month basis.

17–32 Which of the following items does *not* need to be estimated in computing other postretirement employee health benefits?
a. Expected future medical costs.
b. Inflation rate for benefit payments.
c. Number of employees currently covered by benefits.
d. Average life expectancy of employees after retirement.

17–33 The sampling unit in a test of control procedures pertaining to the existence of payroll transactions ordinarily is a(an)
a. Clock card or time card.
b. Employee form W-2.
c. Employee personnel record.
d. Payroll register entry.

17–34 The purpose of segregating the duties of hiring personnel and distributing payroll checks is to separate the
a. Administrative controls from the internal accounting controls.
b. Human resources function from the controllership function.
c. Operational responsibility from the record-keeping responsibility.
d. Authorization of transactions from the custody of related assets.

17–35 An auditor would consider internal control over a client's payroll procedures to be ineffective if the payroll department supervisor is responsible for
a. Hiring subordinate payroll department employees.
b. Having custody over unclaimed paychecks.
c. Updating employee earnings records.
d. Applying pay rates to time cards.

17–36 The auditor may observe the distribution of paychecks to ascertain whether
a. Pay rate authorization is properly separated from the operating function.
b. Deductions from gross pay are calculated correctly and are properly authorized.
c. Employees of record actually exist and are employed by the client.
d. Paychecks agree with the payroll register and the time cards.

Discussion and Research Questions

17–37 (Authorization) The authorization of pay rates, the addition or termination of employees, the capturing of hours worked for the pay period, and the computation of vacation time are some of the more important payroll processes.

Required:
For each of the payroll actions listed below,

a. Identify the party that has the authority to authorize or approve the action.
b. Identify the control procedures that should be implemented to ensure that only properly authorized actions are taken.
c. Indicate the audit implications if the organization does not have sufficient control procedures to ensure the proper authorization of the action listed.

Payroll Actions:

1. An employee is added to the payroll to work in the finishing department as an apprentice.
2. After six months, on the recommendation of the departmental supervisor, the employee's job classification is changed to an experienced apprentice with a corresponding increase in hourly pay.
3. The employee is laid off three months later because of a labor cutback. The employee can collect state unemployment benefits but is not eligible for the union contract–negotiated pay continuance plan that guarantees a 75 percent wage rate for 26 weeks but becomes effective only after five years of employment.
4. An employee with a journeyman classification and seven years of experience was also laid off and applies for the job continuation wage guarantee.
5. Each employee turns in a time card for hours worked each day. These time cards are accumulated for the week and used to calculate payroll. The time cards also indicate the department in which the employee worked.
6. The company has negotiated a new contract with the labor union. The contract calls for a $0.50 across-the-board hourly pay raise for all union employees except for skilled jobs (classification 12), which will receive a $0.75 increase per hour.
7. Each salaried employee is given a specific salary increase based on a combination of merit and an across-the-board component based on overall guidelines set for pay raises.
8. Executive bonuses are scheduled for payment on January 31 for performance during the past year.

17–38 (Control Environment) The following questions are taken from the Control Environment Assessment Questionnaire in Exhibit 17.2.

Required:
For each question,

a. Briefly indicate why the control procedure implied in the question is important. Identify the errors or irregularities that could take place if the control procedure is not present.
b. Briefly describe the audit implication and suggested audit procedures if the answer to the question is *no*.

Control Environment—Selected Questions:

1. Does the personnel department act as an independent check on the payroll processing by
   (a). Screening and authorizing new employee hires?
   (b). Authorizing changes in employee job classification and payrates?
   (c). Maintaining independent records of employee performance?
2. Does the personnel department review all changes made to the major tables (computer files) for employee wage rates to ensure that all changes are made as authorized? Does the personnel department independently receive a printout of the tables after changes are made by payroll and reconcile the changes to the list of authorized changes?
3. Does the human resources department prepare analyses of the expected costs of benefits negotiated during the labor negotiation process? For example, are estimates prepared on the cost of future health costs when postretirement employee benefits are negotiated?
4. Does the human resources or personnel department prepare federal compliance reports on a timely basis? If not, is there any potential liability applicable to late filing of the reports?
5. Is the payroll department sufficiently segregated from the personnel and production functions to ensure that only authorized individuals are added to the payroll and only authorized individuals are paid? Explain.
6. Is there an independent authorization of the hours worked for hourly based employees? If not, does the payroll department provide summary reports of employees and hours worked to departmental supervisors for their review and approval?
7. Do major user groups (personnel, human resources, payroll, and supervisory management) participate in major changes to the payroll and personnel computer applications? Do the user groups exercise authority over changes to the payroll application? Are computer control procedures independently reviewed and tested by users and the internal audit department during the design of the computer applications?
8. Are access controls over computer tables and applications sufficient to ensure that unauthorized parties do not have the ability to change existing records or to input new records?
9. Are exception reports prepared and effectively used by supervisory management?
10. Is the accounting for labor costs periodically reviewed by the accounting department to ensure that labor cost is properly allocated to inventory, overhead, and administrative expense?

17–39 (Fraud Procedures) The following is a list of potential frauds that might occur in connection with payroll.

Required:
For each item listed

a. Identify a control that would have prevented or detected the fraud.

b. Identify specific audit procedures the auditor might utilize to determine the existence of the fraud. Indicate how computerized audit techniques would be useful in performing the fraud investigation.

Potential Payroll Frauds:

1. The payroll clerk added names to the pension database and had monthly checks mailed to one of three post office box numbers for the fictitious individuals. The clerk picked up the checks from the post office.
2. A factory supervisor entered into a scheme with his brother-in-law whereby the brother-in-law was hired and worked in the supervisor's department. The supervisor logged in and out for the brother-in-law, who actually had a different full-time job. The two split the paycheck.
3. A computer programmer developed a code that rounded down the social security withholding from each employee (not more than 1 cent per employee) and added the withholding to his record. Then, at the end of the year, he filed for a refund of excess social security withholdings along with his annual income tax return.
4. A computer programmer built a code into the computer program that utilized an "IF" statement to identify her account. Once identified, a subsequent line of code inflated her monthly pay by 150 percent resulting in compensation one and a half times the authorized rate.
5. Due to a crackdown on the deductibility of travel and entertainment expense, the manager of an organization authorized an increase in his monthly salary of $5,000 to cover the expense that would no longer be reimbursed.
6. The railroad industry had negotiated with the labor union to preserve a number of jobs even though the functions were no longer needed. For example, there is no need for a cabooseperson on many trains. Because not all employees were needed to carry out the necessary functions, employees entered into a scheme in which they covered for each other and worked an average of only three days per week but drew a full week's pay.
7. The payroll supervisor systematically collaborated with good friends to raise their job classifications and thereby increase their pay beyond that authorized for the functions actually performed.
8. A company constructing an addition to the factory properly capitalized labor cost involved in the construction. Due to a poor year, management decided to capitalize all the labor that was involved in maintenance of the existing factory on the grounds that it was part of the remodeling.

*17–40 (Computer-Based Controls for Payroll Application) Talbert Corporation hired an independent computer programmer to develop a simplified payroll application for its newly purchased computer. The programmer developed an on-line, database microcomputer system that minimized the level of knowledge required by the operator. It was based on typing answers to input cues that appeared on the terminal's viewing screen, examples of which follow:

a. Access routine:
   1. Operator access number to payroll file?
   2. Are there new employees?
b. New employees routine:
   1. Employee name?
   2. Employee number?
   3. Social security number?
   4. Rate per hour?
   5. Single or married?
   6. Number of dependents?
   7. Account distribution?
c. Current payroll routine:
   1. Employee number?
   2. Regular hours worked?
   3. Overtime hours worked?
   4. Total employees this payroll period?

The auditor is attempting to verify that certain input validation (edit) checks exist to ensure that errors resulting from omissions, invalid entries, or other inaccuracies will be detected during the typing of answers to the input cues.

Required:
Identify the various types of input validation (edit) checks the auditor would expect to find in the computerized application system. Describe the assurances provided by each identified validation check. Do not discuss the review and evaluation of these controls.

*17–41 (Operational Audit of Personnel Department Functions) The results of a preliminary survey from an operational audit of the personnel function are as follows:

Audit Area	Survey Results
I. Personnel Projections	Policies and procedures for developing personnel projections appeared to be lacking. There was no evidence of communications from top management on new or expanded business opportunities that might affect personnel projections. There was no indication of operating managers having any input regarding projections based on economic trends.

II.	Securing New Personnel	Each department recruits for its open positions without regard to other departments. Policies and procedures pertaining to selection of personnel were not evident. User department satisfaction with the personnel function was not known.
III.	Position Descriptions	Dates of revisions and signatures of approval did not appear on position descriptions sampled in the survey. There was no evidence of job analysis, nor were criteria established to permit subsequent maintenance of descriptions.
IV.	Compensation	No evidence indicating a review of compensation levels for soundness or compliance with established industry standards was found. Compensation levels did not appear to be related to performance. Compensation levels within job classifications were not reviewed or evaluated by the personnel department.

Required:
Develop audit objectives for each audit area in the preliminary operational audit survey described. For each objective developed, identify two audit steps that would be appropriate to follow up on the preliminary survey and one additional procedure that could apply to the overall audit objective.

*17–42 (Operational Audit Findings—Personnel Department) The following is a series of excerpts from the Conditions section of the final report of an operational audit of a firm's personnel department.

Condition I The company's payroll is prepared by the personnel department.

Condition II The firm's personnel manager is the proprietor's son, who has one year of experience in the personnel field.

Condition III The distribution of payroll checks is made by the personnel department.

Condition IV The personnel department makes a quarterly test of all personnel records to ensure that all required documentation is present.

Condition V Personnel hiring is initiated by the personnel department only on the receipt of a request from the user department. The request must be signed by the user department manager or assistant manager.

Condition VI When documentation supporting a particular personnel action is received by the personnel department, a personnel clerk is assigned the task of making the appropriate changes on the file(s) affected. No one, at any time, is assigned the task of verifying that the entries are correctly transcribed.

The internal auditor is preparing a Recommendations section for the report. The following set of internal control characteristics is to be used: (1) competence and integrity of personnel, (2) segregation of incompatible functions, (3) execution of activities as authorized, (4) proper recording of events, (5) appropriate limitation of access to assets, and (6) comparison of existing records with records required. The internal auditor notes that one of each of the six essential characteristics is addressed by each of the six conditions identified.

Required:
For each condition,

a. Identify the essential characteristics of internal control addressed, using one characteristic per condition, with no repeats.
b. State whether that characteristic is violated by the condition.
c. Describe the possible consequences of any such violation.
d. Prescribe one corrective action for any such violation.

*17–43 (Automating Time Collection Function) The internal auditing department was told that two employees were terminated for falsifying their time records. The two employees had altered overtime hours on their time cards after their supervisors had approved the hours actually worked.

Several years ago, the company discontinued the use of time clocks. Since then, the plant supervisors have been responsible for manually posting the time cards and approving the hours for which their employees should be paid. The postings are usually entered in pencil by the supervisors or their secretaries. After the postings for the week are complete, the time cards are approved and placed in the mail racks outside the supervisors' offices for pickup by the timekeepers. Sometimes the timekeepers do not pick up the time cards promptly.

Required:
Assuming that the company does not wish to return to using time clocks, give three recommendations to prevent recurrence of the situation described above. For each recommendation, indicate how it will deter fraudulent reporting of hours worked.

*17–44 (Operational Audit of Employee Benefit Programs) The following are findings resulting from various audits of company employee benefit plans:

1. Piecework accounting.

During an internal audit of a wage incentive plan, an internal auditor found that some of the reported quantities seemed unreasonably high. Employees reported their own piecework production quantities. A comparison of the total employee-reported piecework quantities with independently prepared production reports revealed that totals were as much as 20 percent higher on the employee-reported piecework.

2. Employee health insurance.

   At the request of management, the internal auditing department was conducting an audit of the company's health insurance invoices. Only those charges related to currently enrolled employees should have appeared on the invoices. One thing stood out: the names of some terminated employees were on the invoices.

   A computer run comparing identification numbers of active, eligible employees with those on the insurer's invoices revealed that benefits exceeding $100,000 had been paid on behalf of inactive or former employees. In one instance, an employee who had been terminated for seven years was still receiving benefits.

   One control weakness that the auditors found was the failure of many supervisors to process the forms needed to inform the personnel department of terminations or status changes.

3. Matching contributions.

   A company has an employee savings plan that provides a matching contribution to participating employees' savings accounts. When an employee stops participating in the plan, the company suspends matching contributions. During an audit of the plan, an internal auditor found that the company was still making contributions to the accounts of a number of employees who had ceased to participate. Over $1.2 million in contributions has been made to such accounts.

Required:
For each of the situations discussed above, identify the following:

a. The cause of the problem.
b. The effect of the problem.
c. Recommendations for corrective action to be taken.

*17–45 (Travel and Expense Reimbursements) A corporation operates a chain of several hundred personal computer stores. The company has just ended the first full year of its new direct sales force marketing program. Each member of the new direct sales force is assigned to one of the chain stores as a home base. All sales and reimbursable expenses are reported to a salesperson's home-base store.

In addition to significant recruiting and training expenses, the major new expense created by the program is for travel. Travel reimbursement budgets have been established for each store, based on both the expected sales volume and the number of sales force personnel assigned to each store. Salespeople submit travel reimbursement requests twice each month to the store managers for approval. Each request is to be accompanied by appropriate invoices and receipts. A store manager reviews and approves the travel reimbursement request forms, and submits approved forms and a travel reimbursement voucher for each salesperson to company headquarters. The invoices and receipts are included in the travel reimbursement vouchers, which are prenumbered in a separate series for each store. The store manager indicates the store's budget account code on each travel reimbursement voucher.

At company headquarters, the travel reimbursement vouchers are routed to the accounting department. There clerks compare invoice and receipt details to those shown on the travel reimbursement vouchers and check each voucher for mathematical accuracy. The clerks also account for the numerical sequence of the vouchers, verify the store manager's approval of them, and verify the store's budget account code. Clerks initial the vouchers to indicate completion of their work and forward the vouchers to the accounts payable supervisor. The supervisor reviews the vouchers and prepares a prenumbered batch control form (two copies) for the total dollar amount of the vouchers. The supervisor approves the batch control form, files one copy by date, attaches the second copy of the batch control form to the batch of approved vouchers, and submits the batch to the data processing department for payment.

Reimbursement vouchers are processed twice each month to generate checks and a travel reimbursement expense register. The checks are mailed directly to each salesperson. The travel reimbursement expense register is posted to the general ledger. Monthly reports that show both current period and year-to-date actual versus budgeted travel reimbursement expense for each store are prepared and reviewed by management.

Management has requested that the internal auditing department undertake an audit of the company's internal controls over travel reimbursements for the new direct sales force.

Required:
Develop five audit objectives dealing with the evaluation of internal controls over travel reimbursements and identify four audit procedures for each objective.

17–46 (Analysis of Payroll Control Structure) Kowal Manufacturing Company employs about 50 production workers and has the following payroll procedures: The factory supervisor interviews applicants and on the basis of the interview either hires or does not hire them. When an applicant is hired, he or she prepares a W-4 form (Employee's Withholding Exemption Certificate) and gives it to the supervisor, who writes the hourly rate of pay for the new employee in the corner of the W-4 form and then gives the form to a payroll clerk as notice that the worker has been employed. The supervisor verbally advises the payroll department of rate adjustments.

A supply of blank time cards is kept in a box near the entrance to the factory. Each worker takes a time card on Monday morning, fills in his or her name, and notes in pencil his or her daily arrival and departure times. At the end of the week, the workers drop the time cards in a box near the door to the factory.

On Monday morning, the completed time cards are taken from the box by a payroll clerk. One of the payroll clerks then records the payroll transactions using a microcomputer system, which records all information for the payroll journal that was calculated by the clerk and automatically updates the employees' earnings records and general ledger. Employees are automatically removed from the payroll when they fail to turn in a time card.

The payroll checks are manually signed by the chief accountant and given to the supervisor, who distributes the checks to the workers in the factory and arranges for the delivery of the checks to the workers who are absent. The payroll bank account is reconciled by the chief accountant, who also prepares the various quarterly and annual payroll tax reports.

Required:

a. List the most serious weaknesses in the internal control structure and state the errors that are likely to result from the weaknesses. In your audit of Kowal's payroll, what will you emphasize in your audit tests? Explain.

b. List your suggestion for improving Kowal Manufacturing Company's internal controls for the factory hiring practices and payroll procedures.

17–47 (Standard Payroll Audit Tests) In many companies, labor costs represent a substantial percentage of total dollars expended in any one accounting period. One of the auditor's primary means of verifying payroll transactions is by a detailed payroll test.

You are making an annual examination of Joplin Company, a medium-size manufacturing company. You have selected a number of hourly employees for a detailed payroll test. The following worksheet outline has been prepared.

Column Number	Heading
1	Employee number
2	Employee name
3	Job classification
4	Hours worked:
	Straight time
	Premium time
5	Hourly rate
6	Gross earnings
	Deductions:
7	FICA withheld
8	FIT withheld
9	Union dues
10	Amount of check
11	Account number charged

Required:

a. What factors should the auditor consider in selecting his or her sample of employees to be included in any payroll test?

b. Using the column numbers above as a reference, state the principal way(s) that the information for each heading would be audited.

17–48 (Audit of Other Postretirement Employee Benefits) Jason Company has three types of other postretirement employee benefit plans:

- An union contract benefit program whereby $.50 per hour per employee is remitted to the international union in the employee's name to provide health insurance care on retirement. The union administers the payment of the retirement benefits, and the employer's liability is limited to the contractual remittances to the union. The remittances are due 30 days after the completion of each quarter.
- A defined-benefit plan available to middle-level salaried employees. The plan is contracted to an insurance company. A yearly premium is charged by the insurance company based on the estimated present value of the benefits. The insurance company requires extra premiums due to changes in the plan. According to the contract with the insurance company, the client and insurance company must renegotiate premiums every three years based on experience rates, changes in medical cost, and retiree life expectancy.
- A health plan available only to senior management (division managers, vice presidents, board of directors, and operating officers). The plan provides for complete health insurance coverage for each employee and spouse for the rest of their lives. The plan is not funded but is administered by an insurance company. The insurance company charges the company a premium based on actual benefits claimed during each year, including a processing fee.

Required:

a. Briefly describe the major differences in these three plans and the implications for the audit approach taken.
b. Develop an overall audit program to audit the OPEB expense and liability account for the company.

17–49 (Vacation and Sick Leave) Forestville Company has a vacation and sick leave policy for all its employees as follows:

- One week of vacation for the first year.
- Two weeks of vacation from year 2 to year 10.
- Three weeks of vacation for years 11–15.
- Four weeks of vacation for all employees who have been employed more than 15 years.
- Five sick days (with pay) per year, which can accumulate up to 15 days, but any not taken thereafter are lost.
- Vacation, which is figured on a calendar year basis and can be carried over at a maximum of one week to a subsequent year (the maximum in any year is the defined vacation period plus one week).

A comprehensive database developed by the human resources department contains detailed data about each employee's vacation and sick leave. The company's year-end is September 30. The payroll department estimates that approximately 80 percent of all vacation time is taken by September 30 and uses that basis to make its accrual each year. The payroll department assumes that most employees carry over their sick leave and use an average of seven days of sick leave to estimate the sick leave liability. This is a first-year audit.

Required:

a. Identify the procedures that the auditor should use to determine whether the 80 percent vacation estimate used by the payroll department is reasonable.

b. Briefly discuss the merits of using the 80 percent estimate, given the nature of the client's processing.

c. Briefly identify the procedures the auditor would use to verify the accuracy of the client's accrual of sick leave.

17–50 **(Research)** Manufacturing is becoming more highly automated, and companies are changing the approach they take to allocate labor expense to products. Companies also capture more information about labor performance through automated data collectors located within the factory.

Required:

Review the recent manufacturing or cost accounting literature to identify approaches taken by companies to allocate labor costs to products. Or interview managers from several manufacturing firms in your area to determine their approach to automating the labor-reporting process.

Cases

17–51 (Audit of Pension) Woke-Up-This-Morning (WUTM) Company has a pension program that covers virtually all employees. The company was recently taken over by another company. Shortly after the takeover, the acquiring company performed a detailed audit of WUTM's pension liability and discovered that the pension liability had been substantially understated. The amounts are material and important and the acquiring company wants to renegotiate the acquisition price and is considering suing the previous auditors because the liability had been understated.

WUTM had used an actuary to assist in making the pension expense and liability estimate each year. The acquiring company asserts that the actuary had used optimistic projections on asset returns and had used conservative estimates for growth in pension benefits (based on wages) and on retiree longevity. The actuary claims that the data WUTM provided on its employees, benefit claims, and years to retirement were incorrect and led to the understatement of the liability. At this point, all parties agree that the liability was in fact understated.

Required:

a. What are the relative responsibilities of management, the auditor, and the actuary for the accuracy of the pension expense and liability estimate?

b. What is the responsibility of the auditor in determining the independence and competence of the actuary? What data might the auditor gather to assess the independence and competence of the actuary?

c. What is the auditor's responsibility for

- Determining that the employee descriptive data furnished to the actuary by WUTM was reasonably accurate?
- Evaluating the reasonableness of the assumptions used by the actuary in making the estimates?

d. Briefly describe how the auditor might assess the reasonableness of the two items in part c.

17–52 (Audit of a Highly Automated Manufacturer) Couger, Inc., has a philosophy of automating its production and reporting process. It has three divisions: (1) Jericho is a job-shop manufacturer of customized components built according to customer specifications, (2) Johnstone manufactures automotive subassembly components and has implemented quality circles whereby employees work as a team on assembly, and (3) Jacobsen assembles lawnmowers in a traditional mass production line.

Required:

a. How might Couger implement automated time collection at each of the three divisions?

b. Explain how Couger's internal auditors might implement an integrated test facility to test payroll. What are the advantages of using an ITF in the above situation?

c. Explain how management reports could be used to minimize control risk in recording payroll. For each report identified, briefly discuss how the auditor would evaluate the effectiveness of the report as a control procedure.

End Notes

1. *Overview: OPEB* (Price Waterhouse & Co., 1991), 5.
2. William D. Hall and Arthur J. Renner, "Lessons Auditors Ignore at Their Own Risk: Part 2," *Journal of Accountancy* (June 1991), 66.

CHAPTER

18

Learning Objectives

After studying this chapter, you should be able to:

1. Identify the common audit approaches used to audit long-term assets and many short-term assets such as prepaid accounts.
2. Identify the most efficient approaches to auditing long-term assets and related expenses.
3. Identify the unique issues associated with the audits of intangible assets.
4. Understand the unique audit issues associated with mergers and acquisitions, including those associated with leveraged buy outs (LBOs).

Audit of Long-Lived Assets

Chapter Contents

Mr. Kravis asserts that these intangibles, and the write-offs this goodwill necessitates, are to be ignored, because they are not a cash cost. He should, and undoubtedly does, know better. Specifically, he must know full well that the enormous sum being dumped into the intangibles hopper was not a number that sprang unbidden from the pens of his CPAs; instead, it represents the gigantic gap between the aggregate $26.2 billion paid in the LBO and the relatively minimal tangible book value of the RJR Nabisco net assets being acquired. Accordingly, it represents an actual cost outflow that, for accounting purposes, is attenuated over a period of up to two-score years.[1]

With respect to the carrying amount of investments, a loss in value which is other than a temporary decline should be recognized in the financial statements of an investor. The independent auditor should, therefore, also examine sufficient competent evidential matter to the extent he deems necessary to determine whether such a loss in value has occurred. [AU 332.04]

Chapter Overview

This chapter presents a general discussion of assets not covered in earlier chapters. The long-lived assets include prepaid accounts, property, plant, and equipment, and intangibles. There is a wide variety of long-term assets, but fortunately, there is a commonality in the audit approach to them. Special attention is given to the area of mergers and acquisitions, including the recent development of leveraged buy outs.

These two statements reflect some of the complex issues associated with audits of other assets. A distinguished professor questions the amount (and accounting) of goodwill assigned in the leveraged buy out of RJR Nabisco and in doing so raises important questions about the accounting approach used in accounting for mergers and acquisitions. The second quote identifies the auditor's responsibility to evaluate long-term investments to determine whether more than a temporary decline in value might have occurred. Not all long-term assets, however, are complex to audit. This chapter addresses long-lived assets that are material to the financial statements, including the following:

- Prepaid accounts such as prepaid insurance, rent, and deposits.
- Long-term assets, especially those of property, plant, and equipment, and capitalized leases.
- Long-term investments, such as equity investments in other companies or bonds, and
- intangible assets, such as goodwill, trademarks, or patents.

In addition, we will discuss the transactions leading to the recording of intangibles with a special emphasis on mergers and acquisitions.

Most of the long-lived assets are audited using a balance sheet audit approach. Audit worksheets are developed and used as a basis to verify the balance sheet accounts and to estimate the related expense accounts.

A–AUDITS OF PREPAID ACCOUNTS

Prepaid accounts represent rights to future services from another party and normally include Prepaid Insurance, Prepaid Taxes, and Prepaid Rent. These accounts usually are not material and can be audited efficiently by using analytical procedures to evaluate the related expense accounts (Insurance Expense, Rent Expense, etc.) for reasonableness and supplementing that work by vouching selected cash disbursements and reviewing pertinent contracts.

The overall relationship between the asset and expense account for Prepaid Insurance is shown in Exhibit 18.1. When a client pays for a three-year insurance policy in advance, for example, an amortization schedule is developed to amortize the asset and recognize the associated insurance expense.

Control Structure Considerations

The prepaid accounts are part of the acquisition cycle and normally are subject to the control procedures for that cycle. In addition, a well-designed risk and insurance program will identify organizational assets (tangible and intangible), recognize threats to the assets, develop protection plans, and insure against specific risks. Most large organizations have separate risk and insurance departments responsible for such a program. Because companies without adequate insurance coverage present special risks, most auditors follow the substantive procedures listed below even if the expenditures and expenses are not material to the overall financial statements.

Substantive Tests of Prepaid Insurance

The audit begins with a request to the client to prepare a schedule of insurance, noting beginning and ending account balances, specific coverages, dates of scheduled payments, period of coverage, changes in coverage, current payments, and amortization of the asset. Tests are performed by selecting insurance policies, noting the

Exhibit 18.1

PREPAID ACCOUNT INTERRELATIONSHIPS

Prepaid Insurance	
Beg. Balance	Amortization
Add'l Payments	
End. Balance	

Insurance Expense	
Amortization	
Adjustments	Adjustments
End. Balance	

nature of the coverage and the terms of the policies; testing the client's amortizations, computations, and footings; and tracing totals to the client's general ledger.

The tests address the assertions as follows:

Existence. Coverage is verified through the review of selected client policies. If questions arise about coverage or the validity of the contracts, the auditor considers confirming specific terms with the insurance company (although this is rarely done).

Completeness. Vouching the payments, reviewing the contracts, and recomputing the amortization schedule addresses the completeness assertion.

Rights and obligations. Specific rights or obligations are noted when reviewing the insurance policy. The auditor, particularly in small organizations, normally assesses the adequacy of insurance coverage and communicates concerns to management and the audit committee.

Valuation and allocation. Valuation is tested through the vouching of payments and the testing of the client's amortizations. Insurance claims in process might be confirmed with the insurance company.

Presentation and Disclosure. Prepaid expenses are normally classified as a current asset in the other assets category. Normally, the accounts are not material, and additional disclosure is not needed. Disclosure may be considered if insurance coverage is considered inadequate.*

Analytical Review of Accounts

The balance sheet and related expense accounts often can be efficiently tested using analytical procedures. The procedures can be as simple as comparing expense account balances with the previous few years' balances and adjusting for volume (or size) and inflation. If the balance does not differ materially from expectations, the auditor may conclude the audit testing without expending much time. If the balance does differ materially from expectations, the auditor examines details to determine the reason for the difference and the potential need to adjust the account balances.

Other Assets

Other prepaid assets are addressed using the same types of audit procedure. The accounts include Prepaid Rent, Royalty Advances, and Deposits. As with prepaid insurance, contracts should be reviewed to determine client rights and obligations. Most auditing firms have set up amortization schedules on microcomputers and update the data each year. The auditor also examines the nature of the asset to determine whether there continues to be expected value associated with the asset.

*It is the authors' opinion that a lack of comprehensive insurance plan to ensure the recoverability of the organization from a major (uninsured) catastrophe always ought to be disclosed. This view is directly related to the stewardship function management owes to users. Lending agreements often require certificates of insurance on collateral or the loan will fall in default.

B–AUDITS OF PROPERTY, PLANT, AND EQUIPMENT

Property, plant, and equipment (PPE) often represent the largest single category of assets of manufacturing organizations. An overview of the account relationships is shown in Exhibit 18.2. The asset account (equipment, buildings, or similarly titled assets) represents the culmination of major capital additions. The beginning balance is established in previous year audits (with the exception of first-time audits). The audit thus focuses on material transactions affecting the account balance during the year: additions, disposals, and write-offs of existing assets and the recognition of periodic depreciation or depletion of the asset. A comprehensive audit program for the audit of equipment is shown in Exhibit 18.3. In addition to providing evidence concerning the fairness of the account balance, the audit program is designed to gather information that will assist in auditing tax depreciation and the deferred tax liability.*

First-Time Audits

On the first-time audit of a new client, the auditor may not have the advantage of an audited opening balance for the Property, Plant, and Equipment account. If the client has been audited before, the predecessor auditor should be contacted to determine whether evidence can be gained from their prior audits as to beginning balances. If the auditor cannot use the predecessor auditor's working papers, or if it

Exhibit 18.2

FIXED ASSETS: ACCOUNT INTERRELATIONSHIPS

Equipment	
Beg. Balance Additions	Disposals Write-Offs
End. Balance	

Accumulated Depreciation	
Disposals Write-Offs	Beg. Balance Depreciation
	End. Balance

Depreciation Expense	
Depreciation	
End. Balance	

Gain or Loss on Disposal	
Loss	Gain
End. Balance	End. Balance

*For most companies with computerized information systems, the same computer application computes both book and tax depreciation. The tax computations will differ from the book calculations but will be based on the same property database.

Exhibit 18.3

AUDIT PROGRAM: MANUFACTURING EQUIPMENT

Audit Program Procedures	Done by	W/P Refer
Overall Concerns		
1. Review internal firm manuals and determine whether there are any unique accounting issues associated with the client's industry. For example, special concerns when auditing an electric utility would make the audit different than the audit of a manufacturing company.	______	______
2. Is this a first-year audit? If yes, make arrangements to review the working papers of the predecessor auditor as a basis to establish the validity of the beginning account balances.	______	______
3. Review procedures used by the organization to requisition and approve purchases. Determine whether capital projects are reviewed by a capital budgeting committee and approved by the board of directors.	______	______
4. Make inquiries of the client as to major differences between book and tax depreciation. Evaluate the system the client uses to determine tax accounting and test selected transactions to determine that the depreciation for tax purposes and accumulated depreciation are calculated correctly. Determine that the client has a system to identify and support timing differences that will become a part of the deferred tax liability.	______	______
Existence		
5. Inquire of management as to the existence of significant additions or disposals of property, plant, or equipment during the year.	______	______
6. Request the client to prepare a list of fixed asset additions and disposals for the year. Foot the schedule and trace selected items to entries in the property ledger.	______	______
7. Trace the ending balance per prior year working papers to the beginning balance.	______	______
8. Inquire of management about the existence of significant new leases or the conversion of leases into purchases during the year. Determine management's approach to capitalizing leases.	______	______
9. Tour the client's major manufacturing facilities, noting the following: • Addition of significant new product lines or equipment during the year. • Disposal of significant product lines or equipment. • Equipment that has been discarded, is damaged, or is sitting idly.	______	______
10. Inquire of methods used by the client to identify and classify property no longer used in production. Determine whether management follows the process by reviewing reports by internal auditors or by noting selected idle equipment and tracing the equipment identification numbers to a list of equipment not in use or to the current equipment file.	______	______

(Continued)

Exhibit 18.3

AUDIT PROGRAM: MANUFACTURING EQUIPMENT

	Done by	W/P Refer
11. Inquire of management of methods used to physically observe and count equipment on a periodic basis and reconcile with the property, plant, and equipment ledger.	______	______
Completeness		
12. For selected purchases, examine receiving reports or physically observe the asset. Determine that all items have been recorded in the correct time period.	______	______
13. Review repair and maintenance expense, as well as the Lease Expense account, to determine whether some items should have been capitalized.		
Rights and Obligations		
14. Inquire of assets licensed to the company to determine rights and obligations.	______	______
Inquire as to whether assets have been pledged as collateral or whether obligations have been assumed in connection with purchases.	______	______
Valuation or Allocation		
Equipment account valuation:		
15. If assets no longer have economic value, determine that they have properly been written down to scrap value.	______	______
16. Select a sample of additions over $__________ or a PPS sample and examine invoices, construction billings, work orders, etc., to determine that the assets have been valued at cost and are recorded in the proper account. Determine that all trade-ins have been properly valued and tax liabilities associated with the trade-in have been properly recognized.	______	______
17. Select a sample of asset disposals and examine either a sales or shipping document evidencing disposal of the equipment. Recompute the gain or loss (and tax obligations) on the disposal and trace the gain or loss to the appropriate income or expense account.	______	______
18. Inquire about changes in the estimated useful life of assets. Determine whether changes are recognized in accordance with generally accepted accounting principles. Determine that all new equipment has been properly classified as to its useful life.	______	______
19. Review the accounts for self-constructed assets. Request the client to develop a schedule of capitalized costs. Determine the methods used to		

is the first audit for the client, a statistical sample should be taken to observe existence and to review original invoices to verify cost and ownership. Depreciation and accumulated depreciation should also be recalculated. If the client's records are not adequate, the client may have to take a complete PPE physical inventory.

Exhibit 18.3

AUDIT PROGRAM: MANUFACTURING EQUIPMENT

	Done by	W/P Refer
identify the costs and examine supporting documents for selected entries.	______	______
20. Determine the appropriateness of the company's procedures for capitalizing interest during construction. Review underlying documents, recompute amounts, and determine correctness.	______	______
Depreciation and Accumulated Depreciation:		
21. Review the client's depreciation policy and		
a. Determine whether the overall approach is consistent with the type of equipment purchased. Determine whether there is a need to revise depreciation policies based on technological changes or the client's experience with similar assets.	______	______
b. Determine whether the depreciation approach has been used consistently. Determine appropriate disclosure.	______	______
c. Select a few additions and recompute first-year depreciation according to the proper classification of the property and compare with the client's computation.	______	______
22. Prepare an estimate of first-year depreciation for additions. Update the depreciation worksheet for additions and disposals during the year and estimate depreciation expense. If recorded depreciation differs materially from the estimate, make further inquiries and consider the need for detailed testing of the computer program used to calculate depreciation.	______	______
Presentation and Disclosure		
23. Review classification of property accounts and determine that all items are actively used in producing goods or services and are intended for long-term use in the business.	______	______
24. Review note disclosure to determine that depreciation methods and capitalization methods are adequately disclosed.		
25. Document management's representations concerning the existence and valuation of the assets in the management representation letter.	______	______

Evaluating Control Risk and Control Effectiveness

Many audit procedures contained in Exhibit 18.3 address control procedures to ensure that transactions are properly identified and that recorded assets exist. The control procedures should be designed to

- Identify existing assets, inventory them, and reconcile the physical asset inventory with the property ledger.
- Ensure that all purchases are authorized.
- Appropriately classify new equipment according to the preestablished depreciation categories.
- Identify obsolete or scrapped equipment and write the equipment down to scrap value.

If the client's control procedures are effective, analytical procedures can be used to estimate depreciation expense and accumulated depreciation. If the control procedures are not adequate, a more detailed review of purchases and a recomputation of depreciation will be needed. The existence of a computerized **property ledger** is an important part of the control structure of property, plant, and equipment. The property ledger should uniquely identify each asset with an identification code that corresponds to a physical tag placed on the asset. In addition, the property ledger should provide details on the cost of the property, the acquisition date, the depreciation method used for both book and tax, estimated life, estimated scrap value (if any), and accumulated depreciation to date. Other important control procedures include the following:

- Authorization procedures to acquire new assets. A capital budgeting committee to analyze the potential return on investment is a strong control procedure.
- Periodic physical inventory of the assets and reconciliation with the recorded assets.
- Formal procedures to account for the disposal of assets.
- Periodic review of asset lives and adjustments of depreciation methods to reflect the changes in estimated useful lives.

Tests of Additions and Disposals

If the beginning balance is established through previous audit work, the test of the property accounts can be limited to selected tests of property additions and disposals during the year. The procedures are designed to determine that all additions have been properly

- *Authorized* by examining purchase agreements, board of directors minutes for major acquisitions, and approval by a capital budgeting committee.
- *Classified* based on their function, expected useful life, and established depreciation schedule.
- *Valued* by examining purchase documents such as invoices or construction billings.

The client is asked to prepare a schedule of all additions over a specific amount during the year. The schedule is tested by reviewing entries and determining their correspondence with entries in the property ledger. Selected additions (either all items over the specified amount or a sample) are vouched to vendor invoices and other supporting documentation. An example of a typical working paper is shown in Exhibit 18.4. Although the account balance may be large, the audit work can be done efficiently by concentrating on the additions, recalculating depreciation, and updating the accumulated depreciation account.

The tests contained in the working paper are supplemented by a tour of the factory to observe the general layout and condition of equipment, as well as the existence of idle equipment. The auditor's knowledge of the client's strategic plans and

Exhibit 18.4

INLAY INDUSTRIES
FIXED ASSET WORKING PAPER–EQUIPMENT
DECEMBER 31, 1994

PBC
Worked Performed by________
Date________

Description	Date Purchased	Beginning Balance	Cost Additions	Cost Disposals	Ending Balance	Accumulated Depreciation: Beginning Balance	Depreciation Expense	Disposal —Accumulated Depreciation	Ending Balance
Beginning Balance	Various	124,350			124,350	33,429			33,429
Depreciation on equipment owned at beginning of year							12,435*		12,435
Additions:									
40" lathe	10/30/94	-0-	9,852†		9,852	-0-	1,250‡		1,250
1040 press	3/25/94	-0-	18,956†		18,956	-0-	1,895‡		1,895
60" lathe	5/29/94	-0-	13,903†		13,903	-0-	950‡		950
Disposals:									
Fork lift	6/2/89			7,881§	(7,881)			3,753	(3,753)
Computer	7/2/91			3,300§	(3,300)			2,625	(2,625)
Totals		124,350‖	42,711**	11,181**	155,880**††	33,429‖	16,530**	6,378**	43,581**††

* Estimated from last year, includes one half year depreciation for assets disposed of during the year. See Working Paper PPE-4 for the calculation of the estimate.

† Examined invoice or other supporting document, noting cost and appropriate categorization for depreciation purposes.

‡ Recalculated, noting that depreciation is in accordance with company policy and asset classification.

§ Traced to asset ledger and verified that equipment had been removed. Examined sales document or scrap disposal document for the disposal of the asset.

‖ Traced to December 31, 1993 working papers.

** Footed/crossfooted.

†† Traced to trial balance.

industry changes is used to determine whether additional work should be performed in evaluating whether some classes of equipment should be written down to net realizable value.

Special Examination of Repairs and Maintenance Expense

Some clients might be motivated to record some asset purchases as an expense to reduce taxable income. The most common audit approach to address the completeness of recorded assets is to request a schedule of repair and maintenance expense. All items over a specified amount can be examined to determine whether they are properly classified as an expense or should be capitalized as property, plant, or equipment.

Self-Constructed Assets: Special Issues

Occasionally, organizations use their own personnel to self-construct additions to factories or warehouses. In some cases, an employee works most of the time on regular production work and works sporadically on construction. In other situations, a client may actually own a construction subsidiary that performs most of the client's construction work.

Self-construction presents some unique problems:

1. Identification of specific costs to be assigned to the construction when employees perform multiple tasks during the construction period. The auditor needs to perform detailed tests of payroll to determine that the client has an adequate system to recognize and classify costs.
2. Allocation of overhead. Many companies assign a specific overhead rate to all direct labor hours. Companies often assign these same rates to the construction of property when the components of overhead to be assigned have no applicability to the construction effort.
3. Computing implied interest. The FASB has determined that implied interest should be capitalized during construction. The client must keep detailed records of expenditures and accumulated expenditures at reasonable intervals as a basis for imputing interest.
4. Identifying the cost of raw materials used during construction. In some cases, the client is able to specifically identify raw materials that were requisitioned as part of the construction, but in other cases, the company may use components previously classified as inventory.

Detailed tests of the transactions making up self-constructed assets are usually performed to satisfy the basic audit objectives.

Disposals and Fully Depreciated Equipment

Many organizations have not established the same level of controls over asset disposal or idle assets as they have for the acquisition of assets. For example, equipment might be discarded, but the disposal might not be recorded. Therefore, special procedures are often used to determine whether disposals of fully depreciated equipment has been recorded properly. One approach is to utilize generalized audit software to prepare a printout of fully depreciated (or nearly fully depreciated) equipment, which the auditor can attempt to locate. Or, trade-ins noted during the audit of property additions can be traced to the removal of the old equipment from the books. Alternatively, a sample of property can be taken and traced to the physical assets to determine their existence. The projected sample results, if material, could be used either to book an adjustment or to request the client to perform a physical inventory of property.

Additional Audit Considerations for Capitalized Leases

Depreciation of capitalized leases should reflect the economic or lease life of the asset, whichever is shorter. The more likely problem the auditor will encounter is the existence of leases that should be capitalized but that the client wishes to keep "off the books." The auditor should review all major leases to determine whether some of the leases should be capitalized.

Asset Impairment

In most cases, long-lived assets are used over their expected physical life, or if there is significant technological change, the asset lives may be revised to reflect a shorter expected economic life. In some cases, however, management may believe that a whole class of assets is overvalued, but the company does not wish to dispose of the assets. Quite often this happens when new management takes over and decides that a significant portion of "nonproducing" assets ought to be written down to their fair market value. This is often referred to in the business press as the *Big Bath Theory* by which new management writes off or writes down as many assets as possible, thus decreasing future charges against income. Previous management can be blamed for the **asset impairments** and the write-off can be justified on the dual grounds of asset impairment and previous management's poor stewardship of the assets.

The issue of asset impairment presents two difficult audit problems:

1. The auditor must periodically assess management's approach to identifying impaired assets and writing them down to their current economic value. Normally, management is not interested in identifying and writing down such assets. Thus, the auditor uses an up-to-date knowledge of changes taking place in the client's industry to make preliminary estimates of impaired assets.
2. The auditor must guard against an overzealous management that wants to write every potentially impaired asset down to a minimum realizable value. It is not likely that assets all of a sudden become impaired and need to be written off when new management takes over control of a company.

The FASB has been developing guidelines to assist companies in dealing with asset impairments. The major issue for the auditor is the development of a systematic approach to continuously review the overall composition of an entity's asset base in light of current and planned production and technological and competitive developments in the client's industry.

Depreciation Expense and Accumulated Depreciation

Analytical procedures can be very effective for estimating the reasonableness of depreciation expense and accumulated depreciation. Auditors often develop a computerized spreadsheet to estimate changes in depreciation expense. The spreadsheet categorizes assets by depreciation lives and depreciation method. The current estimate of depreciation on assets continuing in the business is calculated and then modified for assets added or disposed of during the year.

The worksheet should incorporate a number of ratios and an overall test of reasonableness to help determine the reasonableness of the current charges to the accounts. The following are included in these ratios:

- Current depreciation expense as a percentage of the previous year depreciation expense.
- Fixed assets (by class) as a percentage of previous year assets. The relative increase in this percentage can be compared with the relative increase in depreciation as a test of overall reasonableness.
- Depreciation expense (by asset class) as a percentage of assets each year. This ratio can indicate changes in the age of equipment or in depreciation policy, as well as recomputation errors.
- Accumulated depreciation (by class) as a percentage of gross assets each year. This ratio provides information on the overall reasonableness of the account and may indicate problems of accounting for fully depreciated equipment.
- Average age of assets (by class). This ratio provides additional insight on the age of assets and may be useful in modifying depreciation estimates.

The auditor performs similar tests for tax-based depreciation as a basis for determining the reasonableness of temporary tax differences and the deferred tax liability. If questions arise about the client's computations, the auditor follows up with inquiries of the potential differences and detailed tests, which might include these:

- Samples of equipment from the property ledger and calculation of depreciation expense. This is followed by footing the property ledger and agreeing the total to the general ledger accounts. Most of this work is performed using generalized audit software.
- Tests of the application program through either the use of test data or the integrated test facility.

C–AUDITS OF OTHER LONG-LIVED ASSETS

A number of other long-lived assets differ from property, plant, and equipment but use a similar overall audit approach. These other assets include the following:

- *Natural resources* such as oil reserves, timber, and metals that are subject to **depletion.**
- *Patents* with limited monopoly on the design or use of the patented material for a specific period of time determined by the patent laws.
- *Trademarks* identified as a part of the purchase of another organization.
- *Other deferred charges* created as part of the matching process.

Natural Resources

Natural resources presents unique problems for the auditor. First, it is often difficult to identify the costs associated with the discovery of the natural resource. The oil industry debated for years whether all costs incurred in searching for oil (including drilling numerous dry wells) should be capitalized as part of the cost of obtaining a new well (referred to as the *full costing approach*) or whether only the costs associated with drilling a successful well should be capitalized (referred to as the *successful efforts* approach). Second, once the natural resource has been discovered, it is often difficult to estimate the amount of commercially available resources to be used in determining a depletion rate. Third, the company may be responsible for restoring the property to its original condition (reclamation) after the resources are removed. Reclamation costs may be difficult to estimate.

Fortunately, most established natural resource companies have developed sound procedures for identifying costs and use geologists to establish an estimate of the reserves contained in a new discovery. Successful companies find that they need such information to manage the company. The auditor normally has experience with the quality of the client's estimates but may want to use a specialist to review the geological analysis of new discoveries as a basis for establishing the reserves. Most organizations periodically reassess the amount of reserves as more information becomes available during the course of mining, harvesting, or extracting the resources. The auditor should review these estimates and determine their impact on revisions of the depletion rate.

The disclosure of reserves required by the SEC is quite complex and includes an estimate of oil and gas reserves. The auditor must review and test the procedures used by the client in developing such information to determine whether the information complies with the reporting standards established by the SEC. The information is not presently audited, however. Current depletion expense can be audited by: (1) using analytical procedures to compare current depletion as either a percentage of sales or production with that of previous years; and/or (2) by testing the system recording depletion through an analysis of underlying production data. Under the second approach, the auditor will have to determine the reliability of the underlying production data.

Patents

Patents provide a legal monopoly to use a unique product or design for 17 years. The cost of developing the patent may be capitalized when the work is identified with a specific feasible product. Legal costs of successfully defending a patent should also be capitalized. Patents may also be acquired from another entity or may be acquired as part of the acquisition of another entity. The costs of the patent should be amortized over the shorter of the *expected economic life* or the *legal life of the patent.* Like most other **intangible assets,** patents are typically amortized on a straight-line basis. In many instances, an accelerated approach may more directly parallel the expected economic benefit to be received from the patent and should be used. There is a tendency for some companies to establish amortization schedules without periodically reviewing the economic value of the asset. The auditor should review the continued economic viability of patents each year. Pertinent procedures include reviewing trade publications on the competitiveness of the client's products, the use of litigation to fight patent infringement suits, and inquiry of management and production personnel on the continued use of the patent.

Trademarks

Corporate or product trademarks are clearly major assets for many companies. The right to the trademark Coca-Cola is clearly one of the most valuable assets of the Coca-Cola Company. Disney has licensed its Mickey Mouse logo for clothing, glasses, and other souvenirs to the tune of billions of dollars per year.

Unfortunately, the value of a trademark is difficult to estimate. Currently, the fair market values of the assets are not recognized on the financial statements. Since most of the enhancement of a trademark is carried out through advertising, those costs are expensed. Thus, material amounts of trademarks are capitalized only when a company acquires a trademark from another organization or assigns a value to a trademark as part of the acquisition of another entity. In such cases, the auditor verifies the basis for the cost assignments (through independent appraisals) and determines that the costs are amortized over a period of time reflecting the economic benefit to the company, but not to exceed 40 years.

Other Deferred Charges

Deferred charges are often created as part of the matching process and exist only because of it. Examples include deferred charges related to taxes (instead of a credit) and advances on payments of pension obligations. The process leading to the generation of the deferred charge should be reviewed to determine the appropriate amortization or reversal. The client most likely has a detailed schedule of the deferred charge and its expected reversal, which can be analyzed and tested by the auditor by reference to the underlying transaction or asset acquisition.

D–LONG-TERM INVESTMENTS

Long-term investments include holdings of capital stock or other equity interests, bonds and similar debt obligations, and loans and advances. Long-term investments in equity securities are accounted for under the cost or equity method. The portfolio of long-term equity investments should be valued at the lower of cost or market. If a market decline is "temporary," the unrealized loss is reported as a deduction in the stockholder's equity section of the balance sheet. If the decline is "other than temporary," the unrealized loss is reported in the income statement. Auditing problems arise when an attempt is made to determine whether the decline in value is temporary or other than temporary. The auditor can look at the historical trend in values of individual investments and changes in market values, obtain audited financial statements of investees, or obtain appraisals to assist in estimating the decline in value and its permanence.

For an investment accounted for using the equity method, the investor adjusts it by its proportionate share of the investees' profits or losses minus dividends received. Normally, the auditor must rely on the investee's audited financial statements as evidence to support these adjustments. If such statements are not available, the auditor must consider the materiality of the item and make a decision on whether sufficient evidence exists to render an audit opinion. Alternatively, the auditor would have to perform sufficient work on the investee's financial statements to determine that the investor company is recognizing the appropriate gain or loss in its financial statements.

Permanent declines in the value of any long-term investment should be recognized in the accounts. This may occur in a number of circumstances including going concern problems of the investee or a decision made by the investor to sell its equity in the entity.

E–AUDITS OF MERGERS AND ACQUISITIONS

Mergers and acquisitions have become a familiar part of the corporate landscape. During the past few years, we have seen acquisitions of such companies as EDS and Hughes Aerospace by General Motors, leveraged buy outs (acquisitions) of companies such as RJR Nabisco and Beatrice Foods, and mergers of companies in the same industry such as Georgia Pacific and Great Northern Nekoosa in the paper and forest products industry and Bank of America and Security Pacific in the banking industry. By any estimate, merger and acquisition activity represents a significant amount of capital movement and new valuation problems for the client and the auditor.

An Overview of Accounting Issues Associated with Mergers and Acquisitions

The audit approach taken for mergers and acquisitions is dictated by the structure of the transaction and the specific accounting requirements for the transaction. The accounting literature distinguishes between two kinds of business combinations: (1) purchases and (2) poolings of interests. A purchase represents a company's acquisition of another through the purchase of that company's stock on either the open market or in a tender offer to existing shareholders. A pooling of interests represents a merger formed by the exchange of stock between the two entities. Accounting for the two different kinds of combinations is dramatically different.

Purchase Accounting

Purchase accounting treats the acquisition of one company by another company as any other fixed asset purchase, that is, purchase accounting requires the acquisition to be recorded at its cost. The purchase price is measured by the amount of cash tendered and the fair market value of debt or stock issued in making the acquisition. Purchase accounting cannot be used if the acquisition is consummated only by the issuance of stock by the acquiring company.

The acquiring organization is required to allocate the total purchase price to

- The *fair market value of the tangible assets* of the acquired company based on independent appraisals of replacement cost of the assets.
- The *fair market value of the specifically identifiable intangible assets* such as patents or trademarks.
- *Goodwill.*

Existing liabilities are also adjusted to their fair market value. **Goodwill** represents a unique asset that is associated with the acquired entity and exists in addition to those assets that can be specifically identified.

Pooling of Interests

Conceptually, the accounting for a **pooling of interests** originally viewed the transaction as the joining together of two companies in which neither company was necessarily dominant or the acquirer. The assets were thus treated as if they were "pooled" together in the new entity. There is no need to revalue or restate the assets or liabilities of the two companies. Accounting for a pooling carries the existing assets and liabilities forward at their historical cost with no revaluation to fair values.

The accounting advantages of pooling of interests led to abuses of the concept in the 1960s. Due to the difficulty in determining whether a merger was essentially a combination of like-sized entities, the Accounting Principles Board adopted a fairly simple rule in *APB No. 16:* if the acquisition is made through the issuance of common stock only, the combination must be accounted for as a pooling of interests. The acquisition cost is measured by the book value of the assets of the acquired company, not by the fair market value of the stock given up in the merger process. This is true even if the acquiring company is 20, or even 100, times as large as the acquired company or if the market value of the transaction is significantly greater than the historical book value of the acquired company. There is no recognition of goodwill in a pooling.

Leveraged Buy Outs

Accounting for a **leveraged buy out (LBO)** represents an extension of the purchase and pooling concepts. In most LBOs, the purchasing group forms a new entity to acquire an existing company. However, the acquiring entity usually wants to issue debt which is, in turn, to be secured by the assets of the company to be acquired. The new entity becomes a holding company, and the liabilities incurred in the acquisition, such as the new debt offerings, are often "pushed down" to the acquired company and secured by the assets of the acquired company.

An LBO might be accounted for as either a purchase or a pooling of interests. In virtually all cases, however, it is accounted for as a purchase because debt is issued to the shareholders of the acquired company as part of the acquisition. For example, the holding organization structured for the LBO of RJR Nabisco, RJR Holdings, Inc., was incorporated by issuing stock to the acquiring management team. The holding company then secured cash to pay the existing shareholders of RJR Nabisco by borrowing from banks and secured that borrowing by pledging the assets of the acquired company (RJR Nabisco) as collateral. The acquisition of the shares of the acquired company and the issuance of the debt are handled simultaneously so that the lending institutions can secure their debt with the assets of the acquired company. The valuation issues are similar to those of the purchase transaction except that it is often more difficult to determine the exact value of the acquisition because the price of the securities issued is difficult to estimate. Usually, though, the acquiring company determines a set offering price per share of common stock acquired and develops a financial package of debt, cash, and (in some cases) equity to consummate the financial deal.

Audits of Merger and Acquisitions

Acquisitions Accounted for as Purchases

The major audit problems associated with a purchase involve estimating the fair market value of the net assets acquired (including a revaluation of liabilities when applicable). In most cases, the client obtains the services of a reputable, independent appraisal firm to estimate the fair market value of the identifiable tangible and intangible assets. The auditor reviews the work performed by the appraiser utilizing the guidelines in *AU Sec. 336*, which requires the auditor to determine the appraiser's professional reputation, independence, and knowledge of the accounting issues applicable to the engagement. In addition, the auditor should obtain an understanding of the methods used by the appraiser to judge their applicability to the valuation process.

The auditor should determine the reasonableness and reliability of the appraisal. In most cases, that evidence is obtained by reviewing the work of the independent appraiser. In some cases, however, the auditor may wish to select a sample of items included in the appraiser's report (if it is a large appraisal) and engage a second appraisal company to independently appraise the same items.* The auditor is not necessarily looking to determine that the independent appraisal is exactly the same as the client's appraisal but is attempting to determine whether material differences exist between a statistical projection of the appraised values determined by the appraiser engaged by the auditor and the appraisal contracted for by the client.

The appraisal of intangible assets normally includes a specification of assumptions that are associated with the estimate of the value. For example, the appraiser may assume that the economic life of a patent will be eight years and that the revenues directly attributable to the patent will be a specified amount. Auditors must utilize their knowledge of the client and the industry to determine whether such assumptions are reasonable.

In some cases, the liabilities of the acquired company may also change. One common change is the pension liability because the employees' benefits may be changed by the pension program of the acquiring company. Legislation has been recently enacted to help protect the pensions of employees of acquired companies, but there may still be exceptions when employee coverages are changed significantly. Similarly, an acquiring company might change other postretirement employee benefit plans.

Goodwill should be easy to value; it is the net amount left over after all the other assets are valued. The auditor should determine factors that cause the acquirer to pay more than the fair market value for the company's identifiable assets. Is it superior management? Is it some research and development technology that does not exist in the acquiring company? There is usually something present that the acquiring company is attributing value to that should be recognized in determining the timing of the amortization of the goodwill asset. The APB permits the use of a 40-year life in amortizing goodwill, but this is not meant to imply that 40 years is the appropriate choice. The choice should be based on the expected time period over

*Some CPA firms also have independent appraisal units that operate as separate entities within the public accounting firm.

which the entity is expected to receive benefits from the specific advantages acquired in the assets existing at the time of the acquisition.*

The audit of goodwill in years after acquisition is designed to address the following objectives:

1. Goodwill continues to exist. There has been no major change in the economic entity that would jeopardize the expected benefits to be achieved from the purchased goodwill. Goodwill is supposed to represent the superior earning power associated with the entity. The inability to earn a profit would be an indication that the purchased goodwill may not exist.
2. The current amortization of goodwill is reasonable and consistent with that of previous years. Any expected changes in the economic life of the goodwill are accurately reflected in a new amortization schedule. A microcomputer spreadsheet detailing the goodwill amortization assists in the accomplishment of this objective.

The audit of the continued existence of goodwill requires considerable judgment. It is not as simple as using the spreadsheet to calculate the current year amortization. The auditor must understand the business, its current strategy in utilizing assets and adding or disposing of lines of business, and the likelihood of future success in determining whether existing goodwill should be written off. The auditor must also take care to ensure that goodwill is adjusted when the company disposes of an entity, operating division, or a significant amount of property associated with the purchased goodwill. The difficulties associated with these judgments are presented in the Auditing in Practice section.

A significant valuation problem may exist when a company simply overpays for its acquisitions. Because generally accepted accounting principles assume that all transactions are "fair deals," the accountants initially assign the value of this overpayment to goodwill—an asset is created simply by paying more for something than what it is worth. Because it is often difficult to initially determine the actual value of goodwill, the auditor is put in the position of continually monitoring economic factors to determine whether goodwill actually exists or if an asset is carried on the company's book solely because of bad judgment exercised by company management. In such cases, the goodwill should either be written off or written down to its estimated economic value, if any.†

Acquisitions Accounted for as a Pooling of Interests

Because a pooling of interests does not require the revaluation of existing assets, a merger accounted for by the pooling of interests method does not represent any

*Management often argues for the longest amortization period, such as 40 years, based on the argument that (1) any period chosen is arbitrary, thus 40 years is no better and no worse than any other arbitrary choice, and (2) the company continues to build goodwill every year, but the expenditures to build the goodwill are not capitalized. The 40-year period has the advantage of reducing yearly expenses (as compared to shorter amortization periods) and possibly enhancing management bonuses.

†The entity will almost always resist the auditor's attempt to write down goodwill on the grounds that it is not possible to estimate its value. However, most of the unstated arguments may be more germane: the write down of goodwill may put the company in violation of loan covenants or may cause going concern problems. For these reasons, auditors and clients often resist making the hard choices when accounting rules are conceptual in nature but often difficult to explicitly apply.

Auditing in Practice

EVALUATING CONTINUING GOODWILL

XYZ Company was a publicly traded manufacturer of low-cost office-type furniture listed over the counter. Its board decided to diversify and hired new management to lead the diversification. Prior to diversification, the company had assets of approximately $18 million. New management decided to diversify by buying four separate companies—all of which were in the defense industry—over a period of three years. Although the companies were "high tech," most of the technology was well established, including a company that made gyroscopes.

In the first acquisition, the company assigned most of the excess of the purchase price over the fair value of the net assets to an account called Purchased Technology and amortized the intangible asset over a period of nine years. It reasoned that the company had purchased technology that would allow it to compete for the next few years but that new technology would have to be developed to ensure future growth. Only a small amount was allocated to goodwill. The second acquisition, almost identical in cost and nature, allocated the excess cost to goodwill, rather than purchased technology. The rationale used by management was that such an allocation was generally acceptable. The amounts were material in each case with approximately one-half of the total purchase price allocated to either goodwill or purchased technology. For the two other acquisitions, about half of the purchase price was allocated to goodwill. The company's assets grew from $18 million to $32 million.

Recall that goodwill is supposed to represent superior earnings power of the acquired company. Thus, profitability of the acquired company is necessary to show the existence of goodwill. Over a period of five years, only one of the newly acquired companies was profitable (even before considering the amortization of goodwill), and that profit was fairly negligible. The prognosis for future profitability was not good, and the board of directors directed management to look into selling the acquired companies and to concentrate on its furniture business. Management solicited outside investment advice. The investment bankers suggested that the newly acquired businesses could be sold for approximately their book value (before considering corporate goodwill). After a two-year period, the companies were sold at a loss.

The company was sued by an investor who had bought a large amount of the company's stock, both prior to the decision to dispose of the acquired companies and for a period of time after the decision. The investor claimed that income and assets were overstated because goodwill was non-existent. Further, prior year's income was overstated because goodwill was amortized over 40 years when an identical asset, purchased technology, was amortized over nine years. Management argued that it remained optimistic about the future profitability of the companies and that amortization over 40 years was generally accepted. The case was eventually settled out of court but illustrates the fact that auditors face difficult judgments in evaluating the continued value of goodwill, and those judgments will be questioned.

unusual or significant audit problems.* Often, however, a pooling purchase agreement contains a contingent payment dependent on future performance of the acquired entity, and the auditor should have copies of the merger agreement to determine any contingencies associated with the purchase.

*It should be noted, however, that there may be important accounting questions associated with determining whether sufficient criteria have been met to justify the treatment of the acquisition as a pooling.

Auditing in Practice:

THE LEVERAGED BUY OUT OF RJR NABISCO: THE CASE OF GOODWILL

Goodwill Valuation

Throughout 1988, prior to the October takeover proposal, the stock market valued RJR Nabisco's common stock at about $50 a share; hence, it was capitalizing the company's entire shareholder's equity at about $12 billion. The sum was about $6 billion above RJR Nabisco's book value, which meant that the market's valuation of the goodwill inherent in the cigarettes and cookies business was about $10.6 billion (in other words, the $4.6 billion already on the books for goodwill and trademarks, plus the $6 billion tacked on to the company's net worth by the market).

On October 20, without adding a single cigarette or cookie to the company's market potential, RJR Nabisco's management determined that the goodwill factor should be increased by $6 billion over the market valuation. Specifically, management offered to take the company private for $75 a share, or about $25 a share above the market price. This would have brought the intangible to $16.6 billion.

Just one week later, Kohlberg, Kravis & Roberts, (KKR) weighed in with its first offer, pumping up the goodwill from management's $16.6 billion to about $20.5 billion, by din of its $90-a-share bid. The *coup de grace* came in early December with KKR's $108-a-share bid, boosting RJR Nabisco's intangibles to the $24.5 billion figure (in comparison with $8.5 billion of tangible assets).

Financing of the Acquisition

The funding was provided by (1) senior acquisition financing from a syndicate of banks in the amount of $13.6 billion; (2) Drexel Burnham Lambert's sale, as agent, of $5 billion of increasing rate notes for RJR Holdings Capital Corp; (3) partnership debt securities provided by KKR's investor group in the amount of $500 million; and (4) a capital contribution from RJR Holdings Group of $1.5 billion.

Abraham J. Briloff, "Shame on You, Henry Kravis," *Barron's*, March 6, 1989, 18.

Audit Problems Associated with Leveraged Buy Outs

Valuation issues with LBOs tend to be more complex because most of the securities issued in conjunction with the LBO may not have an active market, and thus market value may not be readily determinable. Many LBOs are financed by junk bonds with provisions that the interest rate of the bond be reset to guarantee the owners that the securities will be traded at or near their face value. For example, assume that the acquiring entity issues bonds with an interest rate of 14 percent but the trading value of the bond drops to 83, yielding an effective interest rate of 17 percent. The bond indenture might require the interest rate be changed to 17 percent (or other applicable amount) at specific dates to ensure the trading of the bonds at face value.

Because most LBOs are accounted for using the purchase method, all the problems associated with valuing tangible and intangible assets, including goodwill, apply. An example of the inherent difficulties in dealing with goodwill is contained in the Auditing in Practice discussion of the LBO of RJR Nabisco. The discussion notes the difficulty that auditors face in determining the value of a transaction. The value of RJR Nabisco apparently changed dramatically over a short period of time when a number of different investors became interested in the company. Almost half of the purchase transaction was assigned to goodwill.

Summary

The audit of long-term assets is, for the most part, fairly straightforward. Analytical procedures are generally effective in estimating expense accounts associated with long-lived assets and substantive testing can concentrate on changes that have taken place during the year. A major complicating factor, however, is the existence of contracts that may fundamentally change the client's rights or obligations. In addition, the auditor must be alert to management motivation to keep related liabilities off the books through lease contracts that are substantively purchases of the assets (but may not meet explicit criteria cited by the FASB).

Significant Terms

asset impairment A term used to describe management's recognition that a significant portion of fixed assets is no longer as productive as had originally been expected. When assets are impaired so that it is unlikely that the unamortized cost of the asset is unlikely to be recovered, the assets should be written down to their expected economic value.

depletion The term used to describe the periodic use of natural assets such as oil or minerals as the products are used; represents an estimate of the cost to obtain the product and is measured per unit, such as per barrel of oil or per ton of metal mined. Depletion is a concept similar to depreciation but is always based on a units of production amortization method.

goodwill The excess of the purchase price for an economic entity over the sum of the fair market values of specifically identifiable tangible and intangible assets; can arise only in connection with the purchase of an organization and identifies superior earning power associated with the entity.

intangible asset Assets that convey value either because of exclusive rights associated with their ownership or that represent value of the firm that cannot be specifically identified with specific tangible assets.

leveraged buy out A method of purchasing a company by investing little capital in a new entity that will purchase all, or at least a majority of, outstanding stock of the acquired entity. The buyers issue large amounts of debt to acquire the company. The debt is collateralized by the assets of the acquired company; thus, in a sense, the assets of the company are used to purchase it.

pooling of interests A method whereby one company acquires another company through the issuance of stock for the outstanding stock of the other company. A pooling is viewed as the continuation of existing ownership; thus, the transactions are recorded at the book value of the acquired entity. The stock issued for the transaction is valued at the book value of assets acquired, not the market value of the stock or of the acquired assets.

property ledger A subsidiary ledger listing all items of property, plant, and equipment and their initial cost, depreciation methods, estimated salvage value, and accumulated depreciation.

purchase accounting An accounting method for the acquisition of another entity by a controlling entity whereby the stock of the acquired company is acquired through the issuance of other than 100 percent stock, such as a combination of cash, debt, and equity. The purchased company's assets are revalued at their fair market value, and any excess of the purchase price over the fair market value of the assets acquired is allocated to goodwill.

Review Questions

A–Audit of Prepaid Accounts

18–1 Explain why the audits of accounts such as Prepaid Insurance tend to rely on a balance sheet rather than an income statement approach. Identify the circumstances in which the auditor might want to utilize one approach over the other.

18–2 Assume that a client has insufficient insurance for the risks to which the business is exposed. An uninsured catastrophe loss would be material to the company and would jeopardize the company's ability to operate as a going concern. What are the arguments for and against disclosure of the inadequate insurance in the notes to the company's financial statements? Are such disclosures required by GAAP?

18–3 Assume that a client has a risk and insurance department. How does the existence of such a department affect the auditor's approach to auditing insurance expense and the Prepaid Insurance account?

18–4 What analytical review techniques are most useful in auditing expense accounts associated with the Prepaid Insurance and Prepaid Rent Accounts? Provide an example of two specific analytical review techniques.

18–5 What are the necessary perquisites to effectively using analytical procedures in testing expense accounts? Explain the rationale for each of the prerequisites.

B–Audits of Property, Plant, and Equipment

18–6 Identify the major elements of a good control structure over property, plant, and equipment. For specific control procedures identified, indicate its importance to the audit.

18–7 A staff auditor was assigned the audit of equipment. The audit senior remarked that "this is the easiest account to audit. All you have to do is vouch the major additions and disposals. The client has already scheduled all additions in excess of $5,000 (our specified cutoff) and has pulled the supporting documentation for your review." Indicate the extent of your agreement or disagreement with the senior's comments. Support your answer with specific references to the audit of property, plant, and equipment.

18–8 What particular problems are encountered in the audit of property, plant, and equipment, and goodwill when another entity is purchased? Explain the specific audit implications when the acquisition is accounted for as a purchase.

18–9 Your firm has just been awarded the audit for a major manufacturing company located in your city. The company has been in operation since 1938 and is considered one of the prestigious audits in the community. The company had been audited by a large national firm with a good reputation, but the company liked your firm's audit approach and personal attention. One of your colleagues suggested that the audit is "going to be awful because the client must take a complete physical inventory of property and we will have to verify original cost and depreciation on existing equipment as well as new additions to property." Explain to the colleague why the statement is incorrect for most audits and probably incorrect on this audit. Identify situations in which the statement might be correct.

18–10 Identify the analytical procedures that may be most effective in performing an audit of depreciation expense. Indicate also how the techniques may provide information on the accuracy of the asset accounts. Explain the nature of each analytical procedure and the information gathered by performing the test.

18–11 What is a property ledger? Explain how the auditor would use generalized audit software in auditing a client's property accounts when the accounts are maintained on computerized data files.

18–12 What is meant by *asset impairment?* What are the major audit issues related to asset impairment than must be addressed on an audit?

18–13 What audit procedures does the auditor use to determine that all fully depreciated equipment not used are written off and that all property that are no longer in production have been written down to scrap value?

18–14 Why does an auditor request the client to prepare a schedule of repair and maintenance expenditures that exceed some predetermined limit? Why might a company want to expense an item rather than capitalize it?

18–15 During the audit of a new client, you uncover an accounting policy that states that all purchases of equipment or other items under $500 will be expensed, regardless of their nature. When you inquire of the controller about this policy, she answers that it is a practical and expedient policy to deal with items that are not material. She indicates that such a policy saves a tremendous amount of work because the items are not inventoried, capitalized, or depreciated. How would the existence of such a policy affect the audit?

18–16 What is the relationship of the tests of property, plant, and equipment to the test of transactions performed as part of the acquisition and payment cycle?

18–17 A client has a policy manual that categorizes equipment as to type and assigns a depreciation life based on the categorization to which the equipment are classified. All equipment in a category are depreciated using the same depreciation method, generally, double declining balance. How does the auditor determine the reasonableness of the approach adopted by the client?

18–18 What are the auditing issues associated with the client's self-construction of new property? Identify the audit procedures that would be used to test the construction of an addition to a factory that is being constructed primarily by employees who would have otherwise been laid off.

18–19 What specific procedures should be applied during the course of the audit related to timing differences of depreciation for book and tax purposes?

C–Audits of Long-Lived Assets

18–20 What are the major audit problems associated with the audit of natural resources? To what extent do auditors utilize specialists in the audit of a natural resources company? Explain using a specific example from a natural resources company.

18–21 Explain how the auditor would determine the remaining expected economic life of the following assets that have been on the books for at least three years:

a. Patents.

b. Trademarks.

D–Long-Term Investments

18–22 A client has recorded a debit of $175,000 to an investment in affiliate company. The controller says that it represents 40 percent of the income of an equity method investee. Identify the evidence (and its source) that the auditor would seek to gain satisfaction as to the correctness of the adjustment.

E–Audits of Mergers and Acquisitions

18–23 What are the major accounting differences between purchase accounting and pooling of interests as used in conjunction with acquisitions and mergers? Why might an aggressive management prefer to acquire a company through a pooling rather than a purchase?

18–24 What is goodwill and how is it valued? How do the client and the auditor determine the economic life over which goodwill is to be amortized?

18–25 What is an LBO? What are the accounting and auditing problems associated with a LBO?

18–26 An audit client has acquired another company and accounted for the acquisition as a purchase. An independent real estate appraiser has been hired to value the assets of the acquired company. What are the audit requirements regarding the use of the specialist? Does the auditor need to engage another independent specialist to test the work of the specialist hired by the company? Explain.

Multiple Choice Questions

18–27 The audit of an acquisition accounted for under the purchase method of accounting creates more valuation issues to address in an audit than an acquisition accounted for as a pooling of interests because

a. All specifically identifiable tangible assets must be appraised and valued at their fair market value.

b. All specifically identifiable intangible assets must be appraised and valued at their fair market value.

c. The total purchase price may be difficult to determine if combinations of securities are used in the acquisition.

d. All of the above.

18–28 Analytical procedures are generally considered an effective procedure in auditing insurance and rent expense. Which of the following is not a justification for using analytical procedures to audit these accounts?

a. The expense accounts are expected to be rather stable over periods of time, and differences can be anticipated through reference to size and volume.

b. The techniques are less costly to apply if the conditions for effective use are met.

c. The techniques are more persuasive than direct tests of the accounts.

d. Analytical review techniques can provide direction to the type of substantive tests that should be applied if the accounts differ materially from what is expected.

*18–29 The internal auditor tours the production facility. Which of the errors or questionable practices is most likely to be detected by the audit procedure specified?

a. Insurance coverage on the facility has lapsed.

b. Overhead had been overapplied.

c. Necessary facility maintenance has not been performed.

d. Depreciation expense on fully depreciated machinery has not been recognized.

*18–30 A company keeps its fixed asset records on a computer system. Each record in the file is identified by a unique nine-digit fixed asset identification number. The remaining fields describe the asset, its acquisition date, cost, economic life, depreciation method, and accumulated depreciation. Which of the following audit procedures could not be performed using generalized audit software?

a. Select a sample of assets to be used in verifying existence of the asset.

b. Use parallel simulation capabilities to recompute accumulated depreciation.

c. Use parallel simulation capabilities to compare economic life with accumulated depreciation.

d. Foot the cost and accumulated depreciation fields and trace the totals to the client's general ledger.

*18–31 The auditee has acquired another company by purchase. Which of the following would be the best audit procedure to test the appropriateness of the allocation of cost to tangible assets?

a. Determine whether assets have been recorded at their book value at the date of purchase.

b. Evaluate procedures used to estimate and record fair market values for purchased assets.

c. Evaluate the reasonableness of recorded values by use of replacement cost data for similar new assets.

---

*Adapted from the Uniform CPA examination or the Certified Internal Auditor examination.

d. Evaluate the reasonableness of recorded values by discussion with operating personnel.

*18–32 During an audit of fixed assets, certain machinery is determined to be unusable and of little value, although it is carried on the books at a high value. Which of the following would be the most appropriate recommendation to prevent a recurrence of this finding?

a. Institute a formal, preventive maintenance program.
b. Assign responsibility for machinery to individual line managers.
c. Improve maintenance of perpetual inventory records.
d. Require periodic physical inventory and inspection procedures.

*18–33 An auditor analyzes repairs and maintenance accounts primarily to obtain evidence in support of the audit assertion that all

a. Noncapitalizable expenditures for repairs and maintenance have been properly charged to expense.
b. Expenditures for property and equipment have not been charged to expense.
c. Noncapitalizable expenditures for repairs and maintenance have been recorded in the proper asset account.
d. Expenditures for property and equipment have been recorded in the proper period.

*18–34 The auditor may conclude that depreciation charges are insufficient by noting

a. Large amounts of fully depreciated assets.
b. Continuous trade-ins of relatively new assets.
c. Excessive recurring losses on assets retired.
d. Insured values greatly in excess of book values.

*18–35 When auditing prepaid insurance, an auditor discovers that the original insurance policy on plant equipment is not available for inspection. The policy's absence most likely indicates the possibility of a (an)

a. Insurance premium due but *not* recorded.
b. Deficiency in the coinsurance provision.
c. Lien on the plant equipment.
d. Understatement of insurance expense.

*18–36 To establish the existence and ownership of a long-term investment in the common stock of a publicly traded company, an auditor ordinarily performs a security count or

a. Relies on the client's internal controls if the auditor has reasonable assurance that the control procedures are being applied as described.
b. Confirms the number of shares owned that are held by an independent custodian.
c. Determines the market price per share at the balance sheet date from published quotations.
d. Confirms the number of shares owned with the issuing company.

Discussion and Research Questions

18–37 (Insurance Expense) The audit of the Prepaid Insurance and Insurance Expense accounts typically receive more audit time than might be dictated by their materiality. Auditors often request the client to prepare a complete list of insurance coverage even though neither the asset account nor the related expense account is large.

Required:

a. Explain why the auditor spends more time on the insurance accounts than would seem to be justified by their size.

b. During the course of an audit, the auditor determined that the client depended heavily on its computer data processing facility. The company did not have any formal disaster recovery plans, and in the rare event that the computer center would be wiped out by a disaster, it is unlikely that the company would be able to continue in operation. The client believes that the possibility of such an event is remote and has therefore decided not to insure against the risk. What effect would this finding have on the audit report? Explain the action you would recommend the auditor take.

c. The auditor performs analytical procedures on the insurance expense account and notices a dramatic decrease in the expense during the year. When the controller is queried for this decline, his response was simply that the company had decided to self-insure for most of its major assets because its plants are geographically dispersed. What audit steps would you recommend to finish the audit of the insurance account? Explain the impact of self-insurance on the account.

d. An auditor reviews the client's insurance coverage and notes an apparently large decrease in coverage. The controller explains that the firm changed their insurance company during the year and that the new company indicated that the firm had been overinsured in previous years. What does the auditor need to do to complete the audit of the account?

18–38 (Generalized Audit Software on Equipment Audit) This is the first-year audit of a company that wants to register with the SEC in the near future. The company has been very successful and has implemented a modern computer system to manage its business, including a property, plant, and equipment database. The auditor had received review reports (but not audits), performed by other auditors in previous years, and the auditor did not note unusual fluctuations in either the depreciation or equipment accounts in previous years. The client instituted the computer program only two years ago and has recently taken a physical inventory of property and has used the physical inventory to adjust the database. Because of advanced planning, the auditor was able to observe the taking of the equipment inventory.

The database contains the following information for each asset:

- Property identification number.
- Property description.
- Date acquired.
- Cost.

- Class of assets.
- Depreciation method.
- Salvage value (if applicable).
- Current year depreciation—book.
- Accumulated depreciation—book.
- Current year depreciation—tax.
- Accumulated depreciation—tax.
- Any adjustments such as write-downs or renovations.
- Expected life of asset.
- Location of property.
- Department or person requesting purchase of item.

Required:

a. Write a program to audit the equipment account for the year. Indicate where and how you would use generalized audit software in your audit. (Ignore tax considerations at this point.)

b. Describe how test data might be used in the audit of property for this client.

c. What audit procedures would have been mandated had the client not taken a physical inventory of property?

18–39 (Control over Property, Plant, and Equipment)

Required:

The following represent questions that might be addressed in an evaluation of the control structure for property, plant, and equipment. For each question:

a. Indicate the purpose of the control procedure.

b. Indicate the impact on the audit if the answer to the question is *no*.

Control Structure Questions:

1. Does the client periodically take a physical inventory of property and reconcile to the property ledger?
2. Does the client have a policy manual to classify property and assign an estimated life for depreciation purposes to the class of assets?
3. Does the client have a policy on minimum expenditures before an item is capitalized? If yes, what is the minimum amount?
4. Does the client have a mechanism to identify pieces of equipment that have been designated for scrap? If yes, is it effective?
5. Does the client have an acceptable mechanism to differentiate major renovations from repair and maintenance? If yes, is it effective?
6. Does the client regularly self-construct its own assets? If yes, does the client have an effective procedure to appropriately identify and classify all construction costs?

7. Does the client systematically review major classes of assets for potential impairment?
8. Is management motivated to write down assets for any particular reason? If yes, what is the reason?
9. Does management periodically review asset disposal or the scrapping of assets as a basis for reviewing the assignment of estimated life for depreciation purposes?

18–40 (Analytical Procedures—Depreciation) The audit senior has asked you to perform analytical procedures to estimate the reasonableness of recorded depreciation expense of a manufacturing client. The client has seven different classes of equipment as follows:

(SL = Straight-Line Depreciation, DDB = Double-Declining Balance Depreciation)

• Stamping machines,	10-year life,	SL
• Electronic control units,	6-year life,	DDB
• Materials handling equipment,	8-year life,	DDB
• Office equipment,	6-year life,	SL
• Fork lift trucks,	8-year life,	DDB
• Finishing machines,	4-year life,	DDB
• Trucks,	5-year life,	DDB

Required:

a. Describe in general terms how analytical procedures could be used to estimate the amount of depreciation expense.
b. Identify specific analytical procedures that could be used and indicate how each would be used.

18–41 (Audit Evidence and Conclusions) The following conclusions were taken from a staff auditor's summary worksheet for property, plant, and equipment and the worksheet for prepaid insurance.

Required:

a. For each conclusion or situation listed below, identify the type of audit evidence needed to support the auditor's conclusion.
b. Briefly indicate the audit implications if the auditor's conclusion is justified.

Audit Conclusions or Situations:

1. The choice of eight years for straight-line depreciation of the company's trucks appears unreasonable. I would suggest that the client change to a six-year life and use DDB depreciation.
2. Insurance coverage appears to be inadequate because the client has chosen to carry only liability insurance on the cement trucks. There is no provision for collision or damage done to the trucks.
3. The client acquired a substantial piece of real estate from the town of Baraboo to build a warehouse in the town's new industrial complex. The

land was donated to the company provided it maintains operations for a minimum of 10 years and pays real estate taxes on its appraised value. The land is carried on the books at a fair market value of $250,000.

4. A number of pieces of idle equipment were noted. It is recommended that the equipment be written down to the scrap value of $50,000 from the current net book value of $185,000.
5. The company has self-constructed the warehouse located in the town of Baraboo. It has capitalized all payroll expense that directly related to the construction of the project. The adjusting entry debited Building for $73,000 and credited Payroll Expense for the same amount.
6. The company completely overhauled 10 of its trucks at a significant cost. The overhaul should extend the life of the trucks by at least three years. Because the company performs similar overhauls each year, the cost has been properly charged to repairs and maintenance.
7. The company sold 15 of its old trucks to Virgin Distributors, a new company owned by the brother of the company's chief executive officer. The equipment was old, and a gain of $70,000 on the sale was credited to income.

18–42 (Purchase Accounting) Romenesko Conglomerate Co. recently acquired Teasedale Cosmetic Company through a tender offer for all the common stock of Teasedale Cosmetic. Teasedale stock had been trading on the market at $25 per share, but the tender offer was made at $35 per share for all 2 million of the company's shares. Teasedale had a book value of $17 per share at the time of the acquisition. Romenesko gave each shareholder $10 in cash, 1/2 of a share of Romenesko common stock (trading at $30 per share), and 1/10 of a share of an $8 preferred stock not previously issued. Teasedale's condensed balance sheet consisted of the following before acquisition (in thousands):

Cash	$ 300
Other current assets	3,000
Property and equipment	22,000
Intangibles exclusive of goodwill	2,500
Goodwill	5,000
Total assets	32,800
Current liabilities	4,000
Pension obligation	3,000
Long-term debt	8,000
Deferred taxes	800
Stockholders' equity	17,000
Total liabilities and equity	$ 32,800

Required:

a. What are the unique valuation problems the auditor must address in connection with Romenesko's purchase of Teasedale Cosmetics?

b. How should the auditor use a specialist in the valuation of the purchase transaction?

c. What happens to the goodwill that was on Teasedale's books? Explain.

d. What happens to the other intangibles that were on Teasedale's books? Explain.

e. What happens to the deferred income tax liability on Teasedale's books once the purchase is completed?

f. Assume that the client uses a specialist who does not change the value assigned to current assets or liabilities but reduces the pension obligation to $1,500 and values the property, plant, and equipment at $30 million and other intangibles at $5 million. Additionally, the current market value of Teasedale's long-term debt is $5 million, but its face value remains at $8 million (also its maturity value). What is the amount of goodwill to be recorded?

g. How would the auditor determine the expected economic life over which to amortize the goodwill?

18–43 (Leases) While performing analytical procedures on Merrill Traders, Inc., the auditor discovered a substantial increase in lease expense and a corresponding decrease in both the Property, Plant, and Equipment accounts and related Depreciation. On further inquiry, the auditor discovered that a substantial amount of equipment and one piece of property were sold to an outside leasing company. The company then leased the property back and leased similar equipment from the lessor. The controller shows the auditor that the lease was contractually constructed so that it would not be considered a sale and leaseback. The proceeds of the sale were used to pay down long-term debt.

The auditor is puzzled that economically there appears to be no change in the operations of the company, but the company may have incurred higher future costs because the lease agreement terms do not appear to be as economically favorable as did the past ownership. For example, the company leases equipment for three years when the expected life is five years but is responsible for all maintenance on the equipment.

Required:

a. What role do substance versus form decisions play in the audit of a client and in a situation such as that described?

b. What audit procedures should be performed to finish the analysis of the lease expense account?

18–44 (Audit of Natural Resources Company) Red Lake Mining Co. engages in the search and mining of gold in North America, principally Canada. During the year, it discovered a substantial new source of gold which it estimates holds 15.5 million troy ounces of gold. At the time of discovery, gold was selling for $400 per ounce, and it is estimated that the cost of mining the gold will approximate $250 an ounce. There is no doubt that all of the gold will be sold at market prices. The company estimates that the cost of discovering the ore was approximately $25 million and that it will cost another $225 million to construct a plant to mine the gold.

Required:

a. Because there is a ready market for gold, the controller has proposed that the discovery be valued at the market value, or net market value, of the gold discovered. He says that such a valuation better informs investors as to the real value of the company. Would such a valuation be acceptable?
b. How would the auditor verify the estimate of 15.5 million troy ounces of gold?
c. The controller suggests that a depletion schedule be established based on the $250 million of discovery and plant construction. The audit senior suggests that a depletion allowance be established on the $25 million discovery cost, not the $250 million. Would a depletion allowance based on $250 million be acceptable? Explain.

*18–45 (Analysis of Property Changes) You are doing the audit of Halvorson Fine Foods, Inc., for the year ended December 31, 1995. The following schedule for the property, plant, and equipment and related allowance for depreciation accounts have been prepared by the client. You have compared the opening balances with your prior year audit working papers. The following information is found during your audit.

1. All equipment are depreciated on the straight-line basis (no salvage value taken into consideration) based on the following estimated lives: buildings, 25 years; all other items, 10 years. The corporation's policy is to take one-half year's depreciation on all asset acquisitions and disposals during the year.
2. On April 1, the corporation entered into a 10-year lease contract for a die casting machine with annual rentals of $5,000, payable in advance every April 1. The lease is cancelable by either party (60 days written notice is required), and there is no option to renew the lease or buy the equipment at the end of the lease. The estimated useful life of the machine is 10 years with no salvage value. The corporation recorded the die casting machine in the Machinery and Equipment account at $40,400, the present value at the date of the lease, and $2,020, applicable to the machine, has been included in depreciation expense for the year.
3. The corporation completed the construction of a wing on the plant building on June 30. The useful life of the building was not extended by this addition. The lowest construction bid received was $17,500, the amount recorded in the Buildings account. Company personnel were used to construct the addition at a cost of $16,000 (materials, $7,500; labor, $5,500; and overhead, $3,000).
4. On August 18, Halvorson paid $5,000 for paving and fencing a portion of land owned by the corporation for use as a parking lot for employees. The expenditure was charged to the Land account.

5. The amount shown in the Retirement column for the machinery and equipment asset represents cash received on September 5, on disposal of a machine purchased in July 1991 for $48,000. The bookkeeper recorded depreciation expense of $3,500 on this machine in 1995.
6. Crux City donated land and building appraised at $10,000 and $40,000, respectively, to Halvorson for a plant. On September 1, the corporation began operating the plant. Because no costs were involved, the bookkeeper made no entry for the foregoing transaction.

Halvorson Fine Foods, Inc.
Analysis of Property, Plant, and Equipment
For the Year ended December 31, 1995

Description	Final Balance, December 31, 1994	Additions	Retire-ments	Per Books, December 31, 1985
Assets:				
Land	$ 22,500	$ 5,000		$ 27,500
Buildings	120,000	17,500		137,500
Machinery and equipment	385,000	40,400	$ 26,000	399,400
	$527,000	$62,900	$ 26,000	$564,400
Allowance for depreciation:				
Building	$ 60,000	$ 5,150		$ 65,160
Machinery and equipment	173,200	39,220		212,470
	$233,250	$44,370		$277,620

Required:

a. In addition to inquiring of the client, explain how you found each of the given six items during the audit.
b. Prepare the adjusting journal entries with supporting computations that you would suggest at December 31, 1995, to adjust the accounts for the above transactions. Disregard income tax implications.

18–46 (Permanent Decline in Value of Long-Term Investments) Reid Co. has a significant investment in Red Oak Ltd. carried on the books at cost. The investment is $45 million, but Red Oak Ltd. has fallen on hard times. The current trading price of the stock shows that the market value of Reid's investment is only about $28 million. On the other hand, the problems have been addressed by Red Oak's management. Further, the stock price dip has been made worse by a recession that appears to be ending soon. Thus, it appears that Red Oak will become profitable again, and the long-term outlook for a return to above average profitability is very good. Reid has indicated that it intends to maintain its investment in Red Oak for the long-term, even though Red Oak has presently suspended dividend payments.

Required:

a. What evidence should the auditor evaluate to determine whether the investment in Red Oak should be written down to current market value?

b. Assume that Reid did write down its investment to $28 million and, one year later, its value rose to $35 million. The company wants to write the investment up to $35 million. What audit evidence would be needed to support such an increase in value?

18–47 **(Research: Acquisitions and Goodwill)** During the 1980s, a substantial number of companies were acquired and financed through the issuance of junk bonds. Many of the acquisitions were made through LBOs, some of which have subsequently gone public. Perform a search of either NAARS or Compact Disc Disclosure to determine the amount of goodwill recorded in conjunction with the acquisitions. Evaluate the profitability of the companies and the period of time over which goodwill is amortized. Evaluate the quality of the footnote disclosure associated with goodwill.

18–48 **(Research: Acquisitions and Valuation)** Interview selected CPAs to determine the procedures they use to value assets of a company that had been acquired under purchase accounting. Identify at least five appraisal companies that perform such valuations. Determine what factors auditors use to determine the reliability of appraisals from different companies.

Case

*18–49 (Operational Audit of Fixed Assets) A corporation operates a highly automated flexible manufacturing facility. The capital-intensive nature of the corporation's operations makes internal control over the acquisition and use of fixed assets an important management objective.

A fixed asset budget that indicates planned capital expenditures by department is established at the beginning of each year. Department managers request capital expenditures by completing a fixed asset requisition form, which must be approved by senior management. The firm has a written policy that establishes whether a budget request is to be considered a capital expenditure or a routine maintenance expenditure.

A management committee meets each month to review budget reports that compare actual expenditures made by managers to their budgeted amounts and to authorize any additional expenditures that may be necessary. The committee also reviews and approves as necessary any departmental request for sale, retirement, or scrapping of fixed assets. Copies of the vouchers used to document departmental requests for sale, retirement, or scrapping of fixed assets are forwarded to the accounting department to initiate the removal of the asset from the fixed asset ledger.

The accounting department is responsible for the maintenance of a detailed ledger of fixed assets. When a fixed asset is acquired, it is tagged for identification. The identification number, as well as the cost, location, and other information necessary for depreciation calculations, is entered into the fixed asset ledger. Depreciation calculations are made each quarter and are posted to the general ledger. Periodic physical inventories of fixed assets are taken for purposes of reconciliation to the fixed asset ledger as well as appraisal for insurance purposes.

Required:
Develop four audit objectives and three related work steps for each objective to evaluate internal controls over fixed assets at the corporation.

End Note

1. Abraham J. Briloff, "Shame on You, Henry Kravis," *Barron's*, March 6, 1989, 18.

CHAPTER

19

Learning Objectives

Through studying this chapter, you should be able to:

1. Understand the unique nature of financial institutions and related audit concerns.
2. Understand the risks inherent in financial institutions and the audit approaches needed to address those risks.
3. Evaluate the control structure in financial institutions to determine adjustments to audit programs.
4. Understand the nature of the financing cycle and audit approaches to long-term liabilities.
5. Develop an audit approach for major financing activities applicable to all businesses with a focus on bonds and capital stock.

Audit of Financing Activities: Emphasis on Financial Institutions

Chapter Contents

Chapter Overview

Financial institutions represent unique audit challenges. The failure of many savings and loan institutions in the 1980s; the vulnerability of some insurance companies to large, unexpected redemptions of policies; and the difficulty in estimating the quality of loans all add to the challenges of auditing companies in the financial services sector. Investors expect financial reports to be realistic, not optimistic. As economic conditions change, management and the auditor must consider the effect of the change on the ability of borrowers to repay loans. This chapter addresses factors that are unique to auditing financial institutions and concludes with a brief section on audit ing the financing activities of nonfinancial institutions.

The data clearly show that in recent years bank earnings have varied almost entirely as a result of loan losses and loss provisions. So it's not unreasonable for investors to want to know whether their banks' portfolios contain risky loans that are likely to translate into future losses. But that isn't what the banks tell them. . . . Failures are near a record high among the nation's 13,000 commercial banks. So are loan losses. In the last four years banks charged off $75 billion of bad loans, compared with $28 billion between 1948 and 1981.[1]

In our study of 39 banks which failed in 1988 and 1989, we concluded that flexible accounting rules used to recognize and measure loan losses contributed to banks not accurately reporting these losses in their financial reports prior to failure. . . . The Congress recognized our concerns about bank financial reporting in enacting the Federal Deposit Insurance Corporation Improvement Act of 1991.[2]

The auditor normally should consider the historical experience of the entity in making past estimates as well as the auditor's experience in the industry. However, changes in facts, circumstances, or entity's procedures may cause factors different from those considered in the past to become significant to the accounting estimate. In evaluating reasonableness, the auditor should obtain an understanding of how management developed the estimate. [AU 342.09 and 342.10]

The preceding quotes underline the fundamental audit challenge encountered in audits of financial institutions. The earnings and financial strength of a financial institution are reflected in its loan and investment portfolio. It is difficult, however, to estimate the loans or investments that will turn sour, yet it is management's challenge to do so and the auditor's challenge to determine the reasonableness of those estimates. The financial services sector has been subject to a wide variety of risks, which the auditor must understand to plan and execute an audit for a company in this industry. Fortunately, there are many commonalities across financial services companies, and we will begin with a brief review of those commonalities.

A–NATURE AND AUDIT OF FINANCIAL INSTITUTIONS

Understanding Financial Institutions

Financial institutions solicit outside funds such as demand deposits, savings accounts, and insurance premiums and invest those funds to earn a return. Most financial institutions are heavily leveraged; that is, debt and other liabilities dwarf the amount of equity invested in the business. The institutions have historically been able to operate effectively with such leverage because either (1) their assets and return on them have been fairly predictable or (2) the demands against their accrued liabilities have been fairly predictable. For example, before deregulation, the savings and loan industry invested most of its assets in long-term mortgages, and most of its liabilities were in the form of stable savings accounts. However, the deregulation of the 1980s changed the operations and financial structure of these firms.

The two keys to success in financial institutions are (1) maintaining the stability of capital resources (including debt) and (2) controlling the quality of investment and loan portfolios. Banks and savings and loans are engaged primarily in the business of making loans, most of which are secured by underlying assets such as real estate or securities. Other financial institutions invest heavily in bonds, real estate developments, or marketable equity securities. Insurance companies, for example, are major investors in the bond and stock market, real estate development, and emerging businesses.

Most financial institutions are subject to regulation concerning types of investments and amount of capital that must be maintained. Insurance companies, for example, may be restricted on the types of loans they make or in the percentage of investments in specific risk categories. Regulatory agencies often require financial statements that do not follow GAAP.

The financial statements of financial institutions differ dramatically from those of manufacturing organizations. Exhibit 19.1 presents the income statement and balance sheet of Norwest Bank. The following are the primary differences. Banks do not classify assets and liabilities as current and noncurrent. The bank's assets consist primarily of loans and investments with little property, plant, and equipment. Many banks have sold their buildings and leased them back to keep the asset and related debt off the balance sheet. Loans are usually categorized by type and risk, and the notes to the financial statements describe the risks in significantly greater detail. For example, large international banks have billions of dollars of loans to Third World countries, which many believe are not fully collectible. The amounts of reserves against such loan balances are disclosed.

Customer deposits are the primary liabilities. Federal and state bank regulators set minimum capital requirements, such as six percent of total assets. Violation of the capital requirements can lead to the shut down of the bank and takeover by a regulatory agency.

Exhibit 19.1

NORWEST CORPORATION AND SUBSIDIARIES
CONSOLIDATED BALANCE SHEETS
IN MILLIONS, EXCEPT SHARES

	At December 31, 1992	1991
Assets		
Cash and due from banks	$ 2,388.2	2,589.6
Interest-bearing deposits with banks	47.9	100.1
Federal funds sold and resale agreements	345.7	345.5
Total cash and cash equivalents	2,781.8	3,035.2
Trading account securities	132.0	157.9
Investment securities (market value $926.4 in 1992 and $2,700.1 in 1991)	874.8	2,449.5
Mortgage-backed securities (market value $10,179.9 in 1991)	—	9,892.0
Total investment and mortgage-backed securities	874.8	12,341.5
Investment securities available for sale (market value $1,632.9 in 1992)	1,393.9	—
Mortgage-backed securities available for sale (market value $9,224.7 in 1992)	9,022.7	—
Total investment and mortgage-backed securities available for sale	10,416.6	—
Student loans available for sale	1,158.6	—
Mortgages held for sale	4,727.8	3,007.7
Loans and leases	23,930.3	21,196.5
Unearned discount	(1,002.5)	(971.2)
Allowance for credit losses	(617.8)	(608.1)
Net loans and leases	22,310.0	19,617.2
Premises and equipment, net	640.8	595.6
Interest receivable and other assets	1,514.7	1,538.2
Total assets	$44,557.1	40,293.3
Liabilities and Stockholders' Equity		
Deposits		
Noninterest-bearing	$ 6,588.7	5,815.7
Interest-bearing	20,381.1	20,704.9
Total deposits	26,969.8	26,520.6
Short-term borrowings	8,575.4	5,785.5
Accrued expenses and other liabilities	1,471.0	1,573.2
Long-term debt	4,468.2	3,578.6
Preferred stock–authorized 5,000,000 shares without par value:		
1,137,700 and 1,150,000 shares outstanding in 1992 and 1991, respectively, at $100 stated value, 10.24% cumulative dividends	113.8	115.0
1,143,750 and 1,150,000 shares outstanding in 1992 and 1991, respectively, at $200 stated value, 7.00% cumulative dividends and convertible	228.7	230.0
Common stock, $1 2/3 par value–authorized 300,000,000 shares:		
Issued 141,289,065 and 140,278,855 shares in 1992 and 1991, respectively	235.5	233.8
Surplus	551.8	521.9
Retained earnings	2,008.4	1,768.6
Notes receivable from ESOP	(19.5)	(22.5)
Treasury stock–1,172,940 and 449,492 common shares in 1992 and 1991, respectively	(45.7)	(11.4)
Foreign currency translation	(0.3)	—
Total common stockholders' equity	2,730.2	2,490.4
Total stockholders' equity	3,072.7	2,835.4
Total liabilities and stockholders' equity	$44,557.1	40,293.3

(Continued)

Exhibit 19.1

NORWEST CORPORATION AND SUBSIDIARIES CONSOLIDATED STATEMENTS OF INCOME IN MILLIONS, EXCEPT PER SHARE AMOUNTS

	Year Ended December 31, 1992	1991	1990
Interest Income on			
Loans and leases	$2,191.6	2,394.8	2,466.9
Investment securities	164.3	229.2	265.6
Mortgage-backed securities	557.2	708.8	482.7
Investment securities available for sale	11.6	—	—
Mortgage-backed securities available for sale	157.1	—	—
Student loans available for sale	24.2	—	—
Mortgages held for sale	279.4	192.1	137.8
Money market investments	17.0	53.4	110.4
Trading account securities	23.0	10.7	9.6
Total interest income	3,425.4	3,589.0	3,473.0
Interest Expense on			
Deposits	839.7	1,251.0	1,298.2
Short-term borrowings	269.6	334.9	498.2
Long-term debt	307.1	305.5	261.1
Total interest expense	1,416.4	1,891.4	2,057.5
Net interest income	2,009.0	1,697.6	1,415.5
Provision for credit losses	176.9	330.4	423.8
Net interest income after provision for credit losses	1,832.1	1,367.2	991.7
Non-interest Income			
Trust	155.7	137.6	120.6
Service charges on deposit accounts	161.4	148.0	131.5
Mortgage banking	273.2	185.2	130.7
Data processing	66.1	64.2	65.3
Credit card	134.0	152.2	99.6
Insurance	153.1	138.5	131.5
Other fees and service charges	135.7	122.4	105.7
Net investment and mortgage-backed securities gains	8.9	22.5	6.6
Net venture capital gains (losses)	29.7	(4.6)	10.3
Net investment and mortgage-backed securities available for sale gains	51.0	—	—
Other	33.9	43.5	52.9
Total non-interest income	1,202.7	1,009.5	854.7
Non-interest Expenses			
Salaries and benefits	1,087.1	908.9	775.7
Net occupancy	165.9	148.5	131.5
Equipment rentals, depreciation and maintenance	160.0	139.6	128.1
Business development	111.5	87.8	74.1
Communication	135.6	119.6	99.2
Data processing	85.4	85.9	80.3
FDIC assessment and regulatory examination fees	63.9	58.4	31.0
Intangible asset amortization	65.0	60.5	30.5
Other	460.8	262.5	258.6
Total non-interest expenses	2,335.2	1,871.7	1,609.0

Exhibit 19.1

NORWEST CORPORATION AND SUBSIDIARIES
CONSOLIDATED STATEMENTS OF INCOME
IN MILLIONS, EXCEPT PER SHARE AMOUNTS

	Year Ended December 31, 1992	1991	1990
Income before Income Taxes and Cumulative Effect of a Change in Method in Accounting for Postretirement Medical Benefits	699.6	505.0	237.4
Income tax expense	181.2	82.9	101.6
Income before cumulative effect of a change in accounting for postretirement medical benefits	518.4	422.1	135.8
Cumulative effect on years prior to December 31, 1992 of a change in accounting for postretirement medical benefits, net of tax	(71.7)	—	—
Net Income	$446.7	422.1	135.8
Average Common and Common Equivalent Shares	141.0	138.5	131.2
Per Common Share			
Net Income			
Primary:			
Before cumulative effect of change in accounting for postretirement medical benefits	$ 3.48	2.91	1.02
Cumulative effect on years ended prior to December 31, 1992 of a change in accounting for postretirement medical benefits	(0.51)	—	—
Net Income	$ 2.97	2.91	1.02
Fully Diluted:			
Before cumulative effect of a change in accounting for postretirement medical benefits	$ 3.42	2.89	1.01
Cumulative effect on years ended prior to December 31, 1992 of a change in accounting for postretirement medical benefits	(0.48)	—	—
Net Income	$ 2.94	2.89	1.01
Dividends	$1.080	0.940	0.845

Types of Financial Institutions

Financial institutions have charters that specify the scope of approved activities and other regulatory requirements. The major types of institutions include the following:

Commercial banks must have charters from either a national or state agency. Deposits are generally insured by the Federal Deposit Insurance Corporation (FDIC). Commercial banks are primarily in the business of procuring and lending funds, although there is legislation under consideration to allow commercial banks to provide other services such as brokerage and insurance services. Historically, commercial banks in the United States have been limited as to the geographic areas they may serve, but changes in state banking laws and regulations have led to mergers of large banks into bank holding companies with increased geographic dispersion.

Savings and loans (S&Ls) have either federal or state charters and may be formed as either mutual or stock organizations. Savings and loans were originally chartered by Congress to make home mortgage loans secured by family homes. To finance the mortgages, the S&Ls offered various long-term savings plans for their depositors such as certificates of deposits or savings accounts with rates slightly higher than commercial banks. Most customer deposits were insured by the Federal Savings and Loan Insurance Corporation (FSLIC). The structure worked fine in periods of low inflation but encountered problems during highly inflationary periods because loans were typically long-term with fixed interest (such as 30-year, 8 percent mortgages), but the liabilities carried variable interest rates to compete with other financial institutions for consumer deposits. During the deregulation of the 1980s, many S&Ls sold most of their mortgages and invested in higher return (and higher risk) commercial real estate loans.

Bank holding companies are nonoperating companies formed to provide common ownership and control of nonbanking subsidiary activities permitted by the Bank Holding Company Act of 1956. **Bank holding companies** serve as the parent company for individual banks that retain separate identity but act as one institution. Regulations generally restrict the amount of earnings that can be transferred to the holding company in the form of dividends, advances, and management fees. The regulations are intended to protect the bank and its depositors from mismanaged nonbanking activities of the holding company.

Credit unions have many similarities to savings banks but must share a common base for membership. They are owned by the members much like a mutual company. Deposits may be insured through the National Credit Union Share Insurance Fund (NCUSIF). Credit unions are not subject to income tax and thus may have a competitive advantage in paying returns to their investors, but their charters generally restrict the types of loans and investments they can make.

Life insurance companies manage large sums of assets over the life of the insurance policies issued to their customers. Most are subject to state regulations that prescribe minimum capital ratios and allowable types of investments. Life insurance companies may be either stock or mutual companies.

Property/Casualty insurance companies underwrite specific risks such as those related to health, automobiles, and homes, for example. The success of these companies depends on how well they manage the two major portions of the business: underwriting and investing. The quality of the underwriting influences the frequency and type of claims and the proper pricing for the risks assumed. The quality (safety) of the investments and the returns generated from the investments directly affect the company's competitiveness. Both life insurance and property/casualty insurance companies may be subject to statutory accounting practices (SAP) prescribed by their governing regulatory body.

Although each financial institution is unique, all share common characteristics that influence the audit approach:

- *The companies are all subject to government regulations.* The regulations are designed to protect consumers and depositors from corrupt or overzealous risk taking by management. However, government regulations have decreased in recent years, which many people believe has allowed some financial institutions to assume too many risks.

- Keys to the success of each organization are *the quality of their investment portfolio and the rates of return earned on it.* Some insurance companies, for example, have invested in low-grade, high-yield junk bonds to earn returns that would allow them to price their insurance products competitively. But such high-risk investments can impair operations because they may not be liquid and may be subject to a high degree of volatility.
- *There is a need to manage the assets/liability mix.* **Asset/liability mix** refers to (1) the relative longevity of a company's asset investments compared to its liabilities; (2) the relative stability of the costs associated with the assets/liabilities (for example, investments at fixed interest rates and liabilities containing variable interest rates); and (3) the relative size of the liquid assets versus the liquid liabilities. A financial institution should not support long-term investments with short-term liabilities (as was the case with much of the savings and loan business during the 1970s and 1980s). The ability to manage the asset/liability mix significantly influences the success of the organization.
- *The companies have very few physical assets.* Most of their assets are loans and investments.
- *The companies are heavily computerized.* Reliable, well-controlled computer systems are extremely important to the long-run viability and competitiveness of most financial institutions.
- *Liabilities for insurance companies are extremely difficult to estimate.* Actuarial advice is often sought in estimating the liabilities for insurance coverages. Auditors need to review both actuarial estimates and the history of claims to assess the reasonableness of the recorded liabilities of a property/casualty company.
- *Many financial institutions must prepare financial statements according to a regulatory basis of accounting.* Two sets of financial statements are often prepared, one following regulatory agency requirements and the other following GAAP.
- *Market value accounting has been recommended by the FASB but is resisted by the financial institutions.* The FASB has addressed many financial institution accounting issues and has recommended changes to reflect the current market valuation of investments. Banks have resisted these changes because they are difficult to implement and they might impair their regulatory capital status.
- *The industry uses unique accounting terminology.* For example, the common checking accounts are referred to as *demand deposits* and constitute the primary liabilities of a bank. Insurance companies' liabilities are often referred to as *reserves.*

Unique Risks Inherent in Financial Institutions

The auditor must clearly understand the operating risks of financial institutions to implement a risk-based approach to auditing. The amount of risk in the industry is considerable. Between 1985 and 1988, 689 banks and 499 savings institutions were either closed or given financial subsidies to maintain operations. During 1992 the

Congressional Budget Office predicted that an additional 600 banks would fail or require further assistance in the next five years. Estimates range from $500 billion to as high as $1 trillion to bail out the savings and loans.

Financial institutions are subject to six specific types of risks that should be assessed by the auditor: credit risk, market risk, liquidity risk, interest rate risk, exchange rate risk, and operational risk.

Credit risk. The risk that a debtor may be unable to fulfill its obligation is called **credit risk.** A borrower, for example, may default on a loan. Credit risk can be managed through careful screening of loan applications and diversification of loans across industries and/or geographic regions. The nature of the organization's credit risk should be regularly reviewed by a senior management committee.

Market risk. The risk of fluctuation in current market prices of investments is **market risk.** Market risk can be managed through choices regarding security quality, duration and liquidity.

Liquidity risk. The risk arising when the institution has insufficient resources available at a particular point in time to meet maturing liabilities or obligations is **liquidity risk.** The organization may have sufficient resources, but they may not be liquid when needed.

Interest rate risk. The risk that interest rates earned on assets will be less than the interest rates paid on liabilities is **interest rate risk.** Interest rates may differ in amount and duration. For example, investments may be at fixed (long-term) interest rates, but liabilities may be at flexible (short-term) interest rates.

Exchange rate risk. The risk arising when commitments are made in foreign currencies that fluctuate in value in relationship to the domestic currency is **exchange rate risk.** Many financial institutions compete for funds on a worldwide basis and are affected by significant changes in exchange rates.

Operational risk. The risk that an institution may be unable to process transactions in a timely or accurate manner is **operational risk.** Operational risks often occur when organizations embark on growth strategies but do not pay sufficient attention to building operational support for the new volume or types of transactions. Many of these risks are reflected in "off balance sheet transactions," which may require disclosure.* Many financial institutions, for example, engage in hedging transactions in an effort to offset or mitigate interest or exchange rate risks.

Financial institutions often use hedges, such as buying futures contracts, to offset some risks. The hedging techniques may be difficult to understand and may not be recorded. An organization's plan for dealing with risks should be examined during each audit. Changes in the quality of investments or loans should also be examined and their implications considered in evaluating the riskiness of the client.

*An example of such a transaction is the interest rate swap whereby one institution agrees to pay fixed interest rates on a nominal liability to another institution and receives variable interest rates from the same institution (or another counterparty if arranged by an intermediary). The rationale for such swaps is to better match a financial institution's asset/liability structure. Often the amounts of these transactions or the specific risks associated with them are not shown on the balance sheet. The FASB has proposed changes that will better show the effect of these financial arrangements and portray the risks on the balance sheet.

B–PLANNING AND CONDUCTING THE AUDIT OF FINANCIAL INSTITUTIONS

Once an auditor understands the types of risks associated with financial institutions, attention should be turned to planning the audit engagement. The financial services sector has been studied extensively by the GAO and the Office of the Comptroller of the Currency. Their studies have been helpful in identifying factors that have been associated with failed institutions. The overall audit approach must consider such factors as a basis for assigning personnel to the engagement and determining specific audit procedures to be performed. An analysis of the risk factors begins with an examination of the competitive, economic, and regulatory conditions affecting the client.

Competitive Environment

Expanding world economies have enabled financial institutions to increase their deposits and to sustain rapid growth. During the 1980s, the deregulation of interest rates paid on deposit accounts, the expansion of financial services, and the scaling back of other regulations created a decidedly different competitive environment. Competition for funds intensified. Bank holding companies expanded across state boundaries and mergers, such as those of Chemical Bank with Manufacturer's Hanover and Security Pacific with Bank of America, created mega-size financial institutions to compete on a global basis. The auditor must assess how these changes have affected the client's products or management's propensity to take additional risks.

Economic Environment

Cyclical changes in the economic climate have a direct impact on financial institutions. For example, a recession in a geographic area affects the liquidity of a bank that makes consumer loans in that area. Exhibit 19.2 lists questions designed to assist the auditor in assessing economic risk. The information gathered should be corroborated by an industry background review and interviews with key members of management. Experience and knowledge of the business allows the auditor to analyze company affairs to determine the quality of the responses made by management.

The auditor's assessment of each question directly affects the design of the audit. For example, if the organization has embarked on a growth strategy without implementing needed controls, it is likely that loans will not be well documented or may not have been adequately reviewed by a loan committee. This may expose the company to the risk of experiencing larger losses, and the audit should emphasize the adequacy of loan loss reserves.

Specific Financial Risks

The approach taken to manage the financial structure of the institution may result in risks that should be considered in addressing the adequacy of the firm's recorded

Exhibit 19.2

TYPICAL QUESTIONS ADDRESSING ECONOMIC FACTORS AFFECTING FINANCIAL INSTITUTIONS

1. *New products or services.* To what extent has the client become involved in offering new products or services? Has the institution developed or acquired the expertise to allow it to identify, control, and record provisions for losses associated with these new products or services?
2. *Interest rate changes.* Have interest rate changes affected the client's net interest margins? Has the institution taken measures to hedge its position?
3. *Related-Party transactions.* Are there significant related-party loans or deposits, or significant increases or decreases in those amounts?
4. *Growth without control.* Has there been an emphasis on growth without implementation of corresponding control procedures? Have risks been identified and analyzed in relation to organizational objectives and resources? If yes, describe and identify the specific implications for the audit.
5. *Off balance sheet financing.* Has the organization extensively engaged in off balance sheet transactions such as forward or futures contracts, options, or letters of credit? Has the organization analyzed the risks associated with such financing? Has the organization developed a model for disclosing the risks?
6. *Dependence on single source of funds.* Has the organization become increasingly dependent on large deposits from a few sources or short-term borrowings as a source of funds? Does the organization effectively manage its asset/liability mix? If not, what are the potential effects that should be addressed during the audit?
7. *Management plans and compensation.* (a) Does management have reasonable expectations for (1) changes in interest rates, (2) government support of troubled industries, or (3) volatility in large deposits? (b) To what extent is a significant portion of management compensation tied to earnings or market value of the company's stock? Does management appear to manage earnings, such as using accounting changes to boost earnings or manage the loan loss reserves to meet profit expectations?
8. *Analysis of loan loss reserves:* Does the company incorporate current economic conditions in its analysis of loan loss reserves (i.e., does the analysis consider changes taking place in the economic environment rather than just the aging of the loans)? Is the analysis thorough and does it consider the changes in geographic or global economic factors? Are loan loss reserves reviewed regularly by top management and the board of directors? Does the client use an expert system to assist in its analysis of loan loss reserves?
9. *Loan risk concentration.* Are there concentrations of high-risk loans in specific industries with specific management groups or within specific geographic areas? If so, document and consider the risk on the realizability of the assets.
10. *Overseas loans.* Are there significant loans or investments in less developed countries where the assets may be subjected to abnormal amounts of risk? Document management's approach to managing those investments and the realizability of those investments.
11. *Statutory requirements.* Has the institution failed to meet regulatory reserve, capital, or liquidity requirements? Obtain copies of recent regulatory correspondence and consider the regulatory agencies findings' impact on the audit.
12. *Foreclosed assets.* Has the company foreclosed on significant amounts of assets, or has it restructured a number of significant loans (troubled debt restructuring)? Has the company conservatively assessed the market value of such foreclosures? Has it developed a sound control structure to dispose of the foreclosed assets in a timely manner?

liabilities or the valuation of its assets. Typical questions used by auditors to assess risks associated with management's approach to operations is shown in Exhibit 19.3. The point that should be considered in reviewing the items addressed in Exhibit 19.3 is a simple one: The amount of substantive audit work either expands or contracts, depending on the effectiveness with which management addresses the organization's risks.

The Regulatory Environment

Financial institutions are subject to considerably more regulatory overview than are most other organizations. Many regulatory provisions are aimed at safeguarding a depositor's funds entrusted to a bank or the insurance holder's investment in a policy. Audits by regulatory agencies often focus on the quality of the institution's

Exhibit 19.3

TYPICAL QUESTIONS RELATED TO THE FINANCIAL ANALYSIS OF FINANCIAL INSTITUTIONS

1. *Strategy for managing risk.* Does the company have a specific strategy for managing risk? Is the strategy documented or developed into a formal document? Does management periodically review industry developments as a basis to reassess current strategy?
2. *Existence of asset/liability management policy.* Does the company have a sufficient asset/liability management policy that includes monitoring loan maturities, interest rate structure, and quality of underlying financial instruments and that takes corresponding measures to match interest rates and not engage in interest rate speculation?
3. *Maintenance of interest margin.* How does the company's net interest margin compare to other companies in the same industry and with performance in previous years? Has management sufficiently analyzed and reacted to major changes in interest rates?
4. *Loan and interest rate management.* Has the company experienced unusually high losses associated with past due loans? Does the company effectively manage its past due loans and recognize charge-offs as appropriate? Are variable loans capped at rates that reflect current borrowing rates? Has the organization engaged in excessive short-term borrowing to meet investment and loan demand? Has the board of directors reviewed management's borrowing strategy in relation to long-term market and growth strategy?
5. *Monitoring of off balance sheet transactions.* Do management and the board of directors effectively monitor off balance sheet transactions to identify risks and determine the need for financial statement disclosure?
6. *Financial analysis.* How do the organization's key financial ratios compare to industry averages and to past performance? Does management regularly monitor important ratios such as loan to total borrowings, capital ratio, loan loss ratio, and past due or troubled loan analysis.
7. *Liquidity requirements.* Does the organization effectively analyze and manage its daily liquidity requirements? Does the organization finance long-term loans or investments with short-term borrowings?
8. *Growth and acquisition strategy.* Does the company have a growth and acquisition strategy? Is the strategy well formulated and periodically reviewed by the board of directors? Are profit projections used in developing acquisition or merger plans realistic?

investments and the adequacy of loan loss reserves, the management control structure, and its adherence to regulatory requirements. The auditor should review the most recent report by the regulatory auditors and inquire about the status of any ongoing examination before completing their audit. Regulatory files often contain documentation of the examiner's doubts about management integrity and the safety of investments.

Assessing the Management Control Structure

The auditor's assessment of the management control structure may be the single most important procedure in an audit of a financial institution. Experienced auditors look for answers to common sense questions related to control structure such as these:

- Is management running this organization in the best interests of its shareholders or as if the organization were its personal fiefdom?
- Does the audit committee or board of directors exercise effective independent overview of the management function?
- Has management subjected the organization to unusual or unwarranted risks or increasing amounts of risk? If yes, are there other controls in place to lessen the potential effect associated with the risk?
- Has management paid sufficient attention to processing controls to ensure the protection and safeguarding of the organization's assets?
- Has management engaged in a systematic process to increase earnings through accounting changes as opposed to operations?

Although the questions are simple, court records document numerous cases of financial institution failures because management either ran the organization as if it were designed for personal purposes or management neglected needed controls to run the organization. Furthermore, the payout by many auditing firms associated with the savings and loan failures occurred in large part because the auditors failed to ask such questions or failed to act on the answers.

Other key components of the overall management structure that should be evaluated include the following:

- Competence and functioning of an audit committee.
- Effective oversight by the board of directors.
- Existence of an effective internal audit department.
- Effective oversight by senior management committees, especially the loan review committee and the process by which senior management monitors potential loan losses.
- Overall design and control of computerized information systems.

Effective Audit Committee

Financial institutions have a stewardship function to a broad constituency that includes shareholders, depositors, the business community, government deposit insurance agencies, and the community in which the organization functions.

Regulators are keenly interested in whether the audit committee acts as an independent check and review on management or whether it exists in form only. Governmental agencies, particularly the GAO, have been critical of the effectiveness of supposedly independent audit committees that do not provide effective overview of management activities. Much of that criticism was incorporated into the FDIC Act of 1991 which prohibited major borrowers from serving on a bank's audit committee.

Independent Board of Directors

The GAO has been very critical of financial institutions in which members of the board of directors appeared to have a potential conflict of interest. For example, some members of the board of directors of failed financial institutions were major borrowers from the bank. The FDIC Act of 1991 prohibits such relationships in the future. In addition, boards are required to meet a sufficient number of times to understand the business and have sufficient resources to monitor the organization.

Effective Internal Audit Department

Many financial institutions have large internal audit departments which audit for compliance with the strict laws and regulations under which financial institutions operate, as well as with management's policies and procedures. An effective internal audit department can alert management and the audit committee to operational problems. The internal audit department is likely involved heavily in computer audits. Considering the billions of dollars that flow through the banking system, all controlled by computer applications, it is not surprising that internal auditors in the financial institution sector are the heaviest users of the concurrent audit techniques described in Chapter 10.

Effective Oversight by Senior Management Review Committees

Senior management review committees, such as loan or investment committees, are a crucial element of an organization's control environment. For example, to understand the role of a senior loan committee, it is important to understand that loan officers are often compensated based on the amount of loans they generate. Thus, it is to the loan officer's advantage to make as many loans as possible. Because loan officers are motivated to push as many loans as possible through the process, it is important that a conservative **loan review committee** act as a constraint against overly aggressive approaches by the lending officers. As reported in the best seller, *Inside Job: The Looting of America's Savings and Loans*,[3] many of the failed savings and loans were run without independent analysis by senior management committees or oversight by board of director subcommittees.

Sophisticated Computer Systems

Billions of dollars are transferred electronically through our banking system, and the trend to paperless checking accounts is accelerating. If one can gain unauthorized access to a bank's computer system, there is the potential to transfer millions of dollars to unauthorized accounts. There have been many computer frauds in banking environments. The auditor needs to evaluate the adequacy of computer controls and the existence of concurrent audit techniques to efficiently plan the audit.

Few small banks have the financial resources to develop computer systems needed to interface with the rest of the banking system. Consequently, these small banks have their processing performed by larger banks. If a bank's data processing is performed by another organization, the external auditor normally requests an independent audit report on the service bureau. The service bureau auditor's report describes the important control procedures used by the service bureau and the auditor's tests of the control procedures. The external auditor should consider the service bureau auditor's report in assessing control risk and determining the nature and extent of independent testing to be performed at the service bureau.

Assessing Financial Risk

The auditor should assess the financial risk associated with a particular financial institution as a basis to effectively plan the audit and to tailor procedures to high-risk areas. A recent study by the Office of the Comptroller of the Currency (see Exhibit 19.4) indicated that failed and declining banks had poor asset quality, inadequate operating policies, and poor control systems. Conversely, healthy banks exhibited strengths in the following:

- Controls over key bank officers and departments.
- Management information systems.
- Systems to ensure compliance with policies and laws, lending policy, and problem loan identification systems.

Other problems identified by the Office of the Comptroller of the Currency include nonexistent or inappropriate lending policies, excessive loan growth in relation to the abilities of management, staff, and control systems, undue reliance on volatile liabilities as a capital source, inadequate liquid assets, inept management, excessive credit exceptions, and unwarranted concentrations of credit in one industry. One failed savings and loan institution, for example, had almost 20 percent of its loans to one automobile dealer.

Exhibit 19.4

CONDITIONS LEADING TO DECLINE OF BANKS

	Percent of Banks with Significant Weaknesses	
Problem Areas	Failed Banks	Banks in Rehabilitation (before Recovery)
Poor asset quality	98%	98%
Inadequate policies, planning, and management quality	90	88
Difficult economic environment	35	39
Insider abuse	35	24
Lack of internal audits, poor controls and systems	25	24
Existence of material fraud	11	0
Liquidity and funds management problems	10	6
Nonfunding of expenses	9	4

Source: *Bank Failure—An Evaluation of the Factors Contributing to the Failure of National Banks* (Washington, D.C.: The Office of the Comptroller of the Currency) 1992.

The auditor should perform detailed financial analysis, including ratio analysis and industry comparisons, during the planning process. As an example, Imperial Corporation of America (a failed S&L) recorded a loan loss reserve at a rate well below the industry average when its asset quality was significantly less than the industry average. This knowledge, when coupled with evidence about management integrity, heavy investments in junk bonds, and a short-term management orientation, should serve as a signal to the auditor that inherent and control risk ought to be assessed at a maximum and that audit procedures should be planned accordingly.

Assessing Control Risk and Reporting on Control Structure

The FDIC Act of 1991 was designed to address the significant problems of the banking industry. The bill is far reaching and, among other things, requires a management report stating its responsibility for internal controls and its assessment of controls. The auditor is required to report on management's assertions regarding internal control. The internal control structure is broad based and includes operational areas such as maintaining written documentation for loans, updating reports on collateral, and developing procedures for credit underwriting, as well as the traditional controls associated with the computer processing of transactions. The auditor's report on management's assessment of internal controls will likely lead to greater compliance testing of controls and examination of documentation than would have occurred if such a report were not required. The auditor should meet with management and the audit committee to understand the scope of management's report on controls and to effectively plan the control evaluation work as part of the annual financial statement audit.

Audit of Investment and Loan Assets of Financial Institutions

Loans and Loan Loss Reserves

The primary activity of most banks and S&Ls is making loans. Often a financial institution targets growth areas such as consumer loans, real estate loans, oil and gas development loans, third-country loans, or commercial loans. Small banks, for example, often focus on commercial loans to small businesses, as well as automobile and home loans in the geographic area in which they operate. With the deregulation of the 1980s, many banks expanded their loan portfolio across state and national boundaries. Major banks such as Citicorp and Chase Manhattan made significant loans to less developed countries and participated with other banks in providing funding for leveraged buy outs and other mergers and acquisitions. Other financial institutions expanded with real estate loans in geographic locations far removed from their own locations.

The audit objective for **loan loss reserves** is to evaluate the reasonableness of the reserve recorded by management. Loan loss reserves represent the quantification of management's estimate for uncollectible accounts and the valuation of the collectible asset at its net present value.*

*Most loans are valued at their net present value when the loan is made because the lending rate is usually equal to the current market rate. However, as long-term interest rates change, the net present value of the loan may change. The FASB has recommended that the loan portfolio recognize the change in net present value due to such changes. However, the recommendation is controversial and may change over time.

The audit approach for loan loss reserves does not differ conceptually from the process of estimating the allowance for uncollectible accounts in manufacturing organizations. However, it does differ significantly in the dollar amounts involved, the complexity of the estimation process, and the risks associated with multiple components of the loan portfolio. An overview of an audit approach to estimate loan loss reserves is presented in Exhibit 19.5.

When preparing to audit accounting estimates, the auditor is cautioned by AU 342.04 to exercise the proper amount of professional skepticism:

> The auditor is responsible for evaluating the reasonableness of accounting estimates made by management in the context of the financial statements taken as a whole. As estimates are based on subjective as well as objective factors, it may be difficult for management to establish controls over them. Even when management's estimation process involves competent personnel using relevant and reliable data, there is potential for bias in the subjective factors. Accordingly, when planning and performing procedures to evaluate accounting estimates, the auditor should consider, with an attitude of professional skepticism, both the subjective and objective factors.

Exhibit 19.5

AUDIT APPROACH TO ESTIMATE LOAN LOSS RESERVES

1. Develop an understanding of the risks associated with the client's loan portfolio. Consider such factors as industry concentration, economic conditions affecting the portfolio, the average duration of the portfolio, and the liquidity of the assets.
2. Develop an understanding of the organization's control structure over the lending process and the loan monitoring process for existing loans.
3. Determine the effectiveness of control procedures applicable to the management of the loan portfolio. Determine whether management effectively follows procedures of writing off loans as soon as they are deemed uncollectible.
4. Select a sample of loans using PPS techniques and confirm with the borrowers the existence of the loan, the current loan balance, the claim on collateral, and the major terms of selected loans.
5. Evaluate management's methods for estimating loan losses. Independently test management's methods for making such estimates by evaluating a sample of loans and analyzing the loan loss reserves by industry classification or other relevant categories used by the client.
6. Estimate the net realizable value of the loan portfolio through an analysis of the credit history of borrowers, the current status of collateral securing the loans, the current payment status, and current financial statements of major borrowers. Perform detailed follow-up work on loans that are past due, or loans to companies in troubled industries, to develop an estimate of the collectability of the loans.
7. Determine compliance with government regulations and board policies. Obtain copies of all regulators' reports on the institution and review for loan quality classification.*
8. Review management's preliminary estimate and compare with other financial institutions and previous estimates, taking into consideration the overall quality of the loan portfolio.
9. Reach a conclusion about the overall collectibility of the loan account recorded at net realizable value. Document the conclusion and the basis for the conclusion.

*Most regulatory agencies require the organization to classify its loans into specific categories ranging from write-offs and problem loans to good loans.

Management may show bias in making subjective evaluations about the likelihood of collecting individual loans or may make overly optimistic judgments about factors such as the economic health of customers or the economy affecting the loans. The auditor's professional skepticism should apply to management's optimism regarding economic recovery of individual debtors, the current value of **collateral,** and the likelihood of collecting on past-due loans.

Understand the Control Structure

The auditor must understand the process by which loans are made and approved, as well as senior management's role in reviewing loan strategy and compliance with its loan policies. Of particular importance are the procedures and the documentation required for loan approval and the procedures put in place to secure and evaluate the adequacy of collateral on a continuing basis. Weaknesses in the control structure should be directly linked into the development of the substantive audit program. Failure of top management to review the diversification of loans, for example, would cause the auditor to perform more detailed analysis of the overall loan portfolio.

Determine Effectiveness of Control Procedures

If the preliminary assessment is that control risk is low, the assessment should be corroborated by a test of the effectiveness of specific control procedures. The existence of loan procedures, such as review by a loan committee, the presence and analysis of audited financial statements for large loans, the independent appraisal of collateral, and the economic analysis of the project secured by the loan are important in assessing control risk. Other important control procedures that should be tested include those for computer processing and the integrity of the loan file.

Confirm the Existence of the Loan

The auditor normally confirms the existence of the loan, its current balance, and collateral pledged for the loan with the debtor. The confirmation does not establish collectibility, but it does provide evidence on existence. If the loan is past due, the auditor normally seeks more information, such as current financial statements of the debtor and outside credit reviews, and may want to observe the collateral and ensure that the client has perfected a claim on it. The auditor will normally use a PPS sampling approach supplemented by specific criteria, such as selecting all loans over a specified dollar amount or accounts past due.

Perform Independent Analysis of Loan Collectibility

The auditor's analysis of collectibility and loan risk should address the following factors:

- Industry concentration of loans.
- Geographic concentration of loans.
- Nature of loans (commercial, real estate, LBOs, etc.).
- Current economic conditions affecting major classes of loans.
- Collateral for the loans.
- Age of loans and current payment schedule for past-due loans.

- Loans restructured or in the process of being restructured.
- Loans to related parties (existence and amount).
- Loan compliance with governmental regulations and board policies.
- Overall riskiness of loans and current economic conditions.

Most of the information in the list is contained in the client's database. Therefore, the auditor should be able to use audit software to develop a loan analysis by major loan types and to age the loans based on past-due payments. Many audit firms maintain or have access to analyses of economnic conditions in specific industries that the audit team can review. The audit team should review the client's history of loan write-offs and can use previous data in developing a preliminary assessment of potential loan losses. However, the auditor should be aware that (1) past results are not necessarily a good indicator of the current amount of uncollectible loans because economic conditions do change and the auditing profession has been justifiably criticized for not taking such changes into consideration, (2) the history of loan loss recognitions shows that managements have been very subjective in determining when losses would be recognized,* and (3) the overall estimate of loan losses based on an aggregated model should be corroborated by analysis of individual loans.

Evaluate Management's Methods for Estimating Loan Losses

Management is responsible for developing an accounting information system to estimate loan losses. The system should contain the ability to classify loans by geographic region, industry, age, collateral, current payments, and duration, as well as provide data on loans being restructured and the current economic conditions of borrowers. If such an information system exists, the audit approach should evaluate and test the client's system, including the accuracy of management's classifications, the assumptions used in making the loss estimates, and management's assessment of likely losses on individual loans. Unfortunately, many financial institutions have not developed sophisticated systems to perform the loan loss analysis, and the auditor will need to independently develop a model to estimate loan losses and to compare with management's estimates.

Examine Collateral on Selected Loans

Many commercial and real estate loans are collateralized by the underlying asset for which the loan was made, such as a shopping center under construction. Most banks obtain independent appraisals of the underlying collateral as a requirement for making the loan and will structure it to have first claim on the collateral. The value of the underlying collateral and the priority of the client's claim to the collateral in the event of default are important elements in assessing a minimum value in the event of loan default. Economic conditions do change, however, and it is important that

*For example, often banks such as Citicorp announce a massive loan write-off only to be followed 10 days later by write-offs at other major banks. Some of these write-offs have occurred on third-country debt only days after the issuance of annual financial statements that had classified the loans as good, although there was no appreciable change in the economic conditions of the countries between the issuance of the statements and the write-off.

the financial institution obtain up-to-date independent appraisals of the collateral in making estimates of potential loan losses.*

Evaluate Compliance with Governmental Regulations and Board Policies

Most financial institutions have restrictions—either regulatory or board policy imposed—on the types or amounts of loans or investments they can make. A regional bank, for example, may be prohibited from financing real estate developments outside the geographic region it serves. Loan documentation should show compliance with mandated truth-in-lending requirements. If audit evidence indicates that loans totaling a material amount violate regulations, the auditor should consider the potential effect in either losses, fines, or mandatory disposal of the loans.

Make Preliminary Estimate of Loan Loss and Compare with that for Other Financial Institutions

The estimate of loan loss reserves for the client should be compared with that of other financial institutions operating within the same geographic area or with similar loan portfolios. The purpose of the comparison is not to justify the client's estimate but to determine the reasonableness of major differences.

Loan Loss Reserves—Summary

The approach just described emphasizes the need for an independent and knowledgeable business approach to auditing a highly "judgmental" account. Unfortunately, because of the subjectiveness in making estimates, there is no one "correct" value of loan loss reserves. But the difficulty of obtaining a correct estimate does not relieve the auditor of the duty to make a sound economic estimate of a most probable amount and a likely range of such losses. An example of management's disclosure of loan loss provisions is shown in Exhibit 19.6.

Audits of the Investment Portfolio

The investment portfolio of major banks may be complex with diverse risks. Many of the regulatory restrictions on the investment portfolio were changed with the deregulation of the 1980s, and many companies dramatically changed the nature of their portfolios. Many institutions invested in the vast array of financial instruments discussed in Chapter 18 and engaged in substantial hedging transactions. The audit of the investment portfolio does not differ significantly from that described in Chapter 18 for long-term investments. The approach is summarized here.

*One problem often encountered in the analysis of failures in the savings and loan industry is that the S&Ls did not have appraisals updated for current economic conditions. For example, a number of real estate developments in Arizona were once appraised very high, but when a downturn in the economy occurred, the value of the collateral dropped dramatically and often it was not worth the investments needed to complete the project. Additionally, there were many concerns about the independence and competence of the appraisals. The auditor should be guided by [AU 336] in assessing the competence of the work of specialists when reviewing outside specialists.

Exhibit 19.6

EXAMPLE OF MANAGEMENT'S LOAN LOSS DISCLOSURE

Allowance for Credit Losses

The allowance for credit losses is based on management's evaluation of a number of factors, including credit loss experience, risk analyses of loan portfolios, and current and expected economic conditions.

Charge-offs are loans or portions thereof evaluated as uncollectible. Loans made by the consumer finance subsidiaries, unless fully secured by real estate, are generally charged off when the loan is 90 days or more contractually delinquent and no payment has been received for 90 days. Credit card receivables are generally charged off when they become 180 days past due or sooner upon receipt of a bankruptcy notice. Other consumer loans are generally charged off when they become 120 days past due unless fully secured.

Loans and Leases

Changes in the allowance for credit losses were as follows (amounts in millions):

	1992	1991	1990
Balance at beginning of year	$ 608.1	541.8	374.8
Allowances related to assets acquired	29.5	18.8	54.6
Provision for credit losses	176.9	330.4	423.8
Credit losses	(303.0)	(401.9)	(378.3)
Recoveries	106.3	119.0	66.9
Net credit losses	(196.7)	(282.9)	(311.4)
Balance at end of year	$ 617.8	608.1	541.8

Source: Norwest Corporation, 1992 Annual Report, 36 and 39.

Develop a Meaningful Classification of Investments

The investment portfolio should be classified by type of investment in order to identify and assess the risks associated with the investments. The classification scheme should reflect the nature of the investment, the risks associated with it, other relevant geographic or industry information, duration (long term or short term), and characteristics of the underlying financial instrument. The investments might include stock, equity participation in new companies, foreign currency investments (unhedged), or commercial paper of differing investment grades.

Understand and Analyze the Risks

The classification of loans is a prerequisite to understanding and analyzing the risks associated with the investments. FASB Statement No. 105 requires the disclosure of major risks associated with investments including off balance sheet arrangements for which the company may be contingently liable. Specific investment risks may affect the asset's valuation as economic conditions change and may require financial statement recognition. In particular, the auditor should be alert to transactions that are recorded as hedging transactions that might not be fully hedged.

Determine Current Market Value of Investments

Most financial instruments have a current market value. The SEC requires market value disclosure of most financial instruments. There is considerable discussion about requiring all investments to be "marked to market value" because some bank managements have manipulated reported income by selectively selling long-term investments that have appreciated in value and retaining (but not writing down) similar long-term investments that have declined in value.

Determine the Need for Adjustments

The investment portfolio often needs to be adjusted to reflect changes in its net realizable value. The nature of and the rationale for the adjustments should be documented.

Auditing the Liabilities of Financial Institutions

Auditing the liabilities of some financial institutions is quite complex and requires specialized industry knowledge that extends beyond the scope of this textbook. Two areas—demand deposits and insurance reserves—that demonstrate the complexity are briefly described.

Auditing Demand Deposits and Savings Accounts

Demand deposits (known to most of us as checking accounts) and savings accounts represent the major liabilities of most banks and similar financial institutions. The accounts are subject to a major outside control by customers who conscientiously perform their monthly bank reconciliations. If errors are noted, customers should be able to contact someone independent of the normal account processing to correct the error and discover the cause of the error. Most financial institutions have developed adequate control procedures to ensure the correct processing of customer deposits, transfers, and withdrawals, and most audit approaches concentrate on understanding and testing the effectiveness of the important control procedures such as the following:

- Daily reconciliations of all transactions processed with changes in cash and related obligations.
- Computer access controls.
- Procedures for establishing accounts, writing off dormant account balances, or transferring funds among accounts.
- Independent investigation of customer complaints and corrective actions taken when problems are identified.

Many auditing firms use confirmations to test the existence and valuation of the outstanding liability. However, research has raised questions on the effectiveness of the confirmation procedure to identify individual misstatements and has suggested that the confirmation process be limited to positive confirmations.

Auditing Insurance Reserves

Insurance companies are required to maintain an **insurance reserve** for losses against premiums collected. For example, when an insurance company sells an automobile policy and collects a premium, it expects that a certain percentage of that premium will be paid out in future claims. Accrual accounting requires that an estimate of those future claims be established as a liability at the time the revenue and asset are recognized. The nature of those claims vary by the type of insurance policy written: life insurance reserves differ by the type of policy (whole life or term), medical coverage differs from automobile collision claims, and commercial property claims differ from negligence or common liability claims. The success of an insurance company depends on the skill with which it estimates and manages such claims. Northwestern Mutual Insurance, for example, has a much different mortality rate than does Prudential Insurance because the two target different audiences of policyholders. An automobile insurance company prices its high-risk, under 25-year-old policies differently from its good driver policies. But if the companies do not have data with which to price those policies, they will eventually incur large losses or may even be forced into bankruptcy.

Most life insurance companies use actuaries to make reserve estimates for life insurance policies. The estimates are based on mortality and interest rate assumptions. The problems for property/casualty insurance policies are more complex. Presumably, a well-managed client has a comprehensive information system containing previous claims data that can be used to estimate the needed reserves. If such a system exists, the audit can concentrate on testing the system and estimating the reasonableness of the client's projected reserve.

To better understand the audit issues involved in assessing the reasonableness of such estimates, consider the following information necessary to assess possible claims against an automobile policy with collision, liability, and medical coverage:

- Coverage and limits of the policy held by the claimant.
- Risk class of insured motorist.
- Previous claim data by insured class and automobile.
- Current claims, by class, matched against current coverage.
- Repair cost index by automobile class for various types of repairs.
- Claims in progress.
- Trends in liability settlements and court awards.
- Length of policy coverage.

Based on these data, the company must estimate the expected claims against existing policies. As with loan loss reserves, there is no one right answer. But the approach should be systematic to ensure that management does not subjectively raise or lower the estimate to obtain profit objectives. Deficiencies in the client's information system can lead to errors in estimates such as those detailed in the Auditing in Practice case.

Fraud Exposures

The fraud danger signs for financial institutions are similar to those of other institutions. When there is inadequate segregation of duties, lack of supervision, no action on unusual operating results, and unauthorized access to cash or documents that generate cash, there is a higher than usual probability for fraud. The computerization of financial institutions presents another level of access for sophisticated employees who have knowledge of operations to commit material frauds. The auditor's analysis of an organization's control structure should consider the possibility of fraud within each major operating cycle. Some of the major exposures in financial institutions that should be considered include these:

- Unauthorized electronic transfer of funds.
- Unauthorized manipulation of accounts or interbank transfers.

Auditing in Practice

ESTIMATING INSURANCE RESERVES: RELIABLE INSURANCE CASE

Reliable Insurance Co. of Madison, Wisconsin, introduced a new insurance policy to provide supplemental coverage to Medicare benefits for the elderly. Because there are specific limits to Medicare coverage, the insurance was well received by elderly policyholders, many of whom were in nursing homes. The insurance policy was new, and therefore the company did not have experience with previous claims but did have data about the nature of claims made by senior citizens. The policy was competitively priced and sold very well. The company recognized salesperson commissions as sales were made.

To estimate the reserves, the client used initial claims data to estimate costs and to build a model for reserves. For example, claims data for the first three months could be compared with premiums for the same three months to estimate the needed reserve against future premiums. The model was subsequently adjusted for more information (e.g., information for the first 12 months). The data were sent to an actuarial firm, along with demographic data of the policyholders, to estimate year-end reserves. Unfortunately, the client's accounting system was slow in meeting the unexpected demand for the policies and in recording the claims against them. Consequently, there was a significant delay in processing the initial claims data. As a result, the model was comparing data for different periods; for example, claims data for one month were compared with premiums for three months. The model significantly underestimated the needed reserves for future claims.

Because the company believed that the policy was competitively priced, it moved aggressively to market it and achieved significant sales growth. However, the initial underestimate of costs caused the company to incur substantially greater liabilities than anticipated. In retrospect, the company had significantly underpriced the policies and was forced into bankruptcy when it could not meet policyholder claims. The audit failed to test the accuracy and timeliness of the client's claim processing system and relied on the actuary for the reserve estimate. Had the system been properly tested, the audited financial statements would have been properly presented. But, more important, the company would have had better information on which to base its policy pricing decision and may have been able to stay in business.

- Fraudulent coding in computer programs.
- Fraudulent insurance claims.
- Theft of insurance premiums.

The identification of exposures is not meant to be all-inclusive but to serve as an example of material exposure. The Auditing in Practice case involving State Farm presents an example of a computerized approach to deal with the fraud potential in the insurance industry.

C–AUDIT OF THE FINANCING CYCLE: OTHER COMPANIES

An organization has an almost infinite number of ways to meet its long-term financing needs. The two most common are issuing capital stock (equity) and bonds

Auditing in Practice

COMPUTER AUDITING AT STATE FARM LIFE INSURANCE COMPANY

State Farm Life Insurance Company is a major insurance carrier with more than 3.9 million individual policyholders. Data related to an insurance policy can be input from more than 1,500 terminals or personal computers. During 1989, the computer system handled more than 30 million transactions submitted through regional offices. The internal auditors worked with information systems personnel to identify potential weaknesses in the existing system. They identified unauthorized changes to the policyholder master record followed by a fund withdrawal as one of the most significant areas of exposure for the company.

After considering the major exposures, the internal audit department (with the cooperation of management) installed a system of audit hooks in the computer application. To conduct a fraud and leave the policyholder unaffected, the auditors reasoned that an internal employee would have to change the name, make a claim (and thereby a withdrawal against the policy), and then change the name back to that of the original policyholder. The audit hooks were designed to flag a name change that was followed by a funds withdrawal within a specified period of time. Within one month, the internal auditors found a major pattern of such fraud by one of its employees. Management investigated the fraud and took action against the employee. The internal auditing department is updating the audit program for other exposures that may exist in the system. Thus, the computer, while providing opportunities for the unscrupulous employee, also provides opportunities for auditors to effectively use computer audit techniques to lessen the exposure.

(borrowing). The remainder of this chapter provides a brief overview of audit considerations involved with these two financing methods. However, as discussed earlier with financial instruments, a wide variety of financing instruments are more complex and require extra care should they be encountered. The other accounts the auditor may encounter in auditing financing activities include the following:

- Notes Payable.
- Mortgages Payable or Contracts Payable.
- Special contracts, such as put or take contracts.
- Special bonds:
  - Payment in kind bonds (pays interest in the form of the issuance of more bonds with a stipulated date on which cash interest must be paid).
  - Convertible Bonds which are convertible into equity.
  - Serially retired bonds.
- Preferred Stock.
- Mandatory redeemable preferred stock (preferred stock with a mandatory redemption date).

- Stock options and warrants.
- Stock options as part of a stock compensation scheme.

The internal control and processing considerations for these accounts are similar to those described below for the basic types of bond and capital stock transactions. However, the accounting issues may be significantly more complex if the auditor needs to determine, for example, whether mandatory redeemable stock in substance has more characteristics of debt than equity, or if a convertible bond has more characteristics of equity than debt. The accounting issues cannot be divorced from the audit issues and play an integral part in the audit of financial instruments.

Bonds

Bonds are usually issued to finance major expansions or to refinance existing debt. The transactions are few, but each is highly material to the financial statements. Some of the major considerations in auditing bonds or other long-term debt include the following:

- Is the liability properly recorded and any premium or discount amortized according to the effective interest rate method?
- Are periodic interest payments made and the corresponding interest expense recognized, including the amortization of the discount or premium?
- Are gains or losses on refinancing existing debt appropriately recognized according to GAAP?
- Are major restrictions that are contained in the bond indenture properly disclosed in the financial statements?

Bond Issuance and Amortization Schedule

Most bonds are marketed through an underwriter with the proceeds to go to the issuer after deleting the underwriter's commission. In some cases, the underwriter specifies an interest rate but most often specifies a "best obtainable" rate. The proceeds from the bond issuance can be traced to a deposit in the bank account. The authorization to issue a bond is usually limited to the board of directors, and the proper authorization should be verified during the year of issuance. The bond indenture can be used to set up a bond amortization spreadsheet that the auditor can use each year.

Periodic Payments and Interest Expense

Most companies have agreements with **bond trustees** to handle the registration of current bondholders and to make the periodic interest payments. The bond issuer makes semiannual interest payments to the trustee plus a fee for the trustee's service, and the trustee disburses the individual payments to the bondholders. There is usually no need to verify the existence of the liability with the bondholder. Rather, the auditor may verify the current payments with the trustee or vouch the payments to the trustee and update the amortization schedule spreadsheet.

Disclosure: Examination of Bond Indenture

Bond indentures are written to protect the bondholders against possible financial decline or against the subordination of the value of the debt by the issuance of other debt. Because violation of the bond indenture agreements makes the bonds currently due and payable, the auditor must clearly understand the important provisions of the agreement to determine whether (1) there is violation of the agreement and (2) the material restrictions are disclosed. Common restrictions include maintenance of a minimum level of retained earnings before dividends can be paid, maintenance of a minimum working capital ratio, specification of a maximum debt/equity ratio, and specific callable provisions that specify procedures for calling and retiring debt at prespecified prices and dates. Copies of the bond indenture agreement or its highlights are normally maintained in the permanent file. The importance of such disclosures is shown in the Auditing in Practice case concerning bond indenture disclosure.

Common Stock and Owner's Equity

The following are the major transactions affecting stockholders' equity and should be addressed in the development of an audit program:

- Issuances of stock through a new or secondary offering or through the exercise of a stock option plan.
- Purchase of treasury stock.
- Payment of stock dividends or issuance of new stock through stock splits.
- Sale of treasury stock and recognition of the gain/loss on the sale.
- Addition of donated capital through tax incremental financing or other donation.
- Declaration and payment of dividends.
- Transfer of net income to retained earnings.
- Prior period adjustments to retained earnings.

Auditing in Practice

BOND INDENTURE DISCLOSURE

In the *Adams v. Standard Knitting Mills* case, the auditors were sued because of inadequate disclosure of restrictions associated with a bond indenture. Chadbourne Industries acquired Standard Knitting Mills by offering a new issue of preferred stock for all of Standard's outstanding stock. According to a bond indenture, Chadbourne Industries could not pay dividends that would reduce retained earnings below a specified level. The disclosure contained in the footnotes of Chadbourne Industries disclosed the restriction on the payment of dividends on common stock, at the time the only type of stock outstanding. But the financial statements were issued in conjunction with a proxy statement to issue preferred stock to acquire Standard Knitting Mills. The note disclosure revealed only the restriction on payment of dividends on common stock, not preferred stock. Thus, when the company failed, the former shareholders of Standard Knitting Mills sued the CPA firm, asserting that the financial statements were misleading because of the inadequate disclosure. The judge ruled that the financial statements did not adequately disclose the restrictions on the ability to pay preferred dividends and the investors were damaged because of their reliance on the misleading financial statements.

Although all the assertions apply to the audit of owner's equity, the three assertions of most concern are completeness, valuation, and disclosure.

Completeness

Companies listed on a securities exchange are required to utilize an *independent registrar* to handle stock transactions. The registrar is responsible for signing all newly issued certificates and ensuring that old certificates are received and canceled before new certificates are issued. Most large companies employ a registrar and a **stock transfer agent** to maintain stockholder records, cancel and issue stock certificates, and process dividend payments. The separation from the company is designed to improve efficiency and controls. The auditor should verify the existence of outstanding stock with the registrar as well as the transfer of cash for the payment of dividends to the agent.

If a company does not use a registrar or stock transfer agent, the auditor normally verifies initial existence through examination of certificates or confirmation of the certificates with owners. In subsequent years, the audit work can concentrate on changes in the account, much as the work on fixed assets concentrates on auditing year-to-year changes.

Valuation

Although most stock issuances do not provide valuation problems because the stock is issued for cash, stock is not always issued for cash, and some states have passed laws to guard against "watered stock" whereby the stock is valued at amounts substantially in excess of the value of the assets transferred to the corporation. Valuation difficulties can occur in determining (1) whether the market value of the stock issued or the market value of the asset acquired is a better representation of value, and (2) the proper accounting for an exchange of stock to acquire another business, and (3) whether a merger or acquisition should be accounted for as a purchase or a pooling of interests.

The accounting literature provides guidelines to assist the auditor in dealing with complex transactions. For example, the guidelines are fairly clear on distinguishing between a stock dividend (accounted for at market value) and a stock split (no change in equity). The literature also specifies the accounting for purchase versus pooling accounting. However, purchase accounting can become difficult if a combination of cash, stock, and debt is used to finance an acquisition. The auditor must determine the most appropriate market value to be used for the stock issued in valuing the transaction.

Treasury stock transactions should be examined to determine whether they are recorded in accordance with the board of directors' authorization and state corporation laws and are properly valued. Finally, the auditor should verify that the client has made an accurate distinction between stock and capital in excess of par or stated value.

Disclosure

Disclosure includes a proper description of each class of stock outstanding and the number of shares authorized, issued, and outstanding and special rights associated with each class, stock options outstanding, convertible features, and existence of stock warrants. The potential dilutive effect of convertible debt or preferred stock, stock options, and warrants should be disclosed in accordance with *APB No. 15* in computing primary and fully diluted earnings per share. Any restrictions or appropriations of retained earnings should be disclosed, as well as the existence of prior period adjustments.

An example of a comprehensive audit program for stockholders' equity is shown in Exhibit 19.7.

Exhibit 19.7

LEFLAM MANUFACTURING COMPANY
AUDIT PROGRAM—STOCKHOLDERS' EQUITY
DECEMBER 31, 1994

Assertions:

1. Existence/Occurrence
2. Completeness
3. Rights/Obligations
4. Valuation/Allocation
5. Presentation and disclosure

Objectives:

A. Proper authorization and classification to determine that all transactions and commitments (options, warrants, rights, etc.) are properly authorized and classified. (Assertions 1, 2, 3, 4, and 5)

B. Proper recognition and cutoff to determine that all transactions and commitments are recorded at correct amounts in the proper period. (Assertions 1, 2, and 5)

C. GAAP conformity to determine that all transactions and balances are presented in the financial statements in conformity with generally accepted accounting principles consistently applied and accompanied by adequate disclosures. (Assertion 5)

PROCEDURE	Done by	W/P
I. Stockholders' Equity		
A. Capital stock and additional paid-in capital—substantive test procedures		
1. For each class of stock, identify the number of authorized shares, par or stated value, privileges, and restrictions.	______	______
2. Obtain or prepare an analysis of the activity in the accounts; trace opening balances to the balance sheet as of the close of the year (period) previously audited.	______	______

Exhibit 19.7

3. Examine minutes, bylaws, and articles of incorporation for provisions relating to capital stock and support for all changes in the accounts including authorization per minutes of Board of Directors and stockholders meetings, and correspondence from legal counsel. ______ ______

4. Account for all proceeds from stock issues (including stock issued under stock option and stock purchase plans):

   a. Recompute sales price and applicable proceeds. ______ ______

   b. Determine that proceeds have been properly distributed between capital stock and additional paid-in capital. ______ ______

5. If the company does not keep its own stock record books

   a. Obtain confirmation of shares outstanding from the registrar and transfer agent. ______ ______

   b. Reconcile confirmation with general ledger accounts. ______ ______

6. For stock options and stock option plans, trace the authorization to the minutes of the board of directors meetings and review the plan and the option contracts. Obtain or prepare and test the analyses of stock options that include the following information: ______ ______

   a. *For option plans*, the date of the plan, the number and class of shares reserved for option, the method for determining the option price, the period during which options may be granted, and the identity of persons to whom options may be granted. ______ ______

   b. *For options granted*, the identity of persons to whom granted, the date of grant, the number of shares under option, the option price, the option period, the number of shares as to which options are exercisable, and the market price and value of shares under option as of the date of grant or measurement—first date on which are known both (1) the number of shares the individual is entitled to receive and (2) the option of purchase price, if any. ______ ______

   c. *For options outstanding*, the number of shares subject to option at the beginning of the period, the activity during the period (additional shares subjected to option, the number of shares exercised under options, the number of shares associated with options that expired during the period), and the number of shares subject to option at year-end (period-end). ______ ______

7. Identify all stock rights and warrants outstanding as of the balance sheet date, including the number of shares involved, period during which exercisable, and exercise price; determine that the amounts are properly disclosed. ______ ______

(Continued)

Exhibit 19.7

PROCEDURE	Done by	W/P
8. Obtain or prepare an analysis of the treasury stock account and		
a. Inspect the paid checks and other documentation in support of the treasury stock acquisitions.	______	______
b. Examine the treasury stock certificates; ascertain that the certificates are in the company's name or endorsed to it.	______	______
c. Reconcile treasury stock to the general ledger.	______	______
9. Ascertain amount of dividends in arrears, if any, on cumulative preferred shares.	______	______
B. Retained earnings		
1. Analyze activity during the period; trace the opening balance to the balance sheet as of the end of the year (period) previously audited; trace net income to financial statement assembly sheets; and trace unrealized loss on noncurrent investments to investment working papers.	______	______
2. Determine that dividends paid or declared have been authorized by the board of directors and		
a. Examine paid checks and supporting documents for dividends paid (selected checks to shareholders or to a dividend disbursing agent).	______	______
b. Recompute amounts of dividends paid and/or payable.	______	______
3. Investigate any prior period adjustments and determine whether they were made in accordance with FASB *Statement No. 16.*	______	______
4. Examine supporting documents and authorization for all other transactions in the account, such as treasury stock transactions, considering conformity with generally accepted accounting principles.	______	______
5. Determine the amount of restrictions, if any, on retained earnings at end of period that result from loans, other agreements, or state law.	______	______

Summary

Financial institutions require well-controlled accounting information systems to run their business. Audits of financial institutions present unique challenges for the auditor in auditing accounting estimates, such as loan loss reserves or insurance reserves for which no one correct answer can be reasonably determined. However, a systematic audit approach can be used to determine a reasonable estimate and a reasonable range for the estimate. In addition, auditors are expected to determine that management is not using the estimated accounts to manipulate reported income and is not always choosing the most optimistic estimate. The audits of financial institutions require a considerable amount of unique industry knowledge. This chapter has presented only an overview of the problems associated with financial institution audits, but the principles contained here can be used to audit most financial institutions.

Many financing activities of corporations are fairly straightforward to audit. Most companies have improved their control by contracting with bond trustees or stock transfer agents to handle individual bond and stock transactions. The audit of the major liability accounts concentrates on initial offerings of the securities and significant changes thereafter.

Significant Terms

asset/liability mix An important bank operating concept that serves as a guide to matching the interest rate and maturities of the assets and liabilities.

bank holding company A nonoperating company used to finance and control individual banks that retain separate identities but act as one financial institution.

bond indentures Contractual agreements with bondholders that specify conditions designed to protect the bondholders from default. The agreements often specify restrictions on payment of dividends or conditions in which the loan would be in default and immediately due and payable.

bond trustee An independent organization contracted by a corporation or other entity to maintain individual bondholder records and to disburse periodic interest payments to bondholders.

collateral Specific property designated as a backup to the lending institution should a borrower fail to make interest payments or pay off the principle of a loan; usually free of debt and assigned first claim to the borrower in the event of default on a loan.

credit risk The risk that a debtor may be unable to fulfill its obligation.

demand deposits A liability for banks or savings institutions, usually represented by checking accounts.

exchange rate risk The risk arising when commitments are made in foreign currencies that fluctuate in relationship to the domestic currency.

insurance reserves An insurance company's best estimate of the claims to be made against its policies currently in force; based on past claim history, current demographics and policy coverage, and projected costs of settling policyholder claims.

interest rate risk The risk arising when the interest rates earned on assets are not equivalent to the interest rates paid on liabilities.

liquidity risk The risk arising when the institution has insufficient or illiquid resources available at a particular point in time to meet liabilities or obligations arising or maturing.

loan loss reserves An estimate of uncollectible loan accounts of a bank or savings and loan.

loan review committee A senior management committee that is charged with the task of reviewing loans that have been proposed by a loan officer; serves as an independent check on the actions of individual loan officers.

market risk The fluctuation in current market prices of financial instruments.

operational risk The risk that an institution may be unable to process transactions in a timely or accurate manner.

stock transfer agent An independent entity contracted by a corporation to process stock transfers, issue new stock certificates, cancel existing certificates and possibly be responsible for disbursing dividends to individual shareholders.

Review Questions

A–Nature and Audit of Financial Statements

19–1 What are the major assets of a bank? What are the primary concerns in auditing the major assets of a bank?

19–2 How does the financial structure of a financial institution differ from that of a manufacturing organization? What are the unique audit concerns associated with the financial structure of a financial institution?

19–3 What are the major differences in operations and risks among a bank, a bank holding company, a savings and loan, and a credit union?

19–4 What are the major liabilities of a property/casualty insurance company? What are the difficult audit issues associated with the liabilities of a property/casualty insurance company?

19–5 What is meant by managing the asset/liability mix of a bank? What are the risks to the institution if the asset/liability mix is not properly managed? What are the risks if the asset/liability mix is mismanaged? How would the auditor identify the risks?

19–6 Briefly define the following terms:

- Credit risk.
- Market risk.
- Liquidity risk.
- Interest rate risk.
- Exchange rate risk.
- Operational risk.

19–7 The auditor of Banquet Insurance Company is concerned with the company's liquidity risk. What information should the auditor gather to help assess its liquidity risk?

19–8 What is off balance sheet financing? How does the auditor identify it? What are the disclosure requirements associated with off balance sheet financing?

19–9 How would the auditor become aware of regulatory requirements when auditing a financial institution? Assuming that a client did not meet some important regulatory requirements, what are the disclosure requirements?

19–10 What are the implications for an audit if the auditor determines either that the board of directors does not act as an independent check on management or that the audit committee is ineffective? Provide a specific example of an audit implication.

19–11 Identify how an internal audit department might be effective in implementing concurrent audit techniques within a bank. Cite a specific accounting application for which a concurrent audit technique might be implemented.

B–Planning and Conducting the Audit of Financial Institutions

19–12 Why is it important that a bank establish a loan review committee? What specific information is normally reviewed by a loan review committee in its process of determining whether to approve a loan?

19–13 What is a loan loss reserve? Is management or the auditor responsible for estimating the loan loss reserve? What are the specific audit requirements associated with the estimate of a client's loan loss reserve?

19–14 Explain how a geographic or industry classification helps the auditor assess the adequacy of a client's loan loss reserve.

19–15 Explain how an auditor might utilize a statistical sample in estimating the adequacy of a bank's estimate of its loan loss reserve.

19–16 Where would an auditor find information about the adequacy of the collateral for a specific loan? What information should the auditor gather to assess its adequacy?

19–17 Is it meaningful to compare a client's loan loss reserve as a percentage of loans and its write-offs as a percentage of loans with those for other banks? Explain.

19–18 Identify criteria an auditor might use to classify a client's investment portfolio.

19–19 What is meant by *marking assets to market*? What constitutes a market?

19–20 Would an audit of demand deposits concentrate more on auditing transactions and the control procedures or on sending confirmations to individual customers? What are the relative advantages and disadvantages of sending confirmations to demand deposit customers?

19–21 What is the auditor's responsibility for estimating the adequacy of reserves for a property/casualty insurance company? In formulating your answer, consider an insurer with automobile policies.

C–Audit of the Financing Cycle—Nonfinancial Institutions

19–22 What information should the auditor note when reading a bond indenture? How is the information used in the audit?

19–23 Assume that common stock of a publicly held company is issued to acquire the operating assets of another company (but not the other company). What information should be used to determine the value of the transaction?

19–24 A company declared a five percent stock dividend. Identify the evidence the auditor would examine to determine if the stock dividend were accounted for properly.

19–25 Explain how a bond amortization spreadsheet might be used to audit interest expense over the life of a bond.

Multiple Choice Questions

*19–26 The auditor's program for the examination of long-term debt should include steps that require the

a. Verification of the existence of the bondholders.
b. Examination of the bond trust indenture.
c. Inspection of the accounts payable master file.
d. Investigation of credits to the Bond Interest Income account.

*19–27 An audit program for the examination of the Retained Earnings account should include a step that requires verification of

a. Market value used to charge Retained Earnings to account for a 2-for-1 stock split.
b. Approval of the adjustment to the beginning balance as a result of a write-down of an account receivable.
c. Authorization for both cash and stock dividends.
d. Gain or loss resulting from disposition of treasury shares.

*19–28 An auditor's program to examine long-term debt most likely would include steps that require

a. Comparing the carrying amount of the debt to its year-end market value.
b. Correlating interest expense recorded for the period with outstanding debt.
c. Verifying the existence of the holders of debt by direct confirmation.
d. Inspecting the accounts payable subsidiary ledger for unrecorded long-term debt.

*19–29 When a client company does *not* maintain its own stock records, the auditor should obtain written confirmation from the stock transfer agent and registrar concerning

a. Restrictions on the payment of dividends.
b. The number of shares issued and outstanding.
c. Guarantees of preferred stock liquidation value.
d. The number of shares subject to agreements to repurchase.

19–30 Credit risk is best analyzed by

a. Comparing the client's current rates on loans with the rates charged by other financial institutions.
b. Evaluating the ability of the client to meet its obligations on a timely basis.
c. Evaluating the risk that a debtor may be unable to fulfill its obligation.
d. Comparing interest rates charged on loans with those paid on savings accounts.

19–31 One control objective of the financing/treasury cycle is the proper authorization of company's transactions dealing with debt and equity instruments. Which of the following control procedures would best meet this objective?

*Adapted from the Uniform CPA examination or the Certified Internal Auditor examination.

a. Separation of the responsibility for custody of funds from the recording of the transaction.
b. Written company policies requiring review of major funding/repayment proposals by the board of directors.
c. Use of an underwriter in all cases of new issue of debt or equity instruments.
d. Requiring two signatures on all organization checks of a material amount.

19–32 Which of the following would be the best test of the accuracy of interest accrued for notes receivable for a commercial bank?
a. Statistical sample of notes receivable holders to which positive confirmations will be sent.
b. Statistical sample of notes receivable holders to which negative confirmations will be sent.
c. Recalculation of interest accrued on a sample of notes receivable.
d. Compare loan summary sheets to appropriate accounts in general ledger.

19–33 A middle-level bank manager deposited funds into an account in one branch using the bank's interbranch account settlement process and withdrew funds in excess of the transfer from a different branch. The manager hid the resulting imbalance, which grew over time, by making subsequent fraudulent transfers. A control to prevent or detect this type of fraud is to
a. Require independent interbranch settlement reconciliation on a timely basis.
b. Impose additional higher-level management supervision on middle-level managers.
c. Prohibit middle-level managers from initiating interbranch transfers.
d. Require two middle-level managers to authorize all interbranch transfers.

*19–34 An internal auditor for a broker-dealer matched publicly available files of security quotations to the inventory file of securities held, recording and investigating material differences and proposing adjustments as appropriate. The purpose of this procedure was to
a. Detect and correct quantity errors.
b. Verify ownership status.
c. Determine inventory valuation.
d. Detect and correct pricing errors.

*19–35 A common fraud against banks is to draw checks on accounts which will have insufficient funds by the time the check clears and deposit the checks in accounts in other banks. An audit test that would probably be the most helpful in detecting this is to
a. Investigate all accounts whose average daily balances are low compared to the total deposit level.

b. Confirm accounts requiring a deposit to prevent the account from becoming overdrawn based on the account's opening balance.
c. Institute an automated procedure to identify accounts for further investigation that have attributes associated with kiting.
d. Inspect account activity for accounts with deposits on more than 8 to 10 days per month.

Discussion and Research Questions

19–36 (Audit of Loan Loss Reserves) Two auditors were discussing the process of estimating a client's loan loss reserve. The first auditor stated that she believed that "the best approach is to take a statistical sample of individual loans and to estimate the uncollectible amount from the sample and project that sample to the population as a whole as a best estimate." She added that she also believed that the approach was superior "because it also results in statistical ranges for the estimates."

The second auditor replied that "such an approach misses the global perspective of the loan portfolio. A better approach is to concentrate on the risks inherent in the portfolio and to prepare an aging of the portfolio in terms of principal and interest payments past due." Both auditors agreed that current economic conditions ought to be considered.

Required:
Evaluate the two approaches, citing the advantages and disadvantages associated with each.

*19–37 (Review of Loans) As an internal auditor for the Xenia National Bank, you have been assigned to the audit team reviewing the loan department. Your responsibility is to develop the sampling plan and to complete the audit for the consumer loan division. The audit objective is to determine whether the bank's established loan policies and procedures are being followed.

During your preliminary survey, you obtain the following information:

1. Consumer loans should include installment automobile, home repair, and personal loans only.
2. The current trial balance reflects 6,270 installment loans outstanding with an average unpaid principal balance of $8,525.
3. The average remaining term of the outstanding loans is 26 months. Bank policy is to make this type of loan for no less than 12 months or more than 60 months.
4. The total value of consumer loans represents 14 percent of the total assets of the bank.
5. Previous audits of the consumer loan department disclosed no major discrepancies or policy violations.
6. There have been no major changes in either policies or management of the department since the last audit.

Note: After completion of your review of the consumer loan files, you prepared a summary of those loans on which you noted an apparent exception to established policies (see Table 19–37).

Required:

a. Describe the sampling plan, including the detailed steps you would have used in reviewing the consumer loan files.

b. Identify those exceptions (in Table 19–37) that are the most serious from an audit perspective, the exposure represented by each of these exceptions, and the additional audit steps, if any, to be undertaken in each instance.

Table 19–37
Results of Consumer Loan File Reviews

Exceptions Noted	Affected Loans (Account No. of Each Loan)
1. No properly executed note on file	3,9,14,31,55
2. Note on file not properly authorized	6
3. Note improperly recorded on books	None
4. Note improperly classified on books	23
5. No loan application on file	14
6. Loan application incomplete	None
7. No credit report on file	14
8. No evidence of employment verification in loan file	26,32,54
9. Payments not in accordance with agreement	15,25,40
10. Loan not properly collateralized	14
11. Required liens against collateral not in loan file	14,33
12. Value of collateral not computed correctly	None
13. Unanswered correspondence from borrower in loan file	3,9,27, 44,51,58

*19–38 (Audit of Home Improvement Loans) In your examination of the financial statements of Kay Savings and Loan Association for the year ended December 31, 1994, you find a new account, Home Improvement Loans, in the general ledger. You determine that the account represents unsecured loans not insured by any government agency and made on a discount basis to homeowners who are required to secure life insurance coverage provided by the association under a group life insurance policy for the outstanding amount and duration of the loan. Borrowers are issued coupon books that require monthly installment payments; however, borrowers may prepay the outstanding balance of the loan at any time in accordance with the terms of their loan contract. This account constitutes a material amount of the association's total assets at December 31, 1994.

Required:

a. Prepare an audit program for the examination of the new account, Home Improvement Loans.

b. During your examination of the Home Improvement Loans account, the vice president in charge of the loan department hands you a list of 25 accounts with balances from $30,000 to $145,000, representing approximately 40 percent of the total account balance. The vice president states that confirmation requests are not to be prepared for these 25 accounts because the borrowers have requested no correspondence.

1. Will you comply with the vice president's request? Discuss.
2. Assuming that you complied with the vice president's request and did not send confirmation requests to the no correspondence accounts, what effect, if any, would this compliance have on the audit report?

*19–39 (Loan Evaluation: Sampling Procedures) Management of a fast-growing financial services company is responding to what it believes will be a prolonged contraction of the short-term debt markets. One of management's critical information needs concerns the collectibility of the company's loan portfolio.

The company makes both business loans and personal loans. Business loans always exceed $10,000 in amount; personal loans are generally less than $10,000 in amount.

Management has asked the internal auditing department to provide a current estimate of the collectibility of the company's loan portfolio. The director of internal auditing has recommended the utilization of a stratified statistical sample of the loan portfolio to determine the total amount of collectible loans.

Required:

a. Discuss the reasons that an internal auditor might choose to identify "strata" in a population and then utilize stratified sampling rather than taking a simple random sample of the entire population.
b. Determine the strata that might effectively be used in the company's case.

*19–40 (Defalcation Scheme and Audit Approach) The auditor of a bank is called to a meeting with a senior operations manager because of a customer's report that an auto loan payment was not credited. According to the customer, the payment was made at a teller's window using a check drawn on an account in that bank. The payment was made on its due date, May 5. On May 10, the customer decided to sell the car and called the bank for a payoff on the loan. The payment had not been credited to the loan. The customer came to the bank on May 12 to inquire about the payment and met with the manager. The manager found that the payment had been credited the night before the meeting (May 11); the customer was satisfied because no late charge would be assessed until May 15. The manager asked if the auditor was comfortable with this occurrence.

The auditor located the customer's paid check in the deposit department and found that it had cleared on May 5. The auditor traced the item back through the computer entry records and found that the check had been processed by the teller as a cashed check. The auditor traced the payment through the entry records of May 11 and found that the payment was processed as though the payment had been made with cash instead of a check.

Required:

a. What type of defalcation scheme does this appear to be and how does that scheme operate?

b. What evidence would the auditor accumulate to determine whether such a scheme was being perpetrated?

c. How would the auditor go about determining the extent of the scheme?

19–41 (Fraud: Control Procedures and Audit Techniques) The following is a description of a number of frauds that have taken place in the banking and insurance industry.

Required:

For each fraud identified

a. Identify control procedures that would have been effective in preventing or detecting the fraud.

b. Identify one or two audit procedures that would have been effective in detecting the fraud.

Financial Institution Frauds

1. A programmer at a large midwestern bank changed the computer program that calculated daily interest on savings accounts. The program calculated interest to four decimal places. He truncated the last two digits and had the fraction of cents transferred to his account.
2. A bank teller opened a new account in a friend's name. The teller then accessed selected dormant accounts and made transfers to the friend's account. She forged her friend's name and drew checks on the new account.
3. A commercial bank customer phoned in a request to electronically transfer $25 million from its account in Pittsburgh to its account in Birmingham (all with the same bank). A supervisor in the funds section instead transferred the funds to a Swiss bank and left the country.
4. A claims supervisor in the insurance industry submitted false claims for auto repairs and forged the field representative's signature for them. The claims were all on a policy owned by her brother-in-law. The checks were sent to the brother-in-law and the two split the money.
5. As in part 4, the claims supervisor submitted false claims, but they were made against a valid, in-force policy. The supervisor temporarily changed the mailing address of the policyholder to a post office box number and deposited the proceeds in a series of fictitious accounts that she later consolidated.
6. A bank branch manager inflated profits and personal income by preparing and approving fictitious loans. He used the loan proceeds to partially pay older fictitious loans and pocketed the rest. After six months and with $1.2 million, the manager left the bank and has not been seen since.
7. A clerical bank employee engaged in a scheme to steal one-half of the daily amounts deposited in the bank's automated teller machines (ATMs) (over 75 machines).
8. A bank is a major processor and issuer of Visa cards. Through a clever scheme, a criminal was able to obtain the account numbers of valid

accounts and used them to make purchases through mail-order catalogs.

9. A bank employee gained access to blank credit cards and established accounts in a number of different names. He used the accounts for six months and left the bank.
10. A clever employee in Boston opened a bank account. All personal deposit slips are MICR (magnetic ink character recognition) encoded to speed automated processing. He had a number of blank deposit slips at the counter encoded with his bank number. All the deposits made at the bank for a three-day period by customers using blank deposit slips were deposited to his account. He called the bank to get his balance and had the amounts transferred to a different bank in San Francisco, from which he withdrew the funds and disappeared.

19–42 (Analysis of Loan Loss Reserves) The information in Exhibits 19.1 and 19.6 is taken from the annual report of Norwest Banks, a major bank headquartered in Minneapolis. It has been a major lender to the agriculture industry in the upper Midwest and has expanded its commercial business in the past few years. *Note:* The term *allowance for credit losses* in the exhibits is used instead of *loan loss reserve.*

Required:
After reviewing the information in this exhibit, develop an audit program to estimate the loan loss reserve for Norwest Banks. Assume that the client has a very comprehensive database system and that most customer information is available in computer form or is located in files contained in the loan offices of the 85 individual banks that make up the Norwest Bank Holding Company.

19–43 (Estimating Insurance Reserves) West Bend Mutual is a multiline insurance company specializing in homeowner, boat, and automobile insurance. All insurance is placed through independent insurance agents, but all policies are reviewed before acceptance. The company will not insure high-risk drivers but refers them to a subsidiary for high-risk drivers.

Required:
a. Briefly explain the auditor's responsibility for determining the accuracy of the reserve for insurance losses.
b. Briefly describe an actuary's responsibility for determining the accuracy of the reserve for insurance claims and losses.
c. Assume that the client has a comprehensive system to identify claims data and to match the claims with policies. Also assume that previous experience shows that all the claims are processed efficiently and on a timely basis. Write an audit program to test the client's system for estimating the reserve for insurance losses. Briefly describe the purpose of each audit step.

19–44 (Auditing Demand Deposits) The following audit procedures are often used in connection with the audit of demand deposit accounts (DDAs). DDA accounts meeting specific criteria are paid interest.

Required:
Identify the purpose of each procedure and briefly analyze its effectiveness.

Audit Procedures for Demand Deposits:

1. An attribute sample of existing accounts is taken and a confirmation is sent to the customer requesting a verification of the correctness of the account balance.
2. A PPS sample of the existing accounts is taken and supplemented by selecting all accounts over $50,000. A confirmation is sent to each customer requesting a verification of the correctness of the account balance.
3. Inquiries are made of customer service representatives and documentation of customer problems are reviewed.
4. A sample of recently opened accounts is reviewed to determine that the application form is complete and that the account is initialed by the new accounts manager.
5. The auditor obtains a valid teller password and attempts to establish a new account.
6. A sample of daily teller reconciliations is reviewed for completeness and supervisory approval.
7. A sample of daily processing reconciliations designed to reconcile amounts processed with amounts recorded is reviewed for exceptions.
8. Inquiries are made as to whether exception reports are prepared for various types of unusual transactions on demand deposit accounts. A sample of the reports is reviewed to determine actions taken by supervisory personnel.
9. Audit software is used to create a printout of all DDAs with debit balances.
10. The auditor reviews the internal auditor's working papers documenting the use of an integrated test facility implemented on the DDA application.

19–45 (Bond Indentures and Bond Liabilities) The auditor should review the bond indenture at the time a bond is issued and any time subsequent changes are made to it.

Required:

a. Briefly identify the information the auditor would expect to obtain from a bond indenture agreement. List at least five specific pieces of information that would be relevant to the conduct of the audit.
b. Because auditors are concerned with understatement of liabilities, should they confirm the existence of the liability with individual bondholders? State your rationale.
c. A company issued a bond at a discount. Explain how the amount of the discount is computed and how the auditor could determine whether the amount is properly amortized each year.

d. Explain how the auditor could verify that semiannual interest payments are made on the bond each year.

e. The company has a 15-year, $20 million loan that is due on September 30 of next year. It is the company's intent to refinance the bond before it is due, but it is waiting for the best time to issue new debt. Because its intent is to issue the bond next year, the company believes that the existing $20 million bond need not be classified as a current liability. What evidence should the auditor gather to determine the appropriate classification of the bond?

*19–46 (Bond Covenants and Audit Actions) The following covenants are extracted from the indenture of a bond issue. The indenture provides that failure to comply with its terms in any respect automatically advances the due date of the loan to the date of noncompliance (the maturity date is 20 years hence).

Required:
Identify the audit steps or reporting requirements that should be taken or recognized in connection with each one of the following:

a. The debtor company shall endeavor to maintain a working capital ratio of 2 to 1 at all times, and, in any fiscal year following a failure to maintain said ratio, the company shall restrict compensation of management to a total of $100,000. Management for this purpose shall include the chairman of the board of directors, the president, all vice presidents, the secretary, and the treasurer.

b. The debtor company shall keep all property that is security for this debt insured against loss by fire to the extent of 100 percent of its actual value. Insurance policies securing this protection shall be filed with the trustee.

c. The debtor company shall pay all taxes legally assessed against the property that serves as security for this debt within the time provided by law for payment without penalty and shall deposit receipted tax bills or equally acceptable evidence of payment of same with the trustee.

d. A sinking fund shall be deposited with the trustee by semiannual payments of $300,000, from which the trustee shall, at her discretion, purchase bonds of this issue.

*19–47 (Audit of Stockholders' Equity) A CPA firm is engaged in the examination of the financial statements of Zeitlow Corporation for the year ended December 31, 1994. Zeitlow Corporation's financial statements and records have never been audited by a CPA.

The stockholders' equity section of Zeitlow Corporation's balance sheet at December 31, 1994, follows:

Stockholders' Equity	
Capital stock—10,000 shares of $10 par value authorized:	
5,000 shares issued and outstanding	$50,000
Capital contributed in excess of par value of capital stock	58,800
Retained earnings	105,000
Total stockholders' equity	$213,800

Founded in 1985, Zeitlow Corporation has 10 stockholders and serves as its own registrar and transfer agent. It has no capital stock subscription contracts in effect.

Required:

a. Prepare the detailed audit program for the examination of the three accounts composing the stockholders' equity section of Zeitlow Corporation's balance sheet. (Do not include in the audit program the verification of the results of the current year operations.)

b. After all other figures on the balance sheet have been audited, it might appear that the retained earnings figure is a balancing figure and requires no further verification. Why would an auditor still choose to verify retained earnings? Discuss.

19–48 (Evaluating Loans) A partial trial balance of loans receivable for State Bank of Richfield is shown below. The accounts were identified by the bank as a complete representation of accounts past due.

Customer	Industry	Loan Amount	Past Due
TwinDiscount	Retailer	$ 22.5 million	Yes, but is paying interest
Agranetics	AgriBusiness	$ 14.3 million	Yes, no payments for past year
Grand Dept. Store	Retailer	$ 9.8 million	Yes
Morrisey Mfg.	Manufacturer	$ 12.2 million	Yes
Novel Electronics	Electronics, start-up	$ 4.5 million	Yes, interest deferred

Required:

a. What audit procedures should the auditor use to determine whether the list of all past due accounts is complete?

b. Identify the specific additional information the auditor should seek in assessing the potential loan loss reserve to be associated with each of the above loans. Indicate how the information will be used to make a decision and where the auditor would find it.

c. Identify specific audit procedures that should be performed in conjunction with each loan identified above.

19–49 (Auditing Problem Financial Institutions) A number of problems in financial institutions would not normally show up in an aging of loans receivable or the analysis of investments. For example, each of the following situations has been identified with failed institutions:

1. Outstanding loans appeared to be current. However, the major loans that were kept current were maintained by the financial institution advancing more funds to the borrowers, some of whom were related parties. The recipients used the new loan proceeds to make payments on the old loans.

2. The composition of loans, over time, became concentrated in higher-risk industries and developments. Many of these high-risk loans were predicated on strong economic growth in the industry or geographic region.

3. The value of collateral supporting the loan valuation decreased drastically when a downturn in the economy occurred, but the financial institution did not have current appraisals of the collateral.
4. Large investments in bonds were converted into equity because the borrower could not meet current interest payments. The financial institution valued the equity at the original cost of the bonds.
5. Some large loans were converted into equity ownership in the borrowing company with collateralization by new real estate developments. The equity was valued at the original loan amount.

Required:
For each of the preceding situations, identify the problem the auditor faces in determining the potential change in asset value. Identify the appropriate audit procedures to evaluate the value of the loan or investment.

*19–50 (Audit of Long-Term Debt) The long-term debt working paper (indexed K-1) on pages 928–929 was prepared by client personnel and audited by AA, an audit assistant, during the calendar year 1994 audit of American Widgets, Inc., a continuing audit client. The engagement supervisor is reviewing the working papers thoroughly.

Overall Conclusions
Long-term debt, accrued interest payable, and interest expense are correct and complete at 12/31/94.

Required:
Identify the deficiencies in the working paper that the engagement supervisor should discover.

19–51 **(Research: Expert Systems in Banking Industry)** Expert systems are becoming more widespread in the banking and insurance industries. Review published research to indicate how they have been used for audit purposes in these two industries. Alternatively, review the use of expert systems by public accounting firms for use in these industries and report on their general design.

19–52 **(Research: Banking and Insurance Company Failures)** There have been a number of banking, savings and loan, and insurance company failures during the past decade. Select a sample of newspaper and magazine reports on failures in one of the industries. Analyze their causes and describe the audit implications.

Cases

*19–53 (Evaluation of Control Structure: Segregation of Duties) The internal auditor of a large savings and loan association is concerned about the adequacy of segregation of duties for a wholly owned real estate investment subsidiary. The subsidiary, despite its $10 million in assets, operates out of the main office of its parent. The parent company administers all purchasing, payroll, and personnel functions. The subsidiary's board of directors consists entirely of selected officers.

The real estate investment subsidiary's activities consist primarily of buying, developing, and selling real estate, with some development projects involving joint ventures with contractors. Day-to-day operations are handled by the president and two vice presidents. The president also acts as liaison with the parent. Each vice president has his or her own projects to manage.

All invoices and itemized statements requiring direct payment or reimbursement to contractors or vendors are delivered to one of the two vice presidents for review and approval. After approval, the staff accountant prepares checks and then obtains the signature of one of the vice presidents on them. After they are signed, the checks are returned to the staff accountant for mailing, and supporting documents are filed. All blank checks are kept by the staff accountant.

All customer payments on notes and accounts receivable originating from the sale of real estate are remitted to one of the two vice presidents and then forwarded to the staff accountant, who records the payment and prepares the deposit slip. The deposit may be given to the parent's accounting department or to a teller of the parent.

If the subsidiary experiences a cash shortage, a promissory note is prepared by the staff accountant and is signed by the president or one of the vice presidents. The staff accountant submits the promissory note to the parent in exchange for the cash advance. The staff accountant is responsible for billing customers and advising management when payments are due. The staff accountant reconciles the bank statement once a month.

The staff accountant prepares monthly financial statements, including the accrual of interest receivable and the capitalization of certain interest charges. These financial statements are prepared to reflect the substance of both joint ventures and subsidiary operations. The board of directors reviews the financial statements.

Required:

a. Identify specific areas in which segregation of duties is inadequate. Identify potential alternatives to improve segregation of duties.

b. Assume that adequate segregation of duties is incorporated into the design of the control system. How would the auditor gather evidence to test the actual segregation of duties during normal operations?

19-54 (Bank Reporting) The following quote is taken from "Separating the Sheep from the Goats," *Forbes*, October 1, 1990, 49–50.

> The banks disclose lots of historical information. . . . But, as investors have painfully learned, the historical information doesn't prevent surprise write-offs. Witness the Bank of New England's unexpected $1.4 billion provision for loan losses in December 1989, or Valley National's $348 million provision for loan losses during 1989. Nor does it help investors assess the probability of further charge-offs this year or next.
>
> Kept in the dark and having been burned in the past, investors naturally assume the worst. . . . Viewing this sorry state of affairs, a growing group of banking industry lenders . . . support improving the banks' disclosure of their loan portfolio's quality.

American Widgets, Inc.
Working Papers
December 31, 1994

Index	K-1	
	Initials	Date
Prepared by	AA	3/22/94
Approved by		

Lender	Interest Rate	Payment Terms	Collateral	Balance December 31, 1993	1994 Borrowings	1994 Reductions	Balance December 31, 1994	Interest Paid to	Accrued Interest Payable December 31, 1994	Comments
First Commercal Bank*	12%	Interest only on 25th of month, principal due in full 1/1/98 no prepayment penalty	Inventories	$ 50,000†	$300,000‡ 1/31/94	$100,000§ 6/30/94	$ 250,000‖	12/25/94	$2,500**	Dividend of $80,000 paid 9/2/94 (W/P N-3) violates a provision of the debt agreement, which thereby permits lender to demand immediate payment; lender has refused to waive this violation
Lender's Capital Corp.*	Prime plus 1	Interest only on last day of month, principal due in full 3/5/96	2nd mortgage on Park St. building	100,000†	50,000‡ 2/29/94	—	200,000††	12/31/94	—	Prime rate was 8% to 9% during the year
Gigantic Building & Loan Assoc.*	12%	$5,000 principal plus interest due on 5th of month, due in full 12/31/2005	1st mortgage on Park St. building	720,000†	—	60,000‡‡	660,000††	12/5/94	5,642§§	Reclassification entry for current portion proposed (See RJE-3)

Lender	Interest Rate	Payment Terms	Collateral	Balance December 31, 1993	1994 Borrowings	1994 Reductions	Balance December 31, 1994	Interest Paid to	Accrued Interest Payable December 31, 1994	Comments
J. Lott, majority stockholder*	0%	Due in full 12/31/97	Unsecured	300,000†	—	100,000‖‖ 12/31/94	200,000††	— —	—	Borrowed additional $100,000 from J. Lott on 1/7/95
				$1,170,000† †††	$350,000 †††	$260,000 †††	$1,310,000 †††	T/B	$8,142*** †††	

††† Readded, foots correctly
†† Confirmed without exception, W/P K-2
‖ Confirmed with exception, W/P K-3
** Does not recompute correctly
‡ Agreed to loan agreement, validated bank deposit ticket, and board of directors' authorization, W/P W-7
‡‡ Agreed to canceled checks and lender's monthly statements
‖‖ Agreed to cash disbursements journal and canceled check dated 12/31/94, clearing 1/8/95
*** Traced to working trial balance
† Agreed to 12/31/93 working papers
* Agreed interest rate, term, and collateral to copy of note and loan agreement
§ Agreed to canceled check and board of directors' authorization, W/P W-7

Interest costs from long-term debt

Interest expense for year $ 281,333***

Average loan balance outstanding $1,406,667§§

Five year maturities (for disclosure purposes)

Year end		
	12/31/95	$ 60,000
	12/31/96	260,000
	12/31/97	260,000
	12/31/98	310,000
	12/31/99	60,000
	Thereafter	360,000
		$1,310,000 †††

Snyder plans to ask the country's largest banks to rank the loans they have outstanding along a standardized nine-point scale of riskiness. Snyder will then compare the way the banks rank identical loans—to see if what is considered "minimal risk" by Bank A is considered to be "substandard" by Bank B. He will adjust the rankings of banks that tend to be consistently more optimistic or pessimistic than average, in order to make the rankings comparable. In addition, the banks will be asked to report the rate of return they receive in each of the risk categories.

Required:

a. Explain how "surprises" could occur in the estimate of loan loss reserves. What might lead to them? Explain.
b. Evaluate the proposed plan for additional loan disclosure. What are the advantages and disadvantages of the approaches?
c. Assume that 80 percent of the nation's largest banks are audited by two international CPA firms. Explain how elements of the plan might assist in auditing their banking clients.
d. Would the construction of an internal database on the classification of loans across different banking clients by an auditing firm violate the ethics restriction on confidentiality of information? Explain.

19–55 (Savings and Loan Crisis) There are many criticisms of the way some of the savings and loans were run that directly contributed to their downfall. Two of the more prevalent criticisms were that (1) some S&Ls invested heavily in bonds (often referred to as *junk bonds*) of highly leveraged companies for which there was no market and (2) many S&Ls extended their geographic limit on loans into new areas and new industries and made loans in their pursuit of higher returns that were not adequately collateralized.

Required:

a. Who are the users affected by the integrity of the financial reporting process? (Confine your answers to the savings and loan industry.) To what extent might these users differ from those we typically identify as the users of financial statements?
b. Can public accounting firms be reasonably held responsible for monitoring the actions of their clients (i.e., the stewardship of companies such as the Lincoln Federal S&L or others which stacked the organization with relatives and did not utilize an independent, outside board of directors)?
c. What is the auditor's responsibility to determine the amount of loans that will not be collectible—or even the value of collateral held against the loans—when the company itself does not seem capable of making such estimates?
d. What evidence must an auditor gather to determine that securities classified as marketable securities are really marketable? Explain.

Computer Assisted Problems

Problems for this chapter using the adVenture software are in the Appendix at the end of the book. You should read the introduction and instructions before working the problems. These problems are:

C-14. Using Generalized Audit Software to Test the Commercial Loan Account Balances.

C-15. Using Sampling to Test Controls over Commercial Loans.

C-16. Using Sampling to Perform Substantive Tests on Commercial Loans.

End Notes

1. Dana Wechsler Linden, "Separating the Sheep from the Goats," *Forbes*, October 1, 1990, 49–50.
2. GAO, *Depository Institutions: Flexible Accounting Rules Lead to Inflated Financial Reports*, GAO/AFMD-92-52 (Gaithersburg, Md.: U.S. General Accounting Office, June 1992), 1.
3. Stephen Pizzo, Mary Fricker, and Paul Muolo, *Inside Job: The Looting of America's Savings and Loans* (New York: McGraw-Hill, 1990).

CHAPTER

20

Learning Objectives

Through studying this chapter, you will be able to:

1. Use analytical procedures to provide evidence on income statement items.
2. Understand the usefulness of analytical procedures during the final review of financial statements.
3. Describe the different types of subsequent events and the related audit requirements.
4. Understand the auditor's responsibilities and sources of evidence concerning contingencies, related party disclosures, and going concern issues.
5. Understand the purposes and content of management representation letters.
6. Explain the importance of an internal quality review process.

Completing the Audit and Assessing Overall Risk and Materiality

Chapter Contents

Chapter Overview

This chapter covers several audit activities that complete the audit (Exhibit 20.1). Applying basic analytical procedures to the income statement detail may bring to light unexpected results for which the auditor has not yet obtained sufficient competent evidence. The auditor must make sure that the disclosures are adequate. The auditor should review information that becomes available after the balance sheet date but prior to issuing the audit report to see if amounts should be revised or additional disclosures made. The auditor should make a final assessment of the risk of a material misstatement having gone undetected by all of the substantive procedures that were performed during the audit.

The presentation of financial statements in conformity with generally accepted accounting principles includes adequate disclosure of material matters. These matters relate to the form, arrangement, and content of the financial statements and their appended notes, including, for example, the terminology used, the amount of detail given, the classification of items in the statements, and the bases of amounts set forth. [AU 431.02]

A–ANALYTICAL PROCEDURES

Revenue and Expenses

Analytical procedures help auditors assess the overall presentation of the financial statements. Auditing standards require the use of analytical procedures for both the planning phase and the review phase of the audit for the same reason: to assist in analyzing account relationships that appear to be unusual and may not be justified by the audit evidence gathered so far.

Performing analytical procedures on the income statement detail provides evidence that certain relationships make sense in light of the knowledge obtained about the client throughout the audit. Such procedures may indicate that further audit work needs to be performed before rendering an opinion. Ratio analysis is the most popular analytical procedure and has been covered in previous chapters. In addition to ratio analysis, two other procedures assist in the review phase: common-size analysis and analysis of the dollar and percent change of each income statement item from the previous year.

Common-Size Analysis

Common-size analysis involves the conversion of the income statement dollars to percentages and comparison of the percentages with those for prior years and the industry. Such an income statement is shown in Exhibit 20.2 for LeFlam Manufacturing Company. Each line item is computed as a percent of net sales. This can be

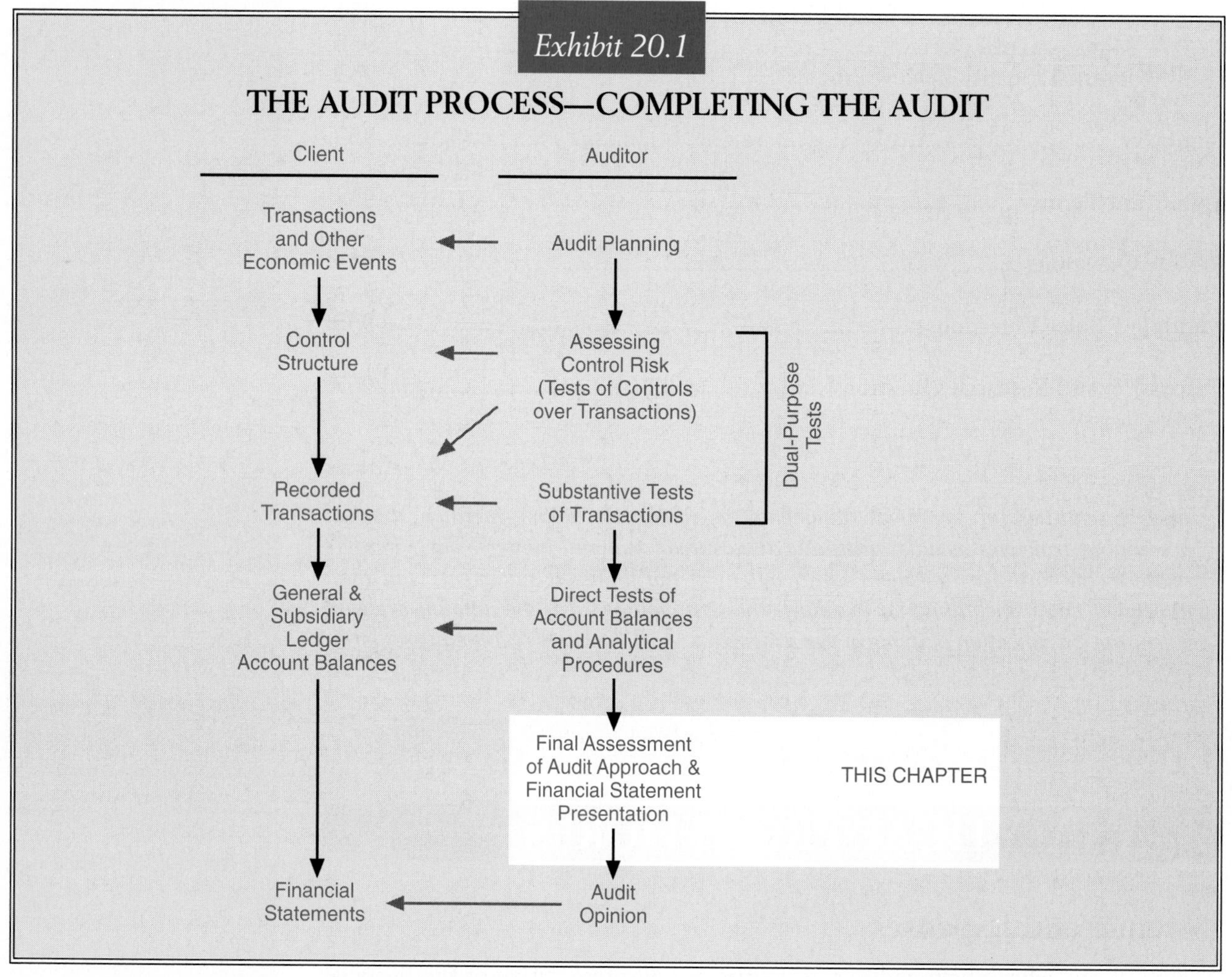

done for the individual selling, general, and administrative expenses as well as the totals. The auditor should be sure that the working papers contain adequate evidence to explain significant variances. For example, LeFlam's operating expenses have declined in dollars as well as a percent of net sales. This was the major cause of the increase in net income. Management may have undertaken a major cost-cutting program during the current year. Evidence of this should be documented in the working papers.

These common-size percentages may be compared with industry data. In the MiniScribe fraud, discussed in previous chapters, the amount of sales returns and allowances as a percent of net sales was significantly less than that for the industry, and gross profit was well above the industry average. Had the auditors taken note of this and obtained proper evidence, they most likely would have suspected that the account was significantly understated. Industry data are published by several federal government agencies, Dun & Bradstreet, Moodys, Standard & Poors, and others (see Chapter 23 for further details about industry data sources). Care must be taken when comparing client and industry ratios to be sure they are calculated the same way. In addition, differences may be caused by using different accounting methods,

Exhibit 20.2

LEFLAM MANUFACTURING COMPANY
COMMON-SIZE INCOME STATEMENT
(IN THOUSANDS)

Account	December 31, 1994	Percent	December 31, 1993	Percent	Industry Averages 1994
Sales	$29,500	102.1%	$24,900	101.6%	102.3%
Sales returns & allowances	600	2.1	400	1.6	2.3
Net sales	28,900	100.0	24,500	100.0	100.0
Cost of goods sold	21,260	73.6	17,800	72.7	74.7
Gross margin	7,640	26.4	6,700	27.3	25.3
Selling expenses	1,742	6.0	1,879	7.7	7.0
General and administrative expenses	1,994	6.9	2,181	8.9	7.9
Total operating expenses	3,736	12.9	4,060	16.6	14.9
Net income from operations	3,904	13.5	2,640	10.8	10.4
Other income (expense)	(924)	(3.2)	(580)	(2.4)	(1.4)
Net income before tax	2,980	10.3	2,060	8.4	9.0
Income taxes	1,190	4.1	950	3.9	4.0
Net income	$ 1,790	6.2%	$ 1,110	4.5%	5.0%

having a different product mix, different customers, or operating in different geographical areas.

Changes from Prior Year

A simple calculation of the dollar and percent change from the prior year for each revenue and expense account can be a useful source of audit evidence. The auditor should have accumulated sufficient competent evidence during the audit to explain any unusual change, such as changes when none are expected, no changes when they are expected, or changes that are not of the expected size or direction. For example, if the client paid more attention to quality control and order processing during the current year than in prior years, sales returns and allowances should have decreased, at least as a percent of sales. Another example is a client that increased its market share by substantially reducing prices for the last three months of the year and undergoing a massive advertising campaign. Without offsetting cost reductions, the auditor should expect sales to increase and the gross profit margin and net income to decline as a percent of net sales. If these expected changes are not reflected in the accounting records, the working papers should contain adequate evidence, supplementing the explanations of management, that corroborates those explanations.

Final Review Stage

The review stands as an analysis of last resort for potential misstatements existing in the financial statements. Typical procedures include reading the financial statements and considering the following:

- The adequacy of evidence gathered in response to unusual or unexpected balances identified in planning the audit or during the course of the audit.
- Unusual or unexpected balances or relationships that were not previously identified.

During the planning stage, for example, the auditor determined that the allowance for doubtful accounts appeared to be too small. During the audit, it was discovered that the client had forgotten to record the current year provision for bad debt expense. The client has now made an adjusting entry to correct this, and the allowance seems reasonable. As another example, during the planning stage, the auditor compared interest expense to the recorded interest bearing debt, and the amounts seemed reasonable. During the audit, however, an unrecorded loan was discovered. A comparison of interest expense to the amount of interest bearing debt now appearing on the financial statements may not look right and may indicate the need for more audit work.

B–AUDIT OF INCOME TAXES

Income tax expense has a major impact on net income. Errors in determining income tax expense have a dollar for dollar effect on reported net income. For example, if the effective income tax rate is 40 percent, a $100 overstatement of sales overstates net income by only $60; a $100 understatement of income tax expense overstates net income by the full $100.

The auditor's assessment of the tax provisions must consider federal, state, and foreign income tax expense and the related current and deferred liabilities. In audits of small and medium-size businesses, the auditor often prepares the tax returns. In other cases, the client or some other professional prepares them. When someone else prepares them, the auditor must review them to be sure that they are proper. When taxable and book income are substantially different due to temporary differences, deferred tax assets and/or liabilities need to be recorded.

The inherent risk is usually quite high for income taxes because of the complexities of the judgments, factors, and calculations that are involved. The auditor often calls on the expertise of someone in the firm's own tax department to assist in evaluating the client's income tax provisions. The auditor usually examines estimated tax returns filed during the year and the canceled checks that accompanied those returns and tests the reasonableness of the current year provision for income tax expense.

The auditor should inquire about the status of IRS audits of prior years and examine the IRS auditor's reports for any disputes or additional assessments. There may be a related contingency that should be recorded and/or disclosed.

C–RELATED-PARTY DISCLOSURES

Most business transactions are carried out on an arm's-length basis between unrelated parties. If the parties are related, the transactions may be subject to manipula-

Historical Perspective

RELATED-PARTY TRANSACTIONS

Related-party transactions are common to businesses of all sizes. Most small businesses regularly engage in related-party transactions, often for tax purposes, but are reluctant to disclose their nature to outside users. Management often sets up a company to lease assets back to the corporation. Perhaps management owns both entities but may want to keep the liability off the books of the corporation, which is seeking an outside loan. In a recent court case, the jury ruled that the financial statements were not fairly presented because management used its joint ownership of two organizations to improve the capital structure of the company that was audited even though it was substantively responsible for debt that had been shifted to a second organization. The transaction was structured as follows:

1. The father and two sons owned a construction company that was incorporated and required outside bonding before it could bid on new jobs. The same individuals, along with their spouses, also owned a partnership that invested in real estate and rented commercial buildings.
2. The construction company was experiencing financial difficulties and could not bid on additional jobs unless there was a reduction in its outstanding debt and an improvement in its debt/equity ratio.
3. Because the construction company did not have any outside sources of funds, the bank would not lend any more to it.
4. Management and the bank agreed to the following transaction (which would not require any money to leave the bank):
   a. The bank would lend $500,000 to the partnership.
   b. The partnership would immediately use the funds to purchase newly issued stock of the corporation.
   c. The construction company would immediately use the funds to pay off $500,000 of its note payable to the bank.
5. The construction company would be responsible for the repayment of the new note to the bank in the event of default by the partnership. At the time the loan was made, the partnership did not have sufficient assets to generate a repayment. In fact, its largest investment was the ownership of the construction company.

The financial statements did not disclose any of these transactions or the obligations of the various parties. The judge ruled that related-party disclosures are necessary so that users can understand the economic substance of the transactions.

Many related-party transactions are cleverly disguised. However, the auditor's review of the economic substance of many transactions usually identifies any material related-party transactions. Users have a right to know whether the financial statements have been manipulated by related-party transactions and the procedures identified here are designed to assist in meeting that obligation.

tion to make the financial statements look better than they otherwise would. Profits can be shifted between related companies. Borrowing and loaning money may be accomplished at other than market rates of interest. The transfer of products or services could be at other than market value. (See Historical Perspective box.)

Users of the financial statements need to be aware of material related-party transactions. The summary to FASB *Statement No. 57*, "Related Parties," states:

> Financial statements shall include disclosures of material related party transactions, other than compensation arrangements, expense allowances, and other similar items in the ordinary course of business. The nature of certain common

control relationships shall be disclosed if the nature of those relationships could significantly affect the reporting enterprise. . . .

Related-party transactions should be considered throughout the entire audit process (refer to AU 334). Auditors should design and perform audits to identify related parties and any significant transactions or common control relationships that should be disclosed and should obtain an understanding of the business purpose of such transactions or relationships.

Identifying Related Parties

Related parties include affiliated companies; principal owners, top management, and its immediate families; entities for which investments are accounted for by the equity method; and any other party whose management or operating policies can be influenced by the client or who can influence the client's management or operating policies. Procedures to identify related parties include the following:

- Asking management to identify related parties.
- Reviewing SEC filings that contain lists of major stockholders, officers, and top management as well as other businesses in which officers and directors occupy directorship or management positions.
- Reviewing stockholder lists or records.
- Reviewing prior year working papers.
- Inquiring of the predecessor auditor or other auditors assisting in the current year audit.
- Determining the names of pension and other trusts established for the benefit of employees and the names of their officers and trustees.
- Reviewing material investment transactions during the audit period to determine whether they resulted in the creation of a related party.

Identifying Related-Party Transactions

The in-charge auditor should be sure that all members of the audit team are provided with the names of related parties so they can be alert for related-party transactions as they perform segments of the audit. The following are specific procedures for identifying such transactions:

- Review the corporate minutes for information about material transactions authorized or discussed.
- Review filings with the SEC and other regulatory agencies.
- Review the extent and nature of business transacted with major customers, suppliers, borrowers, and lenders for indications of previously undisclosed relationships.
- Consider whether related parties are providing products or services that are not given accounting recognition, such as a board member providing free legal counsel, accounting, or management service at no charge; a major stockholder absorbing corporate expenses; or an owner providing space for the client at no charge.

- Review accounting records for large, unusual, or nonrecurring transactions or balances, paying particular attention to transactions recognized at or near the end of the reporting period. For example, a major owner may loan money to the client during the year, the client pays it back shortly before the end of the year, and borrows it again after year-end. The same thing happens at the end of each year. The substance of the transactions is a long-term borrowing that does not appear on the balance sheet.
- Review confirmations of loans receivable and payable for indications of guarantees. Determine the nature and the relationships, if any, of the guarantors to the reporting entity.

Auditing Identified Transactions

Once related-party transactions have been identified, the auditor must understand their nature and business purpose to determine whether they were properly authorized and to test the reasonableness of the amounts to be disclosed. Procedures include these:

- Inquiring of management about the nature and business purpose.
- Examining underlying documents and related accounting records.
- Reviewing the minutes of the board of directors meetings for authorization.
- Arranging for audits of intercompany accounts on concurrent dates.

Disclosure of Related-Party Relationships and Transactions

The auditor should be sure the disclosures are in accordance with FASB *Statement No. 57.* Disclosures should include a description of the nature of the relationships and the transactions (including those for which accounting entries are not made), the dollar amounts, and amounts due from or to related parties and the terms and manner of settlement. Such disclosures should be made for each year for which financial statements are presented. The disclosure should not contain a statement that the related-party transactions were carried out on terms similar to those that would have existed in arm's-length transactions unless the statement can be substantiated.

D–SUBSEQUENT EVENTS

This section presents three situations relating to events occurring after the balance sheet date that require special audit attention:

- Review of events occurring prior to issuance of the audit report, a normal part of each audit.
- Subsequent discovery of facts existing at the date of the auditor's report.
- Consideration of omitted procedures after the report date.

The timeline in Exhibit 20.3 will help understand these situations. Every audit includes procedures to review events and transactions that occur during the subsequent period, which is the period between the balance sheet date and the end of audit field work (period A in Exhibit 20.3). The auditor has no responsibilities to continue obtaining audit evidence after the end of the field work (periods B and C) except when the client is filing a registration statement with the Securities and Exchange Commission preparatory to selling new securities, in which case the auditor must perform a **subsequent events review** up to the effective date of the registration statement. The **effective date** is the date the SEC indicates to the client that it may begin trying to sell the new securities. This date may be several months after the end of the normal field work.

Normal Review of Subsequent Events

Two types of events have been identified in the professional literature [AU 560) as *subsequent events.* The first type applies to evidence about the correctness of the financial statements as of the balance sheet. For example, accounting estimates are an integral part of financial reporting and should be based on the best information available at the time the financial statements are prepared for distribution. The auditor should review events and transactions that occur prior to the end of field work (period A in Exhibit 20.3) to be sure that the estimates are based on the best available information and that other evidence supports recorded book values. The second type of subsequent events occurs after the balance sheet date and does not have a direct effect on the financial statement numbers but should be disclosed in the footnotes to help the users interpret the financial statements.

First Type

The first type of subsequent event provides evidence about conditions that *existed at the balance sheet date.* The financial statement numbers *should be adjusted* to reflect this information. Footnote disclosure may also be necessary to provide additional information. The following are examples:

- A major customer files for bankruptcy during the subsequent period because of a deteriorating financial condition about which the client and auditor were not aware until learning of the bankruptcy filing. This information should be considered in establishing an appropriate amount for the allowance for doubtful accounts and an adjustment to be made if the allowance is not sufficient to cover this potential loss.
- Settlement of a lawsuit for a different amount than was accrued if the event causing the lawsuit occurred before the balance sheet date.

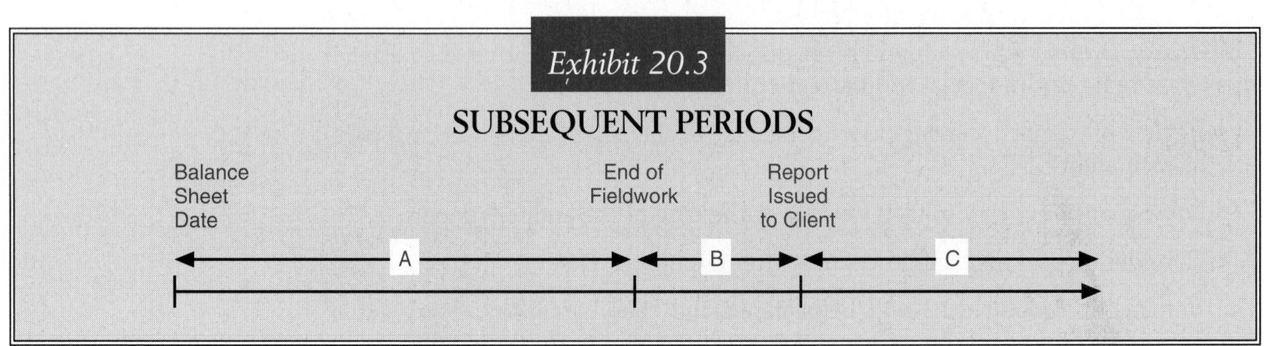

- A stock dividend or split that takes place during the subsequent period should be disclosed. In addition, earnings per share figures should be adjusted to show the retroactive effect of the stock dividend or split.
- Sale of inventory below carrying value.

Second Type

The second type of subsequent event indicates conditions that *did* not *exist at the balance sheet date.* The financial statement numbers *should* not *be adjusted* for these events, but they should be *considered for disclosure.* The following are examples.

- A customer bankruptcy during the subsequent period caused by an uninsured casualty that occurred after the balance sheet date. Because the customer was able to pay at the balance sheet date, the allowance for doubtful accounts should not be adjusted, but the information should be disclosed.
- Initiation of a significant lawsuit relating to an incident that occurred subsequent to the balance sheet date.
- Loss of a major facility due to a natural disaster, such as fire, earthquake, or flood.
- Major decisions made during the subsequent period, such as to merge, discontinue a line of business, or issue new securities.
- A material change in the value of investment securities.

Audit Procedures

Some of the procedures discussed in previous chapters relate to subsequent events, such as cutoff tests, review of subsequent collections of receivables, and the search for unrecorded liabilities. Additional procedures include the following:

- Read the minutes of the meetings of the board of directors, stockholders, and other authoritative groups. The auditor should obtain written assurance that minutes of all such meetings through the end of the field work have been made available. This can be included in the management representation letter described later in this chapter.
- Read interim financial statements and compare them to the audited financial statements, noting significant changes. Investigate significant changes.
- Inquire of management concerning:
  1. Any significant changes noted in the interim statements.
  2. The existence of significant contingent liabilities or commitments at the balance sheet date or date of inquiry, which should be near the end of the field work.
  3. Any significant changes in working capital, long-term debt, or owners' equity.
  4. The current status of items for which tentative conclusions were drawn earlier in the audit.
  5. Any unusual adjustments made to the accounting records after the balance sheet date.

- Inquire of management and its legal counsel concerning contingencies (discussed later in this chapter).
- Obtain a management representation letter (also discussed later in this chapter).

Dual Dating

When the auditor becomes aware of an event that occurs after the end of the field work but before the issuance of the audit report to the client (period B in Exhibit 20.3) and the event is disclosed, the auditor has two options for dating the audit report:

1. Use the date of this event.
2. "Dual date" the report, using the dates of the end of the field work and the event [AU 530].

As an example, consider the situation in which the auditor completed the audit on February 27, 1994, and a fire destroyed the client's main manufacturing plant and warehouse on March 2, 1994. This event is disclosed in Note 14 to the financial statements. The audit report was issued to the client on March 5. The auditor may date the report March 2, 1994, or dual date it as "February 27, 1994, except for Note 14, as to which the date is March 2, 1994." The auditor is assuming less responsibility by dual dating the report. The only event occurring after the end of the field work for which the auditor is taking responsibility is that disclosed in Note 14. The auditor would be taking responsibility for *all* events occurring during period B if the report were dated March 2, 1994, and should perform audit procedures to identify other significant subsequent events that occurred between February 27 and March 2.

Subsequent Discovery of Facts Existing at the Date of the Auditor's Report

Facts may come to the auditor's attention after the audit report has been issued to the client (period C in Exhibit 20.3) that indicate the previously issued financial statements and auditor's report would have been affected had the facts been known at the time of issuance. Such facts may come to the auditor's attention through news reports, performing another service for the client, other business contacts, or a subsequent audit. If such facts would have been investigated had they been known at the report date, the auditor should determine the following:

- Their reliability.
- Whether the development or event had occurred by the report date. Issuance of revised financial statements and audit report is not required when the development or event occurs after the report date.
- Whether users are likely to still be relying on the financial statements. Consideration should be given to the length of time the statements have been outstanding.
- Whether the audit report would have been affected had the facts been known to the auditor at the report date.

Historical Focus

YALE EXPRESS CASE

Auditing standard AU 561, "Subsequent Discovery of Facts Existing at the Date of the Auditor's Report," was the result of a lawsuit against the auditors of Yale Express. During 1963, the auditors were performing a management service related to the manner of recognizing revenues and expenses. While performing that service, they discovered that the prior year audited financial statements contained a material error. An unqualified opinion had been issued on those statements that showed a $1.1 million net income that should have been a $1.9 million net loss. Users were not notified of this until the subsequent year audited financial statements were issued several months later. The stockholders were upset that they had not been notified on a timely basis and sued the auditors. The court held that auditors could be held liable in such situations. This auditing standard was then issued to provide guidance for auditors.

If the auditor decides that steps should be taken to prevent further reliance on the financial statements and audit report, the client is advised to make appropriate and timely disclosure of these new facts. The key action is to notify users as soon as possible so they do not continue to rely on information that is now known to be incorrect (see the Historical Focus discussion). The appropriate action depends on the circumstances:

- If the revised financial statements and audit report can be quickly prepared and distributed, the reasons for the revision should be described in a footnote and referred to in the auditor's report.
- Revision and explanation can be made in the subsequent period audited financial statements if their distribution is imminent.
- If it will take an extended amount of time to develop revised financial statements, the client should immediately notify the users that the previously distributed financial statements and auditor's report should no longer be relied on and that revised statements and report will be issued as soon as possible.

The auditor should be sure that the client takes the appropriate action. If the client will not cooperate, the auditor should:

- Notify the client and any regulatory agency having jurisdiction over it, such as the SEC, that the audit report should no longer be associated with the client's financial statements.
- Notify users known to the auditor that the audit report should no longer be relied on. Auditors typically do not know all of the users who received the report. Therefore, the appropriate regulatory agency should be requested to take whatever steps are needed to disclose this situation.

Consideration of Omitted Procedures after the Report Date

After the audit report has been issued, the auditor may discover that an important audit procedure was not performed. Such an omission may be discovered when working papers are reviewed as part of an external or internal peer review program. According to AU 390, the auditor should decide whether the previously issued audit report can still be supported in light of the omitted procedures. If not, the omitted or alternative procedures should be promptly performed and documented in the working papers. If the results indicate that the previously issued statements and audit report should be modified, the guidance in the previous section of this chapter should be followed. Otherwise, no further action is necessary.

E–CONTINGENCIES AND COMMITMENTS

SFAS No. 5, "Accounting for Contingencies," provides the standards for accruing and disclosing three categories of contingent loss: those for which an unfavorable outcome is (1) probable, (2) reasonably possible, and (3) remote. It requires the accrual and disclosure of probable contingent losses that can be reasonably estimated. It also requires the disclosure of probable contingencies that are not accrued, those that are reasonably possible, and those remote contingencies that are disclosed because of common practice, such as the guarantee of another company's debt. Contingencies include the following:

- Collectibility of receivables and loans.
- Product warranty liability.
- Threat of expropriation of assets in a foreign country.
- Litigation, claims, and assessments.
- Guarantees of debts of others.
- Obligations of banks under standby letters of credit.
- Agreements to repurchase receivables that have been sold.
- Purchase and sale commitments.

Responsibilities Related to Contingencies

Management is responsible for designing and maintaining policies and procedures to identify, evaluate, and account for contingencies. Auditors are responsible for determining that the client has properly disclosed contingencies.

Sources of Evidence of Contingencies

The primary source of information concerning contingencies is the client's management. The auditor should obtain the following from management:

- A description and evaluation of contingencies that existed at the balance sheet date or that arose prior to the end of the field work and the lawyer(s) consulted.

- Assurance in the management representation letter that the disclosure requirements of *SFAS No. 5* have been met.

The auditor should also examine related documents in the client's possession, such as correspondence and invoices from lawyers. Additional sources of evidence are the corporate minutes, contracts, correspondence from governmental agencies, and bank confirmations. While auditing sales and purchases, the auditor should be alert to any commitments that could result in a loss. Management may have signed a purchase commitment for raw materials at a fixed price, for example, and the materials are to be delivered after year-end. If a loss on this commitment exists because of a decline in the market price by year-end, the loss should be accrued and the details disclosed in the footnotes.

Letter of Audit Inquiry

The primary source of corroborative evidence concerning litigation, claims, and assessments is the client's legal counsel. Attorneys are hesitant to provide much information to auditors. They know that the auditors will document that information in the audit working papers, which are, in most states, not protected by privileged communication. Information that is not privileged can be subpoenaed by a court of law and serve as evidence against the client. Attorneys usually have privileged communications with their clients. As a result, the American Bar Association and the AICPA have agreed to the following procedures. The auditor asks the client to send a **letter of audit inquiry** to its legal counsel that includes:

- Identification of the company, its subsidiaries, and the date of the audit.
- Management's list (or a request by management that the lawyer prepare a list) that describes and evaluates the contingencies to which the lawyer has devoted substantial attention.
- A request that the lawyer furnish the auditor with the following:
  1. A comment on the completeness of management's list and evaluations.
  2. For each contingency
     a. A description of the nature of the matter, the progress to date, and the action the company intends to take.
     b. An evaluation of the likelihood of an unfavorable outcome and an estimate of the potential loss or range of loss, if possible.
  3. Any limitations on the lawyer's response, such as not devoting substantial attention to the item or the amounts are not material.

The auditor and client should agree on what is material. It may be desirable to include a materiality scope in the letter of audit inquiry, requesting information only on contingencies that have a maximum potential loss greater than a specified amount. Exhibit 20.4 is an example of a letter of audit inquiry. The lawyer's response should be sent directly to the auditor.

Effect of Contingency on Audit Report

A lawyer's refusal to furnish the requested information either orally or in writing is a scope limitation precluding an unqualified opinion. The lawyer may be unable to form a conclusion on the likelihood of an unfavorable outcome or the amount of

Exhibit 20.4

LETTER OF AUDIT INQUIRY

LeFlam Manufacturing Company
200 Pine Way, Kirkville, WI 53800
January 10, 1995

John Barrington
Barrington, Hunt, & Wibfly
1500 Park Place
Milwaukee, WI 52719

In connection with an audit of our financial statements at December 31, 1994, and for the year then ended, management of the Company has prepared and furnished to our auditors, Rittenberg & Schwieger, CPAs, 5823 Monticello Business Park, Madison WI 53711, a description and evaluation of certain contingencies, including that set forth below involving matters with respect to which you have been engaged and to which you have devoted substantive attention on behalf of the Company in the form of legal consultation or representation. This contingency is regarded by management of the Company as material. Materiality for purposes of this letter includes items involving amounts exceeding $75,000 individually or in the aggregate.

Pending or Threatened Litigation
The Company is being sued by General Materials for failure to pay amounts it claims are due it under a purchase agreement dated March 31, 1992. The suit was filed May 23, 1994, claiming we owe it $140,000 for material we purchased January 29, 1994. This material was defective, and we had received written approval from General Materials to destroy it, which we did. General Materials now claims that the approval was not properly authorized by its management. The case has gone through the deposition stage and trial is set for April 19, 1995. We believe that General Materials' claim is without merit and that we will prevail in the suit.

Please furnish to our auditors such explanation, if any, that you consider necessary to supplement the foregoing information, including an explanation of those matters as to which your views may differ from those stated and an identification of the omission of any pending or threatened litigation, claims, and assessments, or a statement that the list of such matters is complete.

There are no unasserted claims of which we are currently aware. We understand that should you have formed a professional conclusion that we should disclose or consider disclosure concerning an unasserted possible claim or assessment, as a matter of professional responsibility to us, you will so advise us and will consult with us concerning the question of such disclosure and the applicable requirements of *Statement of Financial Accounting Standards No. 5*. Please specifically confirm to our auditors that our understanding is correct.

Response
Your response should include matters that existed as of December 31, 1994 and during the period from that date to the effective date of your response. Please specifically identify the nature of and reasons for any limitation on your response.

Our auditors expect to have the audit completed on February 15, 1995, and would appreciate receiving your reply by that date with a specified effective date no earlier than February 12, 1995.

Other Matters
Please also indicate the amount we were indebted to you for services and expenses on December 31, 1994.

Very truly yours,

Joleen Soyka

Controller
LeFlam Manufacturing Company

potential loss because of inherent uncertainties. If the effect of the matter could be material to the financial statements, the auditor should ordinarily add an explanatory paragraph to the audit report (covered in the next chapter).

F–ADDITIONAL AUDIT ACTIVITIES

Going Concern Issues

Business failures result from a variety of causes, such as inadequate financing, cash flow problems, poor management, product obsolescence, natural disasters, loss of a major customer or supplier, and competition. Investors become upset when a business fails, particularly when it happens shortly after the auditor has issued an unqualified opinion. Such an opinion is not a guarantee that the business is a going concern. Auditors are required, however, to evaluate the likelihood of each client continuing as a going concern for a reasonable period, not to exceed one year from the balance sheet date [AU 341], but they are not responsible for predicting future events. The going concern evaluation is based on information obtained from normal audit procedures performed to test management's assertions; no separate procedures are required unless the auditor believes that there is substantial doubt about the client's ability to continue as a going concern. However, because the public expects auditors to evaluate the going concern assumption, many auditing firms regularly use established bankruptcy prediction models, such as the Altman Z-score (described in Chapter 23), in analyzing whether a particular client might represent a going concern problem. If there is substantial doubt, the auditor should identify and assess management's plans to overcome the problem.

Conditions Indicating a Potential Going Concern Problem

The auditor should be alert to several conditions when performing the audit:

- Negative trends, such as recurring losses, working capital deficiencies, negative cash flows from operating activities, and adverse key financial ratios.
- Internal matters, such as loss of key personnel, employee strike, outdated facilities and products, and uneconomic long-term commitments.
- External matters, such as new legislation, pending litigation, loss of a key franchise or patent, loss of a principal customer or supplier, and uninsured or underinsured casualty loss.
- Other matters, such as default on a loan, inability to pay dividends, restructuring of debt, violation of laws and regulations, and inability to buy from suppliers on credit.

When any of these or similar conditions are identified, the auditor should consider their significance and consider management's plans to solve the problem.

Mitigating Factors

If the auditor concludes that there may be a going concern problem, management's plans to overcome this problem should be identified and assessed. Management may plan to sell nonessential assets, borrow money or restructure existing debt, reduce or delay unnecessary expenditures, and/or increase owner investments. The auditor should identify those factors that are most likely to resolve the problem and audit them. For example, if financial projections are an integral part of the solution, the auditor should ask management to provide that information and the underlying assumptions. The auditor should then consider the adequacy of support for the major assumptions.

Effects on the Financial Statements

If the auditor continues to believe that there is substantial doubt about the client continuing as a going concern for a reasonable period of time, not to exceed one year beyond the date of the financial statements being audited, the adequacy of the related disclosures should be evaluated. Such disclosures might include the conditions causing the going concern doubt, management's evaluation of the significance of those conditions and its plans to overcome the problem, and information about the amounts and classification of assets and liabilities. When the auditor believes that management's plans are likely to alleviate the problem, disclosure of the conditions that initially lead to the going concern doubt should be considered.

Effects on the Audit Report

An explanatory paragraph should be added to the auditor's report when the auditor concludes that substantial doubt about the client's ability to continue as a going concern for a reasonable period of time remains. The paragraph should describe the auditor's concern and refer to a footnote in which management describes the financial problem in more detail.

Summarizing Possible Adjustments

During the course of the audit, misstatements are likely to be detected that individually do not seem to be material to the financial statements, and the auditor will temporarily pass on making those adjustments. They should not be forgotten, however. Most public accounting firms use a working paper to accumulate all of the known and projected misstatements and the carryover effects of prior year uncorrected misstatements (see Exhibit 20.5). Near the end of the audit, these possible adjustments should be reviewed in the aggregate to determine whether their combined effect is material. The auditor compares the total likely misstatements (the sum of known and projected misstatements) to each significant segment of the financial statements, such as total current assets, total noncurrent assets, total current liabilities, total noncurrent liabilities, owners' equity, and pre-tax income.

Planning materiality should be modified for any information that comes to the auditor's attention during the audit to indicate that a different materiality threshold is more appropriate. For example, when planning the audit, the auditor may not have been aware of a bond indenture provision requiring the client to maintain a current ratio of at least 1.75 to 1 at each year-end. If the current ratio is close to that requirement, a misstatement smaller than the planning materiality could cause the client to violate that provision. The auditor should then assess the known and likely misstatements in light of a reduced materiality threshold. It may be necessary to do

Exhibit 20.5

LEFLAM MANUFACTURING COMPANY
SUMMARY OF POSSIBLE ADJUSTMENTS
DECEMBER 31, 1994

SPA

W/P Ref	Acct No.	Description	Debit (Credit) Assets Current	Assets Noncurrent	Liabilities Current	Liabilities Noncurrent	Owners' Equity	Pre-Tax Earnings
		Uncorrected Known Errors						
		Chap 14						
B-4	300	Sales						972
	130	Accounts Receivable	(972)					
		Pricing error						
		Chap 15						
A-1	599	Miscellaneous Expense						500
	100	Cash	(500)					
		Unrecorded bank service charge						
		Chap 16						
AA-6		Miscellaneous Expense						6,500
		Accounts Payable		(6,500)				
		Cutoff error — Christmas party invoice						
C-1	111	Inventory	5,000					
	400	Cost of Goods Sold						(5,000)
		Pricing errors						
H-3	525	Depreciation Expense						94,500
	155	Accumulated Depreciation		(94,500)				
		Understatement of depreciation expense						
		Unknown Projected Errors						
		Chap 14						
B-4	300	Sales						13,493
	130	Accounts Receivable	(13,493)					
		Projected pricing errors from sample.						
C-1	111	Inventory	15,000					
	400	Cost of Goods Sold						(15,000)
		Projected pricing errors from sample						
		Carryover Effect of Prior Year Errors						
U-3	239	Income Taxes Payable			200			
U-3	299	Retained Earnings					300	
	501	Salary Expense						(500)
		Understatement of prior year salary accrual						
		Taxes payable adjustment			38,186			
		Net income adjustment					57,279	
		Total likely error	5,035	(94,500)	31,886	-0-	57,579	95,465
		Final balance from trial balance	19,073,000	1,997,000	(3,346,000)	(13,048,000)	(4,676,000)	(1,678,000)
		Total likely error as % of balance	0.03%	−4.73%	−0.95%	0.0%	−1.23%	−5.69%

Conclusion: In my opinion, the total likely errors are not material to the financial statements taken as a whole, and correcting the above errors is not necessary.

Marginal tax rate 40.00%

PREPARED BY: BJS DATE 2/21/95

REVIEWED BY: LER DATE 2/25/95

more audit work or ask the client to make some correcting entries before an unqualified opinion can be given.

A different materiality threshold may be used for the balance sheet and income statement. A $100,000 overstatement of accounts receivable caused by a bad cash receipts cutoff, for example, is not as important to users as a $100,000 overstatement of receivables caused by a bad cutoff of sales because of the latter's effect on net income.

Adequacy of Disclosures

The auditor's report covers the basic financial statements, which include the balance sheet, income statement, statement of cash flows, a statement of changes in stockholders' equity or retained earnings, and the related footnotes. According to the third standard of reporting, "Informative disclosures in the financial statements are to be regarded as reasonably adequate unless otherwise stated in the report." Disclosures can be made on the face of the financial statements in the form of classifications or parenthetical notations and in the footnotes. Placement of the disclosures should be dictated by the clearest manner of presentation.

The auditor must be sure that the disclosures are adequate, but not so extensive or wordy as to hide the important matters. Confidential information should not be disclosed without the client's permission unless it is required to be disclosed by accounting or auditing standards or is considered for fair presentation. Checklists, such as the partial example in Exhibit 20.6, are available to remind the auditor of matters that should be considered for disclosure. This checklist provides references

Exhibit 20.6

PARTIAL DISCLOSURE CHECKLIST

	Yes	*No*	*N/A*
G. Property and Equipment			
1. For depreciable assets, do the financial statements or notes thereto include disclosure of			
a. Depreciation expense for each period? (*APB No. 12*, par. 5a [AC D40.105a])	___	___	___
b. Balances of major classes of depreciable assets by nature or function? (*APB No. 12*, par. 5b [AC D40.105b])	___	___	___
c. Accumulated depreciation, either by major classes of assets or in total?	___	___	___
d. The method or methods used in computing depreciation with respect to major classes of depreciable assets? (*APB No. 12*, par. 5d [AC D40.105d]); (*APB No. 22*, par. 13 [AC A10.106])	___	___	___

Source: *Disclosure Checklists and Illustrative Financial Statements for Corporations — A Financial Reporting Practice Aid* (New York: AICPA, November 1989) p. 52.

to the source of the disclosure requirements. There may be items that should be disclosed that are not covered by the checklist. The auditor, therefore, should not blindly follow a checklist but should use good audit judgment when there are unusual circumstances of which the users should be aware.

The auditor should consider matters for disclosure while gathering evidence during the course of the audit, not just at the end of the audit. While auditing cash, for example, evidence should be gathered concerning compensating balances or any other restrictions on the use of cash. During the audit of receivables, the auditor should be aware of the need to separately disclose receivables from officers, employees, or other related parties, and the pledging of receivables as collateral for a loan.

Management Representation Letter

Auditors should obtain a **management representation letter** (see Exhibit 20.7) at the end of each audit [AU 333]. Management's failure to provide such a letter is considered a scope limitation sufficient to preclude the issuance of an unqualified opinion. The letter is a part of audit evidence but is not a substitute for audit procedures that can be performed to corroborate the information contained in the letter. The purposes of the letter are as follows:

- It reminds management of its responsibility for the financial statements.
- It confirms oral responses obtained by the auditor earlier in the audit and the continuing appropriateness of those responses.
- It reduces the possibility of misunderstanding concerning the matters that are the subject of the representations.

The letter is typed on the client's letterhead, is addressed to the auditor, is normally signed by the chief executive officer and the chief financial officer, and should be dated as of the audit report date so that it covers all of the matters up to the end of the audit field work. The letter is normally prepared by the auditor for the client to read and sign. The contents depend on the circumstances of the audit and the nature and basis of presentation of the financial statements. It may be limited to matters that are considered material to the statements, with the exception of representations concerning irregularities involving management or employees, which is a qualitative rather than quantitative issue.

The auditor may receive separate representation letters from other corporate officials. The corporate secretary, for example, may be asked to sign a letter representing that all of the corporate minutes (which are usually listed by date) or extracts from recent meetings have been made available to the auditor.

Modifications for Small Business Clients

The content of the letter should be tailored to each audit situation. For example, a small business client may not have retained legal counsel. The auditor normally relies on the review of internally available information and modifies the wording of the management representation letter. The wording of item 7 in Exhibit 20.7 could be changed to read as follows:

> We are not aware of any pending or threatened litigation, claims, or assessments or unasserted claims or assessments that are required to be accrued or disclosed in the financial statements in accordance with *Statement of Financial Accounting*

Exhibit 20.7

MANAGEMENT REPRESENTATION LETTER

LeFlam Manufacturing Company
1200 Express Way
Madison, WI 53710
(608) 255-7820

February 28, 1994 [Audit Report Date]

To Rittenberg and Schwieger, CPAs

In connection with your audit of the balance sheets and the related statements of income and cash flows of LeFlam Manufacturing Company for the years ended December 31, 1994 and 1993, for the purpose of expressing an opinion as to whether the financial statements present fairly, in all material respects, the financial position, results of operations, and cash flows of LeFlam Manufacturing Company in conformity with generally accepted accounting principles, we confirm, to the best of our knowledge and belief, the following representations made to you during your audit.

1. We are responsible for the fair presentation in the financial statements of financial position, results of operations, and cash flows in conformity with generally accepted accounting principles.
2. We have made available to you all:
   a. Financial records and related data.
   b. Minutes of the meetings of stockholders, directors, and committees of directors, or summaries of actions of recent meetings for which minutes have not yet been prepared.
3. There have been no:
   a. Irregularities involving management or employees who have significant roles in the internal control structure.
   b. Irregularities involving other employees that could have a material effect on the financial statements.
   c. Communications from regulatory agencies concerning noncompliance with, or deficiencies in, financial reporting practices that could have a material effect on the financial statements.
4. We have no plans or intentions that may materially affect the carrying value or classification of assets and liabilities.
5. The following have been properly recorded or disclosed in the financial statements:
   a. Related-party transactions and related amounts receivable or payable, including sales, purchases, loans, transfers, leasing arrangements, and guarantees.
   b. Capital stock reserved for options and conversions.
   c. Arrangements with financial institutions involving compensating balances and line of credit.
6. There are no:
   a. Violations or possible violations of laws or regulations whose effects should be considered for disclosure in the financial statements or as a basis for recording a loss contingency.
   b. Other material liabilities or gain or loss contingencies that are required to be accrued or disclosed by Statement of Financial Accounting Standards (SFAS) No. 5.
7. There are no unasserted claims or assessments that our lawyer has advised us are probable of assertion and must be disclosed in accordance with SFAS No. 5.
8. There are no material transactions that have not been properly recorded in the accounting records underlying the financial statements.
9. The company has satisfactory title to all owned assets, and there are no liens or encumbrances on such assets, nor has any asset been pledged.
10. We have complied with all aspects of contractual agreements that would have a material effect on the financial statements in the event of noncompliance.
11. No events have occurred subsequent to the balance sheet date that would require additional adjustment to, or disclosure in, the financial statements.

____
President (CEO)

____
Vice President, Finance (CFO)

Standards No. 5, and we have not consulted a lawyer concerning litigation, claims or assessments.

Other modifications for small business clients include a statement that management has recorded the audit adjustments and that business and personal transactions have been properly segregated.

Management Letter

Auditors often notice things that could help management do a better job. Reporting these observations in a **management letter** is seen by the client as a constructive part of the audit. Such a letter should not be confused with a *management representation letter*. The management letter is not required and it is a letter from the auditor to the client. Staff auditors are encouraged to make notes during the course of the audit on areas of potential improvements. Many of these observations relate directly to control deficiencies or operational matters.

Internal Quality Review Process

Those who work on the audit become very close to the determinations that result in financial statement presentations, to the client personnel, and to the audit procedures. They may not see problems that a knowledgeable auditor who did not work on the audit might see or raise questions that an "outsider" is more likely to raise. Therefore, most firms require that, before an audit report is issued to the client, the audit be subjected to an internal quality review by an audit partner who did not work on the audit. The quality review partner normally reviews the working papers and financial statements to (1) assess the completeness of the audit work and sufficiency of evidence, (2) determine the adequacy of financial statement disclosures, and (3) raise questions about the reasonableness of various financial statement presentations. In this era of seemingly uncontrolled litigation, it is often viewed as a last line of defense, albeit a costly one, for the auditing firm.

One of the membership requirements of the SEC Practice Section of the AICPA is that all audits of publicly held companies must have a review by a partner other than the engagement partner who must concur with the audit report before it can be issued. This is referred to as a **concurring partner review** or a **cold review.**

Small public accounting firms may not have another audit partner. In many of these cases, two such firms come to an agreement to review each other's audits. The reviewer should review the working papers and the draft of the audit report to be sure that there are no major gaps in the audit work performed and that the working papers support the audit opinion.

Summary

Before issuing an audit opinion, the auditor must determine whether the financial statements are presented fairly in all material respects, whether they contain adequate disclosures, and whether they properly reflect events that have occurred up to the end of the field work. The going concern issue must be addressed in each audit. The auditor should be sure that audit risk has been kept at an appropriately low level. An internal quality review program can help ensure that no major audit procedures have been left out and that the working papers support the audit opinion.

Significant Terms

common-size analysis Conversion of financial statement dollars to percentages and comparison of the percentages with those for prior years and the industry.

concurring partner review or **cold review** Review of an audit by an experienced auditor who was not otherwise involved with it.

effective date The date the SEC indicates to the client that it may begin trying to sell the new securities described in a registration statement.

letter of audit inquiry A letter that the auditor asks the client to send to its legal counsel to gather corroborative evidence concerning litigation, claims, and assessments.

management letter A letter from the auditor to the client identifying any problems and suggested solutions that may help management improve its effectiveness or efficiency.

management representation letter A letter to the auditors that is required to be signed by the client's chief executive and chief financial officer for the purpose of reminding management of its responsibility for the financial statements and confirming oral responses given to the auditor during the audit.

subsequent events review A review of events occurring in the period between the balance sheet date and the end of audit field work to determine their possible effect on the financial statements.

Review Questions

20–1 Why should the auditor perform analytical procedures in the final stages of the audit?

20–2 Why is disclosure of related-party transactions so important?

20–3 What sources of information are available to the auditor to help identify related parties?

20–4 What audit procedures will help identify related-party transactions?

20–5 What types of subsequent events should the auditor identify as part of a normal audit? Give an example of each type of subsequent event. How should they be handled in the financial statements?

20–6 With one exception, auditors do not have a responsibility to continue their review of subsequent events beyond the audit report date. What is that exception?

20–7 What audit procedures should be performed to search for subsequent events?

20–8 What is meant by "dual dating"? Explain how dual dating limits the auditor's responsibility for subsequent events.

20–9 Explain the auditor's responsibilities when it is discovered that facts existed at the date of the audit report but were not known to the auditor.

20–10 During a peer review, it was discovered that the auditors failed to perform a significant audit procedure. What steps should the auditors take?

20–11 What is the primary source of information about litigation, claims, and assessments? What is the primary source of corroborative evidence?

20–12 Why are lawyers hesitant to disclose information to auditors?

20–13 Who sends the letter of audit inquiry to the lawyers? To whom should the lawyer send the response to that letter?

20–14 What is the effect on the auditor's report of a lawyer's refusal to furnish the information requested in the letter of audit inquiry?

20–15 Are auditors required to evaluate the likelihood of each audit client being a going concern as a part of each audit? What types of conditions and factors should auditors look for to help make this evaluation?

20–16 How does a summary of possible adjustments working paper help the auditor determine whether the financial statements are fairly presented? What information might it contain?

20–17 Should the auditor always use planning materiality when reviewing the results of the audit and assessing whether the financial statements are fairly presented?

20–18 How is a disclosure checklist helpful? What precautions should the auditor take when using such a checklist?

20–19 What is a management representation letter? Who usually prepares it? Who should sign it? When should it be dated? How does it differ from a management letter?

20–20 What is an internal quality review process? How can a sole proprietor accomplish the objectives of this process?

Multiple Choice Questions

*20–21 Which of the following statements ordinarily is included among the written client representations obtained by the auditor?

a. Management acknowledges that there are *no* material weaknesses in the internal control structure.

b. Sufficient evidential matter has been made available to permit the issuance of an unqualified opinion.

c. Compensating balances and other arrangements involving restrictions on cash balances have been disclosed.

d. Management acknowledges responsibility for illegal actions committed by employees.

*20–22 Which of the following events most likely indicates the existence of related parties?

a. Borrowing a large sum of money at a variable rate of interest.

b. Selling real estate at a price that differs significantly from its book value.

*Adapted from the Uniform CPA examination or the Certified Internal Auditor examination.

c. Making a loan without scheduled terms for repayment of the funds.

d. Discussing merger terms with a company that is a major competitor.

*20–23 Six months after issuing an unqualified opinion on audited financial statements, an auditor discovered that the engagement personnel failed to confirm several of the client's material accounts receivable balances. The auditor should first

a. Request the permission of the client to undertake the confirmation of accounts receivable.

b. Perform alternative procedures to provide a satisfactory basis for the unqualified opinion.

c. Assess the importance of the omitted procedures to the auditor's ability to support the previously expressed opinion.

d. Inquire whether there are persons currently relying, or likely to rely, on the unqualified opinion.

*20–24 Which of the following audit procedures would most likely assist an auditor in identifying conditions and events that may indicate that there could be substantial doubt about an entity's ability to continue as a going concern?

a. Review of compliance with the terms of debt agreements.

b. Confirmation of accounts receivable from principal customers.

c. Reconciliation of interest expense with debt outstanding.

d. Confirmation of bank balances.

*20–25 Auditors should request that an audit client send a letter of inquiry to those attorneys who have been consulted concerning litigation, claims, or assessments. The primary reason for this request is to provide

a. Information concerning the progress of cases to date.

b. Corroborative evidential matter.

c. An estimate of the dollar amount of the probable loss.

d. An expert opinion as to whether a loss is possible, probable, or remote.

*20–26 In an audit of contingent liabilities, which of the following procedures would be *least* effective?

a. Reviewing a bank confirmation letter.

b. Examining customer confirmation replies.

c. Examining invoices for professional services.

d. Reading the minutes of the board of directors.

*20–27 An auditor searching for related-party transactions should obtain an understanding of each subsidiary's relationship to the total entity because

a. This may permit the audit of intercompany account balances to be performed as of concurrent dates.

b. Intercompany transactions may have been consummated on terms equivalent to arm's-length transactions.

c. This may reveal whether particular transactions would have taken place if the parties had *not* been related.

d. The business structure may be deliberately designed to obscure related-party transactions.

*20–28 The development of constructive suggestions to a client for improvements in its internal control structure is

a. Addressed by the auditor only during a special engagement.

b. As important as establishing a basis for reliance on the internal control structure.

c. A requirement of the auditor's consideration of the internal control structure.

d. A desirable by-product of an audit engagement.

*20–29 An auditor accepted an engagement to audit the 1994 financial statements of EFG Corporation and began the field work on September 30, 1994. EFG gave the auditor the 1994 financial statements on January 17, 1995. The auditor completed the field work on February 10, 1995, and delivered the report on February 16, 1995. The management representation letter normally would be dated

a. December 31, 1994.

b. January 17, 1995.

c. February 10, 1995.

d. February 16, 1995.

*20–30 The audit inquiry letter to the client's legal counsel should be mailed only by the

a. Client after the auditor has reviewed it for appropriate content.

b. Auditor after preparation by the client and review by the auditor.

c. Auditor's attorney after preparation by the client and review by the auditor.

d. Client after review by the auditor's attorney.

Discussion and Research Questions

20–31 (Related-Party Transactions)

Required:
Which of the following related-party transactions should be considered for disclosure? Explain your answers.

a. A major shareholder leases a factory building to the client.

b. The client sells 75 percent of its products to an otherwise unrelated discount chain on a just-in-time basis.

c. The principal owner is also the president and receives a salary, travel expense reimbursement, and typical fringe benefits for a president.

d. The client purchases raw materials from an investee for which the investment is properly accounted for using the equity method.

e. The wife of the chief executive officer has loaned money to the client.

20–32 (Related-Party Transactions) The client has prepared a draft of a footnote relating to amounts paid to a construction company for remodeling certain plant facilities. The chairman of the board of the client and his father own the construction company.

Required:

a. What information would the auditors expect to find in the footnote?

b. What audit procedures would the auditor apply to determine the appropriateness of the footnote?

c. Is it appropriate for the client to state that these payments were made on terms similar to those that would have existed in arm's-length transactions? Explain.

*20–33 (Subsequent Events) Milton Green, CPA, is auditing the financial statements of Taylor Corporation for the year ended December 31, 1993. Green plans to complete the field work and sign the auditor's report about March 10, 1994. He is concerned about events and transactions occurring after December 31, 1993, that may affect the 1993 financial statements.

Required:

a. What are the general types of subsequent events that require Green's consideration and evaluation?

b. What are the auditing procedures Green should consider performing to gather evidence concerning subsequent events?

20–34 (Subsequent Events) The auditor is auditing financial statements for the year ended December 31, 1994, and is completing the audit in early March 1995. The following situations came to the auditor's attention:

1. On February 12, 1995, the client agreed to an out-of-court settlement of a property damage suit resulting from an accident caused by one of its delivery trucks. The accident occurred on November 20, 1994. An estimated loss of $30,000 was accrued in the 1994 financial statements. The settlement was for $50,000.
2. Same facts as in 1 except the accident occurred January 1, 1995, and no loss was accrued.
3. The client is a bank. A major commercial loan customer filed for bankruptcy on February 26, 1995. The bankruptcy was caused by an adverse court decision on February 15, 1995, involving a product liability lawsuit initiated in 1994 arising from products sold in 1993.
4. The client purchased raw materials that were received just before year-end. The purchase was recorded based on its estimated value. The invoice was not received until January 31, 1995, and the cost was substantially different than was estimated.
5. On February 2, 1995, the board of directors took the following actions:

   (a). Approved officers' salaries for 1995.

   (b). Approved the sale of a significant bond issue.

   (c). Approved a new union contract containing increased wages and fringe benefits for most of the employees. The employees had been on strike since January 2, 1995.
6. A major customer was killed in a boating accident on January 25, 1995, in Mexico. The customer had pledged his boat as collateral. The boat, which was destroyed in the accident, was not insured. The

allowance for doubtful accounts is not adequate to cover the anticipated loss.

Required:

For each of the preceding independent subsequent events, which are to be considered material

a. Indicate and explain whether the financial statements should be adjusted only, adjusted and disclosed, disclosed only, or neither adjusted nor disclosed.

b. Describe how the auditor would have learned about each of these situations.

20–35 (Subsequent Discovery of Omitted Procedures) During the course of an interoffice quality review, it was discovered that the auditors had failed to consider whether inventory costs of a wholesale client exceeded their market value. Some prices had apparently been falling near year-end. Inventory is a major item in the financial statements, but the auditor does not know whether the market price declines were material.

Required:

a. What procedures could the auditor now perform to resolve this audit problem?

b. What should the auditor do if it turns out that inventory was materially overstated?

20–36 (Contingencies) An audit client is being sued for $500,000 for discriminatory hiring practices.

Required:

Indicate the appropriate action the auditor should take for each of the following independent responses to the letter of audit inquiry:

a. The lawyer stated that the client had a "meritorious defense."

b. The lawyer stated that there is only a remote chance that the client will lose. The client did not accrue any contingent loss or disclose this situation.

c. The lawyer stated the client will probably lose and the amount of loss could be anywhere between $250,000 and $500,000, with no amount within that range being more likely than another. The client disclosed this situation but did not accrue a loss.

d. The lawyer stated that there is a reasonable possibility that the client will lose. The client disclosed this situation but did not accrue a loss.

e. The lawyer stated the client will probably lose between $250,000 and $500,000, but most likely will lose $400,000. The client accrued a $250,000 contingent loss and disclosed the situation.

20–37 (Contingencies) Each of the following is an independent situation related to a contingency.

1. The lawyer refused to furnish the requested information.
2. The lawyer was unable to form an opinion on the probability or amount

of a pending lawsuit, but the auditor believes that the amount could be material.

3. The client stated that it had not consulted lawyers during the past year.
4. The client refuses to accrue for, or disclose, a pending lawsuit related to the infringement of a patent that is the basis of its major product. It is afraid that it will lose customers. The plaintiff is suing for $2,500,000, which represents 50 percent of owners' equity. The lawyer believes that the case can be settled for less than the damages claimed.

Required:
What should the auditor do in each case?

20–38 (Going Concern) A staff auditor has just returned from a continuing professional education workshop on SASs. One of her managers has asked her to prepare a training session for the rest of the staff. In particular, he wants her to discuss the SASs related to the client's ability to continue as a going concern.

Required:
Answer the following, which the auditor could use as the basis for the training session.

a. Describe the auditor's responsibility for assessing each client's ability to continue as a going concern.
b. Describe the effect on the financial statements and on the auditor's report for each of the following independent situations.
   1. The auditor has substantial doubt as to whether the client is a going concern.
   2. The auditor believes the footnote describing the going concern problem is inadequate.
   3. There had been disclosure of a going concern in the prior year statements, which was referred to in the auditor's prior year report, but the uncertainty has been eliminated this year. Comparative statements will be issued.
   4. The auditor concludes that the client is likely to continue in existence for at least one more year. The same conclusion had been reached in prior years.
   5. The client was forced into bankruptcy by creditors after year-end but before the audit was completed.

20–39 (Analytical Procedures) The audit of Humbird Company is almost finished. Gene Beam is the most experienced auditor on this audit and is in charge of performing analytical procedures.

Required:

a. Why is it important that analytical procedures be performed by experienced auditors?
b. What are some of the analytical procedures that Beam might perform?
c. How can these procedures be useful at this stage of the audit?

20–40 (Summary of Possible Adjustments) During the course of the audit of LeFlam for the year ended December 31, 1994, the auditor discovered the following errors (working paper references are in parentheses):

1. The accounts receivable confirmation work revealed one pricing error. The book value of $12,955.68 should be $11,984.00. The projected error based on this difference is $14,465. (B-9)
2. LeFlam had understated the accrued vacation pay by $13,000. (DD-2)
3. A review of the prior year working papers indicates the following uncorrected errors:
   a. Accrued vacation pay was understated by $9,000.
   b. Sales and accounts receivable were overstated by an estimated $60,000 due to cutoff errors.

Required:
Prepare a summary of possible adjustments working paper like the one in Exhibit 20.5 and draw your conclusion about whether the aggregate effect of these errors is material. LeFlam has made no adjustments to the trial balance numbers shown in Exhibit 13.9. The income tax rate is 33 percent for the current and prior year.

20–41 (Concurring Review) Concurring reviews are one of the membership requirements of the SEC Practice Section of the AICPA. Many nonmember CPA firms also require concurring reviews of each audit.

a. What is a concurring review?
b. What are the potential benefits of a concurring review?

20–42 (Audit communications) Several communications involve the client and auditor.

Required:
For each of the following communications, indicate who signs the letter, who receives it, whether it is required or optional, when it should be sent, and its purpose.

a. Lawyer's response to a letter of audit inquiry.
b. Management representation letter.
c. Engagement letter.
d. Management letter.
e. Reportable conditions.
f. Illegal acts.

20–43 **(Research Question—Related Parties)** Using your library, or other resources, select a publicly owned company, study the documents that it has filed with the SEC, and develop a list of related parties.

20–44 **(Research Question—Disclosures)** Obtain a disclosure checklist and the annual report of a public company. For significant accounting policies, leases, pensions, and long-term debt, identify any disclosures that appear to be missing and try to identify why they are missing.

CHAPTER

21

Learning Objectives

Through studying this chapter, you will be able to:

1. Understand the differences among audit, review, and compilation engagements in terms of procedures, the degree of responsibility taken by the accountant, and reports.
2. Describe the various types of audit reports.
3. Identify the circumstances in which the standard audit, review, and compilation reports should be modified and how such reports should be worded.
4. Understand the requirements for reporting on the financial statements of U.S. companies to be used by investors in other countries.

Audit Reports, Compilations, and Reviews

Chapter Contents

Chapter Overview

Public accounting firms provide three levels of service related to historical financial statements: audits, reviews, and compilations. Reviews and compilations are accounting services, not audit services.

In most states, only public accountants licensed by the state are permitted to provide these services. A few states regulate another class of practitioners, often called Registered Accountants, that can perform compilations but not audits or reviews.

The last major step in the audit process is determining the appropriate type of opinion to express (see Exhibit 21.1). Chapter 2 briefly examined the standard audit report. We now cover audit reports in more detail, with emphasis on nonstandard audit reports. The nature of reviews and compilations and the related reports are also covered in this chapter so you can clearly see the differences among these three basic levels of service and reports. Chapter 22 covers several other types of reporting situations.

A number of very significant changes in financial reporting may take place in this decade. Financial reporting finds itself in a state of change–a change in focus that affects display and has implications for reported profitability. . . . Financial statements in the 1990s will be more complicated, more difficult to explain and more difficult to understand.[1]

The objective of the fourth standard is to prevent misinterpretation of the degree of responsibility the auditor is assuming when his name is associated with financial statements. Reference in the fourth reporting standard to the financial statements "taken as a whole" applies equally to a complete set of financial statements and to an individual financial statement. [AU 508.05]

Justification for the expression of the auditor's opinion rests on the conformity of the audit with generally accepted auditing standards and on his findings. [AU 508.04]

A–AUDIT REPORTS

The auditor's report is designed to promote clear communication between the auditor and a financial statement reader by clearly delineating the following:

- What was audited.
- The division of responsibility for the financial statements between the reporting entity's management and the auditor.
- The nature of the audit process.
- The auditor's opinion on the fairness of the financial statements.

An **opinion** can be expressed only after a careful examination of audit evidence that has been gathered in sufficient amounts to be persuasive.

Types of Audit Opinions

Six types of audit opinions may be included in a report to express the auditor's judgment about the fairness of the overall financial statements:

- Standard three-paragraph unqualified opinion.
- Unqualified opinion with an explanatory paragraph *before* the opinion paragraph.

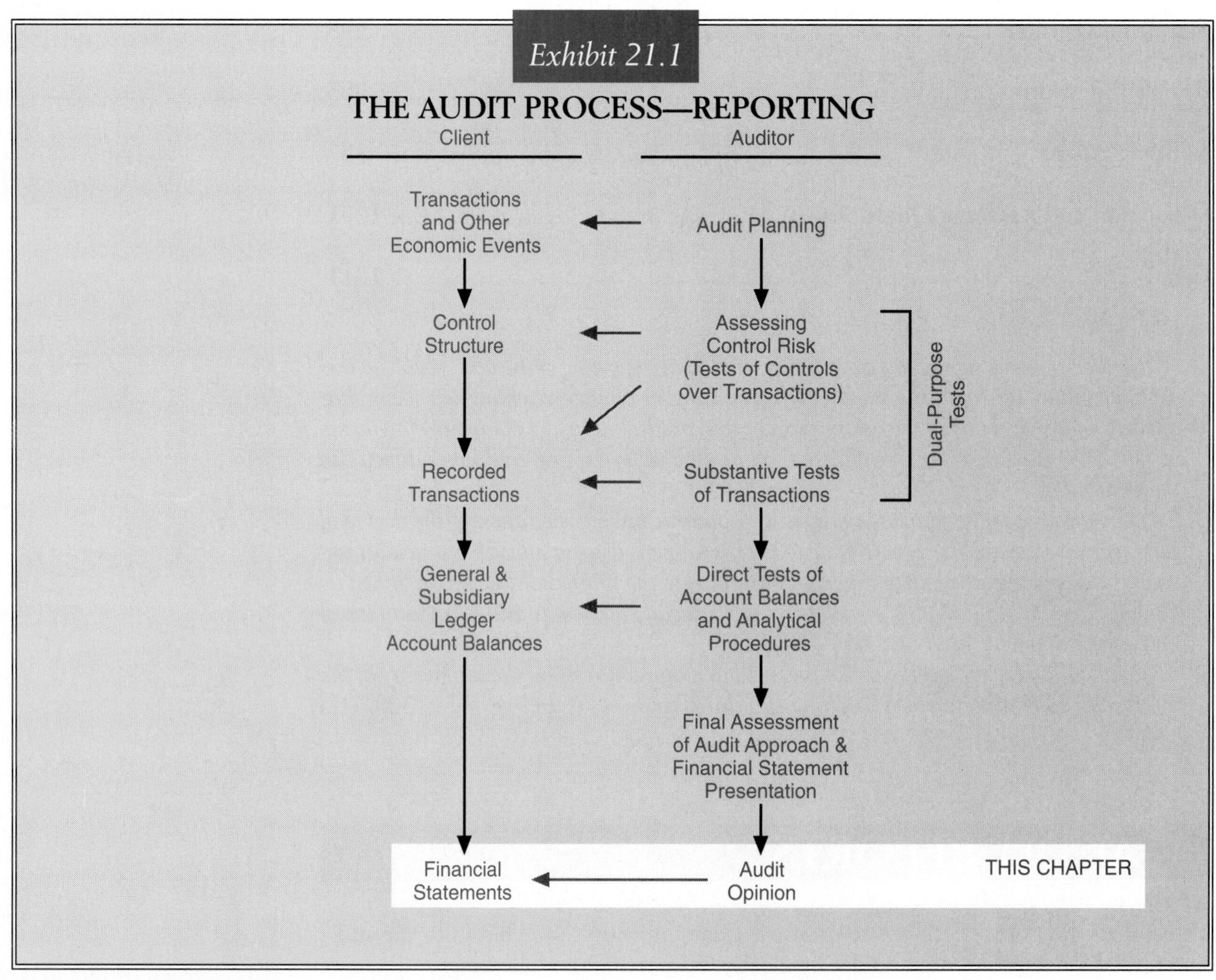

- Unqualified opinion with an explanatory paragraph *after* the opinion paragraph.
- Qualified opinion.
- Adverse opinion.
- Disclaimer of opinion.

Following is an overview of each of these types of opinions. The details are presented later in the chapter.

Standard Unqualified Opinion

A standard three-paragraph **unqualified opinion** is issued when the independent auditor has been able to perform sufficient procedures and believes that the evidence indicates that the financial statements do not contain a material departure from GAAP and that they contain adequate disclosures.

Unqualified Opinion with Explanatory Paragraph before the Opinion Paragraph

When the financial statements contain a material departure from GAAP that, in the auditor's opinion, is justified, a paragraph should be added, normally before the opinion paragraph, that explains the departure and justification. This is followed by the standard opinion paragraph.

Unqualified Opinion with Explanatory Paragraph after the Opinion Paragraph

A fourth paragraph is added after the opinion paragraph in the following circumstances:

- The client has changed an accounting principle or method of application that has a material effect on the financial statements, but such change is in accordance with GAAP. GAAP require proper justification and specify the appropriate accounting and disclosures.
- There are significant uncertainties which are properly disclosed in the footnotes.
- The auditor has significant doubt about whether the client can continue as a going concern.
- The auditor wishes to emphasize some other matter.

Qualified Opinion

A **qualified opinion** may be issued when the auditor has completed the audit and:

- Has concluded that there is a material, unjustified departure from GAAP, but the auditor believes that the financial statements taken as a whole are fairly presented except for this specifically identifiable GAAP departure.
- Has concluded that management's disclosures are not adequate.
- Is comfortable with the overall financial statement presentation but is unable to obtain sufficient competent evidence on a particular area because of scope limitations or the lack of such evidence.

Adverse Opinion

An **adverse opinion** is issued when the auditor has completed the audit and has concluded that the financial statements are materially misleading and therefore, taken as a whole, are not fairly presented due to:

- Material departures from GAAP that pervade the financial statements.
- The lack of important disclosures.

The decision about whether to issue a qualified or adverse opinion is based on the auditor's assessment of the materiality and pervasiveness of the financial statement misstatements. The auditor generally considers the following factors in deciding whether the GAAP departure requires a qualified or an adverse opinion:

- The dollar magnitude of the misstatement.
- The significance of the erroneous item to a particular entity, for example, inventory to a manufacturing company or loan loss reserves to a financial institution.
- The pervasiveness of the misstatement, that is, the number of items and financial statements affected.
- The effect of the misstatement on the financial statements taken as a whole [AU 508.50].
- The potential effect on users.

Disclaimer of Opinion

A **disclaimer of opinion** is issued when the auditor has not been able to obtain sufficient evidence to form an opinion on the overall fairness of the financial statements. This may occur because of a scope limitation, doubt about the client being a going concern, or other uncertainties. A disclaimer must also be issued if the auditor is not independent with respect to the client.

Frequency of Issuance

A review of audit reports of publicly owned companies issued in 1992 contained on the Corporate Disclosure compact disc service disclosed the following frequency of the various types of opinions and causes of modifications (not all modifications were identified, and some reports contain more than one cause):

	Total	Going Concern	Other Uncertainties	GAAP Violation/ Inadequate Disclosure	Scope Limitation	Accounting Change
Unqualified	10,156	1,263	300			7
Qualified	39	7	11	7	10	
Disclaimer	61	46	16		5	
Adverse	1			1		
Total	10,257	1,316	327	8	15	7

It is apparent that the issuance of other than unqualified opinions is unusual. Indeed, the SEC will not accept financial statements on which the opinion is modified because of client-imposed scope limitations, inadequate disclosures, or GAAP violations. As a result, the auditor has significant clout to encourage the client to not limit the scope but to present adequate disclosure and to correct any material violations of GAAP.

The Effect of Materiality on the Type of Opinion

The auditor's assessment of materiality plays an important part in deciding what kind of opinion to issue when there is a GAAP violation or scope limitation.

GAAP Violation. The materiality of a GAAP violation determines whether an unqualified, qualified, or adverse opinion should be issued. For example, if a client expenses an office stapler rather than treating it as a fixed asset and depreciating it over its useful life, the effect is immaterial and an unqualified opinion can be issued. If the client treated a capital lease of a significant piece of equipment as an operating lease, a qualified opinion may be called for. If the leases of the entire fleet of trucks of a trucking company were improperly treated as operating leases, an adverse opinion may be necessary.

Scope Limitation. A difficult decision facing the auditor is determining whether to issue a qualified opinion or a disclaimer of opinion when there is a **scope limitation** that does not permit sufficient evidence to be gathered. The auditor considers the nature of the limitation (imposed by the client or by circumstances), the materiality of the amounts involved, and the auditor's ability to form an opinion on the overall statements in making a judgment between the two alternative opinions. When significant restrictions are *imposed by the client*, the auditor should ordinarily disclaim an opinion [AU 508.42]. The client may, for example, restrict the auditor's observation of inventory or confirmation of accounts receivable. Because these are required procedures, such client-imposed restrictions may increase the risk that the related assets do not exist and, if the amounts are material, the auditor should ordinarily disclaim an opinion. If the client asked the auditor not to confirm one customer's balance because of ongoing dialogue to get the customer to pay its balance and the amount is insignificant, an unqualified opinion could probably be issued after performing limited alternative procedures. If several customers refuse to confirm their balances and the auditor is unable to obtain sufficient persuasive evidence through alternative procedures because of inadequate records, a qualified opinion or disclaimer may be necessary, depending on the materiality of the balances that cannot be substantiated.

Standards of Reporting

First Standard of Reporting

> **The report shall state whether the financial statements are presented in accordance with generally accepted accounting principles** [AU 150.02].

In most audits, it is the intent of management to present financial statements that are in accordance with GAAP. The auditor has several responsibilities in this regard.

General Acceptance. First, it must be determined whether the accounting principles used by management have general acceptance. To make this determination, the auditor turns to a variety of sources, some of which have a higher priority than others.

The most authoritative sources of GAAP are the following:

- FASB and GASB statements and interpretations.
- Accounting Principles Board opinions.
- Accounting Research Bulletins.

Even though the APB opinions and Accounting Research Bulletins were issued before the creation of the FASB and GASB, they continue in effect until superseded or amended by later pronouncements. If the financial statements contain a material departure from any of these authoritative pronouncements, Rule 203 of the Code of Professional Conduct prohibits the auditor from issuing an unqualified opinion except in rare situations, as explained later in this chapter.

If these sources of GAAP do not cover a particular accounting situation, the auditor should look to other sources:

- AICPA industry audit and accounting guides, statements of position, issues papers, and AcSEC practice bulletins.
- Technical bulletins issued by the FASB or GASB.
- Minutes of the FASB Emerging Issues Task Force.
- Concepts Statements of the FASB and GASB.
- International Accounting Standards.
- Industry practice.
- Pronouncements of other professional associations or regulatory agencies, such as the American Accounting Association, Financial Executives Institute, and the SEC.
- Generally accepted textbooks and articles.

If the financial statements contain a departure from these other sources of GAAP, the auditor is not required to modify the audit report if such departure can be justified.

Appropriateness of the Principles. The second responsibility of the auditor is to determine whether the accounting principles selected by management are appropriate in the circumstances. There are several situations in which alternative methods of accounting can be used. In some of these cases, the accounting literature provides criteria for choosing the proper method. For example, the percentage-of-completion method of accounting for long-term construction contracts should be used when it is possible to reasonably estimate the expected profit and the extent of progress toward completion of the project. Otherwise, the completed-contract method should be used. In the case of alternative inventory costing and depreciation methods, the authoritative sources of GAAP do not provide any criteria for choosing the "appropriate" method, and management is free to choose from among those alternatives, such as FIFO/LIFO or straight-line/declining-balance depreciation. Once a method is selected, however, it should be used consistently from year to year.

In some reporting situations, management may choose to use a comprehensive basis of accounting other than GAAP. Examples are the cash basis and income tax basis. These are referred to as special reports, which are covered in the next chapter.

Other Responsibilities. In addition to determining the general acceptance and appropriateness of the accounting principles used by the client, the auditor should consider whether:

- The financial statements, including the related notes, are informative on matters that may affect their use, understanding, and interpretations.
- The information presented is classified and summarized in a reasonable manner, that is, neither too detailed nor too condensed.
- The financial statements reflect the underlying events and transactions in a manner that presents the financial position, results of operations, and cash flows stated within a range of reasonable and practicable limits [AU 411.04].

Second Standard of Reporting

The report shall identify those circumstances in which such principles have not been consistently observed in the current period in relation to the preceding period [AU 150.02].

The auditor should warn the reader when the financial statements have been materially affected by a change in accounting principles. This is done by adding a paragraph after the opinion paragraph that refers to the client's footnote that discloses the nature of the accounting change, the dollar effect of the change (to enhance comparability), and management's justification for the change.

Third Standard of Reporting

Informative disclosures in the financial statements are to be regarded as reasonably adequate unless otherwise stated in the report [AU 150.02].

If the auditor's report does not mention anything about disclosures, the reader may assume that they are adequate for purposes of understanding the financial statements. Disclosure can be provided in the form of a classified balance sheet, descriptive information on the face of the statements, and footnotes. It is sometimes difficult to determine how much detail is "adequate." The auditor is guided by professional accounting pronouncements in many areas, such as leases, pensions, summary of significant accounting policies, and debt. In other situations, the auditor must use judgment to determine whether the disclosure not only technically conforms to the letter of the pronouncements but also clearly communicates to users. For example, contingencies should be adequately described so that the user understands the nature of the contingency and the potential dollar effects involved.

Fourth Standard of Reporting

The report shall either contain an expression of opinion regarding the financial statements, taken as a whole, or an assertion to the effect that an opinion cannot be expressed. When an overall opinion cannot be expressed, the reasons therefor should be stated. In all cases where an auditor's name is associated with financial statements, the report should contain a clear-cut indication of the character of the auditor's examination, if any, and the degree of responsibility he is taking [AU 150.02].

Expressing an Opinion. The auditor is required to express either an unqualified opinion on the entire set of financial statements and related footnotes, including all years presented for comparative purposes, or state the reasons that such an opinion cannot be expressed. Therefore, when the auditor issues a qualified or adverse opinion or disclaims an opinion on one or more of the financial statements, the reason(s) must be stated in the auditor's report. Further, if a qualified or adverse opinion is expressed due to a departure from GAAP, the auditor should explicitly state the nature of the departure and the dollar effects (if such amounts are determinable by the auditor) so that a user could appropriately modify the financial statements to determine the result if they had been fairly presented.

Association with Financial Statements. The standard requires the public accounting firm to provide the client with a report to accompany financial statements any time the firm's name is associated with those statements. This is to prevent any misinterpretation of the nature of the service that was provided or the degree of responsibility the firm assumes. A firm is associated with financial statements by consenting to the use of its name in a report, document, or written communication containing the statements, with the exception of tax returns. A firm is also associated when it submits to the client, or others, financial statements its personnel have prepared or assisted in preparing, even though its name is not appended to the statements [AU 504.03].

Standard Unqualified Audit Report

The standard audit report includes an unqualified opinion; it reflects no reservations or qualifications on the part of the auditor as to the fair presentation of the financial statements. Further, no special conditions exist that need to be brought to the reader's attention. Exhibit 21.2 is an example of a standard unqualified report. Recall that the report is composed of three paragraphs. The introductory paragraph describes what was audited and the division of responsibility between the reporting company's management and the public accounting firm. The scope paragraph describes how the audit was conducted and the nature of the audit process. The opinion paragraph tells the reader whether the auditor believes the statements are fairly presented in conformity with GAAP.

Modifications of the Standard Unqualified Report

There are several situations in which the auditor wishes, or is required, to alter the wording of the standard report. Some of the alterations are informational only; others affect the type of opinion expressed. These require changed wording and many require an additional paragraph. The additional paragraph *precedes* the opinion paragraph if the situation calls for an opinion other than unqualified and usually *follows* the opinion paragraph when the situation does not require opinion modification. The placement of the additional paragraphs is illustrated in Exhibit 21.3. The audit opinion should be modified when:

- The financial statements contain a material, unjustified departure from GAAP,
- The financial statements lack adequate disclosure, or
- The auditor is unable to obtain sufficient, competent evidence.

Exhibit 21.2

STANDARD UNQUALIFIED AUDIT REPORT

INDEPENDENT AUDITORS' REPORT

The Board of Directors and
Stockholders of Norwest Corporation:

We have audited the consolidated balance sheets of Norwest Corporation and subsidiaries as of December 31, 1991 and 1990 and the related consolidated statements of income, cash flows and stockholders' equity for each of the years in the three-year period ended December 31, 1991. These consolidated financial statements are the responsibility of the Company's management. Our responsibility is to express an opinion on these consolidated financial statements based on our audits.

We conducted our audits in accordance with generally accepted auditing standards. Those standards require that we plan and perform the audit to obtain reasonable assurance about whether the financial statements are free of material misstatement. An audit includes examining, on a test basis, evidence supporting the amounts and disclosures in the financial statements. An audit also includes assessing the accounting principles used and significant estimates made by management, as well as evaluating the overall financial statement presentation. We believe that our audits provide a reasonable basis for our opinion.

In our opinion, the consolidated financial statements referred to above present fairly, in all material respects, the financial position of Norwest Corporation and subsidiaries at December 31, 1991 and 1990, and the results of their operations and their cash flows for each of the years in the three-year period ended December 31, 1991, in conformity with generally accepted accounting principles.

/signed/ *KPMG Peat Marwick*
KPMG Peat Marwick
Minneapolis, Minnesota
January 21, 1992

In these three situations, an additional paragraph describing the situation should be added *before* the opinion paragraph, and the opinion paragraph should be appropriately modified.

Modifications Not Affecting the Opinion

In the following situations, the auditor changes the wording of the standard report but still issues an unqualified report:

- Justified departure from GAAP.
- Inconsistent application of GAAP.
- Uncertainties, including going concern doubt.
- Emphasis of a matter.
- Reference to other auditors.

Justified Departure from GAAP

In rare circumstances, the client may have a justified departure from GAAP. Rule 203 of the AICPA Code of Ethics permits the auditor to issue an unqualified opinion

Exhibit 21.3

LOCATION OF ADDITIONAL PARAGRAPHS TO STANDARD UNQUALIFIED REPORT

Heading
Address
Introductory Paragraph
Scope Paragraph
- **Additional Paragraph to Explain Opinion Modification**
- **Justified Departure from GAAP**

Opinion Paragraph
- **Informational Paragraph–Opinion Not Affected**
  - **Inconsistent Application of GAAP**
  - **Uncertainties**
  - **Emphasis of a Matter***

Signature
Date

*Can be placed before the opinion paragraph.

when there has been a material departure from GAAP if the client can demonstrate, and the auditor concurs, that, due to *unusual circumstances*, the financial statements would have been misleading had GAAP been followed.

What constitutes unusual circumstances is a matter of professional judgment. Examples include new legislation or the evolution of a new form of business transaction. An unusual degree of materiality or the existence of a conflicting industry practice does not ordinarily justify a departure from GAAP [ET 203.02].

An informational paragraph should be added* to describe the departure from GAAP, its approximate effects (if they can be practicably determined), and the reasons for which compliance with GAAP would result in misleading statements. An unqualified opinion is appropriate in these circumstances. Exhibit 21.4 shows such a report for Oak Industries.

Inconsistent Application of GAAP

A change in accounting principle includes a change from one GAAP to another–such as from FIFO to LIFO and certain changes in the reporting entity. A change from non–GAAP to GAAP—such as from the cash basis to the accrual basis—is accounted for as a correction of an error, but is treated by the auditor as a change in accounting principles. Changes in accounting estimates and accounting for new transactions are not considered changes in accounting principles. If the client has changed an accounting principle and has followed GAAP in accounting for and disclosing this change, the explanatory paragraph serves as a flag directing the

*The explanatory paragraph seems to logically fit before the opinion paragraph, but the standard does not specify its location [AU 508.15].

Exhibit 21.4

REPORT STATING A JUSTIFIED DEPARTURE FROM GAAP

(Standard introductory and scope paragraphs followed by these explanatory and opinion paragraphs.)

As described in Note 3, in May 1987, the company exchanged shares of its common stock for $5,060,000 of its outstanding public debt. The fair value of the common stock issued exceeded the carrying amount of the debt by $466,000, which has been shown as an extraordinary loss in the 1987 statement of operations. Because a portion of the debt exchanged was convertible debt, a literal application of Statement of Financial Accounting Standards No. 84, "Induced Conversions of Convertible Debt," would have resulted in a further reduction in net income of $3,611,000 which would have been offset by a corresponding $3,611,000 credit to additional paid-in capital; accordingly, there would have been no net effect on stockholders' investment. In the opinion of company management, with which we agree, a literal application of accounting literature would have resulted in misleading financial statements that do not properly portray the economic consequences of the exchange.

In our opinion, the consolidated financial statements referred to above present fairly in all material respects, the financial position of Oak Industries Inc. and subsidiaries as of December 31, 1988 and 1987, and the results of their operations and their cash flows for each of the three years in the period ended December 31, 1988, in conformity with generally accepted accounting principles.

Coopers & Lybrand
San Diego, California
February 10, 1989

reader's attention to the relevant footnote disclosure. This flag can be very useful. For example, a company that reported a 22 percent increase in net income highlighted the increase several times in its annual report to shareholders. But only by noting the additional paragraph in the auditor's report and carefully reading the financial statements and footnotes would the reader have seen that the increase in net income would have been only 6 percent had there not been a change in an accounting principle. The additional paragraph in the auditor's report and the related footnote are shown in Exhibit 21.5. The auditor's reference to the accounting change is brief because the detail is presented in the client's footnotes. This is also true for a reference to uncertainties or going concern doubt.

Uncertainties

Uncertainties refer to situations in which the outcome of some matter cannot be determined as of the end of the audit field work. Uncertainties must be distinguished from scope limitations because material uncertainties result in either an unqualified opinion with an added paragraph or a disclaimer. A scope limitation results in either a qualified opinion or a disclaimer. The resolution of an uncertainty depends on the occurrence of some future event. Examples include pending litigation or serious doubt about the client's ability to continue as a going concern. A scope limitation is a situation in which evidence could have been obtained during the current audit had the client or circumstances permitted.

Unrelated to Going Concern Issue. In uncertainty situations other than a going concern matter, the auditor considers the likelihood that a material loss will result

Exhibit 21.5

REPORT STATING A CHANGE IN AN ACCOUNTING PRINCIPLE

[The audit report on the 1990 financial statements of Phillips Petroleum Company contains the standard introductory, scope, and opinion paragraphs followed by the following explanatory paragraph. An extract from Note 1 to the financial statements is also presented.]

As discussed in Note 1 to the financial statements, effective January 1, 1990 the Company adopted Statement of Financial Accounting Standards No. 96, "Accounting for Income Taxes."

/s/ Ernst & Young
Tulsa, Oklahoma
February 13, 1991

Note 1: Accounting Change
Effective January 1, 1990, the company adopted FASB Statement No. 96, "Accounting for Income Taxes," which requires an asset and liability approach in accounting for income taxes. Under the new method, the amount of deferred tax liabilities or assets is calculated by applying provisions of enacted tax law to determine the amount of taxes payable or refundable currently or in future years. The effect of the change was to increase income before extraordinary item and cumulative effect of a change in accounting principle by $130 million ($.52 per share) for the year. In addition, the cumulative effect of the change on prior years increased net income by $137 million ($.55 per share). Prior years financial statements have not been restated.

from the resolution of the uncertainty. The auditor is more likely to add an explanatory paragraph to the unqualified report as the amount of reasonably possible loss becomes larger or the likelihood of occurrence of a material loss increases [AU 508.26]. The auditor may go so far as to issue a disclaimer.

A paragraph should be added to the report following the opinion paragraph to explain the nature of the uncertainty, indicate that the outcome cannot at present be determined, and refer to the footnote that describes the situation more fully. The financial statements covered by the current auditor's report will not be changed in future years when the uncertainty is resolved because this is an accounting estimate. As long as the client has recorded and/or disclosed the uncertainty using the best available information, a change in any estimated loss will affect only the financial statements of a future year(s). As a result, the auditor may express an unqualified opinion and disclose the uncertainty. The explanatory paragraph in the auditor's report on Black Warrior Wireline Corp read as follows:

> As discussed in Note 4 to the consolidated financial statements, the Company is the subject of a formal investigation by the Securities and Exchange Commission's Branch of Broker-Dealer Enforcement. Also, as discussed in Note 5 to the consolidated financial statements, the company is a defendant in a lawsuit in which an individual asserts that he is due to be compensated for effectuating a financing arrangement for the Company. The ultimate outcome of these uncertainties cannot presently be determined. Accordingly, no provision for any liability that may result upon the ultimate resolution of these matters has been made in the accompanying consolidated financial statements.

Going Concern Consideration. In every audit, the auditor has a responsibility to evaluate whether there is substantial doubt about the client's ability to continue as a going concern for up to one year following the balance sheet date. If there is substantial doubt and the auditor feels comfortable issuing an unqualified opinion, the audit report should contain an explanatory paragraph following the opinion paragraph as illustrated in the following extract from the McGladrey & Pullen's audit report on Bioplasty, Inc.:

> The accompanying consolidated financial statements have been prepared assuming that the Company will continue as a going concern. As discussed in Notes 3 and 9 to the consolidated financial statements, the Company is currently precluded by the FDA from marketing most of its products in the United States and incurred a substantial operating loss and reduction in cash and working capital in fiscal 1992. These circumstances raise substantial doubt about the Company's ability to continue as a going concern. Management's plans in regard to these matters are described in Note 9. The consolidated financial statements do not include any adjustments that might result from the determination that the Company is not a going concern.

There are situations in which the auditor may not feel comfortable issuing any opinion. In such cases, the auditor may issue a disclaimer of opinion. In other situations, the auditor may believe that the client is not a going concern and, if the client does not use liquidation values, the financial statements are not in conformity with GAAP. Both of these situations are covered later in the chapter.

Emphasis of a Matter

The auditor may wish to emphasize a particular event, transaction, or subsequent occurrence that does not affect the opinion on the fair presentation of the financial statements. For example, an agreement made by the client after the balance sheet date to divest itself of a major segment of its business could be described in an additional paragraph.

Other Auditors–Shared Report

The audit client may have branches, warehouses, factories, or subsidiaries at various locations around the country or overseas. Other audit firms may perform part of the audit for convenience or economy. The other firm may be hired by the client or by the principal auditor.

The first decision that must be made is which firm should serve as the principal auditor, that is, who should issue the opinion on the overall financial statements. Among other things, this decision is based on the materiality of the portion of the financial statements the firm has examined, the extent of knowledge of the overall financial statements, and the importance of the components it has examined in relation to the enterprise as a whole [AU 543.03].

The principal auditor needs to decide whether to mention the other auditors in the overall audit report. The firm may choose not to mention them when:

- The other firm is an associated or correspondent firm.*
- The other firm is hired by the principal audit firm that directs the work of the other firm.

*Some CPA firms join together in associations to obtain some of the benefits that large firms have, such as developing common procedures, providing training, and facilitating audits of clients with operations in several locations. Some firms have reciprocal arrangements with firms in foreign countries to provide services for each other.

- The other firm is hired by the client, and the principal auditors are able to satisfy themselves that the work done by the other firm meets their own requirements.
- The amounts audited by the other firm are not material to the combined or consolidated financial statements [AU 543.05].

Whether another auditor is mentioned in the overall audit report, the principal auditor needs to become satisfied with the independence and reputation of the other firm. Each firm is always responsible for its part of the audit work.

If the principal audit firm chooses to mention the other firm in the audit report, the wording of all three paragraphs of the standard report is modified, but no additional paragraph is needed. This is often referred to as a **shared report.** The resulting opinion is unqualified unless there are other reasons for expressing a different opinion. The most extensive change appears at the end of the introductory paragraph to indicate the shared responsibility for the overall opinion, including the magnitude of the amounts audited by the other firm. The wording at the end of the scope paragraph and at the beginning of the opinion paragraph is also modified to show the shared responsibility. The name of the other audit firm is mentioned only with its express permission and if its report is also included in the document. Exhibit 21.6 is an example of a shared report. This report also refers to a change in an accounting principle.

If the other auditor's report is qualified, the principal auditor must consider whether the subject of the qualification is of such nature and significance in relation to the overall financial statements that it would affect the overall opinion. What was material to the segment audited by the other auditor may not be significant to the overall statements.

Modifications Affecting the Opinion

Unjustified Departure from GAAP

If the audit uncovers a material departure from GAAP, the auditor should attempt to have the client correct the financial statements or should express either a qualified or an adverse opinion, depending on the materiality of the misstatement(s) and its pervasiveness in the financial statements. Exhibit 21.7 illustrates an opinion that is qualified because of an unjustified material departure from GAAP. The introductory and scope paragraphs are unaffected.

If, in the auditor's judgment, the financial statements taken as a whole are not presented fairly in conformity with GAAP, the auditor should express an adverse opinion as illustrated in Exhibit 21.8. After the substantive reasons for the adverse opinion have been explained, the opinion paragraph states that the financial statements do not present fairly the company's financial performance.

Inadequate Disclosures

The AICPA's Code of Ethics prohibits an auditor from disclosing confidential information except under certain circumstances. Such information should be disclosed, however, if the auditor believes that the financial statements, including the related footnotes, would otherwise be misleading. If the client refuses to make the disclosures, the auditor should express a qualified or adverse opinion, depending on the

Exhibit 21.6

REPORT REFERRING TO OTHER AUDITORS–SHARED REPORT

To the Shareholders
Donnelly Corporation

We have audited the combined consolidated balance sheets of Donnelly Corporation and Subsidiary as of June 30, 1989 and 1988, and the related combined consolidated statements of income, shareholders' equity, and cash flows for each of the three years in the period ended June 30, 1989. The financial statements are the responsibility of the company's management. Our responsibility is to express an opinion on these financial statements based on our audits. *We did not audit the financial statements of Donnelly Mirrors Limited, the foreign subsidiary, which statements reflect total assets, net sales and net income constituting 11%, 9%, and 24% respectively for 1989, 12%, 10%, and 21% for 1988, and 11% and 22% of net sales and net income, respectively, for 1987, of the related combined consolidated totals. These statements were audited by other auditors whose reports thereon have been furnished to us. Our opinion expressed herein, insofar as it relates to the amounts included for Donnelly Mirrors Limited, is based solely upon the reports of the other auditors.*

We conducted our audits in accordance with generally accepted auditing standards. Those standards require that we plan and perform the audit to obtain reasonable assurance about whether the financial statements are free of material misstatement. An audit includes examining, on a test basis, evidence supporting the amounts and disclosures in the financial statements. An audit also includes assessing the accounting principles used and significant estimates made by management, as well as evaluating the overall financial statement presentation. We believe that our audits *and the reports of other auditors* provide a reasonable basis for our opinion.

In our opinion, *based on our audits and the reports of other auditors*, the combined consolidated financial statements referred to above present fairly, in all material respects, the financial position of Donnelly Corporation and Subsidiary as of June 30, 1989 and 1988, and the results of their operations and cash flows for each of the three years in the period ended June 30, 1989, in conformity with generally accepted accounting principles.

As discussed in Note 1 to the financial statements, the company made a change, with which we concur, in its method of computing depreciation in 1989.

BDO Seidman
Certified Public Accountants
Grand Rapids, Michigan
August 1, 1989

[Emphasis added.]

significance of the omitted disclosures, and provide the information in the audit report, if practicable. The auditor is not, however, required to prepare and present a basic financial statement, such as an omitted cash flow statement or segment information.

The introductory and scope paragraphs are not affected by this situation. The explanatory paragraph should describe the nature of the omitted disclosures, and the opinion paragraph should be modified. Exhibit 21.9 shows such an audit opinion.

Exhibit 21.7

QUALIFIED OPINION DUE TO A GAAP VIOLATION

[Standard introductory and scope paragraphs followed by these explanatory and opinion paragraphs.]

As more fully described in Note 10 to the financial statements, the Company expenses the acquisition of appliances. In our opinion, generally accepted accounting principles require that appliances be capitalized and depreciated over their estimated useful lives.

In our opinion, *except for the effect of the recording of appliances as discussed in the preceding paragraph,* the financial statements referred to above present fairly, in all material respects, the financial position of Knickerbocker Village, Inc., as of December 31, 1991 and 1990 and the results of its operations and its cash flows for the years ended December 31, 1991, 1990, and 1989 in conformity with generally accepted accounting principles. . . .

Held, Kranzler, Friedman & Pincus
February 5, 1992

[Emphasis added.]

Scope Limitation

An unqualified opinion can be given only when the auditor has been able to conduct the audit in accordance with GAAS. Restrictions on the scope of the audit, whether imposed by the client or by circumstances, may require the auditor to qualify the opinion or disclaim an opinion. Examples of circumstances that may limit the audit scope are the timing of the field work, the inability to obtain sufficient competent evidence, or an inadequacy in the accounting records. When a company is audited for the first time, the audit firm is often appointed during the year to be audited. In such a case, the auditor may be unable to obtain sufficient, competent evidence concerning the fairness of the beginning inventory, which affects the current year's income, or of the accounting principles used in the prior year.

Exhibit 21.10 presents an opinion that is qualified because of possible errors that might have been discovered had the scope of the audit not been limited. The scope paragraph refers to the scope limitation, which is then described in an explanatory paragraph. Note that the exception in the opinion paragraph refers to the possible adjustments rather than to the scope limitation itself.

When the *client imposes* substantial restrictions on the scope of the audit, there is a significant risk that the client is trying to hide important evidence, and the auditor should ordinarily disclaim an opinion. If scope limitations caused by *circumstances* are such that it is not possible to form an opinion, a disclaimer should also be issued. In either situation, wording of the introductory paragraph is modified, the scope paragraph is omitted, an additional paragraph is inserted to describe the scope limitation(s), and the last paragraph clearly states that no opinion can be expressed. Exhibit 21.11 illustrates such a disclaimer.

Disclaimer Due to Uncertainties or Going Concern Doubt

In some reporting situations, the magnitude of uncertainties and/or doubt about the client continuing as a going concern is such that the auditor is uncomfortable in issu-

Exhibit 21.8

ADVERSE OPINION

To the Board of Directors
Neco Enterprises Inc.

We have audited the accompanying consolidated balance sheets of NECO Enterprises, Inc. and its subsidiaries as of December 31, 1991 and 1990, and related consolidated statements of loss, deficit and cash flows for the years then ended. These financial statements are the responsibility of the Company's management. Our responsibility is to express an opinion on these financial statements based on our audits.

Except as discussed in the following paragraph, we conducted our audits in accordance with generally accepted auditing standards. Those standards require that we plan and perform the audit to obtain reasonable assurance about whether the financial statements are free of material misstatement. An audit includes examining, on a test basis, evidence supporting the amounts and disclosures in the financial statements. An audit also includes assessing the accounting principles used and significant estimates made by management, as well as evaluating the overall financial statement presentation. We believe that our audits provide a reasonable basis for our opinion.

As discussed in Note 2 to the consolidated financial statements, the Company has presented its consolidated financial statements on the going concern basis, which states assets and liabilities at historical amounts. Because of the magnitude and complexity of the matters discussed in Note 2 (certain of which are not within the direct control of the Company), including the Company's losses from operations, net stockholders' capital deficiency, defaults or other violations of debt covenants, restrictions on its access to the use of a significant proportion of its remaining liquid assets, its present financial inability to complete development of its land held for resale and land held for rental, and the lack of a significant market for its land held for resale and land held for rental, we believe that the Company can no longer carry out its plans and intentions, which are also discussed in Note 2, and cannot convert or otherwise dispose of its assets in the normal course of its business operations. In these circumstances, it is our opinion that generally accepted accounting principles require the Company's assets and liabilities to be stated at their liquidating values. The effect of this departure from generally accepted accounting principles cannot be reasonably determined; however, amounts ultimately received upon liquidation of the assets and amounts ultimately paid to settle liabilities may be different from the amounts stated in the accompanying consolidated financial statements.

In our opinion, *because of the effects of the matters discussed in the preceding paragraph, the consolidated financial statements do not present fairly,* in conformity with generally accepted accounting principles, the financial position of NECO Enterprises, Inc. and its subsidiaries at December 31, 1991 and 1990 or the results of their operations or their cash flows for the years then ended.

Lefkowitz, Garfinkel, Champi & Defrienzo
February 7, 1992

[Emphasis added.]

ing any opinion. In such cases, the auditor may issue a disclaimer of opinion. Such was the case in the auditor's report on the 1991 financial statements of Alloy Computer Products, Inc., that contained the following paragraphs:

> As discussed in Notes 1 and 8 to the financial statements, the Company has suffered recurring losses from operations and negative cash flows and there is

Exhibit 21.9

OPINION QUALIFIED BECAUSE OF INADEQUATE DISCLOSURE

[Standard introductory and scope paragraphs followed by these explanatory and opinion paragraphs.]

The company's consolidated financial statements do not disclose segment information for each of the three years in the period ended September 30, 1988. In our opinion, disclosure of segment information concerning the company's foreign operations and export sales is required by accounting principles generally accepted in the United States of America for a complete presentation of consolidated financial statements.

In our opinion, *except for the omission of segment information as discussed in the preceding paragraph,* the consolidated financial statements audited by us present fairly, in all material respects, the financial position of Pioneer Electronic Corporation and its consolidated subsidiaries at September 30, 1988 and 1987, and the results of their operations and their cash flows for each of the three years in the period ended September 30, 1988, in conformity with accounting principles generally accepted in the United States of America.

Price Waterhouse
November 18, 1988

[Note: This is a Japanese company and the financial statements were stated in Yen.]

[Emphasis added.]

significant outstanding litigation against the Company. These issues raise substantial doubt about the ability of the Company to continue as a going concern.

Because of the significance of the uncertainty regarding the Company's ability to continue as a going concern, *we are unable to express, and do not express, an opinion* on these financial statements. [Emphasis added.]

Auditor Lacks Independence

When auditors lack independence with respect to a client, any procedures they perform are not in accordance with GAAS, and they are precluded from expressing an opinion on such statements. In such cases, a one-paragraph disclaimer should be issued specifically stating their lack of independence but omitting the reasons for it. By omitting the reasons for the lack of independence, the auditor is avoiding the possibility of the reader second guessing the auditor as to independence or lack thereof. Following is an example of such a disclaimer:

> We are not independent with respect to Macro-Vac Company, and the accompanying balance sheet as of December 31, 1993, and the related statements of income, retained earnings, and cash flows for the year then ended were not audited by us and, accordingly, we do not express an opinion on them.

Reports on Comparative Statements

GAAP strongly recommend, but do not require, that the financial statements be presented on a comparative basis. Companies under the jurisdiction of the Securities and Exchange Commission *must* present comparative balance sheets for two

Exhibit 21.10

OPINION QUALIFIED BECAUSE OF A SCOPE LIMITATION

To the Board of Directors
Sound Money Investors Inc.

I have audited the accompanying statement of assets, liabilities and stockholder's equity of Sound Money Investors, Inc. as of December 31, 1991 and the related statements of income, changes in stockholder's equity and cash flows for the year then ended. These financial statements are the responsibility of the Company's management. My responsibility is to express an opinion on these financial statements based on my audits.

Except as discussed in the following paragraph, I conducted my audit in accordance with generally accepted auditing standards. Those standards require that we plan and perform the audit to obtain reasonable assurance about whether the financial statements are free of material misstatement. An audit includes examining, on a test basis, evidence supporting the amounts and disclosures in the financial statements. An audit also includes assessing the accounting principles used and significant estimates made by management, as well as evaluating the overall financial statement presentation. We believe that our audits provide a reasonable basis for our opinion.

As discussed in Notes 5 and 6, the Company has purchased certain assets from a corporation wholly owned by two major stockholders and officers of the Company at management's estimate of their values at the date of acquisition. I have been unable to obtain adequate documentation to support the basis and purchase price of such assets.

In my opinion, *except for the effects of such adjustments, if any, as might have been determined to be necessary had I been able to obtain adequate documentation to support the basis of such assets,* the financial statements referred to above present fairly, in all material respects, the financial position of Sound Money Investors, Inc. as of December 31, 1991 and the results of its operations and its cash flows for the year then ended in conformity with generally accepted accounting principles.

Chaslaur, Inc.
June 2, 1992

[Emphasis added.]

years and the other statements for three years. The fourth reporting standard requires the expression of opinion on the financial statements taken as a whole. If the statements are comparative, the continuing auditors should update their report on the financial statements of the prior year(s) that they had previously audited. **Updating the report** involves considering information that comes to the auditor's attention during the current year's audit but that is related to any prior year statements presented. The report date should be the end of the current year field work.

Occasionally, the opinion on one or more of the prior year financial statements may be different from that on the current year statements. For example, the report in Exhibit 21.12 contains a disclaimer on the 1987 consolidated statements of income, shareholders' equity, and cash flows because of the lack of evidence about the fairness of the 1987 income. It also includes an unqualified opinion on all of the 1988 financial statements. This report is dual dated because the information presented in Note 15 refers to an event that occurred after the end of the field work,

Exhibit 21.11

DISCLAIMER OF OPINION DUE TO SCOPE LIMITATION

We *were engaged to audit* the accompanying consolidated balance sheet of Alternative Distributors Corporation and its Subsidiary as of February 29, 1992 and the related consolidated statements of income, accumulated deficit, cash flows and statement of stockholders' equity (deficit) for the year then ended. These financial statements are the responsibility of the Company's management. **[Reference to the auditor's responsibility to express an opinion is eliminated because no opinion is expressed.]**

[The standard scope paragraph is **omitted.**]

Detailed accounts receivable records have not been maintained and certain records and supporting data were not available for our audit. Therefore, we were not able to satisfy ourselves about the amounts at which accounts receivable and allowance for doubtful accounts are recorded in the accompanying balance sheet at February 29, 1992 (stated at $1,450,000 and $350,000, respectively), and the amount of net sales and bad debt expense for the year then ended (stated at $7,842,778 and $350,244, respectively).

Because of the significance of the matters discussed in the preceding paragraph, the scope of our work was not sufficient to enable us to express, and we do not express, an opinion on the financial statements referred to in the first paragraph.

Gordon, Harrington & Osborn
June 4, 1992, except for note 2 for which the date is June 12, 1992

[Emphasis added.]

which was May 5, 1988. This is an updated report on the financial statements for 1987.

It is also possible that the circumstances related to the prior year(s) statements have changed and the auditor now wishes to give a different opinion from the one expressed in the prior year(s). For example, the auditor may have expressed a qualified opinion on the prior year's statements because of a GAAP violation, but a new management team has revised those statements to bring them into conformity with GAAP. The auditor can now express an unqualified opinion on them. In such a case, the auditor should insert an additional paragraph *before* the opinion paragraph to explain the change in the opinion on the prior year's statements.

When another audit firm (the predecessor) audited one or more of the prior year statements, the client may ask the other firm to **reissue the report** so that all financial statements presented are covered by auditors' reports. Their report is reissued rather than updated because the predecessor firm has done no audit work since the original issuance of its report. Thus, there will be two auditor's reports: the predecessor firm's report that covers the year(s) it audited and the successor firm's report covering the year(s) it audited. However, before reissuing its report, the predecessor firm should:

- Read the financial statements for the current period.
- Compare the prior period statements that it reported on with the prior period amounts included with the current period amounts for comparative purposes to be sure that the same amounts previously reported are being used.

Exhibit 21.12

REPORT EXPRESSING DIFFERENT OPINIONS ON FINANCIAL STATEMENTS OF DIFFERENT YEARS

To the Board of Directors and Shareholders of S.E. Nichols Inc.

We have audited the accompanying consolidated balance sheet of S.E. Nichols Inc. and subsidiaries as of January 30, 1988, and the related consolidated statements of income (loss), shareholders' equity and cash flows for each of the years in the two-year period then ended. These financial statements are the responsibility of the company's management. Our responsibility is to express an opinion on these financial statements based on our audits.

Except as explained in the following paragraph, we conducted our audits in accordance with generally accepted auditing standards. Those standards require [remaining part of scope paragraph is unaffected].

As more fully discussed in Note 15 to the consolidated financial statements, during fiscal 1988, in the course of implementing refinements in its data processing systems, the company discovered a discrepancy between its general ledger and accounts payable subsidiary ledger. After a comprehensive review by management of this matter, it was determined that this discrepancy amounted to approximately $5,500,000. While detailed records no longer exist, company management believes that the discrepancy arose in fiscal 1986, during the conversion from a service bureau facility to an in-house computer system. The company has restated its fiscal 1987 consolidated financial statements to record the effects of this discrepancy and another matter discussed in Note 15, which reduced net income as originally reported by an aggregate of $851,000 ($.19 per share) in fiscal 1987. However, the company has been unable to provide us with sufficient evidence to establish that the approximate $5,500,000 discrepancy arose solely in fiscal 1986, and we have been unable to otherwise satisfy ourselves as to the apportionment of the discrepancy between fiscal 1987 and 1986, although we are satisfied as to the aggregate amount, and that it first arose sometime during those two fiscal years.

Because we have been unable to satisfy ourselves as to the apportionment of the discrepancy between fiscal 1987 and 1986, as discussed above, the scope of our work was not sufficient to enable us to express, and we do not express, an opinion on the accompanying restated consolidated statements of income, shareholders' equity and cash flows for fiscal 1987.

In our opinion, the accompanying consolidated balance sheet as of January 30, 1988 and the consolidated statements of loss, shareholders' equity and cash flows for the year then ended present fairly, in all material respects, the consolidated financial position of S.E. Nichols Inc. and subsidiaries as of January 30, 1988, and the consolidated results of their operations and their cash flows for the year then ended, in conformity with generally accepted accounting principles.

Laventhol & Horwath
May 5, 1988, January 16, 1989 as to Note 15

- Obtain a letter of representation from the successor (current) auditor to ensure that the current audit did not uncover any matters that might have a material effect on the previous statements [AU 508.80].

If the predecessor's report is not presented, the successor should indicate the following in the introductory paragraph of its report:

- The financial statements of the previous period(s) were audited by other auditors.

- The date of that report.
- The type of report previously issued.
- The substantive reasons therefor if the report was other than unqualified [AU 508.83].

Disclaimer for Unaudited Statements of a Public Company

There are situations in which a public accounting firm is associated with unaudited financial statements of a public entity. For example, companies file registration statements with the SEC when they want to sell new securities to the public. Such registration statements contain audited financial statements for the last few fiscal years. In addition, if the most recent audited statements are over 90 days old, unaudited "stub-period" financial statements are to be included to provide more current financial information. The following one-paragraph disclaimer would be issued on such stub-period financial statements:

> The accompanying balance sheet of Portor Co. as of March 31, 1993, and the related statements of income, retained earnings, and cash flows for the three months then ended were not audited by us and, accordingly, we do not express an opinion on them.

International Reporting

Because of the evolution of a global financial market, financial statements of U.S. companies are used by investors in other countries and financial statements of foreign companies are used by investors in the United States. Because different countries have different accounting and auditing standards, it is difficult for investors in the international securities market to compare financial statements and understand the significance of the auditor's opinion. The following discussion applies to U.S. public accounting firms auditing U.S. clients and is based on AU 534, "Financial Statements Prepared for Use in Other Countries."

General and Field Work Standards

When a public accounting firm audits a U.S. client's financial statements that are prepared in conformity with the accounting standards of another country, the audit should be performed in accordance with the general and field work standards of GAAS. For example, the Pillsbury Company, headquartered in the United States, is a subsidiary of a British company and is audited by a U.S. public accounting firm. Pillsbury stock is traded in the U.S. market and, thus, its financial statements are used in the United States as well as Britain. Auditing procedures may need to be modified to accommodate the foreign accounting standards. For example, many countries require some form of inflation accounting, and the auditor will have to develop audit procedures to test that information. The public accounting firm may be requested to apply the auditing standards of another country requiring the performance of certain procedures in addition to those required by GAAS.

Reporting Standards

For Use Solely outside the United States. If the financial statements that are prepared in conformity with another country's accounting standards are to be used solely outside the United States, the auditor may report using either

- A U.S.–style report modified to report on the accounting principles of another country* and following the reporting standards under GAAS (see Exhibit 21.13), or
- The report form of the other country and following the reporting standards of that country (see Exhibit 21.14).

These financial statements and audit report may also be distributed on a limited basis to parties such as banks and institutional investors in the United States that deal directly with the entity if the statements are to be used in a manner that permits such parties to discuss differences from GAAP and their significance with the reporting company's management and/or auditors.

Exhibit 21.13

MODIFIED U.S. REPORT

To the members of The Royal Bank of Scotland

We have audited the accompanying Consolidated Balance Sheets of The Royal Bank of Scotland Group PLC at September 30, 1991 and 1990 and the related Consolidated Statements of Income and Changes in Retained Income and Other Reserves and Cash Flows for each of the three years in the period ended September 30, 1991, all stated in pounds sterling. The financial statements are the responsibility of the Company's management. Our responsibility is to express an opinion on these financial statements based on our audits.

We conducted our audits in accordance with generally accepted auditing standards in the United Kingdom which do not differ in any material respects from auditing standards generally accepted in the United States. Those standards require that. . . .

In our opinion, the financial statements referred to above present fairly, in all material respects, the financial position of The Royal Bank of Scotland Group PLC at September 30, 1991 and 1990, and the results of its operations and its cash flows for each of the three years in the period ended September 30, 1991 in conformity with generally accepted accounting principles in the United Kingdom (which differ in certain material respects from generally accepted accounting principles in the United States–see Note 28).

Coopers & Lybrand Deloitte
November 28, 1991

*The report should include a reference to a footnote that describes the basis of accounting used and an identification of the nationality of the accounting principles. It should also include an opinion on the fairness of the statements in accordance with the basis of accounting described [AU 534.09].

Exhibit 21.14

REPORT FORM OF THE UNITED KINGDOM

To the members of Grand Metropolitan Public Limited Company

We have audited the financial statements on pages 40 to 58 in accordance with Auditing Standards.

In our opinion the financial statements give a true and fair view of the state of affairs of the company at 30th September 1990 and of the profit and source and application of funds of the group for the year then ended and have been properly prepared in accordance with the Companies Act 1985.

KPMG Peat Marwick McLintock
Chartered Accountants
London 7th December 1990

For Use both inside and outside the United States. If financial statements of a company are to be used in both another country and the United States, the auditor may report on dual sets of statements for the client: one prepared in conformity with the accounting standards of the other country and the other prepared in conformity with GAAP. In some instances, the client may choose not to prepare dual financial statements. If such financial statements have more than limited use in the United States, the auditor should modify the opinion for domestic use if there are material GAAP violations. For example, the financial statements of Honda Motor Co., Ltd for 1989 are presented in accordance with Japanese accounting standards. Such standards do not require the disclosure of segment information as required by GAAP. The U.S. auditors issued an audit report that contained the following explanatory and qualified opinion paragraphs:

> The segment information required to be disclosed in financial statements under United States generally accepted accounting principles is not presented in the accompanying consolidated financial statements. Foreign issuers are presently exempted from such disclosure requirement in Securities Exchange Act filings with the Securities and Exchange Commission of the United States.
>
> In our opinion, except for the omission of the segment information referred to in the preceding paragraph, the consolidated financial statements referred to above present fairly, in all material respects, the financial position of Honda Motor Co., Ltd, and subsidiaries . . . in conformity with generally accepted accounting principles.

Summary of Audit Report Modification

Exhibit 21.15 summarizes the major conditions leading to audit report modification. Deciding on the type of opinion is a matter that should not be taken lightly. This is particularly true of the decisions based on the materiality level and pervasiveness of GAAP violations, the significance of scope limitations, and the likelihood of the entity being a going concern. Issuing an inappropriate opinion can lead to legal problems. Because of its importance, the decision is often made after consultation with other professionals within the firm and other firms.

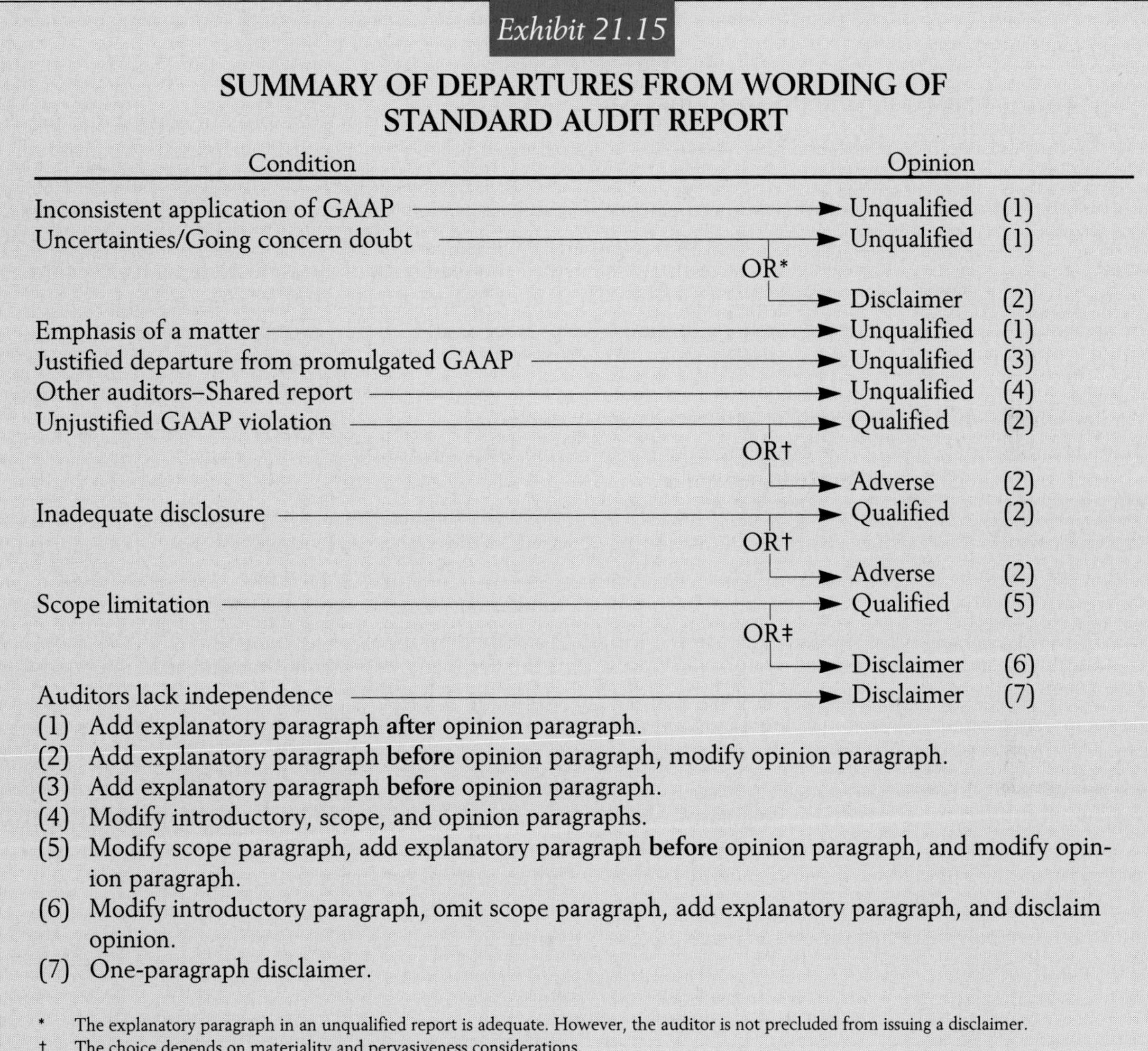

Exhibit 21.15

SUMMARY OF DEPARTURES FROM WORDING OF STANDARD AUDIT REPORT

Condition		Opinion	
Inconsistent application of GAAP		Unqualified	(1)
Uncertainties/Going concern doubt		Unqualified	(1)
	OR*	Disclaimer	(2)
Emphasis of a matter		Unqualified	(1)
Justified departure from promulgated GAAP		Unqualified	(3)
Other auditors–Shared report		Unqualified	(4)
Unjustified GAAP violation		Qualified	(2)
	OR†	Adverse	(2)
Inadequate disclosure		Qualified	(2)
	OR†	Adverse	(2)
Scope limitation		Qualified	(5)
	OR‡	Disclaimer	(6)
Auditors lack independence		Disclaimer	(7)

(1) Add explanatory paragraph **after** opinion paragraph.
(2) Add explanatory paragraph **before** opinion paragraph, modify opinion paragraph.
(3) Add explanatory paragraph **before** opinion paragraph.
(4) Modify introductory, scope, and opinion paragraphs.
(5) Modify scope paragraph, add explanatory paragraph **before** opinion paragraph, and modify opinion paragraph.
(6) Modify introductory paragraph, omit scope paragraph, add explanatory paragraph, and disclaim opinion.
(7) One-paragraph disclaimer.

* The explanatory paragraph in an unqualified report is adequate. However, the auditor is not precluded from issuing a disclaimer.
† The choice depends on materiality and pervasiveness considerations.
‡ The choice depends on the importance of the omitted procedure(s) to the auditor's ability to form an opinion. If it is a significant scope limitation imposed by the client, a disclaimer should ordinarily be issued.

B–COMPILATIONS AND REVIEWS

There are often situations in which a client does not need an audit. In such cases, the public accounting firm can perform fewer procedures and report a lower level of, or no, assurance on the fairness of the financial statements. The most common of these services are referred to as compilations and reviews. Standards for these services were first issued in 1979 (see the Historical Perspective).

Historical Perspective

THE EVOLUTION OF COMPILATION AND REVIEW STANDARDS

Before the issuance of the compilation and review standards in 1979, there were only two levels of assurance a CPA could provide on a company's financial statements: positive assurance (an audit) or no assurance (a disclaimer). In many situations, small, privately held businesses used the financial reports for internal use and to give to the local banker who might be quite familiar with the company and its management. The company may have wanted its financial statements to be looked at by a CPA but did not need a full audit. In some cases, the CPA would do extensive work in analyzing the company's financial reports; in other cases, the CPA simply verified that the financial statements agreed with the general ledger and were put together in good form but did not perform any procedures to gain assurance about the numbers in the financial statements. But both levels of service received the same assurance from the CPA, that is, a disclaimer of opinion.

The compilation and review standards were developed to address this particular constituency and to recognize that CPAs often did a considerable amount of work, although less in scope than an audit, on privately held businesses that received disclaimers of opinions. The work was not sufficient to provide audit assurance, but it was reasoned that the work was sufficient to provide *some assurance*, albeit a negative one, that reflected the limited amount of work performed by the CPA. That negative assurance is now captured in the review report in which a CPA undertakes specific analytic procedures to search for obvious misstatements in a company's financial statements, but not enough work to provide assurance that the statements are fairly presented. Thus, the CPA can communicate only that based on the procedures performed, nothing has come to his or her attention that the financial statements are misstated.

Why would a company and its users be interested in such a report? First, it is less costly. Most reviews cost about one-half of that of an audit. Second, reviews are generally considered higher margin services by the CPA firms. Third, there is less legal liability associated with the report. Thus, if the company has a bank that will accept a review report as a basis for making a loan, it effectively makes the loan less expensive for the company.

As noted in Chapter 4, however, there are danger signals on the horizon. The review standards are not always clear as to when the CPA should expand the scope of work to investigate an item that does not appear to be correctly stated. Nor is it clear in the standards as to whether specific audit procedures are required if the CPA has doubt about the fairness of presentation. Review standards will continue to evolve.

The standards for compilations and reviews of the financial statements of nonpublic entities are called *Statements on Standards for Accounting and Review Services* (SSARSs). A **nonpublic entity** is any entity other than (1) one whose securities trade in a public market either on a stock exchange (domestic or foreign) or in the over-the-counter market, (2) one that makes a filing with a regulatory agency in preparation for the sale of any class of its securities in a public market, or (3) a subsidiary, corporate joint venture, or other entity controlled by an entity covered by (1) or (2) (AR 100.04). These standards are issued by the Accounting and Review Services Committee of the AICPA, which is separate from the Auditing Standards Board (ASB) that develops auditing standards and standards for unaudited statements of public entities.

When a *public entity* does not have its annual financial statements audited, a CPA may be requested to review its annual or interim financial statements. In such a case, the firm may make a review and look to the guidance in the SSARSs for the standards, procedures, and form of report (AU 504.05, note 4). CPAs may also review interim financial information of public entities that have annual audits. Reporting on interim financial information is covered in the next chapter.

Procedures Common to All Levels of Service

It is important that the CPA establish an understanding with the entity, preferably in the form of a written engagement letter, regarding the services to be performed. A written engagement letter will avoid any misunderstanding that may arise, such as happened in the 1136 Tenant's Corporation case described in Chapter 4.

When engaged to provide any service related to financial statements, the CPA should have an appropriate level of knowledge of the accounting principles and practices of the industry in which the entity operates.

Compilations

Compilations can be performed only for *nonpublic entities* and involve presenting, in the form of financial statements, information that is the representation of management (owners) without undertaking to express any assurance on the statements (AR 100.04). The corresponding type of report for *public entities* is a one-paragraph disclaimer of opinion. A client may request its CPA to compile financial statements because it does not have the in-house expertise to prepare the statements or because its banker feels more comfortable with statements prepared by the CPA.

Procedures

The CPA should have a general knowledge of the client's accounting records, the accounting basis to be used (GAAP or another comprehensive basis of accounting), and the form and content of the financial statements. Such an understanding is obtained through experience with the client and inquiry of the client's personnel. The CPA is not required to make inquiries or perform procedures to verify, corroborate, or review information provided by the client. However, if the CPA believes that such information may be incorrect, incomplete, or otherwise unsatisfactory, additional or revised information should be obtained. If the client refuses to provide this information, the CPA should withdraw from the engagement.

Before issuing a compilation report, the CPA should read the financial statements, including footnotes, to make sure that they are appropriate in form and free from obvious material misstatement, such as clerical errors or violations of GAAP.

Standard Compilation Report

The standard compilation report is shown in Exhibit 21.16. The standards referred to in the first paragraph are the *Statements on Standards for Accounting and Review Services* (SSARSs). The second paragraph describes a compilation as taking management's information and putting it into the form of financial statements. The CPA is taking no responsibility for the fairness of the financial statements. Even though no assurance is provided, many users believe that because the CPA's name is associated with the statements, obvious material misstatements would have been mentioned in the CPA's report. Therefore, it is important that the CPA be careful when reading the statements to be alert to any obvious misstatement(s). If there is a material misstatement, it should be described in the report following the disclaimer paragraph.

Exhibit 21.16

STANDARD COMPILATION REPORT

To J. R. Race, President
Race Company

We have compiled the accompanying balance sheet of Race Company as of December 31, 1993, and the related statements of income, retained earnings, and cash flow for the year then ended, in accordance with Statements on Standards for Accounting and Review Services issued by the American Institute of Certified Public Accountants.

A compilation is limited to presenting in the form of financial statements information that is the representation of management. We have not audited or reviewed the accompanying financial statements and, accordingly, *do not express an opinion or any other form of assurance on them.*

Rittenberg & Schwieger, CPAs
January 29, 1994

[Emphasis added.]

Omission of Disclosures for Compilations

The client may request the accountant to compile financial statements that omit substantially all of the required disclosures. This request may be honored if the CPA believes that such omission is not undertaken with the intention of misleading the users. An additional paragraph should be added to the standard compilation report (as directed by AR 100.21) stating:

> The company has elected to omit substantially all of the disclosures required by generally accepted accounting principles. If the omitted disclosures were included in the financial statements, they might influence the user's conclusions about the company's financial position, results of operations, and cash flows. Accordingly, these financial statements are not designed for those who are not informed about such matters.

Omission implies that the CPA is familiar with the users and knows enough about the financial statements to conclude that the omission is not undertaken to mislead users. The major thrust for the omissions comes not in the form of the annual report but in monthly statements that the CPA prepares for the client. The CPA is not expected to provide the missing disclosures in the compilation report unless another comprehensive basis of accounting is used. In that case, the basis used must be disclosed in a footnote or the CPA's report.

CPA Lacks Independence

If the CPA is not independent with respect to the client, a separate paragraph should be added to the compilation report stating "I am [We are] not independent with respect to [client's name]." This does not change the level of assurance provided—none is given. However, if the CPA is not independent with respect to an audit or a review client, the level of assurance is reduced to a disclaimer. Therefore, a CPA lacking independence should ordinarily accept only a compilation engagement.

Reviews

A **review** is an accounting service that involves performing inquiry and analytical procedures to provide a reasonable basis for expressing limited assurance that there are no material modifications that should be made to the financial statements for them to be in conformity with GAAP or, if applicable, with another comprehensive basis of accounting. Reviews are useful to bankers and vendors, for example, who are familiar with the client's business and do not need an audit but want some assurance provided by its CPA but are not willing to demand an audit.

Procedures

A review requires more knowledge and evidence than does a compilation, but is significantly less in scope than an audit. In performing this level of service, the CPA should obtain a general understanding of the entity's organization; operating characteristics; types of transactions, assets, and liabilities; compensation methods; types of products and services; operating locations; and related parties. The CPA should also obtain a management representation letter near the end of the engagement, the content of which is very similar to that illustrated in Chapter 20 for an audit. Basic procedures for conducting a review include the following:

- Inquire concerning actions taken at meetings of the board of directors, stockholders, and other decision-making bodies.
- Inquire about whether the financial statements have been prepared in conformity with GAAP on a consistent basis, any changes in the business activities or accounting principles and practices, events subsequent to the date of the financial statements that would have a material effect on the financial statements, and other matters of concern to the accountant.
- Obtain or prepare a trial balance of the general ledger and foot and reconcile it to the general ledger.
- Trace the financial statement amounts to the trial balance.
- Perform basic analytical procedures such as comparing current financial statement amounts with those of prior period(s) and with anticipated results, such as budgets and forecasts, and studying the relationships of elements of the financial statements that would be expected to conform to a predictable pattern based on the entity's experience, such as interest expense to interest-bearing debt. For any unusual or unexpected results, obtain explanations from management and consider the need for further investigation.
- Read the financial statements to determine whether they appear to conform with GAAP.

Inquiries and analytical procedures should be performed for each of the significant amounts in the financial statements. To give you an idea of these additional procedures, Exhibit 21.17 lists those that might be performed for accounts in the revenue cycle. Note that they are significantly less in scope than the audit procedures. There is no assessment of the internal control structure and no substantive testing of transactions or balances, such as the confirmation of receivables, review of subsequent cash collections, cutoff test, or tests of sales transactions processed during the period. If evidence obtained from such inquiries and analytical procedures does not support

Exhibit 21.17

INQUIRIES AND ANALYTICAL PROCEDURES FOR THE REVENUE CYCLE

Inquiries:
1. Is the revenue recognition policy proper and consistently applied?
2. Has an adequate allowance been made for doubtful accounts?
3. Have receivables considered uncollectible been written off?
4. If appropriate, has interest been reflected?
5. Has a proper cutoff of sales and cash receipts transactions been made?
6. Are there any receivables from employees and related parties?
7. Have receivables been properly classified between current and noncurrent?

Analytical Procedures
1. Compute number of days' sales in ending receivables and compare with that for prior years.
2. Compute aging percentages and compare to those for prior years.
3. Compute bad debt expense as a percent of sales for the year and compare with that for prior years.

the financial statements, the CPA should perform additional procedures and, if the additional evidence indicates material misstatements, have the client correct the statements. Otherwise, the CPA should modify the review report to bring the misstatements to the reader's attention.

Standard Review Report

The standard review report is shown in Exhibit 21.18. It has three paragraphs. The first paragraph identifies what was reviewed. It states that the AICPA's review standards (SSARSs) were followed and that the financial statements are the representations of the company's management. The second paragraph describes a review, states that it is less in scope than an audit, and disclaims an opinion. The third paragraph expresses what is referred to as **limited assurance** or **negative assurance,** which tells the reader that the accountant is not aware of any reporting problems based on the review procedures performed. If there is a reporting problem, such as a departure from GAAP, the limited assurance paragraph should be modified to refer to an additional paragraph that explains the problem.

Distinguishing among Audits, Reviews, and Compilations

A *review* differs significantly from a *compilation* and an *audit.* It differs from a compilation in that inquiry and analytical procedures are performed to provide a reasonable basis for expressing limited assurance. No assurance is expressed in a compilation. A *review* differs from an *audit* in that review procedures do not provide a basis for expressing an opinion. A review does not involve an assessment of control risk or substantive tests of transactions or balances. A review may bring to the CPA's attention matters affecting the financial statements, but it does not provide assurance that the accountant will become aware of all such matters that would be disclosed in an audit.

Exhibit 21.18

STANDARD REVIEW REPORT

To the Shareholders
Apple Grove Company

We have reviewed the accompanying balance sheet of Apple Grove Company as of June 30, 1994, and the related statements of income, retained earnings, and cash flows for the year then ended, in accordance with Statements on Standards for Accounting and Review Services issued by the American Institute of Certified Public Accountants. All information included in these financial statements is the representation of the management of Apple Grove Company.

A review consists principally of inquiries of company personnel and analytical procedures applied to financial data. It is substantially less in scope than an examination in accordance with generally accepted auditing standards, the objective of which is the expression of an opinion regarding the financial statements taken as a whole. Accordingly, *we do not express such an opinion.*

Based on our review, *we are not aware of any material modifications that should be made to the accompanying financial statements in order for them to be in conformity with generally accepted accounting principles.*

Rittenberg & Schwieger, CPAs
August 12, 1994

[Emphasis added.]

Exhibit 21.19 is a summary of the basic procedures performed and standard reports issued in audits, reviews, and compilations.

Summary

Public accounting firms provide three levels of service related to historical financial statements: audits, reviews, and compilations. Audit reports include an opinion about the fairness of the financial statements. Review reports provide a lower level of assurance, called limited assurance, and compilation reports provide no assurance. Users of financial statements see only the reports provided by the firms, not the working papers that document the evidence gathered. It is extremely important that the firms be very careful when reporting on financial statements. Failure to do so can lead to lawsuits against the firms and a loss of public confidence in the public accounting profession.

Significant Terms

adverse opinion Type of audit report issued when the auditor believes that the financial statements are misleading due to material departures from GAAP that pervade the financial statements or to the lack of very important disclosures.

compilation The lowest level of service related to financial statements that is provided by public accounting firms. Not an audit service, it involves presenting, in

Exhibit 21.19

SUMMARY OF BASIC PROCEDURES AND STANDARD REPORTS FOR AUDITS, REVIEWS, AND COMPILATIONS

Procedure	Audit	Review	Compilation
Assess control risk.	X		
Perform substantive tests of transactions and balances.	X		
Perform analytical procedures.	X	X	
Make inquiries of client personnel to verify or corroborate information supplied by the client.	X	X	
Obtain knowledge of client's organization, assets, liabilities, revenues, expenses, operations, locations, and transactions with related parties.	X	X	
Obtain knowledge of the accounting principles and practices of the industry.	X	X	X
Obtain knowledge of the client's transactions, form of accounting records, qualifications of accounting personnel, the accounting basis to be used for the financial statements and the form and content of the statements.	X	X	X
Standard report	Unqualified opinion	Disclaimer and limited assurance	Disclaimer

the form of financial statements, information that is the representation of management and results in a disclaimer—no assurance about the fairness of the financial statements. Such a service can be provided only to nonpublic companies.

disclaimer of opinion A type of audit report issued when the auditor has not been able to obtain sufficient evidence to form an opinion on the overall fairness of the financial statements.

limited assurance A statement by the accountant in a report that nothing has been detected that indicates that the information needs to be changed to bring it into conformity with the appropriate criteria, such as GAAP.

negative assurance See *limited assurance.*

nonpublic entity Any entity other than (1) one whose securities trade in a public market either on a stock exchange (domestic or foreign) or in the over-the-counter market, (2) one that makes a filing with a regulatory agency in preparation for the sale of any class of its securities in a public market, or (3) a subsidiary, corporate joint venture, or other entity controlled by an entity covered by (1) or (2).

opinion The highest level of assurance formed by the auditor after gathering and evaluating an extensive amount of evidence.

qualified opinion A type of audit report issued when the auditor is unable to obtain sufficient competent evidence because of scope limitations or the lack of such evidence; there is a material, unjustified departure from GAAP, or management's disclosures are not adequate, but the auditor has decided not to express an adverse opinion.

reissue the report Reissue a previously issued audit report on which no audit work has been done subsequent to the original report date; it contains the original report date.

review The middle level of service related to financial statements that public accountants provide involving inquiries and analytical procedures and resulting in limited assurance about the fairness of the financial statements.

scope limitation A restriction on the performance of audit procedures caused by the client or the circumstances.

shared report An audit report that indicates that other auditors performed part of the audit.

uncertainties Situations in which the outcome of some matter cannot be determined as of the end of the audit field work, such as the results of pending litigation.

unqualified opinion A type of audit report issued when the auditor has been able to perform sufficient procedures and believes that the evidence indicates that the financial statements do not contain a material, unjustified departure from GAAP or inadequate disclosures.

updating the report Considering information that comes to the auditor's attention during the current year audit but that is related to prior year statements presented for comparative purposes. The report date should be the end of the current year field work.

Review Questions

A–Audit Reports

21–1 Identify the six basic types of audit opinions and explain the circumstances under which each opinion is expressed.

21–2 Explain how materiality affects the type of audit opinion to be expressed.

21–3 What is the difference between a scope limitation and an uncertainty? Give an example of each.

21–4 What types of opinions will the SEC not accept? How does this affect the auditor's reporting environment?

21–5 What factors must the auditor consider when determining whether the financial statements are presented in conformity with generally accepted accounting principles?

21–6 Under what circumstances may an auditor express an unqualified opinion when the related financial statements contain a material departure from a FASB or GASB standard?

21–7 Under what circumstances must the auditor's report refer to the consistency in the application of GAAP or lack thereof? What is the purpose of such reporting?

21–8 When is an audit firm considered to be associated with financial statements? What must the firm do when associated with financial statements?

21–9 Under what circumstances should the auditor put an explanatory paragraph

a. before the opinion paragraph?

b. after the opinion paragraph?

21–10 Why should the auditor ordinarily disclaim an opinion when the client imposes significant limitations on the audit procedures?

21–11 Under what circumstances might the auditor not refer to other auditors who worked on a part of the audit? What is a shared report? If the other auditors did not use due professional care and they are mentioned in the audit report, who is ultimately responsible, the principal auditor or the other auditors?

21–12 Are comparative financial statements required by GAAP? Explain.

21–13 The fourth standard of reporting states that the auditor should express an opinion on the financial statements as a whole.

a. Does this mean that the auditor must express the same opinion on all of the financial statements for a particular year? Explain.

b. Does this mean that the auditor must express an opinion on all of the years presented with the current year for comparative purposes if all years were audited by the same public accounting firm?

c. Explain how the successor's audit report on comparative financial statements should be presented if the predecessor auditor

   1. Reissues the report on prior years.

   2. Does not reissue the report on prior years.

21–14 How should the auditor report on financial statements of a company whose financial statements are prepared in conformity with another country's accounting principles if such statements are to be used

a. Solely outside the United States?

b. Both outside and inside the United States?

B–Compilations and Reviews

21–15 What is

a. A compilation?

b. A review?

21–16 Compare audits, reviews, and compilations in terms of

a. The types of procedures performed.

b. The level of assurance expressed by the accountant.

21–17 In which situation would an accountant's standard report be least affected by a lack of independence–an audit, review, or compilation? Explain.

Multiple Choice Questions

*21–18 Kelsey King, CPA, was engaged to audit the financial statements of Newton Company after its fiscal year had ended. King neither observed the inventory count nor confirmed the receivables by direct communication with debtors but was satisfied concerning both after applying alternative procedures. King's auditor's report most likely contained a(an)

a. Qualified opinion.
b. Disclaimer of opinion.
c. Unqualified opinion.
d. Unqualified opinion with an explanatory paragraph.

*21–19 In which of the following circumstances would an auditor be most likely to express an adverse opinion?

a. Information comes to the auditor's attention that raises substantial doubt about the entity's ability to continue as a going concern.
b. The chief executive officer refuses the auditor access to minutes of board of directors meetings.
c. Tests of controls show that the entity's internal control structure is so poor that it *cannot* be relied on.
d. The financial statements are *not* in conformity with the FASB statements regarding the capitalization of leases.

*21–20 It is *not* appropriate to refer a reader of an auditor's report to a financial statement footnote for details concerning

a. Subsequent events.
b. The pro forma effects of a business combination.
c. Sale of a discontinued operation.
d. The results of confirmation of receivables.

*21–21 Tech Company has disclosed an uncertainty due to pending litigation. The auditor's decision to issue a qualified opinion rather than an unqualified opinion with an explanatory paragraph most likely would be determined by the

a. Lack of sufficient evidence.
b. Inability to estimate the amount of loss.
c. Entity's lack of experience with such litigation.
d. Lack of insurance coverage for possible losses from such litigation.

*21–22 In which of the following situations would an auditor ordinarily issue an unqualified audit opinion without an explanatory paragraph?

a. The auditor wishes to emphasize that the entity had significant related-party transactions.
b. The auditor decides to make reference to the report of another auditor as a basis, in part, for the auditor's opinion.

*Adapted from the Uniform CPA examination or the Certified Internal Auditor examination.

c. The entity issues financial statements that present financial position and results of operations but omits the statement of cash flows.

d. The auditor has substantial doubt about the entity's ability to continue as a going concern, but the circumstances are fully disclosed in the financial statements.

*21–23 When a change in accounting principle has materially affected the comparability of the comparative financial statements presented and the auditor concurs with the change, the auditor should

	Concur Explicitly with the Change	Issue an "except for" Qualified Opinion	Refer to the Change in an Explanatory Paragraph
a.	No	No	Yes
b.	Yes	No	Yes
c.	Yes	Yes	No
d.	No	Yes	No

*21–24 Comparative financial statements include the prior year statements that were audited by a predecessor auditor whose report is not presented. If the predecessor's report was unqualified, the successor should

a. Express an opinion on the current year statements alone and make *no* reference to the prior year statements.

b. Indicate in the auditor's report that the predecessor auditor expressed an unqualified opinion.

c. Obtain a letter of representation from the predecessor concerning any matters that might affect the successor's opinion.

d. Request the predecessor auditor to reissue the prior year report.

*21–25 When reporting on comparative financial statements, which of the following circumstances ordinarily should cause the auditor to change the previously issued opinion on the prior year financial statements?

a. The prior year financial statements are restated following a pooling of interests in the current year.

b. A departure from generally accepted accounting principles caused an adverse opinion on the prior year financial statements and those statements have been properly restated.

c. A change in accounting principle caused the auditor to make a consistency modification in the current year auditor's report.

d. A scope limitation caused a qualified opinion on the prior year financial statements but the current year opinion was properly unqualified.

*21–26 Eagle Company's financial statements contain a departure from generally accepted accounting principles because, due to unusual circumstances, the statements would otherwise be misleading. The auditor should express an opinion that is

a. Unqualified but *not* mention the departure in the auditor's report.

b. Unqualified and describe the departure in a separate paragraph.

c. Qualified and describe the departure in a separate paragraph.

d. Qualified or adverse, depending on materiality, and describe the departure in a separate paragraph.

*21–27 Tread Corp. accounts for the effect of a material accounting change prospectively when the inclusion of the cumulative effect of the change is required in the current year. The auditor would choose between expressing a(an)

a. Qualified opinion or a disclaimer of opinion.
b. Disclaimer of opinion or an unqualified opinion with an explanatory paragraph.
c. Unqualified opinion with an explanatory paragraph and an adverse opinion.
d. Adverse opinion and a qualified opinion.

*21–28 An explanatory paragraph following the opinion paragraph of an auditor's report describes an uncertainty as follows:

> As discussed in Note X to the financial statements, the Company is a defendant in a lawsuit alleging infringement of certain patent rights and claiming damages. Discovery proceedings are in progress. The ultimate outcome of the litigation cannot presently be determined. Accordingly, no provision for any liability that may result upon adjudication has been made in the accompanying financial statements.

What type of opinion should the auditor express under these circumstances?

a. Unqualified.
b. Subject to qualified.
c. Except for qualified.
d. Disclaimer.

*21–29 In which of the following circumstances would an auditor usually choose between issuing a qualified opinion or a disclaimer of opinion?

a. Departure from generally accepted accounting principles.
b. Inadequate disclosure of accounting policies.
c. Inability to obtain sufficient competent evidential matter.
d. Unreasonable justification for a change in accounting principle.

*21–30 Under which of the following circumstances would a disclaimer of opinion *not* be appropriate?

a. The auditor is engaged after fiscal year-end and is unable to observe physical inventories or apply alternative procedures to verify their balances.
b. The auditor is unable to determine the amounts associated with illegal acts committed by the client's management.
c. The financial statements fail to contain adequate disclosure concerning related-party transactions.
d. The client refuses to permit its attorney to furnish information requested in a letter of audit inquiry.

*21–31 During a review of the financial statements of a nonpublic entity, an accountant becomes aware of the lack of adequate disclosure that is material to the financial statements. If management refuses to correct the financial statement presentations, the accountant should

a. Issue an adverse opinion.
b. Issue an except for qualified opinion.
c. Disclose this departure from generally accepted accounting principles in a separate paragraph of the report.
d. Express only limited assurance on the financial statement presentations.

*21–32 Before issuing a report on the compilation of financial statements of a nonpublic entity, the accountant should

a. Apply analytical procedures to selected financial data to discover any material misstatements.
b. Corroborate at least a sample of the assertions management has embodied in the financial statements.
c. Inquire of the client's personnel whether the financial statements omit substantially all disclosures.
d. Read the financial statements to consider whether they are free from obvious material errors.

*21–33 Laura Baker, CPA, was engaged to review the financial statements of Hall Company, a nonpublic entity. Evidence came to Baker's attention that indicated substantial doubt as to Hall's ability to continue as a going concern. The principal conditions and events that caused the substantial doubt have been fully disclosed in the notes to Hall's financial statements. Which of the following statements best describes Baker's reporting responsibility concerning this matter?

a. Baker is *not required* to modify the accountant's review report.
b. Baker is *not permitted* to modify the accountant's review report.
c. Baker should issue an accountant's compilation report instead of a review report.
d. Baker should express a qualified opinion in the accountant's review report.

Discussion and Research Questions

21–34 (Types of Engagements and Reports) The fourth standard of reporting states: "In all cases where an auditor's name is associated with financial statements, the report should contain a clear-cut indication of the character of the auditor's work, if any, and the degree of responsibility the auditor is taking."

Required:
In each of the following independent situations, indicate how the CPA responds to this standard.

a. The CPA is engaged to prepare the financial statements for a nonpublic entity without performing an audit or review.

b. The CPA is engaged to compile *and* review the financial statements of a nonpublic company.

c. The CPA is engaged to prepare the federal and state income tax returns. No other services are provided.

d. The CPA is engaged to audit the annual financial statements of a public company.

e. The CPA's name is contained in the client's registration statement that includes audited financial statements for the year ended December 31, 1993, and unaudited financial statements for the three months ended March 31, 1994. The SEC requires the CPA to include in the registration statement a consent to the use of the public accounting firm's name in that statement.

21–35 (Implications of Risk in Standard Audit Report) What words and phrases in the standard audit report imply that there is a risk that the financial statements may contain a material misstatement?

21–36 (Critique an Audit Report Qualified for a Scope Limitation) You are a senior auditor working for Rittenberg & Schwieger, CPAs. Your staff assistant has drafted the following audit report. You believe the scope limitation is significant enough to qualify the opinion but not to disclaim an opinion.

To Joseph Halberg, Controller
Billings Container Company, Inc.

We have audited the accompanying balance sheet of Billings Container Company and the related statements of income, retained earnings, and statement of changes in financial position as of December 31, 1993. These financial statements are the responsibility of the Company's management.

Except as discussed in the following paragraph, we conducted our audit in accordance with generally accepted accounting principles. Those standards require that we plan and perform the audit to obtain assurance about whether the financial statements are free of misstatement. An audit includes examining evidence supporting the amounts and disclosures in the financial statements. An audit also includes assessing the accounting principles used as well as evaluating the overall financial statement presentation. We believe that our audit provides a reasonable basis for our opinion.

We were unable to obtain sufficient competent evidence of the fair market value of the Company's investment in a real estate venture due to the unique nature of the venture. The investment is accounted for using the equity method and is stated at $450,000 and $398,000 at December 31, 1993 and 1992, respectively.

In our opinion, except for the above-mentioned limitation on the scope of our audit, the financial statements referred to above present fairly the financial position of Billings Container Company as of December 31, 1993 and 1992, and the results of its operations and its cash flows for the year then ended in conformity with generally accepted auditing standards.

/s/Bradley Schwieger, CPA
St. Cloud, MN
December 31, 1993

Required:
Identify the deficiencies in this draft and state how each deficiency should be corrected. Organize your answer around the components of the audit report (introductory paragraph, scope paragraph, etc.).

21–37 (Choosing the Type of Opinion) Several independent audit situations are presented below. Assume that everything *other than what is described* would have resulted in an unqualified opinion.

Required:
Indicate the type of opinion you believe should be expressed in each situation, explain your choice, and, if an explanatory paragraph is needed, indicate whether it should precede or follow the opinion paragraph.

a. The auditor was unable to obtain confirmations from two of the client's major customers that were included in the sample. These customers wrote on the confirmation letters that they were unable to confirm the balances because of their accounting systems. The auditor was able to become satisfied by other audit procedures.
b. The client treated a lease as an operating lease, but the auditor believes it should have been accounted for as a capital lease. The effects are material.
c. The client changed from FIFO to LIFO this year. The effect is material.
    1. The change was properly accounted for, justified, and disclosed.
    2. The change was properly accounted for and disclosed, but was not properly justified.
d. The client restricted the auditor from observing the physical inventory. Inventory is a material item.
e. The client is engaged in a product liability lawsuit that is properly accounted for and adequately described in the footnotes. The lawsuit does not threaten the going concern assumption, but an adverse decision by the court could create a material obligation for the client.
f. The status of the client as a going concern is extremely doubtful. The problems are properly described in the footnotes.
g. One of your client's subsidiaries was audited by another audit firm whose opinion was qualified because of a GAAP violation. You do not believe that the GAAP violation is material to the consolidated financial statements on which you are expressing an opinion.
h. You are convinced that your client is violating another company's patent in the process of manufacturing its only product. The client will not disclose this because it does not want to wave a red flag and bring the other company's attention to this violation.
i. The client has changed its method of accounting for depreciation for all factory and office equipment with reasonable justification. The effect of this change is not material to the current year financial statements but is likely to have a material effect in future years. The client's management will not disclose this change because of the immaterial effect on the current year statements. You have been unable to persuade management to make the disclosure.

*21–38 (Selecting the Proper Audit Opinion) The auditor's report must contain an expression of opinion or a statement to the effect that an opinion cannot be expressed. Six types of opinions that meet these requirements are generally known as

1. A standard three-paragraph unqualified opinion.
2. Unqualified opinion with an explanatory paragraph *before* the opinion paragraph.
3. Unqualified opinion with an explanatory paragraph *after* the opinion paragraph.
4. A qualified opinion.
5. An adverse opinion.
6. A disclaimer of opinion.

Required:
For each of the following situations, indicate the type of opinion that you would render and explain your answer.

a. During the course of the examination, the auditor suspects that a material amount of the assets of the client, Ash Corporation, has been misappropriated through fraud. The corporation refuses to allow the auditor to expand the scope of the examination sufficiently to confirm these suspicions.

b. Balsam Corporation is engaged in a hazardous trade and cannot obtain insurance coverage from any source. A material portion of the corporation's assets could be destroyed by a serious accident. The corporation has an excellent safety record and has never suffered a catastrophe.

c. The auditor is examining Chestnut Corporation's financial statements for the first time. Prior financial statements carry the unqualified opinion of an auditor who is unknown to the current auditor, who believes that the balance sheet presents fairly the corporation's financial position but was not authorized to test the activity of prior periods and is unwilling to assume any responsibility for the work performed by the predecessor auditor.

d. Dogwood Corporation owns properties that have substantially appreciated in value since the date of purchase. The properties were appraised and are reported in the balance sheet at the appraised values with full disclosure. The auditor believes that the values reported in the balance sheet are reasonable but depart from cost.

e. The auditor is examining the financial statements that are to be included in the annual report to the stockholders of Elm Corporation, a regulated company. Elm Corporation's financial statements are prepared as prescribed by a regulatory agency of the U.S. government, and some items are not presented in accordance with generally accepted accounting principles. The amounts involved are material and are adequately disclosed in footnotes to the financial statements.

f. The auditor was engaged to examine FIG Wholesale Corporation's financial statements after the close of its fiscal year. On the completion of his examination, the auditor is satisfied that the corporation's financial statements are presented fairly except for the inventory. The amount of the inventory is material.

g. The auditor has examined Ginkgo Corporation's financial statements for many years. During the year just ended, a service bureau was employed to process Ginkgo's financial data by computer. The auditor knows very little about computers and does not wish to conduct the audit for the year just ended. The auditor and the president of the corporation are old friends, however, and the president persuaded her that she should not withdraw from the engagement. After glancing at the records and comparing the current year statements with those of the prior years, she believes that the statements prepared by the service bureau are stated fairly.

h. Subsequent to the close of Holly Corporation's fiscal year, a major debtor was declared bankrupt due to a rapid series of events. The debtor had confirmed the full amount due to Holly Corporation at the balance sheet date. Because the account was collectible at the balance sheet date, Holly Corporation refuses to disclose any information in relation to this subsequent event. The auditor believes that all accounts were stated fairly at the balance sheet date.

i. Ivy Corporation has a subsidiary company in a foreign country. An independent auditor in that country issued an unqualified opinion on the subsidiary's financial statements. Although Ivy's auditor is unaware of the standards of the practice of public accountancy in the foreign country, she is willing to accept full responsibility for the independent auditor's opinion on the subsidiary company's financial statements because she believes that Ivy Corporation's internal audit staff performed an adequate check on the operations of the subsidiary company during the year. She would be willing to express an unqualified opinion on the financial statements of Ivy Corporation alone, but she must express an opinion on the consolidated financial statements of Ivy Corporation and its subsidiaries.

j. The auditor has examined the financial statements of Juniper Corporation for many years and has always been able to render an unqualified opinion. Seven months ago, the Financial Accounting Standards Board adopted (effective 90 days after adoption) only one of two procedures as proper for reporting a particular financial transaction. Juniper Corporation has applied the previously acceptable procedure for many years and consistently applied that procedure during the year just ended. The corporation disclosed through footnotes to the current financial statements that the procedure employed is now at variance from the one adopted by the FASB. The corporation believes that lack of consistency is an overriding factor because the change in procedure would require it to report a material loss for the current year.

k. Kapok Corporation has used an outside service bureau to process data in years past. During the current year, the client has leased its own computers and no longer uses the service bureau. This change in policy is adequately disclosed in footnotes to the client's financial statements, but uncertainty prohibits either the client or the auditor from assessing the impact of this change on future operations.

l. Linden Corporation has material investments in stocks of subsidiary companies. Stocks of the subsidiary companies are not actively traded in the market, and the auditor's engagement does not extend to any subsidiary company. The auditor is able to satisfy himself that all investments are carried at original cost, and he has no reason to suspect that the amounts are not stated fairly.

m. Maple Corporation has large investments in stocks of subsidiary companies, but the investments are not material in relation to the financial position and results of operations of the corporation. Stocks of the subsidiary companies are not actively traded in the market, and the auditor's engagement does not extend to any subsidiary company. The auditor is able to satisfy herself that all investments are carried at original cost, and she has no reason to suspect that the amounts are not fairly stated.

21–39 (Reporting on Accounting Changes) The accounting and auditing literature discusses several different types of accounting changes:

1. Change from one GAAP to another GAAP.
2. Change in accounting estimate.
3. Change in estimate effected by a change in accounting principle.
4. Correction of an error.
5. Change from non–GAAP to GAAP (a special case of correction of an error).
6. Change in reporting entity (other than a pooling of interest).

Required:

a. For each of these accounting changes, give an example and state the appropriate accounting: restate prior years, show the cumulative effect on the current year income statement, or account for the change in the current and/or future years without changing any opening account balances.

b. For which of these types of changes should the auditor add a paragraph to the audit report assuming that the change had a material effect on the financial statements and was properly justified, accounted for, and disclosed?

*21–40 (Audit Reports and Consistency) Various types of accounting changes can affect the second reporting standard of the generally accepted auditing standards. This standard reads: "The report shall identify those circumstances in which such principles have not been consistently observed in the current period in relation to the preceding period."

Required:

a. Briefly describe the rationale for the standard and the auditor's responsibility in adhering to the standard.

b. For each of the changes listed below, briefly indicate the type of change and its effect on the auditor's report.

Accounting Changes:

1. A change from the completed-contract method to the percentage-of-completion method of accounting for long-term construction contracts.

2. A change in the estimated useful life of previously recorded fixed assets. The change is based on newly acquired information.
3. Correction of a mathematical error in inventory pricing made in a prior period.
4. A change from full absorption costing to direct costing for inventory valuation.
5. A change from presentation of statements of individual companies to presentation of consolidated companies.
6. A change from deferring and amortizing preproduction costs to recording such costs as an expense when incurred because future benefits of the costs have become doubtful. The new accounting method was adopted in recognition of the change in estimated future benefits.
7. A change from capitalizing research and development costs to expensing the costs as incurred. The change was in response to an accounting pronouncement from the FASB.
8. A change to include the employer's share of FICA taxes as retirement benefits on the income statement from including it in other taxes.
9. A company acquired another company during the year and accounted for it as a pooling of interests. The previous year financial statements have been restated to reflect the pooling.

21–41 (Other Auditors) You are in charge of the audit of the financial statements of Parat, Inc., and consolidated subsidiaries covering the two years ended December 31, 1993. Another public accounting firm is auditing Nuam, Inc., a major subsidiary that accounts for total assets, revenue, and net income of 30 percent, 26 percent, and 39 percent, respectively for 1993 and 28 percent, 20 percent, and 33 percent for 1992.

Required:

a. What is meant by the term *principal auditor?*
b. What factors should be considered when determining which public accounting firm should serve as the principal auditor?
c. Under what circumstances might the principal auditor decide not to refer to the other audit firm in the audit report on the consolidated statements?
d. If the principal auditor does not refer to the other auditor in the audit report, who is ultimately responsible to third parties if the other auditor was fraudulent or grossly negligent?
e. Write the audit report referring to the other audit firm and expressing an unqualified opinion.

*21–42 (Critique of Audit Report–Going Concern Doubt) The following auditors' report was drafted by a staff accountant of Turner & Turner, CPAs, at the completion of the audit of the financial statements of Lyon Computers, Inc., for the year ended March 31, 1994. It was submitted to the engagement partner, who reviewed matters thoroughly and properly concluded that Lyon's disclosures concerning its ability to continue as a going concern for a reasonable period of time were adequate.

To the Board of Directors of Lyon Computers, Inc.:

We have audited the accompanying balance sheet of Lyon Computers, Inc. as of March 31, 1994, and the other related financial statements for the year then ended. Our responsibility is to express an opinion on these financial statements based on our audit.

We conducted our audit in accordance with standards that require that we plan and perform the audit to obtain reasonable assurance about whether the financial statements are in conformity with generally accepted accounting principles. An audit includes examining, on a test basis, evidence supporting the amounts and disclosures in the financial statements. An audit also includes assessing the accounting principles used and significant estimates made by management.

The accompanying financial statements have been prepared assuming that the Company will continue as a going concern. As discussed in Note X to the financial statements, the Company has suffered recurring losses from operations and has a net capital deficiency that raises substantial doubt about its ability to continue as a going concern. We believe that management's plans in regard to these matters, which are also described in Note X, will permit the Company to continue as a going concern beyond a reasonable period of time. The financial statements do not include any adjustments that might result from the outcome of this uncertainty.

In our opinion, subject to the effects on the financial statements of such adjustments, if any, as might have been required had the outcome of the uncertainty referred to in the preceding paragraph been known, the financial statements referred to above present fairly, in all material respects, the financial position of Lyon Computers, Inc., and the results of its operations and its cash flows in conformity with generally accepted accounting principles applied on a basis consistent with that of the preceding year.

Turner & Turner, CPAs
April 28, 1994

Required:
Identify the deficiencies contained in the auditor's report as drafted by the staff accountant. Group the deficiencies by paragraph. Do *not* redraft the report.

*21–43 (Selecting the Proper Audit Opinion and Report Modification)

Required:
Items 1 through 8 present various independent factual situations an auditor might encounter in conducting an audit. List A represents the types of opinions the auditor ordinarily would issue and List B represents the report modifications (if any) that would be necessary. For each situation, select one response from List A and one from List B. Select as the *best* answer for each item, the action the auditor normally would take. The types of opinions in List A and the report modifications in List B may be selected once, more than once, or not at all.

Assume the following:

- The auditor is independent.

- The auditor previously expressed an unqualified opinion on the prior year financial statements.
- Only single-year (not comparative) statements are presented for the current year.
- The conditions for an unqualified opinion exist unless contradicted in the factual situations.
- The conditions stated in the factual situations are material.
- No report modifications are to be made except in response to the factual situation.

Audit Situations:

1. The financial statements present fairly, in all material respects, the financial position, results of operations, and cash flows in conformity with GAAP.
2. In auditing the Long-Term Investments account, an auditor is unable to obtain audited financial statements for an investee located in a foreign country. The auditor concludes that sufficient competent evidential matter regarding this investment cannot be obtained but is not significant enough to disclaim an opinion.
3. Due to recurring operating losses and working capital deficiencies, an auditor has substantial doubt about an entity's ability to continue as a going concern for a reasonable period of time. However, the financial statement disclosures concerning these matters are adequate.
4. The principal auditor decides to refer to the work of another auditor who audited a wholly owned subsidiary of the entity and issued an unqualified opinion.
5. An entity issues financial statements that present financial position and results of operations but omits the related statement of cash flows. Management discloses in the notes to the financial statements that it does not believe the statement of cash flows to be a useful statement.
6. An entity changes its depreciation method for production equipment from the straight-line to a units-of-production method based on hours of utilization. The auditor concurs with the change, although it has a material effect on the comparability of the entity's financial statements.
7. An entity is a defendant in a lawsuit alleging infringement of certain patent rights. However, the ultimate outcome of the litigation cannot be reasonably estimated by management. The auditor believes that there is a reasonable possibility of a significant material loss, but the lawsuit is adequately disclosed in the notes to the financial statements.
8. An entity discloses in the notes to the financial statements certain lease obligations. The auditor believes that the failure to capitalize these leases is a departure from GAAP.

List A–Types of Opinions

a. A qualified opinion
b. An unqualified opinion
c. An adverse opinion

List B–Report Modifications

h. Describe the circumstances in an explanatory paragraph *preceding* the opinion paragraph *without modifying* the three standard paragraphs.

d. A disclaimer of opinion
e. Either a qualified opinion or an adverse opinion
f. Either a disclaimer of opinion or a qualified opinion
g. Either an adverse opinion or a disclaimer of opinion
i. Describe the circumstances in an explanatory paragraph *following* the opinion paragraph *without modifying* the three standard paragraphs.
j. Describe the circumstances in an explanatory paragraph *preceding* the opinion paragraph *and modifying the opinion* paragraph.
k. Describe the circumstances in an explanatory paragraph *following* the opinion paragraph *and modifying the opinion* paragraph.
l. Describe the circumstances in an explanatory paragraph *preceding* the opinion paragraph *and modifying the scope and opinion* paragraphs.
m. Describe the circumstances in an explanatory paragraph *following* the opinion paragraph *and modifying the scope and opinion* paragraphs.
n. Describe the circumstances within the *scope* paragraph without adding an explanatory paragraph.
o. Describe the circumstances within the *opinion* paragraph without adding an explanatory paragraph.
p. Describe the circumstances within the *scope and opinion* paragraphs without adding an explanatory paragraph.
q. Describe the circumstances in the *introductory* paragraph without adding an explanatory paragraph and modify the wording of the scope and opinion paragraphs.
r. Issue the *standard* auditor's report *without modification.*

21–44 (Comparison of Procedures for an Audit, Review, and Compilation) Compare and contrast the procedures that should be performed on inventory for an audit, review, and compilation. Assume that the auditor has knowledge of the business and industry. Give specific examples of procedures.

21–45 (Review Report with a GAAP Violation) You have reviewed the financial statements of Classic Company for the year ended June 30, 1994. The only unusual finding is that the company deferred $350,000 of research and development costs rather than expensing them. The costs related to a product that the client believed was certain to be profitable in the future. You are convinced that the product will be profitable but not that the expenses should have been deferred.

Required:
Write the negative assurance and explanatory paragraphs for an appropriate review report.

*21–46 (Critique of a Compilation Report—Auditor Not Independent and Omission of Substantially All Disclosures) The following report was drafted on October 25, 1993, by Russ Major, CPA, at the completion of the engagement to compile the financial statements of Ajax Company for the year ended September 30, 1993. Ajax is a nonpublic entity in which Major's child has a material direct financial interest. Ajax decided to omit substantially all of the disclosures required by generally accepted accounting principles because the financial statements will be for management's use only. The statement of cash flows was also omitted because management does not believe it to be a useful financial statement.

To the Board of Directors of Ajax Company:

I have compiled the accompanying financial statements of Ajax Company as of September 30, 1993, and for the year then ended. I planned and performed the compilation to obtain limited assurance about whether the financial statements are free of material misstatements.

A compilation is limited to presenting information in the form of financial statements. It is substantially less in scope than an audit in accordance with generally accepted auditing standards, the objective of which is the expression of an opinion regarding the financial statements taken as a whole. I have not audited the accompanying financial statements and, accordingly, do not express any opinion on them.

Management has elected to omit substantially all of the disclosures required by generally accepted accounting principles. If the omitted disclosures were included in the financial statements, they might influence the user's conclusions about the Company's financial position, results of operations, and changes in financial position.

I am not independent with respect to Ajax Company. This lack of independence is due to my child's ownership of a material direct financial interest in Ajax Company.

This report is intended solely for the information and use of the Board of Directors and management of Ajax Company and should not be used for any other purpose.

Required:

Identify the deficiencies contained in Major's report on the compiled financial statements. Group the deficiencies by paragraph when applicable. Do *not* redraft the report.

21–47 (Review Program for Inventory) You have been assigned to perform a review of a client's inventory containing microcomputers and related software.

Required:

a. What inquiries and analytical procedures should you perform?

b. What will you do if these procedures do not support the client's inventory values or disclosures?

21–48 (Students' Perceptions of the Effectiveness of Audit, Review, and Compilation Reports) Write a report on your perceptions of the effectiveness of audit, review, and compilation reports in communicating the nature of the service and the degree of assurance provided.

21–49 **(Research–Unusual Reporting Examples)** Using the resources of your library (such as actual annual reports, Total, NAARS, or Disclosure CDROM service), try to find examples of audit reports that

a. Refer to a justified departure from GAAP.

b. Contain an adverse opinion.
c. Contain a scope limitation.
d. Refer to an unjustified departure from GAAP.

21–50 **(Research–Audits, Reviews, and Compilations)** Interview a commercial loan officer of a financial institution and find out under what circumstances it is willing to accept a review or compilation report rather than an audit report before loaning money to a business.

Case

21–51 (Effect on Audit Report of a Foreign Company Violating U.S. GAAP) You are auditing Osakis Electronics USA, Ltd., a subsidiary of a Japanese company, and will issue an audit report covering the balance sheets as of December 31, 1993 and 1992 and the income statements and cash flow statements for the two years then ended. Their common stock is traded on the New York and Tokyo stock exchanges. Each of the following are *independent* audit reporting situations.

1. Osakis does not disclose segment information because Japanese accounting standards do not require it. The Securities and Exchange Commission does not require such disclosures in SEC filings of foreign issuers of securities

Required:
Indicate the effect on your audit report, which will be widely used in the United States.

2. Osakis reports its inventory, fixed assets, depreciation, and cost of goods sold on a current value basis. Such accounting violates the accounting standards of both Japan and the United States. There is disclosure of the pertinent facts, including the effect on key financial statement amounts, in footnote 13.

Required:
a. What factors should you consider in deciding whether to issue a qualified or an adverse opinion?
b. Draft the explanatory and opinion paragraphs for
   1. a qualified opinion.
   2. an adverse opinion.

3. Osakis prepares two sets of financial statements; one set for use in Japan using Japanese accounting principles and the other set for use in the United States using U.S. GAAP. The Japanese set contains a footnote describing the accounting principles used.

Required:
How should you report on these two sets of statements?

End Note

1. Mark Sever and Ronald Boisclair, "Financial Reporting in the 1990's," *Journal of Accountancy*, January, 1990, 41.

CHAPTER

22

Learning Objectives

Through studying this chapter, you will be able to:

1. Understand the audit requirements for reporting on historical financial information other than normal GAAP-based annual financial statements.
2. Understand the various circumstances in which auditors report on internal controls.
3. Understand the reporting requirements for prospective and pro forma financial information.

Special-Purpose Reporting Situations: Expansion of the Attest Function

Chapter Contents

Chapter Overview

The demand for special-purpose reports on financially related data continues to increase. Users are demanding more varied information. At the same time, they want to gain some assurance of the reliability of these data. Thus, auditors are frequently being requested to expand the scope of their work to provide assurance on these new types of reports. This chapter identifies many of these special reporting situations, discusses the demand for such reports, and provides an overview of the standards for attesting to such reports.

The accounting profession was born in the nineteenth century in response to social and economic needs emerging from the Industrial Revolution. As businesses increased in size and significance, and as management gradually separated from owners, employees, and other constituencies, the need for reliable information about the financial affairs of businesses became critical. Accountancy answered those needs by providing a common language to measure and report business activity (accounting principles) and a basis for confidence in the accounting reports (independent reporting).[1]

A client wants help in estimating his personal income taxes for next year. . . . A condominium association needs assistance in developing a budget. A promoter needs help in putting together an offering to sell a real estate limited partnership to a group of doctors. What do these engagements have in common? Each one may involve prospective financial statements.[2]

An independent auditor's judgment concerning the overall presentation of financial statements should be applied within an identifiable framework. Normally, the framework is provided by generally accepted accounting principles, and the auditor's judgment in forming an opinion is applied accordingly. In some circumstances, however, a comprehensive basis of accounting other than generally accepted accounting principles may be used. [AU 623.03]

A–INTRODUCTION

Public accounting firms are increasingly called on to provide new types of attestation services beyond that of typical audits, reviews, and compilations. A small business, for example, may need a bank loan. The bank may require audited financial statements, but the business has maintained its records primarily for tax return purposes. The client may request the auditor to issue an opinion on financial statements prepared on the income tax basis rather than on a GAAP basis. In addition, the Securities and Exchange Commission requires publicly owned companies to prepare quarterly financial statements and has proposed that auditors be required to review those interim financial statements before they are issued.

Some regulatory agencies require management to report its assessment of the effectiveness of its internal control structure and may engage auditors to report on that assessment. Auditors may find reports on the internal accounting controls of a computer service bureau to be useful in understanding and assessing the impact of the service bureau's controls on their audit client.

The basic financial statements covered by the audit opinion are often accompanied by other information provided either by the client or the auditor. In the annual report to shareholders, the president's letter often talks about the company's financial condition and results of operations. Selected financial data, such as a 10-year comparison of key financial information, may be provided. Condensed financial information may be presented in a document that is separate from the complete audited financial statements. There are special requirements for reporting on supplementary or condensed financial information.

A company may be required to provide estimates of its future financial position and results of operations to help the lending institution determine whether or not to approve a loan. Auditors are frequently asked to help prepare or attest to such prospective financial statements.

B–OTHER REPORTS ON HISTORICAL FINANCIAL INFORMATION

Special Reports

The term **special reports** has a specific meaning in the auditing standards and refers to the following types of reporting situations:

- Reporting on financial statements prepared in conformity with a comprehensive basis of accounting other than GAAP, often referred to as OCBOA (other comprehensive basis of accounting) statements.
- Reporting on specified elements, accounts, or items of a financial statement.
- Reporting on the performance of agreed-upon procedures.
- Reporting on compliance with aspects of contractual agreements or regulatory requirements related to audited financial statements.

- Reporting on special-purpose financial presentations to comply with contractual agreements or regulatory provisions.
- Reporting on financial information presented in prescribed forms or schedules.

Comprehensive Basis of Accounting Other than GAAP

The first standard of reporting requires the auditor to state *whether* the financial statements are presented in accordance with GAAP. The Securities and Exchange Commission requires most public companies to follow GAAP.* Some companies, however, prepare their financial statements on an **other comprehensive basis of accounting (OCBOA)** other than GAAP. Some regulatory agencies, such as state insurance commissions, require the preparation of financial statements that conform to prescribed regulatory accounting. Auditing standards permit the auditor to issue opinions on such non–GAAP financial statements as long as the accounting basis used is one of the following:

- A cash or modified cash basis.
- The basis of accounting used for preparing the income tax return.
- The basis of accounting required for reporting to a governmental regulatory agency.
- A basis that has a definite set of criteria that has substantial support and applies to all material items appearing in the financial statements [AU 623.04].

All companies are required by law to maintain financial records so they can prepare proper tax returns. To minimize the cost of record keeping, some companies prepare their financial statements using a cash, modified cash, or income tax basis so they do not have to maintain two sets of records, one for tax reporting and the other for financial reporting. Lending institutions sometimes accept audited financial statements prepared on such a basis because they recognize that it is very expensive for small companies to maintain accounting records that permit preparation of GAAP–basis statements. Some companies have chosen to prepare financial statements adjusted to reflect the changing value of the dollar.

Applicability of GAAS. All 10 of the generally accepted auditing standards apply to audits of OCBOA financial statements. Thus, an audit of an OCBOA financial statement does not differ in approach or concept from that of a GAAP–based financial statement. The major difference is that the auditor first must determine that the client's proposed OCBOA has authoritative support and then the auditor determines whether the financial statements are fairly presented according to the criteria associated with the alternative basis.

Report Requirements. Recall that auditing involves testing assertions in relationship with prescribed criteria. Thus, auditors may issue opinions on the fairness of the financial statements as measured by the other comprehensive basis of accounting used. It is important that the titles of the financial statements clearly indicate that

*There are some exceptions for foreign companies whose securities are traded in the United States.

these are not GAAP-basis statements. This is done by using such titles as Statement of Assets, Liabilities, and Capital—Income Tax Basis and Statement of Revenue and Expenses—Income Tax Basis for the financial statements and in the auditor's report. Using such titles as balance sheet and income statement without modifiers implies the use of GAAP and should be avoided for these special reports.

An example of an audit report on financial statements prepared on a modified cash basis is presented in Exhibit 22.1. The titles of the financial statements are different than for GAAP–basis statements. The scope paragraph is the same as for an unqualified audit report on GAAP–basis statements. There is, however, an added paragraph that refers to a footnote that more fully describes the basis of accounting used and how that basis, in general, departs from GAAP. In the report in the exhibit, the auditors expressed an unqualified opinion that the financial statements are presented fairly, in all material respects, *on the cash basis of accounting as more fully described in the note.*

The last paragraph in Exhibit 22.1 is added because of an uncertainty. The reporting requirements are the same as for audit reports on GAAP–basis statements except for bringing the reader's attention to the basis of accounting used. If there has been a significant change in the accounting principles used or there is a significant uncertainty, an explanatory paragraph should be added. If the auditor is unable to express

Exhibit 22.1

REPORT ON MODIFIED CASH BASIS FINANCIAL STATEMENTS

Independent Auditor's Report

To NCNB Texas National Bank
as Trustee for the Permian Basin Royalty Trust:

We have audited the accompanying statements of assets, liabilities and trust corpus of the Permian Basin Royalty Trust ("Trust") as of December 31, 1988 and 1987, and the related statements of distributable income and changes in trust corpus for each of the three years in the period ended December 31, 1988. These financial statements are the responsibility of the trustee. Our responsibility is to express an opinion on these financial statements based on our audits.

[Standard scope paragraph]

As described in Note 3 to the financial statements, these statements were prepared on a modified cash basis, which is a comprehensive basis of accounting other than generally accepted accounting principles.

In our opinion, such financial statements present fairly, in all material respects, the assets, liabilities and trust corpus of the Permian Basin Royalty Trust as of December 31, 1988 and 1987, and the distributable income and changes in trust corpus for each of the three years in the period ended December 31, 1988 *on the basis of accounting described in Note 3.*

As discussed in Note 5 to the financial statements, the regulatory status of the Waddell Ranch Properties gas from which the Trust receives substantial royalty income is in dispute. The ultimate outcome of the proceedings cannot presently be determined.

/s/ Deloitte Haskins & Sells
Fort Worth, Texas
February 21, 1989

[Emphasis added.]

an unqualified opinion because of a scope limitation, inadequate disclosure, or a violation of the accounting basis used, the auditor should express a qualified or adverse opinion or disclaim an opinion according to the guidelines discussed in Chapter 21. In evaluating the adequacy of the disclosures in OCBOA statements, the auditor should apply essentially the same criteria as for GAAP–basis statements; the statements, including the accompanying notes, should include all informative disclosures that are appropriate. The standards require a note summarizing the comprehensive basis of accounting used and a broad indication of how the statements differ from GAAP. In addition to the summary of significant accounting policies, footnotes typically cover areas such as debt, leases, pensions, related-party transactions, and uncertainties.

Specified Elements, Accounts, or Items

Auditors are sometimes asked to express an opinion on one or more specific elements, accounts, or items of financial statements. Such items may be presented in the auditor's report or in a document accompanying the report. The audit may be undertaken as a separate engagement or in conjunction with the audit of financial statements [AU 623.13]. An audit client may be a retail company, for example, that leases a store. Part of the lease payments are based on the amount of revenues of the store, and the lease agreement may require that an independent auditor provide a report expressing an opinion on whether the revenue is reported to the lessor in accordance with the lease agreement.

Applicability of GAAS. With the exception of the first standard of reporting, all of the auditing standards are applicable to audits of specified elements. The first standard of reporting, which requires that the auditor's report state whether the financial statements are presented in conformity with GAAP is, however, applicable if the subject of the auditor's report is intended to be presented in conformity with GAAP.

Report Requirements. The audit report (see Exhibit 22.2) should identify the specific elements, accounts, or items of a financial statement (the subject) and, if applicable, indicate that the audit was made in conjunction with an audit of the company's financial statements. It should describe the basis on which the item or element is presented and, when applicable, any agreements specifying the basis of presentation if it is not in conformity with GAAP. If considered necessary, the report should include a description of significant interpretations made by the company's management regarding the relevant agreements. If the item or element is prepared to comply with the requirements of a contract or an agreement that results in a presentation that is not in conformity with either GAAP or OCBOA, a paragraph should be added restricting the distribution of the report to those within the entity and the parties to the contract or agreement.

The auditor is not required to do so but may describe specific auditing procedures in a separate paragraph. The other reporting requirements are the same as for audit reports on GAAP–basis financial statements, including the expression of an opinion.

Agreed-Upon Procedures

An accountant may be engaged to apply certain procedures to specific elements, accounts, or items of a financial statement, such procedures being less in scope than is needed for expressing an opinion [AU 622]. Such an engagement is proper as long

Exhibit 22.2

REPORT ON SPECIFIED ELEMENTS OF A FINANCIAL STATEMENT

Independent Auditor's Report

To the Unit Holders of Sabine Royalty Trust:

We have audited the accompanying statements of fees and expenses paid by Sabine Royalty Trust to NCNB Texas National Bank, as trustee and escrow agent, for each of the three years in the period ended December 31, 1988. These statements are the responsibility of the trustee. Our responsibility is to express an opinion on these statements based on our audits.

We conducted our audits in accordance with generally accepted auditing standards. Those standards require that we plan and perform the audit to obtain reasonable assurance about whether the statements of fees and expenses are free of material misstatement. An audit includes examining, on a test basis, evidence supporting the amounts and disclosures in the statements. An audit also includes assessing the accounting principles used and significant estimates made by management, as well as evaluating the overall statement presentation. We believe that our audits provide a reasonable basis for our opinion.

We have read the Sabine Corporation Royalty Trust agreement (the "Trust Agreement"), including Exhibit C thereto entitled "Compensation of Interfirst Bank Dallas, N.A.," which defines fees and expenses payable by Sabine Royalty Trust (the "Trust").

Our audits of the fees and expenses paid included the following tests:

1. On a test basis, we compared the expenses used in the calculation of fees to the underlying expense reports or documents and verified that they were properly included as fees and expenses of the trust.
2. We verified the clerical accuracy of the calculation of fees.

In our opinion, the statements of fees and expenses referred to above present fairly, in all material respects, the fees and expenses paid by the trust to NCNB Texas National Bank, as trustee and escrow agent for each of the three years in the period ended December 31, 1988, in accordance with the trust agreement.

Based on our audits, fees and expenses paid by the trust to the trustee were properly calculated and paid in all material respects in accordance with the trust agreement for the items tested. Further, during the course of our audits, nothing came to our attention to cause us to believe that the fees and expenses paid by the trust to the trustee not tested were not calculated and paid in accordance with the trust agreement.

/s/ Deloitte Haskins & Sells
Dallas, Texas
March 17, 1989

as the parties involved have a clear understanding of the procedures to be performed and the report is distributed only to the named parties involved. A client considering the purchase of another business, for example, may ask its auditor to perform specific procedures, but not an audit, on accounts receivable, inventory, fixed assets, and accounts payable of the other business before deciding to make the purchase. The accountant should be sure that all parties involved understand the scope of the work through direct discussions or review of correspondence with those setting the procedures or distribution of the engagement letter or a draft of the report with a request for their comments before the final report is issued [AU 622.02].

The intent of this understanding is to explicitly identify the procedures that will be used by the auditor, the intended distribution of the report, and the potential usefulness of the reported data to the user requesting the report. It is important to understand that the intent is to carry out the specific procedures, as agreed-upon, and report to specifically identified parties the results of the procedures. Such procedures are not sufficient to render an opinion on the fairness of the item. Therefore, the report (see Exhibit 22.3) should identify the subject of the report, indicate the intended report distribution, identify the procedures performed, state the accountant's findings, disclaim an opinion, and indicate that the report does not extend to the entity's financial statements taken as a whole. If the accountant has no adjustments to propose, the report may include a comment to that effect (such a comment is often referred to as *negative assurance*). It is important that the accountant specifically control the distribution of such reports because they are not intended to be general purpose reports.

Exhibit 22.3

REPORT ON THE APPLICATION OF AGREED-UPON PROCEDURES

To the Board of Directors, Grove Industries

At your request, we have applied certain agreed-upon procedures, as discussed below, to accounting records of Honeycomb, Inc., as of August 31, 1994, solely to assist you in connection with the proposed acquisition of Honeycomb, Inc. It is understood that *this report is solely for your information* and is not to be referred to or distributed for any purpose to anyone who is not a member of management of Grove Industries. Our procedures and findings are as follows:

1. We took a random sample of 100 items from the perpetual inventory record and examined documents evidencing recent purchases to determine whether the records correctly reflect purchase price according to the FIFO basis of accounting. The dollar amount of items sampled was $127,845.53. No errors were found in the sampled items.
2. [A list of other procedures and findings would be inserted here.]

Because the above procedures do not constitute an audit conducted in accordance with generally accepted auditing standards, *we do not express an opinion* on any of the accounts or items referred to above. In connection with the procedures referred to above, *no matters came to our attention that caused us to believe that the specified accounts should be adjusted.* Had we performed additional procedures or had we conducted an audit of the financial statements in accordance with generally accepted auditing standards, matters might have come to our attention that would have been reported to you. This report relates only to the accounts and items specified above and does not extend to any financial statements of Honeycomb, Inc., taken as a whole.

/s/ Rittenberg & Schwieger, CPAs
Madison, WI
September 22, 1994

[Emphasis added.]

Compliance with Contractual Agreements or Regulatory Requirements

Auditors are sometimes required by their client's loan agreement or regulatory agency to furnish a report on the client's compliance with specific regulations [AU 623.19].* Auditors may issue such reports as long as the covenants of the agreement or regulatory requirement are based on information from audited financial statements. In other words, before a compliance report may be issued, the auditor must have assurance that the financial information that is subject to the covenants is fairly presented. A bond indenture, for example, may require the bond issuer to maintain a minimum current ratio, to make minimum payments into a sinking fund, or limit dividends to a certain percent of net income. If such requirements or restrictions are violated, the bonds may become payable on demand of the bondholders rather than at their scheduled maturity date. The auditor cannot express an opinion on covenants relating to unaudited information, for example, maintaining a 2.5 to 1 current ratio at the end of each of the first three quarters of the fiscal year or meeting all pollution standards.

Report Requirements. A compliance report contains *negative assurance* and may be given in a separate report or with the auditor's report accompanying the financial statements. Recall that a negative assurance report simply indicates that the auditor did not find anything that would lead the auditor to conclude that the report is not fairly stated. But the auditor has not performed sufficient audit work to conclude that the report is in fact fairly or accurately presented. The report (see Exhibit 22.4) should include a reference to the audited financial statements, specific covenants, and a statement of negative assurance.

Circumstances Requiring Explanatory Language in a Special Report

Explanatory language should be added to any of the special reports described in the previous sections when:

- There has been a change in accounting principles that materially affected the subject of the report.
- Significant uncertainties affect the subject of the report.
- The auditor has substantial doubt about the organization's ability to continue as a going concern.
- The auditor makes reference to the report of another auditor as a basis, in part, for his or her opinion.

Other Special Report Situations

Auditors are sometimes requested to report on special-purpose financial statements prepared in compliance with a contractual agreement or regulatory provision that may be incomplete presentations or may not be in accordance with GAAP. A real estate company, for example, may be required by a governmental agency to provide an audited schedule of gross income and certain defined expenses but that is not a

*See Chapter 24 for compliance auditing applicable to governmental entities and other recipients of governmental financial assistance.

Exhibit 22.4

REPORT ON COMPLIANCE WITH A CONTRACTUAL AGREEMENT

Independent Auditor's Report

To the Board of Directors and Management
Actup Company and First National Bank of Brace:

We have audited, in accordance with generally accepted auditing standards, the balance sheet of Actup Company as of December 31, 1993, and the related statements of income, retained earnings, and cash flows for the year then ended, and have issued our report thereon dated February 27, 1994.

In connection with our audit, nothing came to our attention that caused us to believe that the Company failed to comply with the terms, covenants, provisions, and conditions of sections 25 to 33, inclusive, of the Indenture dated July 23, 1987, with First National Bank of Brace insofar as they relate to accounting matters. However, our audit was not directed primarily toward obtaining knowledge of such noncompliance.

This report is intended solely for the information and use of the boards of directors and management of Actup Company and First National Bank of Brace and should not be used for any other purpose.

/s/ Rittenberg & Schwieger, CPAs
Madison, WI
March 3, 1994

full GAAP statement. The auditor's report should be carefully worded to alert the reader to these special situations.

Clients are sometimes required to file audited information with regulatory agencies that prescribe the wording of the auditor's report. The prescribed form may not be acceptable because it does not conform to the reporting standards. In such cases, additional wording may be added or complete revision of the form may be needed.

Application of Accounting Principles

Public accountants often seek advice from their colleagues in other public accounting firms concerning such things as how a particular transaction should be recorded or what kind of opinion should be expressed in a specific situation. Because both parties to this consultation are professional accountants, no formal report need accompany such advice. A client may also request such advice from their accountant who has been hired to report on their financial statements. Again, no formal reporting is necessary.

There is a potential problem, however, when public accountants are consulted to determine whether they might take a position contrary to the client's existing auditors. This is often referred to as *opinion shopping* and could lead to adverse conditions for financial statement presentations if public accounting firms used their opinion on an accounting principle as a basis for obtaining new clients. By the same token, clients should have a right to expand their knowledge by seeking outside counsel from experts. To promote the right of free consultation, but at the same time to avoid potential problems of opinion shopping, the profession has responded by developing specific procedures when a firm is contacted by a nonclient or an intermediary (such as an investment banker) on behalf of such an organization, for its opinion on the application of accounting principles to certain transactions. The intent of the procedures (defined below) is to ensure that the auditor contacted is fully aware of all the important issues before issuing an opinion (including knowledge of whether the treatment suggested by the current auditors is in dispute).

Procedures

The auditor contacted needs to gain an understanding of the nature of the transaction and other information to permit an informed opinion. The auditing standards suggest that the accountant should perform the following minimum procedures:

- Obtain an understanding of the form and substance of the transaction(s).
- Review applicable GAAP.
- Consult with other professionals or experts, if appropriate.
- Perform any necessary research or other procedures and consider the existence of creditable precedents or analogies.
- Consult with the current auditor to obtain information not otherwise available, including whether the method suggested by the auditor is in dispute. Permission to talk with the continuing accountant should be obtained from the organization or intermediary.

As an example, an auditor might be contacted by a nonclient with the description of a set of circumstances under which the nonclient believes that it would be appropriate to recognize revenue and seeks the auditor's opinion as to whether the auditor believes that it is appropriate to recognize revenue in such a circumstance. Unless the auditor fully understands all aspects of the situation, such as the nature of the sales contract, the customer's right of return, how the company has handled similar transactions in the past, and so forth, the auditor is not in a position to render an opinion.

Report Requirements

Reports on the application of accounting principle are generally written but in some rare circumstances may be oral. It should describe the transaction or circumstances, state the accountant's conclusion as to the relevant accounting principles or type of opinion to be rendered, and include the reasons for the conclusion. It should also state that responsibility for the proper accounting rests with the preparers of the financial statements and that any difference in the facts, circumstances, or assumptions presented may change the conclusion.

Interim Financial Information

The SEC requires publicly owned companies to (1) file quarterly financial information with the SEC on Form 10-Q within 45 days after the end of each of the first three quarters of the fiscal year and provide their shareholders with quarterly reports and (2) include certain quarterly information in the annual reports to the SEC (Form 10-K) and in the annual reports to shareholders. Some companies engage their public accountants to review this information on a timely basis, that is, before it is issued each quarter. Reviews of this information by auditors are also performed in conjunction with the annual audit. The SEC is weighing the benefits of requiring firms to have their public accountants review the quarterly reports before they are issued. Such a review would improve the credibility of the information. Some companies have requested their auditors to review the quarterly reports to help avoid embarrassing fourth-quarter adjustments uncovered by annual audits.

Review Procedures

The auditor should perform certain review procedures on the quarterly information contained in the annual report to shareholders and when engaged to review the quarterly information issued at the end of each of the first three quarters of the fiscal year [AU 722]. These procedures are much the same as those required by the SSARSs for reviews of financial statements (covered in Chapter 21): making inquiries, performing analytical procedures, reading the minutes of board of directors meetings, and reading the interim information to consider whether it appears to conform with GAAP. In addition, the auditor should obtain written representations from management concerning such things as its responsibility for the financial information, the completeness of the minutes, and subsequent events (not required by the SSARSs).

The standards also require auditors to understand the client's accounting and financial reporting practices and its related internal control structure, normally obtained while auditing the prior year financial statements. If it is a new client, the auditor must perform the necessary procedures to obtain such an understanding.

Reporting on Interim Statements Presented Separately

The standard report on a review of separately issued interim statements is shown in Exhibit 22.5. It identifies the information reviewed, indicates that the standards of the AICPA were followed in performing the review, explains the nature of a review, disclaims an opinion, and provides negative assurance that the auditor is not aware of any material departures from GAAP.

The disclosure and reporting requirements for interim financial statements differ from those for annual statements. Accruals, such as estimates of bad debt expense, are not usually as precise on interim dates as they are at year-end. It is assumed that those who receive the interim statements also received the latest annual statements. Information disclosed in the latest annual statements does not have to be repeated in the interim statements except for continuing contingencies and other uncertainties. There should be disclosures of events that occurred since the latest year-end, such as changes in accounting principles or estimates and significant changes in financial position.

The negative assurance should be modified when there is a material departure from GAAP or inadequate disclosure. In such situations, a paragraph should be added preceding the negative assurance paragraph describing the problem. The negative assurance paragraph would then read as follows:

> Based on our review, *with the exception of the matter described in the preceding paragraph*, we are not aware of any material modifications that should be made to the accompanying financial statements for them to be in conformity with generally accepted accounting principles [AU 722.31]. [Emphasis added.]

Exhibit 22.5

REVIEW REPORT ON INTERIM FINANCIAL STATEMENTS

To the Shareholders of Gressal, Inc.

We have reviewed the balance sheets and statements of income of Gressal, Inc., as of September 30, 1994 and 1993, and for the nine-month periods then ended. These financial statements are the responsibility of the Company's management.

We conducted our review in accordance with standards established by the American Institute of Certified Public Accountants. A review of interim financial information consists principally of applying analytical procedures to financial data and making inquiries of persons responsible for financial and accounting matters. It is substantially less in scope than an audit conducted in accordance with generally accepted auditing standards, the objective of which is the expression of an opinion regarding the financial statements taken as a whole. Accordingly, we do not express such an opinion.

Based on our review, *we are not aware of any material modifications* that should be made to the accompanying financial statements for them to be in conformity with generally accepted accounting principles.

/s/ Rittenberg & Schwieger, CPAs
Madison, WI
April 10, 1994

[Emphasis added.]

Reporting on Interim Financial Information That Accompanies Audited Financial Statements

The SEC requires public companies to present selected quarterly financial information in their annual reports and certain other documents filed with the SEC.* Other companies may voluntarily present such information. The auditor's report on the financial statements ordinarily does not need to be modified to refer to the review of the interim information unless:

- The information is required by the SEC but is omitted or has not been reviewed.
- The information is presented in the footnotes but is not clearly labeled "unaudited."
- The information does not conform to GAAP.
- The information is presented voluntarily, is not reviewed by the auditor, and is not appropriately marked as not reviewed.

Supplementary Information

The **basic financial statements** covered by the auditor's report include the balance sheet, income statement, cash flow statement, statement of changes in owners'

*Item 302(a) of SEC Regulation S-K contains this requirement.

equity (if presented), and related footnotes. These are often accompanied by *supplementary information* required by GAAP or presented voluntarily that may be prepared by the client or the auditor. Auditors are sometimes asked to report on condensed financial statements presented in a document separate from the complete audited financial statements. Auditors may be asked to report on selected financial data contained in a document along with the complete financial statements. The reporting requirements for these situations are described in the following paragraphs.

Information Prepared by the Client—Not Required by GAAP

Many of the documents containing audited financial statements also contain supplementary information prepared by the client. In annual shareholders' reports, for example, management usually reports on the results of the past year and prospects for the future. Financial highlights covering the last several years are often included. The auditor must be sure that such information is not materially inconsistent with that covered by the audit report. The president may, for example, be discussing the growth in earnings using preliminary data that were later corrected in the audited statements.

When there is an inconsistency between the supplementary information and the audited information, the auditor should first determine which is correct. If the audited information is correct, the auditor should attempt to get management to correct the incorrect supplementary information. If management refuses, the auditor should consider other actions such as revising the audit report to include an explanatory paragraph describing the material inconsistency, withholding the use of the report, or withdrawing from the engagement. The action taken will depend on the circumstances and the significance of the inconsistency.

Information Prepared by the Client—Required by GAAP

The FASB and the GASB are authorized to develop standards for financial statements and certain other information supplementary to such statements. *FASB Statement No. 69* requires publicly traded enterprises in the oil and gas industry to disclose the proved gas and oil reserve quantities and other supplementary information. *GASB Statement No. 5* requires presentation of certain 10-year historical trend information relating to pension activities as supplementary information. Such information should either be presented separately from the basic financial statements or, if included as a footnote, should be clearly labeled "unaudited."

The auditor ordinarily makes inquiries about how the information was developed and compares the information with management's responses to those inquiries and to the audited financial statements. Additional procedures may be necessary if the auditor believes this supplementary information may not be properly presented.

The auditor need not mention this supplementary information in the audit report unless:

- It is omitted.
- It departs from prescribed guidelines.
- The auditor is unable to complete the prescribed procedures.
- The auditor cannot remove substantial doubt as to whether the information conforms to prescribed guidelines.

When modifying the audit report for any of these conditions, the auditor's opinion on the basic financial statements is unaffected. An explanatory paragraph should be added to the report, such as this:

> The City of Loonville has not presented the 10-year historical trend information that the Governmental Accounting Standards Board has determined is necessary to supplement, although not required to be part of, the basic financial statements.

Condensed Financial Statements and Selected Financial Data

Occasionally, an audit client wishes to present either condensed or selected financial data derived from previously audited financial statements. As an example, AMAX and McKesson-Robbins experimented with summary annual reports that condensed financial data and presented much of the data in graphic form. They believed that such reports enhanced the ordinary user's understanding of the complexities of the company's financial position and the results of its operations. If the data have previously been audited, then the auditor can report on either condensed financial statements or selected financial data under the circumstances described below.

Condensed Financial Statements. An auditor may be requested to report on condensed financial statements that are derived from, but are presented in a separate document from, audited financial statements. Because such condensed statements are presented in much less detail than complete statements, the auditor should not report in the same manner as for complete statements. To do so might cause the reader to mistakenly believe that the condensed statements include all the disclosures necessary for complete statements.

Condensed financial statements should be labeled as "condensed." Exhibit 22.6 is an example of an auditor's report on such statements.

Selected Financial Data. Selected financial data covering several years are often included in documents containing audited financial statements, such as annual reports to shareholders. If not requested to report on that selected data, the auditor's responsibilities are as described in the previous section under Information Prepared by Client–Not Required by GAAP. If, however, the client engages the auditor to report on such selected financial data, the report should be limited to information that is derived from the audited statements. If the selected data include both financial data derived from audited statements and nonfinancial data, such as number of shareholders or employees, the auditor's report should specifically identify the data covered by the report. The report should indicate:

- That the auditor has audited and expressed an opinion on the complete financial statements.
- The type of opinion expressed.
- Whether, in the auditor's opinion, the information set forth in the selected financial data is fairly stated in all material respects in relation to the complete financial statements from which it has been derived.

Exhibit 22.6

REPORT ON CONDENSED FINANCIAL STATEMENTS

To the Shareholders of Surtic Company:

We have audited, in accordance with generally accepted auditing standards, the consolidated balance sheet of Surtic Company and subsidiaries as of December 31, 1993, and the related consolidated statements of income, retained earnings, and cash flows for the year then ended (not presented herein); and in our report dated February 15, 1994, we expressed an unqualified opinion on those consolidated financial statements.

In our opinion, the information set forth in the accompanying condensed consolidated financial statements is fairly stated, in all material respects, in relation to the consolidated financial statements from which it has been derived.

/s/ Rittenberg & Schwieger, CPAs
Madison, WI
March 22, 1994

Supplementary Information Contained in Auditor-Submitted Documents

Auditors are sometimes requested to prepare and include supplementary information along with the basic financial statements. Such information might include, for example, detailed schedules of selling and administrative expenses, inventory turnover statistics, or an aged accounts receivable trial balance. The auditor's report should cover all of the information contained in an auditor-submitted document. Such documents are sometimes referred to as long-form reports.

The auditor's report should describe the character of the auditor's work and the degree of responsibility the auditor is taking with respect to all of the information contained in the document. Any information that was audited should be covered by an opinion. Information not subjected to audit procedures should be covered by a disclaimer. The report on the supplementary information may be added to the auditor's report on the basic financial statements or may appear separately in the auditor-submitted document. The supplementary information should be clearly identified by referring to page or exhibit numbers, for example, so that the reader knows what is not a required part of the basic financial statements and to what the auditor's report relates. Following is an example of a report disclaiming an opinion on part of the supplemental information:

> Our audit was conducted for the purpose of forming an opinion on the basic financial statements taken as a whole. The information on pages 22–28 is presented for purposes of additional analysis and is not a required part of the basic financial statements. Such information, except for that portion marked "unaudited," on which we express no opinion, has been subjected to the auditing procedures applied in the audit of the basic financial statements; and, in our opinion, the information is fairly stated in all material respects in relation to the basic financial statements taken as a whole.

C–REPORTING ON INTERNAL ACCOUNTING CONTROL

Varying degrees of assurance and types of reports may be provided on an organization's internal control structure. Some reports are formal and widely distributed; other reports convey the auditor's observations on control procedure weaknesses or deficiencies in the design of the control structure to management or the audit committee as uncovered during the audit. Auditors are required to report on the internal control structure and the assessment of control risk when performing a financial audit on governmental units and when performing audits of some financial institutions. The FDIC Improvement Act of 1991 requires management of large banks to issue reports on the internal control structure of the organization and requires auditors to attest to management's representations. The auditors of a service organization's customers may want an opinion on the design or the design and operating effectiveness of the service organization's internal control structure. These reporting situations are discussed in the following sections.

Communication of Internal Control Structure Related Matters Noted in an Audit

In each audit of annual financial statements and each review of interim financial statements, auditors are required by AU 325 to communicate reportable conditions to the company's top management and the audit committee or board of directors. **Reportable conditions** are matters coming to the auditor's attention that represent significant deficiencies in the design or operation of the internal control structure that could adversely affect the organization's ability to record, process, summarize, and report financial data consistent with the assertions of management in the financial statements. Reportable conditions may involve:

- Deficiencies in the design of the system, such as the absence of appropriate segregation of duties.
- Failures in the operation of the controls, such as failure to safeguard assets from misappropriation.
- The absence of a sufficient level of control consciousness within the organization.

The purpose of this reporting is to notify top management so it can decide what to do, if anything, about such conditions.

There are no requirements to perform specific procedures to identify reportable conditions. During the normal course of an audit, such conditions may become apparent when performing procedures to obtain an understanding of the internal control structure or when performing tests of controls or substantive tests. The auditor may be asked to be alert to other situations of particular concern to the client that would not ordinarily be investigated during an audit. The auditor is not precluded from reporting matters other than reportable conditions that would be of value to management.

Material weaknesses may be, but are not required to be, separately identified and communicated from other reportable conditions. A reportable condition may be considered a **material weakness** if the design or operation of the specific internal control structure elements do not reduce to a relatively low level the risk that misstatements in amounts that are material in relation to the financial statements being audited may occur and not be detected within a timely period by employees in the normal course of performing their assigned functions [AU 325.15].

Reportable conditions may be communicated orally or in writing. If done orally, the working papers should document who was told, what they were told, and when they were told. If in writing (see Exhibit 22.7), the report should:

- Indicate that the purpose of the audit was to report on the financial statements and not to provide assurance on the internal control structure.
- Include the definition of reportable conditions.
- Include a restriction on the distribution of the report to the audit committee, management, others within the organization, and, in certain cases, specifically identified regulatory agencies or other third parties.

It should be noted that an audit is not undertaken for the express purpose of reporting on an organization's control structure. In many instances, the auditor will find it economical to perform direct tests of account balances rather than test control procedures. Thus, a report on reportable conditions performed in conjunction with an audit cannot be relied on to cover all conditions that might not have been discovered during the normal course of the audit.

Exhibit 22.7

REPORT ON REPORTABLE CONDITIONS

To the Audit Committee, Crever, Inc.

In planning and performing our audit of the financial statements of Crever, Inc., for the year ended December 31, 1993, we considered its internal control structure in order to determine our auditing procedures for the purpose of expressing our opinion on the financial statements, not to provide assurance on the internal control structure. However, we noted certain matters involving the internal control structure and its operation that we consider to be reportable conditions under standards established by the American Institute of Certified Public Accountants. Reportable conditions involve matters coming to our attention relating to significant deficiencies in the design or operation of the internal control structure that, in our judgment, could adversely affect the organization's ability to record, process, summarize, and report financial data consistent with the assertions of management in the financial statements.

We noted the absence of an effective procedure to account for all shipments. We recommend that you include in your billing program a routine to identify any missing bills of lading numbers and print out a daily exception report to be investigated by someone in the accounting department to ensure that all shipments get billed and recorded.

This report is intended solely for the information and use of the audit committee, management, and others within the organization.

/s/Rittenberg and Schwieger, CPAs
February 28, 1994

Timely communication may be important. Therefore, the auditor may choose to communicate significant matters during the course of the audit rather than wait until its conclusion.

The Auditing Standards Board does not permit auditors to issue a report stating that no reportable conditions were noted during an audit because of the potential for misinterpretation of the limited degree of assurance associated with such a report. Governmental Auditing Standards, however, require a report on internal controls even if reportable conditions are not found.*

In addition to issuing a report on weaknesses in the internal control structure, public accounting firms often issue a separate report, sometimes called a *management letter,* that communicates a variety of observations and suggestions regarding matters not involving the internal control structure. These are constructive suggestions that are intended to help the client become more profitable, for example.

Reporting on a Client's Internal Control Structure over Financial Reporting

Auditors may be engaged to examine and report on management's written assertion about the effectiveness of an entity's internal control structure (ICS) over financial reporting as of a point in time. Such an engagement applies, for example, to auditors of insured depository institutions who examine management's assertions as required by the Federal Deposit Insurance Corporation Improvement Act of 1991. Such an engagement is appropriate when management's assertion is based on reasonable criteria against which it can be evaluated and is capable of reasonably consistent estimates or measurement using those criteria. The proposed standard does not allow the auditor to report directly on the company's ICS *(Statement on Standards for Attestation Services No. 2)*. However, the auditor may issue an opinion on the internal controls of a service organization, covered later in this chapter.

Because the purpose of this report is to express an opinion on management's assertion about the effectiveness of the ICS, the auditor's consideration of the ICS is more extensive than that required for an audit of the financial statements. Knowledge obtained during the audit can be supplemented as needed to form an opinion on management's assertion about the effectiveness of the ICS.

Reasonable Criteria

Criteria issued by the AICPA, regulatory agencies, and other bodies composed of experts are normally considered reasonable criteria for purposes of this report. The specification of criteria is evolving. Broad criteria are contained in AU 319.06, which describes internal controls in terms of policies and procedures that enable the client to record, process, summarize, and report financial data consistent with the assertions embodied in the financial statements. More formal criteria are contained in the report issued by the Committee of Sponsoring Organizations of the Treadway Commission (COSO) titled "Internal Control—Integrated Framework," issued in the fall of 1992. It appears that regulatory agencies may also be issuing statements of criteria.

*See Chapter 24 for a more complete discussion of this report.

Planning the Engagement

The auditor should consider the types of activities of the client that require controls to ensure that the assets are safeguarded against loss and that transactions are properly authorized and recorded to permit the preparation of financial statements in accordance with GAAP. If operations are carried out at multiple locations, the auditor must decide whether to test controls at each location.

Evaluating the Design of the Internal Control Structure

To evaluate the design of the ICS, the auditor should obtain an understanding of the control environment, accounting system, and control procedures by making inquiries, inspecting documents, and observing entity activities and operations as described in Chapter 8. Tests of the effectiveness of the design of a specific ICS policy or procedure are concerned with whether it is suitably designed to prevent or detect material misstatements in specific account balance assertions.

Testing and Evaluating Operating Effectiveness

Before issuing a report on management's assessment of the ICS, auditors must perform tests of controls to determine whether the controls are operating effectively. In a financial statement audit, however, tests of controls need to be performed only on those controls that will allow the auditor to assess control risk at less than the maximum. Tests of controls should be designed to determine how the policy or procedure was applied, how consistently it was applied, and who did it.

The period covered by the tests depends on the nature of the control policy or procedure and the frequency with which they are applied. Some operate continuously, such as credit approval over sales, and others operate only at certain times, such as controls over the taking of physical inventory. The auditor should perform tests of controls over a period of time that is adequate to determine whether the ICS policies and procedures necessary for achieving the objectives of the control criteria are operating effectively.

Forming an Opinion

After obtaining an understanding of the design of the controls and after testing those controls, the auditor should identify any weaknesses in the system and evaluate whether they are material, either individually or together. A weakness may exist, for example, when controls are absent or when a control procedure is not being applied effectively. The accounts payable department, for example, should compare the quantities and prices on vendor invoices with the corresponding purchase order and receiving report. If this procedure is not designed into the system or it is being performed by someone who is lazy or incompetent, the client may pay for products or services that are not received or at prices that are not authorized by the purchasing department.

It should be noted that there may be deficiencies in the ICS but the financial statements may still be fairly presented. A deficiency in the internal control structure does not necessarily mean that financial statements errors will occur but that they are less likely to be prevented by the control structure and if they do occur, they are not likely to be detected. Or, in the example above, the company pays too much for goods and services.

Before issuing the report, the auditor should obtain a written representation letter from management concerning its responsibility for the controls, its performance of an evaluation of the ICS, any irregularities by personnel who have significant roles in the ICS, and whether there were any changes subsequent to the date of management's assessment that might significantly affect the ICS.

Report Requirements

The auditor's report form depends on the manner in which management presents its written assertion. If the written assertion is a separate report that accompanies the auditor's report, the report is considered appropriate for general distribution. The report form is illustrated in Exhibit 22.8.

A different report form is used when management presents its written assertion in a representation letter to the auditor but not in a separate report that accompanies the auditor's report. The board of directors may request the auditor's report without requiring management to present a separate written assertion. The report should be modified to include management's assertion about the effectiveness of the ICS and add a paragraph limiting the distribution of the report to management, others within the entity, and any specified regulatory agency.

Exhibit 22.8

REPORT CONCERNING THE EFFECTIVENESS OF AN ENTITY'S INTERNAL CONTROL STRUCTURE AS OF A SPECIFIED DATE

Independent Accountant's Report

To the Board of Directors and Shareholders of Andreas Company:

We have examined management's assertion that Andreas Company maintained an effective internal control structure over financial reporting as of December 31, 1994, included in the accompanying Management's Assessment of the Internal Control Structure over the preparation of annual financial statements and interim financial statements.

Our examination was made in accordance with standards established by the American Institute of Certified Public Accountants and, accordingly, included obtaining an understanding of the internal control structure over financial reporting, testing and evaluating the design and operating effectiveness of the internal control structure, and such other procedures as we considered necessary in the circumstances. We believe that our examination provides a reasonable basis for our opinion.

Because of inherent limitations in any system of internal control structure, errors or irregularities may occur and not be detected. Also, projections of any evaluation of the internal control structure over financial reporting to future periods are subject to the risk that the internal control structure may become inadequate because of changes in conditions, or that the degree of compliance with the policies or procedures may deteriorate.

In our opinion, management's assertion that Andreas Company maintained an effective internal control structure over financial reporting as of December 31, 1994, is fairly stated, in all material respects, based on criteria of preventing or detecting errors or irregularities in amounts that would be material in relation to the financial statements.

/s/ Rittenberg & Schwieger, CPAs
February 6, 1995

If there are material weaknesses in the ICS that are described in management's assertion, a qualified opinion should be expressed, followed by a separate paragraph describing the weaknesses. If the weaknesses are not described in management's assertion, the weaknesses should be described in a paragraph preceding an adverse opinion.

When reporting on ICS criteria established by a regulatory agency, the report should include material weaknesses coming to the auditor's attention even if not covered by the criteria.

The auditor may be engaged to report on the suitability of the design but not the effectiveness of the ICS. For example, a regulatory agency may require such a report for a new casino before granting a license. In such a case, the report should be modified by referring to the suitability of the design of the ICS in the introductory paragraph and by eliminating reference to testing the effectiveness of the ICS in the scope paragraph. Following is an example of an opinion paragraph:

> In our opinion, management's assertion that Grand Casino's internal control structure over financial reporting is suitably designed to prevent or detect material misstatements in the financial statements on a timely basis as of December 31, 1994, is fairly stated, in all material respects, based on criteria of preventing or detecting errors or irregularities in amounts that would be material in relation to the financial statements.

Reports on the Processing of Transactions by Service Organizations

Some companies use the services of other organizations to process transactions, handle assets, and perform other services. Computer service bureaus provide computing services (such as payroll, general ledger, billing, and inventory control) for their customers. Trust departments of banks may handle pension programs for its customers. There are companies that process mortgage payments for other companies. Auditors of such service organizations **(service auditors)** are sometimes requested to issue *reports on the policies and procedures placed in operation* or on the *policies and procedures placed in operation and tests of operating effectiveness* of the service organization's internal control structure [AU 324]. Such reports are helpful to the auditors of the customers of the service organization **(user auditors)** because part of the customers' control structure often encompasses the controls at the service organization.

Reports covering only the policies and procedures placed in operation can be employed by the user auditors to help obtain an understanding of the client's internal control structure, but such reports should not be relied on for assessing control risk below the maximum because the controls covered by the report were not tested. Reports on policies and procedures placed in operation and *tests of operating effectiveness* may be employed by the user auditor for both obtaining an understanding and, if appropriate, assessing control risk below the maximum.

The service auditor may perform agreed-upon procedures that are substantive in nature for the benefit of user auditors. The results of such procedures may become a part of the evidence necessary to support the user auditor's opinions on the financial statements of their clients. Exhibit 22.9 summarizes the approaches available to the user auditor.

Exhibit 22.9

SUMMARY OF APPROACHES AVAILABLE TO AUDITOR OF A CUSTOMER OF A SERVICE ORGANIZATION

User Auditor	**Service Auditor**
To obtain an understanding of the ICS of the service organization	
May use the service auditor's *Report on Policies and Procedures Placed in Operation*	Issues *Report on Policies and Procedures Placed in Operation* after obtaining an understanding of the ICS but does no testing of controls.
or	
May be able to obtain a sufficient understanding from information available from the client.	
To assess control risk below the maximum:	
May use the service auditor's *Report on Policies and Procedures Placed in Operation and Tests of Operating Effectiveness*	Issues *Report on Policies and Procedures Placed in Operation and Tests of Operating Effectiveness* after testing controls.
or	
User auditor may test client's controls over the activities of the service organization or test controls at the service organization.	
To obtain substantive evidence on user's transactions or assets at the service organization:	
May use service auditor's report	May perform procedures agreed upon by the user organization and its auditor and by the service organization and its auditor and 1. Make specific reference in their report on policies and procedures as having carried out the designated procedures or 2. Provide a separate "special report" on applying agreed-upon procedures (AU 622).
or	
User auditor may perform substantive procedures at the service organization.	

Reports on policies and procedures placed in operation should include a disclaimer of opinion on the operating effectiveness of the ICS and an opinion on whether the description of the ICS that accompanies the report presents fairly, in all material respects, the relevant aspects of the service organization's policies and procedures and on whether they were suitably designed to provide reasonable assurance that the control objectives would be achieved if those policies and procedures were complied with satisfactorily.

Reports on policies and procedures placed in operation and tests of operating effectiveness should include reference to the description of the tests of controls performed and the period covered by such tests; an opinion on whether the policies and procedures that were tested were operating with sufficient effectiveness to provide reasonable, but not absolute, assurance that the related control objectives were achieved during the period specified; a statement that the relative effectiveness and significance of specific service organization policies and procedures and their effect on assessments of control risk at user organizations are dependent on their interaction with the policies, procedures, and other factors present at individual user organizations; and a statement that the service auditor has performed no procedures to evaluate the effectiveness of policies and procedures at individual user organizations.

D–REPORTING ON PROSPECTIVE AND PRO FORMA FINANCIAL STATEMENTS

Prospective Financial Statements

In addition to reporting on historical financial statements, public accountants are sometimes requested to help prepare or to attest to two types of **prospective financial statements**, forecasts and projections. A **forecast** represents an entity's expected financial position, results of operations, and cash flows based on assumptions reflecting conditions expected to exist and the course of action it expects to take. A forecast is appropriate for general use. A **projection** is an entity's expected financial position, results of operations, and cash flows based on one or more hypothetical assumptions. A projection is often used to support a request for a bank loan showing what is likely to happen if the loan is granted, for example, for the development of a shopping center or a new hospital. It shows the expected economic results under certain assumptions. A projection is not appropriate for general use but should be distributed only to the client and those with whom the client is directly negotiating and who can ask questions about the assumptions on which the projection is based.

Statements on Standards for Attestation Engagements include standards for reporting on prospective financial statements [AT 200]. These statements are jointly issued by the Auditing Standards Board, the Accounting and Review Services Committee, and the Management Advisory Services Executive Committee, which have been authorized by the AICPA to issue such standards.

There are three levels of service related to prospective financial statements that a public accountant can provide: compilations, examinations, and applying agreed-upon procedures. The general standards stated in Rule 201 of the Code of Professional Conduct apply to such services: the accountant must be competent, use due professional care, plan the work, supervise any assistants, and perform appropriate procedures before issuing a report.

Compilations of Prospective Financial Statements

A compilation requires the public accountant to review the reasonableness of the assumptions that underlie the prospective statements, test the mechanical accuracy, and otherwise determine that there are not obvious misstatements in the projection.

A compilation, however, does not include testing the validity of the assumptions and is not intended to provide assurance about the accuracy or attainability of the projection. A compilation usually involves reading the statements with their summaries of significant assumptions and accounting policies, and considering whether they appear to be presented in conformity with AICPA guidelines and are not obviously inappropriate. A compilation report is issued describing the broad nature of the accountant's services and disclaiming an opinion on the fairness of the presentation and appropriateness of the assumptions.

A compilation service might be requested by the developer of a proposed new shopping mall. The developer prepares projections based on assumptions regarding demographics of the area, traffic patterns, economic affluence of patrons, and so forth. The accountant performing a compilation tests the mathematical accuracy of the projected statements and reads the assumptions to determine whether they might be obviously inappropriate. The accountant reads the report to determine whether it complies with the applicable accounting standards that specify minimum disclosures, such as a summary of key assumptions.

The standard compilation report on a forecast (Exhibit 22.10) identifies the statements that were compiled by the accountant, states that they were compiled in accordance with the standards established by the AICPA[3], disclaims an opinion, indicates that the prospective results may not be achieved, and states that the accountant does not assume any responsibility to update the report for events and circumstances occurring after the report date. When the presentation is a projection, the report should include a separate paragraph that describes the limitations on the usefulness of the presentation, such as the following:

> The accompanying projection and this report were prepared for the First National Bank of Rhinelander for the purpose of negotiating a loan to expand Jobrace Company's plant and should not be used for any other purpose.

Examinations of Prospective Financial Statements

The examination is the highest level of service an accountant can provide on prospective financial statements. It involves evaluating the support underlying the assumptions, evaluating the prospective financial statements for conformity with AICPA presentation guidelines, and issuing an examination report. The work performed for an examination is much more extensive than for a compilation and is similar to that required in an audit of historical financial statements. In the shopping mall example given above, the accountant would seek evidence on the appropriateness of the assumptions. For example, the accountant might look at census reports and other demographic reports in support of the client's assumptions about traffic and spending patterns expected in the shopping mall. In addition, the accountant must be independent with respect to the client.

The standard examination report on a forecast appears in Exhibit 22.11. In addition to identifying the statements presented, the report includes a statement that the examination was made in accordance with AICPA standards, a brief description of the nature of an examination, and the accountant's opinion that the statements are presented in conformity with AICPA presentation guidelines. Like a compilation report, the examination report also warns the reader that the prospective results may not be achieved and that the accountant has no responsibility to update the report for events occurring after the report date. A report on the examination of a projection includes an additional paragraph restricting the use of the report like that illustrated above for a compilation report.

Exhibit 22.10

COMPILATION REPORT ON FORECASTED FINANCIAL STATEMENTS

We have compiled the accompanying forecasted balance sheet and statements of income, retained earnings, and cash flows of Jobrace Company as of December 31, 1995, and for the year then ending, in accordance with standards established by the American Institute of Certified Public Accountants.

A compilation is limited to presenting in the form of a forecast information that is the representation of management and does not include evaluation of the support for the assumptions underlying the forecast. We have not examined the forecast and, accordingly, do not express an opinion or any other form of assurance on the accompanying statements or assumptions. Furthermore, there will usually be differences between the forecasted and actual results because events and circumstances frequently do not occur as expected, and those differences may be material. We have no responsibility to update this report for events and circumstances occurring after the date of this report.

/s/Rittenberg & Schwieger, CPAs
February 9, 1994

Exhibit 22.11

EXAMINATION REPORT ON A FINANCIAL PROJECTION

We have examined the accompanying projected balance sheet and statements of income, retained earnings, and cash flows of Kavanaugh Company as of December 31, 1995, and for the year then ending. Our examination was made in accordance with standards for an examination of a projection established by the American Institute of Certified Public Accountants and, accordingly, included such procedures as we considered necessary to evaluate both the assumptions used by management and the preparation and presentation of the projection.

The accompanying projection and this report were prepared for the Security National Bank for the purpose of negotiating a loan to build a shopping mall and should not be used for any other purpose.

In our opinion, the accompanying projection is presented in conformity with guidelines for presentation of a projection established by the American Institute of Certified Public Accountants, and the underlying assumptions provide a reasonable basis for management's projection assuming the granting of the requested loan for the purpose of building the Division Fashion Place shopping mall as described in the summary of significant assumptions. However, even if the loan is granted and the mall is built, there will usually be differences between the projected and actual results because events and circumstances frequently do not occur as expected, and those differences may be material. We have no responsibility to update this report for events and circumstances occurring after the date of this report.

/s/Rittenberg & Schwieger, CPAs
November 2, 1994

The accountant should issue a qualified or adverse opinion when the statements depart from AICPA presentation guidelines or when significant assumptions are not disclosed or do not provide a reasonable basis for the prospective statements. The auditor should disclaim an opinion if there is a significant scope limitation.

Applying Agreed-Upon Procedures

In a manner similar to special reports on agreed-upon procedures described earlier in this chapter, the accountant may accept such an engagement in connection with prospective financial statements provided that:

- The users involved have participated in establishing the scope and take responsibility for the adequacy of such procedures.
- The distribution of the report is restricted to the specified users involved.
- The statements include a summary of significant assumptions.

The report should enumerate the procedures performed and indicate that it is intended only for specified users. If such procedures are less in scope than an examination, a disclaimer should be expressed. The report should state the accountant's findings, that the prospective results may not be achieved, and that the accountant has no responsibility to update the report.

Pro Forma Financial Statements

Pro forma financial statements are the profession's version of "what if" statements. That is, they show what the historical financial statements would have been had a consummated or proposed transaction or event occurred at an earlier date [AT 300.04]. They are useful, for example, for proposed business combinations, changes in capitalization, dispositions of segments of business, or sales of securities and the application of proceeds. Pro forma adjustments to historical financial statements should be based on management's assumptions and reflect all significant effects directly attributable to the transaction or event. Such statements should be clearly labeled as pro forma and include a description of the transaction or event. The reporting requirements described below do not apply to circumstances when a transaction consummated after the balance sheet date is reflected in pro forma financial information as required by GAAP.

A public accountant may perform an examination or a review of pro forma financial information under the following conditions:

- The document containing the pro forma information also includes appropriate audited or reviewed historical financial statements.
- The level of assurance provided on the pro forma information is no greater than that provided on the historical financial statements.
- When relevant, the accountant has an appropriate level of knowledge of the accounting and financial reporting practices of each significant constituent part of the combined entity.

Procedures for Pro Forma Statements

In addition to the audit or review procedures applied to the historical financial statements in regard to pro forma statements, the accountant should, among other things:

- Obtain an understanding of the underlying transaction or event by reading the contract and minutes of the board of directors meetings and by making inquiries.

- Discuss with management its assumptions regarding the effects of the transaction or event.
- Evaluate whether pro forma adjustments are included for all significant effects of the transaction or event.
- Obtain sufficient evidence to support such adjustments (the amount and types of evidence needed depend on the level of assurance to be given—an opinion or negative assurance).
- Evaluate the appropriateness of the presentation by management of its assumptions and whether the pro forma adjustments are consistent with each other and with the data used to develop them.
- Determine that the information is properly calculated.

These procedures should be performed for either an examination or a review engagement. However, the accountant would normally obtain more evidence supporting the pro forma adjustments in an examination engagement.

Reports on Pro Forma Statements

The level of assurance given on pro forma statements should be limited to the level of assurance provided on the historical financial statements or, in the case of a business combination, the lowest level of assurance provided on the underlying historical financial statements of any significant constituent part of the combined entity.

A report on the *examination* of pro forma financial information is shown in Exhibit 22.12. The report states that the pro forma information is based on the audited historical financial statements; the objectives of pro forma information; a caveat that the pro forma results might not have been achieved had the transaction or event actually occurred at an earlier date; and an opinion about the reasonableness of management's assumptions, the pro forma adjustments, and the application of the adjustments to the historical financial statements.

Other Attestation Services

As noted in Chapter 2, the scope of attestation services is not limited to financial reports or even to financial data. Public accountants are performing tests of state lotteries, evaluating commercial software to determine whether it performs according to specifications, and reporting on the accuracy of nonfinancial production data governing royalty contracts. The standards for performing such services were discussed in Chapter 2 and closely parallel the standards for the conduct of financial statement audits. The reporting standards provide a framework for reports, but the actual report must specifically note the nature of the assertions examined and the auditor's communication of an opinion on the presentation as judged in relationship to those assertions.

Recall that attestation engagements are intended to result in general-purpose distributions. Thus, the auditor must clearly specify the responsibility taken and whether the assertion is presented in conformity with established or stated criteria against which it was measured. In most situations, the auditor will conduct an examination of the assertion and will issue an attestation report. In some cases, the auditor may not be able to develop sufficient evidence to express a positive opinion and

Exhibit 22.12

EXAMINATION REPORT ON PRO FORMA FINANCIAL INFORMATION

To the Board of Directors of Drycourt Company:

We have examined the pro forma adjustments reflecting the proposed merger described in Note 1 and the application of those adjustments to the historical amounts in the accompanying pro forma condensed balance sheet of Drycourt Company as of December 31, 1993, and the pro forma condensed statement of income for the year then ended. The historical condensed financial statements are derived from the historical financial statements of Drycourt Company, which were audited by us, and of Harden Company, which were audited by other accountants, appearing elsewhere herein. Such pro forma adjustments are based on management's assumptions described in Note 2. Our examination was made in accordance with standards established by the American Institute of Certified Public Accountants and, accordingly, included such procedures as we considered necessary in the circumstances.

The objective of this pro forma financial information is to show what the significant effects on the historical financial information might have been had the proposed merger occurred at an earlier date. However, the pro forma condensed financial statements are not necessarily indicative of the results of operations or related effects on financial position that would have been attained had the above-mentioned merger actually occurred earlier.

In our opinion, management's assumptions provide a reasonable basis for presenting the significant effects directly attributable to the above-mentioned merger described in Note 1, the related pro forma adjustments give appropriate effect to those assumptions, and the pro forma column reflects the proper application of those adjustments to the historical financial statement amounts in the pro forma condensed balance sheet as of December 31, 1993, and the pro forma condensed statement of income for the year then ended.

/s/Rittenberg & Schwieger, CPAs
Madison, WI
June 10, 1994

will express negative assurance. Following is an example of an examination report containing a positive opinion:

To the Board of Directors
XYZ Investment Company

We have examined the accompanying Statement of Investment Performance Statistics of XYZ Fund for the year ended December 31, 1994. Our examination was made in accordance with the standards established by the American Institute of Certified Public Accountants and, accordingly, included such procedures as we considered necessary in the circumstances.

In our opinion, the Statement of Investment Performance Statistics referred to above presents the investment performance of XYZ Fund for the year ended December 31, 1994, in conformity with the measurement and disclosure criteria set forth in Note 1.

/s/ Rittenberg & Schwieger
March 28, 1995

Summary

The arena of attestation activities continually grows. This chapter covered several reporting situations that are summarized in Exhibit 22.13. The nature and extent of procedures and the level of assurance provided vary with each situation. The report must be clear as to the nature of the engagement and the degree of responsibility the accountant is taking.

Exhibit 22.13

SUMMARY OF OTHER REPORTS

Reports on	Level of Assurance	Applicability/Distribution
Special Reports		
Agreed-upon procedures	Disclaimer and negative assurance	GAAP or non-GAAP/Restricted to those knowledgeable about the procedures.
Other comprehensive basis of accounting (OCBOA) (other than GAAP)	Opinion	Must be comprehensive/unrestricted.
Specified elements, accounts, or items of a financial statement	Opinion	Restricted if not in conformity to GAAP or OCBOA.
Compliance with contractual agreements or regulatory provisions	Negative assurance	Restricted to management and the contractor or the regulatory agency.
Application of Accounting Principles	State conclusion concerning the appropriate accounting or type of opinion	GAAP or GAAS/No restrictions per the standards, but normally useful only to the parties requesting the report.
Interim Financial Statements	Negative assurance	GAAP/Unrestricted.
Internal Accounting Control		
At service organizations	Opinion	Unrestricted.
Based solely on a study and evaluation made as part of an audit	Describe reportable conditions	Restricted to management, audit committee, and board of directors.
Opinion on management's assessment of effectiveness	Opinion	Unrestricted.
Supplementary Information		
Prepared by Client		
Not Required by GAAP	Explanatory paragraph if inconsistent with audited information.	GAAP or OCBOA/Unrestricted.

(Continued)

Exhibit 22.13

Reports on	Level of Assurance	Applicability/Distribution
Required by GAAP	Explanatory paragraph under certain circumstances.	GAAP/Unrestricted.
Condensed financial information	Opinion	GAAP/Unrestricted.
Prepared by auditor	Opinion or disclaimer	GAAP or OCBOA/Unrestricted.
Prospective Financial Statements		
Compilation	Disclaimer	GAAP/Forecasts–Unrestricted. Projections–restricted to parties to proposed transaction.
Examination	Opinion	GAAP/Forecasts–Unrestricted. Projections–Restricted to parties to proposed transaction.
Apply agreed-upon procedures	Negative assurance	GAAP/Restricted to those knowledgeable of the procedures.
Pro Forma Financial Information		
Review	Negative assurance	GAAP/Unrestricted.
Examination	Opinion	GAAP/Unrestricted.

Significant Terms

basic financial statements The balance sheet, income statement, cash flow statement, statement of changes in owners' equity, and related footnotes.

forecast An entity's expected financial position, results of operations, and cash flows based on assumptions reflecting conditions expected to exist and the course of action it expects to take.

material weakness A reportable condition that does not reduce to a relatively low level the risk that misstatements in amounts that are material in relation to the financial statements being audited may occur and not be detected within a timely period by employees in the normal course of performing their assigned functions.

other comprehensive basis of accounting (OCBOA) Financial statements not prepared in accordance with GAAP but prepared on a cash or modified cash basis, the basis of accounting used for preparing the income tax return, the basis of accounting required for reporting to a governmental regulatory agency, or some other basis that has a definite set of criteria that have substantial support and apply to all material items appearing in the financial statements.

pro forma financial information Information showing the significant effects on historical financial information had a consummated or proposed transaction occurred at an earlier date.

projection An entity's expected financial position, results of operations, and cash flows based on one or more hypothetical assumptions. A projection is often used to support a request for a bank loan showing what is likely to happen if the loan is granted.

prospective financial statements Financial statements covering one or more future accounting periods. There are two types, forecasts and projections.

reportable conditions Matters coming to the auditor's attention that represent significant deficiencies in the design or operation of the internal control structure that could adversely affect the organization's ability to record, process, summarize, and report financial data consistent with the assertions of management in the financial statements.

service auditors Auditors of service organizations such as a computer service bureau that provide audit reports for user auditors.

special reports Reports on the following types of situations in which the client engages the auditor to perform specific procedures; to report on financial statements prepared in conformity with a comprehensive basis of accounting other than GAAP; to report on specified elements, accounts, or items of a financial statement; or to report on compliance with aspects of contractual agreements or regulatory requirements related to audited financial statements. In addition, they might include some reports based on regulatory requirements.

user auditors Auditors of the customers of the service organization that use audit reports prepared by service auditors.

Review Questions

A–Other Reports on Historical Financial Information

22–1 When might a public accountant be asked to report on agreed-upon procedures? Can the auditor make a statement about the likelihood of misstatements based on agreed-upon procedure engagements?

22–2 What is a special report? When might a special report be issued? What is meant by other comprehensive basis of accounting?

22–3 The distribution of some special reports is restricted. Which ones are restricted? Why are they restricted?

22–4 Can an audit report containing an unqualified opinion be issued on financial statements prepared on the cash basis? How does such a report differ from one issued on GAAP–basis financial statements?

22–5 How does the auditor determine whether a client's proposed statement meets the criteria of an OCBOA?

22–6 Why would a client want to issue OCBOA financial statements when it is specifically noted that they are not prepared in accordance with generally accepted accounting principles?

22–7 Does a public accountant have to follow prescribed procedures and issue a written report when asked to provide advice about the application of an accounting principle or the type of opinion that should be rendered in a specific situation to someone outside the accountant's firm? Explain.

22–8 What level of assurance is provided in a public accountant's review report on interim financial statements?

22–9 How do the disclosure requirements for interim reports differ from those for annual financial statements?

22–10 Under what circumstances would the auditor's report have to be modified because of the interim information contained in the annual report to shareholders?

22–11 What financial statements are normally covered by the audit report on annual financial statements?

22–12 What responsibilities does the auditor have for supplementary information

a. Prepared by the client but not required by GAAP?

b. Prepared by the client and required by GAAP?

c. Prepared by the auditor and included in a document submitted to the client by the auditor?

B–Reporting on Internal Accounting Control

22–13 What are reportable conditions? What is the significance of reportable conditions to the audit of a company's annual financial statements?

22–14 Identify each of the different situations in which the auditor may report on internal control and the type of assurance provided in each case.

22–15 What is a service auditor? Why does the concept of service auditor improve the overall efficiency of the attest function?

C–Reporting on Prospective and Pro Forma Financial Statements

22–16 What are the two types of prospective financial statements? How do they differ? Explain any restrictions on the distribution of such statements.

22–17 How do pro forma financial statements differ from prospective financial statements? What levels of service may the accountant provide related to

a. Prospective financial statements?

b. Pro forma financial statements?

22–18 When are prospective financial statements useful? Of what usefulness is an auditor's report on such statements when they are prospective; that is, the outcome cannot be predicted within a specified limit as are historical financial statements?

22–19 What work is required when the auditor is associated with pro forma financial statements?

22–20 In what reporting situations covered in this chapter can an auditor provide each of the following levels of assurance?

a. An opinion.
b. Negative assurance.

Multiple Choice Questions

*22–21 Accepting an engagement to compile a financial projection for a publicly held company most likely would be inappropriate if the projection were to be distributed to
a. A bank with which the entity is negotiating for a loan.
b. A labor union with which the entity is negotiating a contract.
c. The principal shareholder, to the exclusion of the other shareholders.
d. All shareholders of record as of the report date.

*22–22 An auditor's report on financial statements prepared in accordance with an other comprehensive basis of accounting should include all of the following *except*
a. An opinion as to whether the basis of accounting used is appropriate under the circumstances.
b. An opinion as to whether the financial statements are presented fairly in conformity with the other comprehensive basis of accounting.
c. Reference to the note to the financial statements that describes the basis of presentation.
d. A statement that the basis of presentation is a comprehensive basis of accounting other than generally accepted accounting principles.

*22–23 An accountant who is *not* independent of a client is precluded from issuing a
a. Report on consulting services.
b. Compilation report on historical financial statements.
c. Compilation report on prospective financial statements.
d. Special report on compliance with contractual agreements.

*22–24 An auditor's report would be designated a special report when it is issued in connection with
a. Interim financial information of a publicly held company that is subject to a limited review.
b. Compliance with aspects of regulatory requirements related to audited financial statements.
c. Application of accounting principles to specified transactions.
d. Limited use prospective financial statements such as a financial projection.

*22–25 When reporting on financial statements prepared on the same basis of accounting used for income tax purposes, the auditor should include in the report a paragraph that
a. Emphasizes that the financial statements are *not* intended to have been examined in accordance with generally accepted auditing standards.

*Adapted from the Uniform CPA examination or the Certified Internal Auditor examination.

b. Refers to the authoritative pronouncements that explain the income tax basis of accounting being used.
c. States that the income tax basis of accounting is a comprehensive basis of accounting other than generally accepted accounting principles.
d. Justifies the use of the income tax basis of accounting.

*22–26 Which of the following statements concerning prospective financial statements is correct?
a. Only a financial forecast would normally be appropriate for limited use.
b. Only a financial projection would normally be appropriate for general use.
c. Any type of prospective financial statements would normally be appropriate for limited use.
d. Any type of prospective financial statements would normally be appropriate for general use.

*22–27 If management declines to present supplementary information required by the Governmental Accounting Standards Board (GASB), the auditor should issue a(an)
a. Adverse opinion.
b. Qualified opinion with an explanatory paragraph.
c. Unqualified opinion.
d. Unqualified opinion with an additional explanatory paragraph.

*22–28 When an auditor is requested to express an opinion on the rental and royalty income of an entity, the auditor may
a. Not accept the engagement because to do so would be tantamount to agreeing to issue a piecemeal opinion.
b. Not accept the engagement unless also engaged to audit the full financial statements of the entity.
c. Accept the engagement provided the auditor's opinion is expressed in a special report.
d. Accept the engagement provided distribution of the auditor's report is limited to the entity's management.

*22–29 Negative assurance may be expressed when an accountant is requested to report on the
a. Compilation of prospective financial statements.
b. Compliance with the provisions of the Foreign Corrupt Practices Act.
c. Results of applying agreed-upon procedures to an account within unaudited financial statements.
d. Audit of historical financial statements.

*22–30 When an accountant compiles projected financial statements, the accountant's report should include a separate paragraph that
a. Describes the differences between a projection and a forecast.
b. Identifies the accounting principles used by management.

c. Expresses limited assurance that the actual results may be within the projection's range.

d. Describes the limitations on the projection's usefulness.

*22–31 When an accountant examines a financial forecast that fails to disclose several significant assumptions used to prepare the forecast, the accountant should describe the assumptions in the accountant's report and issue a(an)

a. Qualified opinion.

b. Disclaimer.

c. Unqualified opinion with a separate explanatory paragraph.

d. Adverse opinion.

*22–32 If information accompanying the basic financial statements in an auditor-submitted document has been subjected to auditing procedures, the auditor may express an opinion that the accompanying information is fairly stated in

a. Conformity with generally accepted accounting principles.

b. All material respects in relation to the basic financial statements taken as a whole.

c. Conformity with standards established by the AICPA.

d. Accordance with generally accepted auditing standards.

Discussion and Research Questions

*22–33 (Critique of Report Based on Agreed-Upon Procedures) To obtain information that is necessary to make informed decisions, management often calls on the independent auditor to apply certain audit procedures to specific accounts of a company that is a candidate for acquisition and to report on the results. In such an engagement, the agreed-upon procedures may constitute a scope limitation.

At the completion of an engagement performed at the request of Unclean Corporation, which was limited in scope as explained above, the following report was prepared by an audit assistant and was submitted to the auditor for review:

> To: Board of Directors of Ajax Corporation
>
> We have applied certain agreed-upon procedures, as discussed below, to accounting records of Ajax Corporation, as of December 31, 1993, solely to assist Unclean Corporation in connection with the proposed acquisition of Ajax Corporation.
>
> We have examined the cash in banks and accounts receivable of Ajax Corporation as of December 31, 1993, in accordance with generally accepted auditing standards and, accordingly, included such tests of the accounting records and such other auditing procedures as we considered necessary in the circumstances.
>
> In our opinion, the cash and receivables referred to above are fairly presented as of December 31, 1993, in conformity with generally accepted accounting principles applied on a basis

> consistent with that of the preceding year. We therefore recommend that Unclean Corporation acquire Ajax Corporation pursuant to the proposed agreement.
>
> /s/ CPA firm

Required:
Comment on the proposed report describing those assertions that are

a. Incorrect or should otherwise be deleted.

b. Missing and should be inserted.

22–34 (Critique of Special Report) A staff auditor of Erwachen & Diamond, CPAs, has prepared the following draft of an audit report on cash basis financial statements:

> Accountant's Report To the Shareholders of Halon Company:
>
> We have audited the accompanying balance sheets and the related statement of income as of December 31, 1993 and 1992. These financial statements are the responsibility of the Company's management. Our responsibility is to express an opinion on these financial statements based on our audits.
>
> We conducted our audits in accordance with generally accepted accounting principles. Those principles require that we plan and perform the audit to obtain assurance about whether the financial statements are free of misstatement. An audit includes examining evidence supporting the amounts in the financial statements. An audit also includes assessing the accounting principles used and estimates made by management, as well as evaluating the overall financial statement presentation. We believe that our audits provide a reasonable basis for our opinion.
>
> As described in Note 13, these financial statements were prepared on the basis of cash receipts and disbursements.
>
> In our opinion, the financial statements referred to above present fairly, in all material respects, the financial position of Halon Company as of December 31, 1993, and the results of operations for the year then ended in accordance with generally accepted accounting principles.
>
> /s/ Donald Diamond, CPA
> February 15, 1994

Required:
Identify any deficiencies in the report and explain why they are deficiencies.

*22–35 (Reporting on Income Tax Basis Statements with an Uncertainty) Rose & Co., CPAs, has satisfactorily completed the examination of the financial statements of Bale & Booster, a partnership, for the year ended December 31, 1993. The financial statements, which were prepared on the entity's income tax (cash) basis, include footnotes that indicate that the partnership was involved in continuing litigation of material amounts relating to alleged infringement of a competitor's patent. The amount of damages, if any, resulting from this litigation could not be determined at the time of completion of the engagement. The prior years financial statements were not presented.

Required:
Based on the information presented, prepare an auditor's report that includes appropriate explanatory disclosure of significant facts.

*22–36 (Reporting on Specified Elements, Accounts, or Items) Young & Young, CPAs, completed an examination of the financial statements of XYZ Company, Inc., for the year ended June 30, 1994, and issued a standard unqualified auditor's report dated August 15, 1994. At the time of the engagement, the board of directors of XYZ requested a special report attesting to the adequacy of the provision for federal and state income taxes and the related accruals and deferred income taxes as presented in the June 30, 1994, financial statements.

Young & Young submitted the appropriate special report on August 22, 1994.

Required:
Prepare the special report that Young & Young should have submitted to XYZ Company, Inc.

22–37 (Reporting–Application of Accounting Principles) A public accountant has been asked for her advice on when revenue should be recognized for a specific sales transaction by Terns Manufacturing Company. The product was shipped FOB destination on November 29, 1993, and delivered to the retailer on December 4. The sale is to a retail chain at a fixed price. The buyer has the right to return any unsold product by January 10, 1994, but must pay for any of the product that is sold. The retailer is responsible if the product is lost or damaged while in its possession. The seller has no obligation to help the retailer sell the product. This is the first time the seller has entered into such a contract and does not believe it can develop a reasonable estimate of the amount of product that might be returned in January.

Required:

a. In which of the following cases would a written report be most appropriate? Explain each answer.
    1. The request came from the audit client.
    2. The request came from the seller's auditor.
    3. The request came from the seller's controller, which is audited by another firm.
    4. The request came from an attorney asking the public accountant to serve as an expert witness.
b. What steps should the public accountant take prior to issuing such a written report?
c. Outline the basic sections of such a report and indicate what each section should contain.

22–38 (Internal Control Reports) Compare and contrast the auditor's responsibility for (1) reporting reportable conditions based on an audit of the financial statements and (2) expressing an opinion on management's assessment of its internal control structure over financial reporting in terms of

a. The nature of the engagement.

b. The nature and extent of procedures required before issuing a report.

c. The type of report issued.

22–39 (Reporting on Supplementary Information) When audited financial statements are contained in a document along with supplementary information prepared by the client, explain why the auditor's opinion is not affected when the supplementary information contains a material inconsistency with the audited information. How should the audit report be modified in such a situation?

22-40 (Reporting on Supplementary Information)

Required:
For each of the following independent situations, indicate the auditor's reporting responsibility and, when a report is appropriate, describe the nature of the report.

a. Parate Company's auditor included supplementary statistical information along with the basic financial statements in the document that contains the audited financial statements for the year ended December 31, 1993. The supplementary information is shown in Exhibits A through H in the document and is not audited.

b. Scription Company includes a summary of selected financial data on the first page of its annual report to shareholders covering the years 1984 through 1993. The basic financial statements cover the balance sheets for 1993 and 1992 and the statements of income, retained earnings, and cash flows for each of the three years in the period ended December 31, 1993.

   1. The auditor was *not* asked to report on the selected financial data.

   2. The auditor was asked to report on the selected financial data.

c. Mexcal Oil Company is required by FASB to disclose information about its proven and provable oil and gas reserves. It has done so, and the auditor

   1. Has performed the required procedures and believes the information is

      (a). Presented in conformity with the FASB requirements.

      (b). Is not presented in conformity with the FASB requirements.

   2. Was unable to perform the necessary procedures.

22–41 (Compliance Reports) The auditor is auditing the Inguish Company, which has a bond indenture, dated March 26, 1989, with the Last International Bank of Chicago that contains the following covenants in paragraphs E through I.

Par. E Maintain at least a 2.5:1 current ratio

   i. At the end of each quarter.

   ii. At fiscal year-end.

Par. F Deposit $250,000 into the bond sinking fund by January 1 of each year until the bonds mature.

Par. G Restrict dividend payments to no more than 50 percent of net income each year.

Par. H Make the stated interest payments by the interest dates.

Par. I The company shall conform to all pollution standards.

Required:

a. Under what circumstances is it appropriate for an auditor to report on the compliance of a client with contractual agreements or regulatory requirements?

b. Which of these covenants would it be appropriate to cover in the compliance report to the bond trustee?

c. Give reasons for excluding any of the covenants from the report.

22–42 (Compliance Reports)

Required:

Answer the following concerning the compliance report for the Inguish Company (refer to Question 22–41).

a. Outline the basic elements of a compliance report.

b. Write the paragraph containing negative assurance if

1. All of the covenants have been met.
2. All of the covenants have been met except that the company paid out dividends of $400,000 with net income of only $700,000. The indenture states that if there are any violations of the covenants other than timely interest payments, these are to be reported by the management of the company to the trustee within 45 days of the fiscal year-end, such report to include an explanation of the violation, why it happened, and what management plans to do about it. Management has properly reported this violation, which was caused by the declaration of dividends based on preliminary estimates on net income of $850,000. The decrease in audited net income was the result of an unexpected downturn in the stock market during the last two weeks of the year that created an unrealized loss on decline in the market value of the company's current marketable equity securities.

c. What are the audit implications when the client violates one or more of the bond covenants?

22–43 (General–Other Reports)

Required:

Indicate the level of assurance a public accountant could provide and any restrictions on the distribution of the accountant's report in each of the following independent situations (more than one level may be appropriate):

a. The public accountant has been engaged to

1. Compile a financial forecast.
2. Examine a financial projection.

b. The client has engaged the auditor to report on management's assessment of its ICS over financial reporting.
c. The client has asked the auditor to report on its interim financial statements before they are distributed.
d. The client is engaged in acquisition negotiations with another company. The auditor has been asked to perform certain specified procedures on the accounts receivable, inventory, fixed assets, and accounts payable of the other company.
e. The client has prepared its financial statements on the basis of current values rather than historical cost.

22–44 (Reporting on Interim Financial Information) The auditor has audited the annual financial statements of the Anguishire Company for several years. Management is considering the possibility of having the auditor report on the quarterly financial information for each of the first three quarters of 1994. The report will be distributed to the SEC on Form 10-Q and to shareholders.

Required:

a. Describe the nature of such an engagement and the level of assurance the auditor can provide.
b. Describe the basic procedures the auditor should perform before issuing the report.
c. Contrast the timing of the review procedures (1) when issuing a report to accompany the interim information and (2) when reporting on the quarterly information presented in the annual financial statements without having separately reported on each quarter's financial information.
d. How do the disclosure requirements differ between quarterly and annual financial statements?
e. Outline the basic elements of a report on interim financial information.

22–45 (Reporting on Prospective Financial Information) Systettes Company, an audit client, is planning an expansion program. The National Federal Bank of New London, which will provide the financing, wants a financial projection of Systettes Company's financial position and results of operations for the next five years under the assumption that the bank loan is granted and the proposed expansion occurs. The bank has also requested that the auditor provide the highest level of service that can be provided for projections.

Required:

a. Explain the meaning of the terms *prospective financial statements, financial projections, financial forecasts,* and *pro forma statements.*
b. What types of service may a public accounting firm provide on prospective financial statements? What level of assurance is provided by each type of service?
c. What procedures should the auditor perform before issuing the report?
d. Outline the basic components of the report.

22–46 **(Research–Reporting on the Application of Accounting Principles)** Research the issue in Question 22–37 on revenue recognition and write an appropriate report addressed to Steven Kutil, the controller of Tern's Manufacturing Company.

22–47 **(Research–Supplemental Information Prepared by the Client)** Obtain a recent annual report to shareholders. List the information presented outside the basic financial statements that is related to the audited financial statements and for which the auditor should be sure there are no inconsistencies with the audited information.

Case

22–48 (Attestation Report) The Coalition for Environmentally Responsible Economies (CERES) was formed by the Social Investment Forum and is an alliance of several environmental groups, bankers, and investment fund managers. It was formed to encourage companies to adopt the Valdez Principles (named after the Exxon tanker responsible for the Alaskan oil spill in 1989), which is a set of guidelines for corporate environmental conduct to conserve energy, reduce waste, and market environmentally safe products, for example. CERES intends to sign up companies to adopt these principles, monitor which companies abide by them, and publicize the findings. By doing so, environmentally conscious citizens and investors will be able to decide which firms are best to buy products from, invest in, and work for. Mutual funds have been established to buy shares only in corporations judged to follow the Valdez Principles.

Assume that the AICPA has developed environmental auditing standards. The audit firm has been certified as an environmental auditing company and has done an environmental audit of Exxon Company for the year ended December 31, 1993, in accordance with the environmental auditing standards. Exxon has adopted the Valdez Principles, which are listed in Note 1 to its Environmental Responsibility Report, and the auditor determined that it has abided by those principles.

Required:

Write an attestation report to accompany the Environmental Responsibility Report to be included in the Exxon Company's annual report to shareholders. The Environmental Responsibility Report contains an assertion that the company has followed the Valdez Principles. Be sure that the report conforms to the attestation standards described in Chapter 2.

End Notes

1. *The Future Relevance, Reliability, and Credibility of Financial Information: Recommendations to the AICPA Board of Directors,* signed by the managing partners of the eight largest CPA firms, April 30, 1986.
2. Don Pallais and Robert K. Elliott, "Prospective Financial Statements: Guidelines for a Growing Practice Area," *Journal of Accountancy,* January 1984, 56.
3. Financial Forecasts and Projections Task Force, *Guide for Prospective Financial Statements* (New York: AICPA, 1986).

CHAPTER

23

Learning Objectives

Through studying this chapter, you will be able to:

1. Understand emerging audit tools and techniques designed to increase audit efficiency and effectiveness.
2. Understand how advanced audit procedures are currently implemented by public accounting firms.
3. Develop the ability to use manual and computerized research sources to perform audit and accounting research.
4. Further develop an appreciation of the constantly changing audit environment and how practicing auditors and firms must adapt to advanced technology.

Advanced Audit Techniques and Audit Research

Chapter Contents

Chapter Overview

Auditors regularly use advanced audit tools and techniques and perform practical research on accounting, auditing, and other topics. Several audit tools and techniques have been briefly introduced in previous chapters. In this chapter, more in-depth coverage is provided on analytical procedures, expert systems, automated audit techniques, and accounting and auditing research techniques and sources. All of these tools are designed to enhance the efficiency and effectiveness of audits.

Expert advisers can be expensive, and they're not always available when an urgent call for help goes out. Increasingly, accountants are getting assistance from another source: computer programs that are called expert systems. . . . Aside from providing high-level support on technical issues, a major advantage of expert systems is they allow CPAs to focus on the professional parts of their jobs instead of being distracted by the routine, repetitive tasks.[1]

Analytical procedures are an important part of the audit process and consist of evaluations of financial information made by a study of plausible relationships among both financial and nonfinancial data. Analytical procedures range from simple comparisons to the use of complex models involving many relationships and elements of data. A basic premise underlying the application of analytical procedures is that plausible relationships among data may reasonably be expected to exist and continue in the absence of known conditions to the contrary. [AU 329.02]

A–ANALYTICAL PROCEDURES: ADVANCED TOPICS

Analytical procedures were introduced in Chapter 7 as audit tools that can lead to greater audit efficiency. The term **analytical procedures** is broadly used to signify evidence-gathering procedures that analyze relationships among data items. Synonyms include analytical auditing, analytical review, the business approach to auditing, and performance indicator review. These analytical procedures range from simple comparisons of data for different years to sophisticated computer-based modeling such as regression analysis.

Analytical procedures are used as *attention-directing* procedures and as *substantive audit* procedures. When used as attention-directing devices, the auditor searches for unexpected results that may identify accounts or transactions that merit special audit attention, either alerting the auditor to potential problem areas during the planning stage of an audit or assisting the review partner during the final stages of the audit.

Analytical procedures are also used as substantive audit procedures to address the overall reasonableness of account balances and thereby reduce the extent of other audit tests. Analytical procedures are usually less time consuming than direct tests of account balances. However, the auditor must use caution to assess the reliability of the analytical procedures approach used. They should not be used blindly because their reliability depends on whether a number of important assumptions about the underlying model and data are met. If the analytical procedures support the management assertion being tested, the auditor may reduce or eliminate direct tests of the account balance. If the procedures do not support the assertion tested, more extensive investigation would be warranted.

Research shows that analytical procedures can be highly effective. In a recent study by Wright and Ashton of errors detected during audits, 47.5 percent were initially detected by tests of details, 21.5 percent using expectations from the prior year (such as prior year adjustments), *15.5 percent by analytical procedures*, 13.3 percent through client inquiry, and 2.2 percent by general audit procedures. "Moreover, they [the auditors] believed that analytical review likely would have signaled many errors if some other procedure had not." Comparison with prior year amounts was the analytical procedure that most often signaled the need for adjustment. Experience helps in applying analytical procedures; analytical procedures that were successful in detecting errors were most often performed by auditors with four or more engagements in the client's industry.[2] At the same time, other research shows that analytical procedures, by themselves, especially when used by inexperienced auditors, are *not* very effective in signaling financial statement misstatements. The key to effective use is the ability to form expectations about financial statement balances and to apply healthy skepticism in analyzing the results.

Types of Analytical Procedures: Overview

There are a number of analytical procedures, several of which have been described in previous chapters. For purposes of this discussion, they are classified as

- Trend analysis.
- Ratio analysis.
- Reasonableness tests such as regression analysis.

Trend analysis involves the comparison of an amount for an account for the current year to that of prior years. It is usually calculated as a dollar and/or percent change. A limitation is that it considers only the behavior of a single account and fails to consider account interrelationships. Trend analysis is used primarily to identify potential problems, and the auditor normally looks at trends in related accounts to see if patterns remain the same. A large increase in accounts receivable, for example, may or may not indicate a potential problem, depending on what happened to sales.

Ratio analysis involves the calculation and analysis of relationships between two amounts, such as interest expense and interest-bearing debt. Three types of ratio analysis are frequently used:

- **Financial ratio analysis**—analysis of ratios between financial statement accounts, such as accounts receivable turnover.
- **Common-size statement analysis**—each income statement account balance is shown as a percent of net sales and each balance sheet account balance is shown as a percent of total assets.
- **Nonfinancial ratios**—comparisons of financial and nonfinancial data such as the comparison of number of units produced and production cost, or miles traveled (or gross tonnage hauled) by a trucking company and fuel expense.

A ratio can be compared with that for prior years or other companies or with industry data. Ratio analysis requires analytical thinking by the auditor to determine (1) which amounts are logically related and (2) the significance of the ratio. It can be more effective than trend analysis because it takes into account the logical relationship between accounts.

A reasonableness test involves developing a model to predict an account balance, comparing that prediction with the recorded amount, and determining whether the difference between the predicted value and book value requires investigating. The model can be relatively simple, such as predicting the amount of payroll expense based on the average number of employees and average earnings. More complex models include time-series analysis, cross-sectional analysis, and regression analysis. **Time-series analysis** is the analysis of ratios for a given firm over time. It is a combination of trend and ratio analysis. **Cross-sectional analysis** is the comparison of ratios between firms at a given point in time. **Regression analysis** is a statistical technique used to describe the relationship between the account being audited and other possible predictive factors. These models can be quite reliable, precise, and effective in identifying amounts needing investigation when they are thoughtfully developed and used.

Trend Analysis

Trend analysis includes simple year-to-year comparisons of account balances, graphic presentations, and analysis of financial data, histograms of ratios, and projections of account balances based on the history of changes in that account. It is imperative that the auditor establish *decision rules* in advance to identify unexpected results for additional investigation. One potential decision rule, for example, is that dollar variances that exceed one-third or one-fourth of planning materiality should be investigated. Such a rule is loosely based on the statistical theory of regression models even though regression is not used. Another decision rule is to investigate any change exceeding some percentage. This percent threshold will often be larger for balance sheet accounts than for income statement accounts because balance sheet accounts tend to have larger year-to-year fluctuations.

Simple Year-to-Year Comparisons

Dollar and/or percent changes are calculated for a given account balance (or a grouping of account balances) over one or more periods. Several computer programs, such as the AICPA's *Accountant's Trial Balance,* and spreadsheet programs will automatically calculate these changes for each of the accounts in the trial balance (see Exhibit 23.1).

The auditor can calculate the dollar change, percent change, or both. Using both is most useful in combining percent changes and materiality. A 20 percent increase in telephone expense may be quite insignificant, for example, whereas a 5 percent increase in cost of sales may be very significant when sales has not increased.

Before making these calculations, the auditor should establish a decision rule to determine what dollar and percent change will be considered significant. Professional judgment is required; that is, the auditor considers all pertinent factors, not just the dollar or percentage change. In establishing a decision rule for percentage changes in income statement account balances, for example, the auditor should consider the extent to which each account is likely to change in relationship to the change in sales. Some expenses are relatively fixed, such as depreciation, and would not be expected to vary directly with sales. Others, such as sales commissions, should vary in proportion to the change in sales. When the change is calculated both in dollars and percentage, the auditor may define a significant change as a combination of both, such as a dollar change greater than $50,000 and a percentage change greater than 20 percent. If this decision rule is applied to the changes shown in Exhibit 23.1, it would identify sales returns, overhead and material variances, bad debts, other expenses (interest expense), and income taxes as changing significantly from 1993. The auditor would consider potential explanations for the changes and would, if necessary, modify the audit program to detect whether misstatements exist in the account.

Auditors often use a trend analysis over several years for key accounts, as shown in the following example:

Exhibit 23.1

LEFLAM MANUFACTURING COMPANY
TREND ANALYSIS
($000)

	December 31, 1994	December 31, 1993	Dollar Change	Percent Change
Sales	$29,500	$24,900	$4,601	18.5%
Sales returns & allowances	(600)	(400)	(200)	50.0
Net sales	$28,900	$24,500	$4,400	18.0%
Cost of sales at standard	20,174	17,922	2,252	12.6
Labor variance	108	60	48	80.0
Overhead variance	604	31	573	1830.3
Material variance	(78)	(12)	(66)	530.1
Cost of sales	$20,808	$18,000	$2,808	15.6%
Gross profit	$ 8,092	$ 6,500	$1,592	24.5%
Sales salaries & commissions	811	737	74	10.0
Sales payroll tax	170	155	15	9.5
Employee benefits	162	147	15	10.2
Advertising	347	325	22	6.8
Travel & entertainment	175	160	15	9.6
Promotional literature	95	83	12	14.6
Training	90	110	(20)	−18.1
Misc. selling exp.	29	25	4	15.9
Total selling expenses	$1,879	$1,742	$137	7.9%
Exec/Office salaries	796	711	85	12.0
Admin. payroll tax	210	191	19	9.9
Employee benefits	200	182	18	9.8
Insurance	33	30	3	8.8
Office supplies	15	13	2	17.3
Delivery	23	21	2	10.7
Telephone	9	8	1	12.5
Legal & audit	125	137	(12)	−8.8
Bad debt expense	307	95	212	224.3
Electricity	150	128	22	17.2
Gas	196	174	22	12.4
Travel & entertainment	17	15	2	11.7
Postage	28	20	8	43.0
Depreciation–OB&E	48	47	1	3.1
Off. repair & maint.	4	5	(1)	−16.3
Misc. general exp.	18	17	1	5.5
Total general expenses	$2,181	$1,794	$387	21.6%
Interest expense	924	581	343	59.0
Income taxes	$1,430	$1,097	$333	30.4
Net income	$1,678	$1,287	$391	30.4%

	1994	1993	1992	1991	1990
Gross sales ($000)	$29,500	$24,900	$24,369	$21,700	$17,600
Sales returns ($000)	600	400	300	250	200
Gross margin ($000)	8,093	6,700	6,869	6,450	5,000
Percent of prior year:					
Sales	118.5%	102.2%	112.3%	123.3%	105.2%
Sales returns	150.0	97.5	106.5	129.0	104.6
Gross margin	120.8	133.3	120.0	125.0	100.0
Sales as a percent of 1990 sales	167.6	141.5	138.5	123.3	100

Such analysis provides the auditor with a longer-term perspective of changes in key accounts than is provided in Exhibit 23.1.

Graphic Analysis

Graphic analysis has been shown to be effective in identifying significant or unexpected changes. For example, the sales shown in the preceding example are plotted in Exhibit 23.2 using a microcomputer graphics program. The middle line is drawn freehand to represent an estimate of the trend in sales for the previous four years. The expected value for the current year (1994) can be based on a decision rule. One decision rule is to draw parallel lines on either side of the trend line that encompasses the plotted values for the previous years. Or the lines could represent a variance of one-third or one-fourth of planning materiality. In either case, if the current year value lies within these parallel lines, the procedure does not lead to an expectation of incorrect sales recording. If the book figure lies outside these boundaries, the auditor can determine the significance of the problem by noting the difference between the recorded sales and the closest boundary. If the historical pattern shows significant fluctuations or cycles, this simple graphing procedure will not be as reliable because the boundaries will be relatively far from the trend line. Other common graphic tools include histograms and comparative plotting of accounts. Variation in sales is common, which is why the auditor needs to look at relationships with related accounts such as cost of sales.

Ratio Analysis

Ratio analysis is more effective than simple trend analysis because it takes advantage of economic relationships between two or more accounts. It is widely used because of its power to identify unusual or unexpected changes in relationships. Ratio analysis is useful in identifying whether a significant difference exists between the client results and a norm, such as industry ratios or between auditor expectations of client results and actual results. It is also useful in identifying potential audit problems that may be evidenced in ratio changes between years such as inventory turnover.

Comparison of ratio data over time for the client and its industry can yield useful insights. For example, the percent of sales returns and allowances to net sales for the client may not vary significantly from the industry average for the current period, but comparing the trend over time may provide an unexpected result, as shown in the following example.

	1994	1993	1992	1991	1990
Client	2.1%	2.6%	2.5%	2.7%	2.5%
Industry	2.3%	2.1%	2.2%	2.1%	2.0%

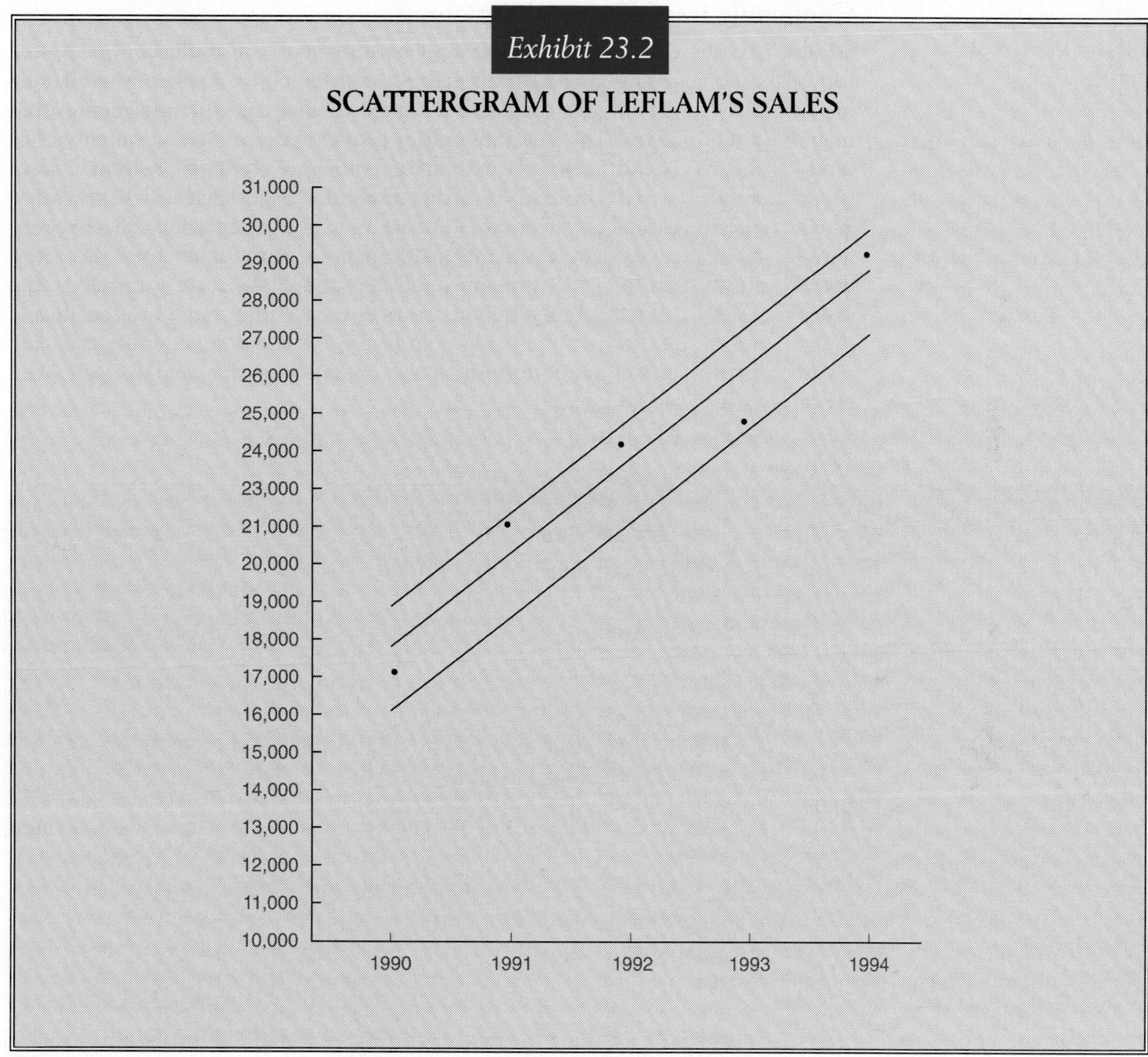

This comparison shows that even though the 1994 percentage of sales returns is close to the industry average, the client's percentage declined significantly from 1993 while the industry's percentage increased. In addition, except for the current year, the client's percentages exceeded the industry average. The result is unexpected, and the alert auditor investigates the potential cause. Possible explanations include the following:

- The client has improved its quality control.
- Sales returns for 1994 were not recorded until 1995.
- Fictitious sales have been recorded in 1994.

The auditor must design audit procedures to identify the cause of this difference to determine whether a material misstatement exists.

Commonly Used Financial Ratios

Exhibit 23.3 shows a number of commonly used financial ratios, the computational formulas, and an example using the financial information for LeFlam Manufacturing Company for 1994. The ratios are designed to elicit specific information that may indicate problems. The first three ratios provide information on potential liquidity problems. The turnover and gross margin ratios are often very helpful in identifying fraudulent activity or items recorded more than once, such as fictitious sales. The leverage and capital turnover ratios are useful in evaluating going concern problems or adherence to debt covenants. Although the auditor chooses the ratios deemed most useful for a client, many auditors routinely calculate and analyze the ratios listed in Exhibit 23.3 on a trend basis over time. Other ratios are specifically designed for an industry. In the banking industry, for example, auditors calculate ratios on percentages of nonperforming loans, operating margin, and average interest rates by loan categories.

Exhibit 23.3

COMMONLY USED RATIOS

Ratio	Formula	LeFlam ($000)
Short-term liquidity ratios:		
Current ratio	Current Assets / Current Liabilities	$19,073 / $3,346 = 5.700
Quick ratio	(Cash + Cash Equivalents + Net Receivables) / Current Liabilities	($100 + $5,444) / $3,346 = 1.657
Current debt to assets ratio	Current Liabilities / Total Assets	$3,346 / $21,070 = .159
Receivable ratios:		
Accounts receivable turnover	Credit Sales / Accounts Receivable	$28,900 / $5,444 = 5.309
Days sales in accounts receivable	365 / Turnover	$365 / $5.309 = 68.75
Inventory ratios:		
Inventory turnover	Cost of Sales / Ending Inventory	$20,808 / $13,385 = 1.555
Days' sales in inventory	365 / Turnover	365 / 1.555 = 234.7
Profitability measures:		
Net profit margin	Net Income / Net Sales	$1,678 / $28,900 = 5.81%
Return on equity	Net Income / Common Stockholders' Equity	$1,678 / $4,676 = 35.89%
Financial leverage ratios:		
Debt to equity ratio	Total Liabilities / Stockholders' Equity	$16,394 / $4,676 = 3.506
Liabilities to assets	Total Liabilities / Total Assets	$16,394 / $21,070 = .778
Capital turnover ratios:		
Asset liquidity	Current Assets / Total Assets	$19,073 / $21,070 = .905
Sales to assets	Net Sales / Total Assets	$28,900 / $21,070 = 1.372
Net worth to sales	Owners' Equity / Net Sales	$4,676 / $28,900 = .162

The ratios in Exhibit 23.3 are the ones most commonly used. The auditor develops specific ratios for the client based on the industry. For example, for a drug company, the auditor analyzes research and development expense as a percent of sales. Financial institutions would emphasize interest rate ratios.

Common-Size Statements

Another useful form of ratio analysis is common-size statements, shown in Exhibit 23.4 for LeFlam's income statement. Net sales is set at 100 percent and all other accounts are shown as a *percent of net sales* for each year presented. A common-size balance sheet can also be prepared, showing each item as a *percent of total assets*. Common-size statements can be prepared in a time-series format with percentages for several years or in a cross-sectional format with comparative percentages for other firms or the industry. Many of the common-size percentages have intrinsic meaning because of their economic relationship, such as gross profit to net sales.

Industry Data Sources

There are a number of sources of individual company and industry data. Several agencies of the federal government, such as the Small Business Administration, the

Exhibit 23.4

LEFLAM MANUFACTURING COMPANY
COMMON-SIZE INCOME STATEMENT

	December 31, 1994	December 31, 1993
Sales	102.1%	101.6%
Sales returns & allowances	−2.1	−1.6
Net sales	100.0%	100.0%
Cost of sales at standard	69.8	73.2
Labor variance	0.4	0.2
Overhead variance	2.1	0.1
Material variance	−0.3	−0.1
Cost of sales	72.0%	73.5%
Gross profit	28.0%	26.5%
Sales salaries & commissions	2.8	3.0
Sales payroll tax	0.6	0.6
Employee benefits	0.6	0.6
Advertising	1.2	1.3
Travel & entertainment	0.6	0.7
Promotional literature	0.3	0.3
Training	0.3	0.4
Misc. selling exp.	0.1	0.1
Total selling expenses	6.5%	7.1%

	December 31, 1994	December 31, 1993
Exec/Office salaries	2.8	2.9
Admin. payroll tax	0.7	0.8
Employee benefits	0.7	0.7
Insurance	0.1	0.1
Office supplies	0.1	0.1
Delivery	0.1	0.1
Telephone	0.0	0.0
Legal & audit	0.4	0.6
Bad debt expense	1.1	0.4
Electricity	0.5	0.5
Gas	0.7	0.7
Travel & entertainment	0.1	0.1
Postage	0.1	0.1
Depreciation–OB&E	0.2	0.2
Off. repair & maint.	0.0	0.0
Misc. general exp.	0.1	0.1
Total general expenses	7.5%	7.3%
Interest expense	3.2	2.4
Income taxes	4.9	4.5
Net income	5.8%	5.3%

Department of Commerce, the Department of the Treasury, and the Federal Trade Commission, provide industry information through the U.S. Government Printing Office. The U.S. Department of Commerce, for example, prepares the *U.S. Industrial Outlook* providing annual prospects for 350 industries.

Businesses such as Dun & Bradstreet, Moody's, Robert Morris Associates, and Standard & Poor's also provide industry information. Dun & Bradstreet publishes *Industry Norms and Key Business Ratios* each year. It is available in paperback and electronic formats and contains 800 lines of business. The norms and ratios are based on the financial statements of over one million private and public companies. Moody's publishes manuals with financial information for specific industries, such as public utilities, municipalities and governments, transportation, banks, and finance companies.

Robert Morris Associates is an association of bank loan officers. It publishes *RMA Annual Statement Studies*, presenting composite financial data based on its loan customers covering over 350 industries. The studies are based on financial statements of companies with loans from the members of the association and do not necessarily represent averages of all companies in a particular industry. The data format includes common-size income statements, balance sheets, and 13 ratios for each industry. The data are presented by company size and the ratios are presented by quartiles for five years. The studies are published each fall with financial information as recent as March 31 of each year. The annual studies contain an appendix that references other sources of composite industry financial data.

Standard and Poor's Corporation Records is published quarterly with daily updates and reports the following information for most publicly owned companies:

- Capitalization.
- Corporate background.
- Major customers.
- Locations.
- Subsidiaries.
- Order backlog.
- Capital expenditures for each of several years.
- Number of employees.
- Classes of stock, number of shares issued, and related information.
- Names of officers and directors.
- Name of auditors.
- History of sales, operating income, and depreciation and amortization expense.
- Three years of income statement information.
- Two years of balance sheet information.

Computer accessible databases containing ratios are also available, such as the Industrial Compustat File. Information about individual firms can be obtained directly from their annual reports and from computerized databases such as DISCLOSURE, the AICPA's National Automated Accounting Research System

(NAARS), and LEXIS/NEXIS. DISCLOSURE and NAARS are described later in this chapter. Many industries have trade associations that publish statistics useful to the auditor.

Caution. Such information is usually unaudited and may not be as reliable as desired. Care should be taken when using ratio analysis on industry data because the data might not be directly comparable for some accounts to that of the client because of

- Different accounting methods.
- Different product mixes.
- Geographic differences.
- Different financial or ownership structures.
- Different types of customers.

Also, industry data are not always calculated the same way as the client does. Some data sources, for example, calculate inventory turnover using cost of sales as a basis, but others use sales as the basis.

Reasonableness Tests

There are several types of **reasonableness tests,** ranging from simple to complex. Usually, most of these techniques involve developing a model to estimate an account balance using other financial or nonfinancial data. The auditor must (1) identify one or more **independent variables** that are likely to have a predictive value for the amount under consideration (the **dependent variable**), (2) develop a model that reflects the relationship between those variables, (3) use the model to estimate what the dependent variable should be, and (4) obtain appropriate evidence for any significant difference between the estimated value and the book value.

Related Factors

A key to the successful use of reasonableness tests is the identification of logical factors related to the dependent variable. Some examples of related factors are shown in Exhibit 23.5. Note that the data used in making the predictions are not limited to financial statement data. With a little imagination and a lot of understanding of the client's operations, auditors can often take advantage of these tests, resulting in a more efficient and effective audit.

Caution. The auditor must determine the reliability of any nonfinancial data used for these tests. Controls over the data should be considered before placing much reliance on the results of tests using those data. Operating data from a well-controlled database, for example, is likely to be reasonably reliable.

Nonstatistical Models

Simple reasonableness tests do not require sophisticated mathematics or statistics. Interest expense, for example, can be estimated using an average interest rate, the average amount of interest-bearing debt outstanding, and the average time such debt was outstanding.

Exhibit 23.5

EXAMPLES OF RELATED FACTORS

Dependent Variable	Independent Variables
Hotel or hospital room revenue, apartment lease revenue	Number of rooms/apartments, average occupancy rate, and average room rate
Professional association membership fee revenue	Number of members by type of fee and the membership fees
Airline revenue	Average load factor and average ticket price
Interest revenue/expense	Average interest rate, average amount of interest-bearing investments/debt, and average time outstanding
Sales commissions	Sales and commission rate
Office salary expense	Average number of office employees and average salary
Wage expense	Average number of employees, average hourly rate, estimated hours worked–regular and overtime
Author royalty expense for a book publisher	Number of books sold, average book price, and average royalty rate
Accrued payroll	Average daily payroll and number of days accrued
Accrued vacation pay	Weekly pay, number of weeks vacation earned, and percent of vacation taken before year-end

Advantages. One advantage of such a simple test is *efficiency*. If the book value of interest expense seems reasonable when compared with the estimated value, the auditor can save time by not having to recalculate interest expense for each interest-bearing debt using actual rates and time. Another advantage is *effectiveness* if the auditor carefully considers all significant factors and their relationships to the balance being modeled.

Regression Analysis

Two problems exist when using reasonableness tests: (1) determining what relationship exists between the dependent and independent variables and (2) determining whether a "significant difference" has occurred. Regression analysis is a statistical technique that can provide information to help solve these two problems. A **simple regression model** includes just one independent variable. A **multiple regression model** includes two or more independent variables. Regression analysis can be used for time-series analysis or cross-sectional analysis. **Time-series regression analysis** is used for predicting a dependent variable based upon the historical relationship between that variable and one or more other financial or nonfinancial independent variables. A *simple time-series regression application* is the prediction of the current year sales by month based on a two- or three-year history of the monthly relationship of sales to cost of sales. Predicted sales are then compared with recorded sales, and any significant differences can be identified. If the auditor does not have adequate evidence to explain the significant differences, additional evidence is needed. A *multiple time-series application* is the prediction of the dependent variable based on a number of independent variables, such as predicting office overhead expense for the current year based on square feet of office space, the age of the building, the number of office employees, and the number of clients served during the previous 10 years. At least 10 periods or data points are needed for a reliable regression model.[3]

Cross-sectional regression analysis is used for predicting an amount, such as an account balance, based on independently predicting variables from the same period: data from other firms, the industry, or across different units of the client's business, such as sales branches or inventory locations. For example, auditors cannot economically observe inventory at each location of a client that has 600 retail outlets. Regression analysis can be used to identify locations that seem out of line with the other stores. Inventory amounts at each store may be predicted based on the sales, floor space, and price-level index at each location. The auditor may choose to observe the inventory at those stores that appear to be out of line or perform additional alternative procedures.

Computer assistance is readily available through most spreadsheets and some graphics computer programs to perform simple regression analysis. Special statistical programs, such as *Statistical Programs for the Social Sciences (SPSS)* or *ANSWERS* (sold by Financial Audit Systems) may be needed for multiple regression models. Many public accounting firms have developed their own regression software. Deloitte & Touche, for example, has a program called *Statistical Techniques for Analytical Review (STAR)*, which is available for microcomputers and can be licensed by other organizations. It is a sophisticated regression program that can be used for time-series or cross-sectional analysis, single or multiple independent variables. It integrates audit decisions about materiality, reliability, and other audit objectives with regression analysis and certain other statistical techniques.[4] Examples of regression analysis applications include predicting

- Monthly sales based on cost of sales and selling expense.
- Airline and truck company fuel expense based on miles driven and fuel cost per gallon.
- Maintenance expense based on production levels.
- Inventory at each branch location of a retail company based on store sales, store square footage, regional economic data, and type of store location.

Simple Time-Series Regression Analysis Illustrated. Sales and cost of sales figures are available for LeFlam Manufacturing Company by month. The auditor wants to predict the current year sales based on the relationship between sales and cost of sales during the previous 24 months. Note that in predicting the monthly sales, the auditor has already established the reliability of the cost of goods sold account for the current period. The simple regression can be used to identify any months during the current year in which there is a significant difference between the predicted sales and recorded sales and to signal the need for more directed investigation.

There has been a close correlation between sales and cost of sales during the past two years, as shown in Exhibit 23.6. Note that the data points fall close to the trend line. The distance between each data point and the trend line represents fluctuations in the dependent variable not explained by fluctuations in the independent variable. Such fluctuations are referred to as **residuals.** That trend line is a physical representation of the regression relationship between the two variables. The formula for that relationship takes the form of

$$y_i = a + bx_i$$

where

y_i = Value of the dependent variable for time period i
a = A constant
b = The regression coefficient
x_i = Value of the independent variable for time period i

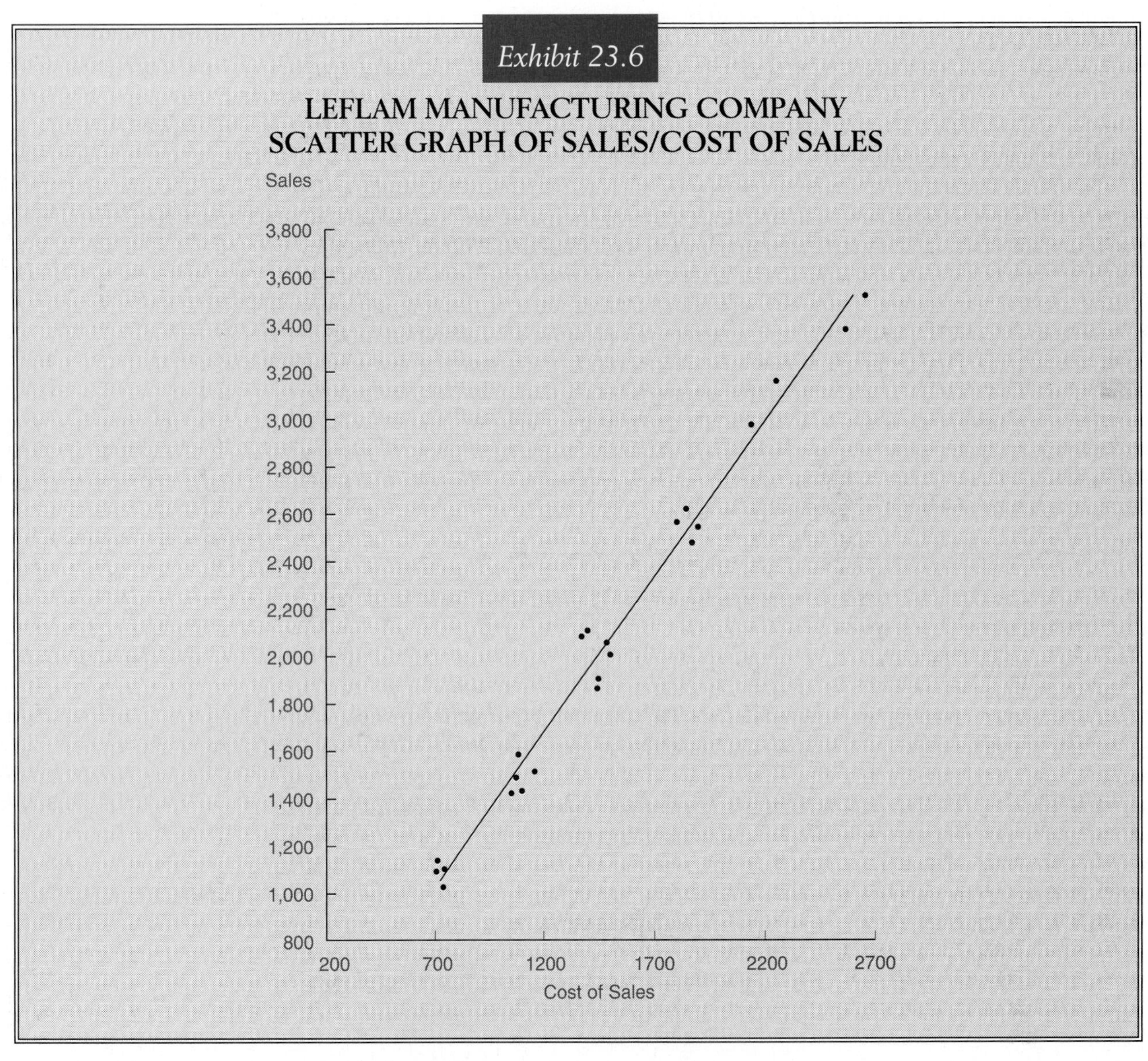

If the line in Exhibit 23.6 were extended down and to the left, it would cross the y axis (vertical axis) at some point. That point is referred to as the *constant* (a). The slope of the curve reflects the coefficient (b) of the relationship between sales (y) and cost of sales (x). The monthly data are entered into a computer program that calculates the values for the constant (a) and regression coefficient (b). The results are shown in Exhibit 23.7. The regression formula is

$$y_i = 80.20622 + (1.332973 \times x_i).$$

A regression formula can be determined for one or more independent variables. The auditor must be sure that there is a significant relationship between the dependent variable and the independent variable(s). The quantitative measure of this relationship is called the *coefficient of determination,* or more simply R^2. R^2 represents the percentage of the total fluctuation in the dependent variable that is explained by the fluctuation in the independent variable. In Exhibit 23.8, R^2 is .984150, which means that the fluctuations in cost of sales explains over 98 percent of the fluctuations in sales. The R^2 relationship is one of correlation, not causation, and the auditor should interpret the changes with some caution. But recall that the auditor has selected variables on the basis of their expected relationships. Some authors suggest that the regression equation should be disregarded if R^2 is less than 70 percent.[5] A significant decrease in R^2 from prior periods also alerts the auditor to the possibility that some other factor is affecting the account balance.

In applying the model to determine whether additional audit investigations are necessary, monthly sales are projected using the computed regression formula. For example, the projected sales for the first month of the current year (month 25) is calculated as follows:

$$\$1,261 = \$80.20622 + (1.332973 \times 886)$$

Differences between projected sales and book sales can be calculated for each month of the current year and analyzed for any significant differences that should be investigated. A *significant difference* should be related to materiality as discussed earlier in this chapter. Planning materiality for LeFlam is $175,000. One decision rule is to consider one-third of planning materiality as a significant difference (approximately $58,000). If such a decision rule is used, the sales recorded in months 26, 29, 31, and 36 should be investigated. Recorded sales for the year exceed predicted sales for the current year by $200,000. The differences can be efficiently investigated by concentrating on the causes of the differences in the four months of deviations noted. For example, possible explanations for the difference in month 36 include

- Special promotion of items with high markups.
- Cutoff errors affecting cost of sales or sales.
- Fictitious sales.
- Double billing of sales.

The auditor prioritizes the most likely explanations and systematically searches for the cause of the unexpected results.

Another approach to identifying a significant difference is to calculate the probability that an individual fluctuation is due to more than a random chance. A reasonable assumption in regression analysis is that each difference from the predicted value is the net effect of many minor unpredictable factors. If any difference is significantly improbable according to the normal probability distribution, there is

Exhibit 23.7

LEFLAM MANUFACTURING COMPANY
REGRESSION ANALYSIS OF 1994 SALES

Month	Cost of Sales	Sales: Actual	Sales: Projected	Sales: Residual
1	$ 709	$ 1,114	$ 1,025	$ 89
2	1,052	1,413	1,482	−69
3	1,781	2,570	2,454	116
4	2,546	3,398	3,474	−76
5	2,130	2,975	2,919	56
6	1,447	1,898	2,009	−111
7	1,402	2,104	1,949	155
8	1,066	1,471	1,501	−30
9	1,088	1,582	1,530	52
10	1,440	1,856	2,000	−144
:	:	:	:	:
23	1,853	2,490	2,550	−60
24	735	1,004	1,060	−56
Total	$35,000	$48,579	$48,579	$ -0-
25	$ 886	$ 1,211	$ 1,261	$−50
26	1,294	1,736	1,805	−69
27	2,185	3,001	2,993	8
28	3,062	4,207	4,162	45
29	2,606	3,613	3,554	59
30	1,762	2,379	2,429	−50
31	1,630	2,321	2,253	68
32	1,309	1,795	1,825	−30
33	1,317	1,828	1,836	−8
34	1,735	2,403	2,393	10
35	2,111	2,924	2,894	30
36	911	1,482	1,295	187*
Total	$20,808	$28,900	$28,700	$ 200

*–This month's sales should be investigated more fully because the residual exceeds the 95% confidence bound for overstatement.

Regression Output:

Constant	80.20622
Std err of Y est	96.58185
R^2	0.984151
No. of observations	24
Degrees of freedom	22
X coefficient(s)	1.332973
Std err of coef.	0.036065

prima facie evidence that some unusual factor, such as a misstatement, may be causing some or all of this difference. A statistically based *decision value* can be calculated as follows:

Decision Value = Standard Error of the Y Estimate × Confidence Coefficient

If a difference between the recorded amount and predicted amount exceeds this value, it should be investigated. The confidence coefficient is based on the desired confidence level and whether the auditor is testing for overstatement, understatement, or both:

	Confidence Coefficient	
Desired Confidence Level	Testing for Overstatement or Understatement	Testing for Both
95%	1.65	1.96
90%	1.28	1.65

The standard error in Exhibit 23.7 is 96.58185. If the auditor is testing for *overstatement only,* the decision value for a 95 percent confidence level is 159.36 (1.65 × 96.58185). There is a 95 percent probability that the residual will be less than 159.36 unless there is an error in that recorded amount. Month 36 (the last month of the current fiscal period) should be investigated because the residual exceeds the decision value. If the auditor is testing for *understatement only,* there are no months during which the decision value is exceeded by a negative residual value. This result tells the auditor that no extra testing of the recorded values needs to be performed. If the auditor is testing for *both overstatements and understatements,* there is a 90 percent probability that any positive or negative residual should be less than 159.36 unless there is an error in the recorded amount. Only the residual for month 36 exceeds the decision value.

Multiple Regression Analysis. Multiple regression involves two or more independent variables, with a formula that takes the form

$$y = a + b_1x_1 + b_2x_2 + \ldots + b_n x_n$$

where:

y = Dependent variable

a = Constant

b_1 = Coefficient of first independent variable

x_1 = First independent variable

b_2 = Coefficient of second independent variable

x_2 = Second independent variable

b_n = Coefficient of last independent variable

x_n = Last independent variable

Some multiple regression programs evaluate each independent variable for its contribution to the model and discard any that are not individually significant for predicting the dependent variable. Other computer programs provide statistics and let the auditor decide whether to drop or add any variables or manipulate the data for time lags and seasonality.

Sources, Independence, and Reliability of Independent Variables. Independent variables for both the base period and current period must be *reasonably accurate* and must be obtained from sources that are independent of the dependent variable. The auditor should be knowledgeable enough about such data to understand what it purports to show and then to decide whether it should be used. Internal sources of data include previously audited data, the basic accounting records and financial statements, production and shipping reports, personnel records, and other operating data. The independence and accuracy of internal sources depend on the internal control structure and whether the internal data have been tested through audit procedures.

The auditor might use multiple regression to predict inventory at each branch location of a retail company based on store sales, store square footage, regional economic data, and type of store location. Using several independent variables is likely to improve the predictive ability over simple regression.

Considerations for Using Regression Analysis. Factors to consider when choosing between regression analysis and other analytical procedures include the following:

- Efficiency.
- Needed levels of precision and reliability.
- Existence of reliable independent variables.
- Whether the dependent variable cannot be predicted with a simpler procedure, such as a simple algebraic calculation.
- Extent that the regression data lend themselves to audit interpretation.
- Extent that the regression assumptions are met.*

Models to Predict Bankruptcy

Auditors are required to consider the possibility that a client will not continue as a going concern. Often the auditor knows that the client is in financial difficulty, but there is a multitude of other factors present that make the decision concerning whether to modify the audit report difficult. Independent, objective, and proven models can assist the auditor in making this assessment. Auditors often use key indicators to predict the likelihood of bankruptcy of their clients. These indicators include the following:

- Excess of current liabilities over current assets.
- Negative net worth.
- Insufficient cash flow from operations to meet debt maturities.
- Loan default.
- Restructuring of debt or leases.

Such indicators, however, do not always indicate potential bankruptcy. Restructuring leases, for example, may be the result of economic changes that allow the client

*The regression assumptions are described in Appendix A.

to obtain more favorable lease terms—a good business decision unrelated to financial difficulties.

A number of studies of bankruptcies have shown that certain combinations of ratios have good predictive power in indicating the likelihood of bankruptcy. Altman developed two combinations of weighted ratios to produce a score of potential bankruptcy (called the **Altman Z-score**), a five-ratio model for publicly owned manufacturing companies and a four-ratio model for public or privately owned manufacturing and service companies.[6] His work has been replicated and newer models represent only slight variations of his original model. The Z-scores are calculated as shown in Exhibit 23.8. Z-scores falling below 1.81 in the five-ratio model or below 1.1 in the four-ratio model indicate high potential for bankruptcy. Scores above 2.99 in the five-ratio model or above 2.6 in the four-ratio model indicate very little potential for bankruptcy.

The formula using the Z-score weights and ratios for public and private companies is applied to the LeFlam Manufacturing Company for 1994 as follows (in thousands of dollars):

Z-score = 6.56 × 0.746, where 0.746 is the ratio of working capital to total assets,
+ 3.26 × 0.170, where 0.170 is the ratio of retained earnings to total assets,
+ 6.72 × 0.191, where 0.191 is the ratio of pre-tax earnings to total assets,
+ 1.05 × 2.725, where 2.725 is the ratio of net worth to total liabilities,
= 9.593.

The resulting score indicates that LeFlam is unlikely to go bankrupt in the near future because the score is well in excess of 2.6. The main factors are (1) the relatively large ratio of working capital to total assets and (2) high earnings before interest and taxes to total assets. The company is very liquid and has good operating results.

Exhibit 23.8

ALTMAN Z-SCORE MODELS

Z-score for Publicly Owned Manufacturing Companies			Z-score for Public and Private Service and Manufacturing Companies	
Weight	Ratio		Weight	Ratio
1.2 ×	Working capital to total assets		6.56 ×	Working capital to total assets
+1.4 ×	Retained earnings to total assets		+3.26 ×	Retained earnings to total assets
+3.3 ×	Return on total assets		+6.72 ×	Earnings before interest and taxes to total assets
+.99 ×	Sales to total assets		+1.05 ×	Net worth to total liabilities
+.6 ×	Market value of equity to total debt			
1.81		High potential for bankruptcy if Z-score <		1.1
2.99		Very little potential for bankruptcy if Z-score >		2.6

Another business risk indicator is called **A Score.**[7] It uses designated values for 17 characteristics of a business related to management and its structure, the information system, company response to changes affecting the business core, major decisions and consequences, and warning signs. The characteristics used are well-known signs that have preceded business failures. They include a chief executive who dominates his or her colleagues (8 points), a passive board of directors (2 points), no budgetary control (3 points), overexpansion (15 points), and creative accounting (4 points). If a company had all of these characteristics, its A Score would be 32. Any combination of characteristics with a total score of 25 or more is a warning of potential business failure. The A Score is a subjective tool that presents a good complement to the Z Score but because of its subjectivity should not be used alone.

Analytical Procedures–Summary

Exhibit 23.9 is a summary of the types of analytical procedures, the focus of the procedures, and a brief explanation. The usefulness and reliability of analytical procedures depends on several factors:

- More reliability can be obtained by applying the procedures to disaggregated data, such as sales by product line, than can be obtained from aggregated data.
- Analytical procedures can be used as an attention-directing tool when the risk of the existence of a material misstatement is high. It can be used as a means to reduce direct tests of an account balance if such risk is low.
- Regression analysis tends to be more reliable than simple trend analysis.

Analytical procedures should be performed by experienced auditors who are in the best position to know what to expect. One of the most exciting and promising tech-

Exhibit 23.9

SUMMARY OF ANALYTICAL PROCEDURES

Type of Analytical Procedure	Focus	Explanation
Trend analysis	A single account balance, such as sales, accounts receivable, or cost of sales	Analyze dollar and/or percent change in account balance from prior year(s).
Ratio analysis: • Financial ratio analysis • Common-size statement analysis	Relationships between balances, such as interest expense and interest-bearing debt or sales and cost of sales	Calculate ratios and compare with prior year, competitor, and industry ratios.
Reasonableness tests: • Simple models • Time-series regression analysis • Cross-sectional regression analysis	Relationships between financial and operating data, such as payroll expense and number of employees and average pay	Estimate what the balance should be based on relationships over time and with other accounting and nonfinancial data.

nological audit developments in recent years is expert systems. A major focus of this development is analytical procedures because (1) they are important in identifying risk areas and detecting misstatements and (2) audit experience is needed to make effective use of such procedures. Expert systems can capture that audit experience for use by less experienced auditors, as discussed in the next section.

B–EXPERT SYSTEMS IN AUDITING

Expert systems represent a branch of computer science more broadly referred to as *artificial intelligence.* Today's development of expert systems for auditing is just one approach to assist auditors in making nonroutine judgments or replacing human judgment with that of the computer program. Other artificial intelligent approaches include neural networks (emulating the thought process of the brain) and knowledge-based systems (systems that will learn from their mistakes). To date, however, most of the auditing applications have been expert system approaches.

The appeal underlying expert systems in auditing is intuitive:

- Some individuals are recognized "experts" in dealing with their subject matter. CPA firms have experts in industry areas such as financial institutions or in functional areas such as statistical sampling and computer auditing. These experts have proven that they have the ability to make consistently superior judgments.
- Computers have become both more powerful and faster. Today's microcomputers can store and process millions of instructions.
- Software packages have been developed to implement rules that can emulate an expert's approach to decision making.
- Auditors have to make a number of complex decisions on most audit engagements. An expert system can serve as a decision aid by pointing out factors that designated experts use in making similar decisions.
- Expert systems can assist in training auditors.

The use of expert systems is not new to auditing. Internal control questionnaires represent a manual form of expert system. The "experts" identified the important control procedures for each cycle or functional area of the business and developed related questions for the auditor to ask when obtaining an understanding of the internal control structure. Strengths and weaknesses could be identified to allow the auditor to tailor substantive audit procedures to the potential misstatements that were identified as being likely to occur. Today's computerized expert systems extend the same concept to other forms of audit decision making.

Ideally, an expert system is capable of learning. Once a decision is recommended, feedback can be used to communicate whether the decision was correct. The new information can be fed back into the system as new knowledge that may be useful in making subsequent recommendations. Most applications of expert system technology have not progressed to the point of "learning," although such technology is expected to emerge by the late 1990s. Expert systems ideally should be developed for ill-structured decision environments, such as estimating the allowance for uncollectible accounts when unique human judgment is required.

Rule-Based Expert Systems

Most of the expert system applications used by auditors are rule-based systems. The designer of the system identifies the pertinent factors considered by an expert in making a decision and links those factors together in a set of decision rules. Most of the systems are arranged in hierarchies of if–then rules and *decision results* to emulate an expert's decision process. An example of the rule linkage of an expert system to evaluate the control environment of a savings and loan client is shown in Exhibit 23.10.

As a review of Exhibit 23.10 indicates, the permutations of rules and potential outcomes can quickly become quite large. With only three simple questions on the existence and effectiveness of audit committees, seven rules were needed to capture the potential outcomes of interest to the auditor (12 combinations of outcomes were possible, but not all were used in the auditor's analysis). The evaluation of audit committee effectiveness would be combined with the evaluation of other control environment factors to assist in formulating an audit assessment of control risk. But the auditor cannot be satisfied with only an assessment of risk. An expert system, like an expert auditor, should consider the possible effect of each answer concerning the audit and suggest modifications of the audit approach due to the specific risks present in the client's environment. One can envision that the development of such an expert system would take considerable time.

Practical Problems with Expert Systems

Capturing Expertise

Who is an expert? What differentiates an expert from other competent auditors in an organization? Can the full thought process of an expert be captured? These are

Exhibit 23.10

DECISION RULES TO EVALUATE CONTROL ENVIRONMENT OF A SAVINGS AND LOAN INSTITUTION

1. Does an independent audit committee exist?	*Yes*	*No*	
2. Is the audit committee considered to be effective?	*Yes*	*Moderately*	*No*
3. Do both the internal auditor and external auditor meet regularly with the audit committee?	*Yes*	*No*	

Rule 1 *If* answers to 1, 2, and 3 are yes, *then* audit committee is evaluated as 1 (low risk).
Rule 2 *If* answer to 1 is no, *then* audit committee is rated as 3 (high risk).
Rule 3 *If* answer to 2 is no, *then* audit committee is rated as 3 (high risk).
Rule 4 *If* answer to 2 is moderate and answer to 3 is yes, *then* audit committee is rated as 2 (moderate risk).
Rule 6 *If* answer to 2 is moderate and answer to 3 is no, *then* audit committee is rated as 3 (high risk).
Rule 7 *If* answers to 1 and 2 are yes and answer to 3 is no, *then* audit committee is rated as 2 (moderate risk).

These rules deal only with one part of the control environment (the existence of an audit committee). The ratings of the audit committee component will be linked with the auditor's evaluation of other control environment factors such as management integrity, financial distress, and so on to formulate an assessment of control environment risk.

the practical problems faced by the developers of expert systems. Various approaches have been utilized. A common approach is to perform protocol analysis whereby the expert is given a problem set and is asked to "think aloud" as he or she solves the problem. The designer then attempts to capture the logic embodied in the thought process. The decision context is expanded for more complex situations and the decision logic is reviewed with the expert after various iterations of the software development. An alternative approach that has been successfully used in developing an expert tax system is to put auditors in front of a one-way mirror and have them explain each step they follow in preparing a tax return and identifying tax planning issues. Experts sitting behind the mirror may add questions. The process and underlying logic are captured by the designer. Although the process of identifying and capturing expertise is improving, it still represents a major limitation: it is difficult to capture all of human expertise and formulate it into a logic system.

Verification

How does one conclude that an expert system is really expert? A number of approaches have been used, but none are considered satisfactory. Three approaches have been most widely used:

1. Compare the expert system's response to that of the original expert using the same set of data. The responses should be consistent.
2. Compare the expert system's responses with that of other experts analyzing the same problem with the same set of data.
3. Compare the expert system's responses with "correct" responses for the same problem set encountered in practice.

The first approach measures internal consistency and should be a "given" for expert systems. The second approach is a step toward validating the thought process of the expert by other experts and should be used. The last approach is preferred, but unfortunately, it is often difficult to tell whether a decision is right or wrong unless there is litigation or some other unforeseen event. Audit committee effectiveness, for example, may have been inappropriately evaluated as high, but the effect on the audit of making the wrong decision may have been minimal because of other compensating factors.

Maintenance

One thing that should be clear is that the audit environment changes rapidly. New accounting and auditing pronouncements seem to be issued on a monthly basis, the client environment changes, and even a firm's audit approach may change. Some of the changes may be significant to an expert system. Like any complex software, the programmer must make the necessary changes without altering the logic of the other decision rules and then verify that the system is still generating "preferred" answers.

Inappropriate Use

At the current stage of development, expert systems are considered a decision aid. Because the systems developed in the audit context are not yet capable of learning, most of the systems are not sufficiently developed to the extent that they should replace human judgment. Expert systems can be useful in ensuring that important factors are considered in a systematic fashion. But there may be something unique about the client's environment not considered by the expert system. It is expected that the auditor will consider the recommended course of action by the expert system but at the same time will consider other information and override the recommendation of the expert system when appropriate. Further, the profession needs to ensure that it will continually develop expertise to face the challenges of an ever-changing environment. If an auditor always subrogates decisions to a computer model, individual expertise will not be developed.*

Potential Role of Expert Systems in Litigation

As discussed in Chapter 3, many audit decisions are made with one eye on potential litigation implications. The decisions of expert systems are no different. Consider the potential courtroom scene in which an auditor is attempting to justify a decision that was different than one recommended by the firm's "experts" as codified in an expert system. Why wasn't the expert system decision used? Alternatively, an auditor could be accused of blindly following an expert system recommendation without considering all the relevant factors applicable to the unique situation of the audit client. These litigation scenarios are not sufficient to completely stifle the development of expert systems, but they are real-world concerns that affect the development and use of many audit tools.

Expert Systems in Use

Expert systems have been developed to assist auditors in preparing corporate tax returns, assessing the adequacy of the allowance for uncollectible accounts, assessing the adequacy of the provision for loan loss reserves in financial institutions, assessing the control risk present in transaction cycles, evaluating the adequacy of computerized controls, and evaluating the financial strength of a savings and loan and assigning a risk factor ranking to it based on criteria established by the FSLIC. Many of these developments involve difficult situations in which the firm has attempted to capture the expertise of an auditor who seems to be better at identifying and solving audit problems.

Three of the most prominent expert systems developed to date by accounting firms are in the tax area, the loan allowance area, and the control assessment area.

Expert-Tax

Coopers & Lybrand has developed *Expert-Tax* to assist its auditors in preparing corporate tax returns and identifying tax planning issues for their clients. Auditors are responsible for identifying and gathering tax information on most audits, and in some situations, are responsible for the initial preparation of the client's tax return. Admittedly, the preparation of a tax return is complex and the rules are constantly changing. Coopers & Lybrand developed *Expert-Tax* at great cost by presenting various tax information to tax experts and having them walk through the development

*Note that the type of expertise discussed here is different than the type using decision aids in structured parts of the audit such as using a computer to calculate the sample size needed for a PPS sampling application or selecting the sample based on criteria furnished by the auditor. The important judgments in sampling (materiality, error definition, and population definition), for example, are still made by the auditor. Sampling formulas and methodologies are well established. The auditor needs to understand the assumptions behind the models but does not have to be an expert at calculating sample size. Similarly, the auditor must develop expertise in recognizing potential problems with receivables collection; such expertise cannot fully be delegated to a computer.

of the tax return and tax planning items. The resulting logic was further reviewed and refined by tax partners into a system that is capable of handling complex tax matters at a highly accurate rate.

LoanProbe

LoanProbe was developed by KPMG Peat Marwick to assist auditors in making the complex decision involving the likely collectability of the outstanding loans of a commercial bank. The system was developed using "expert" commercial loan auditors. The system consolidates all loans made to one entity (or a set of related entities), identifies and evaluates the collateral related to each loan, analyzes changes in the loan customer's industry and other pertinent information about the competitiveness of the customer, and analyzes other financial information about the customer. The expert system evaluates each loan (or set of loans) to a customer and assesses the likelihood of repayment by the customer. The individual loan assessments can be combined into an overall assessment of a loan-loss estimate for the client.

One difficulty in using *LoanProbe* is that it requires the analysis of all individual loans and is time consuming to employ. There is a potential efficiency trade-off between using expert systems and analytical procedures. An analytical model of the adequacy of the loan loss reserve might model past-due accounts, industry economic factors, geographic concentration of loans, the financial health of particular industries or regions, and the value of collateral to estimate the needed loan loss reserve. The analytical model may be accurate over a period of time. The expert system would have required the auditors to explicitly evaluate the economic factors affecting each major customer. One potential, and efficient, use of *LoanProbe* is to have individual financial clients use the system to develop a preliminary estimate of loan loss reserves, which could be evaluated by the auditor.

Control Procedure Evaluation and Control Risk Assessment

Assessing the impact of a wide variety of control procedures that could be implemented in a transaction processing cycle and linking that assessment to specific audit procedures that should be performed is a complex task. Although not formally designated as expert systems, some public accounting firms have developed systems to assist the auditor in making the control risk evaluation and linking that evaluation to specific audit procedures. Many of these systems also capture and document information and the auditor's analysis. It is expected that such expert systems will be used on most large audits on a regular basis.

C–COMPUTERIZED AUDIT TECHNIQUES

Public accounting firms and internal audit departments are increasingly using computer technology to assist in the audit process. Microcomputers that incorporate the latest technology are faster and more powerful than the mainframe computers of a few years ago. Auditors have access to client financial data, computerized libraries of information, and audit assistance software. Microcomputer software can be used to

- Help plan and administer audit engagements.
- Help evaluate risk.
- Customize standard documents.
- Prepare flowcharts.
- Prepare working papers.
- Interact with clients' computers to generate reports and download data for analysis.
- Plan, select, and evaluate samples (covered in Chapter 10).
- Perform common mathematical functions such as calculating depreciation expense, loan and lease amortization, ratios, and other analytical procedures (covered in Chapter 10).
- Help research client and industry background information and accounting and auditing topics.

As noted here, software is available from the AICPA and other software vendors, and large public accounting firms have developed their own software or have worked with vendors to create software. The sections that follow describe some of the more common types of software used by auditors.

Plan and Administer Engagements

Software is available to provide on-the-job project management assistance to analyze, document, and manage the hours expended and the timeliness of an audit engagement. The AICPA markets a program called *Engagement Manager* that can be used to develop time budgets for an engagement, record time and expenses, analyze and revise estimates to complete the engagement, modify the time budget, and print reports. It can be used to provide partners with a weekly executive summary of each engagement to assist them in spotting problems. Many public accounting firms have developed their own engagement administration programs.

Other software provides personnel information to help assign individuals to audit engagements based on such information as their training, types of experience, job evaluations, and years of experience.

Evaluate Risk

Software has been developed to help identify and analyze exposures and risks and to assist in setting audit priorities for an internal audit department. The Institute of Internal Auditors markets a software package called *Audit Master Plan* that assists in risk identification and provides time-reporting and other engagement administration capabilities.

Some public accounting firms have developed software tools to assist in evaluating clients' internal control structure. Using information about the client, risk evaluation programs identify relevant control structure policies and procedures and generate questionnaires tailored to each client. Other programs help identify audit risks in the client's EDP environment based on the auditor's responses to questions about such things as the type of equipment, networking capabilities, and distributed processing.

Customize Standard Documents

Public accounting firms have standard documents such as audit programs, audit reports, confirmation letters, questionnaires, and checklists. In most audits, however, the standard documents require additions, deletions, and modifications to fit a specific client. Software that contains these standard documents and that can be used to make the necessary changes has been developed. The revised documents can be saved for use in the next audit. The AICPA provides a software package called *Audit Program Generator (APG)* that can be used to customize audit programs and, when combined with other electronic library items, can customize

- Checklists for audit planning, engagement review, financial statement disclosures, and tax law compliance.
- Internal control questionnaires.
- Compilation and review programs.

An example of an audit program generated using APG was presented in Exhibit 13.11.

As previously discussed, many large public accounting firms have developed their own audit program software. Coopers & Lybrand, for example, has software called *Automated Audit Program* that not only helps create audit programs but, for each audit procedure, indicates what management assertion(s) the procedure tests and whether it is the primary or secondary test for that assertion. Arthur Andersen & Co. has a program called *Engagement Administration System (EASY)* that includes copies of the firm's standard documents that can be modified using its word processing features. Based on the auditor's answers to key questions, EASY identifies the standard forms relevant for the risk assessment and planning, administrative, and financial reporting areas of the engagement. Standard word processing software is often used for this purpose. Practitioners Publishing Company sells a product called *Guideware* that contains standard documents and word processing capabilities.

Prepare Flowcharts

Manually preparing flowcharts of a client's internal control and accounting systems can be a very tedious task. Auditors can often use flowcharts prepared by the client. When such flowcharts are not available, auditors can use a flowcharting program developed by the public accounting firm or a software company. Commercially available programs have standard flowcharting symbols of various sizes, automatic line connecting features, and automatic centering of words within a symbol. Symbols can be rearranged electronically making it relatively easy to update flowcharts for changes in a client's system.

Prepare Working Papers

Many audit working papers have a standard format. The trial balance may have columns for the account or account grouping title, cross-references, the balance per books, adjustments and reclassifications, the final balance, and the prior year balances. Lead schedules and trial balances have the same columns from year to year. The cash lead schedule, for example, contains balances for each cash account and totals for all cash accounts. These totals also appear on the cash line(s) of the trial balance. Totals on these working papers change when adjusting and reclassifying entries are recorded and they require footing and cross-footing. Software programs are available that create lead schedules from the information entered into the trial balance, post adjusting and reclassification entries to lead schedules and the trial balance, and foot and cross-foot these working papers. Many of these software programs can also calculate ratios and dollar and percent changes from the prior year, prepare consolidated financial statements, and track information to assist in income tax return preparation.

Assist in Sampling Applications

Most firms have computer software to assist in sampling applications. The form can range from relatively simple spreadsheet templates to sophisticated expert systems. This software can assist in planning, selecting, evaluating, and documenting both nonstatistical and statistical samples. The software often includes a random number generator and/or a program to select a dollar interval sample with a random start for PPS sampling.

One example of a decision aid is the expert system developed by McGladrey & Pullen called *Sampling/CPA*. It asks the key questions a statistical expert would ask when deciding what sampling method and sample size to use and what the sample results mean. Two key questions for a statistical substantive test of an account balance, for example, are "Do you anticipate a material error in the population?" and "Do you expect to find any errors of understatement in the population to be sampled?" Based on the auditor's answers to these and other key questions concerning such factors as the audit objective, risk, tolerable error, expected error, and population size, the program suggests a sampling method and sample size.

D–ACCOUNTING AND AUDITING RESEARCH

It is difficult for professional accountants to know or remember all of the accounting and auditing standards of the profession, of different industries, of regulatory agencies, and of their firm. Professionals are often confronted with new accounting, disclosure, and reporting situations, some of which are not covered by the professional literature. Accounting and auditing standards change frequently. Auditing standards require auditors to "study, understand, and apply new pronouncements on accounting principles and auditing procedures as they are developed by authoritative bodies within the accounting profession" [AU 210.04]. New types of businesses, business transactions, and methods of financing evolve over time. One of the main reasons CPAs are required to earn continuing education credits is to keep up-to-date with these changes. Clients and other individuals and organizations often seek technical assistance from professional accountants on the application of new accounting standards, reporting requirements, or business practices. It is, therefore, important to know how and where to do the necessary research, which is an integral part of a professional's activities. This section of the chapter identifies several research sources by topic.

Accounting Issues

Several research sources are available for accounting issues including the accounting standards themselves; agreements reached by the Emerging Issues Task Force; SEC pronouncements; GAAP guides; industry audit and accounting guides; firm specialists, subject files, and publications; financial report surveys; technical "hotlines" to experts at the AICPA or state society of CPAs; and textbooks and published articles. These are explained in the following sections.

Accounting Standards

The primary source of accounting and disclosure requirements for organizations *other than state and local governments* can be found in the *FASB Accounting Standards; Current Text—General Standards, Current Text—Industry Standards,* and Original Pronouncements. They contain the following pronouncements:

- FASB Statements of Financial Accounting Standards.
- FASB Interpretations.
- FASB Technical Bulletins.
- AICPA Accounting Principles Board Opinions.
- AICPA Accounting Research Bulletins.
- AICPA Accounting Interpretations.

The format of the *current text* volumes facilitates research: all of the pronouncements are arranged by subject. The *general standards* volume contains standards generally applicable to all enterprises. More than 27 FASB statements, interpretations, and technical bulletins relating to accounting for leases, for example, are integrated in section L10 of the general standards volume. The *industry standards* volume contains the accounting standards relating to specific industries.

The *original pronouncements* volumes contain all of the pronouncements listed above in their original form and in chronological order. They contain the following information that is not included in the current text volumes:

- Background information.
- Basis for conclusions, including a discussion of factors deemed significant by members of the FASB in reaching their conclusions.
- Dissents or disagreements by members of the FASB with any of its statements or interpretations.

Consensus Views of the Emerging Issues Task Force

The Emerging Issues Task Force (EITF) was established in 1984 by the FASB to help it identify emerging issues. It is made up of 11 members from CPA firms, 4 from industrial companies, an observer from the SEC, and a representative from the

FASB. If a consensus is reached by the task force (15 of the 17 members), no action is usually needed by the FASB, and the consensus views become de facto GAAP. The FASB publishes a summary of the issues considered by the EITF in a loose-leaf service entitled *EITF Abstracts.*

Pronouncements of the Securities and Exchange Commission

The SEC issues several pronouncements that are relevant to publicly owned corporations and their auditors. In 1982, the SEC began issuing *Financial Reporting Releases (FRR)* that cover the SEC's views and interpretations relating to financial reporting. Prior to 1982, such pronouncements were called *Accounting Series Releases (ASRs). Accounting and Auditing Enforcement Releases (AAER)* cover enforcement actions involving accountants. *Staff Accounting Bulletins (SAB)* cover the interpretations of, and practices followed in, the Division of Corporate Finance and the Office of the Chief Accountant of the SEC in administering the disclosure requirements of the federal securities laws. The FRRs, AAERs, and SABs, along with correspondence with the SEC concerning auditor independence, are published by Commerce Clearing House in a volume entitled *SEC Accounting Guide,* which is updated periodically. In that publication, the FRRs are presented in their original form and the ASRs, as modified by FRRs, are codified and organized by topic.

Regulation S-X states the requirements applicable to the form and content of financial statements. It covers such topics as the qualifications and reports of accountants, instructions for specific financial statements, and special provisions concerning financial statements of foreign securities issuers. A companion pronouncement called *Regulation S-K* states the disclosure rules of the SEC. Both of these regulations are quite specific and must be followed by corporations filing with the SEC, requiring accountants and auditors for such corporations to be very familiar with those regulations. *Regulation S-X* and *Regulation S-K* are available from the U.S. Government Printing Office and most of the major printing companies that print the documents filed by corporations with the SEC, such as Pandick, Inc.

State and Local Government Accounting Standards

The Governmental Accounting Standards Board (GASB) has arranged the following material in its publication *Codification of Governmental Accounting and Financial Reporting Standards,* which is updated annually:

- GASB statements, interpretations, technical bulletins, and concepts statements.
- Statements and interpretations by the National Council on Governmental Accounting (NCGA).
- AICPA industry audit guide—*Audits of State and Local Governmental Units*—and related statements of position (SOPs).

Individual pronouncements are available on a subscription, standing order, or individual basis. These pronouncements apply only to state and local governments. Standards for other not-for-profit organizations such as hospitals, colleges and universities, and voluntary health and welfare organizations are issued by their respective associations and the FASB.

Industry Audit and Accounting Guides

The AICPA and many of the large public accounting firms have developed accounting and auditing guides for specific industries. These guides describe the distinctive characteristics of the industry, alert the auditor to unusual problems, and explain regulations and other special factors of the industry. They also illustrate financial statement treatment and the form and wording of auditors' reports when applicable. The AICPA publishes in paperback form, in a loose-leaf subscription service, and in electronic format (described later) auditing and accounting guidelines for a number of industries (see Exhibit 23.11).

Firm Specialists, Subject Files, and Publications

Individuals within a firm are often designated as *specialists* in a particular industry or audit area. One individual may be a specialist in the audit of banks, for example, and another in the audit of utilities. Someone may be the specialist on SEC requirements. The firm may have a person or a group of people designated to help answer accounting and auditing questions on specific subjects and who are available for consultation when needed.

Some public accounting firms maintain a *subject file* containing the firm's experiences with unique accounting, reporting, auditing, and other matters. When auditors are confronted with an unusual situation, they can check the subject file to see whether someone else has already dealt with it. If so, they can learn from the other person's experience. If not, they will have to do additional research, consult with specialists, and try to resolve the situation. They can then add their experience to the subject file to share with others. These subject files take many forms, including microfilm, microfiche, and computer data files on floppy and compact disks.

Many firms publish documents that explain new accounting and auditing standards, some of which include application illustrations.

Financial Report Surveys

The AICPA publishes two series of actual examples of the accounting and audit reporting practices followed in stockholder reports. *Accounting Trends & Techniques*

Exhibit 23.11

AICPA INDUSTRY AUDIT AND ACCOUNTING GUIDES

Guides are available for the following industries:
- Agricultural producers and agricultural cooperatives
- Airlines
- Banks
- Brokers and dealers in securities
- Casinos
- Certain nonprofit organizations
- Colleges and universities
- Construction contractors
- Credit Unions
- Employee benefit plans
- Entities with oil- and gas-producing activities
- Federal government contractors
- Finance companies
- Investment companies
- Property and liability insurance companies
- Providers of health care services
- Savings and loan associations
- State and local governmental units
- Stock life insurance companies
- Voluntary health & welfare organizations

is published annually and contains analyses of 600 stockholders' reports each year. It shows how and to what extent different forms, techniques, and terminology are used in corporate financial statements. It also examines individual elements of the financial statements and auditor's report. Pronouncements of the FASB and SEC are cited along with examples of compliance. Comparative tables show the extent to which specific terminology and techniques are currently used and the trends in reporting practice.

The second series, *Financial Report Surveys*, is designed to supplement the "overview" provided by *Accounting Trends & Techniques*. These surveys include numerous illustrations of actual accounting and audit reporting topics, such as disclosure of related-party transactions, reporting accounting policy changes, and departures from the standard audit report.

Technical Hotlines

The AICPA has a *Technical Information Service (TIS)* to answer technical questions about the application of accounting standards, auditing standards, and the code of professional conduct. This "hotline" service is available to members by telephone. Hundreds of selected inquiries are published under the title *Technical Practice Aids* that are available in paperback and loose-leaf subscription form. This publication also includes AICPA Statements of Position and Practice Bulletins, which provide guidance on issues not covered in the FASB accounting standards or the SASs. In addition, more than 1,300 questions and answers handled by TIS are available in electronic form, described later.

Many state societies of CPAs have a similar hotline service available to their members. A practitioner can call the society's office, describe the nature of the problem, and the society puts the caller in touch with another practitioner who may be able to help.

Auditing and Other Attestation Issues

Many of the research sources described above as relating to accounting issues also relate to auditing and other attestation issues. There are a number of additional research sources including the professional standards, studies and guides concerning auditing procedures, audit manuals and disclosure checklists, and industry audit risk alerts.

Professional Standards

The primary source of auditing and other attestation standards is contained in the AICPA's *Professional Standards*, published as a two-volume paperback and loose-leaf service by Commerce Clearing House. Volume I contains the Statements on Auditing Standards, auditing interpretations, and Statements on Standards for Attestation Engagements, including standards for financial forecasts and projections. The SASs and interpretations have the prefix AU and are arranged in sections generally according to the ordering of GAAS. Volume II contains the code of professional conduct and standards for compilations and reviews, as well as topics related to international accounting and auditing, consulting services, tax practice, quality control, and performance of quality reviews. The Statements on Auditing Standards, Statements on Standards for Attestation Engagements, and Statements on Standards for Accounting and Review Services are each separately published in paperback form and updated periodically.

Auditing Procedures Studies and Guides

The AICPA publishes a paperback series called *Auditing Procedures Studies*. It covers such topics as using the work of internal auditors, auditing the allowance for credit losses of banks, auditor's use of microcomputers, audits of inventories, and the use of confirmations. Guides specifically related to auditing are included in the AICPA series of audit and accounting guides and cover such topics as audit sampling and consideration of the internal control structure.

Audit Manuals and Disclosure Checklists

The AICPA, public accounting firms, and publishing companies have procedures manuals for audit and other services. These manuals often include helpful ideas and references to other sources that can be of assistance in a research project. They cover such topics as compilation and review engagements, audits of small businesses, auditor's reports, and audits of local governments. These guides include references to professional standards, audit programs, checklists, standard forms and letters, and illustrative working papers and reports. Some of these guides are also available in electronic form that allows the user to (1) view such things as standard audit programs, letters, reports, and checklists; (2) load them into a word processor; (3) customize and print them; and (4) save them for the next year using a client extension in the data file name.

There are so many disclosure requirements that a comprehensive checklist is used even by the most experienced auditor or accountant. The large public accounting firms develop their own checklists. The AICPA and commercial companies publish checklists. The AICPA, for example, publishes paperback checklists and illustrative financial statements for corporations in general and for many of the same industries listed in Exhibit 23.11.

Industry Audit Risk Alerts

It is imperative that the auditor knows the current risks that are unique to the client's industry when planning and performing an audit. The AICPA publishes *Industry Audit Risk Alerts* to advise auditors of current economic, industry, and professional developments for most of the same industries listed in Exhibit 23.11. Some public accounting firms develop their own risk alerts.

Indexes to Periodicals

Periodicals often contain useful information, but it is impossible for an individual to subscribe to and read very many of these. Indexes to periodicals, including the *Accountants Index*, the *Business Periodicals Index*, and *The Wall Street Journal Index*, help locate articles relevant to a client, its industry, or a particular topic.

Computer-Assisted Research Sources

The AICPA, public accounting firms, and private businesses are developing a wide variety of computer databases that can be used for research. The following sections describe several of these databases.

Electronic Body of Knowledge Series (EBKS)

The AICPA publishes the *Electronic Body of Knowledge Series (EBKS)* as an alternative to several paperback and loose-leaf services. Publications available in this series on a subscription basis include the following:

- *Audit and Accounting Guides.*
- *Professional Standards,* volumes 1 and 2.
- *Statements of Position (SOPs).*
- *Internal Revenue Code.*
- *Technical Hotline Qs & As,* and
- *Electronic Index to Technical Pronouncements (EITP).*

These run on personal computers and are periodically updated. Information can be accessed using extensive indices and key word search.

The *Electronic Index to Technical Pronouncements* contains references to all authoritative accounting and auditing literature promulgated by the AICPA, FASB, GASB, SEC, Emerging Issues Task Force, International Accounting Standards Committee, and International Auditing Practices Committee. The software allows the user to research topics using key words and locate references to the appropriate literature. The researcher can then retrieve the appropriate pronouncement in electronic, paperback, or loose-leaf form from his or her own library. If the researcher does not have access to the document or a subscription to the appropriate electronic body of knowledge, the full text can be reviewed on screen or retrieved from a database.

The AICPA also has an electronic series called *Paperbacks on Disk Series (PODS),* which does not include updates. This series includes the publications provided in the EBKS except for the audit and accounting guides and SOPs. PODS does include recent editions of *Accounting Trends & Techniques,* which are not in the EBKS.

Total On-Line Tax and Accounting Library (TOTAL)

Mead Data Central, Inc. (Mead), maintains many databases for different professions and organizations. The AICPA has made special arrangements with Mead to provide reduced rate access to the databases relating to accounting, auditing, and tax issues. All of the Big 6 CPA firms, many small firms, and some university libraries and accounting departments subscribe to this service referred to as *Total On-Line Tax and Accounting Library (TOTAL).* Data can be accessed by company, industry, or key words.

National Automated Accounting Research System (NAARS). The *National Automated Accounting Research System (NAARS)* is part of the TOTAL system and contains the full text of annual reports for more than 4,000 corporations that are listed on the American and New York Stock exchanges, traded in the over-the-counter market, or ranked by Fortune. The files include the financial statements, auditor's reports, footnotes, and anything incorporated by reference in the footnotes. The researcher can review alternative financial statement formats, see how other companies in an industry report certain items, locate footnote examples that illustrate disclosure of a particular situation, and review examples of audit reports. NAARS also contains the full text of all authoritative accounting and auditing pronouncements, which are indexed in the *Electronic Index to Technical Pronouncements,* previously described.

LEXIS/NEXIS Libraries. The LEXIS/NEXIS libraries are also part of the TOTAL system and contain the following databases:

- NEXIS—a full text library covering articles in more than 200 newspapers, magazines, and newsletters. It also includes the entire *Encyclopedia Britannica* and *The Federal Register*, a daily publication with the full text of regulations and legal notices issued by the U.S. government.
- Several libraries of decisions of the U.S. Supreme Court, courts of appeals, district courts, and claims courts:

  GENFED—General Federal Law Library.

  BNKG—Federal Banking Library that also includes the Federal Reserve Bulletins.

  BKRTCY—Federal Bankruptcy Library.

  FEDSEC—Federal Securities Library.
- STATES—Individual state law libraries that include decisions from the highest courts in all states.
- COMPNY—Company Library that includes in-depth reports on U.S. and international companies and industries prepared by professional research analysts.

These libraries allow the researcher, for example, to obtain background information on a client and its industry or locate specific laws and regulations relating to that industry. The files also contain cases relevant for reviewing auditor legal liability.

Fedtax Library. Included in TOTAL is the *Fedtax Library*, which includes federal tax laws and regulations, federal tax legislative activity, IRS materials, analysis of tax laws, and other tax-related literature. The researcher can, for example, check a citation or locate the IRS Code section, regulations, revenue rulings, cases, and tax commentary dealing with a specific tax topic.

Other Computer-Assisted Research Sources

Standard computer floppy disks have limited storage capacity. Many of the electronic publications previously described take a substantial portion of the storage capacity of a hard drive. Compact disk read-only memory (CD-ROM) technology significantly expands the storage capacity that can be used for computer-accessible databases. A special CD player is connected to a microcomputer to allow access to the data stored on CD-ROM. One 5-inch CD-ROM can hold over 600 megabytes of information, the equivalent of 300,000 single-spaced typewritten pages. Technological advances will undoubtedly lead to significantly more storage capacity on one of these disks. One company has been working on a CD that will store 12 billion bytes of information.

DISCLOSURE. DISCLOSURE is a compact disk database containing information from SEC filings of over 12,000 publicly held companies whose stock is traded in the United States. It has abstracts of information, whereas NAARS has the full text. The database is updated quarterly. Information available for each company includes type of business according to the Standard Industry Classification (SIC) code; description of the business; name of auditor and type of audit report; financial statements and ratios; names of any affiliated companies; number of shares and employees; names, addresses, ages, titles, and remuneration of owners, officers, and directors; and stock exchange and ticker symbol. It also includes a compilation of auditor changes.

The researcher can use company names or key words to access information in the database. The researcher can find out whether any adverse audit opinions have been issued during the past 18 months, and, if so, the companies and audit firms that were involved. Financial information and ratios for other companies can be accessed on the computer screen or printed out and used for comparison with those of a client.

ABI/Inform. ABI/Inform is a compact disk bibliographic database with abstracts of articles from more than 800 business magazines and journals for several years. It is similar to NEXIS, described previously, but is updated only quarterly. Information is accessed by using key words such as an industry, a company name, a year, or a journal. Key words can be used independently or in combination. ABI/Inform is also available through microcomputers with modems to a database that is continuously updated. The auditor of a car manufacturer, for example, could identify articles relating to the motor vehicle industry during the past year, read the abstracts, and identify the specific magazine or journal and then read the entire article. Copies of articles can be obtained by mail from ABI/Inform by a user who does not have access to the magazine or journal.

Dialogue. Dialogue Information Services, Inc., provides computer access to more than 400 databases. Major newspapers, including *The Wall Street Journal,* are available via modems in full text databases that can be searched using key words.

Newspaper Databases. Many of the major newspapers provide computer databases of articles contained in those newspapers.

Integrated Audit Automation Products

Some public accounting firms have developed integrated audit automation products to further increase the efficiency of auditors. These are usually stored on CD-ROM disks and include such things as the accounting and auditing standards, firm policies and procedures, and several of the proprietary and commercial software programs previously described. Many of these products include communications software that can be used to access LEXIS/NEXIS, to communicate with and/or transfer data files between client locations and the firm's office, between client locations, and between firm offices. Managers and partners can review working papers and other documents, for example, without traveling to the client's office.

Summary

This chapter has covered an assortment of topics. They are related, however, because to be as effective and efficient as possible, modern auditors must be able to use a variety of analytical procedures, computer-assisted auditing tools, and research sources. The connecting theme of this chapter, therefore, is audit effectiveness and efficiency.

Analytical procedures hold great promise for improving the efficiency and effectiveness of audits. As auditors become more knowledgeable about the sophisticated modeling techniques and obtain access to computer assistance, procedures such as regression analysis will likely become more widely used.

Computer-assisted auditing tools will continue to evolve as auditors gain more experience in using them and as microcomputers advance technologically. Research information will continue to become more readily available with the further development of CD-ROM, telecommunication, and similar capabilities. Auditors need to keep abreast of advancements in these areas and take advantage of them.

Appendix A–Multiple Regression Assumptions and Tests

Certain statistical assumptions are implicit in regression models. The primary assumptions are as follows:

- Continuity of relationships among variables throughout the range of observations.
- Constant standard error of residuals from point to point along the regression line (homoscedasticity).
- Independence of residuals from period to period.
- Normal distribution of residuals in the dependent variable.

Regression models assume that the same underlying linear relationship applies throughout the range of observations. *Discontinuity* is typically caused by changes in conditions. The relationship between miles flown and fuel costs for an airline, for example, are affected by a major change in fuel prices during either the base period or between the base period and the current period. If the auditor is using a computer program that does not automatically test for discontinuity, a review of the differences between the book and predicted values may indicate a discontinuity of the variables. When it exists, a new independent variable, such as fuel prices, may eliminate the discontinuity.

Homoscedasticity relates to standard error of the regression residuals. **Standard error** is the standard deviation of data and measures the variability of data. Regression models assume **homoscedasticity,** that is, that the standard error of residuals is constant from point to point along the regression line. Essentially, this assumption means that, for example, the unexplained fluctuations are not larger for larger values of the independent variable than for small values. A review of the distances between the data points and regression line in the scatter graph in Exhibit 23.6 indicates homoscedasticity. Residuals that do not have a constant standard error are said to be **heteroscedastic.** When heteroscedasticity exists in audit applications, the size of the residuals likely varies in proportion to one of the independent variables. To compensate for this, a weighted regression can be performed in which the observations are weighted to compensate for the effect of the independent variable on the standard error.[8] Some regression programs, such as STAR, test for heteroscedasticity and make adjustments to the regression formula if it exists.

Another assumption is that the residuals are statistically independent of each other over time, that the residual in one period is not influenced by the residual in another period. This means that a regression estimate in period i could not be improved by knowledge of what the residual was in period $i - 1$ or any other prior period. A systematic pattern of interdependence over time is known as **autocorrelation** or **serial correlation** of the residuals. When autocorrelation exists, the residual in a period consists of a part that depends on the residual in a prior period and a part that is random. Autocorrelation can be adjusted for by calculating a *generalized regression function* for time-series applications.[9]

Note that if the assumptions do not hold, the statistical inference will likely be in error, possibly by a material amount.

Significant Terms

A Score A weighting of 17 characteristics of a business to predict potential business failure.

Altman Z-score A combination of weighted ratios to produce a score of potential bankruptcy, developed using a regression model to predict companies that are most likely to go bankrupt.

analytical procedures Obtaining evidence by analyzing relationships among financial and nonfinancial data.

autocorrelation Residual in a period consists of a part that depends on the residual in a prior period and a part that is random.

common-size statement analysis A technique that shows each income statement account balance as a percent of net sales and each balance sheet account balance as a percent of total assets.

cross-sectional analysis A technique to compare ratios between firms at a given point in time.

dependent variable The element (variable) being predicted in a model, such as a regression model.

financial ratio analysis Analysis of ratios between financial statement accounts, such as accounts receivable turnover.

heteroscedasticity Standard error of residuals is not constant from point to point along a regression line.

homoscedasticity Standard error of residuals is constant from point to point along a regression line.

independent variables The elements (variables) likely to have a predictive value for a dependent variable.

multiple regression model A regression model that includes two or more independent variables.

nonfinancial ratios Comparisons of financial and nonfinancial data.

R^2 The percentage of the total fluctuation in the dependent variable that is explained by the fluctuation in the independent variable; is also referred to as the coefficient of determination.

ratio analysis The calculation of the relationship between two amounts, such as interest expense and interest-bearing debt.

reasonableness test Developing a model to predict an account balance, comparing that prediction with the recorded amount and determining whether the difference between the predicted value and the book value requires investigating.

regression analysis As used in auditing, a statistical technique used to describe the relationship between the account being audited and other possible predictive factors.

residual Fluctuations in the dependent variable not explained by fluctuations in the independent variable.

serial correlation (See autocorrelation)

simple regression model A regression model with just one independent variable.

standard error The standard deviation of data that measures the variability of that data.

time-series analysis A technique to analyze ratios for a given firm over time; a combination of trend and ratio analysis.

time-series regression analysis A technique used for predicting a dependent variable based on the historical relationship between that variable and one or more other financial or nonfinancial independent variables.

trend analysis The comparison of an amount for the current year with the prior year or years.

Review Questions

A–Analytical Procedures–Advanced Topics

23–1 Explain how analytical procedures can be used as

a. Attention-directing evidence.

b. Substantive evidence.

23–2 Describe and give an example of

a. Trend analysis.

b. Ratio analysis.

c. Reasonableness tests.

23–3 Explain why it is important to develop decision rules when using analytical procedures. Give two examples of decision rules.

23–4 Why might an audit client's information not be comparable to industry information?

23–5 What are indicators of potential bankruptcy?

23–6 Explain the Altman Z-score and how it is used.

23–7 Explain what common-size financial statements are and how they are used.

23–8 Identify the major nongovernmental sources of company and industry financial data.

23–9 Explain how regression analysis can be used as an analytical procedure, including the use of dependent and independent variables. What is the difference between time-series and cross-sectional regression analysis?

23–10 What is the difference between simple and multiple regression analysis?

23–11 Describe two ways of identifying recorded amounts that may contain a material misstatement when using regression analysis.

23–12 What are the primary assumptions implicit in regression models?

23–13 Explain the following terms and their implications when using regression analysis:

a. *Discontinuity*.

b. *Heteroscedasticity*.

c. *Autocorrelation*.

23–14 How can the auditor determine that values for independent variables are reasonably accurate and independent of the amount being predicted? Why is it important for the auditor to make these determinations?

23–15 What are the potential benefits of using regression analysis over other analytical procedures?

23–16 Why is it important that analytical procedures be performed by experienced auditors who are knowledgeable about the client's business and industry?

B–Expert Systems in Auditing

23–17 Explain what an expert system is.

23–18 What are the practical problems involved in the development and use of expert systems?

C–Automated Audit Techniques

23–19 Explain how the microcomputer can be used to assist the auditor in

a. Customizing standard documents.

b. Preparing working papers.

c. Interacting with a client's computer data.

D–Accounting and Auditing Research

23–20 You have been asked to research an accounting question for a publicly owned airline client. What sources could you consult in performing this research? Which of these sources is the most authoritative?

23–21 After you were designated as your office's statistical sampling specialist, you attended several statistical sampling workshops and were involved in sampling applications on several audits. If you were asked a question about the proper use of statistical sampling for which you do not know the answer, what sources might you consult for the appropriate answer?

23–22 You are reviewing the footnotes your audit client is proposing for its annual report to the SEC and stockholders. What sources are available to assist you in determining whether the footnotes are complete?

23–23 What are the main authoritative sources of accounting and auditing requirements related to the audits of state and local governments?

23–24 You are planning the audit of a new client. What sources can you consult to obtain background information about the client, its competition, and the industry?

Discussion and Research Questions

23–25 (Proper Accounting for a New Product) Innovation Corporation is a high-technology firm that relies on the development of new consumer products. Management is excited about the sales potential of its recently developed solar-powered water heater and has initiated a national advertising program promoting this new product. Sales of the water heater during the current year, the first year of sales for this product, are material to the financial statements, and management expects that future sales will increase significantly.

Your review of the sales agreement for the new water heater reveals a three-year return and refund privilege if the unit fails to operate properly. On analysis of the estimated allowance for returns accrued for this product, you find virtually no supporting evidence for management's estimate. Jane Dryden, controller of Innovation, explained that she believed some number was needed for the allowance, but because the product was so new and there was no track record relating to returns, she just picked an amount for the allowance.

Required:

a. What additional facts would you try to obtain before making a decision about the proper accounting and reporting consequences in this case?

b. What basic accounting principles come into play in the analysis of this case?

c. What published accounting standards apply?

d. What do you believe the proper accounting should be in this case?

e. What are the primary audit reporting considerations if the amount of the allowance for returns cannot be substantiated?

23–26 (Accounting for Start-Up Costs—Finance Company Branches) You are an audit senior of a large public accounting firm. You are engaged in your first audit of a finance company. Your audit client, Tofte Finance Company, has set up numerous branch offices during the current year as allowed by a recent change in the state law. In your review of the costs associated with establishing these branches, you noted that certain costs had been capitalized and were being amortized over a 40-year period. Tom Sterling, the controller, maintains that a 40-year amortization period is justifiable under *APB Opinion No. 17, "Intangible Assets."* You recall that the *AICPA Audit Guide—Finance Companies* deals with this subject.

Required:

a. You conclude that you need assistance in determining the appropriate accounting for the costs referred to above. How will you proceed in seeking that assistance?

b. How does it appear that these costs should be accounted for in the financial statements?

c. If the client insists on amortizing these costs over 40 years, and the amounts are material to the financial statements, indicate the effect on your audit report. Support your answer by referencing the appropriate auditing standard(s) and Code of Professional Conduct.

23–27 (Reporting Equity Investee's Decline in Market Value of Long-Term Equity Securities) Your client, Investor, Inc., has an investment of 30 percent of the outstanding voting shares of Investee, Inc., and appropriately accounts for this investment using the equity method. Investee has investments in marketable equity securities, both current and noncurrent assets. Sam August, Investor's controller, has studied FASB *Statement No. 12* (I89 in the Current Text) and has concluded that because the decline in market value of the current portfolio of marketable securities is reflected on Investee's income statement, Investor has appropriately accounted for its share of this decline by recording its share of Investee's net income. However, he has not been successful in determining how Investor should account for its share of the decline in market value of Investee's long-term portfolio of marketable equity securities. August has asked your advice in determining the proper accounting for Investor's share of the decline to market value of Investee's long-term portfolio of marketable equity.

Required:
Review the FASB *Current Text* and determine what advice you should give August.

[*Note:* For questions 23–28 through 23–56, research the issue, develop your answers, and include in your answers the supporting citation(s).]

Accounting-Related Research Questions

*23–28 (Equity Method When Current Direct Ownership Less Than 20 Percent) Company A purchased a 19 percent stock ownership interest in B. The company also made a loan to B, which is convertible into stock of B and is secured by shares of C (B's subsidiary). For as long as the loan is outstanding, Company A will have several seats on B's board. The company also has options to purchase shares of C.

Required:
Is the company required to report its investment in B under the equity method?

*23–29 (Investor's Share of Losses in Excess of Its Investment) Company A's share of the losses of a real estate venture exceeds its investment in the venture.

Required:
How should Company A account for its investment?

*23–30 (Accounting for Teachers' Salaries over a 12-Month Period) Teachers in a public school district teach from September 1 through June 30, a 10-month period. The school district pays these teachers over a 12-month period for the 10 months of service. The school district's fiscal year ends June 30.

Required:
a. What is the appropriate financial statement presentation for the two months of teachers' salaries that have been earned but not yet paid by the school district at the end of the fiscal year?
b. Does the guidance for compensated absences apply?

*Adapted from AICPA's *Technical Hotline Qs & As*.

*23–31 (Uncertainty Arising from Violation of Debt Agreement) At the end of 19X1, a company was in violation of its long-term debt covenant and was unable to obtain a waiver from the bank. It therefore reclassified its debt to current and appropriate footnote disclosures were made. During 19X2, the violation was cured.

Required:
What is the proper classification of the debt in the company's 19X2 comparative financial statements?

*23–32 (Balance Sheet Presentation of Mandatory Redeemable Preferred Stock) A nonpublic audit client has mandatory redeemable preferred stock.

Required:
Should mandatory redeemable preferred stock be reflected in the equity section of the balance sheet?

*23–33 (Accounting for Loan Servicing Fees When Mortgage Loans Are Sold and Seller Retains Servicing Rights) Many thrift institutions that sell mortgage loans and retain the servicing rights have interpreted the AICPA *Industry Audit & Accounting Guide—Savings and Loan Associations*, to allow for gain or loss recognition on the sale of mortgage loans with deferral of an amount equal to the present value of future servicing costs. That accounting treatment differs from the treatment followed in the mortgage banking industry, where a normal servicing fee is deferred under the provisions of FASB *Statement No. 65*.

Required:
Which approach should be followed by savings and loan associations?

*23–34 (Method of Recognizing Revenue from Commissions on Loan Insurance) A finance company receives commissions from independent insurers for getting its borrowers to take out loan insurance.

Required:
How should the company recognize commission revenues?

*23–35 (Accounting for Sale of Property with Option to Repurchase) A corporation sold a parcel of land to a bank. The corporation has an option to repurchase the land for a period of three years. The corporation received the full purchase price at the time of sale.

Required:
What is the proper accounting treatment for this transaction?

*23–36 (Method of Accounting for Sale of Territorial Franchise Right) A client sells territorial franchise rights to region managers for $30,000 with 10 percent taken in cash and the remainder as a note. The region manager in turn sells franchises in his territory. The note is payable at the rate of $1000 per franchise sold in the territory but is due in three years regardless of the number of franchises sold. The collectibility of the notes depends on the performance of the region managers. The company has been able to resell territories of managers who have been unsuccessful, and the down payments have been refunded in these instances.

Required:
What is the proper method of accounting for these franchise fees and the related costs of selling the territories?

*23–37 (Disclosure of Salary Paid to Owner-Manager) Your audit client is a closely held corporation. The principal stockholder is also a member of the company's management.

Required:
Should the salary paid to this principal stockholder be disclosed as a related-party transaction?

Audit-Related Research Questions

*23–38 (Confirmation of Factored Receivables)

Required:
When accounts receivable are sold to a factor under a factoring agreement, is confirmation of these receivables necessary?

*23–39 (Letter of Inquiry to Client's Attorney) When a CPA requested a client to send a letter of inquiry to the client's attorney, the client objected because the attorney would charge for answering it. The client also believed that an inquiry about legal matters was not valid. The client reported that no legal problems were pending for the year under audit but that at the present time litigation is possible.

Required:
Do generally accepted auditing standards require that the client send a letter of inquiry to an attorney?

*23–40 (Statutory Basis Financial Statements Differ from GAAP) Financial statements filed with a state regulatory agency are prepared on a statutory basis that differs from generally accepted accounting principles (GAAP).

Required:
How should the auditor report on the financial statements if she knows they will be distributed to third parties other than the regulatory agency?

*23–41 (State Accounting Guide Differs from GAAP) The guidelines stated in a state department of education accounting guide do not follow those stated in an AICPA *Industry Audit Guide, Audits of Colleges and Universities.*

Required:
Are reports on financial statements conforming to the state accounting guide requirements considered special reports under *SAS No. 62,* "Special Reports"?

*23–42 (Bank Directors' Examination) A CPA firm has been requested by the bank directors to perform specified examination procedures. One of the CPA firm's partners is a director of that bank.

Required:
Can the firm acknowledge in its report that it is not independent and provide the service?

*23–43 (Reliance on State Grain Inspectors for Inventory Measurements) A grain company operates several storage elevators. The company maintains perpetual inventory records for all facilities, both at the elevators and at the home office. State grain inspectors measure the stored grain and in effect perform the same audit functions as the CPA firm. Past experience has been that the differences between the measurements of the state inspectors, the CPA firm, and the perpetual inventory records are immaterial. The state inspectors are qualified with years of experience.

Required:
Can the CPA firm accept the findings of the state inspectors as adequate inventory observation in accordance with generally accepted auditing standards?

*23–44 (Distinctions between Scope Limitations) *SAS No. 58*, "Reports on Audited Financial Statements," paragraph 42, states in part: "When restrictions that significantly limit the scope of the audit are imposed by the client, ordinarily the auditor should disclaim an opinion on the financial statements."

SAS No. 58, paragraph 42, footnote 17, states: "Circumstances such as the timing of his work may make it impracticable or impossible for the auditor to accomplish these procedures. In this case, if he is able to satisfy himself as to inventories or accounts receivable by applying alternative procedures, there is no significant limitation on the scope of his work, and his report need not include a reference to the omission of the procedures or to the use of alternative procedures. . . ."

Required:

a. Based on the preceding excerpts, what is an appropriate auditor's report in each of the following situations:
   1. The auditor is not permitted to confirm receivables but is able to satisfy himself by other means.
   2. The auditor is not permitted to observe inventories but is able to satisfy himself by other means.
b. Is there a distinction between a client-imposed limitation regarding receivables or inventories and other client-imposed scope limitations?

*23–45 (Communication of Internal Control Structure Related Matters Noted in an Audit) In connection with an audit, the auditor did not find any reportable conditions (nor any material weaknesses) in the entity's internal control structure.

Required:

a. May the auditor issue a written report to the client representing that no reportable conditions were noted during the audit?
b. May the auditor issue a written report to the client representing that no material weaknesses were noted during the audit?

*23–46 (Reliance on Observation of Inventories at an Interim Date) Although its fiscal year ends on March 31, a client has always counted its physical inventory on December 31. The March 31 ending inventory has always been calculated by the gross profit method, which has proven over the past to be quite accurate. No perpetual inventory records are kept.

Required:
Can the auditor rely on an observation of inventory that takes place three months prior to the balance sheet date?

*23–47 (Observation of Consignment Inventories Stored in Public Warehouse) Corporation A sells supplies and equipment for manufacturing jewelry. Silver on consignment from a supplier is kept in a vault adjacent to where Corporation A keeps its silver inventory. The supplier employs an independent warehouse firm to protect the consigned silver. The bonded employee of the warehouse firm has sole access to the consignment silver and performs the duties of warehouse manager for Corporation A. The warehouse firm pays the salary of the bonded employee but is reimbursed by Corporation A. Because the possibility for substitutions between Corporation A's silver inventories and the consignment silver exists, the auditors of Corporation A, in conducting a physical observation of Corporation A's silver inventories, also want to conduct a physical observation of the consignment silver.

Required:
Is it necessary for the auditors of Corporation A to observe the consignment silver?

*23–48 (Going Concern Problem—Financial Statements Prepared on the Income Tax Basis of Accounting) A client prepares its financial statements on the income tax basis of accounting. It is experiencing financial difficulties, and its ability to continue in existence is questionable.

Required:
Because the financial statements are prepared on an other comprehensive basis of accounting, is the CPA's audit report required to include an explanatory paragraph that refers to the uncertainty of the company as a going concern?

*23–49 (Failure to Remit Withholding Taxes in Subsequent Period) In the course of an examination of the financial statements, the auditor has discovered that in the period subsequent to the balance sheet date, the company has not remitted to the appropriate agencies the taxes currently withheld from employees' wages.

Required:
Assuming that the amount is material, is it necessary that this matter be disclosed in the auditor's report?

*23–50 (Confirmation of Taxing District's Taxes Receivable) A client, a hospital district, is a taxing authority. The hospital district taxes assessed are collected by the county government with the net proceeds remitted, by the county, to the district. The county maintains all of the tax rolls and related records. In order to render an unqualified opinion on the district's accounts, which would include the tax revenues and the taxes receivable, it would appear necessary to examine the tax rolls of the county government, including selecting properties physically and tracing them to the tax rolls, footing the tax rolls, checking mathematical accuracy of assessment, and so on.

Required:
Are these procedures necessary, or would it be sufficient merely to confirm collections and receivables with the county?

*23–51 (Discovery of Potential Liability in Subsequent Period) In the period subsequent to the balance sheet date, the auditors discovered that an employee of the client had used a company purchase order to obtain merchandise for her personal business. This transaction resulted in a material potential liability of the client. Negotiations with the creditor ensued, and the client's attorney was successful in securing a complete release from any obligation on the part of the client.

Required:
Is it necessary to disclose this matter on the client's financial statements?

*23–52 (Settlements of Pending Litigation in Subsequent Period) The fieldwork for an audit of financial statements for a year ended December 31 was completed on May 22. Pending litigation on December 31, in which the client was the plaintiff, was settled on May 10, resulting in a gain to the client.

Required:
Should the settlement be recognized in the financial statements for the year ended December 31, in accordance with *SAS No. 1,* section 560, "Subsequent Events," as a type I subsequent event?

*23–53 (Compilation of Supplementary Schedules in Audited Financial Statements)

Required:
When an audit has been performed in accordance with generally accepted auditing standards and the client desires supplementary schedules, can these schedules be compiled in accordance with *SSARS 1,* "Compilation and Review of Financial Statements," paragraph 43?

*23–54 (Condensed Financial Statements of a Nonpublic Entity) A client prepares condensed financial statements that name the auditor and state that they have been derived from audited financial statements. The condensed statements incorporate the audited financial statements by reference and indicate that such statements and auditor's report thereon may be obtained.

Required:
Must the auditor report on the condensed financial statements?

23–55 (Applying Analytical Procedures) Analytical procedures are an integral part of planning audits.

Required:
Obtain the financial statements of a publicly owned company, perform appropriate analytical procedures, compare with industry information, and write a report on audit questions raised by your analysis. Identify specific accounts that appear to require special audit attention. Include a copy of the company's financial statements in your report.

23–56 (Bankruptcy Prediction) The Altman Z-score and similar models have been developed to help predict bankruptcy of a company.

Required:
Select one company that has filed for bankruptcy (such as Wang) and another company in the same industry (such as Digital Equipment Company or Compaq), obtain financial statements for each company for the period shortly before the one company filed for bankruptcy, compute the Altman-Z score for each company, and write a report summarizing your findings. Include a copy of each company's financial statements in your report.

Case

23–57 (Term Project—Client and Industry Background Information) Choose a company that is publicly held with stock actively traded on the New York, American or over-the-counter exchange. Each person or team must choose a company that is different from the other individuals' or teams' companies. Obtain a copy of a recent annual report and 10-K for your company.

Required:

a. Answer the following questions:
   1. What is the company's industry?
   2. What are its primary products?
   3. How large is/are the company's
      - Sales?
      - Assets?
      - Number of employees?
   4. Where are the company and its major facilities located?
   5. What other person/companies are closely associated with this company?
   6. Look at the annual report.
      - What image does it intend to convey?
      - What are the segments and functional contents of the annual report?
   7. What is a 10-K and how does it differ from the annual report to shareholders?

b. Obtain outside information about the company and its industry. Answer the following questions:
   1. What are the key economic factors about the industry?
   2. Where is the company in its life cycle?

3. What are the five or six most important factors for success in this business?
4. How does this company stand in respect to these factors?
5. What notable accounting considerations are there for companies in this industry?
6. What social matters are of concern?

c. Analyze the company's financial health:
1. Is this a healthy company?
2. What are its sources of capital and what is the value of its capital?
3. What is the quality of earnings?
4. How has the capital marketplace responded to the company?
5. How does it compare with the rest of its industry?

d. To help plan an audit, answer the following questions:
1. What material types of transactions and transaction cycles are involved?
2. What are the high-risk areas?
3. What are the low-risk areas?
4. What form of auditor's report do you expect will be issued? What does the form mean?

End Notes

1. Mary Ellen Phillips and Carol E. Brown, "Need an Expert? Ask a Computer," *Journal of Accountancy*, November 1991, 91.
2. Arnold Wright and Robert H. Ashton, "Identifying Audit Adjustments with Attention-Directing Procedures," *The Accounting Review* (October 1989), 718–727.
3. Edward Blocher and John J. Willingham, *Analytical Review: A Guide to Analytical Procedures*, 2nd ed. (Colorado Springs: Shepard's/McGraw-Hill, 1988), 321.
4. Kenneth W. Stringer and Trevor R. Stewart, *Statistical Techniques for Analytical Review in Auditing* (New York: John Wiley & Sons, 1986), v.
5. See, for example, Thomas E. McKee, *Modern Analytical Auditing: Practical Guidance for Auditors and Accountants* (New York: Quorum Books, 1989), 129.
6. E. Altman, *Corporate Financial Distress* (New York: John Wiley & Sons, 1983).
7. Developed by John Argenti and discussed in "Predicting Corporate Failure," *Accountant's Digest* (Summer 1983).
8. Stringer, 100–1.
9. Stringer, 95–6.

CHAPTER

24

Learning Objectives

Through studying this chapter, you will be able to:

1. Understand the need for government auditing and distinct government auditing standards.
2. Identify and distinguish between various types of governmental audits.
3. Understand and apply government auditing standards.
4. Understand the auditing and reporting requirements of the Single Audit Act.
5. Understand the scope and importance of internal auditing.
6. Distinguish between operational and financial auditing.
7. Understand and apply the basic steps in an operational audit.
8. Understand how to develop and maintain good relationships with auditees.

Governmental and Operational Auditing

Chapter Contents

An important aspect of GAAP. . . as applied to governments is the recognition of the variety of legal and contractual considerations typical of the government environment. These considerations underlie and are reflected in the fund structure, bases of accounting, and other principles and methods . . . , and are a major factor distinguishing governmental accounting from commercial accounting.[1]

To understand the need for operational audits, one must recognize that boards of directors, elected officials, and senior management are being held to high standards of accountability and responsibility for stewardship. In such an environment, executives and managers frequently request independent evaluation and advice. Although they may have no reason to believe that problems exist, they realize that an objective review and resulting recommendations can benefit the organization.[2]

Chapter Overview

Audits of governmental units and organizations that receive federal financial assistance are an important component of the work of public accountants. Recent studies indicate, however, that a significant percent of such audits are not being performed according to established standards. The first part of this chapter describes the standards appropriate for such audits and some of the unique features of audits of governmental units.

The effectiveness and efficiency of an organization can often be improved when an impartial party takes a critical look at the established policies and procedures and the performance of personnel. This is the primary purpose of operational auditing, which is the subject of the last part of this chapter.

A–GOVERNMENTAL AUDITING

A significant portion of our economy's activities is administered by federal, state, and local governments. Nearly $200 billion is spent each year by the federal government in the form of financial assistance to state and local governments and to not-for-profit entities to provide for transportation; public assistance; education, health, and welfare programs; and job training. This is in addition to expenditures needed to simply run the federal government. **Financial assistance** refers to assistance provided by a federal agency in the form of grants, contracts, loans, loan guarantees, property, cooperative agreements, interest subsidies, insurance, or direct appropriations, but does not include direct federal cash assistance to individuals. Recipients of this assistance include state governments, Indian tribes, cities, towns, counties, school districts, and housing and airport authorities. There are more than 80,000 state and local governmental units and over 900,000 not-for-profit organizations in the United States and its territories. Almost all of the organizational recipients of federal funds may be subject to some form of governmental auditing to ensure that the funds are administered according to the grantor's standards. It is estimated that there are more than 70,000 governmental units and not-for-profit organizations subject to various governmental auditing requirements as contrasted with only 11,000 companies subject to SEC regulation.[3]

The scope of governmental auditing includes not only all departments, functions, and activities of the various levels of government but other organizations receiving government resources through various assistance programs. Such audits are performed by governmental audit agencies and public accounting firms. The U.S. General Accounting Office (GAO) is the largest governmental audit organization in the country. The GAO is known as the Congressional watchdog and is directly responsible to Congress. The Comptroller General of the United States is the head of the GAO and is appointed for a 15-year term, thus helping to ensure that political pressure does not affect the independence of the GAO. The GAO performs financial audits of federal agencies as well as operational and compliance audits of federal agencies and programs. The Department of Defense, the Federal Deposit Insurance Corporation, and other federal agencies have their own audit departments. Most states have legislative auditors and state auditors responsible for auditing state agencies, local governments, and school districts. In some states, local governments and school districts may have a choice of being audited by public accounting firms or the state auditor.

Evolution of Modern Governmental Auditing

Expenditures accounting for approximately one-third of the gross national product is subject to governmental audit requirements. But the audits conducted have not always met required standards. In 1986, the GAO issued a report on its review of the quality of audits of federal financial assistance programs by public accounting firms. The GAO concluded that 34 percent of the 120 randomly selected audits did not satisfactorily comply with applicable auditing standards. The AICPA responded to the need to improve the quality of these audits by forming the Task Force on the Quality of Audits of Governmental Units to develop a comprehensive action plan to improve the quality of governmental audits.

The task force recommended that (1) training in governmental accounting and auditing should be mandatory for persons who perform governmental audits, (2) the quality of guidance for auditors be improved, and (3) a statement on auditing standards should be issued addressing auditing for compliance with laws and regulations. In 1988, the GAO issued a revision of the *Government Auditing Standards (GAS)* in what is referred to as the *Yellow Book*.[4] The standards require those individuals performing governmental audits to complete at least 80 hours of continuing education and training every two years, at least 24 hours of which should be in subjects related to the government environment and governmental auditing. In 1991, the AICPA issued *SAS No. 68*, "Compliance Auditing Applicable to Governmental Entities and Other Recipients of Governmental Financial Assistance" in response to the third recommendation.

Need for Government Auditing Standards

Auditing has become an integral element of government accountability. Public officials, legislators, and private citizens are interested in whether government funds are properly spent in compliance with laws and regulations, are achieving the purposes for which they are authorized, and are doing so economically and efficiently. Thus, audits of governmental organizations and other organizations receiving federal financial assistance are required to evaluate and report on the internal control structure and compliance with laws and regulations of the entity in addition to reporting on the financial results of the entity.

Applicability of Government Auditing Standards

Governmental auditing standards must be followed by government auditors (such as federal inspectors general, GAO auditors, legislative auditors, and state auditors) and public accounting firms *when required by law, regulation, agreement or contract, or policy* of the federal, state, or local governments or agencies thereof. The standards are applicable to audits of government organizations, programs, activities, and functions. They also apply to contractors, nonprofit organizations, and other nongovernment organizations that receive federal financial assistance (subrecipients) or have government contracts requiring the application of these standards. In other words, they have broad applicability to federal, state, and public auditors. Government auditing standards may apply to audits of:

- State, city, county, and Indian tribal governments; school districts; institutions of higher education; and other nonprofit organizations that receive at least $100,000 in money, goods, and/or services from the federal government during the fiscal year.
- Real estate joint ventures or partnerships that receive financial assistance from the U.S. Department of Housing and Urban Development to provide multiple-unit housing for low-income families (HUD audits).
- Finance companies providing mortgages that are federally insured.
- Manufacturing companies providing products to the federal government under contracts that require government auditing standards to be followed.
- Universities providing student loans guaranteed by the federal government.

Types of Government Audits

There are two types of audits covered by government auditing standards: financial audits and performance audits. Financial audits are divided into two types—financial statement audits and financial-related audits. **Financial statement audits** determine (1) the fairness of the financial statements in conformity with GAAP*, and (2) whether the entity has complied with laws and regulations for those transactions and events that may have a material effect on the financial statements. **Financial-related audits** include determining whether (1) financial reports and related items, such as operating statements, are fairly presented, (2) financial information is presented in accordance with established or stated criteria, such as variances between estimated and actual financial performance, and (3) the entity has adhered to specific financial compliance requirements, such as grant requirements.

Performance audits address the economy, efficiency, and program results of a reporting unit. Economy and efficiency audits are performed to determine whether management's objectives are being achieved and to identify opportunities and develop recommendations for improvements. **Program audits** include determining (1) the extent to which the desired results or benefits established by the legislature or other authorizing body are being achieved, (2) the effectiveness of organizations, programs, activities, or functions, and (3) whether the entity has complied with laws and regulations applicable to the program.

The standards described in the next section apply to financial audits. The standards for performance audits are important to improving governmental structure and efficiency and, though not specifically covered in the text, are similar in concept to the principles of operational auditing, covered later in this chapter.

The Government Auditing Standards

Government auditing standards encompass GAAS but are much broader. They contain general standards that apply to both financial and performance audits as well as separate fieldwork and reporting standards for financial and performance audits.

General Standards

The general standards are similar to GAAS in that they require proper qualifications, independence, and the use of due professional care. There are additional independence concerns and an additional standard on quality control.

Independence. Government auditing standards apply to both public accountants and government auditors, some of whom may be employed by the agency being audited. Independence takes on a new meaning under these standards. The auditor must be free from personal and external impairments to independence as well as be organizationally independent. Personal impairments include preconceived ideas toward individuals, groups, organizations, or objectives of a particular program that could bias the audit. It also includes biases potentially induced by political or social convictions that result from employment in, or loyalty to, a particular group, organization, or level of government. Influences external to the audit organization that could impair independence include the following:

*GAAP include the statements and interpretations issued by the Governmental Accounting Standards Board (GASB).

- Unreasonable time restrictions.
- Restrictions on resources provided to the audit organization that would adversely affect its ability to carry out its responsibilities.
- Authority to overrule or to influence the auditor's judgment as to the content of an audit report.

Quality Control. Government auditing standards require each audit organization performing governmental audits to have an appropriate internal quality control system in place and to have an external review performed at least once every three years by an organization not affiliated with the organization being reviewed. Such a requirement now exists for any public accounting firm that is a member of the AICPA. Many state boards of accountancy and state societies of CPAs have similar requirements.

Fieldwork Standards

Government auditing standards incorporate the fieldwork standards of GAAS and have two supplemental standards on planning and working papers.

Planning. Audits of an organization, program, activity, or function are often required by federal, state, and local laws, regulations, and ordinances, but determining the scope of the audit requires special planning. The local school district, for example, receives resources from the city, county, state, and various federal agencies, either directly or indirectly through the state. The U.S. Department of Agriculture may provide food for the school lunch program. The state art commission may provide funding for art programs. The city may provide funds to offset the costs of an adult education program. Each of these programs may require audits. Functions of government are audited because citizens want assurance that the money they pay in taxes is properly spent. But because there are many subrecipients of those funds, the auditor needs to determine what governments are to be served by the audit and plan the audit to efficiently meet the multitude of applicable audit requirements.

Working Papers. This supplemental standard states explicitly what are considered to be proper working paper techniques for any audit, including the following:

- Ensure safe custody and retention for a time sufficient to satisfy legal and administrative requirements.
- Cross-reference audit program to the working papers.
- Contain sufficient information so the supplemental oral explanations are not required.

Reporting Standards

Government auditing standards incorporate the reporting standards of GAAS and three supplemental standards requiring:

- A statement in the auditor's report that the audit was made in accordance with government auditing standards.

- A report on compliance with laws and regulations.
- A report on the internal control structure.

The audit report should state that the audit was conducted in accordance with GAAS and government auditing standards. If any of these standards were not followed, the report should state the omission, the reasons therefore, and indicate the known effect on the results of the audit of not following the standard.

Reporting on Compliance with Laws and Regulations under Government Auditing Standards. GAAS do not require a report on compliance with laws and regulations. Failure to comply with laws and regulations is, however, considered an illegal act and such failures that come to the auditor's attention must be reported to top management and the client's audit committee. Such communication can be either oral or written.

A supplemental reporting standard requires the auditor to prepare a written report on the tests of compliance with laws and regulations. Unfortunately, the laws and regulations are broad and may do the following, for example:

- Require adopting a budget and following procedures that ensure that the budget is adhered to.
- Place limits on local government taxing authority.
- Mandate bidding procedures for purchase orders exceeding a specified dollar limit.
- Place limits on the types of activities or services local governments can perform.
- Place debt-ceiling limitations.

When planning the audit, the auditor should identify and become familiar with the applicable laws and regulations against which compliance should be addressed. Audit procedures should be performed to ensure that the client has complied with the identified requirements. The auditor can identify the relevant laws and regulations by:

- Inquiring of the entity's chief financial officer, legal counsel, or grant administrators.
- Referring to the prior year working papers.
- Reviewing grant and loan agreements.
- Reviewing minutes of meetings of the legislative body of the entity.
- Inquiring of the federal, state, or local audit oversight organization.
- Inquiring of the program administrator of the agency providing the funds.

The compliance report should contain a statement of positive assurance on those items that were tested and negative assurance on those items not tested.* It should include *all material* instances of noncompliance, and *all* instances or indications of illegal acts that could result in criminal prosecution. If the auditor did not test com-

*If a statistically valid and projectable sample of items were tested, an opinion on the relevant universe's compliance may be warranted.

pliance with laws and regulations, the report should so state. This report may be included in either the report on the financial audit or a separate report. A separate report is presented in Exhibit 24.1. The fourth paragraph contains the positive and negative assurances about compliance.

Reporting on Internal Controls under Government Auditing Standards. The auditor's consideration of internal controls under government auditing standards is the same as under GAAS: to obtain an understanding of the internal control structure and to assess control risk. *However, government auditing standards require a written report on reportable conditions, whether or not any reportable conditions are detected.* Material weaknesses should be identified. If no reportable conditions were noted, a written report stating that *no material weaknesses* were found is issued to avoid a conflict with GAAS, which prohibit the auditor from issuing a report saying *no reportable conditions* were detected. The report may be included either in the auditor's report on the financial audit or in a separate report. Materiality is considered at the fund type level under both GAAS and government auditing standards.

In reporting instances of noncompliance with laws and regulations or of reportable conditions, government auditing standards require the auditor to include in the audit report the appropriate elements of an audit finding:

Exhibit 24.1

GOVERNMENT AUDITING STANDARDS REPORT ON COMPLIANCE

To the City Council
City of Star, Minnesota

We have audited the general-purpose financial statements of the City of Star, Minnesota, as of and for the year ended June 30, 1994, and have issued our report thereon dated August 15, 1994.

We conducted our audit in accordance with generally accepted auditing standards and *Government Auditing Standards*, issued by the Comptroller General of the United States. Those standards require that we plan and perform the audit to obtain reasonable assurance about whether the general-purpose financial statements are free of material misstatement.

Compliance with laws, regulations, contracts, and grants applicable to the City of Star, Minnesota, is the responsibility of the City of Star, Minnesota, management. As part of obtaining reasonable assurance about whether the general-purpose financial statements are free of material misstatement, we performed tests of the City's compliance with certain provisions of laws, regulations, contracts, and grants. However, our objective was not to provide an opinion on overall compliance with such provisions.

The results of our tests indicate that, with respect to the items tested, the City of Star, Minnesota, complied, in all material respects, with the provisions referred to in the preceding paragraph. With respect to items not tested, nothing came to our attention that caused us to believe that the City had not complied, in all material respects, with those provisions.

This report is intended for the information of the audit committee, management, and city council. This restriction is not intended to limit the distribution of this report, which is a matter of public record.

Rittenberg and Schwieger, CPAs
August 15, 1994

[Emphasis Added.]

- Criteria—the standards by which the subject of the audit were measured.
- Condition—what the auditor found.
- Cause—the factors that created the problem.
- Effect—the adverse effects on the organization.

An example of reporting a finding is included in Exhibit 24.2.

Single Audit Act of 1984

A local government is likely to receive assistance for a number of projects from a diverse group of federal agencies, either directly or through the state government. Examples of federal assistance are food for school lunch or day-care programs, funds for welfare programs, and funds for low-income housing projects. The **Single Audit Act of 1984** resulted from, among other things, a GAO study of grant recipients that found that the U.S. government did not provide audits for nearly $192 billion of the $240 billion of federal grant funds during the period of 1974 through 1977 (approximately 80 percent of such grants) and that the number of times a recipient was audited ranged from no audits to more than 50.[5] The single audit approach requires many state and local governments to have a single, organization-wide financial and compliance audit. The Single Audit Act is designed to improve the efficiency and effectiveness of audit resources.

The Single Audit Act requires an audit of each state and local government that receives at least $100,000 of federal financial assistance in any fiscal year. State and local governments receiving between $25,000 and $100,000 must have an audit performed under the Single Audit Act or in accordance with federal laws and regulations governing the programs in which they participate. Those receiving less than $25,000 are exempt from compliance with the Single Audit Act and other federal audit requirements. The Single Audit Act specifies that government auditing standards be followed as well as any other auditing and reporting requirements that may relate to particular grants.

The Office of Management and Budget (OMB) is charged under the Single Audit Act to establish regulations to implement the single audit. OMB has issued circulars requiring the Single Audit Act to be followed in audits of state and local governments (Circular No. A-128) and institutions of higher education and other not-for-profit organizations (Circular No. A-133) that receive financial assistance either directly or indirectly from the federal government. The circulars add additional requirements to some audits. Both circulars, for example, hold state and local governments responsible for determining that all subrecipients of the federal grants (state grants of federal funds to other organizations) to which they have provided at least $25,000 of federal financial assistance have met the appropriate audit requirements and spent the funds in accordance with applicable laws and regulations. OMB also has the responsibility to assign a cognizant agency to oversee the single audit of state and larger local governments. A **cognizant agency** is a federal agency assigned by the Director of the OMB to be responsible for implementing the Single Audit Act requirements for a particular state or local government.

Auditing and Reporting on Compliance with Laws and Regulations under the Single Audit Act

GAAS and government auditing standards require testing of compliance at the *financial statement level.* The Single Audit Act has different audit and reporting

Exhibit 24.2

GOVERNMENT AUDITING STANDARDS REPORT ON INTERNAL CONTROL WITH AN AUDIT FINDING

To the City Council
City of Star, Minnesota

We have audited the general-purpose financial statements of the City of Star, Minnesota, as of and for the year ended June 30, 1993, and have issued our report thereon dated August 15, 1993.

We conducted our audit in accordance with generally accepted auditing standards, and *Government Auditing Standards*, issued by the Comptroller General of the United States. Those standards require that we plan and perform the audit to obtain reasonable assurance about whether the general-purpose financial statements are free of material misstatement.

In planning and performing our audit of the general-purpose financial statements of City of Star, Minnesota, for the year ended June 30, 1993, we considered its internal control structure in order to determine our auditing procedures for the purpose of expressing our opinion on the general-purpose financial statements, not to provide assurance on the internal control structure.

The management of City of Star, Minnesota, is responsible for establishing and maintaining an internal control structure. In fulfilling this responsibility, estimates and judgments by management are required to assess the expected benefits and related costs of internal control structure policies and procedures. The objectives of an internal control structure are to provide management with reasonable, but not absolute, assurance that assets are safeguarded against loss from unauthorized use or disposition, and that transactions are executed in accordance with management's authorization and recorded properly to permit the preparation of general-purpose financial statements in accordance with generally accepted accounting principles. Because of inherent limitations in any internal control structure, errors or irregularities may nevertheless occur and not be detected. Also, projection of any evaluation of the structure to future periods is subject to the risk that procedures may become inadequate because of changes in conditions or that the effectiveness of the design and operation of policies and procedures may deteriorate.

For the purpose of this report, we have classified the significant internal control structure policies and procedures in the following categories: financing, revenue, purchases, and external financial reporting.

For all of the internal control structure categories listed above, we obtained an understanding of the design of relevant policies and procedures and whether they have been placed in operation, and we assessed control risk.

We noted the following matter involving the internal control structure and its operation that we consider to be reportable conditions under standards established by the American Institute of Certified Public Accountants. Reportable conditions involve matters coming to our attention relating to significant deficiencies in the design or operation of the internal control structure that, in our judgment, could adversely affect the entity's ability to record, process, summarize, and report financial data consistent with the assertions of management in the general-purpose financial statements.

Processing Tax Collections

Criteria. Timely processing of property tax collections is essential to provide supporting detail for the municipality's financial statements.

Condition. At March 31, 1994, the Property Tax Department had not yet processed collections for the months of October and November 1993.

(Continued)

Exhibit 24.2

Cause. A number of factors have contributed to this problem. These include a hiring freeze compounded by high employee turnover, lack of cross-training for employees, and implementation of a new information system without adequate training and supervision of personnel.
Effect. Processing delays caused misstatements in delinquent property tax accounts to go unresolved because discrepancies between tax bill amounts and payments received have not been reconciled. As a result, timely information on the delinquent tax receivable balance was not prepared. Estimates of unprocessed collections were made for financial reporting purposes. Our test of these estimates indicated they prevented the financial statements from being materially misstated. We consider this to be a reportable condition.*

A material weakness is a reportable condition in which the design or operation of the specific internal control structure elements does not reduce to a relatively low level the risk that errors or irregularities in amounts that would be material in relation to the general-purpose financial statements being audited may occur and not be detected within a timely period by employees in the normal course of performing their assigned functions.

Our consideration of the internal control structure would not necessarily disclose all matters in the internal control structure that might be reportable conditions and, accordingly, would not necessarily disclose all reportable conditions that are also considered to be material weaknesses as defined above. However, we believe the reportable condition described above is not a material weakness.

We also noted other matters involving the internal control structure and its operation that we have reported to the management of City of Star, Minnesota, in a separate letter dated August 15, 1994.

This report is intended for the information of the audit committee, management, and city council. This restriction is not intended to limit the distribution of this report, which is a matter of public record.

Rittenberg & Schwieger, CPAs
August 15, 1994

*This finding is an example from Donald L. Neebes and William A. Broadus, Jr., "GAAS vs. GAGAS: How to Report on Internal Controls," *Journal of Accountancy* (February 1990), 64.

requirements for "major" and "nonmajor" programs and requires intensive testing of compliance at the *major program level.* Dollar guidelines have been established for the purpose of designating major programs. For governments having a total annual expenditure of federal financial assistance up to $1 million, a **major program** is one for which such expenditures exceed the larger of $300,000 or 3 percent of total expenditures for all programs. There are separate guidelines for governments with annual assistance expenditures in excess of $1 million.

The client is responsible for providing the auditor with a schedule of all expenditures of federal financial assistance during the year, whether the assistance was received directly from the federal government or indirectly through another level of government. The schedule should identify each program and the amounts expended. Exhibit 24.3 reports the expenditures of a local government, which had total expenditures of $28 million of which $900,000 was spent on four federal finan-

Exhibit 24.3

EXPENDITURES OF A LOCAL GOVERNMENT

Federal assistance:	
Program 1—Recycling	$ 300,000
Program 2—Scenic river development	25,000
Program 3—Child care	405,000
Program 4—Low-income housing	170,000
	$ 900,000
Other expenditures	27,100,000
	$28,000,000

cial assistance programs. Projects 1 and 3 are major programs; projects 2 and 4 are nonmajor programs.

The Single Audit Act requires an *audit of compliance with specific requirements* applicable to *each major program.* **General requirements** pertain to prohibited political activity, the Davis-Bacon Act (which sets construction contractors' wage requirements), civil rights, cash management, relocation assistance and real property acquisitions, federal financial reports, allowable costs/cost principles, maintaining a drug-free work place, and administrative requirements. This audit report includes positive assurance as to items tested, negative assurances as to items not tested, and a disclaimer of opinion on overall compliance.

The Single Audit Act also requires an audit report on compliance with specific requirements of each major program. **Specific requirements** pertain to the types of services allowed, eligibility of recipients of assistance, matching funds to be provided by the entity, and specific reporting requirements of the agency providing the assistance. The auditor's report includes an opinion on compliance with the specific requirements that may have a material effect on each major federal assistance program. Therefore, in designing tests of compliance, the auditor should set planning materiality based on each major program rather than on the overall financial statements and test a representative number of transactions from each major program. In the situation depicted in Exhibit 24.3, the auditor would establish a separate materiality threshold for programs 1 and 3 and test compliance with the laws and regulations related to each of those programs to be sure the specific requirements were met. This will result in a significant increase in such testing compared to a traditional financial audit.

The Single Audit Act requires the auditor to report *all* instances of noncompliance with laws and regulations and questioned costs related to federal financial assistance. **Questioned costs** include alleged violations of covenants governing the expenditure of funds, costs not supported by adequate documentation, and unnecessary or unreasonable expenditures. The reports under government auditing standards and the Single Audit Act should ordinarily go to appropriate officials of the organization audited and of the organizations requiring or arranging for the audits, including external funding organizations.

Exhibit 24.4 is an overview of the auditing and reporting requirements for compliance with laws and regulations under GAAS, government auditing standards, and the Single Audit Act. The GAAS requirements apply to all audits, including an

Exhibit 24.4

AUDITING AND REPORTING ON COMPLIANCE WITH LAWS AND REGULATIONS

Generally Accepted Auditing Standards

Procedures Performed

Testing of compliance with laws and regulations, in general, in accordance with *SAS No. 54*, "Illegal Acts by Clients." Testing of compliance with laws and regulations applicable to governmental financial assistance in accordance with *SAS No. 68*, "Compliance Auditing Applicable to Governmental Entities and Other Recipients of Governmental Financial Assistance."

Report Issued

Opinion on financial statements.

Government Auditing Standards (GAAS+)

Procedures Performed

Testing of compliance with laws and regulations in accordance with GAAS.

Reports Issued

Statement of positive assurance about transactions tested and negative assurance about transactions not tested; report of nonmaterial instances of noncompliance found.

Single Audit Requirements (Government Auditing Standards +)

Procedures Performed

Major programs: Audit of compliance with specific requirements and tests of compliance with general requirements applicable to major federal financial assistance programs, as defined by the Single Audit Act.

Nonmajor programs: Testing of compliance with laws and regulations applicable to nonmajor federal financial assistance program transactions selected in connection with the audit of the financial statements.

Reports Issued

Major programs: Opinion on compliance, schedule of findings and questioned costs, and report on compliance with general requirements.

Nonmajor programs: Statement of positive assurance about nonmajor federal financial assistance program transactions tested and negative assurance about transactions not tested; schedule of findings and questioned costs.

opinion on the financial statements. An additional report, on compliance, is required in audits for which government auditing standards apply. In audits falling under the Single Audit Act, additional compliance tests and reports are required.

Reporting on Internal Controls under the Single Audit Act

The Single Audit Act requires a written report on the client's internal control systems over the administration of its federal financial assistance programs. Because a full audit of the client's internal control structure is not performed, the report usually contains a disclaimer of opinion on the overall system. If the audit discloses no material weaknesses in the administration of the programs, the report includes negative assurance to that effect. If weaknesses are discovered, they are described.

Summary of Reporting Requirements under GAAS, Government Auditing Standards, and the Single Audit Act

In addition to the GAAS opinion on financial statements, government auditing standards require a written report on compliance with laws and regulations and on internal controls but does not require any auditing procedures not required under GAAS.

The Single Audit Act contains additional audit and reporting requirements, which increases the cost of an audit by around 20 percent, according to many public accountants. These are the additional reports:

- An opinion on the supplementary schedule of federal financial assistance that was prepared by the client.
- A report on internal controls over federal financial assistance.
- An opinion on compliance with specific requirements applicable to major federal financial assistance programs.
- A report on compliance with general requirements applicable to major federal financial assistance programs.
- A report on compliance with specific requirements applicable to nonmajor federal financial assistance program transactions tested.
- A schedule of all findings and questioned costs for both major and nonmajor programs.

The Government Accounting and Audit Committee of the AICPA issued *Statement of Position (SOP)* 89-6 that contains examples of reports to be issued in audits of state and local governmental units.

Determining the Reporting Entity

Determining the reporting entity in a governmental audit may not be a simple task and should be documented before planning the audit. In a typical commercial audit, there is usually no doubt about the scope of the engagement or the units to be included in the financial statements. In the governmental setting, however, the entity is not as clear because there are no voting shares of stock or distinct ownership interests. Does an audit of a city include the school district contained solely within the city's boundaries? Does it include the city owned and operated water or electric utility or the community college? Such questions must be settled in advance. Important factors to consider are the financial interdependency of the governmental unit and the governing authority. The reporting entity should normally include the primary governmental unit and any other governmental entity for which the primary unit is responsible for financing the other entity's deficit, is entitled to its surplus, guarantees its debt, or selects all or a majority of its governing authority. If the city government can appoint three of the five members of the board of directors of the community college, the college should be included in the city's financial statements and in the audit. The components of the reporting entity should be identified in the engagement letter.

Overview of Financial Audit Procedures

Audit and reporting procedures are guided by the SASs, *Audits of State and Local Governmental Units* (an AICPA audit and accounting guide), and related Statements of Position. The following sections discuss several of the audit considerations and procedures that are unique to government auditing standards.

Planning Materiality

The auditor's opinion covers the general-purpose financial statements for state and local governments. These statements provide financial information by fund type—general fund, special funds, debt service funds, capital projects funds, and proprietary funds. Planning materiality should be established by fund type and be related to tolerable misstatements in account balances and classes of transactions within each fund type. A key step in determining planning materiality is to specify the base to be used. The primary objective of accounting for governmental fund types relates to the flow of resources. Therefore, total revenues or expenditures provide an appropriately stable base to determine materiality. For proprietary funds, such as the water utility fund, total assets may be an appropriate base for materiality determination.

Some audit procedures are applied to a particular asset or class of transactions across several funds for efficiency purposes. Audits of cash and payroll are examples. One checking account is often used for several funds. Payroll is usually centralized. It is often most efficient to apply audit procedures for cash and payroll expenditures/expenses for all funds rather than by fund type. In such situations, tolerable misstatement should relate to the smallest fund type covered by the test.

Unique Elements of the Internal Control Structure

Governmental units have many of the same controls as commercial clients, but their internal control structures differ in many ways. Budget, appropriation, and encumbrance systems provide controls over the amount and nature of authorized expenditures. Public budget hearings permit the press and others to comment and report on the activities that are permitted and funded. Legislative enactment may allow little discretion over expenditures. Effective encumbrance systems provide assurance that proposed expenditures are allowed by the budget. Procurement systems are often centralized and separate from the operating departments. Requirements for public notice of proposed acquisitions and bidding procedures may provide effective control over expenditures.

Testing Compliance with Laws and Regulations

More attention and audit time are devoted to testing compliance with laws, regulations, and budget requirements in a governmental audit because government operations are closely regulated and controlled by laws. Events of noncompliance can have material implications for the financial statements. GAAP require that legally adopted budgets be presented in the general-purpose financial statements of a governmental unit as part of the basic financial statements. Thus, the auditor must be sure that the budget information and comparisons with actual amounts are properly presented. A governmental unit's operating activities are closely related to the laws that enable it to raise necessary revenues and provide services to the public.

Auditors should obtain an understanding of the laws and regulations, including the general and specific requirements of federal financial assistance programs, that have a potential direct and material effect on the determination of amounts in the financial statements. The auditor may consider performing procedures like those previously described under government auditing standards.

Once the applicable laws and regulations have been identified, the auditor must design procedures to obtain reasonable assurance of detecting material misstatements resulting from noncompliance. This usually involves testing compliance with specific requirements relating to the types of allowable costs and services and to the eligibility of the recipients of financial assistance. For example, salary and fringe benefit costs may be allocated to a community development block grant for individuals that devote their time to the project being charged. The auditor should determine that the allocation is appropriate and the individuals are working on the project.

Exhibit 24.5 reports the program objective, specific *eligibility* requirements, and suggested compliance audit procedures for funds made available to states under the federal Job Training Partnership Act.

Analytical Procedures

Analytical procedures can be effective in planning and performing governmental audits. Many governmental activities remain relatively stable from year to year. Comparisons of current year information with that of prior years, therefore, can be helpful in spotting unexpected results. Budgeting is more formal than for commercial clients. Comparisons of actual revenues and expenditures with budget are

Exhibit 24.5

PROGRAM OBJECTIVE, SPECIFIC ELIGIBILITY REQUIREMENTS, AND SUGGESTED COMPLIANCE AUDIT PROCEDURES FOR ASSISTANCE RECEIVED UNDER THE FEDERAL JOB TRAINING PARTNERSHIP ACT

Program Objective

The objective of the Job Training Partnership Act (JTPA) is to provide funds to states to use to establish programs to prepare youth and unskilled adults for entry into the labor force. These programs should afford job training to those economically disadvantaged individuals and other individuals facing serious barriers to employment and who are in special need of such training to obtain productive employment.

Eligibility

Compliance Requirement

Each administrative entity is responsible for the eligibility of those enrolled in its programs. Administrative entities may delegate eligibility determinations, if the delegation and related safeguards are included in an approved job training plan.

Suggested Audit Procedures

- Review the eligibility determination system and evaluate for adequacy.
- Review selected participant files and determine the appropriateness of eligibility determinations.

Source: U.S. Office of Management and Budget, *Uniform Requirements for Grants to State and Local Governments—Compliance Supplement (Revised)* (1985), ¶1201A.

particularly effective in identifying areas of risk. Overall tests of reasonableness may replace detailed testing. The auditor can analytically test license fee revenue, for example, by multiplying the average fee by the number of licenses issued and comparing it with the fees recorded during the current and prior years. Any significant fluctuations should be noted and additional testing may be needed, such as confirming a sample from a list of applications filed in the period.

Audit of the Revenue Cycle

Governmental units receive revenue from a variety of sources, such as property and income taxes, licenses, fees, permits, and grants. GAAP require the use of a modified accrual basis of accounting for governmental fund types. Revenues are recognized when they become available and measurable. Revenue is considered available when it is collectible.

Audit emphasis for the revenue cycle is on revenue rather than receivables. Governmental units tend to have relatively large revenue flows and small receivable balances. Verification of the receivable balance is a by-product of verification of revenue rather than the reverse. The auditor often simultaneously confirms total revenues and remaining receivables with outside sources, for example grants from other governmental units. Confirmations are useful for such items as franchise taxes and sales taxes collected by the state and remitted to cities. Normally, the auditor does not confirm receivables for property taxes, special assessments, or other taxes receivable from individual taxpayers because other reliable evidence—analytical procedures, for example, or detailed independent records of recorded deeds and tax assessments—is usually available.

Effective analytical tests often exist to test revenues. The audit program for property taxes, for example, often includes the following procedures:

- Obtain or prepare a schedule summarizing property tax revenue by class of property and compare recorded revenue to the current budget and prior period actual amounts.
- Confirm with the appraisal authority the total assessed valuation of the tax roll, obtain a copy of the ordinance establishing tax rates or confirm the rates, compute the tax levy, and compare to recorded property tax revenue.

Maintenance of the tax roll and determination of the assessed valuation are often the responsibilities of another governmental unit, such as a county appraiser. Because the evidence is generally considered to be independent and persuasive, additional procedures are not usually necessary.

Grant revenues are recognized when the conditions of the grant are met, for example, when the money is spent for a capital improvement. Thus, audit tests of grant revenue focus on compliance with laws and regulations.

Audit of the Expenditures

It is often efficient to stratify the testing of expenditures by classification and test across fund types. Expenditures can be conveniently classified as:

- Personal service expenditures (payroll).
- Current operating expenditures other than for personal services.

- Capital expenditures.
- Debt service expenditures.

Accounts payable and similar liabilities are usually substantiated in conjunction with tests of operating expenditures.

Payroll. The payroll function is usually centralized but is designed to develop a payroll summary for each fund. The funds are charged in amounts to cover gross pay and related employer tax and other contributions, and the total is transferred to the payroll bank account. Individual net payroll checks are written to employees, and payroll deductions and employer's contributions are remitted to the proper agencies for withholdings, FICA, and so on.

The audit of payroll begins with obtaining an understanding of regulations pertinent to wages, salaries, and benefits. Analytical procedures can often be effectively designed to increase audit efficiency. Payroll audit programs often include the following:

- Compare payroll expenditures to prior period actual and current budget by department or function and in total. Determine reasonableness in relation to changes in the number of personnel employed and approved wage rates.
- Compare accruals for compensated absences to prior period actual and current budget, and compare the relation of amounts to gross pay with the same ratio for the prior period.
- Compare pension expenditure to number of covered employees and to the same relationship in the prior period.
- Compare gross pay and related payroll liabilities to comparable totals on Forms 941 filed with the federal government. (The Internal Revenue Service does tie out these forms with individual tax returns within three years. Therefore, it is unlikely that false forms will be filed.)
- Test compliance with laws and regulations relating to payroll, such as allowable fringe benefit costs and pay rates according to the guidelines of the Davis-Bacon Act.

The results of these procedures should be considered in deciding whether it is necessary to sample individual payroll transactions. Observation of payroll distributions is not a common procedure unless there is a serious risk of a padded payroll. However, some states including New York and Illinois require such observation.

Other Operating Expenditures. Major compliance considerations concerning operating expenditures relate to competitive bidding and requirements imposed by ordinances, bond covenants, and grant provisions. The most common audit procedures for operating expenditures are comparisons, tests of details, and search for unrecorded accounts payable. The auditor should compare expenditures to prior period actual and current budget by account for each fund type.

Cash disbursement tests should be performed on a sample basis across fund types, including capital expenditures and debt service. Attribute estimation sampling is useful in determining the appropriate sample size. Selected items should be reviewed for:

- Agreement with supporting documents.
- Correct recording as to account, fund, budget category, and period.
- Approval and compliance with budget and legal requirements, focusing on allowability of the cost and eligibility of the recipient.

Capital Acquisition. Compliance issues relate to restrictions imposed by local regulations, grant requirements, or debt provisions and restrictions on the use of proceeds from disposals. Otherwise, the approach to auditing capital acquisitions is much the same as for commercial clients.

Debt Service Expenditures. Compliance issues that should normally be addressed include these:

- Debt limits imposed by state regulations, the charter, ordinances, or statutes.
- Requirements for voter referendums before issuance of major debt.
- Restrictions imposed in the bond-offering documents, voter referendums, and bond ordinances on the use of the funds.

Confirmations are used extensively to obtain corroborative evidence about the following:

- Principal balances outstanding (with the lender or trustee).
- Interest paid to and cash held by fiscal agents for payment of unpresented bonds and interest coupons.
- Restrictions, terms, and proceeds from sale (with the lender or underwriter).
- Legal compliance of debt sales (with legal counsel or appropriate state authority).
- Compliance with covenants (with the trustee).

Additional audit procedures include examining debt and lease agreements and reviewing legislative minutes or results of a voter referendum for authorization. Interest costs can be analytically tested by relating average rates to average debt outstanding.

Governmental Auditing Summary

Governmental auditing is rapidly evolving and can be complex due to the many federal, state, and local laws and regulations. Exhibit 24.6 is a summary of the audit and reporting requirements under government auditing standards, the Single Audit Act, and OMB Circulars A-128 and A-133. Government auditing standards do not impose additional audit procedure requirements than are already contained in GAAS. The Single Audit Act, however, requires more detailed auditing of, and reporting on, compliance and controls than do GAAS and government auditing standards. The only additional *opinion* required under the Single Audit Act is on compliance with specific requirements of major programs. Several additional reports and schedules, however, are required.

It is imperative that auditors perform quality audits of their governmental audit clients. If they do not, the public will lose confidence in the auditing profession,

Exhibit 24.6

SUMMARY OF THE AUDIT AND REPORTING REQUIREMENTS UNDER GOVERNMENT AUDITING STANDARDS, THE SINGLE AUDIT ACT, AND OMB CIRCULARS A-128 AND A-133

Procedures Performed	Report Issued
1. Audit of the financial statements in accordance with *GAAS*.	• *Opinion* on the financial statements.
2. Audit of the financial statements in accordance with *Government Auditing Standards*.	• Report on compliance with laws and regulations that may have a material effect on the financial statements. • Report on internal control structure-related matters based solely on an assessment of control risk made as part of the audit of the financial statements.
3. Obtain an understanding and assess *control risk* of the internal control structure over *federal financial assistance* and perform tests of controls.	• Report on internal controls over federal financial assistance. • Report on supplementary schedule of federal financial assistance.
4. Test of *compliance* with general requirements applicable to federal financial assistance programs and audit of compliance with specific requirements applicable to major federal financial assistance programs as defined by the *Single Audit Act* or *OMB Circular A-133*.	• Report on compliance with general requirements applicable to federal financial assistance programs. • *Opinion* on compliance with specific requirements applicable to each major federal financial assistance program. • Schedule of findings and questioned costs.
5. Test of compliance with laws and regulations applicable to nonmajor federal financial assistance program transactions selected for testing in connection with 1 or 3.	• Report on compliance with laws and regulations applicable to nonmajor federal financial assistance program transactions tested. • Schedule of findings and questioned costs.

Source: AICPA, *Statement on Auditing Standards No. 68*, "Compliance Auditing Applicable to Governmental Entities and Other Recipients of Governmental Financial Assistance" (New York: AICPA, 1991), Appendix A.

leading to more government involvement, bad publicity, lawsuits, and other unpleasant consequences.

B–OVERVIEW OF INTERNAL AUDITING

Internal auditing has grown from a group of "internal checkers" of 50 years ago to a profession performing complex computer audits, operational audits, analysis of operations, and special investigations for management and the board of directors. Many of today's internal auditors are certified internal auditors (CIAs) and provide a unique service to organizations. In fact, internal auditing is taking on increased importance in many of today's global organizations by assisting management in evaluating controls and operations and thereby providing an important element of global control. The challenge is to identify and meet management expectations; operational auditing is a vehicle to success and survival.

Internal auditing is unique: it is part of the organization, but it must be performed objectively. Internal auditors must also develop competencies in the areas of operations they audit. For this reason, internal auditing is often viewed as a good steppingstone to a management position. The director of internal auditing is often responsible to top management (the chief executive officer or chief financial officer) and to the audit committee. An annual report summarizing the activities of the internal audit department and its reports and findings is normally distributed to and discussed with the audit committee.

External auditors can reduce their audit work by relying on the internal auditors. Internal auditors may test the control procedures in the revenue cycle and routinely confirm customer balances, for example. In addition, internal auditors may provide direct assistance to external auditors by assisting in the observation of physical inventory or in obtaining explanations about confirmation exceptions.

The *scope* of internal auditing seems unlimited. In most organizations, it includes all departments, functions, and activities. The scope of the internal audit function is often formally established in an internal audit department charter or vision and mission statement specifying its authority and responsibilities and providing free access to audit all areas of the organization deemed important by the director, management, or the audit committee. The scope often includes financial audits, the focus of this book, and audits of the effectiveness and efficiency with which management is fulfilling its responsibilities, often referred to as *operational, management,* or *performance audits.* Internal audits may include special projects, investigations, and studies to help management solve problems. The scope can include an evaluation of the effectiveness of inventory control procedures and test the accuracy of the accounting function, of the compliance of a day-care program for employees with federal regulations, of the effectiveness of the personnel department and its compliance with organizational and regulatory requirements, and of pension fund accounting, as well as tests of the controls over the computer center, over compliance with the company's code of conduct, and over the capital acquisition activities.

Competitive Advantages of Internal Auditing

Internal auditing is unique in three respects: (1) its location within the organization, (2) the diversity of functional areas that it examines and types of audits performed on the functional areas, and (3) the diverse backgrounds of individual auditors. Auditors often have backgrounds in data processing, operations management, financing, marketing, and accounting. Some organizations are combining internal auditors and line personnel on problem resolution teams.

Internal auditing can be an effective place to build future managers because operational auditing requires internal auditors to understand operating problems and recommend solutions for operational areas. Once auditors have obtained good operational experience, many of them are returning to the internal audit department, often to manage that department.

A well-managed internal audit department maintains the confidence of management by exceeding professional standards. CIA certificates can be required for promotion to manager positions within the internal audit staff. Risk analysis can be judiciously applied to target audits (1) where there is likely to be a cost-benefit advantage to the organization, (2) where the control structure can be improved, and (3) in areas such as information systems where it has the expertise and time to implement sophisticated audit techniques.

Information Systems Auditing

Information systems auditing, sometimes referred to as *EDP auditing,* has been a major growth area in internal auditing over the past two decades. The Institute of Internal Auditors has sponsored two major research projects referred to as Systems Auditability and Control in 1977 and 1991, which have identified the tremendous growth in information systems topics addressed by auditors. A professional organization, The EDP Auditor's Association, has emerged to specifically address information systems audit concerns. Many internal audit departments have established separate sections of information systems auditors and have staffed these sections with auditors having data processing and auditing backgrounds.

Internal audit departments have a unique competitive advantage in performing information systems auditing. First, because the auditors are present throughout the year, they can effectively perform audits during the systems design process. It is significantly less costly to address control concerns on important applications when they are being developed rather than to correct problems after the system has been implemented. Internal auditors, as control experts, can recommend control standards and/or potential controls as new applications are being developed. Second, the auditors can develop and implement the concurrent audit techniques discussed in Chapter 10. For example, the internal auditor can design and implement an integrated test facility or a snapshot facility into an application as it is being developed. The auditor can then use these facilities to monitor the reliability of the system throughout the year on an efficient basis. Finally, the information systems auditor can assist the remainder of the audit staff in using the computer to perform financial and operational audits or to develop and/or implement some of the advanced audit techniques discussed in Chapter 23.

C–OPERATIONAL AUDITING

In contrast to the financial auditing focus of this text, a significant portion of audit practice is operational auditing performed primarily by internal auditors, but increasingly performed by public accounting firms and governmental auditors. **Operational auditing** is defined as the evaluation of activities, systems, and controls within an enterprise for efficiency, effectiveness, and economy. Governmental auditors call this *program audits.* Operational auditing goes beyond the accounting and financial records to obtain a full understanding of the business and operations under review. The purposes of operational audits are often to assess the quality and efficiency of performance, identify opportunities for improvement, and develop recommendations for improvement. Operational auditing is perceived by many auditees as constructive. Some internal audit departments devote most of their time to operational audits; others concentrate on financial audits.

The Need for Operational Audits

Operational audits are performed for a number of reasons. Managers must objectively establish that their tasks have been accomplished (effectiveness) with the minimum of personnel and time (efficiency) and using the least expensive resources (economy). Top management and audit committees need the help of skilled internal auditors to review the organization's activities and to ensure that operations are well controlled and that normal reports prepared by operational or functional areas are complete, relevant, and reliable. Internal auditing is a staff position, not a line position. Recommendations are made to management and the auditee, but action must come from them.

Internal auditors are looked on as consultants in many organizations because of the diversified background of the staff and their knowledge of the operations of the entire organization, analytical skills, knowledge of what constitutes good internal controls, and independent status* within the organizational structure. Thus, their services are often used for special studies at the request of management.

Activities targeted for operational audits are based on the auditor's analysis of risk and potential benefits to management. More frequent or extensive audits are performed where there is the highest risk that an activity is not accomplishing management's objectives, the failure of which could prevent the enterprise from achieving those objectives. For example, the internal auditors found that the policies for granting loans at a particular branch bank were not being followed. As a result, the internal audit director scheduled that branch for more frequent audits until the problem was solved. The audit committee may have special concerns and request the internal auditors to perform audits related to those concerns.

Comparison of Operational and Financial Auditing

Operational auditing, like financial auditing, tests assertions and gathers audit evidence. But the assertions related to operational auditing pertain to the effectiveness of an operation as measured by (1) compliance with policies, (2) standards of efficient practices for the operation, and (3) the effectiveness of its organization and staffing. In many aspects, operational auditing has always implemented the total quality concepts that are popular today. The operational audit practice of identifying generally accepted "best practices" for an operation is essentially the same as the "benchmarking" concept found in the total quality movement. For example, an operational audit of a company's treasury function begins with an identification of the state of the art procedures for effectively managing cash resources and compares the company's current practices with those "best practices."

Characteristics

Operational auditing has many characteristics similar to those of financial auditing (see Exhibit 24.7). Both must be carefully *planned*. The operational auditor tests

**Internal auditor independence* has a different meaning than *external auditor independence*. An external auditor must be independent in the eyes of people *outside* the organization who rely on the audit opinion. An internal auditor must be independent in the eyes of people *inside* the organization who rely on their work—management and the board of directors.

Exhibit 24.7

CHARACTERISTICS OF FINANCIAL AND OPERATIONAL AUDITING

Characteristic	Financial Auditing	Operational Auditing
Systematic process	Audit is carefully planned before it is performed.	Same
Assertions	Management assertions related to financial reporting—existence, completeness, rights and obligations, valuation and allocation, and presentation and disclosures.	Management assertions related to the organization's operations—whether they are run in an effective, efficient, and economical manner and are in compliance with company policies and governmental regulations.
Criteria	GAAP or comprehensive basis of accounting. Authoritative pronouncements exist.	Vary depending on the audit objectives. Auditor may have to consult textbooks or publications for the definition of "best practices" for the area.
Evidence	Inquiry, observation, confirmations, analytical procedures, documentation, and physical examination.	Same
Objectivity	Auditors must be independent of the organization.	Auditors must be independent of the activity or function being audited.
Reporting	Opinion on the fairness of the financial statements.	Report on audit findings, causes, effects, and recommendations to correct the problem.
Competence	Must have adequate technical training and proficiency as an auditor.	Must have technical proficiency as an auditor and must develop knowledge of the functional area sufficient to permit an objective evaluation.

management's assertions that its area of responsibility is run in an effective, efficient, and economical manner. One major difficulty in operational auditing is identifying the criteria by which operations will be judged; often the criteria are not well defined. The criteria against which the auditor evaluates the activity depends on the nature of the activity being audited and the audit objectives. For example, assume that the auditor is to audit the treasury function. The auditor might visit with internal auditors of other organizations, obtain ideas from members of professional associations such as the Treasurers Management Association, and/or review finance textbooks to identify generally accepted good treasury practices (a form of GAAP for the operation), but if the criteria do not exist, the auditor and auditee should agree on the appropriate criteria before the audit can be performed. When auditing the advertising program of a retailer, there may be no written policies as to when written contracts should be obtained from vendors who participate in a cooperative advertising program. The auditor should meet with management and agree on whether implicit criteria are in existence, even if not formalized. For example, one criterion could be that written contracts are required with all vendors who participate in the cooperative advertising program.

The types of evidence and the procedures used to gather the evidence are similar for both types of audits. The auditor evaluating the treasury function examines documents authorizing cash transfers for both financial and operational audits. However, evidence for the operational audit is expanded to determine the cost of an inefficient procedure—for example, failing to consolidate funds from many bank accounts into one interest-bearing account. Operational audit reports focus on findings, both positive and negative, and include recommendations to correct any audit findings.

Scope and Objectives

Many internal audit departments develop a long-range audit plan that encompasses all or most of the activities within their enterprise. In other departments, operational audits emerge from discussions with management and general awareness of evolving problem areas. Exhibit 24.8 provides some examples of typical operational audits. Some of these activities would not be the subject of a financial audit, such as the audit of cooperative advertising. Other activities may be the subject of both financial and operational audits, but the audit objectives are different. Operational audit objectives for receipts and disbursements, for example, might include determining whether:

- Cash on hand and in the bank is kept at minimum levels.
- Temporary excess cash is safely invested to earn a reasonable rate of return.
- Cash disbursements are made on a timely basis to take advantage of all cash discounts while at the same time not paying the bills too early (see the Auditing in Practice section on Untimely Disbursements).

Auditing in Practice

UNTIMELY DISBURSEMENTS

One auditor discovered that the company was losing more than $350,000 a year because checks were not being mailed soon enough to take advantage of cash discounts. The auditee implemented the auditor's recommendation to pay the bills on a timely basis and, during the next year, bills were indeed paid within the discount period. In fact, during a follow-up audit, the auditors found that checks were being sent an average of four days before they needed to be to take advantage of the discounts. It was estimated that about $1 million of investment income had been lost because of paying the bills too early. Now the bills are being paid just in time to take advantage of the discounts.

Exhibit 24.8

EXAMPLES OF OPERATIONAL AUDITS

Activity or Function	Typical Operational Audits
Inventory	Determine whether inventory is being warehoused efficiently and effectively, whether customer orders are met on a timely basis, and whether duplicate warehouse facilities exist and the related cost of duplication.
Purchasing	Test controls over placement of orders (bidding, reorder point, quantities, etc.). Determine whether the purchasing function responds on a timely basis to requisitions, whether the function uses long-term contracts to build stable supplies, and whether procedures are in compliance with applicable company policies and governmental regulations.
Insurance program	Examine adequacy of coverage (tangible assets, bonding of sensitive positions), study cost/benefit of coverage and consider self-insurance opportunities.
Quality control	Determine whether procedures for testing the quality of purchases are being followed and are effective. Consider whether quality control practices are integrated into the manufacturing function.
Advertising	Determine whether the company is obtaining the advertising for which it is paying, whether cooperative vendors are paying their agreed-upon share of advertising costs, and whether the department has established procedures to evaluate the effectiveness of alternative advertising programs.

Audit Approach

The basic steps in an operational audit are the following:

- Perform a preliminary survey.
- Develop the audit program.
- Perform the fieldwork.
- Prepare working papers.
- Develop a list of, and prioritize, audit findings.
- Discuss findings with auditee.
- Prepare the audit report.
- Meet with auditee and management.
- Follow up to be sure that appropriate action is taken to correct deficiencies.

Perform a Preliminary Survey

A **preliminary survey** is performed to familiarize the auditor with the activity being audited. The preliminary survey is designed to gain an understanding of the nature of the activity, its operating objectives, what is done, how it is done, what it costs, the risks, and that the control structure has been designed to ensure that organizational objectives are met. Some of this information is contained in procedures manuals, but formal procedures may or may not be followed. The auditor should find out how things are really done and should use inquiries, observation, and review of documents to provide most of the information.

The efficiency of the audit depends on how the preliminary survey is conducted. The basic steps in a preliminary survey conducted by an internal auditor are listed in Exhibit 24.9.

Information is available in the internal audit department about the business and activity to be audited, such as prior audit working papers and reports, literature in the library (such as textbooks, research studies, periodicals, and trade magazines), organization charts, and statements of management policies. Questionnaires serve as a reminder list of important topics to discuss at the initial meeting with the auditee. Interviewing skills are extremely important. The auditor must put the auditee at ease, create a cooperative attitude with the auditee, and obtain the necessary information.

Problems may become apparent during the preliminary survey that can provide the basis for a report to management. Findings reported at this stage should be supported by the preliminary survey and documented in the working papers. The preliminary survey serves as a basis for preparing the audit program should management and the auditor decide to proceed to the next stage.

Exhibit 24.9

BASIC STEPS OF A PRELIMINARY SURVEY

- Prepare for the survey by becoming familiar with the nature of the business and activity to be audited, reading reference materials, policy manuals, and previous audit reports and working papers.
- Develop a questionnaire for interviews and discussions.
- Arrange for the initial meeting and interview people involved in the operation.
- Develop an understanding of the objectives, goals, and standards of the operation as seen by top management and operating management.
- Identify and preliminarily evaluate the risks inherent in the operation.
- Observe the facilities, physical layouts, processes, and the flow of materials and documents.
- Document the flow of important activities using flowcharts and/or narrative descriptions.
- Summarize the survey results in the working papers and prepare a memo describing the implications for the audit.

Develop an Audit Program

Audit programs should be prepared on completion of the preliminary survey and should address the objectives, potential problems, risks, and sources of information applicable to the area audited. An example of a partial audit program is shown in Exhibit 24.10 for an audit of the advertising function of a retailer. Many vendors provide for a cooperative advertising program in which the vendors reimburse the company for a specified percentage of the cost of television, radio, and newspaper advertising. The audit program describes the operating and audit objectives, identifies the risks, lists the audit procedures, and provides space to identify the working paper reference where the procedures are documented.

As shown in Exhibit 24.10, the auditor designs the audit program based on the operating objectives, audit objectives, and risks applicable to the functional area. Operating objectives are established by management. They represent the results management seeks to accomplish. Audit objectives are established by the auditor and are designed to determine whether the operating objectives are being achieved. Audit procedures are activities designed to achieve the audit objectives.

Perform the Fieldwork

Fieldwork involves gathering evidence for measuring and evaluating the activity being audited according to preestablished criteria. The criteria for the audit of the cooperative advertising program previously referred to are (1) a written agreement

Exhibit 24.10

SAMPLE AUDIT PROGRAM

Operating objective: Minimize advertising costs through effective use of cooperative advertising programs.

Audit objective: Determine whether written cooperative agreements exist for each participating vendor and whether the company is receiving the correct reimbursements according to those agreements.

Risks	Audit Procedures	W/P Ref.
Loss of vendor payments because no written agreement exists.	Obtain list of all vendors that provide cooperative payments. Determine that a written agreement exists for each of these vendors by examining the agreement.	
Proper amount was not received from vendor.	Select a random sample of advertisements and verify that the correct amount was received by looking at the advertising invoices and contract specifications compared to recorded amount received.	

is to be obtained from each participating vendor and (2) the amounts of advertising reimbursements should agree with the advertisers' invoices and coop agreements. Evaluation of the activity should be based on the established criteria. A deficiency exists, for example, if it is found that no written agreements exist for some of the participating vendors. The auditor should then determine why they do not exist and any dollars lost because the vendors did not reimburse the company.

Prepare Working Papers

The audit working papers facilitate the performance of the audit in an orderly fashion, document the evidence obtained during the preliminary survey and fieldwork, provide the information needed if the conclusions and recommendations are questioned, support the audit report, and serve as a reference for subsequent audits. Most internal audit departments have formal guidelines specifying working paper formats. Working papers reflect on the auditor's competence.

Develop Audit Findings

The auditor should summarize potential audit findings throughout the conduct of the audit to facilitate the report preparation. Some internal audit departments have developed a form on which each audit finding is documented (see Exhibit 24.11). It contains the basic elements that should be included in the audit report: the *criteria* used to evaluate the activity; the *condition*, the *cause*, and the *effect* of the audit finding; any actions already initiated by the auditee to correct the problem; and recommendations to correct the problem. The auditee may disagree with the auditor's recommendations. When this represents an honest difference of opinion, the auditee's comments should also be recorded. Each audit finding should be categorized as major or minor according to its importance and be clearly separated in the audit report. A **major finding** is one that prevents the activity from achieving one of its primary objectives. For example, failure to obtain written agreements that result in the failure of the advertising department to obtain proper reimbursements from vendors may result in significantly increased advertising costs. A **minor finding** does not prevent the activity from achieving a major objective but will continue to have adverse effects if not corrected and should be reported to top management. Inadequate records, for example, may cause the advertising department to overlook an occasional reimbursement opportunity.

Discuss Findings with Auditee

It is useful to meet with the auditee at the end of the fieldwork to discuss the audit findings. This meeting helps ensure the quality of the audit report. The auditee can review the facts for accuracy, inform the auditor of any corrective action taken or planned, and discuss the practicability of recommended corrective actions.

Prepare the Audit Report

The audit report is the principal vehicle for communicating and persuading. A well-written report captures the attention of the reader and is more likely to stimulate corrective action. It should present the facts and rationale for the conclusions and recommendations. Effective audit reports emphasize important findings and include only supported allegations and conclusions and appropriate recommendations. The report should be concise, use active voice and modern technology (such as graphs) to communicate and include all of the information needed to convey the importance of the findings and stimulate action.

Exhibit 24.11

FORM TO SUMMARIZE EACH AUDIT FINDING

Auditee ______________________________ Date ______________

Major Minor W/P Ref ______________

Criteria ____

____

Condition ____

____

Cause ____

____

Effect ____

____

Corrective Action Taken ____

____

Recommendations ____

____

Discussions:

Name	Title	Dept	Date	Auditor

1 ____

Comments ____

2 ____

Comments ____

The *Standards for the Professional Practice of Internal Auditing* issued by The Institute of Internal Auditors contains guidance for reporting the results of audits (see Exhibit 24.12).

During the audit, significant audit findings may be noted that should be corrected as soon as possible. In such cases, interim written or oral reports can be made. The

Exhibit 24.12

STANDARD 430—COMMUNICATING RESULTS

Internal auditors should report the results of their audit work.

1. A signed, written report should be issued after the audit examination is completed. Interim reports may be written or oral and may be transmitted formally or informally.
2. The internal auditor should discuss conclusions and recommendations at appropriate levels of management before issuing final written reports.
3. Reports should be objective, clear, concise, constructive, and timely.
4. Reports should present the purpose, scope, and results of the audit; and, where appropriate, reports should contain an expression of the auditor's opinion.
5. Reports may include recommendations for potential improvements and acknowledge satisfactory performance and corrective action.
6. The auditee's views about audit conclusions or recommendations may be included in the audit report.
7. The director of internal auditing or designee should review and approve the final audit report before issuance and should decide to whom the report will be distributed.

Source: *Standards for the Professional Practice of Internal Auditing* (The Institute of Internal Auditors, Inc., 1978), 400–2.

draft of the written report should be discussed with the auditee before the final report is issued. To facilitate this discussion, it is helpful to put cross-references in the draft so the auditor can find the supporting information in the working papers if questions arise.

The report often contains the following:

- Purpose of the audit.
- Scope of the audit.
- Criteria used.
- Cause(s) of the audit finding.
- Effects of the audit finding.
- Conclusions.
- Recommendations.
- Auditee comments.

The first page of the report should contain an executive summary that captures the most important information if it is a lengthy report. Then the reader can read the detail if he or she wishes.

An abbreviated sample audit report is shown in Exhibit 24.13.

The purpose and scope of the audit should be made clear and set the stage for the remainder of the report. The criteria used establish the authority for the audit findings. The condition states what was found during the audit. Identifying the causes helps management assess the corrective action needed. The effects emphasize the

Exhibit 24.13

SAMPLE OPERATIONAL AUDIT REPORT

November 18, 1994

To: Marketing Vice President
From: Director of Internal Auditing
Subject: Effectiveness of Cooperative Advertising Program

Purpose
The purpose of our audit was to evaluate the effectiveness of the controls over the cooperative advertising program and to determine whether improvements can be made in the operation of the program.

Scope
Our audit covered the cooperative advertising program administered through the home office for all stores. Our audit covered the period from August 1, 1994, to September 30, 1994.

Criteria
At its July 19, 1993, meeting, the Administrative Committee established the requirement that a written contract be obtained for all cooperative agreements.

Condition
Thirty of the 100 cooperative transactions randomly selected for testing did not have supporting contracts. Reimbursements were received according to the contract for the 70 transactions for which a contract existed. Reimbursements were also received in accordance with the understanding of the buyers in 20 of those transactions for which a contract did not exist. In four of the remaining transactions, no reimbursement was received, even after several attempts by the buyers. Amounts less than expected were received for the other six transactions.

Causes
Fifteen of the 30 transactions in noncompliance have been isolated to one staff person. The remaining situations were for smaller vendors and dollar volumes for which the advertising staff did not believe developing a contract was cost justified.

Effects
Advertising costs were increased by $125,600 because of the failure to receive reimbursements in amounts expected. This represents nine percent of the advertising costs tested.

Recommendation
Internal control procedures should be established to ensure that all staff obtain contracts on a timely basis. Standard contracts should be considered for use with small vendors to minimize related legal costs. Training should be provided for the individual associated with most of the problems, or other action taken, as deemed necessary to improve performance.

Auditee Comments
Jim Theme and Jerry Porwall agree that a problem exists regarding obtaining contracts. Corrective action has been initiated for the staff person with the largest volume of transactions, and the policy manual is being updated. They agree that standardized contracts for small vendors was a good idea and they will bring it up at the next Administrative Committee meeting.

importance of the audit finding. The recommendations are just that; the auditor is not in a position to dictate the corrective action. Management may accept the recommendations, develop their own, or decide to accept the risks of not taking corrective action. Including auditee comments helps assure the recipients of the report that the auditees have been consulted. Differences of opinion can be expressed, and the auditee can get credit for any corrective action already initiated.

The final report should be reviewed by the internal audit department director or designee to ensure that it has high quality. It should be issued as quickly as possible, however, so that corrective action can be taken on a timely basis.

Follow-Up on Audit Findings

The effectiveness of operational auditing is enhanced when management requires auditees to respond to internal audit findings and also encourages internal audit to evaluate the adequacy of corrective action. The auditor may perform a follow-up audit to ensure that the problem has in fact been corrected.

Benefits of Operational Audits

Although many operational audits result in cash savings, more benefit is often gained from preventive aspects such as reduced risks, improvements in operations, and strengthened internal controls.

Developing and Maintaining Proper Relationships with Auditees

Operational audits deal mainly with people. Auditors must develop and maintain good relations with auditees in order to obtain the information needed and to ensure that proper corrective action is taken to remedy deficiencies. Many auditees initially resent the intrusion of auditors until they are convinced that the auditors are there to help them do a better job of managing or to reinforce what they are doing well. Overcoming the auditee's fear of criticism, change, and punitive action by superiors is a difficult task. There are several ways to develop and maintain good relationships with auditees.

Auditee Feedback

Many organizations provide a mechanism for the auditee to evaluate the internal auditors. Such an approach has many advantages. It encourages better relations by creating a sense of participation by the auditee and reduces conflicts arising from a defensive attitude against auditors. It also provides a means for evaluating the performance of the auditors and for improving future audits. Such evaluations can be used both by the auditors and senior management to help ensure accountability of the internal audit function. Some internal audit directors call on the auditee to get his or her verbal evaluation of a recent audit.

Seek the Auditees' Input and Keep Them Informed

At the beginning of the audit, ask the auditees what problems they are having and, when appropriate, seek their help in establishing the audit scope and objectives. Keeping the auditees informed of audit findings during the fieldwork is a key to operational audit success. Recommendations should be discussed with the auditees because they may have better ideas on corrective action or difficulties that might be encountered in implementing the auditor's recommendations. The audit report should not contain surprises. Draft reports should be reviewed with the auditees before the final report is distributed unless fraud is suspected.

Do Not Be a Nitpicker

Emphasizing unimportant deficiencies in an audit report will undermine good relations. The auditee will look on the auditor as a nitpicker and disregard the whole report, which may also contain important recommendations. Top management will lose respect for the internal audit function. The audit report should make a clear distinction between major and minor audit findings and other suggestions for improvement.

Report the Good with the Bad and Recognize Auditee Contributions

Audit reports should reflect an objective attitude on the part of the auditors. Good auditors do not just report negative findings; they provide "warm fuzzies" for positive findings to encourage the continuation of the good things done by the auditee. Audit reports should also recognize the auditee's contributions, ideas, and actions taken to correct any deficiencies uncovered by the audit.

Operational Auditing Summary

Managers of modern organizations find operational auditing to be a valuable source of help. Internal auditing can be an exciting career. It allows individuals to become intimately familiar with the many aspects of their organizations, to develop better ways of doing things, to see their ideas implemented, and to interact with top management. It is often considered to be a fast track into an operating management position.

Appendix A–Government Auditing Standards for Financial Audits

General Standards

A. Qualifications: The staff assigned to conduct the audit should collectively possess adequate professional proficiency for the tasks required.

B. Independence: In all matters relating to the audit work, the audit organization and the individual auditors, whether government or public, should be free from personal and external impairments to independence, should be organizationally independent, and should maintain an independent attitude and appearance.

C. Due Professional Care: Due professional care should be used in conducting the audit and in preparing related reports.

D. Quality Control: Audit organizations conducting government audits should have an appropriate internal quality control system in place and participate in an external quality control review program.

Supplemental Fieldwork Standards for Financial Audits

A. Supplemental *planning* fieldwork standards for government financial audits are:

1. Audit Requirements for all Government Levels: Planning should include consideration of the audit requirements of all levels of government.
2. Legal and Regulatory Requirements: A test should be made of compliance with applicable laws and regulations.
   a. In determining compliance with laws and regulations:
      (1) The auditor should design audit steps and procedures to provide reasonable assurance of detecting errors, irregularities, and illegal acts that could have a direct and material effect on the financial statement amounts or the results of financial related audits.
      (2) The auditor should also be aware of the possibility of illegal acts which could have an indirect and material effect on the financial statements or results of financial related audits.

B. Supplemental *working paper* requirements for financial audits are that working papers should:

1. Contain a written audit program cross-referenced to the working papers.
2. Contain the objective, scope, methodology, and results of the audit.
3. Contain sufficient information so that supplementary oral explanations are not required.
4. Be legible with adequate indexing and cross-referencing, and include summaries and lead schedules, as appropriate.
5. Restrict information included to matters that are materially important and relevant to the objectives of the audit.
6. Contain evidence of supervisory reviews of the work conducted.

Supplemental Reporting Standards for Financial Audits

1. Statement on Auditing Standards: A statement should be included in the auditors' report that the audit was made in accordance with generally accepted government auditing standards (government auditing standards). (AICPA standards require that public accountants state that the audit was made in accordance with GAAS. In conducting government audits, public accountants should also state that their audit was conducted in accordance with government auditing standards.)
2. Report on Compliance: The auditors should prepare a written report on their tests of compliance with applicable laws and regulations. This report, which may be included in either the report on the financial audit or a separate report, should contain a statement of positive assurance on those items which were tested for compliance and negative assurance on those items not tested. It should include all material instances of noncompliance, and all instances or indications of illegal acts which could result in criminal prosecution.
3. Report on Internal Controls: The auditors should prepare a written report on their understanding of the entity's internal control structure and the assessment of control risk made as part of a financial statement audit, or a financial related audit. This report may be included in either the auditor's report on the financial

audit or a separate report. The auditor's report should include as a minimum: (a) the scope of the auditor's work in obtaining an understanding of the internal control structure and in assessing the control risk, (b) the entity's significant internal controls or control structure including the controls established to ensure compliance with laws and regulations that have a material impact on the financial statements and the results of the financial-related audit, and (c) the reportable conditions, including the identification of material weaknesses, identified as a result of the auditor's work in understanding and assessing the control risk.

4. Reporting on Financial Related Audits: Written audit reports are to be prepared giving the results of each financial related audit.
5. Privileged and Confidential Information: If certain information is prohibited from general disclosure, the report should state the nature of the information omitted and the requirement that makes the omission necessary.
6. Report Distribution: Written audit reports are to be submitted by the audit organization to the appropriate officials of the organization audited and to the appropriate officials of the organizations requiring or arranging for the audits, including external funding organizations, unless legal restrictions, ethical considerations, or other arrangements prevent it. Copies of the reports should also be sent to other officials who have legal oversight authority or who may be responsible for taking action and to others authorized to receive such reports. Unless restricted by law or regulation, copies should be made available for public inspection.

Source: Extracted from Comptroller General of the United States, United States General Accounting Office, *Government Auditing Standards*, 1988 revision (Washington, D.C.: Government Printing Office, 1988).

Significant Terms

cognizant agency A federal agency assigned by the Director of the OMB to be responsible for implementing the Single Audit Act requirements for a particular government.

financial assistance Assistance provided by a federal agency in the form of grants, contracts, loans, loan guarantees, property, cooperative agreements, interest subsidies, insurance, or direct appropriations but does not include direct federal cash assistance to individuals.

financial-related audits Audits to determine whether (1) financial reports and related items, such as a statement of revenue and expenses, are fairly presented, (2) financial information is presented in accordance with established or stated criteria, such as variances between estimated and actual financial performance, and (3) the entity has adhered to specific financial compliance requirements, such as grant requirements.

financial statement audits Audits to determine (1) the fairness of the financial statements in accordance with GAAP and (2) whether the entity has complied with laws and regulations for those transactions and events that may have a material effect on the financial statements.

general requirements Requirements of federal financial assistance that pertain to prohibited political activity, the Davis-Bacon Act, which sets wage requirements for construction contractors, civil rights, cash management, relocation assistance and real property acquisition, federal financial reports, allowable costs/cost principles, drug-free workplaces, and administrative requirements.

government auditing standards Standards established by the U.S. General Accounting Office to guide audits of state and local government units and recipients of federal financial assistance; incorporate GAAS and provide supplemental standards and are often referred to as the *Yellow Book*.

major finding A finding that prevents the activity from achieving a major objective.

major program A federally assisted program for which expenditures exceed an established threshold. For example, for governments with total annual federal assistance expenditures less than $1 million, the threshold is the larger of $300,000 or 3 percent.

minor finding A finding that does not prevent the activity from achieving a major objective but will continue to have adverse effects if not corrected and should be reported to top management.

operational auditing The evaluation of activities, systems, and controls within an enterprise for efficiency, effectiveness, and economy.

performance audits The evaluation of an organization's economy, efficiency, and programs.

preliminary survey The first step in an operational audit that familiarizes the auditor with the activity being audited by determining the nature of the activity, its operating objectives, what is done, how it is done, what it costs, the risks, and the controls that have been designed to ensure that the objectives are met and risks minimized.

program audits Audits to determine (1) the extent to which the desired results or benefits established by the legislature or other authorizing body are being achieved; (2) the effectiveness of organizations, programs, activities, or functions; and (3) whether the entity has complied with laws and regulations applicable to the program.

questioned costs Costs related to alleged violations of covenants governing the expenditure of funds, costs not supported by adequate documentation, and unnecessary or unreasonable expenditures.

Single Audit Act of 1984 A federal statute that establishes uniform requirements for audits of each state and local government receiving federal financial assistance of at least $100,000 in any fiscal year.

specific requirements Requirements related to federal financial assistance that include the types of services allowed, eligibility, matching, and reporting.

Review Questions

A–Governmental Auditing

24–1 Do government audit standards apply to all audits of governmental operations? Explain.

24–2 Identify and describe the basic types of government audits.

24–3 To what extent are GAAS incorporated into government auditing standards?

24–4 How is the concept of independence different between GAAS and government auditing standards?

24–5 How do the fieldwork standards differ between GAAS and government auditing standards?

24–6 Under what conditions are auditors required to prepare a written report on reportable conditions under GAAS? Government auditing standards?

24–7 What are the major factors to be considered when determining the reporting entity in a governmental audit?

24–8 How does the consideration of planning materiality differ between a commercial and governmental audit? Explain.

24–9 In what basic ways is the internal control structure likely to be different in a governmental entity as compared to a commercial entity?

24–10 Why are more attention and audit time devoted to testing compliance with laws, regulations, and budget requirements in a governmental audit than in a commercial audit? How are problems of noncompliance addressed in reports on government entities?

24–11 What factors led to the Single Audit Act of 1984? What are its objectives?

24–12 What are the auditor's reporting requirements concerning compliance with laws and regulations under GAAS? Government auditing standards? Single Audit Act?

24–13 What are "questioned costs"?

24–14 How does the audit emphasis of the revenue cycle and the expenditure cycle differ in a governmental audit in comparison with a commercial audit? What would explain the difference in emphasis?

C–Operational Auditing

24–15 What are the major objectives of operational auditing? How does operational auditing differ from financial auditing?

24–16 Explain how knowledge of internal controls allows internal auditors to perform useful operational audits of an organization's technical areas, even when the auditor does not have the technical training of the people who work in that area.

24–17 Why do organizations find internal audits useful? In what ways does internal auditing have a competitive advantage over external auditing?

24–18 What is the purpose of a preliminary survey in an operational audit?

24–19 Why should a preliminary survey be performed before writing the audit program?

24–20 Explain the differences among operating objectives, audit objectives, and audit procedures.

24–21 Why is it important for internal auditors to maintain good relations with auditees?

24–22 What are some of the basic techniques for developing and maintaining good relations with auditees?

24–23 Describe the difference between a major and minor finding.

24–24 What information should normally be included in an operational audit report?

24–25 Why is it important to require auditees to respond to reported audit findings?

Multiple Choice Questions

*24–26 Which of the following bodies promulgates standards for audits of federal financial assistance recipients?

a. Governmental Accounting Standards Board.

b. Financial Accounting Standards Board.

c. General Accounting Office.

d. Governmental Auditing Standards Board.

*24–27 A governmental audit may extend beyond an examination leading to the expression of an opinion on the fairness of financial presentation to include

	Program Results	Compliance	Economy and Efficiency
a.	Yes	Yes	No
b.	Yes	Yes	Yes
c.	No	Yes	Yes
d.	Yes	No	Yes

*24–28 When performing an audit of a city that is subject to the requirements of the Single Audit Act of 1984, an auditor should adhere to

a. Governmental Accounting Standards Board's *General Standards*.

b. Governmental Finance Officer's Association's *Governmental Accounting, Auditing, and Financial Reporting Principles*.

c. General Accounting Office's *Governmental Auditing Standards*.

d. Securities and Exchange Commission's *Regulation S-X*.

*24–29 A CPA has performed an examination of the general-purpose financial statements of Big City. The examination scope included the additional requirements of the Single Audit Act. When reporting on Big City's internal accounting and administrative controls used in administering a federal financial assistance program, the CPA should

a. Communicate those weaknesses that are material in relation to the general-purpose financial statements.

*Adapted from the Uniform CPA examination or the Certified Internal Auditor examination.

b. Express an opinion on the systems used to administer major federal financial assistance programs and express negative assurance on the systems used to administer nonmajor federal financial assistance programs.

c. Communicate those weaknesses that are material in relation to the federal financial assistance program.

d. Express negative assurance on the systems used to administer major federal financial assistance programs and express *no* opinion on the systems used to administer nonmajor federal financial assistance programs.

*24–30 The GAO standards of reporting for governmental financial audits incorporate the AICPA standards of reporting and prescribe supplemental standards to satisfy the unique needs of governmental audits. Which of the following is a supplemental reporting standard for government financial audits?

a. A written report on the auditor's understanding of the entity's internal control structure and assessment of control risk should be prepared.

b. Material indications of illegal acts should be reported in a document with distribution restricted to senior officials of the entity audited.

c. Instances of abuse, fraud, mismanagement, and waste should be reported to the organization with legal oversight authority over the entity audited.

d. All privileged and confidential information discovered should be reported to the senior officials of the organization that arranged for the audit.

*24–31 Janice Kent is auditing an entity's compliance with requirements governing a major federal financial assistance program in accordance with the Single Audit Act. Kent detected noncompliance with requirements that have a material effect on that program. Her report on compliance should express a(an)

a. Unqualified opinion with a separate explanatory paragraph.

b. Qualified opinion or an adverse opinion.

c. Adverse opinion or a disclaimer of opinion.

d. Limited assurance on the items tested.

*24–32 Operational auditing is primarily oriented toward

a. Future improvements to accomplish the goals of management.

b. The accuracy of data reflected in management's financial records.

c. The verification that a company's financial statements are fairly presented.

d. Past protection provided by existing internal control.

*24–33 A typical objective of an operational audit is to determine whether an entity's

a. Internal control structure is operating as designed.

b. Operational information is in accordance with governmental auditing standards.

c. Financial statements present fairly the results of operations.

d. Specific operating units are functioning efficiently and effectively.

*24–34 An internal auditor is in the preliminary survey phase of an audit of the firm's purchasing department. The working papers reflect the following audit finding: "Buyers routinely initiate, authorize, and execute both the purchase requisition and purchase order forms for materials ordered for all departments." The discovery is an example of which of the following?

a. Inadequate preventive control: Inappropriate segregation of duties.

b. Inadequate detection control: Inability to determine whether transactions are executed as authorized.

c. Inadequate preventive control: Access to assets is not properly limited.

d. Inadequate directive control: Policies and procedures are not well written.

*24–35 The development of a distribution list for each audit report is important because it

a. Ensures that the audit committee and key company officials are aware of the contribution of internal auditing.

b. Limits circulation of the report to the manager of the audited area and the next higher level of management.

c. Specifies those individuals who have responsibilities with regard to the report.

d. Reinforces the need for audit reports to be complete and well written.

Discussion and Research Questions

24–36 (Applicability of the Single Audit Act) Sherburne County has asked you to do its audit. Before accepting the engagement, you want to know if the Single Audit Act would apply. You determine the following:

- During the year, the county received and recorded as revenue a $50,000 grant from the U.S. Environmental Protection Agency to help start a recycling program in rural areas of the county.
- The school district, which is considered a part of the county reporting entity, received dairy products from the U.S. Department of Agriculture for the schools' lunch program. These products are estimated to have a value of $30,000.
- The U.S. Department of Transportation gave the county a grant of $40,000 to study the need for a rapid rail transit system to the nearby metropolitan area. This money was received and recorded as revenue during the year.

Required:

a. Why is it important for you to know whether the Single Audit Act applies to an audit?

b. Does the Single Audit Act apply in this case? Explain.

c. What are the implications to the planning and conduct of the audit if the Single Audit Act applies?

24–37 (Determining the Reporting Entity) You have been invited to bid for the audit of Sherburne County. The county was recently approached by the local, privately owned, country club because it was having financial difficulties. Because the club was perceived as a benefit to the community, the following agreement was worked out:

- The name was changed to Sherburne County Greens.
- The county agreed to guarantee a new bond issue of $5 million that was needed to upgrade the golf course. The new debt brought the course's total debt to $10 million. The county has no other financial obligations to fund or support the club's operations.
- The county commissioners have the right to appoint three of the club's five members of the board of trustees. The other two members are appointed by the club members. The commissioners closely monitor the performance and positions of its three board members. The county has no other involvement in the day-to-day operations of the club.
- The club has agreed to provide residents of the county reduced membership, lessons, and green fees.

Required:

a. Why is it important for the auditor to determine the reporting entity before making a bid for the audit?

b. Is the country club part of the reporting entity? Explain.

24–38 (Determining Planning Materiality) During the planning stage of your audit of Sherburne County, you are trying to determine the appropriate base to use in establishing planning materiality for each fund type (general, special, debt service, capital projects, and proprietary funds). Some of your colleagues have suggested the following bases: total assets, total revenue, total expenditures, excess of revenues over expenditures, and total fund equity.

Required:

a. What characteristics do you believe are most important in selecting a base for establishing planning materiality?

b. What base do you believe should be used to establish planning materiality for governmental fund types? For proprietary funds? Explain your choice.

24–39 (Analytical Procedures for Property Tax Revenue) The general and debt service funds for Sherburne County show total property tax revenue of $1,798,900. The county appraiser has confirmed a net taxable appraised value of property in the county of $250,000,000. You have received a verified copy of the county ordinance setting the tax levy on each one hundred dollars of appraised value as follows: $0.60 for the general fund and $0.12 for the debt service fund.

Required:

Using analytical procedures, determine whether the recorded property tax revenue is reasonable. Support your answer.

24–40 (Testing Payroll Expenditures) Payroll is one of the largest operating expenditures of governmental organizations.

Required:

a. What factors should the auditor consider when determining whether a detailed test should be performed in addition to analytical procedures to verify payroll expenditures?

b. What analytical procedures might be performed to provide evidence as to the reasonableness of payroll expense?

24–41 (Compliance Tests under the Single Audit Act) Following are examples of reported noncompliance findings from Single Audit Act audits.

a. The City failed to include $32,687 in construction costs potentially eligible for reimbursement from the Federal Aviation Administration in the Construction Contract Estimate supporting the final Outlay Report and Request for Reimbursement for Construction Programs submitted to obtain cost reimbursement on a federally supported airport construction project.

b. The City receives capital assistance annually from the Department of Transportation (DOT), which is used to purchase fixed asset additions. The program requires that when an asset purchased with federal monies is disposed of, a percentage of the funds received on disposition, equal to the percent of the asset's historical cost originally purchased with federal funds, must be refunded to the DOT, thus requiring a separate accounting for the asset's historical cost and related accumulated depreciation. Currently, the City does not have an identifiable/auditable accounting of fixed assets acquired with federal program monies.

c. We tested the Transit Authority's system for compliance with the regulations of the Davis-Bacon Act. The act requires that laborers and mechanics who work on construction projects that are funded with federal funds be paid the prevailing wage as determined by the U.S. Department of Labor. It was determined that the Authority did not maintain a system sufficient to monitor the requirements of the act. Specifically, certified payrolls were not checked against the prevailing wage schedules and payments to individuals were not monitored to determine that those payments were in fact made.

Required:

For each of these findings, indicate the procedures that could have uncovered the noncompliance.

24–42 (Critique of Audit Report on Governmental Entity) The following draft of an audit report was prepared by your assistant for your review. The audit was performed under government auditing standards, but the Single Audit Act did not apply.

To the Chief of Police
Fillmore County, Texas

We have audited the accompanying financial statements of the County of Fillmore, State of Texas, as of June 30, 1993, and for the year then ended. These financial statements are the responsibility of the County's management.

We conducted our audit in accordance with generally accepted auditing standards. Those standards require that we plan and perform the audit to obtain reasonable assurance about whether the general-purpose financial statements are free of misstatement. An audit includes examining, on a test basis, evidence supporting the amounts and disclosures in the general-purpose financial statements. An audit also includes assessing the accounting principles used and significant estimates made by management, as well as evaluating the overall general-purpose financial statement presentation. We believe that our audit provides a reasonable basis for our opinion.

The general-purpose financial statements referred to above present fairly, in all material respects, the financial position of the County of Fillmore, State of Texas, as of June 30, 1993, and the results of its operations and the cash flows of its proprietary and similar trust fund types for the year then ended in conformity with generally accepted accounting principles.

Rittenberg and Schwieger, CPAs
June 30, 1993

Required:

a. Identify the deficiencies in each section of the report draft and explain why they are deficiencies.

b. State what additional reports the auditor should prepare in this situation.

24–43 (Identifying Differences between Audit Reports on a Governmental Entity and a Commercial Entity) The following standard audit report was issued to the commissioners of Sherburne County:

To the Board of Commissioners
Sherburne County, Minnesota

We have audited the accompanying general-purpose financial statements of the County of Sherburne, State of Minnesota, as of June 30, 1993, and for the year then ended. These general-purpose financial statements are the responsibility of the County's management. Our responsibility is to express an opinion on these general-purpose financial statements based on our audit.

We conducted our audit in accordance with generally accepted auditing standards. Those standards require that we plan and perform the audit to obtain reasonable assurance about whether the general-purpose financial statements are free of material misstatement. An audit includes examining, on a test basis, evidence supporting the amounts and disclosures in the general-purpose financial statements. An audit also includes assessing the accounting principles used and significant estimates made by management, as well as evaluating the overall general-purpose financial statement presentation. We believe that our audit provides a reasonable basis for our opinion.

In our opinion, the general-purpose financial statements referred to above present fairly, in all material respects, the financial position of the County of Sherburne, State of Minnesota, as of June 30, 1993, and the results of its operations and the cash flows of its proprietary and similar trust fund types for the year then ended in conformity with generally accepted accounting principles.

Rittenberg and Schwieger, CPAs
August 12, 1993

Required:
Identify three ways in which this report differs from that for a commercial entity.

24–44 (Affect on Audit Planning and Reporting of Expressing an Opinion on a Comprehensive Annual Financial Report as Compared to General-Purpose Financial Statements) Assume that Sherburne County engages you to audit the combining, individual fund, and account group financial statements for inclusion in a comprehensive annual financial report along with audited general-purpose financial statements.

Required:
Compared to an audit of the general-purpose financial statements

a. How would this requirement affect your audit planning?

b. How would this requirement affect your audit report?

24–45 (Preparing for Audit of Purchasing Department) You have been assigned to do an operational audit of the purchasing department to determine whether it is effective, efficient, and economical. The department has been audited before.

Required:

a. Distinguish between effectiveness, efficiency, and economy.

b. When should the audit program be developed?

c. What resources should be available in the internal audit department that will help you prepare for the preliminary survey?

24–46 (Developing Audit Objectives) You are to perform an operational audit of the purchasing activities of your company, which manufactures items for gift shops. Sales are very seasonable.

Required:
Identify four audit objectives that would be appropriate for your audit.

24–47 (Operational Audit Report) The following sentences are to be presented in a report on the operational audit of the customer service department of a business equipment retailer.

a. Our tests of service tickets showed that approximately 10 percent of the 3,250 service tickets processed during the past year were rejected when received from the technicians because of incomplete or incorrect information.

b. The procedures manual requires that service tickets be turned in within seven days of providing the service.

c. We focused our audit on the controls of the service tickets from the time they are filled out by the technicians until they are entered into the computer and invoices are generated.

d. Seventy-four percent of all rejected tickets had the wrong information written on them: wrong serial number, model number, make, or call number.

e. New personnel should be properly informed of company policies and procedures as soon as they are hired.

f. One-third of the technicians interviewed do not verify the serial numbers because the two new dispatchers are not providing that information unless the technicians ask for them.

g. Dispatchers should be required to provide the serial number every time a technician calls in.

h. Service tickets, which are sent to personnel who enter the information into the computer, are located in an office separate from the dispatchers. When the service ticket information is incomplete or inaccurate, the personnel has to contact the dispatchers or technicians personally or by phone to get the necessary information.

i. Forty-two percent of the service tickets were not turned in within seven days of providing the service.

j. Management's standards for incomplete or incorrect service tickets is two percent.

k. Dispatchers should receive the service ticket information and enter it into the computer on the day received. An alternative solution would be to have the data entry personnel relocated to the dispatcher's office.

l. Invoices are not being sent to service customers on a timely basis. Our estimate is that service billings of approximately $275,000 for the past year are being sent an average of four days late, resulting in lost interest income of over $200.

m. Twenty-six percent of the service tickets were incomplete. In most of these cases, the serial number was missing.

n. It takes an average of about 30 minutes per rejected service ticket to obtain the necessary information. In addition, it takes about the same time to follow up on late service tickets. Because average hourly wage plus fringe benefits of the individuals processing these tickets is $9, more than $7,500 of additional payroll-related expense was unnecessarily incurred during the past year.

o. New personnel are not properly informed of company policies and procedures when hired.

p. Records should be kept of which technicians are submitting incomplete, inaccurate, or late service tickets and those who are doing so on a regular basis should be informed that this is against company policy.

q. Management has initiated a program of informing new employees of company policies and procedures. It is considering implementing a monitoring procedure to identify technicians who are not following those policies and procedures.

Required:
Identify the basic sections of an operational audit report and indicate where each of the sentences should be presented in a report.

*24–48 (Elements of Audit Findings) The following are findings resulting from various audits of company employee benefit plans:

a. Piecework accounting.

During an internal audit of a wage incentive plan, an internal auditor found that some of the reported quantities seemed unreasonably high. Employees reported their own piecework production quantities. A comparison of the total employee-reported piecework quantities with independently prepared production reports revealed that totals were as much as 20 percent higher on the employee-reported piecework.

As a result of the auditor's report, management has developed procedures for balancing piecework and production totals. The new controls have eliminated the overstated piecework totals and resulted in reduced production costs.

b. Employee health insurance.

At the request of management, the internal auditing department was conducting an audit of the company's health insurance invoices. Only those charges related to currently enrolled employees should have appeared on the invoices. One thing stood out: The names of some terminated employees were on the invoices.

A computer run comparing identification numbers of active, eligible employees with those on the insurer's invoices revealed that benefits exceeding $100,000 had been paid on behalf of inactive or former employees. In one instance, an employee who had been terminated for seven years was still receiving benefits.

One control weakness that the auditors found was the failure of many supervisors to process the forms needed to inform the personnel department of terminations or status changes.

The computer program used by the auditors to identify ineligible recipients was given to the employee benefits section to be used each quarter to test the validity of insurer invoices.

c. Matching contributions.

A company has an employee savings plan that provides a matching contribution to participating employees' savings accounts. When an employee stops participating in the plan, the company suspends matching contributions. During an audit of the plan, an internal auditor found that the company was still making contributions to the accounts of a number of employees who had ceased to participate. More than $1.2 million has been contributed to such accounts.

Based on suggestions from the auditor, the company developed a procedure for linking its contribution to actual employee deposits. Additionally, efforts are being made to recover erroneous company contributions.

Required:

Develop a point sheet for each finding using the format presented below. In each situation, either write the passage that contains the attribute of the finding or state that the attribute was not covered.

Finding (a, b, or c)

Criteria:

Condition:

Cause:

Effect:

Recommendation or corrective action taken:

24–49 (Operational Audit) An internal auditor of Murry Manufacturing Company has just been assigned to perform an operational audit of the company's inventory warehousing procedures. The company manufactures seven lines of bicycles, four lines of lawn mowers, and three lines of snow blowers. Inventory is kept in four company-owned warehouses located at strategic geographic locations scattered around the country.

The company has a stated objective of shipping all orders within 48 hours of receipt. The company has streamlined production to minimize the number of component parts of each product. However, the company does maintain a 10-year supply of old parts at its central location in Ohio to meet repair needs of its customers.

During the preliminary survey, the internal auditor notes that inventory levels have risen in tandem with sales increases. Sales are up 50 percent over the last five years, but inventory is also up 50 percent over that time. In addition, the last two external audits resulted in significant write-downs of inventory due to shrinkage, spoilage, or obsolescence.

Required:

a. Identify at least four other items of importance the internal auditor might address during the preliminary survey of inventory and warehousing.
b. The director of internal auditing assigns you the task of developing appropriate criteria against which to audit. Identify three potential sources of criteria that should be consulted in developing your response.
c. Identify three potential criteria for the operational audit of inventory and warehousing.
d. Develop an operational audit program for the inventory and warehousing function at Murry Manufacturing.

24–50 (Operational Audit) You are performing an operational audit of DIS, a financial institution. A large part of the correspondence prepared for trust clients (reports, statements, etc.) is sent by express mail, using the following procedure:

1. Each trust plan administrator prepares the express mail package and completes the appropriate airbill, which contains a preprinted number. A file copy of the airbill is kept by the administrator and the package is mailed.
2. Within a week, the express mail firm mails its invoice to Trust Accounting.

3. Trust Accounting partially completes a request, with a copy of the invoice attached, that is sent back to the secretary in Trust Record Keeping. The request asks for the name of the client and who is responsible for the bill payment, DIS or the client.
4. The secretary distributes the documents to the appropriate plan administrator for determination of client name and payor.
5. The plan administrator, using the retained copy of the airbill, completes the information requested.
6. The secretary collects the documents and returns them to Trust Accounting where final disposition is made.

Required:
What would you recommend to improve this procedure?

24–51 **(Research Question)** You have been engaged to audit Sherburne County, including the Sherburne County Hospital, a 50-bed hospital operated by the county. The financial statements of the hospital will be separately issued as well as included in the financial statements of the county. Because the hospital is operated by the county, you are not sure whether to follow the accounting guidance in the AICPA's *Audits of State and Local Governmental Units* or *Hospital Audit Guide*. You are concerned because you believe that different accounting principles might apply, depending on which guide is appropriate to follow.

Required:
Using the government auditing standards, codification of governmental accounting standards, or the AICPA Statements of Position, determine which guide should be followed.

Case

24–52 (Inventory Control—Developing Operational Audit Objectives, Criteria, and Audit Approach) You are planning an operational audit of inventory control for your company, which manufactures electronic equipment such as stereos and televisions. Develop an audit program that identifies the audit objective, appropriate criteria, and your audit approach and tests for each of the following areas:

- Accuracy of perpetual records.
- Purchasing of raw materials and components.
- Efficiency of inventory control.
- Control of scrap and rejects.

End Notes

1. *Codification of Governmental Accounting and Financial Reporting Standards* (Stamford, CT: Governmental Accounting Standards Board, Second Edition, 1987), 39.

2. *Operational Audit Engagements*, Report of the Special Committee on Operational and Management Auditing (New York: AICPA, 1982), 1.
3. Bert T. Edwards, *Impact of the Single Audit Concept on Your Practice*, CPE Participant's Manual (New York: AICPA, 1991), 1–1.
4. United States General Accounting Office, *Government Auditing Standards*, 1988 revision.
5. Comptroller General of the United States, *Grant Auditing: A Maze of Inconsistency, Gaps, and Duplication That Needs Overhauling* (Washington, D.C.: U.S. Government Printing Office, 1980).

Appendix: Computer-Assisted Problems

Contents

USING ADVENTURE

Getting Started

These instructions describe the procedures necessary to run the computer audit software called adVenture that is packaged with the textbook *Auditing: Concepts for a Changing Environment* by Rittenburg and Schwieger. The software is designed to run on DOS-based machines such as the IBM PC and similar Intel-based computers. It is designed to use a mouse although a mouse is not required. Most of the information you need to use the software is contained in the software itself.

Make a Backup

Make a backup copy of the program disk (and data disk if using 5 1/4" disks). Use the copy and save the original. This will help avoid virus problems or accidental damage to the disk. You may want to write-protect these disks and use another formatted disk if you want to save any applications.

Starting the Software

Put the disk containing the adVenture program in the A or B drive of the computer. Be sure you are at the proper drive prompt on the screen (A:> or B:>), then start the software by typing **ADV <Enter>.** (Note: If you are using 5 1/4" disks, the data files are on a second disk. Once the adVenture program has been loaded, replace the program disk with the data file disk. If you are using a nonstandard monochrome monitor you may need to restart the software by typing **ADV/mono <Enter>.**)

Main Screen

The main screen follows the two copyright screens. It allows you to provide information about the project. Enter your name, your instructor's name, the section of the course, the semester/quarter of the course, and a project code. The last character of the project code must always be a number. If a project code is not given by your instructor, use the last four digits of your social security number. When finished inputting this information, press **<Done>** or **<F10>.** You should also enter this information whenever you create a new file. The information is saved with individual projects you save and is printed at the bottom of each printout. You should use the same project code for all applications unless otherwise instructed.

Menu Bar

The menu bar appears on each screen with the following items:

File **Audit Tools** **View** **Status** **Help**

It can be accessed from the main screen by either using the mouse or pressing **<Alt>** and arrow keys. On subsequent screens, you can access Status by pressing **<F2>** and Help by pressing **<F1>**. File, Audit Tools, and View can be accessed only from the main screen.

File: Used to start a new file, to open a file which was previously saved, or to quit the software.

Audit Tools: Identifies the two main tools available in the software: Sampling Methods (Attribute, PPS, and Non-statistical) and Generalized Audit Tools.

View: Allows you to view the contents of any of the nine data files from the main screen by scrolling up and down using the arrow keys.

Status: Provides the file name, project code, and, for sampling applications, information about the sample.

Help: Provides help on using a mouse and the keyboard to move around the screen and on saving a file.

You can use the keyboard to do the following:

<Tab> Move the cursor to the next field. When you have reached the last field on the screen, pressing this key again will return you to

	the first field on the screen and you can continue moving from field to field.
<Esc>	Move back one screen. This is the same as the **<Cancel>** option.
<F1>	Activate the Help screen.
<F2>	Show the status of the current application.
<F10>	Move to the next screen. This is the same as the **<Done>** option.
<Arrow Keys>	Move the cursor up, down, right, and left on the screen and allows you to scroll through the items selected during a sampling procedure.

Saving Applications

You will have several opportunities to save your current application. Use this option frequently to avoid losing information you have entered or samples selected by the software. You can save the application on the same disk as the data files or a separate formatted disk. If the disk is full and you want to delete a file, exit adVenture and use DOS to delete one or more of the files you have previously saved. To save the current application, choose **<Save>,** indicate the drive or directory to which it is to be saved, and give your application a name; up to 8 characters which can be a combination of letters, underscore, and/or numbers. Do not type an extension; the software automatically adds the extension .ADV. Once you have saved an application and you choose **<Save>** again in the same application, be sure you have placed the disk in the computer on which you want to save the application; it will be saved under the original name.

Changing Numerical Entries

If you have entered a number in a field and wish to return to the field to change the number, you will need to delete the old number before entering the new one. Otherwise, the new number will get added to the old number. For example, if you had entered 22 as 220 and went back and typed 22, the result will be 22220 rather than 22. Numeric fields that may need correcting include expected and tolerable deviation rates or amounts, sample sizes, sample failure rates, dollar misstatements, cutoff amounts, and dates.

Opening a Previously Saved Application

You can access a previously saved application by choosing Open in the File option from the menu bar on the main screen. Be sure the disk containing the application is in the disk drive. Choose the drive letter and then the file name. Use **<Tab>** to move between the boxes.

If you reload adVenture after saving an application or if you have worked on a different data file and have now opened the previous application, the disk with the data files must be placed in the disk drive. If you are using a 3 1/2" adVenture disk, the data files are on the same disk as the adVenture program. If you are using 5 1/4" disks, the data files are on a separate disk. You will now be asked to choose the letter of the drive containing the data file. Press **<Enter>** and then **<F10>**.

If you go through the sample selection module again, a new sample will be selected and will replace the old sample. In an attribute sample application in which a sample was previously selected, you can avoid replacing that sample by doing the following: You will be given the option of adding to the previous sample. Choose "YES" but do not change any of the sample selection information. This will retain your previous sample. Otherwise, a completely new sample will be chosen.

Audit Tools

Sampling Methods

Attribute Sampling You must first identify the population on which to perform attribute sampling. The population can be selected by double-clicking the left button of the mouse or using the arrow keys and **<Enter>**. Attribute sampling is designed to select samples to test the effectiveness of control procedures and the completeness of processing. Choose either a 5 percent or 10 percent risk of assessing control risk too low, using either the arrow keys or **<Tab>**. You must type a description of each attribute to be tested (limited to 30 characters), the expected failure rate, and the tolerable failure rate for each attribute. After entering this information, choose **<Done>** or **<F10>** to move to the next screen. If you have reached the bottom of the screen and want to go back and change or add to the attributes already entered, press **<Tab>**. At most times in the application, there are options to Save, Print, or Cancel. You will need to save an application so it can be retrieved later if you are not going to complete it at one time or if your instructor wants you to save it.

The software will compute a suggested sample size for each attribute. You will need to decide whether to use the largest of the suggested sample sizes to test all attributes or enter the desired sample size for each attribute. When you are done with this screen, choose **<Done>** or **<F10>** to select the sample.

The next screen allows you to scroll through the selected sample items. The sample is shown in the random order in which the items were selected. It will show the sample number (for example, 1 of 90, 2 of 90, and so on). You can determine the number of failures for each attribute from a printout of the sample or by scrolling through the sample on the screen. Only the sample items with potential failures will be printed. If you are using different sample sizes for each attribute, you will not use all of the sample items for each attribute. For example, if you have chosen sample sizes of 60 for attribute 1 and 90 for attribute 2, use the sample items numbered 1 to 60 for the first attribute and 1 to 90 for the second attribute. Press **<Done>** or **<F10>** to continue to the evaluation phase.

The sample evaluation module requires you to enter the number of control failures for each attribute. It will then calculate the sample failure rate and the upper failure rate. You will want to print the evaluation. The sample items with possible failures will also be printed at this time. When you are done, return to the main menu by pressing **<Done>** and then **<Esc>**. From the main menu you can select another application or quit the software.

PPS Sampling The design of the PPS Sampling module is similar to that of the attribute sampling module, but requires the input of relevant data to calculate and select the PPS sample. Once the sample has been selected, you should print the sample; only those items with potential misstatements will be printed. Then press **<Done>** or **<F10>** to move to the evaluation module. Determine which of the dollar discrepancies are misstatements. Scroll through the sample on the screen and enter the misstatements for each sample item that you have determined contains a misstatement. When you have entered all of the misstatements, press **<Tab>** to move to **<Done>** or press **<F10>** to move to the evaluation screen. You can now print the evaluation. The sample items you identified with misstatements will be printed with the evaluation.

Nonstatistical Sampling The Nonstatistical Sampling module allows the selection of items on a judgmental basis. The population may be viewed in advance by scrolling through the population from the main menu using the View function. The first screen in the Nonstatistical Sampling module allows you to view a profile of the population by choosing either 5 or 10 strata. You may print the profile.

The next screen allows you to tell the software how to select the sample. You can set a threshold for selecting all items over that amount. If you do not want to select items over a threshold, type 99999999 for the threshold. There are no items in the population over this amount. You then have the option to select a systematic sample of every *n*th item or select your own sample by entering the numbers of the items you wish to include in the sample. When you are done, the sample will be selected. A sample size greater than 200 is not permitted. You should print out the sample (only those with potential misstatements will be printed) and determine the total dollar misstatements in the top stratum (those with book values greater than your threshold) and in the lower stratum.

Two options exist to project misstatements to the population:

1. Based on the percentage of items included in the sample. This method is best when the misstatements are expected to be relatively uniform for all population items.

2. Based on the percent of dollars included in the sample.

Print the evaluation.

Generalized Audit Tools

The Generalized Audit Tools module emulates many of the capabilities of commercial generalized audit software (GAS) but does not require the detailed programming of commercial GAS. Once you have chosen a data file, several report options will be shown on the screen. *Using GAS requires the printer to be on; the report will be printed as soon as you choose one of the options.*

Julian Dates

The dates in the data files are entered as Julian dates (YYDDD or DDD) rather than the MM/DD/YY form. Julian dates in the YYDDD format start with the last two digits of the year and end with the day of that year. For example, the Julian date 94365 represents the 365th day of 1994 (December 31, 1994), 94001 represents the first day of 1994 (January 1, 1994), and so on. Julian dates in the DDD format assume the year 1994 and represent the day in 1994 except for the subsequent disbursements file in which the year 1995 is assumed. This makes it easier for the software to work with the dates for various reports.

COMPUTER-ASSISTED PROBLEMS

General Directions

The following exercises are designed to allow you to simulate an actual audit by making audit decisions using generalized audit software capabilities to analyze client data files, select samples, and evaluate sample results. Each problem provides additional detail on the nature of the accounting population that you are auditing. The accounting populations are contained on the computer disk included with your textbook. Your instructor will furnish you with the following information:

Course section

Project code (This may differ for various groups in the class, but must end in a number.)

If the instructor does not assign a project code for an exercise, use the last four digits of your social security number instead.

There are eight populations contained on the disk that can be used in performing the audit of Brenner Manufacturing Company. They are as follows:

Population 1: **Shipping documents** issued during the year.

Population 2: **Sales invoices** issued during the year.

Population 3: **Sales cutoff invoices:** a list of sales invoices issued during the last 20 days of 1994 and the first 20 days of 1995.

Population 4: **Accounts receivable:** a complete list of unpaid invoices as of year-end.

Population 5: **Cash disbursements:** a list of cash disbursements during the year.

Population 6: **Subsequent year's disbursements:** a list of all cash disbursements made during the first 45 days of 1995.

Population 7: **Receiving reports** prepared during the year.

Population 8: **Perpetual inventory:** a complete list of perpetual inventory records at year-end.

A more complete description of each file is contained with the assignments to be completed in conjunction with specific chapters.

In addition to these eight populations, the ninth file contains commercial loans outstanding at a financial institution. That population is designed to be used in Chapter 19.

Many of the account items selected for examination will contain a misstatement indicator code. Please note, however, that the existence of a code and the associated explanation of the code does not necessarily indicate that the item is misstated. You will have to make a judgment on whether or not specific items noted constitute a misstatement for evaluation purposes.

Introduction to the Problems

The Brenner Manufacturing Company is a continuing audit client. The problems in this appendix are to be used with adVenture to help perform certain audit procedures. Brenner Manufacturing is a maker of electronic instruments that are used with a wide array of sporting goods, ranging from exercise equipment to racing bicycles. Some of its better known products include an electronic "pulse meter" that monitors an athlete's pulse during a workout, an electronic speedometer for bicycles, and an electronic monitor that calculates calories burned. The products are used with Nordic Track ski machines, exercise bicycles, stairsteppers, and other exercise equipment. The company has been active and tries to maintain state-of-the-art equipment but is faced with increasing competition from larger companies such as Casio and Aerodyne. Although the total market is not large, it is growing and is very competitive. The company is constantly looking for new product ideas and areas in which to expand its market.

The president and founder of the company is Fred Palmer. He had formerly worked in research for Hewlett-Packard before leaving to start Brenner Manufacturing. He is 48 years old and has built a competent work force. The research and development department is headed by Mr. Palmer and includes two other associates. The company has been very technology oriented, but in the past few years has started to build up its accounting function. Most of the major functions are now computerized.

For purposes of initial planning, the audit partner has set the following parameters in determining the scope of work to be performed:

Audit risk	5 percent (per firm policy).
Inherent risk	100 percent (per firm policy).
Control risk	50 percent (moderate for all systems based on previous year's audit work; may need to be adjusted based on the results of control testing during the current year's audit).

The accounting department consists of Jerry Trahan, controller, and two assistants, one who works primarily on sales and accounts receivable and the other who processes payroll and disbursements. The company's unaudited balance sheet, statement of changes in retained earnings, and income statement for the current year are as follows:

Brenner Manufacturing Company
Balance Sheet
as of December 31, 1994 and 1993

	1994	1993
Assets:		
Cash	$ 120,046	$ 133,321
Accounts receivable (less an allowance of $42,064 in 1994 and $48,321 in 1993)	1,009,558	916,007
Inventory	1,790,408	1,346,978
Prepaid assets	53,565	63,500
Total current assets	$2,973,577	$2,459,806

Land	365,000	365,000
Equipment, net of depreciation	1,987,000	1,630,000
Building, net of depreciation	1,350,000	1,425,000
Total Assets	$6,675,577	$5,879,806
Liabilities:		
Accounts payable	$ 953,000	$ 815,000
Short-term bank note	1,500,000	1,250,000
Accrued payroll	27,500	20,000
Other accrued expenses	165,000	128,670
Total current liabilities	$2,645,000	$2,213,670
Long-term debt	1,500,000	1,250,000
Total Liabilities	$4,145,500	$3,463,670
Stockholders' Equity:		
Common Stock: $10 par value, issued and outstanding, 100,000 shares	1,000,000	1,000,000
Additional paid-in capital	500,000	500,000
Retained earnings	1,030,077	916,136
Total stockholders' equity	$2,530,077	$2,416,136
Total Liabilities and Equity	$6,675,577	$5,879,806

Brenner Manufacturing Company
Statement of Changes in Retained Earnings
for the Years Ended December 31, 1994 and 1993

	1994	1993
Beginning balance	$ 916,136	$ 848,187
Add: Net income for the year	393,941	337,949
	1,310,077	1,186,136
Less: Dividends declared	280,000	270,000
Ending balance	$1,030,077	$ 916,136

Brenner Manufacturing Company
Income Statement
for the Years Ended December 31, 1994 and 1993

	1994	1993
Sales	$12,598,027	$11,557,876
Less returns & allowances	321,320	259,000
Net sales	$12,276,707	$11,298,876
Cost of goods sold	9,002,231	8,617,331
Gross margin	$ 3,274,476	$ 2,681,545

	1994	1993
Administrative expenses	631,000	497,000
Sales commissions	541,550	499,500
Research & development	636,000	457,000
Warranty expense	575,000	475,000
Interest expense	270,00	225,000
Total administrative & selling expenses	$ 2,653,550	$ 2,153,500
Income before taxes	620,926	528,045
Income tax	226,985	190,096
Net income	$ 393,941	$ 337,949

Problems for Chapter 12: Introduction to Audit Sampling

C-1 (Using Attribute Sampling to Test the Processing of Shipping Documents)

Overview. You have been assigned to the audit of the Brenner Manufacturing Company. During the past year, the company had total sales of $12,598,027 and an unaudited net income of $393,941, an increase of 16.6 percent over the past year. The review of the control structure over the revenue cycle has just been completed, and the senior auditor believes that the structure appears to support a control risk assessment at less than the maximum and has instructed you to perform tests regarding the correctness of the processing of revenue transactions and the operation of key control procedures.

The first audit objective is to test for the completeness of recorded transactions. There is some concern that all shipments may not have been recorded.

Brief Description of Processing. The company uses sales staff to generate orders, which are transmitted to the sales department. In addition, some orders are taken directly by the sales department. Before an item is processed, the sales clerk determines whether inventory is available by checking the perpetual inventory file. The clerk also has the computer calculate the total dollar value of the order and compare it with the existing open credit limit for the customer. If the order exceeds the open credit limit, approval of the sale must be obtained from both the general sales manager and the credit manager. This approval is noted on the order and is entered into the computer system and a shipping document is generated and sent to shipping. The amount shipped is recorded by shipping personnel. Any corrections needed are noted by shipping personnel. The shipping documents are batched and sent to the sales department for further processing and invoice generation. A predefined computer screen is generated for each order, and the clerk enters quantities only when the shipping department has noted a quantity shipped that differs from the quantity ordered. Products are shipped F.O.B. shipping point.

Shipping File Available for Audit Testing. The shipping document file has 500 records that represent sales of $3,544,267. This is less than the full population, but should be treated as if it were the complete population. It should be visualized as approximately 25 percent of the complete population and fully representative of it. For analysis purposes, all materiality decisions ought to be based on the $3,544,267 balance in the file, that is, if misstatements are material to the $3,544,267, you may assume they will also be material to the sales account balance of Brenner Manufacturing Company. The file contains the following fields:

- Shipping document number.
- Shipping date.
- Dollar amount of misstatement noted by your audit work, if any (only known after you sample the population).
- Description of type of misstatement noted in your audit work, if any. The major types of misstatements that will be addressed during the audit test include

  1. Shipments that are not billed.
  2. Invoice at a price greater than the sales order or customer order.
  3. Quantity shipped does not agree with quantity billed.
  4. Item is billed twice.
  5. Item is invoiced before it is shipped.

Required:
Use adVenture and the project code provided by your instructor to select the Attribute Sampling module, the Shipping Document File, and perform the following tasks:

a. Define the attributes you wish to test.

b. Determine the sample size required, assuming the auditor chooses a planned risk of assessing control risk too low of 5 percent. Previous experience shows that misstatements made in properly recording the transactions are quite rare, less than one-half of 1 percent. The auditor decides that a tolerable failure rate of 5 percent is acceptable.

c. Select the sample, evaluate the sample results, and prepare a report specifically addressing the following issues:
   1. For each attribute tested, the most likely failure rate and the achieved upper limit based on the sample results.
   2. A description of the specific account balance misstatements categorized by type of misstatement.
   3. Implications of the misstatements found in your sample including:
      (a) A statement of the probability that material misstatements might be occurring in either Sales or Accounts Receivable.
      (b) The type of misstatements that might be occurring.
      (c) The specific substantive audit procedures that should be designed to test whether material misstatements might be occurring in either the Sales or Accounts Receivable accounts.

   The senior auditor has planned additional auditing procedures that would normally be performed as part of the audit, such as confirming accounts receivable, *at a minimum level* (assumes control risk is low). Thus, any suggestions of additional procedures to the substantive year-end auditing procedures or an expansion of the existing sample is not included in the planned audit budget. Suggestions of additional procedures will add to the total audit costs and will be discouraged by the senior. In addition, the assessment of your performance will be reduced if you specify additional time-consuming and costly procedures that are unnecessary or are not cost justified by the sampling results.

d. Discuss how the penalization of your grade that would occur if you specify procedures that are not justified affected your decision on whether or not to specify additional procedures. Does the time budget set up on an audit have a potentially similar effect? Discuss.

C-2 (Using Attribute Sampling to Perform a Dual-Purpose Test of Sales Transactions) The auditor is expanding the test of controls to ensure that all recorded transactions are valid and have been properly recorded and that important control procedures are operating effectively. The audit procedure is implemented by selecting invoices from the sales invoice file and tracing back through the recording process to the shipping document. The processing system for sales is described in problem C-1. Previous experience shows that misstatements made in properly recording the transactions are quite rare, less than one-half of 1 percent, while control procedure failures have ranged from 1 percent to 2 percent of the transactions tested. The auditor wants to determine that the sales processed contain the proper credit approval, evidence of independent checking of quantities and prices, and that all items were recorded correctly, that is, at the correct price, for the right quantities, and in the correct time period. The sales invoice file contains the audit evidence to assist in your evaluation of each of these attributes.

The sales invoice file has 500 records totaling $3,659,328. This is less than the full population, but should be treated as if it were the complete population. It should be visualized as approximately 25 percent of the complete population and fully representative of it. For analysis purposes all materiality decisions ought to be based on the $3,659,328 balance in the file, that is, if misstatements are material to the $3,659,328, you may assume they will also be material to the sales account balance of Brenner Manufacturing Company. The file contains the following fields:

- Sales invoice number.
- Invoice date.
- Dollar effect of misstatements, if any.
- Description of the nature of misstatements or control procedure failures, if any.

Required:
Use adVenture and the project code provided by your instructor, select the Attribute Sampling module, the Sales Invoice File, and perform the following tasks:

a. The senior auditor has defined the attributes to be tested as:

- All sales items contain proper credit approval.
- There is evidence that quantity and price were independently checked prior to processing.
- There is a customer order for all items invoiced.
- There is a shipping document for all items invoiced.
- The invoice is properly recorded with sales prices equal to the customer order.
- The number of items billed agrees with the items shipped per the shipping document.
- The invoice date does not precede the shipping date.

Write a brief audit program, with the appropriate auditing steps included, to describe the audit work that will be performed in this task. Briefly describe whether your audit program covers tests of control procedures, substantive tests, or both.

b. Determine the sample size required when the auditor chooses a planned risk of assessing control risk too low of 5 percent. The audit firm has previously used a 5 percent tolerable failure rate for the credit approval control, an 8 percent tolerable failure rate for other control procedure failures, and a 4 percent tolerable failure rate for recording or processing misstatements. You may assume the failure rates found in the previous audit are the best estimates for this year. Those rates are:

- 0.5 percent for any processing misstatement.
- 1.5 percent for control procedure failures, including lack of credit approval.

c. Explain why the auditor might choose to use a 5 percent tolerable failure rate for the credit approval test, an 8 percent tolerable failure rate for the other control procedures, but only a 4 percent failure rate for the processing tests.

d. Use the Attribute Sampling module and select a sample using the criteria specified in parts a and b. Once the sample is selected, evaluate the sample results and prepare a report specifically addressing the following issues:

- For each attribute, prepare a description of the specific processing misstatement or control procedure failures found in the sample.
- For each attribute, calculate the most likely failure rate and the achieved upper limit suggested by the sample results.
- Whether the tests support an assessment of control risk below the maximum (either moderate or low).
- The audit implications if the sample results show a failure rate greater than the expected failure rate but less than the tolerable failure rate. For example, do the results suggest that a larger attribute sample

should be taken, that greater substantive audit tests be performed, or that there should be no change in planned audit procedures?

- Implications of the misstatements found or control procedure failures identified in your sample including:
  1. A statement of the probability that material misstatements might be occurring in either Sales or Accounts Receivable.
  2. The type of misstatements that might be occurring.
  3. The specific substantive audit procedures that should be designed to test whether material misstatements might be occurring in either the Sales or Accounts Receivable accounts.

The senior auditor has planned additional auditing procedures that would normally be performed as part of the audit, such as confirming accounts receivable, *at a minimum level* (assumes control risk as low). Thus, any suggestions of additional procedures to the substantive year-end auditing procedures or an expansion of the existing sample is not included in the planned audit budget. Suggestions of additional procedures will add to the total audit costs and will be discouraged by the senior. In addition, the assessment of your performance will be reduced if you specify additional time-consuming and costly procedures that are unnecessary or are not cost justified by the sampling results.

e. For each type of processing misstatement found in your sample, identify a control procedure that should have either prevented or detected it.

Problems for Chapter 14: Sampling for Substantive Tests of Account Balances

C-3 (Using Generalized Audit Software Procedures on Accounts Receivable) You are continuing the work on the Brenner Manufacturing Company and are at the point of determining direct tests of the Accounts Receivable balance. In performing the work, you should use the same project code used in problems C-1 and C-2. This section will use the capabilities of generalized audit software to help analyze the correctness of the Accounts Receivable and Sales account balances.

At year-end, the accounts receivable subsidiary ledger shows 500 unpaid invoices with a balance of $1,051,622 that represents a material amount of total assets and total current assets. There are a number of users of the company's financial statements, including two banks, a potential investment banker, other creditors, and over 100 shareholders.

The accounts receivable file contains unpaid invoices with the following information:

- Invoice number.
- Customer number.
- Credit limit for customer.
- Invoice date.
- Amount of invoice.

The file also indicates any difference between the client's and the customer's records and the reasons for the difference.

(**Note:** When using the Generalized Audit Tools module, your computer must be hooked up to a printer or the program will not work. In addition, all reports will be printed and you will not have an opportunity to review them on the computer screen. Many of the procedures in the generalized audit software routine have been written to minimize the amount of work you will have to perform. For example, most audit software will require you to identify the field you wish to foot. AdVenture does this automatically for you and is thus less complex than the audit software used in practice.)

Required:

Use adVenture and the project code assigned by your instructor. Select the Generalized Audit Tools module and the Accounts Receivable File and perform the following:

a. Create and print an aged trial balance that shows, for each customer, the total balance and related aging as follows:
    - Current accounts.
    - 1–30 days past due.
    - 31–60 days past due.
    - Over 60 days past due.

b. Comment on the implications of the report generated in part a on the selection of accounts receivable for confirmation purposes and its use in evaluating the allowance for doubtful accounts.

c. Perform a further credit analysis of accounts receivable by summarizing all customer balances that exceed their specified credit limit and comment on the implications of the results.

d. Foot the file and see if it agrees with the client's unaudited general ledger balance.

C-4 (Using PPS Sampling to Confirm Accounts Receivable) The audit program calls for the selection of a sample of unpaid invoices to positively confirm accounts receivable. The file layout is described in problem C-3. The audit partner has assessed inherent risk at 100 percent and had initially set control risk at moderate (50 percent). The other substantive procedures risk has been set at 100 percent (not effective). Audit risk, by firm policy, is set at 5 percent. You should adjust the preliminary control risk assessment for the results obtained in problems C-1 through C-3 and determine an appropriate test of details risk for the confirmation task. Previous experience suggests that it is reasonable to expect $15,000 of clerical overstatements in the account balance. During the past year, tolerable misstatement was set at $60,000 for accounts receivable. The senior auditor indicates that you should consider adjusting either or both of these amounts based on the results of your tests of controls. The senior reminds you that the audit is being conducted under a tight time budget this year and anything that would assist in meeting that budget would be appropriately rewarded.

Required:
Use adVenture and the project code, select the PPS Sampling module and the Accounts Receivable File, and do the following:

a. Determine the appropriate test of details risk, tolerable misstatement, and expected misstatement and document your reasons in a working paper. Use adVenture to determine and print the sampling interval and sample size for selecting unpaid invoice items to confirm.

b. Select and print the sample.

c. Determine which, if any, of the differences cited between book value and confirmed value constitute a misstatement of the account balance. Develop a schedule of sampled dollar amounts and misstatements. Use the PPS Sample Evaluation module to evaluate the sample results.

d. Print the statistical evaluation and prepare a working paper to document and analyze the following:
   - Statistical estimate of the most likely misstatement and the upper misstatement limit.
   - Whether the results support the client's reported book value.
   - If the results do not support the recorded book value, indicate the following:
     1. Whether a pattern of misstatements is present.
     2. The auditing procedures that should be performed to complete the audit of accounts receivable.
     3. The most likely cause of the misstatements.
     4. If an extension of the existing sample is suggested,
        (a) Identify the approximate size of the sample to be taken and the approach used to select it.
        (b) Select the additional sample items and document your revised audit evaluation of the confirmation process.

e. Assume that, on average, it costs a CPA firm approximately $15 to complete the audit test for each confirmation selected.
   1. Compute the cost of auditing accounts receivable using the parameters you determined in part a.
   2. If you need to increase your sample size, compute the cost of the additional confirmation work and compare that with the cost of your first sample. What does this tell you about the cost/benefit of good internal control?
   3. Calculate the cost of performing the audit procedures if audit risk is 5 percent (low), tolerable misstatement is $100,000, expected misstatement is $5,000, other substantive procedures risk is 20 percent (very effective), inherent risk is 100 percent, and control risk is 50 percent (moderate).

C-5 (Accounts Receivable Confirmations—Sampling Sensitivity Analysis) Refer to the description of Brenner Manufacturing Company and the nature of the accounts receivable file described in problem C-3 and the analysis performed in problem C-4.

Required:
Use adVenture to do the following:

a. Determine how the sample size would be affected by the auditor's assessment of control risk at the maximum level versus the initial assumption before control testing that control risk was moderate (50 percent).

b. Determine the effect on proposed sample size used in problem C-4 if tolerable misstatement is *decreased* by 25 percent and control risk is moderate (50 percent).

c. Determine the effect on the sample size used in problem C-4 if tolerable misstatement is *increased* by 25 percent and control risk is moderate (50 percent).

d. Perform the same audit tests described in problem C-4, but assume control risk is assessed at the maximum and tolerable misstatement is decreased by 25 percent. Compare the results, including the cost of performing the audit, with that obtained in problem C-4.

C-6 (Using Nonstatistical Sampling to Confirm Accounts Receivable) As an alternative to PPS sampling, the senior auditor wishes to perform the accounts receivable confirmation work using nonstatistical sampling.

Required:
Use adVenture and the project code assigned by your instructor. Select the Nonstatistical Sampling module and the Accounts Receivable File and perform the following:

a. Document your audit judgments about tolerable misstatement, control risk assessment, and detection risk and use those judgments to determine an appropriate sample size. Use adVenture to develop a profile of the population and determine the most appropriate manner to select the sample. Select the sample using techniques such as all items over a specified dollar limit, systematic selection, haphazard selection, or some combination of these. If you choose to use haphazard selection, you will need to print the population so you can identify the items to include in the sample.

b. Develop a schedule of account misstatements and use adVenture to evaluate the sample results including an estimate of the most likely account balance misstatement.

c. After performing your evaluation, summarize the results and comment on:

   - Whether the results support the client's reported book value.
   - If the results do not support recorded book value, indicate the following:

     1. Whether there is a pattern of misstatements present.
     2. The additional auditing procedures you would recommend to complete the audit of Accounts Receivable (above that which would have initially been planned).

3. The most likely cause of the misstatements.

d. Assume that, on average, it costs a CPA firm approximately $15 to complete the audit test for each confirmation selected. Compute the cost of performing the confirmation of accounts receivable using the approach selected above.

e. (Only if either C-4 or C-5 was performed.) Compare the cost of the nonstatistical procedure with the cost of the statistical approach. Briefly comment on your perception of the reliability of the two alternative approaches. Consult with your instructor regarding the correct account balance and comment on the perceived reliability of the two approaches.

C-7 (Accounts Receivable Confirmations: Sampling and Audit Costs) Due to tight time budgets, the senior auditor has set the confirmation scope to select a sample of 25 open invoice items.

Required:
Use adVenture and the project code assigned by your instructor and perform the following:

a. Use the Nonstatistical Sampling module to select and evaluate the sample. How confident are you in the sample result? Compare your audit conclusion obtained from this sample with the conclusion obtained in problems C-4 and C-6. What conclusions can be drawn regarding the effect of sample size using a nonstatistical sampling approach on the reliability of the audit tests on this account? Summarize the conclusions that are justified by the sample and the sampling results.

b. Determine a control risk assessment and tolerable misstatement combination that would be required to justify a PPS sample size of 25. Use these parameters and select a PPS sample for confirmation work and evaluate the results, including:

   - The statistical estimate of most likely misstatement and upper misstatement limit.
   - Whether the results support the client's reported book value.
   - If the results do not support recorded book value, indicate:

     1. Whether there is a pattern of misstatements present.
     2. The additional auditing procedures that should be performed to complete the audit of Accounts Receivable beyond that normally expected.
     3. The most likely cause of the misstatements.

c. Assume that, on average, it costs a CPA firm approximately $15 to complete the audit test for each confirmation selected. Compute the cost of auditing accounts receivable using the nonstatistical approach identified in part a.

C-8 (Using Sampling to Test Sales Cutoff) The senior auditor has asked you to conduct a sales cutoff test in order to complete the accounts receivable and sales work on the Brenner Manufacturing Company. The company has booked a number of unusual sales near the end of the year, and the senior auditor has some concern about whether all of the transactions have been recorded in the correct period.

The client has identified a file of sales that have been recorded near year-end (Cutoff File) that contains a total of 200 invoices representing sales of $947,061, of which 100 had been recorded during the latter part of the fiscal year and 100 had been recorded subsequent to year-end. The file contains the following fields:

- Sales invoice number.
- Invoice date.
- Sales invoice amount.
- Potential misstatement condition and an indication of whether the transaction was recorded in the incorrect period.

The senior auditor has suggested that you determine an appropriate sample size, recognizing that items closer to year-end are more likely to be recorded in error than those further from year-end. The senior auditor has indicated that a total of 30 transactions had been examined last year and a similar amount has been budgeted for this year. If the number of transactions selected differs from the budgeted amount, you are to notify the senior as to the reasons.

Required:
Use adVenture and the project code assigned by your instructor, choose either the PPS Sampling module or the Nonstatistical Sampling module and the Cutoff File, and perform the following:
[Note: If you use the Nonstatistical Sampling module and choose to select the individual items to test, you will need to print the population and enter the item numbers to be included in the sample.]

a. Determine the appropriate sample size and document why you chose that sample size. Assume that items recorded in the wrong year will affect net income by 100 percent of the misstatement.
b. Select, print, and evaluate your sample. Summarize your audit findings and document your conclusion about the correctness of the account balance, and/or the need for an audit adjustment in an audit working paper. Identify implications for either further audit work or financial statement adjustments or disclosures.

Problems for Chapter 16: Audit of Acquisition and Payment Cycle

C-9 (Using Attribute Sampling to Perform a Dual-Purpose Test of Cash Disbursements) You have been assigned to perform tests of disbursements of Brenner Manufacturing Company. The preliminary review of the client's control structure indicates that it should be cost-effective to test controls in operation. Prior year audit work indicated some problems with disbursements being properly supported, but management has indicated that significant improvements have been made in the documentation of all disbursements.

The cash disbursement's file contains 1,000 items totalling $2,750,743. This is less than the full population, but should be treated as if it were the complete population. It should be visualized as approximately 25 percent of the complete population and fully representative of it. For analysis purposes, all materiality decisions ought to be made on the $2,750,743 balance in the file, that is, if misstatements are material to the $2,750,743, you may assume they will also be material to the total disbursements of Brenner Manufacturing Company.

The senior auditor has identified the following areas to be addressed during the disbursements test:

1. Disbursements that are not supported by proper documentation, particularly those which may be related-party transactions.
2. Disbursements that are made for incorrect amounts.
3. Items that have been capitalized but should have been expensed.

In addition, the senior auditor wants you to test the operation of the following control procedures:

4. A comparison is made of the quantity and description of the goods received with the purchase order and invoice before payment is made. There should be evidence of the approval on the disbursement document.
5. All payments have been approved by the controller before payments are made.

Preliminary audit planning indicates that the risk of assessing control risk too low should be set at 5 percent. The expected and tolerable failure rates for each attribute based on prior audits are as follows:

Area	Expected Failure Rate	Tolerable Failure Rate
1	2%	6%
2	0.5	3
3	2	8
4	1	8
5	2	6

Required:

Use adVenture, the project code assigned by your instructor, the Attribute Sampling module and the Current Year's Cash Disbursements File and:

a. Specify the relevant parameters, determine the appropriate sample size for each attribute, select, and print the sample to be used to test each attribute.

b. Evaluate the sample results and determine, for each attribute, the best estimate of the failure rates and the achieved upper limits. Prepare an audit working paper that includes the following:

- Identification of the attributes tested.
- The sample failure rate and achieved upper limit for each of the attributes.
- Your conclusions about the effectiveness of the control procedures or the occurrence of particular types of misstatements noted.
- Specific audit conclusions including an analysis of whether the audit evidence supports a control risk assessment of low.
- If the audit work does not support a control risk assessment of low, identify the specific implications for the design of substantive audit procedures. Indicate the types of misstatements that might be occurring in the account balance and the specific audit procedures that should be performed at year-end to address the potential misstatements.

C-10 (Using Sampling to Test Subsequent Disbursements) You have been assigned the task of reviewing subsequent disbursements to complete the audit of Accounts Payable for Brenner Manufacturing Company. The senior auditor has advised you that the Accounts Payable balance has increased this year from $815,000 to $953,000. Control risk over the disbursements cycle has been assessed as moderate. However, the senior auditor reminds you that the time budget is tight for this area and suggests that you select a sample size sufficient to satisfy you that all material items were recorded, yet small enough to be accomplished within a short time budget. The subsequent disbursements work will be supplemented by analytical review procedures on the expense accounts and a detailed test of cost of goods sold.

The subsequent disbursements file contains the following information:

- Voucher number.
- Invoice date.
- Amount disbursed.
- A description of the misstatement condition, if any.

The file contains the first 200 disbursements of 1995 totaling $411,000.

Required:

Use adVenture and the project code assigned by your instructor. Select the Subsequent Year's Disbursement File and either the PPS Sampling module or the Nonstatistical Sampling module (as assigned by your instructor or as you deem most appropriate) and perform the following:

a. Determine the appropriate sample size and select a sample of subsequent disbursements. Justify the sample size taken in a separate audit memo that will be handed in to your instructor.

b. Select, print, and evaluate the sample and prepare a report covering the following items:

- Misstatements noted in the sample.
- Projected understatement of the Accounts Payable account balance.
- Suggested adjustment to the account balance.

c. If your results suggest that more evidence is needed to form an opinion on the potential understatement of the Accounts Payable balance, indicate the additional audit procedures that should be performed. Be prepared to justify the additional procedures because the time budget for finishing the accounts payable audit does not contemplate the performance of additional procedures.

C-11 (Using Attribute Sampling to Perform a Dual-Purpose Test of Receiving Report Processing) You are now assigned to the task of testing the effectiveness of the control procedures in the purchasing, receiving, and payments functions. The client requires that a valid receiving report be matched with the purchase order before an invoice is approved for payment. The accounts payable is recorded on the computer, but given the size of the organization, the company still manually matches the three documents.

The receiving report file contains 500 records representing purchases of $1,717,769. This is less than the full population, but should be treated as if it were the complete population. It should be visualized as approximately 25 percent of the complete population and fully representative of it. For analysis purposes, all materiality decisions ought to be made on the $1,717,769, that is, if misstatements are material to the $1,717,769, you may assume they will also be material to the total purchases of Brenner Manufacturing Company.

In performing the dual-purpose tests of receiving reports, the senior auditor has instructed you to take a sample of receiving reports and to test for the following:

- The quantity received does not exceed the purchase order quantity unless approved by the purchasing department or the excess was returned and a debit memo was issued for the excess.
- All receipts are recorded in the correct period.

Based on prior audits and the auditor's current study of the control structure, there is reason to expect that approximately 2 percent of the items in the population do not show approval of receipts that differ from the purchase order quantities or the excess is not returned and that approximately 1 percent of the items in the population are recorded in the wrong period. Considering the potential materiality of the items, the senior auditor has suggested a tolerable failure rate of 8 percent for the first attribute and 6 percent for the second attribute.

The Receiving Report File contains the following fields:

- Receiving report number.
- Receiving date.
- Misstatement information (for instance, items received do not match items ordered or there is no evidence that the control procedure has been applied to the transaction).

Required:

Use adVenture and the project code assigned by your instructor. Select the Attribute Sampling module and the Receiving Report File and perform the following:

a. Define the attributes that should be tested to meet the audit objectives identified above.

b. Determine the sample size required when the auditor chooses a planned risk of assessing control risk too low of 5 percent.

c. Select and evaluate a sample using the criteria specified above. Prepare a report specifically addressing the following issues:

   1. The most likely failure rate and the upper misstatement rate for each attribute based on the sample results.
   2. A description of the specific misstatements or control procedures found in the sample.
   3. An assessment of whether the tests support an assessment of control risk below the maximum (either moderate or low).
   4. Implications of the misstatements or control procedure failures found in the sample.
   5. Recommendations for substantive audit tests.

d. For each type of misstatement found in your sample, identify a control procedure that should have either prevented or detected the misstatement.

C-12 (Using Generalized Audit Software to Test Perpetual Inventory) The year-end inventory balance of Brenner Manufacturing Company is $1,790,408, an increase of 32 percent over the previous year, which compares unfavorably with an 8.4 percent increase in sales for the year. Although the company appears to have a strong control environment, the auditor has observed that a number of small misstatements have occurred in the inventory recording in previous years.

The client's Perpetual Inventory File consists of 1,000 items with the following fields:

- Inventory number.
- Stock part number.
- Location code.
- Cost per unit.
- Quantity on hand.
- Extended cost.
- Quantity sold year-to-date.
- Date of last purchase.
- Date of last sale.
- Current sales price.
- Dollar amount of misstatement on sampled items.
- Description of any differences or misstatements on sampled items.

Before performing detailed tests of inventory, the senior auditor suggests that you use the generalized audit software capabilities of adVenture to perform analytical procedures on the current account balance.

(**Note:** When using the Generalized Audit Tools module, your computer must be hooked up to a printer or the program will not work. In addition, all reports will be printed and you will not have an opportunity to review them on the computer screen. Many of the procedures in the generalized audit software routine have been written to minimize the amount of work you will have to perform. For example, most audit software will require you to identify the field you wish to foot. AdVenture does this automatically for you and is thus less complex than the audit software used in practice.)

Required:
Use adVenture and the project code assigned by your instructor. Select the Generalized Audit Tools module and the Perpetual Inventory File and perform the following procedures:

a. Foot the file and determine if it agrees with the balance shown per the general ledger.
b. Assuming that the cost of products has been fairly constant during the year, prepare an estimate of total cost of goods sold for the year. The audit software will do this for you by multiplying quantity sold year-to-date by the current cost-per-unit.
c. Assuming that the sales price has been fairly constant during the year, prepare a report estimating the total amount of recorded sales for the year. The audit software will do this for you by multiplying quantity sold year-to-date by current selling price.
d. Test the recorded extended cost and print out any items for which it appears to be in error. The audit software will multiply quantity-on-hand by cost-per-unit, compare it to the perpetual balance for each item in inventory, and print the items where there is a difference.
e. Test for possible obsolescence by preparing a report of all inventory items with a balance greater than $1,000 that have not had any sales in the last 90 days. Note: the client uses a Julian calendar for recording its sales date, thus the last date of the year would be 94365, or the 365th day of 1994.
f. Calculate the inventory turnover for all items in the inventory and prepare a list of all items for which the inventory turnover is less than 2.5. Identify the auditing procedures you would utilize to follow up on items included in the report.
g. Summarize the total dollar value of inventory at each location to be used in selecting locations to visit to observe inventory.

C-13 (Using Sampling to Test the Perpetual Inventory Account Balance) You have now been assigned the task of completing the substantive testing of the inventory account of Brenner Manufacturing Company. Please refer to question C-12 for a complete description of the inventory account and the perpetual inventory file.

The following tests will require the auditor to select perpetual inventory items for examination and (1) physically observe the quantities on hand to determine whether the recorded quantity is correct and note whether the items appear to be obsolete, and (2) examine purchase invoices and cost records to determine whether the recorded cost is correct.

The senior auditor has assessed inherent risk at 100 percent (per firm policy) and control risk and other substantive procedures risk as moderate (40 percent). Tolerable misstatement is $73,000. You should check with your instructor, however, to determine whether any of these parameters have changed since the beginning of the audit. Your review of the previous year working papers indicate that approximately $13,000 of misstatements were projected to the population, but since only $5,000 of misstatements were actually noted, no adjustments were made to the account balance. The senior auditor indicates there is no reason to expect that this year will be any different.

Required:

Use adVenture and the project code assigned by your instructor. Select either the PPS Sampling module or the Nonstatistical Sampling module, as assigned by your instructor, and the Perpetual Inventory File and perform the following tasks:

a. Determine the sampling interval and appropriate sample size. If you use the Nonstatistical Sampling module, develop a profile of the population before making your selection.

b. Select a sample of items for testing. If nonstatistical sampling is used, prepare an audit working paper noting the sample size used and explaining the rationale and methodology used for sample selection.

c. Select and evaluate the sample. Develop a schedule of potential misstatements dictated by the misstatement codes noted on the sampled items. Evaluate and summarize your sample results in an audit working paper that details the following:

   1. An estimate of the most likely misstatement and, if a PPS sample was chosen, the upper misstatement limit.

   2. Whether the results support the client's recorded book value.

   3. If the results do not support the recorded book value:

      (a) If there is a pattern of misstatements, summarize the pattern and discuss the implications for further testing.

      (b) Identify the most likely cause of the misstatements.

      (c) Identify the auditing procedures that should be performed to address the type of misstatements found in the sample and to determine whether the misstatements are material to the Inventory account balance.

   4. If the results indicate that further auditing procedures of the same nature should be performed, determine the additional sample size needed to be taken, select a second sample, and evaluate the combined sample results. Assume that each additional item selected will cost an additional 20 minutes in audit work (every three items selected cause the audit time to increase by one hour) and calculate the additional time needed to complete the audit task. Justify your decision and the revised results in an audit memo.

d. Perform steps b and c assuming the following:

1. Control risk and other substantive procedures risks are assessed at the maximum.
2. Control risk is assessed at the minimum, the other substantive procedures risk is assessed at the maximum, and tolerable misstatement is changed to $85,000.

Problems for Chapter 19: Audits of Financing Activities: Emphasis on Financial Institutions

C-14 (Using Generalized Audit Software to Test the Commercial Loan Account Balance) You have been assigned to perform the audit tests on the Commercial Loan account of Anchor Savings Bank, a continuing audit client. Anchor Savings Bank has total assets of $187,000,000, of which the Commercial Loan account amounts to $85,498,472.60. The company has most of its computer processing performed by another bank and the auditor has received a report from the other bank's auditors that control procedures are adequately designed and are operating effectively. The auditor's understanding of control procedures at the bank has led to a preliminary assessment of control risk as low. The Commercial Loan File contains 500 records with the following fields:

- Loan number.
- Customer number.
- Date of loan.
- Interest rate on loan.
- Original amount of loan.
- Current loan balance (including past due interest).
- Due date of loan.
- Date of last payment.
- Industry classification of customer.
- Loan officer responsible for originating the loan.
- Description of audit findings (control failure or dollar amount of discrepancy and a code indicating the cause).

Loan payments are to be made quarterly. Your first task is to summarize information that will be useful in helping analyze the account balance and plan further audit work.

Required:
Use adVenture and the project code assigned by your instructor. Select the Generalized Audit Tools module and the Commercial Loan File and perform the following tasks:

(**Note:** When using the Generalized Audit Tools module, your computer must be hooked up to a printer or the program will not work. In addition, all reports will be printed and you will not have an opportunity to review them on the computer screen. Many of the procedures in the generalized audit software routine have been written to minimize the amount of work you will have to perform. For example, most audit software will require you to identify the field you wish to foot. AdVenture does this automatically for you and is thus less complex than the audit software used in practice.)

a. Foot the file and determine if it agrees with the general ledger balance.

b. Print a summary of total loans outstanding by customer. There is more than one loan outstanding for some customers.

c. Print a report classifying loans according to their industry classification and analyze for potential audit implications.

d. Prepare a summary of loans by originating loan officer. Also prepare a detailed report of loans more than 90 days past due by originating loan officer. Evaluate to determine whether there are potential problem loans associated with a particular loan officer.

e. Print a report of all loan balances over $250,000 for subsequent audit testing.

f. Print a listing of all loans with payments not made in the last quarter.

g. Summarize your analysis in a working paper.

C-15 (Using Sampling to Test Controls over Commercial Loans) You have been assigned to test the control procedures over commercial loans of Anchor Savings Bank (see problem C-14) to determine whether:

- The loan was properly authorized.
- The loan file contains evidence of sufficient collateral and up-to-date appraisals of collateral on the loan.
- The loan file contains current credit reports or current financial statements to support the credit decision.
- The interest rate per the books agrees with the interest rate on the approved loan application.

Required:

a. For each control procedure identified above, briefly indicate the importance of the item to the audit.

b. Explain how substantive auditing procedures would be affected if the auditor did not find an acceptable level of compliance with the control procedures.

c. Which sampling method would be best suited for this test? Explain.

d. Use adVenture, the project code assigned by your instructor, and the Commercial Loan File. Select the sampling method you think is best for testing these controls and perform the following:

   1. Identify the decisions that need to be made to determine the appropriate sample size. Document those decisions in an audit planning working paper.

   2. Determine the appropriate sample size and select the sample.

3. Evaluate and summarize your sample results in an audit working paper detailing the following: [Note: For purposes of this problem, ignore indicator codes not related to the control procedures previously listed.]
   (a) The controls that do not seem to be working.
   (b) The impact of control failures on the substantive procedures to be performed.

C-16 (Using Sampling to Perform Substantive Tests on Commercial Loans) You are now going to perform substantive tests of the commercial loans of Anchor Savings Bank (see problems C-14 and C-15) with special emphasis on testing the existence and valuation assertions. As part of these tests, you are to select a representative sample of loans and:

a. Examine the loan documents to determine whether
   1. There is sufficient collateral with up-to-date appraisals.
   2. All supporting documents are present.
   3. The loan payments are up-to-date.
   4. The records reflect a different interest rate than the loan agreement.
b. Confirm the loan balance with the customer.

Previous year's data indicate that control risk should be assessed as high since there were many instances where the loan file could not be located or was incomplete. Previous results lead us to expect no more than $200,000 of misstatements in the account balance. Tolerable misstatement has been set at $1.75 million.

Required:

a. Use adVenture, the project code assigned by your instructor, and the Commercial Loan File. Select the sampling method you think is best for these tests and:
   1. Identify the decisions that need to be made to determine the appropriate sample size. Document those decisions in an audit planning working paper.
   2. Determine the appropriate sample size and select a sample.
   3. Evaluate and summarize your sample results in an audit working paper detailing the following: [Note: For purposes of this problem, ignore indicator codes not related to these tests.]
      (a) Estimate of the most likely misstatement and upper misstatement limit.
      (b) Whether the results support the client's reported book value.
      (c) If the results do not support recorded book value:
         i. Indicate whether there is a pattern of misstatements present. If there is, summarize the pattern and discuss the implications for further testing.
         ii. Identify the most likely cause of the misstatements that were found in the sample.

(d) Whether the results indicate a potential collection problem. If so, indicate what additional procedures need to be performed.

(e) If the results indicate that the sample should be expanded, determine the additional sample size needed to be taken, select a second sample, and evaluate the combined sample results. Assume that each additional item selected will cost the audit an additional 20 minutes in audit work (every 3 items selected cause the audit time to increase by one hour), calculate the additional time needed to complete the audit task in comparison with the greater assurance you expect to obtain, and justify your decision in an audit memo.

b. (Optional; see your instructor.) Perform the audit procedures in part a assuming that control risk is assessed at the minimum and tolerable misstatement is set at $2.5 million.

Glossary

access control software Software designed to limit access to programs or data files to those authorized for such access, comprehensive access control software identifies all users and rules to access data or programs.

accounting application All programs and procedures involved in processing a particular class of transactions, such as the procedures and computer programs involved to process a sales order and to record sales transactions; most accounting applications include both manual and computerized procedures.

Accounting Series Releases (ASRs) Publications by the SEC providing rulings on the appropriate accounting treatment for transactions that have caught the SEC's attention and establishing auditing guidelines for CPA firms practicing before it; as of 1982, ASRs were divided into either *Financial Reporting Releases* or *Auditing Enforcement Releases*.

accounting subsystem or cycle Often referred to as accounting cycles such as sales/collection, acquisition/payment, payroll, inventory, and financing cycles; each subsystem is composed of one or more accounting applications.

accounting system The methods and records established to identify, assemble, analyze, classify, record, and report an entity's transactions and to maintain accountability for the related assets and liabilities; made up of several accounting subsystems.

accounts payable confirmation A confirmation process that seeks a vendor statement as a basis for identifying potential understatement of the accounts payable liability.

achieved precision The precision of an estimate based on the standard deviation of sample items; represents a confidence interval constructed around the point estimate at the confidence level used in constructing the sample. Also referred to as *achieved allowance for sampling error*.

achieved upper limit The maximum likely control procedure failure rate in the population based on an attribute estimation sample.

adverse audit report An audit report whereby the auditor reports an opinion that the financial statements, taken as a whole, are not presented in accordance with generally accepted accounting principles.

adverse opinion Type of audit report issued when the auditor believes that the financial statements are misleading due to material departures from GAAP that pervade the financial statements or to the lack of very important disclosures.

aged receivables trial balance A list of each customer's balance distributed among columns to show the age (time outstanding) of the unpaid invoices.

allowance for sampling error The spread, or difference, between the tolerable and expected control procedure failure rates that represents the precision required in the sample to keep sampling risk at the desired level.

alternative procedures Procedures used to obtain evidence about the existence and valuation of accounts receivable when a positive confirmation is not returned, including examining cash collected after the confirmation date and vouching unpaid invoices to customer's orders, sales orders, shipping documents, and sales invoices.

Altman Z-score A combination of weighted ratios to produce a score of potential bankruptcy, developed using a regression model to predict companies that are most likely to go bankrupt.

American Institute of Certified Public Accountants (AICPA) The primary professional organization for the CPAs, it has a number of committees to develop professional standards for the conduct of audits and other services performed by its members and to self-regulate the profession.

analytical procedure A study of plausible relationships among both financial and nonfinancial data as a basis for identifying potential misstatements in account balances or providing corroborative evidence on the assessment that an account does not contain material misstatements; often uses ratio or trend analysis to identify potential misstatements.

applications programs Written to accomplish specific data-processing tasks such as processing sales and accounts receivable, updating inventory, computing payroll, or developing special management reports, usually are written in higher-level languages such as COBOL, Pascal, or C.

A Score A weighting of 17 characteristics of a business to predict potential business failure.

assertion A positive statement about an action, event, condition, or the performance of an entity or product over a specified period of time; the subject of attestation services.

asset impairment A term used to describe management's recognition that a significant portion of fixed assets is no longer as productive as had originally been expected. When assets are impaired so that it is unlikely that the unamortized cost of the asset will be recovered, the assets should be written down to their expected economic value.

asset/liability mix An important bank operating concept that serves as a guide to matching the interest rate and maturities of the assets and liabilities.

attestation function Any function in which one party is engaged to perform an independent examination of an assertion (representation) made by the first party to a third party, resulting in the communication by the independent party of a conclusion as to the fairness of the representation made by the first party to the third party.

attestation services Provide an expression of an opinion by an auditor to third parties concerning the correctness of assertions contained in financial statements or other reports against which objective criteria can be identified and measured.

attribute A characteristic of the population of interest to the auditor.

attribute estimation sampling A statistical sampling method used to estimate the most likely and maximum rate of control procedure failures based on selecting and auditing one sample.

attribute sampling A family of statistical sampling methods used to estimate the control procedure failure rate in a population; the family of methods includes attribute estimation sampling, discovery sampling, and sequential (stop-or-go) sampling.

audit committee A subcommittee of the board of directors responsible for monitoring audit activities and serving as a surrogate for the interests of shareholders; should preferably be composed of outside members of the board—that is, members who do not hold company management positions.

audit program An auditor-prepared document which lists the specific procedures and audit tests to be performed in gathering evidence to test assertions.

audit risk The risk that the auditors may unknowingly fail to qualify their opinion on financial statements that are materially misstated; audit risk refers to the likelihood that the auditor will issue an unqualified opinion on financial statements that are materially misstated.

audit sampling The application of an audit procedure to less than 100 percent of the items within an account balance or class of transactions for the purpose of evaluating some characteristic of the balance or class [AU 350.01].

audit trail A term used to describe the documents and records that allow a user or auditor to trace a transaction from its origination through to its final disposition or vice versa; must have cross-references to documents or other computer records, may be electronic or paper based.

audit working papers The primary documentation of the work performed by the auditor; documents the items sampled, the work done, the conclusions reached, the auditor performing the tests, the date completed, and the auditor's assessment of potential misstatements in the account balance tested.

auditing A systematic process of objectively obtaining evidence regarding assertions about economic actions and events to ascertain the degree of correspondence between those assertions and established criteria and communicating the results to interested users.

auditor-generated evidence Evidence generated by the auditor, including through the auditor's reasoning process, to substantiate the correctness of account balances. Examples include recomputations, estimates, and analytical analysis.

authentication A means developed for a computer application to determine that the individual requesting the access privilege is who he or she claims to be; popular methods include use of passwords and plastic cards with magnetic strips.

autocorrelation Residual in a period consists of a part that depends on the residual in a prior period and a part that is random.

automated matching A process by which the computer matches a purchase order, receiving information, and a vendor invoice to determine whether the vendor's invoice is correct and should be paid.

bank confirmation A standard confirmation sent to all banks with whom the client had business during the year to obtain information about the year-end cash balance and additional information about loans outstanding.

bank holding company A nonoperating company used to finance and control individual banks that retain separate identities but act as one financial institution.

bank transfer schedule An audit working paper that lists all transfers between client bank accounts starting a short period before year-end and continuing for a short period after year-end; its purpose is to ensure that cash in transit is not recorded twice.

basic financial statements The balance sheet, income statement, cash flow statement, statement of changes in owners' equity, and related footnotes.

basic precision The upper misstatement limit when no misstatements are detected in a PPS sample; computed by multiplying the sampling interval by the reliability factor.

batch processing A method of processing transactions that groups similar transactions (such as accounts receivable payments) into batches, which are then run at one time to update the accounts. Batch controls can then be used to provide assurance that all submitted transactions were processed.

bill of lading A shipping document that describes items being shipped, the shipping terms, and delivery address; a formal legal document that conveys responsibility for the safety and shipment of items to the shipper.

block sampling Selecting a group of adjacent items for testing; not an acceptable method unless several small blocks are randomly chosen because one or a few blocks are not likely to be representative of the entire population.

bond indentures Contractual agreements with bondholders that specify conditions designed to protect the bondholders from default. The agreements often specify restrictions on payment of dividends or conditions in which the loan would be in default and immediately due and payable.

bond trustee An independent organization contracted by a corporation or other entity to maintain individual bondholder records and to disburse periodic interest payments to bondholders.

boundary control procedures Control procedures designed to establish initial control and responsibility for the completeness of transactions, implemented at the point in which an organization enters into transactions with other organizations.

breach of contract Failure to perform a contractual duty that has not been excused; for public accounting firms, the parties to a contract normally include clients and designated "third-party beneficiaries."

cash trace An audit procedure by which the auditor lists cash receipts for some period of time and traces the receipts to deposits in the bank statement to determine whether cash receipts are deposited intact on a timely basis.

class action suits Brought on behalf of a large group of plaintiffs to consolidate suits and to encourage consistent judgments and minimize litigation costs; plaintiff shareholders may bring suit for themselves and all others in a similar situation, that is, all other shareholders of record at a specific date.

classical sampling methods The statistical sampling methods that are based on the normal curve and central limit theorem: mean-per-unit, ratio estimation, and difference estimation sampling.

cognizant agency A federal agency assigned by the Director of the OMB to be responsible for implementing the Single Audit Act requirements for a particular government.

collateral An asset or a claim on an asset usually held by a borrower or an issuer of a debt instrument to serve as a guarantee for the value of a loan or security. If the borrower fails to pay interest or principal, the collateral is available to the lender as a basis to recover the principal amount of the loan or debt instrument.

commercial paper Note issued by major corporations, usually for short periods of time and at rates approximating prime lending rates, usually with high credit rating; its quality may change if the financial strength of the issuer declines.

commission The payment of a fee for selling an item or as a percentage of the fees generated for performing a service, which is generally prohibited by the AICPA but may be allowed in some instances for nonattestation clients; when one is accepted, the CPA must disclose its nature to the user affected by the auditor's service.

common law Developed through court decisions, custom, and usage without written legislation and operating on court precedence; may differ from state to state or by jurisdictions.

common-size analysis Conversion of financial statement dollars to percentages and comparison of the percentages with those for prior years and the industry.

common-size statement analysis A technique that shows each income statement account balance as a percent of net sales and each balance sheet account balance as a percent of total assets.

Companies Causes Consolidation Act of 1945 A British act establishing the requirement for audits that was intended to ensure the fairness of the reporting on a trading company's expeditions and activities by requiring a shareholder to perform an audit of the books of account.

compensatory damages Awarded to clients or third parties to compensate them for losses incurred as a result of reliance on misleading financial statements or breach of contract.

compilation The lowest level of service related to financial statements that is provided by public accounting firms. Not an audit service, it involves presenting, in the form of financial statements, information that is the representation of management and results in a disclaimer—no assurance about the fairness of the financial statements. Such a service can be provided only to nonpublic companies.

compliance audit A systematic process to determine whether or not an entity's activities are carried out in accordance with standards or policies promulgated by management or in some cases by a regulatory agency for the conduct of the entity's activities.

computer audit specialist An individual within a CPA firm who has detailed knowledge in computer auditing, including the ability to implement sophisticated computer audit approaches; most firms support them with advanced training in computer auditing.

computer log The electronic record of all information related to a transaction or attempts to access data files; generated automatically by most operating systems for all transactions.

computer tables (files) A computer file that contains information needed to process transactions that may change frequently; common examples include wage rates for each job classification and employee job history. The tables are efficient because the application program can reference the data to determine current information for processing the transactions without changing the computer program.

concurrent audit techniques Computer audit tools implemented within the client's applications to assist the auditor in testing transactions as they are being regularly processed by the client.

concurring partner review or **cold review** Review of an audit by an experienced auditor who was not otherwise involved with it.

confidential information Information obtained during the conduct of an audit related to the client's business or business plans; the auditor is prohibited from communicating confidential information except in very specific instances defined by the code or with the client's specific authorization.

constructive fraud See *gross negligence.*

contingent fee A fee established for the performance of any service pursuant to an arrangement in which no fee will be charged unless a specified finding or result is attained or in which the amount of the fee otherwise depends on the finding or results of such services.

contingent fee cases Lawsuits brought by plaintiffs with compensation for their attorneys contingent on the outcome of the litigation, usually one-third of the damages awarded (including punitive damages), but could be for any amount negotiated between plaintiff party and the lawyer.

contributory negligence A finding that part of the damages incurred were due to the negligence of the party bringing the lawsuit; presents an important defense for the auditor.

control environment The overall tone of operations of an organization that collectively serves to enhance or mitigate the functioning of specific control policies and procedures; reflects the overall attitude, awareness, and actions of those in control of the organization in creating an atmosphere of control.

control procedures Those policies and procedures that management has established to provide reasonable assurance that specific entity objectives will be achieved.

control risk The risk that a material misstatement could occur but would not be prevented or detected on a timely basis by the organization's control structure, including specific control procedures applied to the recording of financial statement items.

control risk assessment The auditor's assessment of the control risk that is present for each significant account balance and class of transactions and related assertions; assessment is based on the auditor's knowledge of the entity's control environment, accounting system, and control procedures, including the effectiveness of specific controls in operation.

credit risk The risk that a debtor may be unable to fulfill its obligation.

cross-sectional analysis A technique to compare ratios between firms at a given point in time.

custom-designed software A computer program developed by the auditing firm for use in a particular client's operating environment; most often used on highly sophisticated computer applications.

cutoff bank statement A bank statement for a period of time determined by the client and the auditor that is shorter than the regular month-end statements; sent directly to the auditor, who uses it to verify reconciling items on the client's year-end bank reconciliation.

cutoff period The few days just before and just after the balance sheet date; the number of days is chosen by the auditor, depending on the assessment of potential errors made in recording items in the incorrect period (especially sales and receivables).

cutoff tests Procedures applied to transactions selected from those recorded during the cutoff period to provide evidence as to whether the transactions have been recorded in the proper period.

cycle A group of accounts related to a particular processing task; represents a convenient way to look at the interrelationship of account balances. Normally, but not always, a transaction cycle encompasses all aspects of a transaction from its initiation to final disposition.

cycle count Periodic testing of the accuracy of the perpetual inventory record by counting all inventory on a cycle basis.

database management systems A centrally planned and controlled collection of data; the management system includes the software to organize the collection of data into logically similar records and files; it separates the data from application programs, thus creating data independence and allowing greater flexibility in meeting the organization's data needs.

debt covenant An agreement between an entity and its lender that places limitations on the organization; usually associated with debentures or large credit lines, common limitations include restrictions on dividend payments, requirements for a specified working capital or debt/equity ratio, and annual audits of company's financial statements to be furnished to the lender. Failure to satisfy may result in loans or bonds becoming immediately due and payable or redeemable.

decision interval The range of the point estimate plus and minus the achieved precision.

defalcation A type of fraud in which the perpetrator takes assets from the organization for personal gain; the theft of cash is a well-known form of embezzlement.

demand deposits A liability for banks or savings institutions, usually represented by checking accounts.

dependent variable The element (variable) being predicted in a model, such as a regression model.

depletion The term used to describe the periodic use of natural assets such as oil or minerals as the products are used; represents an estimate of the cost to obtain the product and is measured per unit, such as per barrel of oil or per ton of metal mined. Depletion is a concept similar to depreciation but is always based on a units of production amortization method.

desired allowance for sampling error The denominator in the sample size formula for the classical methods; determined by multiplying the tolerable misstatement by a factor based on the risk of incorrect acceptance and the risk of incorrect rejection. If the auditor controls only for the risk of incorrect rejection, it is the same as tolerable misstatement for the account.

detection risk The risk that an auditor's direct test of account balances will lead to the conclusion that the financial statements are free from material misstatement when in fact the statements contain material misstatements.

difference estimation sampling A classical sampling method most effective when frequent misstatements are expected and the sizes of misstatements do not have a close correlation with their related book values. An average difference between book value and audit value is calculated and projected to the population as a whole to determine whether book value might be materially misstated.

directed sampling A nonstatistical sampling application in which the auditor has some idea where to look for problems and wishes to direct the sampling toward those items.

direct tests of account balances An audit approach to testing that focuses on independent evidence to substantiate the year-end balance as opposed to testing the transactions affecting the account balance throughout the year.

directional testing An approach to testing account balances that considers the type of misstatement likely to occur in the account balance and the corresponding evidence provided by other accounts that have been tested. The auditor normally tests assets and expenses for overstatement and liabilities and revenues for understatement because (1) the major risks of misstatements on those accounts are in those directions or (2) tests of other accounts provide evidence of possible misstatements in the other direction.

disclaimer An audit report in which the auditor does not express an opinion on the financial statements.

disclaimer of opinion A type of audit report issued when the auditor has not been able to obtain sufficient evidence to form an opinion on the overall fairness of the financial statements.

discovery sampling An attribute sampling method used to uncover evidence of fraud or potential control failures considered to be critical if they exist at more than a very low occurrence rate; the purpose is to uncover at least one incident for investigation if the attribute exists at more than a relatively low tolerable rate rather than to estimate the maximum likely failure rate.

distributed processing Shifting the processing of transactions to different computing units within a network of computers, depending on size and processing requirements.

Division of Firms A formal division of the AICPA to implement quality control standards for the profession at the firm level; it presently has two divisions: the SEC Practice Section and the Private Companies Practice Section; membership in the former is mandatory for firms with SEC clients. Member firms must adhere to the membership requirements of each division, including those of mandatory peer review.

documentary evidence Evidence obtained through the examination of internally or externally generated documents; includes legal contracts or other evidence supporting the recording of transactions.

dual purpose tests Tests of transactions designed to test both the effectiveness of control procedures and the correctness and completeness of the transaction recording process; it is both a test of controls and a direct test of the account balance.

due diligence defense Proving that reasonable procedures were used, there was reason to believe the financial statements were fairly presented, and that the auditor planned and conducted the audit with "due professional care," can prove that the financial statements were fairly presented, or had a justifiable reason (evidence) to believe the financial statements were fairly presented.

due professional care A standard of care expected to be demonstrated by a competent professional in his or her field of expertise, set by the generally accepted auditing standards but supplemented in specific implementation instances by the standard of care expected by a reasonably prudent auditor.

effective date The date the SEC indicates to the client that it may begin trying to sell the new securities described in a registration statement.

electronic data interchange (EDI) The electronic exchange of documents between organizations, eliminating the development of paper documents and substituting electronic documents for them; prevalent examples include electronic transmission of purchase orders and invoices between customers and vendors.

end-user computing An alternative to traditional systems development methodology whereby the end users use advanced program languages and databases to develop their own applications independent of the data processing assistance.

engagement letter Specifies the understanding between the client and the auditor as to the nature of audit services to be conducted and, in the absence of any other formal contract, is viewed by the courts as a contract between the auditor and the client; generally covers items such as client responsibilities, auditor responsibilities, billing procedures, and the timing and target completion date of the audit.

engagement risk The risk, beyond audit risk, associated with a particular audit client such that the association with the audit client may result in financial losses to the auditing firm; aspects include the likelihood that the client may fail or that the client's senior management lacks integrity.

environmental risk The combination of inherent risk and control risk, referred to thus because it is a risk that the auditor cannot control but can only assess.

error expansion factor A factor used in determining the sampling interval/size for PPS sampling to provide for additional sampling error when some misstatement is expected.

ethical dilemma A situation in which moral duties or obligations conflict, one action is not necessarily the correct action.

ethical problem A situation in which an individual is morally or ethically required to do something that conflicts with his or her immediate self-interest.

evidence The underlying accounting data and all corroborating information utilized by the auditor to gain reasonable assurance as to the fairness of an entity's financial statements. Evidence must be relevant, reliable, and persuasive before an audit can be completed.

exceptions Differences between a customer's records and the client's records reported on positive or negative confirmations.

exchange rate risk The risk arising when commitments are made in foreign currencies that fluctuate in relationship to the domestic currency.

excludable misstatements Misstatements the client has independently detected and corrected within the normal accounting system before the auditor begins substantive testing and misstatements that the auditor will evaluate more fully in some other procedure, such as cutoff errors when there is a separate cutoff test.

expected failure rate The auditor's best estimate of the percentage of transactions processed for which the examined control procedure is not operating effectively.

Federal Trade Commission (FTC) A governmental agency charged with responsibility to oversee and monitor the fairness of competition within U.S. industry; it has been a prime agent in forcing the auditing profession to remove elements of the code of professional conduct that it believed constrained trade. FTC pressure has dramatically influenced the amount of competition among CPA firms for audit clients.

financial assistance Assistance provided by a federal agency in the form of grants, contracts, loans, loan guarantees, property, cooperative agreements, interest subsidies, insurance, or direct appropriations but does not include direct federal cash assistance to individuals.

financial audit A systematic process to determine whether an entity's financial statements or other financial results are fairly presented in accordance with GAAP, if applicable, or another comprehensive basis of accounting.

financial instruments A broad class of instruments—usually debt securities, but also equity or hedges—that represents financial agreements between a party (usually an issuer) and a counterparty (usually an investor) based on either underlying assets or agreements to incur financial obligations or make payments; they range in complexity from a simple bond to highly complex agreements containing puts or options.

financial ratio analysis Analysis of ratios between financial statement accounts, such as accounts receivable turnover.

financial-related audits Audits to determine whether (1) financial reports and related items, such as a statement of revenue and expenses, are fairly presented, (2) financial information is presented in accordance with established or stated criteria, such as variances between estimated and actual financial performance, and (3) the entity has adhered to specific financial compliance requirements, such as grant requirements.

financial statement assertions Management's representations that are embodied in the financial statements reflecting generally accepted accounting principles as applied to the preparation of financial statements. Account balance assertions are classified in five broad categories: existence or occurrence, completeness, rights and obligations, valuation or allocation, and presentation and disclosure. Assertions present a framework for audit testing of account balances and classes of transactions.

financial statement audits Audits to determine (1) the fairness of the financial statements in accordance with GAAP and (2) whether the entity has complied with laws and regulations for those transactions and events that may have a material effect on the financial statements.

finite adjustment factor A formula used to convert sample sizes based on infinitely large populations to those applicable to relatively small populations.

flowchart A graphic representation of an accounting application that normally identifies key controls that are effective in achieving specific control objectives as part of the auditor's preliminary assessment of control risk.

forecast An entity's expected financial position, results of operations, and cash flows based on assumptions reflecting conditions expected to exist and the course of action it expects to take.

foreseeable user Those not known specifically by the auditor to be using the financial statements, but recognized by general knowledge as current and potential creditors and investors who will use them.

foreseen user Individually unknown third parties who are members of a known or intended class of third-party users who the auditor, through knowledge gained from interactions with the client, can foresee will use the statements. Although not identified in the engagement letter, the auditor may have first-hand knowledge that the financial statements will be used to obtain a loan from some bank, for example.

fraud Intentional concealment or misrepresentation of a material fact with the intent to deceive another person, causing damage to the deceived person.

fraudulent financial reporting Preparing and disseminating intentionally misleading financial statements by management as a basis for stock gains or other rewards for management.

General Accounting Office (GAO) Governmental organization directly accountable to the Congress of the United States that performs special investigations for the Congress and establishes broad standards for the conduct of governmental audits.

general controls A term describing computer control procedures that affect more than one application. Examples include control procedures over program changes, access control methods, and application development methodologies.

general requirements Requirements of federal financial assistance that pertain to prohibited political activity, the Davis-Bacon Act, which sets wage requirements for construction contractors, civil rights, cash management, relocation assistance and real property acquisition, federal financial reports, allowable costs/cost principles, drug-free workplaces, and administrative requirements.

generalized audit software (GAS) A computer program that contains general modules to read existing computer files and perform manipulations of the data contained on the files to accomplish audit tasks; designed to build an easy user interface that then translates the user instructions into program code to carry out the desired audit tests by reading the client's file and performing the necessary program steps.

Generally Accepted Auditing Standards (GAAS) Measures adopted by the AICPA to guide the practice of auditing within the public accounting profession in the United States.

going concern report modification A fourth paragraph added to the standard unqualified audit report stating the auditor's substantial doubt about the ability of the client to remain operating as a "going concern"; the nature of the client's problems and management's plans for mitigating the problems must be disclosed in footnotes to the financial statements.

goodwill The excess of the purchase price for an economic entity over the sum of the fair market values of specifically identifiable tangible and intangible assets; can arise only in connection with the purchase of an organization and identifies superior earning power associated with the entity.

government auditing standards Standards established by the U.S. General Accounting Office to guide audits of state and local government units and recipients of federal financial assistance; incorporate GAAS and provide supplemental standards and are often referred to as the *Yellow Book*.

gross negligence Failure to use even minimal care, or evidence of activities that show a "recklessness or careless disregard for the truth"; evidence may not be present but may be inferred by a judge or jury because of the carelessness of the defendant's conduct.

haphazard selection Selection of sample items without any conscious bias; not random based and, therefore, cannot be used for statistical sampling.

heteroscedasticity Standard error of residuals is not constant from point to point along a regression line.

homoscedasticity Standard error of residuals is constant from point to point along a regression line.

human resources department A separate department responsible for negotiating long-term union contracts or developing contracts for employee benefits; may also be responsible for developing reports on compliance with applicable government laws and regulations.

identified user Third-party beneficiaries and other users when the auditor has specific knowledge that known users will be utilizing the financial statements in making specific economic decisions.

illegal acts Acts that violate statute or regulatory law and may subject the company to fines or other penalties.

impress bank account A bank account that normally carries a zero balance and is replenished by the company when checks are to be written against the account; provides additional control over cash. The most widely used imprest bank account is the payroll account to which the company makes a deposit equal to the amount of payroll checks issued.

independence A state of objectivity and impartiality on the part of the auditor (i.e., an independent mental state) required by general auditing standards; auditors are required to maintain an *independence in fact* and *independence in appearance* in the conduct of all audit and attestation engagements.

independent variables The elements (variables) likely to have a predictive value for a dependent variable.

inherent risk The susceptibility of transactions to be recorded in error, assuming there were no related internal accounting controls.

insurance reserves An insurance company's best estimate of the claims to be made against its policies currently in force; based on past claim history, current demographics and policy coverage, and projected costs of settling policyholder claims.

intangible asset Assets that convey value either because of exclusive rights associated with their ownership or that represent value of the firm that cannot be specifically identified with specific tangible assets.

integrated test facility (ITF) A concurrent audit technique by which auditor-submitted transactions are processed concurrently with regular processing to determine whether controls are working properly and processing is correct.

interest rate risk The risk arising when the interest rates earned on assets are not equivalent to the interest rates paid on liabilities.

internal audit An independent appraisal function established within an organization to examine and evaluate the activities of a division or department within it by providing operational, compliance, computer, and financial audits.

internal control structure The elements that operate within an organization to promote adherence to management's control policies and procedures; consists of three elements: (1) the control environment, (2) the accounting system, and (3) the control procedures.

joint and several liability Individual responsibility for an entire judgment against all, when one defendant cannot pay the damages awarded to a plaintiff. Apportions losses among all defendants who have an ability to pay for the damages.

kiting A fraudulent cash scheme to overstate cash assets at year-end by recording deposits in transit in both the account from which the cash is withdrawn and the account to which it is transferred.

lapping A technique used to cover up the embezzlement of cash whereby a cash collection from one customer is stolen by an employee who takes another customer's payment and credits the first customer. This process continues and at any point in time, at least one customer's account is overstated.

lead schedules Working papers that combine similar accounts from the client's general ledger, such as all of the cash accounts; the totals from them appear on a working trial balance.

letter of audit inquiry A letter that the auditor asks the client to send to its legal counsel to gather corroborative evidence concerning litigation, claims, and assessments.

leveraged buyout A method of purchasing a company by investing little capital in a new entity that will purchase all, or at least a majority of, outstanding stock of the acquired entity. The buyers issue large amounts of debt to acquire the company. The debt is collateralized by the assets of the acquired company; thus, in a sense, the assets of the company are used to purchase it.

linked account relationships The effect of the double-entry bookkeeping method whereby specific accounts are directly related; an example is bond interest expense and bond liability. The auditor can gather evidence regarding both accounts by testing one account and estimating the effect on the other account. Most often the auditor tests the asset or liability account balance and uses it as a basis for determining the related expense or revenue account.

limited assurance A statement by the accountant in a report that nothing has been detected that indicates that the information needs to be changed to bring it into conformity with the appropriate criteria, such as GAAP.

liquidity risk The risk arising when the institution has insufficient or illiquid resources available at a particular point in time to meet liabilities or obligations arising or maturing.

loan loss reserves An estimate of uncollectible loan accounts of a bank or savings and loan.

loan review committee A senior management committee that is charged with the task of reviewing loans that have been proposed by a loan officer; serves as an independent check on the actions of individual loan officers.

lockbox A cash management arrangement with a bank whereby an organization's customers send payments directly to a post office box number accessible by the client's bank; the bank opens the cash remittances and directly deposits the money in the client's account.

major finding A finding that prevents the activity from achieving a major objective.

major program A federally assisted program for which expenditures exceed an established threshold. For example, for governments with total annual federal assistance expenditures of less than $1 million, the threshold is the larger of $300,000 or 3 percent.

management integrity The honesty and trustworthiness of management as exemplified by past and current actions; auditors' assessment of management integrity reflects the extent to which the auditors believe they can trust management and its representations to be honest and forthright.

management letter A letter from the auditor to the client identifying any problems and suggested solutions that may help management improve its effectiveness or efficiency.

management representation letter A letter to the auditors that is required to be signed by the client's chief executive and chief financial officer, for the purpose of reminding management of its responsibility for the financial statements and confirming oral responses given to the auditor during the audit.

marketable security A security that is readily marketable and held by the company as an investment.

market risk The fluctuation in current market prices of financial instruments.

materiality The magnitude of an omission or misstatement of accounting information that, in the light of surrounding circumstances, makes it probable that the judgment of a reasonable person relying on the information would have been changed or influenced by the omission or misstatement.

material weakness A reportable condition that does not reduce to a relatively low level the risk that misstatements in amounts that are material in relation to the financial statements being audited may occur and not be detected within a timely period by employees in the normal course of performing their assigned functions.

material weakness in internal accounting control A condition in which the specific control procedures or the degree of compliance with them does not reduce to a relatively low level the risk that the financial statements being audited may contain errors or irregularities in material amounts that will not be detected within a timely period by employees in the normal course of performing their assigned functions.

mean-per-unit sampling A classical sampling method used when few misstatements are expected and the sample is to be selected based on random items rather than random dollars.

minor finding A finding that does not prevent the activity from achieving a major objective but will continue to have adverse effects if not corrected and should be reported to top management.

misstatement For substantive sampling purposes, the differences in recorded values and audited values resulting in either (1) a misstatement of pre-tax income arising from any nonexcludable misstatement(s) (income effect) or (2) a difference that affects the account total (account misstatement).

most likely misstatement In PPS sampling, the sum of the top stratum misstatements and the projection of the lower stratum misstatements. It is the auditor's best estimate of the total misstatement in the population and should be posted to the summary of possible adjustments.

multiple regression model A regression model that includes two or more independent variables.

narrative A written description of an accounting application and the controls within the application.

negative assurance See *limited assurance.*

negative confirmation A request to customers asking them to respond directly to the auditor only if they disagree with the indicated balance.

negligence Failure to exercise reasonable care, thereby causing harm to another or to property.

nonfinancial ratios Comparisons of financial and nonfinancial data.

nonpublic entity Any entity other than (1) one whose securities trade in a public market either on a stock exchange (domestic or foreign) or in the over-the-counter market, (2) one that makes a filing with a regulatory agency in preparation for the sale of any class of its securities in a public market, or (3) a subsidiary, corporate joint venture, or other entity controlled by an entity covered by (1) or (2).

nonsampling risk The risk of improperly auditing sampled items or misjudging inherent or control risk.

open confirmation A request to customers asking them to provide a list of amounts they owe the client; the auditor or client reconciles the customer's output with the client's accounts receivable as a basis for determining the correctness of recorded accounts receivable.

operating system A complex computer program that controls and coordinates the running of the computer and its many functions.

operational audit A systematic appraisal of an entity's operations, usually conducted by an internal auditor, to determine whether an organization's operations are being carried out in an efficient manner and whether constructive recommendations for operational improvements can be made.

operational auditing The evaluation of activities, systems, and controls within an enterprise for efficiency, effectiveness, and economy.

operational risk The risk that an institution may be unable to process transactions in a timely or accurate manner.

opinion The highest level of assurance formed by the auditor after gathering and evaluating an extensive amount of evidence.

other comprehensive basis of accounting (OCBOA) Financial statements not prepared in accordance with GAAP but prepared on a cash or modified cash basis, the basis of accounting used for preparing the income tax return, the basis of accounting required for reporting to a governmental regulatory agency, or some other basis that has a definite set of criteria that have substantial support and apply to all material items appearing in the financial statements.

other postretirement employee benefits Benefits, other than pensions, paid by an organization to its retirees, the most common of which is health insurance. The plans may be formal or informal and may involve a third party such as an insurance company that administers the benefits. The FASB has determined that the cost of providing such benefits should be recognized over the period in which the employee provides productive services for the organization. An expense and liability should be accrued during the period of employment.

other substantive procedures risk (OSPR) The risk that all of the substantive tests, other than the planned sampling test, will fail to detect a material misstatement; professional standards refer to OSPR as *analytical procedures (AP) risk.*

owner/manager controls Controls that operate in small businesses in which the owner-manager provides detailed review and oversight of accounting transactions and performs many of the review procedures that could be attained only through segregation of duties in large organizations.

paperless systems Accounting applications in which key records and documentation are created and stored only in electronic form within computer systems.

parallel simulation A static computer audit approach whereby the auditor develops a computer program intended to simulate an important part of a client's computer program to process live client data, the results of which are compared with the results obtained when the same data were processed by the client's application program.

peer review An independent review of the quality of a public accounting firm or internal audit organization performed by professionals who are not a part of the firm or organization, or review of an audit report and accompanying work papers by a partner or review function, independent of the engagement personnel, before an audit report is issued.

per diem billing rates Standard hourly billing rates that CPA firms establish as the reference billing rate to charge their clients; they vary by responsibility (partner rates are higher than manager rates, which are higher than staff rates).

performance audits The evaluation of an organization's economy, efficiency, and programs.

permanent file A working paper file that contains information that will be of continuing interest to the audit. The file generally contains information such as debt covenants, corporate charters, and highlights of board of directors' meetings.

planning materiality The assessment of materiality by the auditor on the financial statements as a basis for planning the nature, extent, and timing of audit procedures.

point estimate An estimate of the correct value of the population based on a classical sample result. It is the auditor's best estimate of the population value based on sample results and serves as the basis around which confidence intervals can be constructed.

pooling of interests A method whereby one company acquires another company through the issuance of stock for the outstanding stock of the other company. A pooling is viewed as the continuation of existing ownership; thus, the transactions are recorded at the book value of the acquired entity. The stock issued for the transaction is valued at the book value of assets acquired, not the market value of the stock or of the acquired assets.

population The group of transactions or the items that make up an account balance for which the auditor wants to estimate some characteristic, such as the effectiveness of control procedures.

positive confirmation A request to customers asking them to respond directly to the auditor if they agree or disagree with the indicated balance.

precision The spread, or difference, between the tolerable and expected control procedure failure rates.

precision gap widening Provision for additional sampling error when misstatements are detected in a PPS sample. Factors are determined from tables derived from the underlying sampling distribution.

predecessor auditor The immediately previous auditor of the client for which the new auditor is proposing or beginning to serve.

preliminary survey The first step in an operational audit that familiarizes the auditor with the activity being audited by determining the nature of the activity, its operating objectives, what is done, how it is done, what it costs, the risks, and the controls that have been designed to ensure that the objectives are met and risks minimized.

primary benefit test A legal concept requiring the auditor to know of the third party who would primarily benefit from the audited financial statements in order to be held liable to that party for ordinary negligence; established in the *Ultramares* case.

Principles of the Code of Professional Conduct Express the profession's recognition of its responsibilities to the public, clients, and colleagues, guide members in the performance of their professional responsibilities, and express the basic tenets of ethical and professional conduct; they call for an unswerving commitment to honorable behavior, even at the sacrifice of personal advantage.

privileged communication Information about a client that cannot be subpoenaed by a court of law to be used against a client; it allows no exceptions to confidentiality.

privity of contract A mutual relationship between parties to a contract.

probability proportional to size (PPS) sampling A sampling method based on attribute estimation sampling but involving dollar misstatements rather than failure rates; each item in the population has a probability of being included in the sample proportionate to the dollar value of the item. PPS sampling is most effective when auditing for the overstatement of a population and when no or few misstatements are expected.

pro forma financial information Information showing the significant effects on historical financial information had a consummated or proposed transaction occurred at an earlier date.

program audits Audits to determine (1) the extent to which the desired results or benefits established by the legislature or other authorizing body are being achieved; (2) the effectiveness of organizations, programs, activities, or functions; and (3) whether the entity has complied with laws and regulations applicable to the program.

projected misstatement The difference between the point estimate and the book value of the population.

projection An entity's expected financial position, results of operations, and cash flows based on one or more hypothetical assumptions. A projection is often used to support a request for a bank loan showing what is likely to happen if the loan is granted.

proof of cash An audit technique that reconciles beginning and ending balances per the bank with the books and the month's deposits per the bank with the receipts per the books and the bank's withdrawals for the company for the month with the disbursements per the books.

property ledger A subsidiary ledger listing all items of property, plant, and equipment and their initial cost, depreciation methods, estimated salvage value, and accumulated depreciation.

prospective financial statements Financial statements covering one or more future accounting periods. There are two types: forecasts and projections.

prospectus The first part of a registration statement filed with the SEC issued as part of a public offering of debt or equity and used to solicit prospective investors in a new security issue containing, among other items, audited financial statements. Liability for misstatements in a prospectus is imposed by the Securities Act of 1933.

purchase accounting An accounting method for the acquisition of another entity by a controlling entity whereby the stock of the acquired company is acquired through the issuance of other than 100 percent stock, such as a combination of cash, debt, and equity. The purchased company's assets are revalued at their fair market value, and any excess of the purchase price over the fair market value of the assets acquired is allocated to goodwill.

qualified audit report Audit report indicating a significant scope limitation or that the auditor has concluded that the financial statements contain material misstatements or omissions that prevent them from being fairly presented in conformance with GAAP.

qualified opinion A type of audit report issued when the auditor is unable to obtain sufficient competent evidence because of scope limitations or the lack of such evidence; there is a material, unjustified departure from GAAP, or management's disclosures are not adequate, but the auditor has decided not to express an adverse opinion.

quality control An approach by an organization to ensure that high-quality products are produced and high-quality services are provided. The approach specifies quality requirements for processes and products and integrates those concepts into vendor contracts.

quality control standards Encompasses the firm's organizational structure and the policies adopted and procedures established to provide the CPA firm with reasonable assurance of conforming with professional standards. The system of quality control should be suitably designed in relation to the firm's organizational structure, its policies, and the nature of its practice.

questioned costs Costs related to alleged violations of covenants governing the expenditure of funds, costs not supported by adequate documentation, and unnecessary or unreasonable expenditures.

questionnaire An approach to understanding and documenting a client's control structure through answers to prestructured questions designed to depict the client's processing and potential exposures in the client's application system under investigation.

R^2 The percentage of the total fluctuation in the dependent variable that is explained by the fluctuation in the independent variable; is also referred to as the coefficient of determination.

random-based selection Sample selection methods in which each item in the population has an equal chance of being selected; only random-based samples can be statistically evaluated.

ratio analysis The calculation of the relationship between two amounts, such as interest expense and interest-bearing debt.

ratio estimation sampling A classical sampling method that is most effective when frequent misstatements are expected and the sizes of misstatements have a high correlation with the related book values.

reasonableness test Developing a model to predict an account balance, comparing that prediction with the recorded amount and determining whether the difference between the predicted value and the book value requires investigating.

reconciliations Controls that operate by checking for agreement between submitted transactions and processed transactions or between detailed accounts and corresponding control accounts.

red flags Characteristics that research has shown are often associated with fraud, including personal characteristics of top management, organization structure, and economic or financial conditions that provide both the motivation for and the opportunity to commit fraud.

regression analysis As used in auditing, a statistical technique used to describe the relationship between the account being audited and other possible predictive factors.

reissue the report Reissue a previously issued audit report on which no audit work has been done subsequent to the original report date; it contains the original report date.

related-party transaction A transaction with a commonly controlled entity such that the transaction cannot be viewed as an "arm's-length" transaction.

reliability factors Factors related to the test of details risk used to determine the sample interval/size for PPS sampling.

reliability of audit evidence A key characteristic of the evidence that must be evaluated by the auditor in determining the persuasiveness of the evidence-gathering procedures.

reportable conditions Matters coming to the auditor's attention that represent significant deficiencies in the design or operation of the internal control structure which could adversely affect the organization's ability to record, process, summarize, and report financial data consistent with the assertions of management in the financial statements and therefore that, in the auditor's judgment, should be communicated to the audit committee.

requisition A request for the purchase of goods or services by an authorized department or function within the organization; may be documented on a paper or in a computer system.

residual Fluctuations in the dependent variable not explained by fluctuations in the independent variable.

revenue cycle The process of receiving a customer's order, approving credit for a sale, determining whether the goods are available for shipment, shipping the goods, billing the customers, collecting cash, and recognizing the effect of this process on other related accounts such as Accounts Receivable and Inventory.

review The middle level of service related to financial statements that public accountants provide involving inquiries and analytical procedures and resulting in limited assurance about the fairness of the financial statements.

RICO Racketeer Influenced and Corrupt Organizations Act, a federal law passed by Congress to enable the Justice Department and others to bring suits against organized crime that had moved into ostensibly legitimate businesses; provides for treble damages, plus reasonable lawyer fees, as compensation to victims.

rights theory An approach (framework) for addressing ethical problems by identifying a hierarchy of rights that should be considered in solving ethical problems or dilemmas.

risk-based auditing An overall audit approach whereby the auditing firm assesses key factors of risk that may affect a particular audit client and then adjusts the auditing procedures to emphasize these areas. In some cases, the risk-based analysis leads an auditor not to accept a particular client.

risk of assessing control risk too high The risk that the assessed level of control risk based on the sample is greater than the true operating effectiveness of the control structure policy or procedure.

risk of assessing control risk too low The risk that the assessed level of control risk based on the sample is less than the true operating effectiveness of the control structure policy or procedures.

risk of incorrect acceptance The risk of concluding from a sample that the book value is not materially misstated when in fact it is; sometimes referred to as a *Type II statistical error* or the *beta* (β) *risk*.

risk of incorrect rejection The risk of concluding from a sample that the book value is materially misstated when in fact it is not; sometimes referred to as a *Type I statistical error* or the *alpha* (α) *risk*.

roll-forward period The period between an interim date, when a substantive procedure was performed, and the balance sheet date.

roll-forward procedures Procedures performed at or after the balance sheet date to update substantive evidence obtained at an interim date.

rules of professional conduct Detailed guidance to assist the CPA in applying the broad principles contained in the AICPA's Code of Professional Conduct; they have evolved over time as members of the profession have encountered specific ethical dilemmas in complying with the principles of the code.

sampling risk The probability that a sample is not representative of the population, which can lead the auditor to the wrong conclusion about the population; composed of the four immediately preceding risks.

sampling units The individual auditable elements, as defined by the auditor, that constitute the population, such as customers' balances or individual unpaid invoices.

scienter An intent to deceive.

scope limitation A restriction on the performance of audit procedures caused by the client or the circumstances.

Securities Act of 1933 Federal statutory law related to the original issuance of securities, imposes a heavy burden on all parties associated with the issuance of the securities to ensure that full and fair disclosure is obtained in the financial reporting.

Securities and Exchange Commission (SEC) The governmental body with the oversight responsibility to ensure the proper and efficient operation of capital markets in the United States.

Securities Exchange Act of 1934 Congressional act giving the Securities and Exchange Commission broad powers to censure firms practicing before it and to prescribe forms in which information shall be reported to it and the ultimate authority to establish accounting principles for all firms that must file reports with the SEC.

segregation of duties The separation of functions across individuals so that one individual is not put in a situation to both *perpetrate* and *conceal* a fraud or error through the manipulation of accounting records.

sequential (stop-or-go) sampling A multistep process attribute sampling method involving the selection of the smallest possible sample so that the absence of failures allows the auditor to conclude that the tested control procedures are working satisfactorily. If the sample reveals one or more control failures, the auditor must decide whether to expand the sample. Sequential sampling is appropriate for those situations in which it is relatively easy to expand the sample when necessary and few failures are expected.

serial correlation (See autocorrelation)

service auditors Auditors of service organizations such as a computer service bureau that provide audit reports for user auditors.

shared report An audit report that indicates that other auditors performed part of the audit.

simple regression model A regression model with just one independent variable.

Single Audit Act of 1984 A Federal statute that establishes uniform requirements for audits of each state and local government receiving federal financial assistance of at least $100,000 in any fiscal year.

snapshot approach A concurrent audit technique whereby transactions are selected and "tagged" for future identification by the client's application program. When they are processed, specific output is generated to describe the processing to date for the transactions and the files, computations, and so on, that have been made as a function of these data being processed by the application.

special reports Reports on the following types of situations in which the client engages the auditor to perform specific procedures; to report on financial statements prepared in conformity with a comprehensive basis of accounting other than GAAP; to report on specified elements, accounts, or items of a financial statement; or to report on compliance with aspects of contractual agreements or regulatory requirements related to audited financial statements. In addition, they might include some reports based on regulatory requirements.

specific requirements Requirements related to federal financial assistance that include the types of services allowed, eligibility, matching, and reporting.

spreadsheet Software developed initially for microcomputers that allows auditors to emulate manually prepared spreadsheets containing sophisticated mathematical functions; can be used effectively in performing "what-if" analysis and financial statement analysis and in developing significant accounting entries.

stakeholders Those parties that have a vested interest in, or are affected by, the decision resulting from an ethical problem or dilemma.

standard error The standard deviation of data that measures the variability of that data.

statistical sampling The application of probability theory and statistical inference in a sample application to assist the auditor in determining an appropriate sample size and in evaluating the sample results.

statutory law Developed through legislation, such as the Securities Act of 1933 and the Securities Exchange Act of 1934.

stock transfer agent An independent entity contracted by a corporation to process stock transfers, issue new stock certificates, cancel existing certificates and possibly be responsible for disbursing dividends to individual shareholders.

stratification Dividing the population into relatively homogeneous groups called *strata.* Stratification can be performed judgmentally by the auditor but is most often performed with the assistance of generalized audit software to achieve optimum sampling efficiency.

subsequent events review A review of events occurring in the period between the balance sheet date and the end of audit field work to determine their possible effect on the financial statements.

substantive tests Tests of transactions to ensure that they are properly recorded and direct tests of account balances either by performing tests of details making up an account balance or through analytical review techniques to estimate the overall correctness of account balances.

systematic selection Selecting every *n*th item in a population with a random start, where *n* is the number of items in the population divided by the desired sample size.

systems control and audit review facility (SCARF) A concurrent audit technique by which transactions identified by the auditor (either specifically or by preset criteria) are written to a data file for subsequent review by the auditor to determine their completeness, correctness, and authority related to their processing.

tables A commonly used computer term to describe computer files that contain data necessary for the processing of transactions.

tainting percentage In PPS sampling, the amount of misstatement as a percent of the sample item's book value. The tainting percentage is calculated individually for each sampled item.

telecommunications software Software that controls the paths and completeness of all data communications between a computer system, terminals, or other data processing locations; designed to ensure that all data are properly transmitted through authorized media to correct parties and are completely received.

test data approach A static testing approach whereby the auditor develops fictitious transactions to submit for processing by an application of interest to the auditor, the objectives of which are to determine whether (1) computerized controls are operating effectively and (2) computer processing is carried out correctly and completely.

testimonial evidence Evidence based on the written or oral representations of individuals from either inside or outside the organization, often in the form of confirmations; reliability depends heavily on the independence, competence, and care used by the individual furnishing the evidence.

test of details risk A synonym for the risk of incorrect acceptance. It is the part of detection risk related to a sampling application. The other part is the other substantive procedures risk (OSPR).

test of transactions Detailed procedures applied to account balances to determine the validity of the processing of individual transactions throughout the year by tracing the origination of the transaction to its subsequent recording in the accounts and vice versa and to determine the correctness and timeliness of the recording process.

tests of controls Specific audit evidence gathered to determine whether control procedures are operating in the way in which they have been described and documented in the auditor's preliminary understanding of controls; the auditor must determine whether they are operating as posited if the auditor wishes to assess control risk below the maximum.

third-party beneficiary A person who was not a party to a contract but to whom the contracting parties intended benefits be given.

time-series analysis A technique to analyze ratios for a given firm over time; a combination of trend and ratio analysis.

time-series regression analysis A technique used for predicting a dependent variable based on the historical relationship between that variable and one or more other financial or nonfinancial independent variables.

timing difference Confirmation exceptions caused by transactions that are in process at the confirmation date, such as in-transit shipments or payments. These are not misstatements.

tolerable failure rate The auditor's assessment of the maximum rate of control procedure failure that can occur and still allow the auditor to rely on the control.

tolerable misstatement The maximum misstatement in an account balance or class of transactions that the auditor is willing to accept and still conclude that the test results have achieved the audit objective.

top stratum Population items whose book values exceed the sampling interval and are, therefore, all included in the test. The top stratum consists of all account balances exceeding a specific dollar amount.

trend analysis The comparison of an amount for the current year with the prior year or years.

turnaround document A document sent to the customer to be returned with the customer's remittance; may be machine readable and may contain information to improve the efficiency of receipt processing.

uncertainties Situations in which the outcome of some matter cannot be determined as of the end of the audit fieldwork, such as the results of pending litigation.

unqualified audit report Term describing the standard audit report in which the auditor states that the results of the audit indicate that the financial statements are fairly presented in conformance with GAAP; sometimes referred to as a *clean opinion*.

unqualified opinion A type of audit report issued when the auditor has been able to perform sufficient procedures and believes that the evidence indicates that the financial statements do not contain a material, unjustified departure from GAAP or inadequate disclosures.

updating the report Considering information that comes to the auditor's attention during the current year audit but that is related to prior year statements presented for comparative purposes. The report date should be the end of the current year field work.

upper misstatement limit The maximum potential amount of misstatement in a population based on sample results at a specified level of test of details risk.

user auditors Auditors of the customers of the service organization that use audit reports prepared by service auditors.

utilitarian theory An ethical theory (framework) that systematically considers all the potential stakeholders that may be affected by an ethical decision and seeks to measure the effects of the decision on each party; it seeks to assist individuals in making decisions resulting in the greatest amount of good for the greatest number of people.

variables sampling Sampling to estimate a variable, such as the dollar misstatements in a population; variables sampling and classical sampling techniques are used interchangeably in the text.

walk-through An audit approach designed to gain an understanding of the processing that takes place in the accounting system; the auditor "walks" a transaction through its process and inquires of client personnel about the nature of the processing that takes place.

working trial balance A trial balance of the client's general ledger accounts that has similar accounts combined into one total, such as all cash accounts; the individual account detail appears on lead schedules.

Credits

Material from Uniform CPA Examination, Questions and Unofficial Answers, Copyright © 1966, 1967, 1970, 1974, 1975, 1976, 1977, 1979, 1980, 1981, 1982, 1983, 1984, 1985, 1986, 1987, 1988, 1989, 1990, 1991, 1992 American Institute of Certified Public Accountants, Inc., is reprinted and adapted with permission.

CIA exams used throughout the text are reprinted with permission from the Institute of Internal Auditors, Inc., Altamonte Springs, Florida.

Chapter 2

Excerpts from Abraham Briloff, "Standards Without Standards/Principles Without Principles/Fairness without Fairness," *Advances in Accounting,* Vol. 3, 1986, pp. 25–30. Reprinted with permission of JAI Press, Inc.

Chapter 3

Excerpts from an interview with Jose L. Gomez, *The Wall Street Journal,* March 4, 1987. Reprinted with permission of *The Wall Street Journal,* © 1987 Dow Jones & Company, Inc. All rights reserved.

Exhibit 3.4 IIA "Standards of Conduct" from *IIA's Code of Ethics,* copyright 1988 by the Institute of Internal Auditors, Inc., 249 Maitland Avenue, Altamonte Springs, Florida 32710-4201. Reprinted with permission.

Chapter 4

Excerpts from "Accountants' Liability: Coping with the Stampede to the Courtroom," *Journal of Accountancy,* September 1987, p. 119. Copyright © 1987 by American Institute of Certified Public Accountants, Inc. Opinions of the authors are their own and do not necessarily reflect policies of the AICPA. Reprinted with permission of the *Journal of Accountancy.*

Excerpts from "Turning the Tide on Liability," *Accounting Today,* Vol. 6, No. 17, September 7, 1992, p. 1. Copyright Lebhar-Friedman, Inc., 425 Park Avenue, New York, N.Y. 10022. Reprinted with permission of *Accounting Today.*

Excerpts from "Why Didn't Auditors Find Something Wrong with Equity Funding?" *The Wall Street Journal,* May 4, 1973. Reprinted with permission of *The Wall Street Journal,* © 1973 Dow Jones & Company, Inc. All rights reserved.

Poem from "Insurance Men Wax Poetic to Immortalize Equity Funding Case," *The Wall Street Journal,* May 24, 1973, p. 1. Reprinted with permission of *The Wall Street Journal,* © 1973 Dow Jones & Company, Inc. All rights reserved.

Chapter 5

Excerpts from "Cooking the Books: How Pressure to Raise Sales Led Miniscribe to Falsify Numbers," *The Wall Street Journal,* September 11, 1989, p. 1. Reprinted with permission of *The Wall Street Journal,* © 1989 Dow Jones & Company, Inc. All rights reserved.

Comments from "Battle of the Books: Audit Firms Are Hit by More Investor Suits for Not Finding Fraud," *The Wall Street Journal,* January 24, 1989. Reprinted with permission of *The Wall Street Journal,* © 1989 Dow Jones & Company, Inc. All rights reserved worldwide.

John A. Byrne, "How Don Sheelen Made a Mess that Regina Couldn't Clean Up," *Business Week,* February 12, 1990, pp. 46–50. Copyright © 1990 by McGraw-Hill, Inc. Reprinted with special permission.

Daniel Akst, "How Barry Minkow Fooled the Auditors," *Forbes,* October 2, 1989. Copyright © Forbes Inc., 1989. Reprinted with permission of *Forbes* magazine.

Chapter 12

Exhibit 12.5 "Attribute Sample Size Tables," Tables 1 and 2, from *Audit Sampling,* p. 107. Reprinted with permission of the American Institute of Certified Public Accountants, Inc.

Exhibit 12.9 "Attribute Estimation Sample Evaluation Tables," Tables 1 and 2, from *Audit Sampling,* pp. 108–109. Reprinted with permission of the American Institute of Certified Public Accountants, Inc.

Exhibit 12.10 "Sequential Sample Size Table," *Audit Sampling,* p. 112. Reprinted with permission of the American Institute of Certified Public Accountants, Inc.

Chapter 14

Exhibit 14.3 "PPS Sample Design and Evaluation Factors," modified from *Audit Sampling Audit and Accounting Guide.* Reprinted with permission of the American Institute of Certified Public Accountants.

Exhibit 14.13 "Ratio of Desired Allowance for Sampling Error to Tolerable Misstatement," from Donald M. Roberts, *Statistical Auditing* (New York: AICPA, 1978), p. 247. Reprinted with permission of the American Institute of Certified Public Accountants.

Exhibit 14.14 "Probability-Proportional-to-Size Sampling Tables," from *Audit Sampling* (New York: AICPA, 1983), p. 117. Reprinted with permission of the American Institute of Certified Public Accountants.

Chapter 15

"Management Control Considerations for Investors," excerpted from *A Guide to Financial Instruments,* published by Coopers & Lybrand.

Chapter 19

Excerpts from Dana Linden, "Separating the Sheep from the Goats," *Forbes,* October 1, 1990, pp. 49–50. Copyright © 1990 Forbes Inc. Reprinted with permission of *Forbes* magazine.

Chapter 20

Exhibit 20.6 "Partial Disclosure Checklist," from *Disclosure Checklists and Illustrative Financial Statements for Corporations: A Financial Reporting Practice Aid* (New York: AICPA, November 1989 edition), p. 52. Reprinted with permission of the American Institute of Certified Public Accountants.

Chapter 24

Exhibit 24.11 "Standard 430—Communicating Results," from *Standards for the Professional Practice of Internal Auditing.* Copyright 1978 by the Institute of Internal Auditors, Inc. Reprinted with permission of the Institute of Internal Auditors, Inc., 249 Maitland Avenue, Altamonte Springs, Florida 32710-4201.

Index

Boldfaced page numbers indicate where significant terms are discussed.

O

P

Q